HANDBOOK OF
Health Survey Methods

Wiley Handbooks in

SURVEY METHODOLOGY

The *Wiley Handbooks in Survey Methodology* is a series of books that present both established techniques and cutting-edge developments in the field of survey research. The goal of each handbook is to supply a practical, one-stop reference that treats the statistical theory, formulae, and applications that, together, make up the cornerstones of a particular topic in the field. A self-contained presentation allows each volume to serve as a quick reference on ideas and methods for practitioners, while providing an accessible introduction to key concepts for students. The result is a high-quality, comprehensive collection that is sure to serve as a mainstay for novices and professionals alike.

Forthcoming *Wiley Handbooks in Survey Methodology*

De Waal, Pannekoek, and Scholtus · *Handbook of Data Editing and Imputation*

Bethlehem, Cobben, and Schouten · *Handbook of Nonresponse in Household Surveys*

Bethlehem and Biffignandi · *Handbook of Web Surveys*

Johnson · *Handbook of Health Survey Methods*

Sedransk and Nandram · *Handbook of Bayesian Survey Methods*

Larsen and Winkler · *Handbook of Record Linkage Methods*

HANDBOOK OF
Health Survey Methods

Edited by

TIMOTHY P. JOHNSON
Survey Research Laboratory
University of Illinois at Chicago
Chicago, IL, USA

WILEY

Cover Image: ©iStockphoto/adisa

Published by John Wiley & Sons, Inc., Hoboken, New Jersey
Published simultaneously in Canada

Library of Congress Cataloging-in-Publication Data:

Handbook of health survey methods / edited by Timothy P. Johnson.
p. ; cm.
Includes bibliographical references and index.
ISBN 978-1-118-00232-2 (cloth)
I. Johnson, Timothy P., editor.
[DNLM: 1. Health Survey–methods. WA 900.1]
RA407
614.4′2–dc23

2015015374

Printed in the United States of America

10 9 8 7 6 5 4 3 2 1

Contents

PART II

Design and Measurement Issues

PART IV

Health Surveys of Special Populations

List of Contributors

Emily E. Anderson
Neiswanger Institute for Bioethics, Stritch School of Medicine, Loyola University Chicago, Chicago, IL, USA

Michael Battaglia
Battaglia Consulting Group, LLC., Arlington, MA, USA

Paul Beatty
Division of Health Care Statistics, National Center for Health Statistics, Centers for Disease Control and Prevention. Hyattsville, MD, USA

Timothy J. Beebe
Department of Health Sciences Research, Mayo Clinic, Rochester, Minnesota, USA

Maureen R. Benjamins
Sinai Urban Health Institute, Room K437, 1500 South California Avenue, Chicago, IL 60608, USA

Ulrike Boehmer
Department of Community Health Sciences, Boston University, School of Public Health, Boston, MA, USA

Adam C. Carle
University of Cincinnati, Cincinnati, OH, USA

Jarvis T. Chen
Department of Social and Behavioral Sciences, Harvard School of Public Health, Boston, MA, USA

Melissa A. Clark
Department of Epidemiology and Obstetrics & Gynecology, Public Health Program and Warren Alpert Medical School, Brown University, Providence, RI, USA

Kennon R. Copeland
NORC at the University of Chicago, Statistics and Methodology Bethesda, MD, USA

Benjamin Cornwell
Department of Sociology, Cornell University, Ithaca, NY, USA

Michael Davern
NORC at the University of Chicago, Chicago, IL, USA

Elizabeth Dean
RTI International, North Carolina, USA

Ralph DiGaetano
Westat, Rockville, Maryland, USA

Brad Edwards
Westat, Rockville, Maryland, USA

Francis Fullam
Marketing Research, Rush University Medical Center, Chicago, IL, USA; Health Systems Management, Rush University, Chicago, IL, USA

Nadarajasundaram Ganesh
NORC at the University of Chicago, Statistics and Methodology Bethesda, MD, USA

Joe Gfroerer
Center for Behavioral Health Statistics and Quality, Substance Abuse and Mental Health Services Administration, Rockville, MD, USA

Jon R. Gunderson
Assistive Communication and Information Technology Accessibility in the Division of Disability Resources and Education Services (DRES), University of Illinois, Champaign/Urbana, IL, USA

Heidi Guyer
Institute for Social Research, University of Michigan, Ann Arbor, MI, USA

Rooshey Hasnain
Asian American Studies Program and Department of Disability and Human Development, University of Illinois at Chicago, Chicago, IL, USA

Craig A. Hill
Survey, Computing, and Statistical Sciences, RTI International, Chicago, IL, USA

Emily Hoagland
Department of Sociology, Cornell University, Ithaca, NY, USA

Timothy P. Johnson
Survey Research Laboratory, College of Urban Planning and Public Affairs, University of Illinois at Chicago, Illinois, USA

Joel Kennet
Center for Behavioral Health Statistics and Quality, Substance Abuse and Mental Health Services Administration, Rockville, MD, USA

Ronald C. Kessler
Department of Health Care Policy, Harvard Medical School, Boston, Massachusetts, USA

Stanislav (Stas) Kolenikov
Abt SRBI, Silver Spring, MD, USA

Sunghee Lee
Institute for Social Research, University of Michigan, Ann Arbor, MI, USA

John D. Loft
Survey, Computing, and Statistical Sciences, RTI International, Chicago, IL, USA

Liam McKeever
Department of Disability and Human Development, University of Illinois at Chicago, Chicago, IL, USA

Joe Murphy
Survey, Computing, and Statistical Sciences, RTI International, Chicago, IL, USA

Mary B. Ofstedal
Institute for Social Research, University of Michigan, Ann Arbor, MI, USA

Ashmeet Oberoi
Department of Disability and Human Development, University of Illinois at Chicago, Chicago, IL, USA

Jeff Pitblado
Statistical Software, StataCorp LP, College Station, TX, USA

Hadi B. Rangin
Assistive Communication and Information Technology Accessibility in the Division of Disability Resources and Education Services (DRES), University of Illinois, Champaign/Urbana, IL, USA

Safa Rashid
Health Systems Science Department, College of Nursing, University of Illinois at Chicago, Chicago, IL, USA

Ashley Richards
Survey, Computing, and Statistical Sciences, RTI International, Chicago, IL, USA

Marc Roemer
Agency for Healthcare Research and , Quality Survey Statistician formerly at the US Census Bureau, Rockville, MD, USA

Samantha Rosenthal
Department of Epidemiology, Public Health Program, Brown University, Providence, RI, USA

Joseph W. Sakshaug
Department of Statistical Methods, Institute for Employment Research, Nuremberg, Germany. Program in Survey Methodology, Institute for Social Research, University of Michigan, Ann Arbor, Michigan, USA

Mike Scott
Division of Rehabilitation Services of the Illinois Department of Human Services, Chicago, IL, USA

Ami M. Shah
UCLA Center for Health Policy Research10960 Wilshire Blvd, Suite 1550, Los Angeles, CA 00024, USA

Carmit-Noa Shpigelman
Department of Community Mental Health, Faculty of Social Welfare and Health Sciences, University of Haifa, Haifa, Israel

Sandy Slater
Health Policy and Administration Division, School of Public Health, University of Illinois at Chicago, Chicago, IL, USA

Tom W. Smith
NORC at the University of Chicago, USA

Wendy Thomas
Minnesota Population Center, University of Minnesota, Minneapolis, MN, USA

Jonathan B. VanGeest
Department of Health Policy and Management, College of Public Health, Kent State University, Kent, OH, USA

James Wagner
Institute for Social Research, University of Michigan, Ann Arbor, MI, USA

Joseph West
Sinai Urban Health Institute, Room K437, 1500 South California Avenue, Chicago, IL 60608, USA

Steven Whitman
Sinai Urban Health Institute, Room K437, 1500 South California Avenue, Chicago, IL 60608, USA

Gordon Willis
National Cancer Institute, National Institutes of Health, Bethesda, MD, USA

Shannon N. Zenk
Health Systems Science Department, College of Nursing, University of Illinois at Chicago, Chicago, IL, USA

Todd Rockwood
Division of Health Policy and Management, University of Minnesota, Minneapolis, MN, USA

Beth-Ellen Pennell
Survey Research Center, Institute for Social Research, University of Michigan Ann Arbor, Michigan, USA

Preface

Much of what we know about population health comes from quantitative health surveys. This handbook organizes and summarizes current knowledge regarding the design and conduct of health surveys into a single volume. Our goal is to provide a single reference that provides overviews of current issues and which also serves as a gateway to additional resources concerned with each topic. As such, we are hopeful that it will be useful to students, practitioners, and researchers. In the first chapter, I provide a brief overview of the evolution and development of health survey methods over the past two centuries. Subsequent chapters are divided into five sections that address sampling, measurement and field issues, surveys involving special populations, and data management and analysis.

In the section on sampling issues, Michael Battaglia provides an overview of current sampling strategies for community health surveys in Chapter 2. Ralph DiGaetano then discusses, in Chapter 3, procedures for sampling in population-based case–control studies. Approaches to sampling rare and hard-to-reach populations, an increasing focus of researchers concerned with at-risk groups, are reviewed by James Wagner and Sunghee Lee in Chapter 4.

Measurement issues are addressed across eight chapters in the next section. Three of these focus specifically on the development of health measures, including Todd Rockwood's consideration of physical health measures (in Chapter 5), Ron Kessler's and Beth-Ellen Pennell review of mental health measures (in Chapter 6), and Paul Beatty's overview of health behavior and service utilization measures (in Chapter 7). Sunghee Lee reviews commonly employed, albeit poorly understood, subjective health rating measures in Chapter 8, and Gordon Willis provides an overview of current questionnaire pretesting protocols in Chapter 9. The unique and important challenges of cross-cultural health surveys are next considered, in Chapter 10, by Brad Edwards. An important method in health surveys is the use of social network tools and analysis, a topic covered in Chapter 11 by Ben Cornwell and Emily Hoagland. An overview of new technologies becoming available for applications in health survey research is presented by Joe Murphy, Elizabeth Dean, Craig Hill and Ashley Richards in Chapter 12.

Seven chapters address topics relevant to fielding health surveys. Chapter 13, by Steve Whitman, Ami Shah, Maureen Benjamins and Joseph West address strategies for community outreach, collaboration and engagement, a topic that many fail to recognize or appreciate. The challenge of collecting health data from proxy respondents is next addressed by Joe Sakshaug in Chapter 14. Joe Saksaug,

Mary Ofstedal, Heidi Guyer and Tim Beebe provide an overview of current best practices for the collection of various types of biospecimens in Chapter 15, and Shannon Zenk, Sandy Slater and Safa Rashid present strategies for the collection of contextual information during health surveys in Chapter 16. Collection of data regarding sensitive topics is a very common issue in health survey research, and two of these topics are reviewed in handbook chapters. Joe Gforerer and Joel Kennet address measurement of substance use behaviors in Chapter 17 and Tom Smith considers measurement of sexual behavior in Chapter 18. Ethical considerations in the collection of health survey data are reviewed in Chapter 19 by Emily Anderson.

Methods for health surveys of special populations are covered in the next section. Among these are two chapters concerned with surveys of health care professionals and organizations. Chapter 20, by Jonathan VanGeest, Tim Beebe and Tim Johnson examines physician surveys, and Chapter 21, by John Loft, Joe Murphy and Craig Hill discusses surveys of health care organizations. In Chapter 22, Francis Fullam and Jonathan VanGeest review methods for surveying patient populations. Melissa Clark, Samantha Rosenthal and Ulrike Boehmer consider challenges in conducting surveys of sexual minority groups in Chapter 23, and Rooshey Hasnain and colleagues, including Carmit-Noa Shpigelman, Mike Scott, Jon Gunderson, Hadi Bargi Rangin, Ashmeet Oberoi, and Liam McKeever, address issues in surveying persons with disabilities in Chapter 24.

Chapters in the final section of the handbook are devoted to data management and analysis issues. These include Chapter 25, by Adam Carle, which is concerned with assessing the measurement quality of health survey data, and Chapter 26, in which sample weighting for health surveys is reviewed by Ken Copeland and Nadarajasundaram Ganesh. Two chapters consider strategies for merging health surveys with auxiliary data sources. In Chapter 27, Michael Davern, Marc Roemer and Wendy Thomas review the uses of administrative records for this purpose, and Jarvis Chen considers approaches to merging aggregate level information with health survey data in Chapter 28. Finally, in Chapter 29 Stanislav Kolenikov and Jeff Pitblado provide a broad overview of analysis strategies when working with complex health survey data.

With the many public health and health policy issues now being confronted worldwide, it is probably safe to say that there will be a need for health survey research far into our collective future. Health survey methodologies will undoubtedly also continue to improve in quality and rigor, and to evolve to address issues of health and public health that we cannot now anticipate. Our hope is for that research to successfully build upon the foundation of knowledge, experience, and ideas offered in this volume.

Acknowledgments

This handbook is the product of contributions from a talented and highly experienced group of 54 health survey experts. Collectively in 29 chapters, they provide insights and guidance regarding numerous key topics that are relevant to the conduct of evidence-based health survey research. It was a pleasure to work with these professionals and they have my sincere appreciation and gratitude for their contributions and support in developing this handbook. Many of them provided additional support, above and beyond the call, as reviewers of other chapters. The efforts of these and the many other colleagues who also helped review early chapter drafts are also greatly valued and appreciated. Their helpful insights and valuable recommendations improved our final product and for that, I am additionally grateful. Thank you also to my colleagues at the University of Illinois at Chicago Survey Research Laboratory. I learn from them every day and the challenges we confront in conducting our research have found their way into every corner of this volume. I would also like to thank the team at Wiley for inviting me to undertake this project, and their strong support through every stage of its development and production. It is also important to acknowledge that this volume would not exist without my earlier collaborations with Dick Warnecke and the late Seymour Sudman.

Finally, thank you to Lu for putting up with me while this handbook was being completed.

TIM JOHNSON

Chicago
October 2013

CHAPTER ONE

Origins and Development of Health Survey Methods

Timothy P. Johnson
Survey Research Laboratory, College of Urban Planning and Public Affairs, University of Illinois at Chicago, Illinois, USA

1.1 Introduction

The health survey methodologies considered in this handbook have been under continuous development for the past 150 years. The story of their emergence has been one of tools and ideas borrowed from many disciplines, such as demography, economics, medicine, nursing, psychology, public health, social work, sociology, and statistics, to address the concerns of social reformers, health care providers, community advocates, business interests, government planners, policy makers, and academic modelers. Indeed, the statistics derived from health surveys have served multiple purposes and multiple audiences. This chapter provides a brief overview of their origins and development.

1.2 Precursors of Modern Health Surveys

The first recognizable health surveys are no doubt lost to history. It is known, however, that public health problems associated with early industrialization and

Handbook of Health Survey Methods, First Edition. Edited by Timothy P. Johnson.

rapid urbanization during the nineteenth century motivated some of the earliest empirical inquiries that exhibited characteristics not greatly unlike what is now considered modern health survey research (Ackerknecht 1948, Elesh 1972, Rosen 1955). The efforts of Kay (1832) and Booth (1889–1902) to examine poverty conditions in the British cities of Manchester and London, respectively, were in fact early applications of survey methodology to address health-related problems. Booth's *Life and Labour of the People of London*, in particular, was noted for the development of poverty maps, which provided graphical representations of the geographic distribution of poverty indicators across London (Pfautz 1967). Similar efforts were conducted by Villermé (1840), who investigated health conditions among factory workers in France in his volume *Survey of the Physical and Moral Condition of Workers Employed in Cotton, Wool and Silk Factories*, and Johann Peter Frank, who conducted crude surveys of health and social conditions in several Italian provinces in 1786 (Frank 1941). The focus of these early studies on relationships among health, environment, and socioeconomic status became a recurrent and often dominant theme over subsequent decades as health survey tools continued to be developed and refined (cf. Ciocco et al. 1954, Krieger 2011, Sydenstricker 1933a).

Later poverty studies by Rowntree (1910) in York and Bowley and Burnett-Hurst (1915) in Reading and several other English cities each made independent methodological contributions. Rowntree may have been the first to employ a staff of survey interviewers to collect data. Possibly the earliest reported use of systematic random sampling was during the survey conducted in Reading by Bowley, who also included a detailed assessment of the accuracy of his findings that considered each of the sources of error now commonly recognized as part of the total survey error model. Following in the British tradition, poverty surveys, each linking adverse health events with the onset of poverty, were conducted in the U.S. cities of Buffalo in 1887 (Warner 1930), New York City in 1905 (Frankel 1906–1907), and Baltimore in 1916–1917 (Ciocco and Perrott 1957). In none of these efforts, however, were health conditions the central focus of the research but rather one of many factors crudely measured because of their perceived association with poverty and economic status.

Other nineteenth century research focused on urban sanitary conditions and their relationship to population health. One of the earliest such efforts that relied in part on empirical observations was Chadwick's (1842) *Report on the Sanitary Condition of the Labouring Population of Great Britain*, which led to new public health legislation (Rosen 1958). Sanitary research similar to Chadwick's was also undertaken by public health practitioners in the United States concerned with emerging epidemics in rapidly expanding American cities (Bulmer et al. 1991, Peterson 1983, Rosenberg 1962). Most notable were the sanitary surveys conducted in Boston by Shattuck (1850) and in New York by Griscom (1845) and subsequently in numerous other cities. Several such surveys were sponsored by the Russell Sage Foundation, which also supported other early health-related surveys in dozens of communities in the United States and Canada (Department of Surveys and Exhibits 1915). One of the more well-known and comprehensive of these was conducted in Springfield, Illinois, in 1910 (Palmer 1912, Schneider 1915). Sanitary surveys also were conducted by the U.S. Public Health Service, which was reorganized and renamed (formerly known as the *Public Health and Marine Hospital Service*) in 1912 and charged with conducting field research into human disease and public sanitation (Furman and Williams 1973). Between 1914 and 1916, a series of these surveys were conducted by the Public Health Service in rural areas across the nation (Lumsden 1918). The methodologies employed in conducting sanitary surveys were varied, involving numerous approaches to evaluating community conditions. As such, there was at best only partial overlap with what we now consider to be modern health survey research.[1] Although crude approximations by today's standards and widely criticized at the time (Elmer 1914, Schneider 1917), these efforts nonetheless demonstrated the value and importance of systematic observation for the study of health, environment, and related social conditions and contributed to dramatic improvements in public health in the United States and many other nations.

Similar to sanitary surveys in their diversity of methods and focus on action research—but more broadly framed—were the studies conducted as part of the social survey movement in the early years of the twentieth century (Burgess 1916). Covering topics such as housing, adult and child labor, immigration, economics, and criminal justice, in addition to health, these studies perhaps were most accurately described as "social inventories" of communities (Harrison 1912). As with the early sanitary surveys, a variety of practical methods in addition to, or in some cases instead of, household interviews were employed.[2] Perhaps the most well known of these was the Pittsburgh Social Survey, conducted from 1907–1908 (Greenwald and Anderson 1996). Several other important social surveys focused their investigations on specific racial or ethnic groups, including Blacks in Philadelphia (DuBois 1899) and the Polish in Buffalo (Kellogg 1912). Eaton and Harrison (1930) cataloged the vast numbers of social surveys conducted in the first several decades of the last century. Although more broad in their coverage, health remained an important topic in these social surveys; in fact, many of them employed questionnaires to collect health information from respondents. The Pittsburgh social survey, for example, reported on the costs of illness in terms of lost wages, medical bills, medications, hospitalization, and so on (Kellogg 1912), and a survey conducted of residences in the Chicago Stockyards District in 1909–1910 reported information regarding family medical expenditures (Kennedy 1914).

Possibly the first studies specifically designed to collect national health data in the United States were the decennial Censuses of 1880 and 1890, which collected household information regarding persons who were currently "sick or temporarily disabled," "blind," "deaf and dumb," "idiotic," "insane," and "maimed, chrippled [sic], bedridden, or otherwise disabled" (Department of the Interior, Census Office 1888, 1895).[3] Late in the nineteenth century, the U.S. Bureau

[1] The methodology of sanitary surveys is detailed in Horwood (1921).

[2] The methodology of early social surveys is detailed in Aronovici (1916) and Elmer (1920).

[3] Similar sickness and disability data also was collected as part of census activities in Ireland and Australia during the latter half of the nineteenth century (Collins 1951).

of Labor also collected illness data as part of economic canvassing surveys conducted in urban slum areas of four large cities: Baltimore, Chicago, New York, and Philadelphia. This *Special Investigation of the Slums of Great* Cities concluded that rates of sickness were unexpectedly low, given the "wretched conditions" in which these populations lived (Osborn 1895). The Chicago part of the field work for this study was conducted by the noted social activist Florence Kelley under the auspices of Jane Addams' Hull House. Conducting analyses of the Chicago data independently of the Bureau of Labor's official report, Kelley and colleagues developed detailed social and economic maps for slum sections of Chicago similar to Booth's earlier work in London (Holbrook 1895) and consistent with the soon-to-be-popular social survey movement discussed earlier.

1.3 The First Modern Health Surveys

Early in the twentieth century, increases in life expectancy and associated declines in mortality rates also began to render traditional vital statistics less useful for evaluating population health, leading to increased interest in developing methods for assessing population morbidity (National Center for Health Statistics 1981). Research studies for the first time focused on health topics. An early pioneer in this effort was Edward Sydenstricker of the U.S. Public Health Service, who applied survey research methodology to numerous health-related problems (Kasius 1974). An economist by training, Sydenstricker first employed the survey method to collect health information on a periodic basis from employees of cotton mills in seven South Carolina villages (Sydenstricker et al. 1918) and subsequently as part of the Hagerstown Morbidity Survey, which was conducted in Hagerstown, Maryland, in 1923 (Sydenstricker 1926). He also employed surveys as part of his investigations of the population health effects of several notable early twentieth-century events, including the 1918 flu pandemic (Frost and Sydenstricker 1919, Sydenstricker 1931) and the Great Depression (Sydenstricker 1933b). Sydenstricker's health surveys tended to be geographically limited in scope, typically restricted to data collection in a relatively small number of towns and/or cities located mostly along the eastern coast of the United States.

A series of health surveys were also conducted between 1915 and 1917 by the Metropolitan Life Insurance Company, which used its field agents to systematically collect illness information for large numbers of its policy holders in several locations, including Rochester, New York; North Carolina; Boston; Kansas City; the Chelsea neighborhood of New York City; and cities in Pennsylvania and Western Virginia (Stecker et al. 1919). A "sickness census" conducted in Framingham, Massachusetts, in 1917 copied the Metropolitan approach (Armstrong 1917). Further, the Metropolitan Life Insurance Company collaborated with the U.S. Public Health Service on a study designed to track the incidence of minor respiratory diseases via mail surveys sent to convenience samples of university students, university faculties, military medical officers, and families on a biweekly basis over an 18-month period in 1923–1924 (Townsend 1924, Townsend and Sydenstricker 1927).

Other early health surveys included morbidity studies of the "chronic sick" in New York City in 1928 (Jarrett 1933) and of cancer and other chronic diseases in Massachusetts from 1929–1931 (Bigelow and Lombard 1933); the illness surveys completed in Cattaraugus County, New York in 1929–1932 and Syracuse in 1930–1931 (Collins et al. 1955); and the chronic disease survey in the Eastern Health District of Baltimore, fielded from 1938–1943, that addressed the fundamental statistical challenges of differentiating prevalent from incident cases within a population (Downes 1950, Downes and Collins 1940). In 1943, a 20-year follow-up survey of original respondents from Sydenstricker's Morbidity Survey in Hagerstown, Maryland, was also completed (Lawrence 1948).

1.4 The Emergence of National Health Surveys

The first nationwide health survey of the general public conducted in the United States was not government supported. Rather, the *ad hoc* Committee on the Cost of Medical Care Studies, a group of physicians, public officials, and other interested parties, conducted such an effort as the culmination of a series of empirical studies designed to better inform the development of health policy. The national survey of the *Incidence of Illness and the Receipt of Medical Care Among Representative Family Groups* (Falk et al. 1933), was conducted from 1928–1931, during which more than 8000 families in 17 states were interviewed at multiple time points to collect information regarding health conditions and health care expenditures. Similar to Sydenstricker's work in Hagerstown and elsewhere, attempts to confirm respondent self-reports with treating physicians were undertaken.

Shortly thereafter, the U.S. Public Health Service, with support from the Works Project Administration (WPA) and employing staff on public relief, conducted the National Health Survey (Perrott et al. 1939, Weisz 2011), a massive effort that demonstrated the feasibility of collecting national survey data ($n = 83$ urban and 15 rural areas) from large samples of households ($n = 703{,}092$) within relatively brief time periods (i.e., the winter of 1935–1936). Findings from the National Health Survey became the primary source of data regarding the health status and health service use of the American public for the next two decades.

The earliest national survey that employed rigorous probability sampling methods in the United States was conducted in 1939 and primarily designed to estimate unemployment statistics (Frankel and Stock 1942). Shortly thereafter, the first national health survey data collected using probability methods took place when the Census Bureau's *Monthly Report on the Labor Force* was employed to construct nationwide estimates of health-related disabilities in 1943 (Sanders and Federman 1943). Similar estimates were produced by the renamed *Current Population Survey* in 1949 (Woolsey 1950).

1.5 Post-WWII Advances

As core survey methodologies continued to develop after World War II (Susser 1985), the use of these tools to meet demands for more reliable population health statistics, deemed necessary for resource allocation and policy assessment, expanded as well. A bibliography of health survey research, prepared by the Public Health Service in the early 1960s, attests to the scope and variety of health surveys having been conducted by then in the United States (U.S. Public Health Service 1962a). Some of the more notable health surveys conducted in the early post-war years include the Arsenal Health District morbidity survey in Pittsburgh in 1951 (Horvitz 1952), the chronic disease surveys in rural Hunterdon County, New Jersey, from 1952–1955 (Trussell and Elinson 1959) and in Baltimore from 1953–1955 (Commission on Chronic Illness 1957), and the 1954–1955 California Morbidity Survey (Breslow and Mooney 1956). A two-community longitudinal survey that focused on acute respiratory illnesses, rather than chronic disease, was also conducted during 1946–1949 in New York State (Downes 1950). During this period, the first community mental health surveys also were conducted in rural Nova Scotia in 1952 (Leighton et al. 1963) and New York City in 1954 (Srole et al. 1962), along with the first studies demonstrating the usefulness of surveys for the collection of information regarding sensitive topics such as sexual behavior (Kinsey et al. 1948, 1953).

In addition to interviewing the general public directly regarding their health conditions and experiences, surveys became increasing useful for collection of information from various health care providers. Physician surveys, designed to understand practice patterns and other professional behaviors, quickly became common (Ciocco and Altman 1943, Klein 1944, Palmer 1912, Sinai and Mills 1931). The first prospective evidence documenting a link between smoking and lung cancer was in fact a large survey of physicians conducted in England in the early 1950s (Doll and Hill 1954). Surveys of hospitals and other health care facilities (Carpenter 1930; Emerson 1937, Emerson et al. 1930, Jarrett 1933, Peebles 1930), and public health organizations (Schneider 1916) also became commonplace. One of the most comprehensive surveys of health care establishments and facilities was conducted in the province of Ontario, Canada, in 1948 (Mackinnon 1952). Included were all hospitals, mental treatment facilities, nursing homes, dental facilities, public health services, health-related educational facilities, voluntary organizations, organizations supporting disabled persons, and medical services provided in industrial settings. Investigations into the services being provided to patient populations and their assessments of those services also became more common (Ciocco et al. 1950).

Survey methods additionally became an important element of cohort and case–control studies (Kleinbaum et al. 1982, Schlesselman 1982, Scott 2006). Early cohort studies include the still-ongoing Framingham Study, initiated in the late 1940s and designed to examine the natural progression of atherosclerotic disease (Dawber 1980, Oppenheimer 2005). The lifestyle interviews included as part of Framingham's data collection efforts continue to yield valuable findings today (Christakis and Fowler 2008, Rosenquist et al. 2010). Other early examples include the Tecumseh (Michigan) Community Health Study, initiated in 1957 and also designed to investigate heart disease (Napier 1962) and the Alameda County Survey in California, first fielded on a large scale in 1965 (Breslow 1965). Kalton and Piesse (2007) provide an overview of population-based case–control studies that have relied on survey methods to identify and recruit control subjects. Surveys also quickly became useful tools for evaluating health education and other intervention programs (Lombard et al. 1944).

A watershed moment in the development of health survey methods took place when President Dwight Eisenhower signed legislation in 1956 creating the ongoing U.S. National Health Survey, designed to "produce statistics on disease, injury, impairment, disability, and related topics on a uniform basis for the nation as a whole" (U.S. Public Health Service 1958: 1). What is today known as the annual National Health Interview Survey (NHIS) was first fielded the following year, and the currently named National Health and Nutrition Examination Survey (NHANES) became operational in 1959 (U.S. Public Health Service 1962b). Perhaps aware of the various sources of error documented in earlier health surveys (cf. Gray 1955, Kiser 1934), the House of Representatives included language in the National Health Survey Act mandating methodological research be conducted as part of the National Health Survey in order to continually improve its operations (Haywood 1981). Thus encouraged, methodological research was both immediate (cf. Cartwright 1963, Nisselson and Woolsey 1959, Simmons and Bryant 1962, Sanders 1962) and sustained over the ensuing decades (cf. Blumberg and Luke 2013, Cannell et al. 1977, Jabine 1987). This handbook will make reference to much of this research.

1.6 Current Developments

Today, the National Center for Health Statistics, the Agency for Healthcare Research and Quality, and numerous other federal agencies in the United States sponsor a large number of ongoing national survey systems designed to monitor trends in health conditions and behaviors (Madans and Cohen 2005). Many of these are also referenced in subsequent handbook chapters. These surveys continue to develop and experiment with new innovations designed to improve and enhance the information provided. Examples include some of the first assessments of the use of telephones to collect health data (Thornberry 1987), the development of cognitive questionnaire pretesting (Fienberg et al. 1985), and the introduction of computer-assisted survey technologies (Turner et al. 1996). The National Center for Health Statistics also was an early supporter of the development of specialized computer software for variance estimation in complex sample surveys (LaVange and Shah 1988).

Nongovernmental health surveys have also expanded considerably. Suchman (1967) provides an extensive review of survey research applied to public health and medicine during the 1950s and early 1960s by a wide variety of researchers for a wide variety of purposes. Noteworthy for their impact were the nationwide health care utilization surveys conducted by the National Opinion Research

Center over several decades (Anderson and Feldman 1956, Anderson et al. 1963, Anderson and Anderson 1967, Anderson et al. 1975). Today, many academic, business, professional and philanthropic organizations support surveys concerned with population health, population policy, health care utilization, and related topics. The Commonwealth Fund, the Henry J. Kaiser Family Foundation, the Milbank Memorial Fund, and the Robert Wood Johnson Foundation, for example, each actively support broad research programs that focus on health policy issues in the United States and abroad.

Many state and local governments in the United States also now conduct or sponsor surveys to monitor local health conditions. With support from the Centers for Disease Control and Prevention, all 50 U.S. states and several U.S. territories have collected telephone survey data annually regarding health-related risk behaviors as part of the Behavioral Risk Factor Surveillance System (BRFSS) since the early 1980s (Remington et al. 1988). Another ongoing effort is the California Health Interview Survey (2009), first fielded in 2001 and conducted biennially since that time. Other states conduct comprehensive health surveys as well (cf. Nieto et al. 2010), and numerous municipalities have similar efforts. New York City, for example, undertakes a variety of health-related surveys on a regular or periodic basis, including the New York City Community Health Survey and the New York City Health and Nutrition Examination Survey (cf. Norton et al. 2012).

Health surveys in other countries have been equally impressive, with a variety of large national studies of health conditions, behaviors, and risk factors currently operational. Great Britain's first such effort, the Survey of Sickness, began data collection during World War II to examine the effects of wartime stress and pressures on the civilian population (Logan and Brooke 1957). Since 1991, the Health Survey for England has been conducted annually (Mindell et al. 2012). Approximately three dozen other nations now also conduct general and specialized health surveys on a regular basis (National Center for Health Statistics 2005).

Internationally coordinated health survey efforts are also becoming common. One of the earliest such efforts was the World Fertility Survey (WFS), managed and funded by the US Agency for International Development (USAID) with support from several other nations (Lightbourne et al. 1982). The WFS charted declines in childbearing rates across 62 nations between 1974 and 1984. USAID also supported Contraceptive Prevalence Surveys in 37 nations between 1977 and 1985, as well as the current Demographic and Health Surveys program, which has worked with more than 90 nations to conduct population-based health surveys that focus on a variety of health behaviors and outcomes (Corsi et al. 2012). Numerous international health survey programs also are supported by the World Health Organization and the United Nations. Some of the more notable of these are the World Health Survey, conducted from 2002–2004 (Üstün et al. 2003), and the World Mental Health Surveys (Kessler and Üstün 2008). The multinational surveys conducted in support of the International Tobacco Control Policy Evaluation Project are supported by numerous national and international organizations (Fong et al. 2006).

Established health surveys continue to evolve as reflections of the societies they serve. The U.S. NHIS, for example, has shifted its content emphasis, its unit of analysis, and conceptual health framework in response to shifting national priorities over its half-century of operation (Powell-Griner and Madans 2007). Ironically, many of the early surveys, including some of those conducted by the U.S. Public Health Service (Sydenstricker 1926), systematically excluded African-American and other minority population groups. They did so for a variety of reasons, including "to avoid the question of racial differences in employment, income, and sickness" (Perrott and Collins 1935: 597) and because "it was considered that the procedure adopted could not procure satisfactory information from Negro families" (Falk et al. 1933: 5). These practices, some undertaken by employees of the U.S. Public Health Service, are in retrospect a great irony given the current National Institutes of Health emphasis on racial and ethnic health disparities.

In the mid-1970s, a series of professional conferences concerned specifically with health survey research methodology were initiated in the United States, with support from a variety of public and private research organizations (Rice and Rosenthal 1977). To date, 10 such conferences have been held on a periodic basis to review and consider evolving research needs and confront new methodological challenges. An online link to the full set of proceedings from these conferences is provided at the end of this chapter. Several texts concerned specifically with health survey research methodology (Abramson and Abramson 1999, Aday and Cornelius 2006, Cartwright 1983, Cox and Cohen 1985, Witts 1959), measurement (Bowling 2001, McDowell 2006, Streiner and Norman 2008), and analysis (Anderson et al. 1979, Korn and Graubard 1999) have also been published in recent decades. This handbook is intended as a contribution to this body of knowledge, one that focuses on methodological issues that are largely unique to health survey methodology, as well as special considerations when employing common survey methodologies to the study of health-related topics.

REFERENCES

Abramson JH, Abramson ZH. *Survey Methods in Community Medicine*. 5th ed. Edinburgh, England: Churchill Livingstone; 1999.

Ackerknecht EH. Hygiene in France: 1815-1848. Bull Hist Med 1948;22:117–155.

Aday LA, Cornelius LJ. *Designing & Conducting Health Surveys: A Comprehensive Guide*. 3rd ed. San Francisco: Jossey-Bass; 2006.

Anderson OW, Collette P, Feldman JJ. *Changes in Family Medical Care Expenditures and Voluntary Health Insurance: A Five-Year Resurvey*. Cambridge, MA: Harvard University Press; 1963.

Anderson OW, Feldman JJ. *Family Medical Costs and Voluntary Health Insurance: A Nationwide Survey*. New York: McGraw-Hill; 1956.

Anderson RM. National health surveys and the behavioral model of health services use. Med Care 2008;46:647–653.

Anderson R, Anderson OW. *A Decade of Health Services: Social Survey Trends in Use and Expenditure*. Chicago: University of Chicago Press; 1967.

Anderson R, Kasper J, Frankel MR. *Total Survey Error: Applications to Improve Health Surveys*. San Francisco: Jossey-Bass; 1979.

Anderson R, Lion J, Anderson OW. *Two Decades of Health Services: Social Survey Trends in Use and Expenditure*. New York: Ballinger; 1975.

Armstrong DB. *Medical Sickness Census: Framingham Monograph 2*. Framingham, MA: Framingham Community Health and Tuberculosis Demonstration of the National Tuberculosis Association; 1917.

Aronovici C. *The Social Survey*. Philadelphia: The Harper Press; 1916.

Bigelow GH, Lombard HL. *Cancer and Other Chronic Diseases in Massachusetts*. New York: Houghton Mifflin; 1933.

Blumberg SJ, Luke JV. 2013. Wireless substitution: early release of estimates from the National Health Interview Survey, July–December 2012. National Center for Health Statistics. Available at http://www.cdc.gov/nchs/data/nhis/earlyrelease/wireless 201306.pdf. Accessed on August 2013.

Booth C. *Labour and Life of the People of London*. London: Macmillan; 1889–1902.

Bowley AL, Burnett-Hurst AR. *Livelihood and Poverty*. London: G. Bell and Sons; 1915.

Bowling A. *Measuring Disease: A Review of Disease-Specific Quality of Life Measurement Scales*. 2nd ed. Buckingham: Open University Press; 2001.

Breslow L. Alameda and Contra Costa Counties, California. Milbank Mem Fund Q 1965;43(2, Part 2: Comparability in International Epidemiology):317–325.

Breslow L, Mooney HW. The California morbidity survey: a progress report. Calif Med 1956;84:95–97.

Bulmer M, Bales K, Sklar KK. The social survey in historical perspective. In: Bulmer M, Bales K, Sklar KK, editors. *The Social Survey in Historical Perspective 1880–1940*. Cambridge: Cambridge University Press; 1991. p 1–48.

Burgess EW. The social survey: a field for constructive service by departments of sociology. Am J Sociol 1916;21:492–500.

California Health Interview Survey. 2009. CHIS 2007 methodology series: report 2 – data collection methods. Los Angeles, CA: UCLA Center for Health Policy Research. Available at http://healthpolicy.ucla.edu/chis/design/Documents/CHIS2007 _method2.pdf. Accessed on September 2013.

Cannell CF, Marquis KH, Laurent A. A summary of studies of interviewing methodology. Vital and health statistics: series 2, data evaluation and methods research, no. 69. DHEW Publication No. (HRA) 77-1343. National Center for Health Statistics. Washington, DC: U.S. Government Printing Office; 1977.

Carpenter N. *Hospital Service for Patients of Moderate Means: A Study of Certain American Hospitals*. Washington, DC: Committee on the Cost of Medical Care; 1930.

Cartwright A. Memory errors in a morbidity survey. Milbank Mem Fund Q 1963;41:5–24.

Cartwright A. *Health Surveys in Practice and in Potential: A Critical Review of their Scope and Methods*. London: King's Fund Publishing Office; 1983.

Chadwick E. Report on the sanitary condition of the labouring population of Great Britain. London: W. Clowes and Sons; 1842.

Christakis NA, Fowler J. The collective dynamics of smoking in a large social network. N Engl J Med 2008;358:2249–2258.

Ciocco A, Altman I. The patient load of physicians in private practice: a comparative statistical analysis of three areas. Public Health Rep 1943;58:1329–1351.

Ciocco A, Perrott D. Statistics on sickness as a cause of poverty: an historical review of U.S. and English data. Hist Med Allied Sci 1957;12:42–60.

Ciocco A, Densen PM, Thompson DJ. On the association between health and social problems in the population. II. The influence of medical care problems. Milbank Mem Fund Q 1954;32:247–261.

Ciocco A, Hunt GH, Altman I. Statistics on clinical services to new patients in medical groups. Public Health Rep 1950;65:99–115.

Collins SD, Trantham KS, Klehmann JL. Sickness experience in selected areas of the United States. Public Health Monograph No. 25, DHS Publication No. 390. Washington, DC: U.S. Government Printing Office; 1955.

Collins SD. Sickness surveys. pp. 511–535. In H. Emerson, editor. Administrative medicine. Edinburgh: Thomas Nelson and Sons; 1951.

Commission on Chronic Illness. *Chronic Illness in the United States, Volume IV: Chronic Illness in a Large City, The Baltimore Study*. Cambridge, Massachusetts: Harvard University Press; 1957.

Corsi DJ, Neuman M, Finlay JE, Subramanian SV. Demographic and health surveys: a profile. Int J Epidemiol 2012;41:1602–13.

Cox BG, Cohen SB. *Methodological Issues for Health Care Surveys*. New York: Marcel Dekker; 1985.

Dawber TR. *The Framingham Study: The Epidemiology of Atherosclerotic Disease*. London: Harvard University Press; 1980.

Department of the Interior, Census Office. Report on the defective, dependent, and delinquent classes of the population of the United States, as returned at the tenth census (June 1, 1880), by Frederick Howard Wines, special agent. Washington, DC: Government Printing Office; 1888.

Department of the Interior, Census Office. Report on the insane, feeble-minded, deaf and dumb, and blind in the United States at the eleventh census: 1890. Washington, DC: Government Printing Office; 1895.

Department of Surveys and Exhibits. *The Social Survey: A Bibliography*. New York: Russell Sage Foundation; 1915.

Doll R, Hill AB. The mortality of doctors in relation to their smoking habits: a preliminary report. Br Med J 1954;1(4877):1451–1455.

Downes J. Control of acute respiratory illness by ultra-violet lights. Am J Public Health 1950;40:1512–1520.

Downes J. Method of statistical analysis of chronic disease in a longitudinal study of illness. Milbank Mem Fund Q 1951;29:404–422.

Downes J, Collins SD. A study of illness among families in the Eastern Health District of Baltimore. Milbank Mem Fund Q 1940;18:5–26.

DuBois WEB. *The Philadelphia Negro: A Social Study*. Philadelphia: University of Pennsylvania; 1899.

Eaton A, Harrison SM. *A Bibliography of Social Surveys: Reports of Fact-Finding Studies Made as a Basis for Social Action; Arranged by Subjects and Localities*. New York: Russell Sage Foundation; 1930.

Elesh D. The Manchester Statistical Society: a case study of discontinuity in the history of empirical social research. In: Oberschall A, editor. *The Establishment of Empirical Sociology: Studies in Continuity, Discontinuity, and Institutionalization*. New York: Harper & Row; 1972. p 31–72.

Elmer MC. *Social Surveys of Urban Communities*. Menasha, WI: George Banat Publishing Co.; 1914.

Elmer MC. *Technique of Social Surveys* Revised Edition. Minneapolis: University Printing Co.; 1920.

Emerson H. *The Hospital Survey for New York* Volume I. New York: United Hospital Fund; 1937.

Emerson H, Pincus S, Phillips AC. *Philadelphia Hospital and Health Survey, 1929*. Philadelphia: Philadelphia Hospital and Health Survey Committee; 1930.

Falk IS, Klem MC, Sinai N. *The Incidence of Illness and the Receipt and Costs of Medical Care among Representative Families: Experiences in Twelve Consecutive Months During 1928–1931*. Chicago: University of Chicago Press; 1933.

Fienberg SE, Loftus EF, Tanur JM. Cognitive aspects of health survey methodology: an overview. Milbank Mem Fund Q 1985;63:547–564.

Fong GT, Cummings KM, Borland R, Hastings G, Hyland A, Giovino GA, Hammond D, Thompson ME. The conceptual framework of the International Tobacco Control (ITC) Policy Evaluation Project. Tob Control 2006;3(Suppl):iii3–11.

Frank JP. The people's misery: mother of diseases, an address, delivered in 1790 by Johann Peter Frank, translated from the Latin, with an Introduction by Henry E. Sigerist Bull Hist Med 1941;9:81–100.

Frankel LK. The relation between standards of living and standards of compensation. Char Comm 1906–1907;17:304–314.

Frankel LK, Stock JS. On the sample survey of unemployment. J Am Stat Assoc 1942;37:77–80.

Frost WH, Sydenstricker E. Influenza in Maryland: preliminary statistics of certain localities. Public Health Rep 1919;34:491–504.

Furman B, Williams RC. *A Profile of the U.S. Public Health Service: 1798–1948*. Bethesda, MD: National Institutes of Health; 1973.

Greenwald MW, Anderson M. *Pittsburgh Surveyed: Social Science and Social Reform in the Early Twentieth Century*. Pittsburgh: University of Pittsburgh Press; 1996.

Griscom JC. *The Sanitary Condition of the Laboring Population of New York with Suggestions for Its Improvement*. New York: Harper & Brothers; 1845.

Gray PG. The memory factor in social surveys. J Am Stat Assoc 1955;50:344–363.

Harrison SM. A social survey of a typical American city. Proc Acad Polit Sci City N Y 1912;2:18–31.

Haywood A. The National Health Survey–in the beginning. Public Health Rep 1981;96:195–199.

Holbrook AS. *Hull-House Maps and Papers: A Presentation of Nationalities and Wages in a Congested District of Chicago Together with Comments and Essays on Problems Growing Out of the Social Conditions by Residents of Hull-House, A Social Settlement*. New York: Thomas Y. Crowell & Co.; 1895.

Horvitz DG. Sampling and field procedures of the Pittsburgh Morbidity Survey. Public Health Rep 1952;67:1003–102.

Horwood MP. *Public Health Surveys: What They Are, How to Make Them, How to Use Them*. New York: John Wiley & Sons; 1921.

Jabine TB. Reporting chronic conditions in the National Health Interview Survey: a review of findings from evaluation studies and methodological test. Vital and Health Statistics. Series 2, No. 105. DHHS Pub. No. (PHS) 87-1379. Public Health Service. Washington, DC: U.S. Government Printing Office; 1987.

Jarrett MC. *Chronic Illness in New York City, Volume 1: The Problems of Chronic Illness*. New York: Columbia University Press; 1933.

Kalton G, Piesse A. Survey research methods in evaluation and case-control studies. Stat Med 2007;26:1675–1687.

Kasius RV. *The Challenge of Facts: Selected Public Health Papers of Edgar Sydenstricker*. New York: Prodist; 1974.

Kay JP. *The Moral and Physical Condition of the Working Classes Employed in the Cotton Manufacture in Manchester*. London: Ridgway; 1832.

Kellogg PU. The spread of the survey idea. Proc Acad Polit Sci City N Y 1912;2:1–12.

Kennedy JC. *A Study of Chicago's Stockyards Community. III. Wages and Family Budgets in the Chicago Stockyard's District*. Chicago: University of Chicago Press; 1914.

Kessler RC, Üstün TB. *The WHO World Mental Health Surveys: Global Perspectives on the Epidemiology of Mental Disorders*. New York: Cambridge University Press; 2008.

Kinsey AC, Pomeroy WB, Martin CE. *Sexual Behavior in the Human Male*. Philadelphia: Saunders; 1948.

Kinsey AC, Pomeroy WB, Martin CE, Gebhard PH. *Sexual Behavior in the Human Female*. Philadelphia: Saunders; 1953.

Kiser CV. Pitfalls in sampling for population study. J Am Stat Assoc 1934;29:250–256.

Klein H. Civilian dentistry in wartime. J Am Dent Assoc 1944;31:648–661.

Kleinbaum DG, Kupper LL, Morgenstern H. *Epidemiologic Research: Principles and Quantitative Methods*. New York: Van Nostrand Reinhold; 1982.

Korn EL, Graubard BI. *Analysis of Health Surveys*. New York: Wiley; 1999.

Krieger N. *Epidemiology and the People's Health: Theory and Context*. New York: Oxford University Press; 2011.

LaVange LK, Shah BB. A comprehensive software package for survey data analysis. In: *Proceedings of the Bureau of the Census Fourth Annual Research Conference*. Washington, DC: US Department of Commerce; 1988. p 327–336.

Lawrence PS. An estimate of the incidence of chronic disease. Public Health Rep 1948;63:69–82.

Leighton DC, Harding JS, Macklin DB, Hughes CC, Leighton AH. Psychiatric findings of the Stirling County Study. Am J Psych 1963;119:1021–1026.

Lightbourne R, Singh S, Green CP. The World Fertility Survey: charting global childbearing. Popul Bull 1982;37:1–55.

Logan WPD, Brooke EM. The survey of sickness 1943 to 1952. General Register Office Studies in Medical and Population Subjects No. 12. London: HMSO; 1957.

Lombard HL, Tully MR, Potter EA. Evaluation of the cancer educational program in Massachusetts. Hum Biol 1944;16:115–125.

Lumsden LL. Rural sanitation: a report on special studies made in 15 Counties in 1914, 1915, and 1916. Public Health Bulletin No. 94. Washington, DC: Government Printing Office; 1918.

McDowell I. *Measuring Health: A Guide to Rating Scales and Questionnaires*. 3rd ed. Oxford: Oxford University Press; 2006.

Mackinnon P. Report of the Ontario Health Survey Committee, volumes I, II, and III. Toronto: Ontario Ministry of Health; 1952.

Madans JH, Cohen SB. Health surveys: a resource to inform health policy and practice. In: Friedman DJ, Hunter EL, Parrish RG, editors. *Health Statistics: Shaping Policy and Practice to Improve the Population's Health*. Oxford: Oxford University Press; 2005. p 119–128.

Mindell J, Biddulph JP, Hirani V, Stamatakis E, Craig R, Nunn S, Shelton N. Cohort profile: the health survey for England. Int J Epidemiol 2012;41:1585–1593.

Napier JA. Field methods and response rates in the Tecumseh Community Health Survey. Am J Public Health 1962;52:207–216.

National Center for Health Statistics. 1981. Improving the health and nutrition examination survey: an evaluation by a panel of the National Academy of Public Administration. Washington, DC: U.S. Government Printing Office. Available at http://www.cdc.gov/nchs/data/nhanes/nhanesii/improve.pdf. Accessed on 23-June 2013.

National Center for Health Statistics. 2005. International health data reference guide: 2003. DHHS Publication No. (PHS) 2005–1007. Hyattsville, MD: NCHS. Available at http://www.cdc.gov/nchs/data/misc/ihdrg2003.pdf. Accessed on 23-June 2013.

Nieto FJ, Peppard PE, Engelman CD, McElroy JA, Galvao LW, Friedman EM, Bersch AJ, Malecki KC. The survey of the Health of Wisconsin (SHOW), a novel infrastructure for population health research: rationale and methods. BMC Public Health 2010;10:785.

Nisselson H, Woolsey TD. Some problems of the household interview design for the National Health Survey. J Am Stat Assoc 1959;54:69–87.

Norton JM, Sanderson M, Gupta L, Holder-Hayes E, Immerwahr S, Konty K, Olson C, Eisenhower D. 2012. Methodology updates to the New York City Community Health Survey. New York City Department of Health and Mental Hygiene: Epi Research Report, September 2012; 1–12. Available at http://www.nyc.gov/html/doh/downloads/pdf/epi/epiresearch-chsmethods.pdf. Accessed on March 2013.

Oppenheimer GM. Becoming the Framingham study 1947-1950. Am J Public Health 2005;95:602–610.

Osborn C. The slums of great cities. Roy Econ Soc 1895;5:474–476.

Palmer GT. A sanitary and health survey. Proc Acad Polit Sci City N Y 1912;2:32–50.

Peebles A. *A Survey of the Medical Facilities of Shelby County, Indiana: 1929*. Washington, D.C.: Committee on the Cost of Medical Care; 1930.

Perrott GSJ, Collins SD. Relation of sickness to income and income change in 10 surveyed communities. Public Health Rep 1935;50:595–622.

Perrott GSJ, Tibbitts C, Britten RH. The National Health Survey: scope and method of the nation-wide canvass of sickness in relation to its social and economic setting. Public Health Rep 1939;54:1663–1687.

Peterson JA. The impact of sanitary reform upon American urban planning, 1840-1890. In: Krueckeberg DA, editor. *Introduction to Planning History in the United States*. New Brunswick, NJ: Rutgers University Press; 1983. p 13–39.

Pfautz HW. *Charles Booth On the City: Physical Pattern and Social Structure*. Chicago: University of Chicago Press; 1967.

Powell-Griner E, Madans J. History of the National Health Interview survey. Proc Am Stat Assoc Section on Health Policy Statistics 2007:1519–1522.

Remington PL, Smith MY, Williamson DF, Anda RF, Gentry EM, Hogelin GC. Design, characteristics, and usefulness of state-based behavioral risk factor surveillance: 1981–87. Public Health Rep 1988;103:366–375.

Rice DP, Rosenthal G. Advances in health survey research methods: Proceedings of a National Invitational Conference. DHEW Publication No. (HRA) 77-3154. Washington, DC: U.S. Government Printing Office; 1977.

Rosen G. Problems in the application of statistical analysis to questions of health: 1700–1880. Bull Hist Med 1955;30:27–45.

Rosen G. *A History of Public Health*. Baltimore: The Johns Hopkins University Press; 1958.

Rosenberg CE. *The Cholera Years: The United States in 1832, 1849 and 1866*. Chicago: University of Chicago Press; 1962.

Rosenquist JN, Fowler JH, Murabito J, Christakis NA. The spread of alcohol consumption behavior in a large social network. Ann Intern Med 2010;152:426–433.

Rowntree BS. *Poverty: A Study of Town Life*. London: Macmillan; 1910.

Sanders BS. Have morbidity surveys been oversold? Am J Public Health 1962;52: 1648–1659.

Sanders BS, Federman D. The prevalence of disability recorded through four monthly sample surveys. Soc Secur Bull 1943;6(8):5.

Schlesselman JJ. *Case-Control Studies: Design, Conduct, Analysis*. New York: Oxford University Press; 1982.

Schneider F. *Public Health in Springfield, Illinois*. New York: Russell Sage Foundation; 1915.

Schneider F. A survey of the activities of municipal health departments in the United States. Am J Public Health 1916;6:1–17.

Schneider F. Some shortcomings of socio-sanitary investigations. Am J Public Health 1917;7:3–13.

Scott A. Population-based case control studies. Survey Methodol 2006;32:123–132.

Shattuck L. *Report of a General Plan for the Promotion of Public and Personal Health, Devised, Prepared, and Recommended by the Commissioners Appointed under a Resolve of the Legislature of the State*. Boston: Dutton & Wentworth; 1850.

Simmons WR, Bryant EE. An evaluation of hospitalization data from the Health Interview Survey. Am J Public Health 1962;52:1638–1647.

Sinai N, Mills AB. *A Study of Physicians and Dentists in Detroit: 1929*. Washington, DC: Committee on the Cost of Medical Care; 1931.

Srole L, Langer TS, Michael ST, Kirkpatrick P, Opier M, Rennie TAC. *Mental Health in the Metropolis: The Midtown Manhattan Study*. New York: McGraw-Hill; 1962.

Stecker ML, Frankel LK, Dublin LI. *Some Recent Morbidity Data: A Summary of Seven Community Sickness Surveys Made Among Policyholders of the Metropolitan Life Insurance Company, 1915 to 1917*. New York: Metropolitan Life Insurance Company; 1919.

Streiner DL, Norman GR. *Health Measurement Scales: A Practical Guide to their Development and Use*. 4th ed. Oxford: Oxford University Press; 2008.

Suchman EA. The survey method applied to public health and medicine. In: Glock CY, editor. *Survey Research in the Social Sciences*. New York: Russell Sage Foundation; 1967. p 423–519.

Susser M. Epidemiology in the United States after World War II: the evolution of a technique. Epidemiol Rev 1985;7:147–177.

Sydenstricker E. A study of illness in a general population group, Hagerstown morbidity studies, No. 1: the method of study and general results. Public Health Rep 1926;41:2069–2088.

Sydenstricker E. The incidence of influenza among persons of different economic status during the epidemic of 1918. Public Health Rep 1931;46:154–170.

Sydenstricker E. *Health and Environment*. New York: McGraw-Hill; 1933a.

Sydenstricker E. Sickness and the economic depression. Public Health Rep 1933b;48: 1251–1264.

Sydenstricker G, Wheeler GA, Goldberger J. Disabling sickness among the population of seven cotton mill villages of South Carolina in relation to family income. Public Health Rep 1918;33:2038–2051.

Thornberry OT. An experimental comparison of telephone and personal health interview surveys. DHHS Publication No. (PHS) 87-1380. Hyattsville, MD: National Center for Health Statistics; 1987.

Townsend JG. Epidemiological study of the minor respiratory diseases by the public health service. Public Health Rep 1924;43:2669–2680.

Townsend JG, Sydenstricker E. Epidemiological study of minor respiratory diseases. Public Health Rep 1927;42:99–122.

Trussell RE, Elinson J. *Chronic Illness in the United States, Volume III: Chronic Illness in a Rural Area, The Hunterdon Study*. Cambridge, Massachusetts: Harvard University Press; 1959.

Turner CF, Ku L, Sonenstein FL, Pleck JH. Impact of audio-CASI on bias in reporting male-male sexual contacts. In: Warnecke R, editor. *Health Survey Research Methods Conference Proceedings*DHHS Publication No. (PHS) 96-1013. Hyattsville, MD: National Center for Health Statistics; 1996. p 171–176.

U.S. Public Health Service. Origin and program of the U.S. National Health Survey. Public Health Service Publication No. 584-A1. Washington, DC: U.S. Government Printing Office; 1958.

U.S. Public Health Service. Plan and initial program of the health examination survey. Public Health Service Publication No. 584-A4. Washington, DC: U.S. Government Printing Office; 1962a.

U.S. Public Health Service. Health studies of human populations: a selected bibliography. Public Health Bibliography Series No. 38. Washington, DC: U.S. Government Printing Office; 1962b.

Üstün TB, Mechbal A, Murray CJL. The world health surveys. In: Murray CJL, Evans DB, editors. *Health Systems Performance Assessment: Debates, Methods and Empiricism*. Geneva: World Health Organisation; 2003. p 762–796.

Villermé LR. *Tableau de l'état Physique et Moral Dans Ouvriers Employés dans les Manufactures de Coton, de Laine et de Soie*. Paris: Renouard; 1840.

Warner AG. *American Charities and Social Work*. Fourth ed. New York: Thomas Y. Crowell Co.; 1930.

Weisz G. Epidemiology and health care reform: the National Health Survey of 1935–1936. Am J Public Health 2011;101:438–447.

Witts LJ. *Medical Surveys and Clinical Trials: Some Methods and Applications of Group Research in Medicine*. London: Oxford University Press; 1959.

Woolsey TD. Estimates of disabling illness prevalence in the United States: based on the February 1949 Current Population Survey. Public Health Rep 1950;65:163–184.

ONLINE RESOURCES

Proceedings from the first ten conferences on Health Survey Research Methods, dating back to 1975, are available at: www.srl.uic.edu/links/proceedings.html.

PART ONE

Design and Sampling Issues

CHAPTER TWO

Sampling For Community Health Surveys

Michael P. Battaglia
Battaglia Consulting Group, LLC., Arlington, MA, USA

2.1 Introduction

The geographic scope of community health surveys includes states (e.g., the Behavioral Risk Factor Surveillance System), counties, substate regions, cities, and local areas such as neighborhoods (e.g., the New York City Community Health Survey). The populations of interest include households, adults age 18 years and older residing in households, and children age 0–17 years residing in households. The term *general population surveys* is used to describe surveys of these populations. *Subpopulations* or subgroups of interest include households with specific characteristics, and adults and children with specific characteristics. Examples of subpopulations include households below the poverty level, female adults, adults with diabetes, children living in single-parent households, and children without health insurance.

Community health surveys may collect information regarding household characteristics, information on all adults and/or children in the household, or from a sample of one or more adults and/or children in the household. In terms of the structure of the household population, adults and children are nested within households. Therefore, most sample designs for adults and children first select a sample of households and then sample one adult and/or one child residing in the selected households.

Handbook of Health Survey Methods, First Edition. Edited by Timothy P. Johnson.

Sampling procedures for selecting a sample of households are discussed in this chapter. The sampling procedures include *area probability samples*, *random-digit-dialing*, and *address-based* approaches. For each sampling approach, the potential modes of data collection (in-person, telephone, mail, and web) are discussed. *Within-household sampling* procedures for selecting adults and children are also presented. Sampling techniques that are appropriate for subpopulation surveys are illustrated. Differences between sample designs for state versus local surveys are also pointed out.

2.2 Background

Gathering information from all households, adults, and/or children in a population (e.g., within a county) would take a considerable effort in terms of cost and time. At a basic level, a sample is a subset of the entire population. The primary objective of virtually all samples is to be representative of the population. In other words, one seeks to draw inferences from the sample to the entire population. *Probability sampling* is considered the best way to ensure that such inferences can be made (Kish 1965, Yeager et al. 2011). The concepts behind probability sampling underlie statistical theory (Cochran 1977). Probability sampling uses a randomization mechanism to give each member of the population of interest (referred to as the *target population*) a known nonzero probability of selection (Kish 1965). Probability sampling involves the concept of coverage of the target population in the sense that the survey researcher would like all households in the geographic area of interest to have a chance of falling into the selected sample. Population means, proportions, and totals can be estimated from a probability sample and the sampling variability of these estimates as measured by the *standard error* can be calculated directly from the sample (Kish 1965, Cochran 1977).

Returning to the concept of drawing a probability sample of households from a geographic area, we want to give all or almost all households in that area a known nonzero probability of selection using an appropriate probability sampling technique. A cost-efficient method developed for sampling households involves area probability sampling, which serves to cluster households in relatively small areas such as blocks or groups of blocks. This technique is almost always associated with in-person interviewing. It recognizes that no complete list (referred to as a *sampling frame*) of households will typically exist in a geographic area and therefore a *multistage sampling* approach is needed to select a probability sample of households (Kish 1965). Area probability sampling has undergone major changes in recent years with the use of the U.S. Postal Service *Computerized Delivery Sequence File* (CDSF; Iannacchione 2011). The CDSF is basically a list sampling frame of residential delivery point addresses and provides very high coverage of all households in the United States (Iannacchione et al. 2003).

In the 1970s, the concept of conducting household surveys by telephone came into use and the number of telephone surveys greatly expanded because they were less costly and took less time to conduct than in-person surveys (Groves and Kahn 1979). Because no sampling frame of all residential telephone numbers in a geographic area existed, a sampling technique referred to as *list-assisted random-digit-dialing* (RDD) was developed to yield a probability sample of residential telephone numbers (Tucker et al. 2002). This sampling method yields a probability sample of residential landline telephone numbers. Only households without telephone service were excluded from this sampling frame. In 2011, around 2% of households in the United States did not have telephone service (see Figure 2.1). Starting with the beginning of the twenty-first century, personal telecommunications underwent a revolution in the United States. The widespread introduction of cellular telephone service has led more and more households to only have cellular telephone service (Blumberg et al. 2012a). As shown in Figure 2.1, around 32% of adults in the United States lived in households that only have cellular telephone service in 2011. This proportion will almost certainly continue to increase.

In some local geographic areas considerably more than 32% of adults and children lived in cell-only households in 2011. For example, in Arkansas more than 55% of children lived in cell-only households in 2011 (Blumberg et al. 2012b). Cell-only households and adults living in cell-only households are excluded from landline telephone samples. These adults have differing characteristics from adults living in households with landline telephone service (e.g., cell-only adults are more likely to be young adults, to rent rather than own, and to have lower educational attainment). Therefore, in recent years, telephone sampling for community health surveys has undergone a major modification

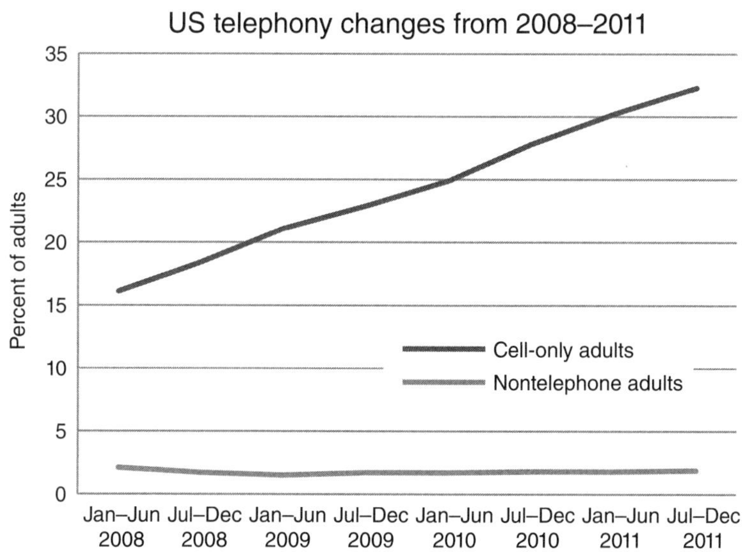

FIGURE 2.1 Percent of adults living in cell-only (wireless only) households and non-telephone households according to the National Health Interview Survey.

commonly referred to as *dual-frame sampling* in an effort to include cell-only households and adults in surveys conducted by telephone (Brick et al. 2011a).

There is a considerable literature on conducting mail surveys with list sampling frames (Dillman 1978). This includes members of organizations such as employees at a company, households receiving a specific type of benefit such as the Supplemental Nutrition Assistance Program (SNAP) children enrolled in a school district, and so on. Mail surveys were rarely used for general population surveys because no complete sampling frame of household addresses within a geographic area existed. The availability of the U.S. Postal Service CDSF has led to an increased use of mail surveys of households, and has led to an even more wide spread use of *multimodality* surveys (Link and Lai 2011). Multimodality surveys use a combination of two or more modes of data collection such as telephone and mail or telephone, mail and web, and so on (Dillman 2000).

In Section 2.3, we provide examples of all of these sampling techniques and discuss their strengths and limitations. Probability sampling is a specialized field of statistics and therefore before embarking on the conduct of a community health survey, the health researcher should give strong consideration to consulting with a sampling statistician who has experience designing samples for local area surveys.

2.3 Theory and Applications

2.3.1 AREA PROBABILITY SAMPLING

Consider a health survey to be conducted using in-person interviewing. The geographic area might be a state, county, city, or neighborhood area. Even though the CDSF address lists from the U.S. Post Office may provide very high coverage of a local area, drawing a simple random sample of housing units from that list would result in a sample of housing units that are geographically dispersed. The cost of sending interviewers to these dispersed housing units would be very costly because multiple attempts are made at most sample housing units in an effort to complete the interview. To address this problem multistage sampling (also referred to as *cluster sampling*) is widely used (Kish 1965). In multistage sampling, one samples housing units at the final stage of sampling. Starting with two-stage sampling, one might first draw a sample of census blocks. Within each sample census block, one then draws a sample of housing units. Because the sample housing units are clustered within blocks, the cost of making multiple attempts on the sample housing units is lower because travel time between sample housing units is reduced. Using three-stage sampling as an example, one might first sample counties in a state. At the second stage of sampling, one might sample census blocks. At the third and final stages of sampling, one would sample housing units within blocks. At the state level, the clustering of census blocks within sample counties reduces interviewer travel costs between census blocks. Figure 2.2 shows an example of how census blocks are nested with census tracts in a section of Cambridge, Massachusetts.

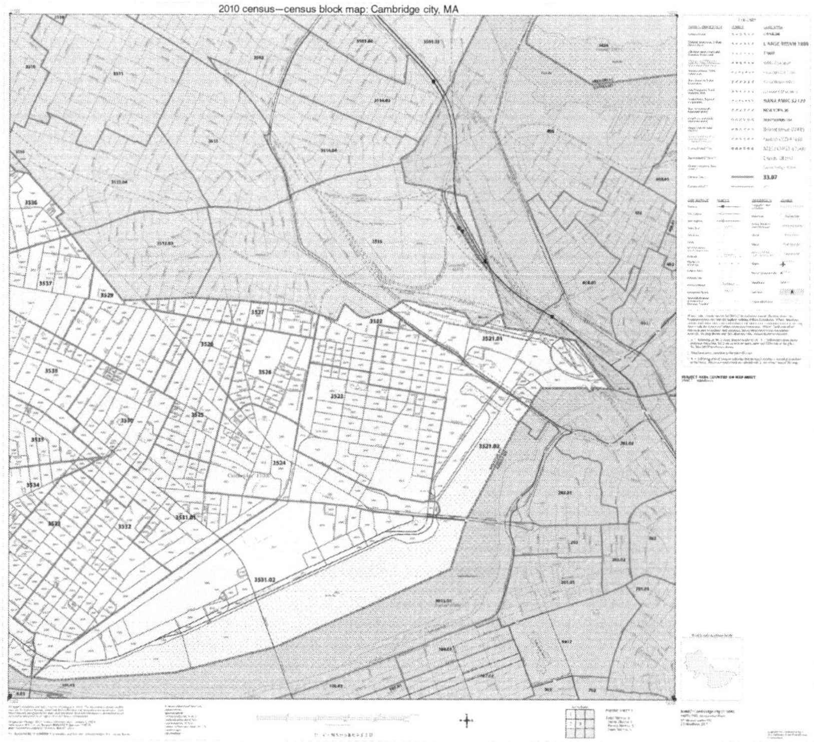

FIGURE 2.2 Census blocks in Cambridge, Massachusetts.

Before the first-stage sampling units are selected, one typically needs to stratify the first-stage units on one or more variables. This stratification helps ensure a representative sample and lowers the sampling variability of the estimates. The actual sampling of the first-stage units is almost always carried out using a technique called *probability proportional to size* (PPS) sampling (Kish 1965). Rather than giving each first-stage unit an equal probability of selection, PPS sampling makes the probability of selection proportional to the measure of size (MOS). The MOS is generally the most recent decennial census count of housing units in the first-stage sampling units. Using two-stage sampling as an example, we would obtain the 2010 Census count of housing units in each census block in the geographic area of interest. After stratification of the blocks, a PPS sample of census blocks is drawn. Then, within each sample block an equal *expected* sample size (also called the *cluster size*) of housing units is drawn. For example, we might set the expected sample size of housing units to 6. So, the expected sample size is 6 housing units from a census block containing 20 housing units and also 6 housing units from a census block containing 50 housing units. Because census blocks were selected using PPS sampling the overall selection probability of a housing unit in the geographic area is a constant for all housing units. It is referred to as a *self-weighting sample of housing units*. The same holds true for a three-stage sample in which the first and second stage sampling units are selected using PPS sampling and the expected sample size of housing units is set to the same value (say six) for each second stage sampling unit (Kish 1965). The term *expected cluster size* is used above because the MOS will not always be accurate. For example, a census block in 2012 might contain 150 housing units compared to the 2010 Census count of 100 housing units due to new construction. In our example above, the *actual* cluster size in such a block would be greater than six housing units.

In our discussion of multistage sampling, one can reduce the cost of the survey by sampling a large number of housing units (say 20) from each census block. There is however a penalty to pay in terms of the larger sample size of housing units per census block increasing the sampling variability of the estimates. Using information from other surveys, a sampling statistician can often estimate this increase in sampling variability relative to a simple random sample, called the *design effect*, and develop a design that attempts to reduce costs without incurring a large design effect and therefore a large increase in sampling variability (Lohr 2010). For example, a design effect of 2.0 means that a sample of 2000 completed interviews has an *effective* sample size of 1000 completed interviews.

The expected sample size of housing units to select from each census block needs to take into account three factors: (i) the desired number of interviews, (ii) the response rate, and (iii) the housing unit vacancy rate.

At the final stage of sampling, one needs to draw a sample of housing units from the selected census blocks. The original approach involved sending specially trained listing staff to the census blocks and have them create a list of housing units for each selected census block. A sample of housing units was then drawn from the list created for each census block. The U.S. Postal Service CDSF has by and large replaced the listing process (Iannacchione et al. 2003). The CDSF is a list of residential delivery points. One can obtain a list of residential delivery points for each sample census block. Most of the addresses in the CDSF are city-style addresses (e.g., 24 Waverly Street or 57 Smith Road, Apartment 1A). There are however some exceptions that cause the CDSF to not offer 100% coverage of the target population. One example would be a newly constructed housing unit that is occupied but has not yet made it into the CDSF. Another example is a housing unit that has mail delivery to a PO Box. When using the CDSF as a housing unit sampling frame for a sample of census blocks one needs to use an appropriate "missed housing unit" technique to give housing units that are not included in the CDSF a chance of entering the sample (McMichael et al. 2008).

In area probability sampling, a within-household sampling technique may be used to randomly select one adult from among all adults living in the household. For households containing one or more children, it is also possible to randomly select a child. The original technique for sampling one adult from the household is known as the *Kish method* (Kish 1949). Graziano (2005) describes all of the techniques in use for selecting one adult from the household. Some surveys attempt to interview all adults in the household or identify a knowledgeable household member who can report on all adults in the household. This approach can result in a larger sample size of adults compared to the sampling of one adult per household, however, if the adults in a household tend to be similar in terms of the key survey questions the *effective* sample size of adults will be less than the actual number of adult interviews. There are also methodological issues that arise when one attempts to interview more than one adult in a household. Most health surveys therefore interview one adult per household.

Most area probability sample designs use in-person interviewing. Other techniques include providing a cell phone to the selected adult that they use to call into the survey research organization's telephone center. One can also provide a uniform resource locator (URL) and log in information to the selected adult for completion of the survey on a secure website.

2.3.2 RANDOM-DIGIT-DIALING

Telephone sampling offers an approach for covering all households with telephone service. There is no complete list of households with telephone service and therefore we must sample telephone numbers and identify those numbers that are residential. Furthermore, we cannot limit our sample to landline telephone numbers, because about 32% of adults in the United States only have cellular telephone service (Blumberg et al. 2012a). To cover households with landline telephone service and households that only have cellular telephone service we must resort to a dual frame sample design.

The sampling of landline telephone numbers using the sampling technique known as *list-assisted random-digit-dialing* has been available for several decades (Tucker et al. 2002). The first step in selecting a list-assisted RDD sample is to identify the landline telephone exchanges (area code—central office code combinations, e.g., 617-492) covering the geographic area of interest. A list of these telephone exchanges is assembled and each telephone exchange is then divided into 100 banks of 100 consecutive telephone numbers:

- 617-492-0000 to 617-492-0099
- 617-492-0100 to 617-492-0199
- 617-492-9900 to 617-492-9999

Using a database of directory-listed residential telephone numbers, we determine the count of listed numbers in each 100 bank. A 100 bank can have anywhere from zero to 100 listed numbers. The banks with zero listed numbers are removed from the sampling frame. The list-assisted sampling frame therefore consists of 100 banks containing one or more listed numbers. These are referred to as the *1+ listed banks*. A simple random sample of complete 10-digit telephone numbers is then drawn from the list-assisted sampling frame for the geographic area of interest. The sample of telephone numbers must be dialed by interviewers to identify the numbers that are residential. In other words, the sample will contain business numbers and unassigned (nonworking) numbers in addition to residential telephone numbers.

The landline list-assisted sample can be used to cover households with landline telephone service. Over 50% of landline households in the United States have one or more working residential cellular telephone numbers, but these dual-service households can be sampled from the landline list-assisted sampling frame. The 32% of households in the United States that only have cellular telephone service are however excluded from the sample. In a nonoverlapping dual frame sample design cell-only households are included in the sample design by sampling from a second sampling frame. That sampling frame consists of dedicated cellular telephone exchange 1000 banks (e.g., 617-417-1000 to 617-417-1999).

For state surveys and for some county and city geographic areas such as Los Angeles County and New York City, it is relatively straightforward to identify the cellular 1000 banks to include in the sampling frame. But, in general, for most county, city, and neighborhood geographic areas, it is difficult to identify specific 1000 banks that cover the geographic area of interest. This is an area of ongoing research with sampling vendors developing different techniques to allow the sample design to identify 1000 banks that potentially overlap with the geographic area of interest. For example, recent research has focused on the construction of cellular sampling frames for local areas based on wire centers, rate centers, and the identification of cellular telephone number billing ZIP Codes (Marketing Systems Group 2012a, 2012b). Regardless of the method used to identify the 1000 banks to include in the sampling frame, during the screening part of the survey one needs to determine if the household is actually located in the geographic area of interest. Landline telephone exchanges, on the other hand, can be assigned to counties and cities and even to neighborhood areas but the match will not be perfect (i.e., some residential telephone numbers will not be located in the neighborhood area). It is therefore also necessary in the screening part of the survey to determine if the household is actually located in the geographic area of interest.

As discussed earlier, our objective is to cover households that only have cellular telephone service. The sample of 10-digit cellular telephone numbers drawn from the sampling frame of 1000 banks must therefore be screened to identify the households that only have cellular telephone service. The landline sample covers landline-only households and dual-service households, while the cell phone screening sample provides coverage of cell-only households. There is no overlap between the two samples, and estimation methods of a two-stratum sample design can be applied. Often the calculation of weights for the respondents involves poststratification of the respondents to control totals for variables such as age, gender, race/ethnicity, education, and so on. For a dual-frame design, the type of telephone service is often also used as a poststratification variable (Brick et al. 2011a). This variable has three categories: (i) landline service only, (ii) cellular telephone service only, and (iii) dual service. Control totals for national surveys can be obtained from the National Health Interview Survey. State-level control totals and control totals for some of the larger counties can also be obtained from the National Health Interview Survey (Blumberg et al. 2012b).

If a sample of adults is being surveyed, one can randomly select one adult from each landline sample household. Most adults use their cell phone as a personal communication device; so in general, adults are linked to their cell phone telephone number and no respondent selection takes place. If one is conducting a survey that collects information on the household from a knowledgeable adult or say on all children in the household, then the selection probability of the household or of each child in the household is a function of the number of landline telephone numbers and the number of adult cell phone telephone numbers associated with the household. This information is not available in the sampling frame and therefore must be determined during the survey.

Today, most dual-frame designs use an overlapping design (Brick et al. 2011a). In the cell phone sample, all adults are included in the survey including those residing in dual-service households. This is referred to as an *overlapping dual-frame design* because dual-service adults are sampled from the landline sample and from the cell phone sample. In many situations, there are advantages to conducting an overlapping dual-frame design. For example, if the cost of conducting a cell phone interview is only somewhat more expensive than the cost of conducting a landline interview, one can consider interviewing dual-service adults in the cell phone sample. Another situation favoring an overlapping dual-frame sample design occurs when dual-service adults who primarily use their cell phone are difficult to reach in a landline sample. The weighting procedures for an overlapping dual-frame sample design are more complex compared to just including cell-only adults from the cell phone sample.

Random-digit-dialing samples have primarily been used to conduct telephone surveys. In some situations the RDD sample is used to make contact with a sample of households for the placement of a diary, for example, to record household food purchases over a fixed time period. For some health surveys that collect information from adults or children on health conditions, a mail questionnaire is sent to persons with a specific health condition in order to collect more detailed information on that health condition.

2.3.3 ADDRESS-BASED SAMPLING

The use of address-based sampling (ABS) for household surveys is a relatively new phenomenon (Link et al. 2006, Link et al. 2008). The initial research related to ABS was based on conducting household surveys using mail questionnaires. As discussed earlier, ABS relies on the CDSF to yield a sampling frame of residential addresses. One can therefore draw a stratified sample of addresses from a geographic area including very small areas such as census tracts. The CDSF classifies addresses as city-style, drop points, PO boxes, throwbacks, vacant, or seasonal. Most addresses in the United States are standard city-style addresses (e.g., 237 Oak Street). Because we are conducting a mail survey, we can include all of the above-mentioned address types in the sampling frame, although seasonal units are often removed from the frame. In some large cities, drop points may account for a significant proportion of the residential addresses. These are typically multi-unit buildings where mail is delivered by the U.S. Postal Service to the building but unit numbers (e.g., apartment numbers) are not included in the CDSF because the mail is distributed internally within the building (Iannacchione 2011).

For a household survey, the questionnaire can be mailed to a sample of residential addresses with instructions for a knowledgeable adult to fill out the questionnaire. Many surveys, however, seek to collect information from a sample of adults. It has proven difficult to provide random respondent instructions to the person opening the mail (Battaglia et al. 2008). The person opening the mail may not understand the directions for randomly selecting one adult or may decide not to follow the instructions. This is in stark contrast to in-person and telephone surveys where the random selection of one adult from the household is a well-established part of the sample design. One approach to dealing with the difficulty of respondent selection in a mail survey is to conduct the survey in two phases (Montaquila and Brick 2012). In the first phase, a brief questionnaire is mailed to the sample addresses with a request to provide a listing of the adults in the household. For each returned questionnaire, one adult is randomly selected and the detailed questionnaire is then mailed directly to that person. The two phases of data collection may result in a lower response rate because there will be nonresponse at each of the two phases. Mail surveys are limited in terms of their length and the need to avoid complex skip patterns in the questionnaire.

Many ABS surveys therefore rely on multimodality data collection (Link and Lai 2011). The most common multimodality designs currently in use include the following:

- Match the ABS sample addresses against a database of directory-listed residential numbers. For the matched addresses, conduct the survey by telephone. For the unmatched addresses, send the household a mail questionnaire.
- Match the ABS sample addresses against a data base of directory-listed residential numbers. For the matched addresses, conduct the survey by telephone. For the unmatched addresses, send the household a letter with an invitation to go to a website URL and fill out the questionnaire.
- Match the ABS sample addresses against a data base of directory-listed residential numbers. For the matched addresses, conduct the survey by telephone. For the unmatched addresses, send a one-page questionnaire with the primary purpose of obtaining a telephone number for the household. For the questionnaires that are returned, conduct the survey by telephone.

ABS is still in the early stages of development as a method for sampling households and/or adults. For surveys considering the use of ABS, a sampling statistician who is familiar with ABS should be consulted.

2.4 Subpopulation Surveys

A subpopulation is a subgroup of the overall population (Kish 1965, Brick et al. 2011b). Examples include households below the poverty level, Asian adults, and children participating in the Women, Infants, and Children (WIC) program. Subpopulations are almost always not preidentified in the sampling frame. For example, a complete list of Asian adults in a geographic area does not exist. One approach that can be used to select a sample of a subpopulation with area probability sampling, random-digit-dialing, and ABS is called a *screening sample design*. In this approach, we first estimate the percent of households in the geographic area that are expected to be eligible (i.e., member of the subpopulation). We then draw a sample large enough to achieve the desired number of interviews with subpopulation members. For example, if 50% of the households are expected to be in the subpopulation or contain one of more persons who belong to the subpopulation, then we need to double our sample size compared to a sample design in which all households are eligible for the survey.

In other situations, we can stratify the sample and reduce the number of households that must be sampled in order to achieve the desired number of interviews with members of the subpopulation (Kalton and Anderson 1986). Stratification is easiest to apply in area probability sampling and ABS. For example, we can use data from the American Community Survey or the 2010 Census to divide a geographic area into neighborhoods (subareas) that differ with respect to, for example, the percent of households below poverty. Table 2.1 shows a hypothetical example of a city divided into three subareas based on the 2010 Census. Stratum A accounts for 40% of the households below poverty in the geographic area. Within stratum A, 50% of households are below poverty. We can take advantage of this concentration of the population by oversampling this stratum relative to the other two strata (Cochran 1977). Oversampling involves allocating a higher percent of the sample to one or more of the strata. For example, we might allocate more than 40% of the sample to stratum A.

If the subpopulation is not concentrated within any of the strata, then oversampling is not appropriate (Kish 1965). Consider the stratification in Table 2.2 where we have divided the geographic area into three subareas based on the percent of the adult population that is Asian. Within stratum A, 70% of adults are Asian so it is tempting to oversample this stratum. However, stratum A only accounts for 15% of the total Asian population and so oversampling this stratum will in most situations lead to high sampling variances due to unequal sampling weights needed to compensate for the undersampling of 85% of the Asian population not located in stratum A.

Stratification can be used with random-digit-dialing but it is less effective because landline telephone exchanges will not cleanly map into local geographic

TABLE 2.1 **A Three-Stratum Design for Households Below Poverty**

Neighborhood	Percent of Total Households Below Poverty	Percent of Households in Stratum Below Poverty
A	40	50
B	50	15
C	10	5

TABLE 2.2 A Three-Stratum Design for Asian Adults

Neighborhood	Percent of Total Adults Who are Asian	Percent of Adults in Stratum Who are Asian
A	15	70
B	40	10
C	45	5

areas. As discussed above, this is even truer for cellular telephone exchanges. For RDD designs, it is often more practical to use the screening sample design approach discussed earlier.

2.5 Sample Size Considerations

One of the first questions directed to sampling statisticians is: "What sample size do I need?" There are two aspects to sample size determination: (i) the size of the sample to be drawn and (ii) the expected number of completed interviews. Typically, the sampling statistician first determines the required number of completed interviews and then divides this number by the expected response rate and in some situations the expected screening eligibility rate. In this section, we focus on the basic aspects of determining the required number of completed interviews. Cochran (1977) and Lohr (2010) provide greater detail on this topic, while Czaja and Blair (2005) provide a layman's discussion on sample size determination.

The required number of completed interviews for descriptive surveys is determined by several factors including: (i) the desired magnitude of standard errors for key survey means, proportions and totals, (ii) the total funds available to conduct the survey, (iii) the need for subgroup estimates, and (iv) the effective sample size based on the expected design effects for key estimates. A sample size calculator website is provided below under "Online Resources" section.

Analytic surveys, on the other hand, may be tied to intervention experiments or may seek to test specific hypotheses, for example, testing the null hypothesis that there is no difference between males and females with respect to a health behavioral risk factor behavior. In this situation sample, size determination should take into account statistical power (1—probability of a Type II error) in addition to the probability of a Type I error (Fleiss 1981). A power and sample size calculator website is provided below under "Online Resources" section.

2.6 Summary

Probability sampling for community health surveys is a well-established field. However, the past 10 years has seen some major modifications. The first major modification has been the use of the CDSF to construct housing unit lists for area probability samples, and the use of the CDSF as a sampling frame for address-based samples. ABS provides a sampling frame that potentially includes almost all housing units in a geographic area. ABS allows for the selection of housing unit addresses from local geographic areas such as census tracts and ZIP codes. The use of ABS has opened up the possibility of using multimodality survey designs where more than one mode of data collection is used. The second major modification has been the switch from landline random-digit-dialing telephone sample designs to dual-frame telephone sample designs. By adding a cell phone sampling frame to the traditional RDD design, coverage of all households except nontelephone households is possible. Dual-frame designs are in wide use for state, county, and city telephone surveys. Dual-frame designs at this point in time are generally not applicable for local neighborhood area surveys because of the difficulty in identifying cellular 1000 banks that overlap with small geographic areas. Nonprobability sampling techniques are also receiving increased attention in part due to the typically lower cost per interview, the potential reduction in the amount of time needed to conduct a survey, and usefulness in sampling very rare populations (Baker et al. 2013).

REFERENCES

Baker R, Brick JM, Bates NA, Battaglia M, Couper MP, Dever JA, Gile KJ and Tourangeau R. 2013. Summary Report of the AAPOR Task Force on Non-probability sampling. Journal of survey statistics and methodology, November 2013;1(2):90–105.

Battaglia MP, Link MW, Frankel MR, Osborn L, Mokdad AH. An evaluation of respondent selection methods for household mail surveys. Public Opin Q 2008;72(3):459–469. Accessed on May 22, 2013.

Blumberg SJ, JV Luke. 2012. Wireless substitution: early release of estimates from the National Health Interview Survey, July-December 2011 National Center for Health Statistics June 2012. Available at http://www.cdc.gov/nchs/nhis.htm.

Blumberg SJ, Luke JV, Ganesh N, Davern ME, Boudreaux MH, Soderberg K. 2012. Wireless substitution: state-level estimates from the National Health Interview Survey, 2010-2011. National Health Statistics Reports, 61, National Center for Health Statistics.

Brick JM, Cervantes IF, Lee S, Norman G. Nonsampling errors in dual frame telephone surveys. Survey Methodol 2011a;37(1):1–12.

Brick JM, Williams D, Montaquila JM. Address-based sampling for subpopulation surveys. Public Opin Q 2011b;75(3):409–428.

Cochran WG. *Sampling Techniques*. 3rd ed. New York: Wiley; 1977.

Czaja R, Blair J. *Designing Surveys: A Guide to decisions and Procedures*. 2nd ed. Thousand Oaks: Pine Forge Press; 2005.

Dillman D. *Mail and Telephone Surveys: The Total Design Method*. New York: Wiley; 1978.

Dillman D. *Mail and Internet Surveys: The Tailored Design Method*. New York: Wiley; 2000.

Fleiss JL. *Statistical Methods for Rates and Proportions*. 2nd ed. New York: Wiley; 1981.

Graziano C. Comparative analysis of within-household respondent selection techniques. Public Opin Q 2005;69:124–157.

Groves RM, Kahn RL. *Surveys By Telephone: A National Comparison With Personal Interviews*. New York: Academic Press; 1979.

Iannacchione VG, Staab JM, Redden DT. Evaluating the use of residential mailing addresses in a metropolitan household survey. Public Opin Q 2003;76(2):202–210.

Iannacchione VG. The changing role of address-based sampling in survey research. Public Opin Q 2011;75(3):556–575.

Kalton G, Anderson DW. Sampling rare populations. J Roy Stat Soc Ser A 1986;149(1):65–82.

Kish L. A procedure for objective respondent selection within the household. J Am Stat Assoc 1949;44:380–387.

Kish L. *Survey Sampling*. New York: Wiley; 1965.

Link MW, Battaglia MP, Frankel MR, Osborn L, Mokdad AH. Address-based versus random-digit dialed surveys: comparison of key health and risk indicators. Am J Epidemiol 2006;164:1019–1025.

Link MW, Battaglia MP, Frankel MR, Osborn L, Mokdad AH. Comparison of address-based sampling versus random-digit dialing for general population surveys. Public Opin Q 2008;72:6–27.

Link MW, Lai JW. Cell-phone-only households and problems of differential nonresponse using an address-based sampling design. Public Opin Q 2011;75(4):613–635.

Lohr SL. *Sampling: Design and Analysis*. 2nd ed. Boston: Brooks/Cole; 2010.

Marketing Systems Group. 2012a. Construction of cellular RDD sampling frames based on switch locations. http://www.m-s-g.com/CMS/ServerGallery/MSGWebNew/Documents/GENESYS/whitepapers/Cellular-RDD-Frame-Construction.pdf.

Marketing Systems Group. 2012b. Cellular number screening & geographic targeting services. http://www.m-s-g.com/CMS/ServerGallery/MSGWebNew/Documents/GENESYS/whitepapers/cns-gts.pdf.

McMichael JP, Ridenhour JL, Skook-Sa BE. A robust procedure to supplement the coverage of address-based sampling frames for household surveys. *Proceedings of the Section on Survey Research Methods*; American Statistical Association; 2008.

Montaquila J, Brick JM. *Transitioning from RDDF to ABS with Mail as the Primary Mode*. San Diego CA: Joint Statistical Meetings; 2012.

Tucker C, Lepkowski JM, Piekarski L. The current efficiency of list-assisted telephone sampling designs. Public Opin Q 2002;75:321–338.

Yeager DS, Krosnick JA, Chang L, Javitz HS, Levendusky MS, Simpser A, Wang R. Comparing the accuracy of RDD telephone surveys and internet surveys conducted with probability and non-probability samples. Public Opin Q 2011;75(4):709–747.

ONLINE RESOURCES

Information from the American Association of Public Opinion Research on best practices in survey research is available at: http://www.aapor.org/Best_Practices1.htm.

The American Association of Public Opinion Research report on calculation of response rates is available at: http://www.aapor.org/AM/Template.cfm?Section=Standard_Definitions2&Template=/CM/ContentDisplay.cfm&ContentID=3156.

The American Association for Public Opinion Research cell phone report evaluating the use of cell phones in survey research is available at: http://www.aapor.org/Cell_Phone_Task_Force_Report.htm.

Information for non-specialists on designing and implementing a sample survey can be found at: http://www.whatisasurvey.info/.

A review of software packages for survey analysis is available at: http://www.hcp.med.harvard.edu/statistics/survey-soft/.

A sample size calculator is available at: http://www.nss.gov.au/nss/home.nsf/pages/Sample+size+calculator.

A power and sample size calculator is available at: http://biostat.mc.vanderbilt.edu/twiki/bin/view/Main/PowerSampleSize.

CHAPTER THREE

Developing a Survey Sample Design for Population-Based Case–Control Studies

Ralph DiGaetano
Westat, Rockville, MD, USA

3.1 Introduction

Case–control studies are widely used in health and epidemiological research to investigate possible causes and correlates of specified diseases or health conditions (see, for example, the reviews by Breslow (2005), Correa et al. (1994), and Knol et al. (2008)). The sample design for a case–control study involves the selection of two samples: a sample of cases with a disease in a given time period and location (often a 100% sample), and a sample of controls—those without the condition—in the same time period and location. The controls are often "frequency matched" to cases on such characteristics as age and sex.

Case–control studies are used when randomized experimentation is not practical. They are the retrospective equivalent of prospective cohort studies. Cohort studies follow a defined group forward in time, collecting data on the possible cause or causes, until some members of the cohort get the disease under study. Case–control studies start with samples of persons with and without the disease and look back in time to examine whether a particular factor or factors are

Handbook of Health Survey Methods, First Edition. Edited by Timothy P. Johnson.

possible causes of the disease. Lacking randomization of the potential cause, both case–control and cohort studies are observational studies, thus requiring control of confounding variables at the design or analysis stage (Cochran 1983).

A number of case–control studies have sampled controls from patients at the same hospitals as the cases or from among friends or neighbors of the cases. However, these methods of sampling controls are at risk of producing invalid findings because of the possible selection biases arising from the special characteristics of these control populations (see Wacholder et al. 1992b). For this reason, a preferred approach is to select the sample of controls from the population from which the cases arise. This chapter discusses some of the statistical design issues and related analytic issues that arise with such population-based case–control studies.

A case–control study is considered population-based if both cases and controls are sampled from the same well-defined population. For example, for a given study that will recruit cases, those with a specified disease, from residents in the state of Connecticut, the control population would consist of all residents of the state without this disease. More formally, the description of the target population for controls might be: those adults in a specified age range residing in Connecticut for the period of time during which cases in the same age range are being accrued. An underlying assumption is that all, or virtually all, of those residing in the state who have the disease in question have a probability for inclusion in the study that can be readily determined as part of the sample selection process.

For logistical and cost reasons, case–control studies are generally limited to specific, well-defined areas (e.g., counties, groups of counties, and small states). If a study is carried out at multiple sites that are somewhat different in nature, a finding that is consistent across all the sites lends greater credence to the general applicability of the finding. Unlike the community health surveys discussed in Chapter 2, where the ultimate focus is on the specific communities being surveyed, the findings from case–control studies are of greatest import if they can be judged to apply more widely.

Population-based case–control studies have many features and requirements that are not generally encountered in survey research. Nevertheless, once the differences are understood, a survey sampling perspective can readily be applied to produce efficient sample designs for such studies. A major purpose of this chapter is to identify how critical requirements of a population-based case–control study can be appropriately met in the sample design so that the key analytic objectives can be achieved in a cost-effective manner. Of course, as with virtually all sample designs, trade-offs will generally be necessary.

Scott and Wild (1986, 1997, 2001, 2002), who have written extensively on sampling and analysis issues in population-based case–control studies (e.g., 1986, 1997, 2001, and 2009), have noted that

> There has also been some work on the choice of sampling design ... but much needs to be done. Because the essence of the problem boils down to estimating two population means ..., it should be possible to transfer a lot of standard survey expertise about efficient design to this problem
>
> (2009, p. 453).

This chapter aims to highlight ways in which researchers conducting population-based case–control studies can take greater advantage of survey sampling methods in both design and analysis.

The remainder of this chapter covers the following topics:

- A "classic" sample design for population-based case–control studies (Section 3.2)
- Concepts and issues of particular relevance to population-based case–control studies (Section 3.3)
- More general sample design considerations (Section 3.4)
- Sample selection of cases (Section 3.5)
- Sample selection of controls (Section 3.6)
- A more efficient method for determining sample weights for population-based case–control studies (Section 3.7)
- Discussion of previously conducted population-based case–control studies focusing on both design and analytic issues (Sections 3.8–3.10)
- Summary (Section 3.11)

3.2 A "Classic" Sample Design for a Population-Based Case–Control Study

Below is a description of what might be characterized as a classic sample design for population-based case–control studies. This design, which has been the basis for many past population-based case–control studies, will serve as a reference point for considering various issues to be addressed in the development of a sample design for such studies.

Suppose that a population-based case–control study is to be carried out in one or several local areas (e.g., counties or groups of counties). A listing that provides high coverage of all cases associated with the area of interest is available or can be constructed (e.g., through the cooperation of hospitals in each area). All eligible cases identified during the case accrual period in the study areas are to be sampled. Controls are to be frequency matched to cases and sampled from listings or other means that provide high coverage of the general population of that area.

For matching purposes, the cells formed by a cross-classification of variables such as age and gender previously identified as risk factors for the disease being studied will serve as strata for the purposes of sampling controls. The matching rate of controls to cases for each stratum is to be 1 to 1 so that the number of controls will be the same as the number of cases for each stratum. An unclustered sample of controls will be selected with equal probability within each stratum, so that the sample design for the selection of controls can be treated as a stratified random sample (Cochran 1977). Interviews of controls are conducted expeditiously so that controls sampled from one age group do not migrate to another age group for analytic purposes (if the reference date is the date of interview), a concern discussed later.

It may be necessary to constrain the definition of controls (or cases) in some way for cost or logistical reasons. For example, if a telephone survey is used to identify controls (limiting costs), households without access to a telephone will have no chance of selection. To maintain strict comparability between cases and controls, the definition of cases eligible for the study must be similarly constrained.

Finally, analyses are to be undertaken without the use of sample weights or variance estimation methods that reflect the sample design.

3.3 Sample Design Concepts and Issues Related to Case–Control Studies

With this background, we now discuss some important concepts and issues that should be understood when undertaking the sample design for a population-based case–control study.

3.3.1 CONCEPTS

Cases. Cases are generally rare populations. Often all, or virtually all, of the incident cases found in a given area during the case accrual period are selected for participation in the study. Arrangements have to be made to ensure that all or virtually all cases within the general population targeted for the study that arise during the time period under study are eligible for sample selection. Sometimes cases are selected from sources such as hospitals that may choose not to participate in the study. If so, analytic adjustments should be made for such nonresponse since different hospitals may serve different subpopulations of the general community and may make differential contributions to the total number and types of cases. Since the control sample is selected from the whole community, without such adjustments the case and control samples will not be comparable, creating the potential for biased results.

Controls. Controls are selected from the same general population as cases but include only those that do not have the disease being studied. The sample design for controls is generally far more complex than that for cases. Controls are often frequency matched to cases on demographic variables such as age, race, and/or gender. This matching implies sampling at higher rates (oversampling) those subgroups that are more prevalent in the case population than the control population. In particular, since diseases tend to be more prevalent among older persons, older members of the general population are often oversampled for the control sample. Obtaining targeted sample sizes for the groups to be oversampled often involves screening a larger sample to identify the members of these groups. Such screening can add substantially to survey costs.

Statistical Inference. The statistical inferences being drawn in a population-based case–control study are not focused on those eligible for sampling during the case accrual period. Rather, inference is being drawn about the population consisting of all members of the target population (cases plus controls) that will continue to be encountered over time. Thus, the set of all the cases occurring in the accrual period can be viewed as a random sample from the corresponding superpopulation of cases and the sample of controls from the corresponding superpopulation of controls (Graubard and Korn 2002, Scott and Wild 2009).

Recognizing that inference is being drawn about a superpopulation is critical in developing analytic plans and, consequently, a sample design for a population-based case–control study. The focus is on the superpopulation distribution, not the sample distribution, when making analytic and design decisions. For example, the distribution of the cases who actually participate in the study may differ from the superpopulation distribution of cases for a number of reasons, such as differential nonresponse across subgroups (e.g., older White males participating at lower rates than other demographic subgroups); sampling case strata at different rates (say, to concentrate survey resources on subgroups of particular analytic importance); or variation in matching rates (perhaps matching some subgroups at a 2 to 1 control to case rate while matching others at a 1 to 1 rate in order to reduce costs and/or increase power for some analyses). Analyses should appropriately account for the extent to which the distribution of participants differs from that of the underlying superpopulation to avoid the risk of bias.

Comparability between Cases and Controls: Strategies for Exclusion. Cases and controls should differ in population definition in only one aspect, that which characterizes a case in the study (e.g., having a particular disease). This has both advantages and disadvantages in developing a sample design for a population-based case–control study. Sometimes use of a particular mode of data collection and sample design results in undercoverage of a particular component of the general population. Excluding from survey eligibility those cases that would have no chance of selection as a control eliminates bias concerns arising from population definitional differences. However, on the downside, this exclusion reduces the sample yield of cases and limits the generalizability of the study findings, thus potentially increasing the risk that the study results will not be fully applicable to a broader population. The possible need to refine the definition of cases and/or controls emphasizes the need to have a well-articulated characterization of the target population initially. Wacholder et al. (1992a) provide an extensive discussion of this issue.

One potential advantage to the maintenance of strict comparability between cases and controls is that it can be used to address immediate coverage concerns. For instance, certain areas of a county may contain only very small percentages of the target population being sampled to serve as controls. This might arise if a study is interested in White, non-Hispanic and Black, non-Hispanic subpopulations and is being carried out in an area of California where large numbers of Hispanics and Asians live. If an area probability sample is being used to sample controls, excluding both controls and cases that live in such areas (e.g., defined by census blocks) could reduce survey costs substantially. Doing so does not raise bias concerns. However, it may limit the extent to which survey results pertain to what might be characterized as the full population of interest.

Care should be taken that such exclusion strategies do not inadvertently remove a large percentage of a subgroup of interest. For instance, suppose the target population for a study is Black and White women aged 20–79 living in Cook County, Illinois, and that controls are to be sampled from listings provided by the Illinois Department of Motor Vehicles (DMV). To retain strict comparability, the target population for both cases and controls can be restricted to those who live in Cook County with a driver's license or ID from the Illinois DMV (cards for identification purposes may be provided by state DMVs to people who do not drive). As long as the only difference in the definition between cases and controls is status of the disease being studied, bias concerns do not arise. However, older individuals may be less likely to have driver's licenses or DMV IDs. If so, the number of cases eligible for the study will be reduced, reducing power to detect differences between cases and controls. Moreover, reduction in coverage leads to greater uncertainty as to whether study findings will pertain to populations beyond those actually studied. Potthoff et al. (2008) provides further discussion of this issue.

Relationship to a Cohort Study. Breslow (2005) points out that in designing a case–control design it can be helpful to imagine how a corresponding cohort study would be planned. In this regard, he discusses cohort definition, nested case–control sampling, and incidence density sampling. Some important sample design aspects emerge from these discussions. Controls should be sampled periodically from the same general population and over the same time period from which cases are being accrued in the study. Thus, an individual may be sampled to serve as a control at each wave of data collection in which he or she is a member of the general control population. Moreover, if an individual sampled as a control later becomes a case, that person should be represented as both a case and control in the analyses.

Reference Population. This term was introduced by Kalton and Piesse (2007) in their discussion of the application of survey research methods to evaluation and case–control studies. Generally, analyses using logistic regression for population-based case–control studies are undertaken perceiving the reference population—the population from which cases and controls are sampled and about which inferences are to be drawn—as the general (super)population eligible for the study (cases and controls combined). Alternatively, the case superpopulation can serve as the reference population, hypothesizing that both cases and controls are selected from the population of cases and determining if there is evidence to indicate that this is not the case.

Viewing the case superpopulation as the reference population is the basis for frequency matching controls to cases. Ideally, one-to-one frequency matching would be achieved exactly. Then, with selection of 100% of the cases and no nonresponse, the control sample distribution is made to look exactly like the case population distribution across what have been deemed critical factors in understanding the case population by the researchers carrying out the study. Recognizing this allows alternative approaches to sample weighting and much greater flexibility in developing sample designs for population-based case–control studies, as will be discussed later.

Absolute Risks. Sample weights that reflect the chance of selection of cases and controls with appropriate adjustments for nonresponse can be used to develop estimates that reflect the general population from which the samples were drawn. This is the basis of the design-based weights generally used in the analysis of survey data. Korn and Graubard (1999) and Scott and Wild (2009) provide discussions of such weights. These population-based weights can be used to estimate absolute risks and other population-based characteristics from the data collected from a population-based case–control study where either frequency matching or no matching at all has been employed. However, if frequency matching of controls to cases has been employed, the variable strata sampling rates for sampling controls from the general population will reduce the precision of estimates of absolute risk, perhaps substantially, compared to that which would have been obtained without frequency matching.

3.3.2 ISSUES

Matching Controls to Cases. Matching is a common feature in population-based case–control studies, with controls matched to cases on some key variables. A number of important issues to consider in applying matching for such studies are reviewed in this section.

There are two types of matching employed in case–control studies: frequency matching and what Korn and Graubard (1999) refer to as "set matching." Frequency matching involves selecting the sample of controls so that their distribution resembles that of cases on one or more variables. Set matching involves individually matching one or more controls to a given case. We only consider frequency matching or unmatched sampling in this chapter, since, as Korn and Graubard point out, set matching has limited potential applications in population-based case–control studies.

Matching has two benefits: increased efficiency and thus power; and reduction in the potential for bias. Korn and Graubard state that matching

> can decrease the variability of estimated associations between risk factors and the disease. It can also lessen the bias of these estimated associations when the matching

> variables are not correctly modeled as covariates in the analysis of an unmatched study.
>
> (1999, p. 307)

Matching can be a useful tool when employing variables that are potential confounders of exposures being investigated. The matching serves to limit or remove the contribution of the matched variables to differences arising between cases and controls, thus increasing the power to identify risk factors among the exposure measures being investigated. However, whether to match and, if so, on what variables requires careful consideration in order to avoid "overmatching" (discussed below).

In frequency matching, matching rates are generally established for each stratum represented by the cross-classification of the matching variables. For instance, if matching on age and gender, one might attempt to obtain the same number of controls as cases for males aged 20–24, 25–29, 30–34, and so on, and use the same strategy for females. In practice, targeted matching rates are goals and are not expected to be achieved exactly. Potential sources of departure include variation in sample yields due to sampling variability; differential response rates across the sampling strata established for both cases and controls; and uncertainty with respect to the response rates that can be achieved or eligibility rates that will be experienced (e.g., cases tend to have higher response rates than controls, but the extent to which this may happen in a particular study cannot be fully anticipated in advance).

To effectively match controls to cases, there must be, of course, some recent information on the case distribution for the target population for the study (registry data, etc.) from which targeted control sample sizes and rates can be estimated.

Breslow (2005) and Cochran (1983) both point out that the gains of matching may be modest, and high monetary costs may be incurred in the oversampling of some subgroups of the general population (basically, the population of controls) in order to achieve targeted matching rates with cases. As discussed later, when sample weights are used, approaches can be developed to vary matching rates to help mitigate costs while getting some of the benefits of a matched design. There may also be analytic/statistical costs if inappropriate or unwarranted matching is undertaken, as described next.

To meet analytic objectives, matching rates can be allowed to vary between strata. For instance, it may be desirable to increase matching rates for some strata substantially (e.g., matching rates of two controls per case for those under the age of 60 and one control per case otherwise). This can help increase power for subgroups of analytic interest while preserving survey resources. Variation in matching rates thus can be an important aspect of a sample design, but it must be appropriately accounted for in the analyses.

With varying matching rates, care must be taken in aggregating the results across the strata. One approach is to perform a stratified analysis and aggregate the results only if they are consistent across strata. Another approach is to perform a weighted analysis where the control sample has been weighted to conform to the population case distribution across the cells defined by the cross-classification of the matching variables such as age and gender (this weighting approach is described in more detail later). A weighted analysis would then produce valid estimates for the overall population, although attention should be paid to the interpretation of these estimates if strata estimates differ to an appreciable extent.

Overmatching. While matching can be beneficial, it can be overdone. Suppose a study is being done to investigate potential causes of bladder cancer, and sources of drinking water are among the possible risk factors. Matching controls and cases by location of residence (e.g., by zip code or area code-exchange) will serve to remove location as a source of variation between cases and controls. Since source of drinking water is correlated with location of residence, the power to detect differences between cases and controls is reduced rather than enhanced because the controls and cases have been "overmatched." In this example, rather than matching controls to cases on geography, a far more useful sample design would employ implicit stratification on geography (through sorting of the strata sample frames by, say, zip code). This would help ensure that the sample distribution of controls across the targeted area of interest is proportionate to the general population distribution. If the location of cases tends to be concentrated in certain geographic areas, perhaps because the constituents of the drinking water have some similarities in these areas, the power to identify this as a potential risk factor would be increased.

There is much discussion on the issue of overmatching (Wacholder et al. 1992c, Breslow 2005). Breslow offers a succinct description: overmatching involves "matching on a factor that is not a confounder of the disease-exposure association." He goes on to identify the three types of overmatching. They involve matching on a "perceived confounding" factor that is, in fact, (i) related only to exposure; (ii) related only to the disease in question; or (iii) an intermediate on the causal pathway.

The first type results in a loss of efficiency, reducing the power to identify existing differences, and, since matching usually involves extra costs, it leads to an unnecessary drain on survey resources. It may be the most common type in population-based case–control studies. The "drinking water" example is of the first type. Breslow discusses in detail an example of this type as well, using fictitious data provided by Rothman et al. (2008). The example involves needlessly matching on gender in a situation where data on the full population show that cases differ substantially from the remainder of the population in terms of a particular exposure—but not differentially by sex. However, exposure numbers differ substantially by gender (this could happen, for example, if males are disproportionately employed in an industry where the exposure commonly arises). Matching on gender and doing an analysis where data are pooled across gender is shown to substantially reduce the power to detect the existing difference between cases and controls.

The second type is regarded as a "case of futility" since the matching factor has no relationship to exposure (Breslow 2005, Miettinen 1970). If such matching is appropriately accounted for in the analyses, it will not affect statistical efficiency, but the cost and effort of attaining such matching will have been wasted.

The third type, described by Breslow as matching on a variable that is "both affected by exposure and a cause of (the) disease" of interest, is the most serious type of overmatching, as it undermines analyses examining the relationship between exposure and disease. This type of overmatching could arise when two-phase sampling is used. With such a sample design (discussed in more detail later) samples of potential controls may be selected and expensive or time-consuming measurements collected. If matching is done using such measurements, care should be taken to ensure that the matching variables do not represent an intermediate on the causal pathway.

Optimal Allocation in a Matching Context: The Sample Allocation of Cases and Controls. Considering the relative cost of sampling cases versus controls in making allocation decisions can help achieve analytic objectives while preserving survey resources.

If one cannot afford to sample all cases, matching rates of controls to cases that are less than one may present a viable option to achieve targeted levels of power.

We will first consider the effect of the matching rate on the precision of the difference in means between cases and controls. Let the overall sample size be fixed at n, divided into np cases and $n(1-p)$ controls, where p indicates the proportion of the total sample represented by cases. Then, assuming the same sample element variance σ^2 for cases and controls (appropriate under the null hypothesis that controls are being sampled from the superpopulation of cases), the variance $V(d)$ of d, the difference between the means of variable y for cases (c) and controls (0), can be expressed as

$$V(\bar{y}_c - \bar{y}_0) = V(d) = \frac{\sigma^2}{np} + \frac{\sigma^2}{n(1-p)} = \frac{\sigma^2}{np(1-p)} \tag{3.1}$$

The matching rate m of controls to cases can be expressed in terms of p as $m = (1-p)/p$, so that $p = 1/(m+1)$ and

$$V(d) = \frac{\sigma^2}{n}\frac{(1+m)^2}{m} \tag{3.2}$$

The minimum value of $V(d)$ occurs when $m = 1$, that is, $V_{\min}(d) = 4\sigma^2/n$. The proportionate increase (PI) in $V(d)$ associated with a matching rate different from 1 is thus

$$\text{PI} = \frac{V(d) - V_{\min}(d)}{V_{\min}(d)} = \frac{(1-m)^2}{4m} \tag{3.3}$$

Table 3.1 shows the proportionate increase in variance and standard error for a range of values of the matching rate m, as determined by specified proportions of the total sample represented by the cases. The table demonstrates that the loss of precision in deviating from a 1-to-1 matching is very small provided the matching rate is not too far from the optimum rate. Even with 1-to-2 or 2-to-1 matching, the proportionate increase in variance is only 12.5%, and the proportionate increase in standard error is 6.1%. Of particular import, note that these results apply irrespective of whether the higher matching rate is used for

TABLE 3.1 Proportionate Increase in Variance and Standard Errors by Matching Rates

Percent of Cases p	Matching Rate m	Proportionate Increase (PI) in $V(d)$	Proportionate Increase (PI) in SE(d)
0.33	2.00	12.5	6.1
0.36	1.75	8.0	3.9
0.40	1.50	4.2	2.1
0.44	1.25	1.3	0.6
0.50	***1.00***	***0.0***	***0.0***
0.56	0.80	1.3	0.6
0.60	0.67	4.2	2.1
0.64	0.57	8.0	3.9
0.67	0.50	12.5	6.1

cases or for controls. For example, a matching rate of 0.50 of controls to cases is equivalent to a 2.00 matching rate of cases to controls. A 2.00 matching rate of cases to controls produces the same proportionate increase in variance (12.5 percent) as a 2.00 matching rate of controls to cases.

The treatment above assumes that the costs of sampling cases and controls are equal. Under this and other assumptions that generally apply to case–control studies, the only rationale for deviating from 1 : 1 matching in a population-based case–control study occurs when the number of cases is limited, as when all eligible cases are to be included in the study. Then, the only way to increase power is to increase the matching rate for controls. Matching rates of up to four controls per case may prove useful under such conditions. Rates that exceed four controls per case generally are inefficient unless it is much cheaper to sample controls than cases (Breslow 2005). Generally, sampling cases is cheaper in a population-based frequency matched case–control study.

When survey resources do not permit the inclusion of all available cases for a study, decisions must be made on how best to allocate the sample of both cases and controls. For instance, in a study focusing on the Black and White populations, all Black cases and a sample of Whites above a certain age might be desired. In a study where cancer cases under a certain age are of particular analytic interest, all cases and controls matched at a rate of 2 to 1 to these cases might be selected, while cases over that age might be sampled to support other, but less critical, analyses while controls are matched to the older cases at a rate of 1 to 1.

It is important, then, to consider that the cost of sampling cases may differ substantially from that of controls. For instance, if controls are randomly selected using area probability sampling (APS), it is generally far more costly to obtain controls than cases. Even if controls are sampled from a list (e.g., from DMV listings), generally, cases will have higher response rates than controls. In addition, there may be a greater degree of screening required to identify controls compared to cases. As a result, for many population-based case–control studies, one may expect a higher cost in terms of fielding controls compared to cases.

When there are cost differentials between sampling cases and controls, the optimum allocation that minimizes $V(d)$ is one that samples more of the less expensive group (see, for example, Cochran 1977). We will consider a simple cost model with the total budget C available, letting the cost per sampled individual be c for cases and kc for controls and assuming no design effect associated with the cases or controls where k may be greater or less than 1. In this situation, the optimum allocation is to employ a matching rate of $\sqrt{k} : 1$ for cases relative to controls. Thus, if the cost per sampled control is four times that of a sampled case, one should sample twice as many cases as controls (that is, the matching rate would be 0.5 controls per case).

Again, note that this applies to strata where cases are not being selected with certainty. Also note that the cost model might differ by strata. For instance, if screening for controls is required, the cost associated with the stratum that drives the size of the screening sample (in an area probability study, the stratum that determines the total number of housing units or addresses to be screened) will have higher cost implications than the costs associated with sampling controls from other strata where cases are being sampled (rather than taken with certainty).

A side consideration for some studies may be that an increased sample size for cases would improve the precision of descriptive estimates for cases such as their treatment regimen and their reactions to the treatment.

Dealing with variable matching rates requires no special efforts if sample weighting is used. In unweighted analyses, it can be addressed in the modeling.

Missing Stratification Data. There are usually some potentially eligible cases and controls with missing data on variables used for assignment to sample strata. For example, race might be a matching variable, and some people are missing race. Dropping people with missing data raises issues of bias since some of them can be expected to be eligible for the survey. Thus, a strategy should be employed for giving such people a chance of selection. When such a person is sampled and later contacted, a final determination of the eligibility criteria obtained directly from the sampled person can be made before proceeding to the main interview. If the person turns out to be ineligible, a slight cost is incurred for undertaking this portion of the interview. This is the trade-off for avoiding the potential bias associated with dropping eligible people.

One strategy might be to assign people with missing data to a stratum with a relatively high sampling rate. For example, if matching on race (Black or White), sex, and age, a 38-year-old female of unknown race could be assigned to the Black, female, 35- to 39-year-old stratum, assuming this stratum has a higher sampling rate than that of White females aged 35–39. This helps assure that the sample size of a "harder to find" group is as large as possible. If the number of people with such missing data is high, those people could be assigned to a different stratum with lower sampling rates. Here the trade-off is lower screening costs versus lower sample sizes. If someone who is White is sampled as Black or vice versa, this is not a problem of bias if sampling weights are employed, as the actual sampling rate will be reflected in the weight. The "penalty" for misclassifications with weighted analyses is variable sampling weights, reducing power and precision. In unweighted analyses, the "penalty" is increased potential for bias that cannot be addressed in the modeling.

3.4 Basic Sample Design Considerations

We will next discuss basic considerations that have to be addressed in the development of any sample design. First, we will discuss two sample design strategies often used for population-based case–control studies: oversampling and two-phase sampling.

3.4.1 TWO SAMPLE DESIGN STRATEGIES

Oversampling. While overmatching is to be avoided, oversampling is a standard sample design feature. Oversampling simply means sampling some subgroups of the population at higher rates than others; its purpose is to increase the precision of estimates of targeted subgroups or the power to detect differences for particular analyses of interest. The downside of oversampling is the reduction of precision (or power to detect differences) for groups not oversampled as well as the target population as a whole. One can calculate "design effects," discussed shortly, to evaluate the impact of oversampling specified subgroups at various rates.

If sample weights that reflect the probabilities of selection are employed in weighted analyses with variance estimates that reflect the sample design, or if unweighted analyses appropriately reflect the oversampling in the modeling, bias will not be incurred. Nevertheless, those unfamiliar with survey sampling often express concerns that oversampling will result in biased results. Since such unwarranted concerns are often expressed and since oversampling strategies are an important element of sample designs not fully taken advantage of in case–control studies, more discussion on this subject is provided.

Consider a sample where all persons in a population are selected with the same probability and survey coverage of the target population is high. Then, the distribution of the characteristics (demographic, geographic, etc.) of the sample is expected to be proportionate to that of the population from which it was selected. For example, if a study is focusing on those aged 20–49 and those aged 20–39 represent about two-thirds of that population, one would expect roughly two-thirds of the persons in an equal probability sample to be aged 20–39. However, suppose some important analyses are to be focused specifically on the age group 20–39. Then, in order to improve the precision of estimates for that subgroup, one might decide to sample that age grouping at a higher rate than the remainder of the target population. In doing so, an oversampled subgroup comprises a higher proportion of the sample than it represents in the general population. Using sample weights that reflect the inverse of the probability of selection ensures that population estimates and analyses are not distorted by a disproportionate contribution from oversampled subgroups. Base sample weights for oversampled groups will be smaller than for the portion of the population not oversampled. For example, if a subgroup is sampled at roughly twice the rate of sample selection for the portion of the population not oversampled, members of the oversampled subgroup will receive base or initial sample weights (prior to nonresponse or poststratification adjustments) that are roughly half the size of the group not oversampled.

The "cost" of oversampling is that power and precision will be reduced for the overall target population and subgroups not oversampled compared to the precision that could have been achieved if the same overall sample size was selected without any oversampling. In developing a sample design, the impact of oversampling specified subgroups can be estimated, permitting an evaluation of its effect on estimates for the oversampled subgroups, other subgroups, and the population as a whole.

The following two points were made earlier but are included here as well for the sake of completeness. First, in population-based case–control studies where frequency matching is employed, the case population distribution generally differs considerably from that of the general population. For example, the case population is often much more heavily concentrated in older age ranges than the general population. When this occurs and if matching on age, controls in older age groups will be heavily oversampled (that is, included in the sample at a higher rate than the proportion these older groups represent of the general population).

Second, the strategy of oversampling can be used to increase power in frequency matched studies by using higher matching rates for sample strata associated with particular analyses of interest. Variable matching rates may also be used in some circumstances to help reduce survey costs.

Two-Phase Sampling. Sometimes information on variables of analytic interest is expensive to collect, and it is of interest to oversample people who are associated with, say, high or low values on one or more such analytic variables. Two-phase sampling (also known as *double sampling* and sometimes referred to as *two-stage* sampling in biostatistical texts) can help in this regard. A large, randomly selected equal probability sample of people can be selected and screened. Among the data collected would be variables correlated with these "difficult to collect" analytic variables (for instance, a screening question might be "Has a physician ever told you that you had high blood pressure?"). Respondents to the first-phase sample can be partitioned into strata based on responses to screener items, including matching variables if employed, and the second phase is then randomly selected within strata, where sampling rates would vary between strata. The difficult or expensive measures to collect would be obtained from this second-phase sample.

Discussion of two-phase sampling can be found in numerous sources, including Rao (1973) and Cochran (1977). Variance estimation methods for properly accounting for such sample designs are discussed by Kim et al. (2006) and Kim and Yu (2011). Discussions in the context of case–control and case–cohort studies can be found in Breslow and Chatterjee (1999), Scott and Wild (2009), and Lumley (2010).

In case–control studies, this two-phase approach is basically the inclusion of an extensive screening component of those potentially eligible for the study. This amounts to obtaining detailed screening information from a sampled person before selecting a stratified sample from among the screened participants. If certain data items are also difficult or expensive to obtain for cases, two-phase sampling could be used in the sample selection of cases as well. This would be an occasion where an optimal allocation strategy to determine matching rates of controls to cases would be worthwhile to consider, assuming potentially higher response rates for cases and, if cases are sampled from listings, the cost of controls being substantially greater than that of cases. As discussed earlier, care should be taken, if matching on data collected in the second phase is undertaken. Specifically, one should avoid matching on a variable that might be both affected by a potential risk factor and a cause of the outcome (disease) being studied. Matching on biological measurements could potentially prove problematic in this regard.

3.4.2 GENERAL CONSIDERATIONS

Variance. Issues of precision and power are prime considerations in developing a sample design. For a population-based case–control study, among the analytic objectives to be specified is the degree of power to detect existing differences between cases and controls. Often the targeted sample sizes of cases and controls are the same, but this is not always the case. If a complex sample design is to be employed (e.g., incorporating clustering or variable sampling rates within strata based on the cross-classification of matching variables), allowance for estimated design effects, described next, should be made. This generally involves increasing targeted sample sizes to compensate for any expected increases in variance resulting from clustering and/or variable sampling rates within strata (matching cells). Without compensating for expected design effects, targeted levels of power may not be attained.

Design Effects. The definition of a design effect is the ratio of the variance of an estimate obtained from data gathered under a specified sample design to the ratio of the variance of that estimate obtained from a simple random sample of the same size (see, for example, Kish 1965). Related to this, the *effective sample size* for an estimate is the ratio of the actual sample size to the design effect associated with the estimate. In developing a sample design where a simple random sample is not employed (virtually all sample designs) and where analyses are carried out using sample weights and variance estimates that reflect the sample design, design effects are estimated to determine the sample sizes required to achieve analytic goals.

There are two major components of design effects. The first, D_1, represents the contribution arising from the variation of sampling rates (and thus sample weights). In planning a sample design, a handy way of estimating the design effect for a population associated with oversampling some strata is based on the proportion of the population in each stratum and the relative (or actual) sampling rates to be used in the strata. Note that this is based on the assumption that variances are equal across strata. (See Kish 1965, pp. 430–431, where the k_h in his discussion corresponds to the k_i below, but he uses the terminology "weight" instead of "oversampling rate" and his W_h corresponds to the p_i below).

Suppose there are I strata. Let

r_i = the sampling rate for stratum i

$r_{\min}$ = the minimum sampling rate across the I strata

$k_i = r_i / r_{\min}$ = the oversampling rate for stratum i

p_i = the proportion of the population found in stratum i.

Then D_1 can be estimated as a product of two sums across the I strata:

$$D_1 = \left(\sum p_i k_i\right)\left(\sum \frac{p_i}{k_i}\right) = \left(\sum p_i r_i\right)\left(\sum \frac{p_i}{r_i}\right) \qquad (3.4)$$

Substituting stratum and population totals for the p_i's and stratum sample sizes and population totals for the r_i's, it is straightforward to reexpress D_1 as

$$D_1 = \left(\frac{n}{N^2}\right)\left(\sum \frac{N_i^2}{n_i}\right) \qquad (3.5)$$

where
n_i = the sample size in stratum i
N_i = the population size for stratum i
N = the population total.

Green (2000) uses this approach in considering sample design and allocation problems.

This latter expression of D_1 is often used at the analysis stage in assessing the contribution to the sample variance from the variation in sample weights, which reflects the overall variation arising from nonresponse adjustments and poststratification as well as varying sample rates. (It may be of interest that this is the method used when estimating D_1 based on the coefficient of variation (CV) of sample weights of respondents, a convenient method available using statistical software such as SAS's PROC UNIVARIATE when a weight variable has already been established. With PROC UNIVARIATE the CV of the weight variable, reported as a percentage, is divided by 100 and the result is squared. Adding the value 1 to the squared value produces the design effect associated with the variability of the weights.)

The second design effect component, D_2, represents the contribution to sample variation arising from clustering the sample, if cluster sampling (Cochran 1977) is employed. Clustering is generally used to limit survey costs and involves the sampling of groupings within which further sampling of different units is usually employed to select members of the ultimate target population for the study. Examples of cluster sampling include sampling census blocks within a county (before sampling addresses within a sampled block and then people within a sampled address) or sampling schools (before sampling students within a school).

For a two-stage sample design (e.g., sampling hospitals and then cases within hospitals), the design effect associated with clustering for a particular estimate can be expressed as

$$D_2 = 1 + \rho(\overline{n} - 1) \qquad (3.6)$$

where
ρ = the intraclass correlation between elements within a cluster for the variable of interest (cases in the example); and

$\overline{n}$ = the average number of responding elements in a cluster across all clusters with at least one responding element ($\overline{n}$ is assumed to be relatively stable for this approach to estimating D_2 to be useful).

Values of ρ range between $[-1/(\overline{n}-1)]$ and 1. Values greater than 0 for a given variable indicate that elements within a cluster tend to be similar for that variable, serving to increase the design effect and thus the variance of the corresponding estimate. For example, people residing on the same block tend to have more similar income levels than people residing on different blocks. Thus, estimates of household income (or estimates correlated with income) where several households are sampled per sampled block can be expected to have lower precision than estimates of income based on a sample where only one household per block is sampled. Of course, gathering data on one household per block is more expensive than selecting several per block.

Generally, the overall design effect D is estimated by computing the product of these two components:

$$D = D_1 D_2 \tag{3.7}$$

(note that $D = D_1$ when no clustering is employed since $\rho = 0$).

The expected value of D is generally larger than 1 for a complex sample design. Effective stratification can serve to reduce the overall design effect D somewhat; however, a conservative approach is often used in developing a sample design, assuming no reduction in sample variation associated with sample stratification unless there is information available to suggest otherwise.

Design Effects and Sample Sizes. In making sample size decisions for population-based case–control studies, initial focus is usually placed on comparisons of interest—that is, the analytic objectives for the full sample and subgroups. Then, the specified level of power to detect existing differences between cases and controls and a Type 1 error α are required for each such comparison in order to determine the needed sample sizes.

There are many references on the determination of sample sizes needed for case–control studies for analyses related to odds ratios (e.g., Breslow and Day 1987, Smith and Day 1987). However, these generally do not incorporate design effects. If a complex sample design is employed, the strata sample sizes determined to achieve a certain level of power should be multiplied by estimated design effects to help ensure that targeted levels of power are obtained.

Bias. There are many potential sources of bias in sample surveys. Survey nonresponse is a critical concern. To the extent that there is differential nonresponse to the survey across subgroups (e.g., by case–control status, age, race, the interaction of age and race, gender, the interaction of age and gender, and site), biased estimates may be incurred, compromising study findings.

Nonresponse is an issue for both cases and controls, and all potential sources of nonresponse should be identified. For instance, if cases are being obtained from hospitals in a local area and some hospitals choose not to participate, this can be an important nonresponse concern. Different hospitals may serve different segments of the general population and may have a relatively large or small percentage of the cases of interest.

Steps may be taken in the estimation or analytic processes to limit the potential effect of nonresponse bias, as will be discussed later. A standard approach in survey research is to adjust sample weights to account for differential nonresponse. If unweighted analyses are undertaken, the model would need to account for this.

Another potential source of bias includes sample misclassification not appropriately accounted for in the analysis. Controls may be misclassified for sampling purposes if they were sampled from one group (stratum) but actually belong to a different group for analysis purposes. Often this may just be a rare occurrence, such as a person being classified as Black for sampling purposes when that same person self-identified as White in the interview. However, a potential source of concern stems from the relationship between age and a study's reference date, the date about which a respondent is asked to focus in terms of providing "prior" data. For example, in a population-based case–control study where age is a matching variable, a woman may be sampled as a control in the age range 35–39, but on the reference date she may actually be in the age range 40–44, the age to be used for analytic purposes. For weighted analyses, this is not a concern, since probabilities of selection are appropriately accounted for. However, a standard assumption for unweighted analyses is that all members of a sample stratum (which would include age groups in this example) have the same chance of selection. This would not be the case for such misclassifications, and there are no adjustments that can be made to deal with them analytically.

Misclassification by age can readily arise in the fielding of a control sample when interviewing takes place a substantial time after sample selection, and, as is often the case, the reference date is defined to be the date of interview. Suppose, for illustration purposes, that in a case–control study where frequency matching on age (in 5-year intervals) was employed, interviews of controls are conducted exactly 6 months after sample selection. Roughly half of those sampled controls aged 39 can be expected to have turned 40 in 6 months. This is about 10 percent of all the controls in the age group 35–39. Often the sampling rates for controls increase nontrivially for older age groups. Analytically, those controls age 39 at the time of sample selection but aged 40 by the time the interview is undertaken will be treated as if frequency matched to cases age 40–44 even though sampled at a substantially lower rate than other 40–44-year olds, incurring the potential for bias in unweighted analyses.

With some sample designs, steps may be taken to help mitigate such misclassification. For instance, if controls are sampled from DMV listings, date of birth will likely be available for determining age. Controls can be assigned to age strata based on their expected age at the time of interview rather than the date of sample selection.

Using date of interview as the reference date helps anchor the response of those selected as controls at a well-defined point in time. Choosing an alternative date as the reference date, which may not be well-established as a point of reference for a respondent (such as the date of sample selection to avoid the "age migration" problem noted above), can result in recall bias if the date has little meaning for the respondent. (Breslow 2005 discusses recall issues in the context of case–control studies; a more detailed discussion of general issues related to recall can be found in Chapters 3 and 4 of Tourangeau et al. (2000)).

A third source of potential bias is the coverage provided by sample frames. If controls are to be sampled from listings that are intended to cover the full population of interest in a study area but some are left off due to programming errors, for example, bias can be incurred. If there are spelling error: systematic omissions from a sample frame, often adjustments can be made to the definition of the case population to deal with this. For instance, a common sample design in the 1980s and 1990s involved sampling controls from listings of telephone numbers. With such a design, cases that could not be reached through a household telephone number were removed from the target population to help maintain comparability between cases and controls.

Cost. For population-based case–control studies, there are a number of important cost considerations. These are indicated here in the form of questions that are typically encountered.

Are cases to be selected from a readily available listing of cases or, perhaps, will such listings be obtained from participating hospitals? What information is readily available to permit the identification of eligible cases? Is the target population such that a large percentage of cases have to be screened out (e.g., the target population might be non-Hispanic Whites and Blacks in Los Angeles county)?

Are population-based controls to be sampled from available listings? If so, will such listings provide all the data needed for sampling, or will further screening be required? If no useful listings are available, is an area probability sample of controls affordable? Are there ways to redefine the population or reduce screening that will make the study less expensive?

What are the planned matching rates? Can they be economically attained even for sample strata (cross-classification of the matching variables) that require very large screening samples to match the expected number of cases?

All of these cost issues enter into the final determination of a sample design. Many potential solutions may be feasible under a complex sample design with clustering and/or the use of variable sampling rates if analyses employ weighted data and variance estimates are developed that reflect the sample design. If unweighted analyses are used and the model does not fully account for components of the sample design employed, there is a risk of incurring bias due to model misspecification.

Analytic Plans and Objectives. The initial determination of the analytic plans and objectives for a study are generally identified prior to other sample design considerations. However, depending upon what can be reasonably undertaken in terms of data collection, some of the initial plans or objectives may need to be modified. Thus, it is important to prioritize study objectives to help ensure that a sample design can be developed to achieve the objectives of greatest importance.

A clear articulation of the target population for the study as well as specific subgroups of analytic interest is a useful starting point. Other considerations include the types of analyses planned (e.g., logistic regression, hierarchical modeling) and whether survey weights will be employed in the analyses.

The reluctance to use complex sample designs for population-based case–control studies in the past may have been due to some extent to the limited availability of software where the sample design could be appropriately reflected. However, this is no longer the case, as software packages such as SUDAAN, STATA, SAS, and M-PLUS all make provision for incorporating sample weights and developing sample variances that reflect the sample design.

Trade-Offs. Generally, in the development of sample designs, trade-offs are made on variance, bias, costs, and the analytic plans and objectives. For instance, use of weighted analyses considerably expands the scope of how a sample design can be developed. One can readily take advantage of standard sample design strategies such as clustering and variable sampling rates within strata to help reduce costs and achieve analytic goals without risking the potential for bias that might be incurred with unweighted analyses arising from model misspecification or Type 1 errors (due to understatement of sample variation). The trade-off when using weighted analyses is that variances are generally larger compared to an unweighted analytic approach, serving to reduce precision and power. To the extent that the increase in variance can be limited, a weighted approach becomes a viable option.

Considering alternative trade-offs can help guide the choice of approaches (area probability, list sampling) and sample frames for sampling controls (Are lists available? What type of screening is necessary?). A paramount consideration is the expected costs of alternative approaches.

3.5 Sample Selection of Cases

Cases may be identified from registry listings, hospitals, or other sources. Regardless of the source, standard survey research procedures apply to the data collection procedures. If nonresponse is encountered in the identification of cases, this nonresponse should be accounted for in the analyses. In addition to person-level nonresponse, this could include hospital nonresponse if cases are identified through hospitals and some choose not to participate. As mentioned earlier, different hospitals may serve different segments of the general population and may have a relatively large or small percentage of the cases of interest, so addressing such nonresponse may not be a trivial task.

If a sample of cases is selected and sample rates vary by strata, this should be accounted for in the analyses (through sample weights or modeling). One source of varying sampling rates is misclassification. Misclassification can arise if matching is undertaken on race, age, and gender, and some cases are misclassified on one or more of these factors. Thus, some cases would be sampled at rates different from others falling in the same matching cell. Again, such variable sampling rates can be accounted for routinely using sample weights but not in unweighted analyses.

For logistical and cost reasons, case–control studies are generally limited to specific, well-defined areas (e.g., counties, groups of counties, and small states). Population-based registries seek to identify all cases within a specific geographic area and report incidence rates and other statistics for these areas. A discussion of cancer registries follows.

3.5.1 CANCER CASES AND REGISTRIES

If cases are individuals with a form of cancer, researchers may be able to take advantage of existing cancer registries. For example, registries maintained as part of the Surveillance Epidemiology and End Results (SEER) program of the National Cancer Institute (NCI) maintain data on cancer cases identified in specified areas across the United States. All U.S. registries (including those in SEER) are members of the North American Association of Central Cancer Registries (NAACCR). A discussion of various registries as well as websites that can be visited to obtain additional information about them is found in the "Online Resources" section at the end of this chapter.

3.6 Sample Selection of Controls

There are three major ways in which the sample selection of population-based controls has been undertaken: telephone screening, APS, and lists. We will consider each.

3.6.1 TELEPHONE SCREENING

For roughly 20 years, from the early 1980s through the early 2000s, the telephone screening approach developed by Waksberg (1998), was a very effective and cost-efficient way of sampling controls for many population-based case–control studies. Response rates were high, and costs were relatively low. A potential drawback was that undercoverage of the poorer components of the general population (those without household phones) could limit the applicability of findings if being a case was correlated with lower socioeconomic status.

However, response rates for telephone surveys have dropped considerably over time (see Curtin et al. (2005) or Battaglia et al. (2008)). Moreover, population-based case–control studies are generally focused on local areas, and with the advent of cell phones and the portability of telephone numbers, telephone surveys do not effectively cover local areas (see Christian et al. (2009) for a detailed discussion of this; Lavrakas et al. (2007) also provides a related discussion). If one were to contemplate using a telephone survey to screen for controls, one could first estimate the coverage of the area to assess the viability of such an approach. For example, one could undertake a screening sample using the same telephone survey methodology planned for the study, collect the county of residence of screened households, and estimate the total number of households in the county represented by the participating households. The ratio of that number to, say, the estimated number of households found in the county based on American Community Survey (ACS) county figures would provide an estimate of the coverage of the target population. If that estimate appears low, this would limit the extent to which survey results would pertain to the county population generally.

Moreover, cases and controls are to be sampled from the same population. Thus, only cases found on the same sampling frame used for sampling controls (representing both land-based phone numbers and cell phone numbers for households with only cell phones) could be eligible for the study. This would add to the work associated with screening cases as well as reduce the number of cases available for analyses.

Telephone screening to identify controls in local areas now has some major disadvantages that would generally remove it as a preferred sample design option. However, its potential use is still being explored (Voigt et al. 2011).

3.6.2 AREA PROBABILITY SAMPLING

APS is a commonly used sample design to concentrate the sample in smaller geographic areas to help reduce survey costs (APS is still costly to implement). It is an oft-used strategy when in-person interviewing is called for. The trade-off for reduced screening costs in this manner is increased variance to the extent that people who live in the same general area are similar in terms of the variables of analytic interest (e.g., measurements correlated with income or the local environs). The degree of similarity is measured by the intraclass correlation coefficient discussed earlier. Useful references on APS include Kish (1965) and Cochran (1977). The discussion below assumes some familiarity with the concepts associated with APS.

For population-based case–control studies, an area sampling approach could potentially be used for local areas such as counties, metropolitan areas, or small states. An approach might be to construct primary sampling units (PSUs) consisting of one or more census blocks or groups of blocks (identified from the latest census files) that cover the area of analytic interest. A sample of these PSUs would be selected with probability proportionate to size, where size might be the number of housing units in an area or a more complex size measure that is related to the demographic groups being sampled (Folsom et al. 1987). All the housing units in a sampled PSU would be listed, and a self-weighting sample of housing units would be selected from each listing so that ultimately all housing units in the area of interest would have the same probability of selection. The sampled housing units would be screened to identify those eligible to serve as controls, and a sample of those eligible would be selected and asked to participate in the study. (Note that what are called *PSUs* here are often referred to as *segments or secondary sampling units* (SSUs) in studies of larger areas, for example, the nation as a whole. The PSUs in a national study are frequently counties or groups of counties, and blocks or groups of blocks often represent the second stage of sample selection.)

The advantage of in-person screening for controls is that high response rates to the household screener can often be attained, certainly much higher than by telephone or mail. The disadvantage is cost. In addition to the screening, there is also the cost of listing each sampled PSU (e.g., block or group of blocks) as well as enhancing coverage of the population in a sampled PSU through the use of "missed structure" procedures. These are implemented to increase coverage (and thus reduce the potential for bias). Coverage concerns can arise, for example, when a new housing development or apartment building has opened after the listing was done but prior to implementing field operations. In addition to increased costs, adding missed structures to the sample adds to the sample size and/or sampling variability (if it is necessary to subsample from the newly added structures).

Many studies cannot afford to undertake an area probability sample. One way in which costs can be mitigated is by increasing cluster sizes—in this case, the average number of responding controls (study participants) per cluster in those clusters with at least one responding control. However, if unweighted analyses are planned, either cluster sizes should be kept small (as with Waksberg's Random Digit Dial (RDD) sample design) or methods such as those discussed by Graubard et al. (1989) and Fears and Gail (2000) should be incorporated to appropriately reflect added variance incurred by clustering.

APS has been used in a number of population-based case–control studies. Brogan et al. (2001) compared sampling controls via APS and telephone screening but did not focus on the impact of clustering on power. Scott and Wild (2009) describe a study of meningitis in New Zealand where APS was employed to sample controls. A population-based case–control study in Puerto Rico, to be discussed soon, used an APS design where the expected number of interviewed controls per cluster (block or group of blocks) was kept small to limit the impact of clustering on the variance—but with higher costs than are typically considered acceptable in studies using an APS design.

3.6.3 ADDRESS-BASED SAMPLING

Address-based sampling (ABS), also discussed in Chapter 2, is a relatively new sampling approach that takes advantage of address listings developed from the U.S. Postal Service (USPS) Computerized Delivery Sequence (CDS) file. Such listings are available publicly through vendors. They have been used successfully for mail surveys (not generally of interest for case–control studies) and are now beginning to be employed for APS designs. Associating addresses with sampled geographic areas (e.g., blocks or groups of blocks) involves geocoding and linking each address to exactly one geographic area for sampling purposes. This linking process is highly accurate but not perfect, so the actual geographic location may occasionally be outside the geographic area targeted. However, it assures that all addresses on the frame have a single chance of selection, so the concerns with such inaccuracies are potential increases in cost and variance, but bias concerns related to probability of selection do not arise.

Traditional APS designs, described above, involve listing a sampled area before selecting addresses within that area, and listing is costly. Using an ABS approach can remove the need for listing. ABS frames generally provide very high coverage of the housing units found in urban areas, where population-based case–control studies are often carried out. Missed structures on a list based on USPS address lists are generally not a major concern, and samples can be designed to ensure that cases and controls are coming from the same population. Specifically, to maintain strict comparability between cases and controls, cases selected for the study in a particular site (e.g., Cook County, Illinois) should be determined to be on the ABS sample frame established for that area. Currently, the USPS CDS file does not provide high coverage of residences in many rural areas. If a portion of the target population for a study is found in a rural area, standard listing operations could be necessary in those areas, adding to survey costs.

Dohrmann et al. (2012) present a detailed discussion of using ABS frames rather than traditional listing methods for area samples. Additional references on ABS include Roth et al. (2012); Iannacchione (2011); Brick et al. (2011); Dohrmann et al. (2006, 2007); and Link et al. (2006, 2008).

3.6.4 LIST SAMPLES AND POTENTIAL LISTS FOR SAMPLE FRAMES

When available, lists of people within the areas of interest represent potential sample frames for sampling controls. Ideally, such lists will contain names, up-to-date addresses, and, to reduce screening costs if matching of controls to cases is to be employed, complete or largely complete data for at least one of the matching variables.

A major issue associated with lists is the coverage they provide of the general population. Unbiased analyses can be undertaken even if they provide relatively low coverage by eliminating from analysis cases that do not appear on a list. However, for example, with telephone surveys, the extent to which study findings pertain more broadly can be called into question when coverage is an issue. Two potentially useful sources of lists to serve as sample frames are lists of people with driver's licenses and lists of Medicare beneficiaries.

Lists from Departments of Motor Vehicles. One possible source of sampling frames is the set of listings of those with driver's licenses or IDs (for those who do not drive) available for a number of states. These would likely be most appropriate for sampling controls for those between the ages of 18 and 64, as coverage may decline for older ages. Walsh et al. (2011) provide a comprehensive evaluation of the availability of driver's license lists from state DMV for use in government-sponsored public health research. In addition, they indicate the extent of coverage provided by the lists for the 16 states where a list was determined to be available for public health researchers at the time of the evaluation (2009–2010).

DMV lists were used for sampling controls under the age of 65 for two population-based case–control studies carried out by the NCI roughly between 2001 and 2005: a population-based case–control study of bladder cancer in northern New England (Colt et al. 2011b), and a population-based case–control study of kidney cancer (Colt et al. 2011a, DiGaetano et al. 2003). It may be of interest that two of the states from which DMV listings were obtained for these studies, Illinois and New Hampshire, are among the states identified by Walsh et al. as not making listings available to researchers in 2009–2010. Thus, it will be important to check with the states under consideration before making decisions about study sites and the possible use of driver's license listings.

In addition to name and address, DMV listings can be expected to provide date of birth and gender, often useful for population-based case–control studies where matching is done on age and sex, eliminating the need for extensive screening. Moreover, since households with Black members or Hispanic members are often found in close proximity to others of the same minority background (Waksberg et al. 1997), sample designs may be developed in some localities to oversample addresses in areas with relatively high concentrations of these minority groups (if of analytic interest). This proved to be a highly effective feature of the sample design for the kidney cancer study to be discussed shortly.

Comparability between cases and controls is maintained by excluding cases that have neither a driver's license nor an ID from their state of residence.

Lists of Medicare Beneficiaries. Lists of Medicare beneficiaries have served as the source of sample frames for controls aged 65 or older for many population-based case–control studies. They are maintained by the Centers for Medicare and Medicaid Services (CMS). However, permission must be obtained to use these lists, and not all studies may qualify to use them. In the "Online Resources" section information is provided on contacting the Research Data Assistance Center (RESDAC) for information on the availability and costs of such lists for a particular study.

The Medicare beneficiaries listings are kept up to date. By way of illustration of what may be available, those used for the Kidney Cancer Study included name, address, date of birth, gender, and race of those in the targeted counties.

Evaluations of the DMV and Medicare Beneficiary Listings. DiGaetano et al. (2003) developed coverage estimates for both DMV and Medicare beneficiary listings for the Chicago and Detroit areas related to a kidney cancer study. These estimates suggest that high, but not complete, coverage can be expected with such frames.

One issue with respect to DMV listings is that driver's licenses have a several year renewal period. Address changes are supposed to be reported in the event of a move, but they may not be. Sampling from DMV or Medicare beneficiary listings from CMS represents sampling of people who must be traced if they are not located at the address obtained from the sample frame. If someone cannot be located or their eligibility status determined (e.g., a family member indicating at the time of household screening that the sampled person had previously moved outside the area of interest), nonresponse is incurred. (Some researchers mistakenly characterize such "unlocatables" as ineligible. In making decisions about such matters, it would be helpful to consult the "Standard Definitions" report for survey disposition code assignments available on the website of the American Association for Public Opinion Research (AAPOR). See the "Online Resources" section for further information on obtaining this AAPOR document).

For these CMS files, those aged 65 in a given calendar year tend to be particularly undercovered as they become eligible for Medicare over the course of that year. If both DMV and CMS listings are being used for sampling controls, an assessment could be made as to whether using DMV listings for age 65 might be preferred to CMS listings. A dual-frame approach might also be considered.

3.7 Sample Weighting for Population-Based Case–Control Studies

Examples will be provided shortly illustrating how trade-offs have been made in the sample design process that have permitted unweighted analyses through judicious choices in handling elements of a complex sample design. These sample design choices have been dictated by the restrictions on how analyses were to be conducted, keeping sample variation low (approximately at the level of a stratified random sample), with trade-offs including increased cost and a greater potential for incurring bias. However, there are analytic approaches readily available that permit cost-saving strategies to be more readily employed, keep variation relatively low, and avoid or reduce the potential for incurring bias. These approaches call for the use of sample weights and estimates of variance that reflect the sample design employed. Such analyses can help provide much greater flexibility in the design process, allowing both cost savings and, in some instances, a greater range of possible analyses.

3.7.1 A NEW APPROACH TO DEVELOPING SAMPLE WEIGHTS FOR CASE–CONTROL STUDIES

The analysis of population-based case–control studies in the past has generally been unweighted, where either the sample design was a stratified random sample or the design was developed in such a way that it could be analyzed as such with little or no concerns about incurring bias or variance unaccounted for in the analyses. The main alternative approach has been one where sample weights have been developed in the standard manner for sample surveys, strictly reflecting the probabilities of selection so that the resulting estimates pertain to the population from which the sample was drawn.

Weighting to the general population has the advantage, as Scott (2006) put it, of "always estimating the linear logistic approximation that we would get if we had data from the whole population." However, unweighted analyses are considerably more efficient than those using such weights, since large design effects can arise in sampling controls, particularly when frequency matching is employed and rarer components of the general population are oversampled (e.g., when cases are heavily concentrated in older age groups and controls are frequency matched to cases on age). Thus, using this weighting approach generally results in far less power to detect existing differences. The downside of unweighted analyses is that model misspecification may arise, resulting in biased results. It can be challenging to appropriately reflect complex sample design features such as variable sampling rates and clustering as well as differential nonresponse using an unweighted analysis. Scott and Wild have done extensive work comparing the two approaches and considering trade-offs between the two (see, for example, 1986, 1997, 2001, 2002, 2009). Korn and Graubard (1999) also provide a useful discussion of the two analytic approaches and the trade-offs involved.

However, there has been a recent development in the sample weighting approach that considerably increases efficiency when using weights while retaining its advantages. It is based on treating cases as the reference population for the analyses, where the sample weights of controls are calibrated (poststratified) so that they reflect the case distribution on the matching variables. This weighting approach is an application of the standardization role that sample weighting can play as described by Kish (1992, 1987), where standardization is achieved by reweighting subclasses of a sample from one population to the domains of the target/reference population.

Li et al. (2011) describe the development of sample weights for both cases and controls. The initial steps involve developing weights that represent the subpopulations from which they were selected (case or control). Standardization is then achieved by reweighting controls to correspond to the case population distribution across strata, where the strata are based on variables used in the matching of controls to cases. They used the following steps broken into components A and B.

A. Weighting to the individual subpopulations (case or control)

  1. Compute the base weight for both cases and controls as the reciprocal of the probabilities of selection (many studies cannot afford to select all available cases in a given study).

  2. Adjust for survey nonresponse (a standard step in survey estimation), utilizing a cross-classification of the matching variables as a framework for the adjustment but also taking advantage of other variables available on both respondents and nonrespondents that may be useful in this regard.

  3. Note that the resulting weighted case distribution of cases eligible for a study in a given area across the cross-classification of the matching variables represents the best available estimate of the distribution of the case superpopulation over the case accrual period.

B. Standardizing the control weights to reflect the case distribution

  1. Poststratify the nonresponse adjusted control weights to the case population distribution across the cross-classification of the matching variables.

The final step, poststratifying the control weights to the sum of the weights for eligible cases within cells based on the cross-classification of the matching variables, achieves exactly what matching is intended to do: make the control population distribution look exactly like the eligible case population distribution across the matching variables. In doing so, considerably greater efficiency is achieved compared to simply weighting back to the general population—the sample weights obtained after completing component A of the weighting process.

In fact, stepping through this weighting process helps highlight something that has generally been obscured: that using general population weights in the analyses after frequency matching controls to cases actually defeats the entire purpose of the matching. The resulting comparisons are between general population characteristics reflected by the controls and the characteristics of cases, usually a rare subpopulation sampled at a much higher rate from listings representing just the subpopulation in question. The matching effort has been entirely undermined since the control estimates simply reflect general population characteristics.

This emphasizes the need to establish analytic plans in advance of the sample design. If analyses are to be undertaken either without weights or with control weights using poststratification to the case distribution and if frequency matching is considered advantageous, then frequency matching should be employed. If analyses are to use sample weights for controls and cases that simply reflect their probabilities of selection with adjustments for nonresponse, no matching should be undertaken since it is more costly and reduces power and precision.

It should be noted that the weighting approach advocated here, poststratifying the general population control weights to the case distribution, is not as efficient as an unweighted approach since there will be variance due to differential sampling rates and clustering (if clustering is employed). However, Li et al. (2011) show that this loss of efficiency is not great, and the gains in flexibility for the sample design are extensive.

Variance estimates (standard errors, confidence intervals) can be obtained using replication or Taylor series linearization methodologies (Korn and Graubard 1999, Wolter 2007, Heeringa et al. 2010). Whichever method is used, care should be taken to ensure that the last step of the weighting, the poststratification of control weights to the case distribution, is fully reflected in the variance estimation process to obtain the full efficiency gains from the weighting process presented here (special steps are needed when a linearization approach is employed).

With an unmatched sample the "poststratification" of the control weights would be achieved simply by scaling the control weights so that they sum to the sum of the weights assigned to the responding eligible cases (the population estimate of the total number of eligible cases encountered during the case accrual period). This is akin to an approach investigated by Scott and Wild (2009) where they show that scaling the sum of the control population weights to the number of sampled controls and the case weights to the number of sampled cases can result in a substantial gain in efficiency.

Developing sample weights in this manner means that variable sampling rates, variable matching rates, clustering, and other elements of complex sample designs can be readily incorporated into the sample design of population-based case–control studies. There are numerous software packages that accommodate sample weights in the analyses of logistic regressions (e.g., SUDAAN, STATA, SAS, and WesVar). If replicate weights are to be employed for variance estimation purposes, analysts should make sure that the software package intended for use in the analyses can accommodate them (see Rust and Rao 1996, Korn and Graubard 1999, Heeringa et al. 2010). SUDAAN, STATA, SAS, and WesVar all can do so. If hierarchical modeling is of interest, M-PLUS accepts survey weights with replicate weights for variance estimation purposes.

There are many references to the development of sample survey weights in statistical literature, including Deville and Sarndal (1992), Brick and Kalton (1996), and Kalton and Flores-Cervantes (2003). In addition, Jiang et al. (2011) discuss adjusting for nonresponse in two-phase sample designs for population-based case–control studies. See also Chapter 26 in this volume.

3.8 The Need to Account for Analytic Plans When Developing a Sample Design: An Example

Brogan et al. (2001) undertook a comparison of telephone and area probability sample designs for case–control studies in the context of the Atlanta component of the Women's Interview Study of Health (or WISH) population-based case–control study for early onset breast cancers, which used a RDD methodology for sampling controls. They identified a number of advantages associated with an area probability approach. However, DiGaetano and Waksberg (2002) pointed out that they did not fully focus on the trade-offs made in developing sample designs for population-based case–control designs in general and the WISH sample design in particular. One concern was the relative costs. Another was that WISH study analyses were to be carried out using an unweighted approach, and Brogan et al. had not factored that into their assessment of the design. Negligible contributions from clusters were required—costly if targeting only two respondents per cluster, where a cluster was one or more census blocks. The average cluster size for their design was a little over 3.5. Moreover, the intraclass correlation coefficient within clusters based on census blocks can generally be expected to be larger than that for clusters of 100 telephone numbers, the WISH sample design.

Brogan et al. carried out analyses using population weights as described by Scott and Wild (2009) and Korn and Graubard (1999), adding considerably to the variance. With the weighting method described in Section 3.7 of this chapter, use of an area probability approach becomes far more viable analytically. Nevertheless, the high survey costs associated with such a sample design remain a concern. Using an ABS approach, discussed earlier, may reduce costs for APS somewhat in urban areas.

Some readers may find it helpful to read Brogan et al. and DiGaetano and Waksberg in learning further about the general decision-making process involved in developing sample designs for population-based case–control studies. However, it should be noted that sampling controls via telephone survey methodologies is unlikely to be considered a viable alternative for most such studies nowadays.

3.9 Sample Designs for Population-Based Case–Control Studies: When Unweighted Analyses Are Planned

The classic sample design for population-based case–control designs was described earlier. Unweighted analyses can be undertaken with such a design, and with a correctly specified model inferences based on the model can be appropriately made (Korn and Graubard 1999). Ideally, analytic models should also incorporate variables to address aspects of sample implementation such as survey nonresponse (which often involve interactions between variables such as lower response rates among older White males).

Unfortunately, the classic design is not usually feasible. Sample frames with all the necessary information for sampling controls (name, contact information, and matching variable data) generally are not available. Moreover, the focus on using unweighted analyses has served as a major constraint on the development of cost-effective designs. An approach for developing complex sample designs for population-based control studies has been to select samples that can be analyzed as if they were selected using a stratified random sample design, the classic design. Two such designs are described below, the second based on the first. The first is the design that was used successfully for many years where population-based controls were recruited using telephone screening.

3.10 Mimicking the Classic Design Using RDD-Based Sampling of Population-Based Controls

3.10.1 SAMPLING CONTROLS USING TELEPHONE SCREENING

Background. A sample design for sampling controls through telephone screening incorporated the RDD methodology developed in the late 1970s. RDD methods for conducting surveys of households that would permit inference to the general population as well as many subgroups of interest were developed by Waksberg and Mitofsky (Waksberg 1978). Working with colleagues from the NCI, Waksberg then developed a basic sample design strategy for sampling people via telephone screening to serve as controls in population-based case–control studies (Hartge et al. 1984, Waksberg 1998). This design was developed specifically to permit unweighted analyses of population-based case–control study data, routinely undertaken at that time. Reviewing this design will help show how trade-offs were made in developing a widely used approach to sampling population-based controls that proved useful for many years.

The Design. The Mitofsky–Waksberg RDD sampling methodology involved sampling clusters of telephone numbers (e.g., the first eight digits of 10-digit phone numbers) and screening a randomly selected phone number within each cluster to assess the expected productivity of sampling within the cluster. Equal probability samples of households with at least one telephone number could be produced with such an approach, and telephone screening is far less costly than in-person screening. It was straightforward to account for households with multiple telephone numbers and to select equal probability samples of controls within strata (e.g., matching cells). Cases with no household telephone were dropped from the study to maintain comparability with the control population eligible for the study.

Perhaps the most innovative aspects of the design dealt with the impact of clustering since it was anticipated that analyses would generally be done without reflecting this aspect of the sample design. To limit the contribution of telephone number clustering to the sample variance to negligible proportions, it was recommended to target an average of 1 or 2 responding controls in those clusters with at least one respondent (respondent to the main interview, not the screening effort). To both reduce respondent burden and limit the contribution to variance associated with "within-household" clustering of respondents, in studies involving both genders, clusters were randomly designated as male or female in advance. Sampled households with no member of the designated gender for the cluster were dropped after screening.

The major trade-offs made with this design can be itemized as follows:

1. Slightly lower response rates at that time (slightly higher potential for bias) for RDD compared to in-person screening but at a much lower cost.
2. With very low cluster sizes more clusters had to be fielded (increased costs) to permit analyses to be undertaken in the usual fashion (satisfying an analytic objective of restricting analyses to software packages users were likely to be familiar with so that important elements of the sample design could be reasonably ignored in the analyses).
3. Unbiased analyses achieved by maintaining comparability between cases and restricted definition of controls, but (as noted by Hartge et al. 1984) potential limitation in terms of a more broad application of survey findings.

This design was often used only to sample controls under the age of 65.

3.10.2 SAMPLING CONTROLS USING AN AREA PROBABILITY SAMPLE

A study of oral cancer in Puerto Rico (Hayes et al. 1999) used a multistage area probability study design for sampling controls under the age of 65 that followed Waksberg's RDD approach—targeting two participating controls per PSU and designating sampled households within PSUs as either male or female to limit the effect of the intraclass correlation within households. Controls age 65 or older were sampled from lists of Medicare beneficiaries (along the lines of the classic design since age, sex, and race were available on these lists).

This sample design for controls under age 65 limited the contribution of clustering to the sample variance, a requirement for the planned unweighted analyses. Of course, it was more expensive to field than would have been the case had more extensive clustering been permitted and appropriately accounted for in the analyses. An RDD approach for sampling controls under 65 was considered but not employed because telephone coverage of households in Puerto Rico was considered undesirably low.

3.10.3 IMPLICATIONS AND CONSIDERATIONS

Unweighted analyses have been the general approach used for population-based case–control study data. If unweighted analyses are planned, care should be taken to ensure that the elements of the sample design and/or its implementation (such as survey nonresponse) are either (i) appropriately reflected in the modeling to limit the potential for bias arising from model misspecification or (ii) of a nature where they can be reasonably ignored, as with Waksberg's sample design for sampling controls using RDD (Waksberg 1998, DiGaetano and Waksberg 2002).

As noted earlier, Potthoff et al. (2008) offers other strategies for developing sample designs (mainly discussed in the context of telephone surveys) where unweighted analyses are planned.

Unfortunately, it is often not feasible to undertake a population-based case–control study that strictly follows or can mimic the classic design. Lists of the target population for controls are often not available. Even when available, if a study calls for frequency matching and one of the matching variables is not on the lists, screening is needed for oversampling purposes to achieve targeted matching rates. Screening increases costs, and the increases might be prohibitive unless alternative sample design strategies are considered. Such strategies could involve oversampling areas where a subpopulation of interest is more heavily concentrated or exclusion of areas where only a small percentage of the target subpopulations are found. Cost savings and operational efficiencies can be obtained through cluster sampling. All of these considerations suggest that advantage should be taken of the full range of sample design options when undertaking a population-based case–control study. Two studies that benefited from such flexibility are described next.

3.11 Examples of the Development of Complex Sample Designs for Population-Based Case–Control Studies Using Weighted Analyses Where Cases Serve as the Reference Population and Variance Estimates Reflect the Sample Design

3.11.1 KIDNEY CANCER STUDY

The U.S. Kidney Cancer Study (KCS) was a frequency matched population-based case–control study carried out by the NCI with case ascertainment from early 2002 through early 2007. The KCS was focused on renal cell cancer primarily in the Detroit area (Wayne, Oakland, and Macomb Counties). Data were also gathered briefly in the Chicago area (Cook County), but the discussion below pertains to the Detroit area in particular.

Controls were to be frequency matched to cases on race (Black and White), age (20–79), and sex. Blacks were of particular analytic interest, but there were far more White cases than Black. Thus, to increase power for this important subgroup, the matching rate for Blacks was 2 to 1 while for Whites it was 1 to 1. In addition, White cases in some older age groups were subsampled to preserve survey resources.

Controls aged 65 and older were selected from lists of Medicare beneficiaries, provided by the CMS, where age, sex, and race were all available. Initially, controls for those aged 20–64 were to be obtained via telephone screening using RDD. However, response rates proved undesirably low and an alternative sample design had to be developed for this age range. It was decided to use DMV listings, available from both the states of Michigan and Illinois at that time. These DMV listings provided both sex and date of birth (age) but not race.

One alternative was to sample controls from DMV listings based on strata representing the cross-classification of the matching variable categories and then screen to find the targeted number of controls for race. However, this was simply too expensive to undertake.

A more cost-efficient design was developed based on the work of Waksberg et al. (1997). They showed that oversampling census block groups with high percentages of Blacks can be a relatively efficient approach to oversampling Blacks in an area sample design. Identifying the block groups associated with addresses found on a DMV file thus has the potential of accomplishing a similar sort of efficiency conditional on a suitable means for linking addresses to block groups. Geocoding provided such a means. Geocoding software was used to link DMV addresses to block groups (block group-level assignments can be expected to be highly accurate).

After completing the geocoding, DMV addresses were partitioned into two groups based on 2000 census data: high Black density (roughly, at least 85%

Black) and low Black density. Thus, the vast majority of people found in the high Black density stratum would be Black. Moreover, this definition of the strata also took into account the percentage of the Black population covered by the high Black density stratum, since a design effect would be incurred when using a different sampling rate for Black controls found living in the low Black density areas. It turned out that approximately 85% of Blacks in the Detroit area in 2000 were found in high Black density areas as defined earlier. The remaining 15% of the Black population found in "low Black density" areas represented only about 5% of the total population in "low density" areas, so such Blacks were to be undersampled for the study. However, since it was planned to use sample weights poststratified to the case population distribution in the analyses, this did not raise bias concerns but would increase sample variability over what was originally planned for using an RDD approach for sampling controls. To compensate for the reduction in precision due to the design effects associated with the variation in sampling rates, sample sizes were increased. The design effects varied by matching cell (age by sex by race) and were expected to range from 1.35 to 1.45. The overall design effect turned out to be about 1.27 for the DMV controls in Detroit.

To limit survey costs, some cases were not selected with certainty—some older age groups were sampled. Sample weights were developed for all cases reflecting both the chance of selection and adjustment for differential nonresponse (response rates varied by such factors as age, race, and gender). These served as the basis for the estimated case population distribution used in the poststratification of control weights.

Additional discussion of the sample design for the KCS can be found in DiGaetano et al. (2003). See Li et al. (2011) for discussion related to the analyses.

3.11.2 CLASSICAL KAPOSI SARCOMA CASE–CONTROL STUDY IN SICILY, ITALY

A frequency matched population-based case–control study of classical Kaposi sarcoma was conducted in Sicily, Italy, from July 2002 through June 2006. In developing the sample design for selecting controls, it was noted that all residents of Sicily have an assigned primary care physician. Thus, sampling physician practices and then patients within practices—a two-stage cluster design—was implemented.

Practices were sampled with probability proportionate to the number of patients on the practice roster with 450 practices sampled in all. Overall strata sample sizes were determined with the goal of matching the expected case distribution across the matching variables, age and sex. Sampling rates were allowed to vary within strata (the cells formed by the cross-classification of the matching variables) since the distribution of people eligible to serve as controls varied across physician practices. With contributions to the variance associated with differential sampling rates and clustering, sample weights (and replicate weights for variance estimation purposes) were used in the analyses (see Li et al. (2011) for more details on both the sample design and analyses).

3.12 Summary

In addition to addressing sample design issues for population-based case–control studies generally, a focus of this chapter has been to encourage the adaptation of a survey sampling perspective when planning the undertaking of such studies. A major concern is the constraint placed on sample designs for these studies by limiting the analyses of study data to unweighted analyses where cases and controls are treated as if selected through stratified random sampling. In so doing, population-based case–control studies are often much more costly than they need to be. Moreover, because this approach often requires a number of assumptions to be made, increased risk of bias can arise (due, for example, to model misspecification or higher than the nominal probability of a Type 1 error).

This chapter has offered several new perspectives on the sample design and analysis of the case–control data. Perhaps paramount is the strategy to treat the case superpopulation as the reference population for analyses. In so doing, a weighting approach providing much greater statistical efficiency than those contemplated in the past can be employed. When frequency matching is used, this weighting approach is designed to ensure that the objective of the frequency matching is achieved exactly. Moreover, adjustments to the weights can be undertaken to help reduce the potential for bias arising from nonresponse, and variance estimates can be routinely developed that reflect the sample design, as they are in other survey sampling efforts. Through optimal allocation considerations, survey resources can be better focused (through, for example, the use of variable matching rates) to help ensure that the highest priority analyses for a study have targeted levels of power. Statistical packages are available to carry out the standard approaches to analyzing case–control data such as logistic regression with weighted data and reflecting the sample design in variance estimation. Bias concerns arising from sample misclassification can be avoided using survey weights (such misclassification can result when matching on age as differences in probabilities of selection for controls in the same analytic age group can occur).

Increasing application of a survey sampling perspective to both the sample design and analysis of population-based case–control studies can help reduce survey costs while improving the quality of the resulting findings.

REFERENCES

Battaglia M, Khare M, Frankel M, Murray M, Buckley P, Peritz S, James M, Lepkowski, Clyde Tucker, Michael Brick J, Edith D. De Leeuw, Lilli Japec, Paul Lavrakas J, Michael Link W, Roberta L. Sangster. Response rates: how have they changed and where are they headed?. In: Lepkowski J et al., editors. *Advances in Telephone Survey Methodology*. Hoboken, NJ: Wiley; 2008. p 529–560.

Breslow NE. Case control studies. In: Ahrens W, Pigeot I, editors. *Handbook of Epidemiology*. Berlin: Springer; 2005. p 287–319.

Breslow NE, Chatterjee N. Design and analysis of two-phase studies with binary outcome applied to Wilms tumour prognosis. J Roy Stat Soc Ser C (Appl Stat) 1999;48:457–468.

Breslow NE, Day NE Statistical methods in cancer research, Vol. 2: the design and analysis of cohort studies, IARC Scientific Publications No. 82; Lyon, France: International Agency of Research on Cancer; 1987. p 305–306.

Brick JM, Kalton G. Handling missing data in survey research. Stat Methods Med Res 1996;5:215–238.

Brick JM, Williams D, Montaquila JM. Address-based sampling for subpopulation surveys. Public Opin Q 2011;75(3):409–428.

Brogan DJ, Denniston MM, Liff JM, Flagg EW, Coates RJ, Brinton LA. Comparison of telephone sampling and area sampling: response rates and within-household coverage. Am J Epidemiol 2001;153:1119–1127.

Christian L, Dimock M, Keeter S. 2009. Accurately locating where wireless respondents live requires more than a phone number. Based on presentation at Annual Meeting of the American Association for Public Opinion Research; 2009 May 14–17; Hollywood, Florida. Available at http://pewresearch.org/pubs/1278/cell-phones-geographic-sampling-problems. Published online: 2009 Jun 9.

Cochran W. *Sampling Techniques*. 3rd ed. New York: Wiley; 1977.

Cochran W. *Planning and Analysis of Observational Studies*. New York: Wiley; 1983.

Colt JS, Karagas MR, Schwenn M, Baris D, Johnson A, Stewart P, Verrill C, Moore LE, Lubin J, Ward MH, Samanic C, Rothman N, Cantor KP, Beane Freeman LE, Schned A, Cherala S, Silverman DT. Occupation and bladder cancer in a population-based case-control study in northern New England. Occup Environ Med 2011a;68(4): 239–249.

Colt JS, Schwartz K, Graubard BI, Davis F, Ruterbusch J, DiGaetano R, Purdue M, Rothman N, Wacholder S, Chow W. Hypertension and risk of renal cell carcinoma among White and Black Americans. Epidemiology 2011b;22:797–804.

Correa A, Stewart WF, Yeh HC, Santos-Burgoa C. Exposure measurement in case-control studies: reported methods and recommendations. Epidemiol Rev 1994; 16(1):18–32.

Curtin R, Presser S, Singer E. Changes in telephone survey nonresponse over the past quarter century. Public Opin Q 2005;69:87–98.

Deville J-C, Sarndal C-E. Calibration estimators in survey sampling. J Am Stat Assoc 1992;87:376–382.

DiGaetano R, Graubard B, Rao S, Severynse J, Wacholder S. 2003. Sampling racially matched population controls for case-control studies: using DMV lists and oversampling minorities. Federal Committee on Statistical Methodology Research Conference 2003, Concurrent Session IX-B. FCSM Statistical Policy Working Paper 37. Available at http://www.fcsm.gov/reports/.

DiGaetano R, Waksberg J. Commentary: trade-offs in the development of a sample design for case-control studies. Am J Epidemiol 2002;155:771–775.

Dohrmann S, Han D, Mohadjer L. Residential address lists vs. traditional listing: enumerating households and group quarters. Proceedings of the American Statistical Association, Section on Survey Research Methods; 2006. p 2959–2964.

Dohrmann S, Han D, Mohadjer L. Improving coverage of residential address lists in multistage area samples. Proceedings of the American Statistical Association, Section on Survey Research Methods; 2007. p 3219–3226.

Dohrmann S, Kalton G, Montaquila J, Good C, Berlin M. Using address based sampling frames in lieu of traditional listing: a new approach. Proceedings of the American Statistical Association, Section on Survey Research Methods; 2012. p 3729–3741.

Fears TR, Gail MH. Analysis of a two-stage case-control study with cluster sampling of controls: application to nonmelanoma skin cancer. Biometrics 2000;56:190–198.

Folsom RE, Potter FJ, Williams SR. Notes on a composite size measure for self-weighting samples in multiple domains. Presented at the meeting of the American Statistical Association, Section on Survey Research Methods; 1987 Aug 17–20; 1987.

Graubard BI, Fears T, Gail M. Effects of cluster sampling on epidemiologic analysis in population-based case-control sampling. Biometrics 1989;45:1053–1071.

Graubard BI, Korn EL. Inference for superpopulation parameters using sample surveys. Stat Sci 2002;17:73–96.

Green JL. Mathematical programming for sample design and allocation problems. Proceedings of the American Statistical Association, Section on Survey Research Methods ; 2000. p 688–692.

Hartge P, Brinton L, Rosenthal J, Cahill J, Hoover R, Waksberg J. Random digit dialing in selecting a population-based control group. Am J Epidemiol 1984;120:825–833.

Hayes RB, Bravo-Otero E, Kleinman DV, Brown LM, Fraumeni JF, Harty LC, Winn DM. Tobacco and alcohol use and oral cancer in Puerto Rico. Cancer Causes Control 1999;10(1):27–33.

Heeringa SG, West BT, Berglund PA. *Applied Survey Data Analysis*. Boca Raton: Chapman & Hall/CRC; 2010.

Iannacchione V. The changing role of address-based sampling in survey research. Public Opin Q 2011;75(3):556–575.

Jiang Y, Scott AJ, Wild CJ. Adjusting for non-response in population-based case control studies. Int Stat Rev 2011;79:145–159.

Kalton G, Flores-Cervantes I. Weighting methods. J Off Stat 2003;19(2):81–97.

Kalton G, Piesse A. Survey research methods in evaluation and case-control studies. Stat Med 2007;26:1675–1687.

Kim JK, Navarro A, Fuller WA. Replicate variance estimation after multi-phase stratified sampling. J Am Stat Assoc 2006;101:312–320.

Kim JK, Yu CL. Replication variance estimation under two-phase sampling. Survey Methodol 2011;37:67–74.

Kish L. *Survey Sampling*. New York: Wiley; 1965.

Kish L. *Statistical Design for Research*. New York: Wiley; 1987.

Kish L. Weighting for unequal pi. J Off Stat 1992;8(2):183–200.

Knol MJ, Vandenbroucke JP, Scott P, Egger M. What do case-control studies estimate? Survey of methods and assumptions in published case-control research. Am J Epidemiol 2008;168:1073–1081.

Korn EL, Graubard BI. *Analysis of Health Surveys*. New York: Wiley; 1999.

Lavrakas PJ, Shuttles CD, Steeh C, Fienberg H. The state of surveying cell phone numbers in the United States: 2007 and beyond. Public Opin Q 2007;71(5):840–854.

Li Y, Graubard BI, DiGaetano R. Weighting methods for population-based case-control studies with complex sampling. J Roy Stat Soc Ser C (Appl Stat) 2011;60(2): 165–185.

Link MW, Battaglia MP, Frankel MR, Osborn L, Mokdad AH. Address-based versus random-digit dialed surveys: comparison of key health and risk indicators. Am J Epidemiol 2006;164:1019–1025.

Link MW, Battaglia MP, Frankel MR, Osborn L, Mokdad AH. Comparison of address based sampling (ABS) versus random-digit dialing (RDD) for general population surveys. Public Opin Q 2008;72(1):6–27.

Lumley T. *Complex Surveys: A Guide to Analysis Using R*. New York: Wiley; 2010.

Miettinen O. Matching and design efficiency in retrospective studies. Am J Epidemiol 1970;91:111–118.

Potthoff RF, Halabi S, Schildkraut JM, Newman BM. Flexible frames and control sampling in case-control studies. Am Stat 2008;62(4):307–313.

Rao JNK. On double sampling for stratification and analytic surveys. Biometrika 1973;6:125–133.

Roth S, Han D, Montaquila J. The ABS frame: quality and considerations. Proceedings of the American Statistical Association, Section on Survey Research Methods; 2012. p 3779–3793.

Rothman KJ, Greenland S, Lash TL. *Modern Epidemiology*. 3rd ed. Philadelphia: Lippincott Williams & Wilkins; 2008.

Rust KF, Rao JNK. Variance estimation for complex surveys using replication techniques. Stat Methods Med Res 1996;5:281–310.

Scott AJ. Population-based case control studies. Survey Methodol 2006;32(2):123–132.

Scott AJ, Wild CJ. Fitting logistic models under case-control or choice based sampling. J Roy Stat Soc Ser B (Methodol) 1986;48:170–182.

Scott AJ, Wild CJ. Fitting regression models to case-control data by maximum likelihood. Biometrika 1997;84:57–71.

Scott AJ, Wild C. Case-control studies with complex sampling. J Roy Stat Soc (Appl Stat) 2001;50:389–401.

Scott AJ, Wild CJ. On the robustness of weighted methods for fitting model to case-control data by maximum likelihood. J Roy Stat Soc Ser B (Methodol) 2002;64:207–220.

Scott AJ, Wild CJ. Population-based case-control studies. In: Pfeffermann D, Rao CR, editors. *Handbook of Statistics, Vol. 29B, Sample Surveys: Inference and Analysis*. Oxford: Elsevier; 2009. p 431–453.

Smith PG, Day NE. Matching and confounding in the design and analysis of epidemiological case-control studies. In: Bithell JF, Coppi R, editors. *Perspectives in Medical Statistics*. London: Academic Press; 1987. p 39–64.

Tourangeau R, Rips LJ, Rasinski K. *The Psychology of Survey Response*. Cambridge: Cambridge University Press; 2000.

Voigt LF, Schwartz SM, Doody DR, Lee SC, Li CI. Effects of cluster sampling on epidemiologic analysis in population-based case-control sampling. Am J Epidemiol 2011;173:118–126.

Wacholder S, McLaughlin JK, Silverman DT, Mandel JS. Selection of controls in case-control studies I. Principles. Am J Epidemiol 1992a;135:1019–1028.

Wacholder S, Silverman DT, McLaughlin JK, Mandel JS. Selection of controls in case-control studies II. Types of controls. Am J Epidemiol 1992b;135: 1029–1041.

Wacholder S, Silverman DT, McLaughlin JK, Mandel JS. Selection of controls in case-control studies III. Design options. Am J Epidemiol 1992c;135:1042–1050.

Waksberg J. Sampling methods for random digit dialing. J Am Stat Assoc 1978;73: 40–46.

Waksberg J. Random digit dialing sampling for case-control studies. In: Armitage P, Colton T, editors. *Encyclopedia of Biostatistics*. New York: Wiley; 1998. p 3678–3682.

Waksberg J, Judkins D, Massey JT. Geographic-based oversampling in demographic surveys of the United States. Survey Methodol 1997;23:61–71.

Walsh MC, Trentham-Dietz A, Palta M. Availability of driver's license master lists for use in government-sponsored public health research. Am J Epidemiol 2011; 173(12):1414–1418.

Wolter K. *Introduction to Variance Estimation*. 2nd ed. New York: Springer; 2007.

ONLINE RESOURCES

Registries maintained as part of the Surveillance Epidemiology and End Results (SEER) program of the National Cancer Institute (NCI) maintain data on cancer cases identified in specified areas across the United States. The quality of information available on cases in terms of both the availability of case-level microdata and the completeness of reporting can be expected to be high in such areas. In addition, arrangements for rapid case ascertainment may be possible to help ensure high coverage of incident cases. Information on SEER can be found at: http://seer.cancer.gov/.

An advantage to SEER data is that microdata are relatively easy for researchers to use, permitting identification of the number of cases of a particular cancer site and histology combination for each SEER site.

The North American Association of Central Cancer Registries (NAACCR) evaluates registry case reporting completeness and other data quality measures and assigns a certification level of gold, 95 percent or higher coverage, or silver, 90 percent or more. Details are at: www.naaccr.org/Certification/USCert2008.aspx

NAACCR also makes microdata available in its CINA Deluxe data set at: www.naaccr.org/Research/CINADeluxe.aspx

Researchers must have an affiliation with a NAACCR member as well as go through an application process to get access to the data. The ability to undertake rapid case ascertainment in a given area would have to be explored.

The Centers for Disease Control and Prevention (CDC) maintains the National Program of Cancer Registries (NPCR), all of which are part of NAACCR. This program also maintains high standards for completeness and data quality. Although the NPCR does not routinely make microdata available to researchers, researchers can contact individual NPCR registries. To obtain access, go to: www.cdc.gov/cancer/npcr.

The National Program of Cancer Registries (NPRC) has funded a website, that includes useful information for researchers on all U.S. cancer registries. This website includes information for all U.S. cancer registries and was developed "to aid cancer epidemiology researchers in navigating the regulatory environment surrounding cancer registries and the specific requirements to obtain data for research purposes and to provide a method for tracking their IRB and other regulatory committee submissions at different States." It can be accessed at: https://www.cancerirbassistance.org

Standard definitions for survey disposition codes are available at the American Association for Public Opinion Research website at: http://www.aapor.org.

The Research Data Assistance Center or RESDAC should be contacted for information on the availability and costs of lists of Medicare Beneficiaries that could serve as population controls for a particular study. Name, address, date of birth, gender, and race are examples of variables that could be made available for sampling purposes. The URL for RESDAC is: www.resdac.org

CHAPTER FOUR

Sampling Rare Populations

James Wagner and Sunghee Lee
Institute for Social Research, University of Michigan, Ann Arbor, MI, USA

4.1 Introduction

This chapter focuses on methods for sampling rare populations in health surveys. Designing a sample for a rare population is a difficult endeavor. Sample designers need to consider the errors and costs associated with alternative designs. The costs associated with the incidence of the rare group are certainly a key consideration, but it is also important to not lose sight of other errors that may be associated with each design. For example, some sampling frames may not include or "cover" important parts of the rare group. If the uncovered portion of the rare group is different with respect to the variables of interest, this undercoverage may lead to bias. Sample design decisions may also have consequences in relation to nonresponse biases as less expensive modes of contact are usually associated with lower response rates. Decisions about sample design may also have an impact on measurement errors. For example, interviewer-administered modes may lead to more socially desirable responses. As a result of these issues, a "total survey error" perspective (Groves 1989) is a useful conceptual tool for considering alternative sample designs.

We begin this chapter with a definition of rare populations, considering reasons why it may be necessary to study rare groups, and then give an overview of some of the issues associated with designing a sample of a rare group. The remainder of this chapter considers a number of design alternatives, beginning

Handbook of Health Survey Methods, First Edition. Edited by Timothy P. Johnson.

with probability sample methods and concluding with a set of designs that may be characterized as nontraditional or nonprobability, depending upon the implementation. Each of the methods is illustrated with a number of example studies, including a more detailed examination of one or two studies in each section. In addition, for each method, there are multiple references that may be useful when designing such samples.

4.1.1 DEFINITION OF RARE POPULATIONS

While the term, *rare populations*, is used in health research generally to indicate subgroups in the total population that are small in size, there is no clear definition. Kalton (2009) uses the proportion of the subgroup in the population and classifies into domains such as major (more than 10%), minor (1–10%), mini- (0.1–1%), and rare (less than 0.01%). On the other hand, Tourangeau (2014), in defining "hard-to-reach" populations, uses a broader set of criteria including elements of data collection operations and introduces different types of hard-to-survey populations, including those that are hard to sample, hard to identify, hard to find/contact, hard to persuade, and hard to interview. In spite of an absence of a clear definition, it can be agreed that locating some subgroups in the general population is very difficult. Consider the Latino gay, bisexual, and transgender population studied in Ramirez-Valles et al. (2005). They are rare in the general population not only ethnically but also sexually and fit Kalton's definition of a minority group in the population and, hence, hard to sample. Moreover, given uncertain social acceptability of sexual minorities, they may wish not to express their sexual orientation, which, in turn, makes them hidden in the general population and, therefore, elusive and hard to find. In this chapter, we will use "rare populations" as a description of the low prevalence of the group of interest. We note that the problem of sampling from rare populations may be further complicated when the rare population is also difficult to identify or interview.

4.1.2 NEED TO STUDY RARE POPULATIONS

Many rare populations are associated with being at high risk for negative health behaviors and outcomes, which has led to an increased demand for data on these populations, for example, racial and ethnic minorities (e.g., Mesch et al. 2008), lesbian, gay, bisexual and transgender (LGBT) populations (e.g., Sanchez et al. 2009), human immunodeficiency virus (HIV)-positive persons (e.g., Dandona et al. 2008) including men who have sex with men (MSM) (e.g., Remafedi 2002), commercial sex workers (CSWs) (e.g., Sarkar et al. 2008), and injection drug users (IDUs) (e.g., Kang et al. (2009)). Although not impossible, studying such rare groups as a cross-section in the general population is challenging, because sample sizes are often far too small to provide reasonable statistical power. If these rare groups are the target population of a study, sampling their members becomes an issue.

4.1.3 DIFFICULTIES SAMPLING RARE POPULATIONS

There is a great deal of research into methods for sampling from rare populations (e.g., Kish 1965 (Section 11.4), Kalsbeek 2003, Kalton 2009, Kalton and Anderson 1986, Sudman et al. 1988). There are two main reasons why sampling for rare populations may be difficult. First, the rarer the group of interest, the higher the screening efforts and costs required to identify members of the group. In some cases, screening may require more resources than conducting actual interviews with eligible persons. Second, depending on the level of social stigma, discrimination and acceptance associated with the characteristics of the rare population of interest, some may misreport their eligibility intentionally in the screening interviews in order not to reveal their identity. For these reasons, traditional probability sampling approaches, although ideal, are sometimes impractical. However, it is worthwhile to note that there are numerous studies of hard-to-reach populations using probability samples such as multistage area probability samples (e.g., Cochran and Mays 2000) and Random Digit Dial (RDD) telephone samples (e.g., Catania et al. 2001). Binson et al. (2007) provide a list of such examples in Table 15.1 in their study.

As a result of these difficulties, there has been a recent spate of development of new methods that are nontraditional and lead to the development of samples for which the probabilities are themselves difficult, if not impossible, to calculate. These also include methods that were developed for purposes other than sampling rare populations. Some examples of these methods include venue-based sampling, time–location sampling, web-based sampling, and respondent-driven sampling.

This chapter provides an overview of traditional, probability methods, and also describes several nontraditional, nonprobability methods for sampling rare populations. In Section 4.2, we will discuss traditional probability sampling methods. In Section 4.3, we will discuss methods that are either not probability methods or may be only considered probability samples if certain assumptions can be made. Other chapters in this volume consider other issues related to sampling. Chapter 2 discusses several probability methods frequently used for general population studies. Chapter 3 considers sampling for the recruitment of controls in case–control studies.

There are several studies that are empirical comparisons of different sampling approaches, including nonprobability and probability methods (e.g., Kendall et al. 2008, Johnston et al. 2006). These studies attempt to evaluate the errors associated with sampling frames and their associated data collection methods. Errors resulting from data collection methods associated with sampling frames include any nonresponse errors resulting from these methods. For this reason, it is difficult to attribute differences to the sampling frame. In addition, since the results depend upon the data collection protocol, they may not generalize well to other settings.

For any study, before considering sampling, it is important to precisely define the study target population. This is even more important for sampling rare populations, because the definitions themselves can be elusive (Meyer and Wilson 2009). One example is the term, *sexual minorities*. This group can be defined very differently across different surveys (e.g., sexual identity, using sexual behavior or sexual attraction discussed in Sell (2007)), and these different definitions may lead to quite different conclusions about the characteristics of the group. Time elements may need to be considered for defining target populations as there may be changes over time. For example, only half of the men who ever had sex with men before the age of 18 did so after 18 (Laumann et al. 1994).

4.2 Traditional Probability Sampling Approaches

Probability sampling is a procedure for randomly selecting a sample such that every member of the population has a known, nonzero probability of being selected (see, e.g., Cochran (1977)). It has an advantage over nonprobability methods in that it allows the researcher to control the sampling bias and variance. Randomization in the selection process solves many of the issues related to sampling bias. Sampling variance is controlled by selecting an appropriate sample size. There has been much research to support unbiased inference from a variety of sample designs that randomly select samples with known probabilities. Methods for estimating variance have been developed for a wide variety of probability sampling designs (Wolter 2007). Many of these have been implemented in commonly available statistical software packages.

Although these methods have been well studied, they may also be expensive, particularly for rare populations. This has led to the search for alternatives. In this section, we describe alternatives that fall within the class of probability samples. At least one of these sample designs may be feasible in a wide range of situations. In the next section, we discuss the methods that may fall outside of probability sampling.

4.2.1 SCREENING STUDIES

One straightforward approach to sampling is to use probability methods for selecting a sample from the general population. The sample is selected from a frame that does not identify members of the target population and, therefore, will include a large proportion of cases that are not part of the group of interest. Since the eligible cases are not identified on the frame, they need to be identified after a sample has been selected. This involves "screening" sampled units to determine eligibility. Each household is contacted and persuaded to respond to a series of questions that are used to determine eligibility. This process can be very expensive, particularly if the proportion of eligible cases in the sample is low. It may be further complicated if the rare population is "hidden," as described earlier.

An example of a study that uses screening to identify a relatively rare group is the Health and Retirement Study (HRS, http://hrsonline.isr.umich.edu/). The HRS is a panel study that recruits a new cohort of persons aged 50–56 every 6 years. This age group has been present in about 9–10% of all households.

The study has selected a national sample using multistage area probability sampling to obtain a sample of all housing units. The final sample is clustered in a sample of counties and further clustered within a sample of neighborhoods within the sampled counties. This clustering reduces travel costs while inducing a correlation among the sampled units that reduces the "effective" sample size (see Kish 1965). The sample of housing units is then screened using face-to-face interviewing techniques to identify households with an eligible person or persons. This screening procedure produces response rates that are quite high. However, this screening procedure is quite expensive to implement.

These methods might be made less expensive if the screening component can be carried out relatively cheaply—for example, in a less expensive mode. A screening questionnaire to identify eligible households or persons might be distributed by mail. Identified eligible households or persons could then be interviewed in other, more expensive modes. The use of the less expensive mode for screening, however, may have negative consequences. For instance, less expensive modes generally produce lower response rates. The errors associated with this nonresponse need to be balanced against other errors.

An example of a study that has experimented with using less-expensive modes for screening is the National Household Education Surveys (NHES) program. These surveys have used a mailed screening survey to identify eligible households (Brick et al. 2011). The experiments have included ways to improve response to the screening survey. The mailed version of the survey can be contrasted with earlier versions of the survey that used RDD sampling. Once eligible persons are identified via the mailed survey, they are contacted by telephone for a detailed interview. The HRS is experimenting with a similar approach. The HRS has used mailed surveys with face-to-face follow-up for nonrespondents as a way to decrease costs while maintaining high response rates (Wagner et al. 2014).

Another option may be to attach the screening to an "omnibus" survey that interviews large numbers of persons from the general population. Under this approach, the screening questions used to identify the rare group would be added to the interview conducted for the general population survey. Identified eligible persons are then asked for consent to release their information to be used by the study interested in the rare population. One problem with this approach is that it may be difficult to find studies that interview large numbers of persons in the general population. Another drawback of this approach is that the quality of the data collected depends upon the procedures of the large survey, which has likely been designed for purposes other than evaluating the rare group of interest.

The Panel Study of Entrepreneurial Dynamics (PSED) Wave I is an example of a survey of a rare group (entrepreneurs) that attached questions to an omnibus survey of the population (Reynolds et al. 2004). The omnibus survey screened 64,622 households. A set of entrepreneurs were identified among this large number of households. A sample of nonentrepreneur "controls" was also identified. From these cases, the PSED survey completed interviews with 830 nascent entrepreneurs and 431 controls. Another example of using an omnibus survey in this way is a study of gay/bisexual men by Xia et al. (2006a, 2006b). They used the 2001 California Health Interview Survey, a large-scale survey targeting the general population, to identify the target group of gay/bisexual men and recontacted 398 such persons in 2002 to collect data about their sexual risk behaviors and HIV history and status.

4.2.2 STRATIFICATION AND OVERSAMPLING

There are methods that may help increase the rates at which eligible households are included in the sample. These methods depend upon the nature of the population of interest. If the population is geographically clustered, it may be possible to create geographic strata with varying rates of eligibility. Then strata with higher rates of eligibility can be "oversampled" relative to strata with lower eligibility rates. It is important to note that the high density stratum needs to include a large proportion of the rare group and have a higher prevalence rate than the low density stratum in order to lead to improved efficiency (Kish 1965, p. 406). If these conditions do not prevail, then large efficiency gains from this approach may not be possible.

Once the strata have been created, and the eligibility rates for each stratum calculated, then basic sample design theory (e.g., Cochran 1977, Kish 1965) can be used to optimally allocate the sample across the strata.

Geographic strata may be used for modest oversampling of racial and ethnic minorities. For other groups, there is infrequently much geographic clustering of groups. An alternative is to use incomplete commercially available lists merged to conventional sampling frames to create strata. Since these lists are incomplete (or else we could use them directly for sampling), sampling from both "likely to be eligible" and "likely ineligible" strata is still required in order to insure complete coverage. In order to be efficient, these methods need to be able to classify most of the rare group into a stratum that includes not too many cases that are not part of the rare group (Kish 1965, p. 406).

A special case of this method might be a list that has nearly complete coverage. The cases not on the list may be part of another stratum, from which no sample is selected. Kish (1965) calls this a "cut-off" stratum. If the undercovered cases are not different than those who are covered, such an approach is more efficient than trying to sample the "cut-off" stratum. Such an approach may produce a lower total mean-squared error since a much larger sample size can be achieved. The difficulty is that any biases due to the undercoverage cannot be directly evaluated.

An example of this disproportionate sampling across strata approach is the Health Information National Trends Survey (HINTS), which uses a geographic stratification of the nation into "high" and "low" concentrations of racial and ethnic minorities (Westat 2012). These areas were defined at the Census Block Group level using American Community Survey (ACS) data. Approximately 23.4% of the population was assigned to the stratum with high concentrations of minorities. This stratum was oversampled such that 53.4% of the sample came from it. This led to an oversample of minorities in the interviewed set.

As already mentioned, commercially available data may be used to stratify samples. These data are often incomplete and sometimes inaccurate. Therefore, they may not be suitable as sampling frames, but can be used to supplement existing sampling frames. For instance, it may be possible to merge data about household members' ages to a sampling frame of housing units. A large proportion of households may have this information to merge to a frame of housing units. A small proportion of the merged cases may have inaccurate information (perhaps due to mobility—that is, the information was correct until the person specified on the commercially available data moved). Although they may not be suitable enough to sample directly from these lists, they can provide information which allows for stratification based on the expected eligibility. For example, if we were interested in households with persons of a specific age, we might use this information to classify all housing units into three strata—merged data indicate an eligible person in household, merged data indicate no eligible person in household, and no merged data available. These three strata might have different expected eligibility rates. As with geographic stratification, these different eligibility rates produce different costs to complete an interview. Using this information, an optimal sample allocation can be designed which, depending upon the proportion of the rare population that is identified and the relative eligibility rates across the strata, may lead to efficiency gains.

The use of commercially available data to create sampling strata is beginning to be explored. An example is the National Survey of Medical Decisions (NSMD), which used such commercially available information to stratify an RDD sample of telephone numbers. The target population for this survey was persons over the age of 40. In order to improve overall eligibility rates, the sample was stratified into three groups: (i) those expected to be eligible based upon information merged onto the telephone number, (ii) those expected to be ineligible, and (iii) those for whom no information was available. Samples were selected from all three strata, however, stratum 1 was oversampled in order to increase the overall, unweighted eligibility rate and, thereby, increase the efficiency of the data collection (Couper et al. 2009). The expected ineligible stratum was sampled at the lowest rate. As was mentioned earlier, in order to realize large gains in efficiency, this kind of information needs to be relatively complete.

4.2.3 MULTIPLE SAMPLING FRAMES

Another option for sampling rare populations involves the use of multiple sampling frames (Hartley 1962, Hartley 1974, Kott et al. 1998, Skinner et al. 1994, Skinner and Rao 1996, Haines and Pollock 1998, Bankier 1986). In general, there may be several sampling frames available for the rare population, but each has its own definite weaknesses and strengths. For instance, one frame (e.g., a list of all housing units in the country) may have complete coverage of the rare group but would be very expensive to use because there are many ineligible units also on the frame. Another frame (e.g., a list of persons in the rare group) might have high eligibility but very low coverage. The multiple frame approach combines the strengths of each frame to overcome their individual weaknesses. In the example, the high coverage frame may be used to provide full coverage, while the low coverage frame is used to improve overall eligibility rates.

After the samples have been selected and interviews conducted, then data from interviews developed from each of the multiple frames need to be combined together in order to produce estimates for the population. Much theory has been developed for combining data from multiple frames (Hartley 1962, Skinner and Rao 1996). Most of these procedures require that membership of the responding unit in each of the frames be ascertained.

Recently, dual-frame surveys have become much more common for telephone surveys. The growth of mobile-only households has led to severe undercoverage of the general population for the RDD landline sampling frame. As a result, many telephone surveys now use a dual-frame approach that samples from the landline RDD sampling frame and the cellular RDD sampling frame (e.g., Hu et al. 2011, Brick et al. 2007). Data from the two frames are then combined using one of several procedures.

For a study of rare populations, a sampling frame that functions as a list of the target population but has less than full coverage would be supplemented with a sampling frame that has full coverage—for example, a list of all housing units in the nation. The higher the proportion of the target population that is on the list frame the better, as this contributes to efficiencies in the design. Obviously, if everyone (or nearly everyone) in the target population were on the list frame, then another frame would not be needed. However, as the coverage of the list frame decreases, the reliance upon the other, more general sampling frame increases.

Srinath et al. (2004) give an example of a dual-frame design for the National Immunization Survey (NIS). This survey was completed in earlier waves as an RDD sample. The target population is households with someone between 19 and 35 months of age. Slightly less than 4% of households meet this eligibility requirement. The dual-frame design combined an RDD sample (with high coverage and low eligibility) with a commercially available list of households expected to be eligible (with low coverage and high eligibility). Srinath et al. (2004) discuss how the sample was allocated across the two frames and methods for weighting the two samples in order to make estimates about the population.

4.3 Nontraditional and Nonprobability Sampling Approaches

Recently, a series of new sampling methods has been proposed. In this section, we describe venue-based, time-location, web-based sampling, snowball sampling, respondent-driven sampling, and multiplicity or network sampling methods separately. Some of these methods may be considered probability methods, but only if certain assumptions are met. For instance, network sampling requires that respondents provide accurate assessments of their network size. For each method, we examine actual applications in the published literature.

4.3.1 VENUE-BASED SAMPLING

When rare populations of interest show a tendency to gather at certain identifiable venues, one may consider using venue-based sampling. "Facility-based sampling" and "site-based sampling" are terms used interchangeably with "venue-based sampling." As the term suggests, these methods sample venues rather than people. A classic example of venue-based sampling is exit polling (Kalton 1991). There are also examples of sampling venues for rare populations: drug treatment centers for IDUs (e.g., Razak et al. 2003), sexually transmitted disease (STD) clinics for MSM and CSWs (e.g., Chys et al. 2002, Risbud et al. 2002), and correctional facilities for those engaged in illegal activities (e.g., Thaisri et al. 2003). Venue-based sampling is a popular method in HIV surveillance systems around the world for sampling MSM (Paquette and De Wit 2010). The venues employed by these systems included social venues (e.g., clubs, bars, gyms), events (e.g., gay parades, LGBT film festivals), venues offering sex on premise (e.g., bath houses, saunas), public cruising (e.g., parks), and social organizations and groups which MSM are likely to frequent. These venues are not necessarily geographic points and some can be mobile.

Venue-based sampling for rare populations starts with formative research that collects sampling-related information from persons who are knowledgeable about the target population through, for example, ethnographic methods (e.g., Meyer et al. 2008). The collected information includes popular venues along with their sizes (i.e., the number of visits). This research is meant to develop a list of all venues to which the target population goes and estimates of the number of rare group members who can be found there. Upon building the frame, venues are sampled as primary sampling units (PSUs) following probability proportionate to estimated sizes (PPeS) in the first stage. Stratification may be considered based on the characteristics of venues (Meyer and Wilson 2009). In the second stage, a sample of visitors to the selected venues is drawn, for example, using systematic sampling. Overall, this resembles the two-stage cluster sampling of exit polls. The difference between sampling for exit polls and venue-based sampling for rare populations is that exit polls are clearly bounded in time, while most rare populations are not. As a result, for sampling rare populations, there is an assumption that all members of the target group will visit the venues on the frame at one point during the data collection.

In order for venue-based sampling to produce a probability sample, the following set of assumptions should be met: (i) all potential venues are covered by the list of venues identified in the formative research; (ii) all population members visit the identified venues in the same pattern across venues; (iii) all the identified venues are accessible; (iv) the size is estimated accurately; and (v) visitors are sampled with a probability sampling approach. A study in Nicaragua by Danel et al. (1996) shows that there are natural settings where populations' venue visit patterns make these assumptions more plausible. However, a desirable property of unbiasedness provided through probability samples is not realized for venue-based sampling when inappropriate procedures or operational limitations are involved. For instance, if the venues are visited by only certain subgroups of the rare population, then this directly violates the second assumption, resulting in a nonprobability sample. In order to compensate for differential visit patterns and to calculate "selection" rates, some studies using venue-based sampling collect data on visit patterns from visitors. This is necessary in order to account for the fact that those who rarely visit the venue have a lower chance of being selected than those who frequently visit the venue. Using such data relies on an implicit assumption that a visitor can reliably say how many times they are likely to visit the venue.

There is no standard procedure for venue-based sampling. Hence, the formative research, when conducted, is not always conducted with a clearly stated, replicable method. Operational issues may limit the ability to select a probability sample at the second stage. If visitors are arriving at a rate faster than field staff are able to select and interview at the specified interval, then probability selections may break down. It is possible to adjust for such issues through weighting, but this assumes that field staff can count all the visitors. While venue-based sampling has the potential to produce probability samples, violating these assumptions will quickly lead to a situation where the probabilities of selection are unknowable, making the replicability of venue-based sample estimates uncertain.

Priorities for Local AIDS Control Efforts (PLACE) is a venue-based assessment tool, developed to provide information about social venues associated with HIV acquisition and transmission to local HIV intervention groups (Weir et al. 2002). It identifies venues where people meet for new sexual partners and examines the characteristics of those socializing at the venues, including formation of new and concurrent partnerships, sexual mixing, and condom use. The end goal of PLACE is to provide information about the social venues where at risk individuals acquire and transmit HIV to local groups for their intervention programs. The target population of the PLACE is clearly restricted to those at social venues in areas at an increased HIV risk.

Weir et al. (2004) provide an example of venue-based sampling. They used PLACE to study those in Karaganda, Kazakhstan in 2002 and 2003 and East London, South Africa in 2000 and 2003. Through formative research with informants who were knowledgeable about the areas, a list of social venues was identified along with names, locations, and sizes. The venues were selected through stratification and with PPeS, and 16 men and 8 women were selected from each venue for an interview. Identified venues differed greatly between data collection years in both locations. In Kazakhstan, the proportion of venues with IDUs socializing and CSWs soliciting clients increased from 15.9% to 35.3% between 2002 and 2003. The population at the selected venues also changed: having two or more sexual partners in the past 4 weeks increased for both genders (40.3% to 49.3% for males and 42.2% to 52.7% for females). Characteristics of the venues and the populations at the selected venues changed in South Africa between 2000 and 2003. HIV-prevention-related characteristics changed dramatically as condom availability at the venues increased from 9.8% to 39.5% and occurrence of AIDS prevention events at the venues increased from 23.4% to 67.2%.

While it may be appealing and convenient to use these changes as general trends in Karaganda and East London, these characteristics and their changes should not be extrapolated to populations beyond those socializing at the venues on the lists compiled during the formative research. If the formative research identified an exhaustive list of venues, then the results may be generalized to all venues. And if sampling individuals at the selected venues followed some type of probability sampling, then the results can be generalized to all individuals socializing at the venues on the list. On the basis of the methodology background, information given in Weir et al. (2004), it is not clear whether these assumptions may be met and whether the changes reflect true trends, differential biases in venue listing during the formative research and in sampling individuals at the venues or differential nonresponse patterns between study years.

4.3.2 TIME–LOCATION SAMPLING

An extension of venue-based sampling that includes a time element is time–location sampling (Kalton 1991). This method has recently been used to sample from rare populations who congregate in specific locations (Kanouse et al. 1999, MacKellar et al. 2007, Stueve et al. 2001). Like venue-based sampling, time–location sampling ultimately selects visits to specified venues, but unlike venue-based sampling, these visits occur over a specified range of times. The sample is selected in two stages. Time–location combinations (e.g., a dance club on Friday, March 15, 2013 from 10 PM–midnight) are selected as PSUs in the first stage. In this stage, PSUs are usually selected with PPeS. These sizes generally involve estimates since they are visits that will occur in the future. As with venue-based sampling, the formative research for defining the frame of PSUs is an important step if coverage of the rare population is to be complete. In the second stage, a sample of visits is selected from the sampled PSUs, usually systematically. If the sampling rate at the second stage is inversely proportional to the first-stage sampling rate, then all visits will have an equal probability of selection. Of course, in practice, this rarely happens and sampling weights are necessary to account for different rates of selection. If inference is to persons (as opposed to visits), then the number of times that persons visit the locations and times that are included on the sampling frame must be known. This can be difficult to reliably report if the number of visits is high (and hence difficult to remember) or because these visits may occur in the future and, therefore, may be speculative.

An example of time and location sampling is a study of female street prostitutes in Los Angeles County (Kanouse et al. 1999). In initial phases of the study design, the goal was to sample from all female prostitutes in LA County. However, this goal proved to be infeasible because it would be too costly to identify off-street prostitutes. Instead, the population was redefined to be street prostitutes since time–location sampling would allow access to this population.

For this study, nearly 200 interviews were conducted with knowledgeable persons in the formative research to identify locations where street prostitutes could be found to be working. The study team attempted to broaden the inclusion of locations by reviewing licensing records for "marker" establishments such as adult entertainment or gambling establishments that might also be associated with prostitution. In the end, the use of "marker" establishments added very little beyond the information obtained from expert interviews. Only about 1% of all interviews were completed in locations identified solely from "marker" establishments. The expert interviews also yielded estimates of the number of working prostitutes in each location. This part of formative research may provide information to assess the assumption about whether the identified venues cover all potential venues.

The second step of the sampling frame construction was to estimate sizes for each location. Two or more on-site visits were made to each location in order to estimate the expected number of eligible persons. These data were then combined with data from the experts in order to create sizes for each time–location. Time-locations were sampled with PPeS. Time–locations with an estimate of fewer than two women were treated as ineligible. The estimated sizes were updated every 2 weeks and the list of locations was updated periodically as well.

In the second stage, only one woman was selected per area. Interviewers went to the selected location at the selected time. They chose a random point within the area from which to start, and then randomly selected a direction to walk. They were to circle the selected location (street segment) so they either walked clockwise or counter-clockwise. They then selected the first woman they saw. If the first woman was not eligible or not interviewed, then they continued in the same direction until they either obtained an interview or returned to the starting point. Once an interview was obtained, the interviewer continued walking around the location, counting the women present, until the time period was over.

The data could be analyzed to represent visits, or a target population of person-time units (akin to visits). Weighting strategies, which involved making some reasonable assumptions, were also developed to analyze the dataset as a set of persons.

Time–location and venue-based sampling, when used to sample persons rather than visits, may be prone to coverage errors and sampling biases. First, there may be undercoverage if all the persons in the target population do not visit the locations that are included in the sampling frame. Frame construction for the National HIV Behavior Surveillance—Men who have Sex with Men (NHBS-MSM) Study (MacKellar et al. 2007) involved developing a list of locations attended by MSM. Knowledgeable persons were interviewed to determine a complete list of locations or venues. Typical venues included bars, dance clubs, businesses, social and religious organizations, parks, beaches, and special events. In an attempt to evaluate the coverage of such a frame, Xia et al. (2006c) used data from the California Health Interview Survey, a survey with a probability sample, to estimate that 83.5% of all MSM in California visit venues like those on the NHBS-MSM sampling frame. However, they also found that those who do not visit such venues are significantly different from those who do. The street prostitute study by Kanouse et al. (1999) addressed this challenge be redefining the target population to those who would likely be covered by a time–location sample. Second, there may be sampling biases if respondents cannot reliably report the number of visits made to the sampled locations over the specified time period of the study. If the survey measures are different for those who are frequent visitors relative to those who rarely visit the locations or venues on the frame, this may lead to biased estimates. Third, it is not unimaginable that the effort to adjust for differential visit patterns through weighting could dampen the efficiency due to difficulties respondents may face in reporting their visit patterns.

4.3.3 WEB-BASED SAMPLING

The web has the potential to be considered a desirable medium for reaching some rare populations, such as MSM, who frequently use the web for contacting other MSM (Benotsch et al. 2002, Bull et al. 2001, Elford et al. 2001, Parsons et al. 2004, Ross et al. 2000). Because the web provides anonymity and sexual partner availability with a lower level of stigmatization or discrimination against the LGBT population, it has accelerated web usage among the sexual minorities, making the web a contributing factor in the spread of HIV (Rosser et al. 2007, Zhang et al. 2008). Web surveys are also typically associated with administrative convenience and lowered costs. Therefore, there is a hope that the web will be useful for studying those populations and building HIV/AIDS behavioral surveillance systems (Chiasson et al. 2006, Zhang et al. 2008).

Sampling rare populations using the web, however, is not simple. In fact, web-based surveys report various sampling approaches. (See Couper (2000, 2007) for an overview of web surveys for the general population.) Most approaches, unfortunately, yield convenience samples where the sampling mechanism is determined by the respondents' self-selection rather than through a randomization under the control of the investigator. Examples of such methods include sampling through email blasts, chat rooms, instant messengers, and banner advertisements (Chiasson et al. 2006, Zhang et al. 2008). There are several studies that have used these approaches, including a study of Latino men who use the Internet to have sex with men (Rosser et al. 2009) and San Francisco Area MSM (Raymond et al. 2010). Although these are popularly used (Paquette and De Wit 2010), since they produce convenience samples, their generalizability is limited. There are a number of studies reporting biased measurement of various characteristics, including demographics, illicit drug use, and risky sexual behaviors, in web-based convenience samples of sexual minorities (e.g., Benotsch et al. 2002, Kim et al. 2001, Liau et al. 2006, Mettey et al. 2003, Ross et al. 2000, Rosser et al. 2007, Taylor et al. 2004, Tikkanene and Ross 2003, Weatherburn et al. 2003).

Pre-recruited web panels have also been considered for sampling rare populations. These panels may be recruited either through probability or through nonprobability methods. Characteristics of panel members are collected at the time of recruitment and used to identify subgroups of interest to various investigators. If the data from the panel includes information for identifying rare populations of interest, the list can be used to build a sampling frame containing only those eligible for the study. However, not all panels are of the same quality. Some recruit panel members only among web users. This may create serious coverage problems if the rare group has a substantial proportion of those who do not use the web. This approach may not be suitable when generalizations beyond web users are desired. If panel members are recruited through web advertisements and self-select into the panel, then this is a nonprobability sample. This self-selection may also create biases if it is selective on characteristics related to the outcomes of interest.

The other type of pre-recruited web panels starts with a probability approach (e.g., RDD telephone surveys) to sample those who are invited to the panels and extends beyond web users by providing web access to web nonusers. If study-specific samples are probability samples of the panel, then these samples are also probability samples. Of course, the panel recruitment may suffer from nonresponse. Any biases resulting from this initial nonresponse may be "inherited" by samples selected from the panel. Because probability of selection is known before the survey operations, the sample design weight can be calculated and further adjusted for potential nonresponse and coverage errors by using auxiliary data collected for the entire panel members. Except for panels such as those maintained by GfK, the Dutch LISS, and the American Life Panel, most web panels use nonprobability methods for sampling as they include web users who voluntarily join the panels and, therefore, provide limited ability to generalize from them.

Herek (2009) provides an example of a pre-recruited panel of more than 40,000 U.S. households that GfK sampled using an RDD sampling frame. Routine panel surveys conducted by GfK collected data on sexual orientation. This allowed the researcher to identify persons self-identified as LGBT. The survey request was sent to 902 English-speaking self-reported LGBT adults. Over the 3 weeks, 775 accessed the questionnaire. After excluding those who changed their self-reported sexual identity to heterosexual and randomly selecting one adult from households with multiple LGBT adults, the final sample size was 662. Because the panel recruitment relies on RDD, this approach does not cover those who do not have a landline telephone. While this is a concern, compared to the nonprobability approach discussed earlier, generalizability is much higher because the sample for panel recruitment is selected probabilistically and those without web access are equipped with a web device. Auxiliary information is available for the entire panel regardless of their response status. This allows not only nonresponse assessment but also nonresponse bias adjustment, although the paper did not include information on whether this was done.

4.3.4 SNOWBALL SAMPLING

Snowball sampling is another type of network sampling using chain referrals. According to Thompson (2012) and Handcock and Gile (2011), snowball sampling describes two very distinctive applications. One is applied to cases for studying rare and hidden populations (e.g., Kalton and Anderson 1986). The sampling typically starts with a convenience sample of the population of interest. Upon the completion of the interview with the first set of respondents, the respondents are asked to identify other members of the same population from their networks. Those identified will be included in the sample and an interview requested. The chain referral continues until the desired sample size is obtained. This approach exploits the fact the chances of a rare group member knowing another member are higher than the chances for a nonmember. Its origin is located in Trow (1957) who clearly indicated that the purpose of this type of sampling was not to produce a representative sample. The chain referral process may also be used to generate a sampling frame, if much of the target population can be reached in this manner.

The other type of "snowball sampling" is due to Goodman's (1961) work, which was based on Coleman (1958). In this application, a probability sample of the target population is initially recruited and the sampling proceeds through chain referrals within their networks, similar to the procedure for the first application. The main purpose of this application of snowball sampling is not to recruit individuals from some type of rare populations but to sample and study relationships. In sampling textbooks (e.g., Lohr 2009), the first application is introduced as snowball sampling. In this context, snowball samples are subject to potential biases unless strong assumptions are met.

Clatts et al. (1995) illustrate the use of snowball sampling. They study homeless youth in New York City. Undoubtedly, sampling such adolescents is difficult. Given that the eligibility was further limited to those with age between 12 and 23 years and being engaged in the street economy or at a substantial risk of becoming involved in the street economy, traditional probability sampling approaches are impractical and nearly impossible because of the absence of information about these difficult-to-locate and rare youth. The study clearly stated, "The use of chain referrals ... had no particular analytic purpose in and of itself," indicating that the snowball sampling was used for recruiting rare and hard-to-reach individuals rather than for studying relationships. They followed the general procedure of snowball sampling described earlier. Since the study goal was not generalizability of the information but its reliability, the nonprobabilistic nature of the sample was not a serious concern. It is worthwhile to note that the initial stage of their snowball sampling was a result of a substantial amount of efforts. They conducted formative research to obtain a basic understanding about the homeless youth, especially those involved in the street economy, and drew the initial sample with an approach that resembled time–location sampling. Therefore, although ultimately a convenience sample, great care was taken to obtain a sample suitable for the study purposes.

4.3.5 RESPONDENT-DRIVEN SAMPLING

Although hidden in the general population from an outsiders' point of view, members of some rare populations are linked to other members of the same group. These links may form an informal network. For instance, drug injection is carried out in group settings where an IDU will inject drugs into another IDU. The chances of an IDU knowing another IDU are much higher than those of a general population, non-IDU knowing any IDUs. First introduced by Heckathorn (1997, 2002), respondent-driven sampling (RDS) exploits the networked nature of specific rare populations for sampling purposes. Researchers first establish contact with a set of rare population members and conduct survey interviews with them. These are the "first wave" of respondents. Researchers utilize these respondents as "seeds" and exploit their social networks for sampling further participants. In RDS practice, these seeds are asked to recruit those who are eligible for the study from their own network. The resulting recruits are considered the second wave of sample. Once these recruits complete the survey, they are asked to recruit the third wave of sample from their network. Recruitment waves continue until the desired sample size is achieved. The overall recruitment/sampling structure follows a chain referral mechanism. One important key in the recruitment is usage of *incentivized* coupons prepared by the research team. Each RDS study respondent is given coupons to distribute to potential recruits in their social network. Other than seeds, recruits are to redeem valid coupons to participate in the survey. The recruiting participants are financially compensated not only for their participation but also by the number of coupons redeemed from among those that they distributed. The usage of coupons also provides information about the linkages among the network of sample units.

RDS claims to produce an unbiased sample of the rare population of interest (Heckathorn 1997, 2002). The claim assumes that the RDS recruitment chain follows a Markov process, which, in turn, allows the overall sample to achieve stationary probabilities. Study participants self-generate the sample in RDS. This eliminates the screening procedure necessary in traditional sampling methods for rare populations and lowers the cost substantially. Moreover, this lowers the concerns of personal privacy. RDS does not require revealing the potentially stigmatized and socially undesirable identity of all members in a study participants' social network as the recruitment is done using coupons. The claimed unbiasedness, economic nature, and lowered privacy concerns of RDS have attracted much attention from the research community.

However, this method requires a set of strong assumptions (Heimer 2005, Gile and Handcock 2008). For instance, the most distinctive element of RDS, compared to traditional probability or adaptive sampling approaches, is that RDS lets study participants control the entire sample selection process while it is controlled by researchers in traditional sampling (Frost et al. 2006). The assumption in this respect is that RDS recruitment is done purely at random. This means that the recruiters do not use systematic criteria for selecting recruits from their networks. Equal homophily is another assumption in RDS. Homophily is the measure of the tendency of individuals to associate with those with similar traits. RDS assumes that the rate of homophily is equal across different subgroups. The tendency of a member of group G recruiting other members of group G is assumed the same as a member of group H recruiting members of group G. In addition, network structure is assumed to have a single component where everyone in the network can be linked through one chain. Reciprocity of the network is also assumed which means if person A reports person B in the network, then person B should also report person A being in the network. Moreover, RDS also assumes 100% response rates. These assumptions may be unrealistic and are difficult to verify. Moreover, the inferences with RDS data are difficult due to the fact that the respondents control the sample selection mechanism. There are a few different estimators proposed for RDS (Heckathorn 1997, 2001,

Sagalnik and Heckathorn 2004, Volz and Heckathorn 2008, Gile 2011). These estimators allow calculation of proportions at best. There is currently no method for computing other statistics, such as population totals with RDS. Moreover, these estimators are based on the satisfaction of the basic assumptions in RDS, such as those examined above.

In contrast to the large volume of research using data collected through RDS (e.g., see articles in *Journal of Urban Health* Vol. 83, Suppl. 1, 2006, Lansky et al. 2007, Lansky and Drake 2009), its methodological assessments are very limited. To date, there have been a handful of studies attempting to address inferential issues (e.g., Sagalnik and Heckathorn 2004, Gile and Handcock 2008, Volz and Heckathorn 2008, Goel and Salganik 2009, Gile 2011, Lu et al. 2012). Moreover, even fewer studies have evaluated the error properties of RDS either theoretically or empirically. Studies that conclude RDS is a valid and effective sampling technique often do not include any verification of the assumptions or use deficient methods to establish comparison criteria (e.g., Heckathorn and Jeffri 2003, Lee et al. 2011). In the survey sampling and methodology literature, very few studies acknowledge RDS. Those that do acknowledge RDS have only considered it as a minor topic and introduced as a variation of snowball sampling (e.g., Kalton 2009, Brick 2011). The best way to empirically evaluate RDS is to compare its estimates with those of traditional samples or population data (Frost et al. 2006). While these types of studies are very scarce, they collectively suggest potentially serious inferential limitations in RDS (e.g., Martin et al. 2003, Wejnert 2009, McCreesh et al. 2012). For example, in a study of students at a specific college by Wejnert (2009), it was apparent that nonresponse does occur and that the report of network/degree size often used in RDS estimators were subject to potentially serious measurement error. These limitations, in turn, imply that the social and behavioral data about the rare populations collected through RDS may mischaracterize these populations in unknown ways. For instance, that measurement error on the network size can lead to variance and bias.

An example of a study using RDS is the Virtual Network Study (VNS) in Bauermeister et al. (2012) which used the WebRDS method introduced by Wejnert and Heckathorn (2008). This method applies RDS sampling through network links on the Internet. VNS targeted young adults aged 18–24 in the United States and its recruitment and data collection were all done over the web. At study onset, VNS participants were given three coupons. This strategy did not foster recruitment chain growth. Qualitative interviews with seeds revealed that the total amount of the potential incentives was not appealing with three coupons; however, once participants were given a chance to earn larger incentives by referring up to 10 people, the recruitment chain started to grow. From 22 seeds a total of 3448 participants were generated. VNS participants were asked, "How many people, ages 18 to 24, have you had contact with in the past 3 months?" Responses ranged between 0 and 2000, and exhibited a skewed distribution with a mean of 72.9 and a median of 40. It seems likely that the network size was measured with error since values like 800 or 2000 are not sensible or difficult to count in the survey setting (hence, likely estimated) and, on the other end of the spectrum, recruits should report a network size of at least one by the assumed reciprocity of the network because their recruiter should be included in the network. These improbable network sizes have been reported by other studies (Wejnert and Heckathorn 2008, Chen 2012, Kappelhof 2012, Schonlau 2012). There is evidence from other studies that reports of network size are very sensitive to the question context (McCreesh et al. 2012, Schonlau 2012). From this, we can speculate that the assumed reciprocal nature of networks may not be realized in practice. In fact, 151 of VNS respondents reported their recruiters as strangers. If the assumptions of RDS are met, this cannot happen because by definition these respondents and their recruiters should know each other. Problems with nonreciprocated network structures as well as multiple component networks were also reported by McCreesh et al. (2012).

4.3.6 MULTIPLICITY/NETWORK SAMPLING

Multiplicity/network sampling is a nontraditional method discussed in the probability sampling literature (Sirken 1970, 1972, 1997, Sirken and Levy 1974). It uses a network of respondents, who are selected using a probability sampling mechanism for a household survey. The multiplicity method collects information about the respondents as well as their networks and samples from the network. While the word, "network," may suggest some similarities between RDS and multiplicity sampling, there are three clear differences between the network sampling proposed by Sirken and RDS. The first difference is perhaps a matter of emphasis. Sirken emphasizes that the networks need to be well specified and easily countable, such as direct family members and biological siblings. RDS, on the other hand, has often been used with networks that are much more loosely defined—for example, intravenous drug users who know each other. Second, in Sirken's network sampling, respondents provide the information about everyone in their networks and researchers draw samples using this network information. On the other hand, RDS lets participants sample on their own from their networks. (This is the reason why RDS may be an attractive option for rare populations who have a strong tendency of being hidden because RDS does not require information of those who wish to hide whereas multiplicity sampling does.) Third, the "seeds" in an RDS sample may be a convenience sample. Multiplicity sampling begins with a probability sample.

The multiplicity approach was used in the National Jewish Population Survey conducted between 1970 and 1973 (Sirken and Goldstein 1973). Although the main part of the survey did not use multiplicity sampling, a section on vital statistics used multiplicity counting of births, deaths, marriages, and divorces that occurred in 1969. Under traditional counting, these events would be counted at the *de jure* residence. However, under multiplicity counting, they were counted at the residence of those in the kinship group. For instance, births were counted not only at the *de jure* residence of the infant but also at the maternal aunts' and grandparents' residence. The reason for using multiplicity counting was to increase the incidence of these events in the collected data. Because vital events, such as death, are not frequent events, the incidence rate is relatively low, which translates into high sampling variance. By increasing the sample size on these measures through multiplicity sampling, the data provide point estimates with greater precision. The multiplicity nature of the sampling in the point estimates were adjusted through weighting (Sirken 1970). However, the study encountered implementation problems in the field, such as decisions to cut multiplicity questions due to increased respondent burden and failure to establish multiplicity enumeration rules for all types of kinships.

4.4 Conclusion

Table 4.1 includes a summary of the advantages and disadvantages of the sampling methods described in this chapter. It should be clear that there are no "pat" answers when sampling rare populations. Finding the appropriate sampling solution for any given study is a highly specific task that needs to consider multiple factors. The incidence of the rare group in the population is a key factor, but the topic of the survey, the coverage error for the key measures of the survey associated with alternative sampling frames, the response and measurement errors associated with alternative modes, and the costs associated with each of these modes are a few of the other important considerations. Time spent considering options, planning, and checking implementation will be rewarded because mistakes can be very costly.

In general, a list frame with complete or nearly complete coverage should be the first choice. Unfortunately, it is often the case that no such list is available. If the coverage of available lists is unacceptably low, then it may make sense to either merge the list to a more traditional sampling frame with high coverage in order to create high and low incidence strata, or to use a dual-frame approach that samples from both the list and the traditional frame. The latter approach requires care when combining data from the two samples. Other data (e.g., population counts from the Census) may also be used to stratify traditional sampling frames, particularly by race and ethnicity for which there is some geographic clustering in the United States. If such strata cannot create a stratum with a high proportion of the target population and few nontarget units, then a screening study might be needed to identify a probability sample of the rare group.

Other methods are available for accessing rare groups. These other methods include both probability and nonprobability methods. Some of the methods we described (e.g., venue-based, time-location, and web-based sampling) do not map very well onto the traditional classification of probability versus nonprobability sampling. Rather, depending on the implementation of the sampling procedure, they have the potential to provide probability samples that allow generalization to the rare population of interest. Other nonprobability methods may be more affordable, but it may be difficult or impossible to generalize the results to a population of interest. The error properties of these other methods should be carefully considered before using them and methods developed for evaluating the validity of the results.

TABLE 4.1 Summary of Sampling Methods

Sampling Method	Advantages	Disadvantages
Screening	Uses probability sampling. May have good coverage depending upon sampling frame	For rare populations this is extremely expensive. Cheaper screening methods may produce lower response rates. May require strong assumptions in the presence of nonresponse
Stratification with oversampling	Uses probability sampling. May have good coverage depending upon sampling frame. Increases the efficiency of screening	May still be very expensive if strata with relatively high coverage and prevalence cannot be created. May require strong assumptions in the presence of nonresponse
Multiple sampling frames	Uses probability sampling. May have good coverage depending upon sampling frame	Estimation may be complex. May be difficult to find suitable frames. May require strong assumptions in the presence of nonresponse
Venue-based sampling	May be less expensive	Difficult to insure coverage of many populations. Inference to persons (as opposed to visits) may be difficult
Time–location sampling	May be less expensive	Difficult to insure coverage of many populations. Inference to persons (as opposed to visits) may be difficult
Web-based sampling	May be less expensive	Difficult to insure coverage of many populations. Many methods produce convenience samples. Requires strong assumptions in analysis
Snowball sampling	May be less expensive	Difficult to insure coverage of many populations. Sampling is out of control of sampler. Requires strong assumptions in analysis
Respondent-driven sampling	May be less expensive. Allows hidden populations the choice of whether to identify themselves to the study	Difficult to insure coverage of many populations. Requires strong assumptions in analysis
Multiplicity sampling	May be less expensive	Difficult to insure coverage of many populations. Requires respondent to correctly specify network size. May still be expensive to identify the initial sample for which the networks will be identified

For all sampling methods, it is important to have a plan for repairing errors caused by coverage, nonresponse, or measurement issues. For the traditional sampling methods outlined earlier and their associated data collection methods, the nonsampling error properties have been examined extensively in the literature and some common characteristics associated with these errors are known. For instance, young males are often associated with nonresponse in all types of probability samples and renters are associated with under-coverage of landline telephone surveys. These characteristics either at the individual or at the aggregate level are used not only to understand the errors but also to make postsurvey adjustments to correct for them.

It is advisable for studies using relatively new sampling methods to provide detailed descriptions about sampling procedures. This will allow readers and data users to understand the error properties and the extent to which the estimates may be generalized. Additionally, it is sensible to collect auxiliary information about those potentially omitted in the formative research and those who do not respond. This information can be used not only to understand the errors but also to compensate for them. Empirical studies that compare methods may also be helpful in better understanding them. Disentangling—where possible—the various sources of error (coverage, nonresponse, measurement error, etc.) is necessary if conclusions from such studies are to be more generalizable than in past studies.

REFERENCES

Bankier MD. Estimators based on several stratified samples with applications to multiple frame surveys. J Am Stat Assoc 1986;81(396):1074–1079.

Bauermeister JA, Zimmerman MA, Johns MM, Glowacki P, Stoddard S, Volz E. Innovative recruitment using online networks: lessons learned from an online study of alcohol and other drug use utilizing a web-based, respondent-driven sampling (webRDS) strategy. J Stud Alcohol Drugs 2012;73(5):834–838.

Benotsch E, Kalichman S, Cage M. Men who have met sex partners via the Internet: prevalence, predictors, and implications for HIV prevention. Arch Sex Behav 2002;31(2):177–183.

Binson D, Blair J, Huebner DM, Woods WJ. Sampling in surveys of lesbian, gay, and bisexual people. In: Meyer IH, Northridge ME, editors. *The Health of Sexual Minorities: Public Health Perspectives on Lesbian, Gay, Bisexual, and Transgender Populations.* New York, NY: Springer; 2007. p 375–418.

Brick JM. The future of survey sampling. Public Opin Q 2011;75(5):872–888.

Brick JM, Edwards WS, Lee S. Sampling telephone numbers and adults, interview length, and weighting in the California Health Interview Survey cell phone pilot study. Public Opin Q 2007;71(5):793–813.

Brick JM, Williams D, Montaquila JM. Address-based sampling for subpopulation surveys. Public Opin Q 2011;75(3):409–428.

Bull S, McFarlane M, Reitmeijer C. HIV and sexually transmitted infection risk behaviors among men seeking sex with men on-line. Am J Public Health 2001;91(6):988–989.

Catania JA, Osmond D, Stall RD, Pollack L, Paul JP, Blower S, Binson D, Canchola JA, Mills TC, Fisher L, Choi KH, Porco T, Turner C, Blair J, Henner J, Bye LL,

Coates T. The continuing HIV epidemic among men who have sex with men. Am J Public Health 2001;91:907–914.

Chen M. The use of respondent-driven sampling to recruit black populations at risk for HIV infection for a behavioral survey in Tanzania and North Carolina, US: effectiveness, challenges and recommendations. Paper presented at the International Conference on Methods for Surveying and Enumerating Hard-to-Reach Populations; New Orleans, LA; 2012.

Chiasson MA, Parsons JT, Tesoriero JM, Carballo-Dieguez A, Hirshfield S, Remien RH. HIV behavioral research online. J Urban Health 2006;83(1):73–85.

Chys PD, Diallo MO, Ettiegne-Traore V, Kale K, Tawil O, Carael M, et al. Increase in condom use and decline in HIV and sexually transmitted diseases among female sex workers in Abidjan, Cote d'Ivoire, 1991–1998. AIDS 2002;16:251–258.

Clatts MC, Davis WR, Atillasoy A. Hitting the moving target: the use of ethnographic methods in the development of sampling strategies for the evaluation of AIDS outreach programs for homeless youth in New York City. In: Lambert EY, Ashery RS, Needle RH, editors. *Qualitative Methods in Drug Abuse and HIV Research. NIDA Research Monograph 157*. Rockville, MD: National Institute of Drug Abuse; 1995. p 117–135.

Cochran WG. *Sampling Techniques*. New York: Wiley & Sons; 1977.

Cochran SD, Mays VM. Relation between psychiatric syndromes and behaviorally defined sexual orientation in a sample of the US population. Am J Epidemiol 2000; 151:516–523.

Coleman JS. Relational analysis: the study of social organizations with survey methods. Hum Organ 1958;17:28–36.

Couper MP. Web surveys: a review of issues and approaches. Public Opin Q 2000;64(4):464–494.

Couper MP. Issues of representation in eHealth research (with a focus on web surveys). Am J Prev Med 2007;32(5):S83–S89.

Couper MP, Zikmund-Fisher BJ, Singer E, Fagerlin A, Ubel PA, Fowler FJ Jr,, Levin C. National survey of medical decisions, 2006–2007: description of methods. 2009. DOI: 10.3886/ICPSR25983.v1.

Danel I, Graham W, Stupp P, Castillo P. Applying the sisterhood method for estimating maternal mortality to a health facility-based sample: a comparison with results from a household-based sample. Int J Epidemiol 1996;25(5):1017–1022.

Dandona L, Dandona R, Kumar GA, Reddy GB, Ameer MA, Ahmed GM, Ramgopal SP, Akbar M, Sudha T, Lakshmi V. Risk factors associated with HIV in a population-based study in Andhra Pradesh State of India. Int J Epidemiol 2008;37(6):1274–1286.

Elford J, Bolding G, Sherr L. Seeking sex on the Internet and sexual risk behavior among gay men using London gyms. AIDS 2001;15(11):1409–1415.

Frost SDW, Brouwer KC, Cruz MAF, Ramos R, Ramos ME, Lozada RM, Magis-Rodriguez C, Strathdee SA. Respondent-driven sampling of injection drug users in two U.S.–Mexico border cities: recruitment dynamics and impact on estimates of HIV and syphilis prevalence. J Urban Health 2006;83(Suppl 1):83–97.

Gile KJ. Improved inference for respondent-driven sampling data with application to HIV prevalence estimation. J Am Stat Assoc 2011;106(493):135–146.

Gile KJ, Handcock MS. Respondent-driven sampling: an assessment of current methodology. Sociol Methodol 2008;40(1):286–327.

Goel S, Salganik MJ. Respondent-driven sampling as Markov Chain Monte Carlo. Stat Med 2009;28(17):2202–2229.

Goodman L. Snowball sampling. Ann Math Stat 1961;32:148–170.

Goodman R, Kish L. Controlled selection—a technique in probability sampling. J Am Stat Assoc 1950;45(251):350–372.

Groves RM. *Survey Errors and Survey Costs*. New York: Wiley; 1989.

Haines DE, Pollock KH. Combining multiple frames to estimate population size and totals. Survey Methodol 1998;24:79–88.

Handcock MS, Gile KJ. Comment: on the concept of snowball sampling. Sociol Methodol 2011;41(1):367–371.

Harter RM, Emmons C-A. The REACH 2010 community-based surveys and their cost issues. Proceedings of Joint Statistical Meeting; American Statistical Association; 2003.

Hartley HO. Multiple frame surveys. Proceedings of the Social Statistics Section; American Statistical Association; 1962.

Hartley HO. Multiple frame methodology and selected applications. Sankhya 1974;36:99–118.

Heckathorn DD. Respondent-driven sampling: a new approach to the study of hidden populations. Soc Probl 1997;44:174–199.

Heckathorn DD. Respondent-driven sampling II: deriving valid population estimates from chain-referral samples of hidden populations. Soc Probl 2002;49(1):11–34.

Heckathorn DD, Jeffri J. Social networks of jazz musicians. In: *Changing the Beat: A Study of the Worklife of Jazz Musicians, Volume III: Respondent-Driven Sampling: Survey Results by the Research Center for Arts and Culture*. Washington, DC: National Endowment for the Arts Research DivisionReport #43; 2003. p 48–61.

Heimer R. Critical issues and further questions about respondent-driven sampling: comment on Ramirez-Valles, et al. AIDS Behav 2005;9(4):403–408.

Herek GM. Hate crimes and stigma-related experiences among sexual minority adults in the United States: prevalence estimates from a national probability sample. J Interpers Violence 2009;24:54–74.

Hu SS, Balluz L, Battaglia MP, Frankel MR. Improving public health surveillance using a dual-frame survey of landline and cell phone numbers. Am J Epidemiol 2011;173(6):703–711.

Johnston L, Sabin K, Hien M, Huong P. Assessment of respondent driven sampling for recruiting female sex workers in two Vietnamese cities: reaching the unseen sex worker. J Urban Health 2006;83(0):16–28.

Kalsbeek WD. Sampling minority groups in health surveys. Stat Med 2003;22: 1527–1549.

Kalton G. Sampling flows of mobile human populations. Survey Methodol 1991; 17(2):183–194.

Kalton G. Methods for oversampling rare subpopulations in social surveys. Survey Methodol 2009;35(2):125–141.

Kalton G, Anderson DW. Sampling rare populations. J Roy Stat Soc, Ser A 1986; 149(1):65–82.

Kang SY, Deren S, Colón H. Gender comparisons of factors associated with drug treatment utilization among Puerto Rican drug users. Am J Drug Alc Abuse 2009;35(2):73–9.

Kanouse DE, Berry SH, Duan N, Lever J, Carson S, Perlman JF, Levitan B. Drawing a probability sample of female street prostitutes in Los Angeles County. J Sex Res 1999;36(1):45–51.

Kappelhof J. The feasibility of conducting a web survey using respondent driven sampling among transgenders in the Netherlands. Paper presented at the International Conference on Methods for Surveying and Enumerating Hard-to-Reach Populations; New Orleans, LA; 2012.

Kendall C, Kerr L, Gondim R, Werneck G, Macena R, Pontes M, Johnston L, Sabin K, McFarland W. An empirical comparison of respondent-driven sampling, time location sampling, and snowball sampling for behavioral surveillance in men who have sex with men, Fortaleza, Brazil. AIDS Behav 2008;12(0):97–104.

Kim A, Kent C, McFarland W, Lkausnet J. Cruising on the Internet highway. K Acqui Immune Defic Syndr 2001;28(1):89–93.

Kish L. *Survey Sampling*. New York: Wiley; 1965.

Kott PS, Amrhein JF, Hicks SD. Sampling and estimation from multiple list frames. Survey Methodol 1998;24:3–10.

Lansky A, Abdul-Quader A, Cribbin M, Hall T, Finlayson TJ, Garfein RS, Lin LS, Sullivan PS. Developing an HIV behavioral surveillance system for injecting drug users: the National HIV Behavioral Surveillance System. Public Health Rep 2007;122:48–55.

Lansky A, Drake A. HIV-associated behaviors among injecting-drug users—23 cities, United States, May 2005–February 2006. Morb Mortal Wkly Rep 2009;58:329–332.

Laumann EO, Gagnon JH, Michael RT, Michaels S. *The Social Organization of Sexuality: Sexual Practices in the United States*. Chicago: University of Chicago Press; 1994.

Lee S. 2009. Understanding respondent driven sampling from a total survey error perspective. *Survey Pract* 2. Available at http://surveypractice.files.wordpress.com/2009/08/lee.pdf.

Lee R, Ranaldi J, Cummings M, Crucetti J, Stratton H, McNutt L-A. Given the increasing bias in random digit dial sampling, could respondent-driven sampling be a practical alternative? Ann Epidemiol 2011;21(4):272–279.

Liau A, Millet G, Marks G. Meta-analytic examination of online sex-seeking and sexual risk behavior among men who have sex with men. Sex Transm Dis 2006;33: 576–584.

Lohr SL. *Sampling: Design and Analysis*. 2nd ed. Pacific Grove, CA: Brooks/Cole; 2009.

MacKellar DA, Gallagher KM, Finlayson T, Sanchez T, Lansky A, Sullivan PS. Surveillance of HIV risk and prevention behaviors of men who have sex with men—a national application of venue-based, time-space sampling. Public Health Rep 2007;122(Suppl 1):39.

Martin JL, Wiley J, Osmond D. Social networks and unobserved heterogeneity in risk for AIDS. Popul Res Pol Rev 2003;22(1):65–90.

McCreesh N, Frost SDW, Seeley J, Katongole J, Tarsh MN, Ndunguse R, Jichi F, Lunel NL, Maher D, Johnston LG, Sonnenberg P, Copas AJ, Hayes RJ, White RG. Evaluation of respondent-driven sampling. Epidemiology 2012;23(1):138–147.

Mesch GS, Turjeman H, Fishman G. Social identity and violence among immigrant adolescents. New Dir Youth Dev 2008;119:129–150.

Mettey A, Crosby R, DiClemente R, Holtgrave D. Associations between Internet sex seeking and STI associated risk behaviours among men who have sex with men. Sex Transm Infec 2003;79:466–468.

Meyer IH, Schwartz S, Frost DM. Social patterning of stress and coping: does disadvantaged status confer excess exposure and fewer coping resources? Soc Sci Med 2008;67:368–379.

Meyer IH, Wilson PA. Sampling lesbian, gay, and bisexual Populations. J Counsel Psych 2009;56(1):23–31.

Paquette D, De Wit J. Sampling methods used in developed countries for behavioural surveillance among men who have sex with men. AIDS Behav 2010;14:1252–1264.

Parsons J, Koken J, Bimbi D. The use of the Internet by gay and bisexual male escorts: sex workers as sex educators. AIDS Care 2004;16(8):1021–1035.

Ramirez-Valles J. The protective effects of community involvement for HIV risk behavior: a conceptual framework. Health Education Res 2002;17:389–403.

Ramirez-Valles J, Heckathorn DD, Vázquez R, Diaz R, Campbell RT. From networks to populations: the development and application of respondent-driven sampling among IDUs and Latino gay men. AIDS Behav 2005;9(4):403–408.

Raymond HF, Rebchook G, Curotto A, Vaudrey J, Amsden M, Levine D, McFarland W. Comparing Internet-based and venue-based methods to sample MSM in the San Francisco Bay Area. AIDS Behav 2010;14:218–224.

Razak MH, Jittiwutikarn J, Suriyanon V, Vongchak T, Srirak N, Beyer C, Kawachi S, Tovanabutra S, Rungruengthanakit K, Sawanpanyalert P, Celentano DD. HIV prevalence and risks among injection and noninjection drug users in northern Thailand: need for comprehensive HIV prevention program. J Acquir Infect Defic Syndr 2003;33:259–266.

Remafedi G. Suicidality in a venue-based sample of young men who have sex with men. J Adolesc Health 2002;31:305–310.

Reynolds PD, Carter NM, Gartner WB, Greene PG. The prevalence of nascent entrepreneurs in the United States: evidence from the panel study of entrepreneurial dynamics. Small Bus Econ 2004;23(4):263–284.

Risbud A, Mehendale S, Basu S, Kulkarni S, Walimbe A, Arankalle V, Gangakhedkar R, Divekar A, Bollinger R, Gadkari D, Paranjape R. Prevalence and incidence of hepatitis B virus infection in STD clinic attendees in Pune, India. Sex Transm Infect 2002;78(3):169–173.

Ross M, Tikkanen R, Mansson D. Differences between Internet sample and conventional samples of men who have sex with men: implications for research and HIV interventions. Soc Sci Med 2000;51:749–758.

Rosser BRS, Miner MH, Bockting WO, Konstan J, Gurak L, Stanton J, Edwards W, Jacoby S, Carballo-Diéguez A, Mazin R, Coleman E. HIV risk and the Internet: results of the Men's INTernet Sex (MINTS) Study. AIDS Behav 2009;13(4):746–756.

Rosser BRS, Oakes JM, Bockting WO, Miner M. Capturing the social demographics of hidden sexual minorities: an Internet study of the transgender population in the United States. Sex Res Social Policy 2007;4:50–64.

Sagalnik M, Heckathorn DD. Sampling and estimation in hidden populations using respondent-driven sampling. Sociol Methodol 2004;34:193–239.

Sanchez NF, Sanchez JP, Danoff A. Health care utilization, barriers to care, and hormone usage among male-to-female transgender persons in New York City. Am J Public Health 2009;99(4):713–719.

Sarkar K, Bal B, Mukherjee R, Chakraborty S, Saha S, Ghosh A, Parsons S. Sex-trafficking, violence, negotiating skill, and HIV infection in brothel-based sex workers of Eastern India, adjoining Nepal, Bhutan, and Bangladesh. J Health Popul Nutr 2008;26(2):223–231.

Schonlau M. Recruiting in an Internet panel using respondent driven sampling. Paper presented at the International Conference on Methods for Surveying and Enumerating Hard-to-Reach Populations; New Orleans, LA; 2012.

Sell R. Defining and measuring sexual orientation for research. In: Meyer IH, Northridge ME, editors. *The Health of Sexual Minorities: Public Health Perspectives on Lesbian, Gay, Bisexual and Transgender Population*. New York: Springer; 2007. p 355–374.

Semaan S, Lauby J, Liebman J. Street and network sampling in evaluation studies of HIV risk-reduction interventions. AIDS Rev 2002;4:213–223.

Sirken MG. Household surveys with multiplicity. J Am Stat Assoc 1970;65:257–266.

Sirken MG. Stratified sample surveys with multiplicity. J Am Stat Assoc 1972;67: 224–227.

Sirken MG. Network sampling. In: Armitage P, Colton T, editors. *Encyclopedia of Biostatistics*. Hoboken, NJ: Wiley & Sons; 1997. p 2977–2986.

Sirken MG, Graubard BI, LaValley RW. Evaluation of census population coverage by network surveys. Proceedings of the Survey Research Methods Section; American Statistical Association; 1978. p 239–244.

Sirken MG, Goldstein S. Use of multiplicity rules in surveys of Jewish populations. Proceedings of the Sixth World Congress of Jewish Studies; Hebrew University, Jerusalem, Israel; 1973. p 47–57.

Sirken MG, Levy PS. Multiplicity estimation of proportions based on ratios of random variables. J Am Stat Assoc 1974;69(345):68–73.

Skinner CJ, Holmes DJ, Holt D. Multiple frame sampling for multivariate stratification. Int Stat Rev /Revue Int Stat 1994;62(3):333–347.

Skinner CJ, Rao JNK. Estimation in dual frame surveys with complex designs. J Am Stat Assoc 1996;91(433):349–356.

Srinath KP, Battaglia MP, Khare M. A dual frame sampling design for an RDD survey that screens for a rare population. Proceedings of the Annual Meeting of the American Statistical Association [CD-ROM]; Alexandria, VA: American Statistical Association; 2004.

Stueve A, O'Donnell L, Duran R, Doval A, Blome J. Methodological issues in time-space sampling in minority communities: results with Latino young men who have sex with men. Am J Public Health 2001;91:922–926.

Sudman S, Sirken MG, Cowan CD. Sampling rare and elusive populations. Science 1988;240:991–996.

Taylor M, Ayanalem G, Smith L, Bemis C, Kenney K, Kerndt P. Correlates of Internet use to meet sex partners among men who have sex with men diagnosed with early syphilis in Los Angeles County. Sex Transm Dis 2004;31:552–556.

Thompson SK. *Sampling*. 3rd ed. Hoboken, NJ: John Wiley & Sons; 2012.

Thaisri H, Lewitworapong J, Vongsheree S, Sawanpanyalert P, Chadbanchachai C, Rojanawiwat A, Kongpromsook W, Paungtubtim W, Sri-ngam P, Jaisue R. HIV infection and risk factors among Bangkok prisoners, Thailand: a prospective cohort study. BMC Infect Dis 2003;3:25.

Tikkanene R, Ross M. Technological tearoom trade: characteristics of Swedish men visiting gay Internet chat rooms. AIDS Educ Prev 2003;15(2):122–132.

Tourangeau R. Defining hard-to-survey populations. In: Tourangeau R, Edwards B, Johnson TP, Wolter KM, Bates N. *Hard-to-Survey Populations*. Forthcoming.

Trow M. *Right-Wing Radicalism and Political Intolerance*. New York: Arno PressReprinted 1980; 1957.

Volz E, Heckathorn DD. Probability based estimation theory for respondent driven sampling. J Off Stat 2008;24:79–97.

Wagner J, Arrieta J, Guyer H, Ofstedal MB. Does Sequence Matter in Multimode Surveys: Results from an Experiment. Field Methods 2014;26(2):141–155.

Weatherburn P, Hickson F, Reid D. *Gay Men's Use of the Internet and Other Settings Where HIV Prevention Occurs*. London: Sigma Research; 2003.

Weir SS, Morroni C, Coetzee N, Spencer J, Boerma JT. A pilot study of a rapid assessment method to identify places for AIDS prevention in Cape Town, South Africa. Sex Transm Infect 2002;78(Suppl I):i106–i113.

Weir SS, Tate JE, Zhusupov B, Boerma JT. Where the action is: monitoring local trends in sexual behavior. Sex Transm Infect 2004;80(Suppl II):ii63–ii68.

Wejnert C. An empirical test of respondent-driven sampling: point estimates, variance, degree measures, and out-of-equilibrium data. Sociol Methodol 2009;39(1):73–116.

Wejnert C, Heckathorn DD. Web-based network sampling: efficiency and efficacy of respondent-driven sampling for online research. Sociol Methods Res 2008;37(1): 105–134.

Westat. 2012. Health Information National Trends Survey 4 (HINTS 4): cycle 1 methodology report. Available at http://hints.cancer.gov/docs/HINTS4_Cycle1_Methods_Report_revised_Jun2012.pdf.

Wolter KM. *Introduction to Variance Estimation*. 2nd ed. New York: Springer; 2007.

Xia Q, Molitor F, Osmond D, Tholandi M, Pollack L, Ruiz J, Catania J. Knowledge of sexual partner's HIV serostatus and serosorting practices in a California population-based sample of men who have sex with men. AIDS 2006a;20: 2081–2089.

Xia Q, Osmond DH, Tholandi M, Pollack LM, Zhou W, Ruiz JD, Catania JA. HIV prevalence and sexual risk behaviors among men who have sex with men: results from a statewide population-based survey in California. J Acquir Immune Defic Syndr 2006b;41(2):38–245.

Xia Q, Tholandi M, Osmond DH, Pollack LM, Zhou W, Ruiz JD, Catania JA. The effect of venue sampling on estimates of HIV prevalence and sexual risk behaviors in men who have sex with men. Sex Transm Dis 2006c;33(9):545.

Zhang D, Bi P, Hiller JE, Lv F. Web-based HIV/AIDS behavioral surveillance among men who have sex with men: potential and challenges. Int J Infect Dis 2008;12:126–131.

ONLINE RESOURCES

Many of the links from Chapter 2 will also be useful for the methods described in this chapter. The Cross-Cultural Survey Guidelines include a chapter on sampling: http://ccsg.isr.umich.edu/sampling.cfm.

The developers of Respondent Driven Sampling (RDS) maintain a website of resources related to this method, including software for the analysis of data collected in this way: www.respondentdrivensampling.org.

The National HIV Behavior Surveillance by the Centers for Disease Control and Prevention targets populations at high risk of HIV infection. Its recruitment process is described at: www.cdc.gov/hiv/bcsb/nhbs/index.htm.

PART TWO

Design and Measurement Issues

CHAPTER FIVE

Assessing Physical Health

Todd Rockwood
Division of Health Policy and Management, University of Minnesota, Minneapolis, MN, USA

5.1 Introduction

The notion of physical health in daily discourse is something that generally has high intersubjectivity. Very often the simple phrase, "How are you?" is taken for granted. Uttered postoperatively to a patient recovering from surgery, this simple phrase has a different meaning than when asked by an interviewer over the telephone to a randomly selected household respondent. In each situation, the context surrounding the conversation dramatically alters the meaning and response. Such contextual factors are integrated into communication (Gorden 1987). For the surgical patient who is likely on pain medication, the meaning of this question is conditioned on having just had surgery and is focused solely on the events that have just occurred. Context in each of these situations defines the meaning of the question. Yet studies are done in which context is altered by study design, such as when baseline measurement is conducted in pre-op and then 3 months later, by a mailed questionnaire.

Surveys are employed to assess physical health diverse ways. In some applications, there is an attempt to use surveys to replace biometric measurement. For example, in joint function, using a survey to establish range of motion is a crude proxy for actually measuring range of motion. Conversely, using a postoperative survey to evaluate the impact of limited range of motion on daily tasks,

Handbook of Health Survey Methods, First Edition. Edited by Timothy P. Johnson.

such as opening a can or bottle, can provide far more information on functional limitation than does assessing range of motion.

At a general level, this intersubjectivity is bound to the fact that all human bodies are more or less similar, with shared physical experiences. However, it is critical to realize that the meanings associated with those experiences may not be universally shared across all situations or with all individuals. An excellent illustration of this can be found in Fadiman's (1997) book, *When the Spirit Catches You and You Fall Down*, which dramatically details differing interpretations about the health of a child (Fadiman 1997). In the Western medical view, the child had a seizure disorder; within the traditional Hmong community, the child was identified as being caught by the spirit and, thus, a religious figure. While this is an extreme example, the principles apply far beyond the interpretation of something from a Western medical versus an Eastern religious paradigm (Tapp 1989). The very notion of what it means to be healthy changes with age, chronic, or serious conditions as well as other factors (Hunt and McEwen 1980). There is a point at which the notion of what it means to be healthy changes, or even more dramatically, changes in which one's identity can change (e.g., cancer survivor (Zebrack 2001, Park et al. 2009)); at this point, it is important to recognize that intersubjectivity regarding physical health may no longer be shared.

In developing survey items to assess physical health, there are situations that are often taken for granted. Yet, there will be many instances in which assumptions about meaning no longer hold true, or the ability of respondents to even comprehend physical health will be challenged. As an illustrative example, in the development of a health-related quality of life scale for individuals with fecal incontinence (FI), ethnographic interviews (differentiated from cognitive interviews in which items were evaluated) with subjects before developing survey items resulted in a fundamental reorientation to understanding health (Rockwood et al. 2000). While this ethnographic work provided valuable insight into what health means to individuals with FI, it was not until the researcher used drugs (laxatives, etc.) for a 3-day period to mimic FI that comprehension of the role the sphincter plays relative to physical health, function, and quality of life, was truly realized. Going to such extremes to develop an instrument is not always possible (e.g., mimicking Parkinson's disease, rheumatoid arthritis, etc.), but when possible it certainly can facilitate the development of items as one begins to recognize the important relationship between knowing the exact location of the nearest bathroom and rectal function.

In developing questions for physical health, there is a universal tendency to just start writing questions, using the assumption that we all have a body and, thus, by extension we all have "physical health" and proceed from that personal experience. The primary risk in this approach is the presumption of shared "experience." For example, everyone has experienced "pain" in their life (e.g., a broken bone, a sliver, slamming a finger in a door, etc.), but the perception of the severity of pain is by no means uniform among individuals (Kane et al. 2002, 2005, McGrath et al. 2000, Von Korff et al. 1990). Furthermore, having experienced "acute" pain in any way does not prepare an individual for developing items to assess chronic pain (Sternbach 1985). Pain is a highly complex phenomenon

(Turk et al. 1987, Cipher and Clifford 2004); for some situations, the simple 0–10 numeric rating scale (NRS) "how would you rate your pain with 0 being no pain at all and 10 being the worst pain imaginable" works well in practice; other situations are more complicated and require measures that include an assessment of whether one's pain is "punishing, grueling, cruel, vicious or killing" (e.g., item 14 in the McGill Pain Questionnaire (Melzack 1975, Von Korff et al. 1990)). If the goal of research is to understand postoperative pain, then the simple 0–10 NRS approach may work quite well. However, if the goal is to understand the psychological impact of pain (Melzack 1975), the distress caused by pain (Zung 1983) or social aspects (Kerns et al. 1985), then other measures of pain must be used.

When writing questions to assess health, it is not only important to understand reality from the respondent's perspective (is a seizure a spiritual or neurological event?), but also how the data will be used. Survey researchers are fundamentally trained to see the world from the respondent's point of view when developing questions; however, this should be simultaneously balanced against the uses to which the data will be put. In health research, the disconnect between meaning to the respondent and the use of the data can become extreme. Clinical definitions are often narrow and rest upon fine distinctions that, while important clinically, may not intrude on a person's daily existence or even be consciously recognized (McDowell and Newell 1996). In other words, we are asking about things that are clinically relevant, but are not relevant in daily life (Barei et al. 2007). The influence of clinical factors can further complicate the survey development in that we are often seduced into thinking about phenomena within a biometric or even classic psychophysic framework (e.g., perceiving one's health is similar to perceiving how loud something is) (Gescheider 1997), which can be antithetical to what a survey is capable of measuring (Hoeymans et al. 1996, McDowell and Newell 1996, Tanur and Social Science Research Council (U.S.). Committee on Cognition 1992, Fowler 1995). Assessing height using a biometric approach works very well (i.e., via a ruler); however, when assessing height using a survey, it is important to understand that response is conditioned on many other factors, which results in short males reporting their height with shoes on, and tall women reporting their height with shoes off. In a clinical setting, a biometric approach to measuring height and weight using a ruler and a scale is completely appropriate. However, in the context of a survey, it is best not to think of height and weight as absolute values determined against an established metric, but rather as a physical state in which there is cognitive reconstruction that is prone to measurement error (Palta et al. 1982, Kuczmarski et al. 2001, Spencer et al. 2002).

The use of surveys to assess physical health is ubiquitous, from the medical history form completed by the patient before a clinic visit, to scales used to inform or make a diagnosis. As a result of this widespread use, information about existing measures as well as what is relevant to consider in developing measures, is spread across diverse disciplines. For example, if one wants to measure basic functional status, a range of tools from orthopedics, occupational therapy, physical therapy, social work, and gerontology exist (Jette et al. 1986). Furthermore, different tools can be found for young versus elderly individuals, the healthy versus the chronically ill, and community dwelling versus institutionalized living, as some examples (McDowell and Newell 1996). While at an abstract level the conceptual meaning of "transfer" is shared among these disciplines and settings, when it comes to writing a question, these differences result in different questions.

It is not within the scope of this chapter to review and compare the full range of issues and existing measures; exercise alone would take volumes to discuss. Rather, the intention is to identify fundamental issues in developing or evaluating existing measures to assess physical health. This chapter will cover four major issues. First, is a review of the research on the use of surveys to assess health behaviors, with a focus on factors that affect response formation and the accuracy of response. Second, is a focus on conceptual issues around developing and evaluating measures of physical health. Third is the importance that psychometric and measurement theories play in evaluating existing scales and developing items. Finally, will be a brief exploration of some important context-based effects.

5.2 Assessing Health: Response Formation and Accuracy

The difficulty in developing items associated with health, especially those associated with the assessment of health behaviors, is not in writing the item. Rather, the difficulty is in writing an item that will yield accurate information in light of the known problems associated with recall, response formation, and context-based effects (Biemer et al. 1991, Schwarz and Sudman 1992, Tanur and Social Science Research Council (U.S.). Committee on Cognition 1992, Schwarz and Sudman 1994, Jobe 2003). Measuring health with a survey is prone to all the problems that any other topic faces when response is dependent upon autobiographical memory (Bradburn et al. 1987, Schwarz and Sudman 1994, Loftus et al. 1992). The last few decades have seen considerable research on questions targeting health and health behavior, which has resulted in an improved understanding of core issues in item development (Menon et al. 1995, Conrad et al. 1998, Schwarz and Oyserman 2001).

Research has identified three primary response formation processes when respondents are presented with an item regarding health or health-related behaviors: (i) direct enumeration, (ii) rate estimation, and (iii) vague estimation (Burton and Blair 1991, Brown 1997, Schwarz and Oyserman 2001, Jobe and Herrmann 1996, Conrad et al. 1998). Direct enumeration occurs when a respondent counts the distinct event(s) that have occurred. Rate estimation is a process by which the respondent does not count distinct events, but uses a process in which the individual determines how often something is done, on "average." Finally, vague estimation differs from rate estimation in that the response formation does not arrive at a "number" but at a vague quantifier (e.g., rarely, sometimes, often, all the time, or a nonnumber quantifier such as "recommended by my provider") (Bradburn and Miles 1979). The immediate value in knowing what response process respondents are likely to use is to know what type of response categories to present them with: open ended for enumeration strategies versus numeric categories for rate estimation and vague estimation strategies.

The research on response to frequency items has spanned a large number of fields, from consumer-oriented research, traditional social science disciplines and public opinion, to health research (Schwarz and Sudman 1994, Schwarz and Oyserman 2001). The model presented in Figure 5.1 is an attempt to synthesize and summarize this diverse literature relative to key characteristics that influence response formation. There are three core aspects to identifying the likely recall strategy and how response is likely to be formed by the respondent: occurrence, routine, and salience.

At the gross level, frequency is characterized as something that occurs rarely or frequently (Schwarz 1990, Schwarz et al. 1991b). Obviously, there is a continuum that ranges between rare and frequent, but in the development of survey items, this gross characterization is the primary framework used. Rare events may include a hospitalization, a broken bone, or an organ transplant (for most individuals). Alternatively, frequent events include walking, eating, talking to

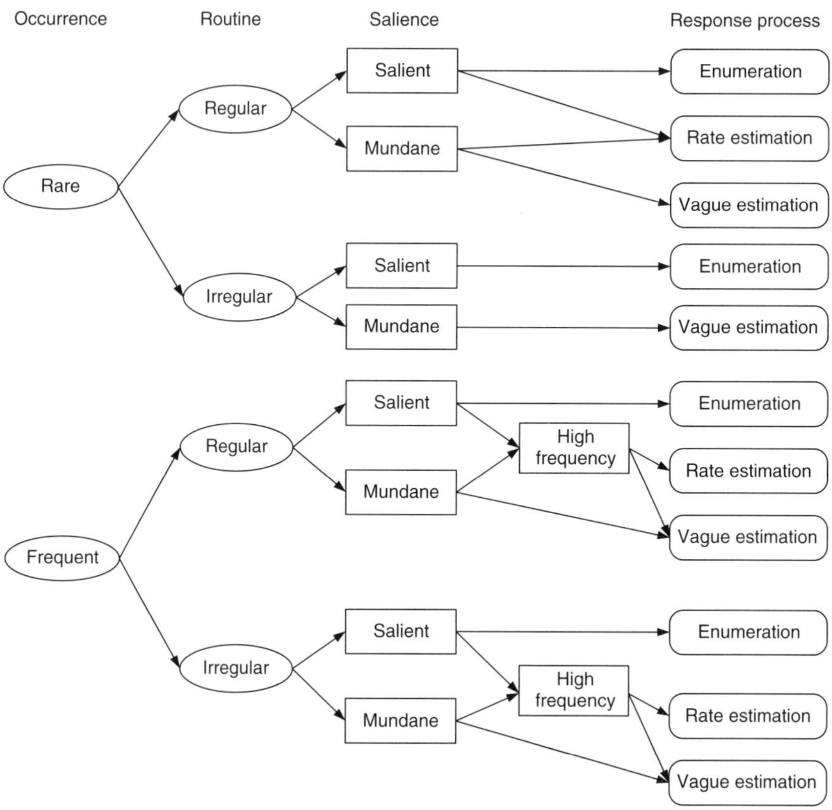

FIGURE 5.1 How attributes and characteristics of survey items lead to a particular type of response formation.

friends/family, or bowel movements. Historically, research in this area has paired these two basic frequencies with the salience aspect, to create a simple dichotomy: rare and salient, frequent and mundane (Schwarz et al. 1991b, Rockwood et al. 1997, Schwarz and Bienias 2006). Over time, this simple framework has been replaced with the recognition that not all rare events are salient and not all frequent events are mundane (Schwarz and Sudman 1996, Sudman et al. 1996).

The second level deals with the routine around the event: does the event occur on a regular schedule or is it irregular in occurrence? Irregular events are those in which the occurrence is episodic, either due to the fact that it is not a planned event (e.g., a car crash) to its occurrence being conditional on other factors (e.g., when I have time, I go to the gym). Alternatively, regularity deals with an established routine and/or periodicity, in which the event occurs habitually (e.g., brush teeth at night before going to bed or go to the gym every Monday, Wednesday, and Friday) (Conrad et al. 1998, Menon et al. 1995, Menon 1997).

The third primary aspect deals with the salience of the event. Again, a gross classification has been used in which events are identified as salient, the occurrence is noteworthy, or mundane, and the occurrence is not noteworthy (Schwarz 1990, Schwarz and Bienias 2006). For salient events, the respondent is likely to be able to localize the event more accurately over time (less subject to telescoping), recall specific and detailed aspects, and be capable of using these recollections to formulate a response; the term *capable* is used intentionally, as the respondent is capable of direct recollection, but doing so is dependent upon the respondent's motivation (Schwarz and Sudman 1994). Conversely, there are mundane events, which are not noted as being unique and particular; the respondent may have vague recollections of particular events, but it is more likely that the response is formulated on an amalgamation of ill-defined and imprecise recollections, or the response could be formulated based on heuristic processes as opposed to direct recall (Brown 1997, Tversky and Kahneman 1973, Schwarz 1990, Schwarz et al. 1991a, Menon 1993, Sudman et al. 1996).

Initial work in this area proceeded from an assumption that events such as hours spent watching television are by definition mundane and other events, such as hospitalizations, are by definition much more salient (Schwarz et al. 1985, Menon 1993, Rockwood et al. 1997). For the general population, such assumptions may hold true, but in health research, we are often dealing with specific and targeted populations in which what is salient could become mundane, such as hospitalizations in the chronic severely ill. Finally, it is important to keep in mind that the definition of what is salient versus mundane can change, due to the passage of time, changes in physical health or even societal changes in beliefs about what is/is not important relative to physical health.

A final mitigating factor is specific to frequent events, in which we are dealing with the tail end of frequency distributions: those events that occur with a high frequency (Menon 1997). The notable characteristic of this is not necessarily literal frequency, but a combination of two factors: something that is habitual and the relationship between the timeframe used to keep track of the event (e.g., I exercise three times per week) and the timeframe used in the question (e.g., in the past month how often have you exercised?). The specific impact of this is to shift the respondent away from enumeration and to the use of rate estimation in response formation (e.g., I exercise three times a week; you want to know how often I exercise in a month? Three times a week, 4 weeks in a month, I exercised 12 times in the past month.) (Conrad et al. 1998, Menon 1993a).

In dealing with the response process, there are critical cognitive and contextual factors that play a significant role in response formation (Sudman and Bradburn 1982, Sirken 1999, Tourangeau et al. 2000). As noted above, the issue of salience can be respondent-dependent, in which what is defined as salient is not uniform across the population; this in and of itself presents a fundamental challenge. A central concern is that, as an event shifts toward the mundane end of the continuum, issues associated with contextual memory, distinguishability, similarity, and exceptions become much more likely to influence response formation and accuracy (Schwarz and Sudman 1992, Menon 1993, Menon 1997, Brown 1997, Conrad et al. 1998, Sudman et al. 1996).

The issue of context memory deals with how much information around the event in question (e.g., when, where, who, what, etc.) is integrated into response formation (Menon 1993, Sudman et al. 1996, Krosnick 1997, Tourangeau et al. 2000). Research has demonstrated that, as more detail about context is brought into processing the respondent, the more likely they are to move away from using estimation and toward using enumeration strategies in response (Menon et al. 1995, Brown 1997). Perhaps one of the most elaborate attempts at establishing context memory is an experiment by Dillman and Tarnai on the impact of asking four items designed to stimulate context memory before asking about seatbelt usage (Dillman and Tarnai 1991). In this study, it was shown that these items designed to produce context memory increase the reported use of seatbelts, although it is not clear if this design increased accuracy or produced over-reporting. Context memory is also affected by distinguishability—that is, can the respondent clearly identify distinct occurrences from one another? This is related to the similarity of events, if the events usually occur in a similar context, then the ability to distinguish is reduced; it is also tied to the regularity of the events, if an event tends to occur regularly then contextual memory tends to be more generally tied to the "class" of the event than to specific events (Conrad et al. 1998, Blair and Burton 1987, Burton and Blair 1991).

Degradation of memory, while primarily identified as an effect associated with the passage of time, involves two processes. First is the basic issue of memorability: is the event something that is explicitly retrievable from memory? (Blair and Burton 1987, Burton and Blair 1991). Before degradation of memory occurs, we have to consider whether or not any given event is retrievable from memory as a distinct occurrence (Tversky and Kahneman 1973, Schwarz and Sudman 1994, Jobe 2003, Harbison et al. 2009). Within health research, we sometimes focus on the narrowly defined events (e.g., tell me about each time you washed your hands yesterday), which in daily life are not likely to be stored as unique events, but in using surveys to study an outbreak of a contagious agent, for example, can be a critical issue. Even if an event does get stored as a distinct memory, we have to deal with the fact that over time the memorability of events degrade (Schwarz and Sudman 1994, Biemer et al. 1991, Sudman et al. 1996). In developing surveys, we have to consider the variable nature of the degradation of memory, which affects the ability to localize an event in time, recall specific aspects and ultimately the ability to recall any specific event at all, and the reliance on heuristics to formulate response as opposed to direct recall (Sudman and Bradburn 1982, Schwarz and Sudman 1992, Schwarz and Sudman 1994, Sudman et al. 1996, Sirken 1999).

There are a number of direct principles that come from Figure 5.1 in terms of writing questions. The following material will highlight some of the basic tools for item development that have been evaluated.

Time bounding of items is a central characteristic of item development in assessing health behavior. Time bounding is often done relative to the purpose of research, identification of the rate of occurrence within a specific time window, but independent of setting rates, it is a central aspect of facilitating response formation even when not attempting to establish rates (Schwarz and Sudman 1994). The time frame has implications for how response is likely to be formed, which has a direct bearing on accuracy. The use of time bounding is predicated on the assumption that it will affect the response formation process used by the respondent. We can move the respondent from using a less accurate response formation process to a more accurate method. For example, if we ask a respondent how many times they ate vegetables in the past year, they will most likely arrive at a vague quantifier (none, a little, some, and a lot); if we ask about the past month, they are likely to estimate how many times a day/week they eat vegetables and multiply it by either 30 or 4, respectively (Menon 1993, Menon et al. 1995, Brown 1997, Schwarz and Oyserman 2001). Finally, if we ask how many times they have eaten vegetables today, they are likely to directly count. It is argued that by appropriately time bounding an item, we can potentially shift the respondent from using vague estimation to using rate estimation or from using rate estimation to enumeration.

Selecting the timeframe to be used for bounding should be directed by what is likely to facilitate shifting the respondent from one response process to another. For frequent events, short timeframes are used; for rare and salient events, timeframes should be long enough to likely include the event, but not so long as to introduce additional error. In developing timeframes, we tend to use those that map to how people keep track of time (e.g., weeks/7 days, month/30 days, year, etc.). In developing timeframes, we should not only consider whether the event is rare (e.g., long timeframes) or frequent (e.g., short timeframes), but should also consider the periodicity of the event: does it occur on a regular schedule or is it irregular? If there is an underlying periodicity associated with the event (e.g., weekly, monthly, and yearly), then the timeframe needs to be organized around that periodicity.

What becomes difficult in time bounding an item is the terminology used. Research has shown first and foremost that "time" is relative; for example, a year can really mean 4 months (Bachman and O'Malley 1981). In our work, cognitive interviewing has shown some basic patterns relative to how time is treated by respondents. Briefly, this work has shown that, at the beginning of a month, the terminology "in the past month" or "in the past 30 days" means the prior calendar month. If asked in the middle of the month, there is a predisposition to answer just based on the calendar month to day, regardless of whether or not past month or 30 days is used. If asked at the end of the month, it refers to the current calendar month. Using the terminology of "the past week" or "past seven days" showed a similar trend; a particularly problematic issue was associated with the week time-frame in that if the question was asked later in the week (on Thursday, Friday, or Saturday) there was the potential for the omission of the weekend. In response to this problem, for our computer-assisted or interviewer-administered surveys, we adopted a methodology of taking the current day, for example, Thursday, and have an automated fill for the question stem that read, "Since last Friday ... ". On the basis of cognitive interviews, this was more likely to include the weekend than the "in the past week" or "7-day" terminology.

Other types of time bounding have been employed in which landmark events are used. The classic example of this is Loftus' work on "Since Mt. St. Helen's erupted ... " (Loftus and Marburger 1983). The use of sentinel events can be effective in reducing forward telescoping (Loftus and Fathi 1985, Loftus and Marburger 1983), but, this is by no means a panacea as the landmark event itself is subject to telescoping and the salience of the event needs to be high and uniform across the study population (Gaskell et al. 2000). Telescoping refers to the movement of an event in time; forward telescoping involves moving an event forward in time (e.g., something that occurred 6 months ago is reported as occurring 3 months ago) and backward telescoping is moving something backward in time (e.g., something that occurred 3 months ago is reported as occurring 6 months ago) (Schwarz and Sudman 1994). Telescoping can also have a synergistic effect with social desirability in which the respondent can consciously push a "negative event" outside the time window (e.g., having five or more drinks on one occasion 2 weeks ago and reporting that it occurred outside the past month time window employed in a question), or a positive behavior is pushed forward to be within the time window (e.g., had their teeth cleaned 7 months ago, but report it as having been done within the past 6 months) (Blair and Burton 1987, Prohaska et al. 1998, Johnson and Schultz 2005). Finally, telescoping can also be unintentional in which respondents fail to accurately localize an event in time due to failure in recall. Generally, shared sentinel events are events that are common across the population (e.g., the Mt. St. Helen's eruption was a shared event in North America). It is possible to use personal sentinel events (e.g., birthday), but the differential time elapse between respondents has to be taken into account when interpreting data.

Another issue that is worth consideration in time bounding is based on the work of Loftus, relative to the use of multiple timeframes; in a classic study, respondents were asked how often they had seen a doctor in the past 6 months and then in the past 3 months (Loftus et al. 1990). The study showed that there was considerable error for the 6-month item, but the 3-month response was fairly accurate. It is important to note that the order of the items is important, the 6-month item had to come first and as noted the data for it are not accurate, but the data for the 3-month item demonstrated significantly improved accuracy (Loftus et al. 1990, Loftus et al. 1992). The increase in accuracy can be attributed to a number of factors: (i) reduction of telescoping effects for the 3-month window, (ii) the 6-month item stimulating relevant memories, and (iii) the potential reduction of social desirability by allowing the respondent to indicate that they had seen a provider in the 6-month item.

While time bounding an item can have significant impact on improving the quality of response formation, it has to be noted that it is not without problems. As noted earlier, the selection of an appropriate time window is critical. If the window is too long, then the effect can be to push the respondent toward using estimation instead of enumeration strategies; if it is too short, it may not provide a long enough window for the event to have occurred. Using a time bound is a conscious choice to trade-off improvement in response formation against introducing error due to telescoping (Schwarz and Sudman 1994, Sudman et al. 1996).

While telescoping is identified as the primary effect associated with time bounding, other effects have been identified in relationship to the use of time bounding. Schwarz and Oyserman (2001) showed that a respondent's interpretation of "severity" was impacted by the length of the time window, in which if asked about the past year, qualifying events were of higher severity than if a shorter time window was used (Menon et al. 1995, Schwarz 1999, Schwarz et al. 1988). Additionally, research by Burton and Blair (1991) noted that using long time frames (e.g., 1 year) can induce the use of rate estimation as opposed to enumeration.

The use of timeframes is one method of attempting to improve response relative to health behaviors. Another strategy used which has a long history in survey methods is decomposition (Bradburn et al. 1987). There are two distinct ways to view decomposition: one is to break the targeted behavior into components, and the other is to focus on situations or times in which the event is likely to occur (Menon et al. 1995, Menon 1997). For the former, alcohol consumption is a classic example in which people are not asked generically about alcohol, but instead are asked separate items for beer, wine, and liquor. In this example, when a class (e.g., alcohol) is broken down into components (e.g., beer, wine, etc.) research points to the conclusion that this type of decomposition leads to over-reporting (Belli et al. 2000, Schwarz 1999). Alternatively, decomposition can take the form of prompting (e.g., did you exercise in the morning, afternoon, evening, weekend, etc.) (Menon 1993, Menon et al. 1995, Menon 1997). Research in this area has converged on recommendations that, if the event occurs regularly (e.g., habitually or is characterized by periodicity) then decomposition contributes to over-reporting; alternatively, if the event occurs irregularly, studies have shown that decomposition can enhance episodic memory, which contributes to an increase in accuracy (Menon et al. 1995, Menon 1997).

A core issue in the assessment of health is the impact of response categories. In developing questions to assess frequency, we generally have three alternatives for the response categories: open-ended, closed ended ranges, or vague quantifiers. For rare and/or salient events, the open-ended (write in the number) alternative is effective and studies have demonstrated that this is the optimal option (Gaskell et al. 1994, Al Baghal 2012, Schwarz and Bienias 2006). When we move away from these items, then the issue of response categories becomes a central concern. Numerous studies have demonstrated across a wide range of issues (from watching TV to exercising), that if closed ended ranges are used, they can significantly impact the inference that is drawn (Schwarz et al. 1985, Schwarz et al. 1991a, 1991b, Rockwood et al. 1997, Courneya et al. 2003, Del Boca and Darkes 2003, Rhodes et al. 2010). In these studies, the experiments focus on differences when presenting a low frequency range (e.g., 0.5 h or less, 0.5–1 h, 1–1.5 h, 1.5–2 h, 2–2.5 h, 2.5 h or more) versus a high frequency range (2.5 h or less, 2.5–3 h, 3–3.5 h, 3.5–4 h, 4–4.5 h, and 4.5 h or more) (Rockwood et al. 1997). Study after study has shown that the ranges presented alters the conclusions drawn—lower ranges produce lower estimates of frequency and higher ranges, higher estimates of frequency (Schwarz et al. 1985, Schwarz et al. 1991a, 1999b, Rockwood et al. 1997, Courneya et al. 2003, Schwarz and Bienias 2006). Work in this area has identified at least three reasons for these differences (Schwarz et al. 1985, Schwarz et al. 1991a, 1991b). First, the response ranges do not accurately reflect the occurrence of the behavior and, thus, distributional differences are due to an inadequate fit between real frequency and options for response. Second, in items that are either frequent, irregular, or mundane, the respondent uses the response categories as cues (e.g., I am average, thus I will select from the middle of the response options; I am above average and will select from those at the top of the scale; or I am below average and will select from those at the bottom). Finally, the scales have a differential susceptibility to social desirability bias. A critical issue relative to the impact of response ranges is that their effect is not uniform between interviewer-administered (telephone) and self-administered (mail) surveys. Both modes demonstrate an effect due to the response ranges, but a low range response scale demonstrates a much stronger effect in the telephone mode (Rockwood et al. 1997). In developing ranges, it is critical to have basic information of the distribution of frequency or duration in the study population, thus developing the response ranges based on that understanding.

A final consideration is the use of vague quantifiers as response alternatives. Most of the research in this area points to serious issues which argue against the use of vague quantifiers. While the intrasubjectivity of vague quantifiers may be acceptable (consistency in the meaning for a respondent across questions), research has demonstrated significant variation in intersubjectivity (consistency in meaning across respondents) about the meaning of vague quantifiers, as noted in the title of Schaeffer's (1991) classic article "Hardly Ever or Constantly." Study after study has demonstrated that the meaning of "often" demonstrates considerable variation between respondents (Robert Pace and Friedlander 1982, McGlone and Reed 1998, Wright et al. 2006). There is a predisposition to assume that numbers are accurate and vague quantifiers are not; in reality, it is just a matter of degree in that neither is totally accurate, and numbers are only marginally more accurate than vague quantifiers.

Figure 5.1, as noted above, is an attempt to summarize a diverse literature into a single framework. Understanding the characteristics of what we are asking about influences the response formation process, and knowing these characteristics is a central consideration in developing questions and response categories. Furthermore, it allows us to understand why some things, such as exercise, are so difficult to assess. Consider that within the general population, for some, exercise is a frequent, regular, salient, high frequency event leading to rate estimation being used in response formation; in others, it is a frequent, irregular, mundane event, in which vague estimation is used, and, finally, for some, it is a rare, irregular and salient event which can lead to direct enumeration. In all instances, a different response formation process occurs; thus, the failure in our ability to accurately measure exercise is, in great part, due to writing an item that works across these diverse response formation processes.

5.3 Conceptual Framework for Developing and Assessing Health

Health-related quality of life (HRQoL) generally proceeds from a framework based on five domains: cognitive, emotional, physical, behavioral, and social. This section will focus primarily on two of these domains: physical and behavioral. In developing items around these two issues, there is a basic framework that underlies the development of any question. Any measure of physical health and/or health behavior is rooted in one or more of three basic issues: capacity, performance, and expectation (see Figure 5.2) (McDowell and Newell 1996). Many survey items concerned with physical health, while seemingly simple, are actually quite complex in that an item is attempting to determine capacity and/or performance during a given period of time at a certain level of intensity.

Capacity should serve as the starting point for any question, regardless of the goal of measurement for the item. Capacity focuses our attention on critical factors that have to be established in order to develop a survey question: is this something that applies to the respondent, and to harmonize our meaning with that of the respondent. One of the most commonly used instruments to assess health status is the SF-36, and many researchers will just adopt the scale for use, without fully considering its appropriateness (Ware et al. 2000). Using the SF-36 in a study to evaluate health status after amputation of a lower extremity due to diabetes or trauma results in a capacity problem. The physical function subscale (Question 3) in the SF-36 is predicated on the lower extremities being intact relative to assessing functional status and, postamputation, the utility of the physical function subscale is compromised. In a study such as this, the Short Musculoskeletal Function Assessment Questionnaire (Barei et al. 2007) is much better at assessing the function. In measuring physical health, capacity is something that can often be overlooked especially when adopting existing measures.

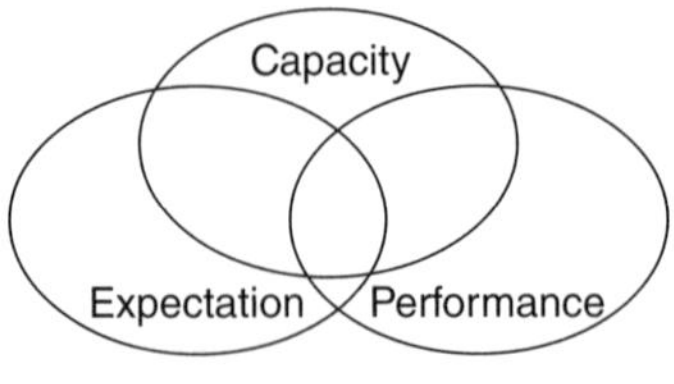

FIGURE 5.2 Basic conceptual framework for physical activities and function.

Thus, the very first step in developing or adopting measures relative to physical health is to determine the nature of capacity in the study population.

The next role of capacity is to enrich our understanding of what we are attempting to assess. What does it mean to walk? Is walking solely the ability to move in which a foot is always on the ground? Or is walking functional, the ability to get from one place to another? If a person has to use an assistive device such as a cane or a walker, does it count as walking? In a study of an elderly population, we asked the question, "Can you walk a block or two?" In evaluating the responses to the item, we found that individuals known to be wheelchair-bound answered the question affirmatively. In postsurvey evaluation, we found that many of the respondents answered the question as a functional item, that is, the ability to get from one place to another. While an extreme example, it does reflect the difference in interpretation between walking as a capacity versus function—a problem that in hindsight could have been solved by adding an "I cannot walk" response category.

Capacity not only defines our ideas about what something is, but also what our goal is relative to measurement. Walking can be about physical ability (e.g., 1 foot in front of the other) or about mobility. Capacity, at first glance, may be considered a simple thing: can the person walk or not? But if we start with capacity when developing an item, we become aware of assumptions about meaning, and refine our understanding of what we want to measure (e.g., walking vs mobility) (MacKenzie et al. 1996). To illustrate the importance of capacity, consider the fundamental issues in measuring disability and impairment. Impairment is focused on physiological limitations; for example, the effect of paralysis from the waist down on walking versus the impact of osteoarthritis in a knee on range of motion, strength, and so on. Impairment deals with whether or not capacity exists at the anatomical and physiological level. Disability is the impact which impairment has on function. It is obvious that paralysis from the waist down removes the capacity to walk, but it does not necessarily limit mobility, only certain types of mobility (MacKenzie et al. 1993). If we use capacity as the initial starting point for developing any survey item, it facilitates our ability to identify what it is that we want to measure and highlights our assumptions.

Capacity is used as the basis for measuring a wide range of issues related to physical health, from developing taxonomic profiles, to measures of functional status (e.g., Activities of Daily Living (ADLs)), to determining diagnosis (McDowell and Newell 1996). Capacity is also a critical issue when considering existing instruments. The first step in evaluating an existing scale should be a question-by-question assessment of capacity: does the item apply to the study population. In the design of instruments, measures of capacity can also serve a similar role to "no-opinion filter" items, in which they serve the purpose of branching respondents around items that are not applicable to them. Capacity is often overlooked or treated casually in assessing physical health. Too many researchers, obsessing about what it means to walk might seem absurd, but a failure to consider capacity results in the inference that a person who answers "no" to the question "Can you walk a block" literally has a mobility impairment. There

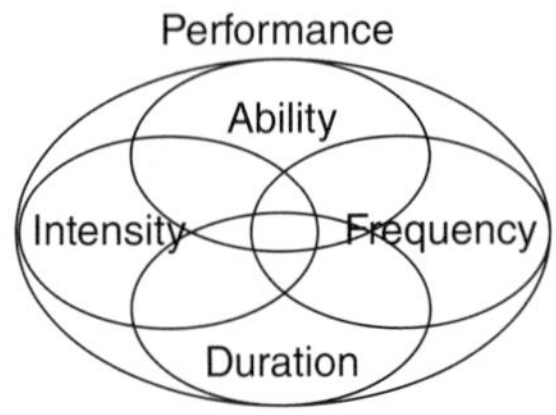

FIGURE 5.3 Conceptual framework associated with performance.

very well may be impairment in mobility, but the question is limited to a certain type of mobility; it does not cover mobility at large.

The second aspect of physical function is performance. When considering performance, there are four aspects that come into play when developing survey items: ability, frequency, duration, and intensity (see Figure 5.3). Measures of performance can range from relatively simple items associated with bending a finger (rheumatoid arthritis), to nonspecific gross indicators such as light, moderate exercise (e.g., take a walk, ride a bike, light yard work, etc.), to detailed instruments that attempt to establish fine gradations, such as metabolic equivalent (MET) expenditure (Hakala et al. 1994, McDowell and Newell 1996, Ainsworth et al. 2000, Richardson et al. 2001, Washburn et al. 2002).

The first aspect to consider relative to performance is ability. Ability can range from a simple step up from capacity, from "can do" to "do," to much more complex multidimensional scales. The change from capacity to ability is not just reflected in the question stem (from "can" to "do"), but is also apparent in the response scale used for a question. For example, shifting a question from "Can you walk up a flight of stairs" to "How easy or difficult is it for you to walk up a flight of stairs" with a Likert response scale (e.g., Very Easy–Very Difficult) demonstrates an incremental change to a capacity item, in which ability is assessed through an intensity indicator. While this represents a minor change to an item, it is a fundamental change in the theory of measurement being drawn on a shift from Guttman to Likert (Summers 1970) and carries with it the need to ensure that the response categories are exhaustive. If a Likert response scale is adopted, the presumption is that a person who cannot walk up a flight of stairs will answer with "very difficult," but this presumption can present difficulty for a respondent, in that "Can't Do" and "Very Difficult" are not the same thing. It is recommended that either a capacity item be used as a branch, (e.g., "can you walk" branches a person into a series of items on "walking") or that an "I can't walk" response option be explicitly included (capacity is used as a no-opinion filter (Schuman and Presser 1996)). In selecting response scales for items, it is important to consider the use of a bipolar scale (e.g., Very Easy–Very Difficult) versus a unipolar scale (e.g., Very Difficult (Or Can't Do)–Not At All Difficult). In the use of a unipolar scale, we focus specifically on either "easy" or "difficult." The use of a unipolar scale should be carefully considered while they can be used to overcome ceiling effects however, if used inappropriately can introduce floor effects (see below for a discussion of floor and ceiling effects).

One of the most frequently used methods to assess ability actually deals with how a set of capacity items are treated. As is discussed later, much of the measurement of physical health and function is treated as a "cumulative" (drawing primarily on the principles of Guttman scaling methods) (Guttman 1944, Guttman 1970, Guralnik et al. 1994, Dotson and Summers 1970). To simply illustrate this principle, the following three items are from the SF-36 (items Q3 g, h, and i) and when treated as a group, represent a continuum of performance.

Q3g Walk more than a mile
Q3h Walk several hundred yards
Q3i Walk one hundred yards

Each item individually is a capacity item, but when treated as a cumulative group, is an indicator of performance.

The second, third, and fourth aspects of performance (i.e., frequency, duration, and intensity) are similar relative to how they impact developing questions. In health assessment, many items combine two or more of these concepts into a single question, taking one of the issues as the task of the question (e.g., how often) and the others as conditional aspects (e.g., for at least 30 min). The meanings of duration and frequency are fairly self-evident (e.g., for how long, how often, etc.), but as pointed out in the section given earlier, obtaining an accurate response is another issue. Intensity plays a central role in the assessment of physical health and does warrant a more detailed discussion.

Intensity is especially prevalent in areas such as exercise and function, but is rarely directly assessed; rather, it is used as a modification to establish a specific meaning for a question. In the assessment of physical health, we often seek to avoid the "whatever it means to you" that is often an interviewer's response when a respondent seeks clarification. In health research, "a serving of fruit" has a specific meaning and the goal is to make sure that the respondent's interpretation is consistent with the researcher's (intensity in this instance referring to a defined amount that represents a serving). The same principles that apply to vague quantifiers as discussed earlier, and as noted by Conrad et al. (1998) apply to vague modifiers in questions (e.g., moderate exercise). Moderate is a level of exercise that has a defined level of intensity associated with it; it is not intended to be left to the respondent to define what moderate means to them personally.

In developing items in which intensity is used, the primary concern is to make sure that it is defined in such a way that its interpretation is uniform in the population. For example, we can draw on either activities or physiological impacts to identify a level of intensity. The following are a series of items all of which are intended to assess moderate activity: The next few questions are about moderate activity you may have done in the past 7 days. Moderate physical activities . . .

Alternative 1: are things that make you breathe just a little harder than normal and your heart rate goes up a little.

Alternative 2: would be something like carrying light loads, bicycling at a regular pace or walking

Alternative 3: would be like walking at a pace such that it would have made it difficult to carry on a conversation?

The first alternative focuses on physiological reactions, the second are example activities, and the third is similar to the first, but expressed in terminology that people will more likely relate to. This question also illustrates how, in health research, questions around physical health or function will utilize multiple aspects of the model underlying their development. In which

Frequency: How many times in the past 7 days ...

Duration: ... for at least 30 minutes ...

Intensity: ... made it difficult to carry on a conversation ...

are all critical to developing the item.

In health research, we often rely on vague quantifiers such as those presented earlier, but can also rely on graphical representations. These can range from the classic graphical response categories used in the Dartmouth CO-OP survey (Beaufait et al. 1992), to the use of images and props in face-to-face surveys. For example, in the assessment of nutrition, survey questions can integrate a picture to represent serving size. In the use of graphics, it is important to give a sense of scale; for example, some studies have used common objects such as a light bulb next to a portion to give the respondent a sense of scale.

When assessing the performance, any given part of the framework can be focused on individually, but the true value of the framework presented in Figure 5.3 is to facilitate the development of items associated with multiple aspects of performance. Explicit recognition of the different aspects of performance ability, frequency, duration, and intensity in item development contributes to developing an item in which all relevant aspects are taken into account.

The application of these principles to the development of performance measures is simple and straightforward, but this simplicity can often hide serious measurement problems. Aside from traditional concerns such as social desirability and the other issues discussed in Section 5.1, the problem of floor and ceiling effects are a central concern in assessing performance (McDowell and Newell 1996, Everitt and Skrondal 2010, Streiner and Norman 1995). A simple way of thinking about floor and ceiling effects is setting the bar too high or low. Floor effects emerge when the measure is assessing a level of function that is above capability (asking a person shortly after hip replacement how often they run) and ceiling effects are due to assessing a level of function that is too low (asking triathlon participants about their ability to walk a mile). Both are concerned with the inability to capture variance in the population. Avoiding floor and ceiling effects requires an understanding of activity in the study population, and identifying appropriate items that will capture the range of capabilities in the study population. The issue of floor and ceiling effects is particularly important in the study of chronic musculoskeletal and neurological conditions, in which we must consider the range of what is and is not possible within the study population, based on condition severity. Measures that are sensitive to assessing function in end-stage Parkinson's disease will demonstrate ceiling effects in early stage and measures that can capture variation in early stage will demonstrate a floor effect in end-stage respondents. This is particularly problematic in cross-sectional studies in which respondents across a wide range of abilities or functioning are being assessed; in longitudinal studies we can transition measures as respondents move from early to late stage. The critical issue is to have at least one point in the "middle" in which measures for both early and late stage are included, which can be used to calibrate the measurement transition.

The final aspect in developing or evaluating physical health measures is expectation. Individuals have underlying expectations about their own physical function and health—that is, what one can do or where one's health status stands in balance against what one wants or expects it to be. It is that "constant comparative" of what is, against what one desires or wants (Sarkisian et al. 2005). The importance of considering expectations is central whenever treatment is being evaluated (e.g., clinical trials or outcomes research) (Mahomed et al. 2002). Respondents are likely to integrate expectation into response formation; thus the answer is a consideration of actual performance relative to expectation. While there is no explicit strategy to remove expectations effects, it is important to recognize that it plays a role in response formation.

The other way in which expectation affects item development is driven by a consideration of the outcomes associated with treatment. For example, after a knee replacement surgery, there are certain clinical expectations about the rate of progress in recovery. At 2 weeks post-surgery, a person should be able to do certain things, and at 6 months other things. These expectations of changes in physical health or function serve to determine what survey items need to be used to assess outcomes. Successful item development requires an understanding of reasonable expectations for performance over time, and using that as the framework for developing items. To be successful often requires collaboration between an expert in survey methodology and a health expert. The health expert knows what are reasonable expectations and can set the range of issues that should be assessed at any given point in time, while it is the job of the survey methodologist to transition these clinical expectations into appropriate survey measures.

The models presented in Figures 5.2 and 5.3 provide a fundamental framework that can guide the development of items to assess physical health and function or for evaluating existing measures. It is often assumed that since an item is about physical health or functioning, which tend to have a basis in physical reality, items are somehow more concrete and easy to develop. While this assumption may be partially correct, it belies the complexity of the questions we tend to ask, how often something is done at a given intensity for a specific time period. The framework presented here facilitates our consideration of what needs to be in the question, how to present the question, and can serve as a gauge to judge the complexity of our questions.

5.4 Measurement Theory

Anyone who has worked with surveys in health research can attest to the frequency with which issues associated with the evaluation of measures, namely reliability and validity, are raised. One of the most frequently encountered questions a survey methodologist in health research will encounter is: Is it valid? The intent of this section is to explore at a basic level the application and use of theories and techniques associated with developing or evaluating measures.

The easiest way to identify and discuss this issue is to start with basic measures of functional status. Any review of measures associated with ADLs, Instrumental Activities of Daily Living (IADLs) or physical function readily demonstrates that there is an underlying assumption that physical health and function is cumulative, we crawl before we walk and we walk before we run (McDowell and Newell 1996). In many of these measures, the principles of Guttman scaling methods are employed (Guralnik et al. 1994, Guttman 1944, Dotson and Summers 1970) and at the current time we are starting to see descendants such as Item Response Theory figure into survey measurement (Hambleton et al. 1991). Even if the goal of any given project is not to develop a standardized scale, the basic principles associated with measurement theory can be useful in developing survey items.

Figure 5.4 provides a simple illustration of how the cumulative principles of Guttman can be used to develop a series of items to evaluate function/activity. A closer inspection of Figure 5.4 illustrates the value of such simple models in developing items. The items at the top of the figure focus on a single type of performance, walking, and allow for an intensity assessment to be generated for that single type of performance. Alternatively, those items on the bottom of the graph allow one to consider different types of performance (stairs, running), which serve as a method of multiple operationalization not only in terms of items, but also in terms of types of function in the assessment of performance.

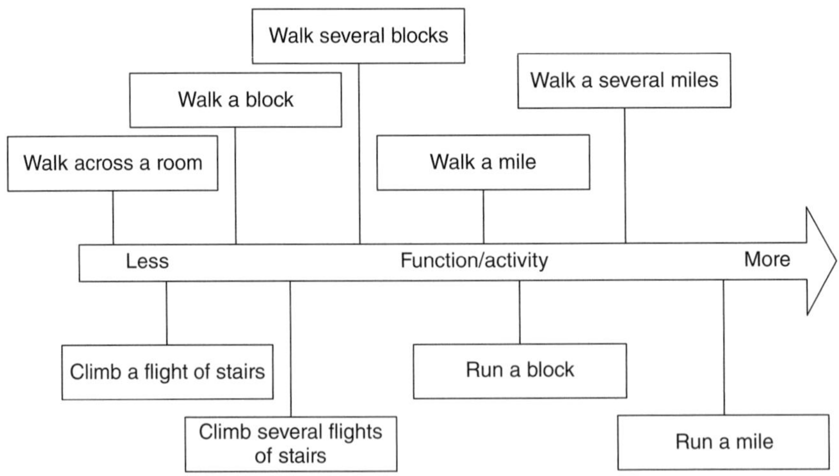

FIGURE 5.4 Illustration of the cumulative nature of function and activity.

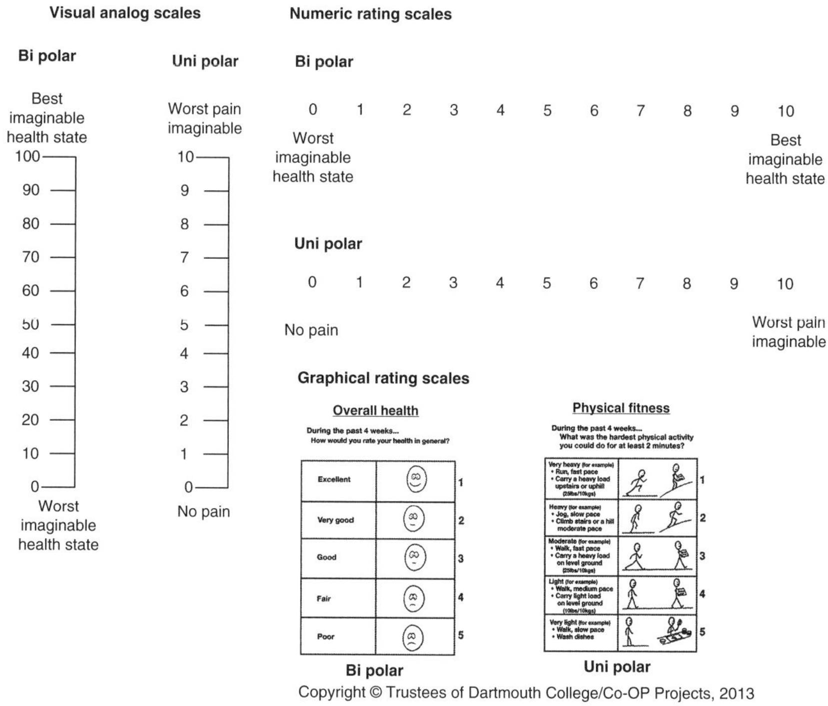

FIGURE 5.5 Examples of uni- and bipolar visual analog, numeric, and graphical rating scales.

Another measurement tool that figures prominently into health research is magnitude estimation (Lodge 1981, Gescheider 1988). The use of magnitude estimation can range from simple applications found in single items, which utilize a visual analog scaling (VAS) or numeric rating scales (NRS), to more complex applications. Figure 5.5 illustrates three basic types of measures that are grounded in magnitude estimation techniques: VAS, NRS, and graphical presentations such as those found in the Dartmouth CO-OP instrument. As is illustrated these scales can be unipolar in which the lower end of the scale is the absence of the phenomena (e.g., no pain) with the scale assessing increasing intensity (e.g., worst pain imaginable) or bipolar in which the scales are anchored with polar opposites (e.g., such as worst/best imaginable health state item in the EuroQol 5D (EQ5D instrument) (Shaw et al. 2005) or a similar semantic differential labeling (Snider and Osgood 1969).

Much more complex applications of magnitude estimation are also utilized in health research. A classic example is the stressful events questionnaire in which different life events are assigned a magnitude score relative to how much stress each induces (Holmes and Rahe 1967). Other applications use magnitude estimation to determine severity of health conditions (FISI, Fecal Incontinence Severity Index) (Rockwood et al. 1999), normed scores (Pain) (Kane et al. 2002), comparison of importance (Kane et al. 1997), and so on. Magnitude estimation is a measurement method that is prone to complex scoring (Lodge 1981). This issue is a particularly important consideration when adopting instruments that utilize magnitude estimation in scoring. For example, if one considers the complexity of scoring the FISI (sum of the weighted value for four types of incontinence for one of five time periods (Rockwood et al. 1999)) as compared to the Wexner score (sum of four items) (Jorge and Wexner 1993), it is clear that the complexity of scoring the FISI limits its application in the clinical setting. Generally speaking, the use of magnitude scaling for an item is clearly a viable option for response options to a question, but developing a scale based on magnitude scaling is outside of the scope for a single use survey, given that it is a moderately complex as well as time and labor-intensive methodology.

Validity and reliability are terms commonly used in health surveys and, in the generally interdisciplinary environment of health research, can lead to difficulties in health surveys. In the interdisciplinary context of health surveys, the meaning of reliability and validity can vary considerably among members of a research team. Those trained in health care rely on an understanding of reliability and validity that is based in a biometric model; as noted above, in this model height is an absolute. Conversely, those trained in the social sciences recognize that the measurement of height, while not perceptual, does have a range of influences that lead to tempering the interpretation of the measurement of height through a survey (e.g., height is accurate within a couple of inches) (Campbell and Overman 1988, Campbell and Russo 2001). The purpose of this material is to highlight fundamental issues associated with validity and reliability in developing items and evaluating scales.

For individuals trained in survey methodology, face validity is a central issue in item development. In the majority of single use surveys, face validity is the only type of validity that is relied on and evaluated. The consideration of what a respondent thinks a question means is the central building block of effective health surveys. As with any survey item development, cognitive interviewing is central to developing and evaluating items (see also Chapter 9) (Willis 2005, Schwarz and Sudman 1996). In working with health surveys, we are often conducting studies targeted at specific populations or settings in which we have limited or potentially no personal experience (e.g., sexual function in women with prolapse) or no experience in a specific setting (e.g., life in a nursing home). In these instances, an iterative approach to cognitive interviewing is recommended. For example, in developing an instrument assessing sexual function in women with prolapse and incontinence, over 40 cognitive interviews were conducted across a 2-month span (Rockwood et al. 2013, Rogers et al. 2013). The cognitive interviews were spread across iterative refinements to the item pool for the study (e.g., 10 cognitive interviews were conducted, the items were revised, another 10 interviews were conducted, and so on). Such an approach to item development can be somewhat more costly and time consuming, but is critical to successful item development in many instances.

In evaluating existing scales for use, the types of validity assessment used in scale development are important to consider. The ubiquity of standardized scales can be both a blessing and a curse, since almost any issue related to physical health has had a "wheel" created; on the other hand, it can be frustrating trying to locate and then select one among all the different "wheels" that are available. Three topics are addressed here: (i) issues to consider when selecting an existing instrument for use, (ii) evaluation of items post-data collection, and (iii) suggestions on how to work with coinvestigators who do not have a background in survey measurement in discussions about scales and scale adoption.

When selecting an instrument for use, the first step is often the most difficult: trying to locate and identify existing scales. There are several excellent resources, such as *Measuring Health* (Bowling 1991, McDowell and Newell 1996) and online resources such as PROQOLID and MAPI institute (http://www.proqolid.org/ and http://www.mapi-institute.com/) but none are comprehensive. The advantage is that they do tend to summarize the most commonly used instruments and will often include the actual instrument and scoring instructions; on the other hand, these resources will not include instruments that are narrowly focused, for example, scales on shoulder function. These latter scales are typically much more difficult to locate and, as noted earlier, require a search across multiple disciplines. In searching for existing scales, it is important to keep in mind the impact of disciplinary background on scales. For example, scales developed by orthopedists will usually have a detailed focus on "physical function" (e.g., how well the shoulder works), scales by physical therapists and, to a greater extent, scales developed by occupational therapists will usually have a greater focus on "life function" (e.g., can you do the things you need to do that involve your shoulder?). An orthopedist is likely to ask, "Can you hold your hand above your head?", while the occupational therapists will ask, "Can you reach up and take a can off a shelf that is above your head?" In evaluating scales, it is critical to assess the fit between the content of the items in the scale relative to the intended use of the scale: physical (orthopedic) or functional performance (OT).

After evaluating the face validity of the scale, the next step is to consider the population used to develop the scale. The assessment needs to focus on the similarity and/or differences between the study population and the population used to develop the scale. All scales are artifacts of the population (sample) they were developed in; had a different sample or population been used there is a chance that a different scale would have emerged. At the extreme, such consideration is readily apparent, such as using a scale developed in college students in the elderly. In health research, given the number of scales that have been developed especially for condition-specific issues, it is important to closely evaluate the population used to develop a scale. Many scales in health research are developed without a serious consideration of external validity and are developed based on a relatively small number of individuals, with a narrow definition (e.g., strict inclusion/exclusion criteria), and from selected settings (e.g., specialty clinics). While these factors do not preclude the validity of the scale, these can be critical factors when selecting among various scales.

After comparing the study population with the population used to develop the scale, the next step is to evaluate the psychometric robustness of the scale (Nunnally and Bernstein 1994). The range of rigor in the psychometric evaluation of scales in health research is bewildering; simply because it has been published as a "valid instrument" does not necessarily warrant treating the instrument as such. When evaluating scales, attention should be paid to processes used for scale evaluation (e.g., classic test theory, IRT, Rasch or Mokken modeling, etc.) and the rigor employed in selecting the final scale item pool (e.g., in factor analysis was a 0.60/0.40 loading rule used) (Nunnally and Bernstein 1994, Bezruczko 2005). While often overlooked, it is important to evaluate this aspect; scales are routinely published in which items are included that have failed to meet standard criteria for inclusion, but are nevertheless retained (for example, see Cotterill et al. (2011)).

The final aspect in the evaluation of existing scales is to determine how the validity of the scale was established. In health research, criterion validity is the dominant method of establishing validity (Nunnally and Bernstein 1994, Streiner and Norman 1995). There are a few key issues to keep in mind. First, the relationship between physiological function and disease and self-reported measures varies considerably dependent upon what is being measured. Functional measures (ADL, joint-specific measures) have relatively high correlation with physiological indicators. However, as one moves to IADLs and ultimately to HRQoL measures, the correlation between physiological or disease indicators declines sharply and in many instances the correlation between a scale and clinical indicators is nonexistent. This is not necessarily a problem; the relationship between disease severity and HRQoL can be mediated by a number of factors (e.g., coping, augmentation, etc.). The critical issue is knowing when such comparisons should be present. A scale on functional status, especially joint-specific function, should involve a comparison to physiological function; if this was not part of the evaluation, then caution should be exercised in selecting the scale. Alternatively, in evaluating HRQoL scales, one should not necessarily expect to see physiological or clinical indicators used as criterion. Rather, one expects to see other scales used as the criterion. For example, the SF-36 and SF-12 are routinely used as criteria for the development of Condition Specific Quality of Life (CSQoL) scales. In these instances, it is critical to understand that although there should be a correlation between the CSQoL and the more general HRQoL (SF-36), there should also be evidence presented that the CSQoL is more sensitive to disease state than the general HRQoL scale (Rockwood et al. 2000, Bordeianou et al. 2008, Rockwood et al. 1999).

For post-data collection, a basic evaluation of the scale should be undertaken before using the data. In conducting this evaluation, it is critical to note that the findings will not likely replicate published results. For example, in scale development an alpha of 0.70 is generally considered to be a lower bound value for items in a scale, but if one has adopted an existing scale for use, it is not unreasonable to see alphas much lower (e.g., ~0.40). A more comprehensive replication of scaling procedures (e.g., exploratory factor analysis) does not need to be undertaken, but can be informative. In health research, many scales are developed using low bars for psychometric robustness; as such, one should not expect the robustness that is found with tests such as the Graduate Record Examination (GRE). The core issue is that, before using the scale in analysis, a basic analysis should be undertaken to determine if the fundamental psychometric properties are sound.

A final note in this area deals with developing a survey in an interdisciplinary environment. Survey methodologists are keenly aware of the standard definition of a survey item, "it allows one to know the distribution of a characteristic in a population"; but as has been noted by many, surveys are blunt instruments. In adopting or developing measures, retaining the notion of the measurement properties of a survey is essential. Some issues are amenable to a blunt measurement (e.g., "can you walk across a room?"), others are not necessarily so amendable (e.g., wellbeing) and as demonstrated in Section 5.2 while it may be a "blunt issue" the problems associated with recall present challenges; at a certain point, the measurement properties of the tool are insufficient for the task and recognizing this is critical. A survey cannot literally determine how many steps a person took during a week (a pedometer can be used for that data point); but by using a survey, we can distinguish those who walked a lot from those who have not walked very much. In a survey, we are dealing with far less certainty in measurement and when we take survey responses and convert them into an MET score, there has to be a healthy consideration of the measurement capabilities of a survey; that is, from a survey, we are inferring a likely MET, rather than literally measuring metabolic expenditure (Ainsworth et al. 2000, Richardson et al. 2001, Washburn et al. 2002).

This issue can be particularly difficult in an interdisciplinary environment. It is the responsibility of the survey methodologist to impress upon collaborators that, with survey items, we do not have a progression that is similar to X-ray, computed tomography (CT), magnetic resonance imagining (MRI), or positron emission tomography (PET) scanning. We can refine the measurement capabilities of a survey through multiple operationalizations, or using multiple scales to some extent (Kaplan 1964, Campbell and Overman 1988, Campbell and Russo 2001). However, the explicit trade-off has to recognized—more detail requires more questions, and this has to be balanced against questionnaire length. In the language of clinicians, many of the things we measure are analogous to soft tissue and a survey is like an X-ray not an MRI or PET scanner.

5.5 Error and Methodology

As with any subject physical health is by no means immune to context-based effects and measurement error (Biemer et al. 1991, Schwarz and Sudman 1992); in fact some of the initial work on social desirability was based on health research (Dohrenwend et al. 1968, Colombotos 1969). Section 5.2 provided a detailed discussion of response formation and context effects associated with factors such as response categories. The following is a brief discussion of two additional issues; by no means the only issues, but two that are important considerations in development of surveys to assess physical health: social desirability (Holtgraves 2004) and issues associated with mode of administration.

One of the best examples of the impact of mode and administration is a study by Fowler in which 50% of a series of questions evaluating health and function postprostrate surgery showed a significant difference between the mail and telephone mode (Fowler et al. 1998). Many studies have demonstrated mode differences for a range of issues, from illicit drug use (Aquilino 1993, Aquilino 1994), disability status (Kelley-Moore 2006, Todorov 2000) to mental health (Epstein et al. 2001) and fundamental issues associated with differences in cognitive processes used by respondents (Jobe and Herrmann 1996). Often mode effects are thought to be synonymous with social desirability and while much of the research on social desirability is dominated by mode comparisons, it is critical to keep in mind that mode of administration interacts with other context-based effects and is not solely a factor associated with social desirability (Tarnai and Dillman 1989, Schwarz et al. 1991c, Dillman et al. 1996, Rockwood et al. 1997, Dillman and Christian 2005).

As the history of survey methods demonstrates, there is no ultimate solution to solving the social desirability and mode effect problems. Methods such as the randomized response technique (RRT; Fox and Tracy 1986), controls for social desirability or other forms of response bias (e.g., Marlow Crowne (Marlow and Crowne 1961), the Balanced Inventory of Desirable Responding (Vispoel and Tao 2012)) are sometimes used; however, their complexity and inability to fully solve this problem have inhibited their widespread use. This does not mean that there are no simple solutions to the issue of social desirability in survey reporting (for example as discussed earlier in Loftus's work on asking about physician visits in the past 6 and 3 months) (Loftus et al. 1990). For example, in the study of smoking behavior, the standard first item is often: "Have you ever smoked a cigarette, even 1 or 2 puffs?" Over time the endorsement of the item has declined at a rate that is in step with the increasing stigma associated with smoking and the decline is relatively uniform across all ages (e.g., individuals over 55 saying "no" who at the age of smoking initiation did not face such negative stigma with smoking). In response to this, we added a standard follow-up to this item in interviewer-administered surveys. If a respondent said "no" to this item, we followed up with the question "Not even one or two puffs?" Across a number of different studies this follow-up item resulted in an increase of 4–15% endorsement of having at least "puffed" once or twice. While this modest increase certainly does not represent a perfect solution to the problem, it does illustrate that simple things can be done to address some of the error.

When writing questions on issues that are subject to social desirability, the problem lies in developing the item such that it makes it acceptable for the person to admit to doing something they perceive they should not, or not report doing something they perceive they should when they have not. As health and public health continue to become more effective at pushing health issues into public awareness, the number of areas that are subject to social desirability effects will continue to increase. Fifty years ago there was little or no social desirability associated with the assessment of smoking; now the negative stigma associated with smoking makes accurate assessment of smoking status much more difficult if not impossible. We are already entering into problems with the assessment of fast food, consumption of high fat foods, and looming over the horizon are a whole host of issues from preventative care to utilization. As the profile and the costs associated with health care continue to grow in the public's awareness, concerns about what is subject to social desirability must be adjusted accordingly.

Given the key role that mode of administration plays relative to social desirability in particular and other context effects in general, careful consideration must be given to mode when designing and conducting studies. If a survey is conducted using the telephone mode, it will generally result in a healthier population than if the same individuals were surveyed by mail. This effect can be dramatic in some populations; Figure 5.6 provides an illustration of the differences in response to the question: "In general, would you say your health is . . . ," between the mail and phone modes. The past several decades have seen a great deal of research and concern about nonresponse error in survey methods as response rates decline (Groves and Couper 1998, Groves 2006). In response to this, the use of mixed-mode designs has become increasingly more common (Dillman et al. 2009). What is not made explicit in such suggestions is the assumption that reduction of nonresponse error is more important than the introduction of measurement error due to mode of administration. Such an approach is reckless. The consideration of the potential reduction of bias due to nonresponse needs to be considered against the potential introduction of measurement error due to mode (see de Leeuw (1992), de Leeuw and Collins (1997), Dillman, et al. (2009), and De Leeuw et al. (2008) for discussion of mixed mode designs.)

Moving beyond the use of mixed mode for a particular administration of a survey is administration in longitudinal surveys. For example, in many clinical studies, patients are recruited in person (either in clinic or via the telephone) and surveys administered using personal interviews. These respondents are then surveyed in the future using self-administered methods (mail or web). Given what is known about mode effects, when designing a longitudinal study to evaluate treatment outcomes, setting up a study in which the baseline administration is done by one mode and follow-up by another can either introduce bias

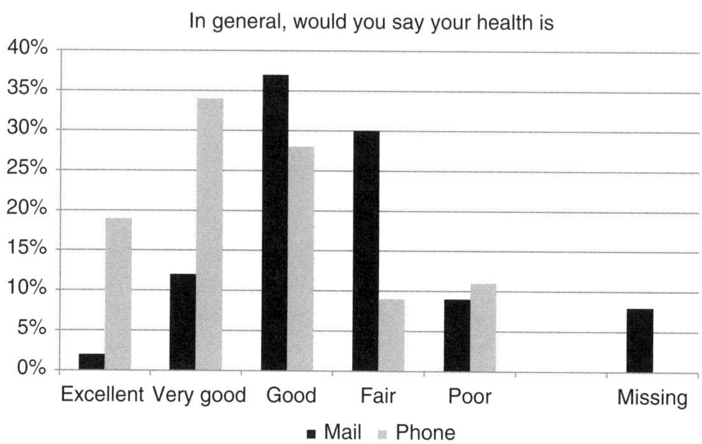

FIGURE 5.6 Comparison of general health rating in patients with fecal incontinence between mail and telephone modes ($p < 0.01$).

and will result in underestimating (e.g., when baseline is done via CATI and follow-up done via mail) or overestimating (e.g., when baseline is done by mail and follow-up by CATI) changes.

5.6 Conclusion

The measurement of physical health and issues related to physical health are simultaneously fraught with difficulty, but can actually produce remarkably accurate information—sometimes. When writing survey items relative to physical issues, there is a tendency to just begin developing items based on personal experience. While it is always beneficial to have first-hand knowledge and experience when writing survey items, the simple models presented in Figures 5.2–5.4 can be useful guides in developing items. At a general level, physical measures are composed of three basic aspects: capacity, performance, and expectation (Figure 5.2): Can they? Do They? Do they think they should be able (respondent expectation)? Should they be able to by now (treatment expectation)? Recognizing which aspect serves as the foundation for a question is critical to writing the right question.

Building on this, the preponderance of measurement in physical health is around the issue of performance (Figure 5.3). In developing items to assess performance there are four basic components that should direct item construction: ability, frequency, duration, and intensity. The assessment of performance often results in what are appearingly simple items, but conceptually are actually complex: How often a week (*frequency*) do you walk at a pace (*ability*) that makes it difficult to carry on a conversation *(intensity)* for at least 20 min *(duration)*? While on the face of it the question appears simple, the question is actually asking the respondent to link four conceptually distinct things together in framing their interpretation of what the question is assessing. The second critical aspect of performance is to keep in mind the cumulative nature of physical things (Figure 5.4). This should be considered in two ways: first, no single item is likely to assess many physical phenomena, multiple items are required; and second, knowing and understanding how to use classic measurement theories such as Guttman can prove to be a valuable tool in development of items (Guttman 1944, Guttman 1970, Guralnik et al. 1994, Dotson and Summers 1970).

A number of works have focused on core mechanical issues around item development and response formation to items assessing issues related to physical health (Loftus et al. 1992, Schwarz and Bienias 2006). This research has demonstrated a number of issues associated with the problems associated with the recall of past behaviors and events. Figure 5.1 is an attempt to distill out the relevant issues identified in the literature and how they point to different recall strategies being used in response formation. A range of factors including context memory, memory degradation, similarity, and distinguishability have been repeatedly demonstrated to affect the respondent's ability to form responses. Furthermore, a number of context-based effects, including leading, telescoping, decomposition, response categories, and social desirability (and the related hello-goodbye effect found in health care in which the severity of symptoms is exaggerated before treatment or at the beginning of a clinical encounter and minimized after to please the clinician (Choi and Pak 2013), which can be found in surveys around health issues as well (Streiner and Norman 1995)) have been demonstrated to influence response. In light of all this research, there is the potential to despair at ever being able to write a question that is error free, but there are tools that we can use to enhance the reduction of error. In developing items, the fundamental goal is to shift respondents to using a response formation process that is likely to produce greater accuracy. This can be simply illustrated by considering the generic question "how often do you exercise?" If asked this way, it is likely to result in a "vague" response (e.g., often, when I can, sometimes, etc.). If we change the item to "how often in the past month did you exercise?", we are likely to push the respondent to using rate estimation (e.g., I exercise three times a week there are 4 weeks in a month, so I exercised 12 times). Finally, if we ask "how often have you exercised today?", the respondent is likely to use direct enumeration (e.g., they literally count what they have done that day).

In developing the items, the goal is to encourage the respondent to use a more accurate method by shifting them from vague estimation toward direct enumeration. The above example illustrates one of the primary methods used to accomplish this through time bounding. Other examples have demonstrated that methods to stimulate relevant cognition, such as decomposition can be useful (Menon 1997), but can also be error inducing (Belli et al. 2000). In addition, asking a series of items to prime memory (Dillman and Tarnai 1991), using multiple time frames (Loftus et al. 1990, Loftus et al. 1992) as well as other methods (e.g., sentinel events (Loftus and Marburger 1983)) have been suggested. None of these methods have demonstrated the ability to solve all the problems, but do identify strategies that can potentially be used in facilitating a more accurate response.

In light of all of this, it is critical to keep in mind the pathways identified in Figure 5.1 and not just focus on the end point of response formation. For some respondents, an event is frequent, regular, mundane and high frequency, in which case decomposition could potentially lead to improved accuracy. But this strategy, when used with a respondent for which the event is frequent, irregular and mundane could lead to over-reporting. It is critical to recognize that the attributes for many of the events assessed around physical health are not universal in the study population. Rather, they differ across respondents and thus any given strategy may promote greater accuracy in some respondents, but induce error in others. In part, much of the problem with the measurement of activities such as exercise, resides in the fact exercise can be rare or frequent, regular or irregular, salient or mundane across different respondents and it becomes fundamentally impossible to develop questions that are capable of working across all of these different pathways leading to different types of response formation.

One of the fundamental advantages in health research is to draw on other measurement modalities. As noted in Chapter 15, we can draw on biological measures. If a study aims to evaluate current smoking status, a saliva, urine, or blood sample can be used for a cotinine test, which if assessed in blood is actually sensitive to exposure levels. A simple pedometer can be an effective means of measuring activity. In health research, there is often access to para-data from a clinic or health plan. These data should be considered for use either as adjunctive to survey data, or even in place of it.

We often think that the measurement of physical function and health are fundamentally different from measuring attitude and opinion. Running is after all an "objective" physical event, and the respondent should be able to indicate whether or not they have done it. Furthermore, given that we often assess response using numbers or ranges of frequency as opposed to vague quantifiers we often assume that the measurement is more accurate. However, measuring issues associated with physical health has more in common with measuring attitudes and opinion than we think and while the use of numbers as opposed to vague quantifiers might provide increased accuracy for some phenomena there are others for which they only present the illusion of greater accuracy. In health research and survey methods Kaplan's (1964: 172) observation of the mystic of quantity in which, a "number is treated as having an intrinsic scientific value" is persistent; assigning a number to represent some aspect of physical health does not mean that physical health has been assessed. In developing survey items to assess physical health Payne's (1950) classic advice on meaningless questions applies also to the development of survey items to assess physical health is no different than any other survey item. What we want to know must be tempered against what the respondent is willing and capable of answering.

REFERENCES

Ainsworth, Haskell WL, Whitt MC, Irwin ML, Swartz AM, Strath SJ, O Brien WL, Bassett DR, Schmitz KH and Emplaincourt PO. Compendium of physical activities: an update of activity codes and MET intensities. Med Sci Sports Exerc 2000;32(9; SUPP/1):498–504.

Al Baghal MT. Numeric estimation and response options: an examination of the measurement properties of numeric and vague quantifier responses [PhD Dissertation]; 2012.

Aquilino WS. Effects of spouse presence during the interview on survey responses concerning marriage. Public Opin Q 1993;57(3):358–376.

Aquilino WS. Interview mode effects in surveys of drug and alcohol use: a field experiment. Public Opin Q 1994;58(2):210–240.

Bachman JG, O'Malley PM. When four months equal a year: inconsistencies in student reports of drug use. Public Opin Q 1981;45:536–548.

Barei DP, Julie Agel and Swiontkowski MF. Current utilization, interpretation, and recommendations: the musculoskeletal function assessments (MFA/SMFA). J Orthop Trauma 2007;21(10):738–742.

Beaufait DW, Nelson EC, Landgraf JM, Hays RD, Kirk JW, Wasson JH and Keller A. COOP measures of functional status. In: Stewart MA, Tudiver F, Bass MJ, Dunn EV, Norton PG, editors. *Tools for Primary Care Research. Research Methods for Primary Care*. Thousand Oaks, CA: Sage Publicastions, Inc.; 1992.

Belli RF, Schwarz N, Singer E and Talarico J. Decomposition can harm the accuracy of behavioural frequency reports. Appl Cogn Psychol 2000;14:295–308.

Bezruczko N. *Rasch Measurement in Health Sciences*. MN: Jam Press Maple Grove; 2005.

Biemer PP, Groves RM, et al. *Measurement Errors in Surveys*. New York: Wiley; 1991.

Blair E, Burton S. Cognitive processes used by survey respondents to answer behavioral frequency questions. J Consum Res 1987;14:280–288.

Bordeianou L, Lee KY, Rockwood T, Baxter NN, Lowry A, Mellgren A and Parker S. Anal resting pressures at manometry correlate with the Fecal Incontinence Severity Index and with presence of sphincter defects on ultrasound. Dis Colon Rectum 2008;51(7):1010–1014.

Bowling A. *Measuring Health: A Review of Quality of Life Measurement Scales*. Philadelphia: Open University Press Buckingham; 1991.

Bradburn NM, Miles C. Vague quantifiers. Public Opin Q 1979;43(1):92–101.

Bradburn NM, Rips LJ and S. K. Shevell. Answering autobiographical questions: the impact of memory and inference on surveys. Science 1987;236(4798):157–161.

Brown NR. Context memory and the selection of frequency estimation strategies. J Exp Psychol Learn Mem Cognit 1997;23(4):898.

Burton S, Blair E. Task conditions, response formulation processes, and response accuracy for behavioral frequency questions in surveys. Public Opin Q 1991;55(1):50–79.

Campbell DT, Overman ES. *Methodology and Epistemology for Social Science: Selected Papers*. Chicago: University of Chicago Press; 1988.

Campbell DT, Russo MJ. *Social Measurement*. Thousand Oaks, CA: Sage Publications; 2001.

Choi BCK, Pak AWP. Hello-goodbye effect. In: Salkind NJ, Rasmussen K, editors. *Encyclopedia of Measurement and Statistics*. Thousand Oaks, CA: Sage Publications, Inc; 2013.

Cipher DJ, Clifford PA. Dementia, pain, depression, behavioral disturbances, and ADLs: toward a comprehensive conceptualization of quality of life in long-term care. Int J Geriatr Psychiatry 2004;19(8):741–748.

Colombotos J. Personal versus telephone interviews: effect on responses. Public Health Rep 1969;84(9):773.

Conrad FG, Brown NR, et al. Strategies for estimating behavioural frequency in survey interviews. Memory 1998;6(4):339–366.

Cotterill N, Norton C, Avery KNL, Abrams P and Donovan JL. Psychometric evaluation of a new patient-completed questionnaire for evaluating anal incontinence symptoms and impact on quality of life: the ICIQ-B. Dis Colon Rectum 2011;54(10):1235–1250.

Courneya KS, Jones LW, et al. Effect of response scales on self-reported exercise frequency. Am J Health Behav 2003;27(6):613–622.

De Leeuw ED. *Data Quality in Mail, Telephone and Face to Face Surveys*. Amsterdam: T. T. Publikaties; 1992.

De Leeuw E, Collins M. Data collection methods and survey quality: an overview. In: Lyberg L, Biemer P, Collins M, et al., editors. *Survey Measurement and Process Quality*. New York: Wiley; 1997. p 199–220.

De Leeuw E, Dillman DA and J. Hox. Mixed mode surveys: when and why. In: *International Handbook of Survey Methodology*. Philadelphia: PA, Lawrence Erlbaum; 2008.

Del Boca FK, Darkes J. The validity of self-reports of alcohol consumption: state of the science and challenges for research. Addiction 2003;98(s2):1–12.

Dillman DA, Christian LM. Survey mode as a source of instability in responses across surveys. Field Methods 2005;17(1):30–52.

Dillman DA, Sangster RL, Tarnai J and Rockwood TH. Understanding differences in people's answers to telephone and mail surveys. In: Braverman MT, Slater JK, editors. *Advances in Survey Research*. San Francisco: Jossey-Bass, Inc.Number 70; 1996. p 110.

Dillman DA, Smyth JD and Christian LM. *Internet, mail, and mixed-mode surveys: the tailored design method*. Hoboken, NJ: Wiley & Sons; 2009.

Dillman DA, Tarnai J. Mode effects of cognitively designed recall questions: a comparison of answers to telephone and mail surveys. In: Biemer PP, Groves RM, Lyberg LE, Mathiowetz NA, Sudman S, editors. *Measurement Errors in Surveys*. New York: Wileyxxxiii; 1991a. p 760.

Dillman DA, Tarnai J. Mode effects of cognitively designed recall questions: a comparison of answers to telephone and mail surveys. In: Biemer PP, Groves RM, Lyberg LE, Mathiowetz NA, Sudman S, editors. *Measurement Errors in Surveys*. New York: Wileyxxxiii; 1991b. p 760.

Dohrenwend BS, Colombotos J and Dohrenwend BP. Social distance and interviewer effects. Public Opin Q 1968;32(3):410–422.

Dotson LE, Summers GF. Elaboration of Guttman scaling techniques. In: Summers G, editor. *Attitude Measurement*. Chicago: Rand McNally & Company; 1970.

Epstein JF, Barker PR and Kroutil LA. Mode effects in self-reported mental health data. Public Opin Q 2001;65(4):529–549.

Everitt B, Skrondal A. *The Cambridge Dictionary of Statistics*. Cambridge, UK; New York: Cambridge University Press; 2010.

Fadiman A. *The Spirit Catches you and you Fall Down : A Hmong Child, Her American Doctors, and the Collision of Two Cultures*. New York: Farrar, Straus, and Giroux; 1997.

Fowler FJ. *Improving Survey Questions : Design and Evaluation*. Thousand Oaks: Sage Publications; 1995.

Fowler FJ Jr, Roman AM and Di ZX. Mode effects in a survey of medicare prostate surgery patients. Pub Opin Q 1998;62(1):29–46.

Fox JA, Tracy PE. *Randomized Response: A Method for Sensitive Surveys*. Beverly Hills: Sage Publications; 1986.

Gaskell GD, O'Muircheartaigh CA and Wright DB. Survey questions about the frequency of vaguely defined events: the effects of response alternatives. Public Opin Q 1994;58(2):241–254.

Gaskell GD, Wright DB and Wright DB. Telescoping of landmark events: implications for survey research. Public Opin Q 2000;64(1):77–89.

Gescheider GA. Psychophysical scaling. Annu Rev Psychol 1988;39(1):169–200.

Gescheider GA. *Psychophysics: The Fundamentals*. Lawrence Erlbaum; 1997.

Gorden RL. *Interviewing: Strategy, Techniques, and Tactics*. Chicago, IL: Dorsey Press; 1987.

Groves RM. Nonresponse rates and nonresponse bias in household surveys. Public Opin Q 2006;70(5):646–675.

Groves RM, Couper M. *Nonresponse in Household Interview Surveys*. New York: Wiley; 1998.

Guralnik JM, Simonsick EM, Ferrucci L, Glynn RJ, Berkman LF, Blazer DG, Scherr PA and Wallace RB. A short physical performance battery assessing lower extremity function: association with self-reported disability and prediction of mortality and nursing home admission. J Gerontol 1994;49(2):M85–M94.

Guttman L. A basis for scaling qualitative data. Am Sociol Rev 1944;9(2):139–150.

Guttman L. The Cornell technique for scale and intensity analysis. In: Summers GF, editor. *Attitude Measurement*. Chicago: Rand McNallyxviii; 1970. p 568.

Hakala M, Nieminen P and J. Manelius. Joint impairment is strongly correlated with disability measured by self-report questionnaires. Functional status assessment of individuals with rheumatoid arthritis in a population based series. J Rheumatol 1994;21(1):64.

Hambleton RK, Swaminathan H, et al. *Fundamentals of Item Response Theory*. Newbury Park, CA: Sage Publications; 1991.

Harbison J, Dougherty MR, Davelaar EJ and Fayyad B. On the lawfulness of the decision to terminate memory search. Cognition 2009;111(3):397–402.

Hoeymans N, Edith JM, Feskens EJ, Geertrudis AM van den Bos and Kromhout D. Measuring functional status: cross-sectional and longitudinal associations between performance and self-report (Zutphen Elderly Study 1990–1993). J Clin Epidemiol 1996;49(10):1103–1110.

Holmes TH, Rahe RH. The social readjustment rating scale. J Psychosom Res 1967;11(2):213–218.

Holtgraves T. Social desirability and self-reports: testing models of socially desirable responding. Pers Soc Psychol Bull 2004;30(2):161–172.

Hunt SM, McEwen J. The development of a subjective health indicator. Sociol Health Illn 1980;2(3):231–246.

Jette AM, Allyson R, Davies AR, et al. The functional status questionnaire. J Gen Intern Med 1986;1(3):143–149.

Jobe JB. Cognitive psychology and self-reports: models and methods. Qual Life Res 2003;12(3):219–227.

Jobe JB, Herrmann DJ. Implications of models of survey cognition for memory theory. Basic Appl Mem Res 1996;2:193–205.

Johnson EO, Schultz L. Forward telescoping bias in reported age of onset: an example from cigarette smoking. Int J Methods Psychiatr Res 2005;14(3):119–129.

Jorge JMN, Wexner SD. Etiology and management of fecal incontinence. Dis Colon Rectum 1993;36(1):77–97.

Kane RL, Bershadsky B, Lin WC, Rockwood T and Wood K. Efforts to standardize the reporting of pain. J Clin Epidemiol 2002;55(2):105–110.

Kane RL, Bershadsky B, et al. Visual Analog Scale pain reporting was standardized. J Clin Epidemiol 2005;58(6):618–623.

Kane RL, Rockwood T, et al. Consumer and professional ratings of the importance of functional status components. Health Care Financ Rev 1997;19(2):11–22.

Kaplan A. *The Conduct of Inquiry: Methodology for Behavioral Science*. San Francisco: Chandler Pub. Co.; 1964.

Kelley-Moore JA. Assessing racial health inequality in older adulthood: comparisons from mixed-mode panel interviews. J Gerontol Ser B Psychol Sci Soc Sci 2006;61B(4):s212–s220.

Kerns RD, Turk DC and Rudy TE. The west haven-yale multidimensional pain inventory (WHYMPI). Pain 1985;23(4):345–356.

Krosnick JA. Thinking about answers: the application of cognitive processes to survey methodology. Public Opin Q 1997;61(4):664–667.

Kuczmarski MF, Kuczmarski RJ and Najjar M. Effects of age on validity of self-reported height, weight, and body mass index: findings from the Third National Health and Nutrition Examination Survey, 1988–1994. J Am Diet Assoc 2001;101(1):28.

Lodge M. *Magnitude scaling, quantitative measurement of opinions*. Beverly Hills: Sage Publications; 1981.

Loftus EF, Fathi DC. Retrieving multiple autobiographical memories. Soc Cognit 1985;3(3):280–295.

Loftus EF, Klinger MR, et al. A tale of two questions: benefits of asking more than one question. Public Opin Q 1990;54(3):330–345.

Loftus EF, Marburger W. Since the eruption of Mt. St. Helens, has anyone beaten you up? Improving the accuracy of retrospective reports with landmarkevents. Mem Cognit 1983;11(2):114–120.

Loftus EF, Smith KD, et al. Memory and mismemory for health events. In: Tanur JM, S. S. R. C. U. S. C. o. Cognition, editors. *Questions about Questions: Inquiries into the Cognitive Bases of Surveys*. New York: Russell Sage Foundationxxi; 1992. p 306.

MacKenzie EJ, Cushing BM, Jurkovich GJ, Morris Jr. JA, Burgess AR, deLateur BJ, McAndrew MP and Swiontkowski MF. Physical impairment and functional outcomes six months after severe lower extremity fractures. J Trauma 1993;34(4):528.

MacKenzie EJ, Damiano A, Miller T and Luchter S. The development of the functional capacity index. J Trauma Acute Care Surg 1996;41(5):799–807.

Mahomed NN, Liang MH, Cook EF, Daltroy LH, Fortin PR, Fossel AH and Katz JN. The importance of patient expectations in predicting functional outcomes after total joint arthroplasty. J Rheumatol 2002;29(6):1273–1279.

Marlow D, Crowne DP. Social desirability and response to perceived situational demands. J Consult Psychol 1961;25(2):109.

McDowell I, Newell C. *Measuring Health: A Guide to Rating Scales and Questionnaires*. New York: Oxford University Press; 1996.

McGlone MS, Reed AB. Anchoring in the interpretation of probability expressions. J Pragmat 1998;30(6):723–733.

McGrath PA, Speechley KN, et al. A survey of children's acute, recurrent, and chronic pain: validation of the Pain Experience Interview. Pain 2000;87(1):59–73.

Melzack R. The McGill Pain Questionnaire: major properties and scoring methods. Pain 1975;1(3):277–299.

Menon G. The effects of accessibility of information in memory on judgments of behavioral frequencies. J Consum Res 1993;20(3):431–440.

Menon G. Are the parts better than the whole? The effects of decompositional questions on judgments of frequent behaviors. J Market Res: 1997;34:335–346.

Menon G, Raghubir P and Schwarz N. Behavioral frequency judgments: an accessibility-diagnosticity framework. J Consum Res 1995:212–228.

Nunnally JC, Bernstein IH. *Psychometric Theory*. New York: McGraw-Hill; 1994.

Palta M, Prineas RJ, Berman R and Hannan P. Comparison of self-reported and measured height and weight. Am J Epidemiol 1982;115(2):223–230.

Park CL, Zlateva I and Blank TO. Self-identity after cancer: "survivor", "victim", "patient", and "person with cancer". J Gen Intern Med 2009;24:430–435.

Payne SL. Thoughts about meaningless questions. Public Opin Q 1950;14(4):687–696.

Prohaska V, Brown NR, et al. Forward telescoping: the question matters. Memory 1998;6(4):455–465.

Rhodes RE, Matheson DH and Mark R. Evaluation of social cognitive scaling response options in the physical activity domain. Meas Phys Educ Exerc Sci 2010;14(3):137–150.

Richardson MT, Ainsworth BE, Jacobs DR and Leon AS. Validation of the Stanford 7-day recall to assess habitual physical activity. Ann Epidemiol 2001;11(2):145–153.

Robert Pace C, Friedlander J. The meaning of response categories: how often is "occasionally," "often," and "very often"? Res High Educ 1982;17(3):267–281.

Rockwood T, Constantine M, et al. The PISQ-IR: considerations in scale scoring and development. Int Urogynec J Forthcoming. 24(7):1105–1122.

Rockwood TH, Church JM, et al. Patient and surgeon ranking of the severity of symptoms associated with fecal incontinence: the fecal incontinence severity index. Dis Colon Rectum 1999;42(12):1525–1532.

Rockwood TH, Church JM, et al. Fecal incontinence quality of life scale: quality of life instrument for patients with fecal incontinence. Dis Colon Rect 2000;43(1):9–16discussion 16–17.

Rockwood TH, Sangster RL, et al. The effect of response categories on questionnaire answers: context and mode effects. Sociol Methods Res 1997;26(1):118–140.

Rogers R, Rockwood T, et al. A revised measure of sexual function in women with pelvic floor disorders (PFD); the pelvic organ prolapse incontinence sexual questionnaire, IUGA-revised (PISQ-IR). Int Urogynecol J Forthcoming. 1–13.

Sarkisian CA, Prohaska TR, et al. The relationship between expectations for aging and physical activity among older adults. J Gen Intern Med 2005;20(10):911–915.

Schaeffer NC. Hardly ever or constantly? Group comparisons using value quantitifers. Public Opin Q 1991;55(3):395–423.

Schuman H, Presser S. *Questions and Answers in Attitude Surveys : Experiments on Question Form, Wording, and Context*. Thousand Oaks, CA: Sage Publications; 1996.

Schwarz N. Assessing frequency reports of mundane behaviors: contributions of cognitive psychology to questionnaire construction. In: Hendrick C, Clark MS, editors. *Research Methods in Personality and Social Psychology*. Thousand Oaks, CA: Sage Publications, Inc.**11**; 1990.

Schwarz N. Self-reports: how the questions shape the answers. Am Psychol 1999;54(2):93.

Schwarz N, Bienias J. What mediates the impact of response alternatives on frequency reports of mundane behaviors? Appl Cognit Psychol 2006;4(1):61–72.

Schwarz N, Bless H, et al. Response scales as frames of reference: the impact of frequency range on diagnostic judgements. Appl Cognit Psychol 1991a;5:37–49.

Schwarz N, Hippler H-J, et al. Response scales: effects of category range on reported behavior and comparative judgments. Public Opin Q 1985;49:388–395.

Schwarz N, Knauper B, et al. Rating scales: numeric values may change the meaning of scale labels. Public Opin Q 1991b;55(4):570–582.

Schwarz N, Oyserman D. Asking questions about behavior: cognition, communication, and questionnaire construction. Am J Eval 2001;22(2):127–160.

Schwarz N, Strack F, et al. The impact of administration mode on response effects in survey measurement. Appl Cognit Psychol 1991c;5(3):193–212.

Schwarz N, Strack F, et al. The range of response alternatives may determine the meaning of the question: further evidence on informative functions of response alternatives. Soc Cognit 1988;6(2):107–117.

Schwarz N, Sudman S. *Context Effects in Social and Psychological Research*. New York: Springer-Verlag; 1992.

Schwarz N, Sudman S. *Autobiographical Memory and the Validity of Retrospective Reports*. New York, NY: Springer-Verlag; 1994.

Schwarz N, Sudman S. *Answering Questions: Methodology for Determining Cognitive and Communicative Processes in Survey Research*. San Francisco: Jossey-Bass Publishers; 1996.

Shaw JW, Johnson JA, et al. US valuation of the EQ-5D health states: development and testing of the D1 valuation model. Med Care 2005;43(3):203–220.

Sirken MG. *Cognition and Survey Research*. New York: Wiley; 1999.

Snider JG, Osgood CE. *Semantic Differential Technique: A Sourcebook*. Chicago: Aldine Pub. Co.; 1969.

Spencer EA, Appleby PN, et al. Validity of self-reported height and weight in 4808 EPIC–Oxford participants. Public Health Nutr 2002;5(04):561–565.

Sternbach RA. Acute versus chronic pain. In: Wall PD, Melzack R, editors. *Textbook of Pain*. Edinburgh: Churchill Livingstone; 1985.

Streiner DL, Norman GR. *Health Measurement Scales: A Practical Guide to their Development and Use*. Oxford; New York: Oxford University Press; 1995.

Sudman S, Bradburn NM. *Asking Questions*. San Francisco: Jossey-Bass; 1982.

Sudman S, Bradburn NM, et al. *Thinking About Answers: The Application of Cognitive Processes to Survey Methodology*. San Francisco: Jossey-Bass Publishers; 1996.

Summers GF. *Attitude Measurement*. Chicago: Rand McNally; 1970.

Tanur JM, Social Science Research Council (U.S.). Committee on Cognition. *Questions About Questions: Inquiries into the Cognitive Bases of Surveys*. New York: Russell Sage Foundation; 1992.

Tapp N. Hmong religion. Asian Folklore Stud 1989;48(1):59–94.

Tarnai J, Dillman DA. Questionnaire context in mail and telephone surveys. First Nags Head Conference on Cognition and Survey Research; Nags Head, NC; 1989.

Todorov A. Context effects in National Health Surveys: effects of preceding questions on reporting serious difficulty seeing and legal blindness. Public Opin Q 2000;64(1):65–76.

Tourangeau R, Rips LJ, et al. *The Psychology of Survey Response*. Cambridge: Cambridge University Press; 2000.

Turk DC, Meichenbaum D, et al. *Pain and Behavioral Medicine: A Cognitive-Behavioral Perspective*. The Guilford Press; 1987.

Tversky A, Kahneman D. Availability: a heuristic for judging frequency and probability. Cogn Psychol 1973;5(2):207–232.

Vispoel W, Tao S. A generalizability analysis of score consistency for the balanced inventory of desirable responding. Psychol Assess 2012;25:94–104.

Von Korff M, Dworkin SF, Le Resche L, et al. Graded chronic pain status: an epidemiologic evaluation. Pain 1990;40(3):279–291.

Ware JEJ, Kosinski M, et al. *How to Score Version 2 of the SF-36 Health Survey*. Lincoln, RI, QualityMetric Incorporated; 2000.

Washburn RA, Zhu W, et al. The physical activity scale for individuals with physical disabilities: development and evaluation. Arch Phys Med Rehabil 2002;83(2):193–200.

Willis GB. *Cognitive Interviewing : A Tool for Improving Questionnaire Design*. Thousand Oaks, CA: Sage Publications; 2005.

Wright DB, Gaskell GD, et al. How much is 'quite a bit'? Mapping between numerical values and vague quantifiers. Appl Cognit Psychol 2006;8(5):479–496.

Zebrack BJ. Cancer survivor identity and quality of life. Cancer Pract 2001;8(5):238–242.

Zung WK. A self-rating pain and distress scale. Psychosomatics 1983;24(10):887–894.

ONLINE RESOURCES

Patient-Reported Outcome and Quality of Life Instruments Database (PROQOLID), a diverse collection of instruments to assess outcomes and quality of life can be accessed at: http://www.proqolid.org.

The MAPI Research Trust parent of PROQOLID contains similar instruments as well as translated instruments and translation assistance: http://www.mapi-trust.org.

Information on the World Health Organization Composite International Diagnostic Interview (CIDI), including a PDF of the instrument and training requirements is available at: http://www.hcp.med.harvard.edu/wmhcidi.

Information on the World Health Organization World Mental Health Survey Initiative, an ongoing initiative that has thus far implemented mental health needs assessment surveys in 28 countries can be found at: http://www.hcp.med.harvard.edu/wmh.

US surveys that contain the K6 scale include the CDC Behavioral Risk Factors Surveillance Survey, the SAMHSA National Household Survey on Drug Use and Health, and the National Health Interview Survey. These can be accessed at the following URL addresses: http://www.cdc.gov/BRFSS, http://www.oas.samhsa.gov/nhsda.htm, http://www.cdc.gov/nchs/nhis.htm.

An example of a computerized self-administered mental health assessment is the Army Study to Assess Rick and Resilience in Servicemembers (Army STARRS). Army STARRS is a large prospective study of suicide risk among US Army personnel: http://www.armystarrs.org.

Information on the US National Institutes of Health's network of researchers developing a comprehensive battery of patient self-report outcome scales called the Patient-Reported Outcomes Measurement Information System (PROMIS) can be found at: http://www.nihpromis.org.

The National Center for Health Statistics descriptions of health related surveys and data collection systems in the U.S. Federal system can be accessed at: http://www.cdc.gov/nchs/surveys.htm and http://www.cdc.gov/nchs/measures_catalog.htm.

CHAPTER SIX

Developing and Selecting Mental Health Measures

Ronald C. Kessler
Department of Health Care Policy, Harvard Medical School, Boston, Massachusetts, USA

Beth-Ellen Pennell
Survey Research Center, Institute for Social Research, University of Michigan, Ann Arbor, Michigan, USA

6.1 Introduction

This chapter presents an overview of measurement approaches in surveys of mental illness. Although up through the 1980s most survey research on mental illness focused on dimensional measures of nonspecific psychological distress (Gove and Tudor 1973, Mirowsky 1999), more recent research has been interested in specific syndromes, such as depression (Dowrick et al. 2011), eating disorders (Roberto et al. 2010), and post-traumatic stress disorder (Hauffa et al. 2011). Categorical (i.e., yes–no) measures of disorder presence and dimensional measures of symptom severity are both used in these more recent studies. We begin by presenting a brief historical overview of the progression of survey research on mental illness and then present overviews of the most widely used categorical measures of mental disorders and dimensional measures of symptom severity. The chapter closes with a discussion of emerging issues in the survey assessment of mental illness.

Handbook of Health Survey Methods, First Edition. Edited by Timothy P. Johnson.

6.2 Historical Background

6.2.1 POST WORLD WAR II SCREENING SCALE STUDIES

The beginning of modern survey research on mental disorders can be traced to the growing concern about the prevalence of mental illness shortly after World War II. This concern occurred because many returning veterans suffered from what is now known as *post-traumatic stress disorder*. One response was the initiation of several surveys of mental disorders based on direct interviews with representative community samples. The earliest such surveys were carried out by clinicians or used lay interview data in combination with record data as input to clinician evaluations (e.g., Leighton 1959, Srole et al. 1962). In later surveys, clinician judgment was abandoned in favor of less expensive self-report symptom rating scales that assigned each respondent a score on a continuous dimension of nonspecific psychological distress (e.g., Gurinet al. 1960). Controversy surrounded the use of these rating scales, focusing on item bias, insensitivity, and restriction of symptom coverage (e.g., Dohrenwend and Dohrenwend 1965, Seiler 1973). Nonetheless, symptom rating scales continued to be the mainstay of community surveys of mental illness through the 1970s.

Three factors accounted for the attraction of symptom rating scales. First, they were much less expensive than clinician interviews. Second, symptom scales dealt directly with the actual constellations of symptoms in the population rather than with classifications imposed on by clinicians. Third, the clinician-based diagnostic interviews available at that time did not have good psychometric properties in community samples (Dohrenwend et al. 1978).

The most important disadvantage of working with rating scales was that these scales did not allow researchers to determine which respondents had clinically significant emotional problems. This was not as important to social scientists, whose main concern was to characterize the distress associated with structural variations, than as it was to clinicians and social policy analysts who wanted to make decisions regarding such things as the number of people in need of mental health services. A division consequently arose between social scientists, who focused much of their research on studies of dimensional distress, and psychiatric epidemiologists, who focused their research on studies of dichotomous caseness designations.

A middle ground between these two positions was sought by some researchers who developed rules for classifying people with scores above a certain threshold on distress scales as psychiatric "cases" (e.g., Radloff 1977) and studied both continuous and dichotomous outcomes. The precise cut-points used in this research were usually based on statistical analyses to discriminate optimally between scores of patients and community residents. However, as noted above, considerable controversy surrounded the decision of exactly where to draw cut-points. Dichotomous diagnostic measures allowed this sort of discrimination to be made directly based on evaluations of diagnostic criteria, but these interviews were not precise due to lack of agreement on appropriate research diagnostic criteria and absence of valid instruments for carrying out diagnostic interviews.

6.2.2 THE RISE OF FULLY STRUCTURED DIAGNOSTIC INTERVIEWS

It was not until the late 1970s that this controversy was resolved with the establishment of clear research diagnostic criteria (Feighner et al. 1972) and development of systematic research diagnostic interviews (Endicott and Spitzer 1978). Early interviews of this type required administration by clinicians, which yielded rich data but limited their use in epidemiologic surveys because of the high costs associated with large-scale use of clinicians as interviewers. Because of these high costs and logistic complications, only a handful of such studies were carried out. These studies were generally quite small and based on local samples (e.g., Weissman and Myers 1978).

Two responses to this situation occurred in the late 1970s. The first was the refinement of two-stage screening methods in which a first-stage screening scale was administered by a lay interviewer to a large community sample followed with more expensive second-stage clinician-administered interviews to the subsample of respondents who screened positive plus a small subsample of those who screened negative (Newman et al. 1990). The second response was the development of fully-structured research diagnostic interviews that could be administered by lay interviewers. The first instrument of this type was the Diagnostic Interview Schedule (DIS; Robins et al. 1981), which was developed with support from the National Institute of Mental Health for use in the Epidemiologic Catchment Area (ECA) Study (Robins and Regier 1991). Several other interviews, most of them based on the DIS, were subsequently developed. The most widely used of these is the World Health Organization's (WHO's) *Composite International Diagnostic Interview* (CIDI; World Health Organization 1990), which was used in the two major national household surveys of mental disorders carried out in the United States over the past two decades: the National Comorbidity Survey (NCS; (Kessler et al. 1994) and the National Comorbidity Survey Replication (NCS-R; Kessler et al. 2004).

6.2.3 THE USE OF BLENDED CATEGORICAL AND DIMENSIONAL ASSESSMENTS

One of the most striking and consistent results of the surveys carried out since the 1980s using fully-structured diagnostic interviews is that roughly 50% of the general population is found to meet criteria for one or more of the commonly occurring mental disorders assessed in these surveys at some time in their life and roughly 30% meet criteria in the year of interview (Regier et al. 1993, Kessler et al. 1994, Regier et al. 1998, Kessler et al. 2005b, 2005c). Long-term longitudinal studies show that the high lifetime prevalence estimates are, if anything, under-estimates (Moffitt et al. 2010). These high prevalence estimates have been criticized as implausible (Narrow et al. 2002). Yet clinical reappraisal by blinded clinical interviewers confirms that most respondents judged to have mental disorders in the surveys are, in fact, confirmed as having these disorders by mental health professionals (Kessler et al. 1998, Haro et al. 2006).

This high prevalence reflects the wide and growing range of emotional difficulties included in successive editions of the American Psychiatric Association's *Diagnostic and Statistical Manual of Mental Disorders* (American Psychiatric Association 1980, 1987, 1994). Not all of these disorders are severely impairing. Not all of them require treatment (Wakefield and Spitzer 2002). This is, of course, also true of many minor physical health problems, but many lay people find it surprising that the same wide variation in severity is found among mental disorders. As a result of this high prevalence of mental disorders in the community, commentators have argued that it is important for surveys of mental disorders to go beyond simple yes–no categorical classifications to include dimensional information about symptom severity (Maser and Patterson 2002, Kessler et al. 2003c, Narrow et al. 2009). A number of widely used clinical severity measures exist for this purpose (Rush et al. 2007), but these measures were largely developed for use in clinical samples of patients and many of these measures are what clinical researchers refer to as *semistructured*; that is, although they use a standard set of questions to elicit open-ended respondent reports, the response ratings are based on clinical judgments of these open-ended reports and consequently require a good deal of training and clinical expertise to use (Brugha et al. 1999). Scales of the sort more typically used in surveys, where fixed-choice response options are presented to respondents and respondents choose among those options for their responses, in comparison, are referred to as *fully-structured*.

Recognizing the considerable time, money, and logistic complications involved in using semistructured scales in large-scale clinical administration, a number of clinical researchers have developed fully structured approximations of standard semistructured dimensional symptom severity scales. A good example is modification of the *Hamilton Rating Scale for Depression* (HRSD; Hamilton 1960, 1967), a semistructured measure of depression symptom severity that has been the gold standard measure of depression treatment effectiveness for many years. The HRSD is also commonly used to help make clinical triage decisions based on guidelines that have developed over time regarding the meaning of scores in different parts of the scale range (Ruhe et al. 2005, Furukawa et al. 2007). But the HRSD can only be administered by carefully trained clinicians and takes 20–45 minutes to administer, making it infeasible to use either in general medical settings or as a symptom tracking instrument in routine mental health specialty settings. As a result, self-report approximations of the HRSD have been developed (e.g., Carroll et al. 1981, Rush et al. 2000). One of these self-report scales, the *Quick Inventory of Depressive Symptomatology Self-Report* (QIDS-SR), takes only 3–4 minutes to self-administer, has a Pearson correlation of 0.86 with clinician-administered HRSD scores among patients in treatment for depression, and is as sensitive to symptom improvement during the course of treatment as the HRSD (Rush et al. 2003).

Disorder-specific symptom severity scales such as the QIDS-SR are not designed to be administered to unrestricted samples of the general population, but to people who have already been judged to meet criteria for a particular mental disorder. As a result, the most recent development in survey assessment of mental disorders is to use a fully structured diagnostic interview such as the

CIDI to determine whether respondents meet criteria for a given mental disorder and then use a fully-structured approximation of clinical symptom severity scales to assess symptom severity among respondents who meet criteria for a disorder of interest. This kind of blended approach to assessment is the one used in the WHO's World Mental Health (WMH) Survey Initiative (Kessler et al. 2006c, Kessler and Üstün 2008).

6.3 Fully Structured Diagnostic Interviews

6.3.1 THE FIRST GENERATION

As noted above, the first fully structured psychiatric diagnostic interview was the DIS (Robins et al. 1981). The DIS was developed for use in the ECA Study (Robins and Regier 1991), a landmark survey of mental disorders carried out in selected neighborhoods in five U.S. communities in the 1980s. The DIS operationalized the diagnostic criteria of the DSM-III diagnostic system (American Psychiatric Association 1980) by developing questions that held as closely as possible to the wording of the DSM and used consistently understandable terms to operationalize intensity words in the DSM that respondents were not likely to understand such as *persistent, excessive, recurrent*, and *markedly* (Robins and Cottler 2004). Clinical reappraisal studies yielded mixed evidence about the concordance of resulting diagnoses with independent diagnoses made by trained clinical interviewers (Anthony et al. 1985, Helzer et al. 1985).

The wide dissemination of ECA results led to replications in other countries (Weissman et al. 1996a, 1996b, 1997). However, the DIS generated diagnoses only according to DSM criteria, not according to the criteria of the WHO International Classification of Diseases ICD; (Sartorius 1995). This limited use of the DIS, as more than half the countries in the world use the ICD system to diagnose mental disorders. WHO addressed this limitation by establishing a task force to expand the DIS to include ICD criteria. The resulting instrument was called the *CIDI* (Robins et al. 1988).

This first version of the CIDI was very similar to the DIS other than for inclusion of expanded ICD symptom questions. CIDI validity studies showed that CIDI diagnoses were significantly related to independent clinical diagnoses but that individual-level concordance was far from perfect (Wittchen 1994). Nonetheless, demand was so high that the CIDI, which was translated by WHO into many different languages, became widely used during the first half of the 1990s. An important problem with this first generation of CIDI surveys with regard to systematic comparison, though, was that the interview contained no information about risk factors, consequences, or treatment, leading to lack of comparability in measures that hampered efforts to make cross-national comparisons of these correlates (Kessler 1999).

Recognizing the value of coordinating the measurement of broader areas of assessment, WHO launched an initiative to expand the CIDI that brought together the senior scientists responsible for planned CIDI surveys across the world in an effort to develop a joint battery to measure risk factors, consequences, and treatment. Within a short period of time, research groups in over a dozen countries joined this initiative, which came to be known as the *WMH Survey Initiative*. The number of participating WMH countries has since expanded to 28. These WMH collaborators developed a new version of the CIDI (Kessler and Üstün 2004) that has subsequently become the international standard for large-scale community surveys of mental disorders.

6.3.2 THE REVISED CIDI

On the basis of the concerns about evidence of limited clinical validity of the first version of the CIDI, the WMH collaborators modified the instrument in a number of ways to improve validity (Kessler and Üstün 2004). This work was facilitated by previous evaluations of the CIDI by survey methodologists in preparation for the NCS in the United States (Kessler et al. 1998, 1999, 2000) as well as by methodological research carried out by survey researchers to address methodological problems of the type detected in initial evaluations of the CIDI (e.g., Turner and Martin 1985, Oksenberg et al. 1991, Tanur 1992, Sudman et al. 1996, Tourangeau and Yan 2007, Wittenbrink and Schwarz 2007). An experimental study showed that the CIDI modifications put in place by WMH led to substantial increases in lifetime recall of mental disorders and significantly improved concordance of diagnoses based on the CIDI with independent clinical evaluations (Kessler et al. 1998). Subsequent clinical reappraisal studies replicated these findings and showed that diagnoses based on the modified CIDI have generally good concordance with independent clinical diagnoses for a wide range of disorders over a number of countries (Haro et al. 2006).

The CIDI is available in modular form, which means that it can be used to assess a small number of diagnoses or even a single diagnosis. Use of the CIDI requires successful completion of a training program offered by a WHO CIDI Training and Research Centre based on a 40-hour interactive CD-ROM based CIDI training course and 3-day face-to-face training program. Remedial training elements are embedded in the CD-ROM whenever a trainee fails an embedded test. Trainees who successfully complete the certification process at the end of this program are given access to all CIDI training materials for use in training interviewers and supervisors along with CIDI programs and computerized diagnostic algorithms. A PDF copy of the CIDI along with contact information for CIDI training is available at www.hcp.med.harvard.edu/wmhcidi.

6.4 Dimensional Measures of Symptom Severity

6.4.1 SCREENING FOR NONSPECIFIC PSYCHOLOGICAL DISTRESS

As noted in Subsection 6.2.2, dimensional scales of nonspecific psychological distress have been used in community epidemiological surveys since the end of

World War II. The first of these scales were based on the Neuropsychiatric Screening Adjunct developed by Star (1950) for selective service screening in World War II. Although the original Star scale was scored as a simple count of endorsed items, factor analysis showed related scales to be multidimensional, leading to the development of multidimensional screening tools for common mental disorders in primary care settings (Goldberg 1972, Lipman et al. 1977). These scales have been widely promoted in conjunction with treatment quality improvement initiatives (Tansella and Thornicroft 1999). However, some of these scales are quite long, such as the 90-item Hopkins Symptom Checklist (HSCL-90; Lipman et al. 1977, 1979) and the 60-item General Health Questionnaire (GHQ; Goldberg 1972). A variety of shorter versions of these scales were developed to address this problem of length (e.g., Derogatis et al. 1974, Goldberg and Hillier 1979, Vieweg and Hedlund 1983, Strand et al. 2003).

Even though the original long-form scales were mostly multidimensional, most short versions are unidimensional. This transformation was supported by the finding that the multidimensional information in the original scales was generally not helpful in primary care settings, where clinician interest is in a yes–no distinction between patients who do or do not have clinically significant emotional problems that should be followed up with more in-depth semistructured questioning (Cleary et al. 1982). On the basis of this thinking, very short scales, such as the 12-item version of the GHQ (GHQ-12), became much more popular than the original longer scales (Goldberg and Williams 1988). It is noteworthy that long multidimensional scales such as the HSCL-90 and GHQ-60 could be reduced efficiently to short unidimensional scales because factor analysis always found a very strong first principal factor in the long scales (Dohrenwend et al. 1980).

6.4.2 SCREENING FOR SERIOUS MENTAL ILLNESS (SMI)

As noted above in Subsection 6.2.3, dimensional symptom scales have taken on new importance in the context of the movement to distinguish cases based on severity rather than purely on the basis of diagnosis. In particular, a number of recent large-scale community epidemiologic surveys have included brief screening scales to provide a rapid assessment of the prevalence of serious mental illness (SMI). The most widely used screening scale of SMI in these studies is the K6 scale (Kessler et al. 2002, Furukawa et al. 2003, Kessler et al. 2003a), a six-question scale that was developed explicitly to estimate the prevalence of SMI as defined by U.S. Public Law (PL) 102-321, the Alcohol, Drug Abuse, and Mental Health Administration (ADAMHA) Reorganization Act. This law established a U.S. federal Block Grant for states to fund Community Mental Health Services for adults with SMI and the law required states to include incidence and prevalence estimates in their annual applications for Block Grant funds. The law also required the U.S. Substance Abuse and Mental Health Services Administration (SAMHSA) to develop an operational definition of SMI and to create an estimation methodology based on this definition for use by the states. The definition of SMI stipulated in PL 102-321 requires the person to have at least one 12-month DSM disorder, other than a substance use disorder, and to have "serious impairment."

Given the importance for policy planning purposes of knowing the prevalence and sociodemographic distribution of SMI in the population of United States for purposes of allocating Block Grant funds (which are in excess of $1 billion each year), the architects of all major U.S. federal health tracking surveys decided to include a measure of SMI in their interviews shortly after the ADAMHA Reorganization Act was published. The K6 was developed for this purpose to be included in the U.S. National Health Interview Survey (NHIS), a national survey of close to 50,000 households that has been carried out on an ongoing basis in the United States for more than half a century (www.cdc.gov/nchs/nhis.htm). The goal was to create a very brief (6–10 items) scale that would provide accurate aggregate estimates of SMI prevalence and correlates. Although a number of distress scales existed that had been used for many years at of the time the K6 was developed (e.g., Gurin et al. 1960, Dohrenwend et al. 1980, Derogatis 1983), only a few of them were brief enough to meet this time requirement (Pearlin et al. 1981, Ware and Sherbourne 1992) and none was developed using modern psychometric methods to maximize precision in the clinical range of the population distribution (van der Linden and Hambleton 1997). On the basis of these considerations, the decision was made to develop a new screening scale for use in the redesigned NHIS.

The conceptualization of this task relied importantly on the finding noted above that questions about a heterogeneous set of cognitive, behavioral, emotional, and psychophysiological symptoms are elevated among people with a wide range of different mental disorders, leading to a strong first principal factor in the structure of nonspecific psychological distress (Dohrenwend et al. 1980, Link and Dohrenwend 1980). This core dimension of nonspecific psychological distress was taken as the focus of the K6. The K6 was developed using item response theory methods to select questions with the maximum precision at the clinical threshold of the scale. On the basis of the fact that no more than 10%, and probably closer to 6%, of the U.S. population meet criteria for SMI in a given year (Kessler et al. 1996), the decision was made to seek maximum precision of the K6 in the 85th–95th percentile range of the population distribution.

A number of independent clinical validation studies have shown that the K6 has very good concordance with blinded clinical diagnoses of SMI in general population samples of the United States (Kessler et al. 2002, 2003a) and a number of other countries throughout the world (Furukawa et al. 2003, 2008, Gill et al. 2007, Patel et al. 2008, Fassaert et al. 2009). Additional studies found similarly good concordance in special patient populations that included primary care attenders (Haller et al. 2009), postnatal females (Baggaley et al. 2007, Tesfaye et al. 2010), and patients with substance use disorders (Swartz and Lurigio 2006, Hides et al. 2007). Methodological research also showed that the K6 has little bias with regard to sex and education (Baillie 2005), a feature that was built into the scale from the onset, as items were selected for the K6 based on formal comparisons of differential item functioning by age, sex, and education to minimize biases with regard to these variables (Kessler et al. 2002). The K6 was also included in the WHO WMH Surveys and was shown to have good concordance across a wide range of countries with diagnoses of SMI based on the CIDI (Kessler et al. 2010).

6.4.3 SCREENING FOR PARTICULAR DISORDERS

A number of screening scales have also been developed for particular mental disorders such as attention-deficit/hyperactivity disorder (ADHD; Kessler et al. 2005a), bipolar disorder (Hirschfeld et al. 2000), generalized anxiety disorder (Spitzer et al. 2006), major depressive disorder (Kroenke et al. 2001), and post-traumatic stress disorder (Breslau et al. 1999). Coordinated sets of such scales have proliferated in recent years for use either as web-based self-diagnosis tools (Farvolden et al. 2003, Donker et al. 2009) or primary care screening tools (Broadhead et al. 1995, Hunter et al. 2005, Gaynes et al. 2010). Some of these scale sets are listed in Table 6.1 along with information about the disorders they assess. (Table 6.1). A number of other stand-alone screening scales have been developed for particular disorders, such as the ADHD Self-Report Scale (ASRS) screening scale of ADHD (Kessler et al. 2007a) and the CIDI screening scale for bipolar disorder (Kessler et al. 2006a).

Results of clinical reappraisal studies of these screening scales are shown in Table 6.1 for dichotomous versions of the screening scales created by the scale developers to maximize concordance with clinical diagnoses. The coefficients presented are sensitivity (SN; the proportion of clinical cases detected in the screening scale), specificity (SP; the proportion of clinical noncases correctly classified as noncases by the screening scale), and area under the receiver operating characteristic curve (AUC, area under the curve), a standard measure of diagnostic concordance that can be interpreted as the probability of correctly identifying a clinically-defined case in a series of paired comparison tests in which scores on the screening scale are compared between one randomly selected respondent with a clinical diagnosis and one randomly selected respondent without a clinical diagnosis and the respondent with the higher score is estimated to be the one with the disorder (Pepe 2003). AUC is 0.50 when the screening scale is completely unrelated to clinical diagnosis and 1.0 when the two are perfectly related. AUC scores between these two extremes are often interpreted in parallel with the interpretation of Cohen's K (Landis and Koch 1977) as *slight* (0.5–0.6), *fair* (0.6–0.7), *moderate* (0.7–0.8), *substantial* (0.8–0.9), or *almost perfect* (0.9+). As shown in Table 6.1, many of the screening scales in the coordinated sets shown here have *substantial* concordance with clinical diagnoses. Even better performance has been found for some standalone screening scales that have been developed for particular disorders, such as the *almost perfect* values of AUC found for the ASRS screening scale of adult ADHD (Kessler et al. 2007a) and the CIDI screening scale for bipolar disorder (Kessler et al. 2006a).

TABLE 6.1 **Some Integrated Sets of Screening Scales for Common DSM-IV Mental Disorders**

			DSM-IV Diagnosis[a]								
	Validator[b]	Sample[c]	MDD	BPD	SoP	SP	GAD	OCD	PTSD	PD	AA/AD
I. WB-DAT[d]	SCID	MHS									
SN[e]			0.79		0.74		0.63	0.71	0.95	0.75	
SP[e]			0.89		0.94		0.94	0.97	0.93	0.94	
AUC[e]			0.84		0.84		0.73	0.84	0.94	0.84	
II. SDDS-PC[d]	SCID	PC									
SN[e]			0.90				0.90	0.64		0.78	0.62
SP[e]			0.77				0.54	0.72		0.80	0.98
AUC[e]			0.84				0.72	0.68		0.79	0.80
III. WSQ[d]	CIDI	WEB									
SN[e]			0.85		0.72	0.80	0.93	0.80	0.83	0.90	0.83
SP[e]			0.59		0.73	0.47	0.45	0.69	0.47	0.44	0.72
AUC[e]			0.72		0.72	0.63	0.69	0.74	0.65	0.67	0.77
IV. M-3[d]	MINI	PC									
SN[e]			0.84	0.88	0.82[f]		0.82[f]	0.82[f]	0.88[f]	0.82[f]	
SP[e]			0.80	0.70	0.78[f]		0.78[f]	0.78[f]	0.76[f]	0.78[f]	
AUC[e]			0.82	0.79	0.80		0.80	0.80	0.82	0.80	

V. SCL-90DS[d]	PDI	MHS						
SN[e]			0.79	0.75	0.75[f]	0.75[f]	0.78	0.79
SP[e]			0.66	0.58	0.64[f]	0.64[f]	0.64	0.73
AUC[e]			0.72	0.66	0.69	0.69	0.71	0.76

[a]MDD, major depressive disorder; BPD, bipolar disorder; SoP, social phobia; SP, specific phobia; GAD, generalized anxiety disorder; OCD, obsessive–compulsive disorder; PTSD, post-traumatic stress disorder; PD, panic disorder; AA/AD, alcohol abuse/dependence.

[b]The screening scales were evaluated by comparing diagnoses based on the screening scales against independent diagnoses based on more in-depth clinical reappraisal interviews. Four different validator interviews of this sort were used in the five studies: SCID, Structured Clinical Interview for DSM-IV Axis I disorders patient edition (SCID-I/P, Version 2.0; First et al. 1995); CIDI, Composite International Diagnostic Interview, Version 3.0. (Kessler and Üstün 2004); PDI, Psychiatric Diagnostic Interview (Othmer et al. 2000).

[c]The samples used to validate the screening scales were as follows: MHS, patients in an outpatient mental health specialty treatment setting; PC, patients in a primary care treatment setting; WEB, an Internet sample of Dutch adults with Internet access who responded to Internet banners seeking people who "felt anxious, depressed, or thought of themselves as drinking too much alcohol."

[d]WB-DAT, Web-Based Anxiety and Depression Test (Farvolden et al. 2003); SDDS-PC, Symptom-Driven Diagnostic System for Primary Care (Broadhead et al. 1995); WSQ, Web-Based Screening Questionnaire for Common Mental Disorders (Donker et al. 2009); M-3, My Mood Monitor (Gaynes et al. 2010); SCL-90DS, SCL-90 Diagnostic Scales (Hunter et al. 2005).

[e]SN, Sensitivity (the proportion of cases defined by the validator ["clinical cases"] that are classified as cases by the screening scale); SP, Specificity (the percent of clinical noncases that are classified as noncases by the screening scale); AUC, area under the receiver operating characteristic curve (the probability of correctly identifying a clinical case in a series of paired comparison tests in which scores on the screening scale are compared between one randomly selected clinical case and one randomly selected clinical noncase and the respondent with the higher score is estimated to be the one with the disorder. In calculating AUC in pairs where the screening scale scores are identical for the clinical case and noncase, the estimate of which one has the disorder is based on random assignment. AUC has an expected value of 0.50 when the screening scale is completely unrelated to clinical diagnosis and an expected value of 1.0 when the screening scale is perfectly related to clinical diagnosis.)

[f]Combined in a single category.

6.4.4 SCORING SCREENING SCALES FOR PARTICULAR DISORDERS

The screening scales described in the last three subsections are all dimensional scales that are dichotomized in clinical practice to estimate presence of a particular disorder. Survey applications can also use dichotomization. This can be done in several different ways depending on the purpose of the study. In some cases, the screening scale is dichotomized to maximize total classification accuracy, but in cases of rare disorders, this can lead to a rule that classifies all respondents as noncases. At other times dichotomization is done to equalize SN and SP (as in the M-3 scales in Table 6.1) or to equalize the number of false positives and false negatives (as in several other scales in Table 6.1). The latter rule will generally mean that SN will be lower than SP at the optimal cut-point, as noncases are typically more common than cases. In still other cases, a weight is applied to the relative importance of false positives and false negatives and an optimal scoring rule is developed to maximize the weighted total classification accuracy. Using this approach leads to a rule that creates many more false positives than false negatives, as when the public health importance of detecting a high proportion of people with a communicable disease is so high that public health officials might be willing to bear the expense of working up many false positives to detect a single true case (Kraemer 1992).

But dichotomous classification is not necessary in surveys, as no decision about whether or not to treat is made with survey respondents. This being the case, a transformation that retains more information is to convert K6 scores into continuous probability-of-SMI scores. This can be done by embedding a clinical calibration study into a subsample of a survey sample to estimate predicted probability of SMI at each value of the K6 scale. This is a common feature of psychiatric epidemiological surveys (e.g., Kessler and Üstün 2004, Haro et al. 2006), where a probability subsample of survey respondents that oversamples screened positives is reinterviewed by clinical interviewers who make diagnoses blinded to the K6 scores in the main survey. Once data of this sort are available, K6 scores along with measures of other predictors of SMI, such as sociodemographic variables, can be included as predictors in a multiple regression analysis within the clinical calibration subsample (appropriately weighted to adjust for the oversampling of respondents with high K6 scores) to establish the functional form of the association between K6 scores and SMI and to explore the possibility that this association varies as a function of the respondent's age, sex, education, or other characteristics. When a best-fitting model is found, a predicted probability of SMI based on this model can be assigned to each sample respondent in the entire sample (not just the clinical calibration subsample). Scoring rules have been developed and published for the K6 based on such analyses of general population survey data obtained in the WMH surveys (Kessler et al. 2010).

In providing these transformation rules, it is important to recognize that the uncertainty of inference from the prediction equations needs to be taken into consideration in analyzing estimates of the prevalence and correlates of SMI based on transformed K6 data. Conventional significance testing would treat the individual-level predicted probabilities of SMI as known rather than estimated from a model. The method of multiple imputation (MI; Rubin 1987) can be used to overcome this limitation by generating a number of different estimates of the predicted probability of SMI for each respondent and using information about variation across these predictions to adjust estimates of standard errors for imprecision. In order to allow researchers to implement this MI approach to estimation when they use published transformation rules to score K6 responses, pseudosample coefficients for best-fitting prediction equations have been published (Kessler et al. 2010).

6.4.5 SCREENING SCALES OF DISORDER SEVERITY

As noted above in Subsection 6.2.3, clinical studies of patients typically use semistructured dimensional scales to assess disorder severity. The HRSD (Hamilton 1960, 1967) was mentioned as an example, but there are many others, such as the Yale–Brown Obsessive Compulsive Scales (YBOCS) to assess the severity of obsessive–compulsive disorder (Goodman et al. 1989), the Panic Disorder Severity Scale (PDSS) to assess the severity of panic disorder (Shear et al. 1997), and the Generalized Anxiety Disorder Severity Scale (GADSS; Shear et al. 2006). These clinical severity scales are the measures typically used in clinical trials to evaluate the effectiveness of treatment. They can also be used in routine clinical practice to monitor treatment response, although the substantial time and effort typically needed to administer these scales usually make them impractical for routine clinical use.

The need for alternative self-report versions of these scales to monitor treatment response has increased greatly in recent years in response to demands for treatment quality improvement initiatives using evidence-based methods that require symptom monitoring (Baldassano et al. 2011, Davis et al. 2011) and the development of computerized adaptive treatment algorithms for modifying treatment based on evidence about initial treatment response (Pineau et al. 2007). Fully-structured versions of numerous symptom severity scales have been developed to meet this need. We noted in Subsection 6.2.3 that the QIDS-SR was developed for this purpose to provide a quick self-administered assessment of depressive symptoms that closely approximates the ratings obtained in the much more labor-intensive semistructured clinician-administered HRSD. Other fully structured symptom severity scales include the Panic Disorder Self-Report Scale as an approximation of the PDSS (Houck et al. 2002), computerized self-administered versions of the Hamilton anxiety and depression scales (Kobak et al. 1999, Williams et al. 2008), the Addiction Severity Index (Brodey et al. 2004), and the ChronoRecord system (Whybrow et al. 2003) to approximate the rating of mood fluctuation in bipolar disorders obtained in the clinician-administered Young Mania Rating Scale (Young et al. 1978) and Hamilton Depression Rating Scale (Hamilton 1960).

As noted above in Subsection 6.2.3, the most recent version of the CIDI (Kessler and Üstün 2004) includes a number of these fully structured versions of disorder-specific severity scales. This blending of community epidemiological data on disorder prevalence with clinical data on disorder severity is useful in creating a crosswalk between community and clinical studies. We know based on this crosswalk, for example, that well over 80% of the people in community samples who meet criteria for panic disorder have levels of severity that clinicians would judge to be moderate-to-severe (Kessler et al. 2006b) and that while many people with major depressive disorder fail to seek treatment the severity of those untreated cases as judged by standard clinical severity measures is much lower than that of depressed people who obtain treatment (Kessler et al. 2003b).

6.5 Emerging Issues in Survey Assessments of Mental Disorders

6.5.1 NONREPORTING BIAS

Mental disorders are stigmatized and likely to be under-reported in surveys. Methods exist to help reduce this bias (Tourangeau and Yan 2007). The most common approach is to increase the respondent's sense of privacy, using or supplementing interviews with self-administered modes, guaranteeing confidentiality, and instructing interviewers to conduct their interviews in a private setting (without the presence of a third party). Most methodological research on these methods has focused on administration mode. This literature suggests that sensitive items should be self-administered and that self-administration may be even more important in contexts where interview privacy cannot be controlled or is culturally inappropriate (Davis et al. 2010). Computerized interviews, computer-assisted self-interviews (CASI), and audio computer-assisted self-interviews (ACASI) lead to even greater increases in reporting sensitive behaviors (Turner et al. 1998, Richman et al. 1999, Tourangeau and Yan 2007). Computerized self-administration has the added benefit of reducing administration errors and guiding respondents through more complex routing than could be used in paper questionnaires (Langhaug et al. 2010).

The literature on the effects of interview privacy on reporting sensitive information is limited and results more mixed (Pollner and Adams 1994, Aquilino 1997, Aquilino et al. 2000, Tourangeau and Yan 2007). We are aware of only one study that systematically evaluated privacy effects on reports of mental illness. That study, carried out in the WMH Surveys, found that lack of interview privacy was associated with significant reduction in reported mental disorders, particularly in low and middle income countries (Mneimneh and Pennell 2011), although presence of another adult during the interview was consistently associated with increased reporting of suicidal behaviors, possibly reflecting greater respondent willingness to admit suicidal behaviors in front of someone who has independent knowledge of those behaviors.

Given rapid advances in computer technology in surveys, new approaches are likely to be developed to increase reporting of mental disorders. One intriguing recent study illustrates the possibilities. In this study, researchers tackled the difficult problem of assessing suicidal ideation in a sample of emotionally distressed people who might be motivated to conceal their suicidality from interviewers

(Cha et al. 2010). The researchers reasoned that such individuals might have an attentional bias toward suicide-related words and, if so, that a neurocognitive test that measured reaction time in a word identification task might be able to detect this bias and infer suicidality in the absence of respondents admitting their suicidality to interviewers. The study to test this hypothesis was carried out in a sample of individuals seeking treatment for emotional problems in the waiting room before their initial evaluation visit. The task involved showing each respondent a series of 48 words on as many computer screens, each word printed in either red or blue, and asking respondents to indicate the word as quickly as possible by pressing a red or blue computer key. Suicide-related words (e.g., suicide, dead, funeral) were interspersed with other words. Each respondent was then evaluated by a clinician blinded to test results. This evaluation included questions asked of the respondent about suicidality as well as a clinician rating of patient suicide risk in the next 6 months. Respondents were then followed for 6 months to monitor suicide attempts. Information about differential response latencies to the suicide-related words compared to other words in the color identification tasks significantly predicted suicide attempts after controlling for baseline respondent reports of suicidality as well as for clinician assessments of suicide risk.

It would be an easy matter to include this kind of neurocognitive assessment in a CASI survey to augment standard self-report questions. Indeed, this is currently being done as part of the Army Study to Assess Risk and Resilience in Servicemembers, a large prospective study of suicide risk among U.S. Army personnel (www.armystarrs.org). Approximately 30,000 new Soldiers are being administered a CASI survey during their first week of basic training and then are being followed for a number of years to determine the extent to which baseline assessments predict subsequent suicides. On the basis of the concern that new Soldiers might be reluctant to admit suicidality even in a CASI format, the Cha et al. neurocognitive word response latency test is being included along with more standard self-report survey questions about suicidality.

6.5.2 RECALL BIAS

Many surveys of mental illness ask respondents to report lifetime mental disorders (Kessler et al. 2007b). Methodological studies show that these reports are often downwardly biased (Andrews et al. 1999, Patten 2009, Patten et al. 2012). The most obvious way to address this problem is to reduce recall periods based on evidence about the time windows over which recall error begins to occur. For example, evidence that failure to recall nonserious injuries begins to emerge for recall periods longer than 3 months has led to the recommendation that estimates of prevalence based on self-report injury questions be based on no more than a 3-month recall period (Smith et al. 2005, Warner et al. 2005). Another way to address the problem of recall failure is to use repeat assessments with short recall time windows for each assessment to reduce recall bias. Health diaries have been used for this purpose (Finnell and Ditz 2007, Zanni 2007). Although evidence exists that respondent burden in repeat assessments can lead to under-reporting (McNamee et al. 2010), this typically does not occur until after a relatively large number of replications, making it possible to use this approach for multiple assessments without bias.

Innovations in mobile communications technology developed for clinical purposes (Visvanathan et al. 2011) are now making repeat assessments increasingly feasible. For example, short repeat e-surveys using mobile phones have been used to monitor emotional functioning of patients with mental disorders (Prociow and Crowe 2010). This approach could be used in conjunction with more conventional community surveys to obtain follow-up data on prevalence and correlates of mental disorders over a series of short-recall follow-up periods. Several challenges have to be resolved to make such surveys practical, but methodological research is currently underway that will hopefully lead to practical large-scale applications in the coming years (Fukuoka et al. 2011).

6.5.3 RESPONDENT BURDEN

Another problem with assessments of mental disorders is that they are quite often lengthy. The CIDI, for example, takes between 45 and 90 minutes to administer and assesses close to two dozen different mental disorders. Respondent burden is a challenge in situations of this sort and is multiplied when multiple assessments are considered. Although screening scales can be used to speed up diagnosis, screening scales inevitably trade off speed with precision. The use of computer adaptive testing (CAT) holds the most promise for addressing this problem. CAT is a form of computer-based testing that selects a subset of questions from a larger set to minimize the number of questions needed to assign accurate total-scale scores by starting with a set of seed questions for all respondents and then customizing subsequent questions based on prior response patterns (Wainer 2000).

The U.S. National Institutes of Health has funded a network of researchers to use CAT to develop a comprehensive battery of patient self-report outcome scales called the *Patient-Reported Outcomes Measurement Information System* (PROMIS) (www.nihpromis.org). Scales of anxiety, depression, and anger are included among the PROMIS scales (Pilkonis et al. 2011). A separate set of CAT scales was developed by Gibbons and associates (Gibbons et al. 2008) to shorten administration time for the 626-item Mood and Anxiety Spectrum Scales (MASS; Dell'Osso et al. 2002). The enormous potential value of CAT is well-illustrated in this study, as administration of the full MASS to a sample of psychiatric outpatients and subsequent implementation of a CAT algorithm showed that excellent concordance with total-scale scores (Pearson correlation > 0.90) could be achieved by administering an average of only about 5% of the full set of MASS questions to respondents.

In considering this extraordinary success of CAT with the MASS, it has to be noted that the MASS contains highly redundant items. Efficiency will be much lower in applying CAT to the much shorter scales used to diagnose mental disorders. A good case in point is a recently developed 61-item CAT test for the assessment of DSM-IV major depression known as the *D-CAT* (Fliege et al. 2005). While the D-CAT has been shown to generate very good concordance with much longer dimensional scales of depression with as few as 6–10 items per respondent and to have the same level of concordance as these longer scales with the diagnosis of DSM-IV major depression as assessed by the CIDI, this concordance is only moderate even though the CIDI assessment of major depression is itself not much longer than the number of items that typically have to be administered from the D-CAT (Fliege et al. 2009). On the basis of this result, caution is needed in considering the potential value of CAT for making diagnoses of mental disorders either in clinical settings or in computerized surveys. Despite this caution, though, it is likely that future research will show that CAT has value in making meaningful reductions in the amount of time needed to diagnose some mental disorders and substantial reductions in the amount of time needed to assess the distress and impairment associated with mental disorders.

6.6 Conclusion

This chapter has presented an overview of the measurement of mental illness in health surveys. We have shown that a number of psychometrically sound screening scales exist of nonspecific psychological distress and specific mental disorders. We also described disorder severity scales. And we described the fully structured psychiatric diagnostic interviews. Finally, we discussed emerging issues in the survey assessment of mental disorders, with a special emphasis on the problems of nonreporting bias, recall bias, and respondent burden. While much methodological work remains to be done to resolve these problems, our review pointed to a number of promising new directions and encouraging preliminary findings that lead to optimism about future improvements in the already impressive set of measurement tools and implementation strategies available to assess mental disorders in surveys.

REFERENCES

American Psychiatric Association. *Diagnostic and Statistical Manual of Mental Disorders, (DSM-III)*. 3rd ed. Washington, DC: American Psychiatric Association; 1980.

American Psychiatric Association. *Diagnostic and Statistical Manual of Mental Disorders, (DSM-III-R)*. 3rd revised ed. Washington, DC: American Psychiatric Association; 1987.

American Psychiatric Association. *Diagnostic and Statistical Manual of Mental Disorders, (DSM-IV)*. 4th ed. Washington, DC: American Psychiatric Association; 1994.

Andrews G, Anstey K, Brodaty H, Issakidis C, Luscombe G. Recall of depressive episode 25 years previously. Psychol Med 1999;29:787–791.

Anthony JC, Folstein M, Romanoski AJ, Von Korff MR, Nestadt GR, Chahal R, Merchant A, Brown CH, Shapiro S, Kramer M. Comparison of the lay Diagnostic Interview Schedule and a standardized psychiatric diagnosis. Experience in eastern Baltimore. Arch Gen Psych 1985;42:667–675.

Aquilino WS. Privacy on self-reported drug use: interactions with survey mode and respondent characteristics. In: Harrison L, Hughes A, editors. *The Validity of*

Self-Reported Drug Use: Improving the Accuracy of Survey Estimates (National Institute on Drug Abuse, Monograph 167). Washington, DC: National Institute of Health, Department of Health and Human Services; 1997. p 383–415.

Aquilino WS, Wright DL, Supple AJ. Response effects due to bystander presence in CASI and paper-and-pencil surveys of drug use and alcohol use. Subst Use Misuse 2000;35:845–867.

Baillie AJ. Predictive gender and education bias in Kessler's psychological distress Scale (k10). Social psychiatry and psychiatric epidemiology 2005;40:743–748.

Baggaley RF, Ganaba R, Filippi V, Kere M, Marshall T, Sombie I, Storeng KT, Patel V. Detecting depression after pregnancy: the validity of the K10 and K6 in Burkina Faso. Trop Med Int Health 2007;12:1225–1229.

Baldassano CF, Hosey A, Coello J. Bipolar depression: an evidence-based approach. Curr Psychiatry Rep 2011;13:483–487.

Breslau N, Peterson EL, Kessler RC, Schultz LR. Short screening scale for DSM-IV posttraumatic stress disorder. Am J Psych 1999;156:908–911.

Broadhead WE, Leon AC, Weissman MM, Barrett JE, Blacklow RS, Gilbert TT, Keller MB, Olfson M, Higgins ES. Development and validation of the SDDS-PC screen for multiple mental disorders in primary care. Arch Fam Med 1995;4:211–219.

Brodey BB, Rosen CS, Brodey IS, Sheetz BM, Steinfeld RR, Gastfriend DR. Validation of the Addiction Severity Index (ASI) for internet and automated telephone self-report administration. J Subst Abuse Treat 2004;26:253–259.

Brugha TS, Bebbington PE, Jenkins R. A difference that matters: comparisons of structured and semi-structured psychiatric diagnostic interviews in the general population. Psychol Med 1999;29:1013–1020.

Carroll BJ, Feinberg M, Smouse PE, Rawson SG, Greden JF. The Carroll rating scale for depression. I. Development, reliability and validation. Br J Psych 1981;138:194–200.

Cha CB, Najmi S, Park JM, Finn CT, Nock MK. Attentional bias toward suicide-related stimuli predicts suicidal behavior. J Abnorm Psychol 2010;119:616–622.

Cleary PD, Goldberg ID, Kessler LG, Nycz GR. Screening for mental disorder among primary care patients. Usefulness of the General Health Questionnaire. Arch Gen Psych 1982;39:837–840.

Davis RE, Couper MP, Janz NK, Caldwell CH, Resnicow K. Interviewer effects in public health surveys. Health Educ Res 2010;25:14–26.

Davis TE 3rd, May A, Whiting SE. Evidence-based treatment of anxiety and phobia in children and adolescents: current status and effects on the emotional response. Clin Psychol Rev 2011;31:592–602.

Dell'Osso L, Armani A, Rucci P, Frank E, Fagiolini A, Corretti G, Shear MK, Grochocinski VJ, Maser JD, Endicott J, Cassano GB. Measuring mood spectrum: comparison of interview (SCI-MOODS) and self-report (MOODS-SR) instruments. Compr Psychiatry 2002;43:69–73.

Derogatis LR. *SCL-90-R Revised Manual*. Baltimore, MD: Johns Hopkins School of Medicine; 1983.

Derogatis LR, Lipman RS, Rickels K, Uhlenhuth EH, Covi L. The Hopkins Symptom Checklist (HSCL): a self-report symptom inventory. Behav Sci 1974;19:1–15.

Dohrenwend BP, Dohrenwend BS. The problem of validity in field studies of psychological disorder. J Abnorm Psychol 1965;70:52–69.

Dohrenwend BP, Shrout PE, Egri G, Mendelsohn FS. Nonspecific psychological distress and other dimensions of psychopathology. Measures for use in the general population. Arch Gen Psych 1980;37:1229–1236.

Dohrenwend BP, Yager TJ, Egri G, Mendelsohn FS. The psychiatric status schedule as a measure of dimensions of psychopathology in the general population. Arch Gen Psychiatry 1978;35:731–737.

Donker T, van Straten A, Marks I, Cuijpers P. A brief Web-based screening questionnaire for common mental disorders: development and validation. J Med Internet Res 2009;11:e19.

Dowrick C, Shiels C, Page H, Ayuso-Mateos JL, Casey P, Dalgard OS, Dunn G, Lehtinen V, Salmon P, Whitehead M. Predicting long-term recovery from depression in community settings in Western Europe: evidence from ODIN. Soc Psychiatry Psychiatr Epidemiol 2011;46:119–126.

Endicott J, Spitzer RL. A diagnostic interview: the schedule for affective disorders and schizophrenia. Arch Gen Psychiatry 1978;35:837–844.

Farvolden P, McBride C, Bagby RM, Ravitz P. A Web-based screening instrument for depression and anxiety disorders in primary care. J Med Internet Res 2003;5:e23.

Fassaert T, De Wit MA, Tuinebreijer WC, Wouters H, Verhoeff AP, Beekman AT, Dekker J. Psychometric properties of an interviewer-administered version of the Kessler Psychological Distress scale (K10) among Dutch, Moroccan and Turkish respondents. Int J Methods Psychiatr Res 2009;18:159–168.

Feighner JP, Robins E, Guze SB, Woodruff RA Jr, Winokur G, Munoz R. Diagnostic criteria for use in psychiatric research. Arch Gen Psychiatry 1972;26:57–63.

Finnell D, Ditz KA. Health diaries for self-monitoring and self-regulation: applications to individuals with serious mental illness. Issues Ment Health Nurs 2007;28:1293–1307.

First MB, Spitzer RL, Gibbon M, Williams JBW. *Structured Clinical Interview for Axis I DSM-IV Disorders—Patient Edition (SCID-I/P)*. New York: Biometrics Research, New York State Psychiatric Institute; 1995.

Fliege H, Becker J, Walter OB, Bjorner JB, Klapp BF, Rose M. Development of a computer-adaptive test for depression (D-CAT). Qual Life Res 2005;14: 2277–2291.

Fliege H, Becker J, Walter OB, Rose M, Bjorner JB, Klapp BF. Evaluation of a computer-adaptive test for the assessment of depression (D-CAT) in clinical application. Int J Methods Psychiatr Res 2009;18:23–36.

Fukuoka Y, Kamitani E, Dracup K, Jong SS. New insights into compliance with a mobile phone diary and pedometer use in sedentary women. J Phys Activ Health 2011;8:398–403.

Furukawa TA, Akechi T, Azuma H, Okuyama T, Higuchi T. Evidence-based guidelines for interpretation of the Hamilton Rating Scale for Depression. J Clin Psychopharmacol 2007;27:531–534.

Furukawa TA, Kawakami N, Saitoh M, Ono Y, Nakane Y, Nakamura Y, Tachimori H, Iwata N, Uda H, Nakane H, Watanabe M, Naganuma Y, Hata Y, Kobayashi M, Miyake Y, Takeshima T, Kikkawa T. The performance of the Japanese version of the K6 and K10 in the World Mental Health Survey Japan. Int J Methods Psychiatr Res 2008;17:152–158.

Furukawa TA, Kessler RC, Slade T, Andrews G. The performance of the K6 and K10 screening scales for psychological distress in the Australian National Survey of Mental Health and Well-Being. Psychol Med 2003;33:357–362.

Gaynes BN, DeVeaugh-Geiss J, Weir S, Gu H, MacPherson C, Schulberg HC, Culpepper L, Rubinow DR. Feasibility and diagnostic validity of the M-3 checklist: a brief, self-rated screen for depressive, bipolar, anxiety, and post-traumatic stress disorders in primary care. Ann Fam Med 2010;8:160–169.

Gibbons RD, Weiss DJ, Kupfer DJ, Frank E, Fagiolini A, Grochocinski VJ, Bhaumik DK, Stover A, Bock RD, Immekus JC. Using computerized adaptive testing to reduce the burden of mental health assessment. Psychiatr Serv 2008;59:361–368.

Gill SC, Butterworth P, Rodgers B, Mackinnon A. Validity of the mental health component scale of the 12-item Short-Form Health Survey (MCS-12) as measure of common mental disorders in the general population. Psychiatry Res 2007;152:63–71.

Goldberg DP. *The Detection of Psychiatric Illness by Questionnaire*. Oxford, UK: Oxford University Press; 1972.

Goldberg DP, Hillier VF. A scaled version of the General Health Questionnaire. Psychol Med 1979;9:139–145.

Goldberg D, Williams P. *A User's Guide to the General Health Questionnaire*. Slough, UK: NFER-Nelson; 1988.

Goodman WK, Price LH, Rasmussen SA, Mazure C, Delgado P, Heninger GR, Charney DS. The Yale-Brown Obsessive Compulsive Scale. II Validity. Arch Gen Psych 1989;46:1012–1016.

Gove WR, Tudor JF. Adult sex roles and mental illness. Am J Sociol 1973;78:812–835.

Gurin G, Veroff J, Feld SC. *Americans View Their Mental Health*. New York: Basic Books Inc.; 1960.

Haller DM, Sanci LA, Sawyer SM, Patton GC. The identification of young people's emotional distress: a study in primary care. Br J Gen Pract 2009;59:e61–70.

Hamilton M. A rating scale for depression. J Neurol Neurosurg Psychiatry 1960; 23:56–62.

Hamilton M. Development of a rating scale for primary depressive illness. Br J Soc Clin Psychol 1967;6:278–296.

Haro JM, Arbabzadeh-Bouchez S, Brugha TS, de Girolamo G, Guyer ME, Jin R, Lepine JP, Mazzi F, Reneses B, Vilagut G, Sampson NA, Kessler RC. Concordance of the Composite International Diagnostic Interview Version 3.0 (CIDI 3.0) with standardized clinical assessments in the WHO World Mental Health surveys. Int J Methods Psychiatr Res 2006;15:167–180.

Hauffa R, Rief W, Brahler E, Martin A, Mewes R, Glaesmer H. Lifetime traumatic experiences and posttraumatic stress disorder in the German population: results of a representative population survey. J Nerv Ment Dis 2011;199:934–939.

Helzer JE, Robins LN, McEvoy LT, Spitznagel EL, Stoltzman RK, Farmer A, Brockington IF. A comparison of clinical and diagnostic interview schedule diagnoses. Physician reexamination of lay-interviewed cases in the general population. Arch Gen Psych 1985;42:657–666.

Hides L, Lubman DI, Devlin H, Cotton S, Aitken C, Gibbie T, Hellard M. Reliability and validity of the Kessler 10 and Patient Health Questionnaire among injecting drug users. Aust New Zeal J Psych 2007;41:166–168.

Hirschfeld RM, Williams JB, Spitzer RL, Calabrese JR, Flynn L, Keck PE Jr, Lewis L, McElroy SL, Post RM, Rapport DJ, Russell JM, Sachs GS, Zajecka J. Development and validation of a screening instrument for bipolar spectrum disorder: the Mood Disorder Questionnaire. Am J Psych 2000;157:1873–1875.

Houck PR, Spiegel DA, Shear MK, Rucci P. Reliability of the self-report version of the panic disorder severity scale. Depress Anxiety 2002;15:183–185.

Hunter EE, Penick EC, Powell BJ, Othmer E, Nickel EJ, Desouza C. Development of scales to screen for eight common psychiatric disorders. J Nerv Ment Dis 2005;193:131–135.

Kessler RC. The World Health Organization International Consortium in Psychiatric Epidemiology (ICPE): initial work and future directions—the NAPE Lecture 1998. Nordic Association for Psychiatric Epidemiology. Acta Psych Scand 1999;99:2–9.

Kessler RC, Adler L, Ames M, Demler O, Faraone S, Hiripi E, Howes MJ, Jin R, Secnik K, Spencer T, Ustun TB, Walters EE. The World Health Organization Adult ADHD Self-Report Scale (ASRS): a short screening scale for use in the general population. Psychol Med 2005a;35:245–256.

Kessler RC, Adler LA, Gruber MJ, Sarawate CA, Spencer T, Van Brunt DL. Validity of the World Health Organization Adult ADHD Self-Report Scale (ASRS) Screener in a representative sample of health plan members. Int J Methods Psychiatr Res 2007a;16:52–65.

Kessler RC, Akiskal HS, Angst J, Guyer M, Hirschfeld RM, Merikangas KR, Stang PE. Validity of the assessment of bipolar spectrum disorders in the WHO CIDI 3.0. Journal of Affective Disorders 2006a;96:259–269.

Kessler RC, Andrews G, Colpe LJ, Hiripi E, Mroczek DK, Normand SL, Walters EE, Zaslavsky AM. Short screening scales to monitor population prevalences and trends in non-specific psychological distress. Psychol Med 2002;32:959–976.

Kessler RC, Angermeyer M, Anthony JC, De Graaf R, Demyttenaere K, Gasquet I, de Girolamo G, Gluzman S, Gureje O, Haro JM, Kawakami N, Karam A, Levinson D, Medina Mora ME, Oakley Browne MA, Posada-Villa J, Stein DJ, Adley Tsang CH, Aguilar-Gaxiola S, Alonso J, Lee S, Heeringa S, Pennell BE, Berglund P, Gruber MJ, Petukhova M, Chatterji S, Ustun TB. Lifetime prevalence and age-of-onset distributions of mental disorders in the World Health Organization's World Mental Health Survey Initiative. World Psych 2007b;6:168–176.

Kessler RC, Barker PR, Colpe LJ, Epstein JF, Gfroerer JC, Hiripi E, Howes MJ, Normand SL, Manderscheid RW, Walters EE, Zaslavsky AM. Screening for serious mental illness in the general population. Arch Gen Psych 2003a;60:184–189.

Kessler RC, Berglund P, Chiu WT, Demler O, Heeringa S, Hiripi E, Jin R, Pennell BE, Walters EE, Zaslavsky A, Zheng H. The US National Comorbidity Survey Replication (NCS-R): design and field procedures. Int J Methods Psychiatr Res 2004;13:69–92.

Kessler RC, Berglund P, Demler O, Jin R, Koretz D, Merikangas KR, Rush AJ, Walters EE, Wang PS. The epidemiology of major depressive disorder: results from the National Comorbidity Survey Replication (NCS-R). JAMA 2003b;289:3095–3105.

Kessler RC, Berglund P, Demler O, Jin R, Merikangas KR, Walters EE. Lifetime prevalence and age-of-onset distributions of DSM-IV disorders in the National Comorbidity Survey Replication. Arch Gen Psychiatry 2005b;62:593–602.

Kessler RC, Berglund PA, Zhao S, Leaf PJ, Kouzis AC, Bruce ML, Friedman RM, Grosser RC, Kennedy C, Kuehnel TG, Laska EM, Manderscheid RW, Narrow WE,

Rosenheck RA, Santoni TW, Schneier M. The 12-month prevalence and correlates of Serious Mental Illness (SMI). In: Manderscheid RW, Sonnenschein MA, editors. *Mental Health, United States 1996*. Washington, DC: U.S. Government Printing Office; 1996. p 59–70.

Kessler RC, Chiu WT, Demler O, Merikangas KR, Walters EE. Prevalence, severity, and comorbidity of 12-month DSM-IV disorders in the National Comorbidity Survey Replication. Arch Gen Psychiatry 2005c;62:617–627.

Kessler RC, Chiu WT, Jin R, Ruscio AM, Shear K, Walters EE. The epidemiology of panic attacks, panic disorder, and agoraphobia in the National Comorbidity Survey Replication. Arch Gen Psychiatry 2006b;63:415–424.

Kessler RC, Green JG, Gruber MJ, Sampson NA, Bromet E, Cuitan M, Furukawa TA, Gureje O, Hinkov H, Hu CY, Lara C, Lee S, Mneimneh Z, Myer L, Oakley-Browne M, Posada-Villa J, Sagar R, Viana MC, Zaslavsky AM. Screening for serious mental illness in the general population with the K6 screening scale: results from the WHO World Mental Health (WMH) survey initiative. Int J Methods Psychiatr Res 2010;19(Suppl 1):4–22.

Kessler RC, Haro JM, Heeringa SG, Pennell BE, Üstün TB. The World Health Organization World Mental Health Survey Initiative. Epidemiol Psichiatr Soc 2006c;15:161–166.

Kessler RC, McGonagle KA, Zhao S, Nelson CB, Hughes M, Eshleman S, Wittchen HU, Kendler KS. Lifetime and 12-month prevalence of DSM-III-R psychiatric disorders in the United States. Results from the National Comorbidity Survey. Arch Gen Psych 1994;51:8–19.

Kessler RC, Merikangas K, Berglund P, Eaton WW, Koretz DS, Walters EE. Mild disorders should not be eliminated from the DSM-V. Arch Gen Psychiatry 2003c;60:1117–1122.

Kessler RC, Mroczek DK, Belli RF. Retrospective adult assessment of childhood psychopathology. In: Shaffer D, Lucas CP, Richters JE, editors. *Diagnostic Assessment in Child and Adolescent Psychopathology*. New York: Guilford Press; 1999. p 256–284.

Kessler RC, Üstün TB. The World Mental Health (WMH) Survey Initiative Version of the World Health Organization (WHO) Composite International Diagnostic Interview (CIDI). Int J Methods Psychiatr Res 2004;13:93–121.

Kessler RC, Üstün TB. *The WHO World Mental Health Surveys: Global Perspectives on the Epidemiology of Mental Disorders*. New York: Cambridge University Press; 2008.

Kessler RC, Wittchen H-U, Abelson JM, McGonagle KA, Schwarz N, Kendler KS, Knäuper B, Zhao S. Methodological studies of the Composite International Diagnostic Interview (CIDI) in the US National Comorbidity Survey. Int J Methods Psychiatr Res 1998;7:33–55.

Kessler RC, Wittchen H-U, Abelson JM, Zhao S. Methodological issues in assessing psychiatric disorder with self-reports. In: Stone AA, Turrkan JS, Bachrach CA, Jobe JB, Kurtzman HS, Cain VS, editors. *The Science of Self-Report: Implications for Research and Practice*. Mahwah, NJ: Lawrence Erlbaum Associates; 2000. p 229–255.

Kobak KA, Greist JH, Jefferson JW, Mundt JC, Katzelnick DJ. Computerized assessment of depression and anxiety over the telephone using interactive voice response. M.D. Comput 1999;16:64–68.

Kraemer HC. *Evaluating Medical Tests*. Newbury Park, CA: Sage Publications; 1992.

Kroenke K, Spitzer RL, Williams JB. The PHQ-9: validity of a brief depression severity measure. J Gen Intern Med 2001;16:606–613.

Landis JR, Koch GG. The measurement of observer agreement for categorical data. Biometrics 1977;33:159–174.

Langhaug LF, Sherr L, Cowan FM. How to improve the validity of sexual behaviour reporting: systematic review of questionnaire delivery modes in developing countries. Trop Med Int Health 2010;15:362–381.

Leighton AH. *My Name is Legion. Volume I of the Stirling County Study*. New York: Basic Books; 1959.

Link BG, Dohrenwend BP. Formulation of hypotheses about the true relevance of demoralization in the United States. In: Dohrenwend BP, Dohrenwend BS, Gould MS, Link B, Neugebauer R, Wunsch-Hitzig R, editors. *Mental Illness in the United States: Epidemiological Estimates*. New York: Praeger; 1980. p 114–132.

Lipman RS, Covi L, Shapiro AK. The Hopkins Symptom Checklist (HSCL): factors derived from the HSCL-90 [proceedings]. Psychopharm Bull 1977;13:43–45.

Lipman RS, Covi L, Shapiro AK. The Hopkins Symptom Checklist (HSCL)—factors derived from the HSCL-90. J Affect Disord 1979;1:9–24.

Maser JD, Patterson T. Spectrum and nosology: implications for DSM-V. Psych Clin North America 2002;25:855–885 viii-ix.

McNamee R, Chen Y, Hussey L, Agius R. Time-sampled versus continuous-time reporting for measuring incidence. Epidemiology 2010;21:376–378.

Mirowsky J. Analyzing associations between mental health and social circumstances. In: Aneshensel CS, Phelan JC, editors. *Handbook of the Sociology of Mental Health*. New York: Springer; 1999. p 105–123.

Mneimneh ZN, Pennell BE. Interview privacy and social desirability effects on reporting sensitive outcomes. Presentation at the American Association for Public Opinion Research; Phoenix, AZ; 2011.

Moffitt TE, Caspi A, Taylor A, Kokaua J, Milne BJ, Polanczyk G, Poulton R. How common are common mental disorders? Evidence that lifetime prevalence rates are doubled by prospective versus retrospective ascertainment. Psychol Med 2010;40:899–909.

Narrow WE, Kuhl EA, Regier DA. DSM-V perspectives on disentangling disability from clinical significance. World Psych 2009;8:88–89.

Narrow WE, Rae DS, Robins LN, Regier DA. Revised prevalence estimates of mental disorders in the United States: using a clinical significance criterion to reconcile 2 surveys' estimates. Arch Gen Psychiatry 2002;59:115–123.

Newman SC, Shrout PE, Bland RC. The efficiency of two-phase designs in prevalence surveys of mental disorders. Psychol Med 1990;20:183–193.

Oksenberg L, Cannell CF, Kanton G. New strategies for pretesting survey questions. J Off Stat 1991;7:349–365.

Othmer E, Penivk ED, Powell BJ, Read MR, Othmer SC. *Psychiatric Diagnostic Interview IV*. Los Angeles, CA: Western Psychological Services; 2000.

Patel V, Araya R, Chowdhary N, King M, Kirkwood B, Nayak S, Simon G, Weiss HA. Detecting common mental disorders in primary care in India: a comparison of five screening questionnaires. Psychol Med 2008;38:221–228.

Patten SB. Accumulation of major depressive episodes over time in a prospective study indicates that retrospectively assessed lifetime prevalence estimates are too low. BMC Psychiatry 2009;9:19.

Patten SB, Williams JV, Lavorato DH, Bulloch AG, D'Arcy C, Streiner DL. Recall of recent and more remote depressive episodes in a prospective cohort study. Soc Psychiatry Psychiatr Epidemiol 2012;47(5):691–696.

Pearlin LI, Lieberman MA, Menaghan EG, Mullan JT. The stress process. J Health Soc Behav 1981;22:337–356.

Pepe MS. *Statistical Analysis of Medical Tests for Classification and Prediction*. Oxford, UK: Oxford University Press; 2003.

Pilkonis PA, Choi SW, Reise SP, Stover AM, Riley WT, Cella D. Item banks for measuring emotional distress from the Patient-Reported Outcomes Measurement Information System (PROMIS(R)): depression, anxiety, and anger. Assessment 2011;18:263–283.

Pineau J, Bellemare MG, Rush AJ, Ghizaru A, Murphy SA. Constructing evidence-based treatment strategies using methods from computer science. Drug Alcohol Depend 2007;88(Suppl. 2):S52–60.

Pollner M, Adams RE. The interpersonal context of mental health interviews. J Health Soc Behav 1994;35:283–290.

Prociow PA, Crowe JA. Towards personalised ambient monitoring of mental health via mobile technologies. Technol Health Care 2010;18:275–284.

Radloff LS. The CES-D Scale: a self-report depression scale for research in the general population. Appl Psychol Measure 1977;1:385–401.

Regier DA, Kaelber CT, Rae DS, Farmer ME, Knauper B, Kessler RC, Norquist GS. Limitations of diagnostic criteria and assessment instruments for mental disorders. Implications for research and policy. Arch Gen Psych 1998;55:109–115.

Regier DA, Narrow WE, Rae DS, Manderscheid RW, Locke BZ, Goodwin FK. The de facto US mental and addictive disorders service system. Epidemiologic catchment area prospective 1-year prevalence rates of disorders and services. Arch Gen Psych 1993;50:85–94.

Richman WL, Keisler S, Weisband S, Drasgow F. A meta-analytic study of social desirability distortion in computer-administered questionnaires, traditional questionnaires, and interviews. J Appl Psychol 1999;84:754–775.

Roberto CA, Grilo CM, Masheb RM, White MA. Binge eating, purging, or both: eating disorder psychopathology findings from an internet community survey. Int J Eat Disord 2010;43:724–731.

Robins LN, Cottler LB. Making a structured psychiatric diagnostic interview faithful to the nomenclature. Am J Epidemiol 2004;160:808–813.

Robins LN, Helzer JE, Croughan J, Ratcliff KS. National Institute of Mental Health Diagnostic Interview Schedule. Its history, characteristics, and validity. Arch Gen Psych 1981;38:381–389.

Robins LN, Regier DA. *Psychiatric Disorders in America: The Epidemiologic Catchment Area Study*. New York: Free Press; 1991.

Robins LN, Wing J, Wittchen HU, Helzer JE, Babor TF, Burke J, Farmer A, Jablenski A, Pickens R, Regier DA, Sartorius N, Towle LH. The Composite International Diagnostic Interview. An epidemiologic instrument suitable for use in conjunction with different diagnostic systems and in different cultures. Arch Gen Psych 1988;45:1069–1077.

Rubin DB. *Multiple Imputation for Nonresponse in Surveys*. New York: John Wiley & Sons; 1987.

Ruhe HG, Dekker JJ, Peen J, Holman R, de Jonghe F. Clinical use of the Hamilton Depression Rating Scale: is increased efficiency possible? A post hoc comparison of Hamilton Depression Rating Scale, Maier and Bech subscales, Clinical Global Impression, and Symptom Checklist-90 scores. Compr Psychiatry 2005;46: 417–427.

Rush AJ, Carmody T, Reimitz PE. The Inventory of Depressive Symptomatology (IDS): clinician (IDS-C) and self-report (IDS-SR) ratings of depressive symptoms. Int J Methods Psychiatr Res 2000;9:45–59.

Rush AJ, First MB, Blacker D. *Handbook of Psychiatric Measures*. 2nd ed. Washington, DC: American Psychiatric Association; 2007.

Rush AJ, Trivedi MH, Ibrahim HM, Carmody TJ, Arnow B, Klein DN, Markowitz JC, Ninan PT, Kornstein S, Manber R, Thase ME, Kocsis JH, Keller MB. The 16-Item Quick Inventory of Depressive Symptomatology (QIDS), clinician rating (QIDS-C), and self-report (QIDS-SR): a psychometric evaluation in patients with chronic major depression. Biol Psychiatry 2003;54:573–583.

Sartorius N. *Understanding the ICD 10 Classification of Mental Disorders: A Pocket Reference*. In: *Science Press, Ltd*. Shanghai: China; 1995.

Seiler LH. The 22-item scale used in field studies of mental illness: a question of method, a question of substance, and a question of theory. J Health Soc Behav 1973;14:252–264.

Shear K, Belnap BH, Mazumdar S, Houck P, Rollman BL. Generalized anxiety disorder severity scale (GADSS): a preliminary validation study. Depress Anxiety 2006;23:77–82.

Shear MK, Brown TA, Barlow DH, Money R, Sholomskas DE, Woods SW, Gorman JM, Papp LA. Multicenter collaborative panic disorder severity scale. Am J Psych 1997;154:1571–1575.

Smith GS, Wellman HM, Sorock GS, Warner M, Courtney TK, Pransky GS, Fingerhut LA. Injuries at work in the US adult population: contributions to the total injury burden. Am J Public Health 2005;95:1213–1219.

Spitzer RL, Kroenke K, Williams JB, Lowe B. A brief measure for assessing generalized anxiety disorder: the GAD-7. Arch Intern Med 2006;166:1092–1097.

Srole L, Langner TS, Michael ST, Opler MK, Rennie TA. *Mental Health in the Metropolis: The Midtown Manhattan Study*. New York: McGraw-Hill; 1962.

Star SA. The screening of psychoneurotics in the Army: technical development of tests. In: Stouffer S, Guttman L, Suchman E, editors. *The American Soldier: Measurement and Prediction*. Princeton, NJ: Princeton University Press; 1950. p 486–547.

Strand BH, Dalgard OS, Tambs K, Rognerud M. Measuring the mental health status of the Norwegian population: a comparison of the instruments SCL-25, SCL-10, SCL-5 and MHI-5 (SF-36). Nord J Psychiatry 2003;57:113–118.

Sudman S, Bradburn N, Schwarz N. *Thinking About Answers: The Application of Cognitive Processes to Survey Methodology*. San Francisco, CA: Jossey-Bass; 1996.

Swartz JA, Lurigio AJ. Screening for serious mental illness in populations with co-occurring substance use disorders: performance of the K6 scale. J Subst Abuse Treat 2006;31:287–296.

Tansella M, Thornicroft G, editors. *Common Mental Disorders in Primary Care: Essays in honour of Professor Sir David Goldberg*. London, UK: Routledge; 1999.

Tanur JM. *Questions about Questions: Inquiries Into the Cognitive Bases of Surveys*. New York: Russell Sage Foundation; 1992.

Tesfaye M, Hanlon C, Wondimagegn D, Alem A. Detecting postnatal common mental disorders in Addis Ababa, Ethiopia: validation of the Edinburgh Postnatal Depression Scale and Kessler Scales. J Affect Disord 2010;122:102–108.

Tourangeau R, Yan T. Sensitive questions in surveys. Psychol Bull 2007;133:859–883.

Turner C, Martin E. *Surveying Subjective Phenomena*. New York: Russell Sage Foundation; 1985.

Turner CF, Ku L, Rogers SM, Lindberg LD, Pleck JH, Sonenstein FL. Adolescent sexual behavior, drug use, and violence: increased reporting with computer survey technology. Science 1998;280:867–873.

van der Linden WJ, Hambleton RK. *Handbook of Modern Item Response Theory*. New York: Springer Verlag; 1997.

Vieweg BW, Hedlund JL. The General Health Questionnaire (GHQ): a comprehensive review. J Operat Psych 1983;14:74–81.

Visvanathan A, Gibb AP, Brady RR. Increasing clinical presence of mobile communication technology: avoiding the pitfalls. Telemed J E-Health 2011;17:656–661.

Wainer H. *Computer Adaptive Testing: A Primer*. Wahwah, NJ: Lawrence Erlbaum Associates; 2000.

Wakefield JC, Spitzer RL. Lowered estimates—but of what? Arch Gen Psychiatry 2002;59:129–130.

Ware JE, Sherbourne CD. The MOS 36-item short-form health survey (SF-36). I. Conceptual framework and item selection. Med Care 1992;30:473–483.

Warner M, Schenker N, Heinen MA, Fingerhut LA. The effects of recall on reporting injury and poisoning episodes in the National Health Interview Survey. Inj Prev 2005;11:282–287.

Weissman MM, Bland RC, Canino GJ, Faravelli C, Greenwald S, Hwu HG, Joyce PR, Karam EG, Lee CK, Lellouch J, Lepine JP, Newman SC, Oakley-Browne MA, Rubio-Stipec M, Wells JE, Wickramaratne PJ, Wittchen HU, Yeh EK. The cross-national epidemiology of panic disorder. Arch Gen Psychiatry 1997;54:305–309.

Weissman MM, Bland RC, Canino GJ, Faravelli C, Greenwald S, Hwu HG, Joyce PR, Karam EG, Lee CK, Lellouch J, Lepine JP, Newman SC, Rubio-Stipec M, Wells JE, Wickramaratne PJ, Wittchen H, Yeh EK. Cross-national epidemiology of major depression and bipolar disorder. JAMA 1996a;276:293–299.

Weissman MM, Bland RC, Canino GJ, Greenwald S, Lee CK, Newman SC, Rubio-Stipec M, Wickramaratne PJ. The cross-national epidemiology of social phobia: a preliminary report. Int Clin Psychopharmacol 1996b;11(Suppl 3):9–14.

Weissman MM, Myers JK. Affective disorders in a US urban community: the use of research diagnostic criteria in an epidemiological survey. Arch Gen Psychiatry 1978;35:1304–1311.

Whybrow PC, Grof P, Gyulai L, Rasgon N, Glenn T, Bauer M. The electronic assessment of the longitudinal course of bipolar disorder: the ChronoRecord software. Pharmacopsychiatry 2003;36(Suppl 3):S244–249.

Williams JB, Kobak KA, Bech P, Engelhardt N, Evans K, Lipsitz J, Olin J, Pearson J, Kalali A. The GRID-HAMD: standardization of the Hamilton Depression Rating Scale. Int Clin Psychopharmacol 2008;23:120–129.

Wittchen HU. Reliability and validity studies of the WHO-Composite International Diagnostic Interview (CIDI): a critical review. J Psychiatr Res 1994;28:57–84.

Wittenbrink B, Schwarz N, editors. *Implicit Measures of Attitudes: Procedures and Controversies*. New York: Guilford; 2007.

World Health Organization. *Composite International Diagnostic Interview (CIDI, Version 1.0)*. Geneva, Switzerland: World Health Organization; 1990.

Young RC, Biggs JT, Ziegler VE, Meyer DA. A rating scale for mania: reliability, validity and sensitivity. Br J Psych 1978;133:429–435.

Zanni GR. Patient diaries: charting the course. The Consulting Pharmacist 2007;22: 472–476479–482.

ONLINE RESOURCES

Information on the World Health Organization Composite International Diagnostic Interview (CIDI), including a PDF of the instrument and training requirements is available at: www.hcp.med.harvard.edu/wmhcidi/.

Information on the World Health Organization World Mental Health Survey Initiative, an ongoing initiative that has thus far implemented mental health needs assessment surveys in 28 countries can be found at: www.hcp.med.harvard.edu/wmh/.

US surveys that contain the K6 scale include the CDC Behavioral Risk Factors Surveillance Survey, the SAMHSA National Household Survey on Drug Use and Health, and the National Health Interview Survey. These can be accessed at: www.cdc.gov/BRFSS, www.oas.samhsa.gov/nhsda.htm, www.cdc.gov/nchs/nhis.htm.

An example of a computerized self-administered mental health assessment is the Army Study to Assess Rick and Resilience in Servicemembers (Army STARRS). Army STARRS is a large prospective study of suicide risk among US Army personnel: www.armystarrs.org.

Information on the US National Institutes of Health's network of researchers developing a comprehensive battery of patient self-report outcome scales called the Patient-Reported Outcomes Measurement Information System (PROMIS) is at: www.nihpromis.org.

CHAPTER SEVEN

Developing Measures of Health Behavior and Health Service Utilization

Paul Beatty
Division of Health Care Statistics, National Center for Health Statistics, Centers for Disease Control and Prevention, Hyattsville, MD, USA

7.1 Introduction

Self-reports are a critical source of behavioral health data because, quite simply, there is often no other feasible way to obtain information about what people actually do. This is certainly the case regarding day-to-day activities such as what people eat, or how often they exercise—generally no records are made of such events. Records may be available for more notable health behaviors, such as frequency or outcome of medical visits, but even so, there are limitations to the accessibility of such information, and such records may not meet research needs if they were created for administrative purposes. Even if records exist and adequately address research questions, self-reports are often used to find and access them. In some cases, health behaviors may be directly observable, but making observations across sufficient people and times to create behavioral data representative of a population may be challenging.

Fortunately, asking questions about what people do is a ubiquitous part of daily conversation (Schuman and Kalton 1985). Nevertheless, behavioral survey questions are odd communicative events. They often ask people about things

Handbook of Health Survey Methods, First Edition. Edited by Timothy P. Johnson.

that have little personal importance or memorability, however interesting the behaviors may be to survey researchers. They are different than most everyday exchanges in that they tend to be heavily scripted, a consequence of the objective of measuring behavior in a standardized manner. And whereas misunderstandings in everyday communication can be worked out through improvized discussions, such interactions are generally restricted in survey communication (Schaeffer 1991, Schober and Conrad 2002, Bradburn et al. 2004, p. 4) largely because they introduce unwanted variation into the administration of questions (Fowler and Mangione 1990). This means that it is desirable for questions to be self-evident in meaning for all respondents—regardless of their age, education, linguistic competence, or particular experience with the research topic.

The challenge of crafting survey questions that approach this standard is considerable, and may take more time and effort than is generally appreciated. It is easy for question authors to conclude that since a question makes sense to them, it will make sense to others in a consistent manner. Unfortunately, testing questions on small groups of individuals may reveal confusion, different interpretations, or trouble providing the desired information (Belson 1981). However, it is often possible to meet the challenge of crafting *reliable* and *valid* behavioral survey questions, if one devotes adequate time and attention to the process.

This chapter examines the optimal development of measures of health behavior and health service utilization. The process entails several stages:

- A *conceptual* phase, in which researchers flesh out what they want specific items to measure
- An *item development* phase, in which researchers craft specific questions
- A *questionnaire assembly* stage, in which researchers consider how individual items will work together as a cohesive data collection instrument
- And, a *testing and evaluation* stage, in which researchers determine how well the instrument meets data needs, and make adjustments as needed.

Most of this chapter will focus on the item development phase, with particular attention to the attributes of good questions and questionnaires. However, it will be useful to touch upon the other phases, to put the development process into context. In addition, this chapter will usually assume that questions are being developed from scratch. This is not always the case in reality, as many previously administered questionnaires are readily available and may be successfully adapted into new surveys (Bradburn et al. 2004, p. 23, Aday and Cornelius 2006, p. 50). Toward the end of the chapter, some considerations for adapting items from existing questionnaires are presented.

7.2 The Conceptual Phase of Questionnaire Development

Before attempting to write specific questions (or select questions from other surveys), it is important to carefully assess what data are really needed—and *then* to think systematically about what questions would meet those objectives (Bradburn et al. 2004, pp. xii, 22). This might seem obvious, but if researchers are impatient to get into the field, it is easy to give short-shrift to this initial phase. Engaging subject matter experts and analysts can be extremely useful in these early stages, helping to ensure that content needs are well specified (Converse and Presser 1986). It can be useful to develop mock analytic tables specifying proposed relationships between variables, and to take specific hypotheses as a starting point for defining which concepts need to be reflected within individual questions (Aday and Cornelius 2006, pp. 92–97). Doing this can be time consuming, but it can prevent a great deal of frustration later, when it may be discovered that questions match poorly with analytic objectives, or that important aspects were never adequately captured.

It is also problematic to confuse the act of defining objectives with the act of writing questions. Questions do not always directly correspond to desired data points (Bradburn et al. 2004, p. 20, Aday and Cornelius 2006, pp. 50–53). For example, a researcher might want to know how many calories a person consumed in a week, but it is unlikely that respondents would be able to directly report that—more specific questions about food consumption may perform better. Crafting a reasonable question from a data objective is sometimes a matter of reworking language, and sometimes a matter of parsing the objective into multiple questions. For example, Fowler and Cosenza (2008) propose that the optimal way to determine how many doctors have been seen in the last 12 months is to ask multiple questions about different types of doctors (primary care, specialists, psychiatrists, and others). This might be simpler to understand and might pose simpler memory tasks than a single, broad question on the topic (p. 146; see also Dillman 2007, p. 77). It can therefore be quite useful to spend some time carefully defining data points, and then deliberately changing the focus on ways to best *operationalize* those concepts into questions.

7.3 Development of Particular Questions

Most of this chapter focuses on guidance for writing survey questions to collect data about behaviors or events, guidance which is informed by both scientific evidence and accumulated practical wisdom (Krosnick and Presser 2010). It is beyond the scope of this chapter to fully review the voluminous scientific literature on this topic, or the numerous practical guides available; what follows is an attempt to incorporate selected ideas from both that will hopefully serve as a useful overview of key principles and ideas. These principles offer no foolproof formulas or easy checklists that lead to optimal questions—translating concepts into questions is an effortful process, and still very much a craft that requires time and practice. It is also a practice that requires consideration of tradeoffs, as there may not be one question (or questions) that are optimal for capturing a particular concept. One rendition might be a bit vague; an alternative might eliminate ambiguity while adding complexity and response burden. Investigator judgment is needed to assess the relative merits among potential variations, ideally by adding the insights of methodologists to the foundation laid by subject matter experts. Also, while these principles serve as useful guides, the actual fit of a question with its data collection objective is best evaluated through empirical testing (discussed further at the end of this chapter).

7.3.1 USING BROADLY UNDERSTOOD WORDS AND AVOIDING TECHNICAL TERMS

This is probably the most common (and common sense) guideline, one that appears in virtually every questionnaire design guide. Keeping in mind that survey questions generally must be comprehensible to a wide range of respondents, it makes sense to use language that is as straightforward as possible. While nuanced words can convey specific meanings, sometimes these produce no obvious advantage—for example, there does not seem to be much benefit to using "principal" when "main" works just as well (Converse and Presser 1986).

Researchers may also overestimate respondents' knowledge of particular terms. It may be quite natural for health services researchers to want to determine whether patients were "seen on an outpatient basis," but some respondents may simply know that they saw a physician "in an office," or conversely that they "stayed overnight" in a hospital. Sometimes, a term may be misunderstood even though it is appropriate and accurate, such as a "dental sealant" (Willis 2005). In such cases, it may be necessary for the question to provide a brief definition or clarifying remark.

Interestingly, technical terms can even cause problems with individuals who have very specialized experience. The question "Have you ever donated platelets using an apheresis device" is more confusing than necessary—although platelet donation routinely uses this device, some donors do not know it by name. Since the real point of the question was whether they had donated, the question is more straightforward when the name of the device is dropped (i.e., "have you ever donated platelets?")

7.3.2 AVOIDING AMBIGUOUS WORDS OR CONCEPTS

Another problem with words is that even if they are generally understood, they can have multiple meanings—and the way that they are interpreted is not always as intended. Consider the following question:

- In the past year, how many times have you telephoned your doctor?

This seems relatively straightforward, but does "your doctor" mean *primary care* doctor, or any physician that the respondent has interacted with? Would another health professional in the doctor's office qualify, such as a nurse practitioner? Does the call need to be about something explicitly medical, or should it count if the call was about billing or logistical matters? Does the call need to be with regard to oneself, or could it have been on behalf of other family members? By "the past year" do we mean this calendar year, or the last 365 days, which could represent different lengths of time?

Other survey questions have asked about time spent "working near a large electrical machine" (what qualifies as working near, or as large?) or whether "immediate blood relatives" have diseases such as diabetes (do cousins count?) One of the most infamous of ambiguous terms is "have sex"—for some, this includes only intercourse, while for others it includes other forms of sexual contact (Sanders and Reinisch 1999). Interestingly, respondents are not always consistent in their own use of the term: in some tests of questions on sexual behavior, respondents defined the term one way, and answered behavioral questions with a different definition in mind (Beatty 2002).

Ambiguous words or concepts are unfortunately very common in everyday language, and are therefore difficult to escape in survey questions. As noted earlier, it is generally possible to figure out what someone means in the course of everyday interaction, but some conversational resources are restricted when responding to surveys. The result can be that respondents in the same situation could answer questions quite differently, thereby creating a great deal of uncertainty about what the data really mean. It is, of course, impossible to avoid all ambiguity, and attempts to do so can create questions that are truly unwieldy (Fowler 1995, p. 17). Nevertheless, it is important to keep in mind that such ambiguities exist, and to be on the lookout for them, choosing terms and phrases that minimize the potential for a high variety of interpretations.

7.3.3 BE CAREFUL OF UNWARRANTED ASSUMPTIONS

Another question that seems straightforward is "When riding in the back seat of a car, how often do you wear a seatbelt?" However the question is confusing for respondents who always wear a seat belt, but never sit in the back seat of a car. Or, if one usually wears a seat belt but rarely sits in the back seat, what answer makes the most sense? One solution, which is often appropriate when unwarranted assumptions are discovered, is to ask two questions—for example, one about whether they sit in the back seat, and if they do, another about their behavior there (Fowler 2004). There is a similar problem with the question "What sort of place do you usually go for routine medical care?"—the question makes the possible erroneous assumption that the respondent actually has such a place. Again, a common solution to the problem is asking multiple questions, the first of which generally addresses the assumption.

A special case of unwarranted assumptions (although a common one) is referred to as a *double-barreled* question. These are questions that essentially ask respondents to answer two questions at once. For example, "do you have health insurance and a usual place to receive routine care" is double-barreled because for some respondents, the answer will be "yes" to one part and "no" to another (see Fowler 1995, p. 82, Bradburn et al. 2004, pp. 142–145, and Dillman 2007, pp. 73–74 for additional examples). Some analysts reason that double-barreled questions are not really a problem, figuring that respondents can simply answer "no" unless all parts of the question are true. This ignores the fact that respondents may be confused by the intent of the question, frustrated that any answer they provide will seem to be only partially correct, and might respond differently depending upon which component of the question seems more important.

This problem is taken to an even higher degree in the following question: "Do you have any difficulty hearing, seeing, communicating, walking, climbing stairs, bending, learning, or doing any similar activities?" This is intended to be a general screener to determine whether respondents had anything that could be considered to be a disability or condition that could limit activities; those who said "no" could skip a wide range of follow-up questions. Because the objective was to determine if the answer to *any* of these was "yes," it seems efficient to ask a single question. However, some respondents have difficulty understanding the question, either because it is overwhelming in scope (Miller 2003) or seems illogical to respondents: if they have problems with only one of these activities, a positive response may feel like it is conveying the wrong overall picture of their limitations. Respondents are likely to assume that certain conventions of everyday communication apply in surveys as well, including that information they provide should be relevant, accurate, and informative (Grice 1975; summarized in Sudman et al. 1996, pp. 62–64). In that context, respondents might see a blunt "yes" response as inadequate. Breaking such large items into multiple questions is more straightforward for respondents, even if one ultimately only cares about the aggregate response. Researchers are, of course, free to aggregate such responses into a single variable after data are collected.

7.3.4 MAINTAIN A REASONABLE LEVEL OF OVERALL QUESTION COMPLEXITY

As mentioned earlier, question construction often involves tradeoffs in the level of specificity. Questions that are not specific enough are vague, but questions that are very specific can be so complex that respondents lose track of important details. Consider the following question:

- What kind of health insurance or health care coverage do you have? Include those that pay for only one type of service, such as nursing home care, accidents, or dental care. Exclude private plans that only provide extra cash while hospitalized.

The motivation behind such questions is simply to obtain needed information in an efficient manner; however, this is a lot of material to keep straight at one time. Error is more likely when overall complexity makes it very challenging for respondents to keep track of all of these nuances (Tourangeau et al. 2000, pp. 38–40, Fowler 1992). If details are forgotten or misunderstood, respondents might underreport or overreport. Even more dangerously, respondents could miss the overall intent of the question.

Such a problem was observed with the following question: "In the past 12 months, how many times have you seen or talked on the telephone about your physical or mental health with a family doctor or general practitioner?" Results of cognitive interviews suggested that respondents did not hear the word "seen" and thought the question was only about *talking on the telephone* to the doctor. In a subsequent experiment, a version of the question which dropped "or talked on the telephone" produced significantly fewer reports of respondents reporting "zero" than the original question. In other words, even though the inclusion of telephone calls was designed to capture more contact with physicians, it actually had the opposite effect. The complexity of the question obscured its intended meaning (Beatty et al. 2007).

One additional point worth mentioning is that length and complexity are not necessarily synonymous. Lengthening questions through *additional examples and prompts* can actually help with complex recall tasks. This additional material should be illustrative or clarifying, rather than introducing additional complexity. For example, in addition to simply asking whether a respondent drank wine or champagne in the past year, additional material in the question could provide examples (table wine, sparkling wine) or prompted about various occasions ("you might have drunk wine to accompany dinner, to celebrate an occasion, to enjoy a party, or for some other reason") (Bradburn et al. 2004, p. 74). Some research also suggests that adding innocuous and repetitive content can improve completeness of reports, presumably because it encourages respondents to spend more time recalling information (Laurent 1972, Cannell et al. 1981). An important distinction is that this additional material should be either illustrative or repetitive, rather than introducing new complexities to be considered (e.g., include one factor but exclude another while answering).

Questionnaire designers may need to convey very specific details to respondents. In aiming for this, they may craft individual questions that are too ambitious to be effective. Often, question complexity can be managed by asking multiple questions. When that is impractical, questionnaire designers need to weigh the importance of each component of the question, and construct the question in a way that is most likely to be readily understood. The "enduring counsel for simplicity" of individual questions remains one of the key tenets for questionnaire designers (Converse and Presser 1986, p. 9, Willis 2005, p. 17).

7.3.5 CHOOSING AN APPROPRIATE REFERENCE PERIOD

Most of the factors considered up to this point have focused on *comprehension* of survey questions. But even if a question is comprehended as intended, responding still involves several additional steps, including *retrieval* of relevant information from memory, *judgments* about the relevance and completeness of this information, and *selection of a response* from the available options (outlined in greater detail in Tourangeau et al. 2000, pp. 7–14). Each of these steps has implications for questionnaire design.

Every question about past behavior poses a recall task of some type—in some cases, *whether* a particular event occurred (perhaps within a particular timeframe), or how *often* something occurred, or *details* or descriptive information about some event. Memory must be consulted in each case to provide the information necessary for response. The specific memory task is driven by the particulars of the question—and the reasonableness of the response task may vary accordingly.

One component of questions that ask whether (or how often) an event occurred is the *reference period*—for example:

- *In the past year,* have you had a routine medical checkup with a doctor or other health care professional?
- *In the past 30 days,* how often did you eat hot or cold cereals?
- *In the past 7 days,* how many times have you taken aspirin or any medicine that had aspirin in it?

Reference periods are sometimes selected to cover a particular amount of variation of a behavior in question. For example, respondents are more likely to report having a routine medical exam in the past *year* than the past *month.* Behaviors such as alcohol consumption might vary at different times of the week, possibly dictating that questions about the *past week* would be more stable than the *past 24 hours.* It is also possible that reports in short reference periods are not good representations of typical behavior (Fowler 1995, p. 157, Dillman 2007, pp. 67–70). Researchers need to determine what span of time is meaningful for individual-level responses in selecting what reference period to ask about.

The choice of reference period may also be influenced by whether events or behaviors are likely to be *counted* or *estimated.* Counting is more likely when the event or behavior in question is uncommon, or takes place at irregular intervals—for example, having surgery (at least for most people). Common or indistinctive events and behaviors, and those that take place at regular intervals, are less individually memorable, and are therefore likely to be estimated based on general patterns—for example, if someone generally takes medication on a daily basis, they are likely to report taking medications *seven times in 1 week* based on the pattern, rather than remembering individual instances. It is tempting to conclude that counting is more precise than estimation, and that counting should therefore be encouraged by utilizing short reference periods that would make individual instances of an event stand out more. In reality, neither counting nor estimating is always more accurate—both can include errors, and in any case it is difficult to control what strategy respondents use (Sudman et al. 1996, p. 223).

Still, the choice of reference period can affect the likely accuracy of reports. Relatively short reference periods are likely to be best for events or behaviors that are estimated, since longer reference periods can increase the risk of computational error. However, longer reference periods may be better for uncommon and irregular events because they reduce the risk of bias from *telescoping,* that is, incorrectly remembering events as taking place in the reference period (Bradburn et al. 2004, pp. 66–67, Sudman et al. 1996, pp. 223–224).

7.3.6 MAXIMIZING THE QUALITY OF RECALL

Regardless of the length of the reference period, questionnaire designers can facilitate recall by clearly specifying the intended timeframe (e.g., "in the last seven days, that is, between January 1 and January 7, 2013"). Questions can also include *retrieval cues* that help stimulate recall. This can include examples of a particular concept—for example, when asking about medical exams received from "health care professionals," it can be useful to mention that this can include physicians, nurses, nurse practitioners, physician assistants, and others. As noted earlier, such examples can help to clarify the intent of the question, but they can also help to nudge memories to the surface by explicitly mentioning specifics that respondents might not have automatically considered. Care should be taken that examples offer a reasonable range of what should be considered, rather than a subset that could be biasing (Bradburn et al. 2004, p. 58). For example, if a question asks about physical activity but examples focus only on formal exercise, reports could be limited to such activities at the expense of other activities of interest. Cues can also prompt respondents to think about particular details that might be helpful—for example, if asking whether a respondent received a particular test during a recent visit to a physician, it might help to ask respondents to think of other aspects of the appointment, such as who accompanied the respondent and the overall purpose of the visit (Tourangeau et al. 2000, p. 96). Perhaps the most elaborate use of cuing takes place in an *event history calendar*, which asks respondents to record details about the timing and location of various life events, and uses these landmarks to facilitate the recall of other memories (Belli et al. 2001); however, administering such tools can be more complicated and effortful than typical survey questionnaires.

Perhaps the most useful way to maximize quality of recall is to pose a response task that lines up with information that can be retrieved from memory most easily. Often, this means asking about something simple and specific—for example, a question about times swimming in the past week should be easier than a question about exercise more generally (Sudman et al. 1996, p. 225). Still, the most specific questions are not always best. Menon (1997) found that responses to broad questions were more accurate than responses to questions that had been "decomposed" into more specific ones, at least when estimation was the likely response strategy. Beatty and Maitland (2008), finding mixed results along those lines, concluded that decomposing questions sometimes brought the response task more closely into line with available memories, but sometimes made it less so; optimal questionnaire design may benefit from an understanding of how memories on a particular topic are organized, although this might also vary across respondents.

Finally, it is important to note that in some cases, self-reports may be inadequate for our research needs because the information is simply not known. For example, studies have shown that even with a variety of recall aids, some parents simply cannot provide meaningful detail about which shots their children received and when, because they never really knew (Lee et al. 1999). Similarly, some respondents may have little knowledge of details such as the doses of medications; if it was never necessary for them to know such information, it would never have been encoded in memory. In some cases, it may be necessary to accept that external data sources may be needed to answer particular research questions, rather than relying primarily upon respondent recall.

7.3.7 AVOIDING UNINTENTIONAL INFLUENCES ON RESPONSES

Skilled questionnaire designers choose their words carefully to present concepts clearly and to pose a reasonable response task. Still, the response process can be subject to a variety of biases and influences that can affect responses, even when the meaning of a question seems clear at face value. A common example of this is a "loaded" question, containing words that may lead respondents toward a particular answer (cf. Bradburn et al. 2004, pp. 5–8). While commonly seen as a problem with attitudinal questions, loaded words and phrases can affect responses to behavioral questions as well. For example, asking someone whether they "follow recommended guidelines" regarding a particular behavior is likely to encourage positive responses, just as asking whether someone performed an "illegal" behavior is likely to encourage negative responses (Dillman 2007, pp. 75–76). In both cases, the descriptors are unnecessary and tend to be leading.

Interestingly, this can be a problem that goes beyond behaviors that are clearly sensitive such as sexual activity and drug use. Respondents might also feel that there are more desirable answers to questions on relatively innocuous topics such as eating, getting exercise, and getting routine checkups. One way to minimize potential bias is to present alternative answers with equal emphasis—for example, "Did you happen to jog, or not?" The presentation of two alternative responses, with both given comparable emphasis, suggests that both could be acceptable answers (Bradburn et al. 2004, p. 38, Fowler 1995, pp. 29, 36).

Not all unintentional influences are related to concerns about positive self-presentation. Because survey response is a social interaction, respondents attempt to bring "common sense" interpretations to response tasks, even though this may at times run contrary to the researcher's wishes. For example, one of the commonly held understandings of everyday communication is that participants should say things that they believe to be relevant to the purpose of the conversation (Grice 1975, summarized in Sudman et al. 1996, pp. 62–64). In a survey context, this means that respondents will commonly interpret questions based on what they perceive the researcher really wants to know. For example, if a question asks about behavior in the last week, but the last week was atypical, the respondent might reason that the researcher really wants to know about *usual* behavior—and would report typical behavior rather than literally accurate information. The respondent would not do this out of a desire to deceive, but rather to be more faithful to the perceived spirit of the request for information. It might be possible to counteract this tendency by allowing the respondent to also indicate whether the recent behavior was typical or not (Fowler 1995, pp. 37–38).

Juxtaposition of topics can also have an unintended influence on response judgments. The following question combines some rather different ideas within the same item: "Have you had an accidental needle-stick, or come into contact with anyone else's blood?" The question was intended to capture a broad range of exposures to blood, some riskier than others, but in doing so it mixed a very specific clinical event with something much more general that could happen in a playground. The inclusion of the specific clinical example suggested to some respondents that the real intent of the question was to capture dangerous medical exposures to blood, which was much narrower than intended. Separating these two components encourages broader interpretations (Beatty 2002).

Juxtaposition of topics across questions can also create *context effects*, where the process of responding to one question affects interpretations of a subsequent one. This is something considered in more detail in the subsequent discussion of questionnaire assembly.

7.3.8 PRESENTING APPROPRIATE RESPONSE CATEGORIES

Even if the respondent adequately understands the question, can recall relevant information, and makes judgments relatively free of unintended influences, one critical step remains: they must actually provide the response (Tourangeau et al. 2000, pp. 230–254). As with other aspects of the question, designers select response categories that meet their analytic needs, but also present appropriate choices for respondents to adequately express their answers. There are a number of different forms of response options, and considerations for designers to keep in mind for each.

Many behavioral survey questions provide *closed-ended* response options—that is, specific answer categories that we ask the respondent to choose from. A "yes/no" question is the simplest example of this, for example, "During the past three months, did you have an injury where any part of your body was hurt?" Sometimes, the basic distinction (did this happen or not) is the only information researchers need to know, although it may also be used to determine whether more detailed follow-up questions are appropriate (in this case, details about the frequency, severity, and circumstances of any injuries). Yes/no responses work well for determining whether a particular event occurred, provided that the event is well defined. They can be more problematic as more subjectivity is introduced. For example, when asking whether a respondent "usually" does something, the answer might be "it depends" (Fowler 1995, p. 27), which is difficult to map onto a simple response. Questionnaire designers need to evaluate whether a question really asks something that can be dichotomized in terms of yes and no.

More detailed information may be obtained through the use of a longer set of *categorical response options*. For example, the researcher might want to know "In what way was your body hurt?" and provide response options such as broken bone, sprain, cut, bruise, burn, and so forth. If categories are well chosen, they have the potential to ease the burden on respondents and improve the quality of responses by providing a clear sense of the distinctions that are meaningful to researchers. In some cases, respondents are asked to select the one response that best applies. In others, it might be appropriate for respondents to select *all* that apply (e.g., respondents might be covered by several different sources of health insurance, and when asking about their types of health insurance coverage it would be appropriate to accept multiple responses). In either case, the researcher should ensure that the response options are *exhaustive*, not omitting reasonable answers, so that the respondent's situation is actually reflected as one of the response options. Also, particularly when soliciting one "best" response, the options should be *mutually exclusive*, such that a respondent's situation can be adequately recorded through one response. Consider a question about marital status that includes the response categories of single, married, divorced, widowed, and living with a partner. This list would not be exhaustive, because people who are separated from a spouse might feel that neither "married" nor "divorced" fully applies. The list is also not mutually exclusive, because some divorced and widowed people might consider themselves to be single. It would therefore be better to replace "single" with "never married," which makes the meaning of each category distinct (Bradburn et al. 2004, p. 268).

At the same time, completeness needs to be balanced by presenting a manageable level of detail. For example, there are potentially dozens of legitimate distinctions that one could make about various types of public and private health insurance. A single question that included all of these would be unwieldy. One solution is to use multiple questions, with the first capturing broad categories, and subsequent questions digging into greater detail (Fowler 1995, p. 86), although care must be taken that these initial questions reflect distinctions that are actually meaningful to respondents. Also, depending upon the mode of administration, it may be possible to include visual aids, so that respondents can see the range of options that are being presented (Bradburn et al. 2004, pp. 173–174). It is important to note that even with visual aids, there are limits to the amount of detail that respondents can keep straight.

Researchers may choose to ask questions in an open-ended manner, accepting verbatim responses rather than channeling responses into closed categories. Sometimes this is done because rich description is desired by the researcher, or because the topic asked about is too complex to capture in a standardized manner, or because researchers do not have enough knowledge to construct reasonable response categories. The use of open-ended questions requires some sort of coding or data reduction after the fact, so relying upon them shifts some conceptual work to later in the research process (Bradburn et al. 2004, pp. 153–156). Also, as noted earlier, respondents may use answer categories to help understand the intent of the question—therefore, the words in open-ended questions may need to be even clearer to fully convey intended meaning.

7.3.9 CAPTURING QUANTITATIVE RESPONSES (INCLUDING VAGUE QUANTIFIERS)

As we have seen throughout this chapter, many behavioral questions assess the frequency of events or behaviors. Sometimes this entails reporting a simple quantity: "How many days of work did you miss as a result of this injury?" The most common advice is to pose such questions in an open-ended manner, largely because this is the simplest way to collect such data (Krosnick and Presser 2010), and also because response categories can have a strong effect on respondent reports, if they use response categories as a frame of reference for estimation. As one example, respondents may think of their own behavior as moderate or average, and might therefore be drawn to middle response options (Schwarz et al. 1985, Sudman et al. 1996, p. 218–221). Open-ended questions avoid such effects. Still, it may still be use useful to explicitly offer flexible response units: the question "In the last 30 days, how many times per day, week, or month did you do exercises to strengthen your muscles?" accommodates a variety of experiences, whether respondents exercise twice a day, three times a week, or just once a month.

However, some survey questions do rely upon categories of frequencies, presumably due to concerns about respondents' ability or willingness to provide open-ended responses. One example is a question about number of days that a respondent has used marijuana (categories included never, 1–2 days, 3–5 days, 6–10 days, 11–49 days, 50–99 days, continuing in 100-day increments). Open-ended responses might be difficult or embarrassing, particularly in higher ranges, but selecting a category might pose a more manageable task and lead to analytically useful data (Turner et al. 1992; cited in Bradburn et al. 2004).

Another approach to measuring frequency is the use of *vague quantifiers* such as "often, sometimes, rarely, or never." The major criticism of vague quantifiers is that individual interpretations can vary greatly, and they can have different meanings in different domains—for example, "often" eating vegetables is unlikely to be comparable to "often" visiting a doctor (Sudman et al. 1996, p. 225). These problems can make results difficult to interpret. However, vague quantifiers are sometimes used when impressionistic reports are acceptable to a researcher, and when actual quantification would be more effortful than desired—for example, in the case of proportions that would require multiple questions (Fowler 1995, p. 158). Still, in one study, Miller (2004) identified various problems interpreting response scales based on vague quantifiers. In one instance, a respondent failed to understand the progressive meaning of terms such as "moderate, severe, and extreme." In another, response categories regarding currently smoking cigarettes "daily, occasionally, or not at all" were misunderstood; although "occasionally" was intended as a middle point between other extremes, someone who scaled back smoking to only a couple times a day selected "occasionally" as literally correct. Some variety of interpretation may be inevitable when using vague quantifiers, but misunderstandings of the overall intent of the scale are problematic.

Another common objective of survey questions is to identify when a particular behavior or event occurred. In open-ended questions about timing, it is important to specify the desired response format—for example, *how many months ago* an event occurred. If simply asked when an event occurred, a respondent could reply with a date (on January 15), an age (when I was 30), time from the present (about 6 months ago), or time from another landmark event (a week after the previous occasion) (Fowler 1995, p. 3). In general, respondents find it easier to report how long ago an event occurred rather than to provide particular dates (Huttenlocher et al. 1990). Dating of events is a particularly difficult response task (see Sudman et al. 1996, pp. 185–196 and Tourangeau et al. 2000, pp. 100–135 for overviews), and uncertainty about dating increases the longer ago the event in question occurred. The use of closed response categories may provide a simpler response task, provided the ranges provide an acceptable level of detail to the researcher—for example, less than 6 months ago, between 6 months and a year, and more than a year ago (Bradburn et al. 2004, p. 41). If used, care should be taken to ensure that categories are mutually exclusive, and researchers should be aware of the potential for telescoping errors, as described earlier.

7.4 Overall Questionnaire Construction

Up to this point, this chapter has treated questions as individual units, and has presented a number of considerations to maximize their quality. Ultimately, however, respondents experience a questionnaire as a complete entity. Schuman (1992) suggested that this experience is less like viewing a series of independent snapshots than watching a movie, with respondents looking for an overall logical arc, and with early items potentially affecting interpretations of later ones. One implication of this is that it is important to organize questions into coherent topics. As discussed earlier, respondents rely on various conventions of everyday communication (cf. Grice 1975) in making sense of the survey task; one such convention is that there is an underlying logic behind what the researcher is asking them to do. Haphazard juxtaposition of topics works against that expectation, leading not only to potential confusion, but also to response burden. It is also helpful to mark transitions with brief statements ("I'd now like to ask you some questions on a different topic.") Strategic organization can also help to maximize respondent motivation, for example, by beginning with relatively interesting and unthreatening questions before moving to more challenging material (Bradburn et al. 2004, p. 332).

Consistency in terms of format and overall level of language is also important. If individual questions are drafted by different people or drawn from different sources, they may include stylistic differences that serve no substantive purpose—for example, inconsistent response categories that are intended to measure the same thing, or general differences of style or tone. Again, respondents may notice such differences and assume that there is some underlying reason for them under norms of everyday communication, which could affect judgment processes in an unintended manner. For that reason, stylistic and formatting differences should be smoothed over so that the questionnaire as written appears to be presented in a standard voice. Still, keep in mind that some inconsistencies may be perfectly appropriate (if, for example, a change in response categories was deliberate for a particular analytic purpose).

The overall order of question presentation is also important, because the content of preceding questions can influence responses to subsequent ones. One way this can happen is through the cueing of respondent memories, bringing facts or judgments to the surface that may be drawn upon in subsequent questions. Consider, for example, a question about overall health. If the question is preceded by a series of questions about various health conditions, the issues raised in these questions are more likely to be taken into account when formulating the response to an overall health question. Note that this may or may not be desirable: the researcher may prefer that the respondent consider only those issues that come to mind spontaneously, or may actually want the respondent to think about particular issues. Previous questions can also affect judgments about the *relevance* of information already discussed. For example, if a questionnaire asks about consumption of alcoholic beverages, and later asks about consumption of beverages in general, respondents could commonly infer that the latter question referred to *beverages other than* alcoholic ones—since those have already been addressed, and according to standard conventions of communication, respondents might infer that the researcher would not be asking about information that was already provided (cf. Grice 1975). Generally, research on *context effects* of earlier questions on subsequent ones has focused on attitudinal research (see Sudman et al. 1996, pp. 80–129; and Tourangeau et al. 2000, pp. 197–229 for overviews), but clearly some of the same memory and judgment issues can apply to behavioral questions. More generally, researchers should be mindful of how topics are organized into the questionnaire, and consider whether the progression of ideas is consistent with research objectives.

The *overall length* of a questionnaire bears some consideration as well. As researchers compile all potentially interesting items into an instrument, overall volume can expand quickly. However, there are limits to both the breadth of depth of topics that can be fruitfully incorporated into a single questionnaire. There is some evidence that respondents put less effort into responses as questionnaire length increases (Herzog and Bachman 1981), choose responses that they perceive will end the survey more quickly (Kreuter et al. 2011), and possibly decline to participate altogether, although the relationship between interview length and willingness to participate is not always clear (Bogen 1996). The clearest negative effects of questionnaire length occur with self-administered questionnaires—that is, mail survey respondents are less likely to complete large booklets than questionnaires limited to a few pages (Dillman et al. 1996, Leslie 1996, cited in Dillman 2007). On the whole, it is important to recognize that respondent willingness to participate is finite, and it is useful to evaluate whether overall length, burden, and level of detail in the questionnaire are within bounds that respondents are likely to find acceptable.

Finally, we should briefly consider the importance of taking into account the intended *mode of administration*. This topic is too vast for comprehensive treatment here, but it is worth considering a few points. Generally, interviewer-administered face-to-face surveys put the lightest burden on overall questionnaire design, as interviewers can help to compensate for some weaknesses by helping to motivate respondents or by clarifying difficult aspects of questions (Fowler 1995, pp. 31–32). However, for various reasons including cost and efficiency, face-to-face interviewing has become less common than data collection through other modes—initially the telephone, and more recently self-administered modes including mail, Internet, personal electronic devices, or combinations of these (Dillman 2007, pp. 7, 450). The choice of mode has various implications for questionnaire design. For example, oral administration of questions over the telephone eliminates some of the communication resources available in face-to-face administration, which could have implications for the maximum complexity of telephone survey questions (Groves 1990). Self-administered questionnaires on paper must be designed so that respondents can navigate them without external assistance, which has implications for the overall complexity of skip patterns (Jenkins and Dillman 1997). Web surveys can make it feasible to present a great deal of visual information and include complex skip logic, but lack the presence of an interviewer for clarification and motivation (Couper et al. 2001). There is also a variety of evidence that self-administered questionnaires encourage more complete reporting of sensitive behaviors (e.g., Tourangeau and Smith 1996). For a general review of the relationship between mode and responses to questions, see Dillman (2007, pp. 224–232). In short, questions that are feasible in one mode may run into difficulties in others. Questionnaire designers need to be sensitive to these various limitations when assembling their instruments.

7.5 Questionnaire Testing and Evaluation

The topic of questionnaire testing is given more complete treatment elsewhere in this volume (see Chapter 9), but a few general points are worth considering here. Most importantly, it should be obvious that writing questions and constructing questionnaires is difficult work. Bradburn et al. (2004) propose an 18-step process for questionnaire development, involving various stages of drafting, testing, and revising questions, sometimes with multiple iterations (pp. 315–316). One reason for devoting this level of attention to design is that the communicative burden on survey questions is high, and difficult to meet in practice. Another is that questionnaire design rules, though helpful, are often not specific enough to inform the design of individual questions (Krosnick and Presser 2010, Willis 2005, pp. 27–28).

The potential arsenal of questionnaire evaluation activities is vast, including activities that require data collection and those that rely on judgment without data collection; evaluation methods involving data collection may be quantitative or qualitative (Krosnick and Presser 2010). Several recent volumes discuss the range of possibilities in depth (Presser et al. 2004, Madans et al. 2011). The choice of evaluation methods used may depend upon resources available as well as investigator expertise. Two particularly common and complementary approaches include cognitive interviewing, which entails administrating draft questions while soliciting additional self-reports about respondent interpretations and thought-processes (Beatty and Willis 2007); and field pretesting, which entails administering questions on a small scale as the survey will be actually administered (Converse and Presser 1986). The combination of approaches seems particularly useful for producing both in-depth analysis of measurement quality and practical performance in the field.

7.6 Using Questions from Previously Administered Questionnaires

As surveys have proliferated over the last several decades, it is increasingly likely that questions on virtually any health-related topic have been asked at some point in the past. Rather than crafting questions from scratch, it is often possible to use previously administered questions on new surveys (cf. Converse and Presser 1986, pp. 50–51, Bradburn et al. 2004, pp. 23–26, Aday and Cornelius 2006, pp. 50, 195). Questionnaires are generally easy to find, and in fact, it is considered good practice to make specific questions available for data that are publicly presented (American Association for Public Opinion Research (AAPOR) 2010).

Still, some cautions are in order. Questions drawn from other instruments may almost meet specific data needs, but still require adaptation of wording or responses. Also, keep in mind that when borrowing questions, many of the questionnaire-level issues discussed above are especially pertinent. Taking a question out of one survey and putting it into another could change its context—so even if the wording is identical, it might not capture exactly the same thing. The flow of topics still needs to be considered. Sometimes format consistency needs to be imposed on the borrowed question.

Perhaps most importantly, keep in mind that just because a question has been administered in a past survey does not guarantee its quality—it is still necessary to evaluate how well it meets particular data needs. Testing questions is still important, as differences in question objectives can be subtle, and the meanings of questions can easily fluctuate across instruments and over time. Still, there are many advantages to building upon the work done by others, and a review of previously used survey questions on the same topic is generally an excellent investment of time.

7.7 Conclusion

Good questionnaire design is a difficult and a time consuming task. It is guided by a great deal of scientific evidence, but remains largely a craft. Hopefully the issues and examples provided in this chapter reveal some useful strategies for measuring health behavior and health service utilization. Unfortunately, there are no easy formulas for writing good questions. The purpose of this chapter is merely to sensitize the reader to various issues that should be considered. With these issues in mind, researchers interested in measuring events and behaviors must carefully consider the words used while doing everything possible to maximize the clarity of language and reasonableness of the response tasks. Inevitably, this requires a great deal of judgment. It is also most likely to be successful when viewed as an iterative process, with questions drafted, modified to make them as answerable as possible, tested, and most likely, revised and retested. This effortful process is ultimately rewarded by high quality data that help to address a variety of important research needs.

REFERENCES

Aday LA, Cornelius LJ. *Designing and Conducting Health Surveys: A Comprehensive Guide*. 3rd ed. San Francisco, CA: Jossey-Bass; 2006.

American Association for Public Opinion Research (AAPOR). 2010. AAPOR code of professional ethics and practices, Revised May 2010. http://www.aapor.org/Standards_and_Ethics.htm. Accessed on July 16, 2014.

Beatty P. Cognitive interview evaluation of the blood donor history screening questionnaire. Final Report of the AABB Task Force to Redesign the Blood Donor Screening Questionnaire. Report submitted to the U.S. Food and Drug Administration; 2002.

Beatty P, Cosenza C, Fowler FJ. New experiments on the optimal structure of complex survey questions. Paper presented at the European Survey Research Association Conference, Prague, Czech Republic; 2007 Jun 25–29; 2007.

Beatty P; Maitland A. The accuracy of decomposed vs. global behavioral frequency questions. Paper presented at the American Association for Public Opinion Research Conference; New Orleans, LA; 2008.

Beatty P, Willis GB. Research synthesis: the practice of cognitive interviewing. Public Opin Q 2007;71:287–311.

Belli R, Shay W, Stafford F. Event history calendars and question lists. Public Opin Q 2001;65:45–74.

Belson WA. *The Design and Understanding of Survey Questions*. London, UK: Gower; 1981.

Bogen K. The effect of questionnaire length on response rates—a review of the literature. Proceedings of the Section on Survey Research Methods. Alexandria, VA: American Statistical Association; 1996. p 1020–1025.

Bradburn N, Sudman S, Wansink B. *Asking Questions: The Definitive Guide to Questionnaire Design—For Market Research, Political Polls, and Social and Health Questionnaires*. San Francisco, CA: Jossey-Bass; 2004.

Cannell CF, Miller PV, Oksenberg L. Research on interviewing techniques. In: Leinhardt S, editor. *Sociological Methodology*. San Francisco: Jossey-Bass; 1981.

Converse JM, Presser S. *Survey Questions: Handcrafting the Survey Questionnaire*. Beverly Hills, CA: Sage; 1986.

Couper MP, Traugott MW, Lamias MJ. Web survey design and administration. Public Opin Q 2001;65:230–253.

Dillman DA. *Mail and Internet Surveys: The Tailored Design Method*. 2nd ed. Hoboken, NJ: John Wiley and Sons; 2007.

Dillman DA, Singer E, Clark JR, Treat JB. Effects of benefit appeals, mandatory appeals, and variations in confidentiality on completion rates for census questionnaires. Public Opin Q 1996;60:376–389.

Fowler FJ. How unclear terms affect survey data. Public Opin Q 1992;56:218–231.

Fowler FJ. *Improving Survey Questions: Design and Evaluation*. Thousand Oaks, CA: Sage; 1995.

Fowler FJ. The case for more split-ballot experiments in developing survey instruments. In: Presser S, Rothgeb JM, Couper MP, Lessler JT, Martin E, Martin J, Singer E, editors. *Methods for Testing and Evaluating Survey Questionnaires*. Hoboken, NJ: Wiley Interscience; 2004.

Fowler FJ, Cosenza C. Writing effective questions. In: de Leeuw ED, Hox JJ, Dillman DA, editors. *International Handbook of Survey Methodology*. London, UK: Psychological Press; 2008.

Fowler FJ, Mangione TW. *Standardized Survey Interviewing*. Newbury Park, CA: Sage; 1990.

Grice HP. Logic and conversation. In: Cole P, Morgan JL, editors. *Syntax and Semantics. 3: Speech Acts*. New York: Academic Press; 1975.

Groves RM. Theories and methods of telephone surveys. Annu Rev Sociol 1990;16:221–240.

Herzog AR, Bachman JG. Effects of questionnaire length on response quality. Public Opin Q 1981;45:549–559.

Huttenlocher J, Hedges LV, Bradburn NM. Reports of elapsed time: bounding and rounding processes in estimation. J Exp Psychol Learn Mem Cogn 1990;16:196–213.

Jenkins C, Dillman DA. Towards a theory of self-administered questionnaire design. In: Lyberg L, Biemer P, Collins M, Decker L, deLeeuw E, Dippo C, Schwarz N, Trewin D, editors. *Survey Measurement and Process Quality*. New York: Wiley Interscience; 1997.

Kreuter F, McCulloch S, Presser S, Tourangeau R. Filter questions in interleafed versus grouped format: effects on respondents and interviewers. Sociol Meth Res 2011;40:88–104.

Krosnick JA, Presser S. Questionnaire design. In: Wright JD, Marsden PV, editors. *Handbook of Survey Research*. 2nd ed. West Yorkshire, UK: Emerald Group; 2010.

Laurent A. Effects of question length on reporting behavior in the survey interview. J Am Stat Assoc 1972;67:298–305.

Lee L, Brittingham A, Tourangeau R, Willis G, Ching P, Jobe J, Black S. Are reporting errors due to encoding limitations or retrieval failure? Surveys of child vaccination as a case study. Appl Cognit Psychol 1999;13:43–63.

Leslie TF. *1996 National Content Survey Results. Internal DSSD Memorandum No 3*. Washington, DC: U.S. Bureau of the Census; 1996.

Madans J, Miller K, Maitland A, Willis GB. *Question Evaluation Methods: Contributing to the Science of Data Quality*. Hoboken, NJ: John Wiley and Sons; 2011.

Menon G. Are the parts better than the whole? The effect of decompositional questions on judgments with frequent behaviors. J Market Res 1997;24:335–346.

Miller K. Conducting cognitive interviews to understand question-response limitations. Am J Health Behav 2003;27(Suppl. 3):S264–S272.

Miller K. Cognitive interviewing at the National Center for Health Statistics: cross-cultural and translation issues. Presented at the National Center for Health Statistics Data Users Conference; Washington, DC; August 2004.

Presser S, Rothgeb JM, Couper MP, Lessler JT, Martin E, Martin J, Singer E. *Methods for Testing and Evaluating Survey Questionnaires*. Hoboken, NJ: Wiley Interscience; 2004.

Sanders SA, Reinisch JM. Would you say you 'had sex' if.... JAMA 1999;281(3):275–277.

Schaeffer NC. Conversation with a Purpose—or Conversation? Interaction in the Standardized Interview. In: Biemer PP, Groves RM, Lyberg LE, Mathiowetz NA, Sudman S, editors. *Measurement Error in Surveys*. New York: John Wiley; 1991.

Schober MF, Conrad FG. A collaborative view of standardized survey interviews. In: Maynard D, Houtkoop-Steenstra H, Schaeffer NC, van der Zouwen J, editors. *Standardization and Tacit Knowledge: Interaction and Practice in the Survey Interview*. New York: John Wiley; 2002.

Schuman H. Context effects: state of the art/state of the past. In: Schwarz N, Sudman S, editors. *Context Effects in Social and Psychological Research*. New York: Springer-Verlag; 1992.

Schuman H, Kalton G. Survey methods. In: Lindzey G, Aronson E, editors. *Handbook of Social Psychology* Vol 1. New York: Random House; 1985.

Schwarz N, Hippler HJ, Deutsch B, Strack F. Response categories: effects on behavioral reports and comparative judgments. Public Opin Q 1985;49:388–395.

Sudman S, Bradburn N, Schwarz N. *Thinking About Answers: The Application of Cognitive Processes to Survey Methodology*. San Francisco, CA: Jossey-Bass; 1996.

Tourangeau R, Rips LJ, Rasinski K. *The Psychology of Survey Response*. Cambridge, UK: Cambridge University Press; 2000.

Tourangeau R, Smith T. Asking sensitive questions: the impact of data collection, question format, and question context. Public Opin Q 1996;60:275–304.

Turner CF, Lessler JT, Gfroerer JC. *Survey Measurement of Drug Use: Methodological Studies*. Washington, DC: U.S. Department of Health and Human Services; 1992.

Willis GB. *Cognitive Interviewing: A Tool for Improving Questionnaire Design*. Thousand Oaks, CA: Sage; 2005.

ONLINE RESOURCES

The National Health Interview Survey, conducted by the National Center for Health Statistics, has asked questions about a variety of health behavior and health care utilization topics for the past half-century. Questionnaires and related documentation from the survey can be found at: www.cdc.gov/nchs/nhis/nhis_questionnaires.htm.

The Survey Question Bank includes questionnaires and documentation for a wide variety of health surveys conducted in the United Kingdom. It can be accessed at: http://surveynet.ac.uk/sqb/topics/health.asp#majorsurveys.

A variety of other institutions conduct surveys on health and health care, making recently administered questions and resulting datasets available. Two useful examples are from the Gallup Organization. One of these can be accessed at: www.gallup.com/poll/wellbeing.aspx?ref=f.

A second is the Pew Internet and American Life Project, which can be found at: http://pewinternet.org/topics/Health.aspx?typeFilter=5.

The Q-Bank of the National Center for Health Statistics is an archive of results of question evaluation studies, and includes many questions on health behaviors and health care utilization. This is not an archive of questions to necessarily use "off the shelf," but the database provides detailed analysis of what the questions actually measure, including both strengths and weaknesses. It can be found at: wwwn.cdc.gov/qbank/home.aspx.

Also, there are many on-line resources to assist researchers with all phases of surveys, often with specific guidance on writing and evaluating questions. One particularly useful guide can be found at: http://oqi.wisc.edu/resourcelibrary/uploads/resources/Survey_Guide.pdf.

CHAPTER EIGHT

Self-Rated Health in Health Surveys

Sunghee Lee
Institute for Social Research, University of Michigan, Ann Arbor, MI, USA

8.1 Introduction

8.1.1 POPULARITY OF SRH

Global self-rated health (SRH) is defined as an individual's perceived overall health and is both a concept frequently used in research and a popular measurement item in health surveys. Depending on the field, SRH is termed differently: self-assessed health, self-ratings of health, self-assessments of health, perceived health, self-perceptions of health, subjective health, self-evaluated health, self-evaluations of health, global health, self-reported health, to name a few. Elinson (1994) recounted the intriguing origin of SRH. In the 1940s and 1950s when systematic efforts for developing health-related surveys were about to grow, SRH was introduced not as a scientific measurement item but as a conversation starter for health survey interviewers. Because health surveys included topics that were personal and potentially unpleasant, the nonthreatening nature of the SRH content was viewed as a way to build rapport between interviewers and respondents before starting actual interviews. Over the years, researchers have analyzed SRH and provided evidence for its utility, which led to its popular use in health research.

Handbook of Health Survey Methods, First Edition. Edited by Timothy P. Johnson.

As a research concept, SRH is used for understanding population health and monitoring trends. It can be found not only in health research (e.g., Hays et al. 1996, Jylhä et al. 2006, Maddox 1964, McGee et al. 1999), but also in other social sciences, including demography (e.g., Bratter and Gorman 2011, Liu and Zhang 2004), sociology (e.g., Borg and Kristensen 2000), and economics (e.g., Dwyer and Mitchell 1999, Jürges 2007). It is also used as a comparative research tool (e.g., Appels et al. 1996, Bardage et al. 2005, Eurostat 1997, OECD 2010) and, consequently, as a means for studying health disparities (e.g., Borrell and Dallo 2008, Ferraro 1993, Goodman 1999, Idler 2003, Spencer et al. 2009). In sum, SRH serves as an important tool for understanding society and shaping policy decisions.

The popularity of SRH as a research concept is supported by ample empirical evidence indicating that SRH is a strong correlate of objective health conditions (e.g., Idler and Kasl 1995, La Rue et al. 1979, Linn and Linn 1980, Maddox and Douglas 1973) as well as a strong predictor of subsequent morbidity, mortality (e.g., Benyamini and Idler 1999, Bergner and Rothman 1987, Franks et al. 2003, Idler and Angel 1990, Idler and Benyamini 1997, Lima-Costa et al. 2012, McGee et al. 1999, Mossey and Shapiro 1982, Vuorisalmi et al. 2005) and heath care utilization (e.g., DeSalvo et al. 2005, Menec and Chipperfield 2001, Miilunpalo et al. 1997). It is notable that the predictive power of SRH is found to hold even after controlling for socio-demographic characteristics, objective health measures, and clinical medical risk factors that also influence health outcomes and utilization.

8.1.2 SRH IN HEALTH SURVEY PRACTICE

Because of its many desirable properties, virtually all health-related surveys ask SRH. As a survey item, SRH is typically measured in a single question with simple wording. Table 1 in Idler and Benyamini (1997) lists a range of actual SRH question wordings from various studies. The standard version of SRH asks about one's health directly and often reads as some variation of, "In general, how would you rate your health: excellent, very good, good, fair, or poor?" Other versions of direct SRH include "How would you characterize your health overall?" "How is your health in general?" and "How would you rate your health at the present time/these days/right now?" An alternative to this standard version is to ask SRH comparatively. There are two types of comparative SRH. First, health is measured in comparison to other people, for example, asking "Compared to other people your age, would you say your health is excellent, very good, good, fair or poor?" The second comparative version of SRH asks about health transition by comparing the current and past health status as, "Is your health better, worse, about the same as it was 10 years ago?" This version does not appear explicitly as SRH, although it does attempt to measure one's general health state.

The standard and the first comparative versions are reported to be similar in their psychometric properties, including reproducibility, reliability, and validity, with both physical and emotional function measures and it is suggested that they can be used interchangeably (DeSalvo et al. 2006). There is, however, contradictory evidence indicating that older people tend to rate their health better with the comparative version than with the standard version, whereas younger people show the opposite (Baron-Epel and Kaplan 2001). While the same construct is sought to be measured across these three versions, the operational items are not identical and, hence, are likely to elicit slightly different constructs.

Administration of SRH is fairly easy. It requires minimal space on questionnaires and minimal interview time. Combined with its impressive utility, the administration convenience of SRH has promoted its visibility in survey practice. SRH is found in various health surveys around the world (e.g., the U.S. National Health Interview Survey (NHIS), the Health Survey for England, the Canadian Community Health Survey, the World Health Survey, the Survey of Health and Living Status of the Middle Aged and the Elderly in Taiwan, the Australian Longitudinal Study on Women's Health, the National Population Health Survey in Canada, and the Survey of Health, Ageing and Retirement in Europe). SRH is also a crucial item in quality-of-life batteries, such as the Short Form health surveys (e.g., SF-36, SF-12, and SF-8) from the Medical Outcomes Study, the Quality of Life Questionnaire (QLQ-C30) by the European Organization for Research and Treatment of Cancer Quality, and the EQ-5D by the EuroQol Group. These make SRH arguably one of the most popular survey items (Bowling 2005). In 1993, there was a conference solely dedicated to this item organized by the U.S. National Center for Health Statistics (NCHS), the *NCHS Conference on the Cognitive Aspect of Self-Reported Health Status* (National Center for Health Statistics 1994).

8.2 Utility of Self-Rated Health

In this section, we first examine the utility of SRH in the public health literature and then provide its theoretical underpinnings deduced from cognitive psychology as popularly used in the survey methodology literature. The order of this discussion may seem reversed. Unlike the traditional measurement approach where an item is developed to test theory, SRH as a survey item was not developed from theories as noted above. Instead, it was first used as a conversational starter and then its theoretical value was discovered. Therefore, our discussion follows this order.

8.2.1 EMPIRICAL EVIDENCE: PUBLIC HEALTH LITERATURE

In the public health literature, the utility of SRH is discussed in two ways depending on the causal direction of its relationship with health status. On one hand, current objective health conditions are important determinants of SRH. On the other, reports to SRH questions are a significant predictor of subsequent health conditions. Therefore, the causal direction in the relationship between SRH and objective health measures, such as morbidity, mortality, and health care utilization status, is not necessarily uniform.

Literature suggests a wide array of determinants of SRH. While these determinants are not completely mutually exclusive or independent, they provide an overview of what contributes to one's report of SRH. Also, note that the casual direction in the relationship between the determinants and SRH is not always clear cut. The first set of determinants of SRH includes biomedical factors, including both objective clinical and subjective self-reported measures. Both current and previous diseases, physical ability and performance, functional limitations and disabilities are related to current SRH (Cott et al. 1999, Mavaddat et al. 2011, Singh-Manoux et al. 2006). Various health measures, such as mobility, chronic pain, speed during daily activities, and energy levels, differentiate reports to SRH (Christian et al. 2011, Mäntyselkä et al. 2003). Mental health is also an important determinant of SRH. Indicators of distress, mood, and depression, such as those measured by the Center for Epidemiologic Study Depression (CES-D) scale, have all been shown to influence SRH (Andrew and Dulin 2007, Farkas et al. 2009).

Demographic and socioeconomic factors are a second set of correlates of SRH. Age, gender, race, education, income, and social class all have effects on SRH (Damián et al. 2008, Kaplan and Camacho 1983, Pinquart 2001). Typically, women report poorer health than men, as do older people than younger people, and non-Whites compared to Whites. Not surprisingly, lower social class, measured with educational attainment, employment, literacy level, and income, is also linked to poorer health (Subramanian et al. 2005).

Additionally, social environment and social networks also play a role in determining one's report of SRH after removing the effects of individual-level characteristics (Cheng and Chan 2006, Gele and Harsløf 2010, Kawachi et al. 1999, Litwin 2006). For instance, residence in rural and economically deprived areas is shown to be an independent correlate of negative health. An increase in social capital, trust, and support in the community where a person lives, in contrast, produce positive responses to the SRH question (Baron-Epel et al. 2008, Subramanian et al. 2005, Yip et al. 2007).

The determinants of SRH examined earlier have an independent effect on SRH apart from other variables. Some show a stronger effect than others. Physical health symptoms, among all determinants, are reported to play a more important role than other biomedical factors in shaping answers to SRH (Bailis et al. 2001, Davies and Ware 1981). However, there is no coherent agreement, as Johnson et al. (1990) reported that both physical and psychological factors were significant independent components of SRH. It also appears that SRH is relatively stable, reflecting chronic rather than acute illness and disabilities (Gold et al. 1996, Goldstein et al. 1984). Of course, these determinants play differential roles depending on the population. Krause and Jay (1994), for example, showed that non-Whites may use health problems to determine SRH, whereas Whites may use general physical functioning.

Obviously, the list of determinants is long. Still, these determinants in combination are shown to explain at most 40% of the variance in SRH (Baron-Epel 2004). This means that SRH includes characteristics much wider than what research has examined thus far (Jylhä 2011, Kaplan and Camacho 1983, Mossey and Shapiro 1982). However, understanding these determinants is important, because they can be used as a mitigating tool for improving health. For instance, social capital has been suggested as a way to reduce health inequality by shifting focus onto structurally imposed unequal opportunities to access social capital (Subramanian et al. 2005, Yip et al. 2007).

The single most important reason for the accelerated visibility of SRH in the health research literature is its utility as a predictor for future mortality and health outcomes (Benyamini et al. 1999, Ford et al. 2008, Idler and Benyamini 1997, Idler et al. 1990, Thorslund and Lundberg 1994, Wolinsk and Johnson 1992). Specific physical disabilities, functional limitations, and cognitive impairments are also shown to be predicted by previous reports to SRH (Bond et al. 2006, Ferraro et al. 1997, Idler and Kasl 1995). Moreover, SRH significantly predicts future health care utilization, such as the number of physician visits and hospitalizations (DeSalvo et al. 2005, Menec and Chipperfield 2001, Miilunpalo et al. 1997). The literature indicates that SRH is a useful measure for predicting future survival for the elderly and general populations alike, Western and Eastern populations alike, and those with different types of health conditions (Ben-Ezra and Shmotkin 2006, Dzekedzeke et al. 2008, Frankenberg and Jones 2004, Jylhä et al. 1998, Larsson et al. 2002, Lesser 2000, McGee et al. 1999, Nybo et al. 2003, Pu et al. 2011, Shadbolt et al. 2002, Walker et al. 2004, Yu et al. 1998).

Given the ample amount of research suggesting SRH as a reliable measure of health and its relevance for policy implications, SRH has been recommended by the World Health Organization (WHO) (DeBruin et al. 1996), the U.S. Centers for Disease Control (Hennessy et al. 1994), and the European Commission (Kramers 2003) to study population health. Moreover, SRH is used for comparative studies. For instance, using the data on SRH from the European Community Household Panel Survey, Eurostat (1997) compared the health status of 12 European countries. Likewise, the Organization for Economic Cooperation and Development (OECD) examined the health status of 31 European Union countries, although it made a cautionary remark for cross-national comparability (Organization for Economic Co-operation and Development 2010). Using SRH, Bardage et al. (2005) compared older adult health across Finland, Sweden, the Netherlands, Spain, and Israel. SRH has also been used for comparisons among various population subgroups associated with gender (e.g., Idler 2003), race (e.g., Ferraro et al. 1997), educational attainment (e.g., Subramanian, et al. 2010), socioeconomic status (e.g., Dowd and Zajacova 2007, Goodman 1999), poverty status (e.g., McDonough and Berglund 2003), and immigration status (e.g., Kulla et al. 2010). These studies further discussed SRH as a measure for health disparities across comparison groups.

8.3 Theoretical Evidence: Cognitive Processes Pertinent to Responding to SRH in Surveys

While the practical utility of SRH is supported by empirical evidence, its theoretical understanding is limited (Davies and Ware 1981, Jylhä 2009, 2011). In this section, we examine the measurement process of SRH as potential grounds for understanding SRH's utility. Because information on SRH comes from respondents directly, examining the cognitive strategies required to respond to SRH will provide insight into how SRH exhibits such a powerful measurement utility (Jylhä 2009, 2011). It may appear that cognitive psychology and the measurement of SRH are far apart from each other. However, survey respondents carry out cognitive tasks of judging what a given question intends to ask and what appropriate answers may be. Consequently, cognitive psychology has been employed as a major tool for systematically understanding measurement properties of survey items through the Cognitive Aspects of Survey Methodology (CASM) movement over the last several decades (Belli et al. 2007, Jabine et al. 1984, Jobe and Mingay 1991, Schwarz 2007, Tourangeau 2004). The CASM integrates preexisting cognitive psychology theories into survey methodology. The most important framework from the CASM is the four-step model which illustrates the following steps in survey respondent's cognitive processes (Hastie and Carlston 1980, Tourangeau 1984): (i) question comprehension, (ii) memory retrieval, (iii) judgment between information sought and retrieved, and (iv) reporting/editing a response. This model was specifically suggested for methodological studies of SRH by Schechter (1994) and Singer (1994). Jylhä (2009) also suggested a similar model for SRH.

The first cognitive step, question comprehension, requires understanding of health as a concept, the meaning of health status and the response scale being employed. Conceptualization of health is an essential element to understand this cognitive step. Although health is not an unusual topic in everyday conversations, how one defines health may very well differ from how the next person defines it. There have been a number of models attempting to conceptualize health, where each model has a different emphasis. We will examine a few models from Larson (1999). The first is the medical model, an older but widely used approach. Under this model, health is defined as the absence of disease or disability. While this model appears to incorporate narrow aspects of health, this is dominantly held in the United States. The second and newer model is proposed by the WHO and describes health as "a state of complete physical, mental, and social well-being and not merely the absence of disease or infirmity" (World Health Organization 1948). It takes a holistic approach to health by reflecting what surrounds a person. Additionally, there are the wellness model and the environmental model that give rise to other aspects of health (Larson 1999). These models can be understood with Figure 8.1, where medical, psychological, social, economic, and spiritual conditions all influence health status. Of course, these conditions interact and overlap with one another, and multiple layers of components under each condition further complicate the conceptualization. Also, note

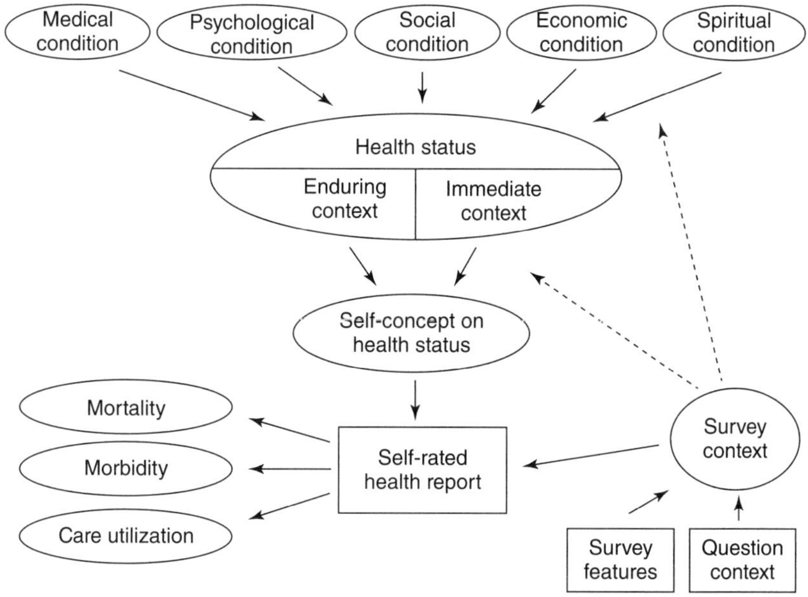

FIGURE 8.1 Survey measurement process of self-rated health.

that SRH itself influences these conditions. Each model places differing levels of importance on each condition in determining health. However, these models individually or collectively do not explain what the reality of health encompasses completely. This corresponds to the previous discussion that all determinants of SRH in combination can explain only a fraction of its variance.

Another necessary element in comprehending the SRH question is the meaning of health status. It has been hypothesized that there are two different views that explain how people interpret the meaning of health status (Bailis et al. 2003). The first view relevant to health perceptions is enduring and static. The SRH literature indicates that major negative medical incidents do not necessarily lead people to lower the rating of their own health status (Wilcox et al. 1996). The fact that objective health measures cannot explain SRH successfully and that the predictability of SRH for one's survival is higher than that of objective measures suggest that respondents hold certain views about their health status that helps maintain stable responses to SRH over time. In this view, beliefs about one's own health and future plans for health behaviors can affect how people perceive their health status.

Alternatively, health status reflects an immediate and spontaneous view used in medical sociology (Potter and Wetherell 1987). Literature cited earlier has linked verifiable objective medical factors with health status and shown that changes in those factors may cause changes in health status reports to a certain degree. Under this context, beliefs about health or expectations about future health do not influence what people perceive as their health status. In reality, these two views are used simultaneously (Bailis et al. 2003, Jylhä 1994).

Of course, each contributes to determining health status at differing levels that also differ from one person to another.

SRH can be understood as a type of self-concept, a theory about one's own self (Epstein 1973). This reflects how an individual sees him- or herself, how other people actually see the individual, and how the individual believes others see him or her (Rosenberg 1990). (Although Bailis and his colleagues (2003) linked the self-concept only with the enduring context of health, we deviate from it here to reflect the self-concept literature that defines the self as fluid yet consistent (Rogers 1951)). Under this perspective, a person first establishes a self-perception on his or her own health status with stable attributes. As people often feel a basic need to keep this self-concept consistent, this perception is not likely to fluctuate much. However, this perception may change over time as new information provides sufficient evidence to warrant a reorganization of one's self-concept of personal health.

Answering the SRH question also requires respondents to comprehend the meaning of its response categories. While there is no universally agreed response scale for SRH, we will use the excellent-to-poor scale as an example. It is obvious that how one defines excellent health does not necessarily correspond to how the next person defines it, as responses are likely to be influenced by individual characteristics, as well as cultural background. Comprehension and interpretation of the response scale is tightly linked to reporting, the final cognitive step. We will discuss more on this with the reporting step later.

Conceptualizing health and comprehending the SRH question are prerequisites for a memory search for relevant experiences and other information. Searching for information corresponds to the second cognitive step: retrieval. On the basis of respondents' understanding of the information sought by the question, they search through their cognitive space for the relevant information. This is likely to be the step where the richness of the health information that respondents incorporate in assessing their health is determined. As indicated through its strong utility in predicting survival, the breadth and depth of information SRH provides can be fuller than what objective or clinical health measures alone can provide.

Once relevant information is retrieved, respondents weigh and integrate it to make a decision about their current health. This is the third cognitive step involving judgment. At this stage, respondents may not have a crystallized idea about their answers but are likely to have some vague idea about what to report. There are limited and inconclusive findings about what criteria respondents use to judge their health. Some suggest that respondents base their SRH reporting on negative health, its severity and duration, and restrictions imposed by negative health (Manderbacka 1998). Physical health has been suggested as being a more important criterion than other types of health in doing so (Groves et al. 1992). Yet, others suggest SRH involves a complex process of identification and adaptation using various criteria (McMullen and Luborsky 2006). There is also discussion on whether respondents assess their health in comparison to other people. With elderly persons, SRH rates are not as sensitive to increases in objective health problems (Heller et al. 2009, Liang et al. 2005). This suggests that older people are more likely to compare themselves to their age peers when evaluating their health (Cheng et al. 2007, Idler et al. 2004). These can be further explained with the belief-sampling model (Tourangeau et al. 2000), which assumes that people are likely to have a pool of considerations or beliefs for a given topic. When asked about the topic in a survey setting, they consult with a sample of these considerations, instead of all considerations, in formulating their response. For SRH, respondents may consider a wide range of the components discussed earlier, sample those most relevant to their personal belief-system or the given question, and then construct their answers.

The final cognitive step comes as respondents edit and report their answers. The information from the judgment step should be constructed into an acceptable form that can be mapped onto one of the given response categories. For SRH, respondents are limited to a set of response categories such as: "excellent," "very good," "good," "fair," and "poor." These simple classifications of health status certainly do not represent the full spectrum of how people assess their health, and respondents will often need to edit their answers in order to connect them to the most proximate available answer category through complex cognitive processing (Jylhä 1994). If a different scale is employed, they may be engaged in different editing tasks. In certain cases, such as a survey of new employees, respondents may edit their answers to SRH in order to present themselves more desirably to the researcher.

As examined earlier, although it may appear as a simple task, respondents are engaged in complex cognitive steps when answering questions about their health, although it may not be done deliberately or consciously (Jylhä 2009, 2011). Of course, the level of effort for the tasks differs by the level of saliency and importance assigned to various aspects of health as suggested in Figure 8.1. Additionally, the level of saliency and importance of detailed components of health are likely reflected in the response. For example, if a respondent views physical health, compared to mental health, as a more influential factor for evaluating overall health, he or she is likely to make an effort to tap into information related to his or her physical health and use that information more than information related to mental health. The fact that respondents proceed with such complex processes to integrate all health information relevant for the question and also to themselves may be the reason why SRH provides such strong utility for understanding overall health status.

8.4 Measurement Issues for Self-Rated Health

From a survey measurement perspective, SRH is the type of question that is not expected to provide ideal measurement properties, not only because it deals with a general concept but also because it relies on self-reports, all of which make the item highly susceptible to subjective interpretations as examined above. Fienberg et al. (1985) have noted that "No other single question provokes so much discussion among analysts." In light of this, SRH can be viewed as an incomplete source of data in spite of its utility. In this section, we will examine measurement issues of SRH arising due to the survey context and will link back to the cognitive processes discussed above. While this by no means is an exhaustive list, it covers a wide range of issues.

8.4.1 GLOBAL HEALTH MEASURE VERSUS SPECIFIC HEALTH DOMAIN MEASURE

SRH has been discussed as a single global measure thus far. Some surveys, while still using the same general rating scale, ask about specific domains of health using a form of SRH that employs multiple items. For example, the National Latino and Asian American Study (NLAAS) includes separate items on general physical and mental health. They ask, "How would you rate your overall physical health?" and then "How would you rate your overall mental health?" Also, the Consumer Assessment of Healthcare Providers and Systems (CAHPS) Clinician and Group Survey asks mental health questions separately from general health by adding "In general, how would you rate your overall mental or emotional health?" after the global SRH question that does not specify a certain health domain.

Certainly, asking questions on specific domains may appear attractive given that it may reduce the level of subjectivity in the global health measure. The practice in NLAAS, in particular, may have been motivated by the fact that respondents tend to place greater importance on physical health than mental health when evaluating overall health with SRH, because this practice does not let a specific domain of health dominate the assessment of overall health. However, using these measures on specific health domains is likely to limit understanding of someone's overall health, because these measures combined together may still capture a narrower aspect of health than the global health measure may capture (Maddox and Douglass 1973, Mossey and Shapiro 1982, Verbrugge and Ascione 1987). Asking the status of specific health domains separately may impose artificial restrictions on respondents' health-related cognitive space, limiting their interpretation of health and retrieval of related information. Consequently, the combined utility of ratings on separate health domains may not be as comprehensive as, and comparable to, the value of the global measure for predicting subsequent mortality.

8.4.2 RESPONSE SCALE

The five-point Likert-type scale is the standard choice for SRH, although some studies have used a four-point scale instead, especially those conducted before SRH established its popularity as a survey item (see Table 1 in Idler and Benyamini 1997). The five-point scale ranging from "excellent" to "poor" is popular among surveys conducted in the United States. Some surveys, those conducted outside of the United States in particular, tend to use some other variations of the five-point scale, such as "very good," "good," "neither good nor bad," "bad," and "very bad," which is supported by the WHO. Although the WHO version may appear preferable given its obvious balance in the categories, there is no empirical evidence demonstrating it (Jürges et al. 2008). Summarizing one's health status into one of these preset categories is not an easy task, as one's interpretation of, for example, "excellent" health may mean something completely different from the next person's interpretation. One may think that his or her health cannot be excellent unless he or she can set a new marathon record, while another person thinks that his or her health is excellent because he or she does not have any illness, works out regularly and maintains a healthy diet.

Likert-type SRH response scales, regardless of their specificity, implicitly assume some form of linearity across categories. However, the cognitive spacing between two adjacent categories may not be the same, unlike numeric rating scales. For example, Johnson et al. (1997) showed that the gap between "fair" and "poor" health was larger than the gap between "good" and "fair" health within respondents' cognitions across multiple race/ethnic groups.

Alternatively, there is a different measure of health status used in EQ-5D which uses a category rating thermometer. On a scale from 0 to 100, where 0 means the worst imaginable health state and 100 means the best, respondents are asked to rate their health. While this response scale is numeric and linear, it is likely to come with its own measurement challenges. This scale may appear foreign especially to those who have lower numeracy skills, causing additional cognitive difficulties.

8.4.3 SELF-REPORTS VERSUS PROXY REPORTS

By definition, SRH implies self-reports as an information source. In survey practice, however, respondents are often asked to report for someone else in the family or household. For example, the NHIS household module includes questions about all household members, but interviews only the household informant. This makes the informant a proxy respondent for other household members. In the NHIS, SRH is included in this household module. The informant provides information about his or her own general health as a self-respondent and about all other household members as a proxy respondent. The nature, amount, breadth, and depth of information about the informant himself or herself are likely to be vastly different than the information about someone else. Because of this, whether the needed information is about the general health of one's own self or someone else affects the retrieval process directly.

There are studies supporting proxy response. Spouses or close family members appear to be able to provide valid health-related information (Lee et al. 2004). Brissette et al. (2003) used interviewers' rating of the respondents' general health status to predict mortality and found the prediction to be successful. However, the response scale used by the interviewers was different from that of a typical SRH measure, which limits its applicability for proxy responses on SRH. The utility of proxy response to SRH will require additional research (see also Chapter 14).

8.4.4 QUESTION CONTEXT

All human judgment is dependent on a context (Schwarz 1999). In a survey setting, respondents typically make judgments about question items on the spot.

Anything related to the setting up to the point when a specific question is asked may contribute to the context. We define this as the question context. It can include survey features, such as interview mode, the presence and attributes of an interviewer, survey topics, preceding questions, question wordings, and response scales, as well as external factors such as the environmental setting and the historical background of an interview, and respondents' characteristics (Braun 2003, Schuman 1992, Schwarz 1994, 1996, Schwarz and Clore 1983).

While there is a myriad of elements that can be discussed under question context, we will focus on the question order because this is the feature that can be experimented with and controlled within a given survey condition. In this sense, question contexts are created by preceding questions that are semantically related. Hence, it is not surprising to find that the terms, "context effects" and "order effects," are used interchangeably in the survey research literature (e.g., Schuman and Presser 1981, Part II of Schwarz and Sudman 1992).

Typically, survey questions asking about a general concept are open to subjective interpretations and hence are more prone to survey context (Payne 1951, Schwarz 1999, Schwarz et al. 1991, Tourangeau et al. 1991). SRH fits into this class. As shown in Figure 8.1, the survey context can potentially affect all SRH measurement processes. Respondents may not always have preformed ideas about what health means or their health status, and the particular context in which an SRH question is presented may serve as a cue as to how to cognitively process the SRH response task.

Currently, the literature recommends placing SRH before specific and objective health questions in order to avoid the potential context effects that these items might create (e.g., Bowling 2005, Keller and Ware 1996, McColl et al. 2001). This is practiced in many surveys, including the U.S. Behavioral Risk Factor Surveillance System (BRFSS) and various quality-of-life measures, such as the SF-12 and SF-36. This coincides with the general notion held in the survey methodology literature that it is advantageous to place a question about a general concept before specific ones (McFarland 1981). There is also an opposing view. As discussed by Fayers and Sprangers (2002), the European Organization for Research and Treatment of Cancer (EORTC) QLQ-C30, a quality-of-life instrument for cancer patients introduced by Aaronson et al. (1993), locates SRH at the end of the questionnaire. This is done intentionally to promote the use of answers to preceding questions as a frame of reference for answering SRH. However, the existing literature on the SRH question context does not provide clear guidance, as they fail to show meaningful context effects (e.g., Barry et al. 1996, Bowling and Windsor 2008, Crossley and Kennedy 2002).

The existence of question context effects suggests that respondents are not only a provider of elicited information but also a user of accumulated information in the survey process. Respondents are likely to use the most accessible information in their cognitive space to answer SRH, regardless of the source. It may come from their memories pertinent to health or the subtle nonhealth-related elements in their interactions with the interviewer. Jylhä (1994) qualitatively showed that SRH reports are a context-bound phenomenon.

As discussed earlier, it has also been suggested that the contexts include a broader spectrum of elements surrounding a question echoing the salience model (Schuman and Presser 1981). Couper et al. (2007) showed that question contexts created by visual cues in a web survey affected SRH reports. Specifically, when SRH was accompanied by an image of a healthy person jogging, respondents in their experiment reported poorer health than when the SRH question was asked while presenting an image of a sick person in a hospital bed.

Cross-Cultural Comparability. SRH has been administered to people from a wide range of cultural backgrounds and translated into many different languages. This certainly provides researchers an opportunity to compare health status across multiple populations conveniently (Appels et al. 1996, Bardage et al. 2005, Borrell and Dallo 2008, Eurostat 1997, Ferraro 1993, Goodman 1999, Idler 2003, OECD 2010). However, the measurement properties of SRH have been examined mostly with English-speaking populations (e.g., Barry et al. 1996, Bowling and Windsor 2008, Crossley and Kennedy 2002) or with rather homogeneous groups of northern Europeans, such as Finns (e.g., Miilunpalo et al. 1997, Vuorisalmi et al. 2005), Swedes (e.g., Burström and Fredlund 2001), Dutch and Lithuanians (e.g., Appels et al. 1996). Therefore, whether the strong utility of SRH in the current literature is applicable beyond these populations is uncertain, and cross-cultural and cross-linguistic comparability of SRH cannot be guaranteed. As discussed previously, understanding the SRH measurement mechanism is not a trivial task, and adding a cross-cultural dimension makes the task more complicated (Landrine and Klonoff 1994, Pachter 1994).

Various measurement issues examined above are of concern in their own right, but when they interact with respondents' cultural background or interview language, they become even more important, because they introduce noncomparability among study populations. There are many layers of issues with SRH when it comes to its implementation with diverse populations. All elements in Figure 8.1, as well as survey response cognitive processes, become hurdles for comparability. It is likely that health is conceptualized differently across cultures and is a more salient topic or includes a wider spectrum of considerations in some cultures than in others (Bailis, et al. 2003, Idler et al. 1999, Kazarian and Evans 2001, Krause and Jay 1994, Larson 1999, Nisbett 2003, Pannenborg 1979, Pachter 1994). What is perceived as fair health in one cultural group may be perceived as poor health by a different group. Moreover, if the SRH item is to be translated, there may be no comparable words for the response categories to retain the same measurement properties. Given these issues, it is not surprising to find that studies examining the cross-cultural validity of SRH provide inconclusive findings (e.g., Jürges et al. 2008, Jylhä et al. 1998, Leung et al. 2006, Liu and Zhang 2004, McGee et al. 1999, Pu et al. 2011, Sadana et al. 2002, Wagner et al. 1998).

In the United States, SRH has been used to study health disparities of racial/ethnic minorities, such as the Hispanic population (e.g., Borrell and Dallo 2008, Kandula et al. 2007, Nelson et al. 2003, Salomon et al. 2004, Shaw and Pickett 2011, Shetterly et al. 1996). There are very few methodological studies examining the utility of SRH with Hispanics, and those that are available provide evidence against comparability (e.g., Finch et al. 2002, Nelson et al. 2003, Viruell-Fuentes et al. 2010). Unfortunately, the data in these studies are methodologically limited, because some included only English-speaking Hispanics. The utility of SRH for the United States Hispanic population is yet to be verified.

It has been shown that simple changes in the question context may interact with survey interview language. In experiments conducted by Lee and Grant (2009) and Lee et al. (2014), those interviewed in Spanish due to limited English proficiency reported much better health when SRH was asked after a series of specific health condition questions (hence, within a health context) than when asked as the first health-related question (hence, without a health context). However, the question contexts did not influence reports of English-speaking respondents. Lee and Schwarz (2014) further examined this with the Hispanic and non-Hispanic population aged 50 years and older and found the same phenomenon: Hispanic ethnicity interacted with SRH question contexts as the Hispanic respondents reported significantly better health on SRH within, rather than without a health context, while the non-Hispanic respondents reported consistently regardless of contexts. Therefore, the difference in health status between Hispanics and non-Hispanics changed depending on the contexts. The SRH question context also affected the mortality prediction for Hispanics. For non-Hispanics, those who reported positive health on SRH were more likely to survive in subsequent time points than those who reported negative health regardless of SRH contexts. This confirms SRH's utility as a predictor of subsequent mortality. However, for Hispanics, the context mattered. When SRH was asked within a health context, the mortality rates differed between those who reported positive and negative health. When SRH was asked without a health context, on the other hand, subsequent mortality was not different between those who reported positive and negative health. In sum, depending on the SRH question context, not only the conclusions on group-level health status differed but also the magnitudes of health disparities were found to be artificially increased or decreased. Additionally, the utility of SRH to predict mortality may not be realized. This means that the cross-cultural comparability of SRH can be dampened by simple changes in question context. See Chapter 10 for additional discussion of cross-cultural measurement issues.

8.5 Conclusion

While being exposed to many sources of measurement errors, SRH still is a useful tool with impressive properties for understanding the general health of the population. It is simple, easy, and convenient to administer, yet it appears to capture a more inclusive range of domains relevant to health than do numerous classical objective health risk factor questions. Moreover, it allows us to predict future health outcomes and health care utilization. In sum, it provides sustained and relevant health information to researchers and policy makers.

Nevertheless, what SRH really measures is still unclear (e.g., Bailis et al. 2003, Fylkesnes and Forde 1992, Krause and Jay 1994) and current survey design practices for SRH are disorganized and disjointed. Obviously, naïvely assuming that measurement properties will be equivalent without considering specifically how, and within which context, SRH is asked will be problematic. On the basis of the measurement issues examined earlier, it appears that SRH may function best when asked (i) as a global item rather than as multiple items concerned with separate health domains, (ii) about respondents themselves rather than someone else, and (iii) within a health context. However, note that this is a limited view bounded by what has been examined in the literature. Whether to use a balanced or unbalanced response scale for the standard version of SRH does not appear critical. While there is no best practice that can be recommended for administering SRH in surveys as of yet, there are research venues that may serve as a stepping stone for improving our understanding of SRH as a measurement tool. Examining respondents' understanding of SRH as a survey question and how they formulate answers, and how these processes may potentially vary across various populations continue to be important foci for future research (Jylhä 2009, 2011 Lee et al. 2014). Continued research will not only allow us to better utilize the measurement qualities of SRH but also further enhance our understanding of population health in general.

REFERENCES

Aaronson N, Ahmedzai S, Bergman B, Bullinger M, Cull A, Duez NJ, Filiberti A, Flechtner H, Fleishman SB, de Haes JC. The European Organization for Research and Treatment of Cancer QLQ-C30: a quality-of-life instrument for use in international clinical trials in oncology. J Natl Cancer Inst 1993;85(5):365–376.

Andrew DH, Dulin PL. The relationship between self-reported health and mental health problems among older adults in New Zealand: experiential avoidance as a moderator. Aging Ment Health 2007;11(5):596–603.

Appels A, Bosma H, Graubauskas V, Gostautas A, Sturmans F. Self-rated health and mortality in a Lithuanian and a Dutch population. Soc Sci Med 1996;42(5):681–689.

Bailis D, Segall A, Chipperfield J. Two views of self-rated general health status. Soc Sci Med 2003;56:203–217.

Bailis DS, Segall A, Mahon MJ, Chipperfield JG, Dunn EM. Perceived control in relation to socioeconomic and behavioural resources for health. Soc Sci Med 2001;52:1661–1676.

Bardage C, Pluijm SMF, Pedersen NL, Deeg DJH, Jylhä M, Noale M, Blumstein T, Otero A. Self-rated health among older adults: a cross-national comparison. Eur J Aging 2005;2:149–158.

Baron-Epel O. Self-rated health. In: Anderson NB, editor. *Encyclopedia of Health and Behavior*. Thousand Oaks, CA: Sage; 2004. p 714–719.

Baron-Epel O, Kaplan G. General subjective health status or age-related health status: does it make a difference? Soc Sci Med 2001;53:1373–1381.

Baron-Epel O, Weinstein R, Haviv-Mesika A, Garty-Sandalon N, Green MS. Individual-level analysis of social capital and health: a comparison of Arab and Jewish Israelis. Soc Sci Med 2008;66(4):900–910.

Barry M, Walker-Corkery E, Chang Y, Tyll L, Cherkin D, Fowler F. Measurement of overall and disease-specific health status: does the order of questionnaires make a difference? J Health Ser Res Polic 1996;1:20–27.

Belli RF, Conrad FG, Wright DB. Cognitive psychology and survey methodology: nurturing the continuing dialogue between disciplines. Appl Cognitive Psychol 2007;21(2):141–144.

Ben-Ezra M, Shmotkin D. Predictors of mortality in the old-old in Israel: the cross-sectional and longitudinal aging study. J Am Geriatr Soc 2006;54(6):906–911.

Benyamini Y, Idler E. Community studies reporting association between self rated health and mortality: additional studies, 1995–1998. Res Aging 1999;21(3):392–401.

Benyamini Y, Leventhal E, Leventhal H. Self-assessments of health: what do people know that predicts their mortality? Res Aging 1999;221(3):457–500.

Bergner M, Rothman ML. Health status measures: an overview and guide for selection. Ann Rev Public Health 1987;8:191–210.

Bond J, Dickinson H, Matthews F, Jagger C, Brayne C. Self-rated health status as a predictor of health, functional and cognitive impairments: a longitudinal cohort study. Eur J Aging 2006;3:193–206.

Borg W, Kristensen TS. Social class and self-rated health: can the gradient be explained by differences in life style or work environment? Soc Sci Med 2000;51:1019–1030.

Borrell L, Dallo F. Self-rated health and race among Hispanic and non-Hispanic adults. J Immigr Minor Health 2008;10(3):229–238.

Bowling A. Techniques of questionnaire design. In: Bowing A, Shah E, editors. *Handbook of Health Research Methods: Investigation, Measurement and Analysis*. Berkshire, UK: McGraw-Hill; 2005. p 394–427.

Bowling A, Windsor J. The effects of question order and response-choice on self-rated health status in the English Longitudinal Study of Aging (ELSA). *J Epidemiol & Comm Health* 2008;62:81–85.

Braun M. Communication and social cognition. In: Harkenss JA, Van de Vijver FJR, Mohler PP, editors. *Cross-Cultural Survey Methods*. Hoboken, NJ: John Wiley & Sons; 2003. p 57–67.

Bratter JL, Gorman BK. Does multiracial matter? A study of racial disparities in self-rated health. Demography 2011;48(1):127–152.

Brissette I, Leventhal H, Leventhal EA. Observer ratings of health and sickness: can other people tell us anything about our health that we don't already know? Health Psychol 2003;22(5):471–478.

Burström B, Fredlund P. Self-rated health: is it a good predictor of subsequent mortality among adults in lower as well as in higher social classes? J Epidemiol Commun Health 2001;55:836–840.

Cheng ST, Chan ACM. Filial piety and psychological well-being in well older Chinese. J Gerontol B Psychol Sci Soc Sci 2006;61(5):P262–P269.

Cheng S, Fung H, Chan A. Maintaining self-rated health through socla comparison in old age. J Gerontol B Psychol Sci Soc Sci 2007;62(5):P277–P285.

Christian LM, Glaser R, Porter K, Malarkey WB, Beversdorf D, Kiecolt-Glaser JK. Poorer self-rated health is associated with elevated inflammatory markers among older adults. Psychoneuroendocrinology 2011;36:1495–1504.

Cott CA, Gignac MAM, Badley EM. Determinants of self-rated health for Canadians with chronic disease and disability. J Epidemiol Community Health 1999;53:732–736.

Couper MC, Conrad F, Tourangeau T. Visual context effects in Web surveys. Public Opin Q 2007;71(4):623–634.

Crossley T, Kennedy S. The reliability of self-assessed health status. J Health Econ 2002;21(4):643–658.

Damián J, Pastor-Barriuso R, Valderrama-Gama E. Factors associated with self-rated health in older people living in institutions. BMC Geriatr 2008;8:5.

Davies AR, Ware JE. *Measuring Health Perceptions in the Health Insurance Experiments.* Rand: Santa Monica, CA; 1981.

DeBruin A, Picavet H, Nossikov A. Health interview surveys. In: *Towards International Harmonization of Methods and Instruments.* Regional Publication European Series No. 58. Geneva, Switzerland: World Health Organization; 1996.

DeSalvo K, Fan V, McDonell M, Fihn S. Predicting mortality and health care utilization with a single question. Health Services Res 2005;40(4):1234–1246.

DeSalvo KB, Fisher WP, Tran K, Bloser N, Merrill W, Peabody J. Assessing measurement properties of two single-item general health measures. Qual Life Res 2006;15:191–201.

Dowd JB, Zajacova A. Does the predictive power of self-rated health for subsequent mortality risk vary by socioeconomic status in the US? Int J Epidemiol 2007;36(6):1214–1221.

Dwyer DS, Mitchell OS. Health problems as determinants of retirement: are self-rated measures endogenous? J Health Econ 1999;18(2):173–193.

Dzekedzeke K, Siziya S, Fylkesnes K. The impact of HIV infection and adult mortality in some communities in Zambia: a cohort study. Trop Med Int Health 2008;13(2):152–161.

Elinson J. Introductory remarks. Paper presented at the 1993 NCHS Conference on the Cognitive Aspects of Self-Reported Health Status; Hyattsville, MD; 1994.

Epstein S. The self-concept revisited, or a theory of a theory. Am Psychol 1973;28:404–416.

Eurostat. *Self-Reported Health in the European Community. Statistics in Focus, Population and Social Conditions.* 1024-4352. 1997.

Farkas J, Kosnik M, Zaletel-Kragelj L, Flezar M, Suskovic S, Lainscak M. Distribution of self-rated health and association with clinical parameters in patients with chronic obstructive pulmonary disease. Wien Klin Wochenschr 2009;121:297–302.

Fayers P, Sprangers M. Understanding self-rated health. Lancet 2002;359:187–188.

Fienberg SE, Loftus EF, Tanur JM. Cognitive aspects of health survey methodology: an overview. Milbank Q 1985;63:547–564.

Ferraro KF. Are black older adults health-pessimistic? J Health Soc Behav 1993;34:201–214.

Ferraro K, Farmer M, Wybraniec J. Health trajectories: long term dynamics among black and white adults. J Health Soc Behav 1997;38:38–54.

Finch B, Hummer R, Reindl M, Vega W. Validity of self-rated health among Latino(a)s. Am J Epidemiol 2002;155(8):755–759.

Ford J, Spallek M, Dobson A. Self-rated health and a healthy lifestyle are the most important predictors of survival in elderly women. Age Ageing 2008;37:194–200.

Frankenberg E, Jones NR. Self-rated health and mortality: does the relationship extend to a low income setting? J Health Soc Behav 2004;45(4):441–452.

Franks P, Gold MR, Fiscella K. Sociodemographics, self-rated health, and mortality in the US. Soc Sci Med 2003;56(12):2505–2514.

Fylkesnes K, Forde OH. Determinants and dimensions involved in self-evaluation of health. Soc Sci Med 1992;35(3):271–279.

Gele AA, Harsløf I. Types of social capital resources and self-rated health among the Norwegian adult population. I J Equity Health 2010;9:8.

Gold M, Franks P, Erickson P. Assessing the health of a nation: the predictive validity of a preference-based measure and self-rated health. Med Care 1996;34(2):163–177.

Goldstein MS, Siegel JM, Boyer R. Predicting changes in perceived health status. Am J Public Health 1984;74:611–614.

Goodman E. The role of socioeconomic status gradients in explaining differences in US adolescents' health. Am J Public Health 1999;89(10):1522–1528.

Groves RM, Fultz NH, Martin E. Direct questioning about comprehension in a survey setting. In: Tanur JM, editor. *Questions About Questions: Iniquties into the Cognitive Bases of Surveys*. New York: Russell Sage; 1992. p 49–61.

Hastie R, Carlston DE. Theoretical issues in person memory. In: Hastie R, Ostrom TM, Ebbesen EB, Wyer Jr. RS, Hamilton DL, Carlston DE, eds. *Person Memory: The Cognitive Basis of Social Perception*. Hillsdale, New Jersey: Erlbaum; 1980. pp. 1–54.

Hays RD, Kallich JD, Mapes DL, Coons SJ, Amin N, Carter WB, Kamberg C. *Kidney Disease Quality of Life Short Form (KDQOLSFTM). Version 1.2: A Manual for Use and Scoring*. Rand: Santa Monica, CA; 1996.

Heller DA, Ahern FM, Pringle KE, Brown TV. Among older adults, the responsiveness of self-rated health changes in Carlson Comorbidity was moderated by age and baseline comorbidity. J Clin Epidemiol 2009;62(2):177–187.

Hennessy C, Moriatry D, Zack M, Sherr P, Brackbill R. Measuring health-related quality of life for public health surveillance. Public Health Rep 1994;109(5):665–672.

Idler E. Discussion: gender differences in self-rated health, in mortality, and in the relationship between the two. Gerontologist 2003;43(3):372–375.

Idler E, Angel RJ. Self-rated health and mortality in the NHANES-I epidemiologic follow-up study. Am J Public Health 1990;80:446–452.

Idler E, Benyamini Y. Self-rated health and mortality: a review of twenty-seven community studies. J Health Soc Behav 1997;38(1):21–37.

Idler E, Hudson S, Leventhal H. The meanings of self-ratings of health: a qualitative and quantitative approach. Res Aging 1999;21:458–476.

Idler EL, Kasl SV. Self-ratings of health: do they also predict change in functional ability? J Gerontol B Psychol Sci Soc Sci 1995;50B(6):S344–S353.

Idler E, Kasl S, Lemke J. Self-evaluated health and mortality among the elderly in New Haven, Connecticut, and Iowa and Washington counties, Iowa, 1982–1986. Am J Epidemiol 1990;131(1):91–103.

Idler E, Leventhal H, McLaughlin J, Leventhal E. In sickeness by not in health: self-ratings, identity, and mortality. J Health Soc Behav 2004;45(4):336–356.

Jabine TB, Straf ML, Tanur JM, Tourangeau R. *Cognitive Aspects of Survey Methodology: Building a Bridge Between Disciplines*. Washington, DC: National Academy Press; 1984. p 73–100.

Jobe JB, Mingay DJ. Cognition and survey measurement: history and overview. App Cognit Psychol 1991;5:172–192.

Johnson TP, O'Rourke D, Chavez N, Sudman S, Warnecke R, Lacey L, Horm J. Social cognition and response to survey question among culturally diverse populations. In: Lyberg LE, Biemer PP, Collins M, et al., editors. *Survey Measurement and Process Quality*. New York: John Wiley & Sons; 1997. p 87–114.

Johnson TP, Stallones L, Garrity TF, Marx MB. Components of self-rated health among adults: analysis of multiple data sources. Int Q Community Health Educ 1990;11(1):29–41.

Jürges H. True health vs response styles: exploring cross-country differences in self-reported health. Health Econ 2007;16(2):163–178.

Jürges H, Avendano M, Mackenbach JP. Are different measures of self-rated health comparable? An assessment in five European countries. Eur J Epidemiol 2008;23:773–781.

Jylhä M. Self-rated health revisited: exploring survey interview episodes with elderly respondents. Soc Sci Med 1994;39(7):983–990.

Jylhä M. What is self-rated health and why does it predict morality? Towards a unified conceptual model. Soc Sci Med 2009;69:307–316.

Jylhä M. Self-rated health and subjective survival probabilities as predictors of mortality. In: Rogers RG, Crimmins EM, editors. *International Handbook of Adult Mortality. International Handbooks of Population 2*. New York: Springer Science + Business Media; 2011. p 329–344.

Jylhä M, Guralnik JM, Ferrucci L, Jokela J, Heikkinen E. Is self-rated health comparable across cultures and genders? J Gerontol Ser B 1998;53(3):S144–S152.

Jylhä M, Volpato S, Guralnik JA. Self-rated health showed a graded association with frequently used biomarkers in a large population sample. J Clin Epidemiol 2006;59(5):465–471.

Kandula N, Lauderdale D, Baker D. Differences in self-rated health among Asians, Latinos, and non-Hispanic whites: the role of language and nativity. Ann Epidemiol 2007;17(3):191–198.

Kaplan GA, Camacho T. Perceived health and mortality: a nine-year follow-up of the human population laboratory cohort. Am J Epidemiol 1983;117(3):292–304.

Kawachi I, Kennedy BP, Glass R. Social capital and self-rated health: a contextual analysis. Am J Public Health 1999;89:1187–1193.

Kazarian SS, Evans DR. *Handbook of Cultural Health Psychology*. San Diego, CA: Academic Press; 2001.

Keller S, Ware J. Questions and answers about SF-36 and SF-12. Medical Outcomes Trust Bull 1996;4:3.

Kramers PG. The ECHI project: health indicators for the European Community. Eur J Public Health 2003;13(suppl 3):101–106.

Krause N, Jay G. What global self-rated health items measure. Med Care 1994;32(9):930–942.

Kulla GE, Ekman S-L, Heikkilä AK, Sarvimäki AM. Differences in self-rated health among older immigrants—a comparison between older Finland-Swedes and Finns in Sweden. Scand J Public Health 2010;38(1):25–31.

Larson JS. The conceptualization of health. Med Care Res Rev 1999;56(2):123–136.

Larsson D, Hemmingsson T, Allebeck P, Lundberg I. Self-rated health and mortality among young men: what is the relation and how may it be explained? Scand J Public Health 2002;30(4):259–266.

Landrine H, Klonoff EA. The African American Acculturation Scale: development, reliability, and validity. J Black Psychol 1994;20(2):104–127.

La Rue A, Bank L, Jarvik U, Hetland M. Health in old age: how do physicians' ratings and self-ratings compare? J Gerontol 1979;34(5):687–691.

Lee S, Grant D. The effect of question order on self-rated general health status in multilingual survey context. Am J Epidemiol 2009;169(12):1525–1530.

Lee S, Mathiowetz N, Tourangeau R. Perceptions of disability: the effect of self- and proxy response. J Official Statist 2004;20(4):671–686.

Lee S, Schwarz N. Question context and priming meaning of health: effect on differences in self-rated health between Hispanics and non-Hispanic Whites. Am J Public Health 2014;104(1):179–185.

Lee S, Schwarz N, Streja L. Culture-sensitive question order effects of self-rated health between older Hispanic and non-Hispanic adults in the United States. J Aging Health 2014. Published online before print.

Lesser GT. Social and productive activities in elderly people. Self rated health is important predictor of mortality. Br Med J 2000;320(7228):185.

Leung PW, Kwong SL, Tang CP, Ho TP, Hung SF, Lee CC, Hong SL, Chiu CM, Liu WS. Test-retest reliability and criterion validity of the Chinese version of the CBCL, TRF, and YSR. J Child Psychol Psychiatry 2006;47:970–973.

Liang J, Shaw BA, Krause N, Bennett JM, Kobayashi E, Fukata T, Sugihara Y. How does self-assessed health change with age? A study of older adults in Japan. J Gerontol B Psychol Sci Soc Sci 2005;60(4):S224–S232.

Lima-Costa MF, Cesar CC, Chor D, Proietti FA. Self-rated health compared with objectively measured health status as a tool for mortality risk screening in older adults: 10-year follow-up of the Bambuí Cohort Study of Aging. Am J Epidemiol 2012;175(3):228–235.

Linn BS, Linn MW. Objective and self-assessed health in the old and very old. Soc Sci Med 1980;14(4):311–315.

Litwin H. Social networks and self-rated health: a cross-cultural examination among older Israelis. J Ageing Health 2006;18(3):335–358.

Liu G, Zhang Z. Sociodemographic differentials of the self-rated health of the oldest-old Chinese. Pop Res Policy Rev 2004;23:117–133.

Maddox G. Self assessment of health. J Chron Dis 1964:449–460.

Maddox GL, Douglas EB. Self assessment of health: a longitudinal study. J Health Soc Behav 1973;14(1):87–93.

Manderbacka K. Examining what self-rated health question is understood to mean by respondents. Scand J Soc Med 1998;26(2):145–153.

Mäntyselkä PT, Turunen JH, Ahonen RS, Kumpusalo EA. Chronic pain and poor self-rated health. J Am Med Assoc 2003;290(18):2435–2442.

Mavaddat N, Kinmonth AL, Sanderson S, Surtees P, Bingham S, Khaw KT. What determines Self-Rated Health (SRH)? A cross-sectional study of SF-36 health domains in the EPIC-Norfolk cohort. J Epidemiol Commun Health 2011;65(9):800–806.

McColl E, Jacoby A, Thomas L, et al. Design and use of questionnaires: a review of best practice applicable to surveys of health service staff and patients. Health Technol Assess 2001;5(31):1–256.

McDonough P, Berglund P. Histories of poverty and self-rated health trajectories. J Health Soc Behav 2003;44:200–216.

McFarland S. Effects of question order on survey response. Public Opin Q 1981;45:208–215.

McGee DL, Liao Y, Cao G, Cooper RS. Self-reported health status and mortality in a muiltiethnic US cohort. Am J Epidemiol 1999;149(1):41–46.

McMullen CK, Luborsky MR. Self-rated health appraisal as cultural and identity process: African American elders' health evaluative rationales. Gerontologist 2006;46(4):431–438.

Menec V, Chipperfield J. A prospective analysis of the relation between self-rated health and health care use among elderly Canadians. Canadian J Aging 2001;20:293–306.

Miilunpalo S, Vuori I, Oja P, Pasanen M, Urponen H. Self-rated health status as a health measure: the predictive values of self-reported health status on the use of physician services and on mortality in the working-age population. J Clin Epidemiol 1997;50(5):517–528.

Mossey J, Shapiro E. Self-rated health: a predictor of mortality among the elderly. Am J Public Health 1982;72(8):800–808.

National Center for Health Statistics. Proceedings of the 1993 NCHS Conference on the Cognitive Aspects of Self-Reported Health Status; Hyattsville, MD; 1994.

Nelson DE, Powell-Grinder E, Town M, Kovar M. A comparison of national estimates from the National Health Interview Survey and the Behavioral Risk Factor Surveillance System. Am J Public Health 2003;93(8):1335–1341.

Nisbett RE. *The Geography of Thought: How Asians and Westerners Think Differently and Why*. New York: The Free Press; 2003.

Nybo H, Petersen HC, Gaist D, Jeune B, Andersen K, McGue M, Vaupel JW, Christensen K. Predictors of mortality in 2,249 Nonagenarians: the Danish 1905 Cohort Survey. J Am Geriat Soc 2003;51(10):1365–1373.

Organization for Economic Co-operation and Development. 2010. Health at a glance: Europe 2010. OECD Publishing. Accessed on 7/3/2014 from http://dx.doi.org/10.1787/health_glance-2010-en.

Pannenborg C. *A New International Health Order: An Inquiry into the International Relations of World Health and Medical Care*. Sijthoff and Boordhoff: The Netherlands; 1979.

Pachter L. Culture and clinical care: folk illness beliefs and behaviors and their implications for health care delivery. J Am Med Assoc 1994;271:690–694.

Payne S. *The Art of Asking Questions*. Princeton, NJ: Princeton University Press; 1951.

Pinquart M. Correlates of subjective health in older adults: a meta-analysis. Psychol Aging 2001;16:414–426.

Potter J, Wetherell M. *Discourse and Social Psychology. Beyond Attitudes and Behavior*. London: Sage Publications; 1987.

Pu C, Tang G-J, Huang N, Chou YJ. Predictive power of self-rated health for subsequent mortality risk during old age: analysis of data from a nationally representative survey of elderly adults in Taiwan. J Epidemiol 2011;21(4):278–284.

Rogers CR. *Client-Centered Therapy*. New York: Houghton Mifflin; 1951.

Rosenberg M. The self-concept: social product and social force. In: Rosenberg M, Turner R, editors. *Social Psychology: Sociological Perspectives*. New Brunswick, NJ: Transaction Publishers; 1990.

Sadana R, Mathers C, Lopez A, Murray C, Iburg K. Comparative analyses of more than 50 household surveys on health status. In: Murray C, Salomon J, Mathers D, Lopez A, editors. *Summary Measure of Population Health: Concepts, Ethics, Measurement and Applications*. Geneva, Switzerland: World Health Organization; 2002. p 369–386.

Salomon J, Tandon A, Murray C. Comparability of self-rated health: cross sectional multi-country survey using anchoring vignettes. Bri Med J 2004;328(7434):258–261.

Schechter S. The relevance of cognition in survey research. Paper presented at The 1993 NCHS Conference on the Cognitive Aspects of Self-Reported Health Status; Hyattsville, MD; 1994.

Schuman H. Context effects: state of the past/state of the art. In: Schwarz N, Sudman S, editors. *Context Effects in Social and Psychological Research*. New York: Springer-Verlag; 1992. p 5–20.

Schuman H, Presser S. *Questions and Answers in Attitude surveys: experiments on question form, wording, and context*. New York: Academic Press; 1981.

Schwarz N. Attitude construction: evaluation in context. Soc Cognit 2007;25:638–656.

Schwarz N. Self-reports: how the questions shape the answers. Am Psychol 1999;54(2):93–105.

Schwarz N. *Cognition and Communication: Judgmental Biases, Research Methods, and the Logic of Conversation*. Hillsdale, NJ: Erlbaum; 1996.

Schwarz N. Judgment in a social context: biases, shortcomings, and the logic of conversation. In: Zanna M, editor. *Advances in Experimental Social Psychology*. San Diego, CA: Academic Press; 1994. p 123–162.

Schwarz N, Clore GL. Mood, misattribution, and judgments of well-being: informative and directive functions of affective states. J Pers Soc Psychol 1983;45(3):513–523.

Schwarz N, Strack F, Mai H. Assimilation and contrast effects in part-whole questions sequences: a conversational logic analysis. Public Opin Q 1991;55(1):3–23.

Schwarz N, Sudman S, editors. *Context Effects in Social and Psychological Research*. New York: Springer-Velag; 1992.

Shadbolt B, Barresi J, Craft P. Self-rated health as a predictor of survival among patients with advanced cancer. J Clin Oncol 2002;20(10):2514–2519.

Shaw RJ, Pickett KE. The association between ethnic density and poor self-rated health among US Black and Hispanic people. Ethnic Health 2011;16(3):225–244.

Shetterly S, Baxter J, Mason L, Hamman R. Self-rated health among Hispanic vs non-Hispanic white adults: the San Luis Valley Health and Aging Study. Am J Public Health 1996;86(12):1798–1801.

Singer E. Self-rated health: how are judgments made? Paper presented at: the 1993 NCHS Conference on the Cognitive Aspects of Self-Reported Health Status; Hyattsville, MD; 1994.

Singh-Manoux A, Martikainen P, Ferrie J, Zins M, Marmot M, Goldberg M. What does self rated health measure? Results from the British Whitehall II and French Cazel cohort studies. J Epidemiol Community Health 2006;60:364–372.

Spencer SM, Schulz R, Rooks R, Albert S, Thorpe R, Brenes G, Harris T, Koster A, Satterfield S, Ayonayon H, Newman A. Racial differences in self-rated health at similar levels of physical functioning: an examination of health pessimism in the Health, Aging and Body Composition Study. J Gerontol Soc Sci 2009;64(1):87–94.

Subramanian SV, Huijts T, Avendano M. Self-reported health assessments in the 2002. World Health Survey: how do they correlate with education? Bull World Health Organ 2010;88(2):131ISSN: 0042-9686.

Subramanian SV, Kim D, Kawachi I. Covariation in the socioeconomic determinants of self rated health and happiness: a multivariate multilevel analysis of individuals and communities in the USA. J Epidemiol Community Health 2005;59:664–669.

Thorslund M, Lundberg O. Health and inequalities among the oldest-old. J Aging Health 1994;6:51–69.

Tourangeau R. Survey research and societal change. Ann Rev Psychol 2004;55:775–801.

Tourangeau R. Cognitive science and survey methods. In: Jabine TB, Straf ML, Tanur JM, Tourangeau R, editors. *Cognitive Aspects of Survey Methodology: Building a Bridge Between Disciplines*. Washington, DC: National Academy Press; 1984. p 73–100.

Tourangeau R, Rasinski K, Bradburn N. Measuring happiness in surveys: a test of the subtraction hypothesis. Public Opin Q 1991;55(2):255–266.

Tourangeau R, Rips L, Rasinski KJ. *The psychology of survey response*. New York, NY: Cambridge University Press. 2000.

Verbrugge LM, Ascione FJ. Exploring the iceberg: common symptoms and how people care for them. Med Care 1987;25(6):539–569.

Viruell-Fuentes E, Morenoff J, Williams D, House J. Language of interview, self-rated health, and other Latino health puzzle. Am J Public Health 2010;101(7):1306–1313.

Vuorisalmi M, Lintonen T, Jylhä M. Global self-rated health data from a longitudinal study predicted mortality better than comparative self-rated health in old age. J Clin Epidemiol 2005;58(7):680–687.

Wagner A, Gandek B, Aaronson N, Acquadro C, Alonso J, Apolone G, Bullinger M, Bjorner J, Fukuhara S, Kaasa S, Leplège A, Sullivan M, Wood-Dauphinee S, Ware JE Jr. Cross-cultural comparisons of the content of SF-36 translations across 10 countries: results from the IQOLA project. J Clin Epidemiol 1998;51:925–932.

Walker JD, Maxwell CJ, Hogan DB, Ebly EM. Does self-rated health predict survival in older persons with cognitive impairment? J Am Geriat Soc 2004;52(11):1895–1900.

Wilcox VL, Kasl SV, Ilder EL. Self-rated health and physical disability in elderly survivors of a major medical event. J Gerontol B Psychol Sci Soc Sci 1996;51B(2):S96–S104.

Wolinsk F, Johnson R. Perceives health status and mortality among older men and women. J GerontolSoc Sci 1992;47(6):S304–S312.

World Health Organization. *Constitution of the World Health Organization*. Geneva, Switzerland: World Health Organization; 1948.

Yu ES, Kean YM, Slymen DJ, Liu WT, Zhang M, Katzman R. Self-perceived health and 5-year mortality risks among the elderly in Shanghai. China Am J Epidemiol 1998;147(9):880–890.

Yip W, Subramanian SV, Mitchell AD, Lee DTS, Wang J, Kawachi I. Does social capital enhance health and well-being? Evidence from rural China. Soc Sci Med 2007;64:35–49.

ONLINE RESOURCES

Measures of self-reported health (SRH) are included in the Short-Form (SF) Health Survey designed by the Medical Outcomes Study for data collection for clinical practice and research. There are various versions, such as SF-36, SF-12, and SF-8, each corresponding to the number of items included in the instrument. In general population surveys, SF is often used as a part of questionnaires rather than as a stand-alone instrument. Information on various versions is available at: www.sf-36.org/?id=0.

The SF-36 instrument, scoring instructions and related-documents can be located at: www.rand.org/health/surveys_tools/mos/mos_core_36item.html.

A psychometric evaluation of the English-version of SRH is available at: http://patienteducation.stanford.edu/research/generalhealth.html.

A psychometric evaluation of the Spanish-version of SRH is available at: http://patienteducation.stanford.edu/research/generalhealthesp.html.

An example of the use of SRH for public policy goals as part of the Healthy People 2020 in the United States: www.healthypeople.gov/2020/about/GenHealthAbout.aspx#self.

The use of SRH as a key indicator of the National Health Interview Survey in the United States is presented in: www.cdc.gov/nchs/nhis/released201306.htm#11.

An example of the use of SRH as an indicator of well-being in Canada can be found at: www4.hrsdc.gc.ca/.3ndic.1t.4r@-eng.jsp?iid=10.

The use of SRH for cross-national comparisons by the Organisation for Economic Co-operation and Development (OECD) is available at: www.oecd.org/edu/research/45760738.pdf.

CHAPTER NINE

Pretesting of Health Survey Questionnaires: Cognitive Interviewing, Usability Testing, and Behavior Coding

Gordon Willis
National Cancer Institute, National Institutes of Health, Bethesda, MD, USA

9.1 Introduction

Prior to undertaking a particularly complex or multifaceted endeavor, it is sometimes customary to conduct a *dry run.* According to The Word Detective (http://www.word-detective.com/2009/07/dry-run/):

> Beginning in the late 19th century, fire departments in the US began conducting practice sessions where engines were dispatched and hoses deployed, but water was not pumped, thus making the exercises literally "dry" runs ... Just when the term came into more general use meaning "practice session" is uncertain, but it seems to have been after the term "dry run" was widely used in the US Armed Services during World War II.

A pretest of a survey questionnaire can be seen as a sophisticated form of dry run: Despite our best efforts in applying effective questionnaire-design rules, enlisting experts to anticipate difficulties, and heading off these anticipated challenges, there is no substitute for putting the system to an exhaustive test,

Handbook of Health Survey Methods, First Edition. Edited by Timothy P. Johnson.

prior to the administration of our field survey. As such, this chapter describes several varieties of such pretests of health surveys, with a view toward recommending approaches that are effective and efficient for identifying difficulties that potentially lead to survey response error, and for setting the stage for their remediation.

The term *pretesting* subsumes a number of specific procedures, ranging from a preliminary and informal review, to a complex formal field test that attempts to replicate the field environment as closely as possible. As a matter of definition, I consider a pretest as an empirical evaluation of a questionnaire—conducted prior to fielding—that involves the administration of the instrument to individuals uninvolved in the design process, and who are regarded as reasonable "stand-ins" for field survey respondents (and who are referred to as either *subjects, participants,* or *pretest respondents*). I discuss three common forms of pretesting: *Cognitive Interviewing, Usability Testing, and Behavior Coding.*

9.2 Historical Background and Theory of Pretesting

The empirical pretesting of survey questionnaires has become widespread over the past 30 years, but has a much more extensive history—as designers have long felt that writing survey questions, or answering them, is not always (or even normally) a straightforward process. It is likely that for as long as large-scale surveys have been conducted, administrators have conducted some form of what Presser et al. (2004) label a *Conventional Pretest,* which is typically conducted as a true dry run, in the sense that it replicates survey administrative elements exceeding the administration of the questionnaire itself, including respondent contact, interviewer assignment, and data processing. However, beyond perhaps convening of field interviewers for a debriefing to discuss the functioning of the survey questions, the conventional field pretest did not spawn any particularly sophisticated approach to the systematic evaluation of the questionnaire as a measurement instrument. Nor did it engage heavily in either developing or applying either psychological, linguistic, or sociological theory.

At some point in the largely uncharted history of survey research, practitioners began to engage in activities that would today be recognized as bona fide pretests that explicitly address the questionnaire instrument, and that endeavor to illuminate and eliminate potential sources of measurement error. Cantril and Fried (1944) conducted what modern methodologists would label cognitive pretesting. It was only in the 1980s, however, that pretesting came to be viewed as a set of special-purpose procedures embodying characteristics that specifically target the quality of the survey questionnaire, and that depart from strict field survey methods, as opposed to simply serving as a dry run in the more traditional sense. A review by Jobe and Mingay (1991) notes that several strands contributed to this development, beginning at the United Kingdom's Royal Statistical Society and the Social Science Research Council (Moss and Goldstein 1979), then at the U.S. Census Bureau and Bureau of Justice Statistics (Biderman 1980), and later at ZUMA in Germany (Hippler et al. 1987). However, the most direct triggering event for a fairly explosive increase in the view of pretesting as a science unto itself may have been the introduction of the four-stage model of the survey response process, by Tourangeau (1984). The Tourangeau model was a major facet of the 1983 seminar on the Cognitive Aspects of Survey Methodology, or CASM I, which explored the interdiscipline between cognitive psychology and survey research methods (Sirken et al. 1999). Tourangeau provided a simple yet elegant depiction of the respondent's task when presented an individual survey item, consisting of (i) comprehension of the item (interpretation), (ii) retrieval (recall from memory) of information, (iii) judgment and estimation processes, and (iv) a final response process. Although this basic cognitive model has since its inception been expanded upon, modified, or incorporated into a more extensive description, it has stood the test of time and remains the dominant theoretical basis for the survey response process.

As a further result of CASM I, the theoretically based notion that complex psychological processes underlie the answering of survey questions was enjoined to a second development: the adaptation of procedures then in vogue within experimental psychology for the purposes of externalizing cognitive processes, and making them evident to the researcher. The initial procedure borrowed in this manner was the "think-aloud" interview, introduced and advocated by Ericsson and Simon (1980, 1984), and implemented as a potential means for formulating survey questions. In the late 1980s, subsequent to the introduction of the cognitive model and the introduction of the think-aloud, a further, critical development occurred: survey practitioners began to recognize that these procedures could be applied in the pretesting of draft questionnaires, such as within the Questionnaire Design Research Laboratory at the National Center for Health Statistics (e.g., Royston 1989). The *cognitive interview* (CI) emerged from these developments as an institutionalized procedure embedded into the evaluation of survey questionnaires, and since that era has largely become the face of pretesting.

In addition to the CI, a separate development in pretesting science was motivated by the advent and widespread adoption by the survey industry of a key piece of technology—the digital computer. As questionnaires began a conversion from paper to computer-based administration, and as organizations such as the U.S. Census Bureau (2003) began to rely on interviewer-administration of questions via CAPI (Computer-Assisted Personal Interviewing) or CATI (Computer-Assisted Telephone Interviewing) instruments, a view emerged that these systems need to exhibit the important characteristic of operator *usability* (Couper 1999, Couper et al. 1998). Usability testing (UT) as adopted from computer science more generally, was therefore adapted to computerized surveys as a separate pretesting technique. Soon afterward, as computers began to be programmed with self-administered questionnaires, the realm of usability came to involve the respondent, rather than only the interviewer. Finally, as the Internet and World Wide Web surveys took off in popularity, UT emerged as a vital means for pretesting these computerized forms as well (Baker et al. 2004). There does not appear to be an extensively developed model or theory of the cognitive processes associated with UT. However, several authors have been concerned with the manner in which tendencies of the human visual processing system impact behavior in web surveys (Dillman 2007). Tourangeau et al. (2000b) have emphasized the cognitive underpinnings of web survey design, and the University of Maryland Department of Psychology (http://lap.umd.edu/survey_design/) has produced a guide that makes use of cognitive concepts such as figure-ground relationships, and Gestalt principles of perception. Further, there have been efforts to apply related notions of culturally derived meaning to human-computer interaction (see http://citeseerx.ist.psu.edu/viewdoc/summary?doi=10.1.1.84.5946).

The third major pretesting technique included in the current triumvirate is *behavior coding* (BC), which departs from cognitive interviewing in particular by adopting an explicit focus on the role of the interviewer within telephone and in-person surveys. Beginning in the 1960s, Cannell and colleagues at the University of Michigan considered the three-way interaction between interviewers, respondents, and survey questionnaire, and developed BC (also known as *interaction analysis*) as a formal means for evaluating survey questions (Cannell et al. 1968). Behaviors that are generally coded include misreading of survey questions by the interviewer, and indications by the respondents that they are experiencing difficulties, such as requests for clarification of question meaning, or providing responses that the interviewer is unable to record. Although BC has not consistently relied upon a large body of theory, and has not given rise to entities devoted to its practice akin to cognitive laboratories, it nevertheless has persisted as an influential means for critically evaluating survey items, often through its placement within the conventional, dry run form of survey pretesting, as a valuable adjunct.

As a result of each of these historical developments, Cognitive Interviewing, UT, and BC are considered to be state-of-the-science methods, and are themselves increasingly the focus of significant methodological work attempting to evaluate their effectiveness, and to hone these techniques in the interest of development of a set of "minimal" or even "best" practices. The next sections consider these major pretesting variants in turn, by illustrating their major features, as well as their unique strengths and limitations.

9.3 Cognitive Interviewing

As noted above, the CASM I conference was instrumental in launching the interdiscipline between survey methodology and cognitive psychology, with respect to questionnaire design (Tourangeau et al. 2000a). Several authors (e.g., Loftus 1984) recognized that in addition to the theory derived from cognitive psychology, its methods as well might be profitably applied to the domain of survey question testing. Loftus (1984) initially proposed that the think-aloud procedure explicated by Ericsson and Simon (1980) could be applied to the intensive study of survey questions, by requesting that test subjects voice their thoughts aloud as they answer a set of targeted survey question. The investigator would then examine the resultant "protocol," or record of the verbal stream produced, for indications of how the cognitive processes that influence the survey response themselves operate. On the basis of this knowledge, one could presumably frame superior survey questions that optimized cognitive processing tendencies. For example, Loftus chronicled the tendencies of survey respondents to recall past medical visits in a forward chronological order, in reverse order, or in neither of these. In fact, she found evidence for the use of all of these strategies, rather than a single variant, and concluded that there appeared to be no one best approach to guide such information retrieval. It is because of the initial focus on think-aloud that cognitive interviewing has sometimes been referred to as simply *the think-aloud*.

9.3.1 CURRENT CONCEPTUALIZATIONS OF THE COGNITIVE INTERVIEW

An important departure from the think-aloud approach, however, emerged early in the history of usage of the CI. The alternative procedure, best represented by Belson's (1981) work, was the probed interview. *Verbal probing* or in essence "asking questions of the respondent about the survey question," was the basic procedure used by Cantril and Fried over a half-century ago, and therefore pre-dates the think-aloud. Probing has come to largely characterize cognitive interviewing, and involves a range of queries of the participant, ranging from the very general and nondirective ("You said your health in general is 'fair', tell me more about that") to the very targeted and precise ("What does the term 'dental sealant' mean to you?"). If such probing reveals signs of misinterpretation or other difficulties (e.g., the finding described by Willis (2005) that CI subjects erroneously consider dental sealants to be fillings), then this constitutes evidence that a tested item may require revision. Probing has received a considerable degree of discussion in the survey research literature (Collins 2003), and has been reviewed extensively by Willis (2005) in a book specifically devoted to cognitive interviewing practices. For current purposes, it will suffice to note that as the field of cognitive interviewing has developed, probing has increasingly been combined with the use of the think-aloud, so that both have come to be incorporated, procedurally. Cognitive interviewing in this form has been applied widely to both interviewer-administered and self-administered questionnaires, whether paper-based or computerized, and whether administered to the general population or to special populations.

9.3.2 SOCIOCULTURAL ASPECTS OF COGNITIVE TESTING

Although emergent forms of pretesting were inspired by the cognitive paradigm from psychology, they have always had a strong implicit *sociocultural focus* as well, especially as survey questions typically focus on the social location of the individual within the world, and his/her conception of that location. As a concrete example, asking the respondent to report the basic demographic characteristics of race and ethnicity invokes concepts of self-identity within a social context, as one's report of group membership may depend on the context in which the question is asked, the identity of the interviewer, the perceived objective of the survey administrator, and so on. Within the past decade, the sociocultural focus has become more explicit and pronounced such that the disciplinary underpinnings of pretesting (and of cognitive interviewing in particular) are no longer as closely connected to the pure cognitive model (Collins 2007, Miller 2011). This trend has been furthered by the increased tendency to include in population surveys members of diverse cultural subpopulations, and to draw the attention of researchers who were trained in qualitative research traditions, emanating from sociology and anthropology, which emphasize elements other than individual-level cognition in a mechanistic sense.

Hence, a second wave of theoretical tradition has impacted the conduct of pretesting, involving the concepts, theories, and methods of qualitative research. Gerber (1999) in particular set the stage by making the case that cognitive interviewing implicitly incorporates concepts related to the culturally defined striving for meaning, in the manner long studied by anthropologists and sociologists. Within the past 10 years, Miller (2011) and colleagues at the National Center for Health Statistics have introduced key concepts from the classical qualitative research tradition, such as Grounded Theory (Glaser and Strauss 1967) and the Constant Comparison Method for qualitative analysis, in refocusing the researcher perspective. Most importantly, they have reconceptualized the purpose of pretesting and question evaluation, and rather than focusing on diagnosis and remediation, strive for a basic understanding of "what the question captures," in terms of the range of interpretations that may influence the use of the item. For example, study of the concept of "disability" has determined that the term carries a range of interpretations, based on one's position in society, and based on the particular social context in which a survey question containing the term is administered (Miller et al. 2010). However, the basic procedures that derive from this perspective are, at least in basic form, similar to those of the cognitive approach. Overall, cognitive interviewing can therefore be considered to depend on several strands, with respect to disciplinary perspective (cognitive psychology, sociology–anthropology), and dominant methods (think-aloud, verbal probing).

9.3.3 PROCEDURAL ASPECTS OF CI

Cognitive interviewing as a questionnaire pretesting and evaluation method is now practiced at several United States Government laboratories (the U.S. Census Bureau, NCHS, Bureau of Labor Statistics); at contract research organization laboratories (Abt Associates, Research Triangle Institute, Westat), at several non-U.S. locations (Statistics Netherlands, Statistics Sweden, Statistics Finland), as well as by many academic and applied researchers. CIs are conducted to pretest a wide range of questionnaire topics, including but not limited to health (e.g., employment, income, Federal program participation, labor force dynamics, transportation, Internet use, and so on). The approaches used are generally applicable across topic (for a recent overview, see Madans et al. (2011)). Procedurally, cognitive interviewing involves the following elements (see Willis (2005) for extensive discussion of each):

1. *Small-scale iterative testing* of volunteer subjects: A "round" of testing may consist of only 8–12 subjects—this would be the number of times the questions are administered prior to review of results, modification, and then potentially a further cycle of testing to determine whether proposed changes are adequate—or else are found to produce unanticipated new problems. Normally, one to three rounds are conducted with modifications made subsequent to each. A distinct advantage to the conduct of more than one round is that this affords the developers an opportunity to evaluate modifications that represent attempts at problem resolution. Additional rounds also provide further testing of unchanged items that have to that point not been identified as problematic.
2. *Use of targeted probing* approaches that are tailored to the testing situation: Cognitive testing that involves interviewer-based probing has involved two major varieties: Concurrent and Retrospective probing. Concurrent probing involves a back-and-forth exchange between interviewer and subject, such that subsequent to the interviewer asking the evaluated question and the subject answering it, the interviewer immediately follows up with additional probing questions to delve more fully into the subject's response. As an example that pertains to an interviewer-administered questionnaire:

   Interviewer (asks targeted survey question) In the past 7 days, on how many days did you walk for exercise.

   Subject Uh, three.

   Interviewer (probe) Tell me about those times.

   Subject Well, I probably went to the gym twice, and I also walked to the store yesterday. I'm assuming you want to include that – it's uphill and I did get some real exercise carrying those bags.

   Interviewer (probe) How sure are you that these were all in the past 7 days?

   Subject I don't know – I usually go to the gym twice a week. I don't remember anything different about this last week, you know, in that regard.

   The advantage to this exchange is that it unfolds as a naturalistic type of conversation. On the basis of probing, several details emerge beyond simply the initial answer of "three": (i) The subject assumes that walking to a shop is intended to count (which may not necessarily fit the researcher's intent); and (ii) he/she is making a judgment based on usual behavior, as opposed to recalling enumerated episodes.

   On the other hand, retrospective probing—sometimes simply referred to as a *debriefing*—defers all probing to the end of the interview, after the evaluated survey questions have been administered. An exchange analogous to that above would proceed somewhat differently:

Interviewer: Earlier I asked you the question: In the past 7 days, on how many days did you walk for exercise? Do you remember how you answered that?

Subject Uh, yeah, I think I said three times.

From this point on, probing (and presumably, subject responses) could unfold just as for the example involving concurrent probing. Note the fundamental difference introduced by the debriefing approach: (i) The interviewer must re-read (or otherwise present) each question to be probed; and (ii) as the response is no longer in the subject's short-term memory, the interviewer must then either ask again for the previous answer, or else remind the subject of it. Parenthetically, the above example illustrates the former (reasking); as the latter (reminding) would involve stating instead "You told me three times … Tell me more about those times?" This procedural difference clearly creates different cognitive demands, but does not appear to have been discussed within the scientific literature.

The relative merits and drawbacks of each approach are summarized elsewhere (Willis 2005), but in brief, concurrent probing appears to be especially efficient and useful for interviewer-administered questionnaires, where the usual ask-and-respond sequence is embellished by probe questions, which simply expand the ongoing conversational interaction in a natural way. Retrospective probing is especially useful in testing of self-administered questionnaires, where the subject can be left to complete the instrument and to navigate his/her way through it, without interference. Subsequent to the interview, a debriefing discussion between the pair that involves verbal probing (but not, in this case, think-aloud) can rely upon the completed questionnaire as a guide.

3. As a second key feature, CI data collection is *overwhelmingly qualitative* in nature: The data from CIs largely consist of written comments made either during or after the interview, by the cognitive interviewer. There is some debate about how much quantification should be conducted within the interview (Beatty and Willis 2007, Willis 2005). At one extreme, cognitive interviewers may be tempted to record every answer given to tested questions, as well as answers to all probe questions, for purposes of tallying and perhaps cross-classifying these (e.g., answers of "yes" to item "Do you now have ANY type of disability?" may be associated with different responses to probe questions than are "no" answers to that item). At the other extreme, interviewers may simply note in a global, qualitative sense that a particular phrasing appeared to produce problems, on an interview-specific basis.
4. *Analysis of the CI* involves qualitative analysis of text-based data. There appear to be two basic approaches to analysis. The most common approach, applied for several decades, is one of data reduction through *successive aggregation*—in which written comments on individual interviews are first

summarized across all interviews conducted by a particular interviewer; then across interviewers, and then perhaps even across organizations, to produce one overall summary of each item's functioning. An alternative to this would be what Miller (2011) terms a Joint Analysis, in which all lower level findings are reviewed by all analysts: Rather than interpretation occurring according to a clustered, hierarchical format, a more in-depth approach leads all analysts to simultaneously consider all of the lowest level evidence, prior to making conclusions.

A key issue critical to any type of CI analysis is the extent and nature of data coding. Often, *uncoded analysis* is done, where no explicit codes are used to guide data reduction and organization of the findings. In such cases, the cognitive interviewers simply summarize their conclusions concerning question function (e.g., "The term 'dental sealant' should be defined because it tends to be misunderstood"). A higher level of coding is attained when the investigators group their findings according to the four processes that comprise the Tourangeau cognitive model (e.g., grouping comprehension problems separately from retrieval problems). Alternately, an analysis approach that is motivated by commonly accepted qualitative research methods builds codes directly from the data. Rather than imposing an *a priori* coding scheme or model (e.g., comprehension, recall …), this approach eschews such predetermination, and instead processes the reactions of survey respondents to an evaluated set of items in an inductive manner which develops coding and conceptual categories from the low level (text-based) data. As such, coding categories are developed for each investigation anew, based on the results of intensive qualitative analysis. Such analysis tends to be time consuming, but may be facilitated by the use of several computerized qualitative analysis programs (for a review of these see Banner and Albarran (2009))

Hence, in evaluation of the question "How many hours did you watch television yesterday?," the cognitive model leads one to establish whether the question produced cognitive problems with respect to comprehension of key terms ("television"; "watch"; "yesterday"); recall (of frequency), decision (whether subjects appear to under- or over-report due to the element of social desirability), and so on. The qualitative analysis model, on the other hand, leads the researcher to instead develop a compilation of the discrete set of ways the question is interpreted (e.g., television watching by the individual who is focused on the show; as a shared activity occurring in the background, etc.). Either approach can lead to a conclusion that the question either exhibits cognitive defects, or else fails to capture the phenomenon intended by the investigator. In fact, these conclusions may be only subtly different, and need not be in conflict. Either way, the researchers carrying out the pretest can make decisions concerning the adequacy of the item, and whether revision is in order.

9.3.4 ILLUSTRATIVE EXAMPLES

Applications of CI can best be illustrated through specific case studies demonstrating its use. Here's an example that represents a "remediation" model, in which the objective is to rectify observed problems, prior to question finalization and fielding. The second example will illustrate the use of cognitive testing mainly for purposes of conceptual understanding—that is, determining what it is that the item is measuring—rather than an emphasis on "finding-and-fixing."

EXAMPLE 9.1 Identifying and remediating problems

A paper-based self-administered questionnaire on perceptions of cancer risk was submitted to cognitive testing (Figure 9.1). The instrument embodied a table or matrix format, with an instruction and header at the top indicating that the respondent should indicate, for each of 21 vertically listed items, " … how concerned you feel right now about the following things." For each item, the respondent is to circle a number between 1 (not at all) to 5 (extremely). Cognitive testing relied on a retrospective approach, in which the subject completed the questionnaire unassisted and unprobed, and the debriefing probing was then conducted. Probing ranged from the very specific ("why did you choose [1-5]?" to more general items asking about their perceptions concerning breast cancer risk. Testing was conducted across four languages: English, Spanish, Chinese, and Korean, and across four independent testing laboratories, for a total of 148 interviews—a large CI project.

Please circle the single number (on a scale from 1 to 5) that best describes ***how concerned you feel right now*** about the following things:

	FEELINGS OF CONCERN NOW				
	Not at all	Hardly	Somewhat	Very much	Extremely
1. Breast cancer occurring in me	1	2	3	4	5
2. My family's history of cancer	1	2	3	4	5
3. What I can do to prevent breast cancer	1	2	3	4	5
.					
12. What having breast cancer would do to my body	1	2	3	4	5
13. Symptoms or signs of breast cancer in me	1	2	3	4	5
14. My chances of dying of breast cancer	1	2	3	4	5
.					

FIGURE 9.1 Self-administered Cancer Risk Scale evaluated through cognitive interviewing.

The basic results were somewhat unexpected, but compelling. On the basis of a range of types of probes requesting that subjects simply explain their answer, each set of researchers made the identical observation: Despite efforts to highlight the critical concept of current concern about each item, subjects had an overwhelming tendency to ignore this instruction and to overlook the additional element of *feelings of concern now*. As a result, they simply responded to each item according to a separate interpretation implied by the response categories—in effect, "to what degree this is true." For example, when presented with the item "Breast cancer occurring in me," answers tended to be based on self-perceived risk (none to extreme), as opposed to how concerned they were about this outcome. Similarly, answers given to "What breast cancer would do to my body" elicited responses concerning the degree that this cancer would hypothetically affect the body (e.g., 5 = an extreme amount)—again, not necessarily related to current concerns. The researchers were unanimous in concluding that the instrument had failed in communicating the interpretation intended, and that it would be necessary to return to the proverbial drawing board. Interestingly, this example well-exhibits a case where a severe problem was not predicted before the fact, yet was easily (and reliably) uncovered through empirical testing.

EXAMPLE 9.2 **Obtaining insights into conceptual understanding:**

A common question within health surveys that has achieved almost mythical status (and which has had at least one entire Workshop and resulting publication devoted to it (Schechter 1995)) is the general health question: *Would you say your health in general is excellent, very good, good, fair, or poor?* The item has a long history, especially due to its demonstrated utility as a predictor of morbidity and mortality. Cognitive testing, however, has revealed several consistent findings concerning its interpretation. Most significantly, the general form of the item fails to differentiate between multiple concepts of health. When the cognitive interviewer engages in probing in order to obtain in-depth information on how the item is interpreted and processed (e.g., "What does this question make you think of?"; "Why do you say [Excellent ... Poor]?") it has repeatedly been found to elicit thoughts of several varieties including physical (somatic) health, mental health, emotional health, spiritual health, and even financial health. As such, for use in the general population, some surveys (e.g., the Behavioral Risk Factor Surveillance System survey, or BRFSS) have chosen to subdivide the item into (i) physical and (ii) mental/emotional health. Further, it has been determined through cognitive testing that the emphasis of one or another of these implicit subcategories varies by culture. Miller et al. (2005) found this variation to be dependent on both gender and ethnicity, such that White males tended to interpret "health in general" as limited to physical health (e.g., "I haven't had a heart attack or stroke"), whereas Hispanic females voiced a much wider conceptualization that encompassed a range of health attributes, including the emotional and spiritual. Such a finding does not necessarily invalidate the item, or demand that it be altered, but rather provides more understanding of what it measures. Of course, the recognition of such variance might lead the investigators to further subdivide the item, as for the BRFSS. ■

9.3.5 CURRENT ISSUES IN COGNITIVE TESTING

Although CI is fairly well established, it is not currently characterized by a commonly accepted set of best practices (Blair and Brick 2010). In fact, the procedural aspects of this pretesting method vary widely among practitioners, and several issues are unsettled, and may even be somewhat contentious. Several of the most pressing methodological problems are as follows:

1. *How many interviews are needed to identify problems?* As discussed earlier, it has been typical to rely on small iterative testing rounds to identify problems in survey questions. In part, this has been based on the presumption that cognitive testing, due to its intensive nature, relies more on quality than on quantity, and that *saturation* (that is, the state in which major problems are no longer identified by conducting additional interviews) can be achieved relatively quickly. There is some evidence that cognitive testing conducted in this way has in fact produced positive results (Willis and Schechter 1997). However, Blair and Conrad (2011) have more recently conducted an extensive CI study which chronicled the natural history of identification of problems, as sample size increased to 50 cases and beyond. They found a generally positive monotonic relationship between number of interviews and number of problems found, suggesting that saturation is not achieved given the small sample sizes typically used. Miller (2011) as well has pointed out that in order to fully study the interpretation of items across multiple sociocultural groups, many more interviews may be necessary. It is likely that there is no general answer to the question "How many interviews are necessary?" as this may depend on the nature of the investigation, the extent and nature of problematic items, the resources one may bring to bear, and of course whether the researcher's objective is to "find problems" in the first place.
2. *How should analysis be conducted?* As stated, analysis of CIs is a second area where procedures vary. Given that there is no single commonly accepted best practice in this regard, what may be most important is that practitioners are transparent about and document the nature of the analysis conducted. In particular, it is necessary to make clear what evidence from the interviews was used to determine that a problem existed, in particular to differentiate these from opinions concerning question functioning.
3. *How much intensive verbal probing should be done?* In some ways this issue recapitulates a longstanding tension between think-aloud and verbal probing. On the one hand, one could argue that the introduction of probes may contaminate the survey interaction, or produce *reactivity effects*; that is, their use may influence the respondent's thinking in a way that is artificial, and is not representative of unprobed behavior (e.g., an interesting probe could lead the person to think about a topic more deeply than they otherwise would when simply answering a series of survey questions). Hence, one might decide to probe only judiciously or conservatively, and Conrad and Blair (2001), in particular, have advocated this approach. The opposite view, which has largely been adopted by cognitive interviewers, is that think-aloud cannot

itself be relied upon to provide useful results, as it puts too much of the burden on the subject; may itself introduce reactivity as it interferes with normal cognitive processing of survey questions; and may fail to investigate key issues that can be targeted by an experienced and skilled cognitive interviewer. This issue has perennially stood at the forefront of the field, but is becoming even more pronounced, as some practitioners have begun to develop the capacity for unmoderated CIs (that is, those that do not include any interviewer, but simply automated recording of responses, with subsequent analysis) for the pretesting of self-administered items Murphy, Edgar, and Keating (2014). Such interviews may be less expensive, and also provide significantly increased sample sizes to the levels advocated by Blair and Conrad (2011). Hence, the establishment that such interviews are productive could result in a reduction in the intensity of verbal probing.

4. *How can one demonstrate the reliability and validity of CI?* Conrad and Blair (2004) presented a research agenda for CI that addresses the complex issues involved in demonstrating method validity. Further, Willis (2005) examines, in depth, the science of evaluation concerning CI, from a number of perspectives. At this point, no clear body of evidence exists which will unambiguously support a conclusively positive outcome evaluation—that is, the demonstration that this method exhibits sufficient reliability or validity. Rather, as a requisite condition, a useful step in that direction would be to accumulate information that addresses the requirements of an initial, process evaluation. In particular, rather than simply stating that we have conducted cognitive interviewing, it is imperative that practitioners begin to specify, in a systematic way, the procedural variants they are using, and exactly what result each set of selected features has produced. To this end, Boeije and Willis (2011) have developed the Cognitive Interviewing Reporting Framework (CIRF), a detailed checklist specifying the categories of information that should be included in any cognitive testing report. Closely related to this initiative, Miller and colleagues (Miller et al. 2003) describe Q-Bank, an online database for storage and retrieval of cognitive testing reports, which could provide precisely the types of information needed to work toward resolution of questions concerning optimal practices.

9.4 Usability Testing

Similar to cognitive interviewing, UT has become pronounced in application over the last two decades. This is unsurprising, as the focus of UT is computerized instruments, which have been in widespread use since the 1990s, initially as large surveys such as the National Center for Health Statistics' National Health Interview Survey were converted from paper to CAPI or CATI format. A basic issue regarding UT of questionnaires has been that of who the human target is. Initially, the focus was the interviewer, as computerized questionnaires were interviewer-administered, typically embedded within stand-alone computers. Issues concerning whether the instruments were "usable" largely related to how well they could be navigated by the interviewer. More recently, as surveys have migrated to self-administration, and especially to Internet-based delivery, a shift has occurred to the perspective of the survey respondent. In this case—as there exists no interviewer—the issue at hand is whether the respondent can both process the survey questions, in classic sense; but also how well he/she can navigate and understand the instrument as a whole, as it is administered by the computer.

9.4.1 EXAMPLE: USABILITY TESTING OF A DIETARY QUESTIONNAIRE

Figure 9.2 illustrates one screenshot from the formative version of a complex Internet-based (web) dietary survey developed by NCI to collect information on foods consumed during the past year. Unlike a traditional, linear, question-by-question instrument, it exhibits a flexible data-entry approach containing a number of elements that demand navigational and problem-solving behavior by users, including a navigation panel at the left, indicating where in

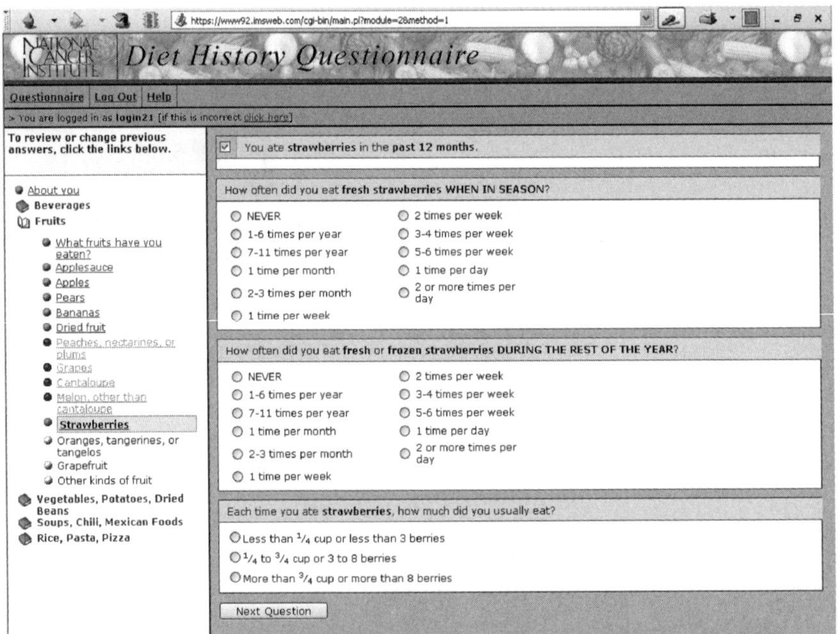

FIGURE 9.2 Example screen from Internet-based dietary assessment survey evaluated through usability testing. Note: The Internet version uses multiple colors: In the left panel, bullets associated with applesauce, apples, pears, bananas, and dried fruit are in green; bullets associated with peaches, grapes, cantaloupe, and melon are red.

the instrument the user is, and which sections have been completed. When evaluated via UT, several potentially problematic features can be investigated:

1. Is it clear where to look when each new screen is presented? Note that the questions to be answered (e.g., "How often did you eat fresh strawberries ... ") are not in the upper left, where one's vision is typically first drawn.
2. Is the use of colors for conveying information appropriate and well understood?
3. Do the survey questions embedded within the instrument themselves pose classical questionnaire-design problems, especially related to comprehension and recall?

UT of this food-frequency questionnaire (unpublished), based on two rounds of nine individuals, suggested that respondents were able to grasp the functioning of the physical layout, and to determine that the purpose of the left panel was to indicate which sections had been completed. Because the web version represented a conversion of a paper questionnaire, the investigators did not focus on questionnaire-design problems, and few were identified. However, the use of color on the left-side panel was found to be problematic. For example, the color red often indicates a problem or error in computer applications, and this caused respondents undue concern, given that the use of that color within this panel was only intended to indicate that a section was yet to be completed. As a result, the investigators chose to use only green and gray.

Given the commonality of key elements between CI and UT, one might wonder how much these actually differ in practice. In an earlier work (Willis 2005), I considered the relationship between these, and concluded that despite these having very different histories, they have considerable overlap and have often converged in cases where computerized instruments are tested. The major difference between cognitive interviewing and UT seems to be a matter of emphasis. Cognitive testing tends to focus more on the mental processing of survey questions, whereas UT considers whether those questions are presented in a manner that is user-friendly and functional. It is, however, very difficult in practice for either interviewers or subjects/users to disentangle content from the vehicle which carries that content. As such, although the major aim in UT might be to establish whether the user knows where to look on the screen to continue, it may be imperative to additionally ascertain whether the user can comprehend the questions being presented. An item presenting classical cognitive issues, such as the one previously mentioned—*Would you say your health in general is excellent, very good, good, fair, or poor?*—does not cease to present such issues once it is embedded in a web survey. Hence, a usability test may include a user who spontaneously comments that "I don't know whether you are just talking about physical health, or including mental things like depression." Usability testers do tend to pay attention to such issues—as these may clearly affect the ultimate aim of attaining high quality data—even absent the nominal intent to seek insights of this nature. Similarly, a cognitive test of a self-administered instrument (whether paper-based or computerized) would be remiss if it failed to note usability problems related to navigation of that instrument. A review of the few in-depth descriptions in the literature concerning how UT of web surveys is accomplished suggests that the methods are not much different from those of CI. For example, Baker et al. (2004) describes a practice in which:

> We first ask the respondent to complete the web interview while we observe and answer any questions that he or she may have, noting areas of confusion. When the respondent has completed the interview, we ask a few standard questions aimed at uncovering especially difficult questions or sections, or cumbersome tasks. We then go back to the beginning of the questionnaire and proceed through each screen with the respondent noting any ambiguities or difficulties that he or she may have encountered. We typically follow this process with 10 to 12 respondents, or until we feel that the respondents' reactions suggest that we are unlikely to encounter major usability problems in actual field use.

What is most remarkable about this description is how closely it follows the fundamental elements of cognitive testing of a paper-based questionnaire.

9.4.2 CURRENT ISSUES IN USABILITY TESTING

In some ways, the pertinent methodologically oriented questions of interest overlap greatly with those concerning cognitive interviewing cited earlier: (i) should these engage heavily in think-aloud or depend on verbal probing? (ii) what sample sizes should be selected, and (iii) how can reliability and validity be ascertained? Each of these research questions is ripe for attention.

9.5 Behavior Coding

BC can be conceived, most fundamentally, as eavesdropping on a fielded interview to identify instances where the interviewer has difficulty asking questions, the respondent has difficulty answering them, or both (Fowler 2011). BC was initially implemented to monitor interviewer performance, by identifying instances in which an interviewer read a question in a way that altered its intent or meaning. Such difficulties could be used to diagnose a problem with either the interviewer (who chose not to read questions in a standardized manner) or the item (which may be phrased in a way that renders it difficult, or counterproductive, to be read as scripted). It soon became evident, however, that BC as well has value in identifying problems that respondents have in answering questions, and in fact the respondent side of the interaction has increasingly been relied upon as an indicator of survey question flaws. In contrast to cognitive interviewing, BC has been considered a quantitative technique, in that a relatively large sample of interviews is coded to produce qualitative distributions of problem frequencies (e.g., for a particular item, 25% of interviews produce reading errors).

BC in its normal form is only applicable to interviewer-administered instruments (it is possible to observe and code behaviors by those completing self-report instruments, but this would constitute a different type of procedure). Further, BC is usually applied at a later point in the development of a survey questionnaire than is cognitive interviewing, as the focus is on questions that have been sufficiently developed that they can be administered by an interviewer under field conditions (although BC has been carried out prior to fielding, even within a cognitive lab). Because BC does typically involve a relatively large numbers of interviews, and normally involves a field environment, it is often conducted as part of a conventional pretest (i.e., a dry run). Or, BC can be conducted as a form of quality assessment of an ongoing field survey. Such results can be used to assess interviewer and instrument performance to either provide the basis for changes to be made over the course of data collection, or to provide information that may provide valuable context for data analysis or planning of further survey cycles (i.e., the fielded survey is viewed as a pretest of the subsequent cycle).

The most significant operational difference between cognitive interviewing and BC is that, whereas the former is accomplished through active procedures that depart from the usual interactional exchange (probing and think-aloud), BC is passive and effectively transparent to the respondent. This departure in basic procedure is in turn tied to fundamental differences in the nature of the data obtained from each. CI relies on probing in order to unearth covert problems not obvious in the exchange, whereas BC observes what has occurred overtly—that is, where there are unprompted problems that may be detected by observation of the question–answer exchange between interviewer and respondent during the interview. Further, because BC explicitly codes the behaviors of interviewers, it places a much greater emphasis on the role of the survey interviewer than does CI, where the contribution of the interviewer is normally viewed mainly with respect to probing behavior, and interviewer performance in delivering the evaluated items is not an explicit area of focus (although this distinction is certainly not absolute, as a cognitive interviewer can note questions that seem difficult to read or otherwise administer).

9.5.1 PROCEDURAL ASPECTS OF BEHAVIOR CODING

In brief, BC generally consists of the following steps and elements:

1. *Determination of sequences to be coded.* It is not imperative to code an entire survey—sometimes a critical segment of the questionnaire is selected.
2. *Development of coding scheme.* A range of codes of varying specificity have been developed; a basic set is presented in Figure 9.3.
3. *Development of system for recording and processing results.* For administration procedures that rely on centralized control systems, such as CATI stations, recording of audio segments may be incorporated into a standing monitoring system developed for quality control purposes. More recently, for in-household or other environments making use of laptop computers, a Computer Audio-Recorded Interview (CARI) system relies on the laptop to record the interview, and to store appropriate files (Thissen et al. 2008).

Interviewer-oriented codes

1) Interviewer reads question **incorrectly**

2) Interviewer **probes** incorrectly

Respondent-oriented codes

1) Respondent **interrupts** reading of question

2) Respondent **requests clarification**of question meaning

3) Respondent expresses **uncertainty** in answering

4) Respondent provides **uncodeable** answer

FIGURE 9.3 **Basic codes used to study the interviewer–respondent interaction in behavior coding studies.**

4. *Collection of audio data.* A set number of interviews are normally recorded, perhaps according to a sampling plan that endeavors to include important demographic strata (e.g., age) or, for studies comparing question versions, different item variants. Normally respondents are asked to provide approval for audio recording of their interview, which is described by the interviewer at the outset as necessary for purposes of quality control.
5. *Coder training and coding of interviews.* Before reviewing recorded interviews, coders must be trained to understand the basic purpose of BC, and to apply the coding system. Sometimes experienced field interviewers can be used for this purpose.
6. *Compilation of codes, for each item.* A summary table can be produced which displays frequencies of each coded item, over all interviews, and for each relevant respondent characteristic or instrument version. A criterion can be set for problem frequencies to identify particularly problematic items—typically around 15% as suggested by Fowler (2011), but sometimes determined in the context of observed frequencies within the current investigation (Willis 2005).
7. *Conduct of coder debriefing.* A qualitative enhancement to the quantitative processing of data is a debriefing of coders, in which these individuals meet with the questionnaire designers and describe what they heard occurring for individual items, in terms of problems in the interaction that may diagnose questionnaire defects (or need for modification to interviewer training). This meeting can be guided by a listing of code frequencies that draw attention to the most problematic items.
8. *Question modification.* On the basis of the accumulated quantitative and qualitative data, researchers can determine which items have produced problems, and why, and this may lead to modification, similarly to CI or UT approaches already described.

9.5.2 ILLUSTRATION OF BEHAVIOR CODING

Stapleton Kudela et al. (2009) relied on multifaceted application of BC within a health-related context to evaluate the functioning of an instrument designed to assess the potential adverse health effects of racial and ethnic discrimination. Item functioning was determined according to questionnaire version, and across multiple racial-ethnic groups. One version first asked about unfair treatment in general: *In your entire life, have you been treated unfairly in [restaurants/stores/ . . .]*, before proceeding to ask the respondent to attribute this to either race/ethnicity or to some other characteristic (i.e., age, gender, speaking accent, and weight). The second version directly asked the respondent to directly attribute cause to racial/ethnic discrimination, asking: *In your entire life, have you been treated unfairly in [restaurants/stores/ . . .] because you are [Black/White/Hispanic/Asian/American Indian – Native American]?*

BC results revealed that, for multiple contexts in which unfair treatment could occur, frequencies of codes that assessed respondent difficulties were generally higher for the first than for the second version. The investigators concluded that the greater level of specificity of the version attributing the cause of unfair treatment directly to racial/ethnic discrimination resulted in less ambiguity of meaning. Interestingly, code frequencies were also found to be higher for White non-Hispanics than for other groups. This finding was explored through a coder debriefing, which suggested that Whites tended to object that the questions did not pertain to them, as they had rarely experienced such events. These findings had been more difficult to observe in earlier CI, largely because of limits in sample size and difficulties in systematic assignment to questionnaire version.

BC has also been applied within the context of multilingual investigations which attempt to determine whether items exhibit the key characteristic of cross-cultural comparability once translated. For purposes of evaluating the functioning of a set of tobacco-survey questions, Willis et al. (2008) conducted a BC investigation of items that had been translated into Spanish, Chinese (Mandarin and Cantonese), Korean, and Vietnamese. The item: *In your entire life, have you smoked 100 or more cigarettes,* was found to be particularly problematic in Asian-language interviews, as evidenced by a high frequency of behavior codes reflecting requests for clarification, but appeared to function well in English. This puzzling result was examined by conducting a debriefing session in which coders explained why they had assigned codes more frequently to Asians. Interestingly, the difficulty was found to have derived from the very literal translation from English of "In your entire life"—which came across to speakers of multiple Asian languages as the equivalent of "In your ENTIRE life—that is, from birth to death, have you smoked 100 or more cigarettes"). The erroneous formulation introduced an element (future behavior) that was clearly not implied by the original English version. The defective translation turned out to be simple to resolve by selecting an expression for each Asian language that in effect asks "Up to this point in your life, have you smoked 100 or more cigarettes".

The above example illustrates a number of critical points concerning question translation and pretesting, but for current purposes what is significant is that (i) BC was useful as a means for identifying a previously overlooked translation problem, that produced a clear "red flag" when the item was administered to actual respondents; and (ii) The introduction of the qualitative element of the coder debriefing was instrumental in identifying the nature of the problem, after quantitative evidence based on BC frequencies first established its seriousness. Hence, BC can be especially useful in providing a means for identifying cross-cultural issues that surface only once when a sufficiently wide range of respondents are engaged. Although one might argue that these problems should have been identified earlier, during either the translation process, or perhaps within cognitive interviewing (which had also been conducted), the fact is that they were not. BC may therefore be useful as a check to identify problems that have otherwise escaped detection.

9.5.3 CURRENT ISSUES IN BEHAVIOR CODING

1. *Number/depth of behavior codes.* Schaeffer and Dykema (2004) have argued that after a half-century of usage of BC, researchers still lack a good understanding of which particular respondent behaviors serve as effective indices of interactional problems that adversely affect data quality. Hence, it is unknown whether we should rely on a few simple codes (e.g., respondent had some problems vs no evidence of a problem); or whether an extensive set of more detailed codes should be applied.
2. *Applications to cross-cultural realm.* Schoua-Glusberg (2004) has summarized issues deriving from the unavoidable fact that all interactions between interviewer and respondent occur within a sociocultural context, and that this context likely influences codeable behavior. Most troublesome is the possibility that behaviors that are elicited by respondents vary cross-culturally, so that counts of coding frequencies are themselves nonequivalent across group (Pan et al. 2010). Certainly, members of varied groups may exhibit different tendencies to interrupt the interview, to request clarification, or to express uncertainty—even at a set level of item comprehension. On the other hand, Johnson et al. (2011) found that respondents from different cultures were equally likely to elicit codeable behaviors illustrative of interactional problems in reaction to items that were intentionally flawed, suggesting some degree of cross-cultural commonality in the nature of the interviewer–respondent interaction.

9.6 Summary

The basic objective underlying the conduct of pretesting through Cognitive Interviews, UT, and BC, is to iron out both covert and overt problems prior to survey fielding. Each method has particular strengths and limitations (Presser and Blair 1994). Some of the respective advantages versus disadvantages relate to classic tensions between quantitative and qualitative research: CI and UT embody the benefit of intensive investigation that enhances explanatory power, and provide a richness that makes quantified data seem somewhat limited by comparison. On the other hand, qualitative procedures can appear unsystematic and idiosyncratic, and method reliability is difficult to establish. Further, CI and UT present high demands with respect to training and prior experience, and the activities are labor-intensive, with few effective shortcuts or scales of economy. Because BC, on the other hand, exhibits a greater degree of quantification, it is more effective in providing information on the extent of a problem, as evidenced by the observed distributions of problem coding categories. In truth, the strict standardization and quantification provided by BC may often be somewhat illusory in nature, as much of the obtained value lies with the free-flowing, qualitative explanations provided through coder debriefings. Further, BC coding systems differ significantly across practitioners, and it is not clear which variant leads to higher reliability and validity.

It is important to recognize that pretesting procedures are not independent, but feature considerable overlap. As discussed, CI and UT share a number of key features. Even CI and BC, although in principle very different, may tend to identify similar issues in the questionnaire—as cognitive problems for respondents often do produce overt indications of interactional difficulty. One possible view regarding the relationships among pretesting methods is that these can be regarded as a set of overlapping sieves that "catch" problems as the questionnaire is successively evaluated. Although it would seem ideal to therefore include multiple methods within a pretesting evaluation, it is common to select just one, due to practical considerations such as survey administration mode (as computerized self-administered questionnaires are amenable to UT), or point in questionnaire development (as draft questionnaires will be evaluated via CI, and later versions contained within a field test or pilot study will more naturally be evaluated through BC). Increasingly, pretesting procedures are being used in *mixed-method* combinations that incorporate both qualitative and quantitative components (Schaeffer and Dykema 2004). Where possible, investigators are increasingly also incorporating classical psychometric evaluation (Nunnally 1978), and modern measurement theory applications such as Item Response Theory (van der Linden and Hambleton 1997). As such, a promising future direction lies not only in the combination of standard forms of pretesting, but also in the combination of these with psychometrically oriented evaluation.

Finally, the coverage of pretesting within this chapter is not exhaustive, and other means for evaluating survey questions exist (see Madans et al. 2011). Some of these are less empirical in nature; for example, Expert Review consists of a critique of survey questions by either topic-related (substantive) or questionnaire design experts (Willis 2005). Alternatively, Focus Groups involve discussion of formative survey material by a group of individuals who resemble cognitive interviewing participants (Krueger 1994). Within the area of cognitive interviewing, or closely aligned with it, several very specialized procedures exist (e.g., card sorting, vignette studies, or response latency analysis; see Willis 2005); as are methods that reflect Esposito and Rothgeb's (1997) notion of *quality assessment,* as opposed to pretesting (e.g., embedding of cognitive probes within a fielded survey). Readers can find additional details by consulting a range of existing references (Bassili and Scott 1996, DeMaio and Rothgeb 1996, Forsyth and Lessler 1991, Martin 2004, Presser et al. 2004, Willis 1999, 2005).

As is frequently the case within an applied science that is intended to exhibit practical usability, the most significant challenge to pretesting practice is the development of a useful mix of well-developed, credible methods that questionnaire developers can confidently devote resources to, and rely upon, as means for achieving the ultimate goal of improving survey quality. As a more general conclusion, though, no matter what mix of pretesting methods result in the optimal outcome, careful attention to pretesting is a vital practice for any survey questionnaire. Sending the proverbial fire truck to put out a conflagration, in the absence of a dry run, is certainly a risky approach.

REFERENCES

Baker RP, Crawford S, Swinehart J. Development and testing of web questionnaires. In: Presser S, Rothgeb J, Couper M, Lessler J, Martin E, Martin J, Singer E, editors. *Methods for Testing and Evaluating Survey Questions*. New York: Wiley; 2004. p 361–384.

Bassili JN, Scott BS. Response latency as a signal to question problems in survey research. Public Opin Q 1996;60:390–399.

Banner DJ, Albarran JW. Computer-assisted qualitative data analysis software: a review. Can J Cardiovasc Nurs 2009;19(3):24–27.

Beatty PC, Willis GB. Research synthesis: the practice of cognitive interviewing. Public Opin Q 2007;71(2):287–311.

Belson WA. *The Design and Understanding of Survey Questions*. Aldershot, UK: Gower; 1981.

Biderman AD. Report of the workshop on applying cognitive psychology to recall problems of the National Crime Survey. Washington, D.C.: Bureau of Social Science Research; 1980.

Blair J, Brick P. Methods for the analysis of cognitive interviews. *Proceedings of the Section on Survey Research Methods, American Statistical Association*. American Statistical Association: Alexandria, VA; 2010. p 3739–3748.

Blair J, Conrad FG. Sample size for cognitive interview pretesting. Public Opin Q 2011;75(4):636–658.

Boeije H, Willis G. The cognitive interviewing reporting framework (CIRF): incorporating the principles of qualitative research. Paper presented at the meeting of the European Survey Research Association. Lausanne, Switzerland; 2011.

Cannell CF, Fowler FJ, Marquis K. *The Influence of Interviewer and Respondent Psychological and Behavioral Variables on the Reporting in Household Interviews*. Vital and Health Statistics, Series 2, No. 26 (PHS No. 1000, PB80-128275). Washington, DC: U.S. Government Printing Office; 1968.

Cantril H, Fried E. The meaning of questions. In: Cantril H, editor. *Gauging Public Opinion*. Princeton, NJ: Princeton University Press; 1944.

Census Bureau. *Census Bureau Standard: Pretesting Questionnaires and Related Methods for Surveys and Censuses*. Washington, DC: US Census Bureau; 2003.

Collins D. Pretesting survey instruments: an overview of cognitive methods. Qual Life Res 2003;12:229–238.

Collins D. Analysing and interpreting cognitive interview data. *Proceedings of the 2007 QUEST Conference*; Ottawa, CA; 2007. p 64–73.

Conrad F, Blair J. Interpreting verbal reports in cognitive interviews: probes matter. *Proceedings of the Annual Meeting of the American Statistical Association Proceedings of the Section on Survey Research Methods*; American Statistical Association; 2001.

Conrad F, Blair J. Data quality in cognitive interviews: the case of verbal reports. In: Presser S, Rothgeb J, Couper M, Lessler J, Martin E, Martin J, Singer E, editors. *Methods for Testing and Evaluating Survey Questionnaires*. Hoboken, NJ: Wiley; 2004. p 67–87.

Couper MP. The application of cognitive science to computer assisted interviewing. In: Sirken M, Herrmann D, Schechter S, Schwarz N, Tanur J, Tourangeau R, editors. *Cognition and Survey Research*. New York: Wiley; 1999. p 277–300.

Couper MP, Baker RP, Bethlehem J, Clark CZF, Martin J, Nicholls WL, O'Reilly JM. *Computer Assisted Survey Information Collection*. New York: Wiley; 1998.

DeMaio TJ, Rothgeb JM. Cognitive interviewing techniques: in the lab and in the field. In: Schwarz N, Sudman S, editors. *Answering Questions: Methodology for Determining Cognitive and Communicative Processes in Survey Research*. San Francisco: Jossey-Bass; 1996. p 175–195.

Dillman DA. *Mail and Internet Surveys: The Tailored Design Method*. 2nd ed. New York: Wiley; 2007.

Ericsson KA, Simon HA. Verbal reports as data. Psychol Rev 1980;87:215–251.

Ericsson KA, Simon HA. *Protocol Analysis: Verbal Reports as Data*. Cambridge: MIT Press; 1984.

Esposito JL, Rothgeb JM. Evaluating survey data: making the transition from pretesting to quality assessment. In: Lyberg L, Biemer P, Collins M, de Leeuw E, Dippo C, Schwarz N, Trewin D, editors. *Survey Measurement and Process Quality*. New York: Wiley; 1997. p 541–571.

Forsyth BH, Lessler JT. Cognitive laboratory methods: a taxonomy. In: Biemer PP, Groves RM, Lyberg LE, Mathiowetz NA, Sudman S, editors. *Measurement Errors in Surveys*. New York: Wiley; 1991. p 393–418.

Fowler FJ. Coding the behavior of interviewers and respondents to evaluate survey questions. In: Madans J, Miller K, Maitland A, Willis G, editors. *Question Evaluation Methods*. Hoboken, NJ: Wiley; 2011. p 7–21.

Gerber ER. The view from anthropology: ethnography and the cognitive interview. In: Sirken M, Herrmann D, Schechter S, Schwarz N, Tanur J, Tourangeau R, editors. *Cognition and Survey Research*. New York: Wiley; 1999. p 217–234.

Glaser BG, Strauss AL. *The Discovery of Grounded Theory: Strategies for Qualitative Research*. Chicago: Aldine; 1967.

Hippler HJ, Schwarz N, Sudman S, editors. *Social Information Processing and Survey Methodology*. New York: Springer-Verlag; 1987.

Jobe JB, Mingay DJ. Cognition and survey measurement: history and overview. Appl Cognit Psychol 1991;5:175–192.

Johnson TP, Holbrook AL, Shavitt S, Cho YI, Chavez N, Weiner S. Cross-cultural validity of behavior codes. Paper presented at the 66th Annual Meeting of the American Association for Public Opinion Research; 2011.

Krueger RA. *Focus Groups: A Practical Guide for Applied Research*. 2nd ed. Thousand Oaks, CA: Sage; 1994.

Loftus E. Protocol analysis of responses to survey recall questions. In: Jabine TB, Straf ML, Tanur JM, Tourangeau R, editors. *Cognitive Aspects of Survey Methodology: Building a Bridge Between Disciplines*. Washington, DC: National Academy Press; 1984. p 61–64.

Madans J, Miller K, Maitland A, Willis G. *Question Evaluation Methods: Contributing to the Science of Data Quality*. Hoboken, NJ: Wiley; 2011.

Martin E. Vignettes and respondent debriefing for questionnaire design and evaluation. In: Presser S, Rothgeb J, Couper M, Lessler J, Martin E, Martin J, et al., editors. *Methods for Testing and Evaluating Survey Questions*. New York: John Wiley and Sons; 2004. p 149–171.

Miller K. Cognitive interviewing. In: Madans J, Miller K, Maitland A, Willis G, editors. *Question Evaluation Methods*. Hoboken, NJ: Wiley; 2011. p 51–75.

Miller K, Canfield B, Beatty P, Whitaker K, Wilson B. Q-BANK: development and implementation of an evaluated-question database. Paper presented at the 2003 Federal Committee on Statistical Methodology Research Conference; Arlington, VA; 2003.

Miller K, Mont D, Maitland A, Altman B, Madans J. Results of a cross-national structured cognitive interviewing protocol to test measures of disability. Quality and quantity; 2010.

Miller K, Willis G, Eason C, Moses L, Canfield B. Interpreting the results of cross-cultural cognitive interviews: a mixed-method approach. ZUMA-Nachrichten Spezial Issue #11 2005:79–92.

Nunnally JC. *Psychometric Theory*. New York: McGraw-Hill; 1978.

Moss L, Goldstein H, editors. *The Recall Method in Social Surveys*. London: NFER; 1979.

Murphy J, Edgar J, Keating M. Crowdsourcing in the cognitive interviewing process. *Paper presented at the Annual Meeting of the American Association for Public Opinion Research*, Anaheim, CA; 2014.

Pan Y, Landreth A, Park H, Hinsdale-Shouse M, Schoua-Glusberg A. Cognitive interviewing in non-English languages: a cross-cultural perspective. In: Harkness JA, Braun M, Edwards B, Johnson TP, Lyberg L, Mohler PP, Pennell B-E, Smith TW, editors. *Survey Methods in Multinational, Multiregional, and Multicultural Contexts*. Hoboken, NJ: Wiley; 2010. p 91–113.

Presser S, Blair J. Survey pretesting: do different methods produce different results?. In: Marsden PV, editor. *Sociological Methodology*Vol. 24. Washington, DC: American Sociological Association; 1994. p 73–104.

Presser S, Rothgeb J, Couper M, Lessler J, Martin E, Martin J, Singer E. *Methods for Testing and Evaluating Survey Questionnaires*. Hoboken, NJ: Wiley; 2004.

Royston PN. Using intensive interviews to evaluate questions. In: Jr. Fowler FJ, editor. *Health Survey Research Methods*. Washington, DC: U.S. Government Printing Office; 1989. p 3–7(DHHS Publication No. PHS 89–3447).

Schaeffer NC, Dykema JL. A multiple-method approach to improving the clarity of closely related concepts: distinguishing legal and physical custody of children. In: Presser S, Rothgeb J, Couper M, Lessler J, Martin E, Martin J, Singer E, editors. *Methods for Testing and Evaluating Survey Questions*. New York: Wiley; 2004.

Schechter S. Proceedings of the 1993 NCHS conference on the cognitive aspects of self-reported health status (Cognitive Methods Staff Working Paper No. 10). Hyattsville MD, editor. *Centers for Disease Control and Prevention/National Center for Health Statistics*. 1994.

Schoua-Glusberg A. Response 2 to Fowler's chapter: coding the behavior of interviewers and respondents to evaluate survey questions. In: Madans J, Miller K, Maitland A, Willis G, editors. *Question Evaluation Methods*. Hoboken, NJ: Wiley; 2004. p 41–48.

Sirken MG, Herrmann DJ, Schechter S, Schwarz N, Tanur JM, Tourangeau R. *Cognition and Survey Research*. New York: Wiley; 1999.

Stapleton Kudela M, Stark D, Hantmann J, Deak MA, Newsome J. *Behavior Coding of the 2007 CHIS Discrimination Module: Final Report*. Westat; 2009.

Thissen MR, Fisher C, Barber L, Sattaluri S. Computer audio-recorded interviewing (CARI). A tool for monitoring field interviewers and improving field data collection. *Proceedings of Statistics Canada Symposium in Data Collection: Challenges, Achievements and New Directions*; 2008.

Tourangeau R. Cognitive sciences and survey methods. In: Jabine TB, Straf ML, Tanur JM, Tourangeau R, editors. *Cognitive Aspects of Survey Methodology: Building a Bridge Between Disciplines*. Washington, DC: National Academy Press; 1984. p 73–100.

Tourangeau R, Rips LJ, Rasinski K. *The Psychology of Survey Response*. Cambridge: Cambridge University Press; 2000a.

Tourangeau R, Couper MP, Tortora R, Miller-Steiger D. Cognitive issues in the design of web surveys. *Proceedings of the Section on Survey Methods Research*; American Statistical Association; 2000b. p 476–480.

van der Linden W, Hambleton RK. *Handbook of Modern Item Response Theory*. New York: Springer-Verlag; 1997.

Willis GB. *Cognitive Interviewing: A Tool for Improving Questionnaire Design*. Thousand Oak, CA: Sage; 2005.

Willis G, Lawrence D, Hartman A, Kudela M, Levin K, Forsyth B. Translation of a tobacco survey into Spanish and Asian languages: the tobacco use supplement to the current population survey. Nicotine Tob Res 2008;10(6):1075–1084.

Willis G, Schechter S. Evaluation of cognitive interviewing techniques: do the results generalize to the field? Bull Am Meteorol Soc 1997;55:40–66.

ONLINE RESOURCES

A short guide to pretesting can be found at: www.whatisasurvey.info/chapters/chapter7.htm.

An overview of cognitive interviewing is available in: Willis GB. (1999). *Cognitive Interviewing: A How-To Guide*, which is downloadable from: http://appliedresearch.cancer.gov/areas/cognitive/interview.pdf.

General resources and bibliography for web survey methodology are available at www.websm.org.

The University of Maryland *Online Survey Design Guide* can be found at: http://lap.umd.edu/survey_design/.

A brief guide labeled *Quality Web Content* is at: www.webpagecontent.com/arc_archive/124/5/.

For behavior coding, see Jack Fowler's 2011 presentation at the Question Evaluation Methods Workshop: http://wwwn.cdc.gov/qbank/QEM/Fowler_BehaviorCoding_QEM_Primary_Paper.pdf.

CHAPTER TEN

Cross-Cultural Considerations in Health Surveys

Brad Edwards
Westat, Rockville, Maryland, USA

10.1 Introduction

The origins of what we think of as "culture" in the social sciences today are classical. Cicero used *cultura* to refer to the "cultivation" or development of thought and emotions. In the seventeenth century, Samuel Pufendorf wrote that culture "referred to all the ways in which human beings overcome their original barbarism, and through artifice, become fully human" (Velkley 2002). Germans in the next century refined this to mean the ways a people can be distinguished from other groups, giving rise to the fields of cultural anthropology and ethnography. Inherent in this concept is the notion that the distinct worldview of a people contains many aspects that have been expressed in local ("folk") ways (Bastian 1860). Language "encodes" culture. Linguistic structuralists began to focus on the formal elements of language, stripped of its content. Levi-Straus (1955) applied their approach to culture, and found that structural elements of cultural aspects like kinship systems and creation myths could be mapped across cultures into basic elements that are universal in all human societies. Identifying, quantifying, and comparing distinctions among groups have become a core

Handbook of Health Survey Methods, First Edition. Edited by Timothy P. Johnson.

purpose of survey research in the last century, but often without regard to the underlying structures within each group.

Cultural differences have long been a concern in health and health care, as reflected in surveys for at least half a century. The earliest studies often focused on comparison of groups within country in one language, but as methods became more powerful and sophisticated, multilingual surveys became easier to implement, and multinational studies were attempted. One of the earliest examples is a study comparing health care systems in the United States and Sweden (Andersen et al. 1970). Interest in survey methods for comparing health status, use of health care services, and health outcomes among population groups and across countries has increased greatly in the past two decades. This field is often called *3MC*, from the title of a seminal 2008 conference in Berlin (International Conference on Survey Methods in Multinational, Multiregional, and Multicultural Contexts (3MC) 2008).

In this chapter, we outline the development and growth of comparative surveys, of comparative methods in survey research, and of culture and language issues in health and health care. A summary of cross-cultural considerations in the survey life cycle is followed by a more detailed discussion of theory and practice in instrument design, translation, survey operations, quality assessment, and analysis. We draw examples from a number of national and multinational health surveys.

10.1.1 COMPARABILITY AND COMPARATIVE SURVEYS

Harkness defines comparative surveys as those surveys explicitly designed to compare two or more groups (Harkness et al. 2010a). Although one could interpret this very broadly—almost all survey data are intended to be used for group comparisons—the emphasis is on "designed to compare," and the design usually requires careful planning. Comparative surveys collect data from different cultural, linguistic, or ethnic population groups, regions or nations, and the goal of comparison drives much of their design. They are often (but not necessarily) multilingual.

The concept of comparability in cross-cultural surveys is subtle. In medicine, practitioners have accepted English as their international language; it is used in almost all international conferences and professional journals, and has acquired the status that medical Latin enjoyed 2000 years ago. Non-English-speaking countries can choose to use the English terms or translate them into their own language (e.g., bypass is "bypass" in German and Italian, but *pontage* in French and *shuntirovanie* in Russian) (Wulff 2004). Physicians who do not speak a *lingua franca* can still use the English terms for body parts or health conditions, drawn from Greek or Latin. But in most realms, communication between two people who do not speak or read the same language is facilitated by an interpreter or translator (human or machine). The process of communicating between languages can vary greatly in quality, but even the best translation cannot be exact. This is clear to any reader who has read the same book in two translations. Languages don't have exact equivalents for all words and phrases. Some words and phrases can be expressed in more or less standard language that moves easily across cultures (e.g., "hand," "sun," and "eat"), but many others are more localized, embedded within a culture ("How often in the past month have you felt blue?" in American English or "How old is your father's older brother by birth?" in Mandarin Chinese) and more difficult to resolve in translation. Some concepts are unique to a culture; identical concepts do not exist elsewhere. Other concepts are shared by many but not all cultures. For example, a medical device common in the United States and Europe may not exist in Samoa, and it would be folly to craft a question in Samoan about it.

What makes cross-cultural surveys so different? More than 40 years ago Verba wrote, " ... there is nothing unique about cross-cultural studies ... [*but*] ... the problems are more severe and more easily recognizable" (Verba 1969). Harkness and colleagues reviewed the more recent literature and found a consensus that cross-cultural surveys are more complex than mono-cultural surveys. "Special difficulties ... include challenges to 'equivalence,' multiple language and meaning difficulties, conceptual and indicator issues, obtaining good sample frames, practical problems in data collection, as well as the sheer expense and effort involved" (Harkness et al. 2010b). The unique aspects of the various cultures along the dimensions of the study objectives must be addressed from the outset and can affect every subsequent stage of the project. This creates a complexity layered on top of general survey design requirements that makes cross-cultural surveys special. They require not just more effort, but a different kind of effort, than general surveys.

In cross-cultural studies, it is easy to find many references to *equivalence*, a concept borrowed from psychology and psychometrics that develop "equivalent" scales from a series of items that perform in the same way with different groups. In the cross-cultural literature, Johnson reported more than 50 unique uses of the term (Johnson 1998). If exact equivalence is elusive in surveys, what about *functional* equivalence? Functional equivalence might exist in a survey of two countries or groups within country that are very similar in most respects. They may not use a single word or phrase to describe a concept, but the concept exists in both cultures and a cluster of words in each culture might be used to describe it. However, the farther apart the two cultures are, the greater the dissimilarity, and the less likely that anything like functional equivalence exists. Almond and Verba (1963) concluded that complete equivalence is never achievable in practice.

The problem with equivalence is that it is an absolute, an ideal concept. A survey questionnaire is a rather blunt instrument in many respects, designed to work in a quantitative, probabilistic context. Mohler and Johnson have proposed *comparability* as a heuristic way to think about the issue, and *similarity* as a useful term for measuring comparability at the construct, variable, and question level (Mohler and Johnson 2010).

The Cross-Cultural Survey Guidelines offer this definition of comparability: "The extent to which differences between survey statistics from different countries, regions, cultures, time periods, and so on, can be attributable to differences in population true values" (Survey Research Center 2010).

10.1.2 BRIEF HISTORY OF WORK ON COMPARATIVE METHODS IN SURVEY RESEARCH

In the postwar dawn of multicountry survey research, a number of comparability problems surfaced. Team members from different countries spoke different languages and had difficulty communicating. Questionnaire translation standards did not exist. It was difficult to determine if a question measured opinions or behavior or demographics in the same way in different countries (Almond and Verba 1969). Similar problems were encountered in early multicultural work within countries. For example, during the polio epidemic in the United States in the mid-twentieth century, research on incidence revealed differences between Blacks and Whites, but it was unclear whether the measures were biased. "There is the possibility ... that reports from the colored were not ... comparable with those from the white" (Collins 1946, as quoted in Mohler and Johnson 2010). Rigorous methodological work on basic, monocultural surveys was slow to develop, with the exception of sampling (Kish 1965, Deming 1966). Nonsampling error was a black box through the 1950s, and questionnaire design was considered an art, not a science (Payne 1951).

As general survey methods developed in the 1970s and 1980s (Dillman 1978, Sudman and Bradburn 1982, Converse and Presser 1986), the number of multinational studies expanded and the surveys became less *ad hoc*. For example, the International Social Survey Program (ISSP) began in 1985 in six countries, to provide comparative data on a wide range of societal values and attitudes. The World Health Organization began the cross-national Health Behaviour in School-Aged Children (HBSC) in the mid-1980s (Honkala 2013). The U.S. Agency for International Development created the Demographic and Health Surveys program in 1984; since then the program has conducted 260 surveys in 90 countries (Demographic and Health Surveys). Chen demonstrated the richness of these data in describing how he explored the relationship between language type (i.e., whether or not the present is distinguished from the future) and household savings rates, using data from the DHS and official statistics (Chen 2013).

Six generic health status instruments (the Quality of Life Index, the Nottingham Health Profile, the Functional Status Questionnaire, the Charts for Primary Care Practice, the Duke Health Profile, and the Short-Form 36 Health Survey) came into use in multiple countries between 1981 and 1992 (Sadana et al. 2000). Within-country surveys began to focus on cultural, racial, and ethnic groups and issues. The General Social Survey (GSS), the U.S. component of the ISSP since it began, has created many cross-sectional data series on attitudes toward race, on access to health care, and on vignettes of various health care situations in English and Spanish (NORC). The National Health Interview Survey (NHIS), begun in 1957, collected race by interviewer observation until 1982, when questions were added to collect race and Hispanic origin from all household members (Centers for Disease Control and Prevention). The National Medical Expenditure Survey (NMES) included a parallel Survey of American Indians and Alaska Natives (SAIAN) in 1986 (Interuniversity Consortium for Political and Social Research).

As Smith (2010) notes, this period continued through the end of the twentieth century. During these three decades, multinational survey methods were viewed as no different in kind from monocultural methods. Rather, multinational surveys were considered presenting a degree of greater difficulty in comparability, operations, and management. Multicultural issues in surveys within country often went unrecognized, except in special studies of minority populations such as the 1979 Chicano Survey (Interuniversity Consortium for Political and Social Research). The Third National Health and Nutrition Examination Survey (NHANES), conducted from 1988 to 1994, is another exception. It sampled Mexican Americans (but not other Hispanics) at a higher rate, in recognition of the cultural differences among Hispanic groups as well as the difficulty of screening enough other Hispanics in the United States to meet analytic needs (Ezzati and Massey 1992). A number of recent studies have recognized differences among various Hispanic groups, and researchers increasingly regard them as too culturally distinct from one another to aggregate.

The current era is characterized by the recognition that survey methods for comparative surveys are not just extensions of general survey methods, but have qualitative differences from them. Multicultural and multinational studies begun since then are generally more attentive to comparative survey methods, and they contribute to and draw upon a growing literature. For example, the European Social Survey (ESS) pioneered the application of translation research to cross-cultural surveys. These efforts were spearheaded by Harkness, the ESS leader for translation and questionnaire design. *Cross-Cultural Survey Methods* (Harkness et al. 2003) was her first volume collecting work in this field. It was followed by an annual workshop series sponsored by a group known as *Comparative Survey Design and Implementation* (CSDI). The CSDI organizers convened the Berlin 3MC conference in 2008. A major product was the volume *Survey Methods in Multinational, Multiregional, and Multicultural Contexts* (Harkness et al. 2010a). Another CSDI effort was the development of *Cross-Cultural Survey Guidelines*, an online resource maintained at the University of Michigan's Survey Research Center (Survey Research Center 2010)

The Survey of Health, Ageing, and Retirement in Europe (SHARE) is an example of a project developed in the current era. Building on the framework of the Health and Retirement Survey in the United States and the English Longitudinal Survey of Ageing in the United Kingdom, SHARE has established a model for pilot testing and for collecting data from physical and cognitive assessments in cross-cultural contexts (Borsch-Supan et al. 2010).

The history of the concept of informed consent in medicine and research parallels and informs the development of cross-cultural survey methods. The Nuremburg Code in 1947 was created to ensure people were never again subjected to the horrific experiments conducted by the Nazi regime using Jews, Roma, homosexuals, and other ethnic and cultural groups throughout Europe. "Although the United States was condemning the Nazi experiments ... an unethical and inhumane experiment was going on in Tuskegee, Alabama" (Osman 2001). The U.S. Public Health Service began studying the effects of syphilis on low income Black men in 1932, and continued the study for decades, until it was stopped in 1972 with the publication of a New York Times article. Men were not informed that there was an effective treatment for the disease (penicillin), and were discouraged from seeking other medical advice. The Belmont Report (U.S. Department of Health and Human Services, Office of the Secretary 1979) held that medicine and research involving human subjects must attend to these moral elements: disclosure, understanding, voluntariness, competence, and consent.

Of these, *understanding* is perhaps the most relevant for cross-cultural survey research. At the most basic level in the United States, it means if the subject has difficulty understanding English (or Spanish, if the protocol is presented in that language), an interpreter must be provided to make sure the subject has the opportunity to ask questions about the study. But awareness is increasing that the context of survey research is not universally shared across cultures, and the informed consent process must be adapted in order to communicate effectively with members of each culture (Pan et al. 2010).

10.1.3 CULTURE AND LANGUAGE ISSUES IN HEALTH AND HEALTH CARE

Until the last century, health was culturally determined. Each culture in each part of its history defined health in its own particular way, and these ways varied greatly. For instance, concepts of healthy weight and nutrition, or life expectancy and disease can be quite different from one culture to another and within a culture over time.

But as the public health movement grew in the nineteenth and early twentieth centuries, a more universal notion of health gained currency. Proper sanitation, access to adequate health care, and the development of norms for height and weight became common elements. Along with this came a need to assess the health of a population, to compare populations, and to assess a population over time. With the development of probability sampling in the 1930s, survey research became an essential tool for assessing population health (see also Chapter 1).

Although generally well-meaning, the public health movement often failed to recognize or address cultural differences. For example, through at least the mid-twentieth century in the United States for example, a paternalistic approach was applied to improving the health of Native Americans. This "one size fits all" approach dismissed the Native cultures and their traditional medicines and attempted to impose a Western model, but failed to improve health outcomes in these widely dispersed, extremely poor populations. Similarly, Irish Travelers, a distinct ethnic group with nomadic traditions, its own language, and high levels of illiteracy and poverty in the Republic of Ireland and Northern Ireland, were encouraged to move into permanent settlements in towns and to integrate into the general culture; data were not collected on them as a distinct group, hence their health could not be measured. These policies were generally unsuccessful in improving the population's health, but were not discontinued until early in the twenty-first century (Kelleher and Quirke 2014).

Such gaps in public health systems can lead to tragedies in the provision of health care services. Consider the following example:

> Thirteen-year-old Graciela Zamora was like many children whose parents speak limited English: she served as her family's interpreter. When she developed severe abdominal pain, her parents took her to the hospital. Unfortunately, Graciela was too sick to interpret for herself, and the hospital did not provide an interpreter. … [H]er Spanish-speaking parents were told, without … an interpreter, to bring her back immediately if her symptoms worsened, and otherwise to follow-up with a doctor in three days. However, … her parents understood … that they should wait three days to see the doctor. After two days … they felt they could no longer wait, and rushed her back to the emergency department. … [S]he had a ruptured appendix. She was airlifted to a nearby medical center in Phoenix, where she died a few hours later.
>
> (Chen et al. 2007)

Although the great majority of problematic cultural and language encounters in provider settings do not risk the patient's life, they often result in misunderstandings about symptoms and treatment, improper consent procedures, inadequate follow-up, and poor health outcomes. Health literacy is "the degree to which individuals have the capacity to obtain, process, and understand basic health information and services needed to make appropriate health decisions" (Ratzan and Parker 2000). Speaking the same language as the provider should not be a prerequisite for health literacy or for equal access and fair treatment.

In the United States in 2011, those who do not speak English "very well" numbered about 25,000,000, nearly 9% of the population. Between 1980 and 2010, this limited English proficiency (LEP) group increased 158% between 1980 and 2010, primarily because of a large wave of immigration from developing countries (Ryan 2013).

Spanish is spoken by about 13% of the U.S. population (Ryan 2013). In 10 articles examining language barriers in Hispanic populations and published in biomedical journals, Timmins (2002) found evidence for adverse effects of language on access to care, quality of care, and adverse outcomes.

The legal basis for providing access to medical care for all, including those from minority cultures and those who don't speak English, is Title VI of the 1964 Civil Rights Act:

> No person in the United States shall, on the grounds of race, color, or national origin, be excluded from participation in, be denied the benefits of, or be subjected to discrimination under any program or activity receiving federal financial assistance.
>
> (42 U.S.C. 2000d 1964)

The U.S. courts have held that language is covered by national origin. In 1980, the Department of Human Services made clear this applied to health care providers, banning discrimination "in health and human services programs because they have a primary language other than English" (U.S. Government 1980). The HHS Office for Civil Rights (OCR) is charged with oversight, and its pursuit of complaints from patients on the basis of language in several major hospitals led to the development of major hospital-based interpreter services programs (Chen). The OCR issued a Policy Guidance document (August 2003) that offers four factors for determining the extent and types of language services expected of providers: number or proportion of LEP persons served or eligible for services; frequency of contact; importance of the service; and provider resources and costs (Chen et al. 2007).

In the United States today, health care providers are expected to ensure language access to all patients; large hospitals and other providers must provide language assistance services. Some states (e.g., California, New Jersey, Washington) have gone farther, stipulating translation and interpretation requirements for specific services, documents, and languages (Youdelman 2007, Chen et al. 2007). Some government agencies and hospitals have been developing innovative methods for reaching LEP patients (e.g., Agency for Healthcare Research and Quality 2012, Hahn 2012). However, these are *best* practices. There is very little enforcement. Rose and colleagues (Rose et al. 2010) reported that two-thirds of physicians treating cancer patients in Los Angeles County said that availability of trained medical interpreters was poor. In common practice, smaller providers only invest in improving language access and services when confronted with a complaint. "The reality is that many health care providers are not aware of their responsibility, have not prioritized the issue, or have not been held accountable through consistent enforcement of these laws" (Chen et al. 2007).

Disparities. Concerns about disparities in health and health care have moved to the top of the health policy agenda as more data have been produced that allow group comparisons—by race and ethnicity, language, gender, income, age, sexual orientation, and geography (LaViest 2005). In the United States, Healthy People 2020 strives to improve the health of all groups. It defines disparity as "a particular type of health difference that is closely linked with social, economic, and environmental disadvantage. Health disparities adversely affect groups of people who have systematically experienced greater obstacles to health based on … characteristics historically linked to discrimination or exclusion" (U.S. Department of Health and Human Services). The Agency for Healthcare Research and Quality issues the National Healthcare Disparities Report annually. The 2012 report found barriers and restricted access to care for 26% of Americans, disproportionately Blacks and Hispanics. Blacks and Hispanics receive worse care than Whites on about 40% of quality measures (Clancy 2013). Many surveys over the past decade have documented these disparities and their consequences for minority health (Timmins 2002, Van Wieren et al. 2011, Pampel and Denney 2011, Mulia et al. 2009, Nyaronga et al. 2009, Ai et al. 2013).

At the international level, many countries and organizations recognize that health is a global concern, intrinsically linked to security, economic growth, and well-being. Researchers and policy makers are striving to measure and reduce disparities across countries and regions, for minority groups and between women and men. Some of these are disease specific, especially focused on infectious diseases, while others are focused on substance abuse and mental health, or health determinants (Room et al. 2012, Breslau et al. 2011, Setia et al. 2011, Dunn and Dyck 2000).

Interpretation and Translation. The meanings of interpretation and translation are often confused. Here we refer to interpretation as the act of converting speech from the speaker's language to the listener's language. Translation is the act of converting text from one language to another. In the interpretation and translation literature, the former is referred to as the *source language*, and the latter is known as the *target language*. Translation studies encompass the theory and application of both language interpretation and translation.

Professional schools and associations for interpreters have long maintained clear ethical standards. These include avoiding injecting oneself into a conversation. When the speaker uses the first person, the interpreter uses the first person ("Tell me what's bothering you?," not "He wants to know what's bothering you."). Conflicts of interest are to be avoided. In the Zamora case discussed earlier, although Graciela was often pressed into playing the role of interpreter in the family system, there would be an obvious conflict of interest in medical provider settings. This conflict might result in missing information and degraded quality of care. Parents might be embarrassed to report certain problems in the child's presence, and children who interpret might be privy to information they might not otherwise obtain.

Fluency in two languages is not sufficient for interpreting. Interpreters must be able to move easily from one language to another, often quickly in real time, a very complex task. They must be able to infer context of language in the two cultures in order to convey the speaker's intent in a way that can be understood by the listener—preserving tone, register and feeling. Medical interpreters also require some special knowledge, such as: terms for symptoms, conditions, procedures, parts of the body; ethical issues and informed consent procedures in a clinical setting; and structure of the health care system. Some states and many health care systems have adopted a requirement that medical interpreters be certified as meeting certain standards.

Use of professional interpretation services by telephone or through a video connection is a common solution, especially for situations where the number of patients speaking the language is very small.

Translation is almost never performed in "real time" and can take advantage of dictionaries and other language aids, including previous translations of similar material. A translator's work can be edited by other translators. Translation of medical terminology has a long historical record, dating back at least to the twelfth century and the Toledo School of Translation (Moore 2010). Translation has some advantages over interpretation. It can assure that messages about a program or a disease or a program of care are delivered in a uniform way. It can be tailored to the provider's needs, in ways that a professional interpreting service using many staff by phone worldwide cannot. It is also less expensive than using professional interpreters.

Cultural Competency. As noted earlier, culture and language are closely linked but culture is also manifested in many other ways. The notion of "competence" in addressing cultural differences originated about 25 years ago in health care research, and a subfield of research in cultural competency has developed since then (Betancourt et al. 2001). The HHS Office for Minority Affairs has published standards for Culturally and Linguistically Appropriate Services (CLAS) in health care (U.S. Government). A number of tools are available for developing and assessing cultural competency—the ability to communicate well with people of different cultures, respecting their traditions and beliefs (e.g., the Cultural Competence Health Practitioner Assessment) (Center for Child and Human Development, Georgetown University).

The Consumer Assessment of Healthcare Providers and Systems (CAHPS) collects data on patients' perceptions of the cultural competence of their providers. Seligman et al. (2012) found race and ethnic differences in these assessments were insignificant, and recommended that cultural competency should be implemented across populations, rather than targeted at specific groups. Coelho and Galan (2012) reported physicians, regardless of ethnicity, were more accurate at rating White faces and verbal tones.

In health survey research, "building cultural competence requires the development of awareness, knowledge, and skills" (Jin et al. 2011). Of particular relevance to health survey design are idioms of distress (ways cultures express, experience, and cope with distress) and culture-bound symptoms (clusters of symptoms much more common in some cultures than others) (U.S. Department of Health and Human Services 2001). Somatization is an example of an idiom of distress. Stomach and chest pains are common among Whites and some Hispanic groups (Escobar et al. 1987); dizziness, blurred vision, and vertigo are common among some Asian groups (Hsu and Folstein 1997); and sensations of burning extremities, worms in the head, or ants under the skin are common in Africa and South Asia (American Psychiatric Association 1994). Some examples of culture-bound symptoms are: *taijin kyofusho* in Japan, an intense fear that one's body or body functions are offensive to others; and *ataque de nervios* in some Hispanic and Caribbean groups, attacks of screaming, crying, trembling, and aggression. Ethno- or cultural psychiatry studies how culture interacts with biology to "shape illnesses and reactions to them" (U.S. Department of Health and Human Services 2001). Integrative neuroscience and genetics study the role of culture in mental health and illness, related to the structure and function of the brain (Hyman 2000).

Although cross-cultural issues are often associated with household surveys, they can present themselves in establishment surveys as well. For example, to reach health care providers, one may be required to reach into or through hospitals, agencies, or practices to collect data from a specific provider, and establishment surveys often require multiple respondents and access to records. It is not a very significant stretch of the concept of culture to understand its relevance to comparative studies of different provider types (Edwards et al. 2009). And patient safety studies have adopted the word "culture" to describe how hospitals incorporate safety objectives and best practices in rules and language.

10.1.4 CROSS-CULTURAL CONSIDERATIONS IN THE SURVEY LIFE-CYCLE

Cross-cultural issues are encountered at each stage of the survey life-cycle. Figure 10.1, drawn from the Cross-Cultural Survey Guidelines (Survey Research Center 2010), illustrates these stages in detail.

Study, Organizational, and Operational Structure. In the beginning, cross-cultural and multinational surveys employed simple forms of organization. Either a single entity (a government agency or research institution in one country) held responsibility for all the planning, design, and implementation of the survey (as the U.S. State Department did in the post-war surveys of the effect of bombing on civilians in Germany, the United Kingdom, and Japan) (U.S. Strategic Bombing Survey 1947a and 1947b; Janis 1951), or responsibility was divided among a number of entities, one in each country (as in the case of the Verba studies cited earlier). As the methodology has advanced and the complexities have increased, these two alternative structures persist, but in altered forms. If responsibility is maintained in one organization (either in

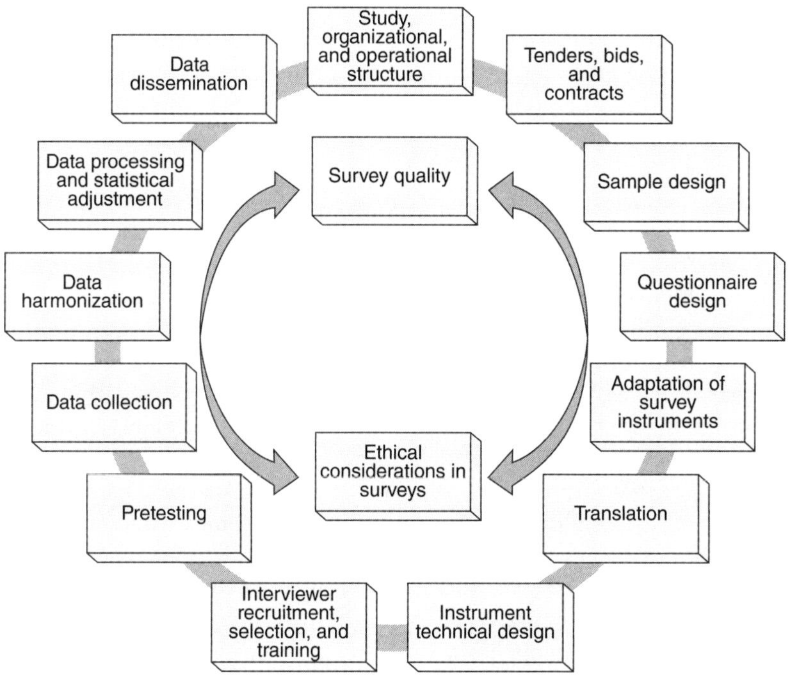

FIGURE 10.1 Survey project life cycle (Survey Research Center 2010). Reprinted with permission from the Survey Research Center, Institute for Social Research, University of Michigan.

a multinational survey or in a cross-cultural survey within-country), greater control and efficiency may be achieved, but there is considerable risk that cultural differences will be overlooked. Many have recognized the critical importance of including members of each culture in the research team for this model. If the responsibility is spread among participating countries or groups, the risk is that insufficient attention will be paid to ensuring that research goals and quality standards are met, and attempts have been made to document specifications and performance to compensate for these tendencies.

Sample Design. Sampling issues in cross-cultural and multinational surveys are perhaps the best understood part of the survey process. The literature on rare and elusive populations is extensive, and the topic was addressed comprehensively at the 2012 International Conference on Hard-to-Reach Populations and a monograph (Tourangeau et al. 2014).

Questionnaire Design, Adaptation, Translation, and Pretesting. These stages pose some of the greatest challenges and risks in surveys that are conducted in more than one language. All too often the design starts with questions in the source language rather than with concepts that take the various cultures to be compared into account. Little effort is made to adapt questions borrowed from other monocultural instruments, or to pretest the instrument and survey protocol with the groups to be compared. And the design often ends with the finalization of the questionnaire in the source language, even though many problems with the questionnaire may only become visible in the attempt to translate the questions into another language.

Instrument Technical Design refers to the process of transforming question text into programming specifications. Decisions about orientation of text on the computer screen, the use of color, the display of response options, and many other technical issues need cultural and linguistic input and review.

Interviewer Recruitment, Selection, and Training, Data Collection, and Data Processing are major operations that occur between the design stage and the product stage. They are often heavily dependent on the infrastructure within the cultures to be surveyed, and may rely on many hidden assumptions. Practice and experience can vary greatly from one country to another.

Harmonization improves the comparability of cross-national data. It may do this at any stage of the life cycle. For example, it may compare question wording and response categories across countries, find some differences, and attempt to adjust for the differences. Data from different surveys may also be harmonized, if the surveys are comparable (Granda et al. 2010).

Statistical adjustment applies weights created from the probabilities of selection, and adjusts these weights to represent nonresponders. It may include bias analysis if nonresponse is great, and it may compare nonresponse across groups and countries.

Data dissemination has received increasing attention as an important part of overall survey quality. The speed of data release, its accessibility, its comparative value and level of documentation are often determinants of survey success.

The following section discusses several of these stages at greater length: instrument design, translation and interpretation, survey operations and process quality, and analysis.

10.2 Theory and Practice

This section discusses theoretical development in cross-cultural instrument design, translation, survey operations, process quality, and analysis. For each area, we offer examples of ways the theory has been applied in health surveys, primarily in the United States, but also on some cross-national health surveys.

10.2.1 INSTRUMENT DESIGN

For any survey, the instrument design process is understood to include theoretical concepts, latent constructs, indicators, and questions (Harkness et al. 2010c). Naïve designers may begin with a set of questions, but this approach is particularly inappropriate for cross-cultural studies. For comparative instruments, it is helpful to begin with a theoretical framework. Articulate how concepts relate to each other in the framework. Define or describe the concepts. Incorporate cross-cultural review at this beginning stage, and identify issues that, if undetected, could jeopardize comparability. Smith (2003, 2004) gives examples of questionnaire design considerations in a multilingual context.

Of necessity, researchers consider concepts that are grounded in their experience and knowledge of their own culture. But this perspective comes with blinders that make it extremely difficult to determine if these same concepts are present in the other cultures of interest. This tension between the emic (what is internal to a culture) and the etic (that which is external to the culture) has long been a focus of cultural anthropology and ethnography. Even when the same concept is present in multiple cultures, the way it is mapped in cognitive space (i.e., the indicators) may be quite different. Participation, review, or input by other researchers who are insiders or have considerable experience in other cultures can be critical. If a concept is not present in another culture, no cross-cultural comparison is possible.

For example, consider the concept of religiosity. This is often confused with its most popular indicator in the West, the frequency of attendance at religious services. But in many Eastern cultures, religion and spirituality are more integrated into daily life, and religiosity cannot be measured by this indicator. Is the concept of religiosity universal? Some have attempted to compare cultures on this dimension by selecting other indicators in Eastern cultures, but the effort requires a keen understanding of cultural differences.

Concept coverage has become a core concern in cross-cultural psychology and educational testing, but it is often ignored in the general field of health surveys, with the exception of quality of life research (Harkness et al. 2010c, Fox-Rushby and Parker 1995). Addressing concept coverage moves the researcher closer to participant- or respondent-centered design. Respect for the human research subject implies one should avoid asking questions that have no meaning to the subject. But because almost all cross-cultural researchers begin their careers in mono- or dominant-culture environments, it can be difficult to acknowledge a gap in understanding other cultures that can only be bridged by assembling a team that can represent the cultures of interest for comparison.

Designing data collection instruments for cross-cultural studies is challenging to say the least. Some questions have a strong pedigree, having been used on many predecessor studies. A pedigree suggests the question should be used "as is" in a new design, even though it may not be the best choice in a multicultural context. With regard to testing, it is desirable to test each question or scale with each culture that will be compared, but in practice this can be quite difficult to achieve because of schedule and resource constraints.

Different design approaches have developed within disciplines for various types of questions and modes. In health surveys, the most common questions are about facts or behaviors ("Do you have any vision problems?"), or medical history ("Have you seen a doctor or other medical professional in the last 12 months?"). Less common are questions about psychological states, attitudes or opinions, or about knowledge and skills ("Here is a label from a prescribed medicine bottle. What is the strength of the tablets?"). Many constructs are measured by only one or two items, but scales are more commonly used for assessing mental states and program knowledge.

Basic design principles for comparative surveys are no different than for general surveys, except for the need to address comparability at each stage. The most critical stage is at the very beginning of the survey life cycle, in identifying the concepts and the groups for comparison. Many multicultural studies are not designed at the outset to compare concepts across cultures, but they are not the focus of this chapter. Rather, here we are concerned with surveys that are intended to compare data across cultures. For multicultural surveys, one cannot rely solely on the topic literature and repeat approaches that have been used on many studies. Conventions that are implicit in monocultural studies, such as a focus on the individual's opinions or the use of a scale of a certain length, may not perform as expected in other cultural contexts (Park et al. 1988, Schwarz et al. 2010, Yang et al. 2010, Johnson et al. 2010, Van Vaerenbergh and Thomas 2013). The domain of health and all its concepts varies greatly from culture to culture (Harkness 2004). Unfortunately, experience and guidance in comparative survey design has not reached the level of development one finds today in general survey research. Finding competent experts can be difficult. Much of the existing knowledge comes from trial and error, and is reported in professional conferences but may not always make its way into peer-reviewed journals.

Without a conceptual framework, it is difficult to identify design gaps or evaluate proposed additions. In health services research, a common framework has its origins in Andersen's behavioral model in the 1960s and early 1970s, and has become the basis for work in disparities, access to care, and many other components of the field (Andersen 1995). A common conceptual framework also helps the research team share knowledge about cultural variations and develop an approach for addressing multicultural issues.

A *quality assurance and control plan* can spotlight issues with multicultural aspects in design, translation, pretesting, survey operations, and processing. The plan can focus on product quality, process quality, and organizational quality (Lyberg and Stukel 2010).

Standardization has been a dominant paradigm in general survey research over the past half century, and some research teams have extended the paradigm to cross-cultural studies. For instance, a specific objective of CHIS (the California Health Interview Survey) is to support comparisons across a number of racial and ethnic groups. Telephone (CATI) is the mode of data collection. Translations are produced in five languages. Interviewers are hired who speak those languages fluently (as evidenced by a standardized test developed by Westat), and interviews are monitored in real time to assure that the CATI instrument is administered exactly as intended, across all groups. However, some recent researchers have argued that more adaptation is needed to address the contexts of different cultures (e.g., Pan and Lubkemann 2014).

Ideally, instrument *design experts and teams* should include people who have cultural expertise in each group that will be compared in the survey. When this is not possible, the team should reach out to reviewers who have this cultural knowledge. English is typically the source language and the lingua franca in design activities, so the team must develop sensitivity to those members who may not have English as their primary language, in order to encourage their full participation in the design. Advance translation is a term that has surfaced in recent literature. It means developing a translation of the draft source (English) language questionnaire in order to identify concepts that are difficult to translate and that therefore may not be comparable across cultures, or question wording that is too vernacular or colloquial (e.g., "How often in the past month have you felt downhearted or blue?").

Instrument Design Fundamentals. Questions are measurement tools that allow researchers to conduct studies of indicators, which can give insight into latent constructs and the theoretical concepts behind them. This design hierarchy helps identify issues in cross-cultural surveys. Identifying indicators that tap into a construct allows one to assess whether these indicators are appropriate across cultures, before questions are formulated. This is a critical step, because indicators can vary widely. Sometimes, a construct that can be adequately represented by only two or three indicators in one culture, may require many more indicators in another culture. Consider health insurance coverage, for instance. In countries with a single party payer, such as France, nearly everyone has coverage and all have the same coverage. But in the United States, with its Balkanized system of coverage and noncoverage and mix of different public and private plans (all dimly understood by most citizens), many items are required. Thus, the insurance section of the Medical Expenditure Panel Survey (MEPS) in the United States contains many questions to determine an individual's coverage.

Can the questions be answered? Questions that may seem straightforward in one cultural context (e.g., the race question in the U.S. dominant culture) make little sense in another culture (e.g., the race question for Hispanic immigrants in the United States). Some questions can be sensitive in some cultures but not others. It is easy for misunderstandings to arise between the intended meaning of a question and the perceived meaning. This is one of the largest sources of nonsampling error in surveys. It is a particular concern in cross-cultural research, and often requires careful testing in each culture.

Mode. Mixed-mode surveys are becoming increasingly common. Cross-cultural issues may be related to mode, and should be considered in early stages of design. For example, surveys in the United States that begin with a web interview and move to telephone for those who don't respond to the web are likely to find a lower take up rate for the web among racial and ethnic minorities. If there are mode effects, data from minorities might not be comparable to data from the rest of the population.

Key Decisions on Instrument Design. Cross-cultural studies face three key decisions in instrument design.

- To what extent do the cultures share common understandings of the questions? Assuming that there is a common understanding implies there are common indicators, constructs, and concepts. If understandings differ at the question level, but there are common indicators, questions could be adapted, or added for each culture.
- Where do the questions come from? A study may choose to use existing questions, adapt questions others have used, or develop new questions. Many surveys use all three approaches. The source of the questions is important in developing translation and pretesting plans.
- How can comparability and validity be established across cultures? The answer to this question depends largely on what stage cross-cultural input is sought. Many health surveys take a sequential approach (drafting the questions in the context of the dominant culture, and only obtaining cross-cultural input in the translation stage). Others develop in parallel, and attempt to get cross-cultural input at virtually every stage of the design process. The most elaborate and costly approach would be to develop the instrument simultaneously within each cultural context, an approach that is very rarely undertaken.

Most cross-cultural designs for health surveys ask everyone the same questions. This has many advantages. In analysis populations can be compared at the question (rather than the indicator) level. Translation allows all the questions to be replicated. It is easy to replicate questions from other surveys, and it is easy to implement them. The approach is easy to understand: "keep everything the same."

In some cases, most questions may be appropriate for all groups, but some aspects of some of the groups may not be captured by the common questions. A frequent solution is to add a supplement or section of questions for just those groups. This is a common approach on multinational studies.

Asking the same question in a sequential design draws criticism from those who believe strongly that cross-cultural issues must be addressed throughout the design process. Typically, questions are developed in the source language (Standard American English in the United States), then the final version of the instrument is translated into other languages. Translators are expected to keep the meaning of each question the same. But meaning is not only conveyed by words. Context plays a large role. Translation difficulties are often markers for design problems in the source questions (or indicators, constructs, or concepts).

Asking a different question (ADQ) in a parallel design is postulated as an alternative. Separate research teams working in different languages can begin with concepts that are believed to exist across the cultures and then identify constructs, choose indicators, and develop questions that are likely to be different in specific meaning and context, because they are tailored for each culture. In practice, the ADQ approach is very difficult and could be quite costly to implement, and few examples exist. It is impractical when a survey will be done in many languages (because of the number and size of the research teams required), and even in countries like Canada and Belgium with two official languages spoken by most of the population, it requires a high level of coordination and cooperation.

To help researchers take advantage of the body of work in health survey development, the National Center for Health Statistics (NCHS) established Q-Bank, a repository of questions that have been used on official statistical surveys in the United States, with each item's history and evidence from testing. To illustrate its breadth, one can find 108 questions on disability, drawn from six surveys; each is presented with its exact wording, date, testing agency, and a link to the report that discusses its evaluation (National Center for Health Statistics).

Pretesting has become almost synonymous with cognitive testing, but there are many ways to pretest besides conducting cognitive interviews (Harkness et al. 2010c) (see also chapter 9). Foremost among them is field testing. The Early Childhood Longitudinal Study—Birth Cohort (ECLS-B) made extensive use of field testing to refine the design for the first 2 years of data collection. A number of mini-pretests and large-scale pilot tests were conducted using field interviewers and abridged protocols to assess comparability of items across Black, Hispanic, and American Indian/Alaska Native populations. These tests allowed researchers to assess comparability in the context of field interviewing, outside the lab, in time to alter the design to improve comparability.

The total survey error (TSE) paradigm has recently been expanded to incorporate the notion of comparability error (Smith 2011, Edwards and Smith 2013). TSE can be especially useful in evaluating questions in cross-cultural surveys. Recent technical innovations such as using CARI (Computer-Assisted Audio Recorded Interviewing) behavior coding to capture paradata about interviewer-respondent interactions allow measurement of questionnaire performance and interviewer performance across population groups (Hicks et al. 2010).

10.2.2 TRANSLATION AND INTERPRETATION

Language and translation have long been recognized as major challenges in cross-cultural surveys. However, until recently these concerns have been insular, without reference to advances in the translation sciences, or even to basic translation terminology. In translatology, standard starting points are "a definition of the translation goal (purpose or function), genre, medium (audio-visual, paper, aural), and the intended audience" (Harkness et al. 2010d). Context is all-important. In contrast, survey methodologists have focused at the level of words, often starting with the notion that a translation should be "word-for-word," "close," "conceptually equivalent." Translation theory and cognitive models in survey research have yet not been integrated.

In the translation sciences, translation (from written form to written form) is distinguished from interpretation (speech to speech), and interpretation is understood to require much more skill than translation. Translators can use references and reviewers, and can ponder options with the luxury of time. Both translation and interpretation require skills beyond merely facility in two languages. Academic programs grant degrees in translation and interpretation and emphasize meaning and context, roles, and ethics.

Although survey translation has long been recognized as important in survey research, especially with the rise in multicultural and multinational studies, it is often isolated from the design, testing, and implementation processes. Techniques for translation in the survey world are often justified by reference to what others have done, and established practice is often far from best practice (Harkness et al. 2010d). For example, back-translation was recognized for decades as the gold standard for assessing translation quality (starting with work by Brislin 1970), though its focus is on producing information for the monolingual researcher who created the questions in the source language, rather than producing the best possible text for the interviewer and respondent in the target language. More recent work has established approaches for translation by committee and successive iterations by a team, so that the draft translation is edited by translation experts (Harkness et al. 2010d, Willis et al. 2010, Dept et al. 2010). Standards for translation procedures and quality assurance have been developed in major survey programs and organizations (e.g., the U.S. Bureau of the Census, 2004 Guidelines) (Pan and de la Puente 2005; Census, U. B. 2004).

Willis and colleagues (2010) discuss examples of team-based translation on five health studies, including the tobacco use supplement to the Current Population Survey, the Cancer Control Module in the NHIS, and two sets of questions for the National Cancer Institute. The translations in these studies covered five languages: Spanish, Korean, Vietnamese, Cantonese, and Mandarin Chinese. They used a mixed-method design to evaluate the five-step process developed by Harkness: translation, review, adjudicate, pretest, and document (TRAPD; Harkness, van de Vijver, Mohler 2003). They measured improvements that occurred at each stage. A key finding was that each stage finds errors, and different kinds of errors.

The Willis project was focused on improving the quality of the target document, but many designers have found that translation and pretesting often surface problems in the source document as well. Often these discoveries come too late to inform the overall design, hence many experts advocate a pretranslation review to assess "translatability." Difficulty in translating items can be a signal that indicators, constructs, or even concepts may not line up across cultures, so it is more efficient in cross-cultural studies to build this into earlier stages in the design process.

The use of interpreters in survey interviews has received some attention recently. Interpreter services are widely used by telephone in medical settings to improve quality of care, and automated services (developed first for military applications) are now in common use commercially on mobile devices. A long-standing but covert practice in many survey organizations conducting face-to-face interviews in households has been to use family members as interpreters, but such practice is roundly condemned in professional interpreting circles on ethical and role conflict grounds. Edwards (2003) reported behavior coding of interviews conducted using interpreters in household settings, and found the frequency of problematic behaviors ranged widely. In one case, the interpreter was heard telling the respondent that the question was difficult, so it was best to just answer "no" (without even hearing the question in the target language). Harkness et al. (2009) found very low quality in interviews conducted by phone with interpreters, compared to interviews conducted by native speakers working with a translation.

Another common practice in survey organizations has been to use bilingual interviewers to interpret "on the fly"—looking at the English question text but expressing it to the respondent in the target language, hearing the answer in the target language, and recording the answer in English (or with English category labels). This has been found to impose a very heavy cognitive burden on interviewers, and is almost impossible to do without making major changes in meaning for many questions (Harkness et al. 2008).

10.2.3 SURVEY OPERATIONS, PROCESS QUALITY, AND HARMONIZATION

Data collection activities are typically the component that drives survey costs, at least for interviewer-administered modes. Collecting data from people is challenging and requires careful planning. To be effective, it must be subjected to process controls to assure it meets quality standards or objectives. Pennell et al. (2010) note surprisingly little attention has been given to data collection issues in multicultural and multilingual surveys. Lyberg and Stukel (2010) observe "... comparative studies are becoming increasingly important but they are still very difficult to design and control."

Two organizational considerations deserve attention. The first is the degree of standardization versus accommodation. Most researchers would agree standardized protocols are desirable, all else being equal. However, depending on the study design, some aspects of a standardized protocol may be inappropriate for all groups in a comparative survey. For example, suppose a decision is made to create advance letters in English using a 10th grade reading level and send them to the entire sample in a U.S. city. Because the sample contains many households occupied by recent immigrants from Central America who do not speak English very well, the letter is translated into Spanish. But the immigrants average less than 8 years of education in Spanish. Should the translation be at the 10th-grade level to parallel the English version, or something lower? For another example, consider a national U.S. survey that makes extensive use of traveling interviewers. The sample includes an oversample of American Indians on tribal lands and native Alaskans. It might be appropriate to accommodate the requirements of these subgroups by hiring and training local interviewers in those locations.

The second organizational consideration is when and how to collaborate. Section 10.2.1 discussed collaboration in the design phase. In data collection planning, many believe it is helpful to engage researchers from the groups to be studied, who are familiar with the population and have conducted similar research. This can help identify potential problems in time to make adjustments in the protocol, and enhance perceptions of legitimacy.

The choice of mode has important implications for survey quality and costs. Most surveys do not vary mode by group, but a mode that is suitable for the general population may not be optimal for a specific comparison population. These mode differences by groups are discussed in the survey mode literature; see summaries in de Leeuw (2008) and Groves et al. (2009). Comparative studies that use mixed-mode designs must give special attention to the possibility of mode effects. Most multinational studies adopt a unimode design.

For surveys conducted in modes that require interviewers, language is an obvious consideration in developing a staffing plan. If the survey will be conducted in more than one language, data collection staff with skills in those languages are required. For most U.S. national surveys conducted in person, Spanish and English language instruments are used, but interviewers who are *bilingual* in English and Spanish are hired to conduct the interviews in Spanish, as well as at least some interviews in English. The distribution of Spanish speakers is such that it is usually impractical to form an assignment that consists solely of interviews conducted in Spanish. In contrast, telephone surveys conducted in a phone center can hire monolingual interviewers (broadening the labor pool) to cover the other languages, assuming a bilingual supervisor can be hired with skills in both English and the other language. This approach has been implemented successfully on CHIS, which conducts interviews in English, Spanish, Korean, Vietnamese, and Mandarin and Cantonese Chinese.

California is not a typical U.S. state. In representative household samples for national U.S. surveys, beyond English and Spanish, no other language is spoken by more than 0.6% of the sampled households (census). The National Epidemiologic Survey on Alcohol and Related Conditions (NESARC), a face-to-face field survey conducted in 2012, took a similar approach to CHIS, translating the instruments into a number of Asian languages and hiring field interviewers who spoke those languages fluently. Of the 35,000 completed NESARC interviews, only about 1% were conducted in any of these Asian languages. Asian as a group label includes many ethnic subgroups speaking different languages. Even Mandarin, the most commonly spoken, was used in NESARC only 0.5% of the time. Survey designers must make tradeoffs between survey costs and the value of conducting interviews with members of those groups who do not speak English or

Spanish. The translation is a minor component of costs; data collection infrastructure and systems enhancements are much more significant.

Community engagement can help data collection efforts with many cultural groups (see also Chapter 13). It can take many forms: meetings with public officials, community representatives, or stakeholders; alliances with community groups; media campaigns; and letters of endorsement. In the 2010 census in the United States, hundreds of thousands of partnerships were created between the Bureau and local organizations. Evans et al. (2014) evaluated the utility of this massive effort. On NHANES, targeted media campaigns are used when a sampled county has a large number of households in a single minority ethnic or racial group. Newspapers and radio stations that serve the group are targeted for press releases and interviews with research staff. Thousands of journal articles have been written based on NHANES data, and some of these articles focus on health conditions or other data that are especially relevant to the group, so interviewers are armed with copies of these articles to aid in gaining cooperation (Montalvan et al. 2008).

Biomarkers (samples of saliva, urine, blood, hair, etc.) and physical measures (height, weight, waist circumference, walking speed, lung capacity, etc.) have become increasingly common in health surveys, as an addition to or a replacement for self-reported data (see also Chapter 15). Because survey costs have risen, there is a need to increase the value of the survey data, and data from biomarkers and taking physical measures can greatly enhance the self-reported data. Also, in the past decade the cost of kits for collecting biomarker data has dropped and many more kits are on the market, so it is now much more feasible to consider these as part of the study protocol. However, acceptance of biomarker collection and physical measurements may vary by cultural group, and some tailored strategies may help to increase acceptance in specific groups.

Quality Assurance. Cross-cultural surveys have additional complexity associated with the comparability objective, and this should be reflected in a quality assurance plan. The quality assurance plan should address ways the survey will measure quality for each group. The plan can encompass all stages in the survey, from initial design and sample selection, through instrument design, data collector recruitment and training, data collection, processing, and analysis. Pretesting protocols with each comparison group is best practice, and can be viewed as an important quality checkpoint. Quality control procedures measure how well the plan is implemented, and statistical process control charts and other visualization tools help managers identify errors that are not just random noise.

In practice, these plans are much easier to develop and implement for within-country surveys than for multinational surveys. When multiple countries participate, the plan must cross survey organizations and survey infrastructures, and this can become exceedingly problematic with surveys in many countries. The Programme for International Assessment of Adult Competencies (PIAAC) has addressed this problem in a novel way, with monthly text and telephone reports to a central coordinator, based on goals and standard operating procedures.

Often data from more than one survey are needed to address a research question. *Harmonization* can improve comparability between the surveys. It can take many forms and can be implemented at any stage in a project's lifecycle. In the simplest case, two or more surveys that are both in a design stage and have some constructs in common might join forces to choose indicators or develop question wording. For example, in reviewing a 2013 request from the National Institute on Drug Abuse to approve the baseline Population Assessment of Tobacco and Health, the Office of Management and Budget convened a meeting to harmonize items across tobacco surveys in the United States. This is referred to as *input* harmonization.

Granda et al. (2010) contrast input harmonization with *ex-ante* harmonization (which defines the variables the studies will produce, without prescribing how the variables are created) and *ex-post* harmonization (for existing data from surveys). Ex-post harmonization presupposes that comparability exists; tests may be necessary to establish it, as described in the next section.

Another strategy is to rely on standard classification schemes such as the *International Classification of Diseases* (World Health Organization 2010) or the *Physician's Desk Reference* (PDR Staff 2012) for prescribed medicines. As long as two surveys use the same scheme, it may not matter what items were used to obtain the raw data. A variation on this approach is when a scale or set of questions has been developed to produce a core set of variables, and the scale or set of questions are used across surveys. The Short-Form Health Survey 36 (SF36) is one example (Ware et al. 1994). Another is the Washington Group Short Set of six questions on disability, recently developed at the NCHS and promoted as core disability items for all federally sponsored U.S. health surveys (Washington Group on Disability Statistics).

Anchoring vignettes might be viewed as a type of input harmonization. King and colleagues developed this technique to achieve comparability on the World Health Survey. A number of scenarios are posed to each respondent, and they rate each scenario on a given dimension, then are asked to rate themselves. In this way an adjustment can be made for each respondent within the culture, and cultures can be compared with each other (King et al. 2004, Salomon et al. 2001). The technique can be a powerful tool in creating comparable data sets, but some research teams view them as unwieldy because a vignette requires a significant amount of time to administer and only produces one or two analytic variables.

10.2.4 ANALYSIS

Analysis of cross-cultural health survey data is distinguished by the need to address the possibility of cultural bias. This bias may have been introduced at any stage in the project life cycle. Comparative error can be found at any stage in the survey process, including analysis, but it is typically treated as a type of measurement error in the TSE paradigm. It can apply to items or scales.

Methods for detecting comparative error range from relatively simple ways to gain a quick overview of the data to more complex techniques that allow comparison of many groups and produce summary measures across groups. Braun and Johnson (2010) discuss seven classes of methods:

- Comparisons of distributions across response categories, including nonresponse, means; correlations with benchmark items and with explanatory variables; and interaction plots
- Exploratory factor analyses
- Reliability comparisons
- Multiple correspondence analysis (MCA) and multidimensional scaling (MDS)
- Multigroup confirmatory factor analysis (CFA)
- Multilevel modeling, and
- Item response theory (IRT) models

They provide a table summarizing the advantages and disadvantages of each. Although their context is multinational surveys, the summary of analytic methods applies equally well to cross-cultural surveys within one country.

In psychometrics, measurement error at the item level is known as *differential item functioning*, or DIF. An item shows DIF if people in two groups who share the same latent ability or trait, have a different probability of response to an item solely because of membership in their group. The most common ways to measure DIF are Mantel–Haenszel, logistic regression, and IRT methods. IRT methods are often used in creating and refining scales to eliminate DIF. IRT was developed in the 1950s and 1960s by Lord (a psychometrician), Rasch (a mathematician), and Lazarsfeld (the sociologist), working in separate fields on parallel tracks (Lazarsfeld's work on latent trait models is essentially identical to IRT.) (Lord 1980, Rasch 1960, Lazarsfeld and Henry 1968). IRT methods are most useful in assessing comparability of data from several groups, such as those encountered in surveys within a single country. They are less appropriate for work with data from a large number of countries.

More advanced methods for analyzing multicultural data include the following:

- Multigroup structural equation modeling (MGSEM)
- Multilevel structural equation modeling (MLSEM)
- Multilevel latent class analysis
- Multitrait-multimethod (MTMM) analysis

Hox et al. (2010) elaborate on multilevel and structural equation modeling, and Oberski et al. (2010) discuss MTMM designs.

None of these analytic methods provide more than circumstantial evidence of multicultural bias, but they can suggest the possibility of comparative error.

These possibilities warrant deeper investigation of stages in the project that could have introduced cultural bias. (For example, on a multinational assessment of literacy, one country's data were found to be markedly different from all others; investigation revealed a systematic difference in coding procedures in that country.) Furthermore, some degree of comparative error undoubtedly exists in all multicultural surveys, but the TSE model encourages understanding the errors, making explicit tradeoffs between errors, and seeking to minimize or reduce total error.

10.3 Conclusion

Cross-cultural health surveys have a critical role in public health, health care, and health care financing. They are essential for research on health disparities, policy evaluations, and health communications research. They are part of a fast-growing class of surveys designed to compare groups in meaningful ways. Methods for designing, implementing, and analyzing data from multicultural and multinational surveys have become much stronger in the twenty-first century. Much of this progress in cross-cultural methods work has sprung from the needs of multinational surveys, but it applies equally well to distinct cultures within one country. It emphasizes the need to assess comparability at all stages in the project life cycle.

For health surveys intended to compare cultural groups, the design process must incorporate input from the cultures of interest, and ensure the study's concepts are shared across all groups. Translation procedures should build on advances in the translation sciences, and become an important part of initial design activities. Survey operations must adapt to cultural differences but maintain procedural standards in most activities. Process quality can be applied to all facets of operations activities. Many analytic tools are available to assess comparability and detect meaningful differences across groups.

The health field holds a special place in cross-cultural discussions. In both medicine and public health, general well-being and even vital status are often dependent on a deep understanding of cultural differences in the population. Cultural competency has become an essential health care skill. In diverse communities, hospitals are expected to provide services in the language of their patients. Some of the most notorious disasters in public health have occurred where respect for cultural differences was lacking; the Tuskegee Syphillis Study is perhaps the best example (Jones 1993). No health survey designed to compare cultural groups can afford to ignore cross-cultural considerations.

REFERENCES

n.d. Available at www.CSDIworkshop.org/. Retrieved 2013 Sept 30 from Comparative Survey Design and Implementation.

42 U.S.C., 2000d. U.S. Civil Rights Act, Title VI; 1964.

Agency for Healthcare Research and Quality. *TeamSTEPPS: Limited English Proficiency*. Rockville, MD: Agency for Healthcare Research and Quality; 2012.

Ai A, Appel H, Huang B, Hefley W. Overall health and health care utilization among Latino American men in the United States. Am J Mens Health 2013;7(1):6–17.

Almond G, Verba S. *The Civic Culture: Political Attitudes and Democracy in Five Nations*. Princeton: Princeton University Press; 1963.

American Psychiatric Association. *The Diagnostic and Statistical Manual of Mental Disorders*. Washington, DC: American Psychiatric Association; 1994.

Andersen R. Revisiting the behavioral model and access to care: does it matter? J Health Soc Behav 1995;36:1–10.

Andersen R, Smedby B, Anderson O. Medical Care Use in Sweden and the United States *(Vol. Research Series No. 27)*. Baltimore, Maryland: Center for Health Administration Studies; 1970.

Bastian A. *Der Mensch in der Geschichte*. Leipzig; Otto Wigand; 1860.

Betancourt J, Green A, Carrillo J. *Cultural Competence in Health Care: Emerging Frameworks and Practical Approaches*. New York: The Commonwealth Fund; 2001.

Borsch-Supan A, Hank R, Jurges H, Schroder M. Longitudinal data collection in continental Europe: experiences from the Survey of Health, Ageing, and Retirement in Europe (SHARE). In: Harkness JA, Braun M, Edwards B, Johnson TP, Lyberg L, Mohler PP, Pennell B-E, Smith TW., editors. *Survey Methods in Multinational, Multiregional, and Multicultural Contexts*. Hoboken: Wiley; 2010. p 507–514.

Braun M, Johnson TP. An illustrative review of techniques for detecting in equivalences. In: Harkness JA, Braun M, Edwards B, Johnson TP, Lyberg L, Mohler PP, Pennell B-E, Smith TW., editors. *Survey Methods in Multinational, Multiregional, and Multicultural Contexts*. Hoboken, NJ: Wiley; 2010. p 375–394.

Breslau J, Miller E, Jin R, Sampson N, Alonso J, Andrade L, et al. A multinational study of mental disorders, marriage, and divorce. Acta Psychiatr Scand 2011;124:474–486.

Brislin R. Back translation for cross-cultural research. J Cross-Cult Psychol 1970; 1:185–216.

Census, U. B. 2004. Language translation guidelines. Retrieved 2013 Sept 30 from United States Bureau of the Census.

Center for Child and Human Development, Georgetown University. n.d. Cultural competence health practitioner assessment. Available at http://nccc.georgetown.edu/features/CCHPA.html. Retrieved 2013 Oct 4 from National Center for Cultural Competence.

Centers for Disease Control and Prevention. n.d. National Health Interview Survey. Available at www.cdc.gov/nchs/nhis.htm. Retrieved 2013 Sept 30 from National Center for Health Statistics.

Chen K. *Could your Language Affect your Ability to Save Money?* Edinburgh, Scotland, U.K.: TED Global; 2013. Available at http://www.ted.com/talks/keith_chen_could_your_language_affect_your_ability_to_save_money.html. Retrieved 2013 Oct 4.

Chen AH, Youdelman MK, Brooks J. The legal framework for language access in healthcare settings: title VI and beyond. J Gen Intern Med 2007;22:362–367.

Clancy C. 2013. From the director. *Research Activities*; p. 2.

Coelho K, Galan C. Physician cross-cultural nonverbal communication skills, patient satisfaction and health outcomes in the physician-patient relationship. Int J Fam Med 2012;2012 Epub 2012 June 25.

Collins S. The incidence of poliomyelitis and its crippling effects, as recorded in family surveys. Public Health Rep 1946;61:327–355.

Converse JM, Presser S. *Survey Questions: Handcrafting the Standardized Questionnaire*. SAGE; 1986.

de Leeuw E. Choosing the method of data collection. In: de Leeuw E, Hox J, Dillman D, editors. *International Handbook of Survey Methodology*. New York: Lawrence Erlbaum; 2008. p 233–235.

Deming WE. *Some Theory of Sampling*. New York: Dover Publications; 1966.

Demographic and Health Surveys. n.d. Available at http://www.measuredhs.com/. Retrieved 2013 Oct 4 from Measure DHS: Demographic and Health Surveys.

Dept S, Ferrari A, Wayrynen L. Developments in translation verification procedures in three multilingual assessments: a plea for an integrated translation and adaptation monitoring tool. In: Harkness JA, Braun M, Edwards B, Johnson TP, Lyberg L, Mohler PP, Pennell B-E, Smith TW., editors. *Survey Methods in Multinational, Multiregional, and Multicultural Contexts*. Hoboken, NJ: Wiley; 2010. p 157–173.

Dillman DA. *Mail and Telephone Surveys: The Total Design Method*. New York: Wiley; 1978.

Dunn JR, Dyck I. Social determinants of health in Canada's immigrant population: results from the National Population Health Survey. Soc Sci Med 2000;51:1573–1593.

Edwards B. *Examining the role of interpreters in surveys*. Mannheim, Germany: ZUMA; 2003.

Edwards B, Hicks W, Tourangeau K, Harris-Kojetin L, Moss A. *Computer-Assisted Audio Recording (CARI): Repurposing a Tool for Evaluating Comparative Instrument Design*. Warsaw, Poland: ; 2009.

Edwards B, Smith T. *Comparative Error and Total Survey Error.* 2013 Workshop. Stockholm: CSDI; 2013.

Escobar J, Burnam M, Karno M, Forsythe A, Golding J. Somatization in the community. Arch Gen Psychiatry 1987;44:713–718.

Evans D, Datta A, Yan T. Paid media: lessons from the 2010 census. In: Tourangeau R, Edwards B, Johnson T, Wolter K, Bates N, editors. *Hard-to-Survey Populations*. Cambridge: Cambridge University Press; 2014.

Ezzati TM, Massey JT. *Sample Design: Third National Health and Nutrition Examination Survey*. Hyattsville: National Center for Health Statistics, Centers for Disease Control and Prevention, U.S. Department of Health and Human Services; 1992.

Fox-Rushby J, Parker M. Culture and the measurement of health-related quality of life. Eur Rev Appl Psychol 1995;45:257–263.

Granda P, Wolf C, Hadorn R. Harmonizing survey data. In: Harkness JA, Braun M, Edwards B, Johnson TP, Lyberg L, Mohler PP, et al., editors. *Survey Methods in Multinational, Multiregional, and Multicultural Contexts*. Hoboken: Wiley; 2010. p 315–332.

Groves R, Fowler F, Couper M, Lepkowski J, Singer E, Tourangeau R. *Survey Methodology*. 2nd ed. Hoboken, NJ: Wiley; 2009.

Hahn E. The talking touchscreen (La Pantalla Parlanchina): innovative multimedia methods for health outcomes assessment and patient education in underserved populations. *International Conference on Survey Methods for Hard-to-Reach Populations: 2012 Proceedings*; Alexandria, Virginia: American Statistical Association; 2012.

Harkness JA. Overview of problems in establishing conceptually equivalent health definitions across multiple cultural groups. In: Cohen SB, Lepkowski JM, editors. *Eighth Conference on Health Survey Research Methods: Proceedings*. Hyattsville: U.S. Department of Health and Human Services, Centers for Disease Control and Prevention, National Center for Health Statistics; 2004.

Harkness JA, Braun M, Edwards B, Johnson TP, Lyberg L, Mohler PP, Pennell B-E, Smith TW. Survey Methods in Multinational, Multiregional, and Multicultural Contexts. Hoboken: Wiley; 2010a.

Harkness JA, Braun M, Edwards B, Johnson T, Lyberg L, Mohler P, Pennell B-E, Smith TW. Comparative survey methodology. In: Harkness J, Braun M, Edwards B, Johnson T, Lyberg L, Mohler P, Pennell B-E, Smith TW., editors. *Survey Methods in Multinational, Multiregional, and Multicultural Contexts*. Hoboken, NJ: Wiley; 2010b. p 3–16.

Harkness JA, Edwards B, Hansen S, Miller D, Villar A. Designing questionnaires for multipopulation research. In: Harkness JA, Braun M, Edwards B, Johnson T, Lyberg L, Mohler P, Pennell B-E, Smith TW., editors. *Survey Methods in Multinational, Multiregional, and Multicultural Contexts*. Hoboken, NJ: Wiley; 2010c. p 33–57.

Harkness JA, Schoebi N, Joye D, Mohler P, Faass T, Behr D. Oral translation in telephone surveys. In: Lepkowski J, Tucker C, Brick J, de Leeuw E, Japec L, Lavrakas P, editors. *Advances in Telephone Survey Methodology*. Hoboken, NJ: Wiley; 2008. p 231–249.

Harkness JA, van de Vijver FJ, Mohler PP. *Cross-Cultural Survey Methods*. Hoboken: Wiley; 2003.

Harkness JA, Villar A, Edwards B. Translation, adaptation, and design. In: Harkness JA, Braun M, Edwards B, Johnson T, Lyberg L, Mohler P, Pennell B-E, Smith TW., editors. *Survey Methods in Multinational, Multiregional, and Multicultural Contexts*. Hoboken, NJ: Wiley; 2010d. p 117–140.

Harkness JA, Villar A, Kruse Y, Branden L, Edwards B, Steele C, et al. *Using Interpreters in Telephone Surveys.* 2009 Workshop. Ann Arbor, MI: CSDI; 2009.

Hicks W, Edwards B, Tourangeau K, McBride B, Harris-Kojetin L, Moss A. Using CARI tools to understand measurement error. Public Opin Q 2010;74:985–1003.

Honkala S. World Health Organization approaches for surveys of health behaviour among schoolchildren and for health-promoting schools. Med Princ Pract 2013;23:1–8.

Hox J, de Leeuw E, Brinkhuis M. Analysis models for comparative surveys. In: Harkness JA, Braun M, Edwards B, Johnson TP, Lyberg L, Mohler PP, Pennell B-E, Smith TW., editors. *Survey Methods for Multinational, Multiregional, and Multicultural Contexts*. Hoboken, NJ: Wiley; 2010. p 395–418.

Hsu L, Folstein M. Somatoform disorders in Caucasian and Chinese Americans. J Nerv Ment Dis 1997;185:382–387.

Hyman S. The genetics of mental illness: implications for practice. Bull World Health Organ 2000;78:455–463 Geneva, Switzerland.

International Conference on Survey Methods in Multinational, Multiregional, and Multicultural Contexts (3MC); 2008 Jun 25–28; 2008. Available at

CSDIworkshop.org/v2/index.php/2008-3mc-conference. Retrieved 2013 Sept 30 from Comparative Survey Design and Implementation (CSDI).

Inter-university Consortium for Political and Social Research. n.d.-a Mexican origin people in the United States: the 1979 Chicano Survey (ICPSR 8436). Available at www.icpsr.umich.edu/icpsrweb/ICPSR/studies/8436. Retrieved 2013 Sept 30 from ICPSR.

Inter-university Consortium for Political and Social Research. n.d.-b National medical expenditure survey series. Available at www.icpsr.umich.edu/icpsrweb/ICPSR/series/45. Retrieved 2013 Sept 30 from ICPSR.

Janis I. *Air War and Emotional Stress: Psychological Studies of Bombing and Civilian Defense*. New York: McGraw Hill; 1951.

Jin T, Bailey JT, Bristol K, Link MW. Design considerations for a cross-cultural enumeration survey. *Proceedings of the 66th Annual Conference of the American Association for Public Opinion Research.* Phoenix: American Statistical Association; 2011.

Johnson TP. Approaches to establishing equivalence in cross-cultural and cross-national research. In: Harkness J, editor. *Cross-Cultural Survey Equivalence*Vol. Nachrichten Spezial. Mannheim: ZUMA; 1998. p 1–40.

Johnson T, Shavitt S, Holbrook A. Survey response styles across cultures. In: Matsumoto D, van de Vijver FJR, Holbrook A, editors. *Cross-Cultural Research Methods in Psychology*. Cambridge: Cambridge University Press; 2010. p 130–176.

Jones J. *Bad Blood: The Tuskegee Syphilis Experiment, New and Expanded Edition* ed. New York: Free Press; 1993.

Kelleher C, Quirke B. The All Ireland Traveller health study 2007-2011. In: Tourangeau R, Edwards B, Johnson T, Wolter K, Bates N, editors. *Hard-to-Survey Populations.* Cambridge: Cambridge University Press; 2014.

King G, Murray C, Salomaon J, Tandon A. Anchoring vignettes. Am Polit Sci Rev 2004;98(1):191–207.

Kish JL. *Survey Sampling*. New York: Wiley; 1965.

LaViest T. *Minority Populations and Health: An Introduction to Health Disparities in the United States*. San Francisco: Jossey-Bass; 2005.

Lazarsfeld P, Henry N. *Latent Structure Analysis*. Boston: Houghton Mifflin; 1968.

Levi-Straus C. *Tristes Tropiques*(1973 Translation ed.). (J. A. Weightman, Trans.). New York, NY: Atheneum; 1955.

Lord F. *Applications of Item Response Theory to Practical Testing Problems*. Mahwah, NJ: Erlbaum; 1980.

Lyberg L, Stukel DM. Quality assurance and quality control in cross-national comparative studies. In: Harkness JA, Braun M, Edwards B, Johnson TP, Lyberg L, Mohler PP, Pennell B-E, Smith TW., editors. *Survey Methods in Multinational, Multiregional, and Multicultural Contexts*. Hoboken: Wiley; 2010. p 227–249.

Mohler PP, Johnson TP. Equivalence, comparability, and methodological progress. In: Harkness JA, Braun M, Edwards B, Johnson TP, Lyberg L, Mohler PP, et al., editors. *Survey Methods in Multinational, Multiregional, and Multicultural Contexts*. Hoboken, NJ: John Wiley & Sons, Inc.; 2010. p 17–29.

Montalvan P, Pinder G, Kottiri B, Petty-Martin C. 2008. Attaining high survey participation in an era of growing public antagonism: NHANES experience. *Proceedings of the Annual Conference of the American Association for Public Opinion Research.*

Moore M. (2010). (blog) Medical Translation. New York. Retrieved 2013 Sept 30.

Mulia N, Ye Y, Greenfield T, Zemore S. Disparities in alcohol-related problems among white, black, and Hispanic Americans. Alcohol Clin Exp Res 2009;33(4):654–662.

National Center for Health Statistics. n.d. Q-Bank. Available at www.cdc.gov/qbank/home.aspx. Retrieved 2013 Sept 30 from Centers for Disease Control and Prevention.

NORC. n.d. GSS: General Social Survey. Available at www3.norc.org/gss+website. Retrieved 2013 Sept 30 from NORC.

Nyaronga D, Greenfield T, McDaniel P. Drinking context and drinking problems among black, white, and Hispanic men and women in the 1984, 1995, and 2005 U.S. National Alcohol Surveys. J Stud Alcohol Drugs 2009;70(1):16–26.

Oberski D, Saris W, Hagenaars J. Categorization errors and differences in the quality of questions in comparative surveys. In: Harkness J, Braun M, Edwards B, Johnson T, Lyberg L, Mohler P, et al., editors. *Survey Methods in Multinational, Multiregional, and Multicultural Contexts*. Hoboken, NJ: Wiley; 2010. p 435–454.

Osman H. History and development of the doctrine of informed consent. Int Electron J Health Educ 2001;4:41–47.

Pampel F, Denney J. Cross-national sources of health inequality: education and tobacco use in the World Health Survey. Demography 2011;48(2):653–674.

Pan Y, Landreth A, Park H, Hinsdale-Shouse M, Schoua-Glusberg A. Cognitive interviewing in non-English languages: a cross-cultural perspective. In: Harkness JA, Braun M, Edwards B, Johnson TP, Lyberg L, Mohler PP, Pennell B-E, Smith TW., editors. *Survey Methods in Multinational, Multiregional, and Multicultural Contexts*. Hoboken: Wiley; 2010. p 91–113.

Pan Y, Lubkemann S. Standardization and meaning in the survey of linguistically-diversified populations: insights from the ethnographic observation of linguistic minorities in 2010 census interviews. In: Tourangeau R, Edwards B, Johnson T, Wolter K, Bates N, editors. *Hard-to-Survey Populations*. Cambridge, England, U.K.: Cambridge University Press; 2014.

Pan Y, de la Puente M 2005. Census Bureau guideline for the translation of data collection instruments and supporting materials: documentation on how the guideline was developed. Available at http://www.census.gov/srd/papers/pdf/rsm2005-06.pdf. Retrieved 2013 Sept 30 from United States Bureau of the Census.

Park K, Upshaw H, Koh S. East Asians' responses to western health items. J Cross-Cult Psychol 1988:51–64.

Payne SL. *The Art of Asking Questions*. Princeton: Princeton University Press; 1951.

PDR Staff. *Physician's Desk Reference*. Montvale, NJ: PDR Network; 2012.

Pennell B-E, Harkness J, Levenstein R, Quaglia M. Challenges in cross-national data collection. In: Harkness J, Braun M, Edwards B, Johnson T, Lyberg L, Mohler P, et al., editors. *Survey Methods in Multinational, Multiregional, and Multicultural Contexts*. Hoboken, NJ: Wiley; 2010. p 269–298.

Rasch G. *Probabilistic Models for Some Intelligence and Attainment Tests*. Copenhagen: Danish Institute for Educational Research; 1960.

Ratzan S, Parker R. Introduction. In: Selden C, Zorn M, Ratzan S, Parker R, editors. *National Library of Medicine Current Bibliographies in Medicine: Health Literacy*. Bethesda, MD: National Institutes of Health, U.S. Department of Health and Human Services; 2000. p 537–541.

Room R, Makela P, Benegal V, Greenfield T, Hettige S, Tumwesigye N, et al. Times to drink: cross-cultural variations in drinking in the rhythm of the week. Int J Public Health 2012;57(1):107–117.

Rose DE, Tisnado DM, Malin J, Tao ML, Maggard MA, Adams JL, et al. Use of interpreters by physicians treating limited English proficient women with breast cancer: results from the provider survey of the Los Angeles Women's Health study. Health Serv Res 2010;45(1):172–194.

Ryan C. *Language Use in the United States: 2011*. Suitland, Maryland: U.S. Census Bureau, U.S. Department of Commerce; 2013.

Sadana R, Mathers CD, Lopez AD, Murray CJ, Iburg K. *Comparative Analyses of More than 50 Household Surveys on Health Status*. Geneva: World Health Organization; 2000.

Salomon, J., Tandon, A., & Murray, C. (2001). Using vignettes to improve cross-population comparability of health surveys: concepts, design, and evaluation techniques. *Global Programme on Evidence for Health Policy Discussion Paper No.41*. World Health Organization.

Schwarz N, Oyserman D, Peytcheva E. Cognition, communication, and culture: implications for the survey response process. In: Harkness JA, Braun M, Edwards B, Johnston TP, Lyberg L, Mohler PP, Pennell B-E, Smith TW., editors. *Survey Methods in Multinational, Multiregional, and Multicultural Contexts*. Hoboken: Wiley; 2010. p 177–190.

Seligman H, Fernandez A, Stern R, Weech-Maldonado R, Quan JJ. Risk factors for reporting poor cultural competency among patients with diabetes in safety net clinics. Med Care 2012;S56–61.

Setia MS, Quesnel-Vallee A, Abrahamowicz M, Tousignant P. Access to health-care in Canadian immigrants: a longitudinal study of the National Population Health Survey. Health Soc Care Commun 2011;19(1):70–79.

Smith TW. Refining the total survey error perspective. Int J Pub Opin Res 2011:464–484.

Smith TW. Developing and evaluating cross-national survey instruments. In: Presser S, Rothgeb J, Couper M, Lessler JT, Martin J, Singer E, editors. *Methods for Testing and Evaluating Survey Questionnaires*. Hoboken: Wiley; 2004.

Smith TW. The globalization of survey research. In: Harkness JA, Braun M, Edwards B, Johnson TP, Lybereg L, Mohler PP, et al., editors. *Survey Methods in Multinational, Multiregional, and Multicultural Contexts*. Hoboken: Wiley; 2010. p 477–484.

Smith TW. Developing comparable questions in cross-national surveys. In: Harkness JA, Van de Vijver FJR, Mohler PP, editors. *Cross-Cultural Survey Methods*. Hoboken: Wiley; 2003. pp. 69–91.

Sudman S, Bradburn NM. *Asking Questions*. San Francisco: Jossey-Bass; 1982.

Survey Research Center. 2010. Available at http://www.ccsg.isr.umich.edu/. Retrieved 2013 Jan 5 from Guidelines for Best Practice in Cross-Cultural Surveys.

Timmins CL. The impact of language barriers on the health care of Latinos in the United States: a review of the literature and guidelines for practice. J Midwifery Womens Health 2002;47(2):80–96.

Tourangeau R, Edwards B, Johnson T, Wolter K, Bates N, editors. *Hard-to-Survey Populations*. Cambridge: Cambridge University Press; 2014.

U.S. Department of Health and Human Services. *Mental Health: Culture, Race, and Ethnicity—A Supplement to Mental Health: A Report of the Surgeon General*.

Rockville, Maryland: U.S. Department of Health and Human Services, Substance Abuse and Mental Health Administration, Center for Mental Health Services; 2001.

U.S. Department of Health and Human Services. n.d. Disparities. Available at healthypeople.gov/2020/about/DisparitiesAbout.aspx. Retrieved 2013 Sept 30 from Healthy People 2020.

U.S. Department of Health and Human Services, Office of the Secretary. *The Belmont Report*. Washington, DC: U.S. Government; 1979.

U.S. Government. *Notice.* 45 Federal Register 82972. Washington, DC: U.S. Government Printing Office; 1980.

U.S. Government. n.d. The National CLAS standards. Available at http://www.minority health.hhs.gov/templates/browse.aspx?lvl=2&lvlID=15. Retrieved 2013 Sept 30 from The Office of Minority Health.

U.S. Strategic Bombing Survey. The Effects of Strategic Bombing on German Morale *(Vol. 1)*. Washington, DC, USA: U.S. Government Printing Office; 1947a.

U.S. Strategic Bombing Survey. The Effects of Strategic Bombing on Japanese Morale *(Vol. 1)*. Washington, DC, U.S.: U.S. Government Printing Office; 1947b.

Van Vaerenbergh Y, Thomas T. Response styles in survey research: a literature review of antecedents, consequences, and remedies. Int J Pub Opin Res 2013:195–217.

Van Wieren A, Roberts M, Arellano N, Feller E, Diaz J. Acculturation and cardiovascular behaviors among Latinos in California by country/region of origin. J Immigr Minor Health 2011;13(6):975–981.

Velkley R. The tension in the beautiful: on culture and civilization in Rousseau and German philosophy. In: Velkley R, editor. *Being after Rouseau: Philosophy and Culture in Question*. Chicago: The University of Chicago Press; 2002. p 11–30.

Verba S. The uses of survey research in the study of comparative politics: issues and strategies. In: Rokkan S, Verba S, Viet J, Amasy E, editors. *Comparative Survey Analysis*. The Hague: Mouton; 1969. p 56–106.

Ware J, Kosinski M, Keller S. *SF-36 Physical and Mental Health Summary Scales: A User's Manual*. Boston, MA: The Health Institute; 1994.

Washington Group on Disability Statistics. n.d. Available at www.cdc.gov/nchs/washington_group/wg_questions.html. Retrieved 2013 Sept 30 from Centers for Disease Control and Prevention.

Willis G, Kudela M, Levin K, Norberg A, Stark D, Forsythe B, et al. Evaluation of a multistep survey translation process. In: Harkness JA, Braun M, Edwards B, Johnson TP, Lyberg L, Mohler PP, Pennell B-E, Smith TW., editors. *Survey Methods in Multinational, Multiregional, and Multicultural Contexts*. Hoboken, NJ: Wiley; 2010. p 141–156.

World Health Organization. 2010. International statistical classification of diseases and related health problems tenth revision: version 2010. Available at http://apps.who.int/classifications/icd10/browse/2010/en. Retrieved 2013 Oct 4 from World Health Organization.

Wulff HR. The language of medicine. J Roy Soc Med 2004;97:187–188.

Yang Y, Harkness JA, Chin T-Y, Villar A. Response styles and culture. In: Harkness JA, Braun M, Edwards B, Johnson TP, Lyberg L, Mohler PP, Pennell B-E, Smith TW., editors. *Survey Methods in Multinational, Multiregional, and Multicultural Contexts*. Hoboken: Wiley; 2010. p 203–223.

Youdelman M, Yang Y, Harkness JA, Chin T-Y, Villar A. *Medicaid and SCHIP Reimbursement Models for Language Services*. Washington: National Health Law Program; 2007.

ONLINE RESOURCES

Information on anchoring Vignettes is available at: http://gking.harvard.edu/vign.

California Health Interview Survey resources are available at: http://healthpolicy.ucla.edu/chis/Pages/default.aspx.

Information regarding the Comparative Design and Implementation (CSDI) Workshops can be found at: www.CSDIworkshop.org.

The Cross-Cultural Survey Guidelines can be accessed at: www.ccsg.isr.umich.edu/.

The Cultural Competence Health Practitioner Assessment website is at: http://nccc.georgetown.edu/features/CCHPA.html.

The website of the European Social Survey is at: www.europeansocialsurvey.org/

Presentations from the 2008 International Conference on Survey Methods in Multinational, Multilingual, and Multicultural Contexts can be found at: www.csdiworkshop.org/v2/index.php/2008-3mc-conference/2008-presentations.

The website of the International Social Survey Program is at: www.issp.org.

The Q-Bank at the National Center for Health Statistics is at: www.cdc.gov/qbank/home.aspx.

The website for the Survey of Health, Ageing, and Retirement in Europe (SHARE) is at: www.share-project.org/.

Information regarding World Health Organisation Surveys is at: http://www.who.int/topics/health_surveys/en/.

The U.S. Agency for International Development's Demographic and Health Surveys website is at: http://www.measuredhs.com/.

The U.S. Census Bureau's language translation guidelines are available at: www.census.gov/srd/papers/pdf/rsm2005-06.pdf.

CHAPTER ELEVEN

Survey Methods for Social Network Research

Benjamin Cornwell and Emily Hoagland
Department of Sociology, Cornell University, Ithaca, NY, USA

11.1 Introduction

Research on the relationship between social networks and health-related processes continues to grow rapidly. With a few important caveats, research on how social networks affect individual health generally emphasizes the health benefits of being socially connected (see Berkman and Kawachi (2000), Kawachi et al. (2008), Thoits (2011), Umberson and Montez (2010), York Cornwell and Waite (2009)). Social networks that are rich in strong ties are critical for providing the social capital, social support, and informal social control efforts that can be beneficial for health (Ashida and Heaney 2008, Umberson 1987). Network ties serve as coping resources that buffer against the negative effects of stressful life events, such as bereavement, and have enduring benefits in terms of self-esteem, sense of control, and sense of belonging (e.g., Hawkley and Cacioppo 2010, Thoits 2011). These things, in turn, have downstream benefits for cardiovascular, neuroendocrine, and immune function (for a review, see Uchino (2006)). Beyond this, social networks play a major role in shaping individuals' access to health-related information and health care (e.g., York Cornwell and Waite 2012), a wide variety of health-related behaviors (e.g., Christakis and Fowler 2008), and exposure to

Handbook of Health Survey Methods, First Edition. Edited by Timothy P. Johnson.

health risks (e.g., Friedman et al. 1997). Finally, beyond the individual level, social networks shape the spread of infection within populations (Morris 2004), the diffusion of medical innovations and treatments among physicians (Burt 1987b, Valente 2010), and coordination and influence among health-related organizations (e.g., Harris et al. 2008, Laumann and Knoke 1987).

Most network-oriented research in the area of health studies is concerned with the link between individuals' social networks and their health-related outcomes such as exposure to risk, access to healthcare, health-related behavior, or one of many measures of physical or mental health. Due in part to the growing influence of this relational perspective on health, there is an increasing call for health researchers to take into account various structural features of individuals' social networks (e.g., Ikeda and Kawachi 2010, Morris 2004, Smith and Christakis 2008, Valente 2010), and likewise for network researchers to take health into account (e.g., Cornwell 2009, Haas et al. 2010). Scholars have shown that different aspects of social networks are relevant for understanding different health phenomena (e.g., Ashida and Heaney 2008, Smith and Christakis 2008, Valente 2010, York Cornwell and Waite 2009). This has increased the need for high quality data on specific features of social networks that are relevant to a wide variety of health phenomena.

One of the goals of this chapter is to provide an overview of this work, to describe some key aspects of social networks that are relevant to health, and also to provide a primer on survey research methods in particular that can be employed to collect valuable data of this sort. To be sure, social network data can be collected in a number of ways. Direct physical observation is one approach, which may involve recording a person's physical contacts during a given period of time. Owing to the time and effort required, this is rarely done. Other scholars make use of archival records, such as rolodexes, personnel files, news reports, or biographical records (e.g., see Burt (1992), Burt and Lin (1977), Galaskiewicz (1985), Padgett and Ansell (1993), Rosenthal et al. (1985)). These approaches are more appropriate for the study of special populations (e.g., public figures).[1] Some researchers have also begun to use sensory and monitoring devices to track real-time social contact dynamics (e.g., Read et al. 2012), while others have turned to electronic networks to explore social networks, particularly to understand flows of health-related information (e.g., Newman et al. 2011).

But the most popular approach to gathering detailed information about individuals' social network connections—especially in the context of health research—has been to ask individuals directly about who their network members are and about other important aspects of their social networks in the context of an interview or a questionnaire (McCarty et al. 1997, Valente 2010). The survey

[1] However, one recent string of studies (see Christakis and Fowler 2007, 2008, Fowler and Christakis 2008) has made clever use of archival material from the Framingham Heart Study. Respondents had provided names of contacts decades ago when interviewers asked whom they could contact in the event that they needed to get in touch with the respondent but could not get find them. Christakis and Fowler used this information to reconstruct the social network of the entire Framingham community.

approach is often favored over other methods because it is less time-intensive than observational techniques, and they allow for data to be collected in a wider variety of settings and for more representative samples. The remainder of this chapter focuses on this survey approach to network data collection. We will discuss the types of social network data one can collect via surveys, the strengths and limitations of network data that are gathered using various survey approaches, as well as recent methodological and technological developments that stand to improve the quality and range of survey-based network data.

11.2 Respondents as Social Network Informants

The focus of this chapter will be on using survey methods for eliciting information about the social networks of individuals to aid in analyses of health outcomes. It is useful at this point to address one criticism of survey research on social networks, which is that respondents are not reliable sources of information about their social networks. A series of early studies by Bernard et al. (e.g., Bernard and Killworth 1979, Bernard et al. 1980), for example, compared respondents' reports of who their network members are with the researchers' own observations of whom respondents interacted with during the study period. They found that roughly half of what people reported about their contacts in specific contexts was incorrect in one way or another (see also Adams and Moody 2007, Casciaro 1998, Wasserman and Faust 1994). Scholars have responded to this concern by noting that it is actually more useful to ask respondents about their social network ties because their personal impressions provide better information about durable patterns of social interaction that emerge over a long period of time than observations of specific interactions during some restricted observational period (Freeman et al. 1987, Romney and Faust 1982). In addition, even when respondents' perceptions of their social networks or resources (e.g., the number of friends they have, access to social support, aspects of network members' behavior) are inaccurate or biased in some way, those perceptions are often more consequential for things such as sense of belonging, isolation, and health-related behavior than actual observed patterns (e.g., see Chernoff and Davison (2005), Krackhardt (1987), McDowell and Serovich (2007), Perkins (2002), Wethington and Kessler (1986), York Cornwell and Waite 2009). For these reasons, survey-based social network data—especially data on the stronger kinds of social ties that are closely associated with health—are often regarded as both more accurate and more meaningful than data gathered through other methods.

11.3 Whole, Egocentric, and Mixed Designs

The most fundamental tasks in such a data collection effort is usually to identify the members of the target population and then to ascertain who these individuals'

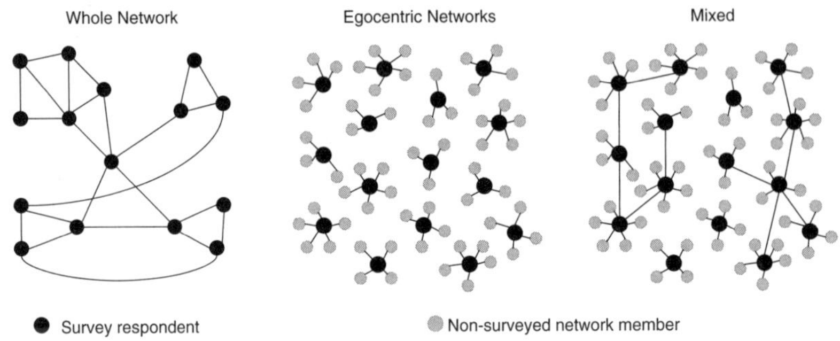

FIGURE 11.1 **Hypothetical social network data structures from whole, egocentric, and mixed designs. The circles, or "nodes," in the diagrams given in this figure represent individuals. Note that the networks depicted in each of the three panels suggest a sample of 15 respondents. The straight and curved lines that connect the nodes together represent social relationships of some kind (e.g., friendship, kinship, and familiarity) that tie the individuals together. These network structures are not drawn from any empirical data, and are presented here merely to depict the types of network structures that a researcher can produce when using different types of survey designs.**

social network members are—that is, to define the boundaries of the social networks in question (Laumann et al. 1983). At this stage, one of the first questions that faces a researcher who wishes to collect social network data is whether to collect whole or egocentric network data, or both. A whole network is comprised of a bounded social collectivity in which respondents are connected *to each other* in some way. An egocentric network, on the other hand, centers on a focal actor and his or her network contacts, regardless of whether the latter are also survey respondents (see Figure 11.1). Both whole and egocentric network data can be collected using survey methods—but they involve different data collection strategies, they have different advantages and disadvantages, and they make different types of analyses possible. The decision to choose one design over the other is usually determined by the research aims, the context of the study resource constraints, and the researcher's level of access to the individuals in the setting of interest. We cover some of the key principles of these approaches below, and address recent approaches that combine elements of whole and egocentric network designs.

11.3.1 WHOLE NETWORKS

The primary advantage of a whole network design is that the researcher can detect network ties among respondents and therefore directly derive measures of network members' attributes, behaviors, beliefs, and anything else that is collected in other segments of the survey. In addition, one can examine the whole network to develop measures of things such as the respondent's centrality in the larger network, his or her ability to access information or resources in different regions of the network, as well as the extent to which he or she is structurally proximate or similar to another respondent with respect to the patterns of ties they maintain within the larger community (see Wasserman and Faust 1994). Whole network designs are often difficult to execute, however, except in bounded settings such as classrooms, schools, apartments or dorms, and organizations.

To collect whole networks, researchers often compile a roster of the universe of respondents before data collection. This roster is then used both as the sampling frame and as a list that respondents themselves can reference when identifying who their network members are. Perhaps the largest-scale and most widely used whole network design was carried out by the National Longitudinal Study of Adolescent Health (AddHealth), which surveyed students in 132 schools throughout the United States. In one part of the study, the researchers provided each student with a roster that listed every student in the school and asked the students to identify up to ten friends from that roster (up to five boys and five girls).

One advantage of supplying respondents with a roster is that it allows them to recognize rather than report relationships, which can reduce bias associated with memory. This also makes the network data precise and obviates the need to confirm network members' identities. One problem with supplying respondents with a roster is that in some cases it reveals the identities of other survey participants, which raises ethical issues regarding protection of human subjects. Such concerns are amplified by the fact that many network studies are interested in the spread of disease or social influences on sexual, drug use, deviance, and other risk-related behaviors (e.g., see Morris 2004). If a researcher wishes to ask respondents to report which of their network members engage in risky or illegal behavior, the researchers may be required by an IRB to take steps to protect those network members as "secondary subjects" of the study (Woodhouse et al. 1995). This is more likely to be a problem in situations where those other network members are directly identifiable, such as in a whole network design. See also the discussion in Chapter 19.

Another disadvantage of supplying respondents with a fixed roster is that it pre-specifies the boundaries of the network, meaning that some potentially consequential network members who do not appear on the supplied roster will be ignored. Thus, some researchers leave the task of identifying the most relevant network members over to the respondent, as his or her subjective sense of who constitutes an important network tie may be more accurate than the researcher's (Laumann et al. 1983). Such an approach can still yield whole network structures, especially if this information is being collected within a bounded setting such as a school or a small village or community. Inevitably, respondents' lists of network members will include other respondents in that setting, thus providing a sense of their connectedness to each other.

11.3.2 EGOCENTRIC NETWORKS

Due to the greater demands and difficulties associated with collecting whole network data (e.g., compiling a complete roster of relevant actors, getting IRB approval for collecting network data using whole rosters), most researchers collect *egocentric* social network data. In this approach, researchers have no preconceived notions about who is in the respondent's social network. Rather, respondents are asked to provide the names of their network members (typically using only their first names, nicknames, or initials to protect network members' identities), and these are then recorded by the researcher in a personalized "roster" which can be referred to later by the respondent and the interviewer. In egocentric studies, network members are rarely interviewed. Rather, the researcher relies on the respondent to provide any information he or she wants to know about those network members, including network members' attributes, behaviors, and their relationships with each other (see Section 11.6).

Egocentric designs are more appropriate for samples in which respondents are unlikely to know each other, such as large nationally representative surveys. The main disadvantage of using an egocentric design is that it entails a sacrifice in the breadth and quality of the network data, as it is entirely dependent upon respondent recall, comprehensiveness, and accuracy. But egocentric network data can still be used to calculate a wide variety of network structural measures, including ego network composition, heterogeneity, and density, as well as positional measures such as network betweenness, centrality and bridging and brokerage potential (e.g., see Burt (1992), Cornwell (2009), Everett and Borgatti (2005), Marsden (2002)).

11.3.3 MIXED DESIGNS

A growing practice in health research is to develop egocentric network data within the context of a sample of respondents who *might* also be linked to each other. A major advantage of such a design is that one can directly compare the influence of perceived and actual social network characteristics. The most comprehensive way to do this is to interview a set of people within a given context and ask those respondents to name the other respondents to whom they are connected, and then proceed to ask each respondent about his or her contacts' behaviors/attitudes. Respondents' reports of their network members' characteristics can then be compared to those network members' actual reports. This approach is especially useful in cases where researchers are interested in characteristics of social network members that may be "hidden" from respondents, such as risky or illegal behavior (e.g., drug use) and behavior that carries a social stigma (e.g., unprotected anal sex). Respondents still provide data about their egocentric network members' (perceived) characteristics, and researchers will know which of those egocentric network members correspond to which of the other respondents. However, there still may be some members of a given respondent's egocentric network who do not appear in the sample.

A common obstacle to developing whole network data in which respondents are connected to each other involves human subjects concerns associated with revealing the names of other study participants to respondents. This is especially problematic in studies of health-related issues such as the spread of sexually transmitted diseases (STDs) such as HIV/AIDS and associated high risk behaviors such as needle sharing. A growing number of researchers in the field of epidemiology develop samples to study these issues using a technique known as *respondent-driven sampling* (RDS). RDS is a chain-referral design in which a small initial set of "seed" participants are asked to recruit subsequent participants, who are also asked to recruit additional participants, and so on in multiple waves until a large sample is obtained. RDS is preferable to simpler snowball sampling designs for a number of reasons. For one, RDS uses respondents' network connections to generate a sample that approximates a probability sample allowing for valid statistical analysis when its assumptions are met (Gile and Handcock 2010, Heckathorn 1997, 2002, Wejnert and Heckathorn 2011). RDS uses information about how well connected each respondent is to weight his or her influence in statistical estimates—specifically, to reduce bias in statistical estimates that may be caused by better-connected respondents' disproportionate impact on the composition of the recruited sample. Each respondent's influence on the sample's composition is also constrained by allowing each participant to recruit only three or four participants, which ensures that with enough waves of recruitment, the sample will eventually reflect the composition of the larger target population (Heckathorn 1997). Furthermore, by tracking who recruits whom via coded vouchers, RDS allows researchers to adjust for nonindependence among observations. Overall, the RDS method is easier and less expensive to implement than probability sampling, and more representative of the target population than convenience or simple snowball sampling. The approach is best suited to the task of sampling members of hidden or hard-to-reach populations.

Chain-referral designs such as RDS are also valuable because they can be used to reconstruct a partial picture of respondents' connections to each other without actually revealing a list of study participants' names. Because respondents recruit each other, researchers have some information about which respondents are connected to each other. This information can be used not only to correct for nonindependence among the observations, but also to derive direct measures of at least a portion of a given respondent's network members' characteristics. A researcher can do this by measuring the characteristics of respondents who are only one or two steps removed from the respondent in question in the referral chain. When doing so, researchers need to remain cognizant of the fact that respondents typically recruit only three or four other respondents into RDS samples, and those who appear at the beginning or end of a given referral chain (e.g., "seed" participants) will have truncated networks. More importantly, because people can be recruited into the sample only once, the referral chain cannot be used to determine whether there are connections between respondents who did not directly recruit each other, even though such connections are likely to exist (see Granovetter 1973). Therefore, summary measures that refer to the characteristics of the respondents to whom a given respondent is linked may not be accurate representations of all of the study participants who are in the respondent's network. Researchers can get around this problem by asking respondents to provide as much detail as possible about their egocentric network members, and then cross-referencing that information with other respondents' data to identify probable matches. One problem with this approach is that one has to elicit a great deal of descriptive information about each egocentric network member (e.g., race, sex, age, initials, distinctive features) to make matches with a reasonable degree of certainty. Furthermore, this approach is only feasible within bounded settings in which it is reasonable to assume that respondents could know each other. See also the discussion in Chapter 4.

11.3.4 AFFILIATION NETWORKS

There is at least one other way one can use survey techniques to ascertain connections between respondents without having to ask them directly and without revealing the identities of other study participants. This involves constructing respondents' affiliation networks (see Borgatti and Everett 1997; also see Chapter 8 in Wasserman and Faust 1994)—that is, recording their connections to specific events, meetings, workplaces, or other contexts in a given area that might reasonably be assumed to have given rise to a (or arise from a preexisting) connection between the respondents. Given the assumption that people who are affiliated with several of the same events or contexts are socially connected, one can ascertain network ties between respondents by asking a set of questions to identify the places or events a person has been associated with during some bounded period of time. Once this information is developed, one can then use "two-mode" network analysis techniques (see Borgatti and Halgin 2011) to quantify the extent to which respondents' affiliations overlap. This provides a basis for determining which respondents have at least some capacity to influence each other or access similar pools of resources. For example, Schneider et al. (2012) asked a sample of Chicago men who have sex with men (MSM) about which of nine area health centers offering HIV services they had heard of and/or been to. They then used that information to ascertain the extent to which different risk groups are segregated with respect to health service utilization patterns.

11.4 Name Generators

After a study design has been decided upon and survey respondents have been identified, the primary task is to identify each respondent's social network members. In some network studies, respondents can identify their network members from an existing roster. Oftentimes this is not possible, and sometimes researchers are mainly interested in those network members who are foremost in respondents' minds. The most common way to generate a list, or roster, of a respondent's social network members—especially in egocentric network studies—is to ask him or her to list their names. The questions that are used to elicit names of network members from respondents are called *name generators*. A list of name generators that have been used in several influential egocentric social network studies is provided in Table 11.1.

Most health researchers who are interested in social network effects focus on the role of social influence, social support, access to valuable resources, and other social processes that unfold over a period of time and have lasting impacts on health. Therefore, a researcher has to be careful to choose a name generator that elicits names of relatively close, regular social contacts. Research suggests that

TABLE 11.1 Some Examples of Name Generators that Have Been Used to Generate Egocentric Social Network Data in Recent Health-Related Research

Name Generators	Main Data Source	Examples of Recent Health-Related Applications
"From time to time, most people discuss important matters with other people. Looking back over the last 6 months, who are the people with whom you discussed matters important to you? Just tell me their first names or initials."	The General Social Survey (GSS)	Askelson et al. (2011), Song (2011)
"From time to time, most people discuss things that are important to them with others. For example, these may include good or bad things that happen to you, problems you are having, or important concerns you may have. Looking back over the last 12 months, who are the people with whom you most often discussed things that were important to you?" (*Prompt if do not know*: "This could be a person you tend to talk to about things that are important to you.")	The National Social Life, Health, and Aging Project (NSHAP)	Cornwell and Laumann (2011), York Cornwell and Waite (2009)
"I'm interested in who, among all of the people in your life, you talk to about health problems when they come up. Who are the people that you discuss your health with or you can really count on when you have physical or emotional problems?"	Indianapolis Network Mental Health Study (INMHS)	Perry (2012), Perry and Pescosolido (2010)
"In the past year, when you have encountered difficulties in life (e.g., work, finance, family, law, or illness), who did you turn to for actual help or information?"	Taiwan Social Change Survey (TSCS)	Son et al. (2008)
"During the last 3 months, who did you get together to hang out with or socialize?"	N/A	Latkin et al. (2011, 2012); see also Haines et al. (2011)
"Who are the people to whom you currently feel the closest?"	N/A	Nahum-Shani et al. (2011)

individuals can come into contact with thousands of people over a period of several months (see Fu 2005). Such an expansive contact network is only relevant in specific research contexts, such as in studies of the spread of diseases such as influenza (e.g., Mikolajczyk and Kretzschmar 2008). At the same time, a given individual is likely to "know" (i.e., be familiar with or be able to recognize) thousands of people (Bernard et al. 1990). Research suggests that the "active" social networks of most individuals contain hundreds of people (Roberts et al. 2009). But only some of these people are important or relevant to the kinds of influence and/or support processes that are thought to influence health. Therefore, to identify these people, a researcher has to select a name generator that helps respondents cut through the fog of everyday life and call to mind only the most pertinent network members.

Name generators can employ different cognitive cues and can be worded in different ways to elicit different types of network ties. Marin and Hampton (2007) distinguish between four types of name generators that can be useful in zeroing in on relevant network members: *role-relation, interaction, affective, and exchange*. The rationale for using the "role-relation" approach is that different types of relationships (e.g., friendships ties, kin ties) involve different bundles of social obligations and expectations. If a researcher believes that it is most important to assess respondents' access to friends, for example, he or she might use a name generator such as: "Who are your closest friends?" It is important to note that this method makes assumptions about roles that can be problematic—for example, not everyone defines "friend" in the same way, and not everyone is close to their family members. The "interaction" approach avoids this focus on the type of social contact and instead asks respondents to produce names of contacts in accordance with some feature of interaction. For example, one might ask the respondent to simply list the contacts he or she most recently had. This can also be done via a time diary. (Retrospective accounts are sometimes less accurate.) This approach may be more useful to assessing the respondent's typical social environment, but it is not as effective at tapping his or her access to certain types of ties. "Affective" name generators allow the respondent to subjectively determine the value of a tie. Such name generators typically ask respondents to name those people who support them, to whom they feel close, or those who are most important to them (Milardo 1988). "Exchange"-focused name generators assume that the most important ties are those with whom one can potentially trade potentially valuable resources, and might include questions such as: "Whom do you rely upon for help with everyday tasks?" or "From whom could you borrow a large sum of money?" (Marin and Hampton 2007; see also McCallister and Fischer 1978). These name generators tend to produce names of respondents who are embedded in reciprocal relationships, but may not be as effective at identifying the people with whom one has the most, or most rewarding, social contact.

Perhaps the most widely used and empirically validated name generator in the social sciences asks respondents to name people with whom they "discuss [personal/important] matters," which combines interactive and affective elements. This item was first used by McCallister and Fischer (1978), and then gained widespread exposure thanks to its inclusion in the 1985 and 2004 General Social Surveys (GSS). It has since been used in hundreds of studies, and was recently included in two waves (2006 and 2011) of the National Social Life, Health, and Aging Project (NSHAP) to develop data on change in the egocentric social networks of older adults. Respondents are typically asked to name up to five network members in response to this question. This procedure tends to elicit "core" or strong social network ties—ties through which social influence and resources (such as social support) are most likely to flow (see Bailey and Marsden 1999, Ruan 1998, Straits 2000, c. f. Bearman and Parigi 2004). Therefore, name generators like this are well-suited to the study of health-related outcomes. Perry and Pescosolido (2010) find substantial overlap between names elicited in response to the "personal/important matters" name generator and a similar question that asked respondents to name people with whom they discussed "health matters," but they also find that the health matters network is more closely associated with mental health–related outcomes.

11.4.1 MULTIPLE NAME GENERATORS

To avoid underreporting of network members, some researchers intentionally use broader name generators that encompass a wide range of both strong and weak network ties. For example, multiple name generators can be used to ask respondents to name people they turn to for a number of different types of social support (e.g., see Fischer 1982, Sarason et al. 1983). Another approach is to use separate name generators for each of a number of different types of contexts or foci (e.g., home, neighborhood, workplace, home, organizations, and informal groups), and then ask follow-up questions (e.g., "Is this person important to you?") to zero in on the most relevant contacts in each context (Bidart and Charbonneau 2011).

Bernard et al. (1990) compared the results of the "important matters" name generator and a social support instrument that asks 11 name-generating questions, and found that the important matters instrument produced smaller networks that are composed of relatively close contacts. Similarly, Marin and Hampton (2007) compared the effectiveness of using single and multiple name generators and, in addition, examined two alternative name generators: A modified multiple generator (MMG), and a multiple generator random interpreter (MGRI). The MMG included the "important matters" item as well as the "Who do you enjoy socializing with?" name generator, while the MGRI included a set of six name generators. The study found that no single name generator provided as reliable an estimate of network size as the multiple name generator, though the network measures based on the combined "important matters" and "socializing" questions were moderately to strongly correlated with measures derived from the multiple name generators. They recommend using at least two (but preferably more) name generators. An additional advantage of using multiple name generators is that it allows researchers to assess the extent to which respondents' networks are partitioned into separate clusters of people who provide different types of resources, as opposed to a single set of network members upon whom they rely for multiple things.

If one is concerned about obtaining information about a broad range of ties but does not want to employ multiple name generators, one can also simply use name generators that intentionally tap a wide range of ties. Interaction-based name generators are capable of doing this. McCarty et al. (1997) measured features of "total personal networks," which included anyone who would recognize the respondent. Others employ multiple name generators in succession. However, researchers must balance concerns over recall bias or underreporting due to respondent uncertainty with concerns over *expansiveness bias*, or the overreporting of ties due to the use of overly ambiguous name generators (Feld and Carter 2002). In addition, the use of multiple name generators is more costly for interviewers and places a greater burden on respondents.

11.5 Free Versus Fixed Choice

A key decision that has to be made when designing any network instrument—regardless of whether preset rosters or name generators are used—is whether and how to restrict respondents' reports of their social network connections. One can either let respondents list as many network members or relationships as they can and want on an existing roster or in response to a name generator—the "free choice" approach—or one can restrict respondents' responses to some maximum number of network members or connections or cut respondents off once some other threshold has been reached—the "fixed choice" approach (Wasserman and Faust 1994). The practice of supplying participants with rosters of potential alters can be seen as a variant of the fixed choice approach, because a respondent's network cannot exceed the size of the roster. There are advantages and disadvantages associated with both of these approaches. Free choice produces larger networks and therefore makes it possible to identify a wider range of potential network influences and resources of different types (e.g., weak ties as well as strong ties). On the other hand, if one then wants to ask follow-up questions about each network member who is named, this approach can be prohibitive and costly. Some researchers get around this by letting respondents list as many network members as they like, but then asking follow-up questions about a limited subset of the alters who were named (usually either the first ones who were named).

In survey research, most researchers adopt the fixed-choice approach. Some studies allow respondents to name up to some large number (e.g., dozens) of network members. Most, however, restrict the number of network members a respondent can name to between three and ten. The GSS allows respondents to list up to five people with whom they discuss important matters, while the NSHAP restricts the roster to five such discussion partners as well as one other "close" contact. The AddHealth study limited the number of friends adolescents could list at Wave 1 to five girls and five boys apiece.

While upon first impression these limits may seem overly restrictive—given that most people have much larger networks—research shows that asking about five network members yields enough data to generate reliable estimates of network properties such as network composition and density (see Marsden 1993).

And there is mixed evidence regarding whether respondents are restricted by fixed-choice designs. In the 1985 GSS, for example, 24.7% of respondents reached the maximum of five discussion network members named, but only 5.5% indicated that they would have named more network members if allowed (Marsden 1987). The primary attraction of the fixed-choice approach is that it can drastically reduce survey time for a subset of respondents who have large networks, especially if many follow-up questions are to be looped over each network member who is named (see Section 11.6). If a researcher is primarily interested in gathering data about the types of network members who are likely to exercise an influence on heath or health-related behavior, or wants to understand the structure of one's core support network, the fixed-choice approach is effective at limiting the network to the most relevant network ties, as respondents tend to name closer contacts first (Burt 1986). On the other hand, if one is interested in a respondent's access to weaker ties or in assessing the range of contacts a person maintains, a free-choice design may be more appropriate.

11.6 Name Interpreters

The goal in many social network studies is to assess associations between a given respondent's social network members' attributes, behaviors, attitudes, or other characteristics, on one hand, and the respondent's own characteristics, on the other. There is also often an interest in qualities of respondents' relationships with their network members (e.g., tie strength). Therefore, lists of respondents' social network members are only useful insofar as a researcher also develops information about those network members and respondents' relationships with them. In whole network designs such as the AddHealth study, where researchers also survey the network members who are named by a given respondent (e.g., other students in the respondent's school), researchers get direct information about a given respondent's network members (e.g., their health, their social behaviors, etc.) by cross-referencing the interview or questionnaire data that were gathered from those people. (One can also supplement this information by gathering data from respondents regarding their *perceptions* of alters' behavior, assessments of the nature and quality of their relationships with those network members, or other relevant information.) But in egocentric designs, where respondents name network members who are not themselves respondents, researchers must rely solely on information respondents provide about their network members. This information is usually drawn out of respondents via follow-up questions that are referred to as *name interpreters.*

Name interpreters are often employed to develop information about network members' attributes, the nature of their relationships with network members (e.g., tie strength, duration, positively vs negatively valenced interactions), network members' behaviors and attitudes (e.g., health statuses, health-related behaviors), and the nature of network members' relationships with each other. One can ask respondents to estimate a given network characteristic by asking a single question (e.g., "What proportion of your network members are kin?"). But due to the cognitive demands of generating such estimates, a better approach is to measure network characteristics using multiple-item instruments that ask respondents for one datum at a time, looped over each of their network members one by one.

11.7 Social Network Measures

The issue of what aspects of networks to measure—or what to ask respondents about their network members in egocentric designs—depends on the study aims. In the following sections, we describe some of the characteristics of network members that researchers often collect via name interpreters.

11.7.1 NETWORK COMPOSITION

Social network researchers often stress the importance of network composition for individual outcomes such as health. Accordingly, a common first name interpreter following the use of a name generator (in egocentric designs) is: "What is the nature of your relationship with [Name]?" This question is typically followed by a list of options, including "spouse/partner," "child," "friend," "neighbor," "coworker," and so on. This question allows researchers to assess not only network composition (e.g., proportion kin), but also range (e.g., number of roles played by the respondent). If respondents are allowed to choose more than one relationship type category for each network member, then the researcher can also assess relationship *multiplexity*, which reflects the number of different ways in which a network member is connected to the respondent and therefore is often used to measure tie strength or durability (Verbrugge 1979). Other features of network composition that are of interest to researchers include network members' race, sex/gender, and age. These can be assessed by asking straightforward questions such as: "Is [NAME] male or female?"

Network composition—especially in terms of the prevalence of kin in one's network—is often seen as important because it reflects the extent to which one's network is comprised of durable social connections that have wide-ranging social obligations encoded into them. Research has found that measures of kin composition and network range affect levels of stress, for example (e.g., Haines and Hurlbert 1992, Kana'Iaupuni et al. 2005). Network composition is also important in that research suggests that different types of network ties play different roles in shaping health and health-related behavior (e.g., see Christakis and Fowler 2007). Network composition can also be used to measure the degree of *homophily* in a person's network, or the extent to which people become connected to others who are similar in some way, such as with respect to race/ethnicity (McPherson et al. 2001). In social networks, homogeneity is thought to increase ease of communication and coordination among members, and thus may have some benefits in terms of support and social capital (e.g., Lin et al. 1985). At the same time, it also implies reduced network range. Research on risk networks highlights different implications of homophily. Being similar to each other generally increases network members' capacities to influence each other

(McPherson et al. 2001), which has implications for key health-related behaviors. On the other hand, research in network epidemiology suggests that homophilous risk network ties (e.g., reflecting assortative mating) reduce rates of transmission of infection, in part because risk network ties between dissimilar individuals (e.g., dissimilar with respect to race, geographic location, sexual orientation, or serostatus) constitute "bridges" through which infections might spread between disparate groups (e.g., Aral 2000).

11.7.2 NETWORK MEMBERS' ATTITUDES AND BEHAVIORS

Following social influence perspectives, many researchers collect information about individuals' social network members' behaviors, attitudes, and experiences because those attributes are thought to affect individuals in some way. Numerous studies have shown that people's health-related statuses and behaviors mirror those of their network members. Health statuses such as obesity and health-related behaviors such as smoking diffuse along network pathways through numerous subtle mechanisms of influence (e.g., see Christakis and Fowler 2007, 2008, Valente 2010), so network researchers are often interested in network members' attitudes and behaviors. One way to learn about respondents' normative environments in egocentric studies is to ask them directly about their network members' health-related attributes. Studies of smoking and drinking, for example, often ask respondents about the extent to which their friends engage in those behaviors. As discussed elsewhere in this chapter, one has to be careful when asking name interpreters to capture these kinds of alter attributes, as answers may be affected by projection bias, recall bias, or simple lack of information (see the Section 11.10). Whole network data are often necessary to assess the actual behaviors of one's network members.

11.7.3 RELATIONSHIP CHARACTERISTICS

To understand how a person's social network functions, information about the nature of his or her network relationships is invaluable. Research shows that well-being is related to subjective, qualitative aspects of network ties, such as emotional closeness (which is related to self-esteem and happiness), as well as to more objective features of relationships, such as frequency of contact, duration, and content of discussions or exchanges (e.g., see York Cornwell and Waite 2009, Wellman and Wortley 1990). Information about tie strength is particularly important because it provides clues about the types of resources respondents have access to through their networks. Whereas strong ties are associated with wide-ranging and unconditional social support and social capital, weak ties often signal connectedness to diverse regions of social networks, mobility, and independence (see Burt 2005, Cornwell 2011b, Granovetter 1973). Network researchers have begun to urge researchers to examine the "functional specificity" of network ties, pointing out that having network ties—even strong ones—does not guarantee that they are relevant to health. They therefore argue that health researchers should attempt to understand how relevant one's network ties are to certain health outcomes or behaviors specifically (Perry and Pescosolido 2010). For example, the

NSHAP study uses a name interpreter to assess the likely involvement of each network member in respondents' health-related behaviors, medical treatment, and advice (Cornwell et al. 2009). The name interpreter is worded as: "Suppose you had a health problem that you were concerned about, or needed to make an important decision about your own medical treatment. How likely is it that you would talk with [NAME] about this? Would you say very likely, somewhat likely, or not likely?" Recent work suggests that this information provides crucial context for understanding the relevance of networks to important health outcomes. Older adults who had larger confidant networks were less likely to have uncontrolled or undiagnosed hypertension, but only if they tended to discuss health and medical matters with their network members—otherwise, they were more likely to suffer from uncontrolled or undiagnosed hypertension (York Cornwell and Waite 2012). Because the respondent is party to each relationship, questions about these kinds of relationship featured are often reliably answered by respondents.

11.7.4 NETWORK DENSITY

Social network data are powerful because they capture important dimensions of individuals' positions within larger social structure (see Wasserman and Faust 1994). One of the most important structural features of social networks in this respect is network density. This refers to the extent to which one's network members are connected to *each other*. Network density is important because it captures network members' capacity for coordination and control. Denser networks are thought to be more effective at providing support and at controlling health-related behavior because they allow for direct and indirect means of contact between network members (see Ashida and Heaney 2008, DiMatteo 2004, Haines et al. 1996). Like network composition, network density can be calculated directly in whole network designs. In egocentric designs, network density can be assessed by asking respondents a series of name interpreters that ask them to either indicate whether each network member knows each of the other network members or about the nature, frequency, or quality of the relationship between each pair of network members (McCarty 2002). This is typically done via a loop of questions that asks about the nature of the relationship (e.g., frequency of contact) between network members A and B, A and C, A and D, and so on, for all $n(n-1)/2$ pairs of network members.[2] These designs yield what are sometimes called *cognitive social structures*, because they are network structures that respondents perceive (see Krackhardt 1987). There is some evidence that respondents are biased toward reporting closer (or a larger number of) relationships among network members

[2]This type of question is appropriate if the relationship between network members A and B is conceptualized as symmetric (e.g., "Do Michael and Maria like each other?"). In some cases, researchers might be interested in assessing asymmetry in the relationship between alters. This would require asking something like "Does Michael like Maria?" in addition to the reverse, "Does Maria like Michael?" This is rarely done in survey-based network research, in part because it doubles the number of questions required to assess network density $n(n-1)$. However, an asymmetric matrix like this could be useful for detecting dysfunctional networks that could obstruct the flow of support resources or hamper the coordination of support among network members.

(see Freeman et al. 1987, Janicik and Larrick 2005), so researchers need to remain cognizant of the fact that measures of network density are merely estimates. A small number of studies have sought to reduce the number of questions required to estimate network density by asking respondents a single general question such as "What proportion of your network members know each other?" This approach yields almost completely unreliable estimates (Burt 1987a), so most researchers opt to ask the series of name interpreters.

11.7.5 CENTRALITY

Other measures of social network structure can also be derived from survey-based social network data. Some social networks researchers underscore the importance of *centrality* within social networks (Wasserman and Faust 1994). There are different dimensions of centrality. Degree centrality refers to the number of connections a person has within a network. Closeness centrality reflects the average number of steps it takes for a given actor to "reach" or access the other members of the network (Freeman 1979). And eigenvector centrality captures the extent to which a person is connected to network members who are themselves central (Bonacich 2007). Regardless, centrality generally means greater social status and more exposure to and influence over the flow of information and resources within a network. Likewise, it signals a high level of embeddedness within that setting, as opposed to marginalization somewhere in its periphery. In these senses, centrality may often have a variety of benefits for individuals. Fowler and Christakis (2008), for example, showed that people who are central in friendship and kinship networks are more likely to be happy. But it is important to note that the relevance of centrality to health depends on the health process being examined and the type of network being considered. Network-epidemiological research has shown that people who are more central in risk networks (e.g., sexual or drug-sharing networks) are at greater risk for infection because of their lower overall distance from infected individuals in the network (e.g., Christley et al. 2005). Measure of closeness and eigenvector centrality are usually only available in whole networks, although one can get some sense of centrality using egocentric data regarding network members' (perceived) relationships with each other (see Marsden 2002).

11.7.6 BETWEENNESS AND BRIDGING

A closely related class of structural features of networks that are increasingly used in health research relate to betweenness and bridging. These concepts generally refer to the extent to which a given actor connects other network members who would otherwise be unconnected, or connected only through a longer, more roundabout chain of contacts (Burt 1992, Freeman 1979). An individual who has high betweenness or bridging potential in a network has greater influence over the flow of resources or information between other network members. Thus, in some areas of research, betweenness and bridging are emphasized for the advantages they confer upon individuals in terms of gatekeeping, brokerage, and other strategic opportunities (e.g., Burt 1992, Gould and Fernandez 1989). With respect to health, some research argues that occupying this kind of structural position provides a sense of independence or autonomy that is beneficial for psychological well-being (Cornwell 2011b, Cornwell and Laumann 2011). At a more global level, betweenness has been used in health research for purposes such as assessing an individual's risk of infection (Christley et al. 2005). Similarly, research shows that individuals who occupy bridging positions (e.g., structural holes, or gaps) between different unconnected groups often play a key role in whether a given disease, behavior, or piece of information spreads between those groups (see Burt 2004, Luke and Harris 2007, Morris 2004). As is the case with centrality, betweenness and bridging are best ascertained using global network data. This is partly due to the fact that egocentric network data rarely provide data on third parties outside of ego's first-order network who might provide indirect paths around ego. Nonetheless, one can get some sense of bridging potential using information from egocentric networks (Cornwell 2009, Everett and Borgatti 2005, Kalish and Robins 2006).

11.8 Other Approaches to Collecting Network-Like Data

Most network researchers collect detailed information on respondents' social network members using either a whole or egocentric network design. But researchers can also infer some properties of respondents' social networks without having to record an entire roster and information about each network member who appears in it. These approaches do not yield traditional network data, but they can provide insight into aspects of social connectedness—particularly as it relates to access to socioemotional resources, social support, and social capital—that are closely associated with health. We will briefly describe two of these approaches.

11.8.1 POSITION AND RESOURCE GENERATORS

Some researchers who are interested in assessing the variety of resources respondents have access to their networks or the range of contacts they maintain ask *position generators* (see Erickson 1996, Lin et al. 2001) and/or *resource generators* (see Van Der Gaag and Snijders 2005) instead of name generators. These instruments do not elicit information about specific alters in an individual's ego-network, but focus instead on the types of alters the individual has access to. Position generators typically appear as a series of parallel questions that ask respondents if they know people who occupy various hierarchically ordered positions—usually occupations (e.g., "Do you know someone who is a [social worker/doctor]?"). Resource generators combine some aspects of name generators/interpreters and position generators (Snijders 1999). These measurement instruments query respondents about whether they know someone through whom they can access some theoretically relevant resource, such as specific types of social support, money, or information (e.g., "Do you know anyone who can give legal advice?"). Researchers who use these instruments typically ask a string of questions to cover different types of positions/resources, and sometimes ask follow-up questions about the strongest or most frequently accessed contact in each category (e.g., the specific nature of the respondent's relationship with that person). The Survey on the Social Networks of the Dutch (SSND), for example, asked about respondents' connections to people in 30 different occupations and their access to 33 different types of social resources (see Röper et al. 2009, Van Der Gaag and Snijders 2005).

Position and resource generators are often used to gauge respondents' extensity of access to different structurally embedded resources, or social capital (Lin 2001). For example, researchers can use the data from position generators to assess the "highest upward reach" of a respondent's network in terms of social hierarchy. These types of questions often take less time than the name generator/interpreter approach. Unless combined with name generators, however, position and resource generators do not usually result in an actual list of network members. As such, they yield no information about key features of social network structure, such as network composition and density. Furthermore, they tend to overlook ties to people who do not occupy key positions (e.g., retirees, students) and/or do not possess many resources. There is also some question as to respondents' abilities to accurately report the occupations (Laumann 1966) and the resources of their network members. When employing resource generators in particular, one needs to exercise caution in distinguishing between respondents who do not have any network members who possess certain resources from respondents who simply have not had to search for those resources. Some examples of position and resources generators that may be relevant in health research are provided in Table 11.2.

11.8.2 SOCIAL NETWORK INDICES

Some of the most influential studies of the relationship between social networks and health have employed so-called social network indices (SNIs). The key feature of a social network index is that it collects information about a number of interrelated dimensions of one's social network and then combines them into a single measure. Perhaps the earliest and most influential SNI was developed by Berkman (1977) and then used by Berkman and Syme (1979) in a seminal study that demonstrated a substantial relationship between social isolation and mortality risk. Respondents were asked if they were married, how many close friends and relatives they had, as well as their involvement in church and other community groups. The researchers then categorized respondents according to which combinations of ties they had, and gave greater weight to relationship categories that contained more intimate types of contacts.

Many subsequent studies have utilized similar measures in studies of various health outcomes in different contexts (e.g., Cannuscio et al. 2004, Cohen et al. 1997). SNIs vary with respect to the number and types of social ties that are included and how different types of ties are weighted. Regardless, most SNIs essentially measure the range of a given individual's active network in terms of the

TABLE 11.2 Examples of Potentially Heath-Relevant Position and Resource Generators

Position Generators

Do you know anyone who is a …

… doctor[a]
… nurse[a]
… pharmacist[a]
… social worker[a]
… physical therapist[a]
… dentist … psychologist or psychiatrist
… other health care professional
… lawyer[a]
… minister, priest, or rabbi[a]

Resource Generators

Do you know anyone who …

… owns a car[b]
… has a professional degree
… is handy repairing household equipment[b]
… can help with small jobs around the house (carpenting, painting)[b]
… can do your shopping when you (and your household members) are ill[b]
… can give medical advice when you are dissatisfied with your doctor[b]
… has knowledge about financial matters (taxes, subsidies)[b]
… can loan you a large sum of money[b]
… can give advice concerning a conflict with family members[b]
… can discuss health/medical matters with you
… is familiar with Medicare/Medicaid
… you can rely on for help/support if you need it

[a]Indicates a position generator that appears in the position generator instrument developed by Lin (e.g., Lin et al. 2001).
[b]Indicates a resource generator that appears in the SSND (see Röper et al. 2009, Van Der Gaag and Snijders 2005).

number of different role-domains (of varying importance) in which the individual is involved.

The use of SNIs is not common within the field of social network analysis. The primary strength of SNIs is that they are (usually) more parsimonious and require fewer items to construct than instruments that are used to capture features of social network structure (e.g., via loops of name interpreters). A weakness of SNIs is that they predetermine which types of social ties are most relevant to health, and therefore ignore underlying variation in what individuals get out of different types of relationships. More importantly, because SNIs combine numerous dimensions of social network connectedness into a single measure, they preclude identification of the specific mechanisms through which social relationships affect health outcomes. Exceptions can be found in studies that separate network indices into subscales or separate measures that capture different dimensions of social networks (e.g., York Cornwell and Waite 2009). Relatedly, because SNIs are designed to capture overall social integration, they are not well suited to the analysis of specific types of network change (see below).

11.9 Modes of Data Collection and Survey Logistics

Social network data can be collected using different survey modes. Most social network data are collected during in-person or telephone interviews, and usually with the help of computer-assisted personal interviewing (CAPI) or computer-assisted telephone interviewing (CATI) systems. These are particularly useful in the case of studies that require respondents to provide lists of network members as well as data in response to subsequent name interpreters. Because social networks vary in size, it is impossible to know beforehand how many names will be provided and, therefore, how many follow-up questions a given respondent will be asked. For this reason, it is difficult to administer social network instruments on paper-and-pencil questionnaires. For ease of reference, questions that are to be looped over each network member—e.g., "How close are you and [NAME]?"—require names to be filled in beforehand. CAPI and CATI systems automate. (If, on the other hand, the social network data component of a survey merely consists of respondents checking off names on a pre-printed roster with no subsequent name interpreters, a paper-and-pencil survey may suffice.)

The logistical advantages of using both an interviewer and a computer together to guide respondents through the network instruments are most apparent when considering the challenges of collecting data on changes in respondents' networks over time. In these instances, it may be helpful for interviewers to reference or to present respondents with the social network rosters that were provided to (or generated by) them at previous waves. This also helps to ensure that respondents see these previous rosters at the correct time, not before they have provided the roster for the current wave. (It would be next to impossible to do this in a paper-and-pencil survey. While one could send the respondent a list of the people he or she named at an earlier wave, it would be difficult to guard against cross-wave contamination by making sure that the respondent does not see the roster from a previous wave until after providing his or her current social network data.)

11.9.1 INTERNET SURVEYS

While most researchers still prefer to collect egocentric network data through phone or in-person interviews, web-survey collection methods are becoming increasingly popular. This typically involves having respondents complete a series of network-oriented questions—such as name generators and interpreters—that are administered and automatically recorded using online survey software (e.g., see Vehovar et al. 2008). This speeds up data collection and delivery, and drastically reduces survey administration costs. Major drawbacks include low response rates and nonrepresentative samples that are typical of web-based surveys (see Fan and Yan 2010). Some scholars also argue that web-based surveys place a greater cognitive burden on the respondents and yield less reliable data on basic network features like tie strength (Vehovar et al. 2008; see also Coromina and Coenders 2006, Matzat and Snijders 2010).

11.9.2 MOBILE DEVICE SURVEYS

Other researchers are turning to microelectronic communication devices—especially smartphones—to overcome some of the limitations of other survey methods. For example, because in-person and telephone survey data collection is often such a mammoth task, respondents are usually only surveyed once during a given period of time—and any follow-ups typically occur months or years later. This limits the capacity to track short-term changes in both health and social network measures. This extended time frame may be ill-suited to the study of some health-related behaviors and outcomes—such as stress, happiness, and substance abuse—that vary on smaller time scales (Cornwell 2011a). Therefore, some researchers have begun to equip respondents with smartphones, through which they can administer survey questions that respondents answer remotely using their device's touch screen function (e.g., Cohn et al. 2011, Jones and Johnston 2011). If the researcher is asking a limited number of straightforward questions (e.g., "Who are you with?" and "How do you feel?"), he or she can "ping" respondents and administer the survey multiple times during the course of several hours or weeks.

This approach, which is referred to as *ecological momentary assessment* (ESA), is useful for providing assessments of short-term health status, mood, activity, social context, and other factors within respondents' natural environments (see Shiffman 2009, Shiffman et al. 2008). Researchers can also synchronize these data with real-time data on respondents' whereabouts, which can be collected via the Global Positioning System (GPS) and recorded remotely for later analysis. This is a promising approach to obtaining high resolution social affiliation data which can be used to link respondents to each other (e.g., Eagle et al. 2009). One disadvantage of this approach is that it increases respondent burden, reduces respondent privacy, and severely limits the number of questions that can be asked at a given time. To address the last of these issues, ESA studies are most informative when accompanied with a longer initial and/or exit interview that is conducted using traditional survey methods.

11.10 Avoiding Endogeneity in Survey-Based Network Data

Survey researchers need to be attentive to several issues when designing and analyzing survey-based social network data. In particular, there are several sources of endogeneity in these data that can severely bias estimates of network characteristics in, for example, analyses that regress some health outcome on some set of social network variables. Endogeneity in this context occurs whenever a regressor is correlated with the error term, and it can arise for a number of reasons. Some forms of bias can be avoided through careful selection and wording of name generators, and some can be attenuated by gathering data on potential confounders and covariates. For example, key sociodemographic factors that have strong associations with various social network measures (e.g., size, composition, and density) include age, race/ethnicity, gender, education (e.g., see Cornwell et al. 2008, McPherson et al. 2006), as well as personality (Burt et al. 1998, Casciaro 1998). Other factors that scholars should take into account are discussed below.

11.10.1 INSTRUMENT BIAS

Research shows that different respondents read name generator prompts and define various types of relationships in different ways (see Batchelder 1989, Bearman and Parigi 2004). For example, role-relation name generators can generate confusion for respondents due to the ambiguity of terms/concepts such as "friend" (Marin and Hampton 2007). Likewise, affective name generators can be problematic due to the subjective nature of qualifiers such as "especially significant" or "close." A problem with name generators that focus on a specific action, such as exchange—for example, "With whom do you discuss important matters?" or "Whom could you turn to for a loan if you needed it?"—is that they are unable to distinguish between respondents who have few such contacts and those who have not had the need or occasion to utilize them for whatever reason within the specific time period (see Bearman and Parigi 2004). Some researchers therefore recommend asking respondents about network members who come to mind relative to very specific types of activities, resources, and contexts—for example, asking "With whom do you discuss health matters?" instead of "With whom do you discuss important matters?" (Perry and Pescosolido 2010).

11.10.2 RECALL BIAS

There is considerable evidence that when general name generators such as the "important matters" item are asked, a nontrivial number of respondents fail to name the types of network members who are of greatest interest to the researcher, even when respondents maintain such relationships. For example, people sometimes forget some of their closest friends when asked to name them (Brewer and Webster 1999). Many respondents even fail to mention their spouses when asked to name their closest contacts (see Bell et al. 2007, Liao and Stevens 1994). Some of this may be due to memory or recall issues, time pressure, or other factors. Therefore, following the completion of a social network roster, some surveys ask one or two questions to pick up any additional contacts. For example, in the NSHAP study, if respondents do not name a spouse or partner in response to the "important matters" item, they are asked whether they have a spouse or partner (Cornwell et al. 2009). Surprisingly, 15% of all respondents (and 23% of those who had a spouse or partner) did not mention a spouse or partner until this follow-up question was asked.

Some researchers use visual diagrams to increase the accuracy of respondents' reports of who their network members are, how important they are to them, and how they are connected to each other (see McCarty et al. 2007). One approach, which was developed for research on "convoys" of social relations (see Antonucci et al. 2010), is known as the *hierarchical mapping* technique (see Ajrouch et al. 2001, Antonucci 1986). This involves presenting respondents with three concentric circles, with the word "You" appearing in the center of the innermost circle. The respondent is asked to write the first names or nicknames of alters at various places within the diagram, with the instruction that they place people whom "it would be hard to imagine life without" in the innermost circle, other close contacts in the middle circle, and any additional (less intimate) network members in the outermost circle. A similar approach is to construct participant-aided sociograms during the course of the interview. These are visualizations of egocentric networks that are actually created in the field with the help of the participant rather than being constructed afterwards by the researcher. Some studies—see, for example, Hogan et al. (2007)—employ elaborate organizational props, while McCarty et al. (2007) simply ask respondents to draw their own social networks. These approaches can be useful for checking the reliability of respondents' reports of their network members' connections to each other.

11.10.3 PROJECTION BIAS

In egocentric designs, every bit of information about network members—including their basic attributes such as sex and race—is provided by respondents. As such, researchers must be attentive to issues surrounding informant accuracy and bias. Questions about network members' basic attributes (e.g., "What is [NAME]'s sex?") are rarely problematic. In many studies, however, researchers are interested in the relationship between respondents' experiences/behaviors/attitudes and their network members' experiences/behaviors/attitudes. In egocentric designs, all of this information comes directly from respondents through their responses to name interpreters (i.e., proxy reporting). One problem with this is that respondents tend to project their own attributes onto their network members (e.g., see Goel et al. 2010, Hogset and Barrett 2010), which can lead to a disjuncture between respondents' reports and network members' actual attributes (e.g., Goel et al. 2010). The severity of this bias can be assessed only if one has whole network data, or at least a sense of some network members' actual attributes (e.g., as in RDS studies). Recent work suggests that the effects of any projection bias in technology adoption studies (e.g., studies that ask respondents whether their network members use certain technologies) is minimal, but that in many cases it does account for associations that are otherwise interpreted as network contagion or social influence effects (Hogset and Barrett 2010).

We could find no studies of the extent to which projection bias varies according to the type of network characteristics being reported by respondents. Therefore, in general, researchers should be wary of asking respondents about the extent to which their network members engage in behaviors that carry some social stigma (e.g., overeating, smoking, engaging in risky sex or drug use) unless they have some way to confirm or disconfirm their reports. Also, as discussed at the beginning of this chapter, bear in mind that respondents' perceptions of network members' behavior are often just as important in predicting respondents' behavior as actual observed patterns are (Chernoff and Davison 2005, Perkins 2002). In this sense, it is not always the case that one needs to ascertain network members' actual behaviors.

11.10.4 RESPONDENT AND INTERVIEWER FATIGUE

Respondent fatigue can also affect the number of alters respondents list in response to a name generator (see Pustejovsky and Spillane 2009). Some respondents learn through the course of an interview that if they provide long lists of items in response to a question, this can increase the number of looped follow-up questions they will have to answer. This "training effect" may induce some respondents to truncate the number of network members they provide in response to a name generator (McPherson et al. 2006). Similar interviewer effects have been detected in egocentric social network data (Marsden 2003, Van Tilburg 1998). Interviewer fatigue may lead to variation in interviewers' efforts to probe for additional names in response to name generators. These are good reasons to use a fixed-choice design, to minimize the number of network members about which respondents must provide information. It is also important to make sure that interviewers are well trained. In addition, some surveys have begun to ask social network questions at the beginning of the interview so as to attenuate such respondent and interviewer effects (see Cornwell et al. 2009).

11.10.5 REVERSE CAUSALITY

It is beyond the scope of this chapter to address statistical concerns associated with causal order issues or methods for attenuating resulting endogeneity. However, it is an important issue to bring up in the context of a discussion of surveys that are oriented toward both health and social network data, as it is an issue that needs to be taken into account at the survey design stage. The vast majority of research that examines associations between health and social network measures such as network size, composition, density, or access to social support is oriented toward ways in which such aspects of networks affect health. But lately more researchers have become interested in identifying ways in which health affects individuals' abilities to establish and maintain network ties, especially weak ties and peripheral contacts (Aartsen et al. 2004, Cornwell 2009, Haas et al. 2010, McLaughlin et al. 2011). The issue of causal order can only be appropriately dealt with via a longitudinal design in which baseline health and network data are collected. Researchers who are limited to cross-sectional designs might at the very least consider including questions to ascertain the approximate dates of both the onset of any illnesses or conditions of interest and the beginnings of relationships that are reported in the social network module (including relationships among network members, if network density is a variable of interest). Such data could be used to roughly assess temporal order. If the network variable of interest concerns network members attributes, behaviors, or other characteristics, selection issues are also a concern, as discussed later.

11.11 Selection Issues

The issue of selection bias is rapidly emerging as a hot topic within the field of social network research. For one, an emerging body of sociological research documents a variety of contextual influences on measures of social network connectedness and support (e.g., see Fiori et al. 2008, Entwisle et al. 2007). The same network survey can yield vastly different distributions of network structural characteristics when fielded in different neighborhoods or villages, let alone regions or countries where different languages dominate. It is important to take these factors into account not only because they may be confounded with key network measures, but also because contextual factors can condition the association between social networks and health (Litwin 2010, Mansyur et al. 2008; Son et al. 2008). It is important, therefore, to carefully choose the study site and sample.

11.11.1 HOMOPHILY

Apart from the usual issues surrounding sample selection (which plague all aspects of survey data), selection also affects social network data directly. This is particularly true in research that examines how social network members' health and health-related behaviors affect respondents' health outcomes (Smith and Christakis 2008, Valente 2010). For example, Christakis and Fowler (2007) used longitudinal survey data to show that, over time and through various mechanisms, an individual's body mass index (BMI) is affected by the BMIs of his or her network members. A common counter-argument to this kind of finding is that such an association may in part be an artifact of the process of "homophily" (McPherson et al. 2001), whereby people who are similar to each other (i.e., with respect to BMI) are disproportionately more likely to become (and remain) connected to each other (e.g., because they have similar habits, desires, and interests).

Research on this issue shows that social influence does operate in networks, but that homophily based network selection can inflate observed associations between a given individual's characteristics and the characteristics of his or her network members (e.g., Ennett and Bauman 1993, Schaefer et al. 2011, Shalizi and Thomas 2011, VanderWeele 2011). With longitudinal data, one can sidestep this issue by examining whether influence operates over time within stable social relationships (e.g., Fisher and Bauman 1988). If one is using cross-sectional, but whole, social network data, Hall and Valente (2007) suggest that the characteristics of people who named the respondent can be used to model influence effects, while the characteristics of people whom the respondent named can be treated as selection controls. If all one has are cross-sectional egocentric social network data, then one must take extra care in interpreting associations between respondents' and their network members' characteristics.

11.12 New Directions: Measuring Social Network Dynamics

Growing concerns in social network-oriented health research over issues of reverse causality and selection have contributed to a recent explosion of research on social network change, or *network dynamics*. Research shows that over-time changes in different aspects of social networks—including network size, rate of contact with network members, access to weak ties, and network members' health—have health effects above and beyond baseline levels (Aartsen et al. 2004, Christakis and Fowler 2007, Eng et al. 2002, Giordano and Lindstrom 2010, Zhang et al. 2011). For example, changes in individuals' social networks may disrupt the internal support functions of a network, including established routines of coordination and communication among one's network members that facilitate monitoring and aid. Research in this area signals a shift in the emphasis of health research from static measures of overall social connectedness toward the dynamic processes through which social network resources are lost and cultivated.

11.12.1 BETWEEN- VERSUS WITHIN-NETWORK CHANGES

The prospect of social network change poses several challenges to survey-based social network research. First and foremost is the need to use multiple observations to track changes in social networks over time, which can only be done in the context of a longitudinal study design. Perhaps the most important (and also most frequently overlooked) issue is that there are two primary sources of social network change: (i) changes with respect to which network members/ties are included in one's network, which can be thought of as *between*-network changes; and (ii) changes with respect to the (connections to) network members who are present throughout the period in question, which can be thought of as *within*-network changes (Feld et al. 2007). If one does not employ an appropriate survey instrument, it is difficult to distinguish between these very different types of network change.

For example, assume we are interested in the potential health impacts of changes in the amount of social support a person receives from their social network members. One way to do this is to quantify one's levels of access to support both at time t and later at time $t + 1$, and then subtract the former quantity from the latter to generate a measure of overall change in access to support. Positive values would reflect an increase in overall access to support, whereas negative values reflect a decrease. Without knowing whether the composition of one's network changed between waves (i.e., whether the respondent has the exact same roster of network members at $t + 1$ as they did at t), however, it is impossible to distinguish between cases in which a respondent's network members *became less supportive* between waves from those in which a respondent lost supportive network members and/or gained unsupportive network members between waves. These are inherently different social scenarios that involve different mechanisms. In the former case, the nature of the respondent's relationships with his or her network members changed (within-network change), whereas in the latter case the respondent experienced between-network changes (e.g., due to bereavement) that may exert independent influences on health. Similarly, a simple comparison of aggregate measures of network size at times t and $t + 1$ often masks considerable internal turnover in network composition.

As such, when designing an instrument to capture change in respondents' social networks over time, the optimum approach is to track changes in respondents' actual social network rosters—that is, changes in whom, exactly, they identify as members of their social networks at different time points. This can be done in the context of both whole network and egocentric network designs. (It is important to note, however, that it is not possible to distinguish within- from between-network changes when one employs only position generators, resource generators, or SNIs.)

11.12.2 TRACKING CHANGES IN WHOLE AND EGOCENTRIC NETWORKS

Unique issues arise when attempting to track roster composition change in the context of different research designs. In a study that is examining whole networks, the boundaries of the baseline social network are often restricted to the initial pool of respondents. Because attrition at $t + 1$ may be due to a variety of causes, including non-response, it is a good idea to ensure that respondents can name those attrited respondents as network members at $t + 1$. This will allow researchers to detect indirect connections that may exist between respondents who remain in the study at $t + 1$ but who are only connected to each other through attrited respondents. To avoid biasing respondents' reports of who their network members are at $t + 1$, researchers must not allow respondents to see or remind them of whom they listed at time t until after respondents have provided that information for time $t + 1$.

In the context of egocentric data collection, interviewers must rely entirely upon respondents' reports of whom their network members are to construct their network rosters for multiple time periods, and then cross-check rosters from those periods to detect any changes. Several procedures can be used to maximize the accuracy of respondents' reports of network change. First, at both times t and $t + 1$, respondents should be asked to provide enough identifying information about network members to make them clearly recognizable to respondents (and yet not enough information to allow for deductive disclosure of network members' identities). This often involves asking for and recording a first name (and perhaps last initial), as well as information about each alter from subsequent name interpreters (e.g., race, sex, approximate age, and the nature of the relationship). This information will help respondents remember their time t network members at time $t + 1$. Once respondents have provided data in response to name interpreters and name generators at $t + 1$, respondents can then be shown the rosters they provided at time t (e.g., on a computer screen or using a hand card), and asked to identify matches between them. This *roster matching* technique was pioneered in Wave 2 (W2) of the NSHAP study. After a given respondent provided his or her W2 egocentric network roster and answered a series of name interpreters, the computer

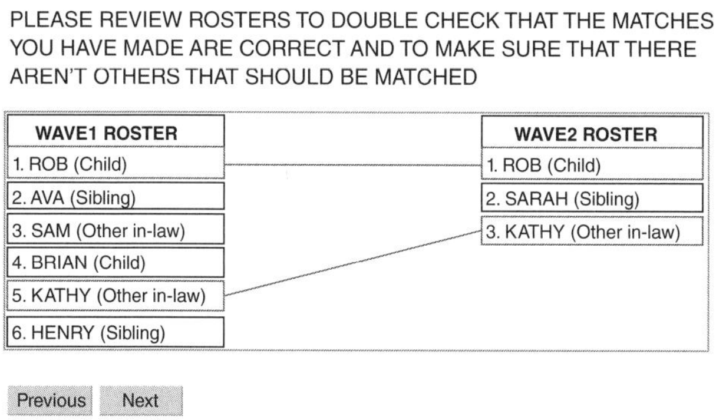

FIGURE 11.2 **Screenshot from NSHAP's egocentric network roster matching exercise. The names that appeared in the original screenshot of the rosters above have been replaced with pseudonyms. However, during an actual interview, respondents are shown the names they provided at both times t and $t + 1$. The names of and other information concerning respondents' network members at time t are preloaded from their original time t survey responses stored in the CATI system.**

screen displayed the respondent's W1 and W2 network rosters next to each other (see Figure 11.2). He or she was then asked where, if anywhere, the people named at W2 appeared in the W1 rosters. Respondents answered using a touch screen interface with which they were able to draw lines on the screen directly between matching W1 and W2 confidants. The W1 roster line corresponding to a given W2 network member was automatically recorded, where applicable.

Asking respondents to directly match roster members across time points is useful for two reasons. First, it obviates the need for researchers to infer which network members who were listed at time t correspond to the network members who were listed at time $t + 1$. Second, and perhaps more importantly, it allows researchers to ask respondents follow-up questions to explain discrepancies between the times t and $t + 1$ rosters. With this approach, a researcher can determine whether someone who was named at time t but not at $t + 1$ has died, moved, had a falling out with the respondent, or a number of other health-relevant causes. Likewise, researchers can probe to learn more about the circumstances under which respondents gained any new contacts at time $t + 1$ who were not named at time t. These measures provide crucial context for understanding the qualitative nature, and thus the health relevance, of network changes that are reported by survey respondents. Finally, these follow-up probes allow researchers to detect bias in measures of social network change that may arise from limitations in the survey's network instruments. For example, in fixed choice designs that limit respondents to naming five network members, changes in roster membership between t and $t + 1$ may be an artifact of respondents having been restricted to naming fewer network members than they actually had at either wave, thus increasing the likelihood that they would (randomly) substitute one for another.

11.13 Further Reading

This chapter provided a basic overview of survey-based approaches to collecting social network data. We did not attempt to provide an account of the evolution of these approaches over the past few decades, nor did we address the full range of social network measures or visualization techniques, nonsurvey-based approaches, software options, and other aspects of social network analysis. There are a number of excellent sources that provide detailed information about specific aspects of social network analysis, including an account of the historical development of the method (Freeman 2005), overviews of specific applications in health studies (Valente 2010) and network epidemiology (Morris 2004), other discussions of social network survey methods (Marsden 2011), as well as comprehensive accounts of a wide variety of general social network measures and methods that can be used in different fields (Carrington et al. 2005, Kadushin 2012, Knoke and Yang 2008; and see especially Wasserman and Faust 1994).

Acknowledgments

We wish to thank Erin York Cornwell for making valuable suggestions and comments on this chapter.

REFERENCES

Aartsen MJ, van Tilburg T, Smits CHM, Knipscheer KCRM. A longitudinal study of the impact of physical and cognitive decline on the personal network in old age. J Soc Pers Relat 2004;21:249–266.

Adams J, Moody J. To tell the truth: measuring concordance in multiply reported network data. Soc Netw 2007;29:44–58.

Ajrouch KK, Antonucci TC, Janevic MR. Social networks among Blacks and Whites: the interaction between race and age. J Gerontol Ser B Psychol Sci Soc Sci 2001;56:S112–S118.

Antonucci TC. Social support networks: hierarchical mapping technique. Generations 1986;10:10–12.

Antonucci TC, Fiori KL, Birditt KS, Jackey LMH. Convoys of social relations: integrating life-Span and life-course perspectives. In: Lerner RM, Lamb ME, Freund AM, editors. *The Handbook of Life-Span Development* Vol 2. Hoboken, NJ: Wiley; 2010. p 434–473.

Aral SO. Behavioral aspects of sexually transmitted diseases: core groups and bridge populations. Sex Transm Dis 2000;27:327–328.

Ashida S, Heaney CA. Differential associations of social support and social connectedness with structural features of social networks and the health status of older adults. J Aging Health 2008;20:872–893.

Askelson NM, Campo S, Carter KD. Completely isolated? Health information seeking among social isolated. Health Educ Behav 2011;38:116–122.

Bailey S, Marsden PV. Interpretation and interview context: examining the General Social Suvey generator using cognitive methods. Social Netw 1999;21:287–309.

Batchelder WH. Inferring meaningful global properties from individual actors' measurement scales. In: Freeman LC, White DR, Romney AK, editors. *Research Methods in Social Network Analysis*. VA: George Mason University Press; 1989.

Bearman P, Parigi P. Cloning headless frogs and other important matters: conversation topics and network structure. Soc Forces 2004;83:535–557.

Bell DC, Benedetta B-MQ, Haider A. Partner naming and forgetting: recall of network members. Soc Netw 2007;29:279–299.

Berkman LF. Social networks, host resistance, and mortality: a follow-up study of Alameda County residents [Doctoral dissertation]. University of California, Berkeley; 1977.

Berkman LF, Kawachi I. *Social Epidemiology*. New York: Oxford University Press; 2000.

Berkman LF, Syme SL. Social networks, host resistance, and mortality: a nine-year follow-up study of Alameda County residents. Am J Epidemiol 1979;109:186–204.

Bernard HR, Killworth PD. Informant accuracy in social network data II. Hum Commun Res 1979;4:3–18.

Bernard HR, Johnsen EC, Killworth PD, McCarty C, Shelley GA, Robinson S. Comparing four different methods for measuring personal social networks. Soc Netw 1990;12:179–215.

Bernard HR, Killworth PD, Sailer L. Informant accuracy in social network research IV: a comparison of clique-level structure in behavioral and cognitive data. Soc Netw 1980;2:191–218.

Bidart C, Charbonneau J. How to generate personal networks: issues and tools for a sociological perspective. Field Meth 2011;23:266–286.

Bonacich P. Some unique properties of eigenvector centrality. Soc Netw 2007;29: 555–564.

Borgatti SP, Everett MG. Network analysis of 2-mode data. Soc Netw 1997;19:243–269.

Borgatti SP, Halgin DS. Analyzing affiliation networks. In: Carrington P, Scott J, editors. *The Sage Handbook of Social Network Analysis*. Sage; 2011.

Brewer DD, Webster CM. Forgetting of friends and its effects on measuring friendship networks. Social Netw 1999;21:29–43.

Burt RS. A note on socio-metric order in the general social survey data. Social Netw 1986;8:149–174.

Burt RS. A note on the general social survey's ersatz network density item. Soc Netw 1987a;9:75–85.

Burt RS. Social contagion and innovation: cohesion versus structural equivalence. Am J Sociol 1987b;92:1287–1335.

Burt RS. *Structural Holes: The Social Structure of Competition*. Cambridge: Harvard University Press; 1992.

Burt RS. Structural holes and good ideas. Am J Sociol 2004;110:349–399.

Burt RS. *Brokerage and Closure: An Introduction to Social Capital*. New York: Oxford University Press; 2005.

Burt RS, Jannotta JE, Mahoney JT. Personality correlates of structural holes. Social Netw 1998;20:63–87.

Burt RS, Lin N. Network time series from archival records. Sociol Methodol 1977;8:224–254.

Cannuscio CC, Colditz GA, Rimm EB. Employment status, social ties, and caregivers' mental health. Soc Sci Med 2004;58:1247–1256.

Carrington PJ, Scott J, Wasserman S, editors. *Models and Methods in Social Network Analysis*. Cambridge: Cambridge University Press; 2005.

Casciaro T. Seeing things clearly: social structure, personality, and accuracy in social network perception. Soc Netw 1998;20:331–351.

Chernoff RA, Davison GC. An evaluation of a brief HIV/AIDS prevention intervention for college students using normative feedback and goal setting. AIDS Educ Prev 2005;17:91–104.

Christakis NA, Fowler JH. The spread of obesity in a large social network over 32 years. N Engl J Med 2007;357:370–379.

Christakis NA, Fowler JH. The collective dynamics of smoking in a large social network. N Engl J Med 2008;358:2249–2258.

Christley RM, Pinchbeck GL, Bowers RG, Clancy D, French NP, Bennett R, Turner J. Infection in social networks: using network analysis to identify high risk individuals. Am J Epidemiol 2005;162:1024–1031.

Cohen S, Doyle WJ, Skoner DP, Rabin BS, Gwaltney JM Jr,. Social ties and susceptibility to the common cold. JAMA 1997;277:1940–1944.

Cohn AM, Hunter-Reel D, Hagman BT, Mitchell J. Promoting behavior change from alcohol use through mobile technology: the future of ecological momentary assessment. Alcohol Clin Exp Res 2011;35:2209–2215.

Cornwell B. Good health and the bridging of structural holes. Soc Netw 2009;31:92–103.

Cornwell B. Age trends in daily social contact patterns. Res Aging 2011a;33:598–631.

Cornwell B. Independence through social networks: a comparison of older men's and women's bridging potential. J Gerontol B Psychol Soc Sci 2011b;66B:782–794.

Cornwell B, Laumann EO. Network position and sexual dysfunction: implications of partner betweenness for men. Am J Sociol 2011;117:172–208.

Cornwell B, Laumann EO, Philip Schumm L. The social connectedness of older adults: a national profile. Am Sociol Rev 2008;73:185–203.

Cornwell B, Laumann EO, Schumm LP, Graber J. Social networks in the NSHAP study: rationale, measurement, and preliminary findings. J Gerontol Ser B Soc Sci 2009;64B(S1):i47–i55.

Coromina L, Coenders G. Reliability and validity of egocentered network data collected via web. A meta-analysis of multilevel multitrait multimethod studies. Soc Netw 2006;28:209–231.

DiMatteo MR. Social support and patient adherence to medical treatment: a meta-analysis. Health Psychol 2004;23:207–218.

Eagle N, Pentland A, Lazer D. Inferring friendship network structure by using mobile phone data. Proc Natl Acad Sci 2009;106:15274.

Eng PM, Rimm EB, Fitzmaurice G, Kawachi I. Social ties and change in social ties in relation to subsequent total and cause-specific mortality and coronary heart disease incidence in men. Am J Epidemiol 2002;155:700–709.

Ennett ST, Bauman KE. Peer group structure and adolescent cigarette smoking: a social network analysis. J Health Soc Behav 1993;34:226–236.

Entwisle B, Faust K, Rindfuss RR, Kaneda T. Networks and contexts: variation in the structure of social ties. Am J Sociol 2007;112:1495–1533.

Erickson B. Culture, class and connections. Am J Sociol 1996;102:217–251.

Everett M, Borgatti SP. Ego network betweenness. Soc Netw 2005;27:31–38.

Fan W, Yan Z. Factors affecting response rates of the web survey: a systematic review. Comput Hum Behav 2010;26:132–139.

Feld S, Carter WC. Detecting measurement bias in respondent reports of personal networks. Soc Netw 2002;24:365–383.

Feld SL, Jill Suitor J, Hoegh JG. Describing changes in personal networks over time. Field Meth 2007;19:218–236.

Fiori KL, Antonucci TC, Akiyama H. Profiles of social relations among older adults: a cross-cultural approach. Ageing Soc 2008;28:203–231.

Fischer CS. *To Dwell Among Friends: Personal Networks in Town and City*. Chicago: University of Chicago Press; 1982.

Fisher LA, Bauman KE. Influence and selection in the friend-adolescent relationship: findings from studies of adolescent smoking and drinking. J Appl Soc Psychol 1988;18:289–314.

Fowler JH, Christakis NA. The dynamic spread of happiness in a large social network: longitudinal analysis over 20 years in the Framingham heart study. Br Med J 2008;337:a2338.

Freeman LC. Centrality in social networks: conceptual clarification. Social Netw 1979;1:215–239.

Freeman LC. *The Development of Social Network Analysis*. Vancouver: Empirical Press; 2005.

Freeman LC, Romney AK, Freeman SC. Cognitive structure and informant accuracy. Am Anthropol 1987;89:310–325.

Friedman SR, Neaigus A, Jose B, Curtis R, Goldstein M, Ildefonso G, Rothenberg RG, Des Jarlais DC. Sociometric risk networks and risk for HIV infection. Am J Public Health 1997;87:1289–1296.

Fu Y-c. Measuring personal networks with daily contacts: a single-item survey question and the contact diary. Soc Netw 2005;27:169–186.

Galaskiewicz J. *Social Organization of an Urban Grants Economy*. New York: Academic Press; 1985.

Gile KJ, Handcock MS. Respondent-driven sampling: an assessment of current methodology. Sociol Methodol 2010;40:285–327.

Giordano GN, Lindstrom M. The impact of changes in different aspects of social capital and material conditions on self-rated health over time: a longitudinal cohort study. Soc Sci Med 2010;70:700–710.

Goel S, Mason W, Watts DJ. Real and perceived attitude agreement in social networks. J Pers Soc Psychol 2010;99:611–621.

Gould RV, Fernandez RM. Structures of mediation: a formal approach to brokerage in transaction networks. Sociol Methodol 1989;19:89–126.

Granovetter MS. The strength of weak ties. Am J Sociol 1973;78:1360–1380.

Haas SA, Schaefer DR, Kornienko O. Health and the structure of adolescent social networks. J Health Soc Behav 2010;51:424–439.

Haines VA, Beggs JJ, Hurlbert JS. Neighborhood disadvantage, network social capital, and depressive symptoms. J Health Soc Behav 2011;52:58–73.

Haines VA, Hurlbert JS. Network range and health. J Health Soc Behav 1992;33:254–266.

Haines VA, Hurlbert JS, Beggs JJ. Exploring the determinants of support provision: provider characteristics, personal networks, community contexts, and support following life events. J Health Soc Behav 1996;37:252–264.

Hall J, Valente TW. Adolescent smoking networks: the effects of influence and selection on future smoking. Addict Behav 2007;32:3054–3059.

Harris JK, Luke DA, Burke RC, Mueller NB. Seeing the forest and the trees: using network analysis to develop an organizational blueprint of state tobacco control systems. Soc Sci Med 2008;67:1669–1678.

Hawkley LC, Cacioppo JT. Loneliness matters: a theoretical and empirical review of consequences and mechanisms. Ann Behav Med 2010;40:218–227.

Heckathorn DD. Respondent-driven sampling: a new approach to the study of hidden populations. Soc Probl 1997;44:174–199.

Heckathorn DD. Respondent-driven sampling II: deriving valid population estimates from chain-referral samples of hidden populations. Soc Probl 2002;49:11–34.

Hogan B, Carrasco JA, Wellman B. Visualizing personal networks: working with participant-aided sociograms. Field Meth 2007;19:116–144.

Hogset H, Barrett CB. Social learning, social influence, and projection bias: a caution on inferences based on proxy reporting of peer behavior. Econ Dev Cult Change 2010;58:563–589.

Ikeda A, Kawachi I. Social networks and health. In: Steptoe A, Freedland K, Jennings JR, Llabre MM, Manuck SB, Susman EJ, editors. *Handbook of Behavioral Medicine: Methods and Applications*. New York: Springer; 2010. p 237–262.

Janicik GA, Larrick RP. Social network schemas and the learning of incomplete networks. J Pers Soc Psychol 2005;88:348–364.

Jones M, Johnston D. Understanding phenomena in the real world: the case for real time data collection in health services research. J Health Serv Res Policy 2011;16:172–176.

Kadushin C. *Understanding Social Networks: Theories, Concepts, and Findings*. Oxford: Oxford University Press; 2012.

Kalish Y, Robins G. Psychological predispositions and network structure: the relationship between individual predispositions, structural holes and network closure. Soc Netw 2006;28:56–84.

Kana'Iaupuni SM, Donato KM, Thompson-Col'on T, Stainback M. Counting on kin: social networks, social support, and child health status. Soc Forces 2005;83:1137–1164.

Kawachi I, Subramanian S, Kim D. Social capital and physical health: a systematic review of the literature. In: Kawachi I, Subramanian SV, Kim D, editors. *Social Capital and Health*. New York: Springer; 2008. p 1–26.

Knoke D, Yang S. *Social Network Analysis*. 2nd ed. Thousand Oaks, CA: Sage Publications, Inc.; 2008.

Krackhardt D. Cognitive social structures. Soc Netw 1987;9:109–134.

Latkin C, Yang C, Tobin K, Penniman T, Patterson J, Spikes P. Differences in the social networks of African American men who have sex with men only and those who have sex with men and women. Am J Public Health 2011;101:e18–e23.

Latkin C, Yang C, Tobin K, Roebuck G, Spikes P, Patterson J. Social network predictors of disclosure of MSM behavior and HIV-positive serostatus among African American MSM in Baltimore, Maryland. AIDS Behav 2012;16:535–542.

Laumann EO. *Prestige and Association in an Urban Community*. New York: Bobbs-Merrill; 1966.

Laumann EO, Knoke D. *The Organizational State: Social Choice in National Policy Domains*. Madison: University of Wisconsin Press; 1987.

Laumann EO, Marsden PV, Prensky D. The boundary specification problem in network analysis. In: Burt RS, Minor MJ, editors. *Applied Network Analysis: A Methodological Introduction*. Beverly Hills, CA: Sage; 1983. p 18–34.

Liao TF, Stevens G. Spouses, homogamy, and social networks. Soc Forces 1994; 73:693–707.

Lin N. *Social Capital: A Theory of Social Structure and Action*. New York: University of Cambridge Press; 2001.

Lin N, Fu Y, Hsung R. The position generator: measurement techniques for social capital. In: Lin N, Cook K, Burt RS, editors. *Social Capital: Theory and Research*. New York: Aldine De Gruyter; 2001. p 57–84.

Lin N, Woelfel MW, Light SC. The buffering effect of social support subsequent to an important life event. J Health Soc Behav 1985;26:247–263.

Litwin H. Social networks and well-being: a comparison of older people in Mediterranean and non-Mediterranean countries. J Gerontol B Psychol Sci Soc Sci 2010; 65B:599–608.

Luke DA, Harris JK. Network analysis in public health: history, methods, and applications. Annu Rev Public Health 2007;28:69–93.

Mansyur C, Amick BC, Harrist RB, Franzini L. Social capital, income inequality, and self-rated health in 45 countries. Soc Sci Med 2008;66:43–56.

Marin A, Hampton K. Simplifying the personal network name generator: alternatives to traditional multiple and single name generators. Field Meth 2007;19:163–193.

Marsden PV. The reliability of network density and composition measures. Social Netw 1993;15:399–421.

Marsden PV. Egocentric and sociocentric measures of network centrality. Social Netw 2002;24:407–422.

Marsden PV. Interviewer effects in measuring network size using a single name generator. Social Netw 2003;25:1–16.

Marsden PV. Survey methods for network data. In: Scott J, Carrington PJ, editors. *The Sage Handbook of Social Network Analysis*. London: Sage; 2011. p 370–388.

Marsden, Peter V. Core Discussion Networks of Americans. *American Sociological Review* 1983;52:122–131.

Matzat U, Snijders C. Does the online collection of ego-centered network data reduce data quality? An experimental comparison. Social Netw 2010;32:105–111.

McCallister L, Fischer CS. A procedure for surveying personal networks. Sociol Meth Res 1978;7:131–148.

McCarty C. Measuring structure in personal networks. J Soc Struct 2002;3:1.

McCarty C, Bernard HR, Killworth PD, Shelley GA, Johnson EC. Eliciting representative samples of personal networks. Social Netw 1997;19:303–323.

McCarty C, Molina JL, Aguilar C, Rota L. A comparison of social network mapping and personal network visualization. Field Meth 2007;19:145–162.

McDowell TL, Serovich JM. The effect of perceived and actual social support on the mental health of HIV-positive persons. AIDS Care 2007;19:1223–1229.

McLaughlin D, Adams J, Vagenas D, Dobson A. Factors which enhance or inhibit social support: a mixed-methods analysis of social networks in older women. Ageing Soc 2011;31:18–33.

McPherson M, Smith-Lovin L, Cook JM. Birds of a feather: homophily in social networks. Annu Rev Sociol 2001;27:415–444.

McPherson M, Smith-Lovin L, Brashears ME. Social isolation in America: changes in core discussion networks over two decades. Am Sociol Rev 2006;71:353–375.

Mikolajczyk RT, Kretzschmar M. Collecting social contact data in the context of disease transmission: prospective and retrospective study designs. Social Netw 2008;30:127–135.

Milardo R. Families and social networks: an overview of theory and methodology. In: Milardo R, editor. *Families and Social Networks*. Newbury Park, CA: Sage; 1988. p 13–47.

Morris M, editor. *Network Epidemiology: A Handbook for Survey Design and Data Collection*. Oxford: Oxford University Press; 2004.

Nahum-Shani I, Bamberger PA, Bacharach SB. Social support and employees well being: the conditioning effect of perceived patterns of supportive exchange. J Health Soc Behav 2011;52:123–139.

Newman MW, D Lauterbach, SA Munson, P Resnick, ME Morris. It's not that I don't have problems, I'm just not putting them on Facebook': challenges and opportunities in using online social networks for health. *Proceedings of the ACM 2011 Conference on Computer Supported Cooperative Working 2011*; 2011. p 341–350.

Padgett JF, Ansell CK. Robust action and the rise of the Medici, 1400–1434. Am J Sociol 1993;98:1259–1319.

Perkins HW. Social norms and the prevention of alcohol misuse in collegiate contexts. J Stud Alc 2002;14(Suppl):164–172.

Perry Brea L. Coming untied? Narrative accounts of social network dynamics from first-time mental health clients. Sociology of Health & Illness 2012;34:1125–1139.

Perry BL, Pescosolido BA. Functional specificity in discussion networks: the influence of general and problem-specific networks on health outcomes. Soc Netw 2010;32:345–357.

Pustejovsky JE, Spillane JP. Question-order effects in social network name generators. Social Netw 2009;31:221–229.

Read JM, Edmunds WJ, Riley S, Lessler J, Cummings DAT. Close encounters of the infectious kind: methods to measure social mixing behaviour. Epidemiol Infect*First view available online:* 2012. DOI: 10.1017/S0950268812000842.

Roberts SGB, Dunbar RIM, Pollet TV, Kuppens T. Exploring variation in active network size: constraints and ego characteristics. Soc Netw 2009;31:138–146.

Romney AK, Faust K. Predicting the structure of a communications network from recalled data. Soc Netw 1982;4:285–304.

Röper A, Völker B, Flap H. Social networks and getting a home: do contacts matter? Social Netw 2009;31:40–51.

Rosenthal N, Fingrutd M, Ethier M, Karant R, McDonald D. Social movements and network analysis: a case study of nineteenth-century women's reform in New York state. American J Sociol 1985;90:1022–1054.

Ruan D. The content of the General Social Survey discussion networks: an exploration of General Social Survey discussion name generator in a Chinese context. Social Netw 1998;20:247–264.

Sarason IG, Levine HM, Basham RB, Sarason BR. Assessing social support: the social support questionnaire. J Pers Soc Psychol 1983;48:1162–1172.

Schaefer DR, Kornienko O, Fox AM. Misery does not love company: network selection mechanisms and depression homophily. Am Sociol Rev 2011;76:764–785.

Schneider JA, Walsh T, Ostrow D, Cornwell B, Michaels S, Friedman S, Laumann E. Health center affiliation networks of Black men who have sex with men: disentangling fragmented patterns of HIV prevention and treatment utilization. Sex Transm Dis 2012;39:598–604.

Shalizi CR, Thomas AC. Homophily and contagion are generically confounded in observational social network studies. Sociol Meth Res 2011;40:211–239.

Shiffman S. How many cigarettes did you smoke? Assessing cigarette consumption by global report, time-line follow-back, and ecological momentary assessment. Health Psychol 2009;28:519–526.

Shiffman S, Stone AA, Hufford MR. Ecological momentary assessment. Annu Rev Clin Psychol 2008;4:1–32.

Smith KP, Christakis NA. Social networks and health. Annu Rev Sociol 2008;34: 405–429.

Snijders TAB. Prologue to the measurement of social capital. La Rev Tocque 1999; 20:27–44.

Son J, Lin N, George LK. Cross-national comparison of social support structures between Taiwan and the United States. J Health Soc Behav 2008;49:104–118.

Song L. Social capital and psychological distress. J Health Soc Behav 2011;52:478–492.

Straits BC. Ego's important discussants or significant people: an experiment in varying the wording of personal network name generators. Soc Netw 2000;22:123–140.

Thoits PA. Mechanisms linking social ties and support to physical and mental health. J Health Soc Behav 2011;52:145–161.

Uchino BN. Social support and health: a review of physiological processes potentially underlying links to disease outcomes. J Behav Med 2006;29:377–387.

Umberson D. Family status and health behaviors: social control as a dimension of social integration. J Health Soc Behav 1987;28:306–319.

Umberson D, Montez JK. Social relationships and health: a flashpoint for health policy. J Health Soc Behav 2010;51:S54–S66.

Valente TW. *Social Networks and Health*. Oxford: Oxford University Press; 2010.

Van Der Gaag M, Snijders TAB. The resource generator: social capital quantification with concrete items. Social Networks 2005;27:1–29.

VanderWeele TJ. Sensitivity analysis for contagion effects in social networks. Sociol Meth Res 2011;40:240–255.

Van Tilburg T. Interviewer effects in the measurement of personal network size. Sociol Meth Res 1998;26:300–328.

Vehovar V, Manfreda KL, Koren G, Hlebec V. Measuring ego-centered social networks on the web: questionnaire design issues. Social Netw 2008;30:213–222.

Verbrugge LM. Multiplexity in adult friendships. Soc Forces 1979;57:1286–1309.

Wasserman S, Faust K. *Social Network Analysis: Methods and Applications*. Cambridge: Cambridge University Press; 1994.

Wellman B, Wortley S. Different strokes from different folks: community ties and social support. Am J Sociol 1990;96:558–588.

Wejnert C, Heckathorn D. Respondent-driven sampling: operational procedures, evolution of estimators, and topics for future research. In: Williams M, Vogt P, editors. *The SAGE Handbook of Innovation in Social Research Methods*. London: SAGE Publications; 2011. p 473–497.

Wethington E, Kessler RC. Perceived support, received support, and adjustment to stressful life events. J Health Soc Behav 1986;27:78–89.

Woodhouse DE, Potterat JJ, Rothenberg RB, Darrow WW, Klovdahl AS, Muth SQ. Ethical and legal issues in social network research: the real and the ideal. In: Needle RH, Coyle SL, Trotter RR, editors. *Social Networks, Drug Abuse, and HIV Transmission*. 1995. p 131–143.

York Cornwell E, Waite LJ. Social disconnectedness, perceived isolation, and health among older adults. J Health Soc Behav 2009;50:31–48.

York Cornwell E, Waite LJ. Social network resources and management of hypertension. J Health Soc Behav 2012;53:215–231.

Zhang X, Yeung DY, Fung HH, Lang FR. Changes in peripheral social partners and loneliness over time: the moderating role of interdependence. Psychol Aging 2011;26:823–829.

ONLINE RESOURCES

The website of the International Network for Social Network Analysis (INSNA), a professional organization that organizes annual conferences and publications, provides access to social network resources, and serves as a general networking source for social network researchers: www.insna.org/.

A free online social network analysis introductory textbook that covers basic concepts, methods and measures, by Robert A. Hanneman and Mark Riddle can be accessed at: http://faculty.ucr.edu/~hanneman/nettext/.

Free software (E-Net) for the analysis of egocentric social networks, including sample datasets, documentation, and related external links is available at: https://sites.google.com/site/enetsoftware1/Home.

Free software (Pajek) for the analysis of large social networks, as well as a wiki site providing advice, FAQs, and access to other online resources can be obtained at: http://pajek.imfm.si/doku.php?id=pajek.

A suite of software packages for social network analysis (statnet), focusing on statistical modeling of large networks, which runs with R, is available at: www.statnetproject.org/.

The home page of *the Journal of Social Structure*, an electronic journal of (INSNA), which publishes original research using social network analysis is at: www.cmu.edu/joss/index.html.

Information about the survey items that are needed to construct Cohen's social network index and instructions regarding how to score it, are available at the following URL addresses: www.psy.cmu.edu/~scohen/SNI.html and www.psy.cmu.edu/~scohen/SNIscore.html.

CHAPTER TWELVE

New Technologies for Health Survey Research

Joe Murphy, Elizabeth Dean, Craig A. Hill, and Ashley Richards
RTI International, North Carolina, USA

12.1 Introduction

This chapter provides an overview of the difficulties health survey researchers face in efficiently collecting high quality data using traditional methods and the promise and pitfalls of new communication vehicles and platforms. With the decline in coverage (and response) of traditional modes and the increase in coverage (and potential for response) with new modes, numerous possibilities exist, including text message surveys, multimedia survey invitations sent to cell phones, and surveys conducted through social networking sites (SNSs). Paradoxically, while many people rely on technologies like caller ID to avoid being contacted and sharing information about themselves in surveys, they are simultaneously willing to share massive amounts of personal information on SNSs. Any given Facebook newsfeed, Twitter posting, or blog entry is likely to include reports of an individual's mood, health status, dietary intake, and physical activity—exactly the kinds of health-related information that survey researchers try to collect. Many of the new communication modes are based on social networks, where individuals are connected as "friends" and share information, interests, and other methods of interaction, and at the extreme, the information being shared on these platforms

Handbook of Health Survey Methods, First Edition. Edited by Timothy P. Johnson.

can be utilized with no survey interaction to answer health-related questions. Here, we summarize current uses of new technologies in health survey research and consider the roles that new technologies and social media, such as Facebook, Twitter, and Second Life (SL), can play in supplementing traditional survey research methods.

12.2 Background

Health survey research has adapted over the years in response to technological innovation. Until the 1990s, health surveys were conducted via face-to-face interview, by paper-and-pencil (PAPI), or on the telephone. With the widespread popularity of the personal computer and then the Internet, additional modes of health survey data collection became viable, including computer-assisted personal interviewing (CAPI), audio computer-assisted self-interviewing (ACASI), interactive voice response (IVR) systems, and web surveys (Turner et al. 1998). In the twenty-first century, mobile technologies and social media platforms have boomed, outgrowing and supplanting more traditional means of communication. For example, the largest and most popular social media site, Facebook, claims 1.15 billion monthly active users as of June 2013 (Facebook 2013). In a dual-frame survey, the Pew Internet and American Life Project found that 57% of adults and 67% of online adults use Facebook in the United States (Pew Internet and American Life Project 2013, Rainie et al. 2013). However, these new technologies are not yet being utilized on a majority of health surveys. Surveys are just beginning to realize and utilize the flexibility and efficiency available with new technologies and means of communication.

The need for new survey methods drawing from advances in technology is evident. Surveys are becoming most costly and more prone to error as a result of undercoverage and nonresponse. In addition, there is a need in many cases for more timely or real-time data and different types of data (e.g., motions, locations, and images) that traditional survey approaches cannot supply. Regarding cost and error, health survey response rates have been declining since the 1990s (de Heer 1999, Steeh et al. 2001, Tortora 2004, Curtin et al. 2005), driving up the costs of data collection and calling into question the quality of such data. One of the major concerns with declining response rates is the threat of nonresponse bias. The inability to reach respondents makes securing their answers less likely and more costly. Although the relationship between response rate and nonresponse bias is not straightforward, the threat of nonresponse bias increases when response rates decrease if the reason for nonresponse is correlated with the key survey estimates (Groves 2006). In the United States, for example, the Office of Management and Budget (OMB) requires that federally funded surveys with a response rate under 80% conduct a nonresponse bias analysis (Office of Management and Budget 2006).

Several factors are contributing to declining response rates for health surveys, including increased mistrust in requests for personal information, or, in some cases, biological samples, from both government and survey organizations and increased reluctance to share personal information with unknown persons or entities (e.g., Kim et al. 2011). With the rise of telemarketing prior to the advent of the Do Not Call list early in the twenty-first century, Americans were inundated with calls that could be indiscernible at first from survey requests (Remington 1992, Tourangeau 2004). Junk mail and spam e-mail were also more prevalent than ever during this time (Kim et al. 2010, Tynan 2002). In field surveys, controlled access housing units with features such as gates, guards, and buzzer systems make it harder for individuals to be contacted at their door, thus producing higher rates of nonresponse (Cunningham et al. 2005, Best and Radcliff 2005). These impediments must be overcome to successfully complete field data collection operations (Keesling 2008). Because individuals have restricted access in these ways, reaching them and collecting quality health survey data has become more difficult and more costly (Curtin et al. 2005). Technological advances, such as caller ID on both landlines and mobile phones, likely contribute to declining cooperation and response rates (Kempf and Remington 2007). Furthermore, the threat of computer viruses from unknown sources and news stories about identity theft and stolen laptops containing individuals' confidential information likely led to people becoming more protective of their personal information.

Another major issue facing health survey data collection is the reduction in landline telephone coverage (Blumberg and Luke 2009). Surveys conducted by telephone, for example, run the risk of missing entire—but important—segments of the population of interest if the "traditional" landline-based telephone sampling methods are not conjoined with (or replaced by) a cell phone frame. This is an especially important consideration when conducting health surveys of young people or low income adults, for which landline coverage is especially low. A decade ago, Holbrook et al. (2003) suggested that telephone numbers can no longer be relied upon for survey sampling. Henning (2009) argues that telephone surveys are in decline, due in part to the rise in "cord cutters"—households with no landline telephone but with only cell phones and that "phone surveys with random digit dialing are no longer representative of the U.S. population." The survey research discipline has been focused on trying to plug the holes in landline sampling methods by adjusting its techniques, by introducing dual-frame sampling methodologies, or by replacing it with address-based sampling (ABS) (Iannacchione 2011). While these approaches have addressed the fact that more respondents are moving away from their landlines, these techniques can still be costly and time consuming. Furthermore, they do not address the underlying notion that many respondents may simply no longer be willing to participate in activities like a survey interview under the traditional model.

Data needs also require study results to be supplied as quickly as possible and often quicker than can be obtained with a traditional survey approach. For instance, the U.S. Centers for Disease Control collect data on influenza rates via various survey methods but by the time the results are obtained and compiled, they may not be actionable—for example, flu season may have passed. A finger on the pulse of the general population, so to speak, is needed when the cycle of acting on information must be rapid.

The need for supplementation of survey data with other data types is also a challenge to traditional survey methods and technology. When interacting with a survey respondent, it may be necessary to know features of the physical environment that can be either passively captured through a device (e.g., GPS, Global Positioning System) or captured by the interviewer or respondent in a systematic way (e.g., photo imagery or biological/environmental data). Another source of information may come in the form of "organic" data created by individuals but not in response to "designed" data collection activities (Groves 2011). These may come in the form of posts on SNSs or other electronic media that can be "harvested" to draw insights on health topics.

This chapter explores the ways in which new technologies and means of communication may address some of the existing deficiencies in health survey data collection. The options range from active protocols in which the respondent is actively providing information to the researcher through passive methods that rely on mining or "scraping" information from existing digital resources such as online SNSs. While the adaptation of these new technologies is still in its infancy, and major gaps exist in addressing all the challenges present in health survey research, there are indications that emerging technologies can help resolve some of the current problems with health survey data collection. As with any new methods or technologies, it is important to think creatively about the potential for research, but at the same time retain objectivity and rigor in evaluating whether they are "fit for use."

12.3 Theory and Applications

To understand how new technologies and modes of communication can improve health survey data collection, we must first consider the nature of these systems. The most useful survey research technologies are those that are already common in everyday life. In Figure 12.1, we define several new technologies and their potential areas of application in health survey research. This is just a sample of the new technologies that may have some application for health survey research, and new ones are coming about seemingly daily. Several of these technologies have real potential for application in different stages of the survey process or related activities, including recruitment; registry building; cognitive interviewing; data collection (both active and passive); panel maintenance; and the supply of organic data.

Technology	Description	Recruitment	Registry building	Cognitive interviewing	Data collection	Passive data collection	Panel maintenance	"Organic" data
Social networking sites	Online information-sharing communities, including Facebook, Twitter, and LinkedIn	•	•		•	•	•	•
Craigslist	A free online network of classified advertisements	•						
Second Life	An online virtual world in which users interact with each other through avatars	•		•	•			•
Google Trends	A tool that compares Google search volume patterns across specific regions, categories, time frames, and properties					•		
Text messaging	An electronic communication sent and received by cellular phone that can include text, picture, video, and/or sound				•		•	
Smartphone	A high-end mobile phone that combines the functions of a personal digital assistant (PDA) and a mobile phone				•	•	•	•

FIGURE 12.1 New technologies and their primary applications for health survey research.

We next look at several of these technologies in more detail to discuss their relevance for health survey research.

12.3.1 FACEBOOK

Facebook is one of the most popular SNSs on the Internet. Users can enroll for free, complete a profile, and share information about themselves, such as their hometown, current city, education, employment, interests, and favorites. Users post photos, videos, notes, and status updates with the intention that their personal contacts (referred to as *friends* on Facebook) will view and comment on these communications. Facebook is also used to make new contacts and follow, or "like," different groups, organizations, or products. Facebook was launched in February 2004 and currently claims 1.15 billion monthly active users (Facebook 2013), although there have been reports that up to one-third of these user accounts may not represent real individuals (Nyberg 2010). Facebook has also acknowledged the prevalence of fake accounts, although its estimates are much lower at 8.7% as of June, 2012 (United States Securities and Exchange Commission 2012). A December 2012 Pew Internet and American Life Project poll conducted with a dual-frame sample found that 67% of online adults in the United States use Facebook (Pew Internet and American Life Project 2013), which is up from 43% of adults reported by *USA Today*/Gallup in 2011. The *USA Today*/Gallup survey found that Facebook use is highest among young

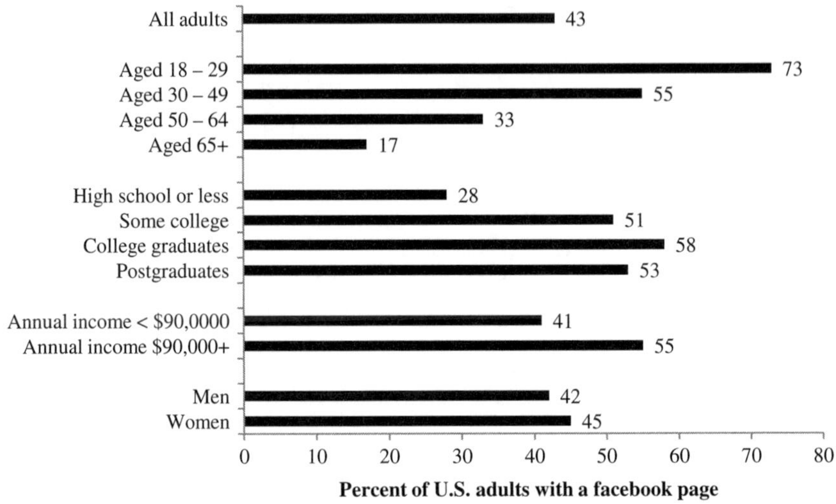

FIGURE 12.2 Facebook coverage in the United States, 2011.

adults, college graduates, and those with an income of over $90,000 (Morales 2011). Figure 12.2 presents a demographic summary of United States Facebook coverage and users based on the *USA Today*/Gallup data.

The most common current application for Facebook in survey research is locating sample members. Facebook has been used for tracing sample members by the National Longitudinal Study of Adolescent Health (Add Health) (Perkins et al. 2009) and the Longitudinal Studies of Child Abuse and Neglect (LONGSCAN) (Nwadiuko et al. 2011). Rhodes and Marks (2011) outline the procedure that is becoming more common on longitudinal surveys where some prior information about sample members has been collected: Survey project staff enter basic information about sample members including full name, best known address, age, e-mail address, and child's name into Facebook's built-in search feature to locate sample members. Once a profile is found that is a likely match with the sample member, a private message is sent requesting the sample member to contact the study to complete the survey. Using this method, Rhodes and Marks found and contacted 32% of sample members who had not responded to previous contact attempts through mail, e-mail, and telephone. The effect of Facebook alone is difficult to disentangle because other contact attempts continued as Facebook was utilized; however, Facebook appears to have increased response. Facebook was the last contact method used by 31% of the messaged participants who completed an interview. A total of 73% who were contacted on Facebook ultimately completed the interview, which was greater than the response rate for sample members who were not located on Facebook. Other applications for survey research have been hampered by the fact that Facebook currently lacks a sampling frame, meaning representative samples of its user population may be infeasible at the moment. There have been efforts to compile and make available a frame of Facebook users (Boges 2010), but the quality and completeness of such data would require extensive evaluation before claims of representation could be made. Some convenience sample surveys have been conducted on Facebook, such as a large-scale survey of Catholics enabled by Facebook snowball sampling (Brickman Bhutta 2012). Another example is the Facebook application MyType. MyType (2011) conducted personality tests and opinion surveys, and administered 700,000 completed interviews through self-administered web questionnaires on a third-party application within Facebook. Of those who have completed MyType surveys, 100,000 opted to publish their results on their personal Facebook pages. Contrary to the traditional thinking about surveys and confidentiality, some respondents may be motivated by the prospect of sharing their opinions with friends online. In fact, one study of undergraduates found that even among those with a high level of concern about privacy, most have joined online social networks (Acquisti and Gross 2006). Part of the appeal of online social media is "empowering exhibitionism"—the ability to reveal aspects of one's personal life without shame (Koskela 2004). It is a means of counteracting top-down, vertical communication styles and rebelling against authoritarian sources of information. Also empowering is the ability to construct one's online identity through the choice of what to share, including activities, beliefs, locations, preferences, and so on. (Albrechtslund 2008).

Facebook may also have a utility for pretest recruitment. Prior research has focused on the utility of online classified systems, such as Craigslist, for efficiently recruiting research subjects for pretesting activities such as cognitive interviews (Murphy et al. 2007a), and Facebook, with its expanding reach, may allow for recruitment in similar ways. By advertising opportunities to participate in pretesting activities to individuals with selected demographic characteristics, users would have the opportunity to simply click on an ad and be put in touch with the survey organization. Facebook was successfully used to recruit users of an online virtual world to complete cognitive interviews. Over 1600 responded to an advertisement and screening survey—vastly more than typically responds to a Craigslist or classified ad (Dean et al. 2013).

The web of socially linked friends and acquaintances that comprise Facebook also lends itself well to registry building, which is an important activity in many health studies. For instance, the World Trade Center Health Registry aimed to contact approximately 400,000 individuals who were in the vicinity of the World Trade Center in New York City during the attacks of September 11, 2001 or during the cleanup operation (Murphy et al. 2007b). Although a multifaceted approach was successful in compiling the registry (Pulliam et al. 2010), it is likely that much of this work could have been streamlined by allowing for respondent-driven sample generation through spreading the word on Facebook. There is, for example, a National Bone Marrow Registry that has over 221,000 "likes."

In the adjacent field of market research, social media platforms like Facebook are used to measure "buzz" about brands and to follow and track consumer behavior around the clock (Asberg 2009; Jansen 2009). One approach to tracking public opinion via Facebook is to analyze group wall posts using speech content analysis (Casteleyen et al. 2009). In addition to content analysis of wall posts, market research data can also be collected by engaging Facebook users in social media conversation. For example, engaging Facebook users with brands is best driven by encouraging a community of consumers that is focused around a particular brand (Smith 2009).

Researchers are finding additional creative ways to utilize Facebook for health survey research purposes. For instance, Moreno et al. (2011) conducted surveys of undergraduate students at two universities and examined the associations between their displayed alcohol use references on Facebook and self-reported survey responses using a clinical scale for problem drinking. They found positive associations between problem drinking and alcohol-related injury between Facebook pages and the surveys, suggesting that clinical criteria for problem drinking, and possibly other health behaviors, can be applied to information shared on Facebook or other SNSs.

12.3.2 TWITTER

Twitter was launched in July 2006 and by 2012 was estimated to have over half a billion accounts, including 140 million in the United States (Semiocast 2012). Twitter is another emerging source of data on people's health behaviors and attitudes. It is a widely used microblogging service, similar to the status update function of Facebook. Twitter users submit short messages ("Tweets") of 140 characters or less. Tweets appear on the users' profile pages and the profiles of their followers. The Pew Research Center's Internet and the American Life Project reports that 18% of online adults in the United States use Twitter (Brenner and Smith 2013). Twitter is frequently accessed on phones, as 16% of all smartphone owners use Twitter on their phones (Smith and Brenner 2012). Most Twitter users Tweet about personal life (72%), work life (62%), news (55%), and "humorous or philosophical observations" (54%) (Smith and Rainie 2010). Fewer, but significant numbers, use Twitter to share photos (40%), videos (28%), or their location (24%). As shown in Figure 12.3, in the United States, Twitter is used disproportionately by younger, non-White, and more urban individuals (Duggan and Brenner 2013).

As opinion-rich data sources like Twitter grow in popularity, they can be used to actively seek out and understand public opinions. Opinion mining and sentiment analysis methods have been developed to address the computational treatment of opinion, sentiment, and subjectivity in such information sources (Pang and Lee 2008). For instance, Chew and Eysenbach (2010) argued that while surveys are popular in measuring public perceptions in emergencies, they can be costly and time consuming. They illustrated an "infoveillance" approach that analyzed Tweets using the terms "H1N1" and "swine flu" during the 2009 H1N1 pandemic. They conducted a content analysis of Tweets, and, through this process, validated Twitter as a real-time, health-trend tracking tool. They found that while H1N1-related Tweets were primarily used to disseminate

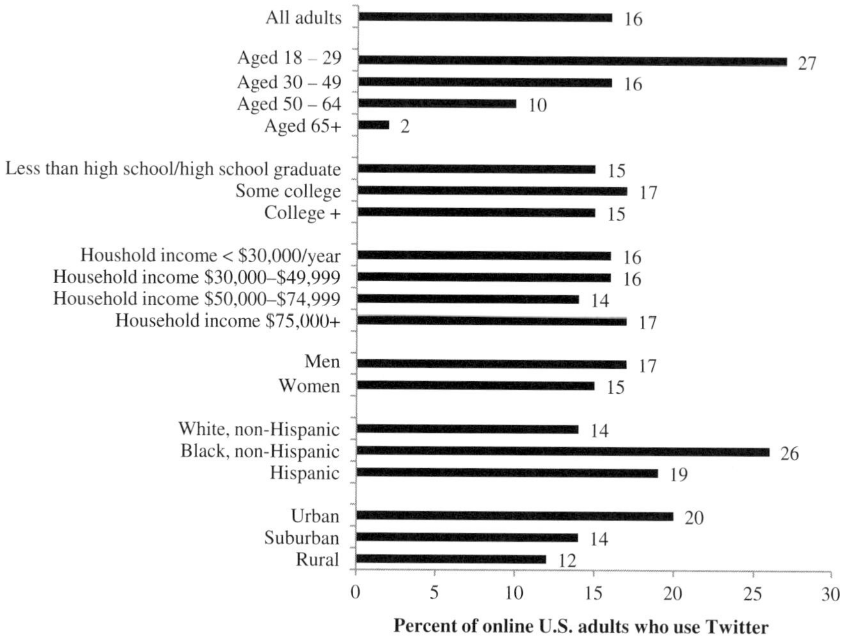

FIGURE 12.3 Twitter coverage in the United States, 2012.

information from credible sources, they were also a source of attitudinal data and experiences. The authors suggested that Tweets can be used for real-time content monitoring and may help health authorities respond to public concerns.

Squiers et al. (2011) supplemented a survey of women aged 40–74 with an analysis of social media posts around the time of the controversy surrounding the U.S. Preventive Services Task Force (USPSTF) revised breast cancer screening recommendations, developing a search syntax using keywords to identify relevant blog posts and Tweets. They found that, by this measure of public sentiment, the majority of mentions related to the revised screening recommendations were either unsupportive or neutral about the new USPSTF guidelines. Although this study did not compare Tweet content and survey results directly, it did demonstrate how the former can supplement the latter when investigating reactions to health guidelines.

Murphy et al. (2011) tracked mentions of the term *salvia* on Twitter from 2008–2011 and compared trends to self-reported use of *Salvia divinorum* from the National Survey on Drug Use and Health. The authors also coded the sentiment of Tweets about salvia use to determine whether discussion about the substance was being portrayed in a positive, neutral, or negative light on Twitter. This analysis found some evidence that information sharing about salvia on Twitter may be associated with actual self-reported salvia use, although more research into the nature of trends and causality is needed to determine how the two sources of data relate to one another.

From adjacent fields of research, we find examples of utilizing social media to predict election outcomes or match survey results. O'Connor et al. (2010) compared Tweet sentiments with consumer confidence and political opinion, and while the results varied, they found correlations are as high as 80% for some comparisons. Tumasjan et al. (2010) found that the mere number of Tweets mentioning a political party reflected the election result in the 2010 German federal election. More generally, a content analysis suggests that Tweets can be used to measure political sentiment.

In addition to tracking trends and sentiments, Twitter can also be used as a simple diary to track behaviors. TweetWhatYouEat.com allows users to document their meals and caloric consumption. Alex Ressi, who launched the website, suggests that Tweeting is effective for improving behaviors because it adds a "component of shame" by documenting behaviors and making them publicly available (Heussner 2009). Qwitter was a similar concept to TweetWhatYouEat. Launched in 2008 by Tobacco Free Florida, Qwitter users Tweeted the number of cigarettes they smoked each day and viewed graphs of their use over time as they tried to quit (Heussner 2009).

Researchers could benefit in several ways from conducting studies using Twitter diary methods. If the sample members were already active Twitter users, respondents would presumably enjoy Tweeting and would be accustomed to using this method of reporting information about themselves. Thus, response rates might be higher and responses more candid. Twitter responses would probably be more timely and accurate than retrospective PAPI diary responses, because respondents could be prompted about how they are feeling or what they are doing at a particular moment. For instance, a pilot test by Richards et al. (2012) found that Twitter diary respondents answered questions asked around the clock in 2.6 h, on average. Other advantages include access to timestamp data for all entries, instant data transmission to researchers, and reduced equipment and training costs. Twitter diaries would not be without limitation, however. Researchers would be limited by the capabilities of Twitter, including the current 140 character limit. In addition, because Twitter might not be novel to respondents, it is possible that they would be more likely to forget to update their diary for the study. However, this could be compensated for by having the researchers prompt users with reminder Tweets.

12.3.3 SECOND LIFE

Advances in technology in recent years have introduced additional possibilities of survey modes and methods of administration. One of the more futuristic possibilities is conducting interviews with embodied conversational agents (ECAs), which are graphical depictions of humans that can interact with respondents in human-like ways. Though this method is feasible, it is rarely used for survey interviews because, as ECAs become more human-like, they become vulnerable to human-like social influence, like social desirability effects (Cassell and Miller 2008).

Second Life (SL) is an online three-dimensional environment in which users ("residents") create avatars through which they interact with the virtual world. SL residents are able to communicate via instant messaging and voice chat, but compared with other social networking technologies, the purpose of SL is more for entertainment than communication with persons known in real life. Unlike Facebook and Twitter, which are generally used to augment one's real-life persona and relationships, SL users represent themselves in ways that may be a complete departure from their real-life appearance and personality.

SL was launched in 2003 and in that year 50,000 user hours were logged in-world. User hours peaked at 481 million in 2009, but resident activity holds steady. Each month, SL has over a million monthly active users (the total number of users who log in in any given month). Residents in SL come from more than 100 countries; about 40% of SL avatars are from the United States. In November 2008, the most active users were 25–44 years old (64% of hours logged) and male (59% of hours logged) (Linden Lab 2009, 2011).

Epidemiology was one of the first fields to start conducting research in virtual worlds. Since research shows that people with avatars in virtual worlds tend to consider the avatar as part of their identity (Taylor 2002), virtual worlds can provide a realm to understand people's disease response behaviors. The outbreak of the World of Warcraft "corrupted blood" virus validated and inspired the use of virtual worlds for epidemiologic modeling (Lofgren and Fefferman 2007; Balicer 2007). Epidemics have broken out in virtual worlds, and remarkably, avatar behavior in response to these virtual epidemics has been similar to human behavior in real-life epidemics: they try to avoid the infected. For this reason, SL is a useful tool for modeling epidemics like HIV/AIDS (Gordon et al. 2009).

Preliminary research indicates that SL may provide a context-rich environment for conducting cognitive interviews (Dean et al. 2009, Murphy et al. 2010). Advantages of both text-based chat and voice chat could be harnessed. With a text-based chat, full transcripts of cognitive interviews could be generated. Using voice chat, respondents' emotive cues could be captured. The only element from an in-person cognitive interview that would be missing would be the facial and physical expressions, although SL users can manipulate these for their avatars to a certain extent. An additional advantage of cognitive interviews in SL is the efficiency with which avatar respondents are recruited in the virtual world. Recruitment of a convenience sample of cognitive interview participants in SL can mirror traditional in-person recruitment methods (such as public flyers, classified ads and word-of-mouth) in the virtual world, accessing a geographically diverse population at lower costs than real world recruitment (Dean et al. 2012, Dean et al. 2013). This may be particularly true for recruitment of special populations that are more accessible in SL. For instance, compared to survey respondents in real life, SL respondents may be in poorer health (Castronova and Wagner 2011).

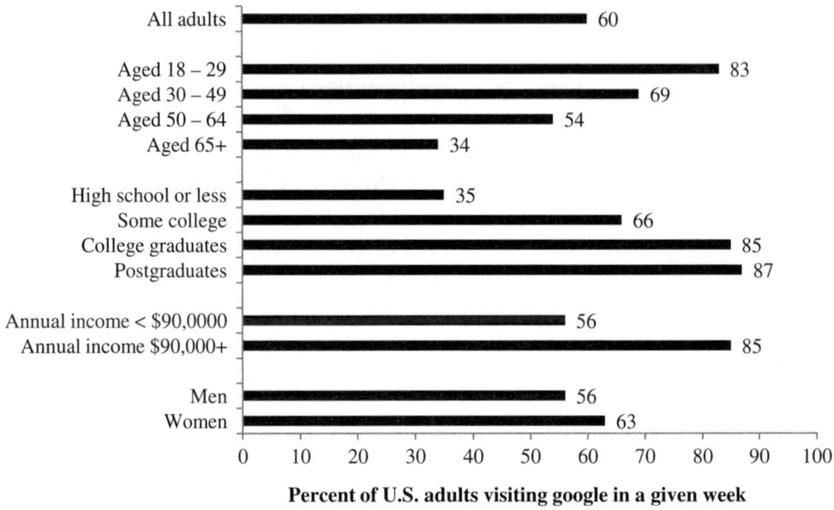

FIGURE 12.4 Use of Google in the United States, 2011.

12.3.4 GOOGLE AND INTERNET SEARCH QUERIES

The widespread use of the Internet in today's society is well documented. One of the most common uses of the Internet is to search for particular websites or information. And, one of the most popular sites for search is Google, for which 83% of users are from the United States. (Purcell et al. 2012). Like Facebook, Google tends to attract younger, more educated, and more affluent users, as shown in Figure 12.4 (Morales 2011).

Google makes available statistics regarding the volume of search queries over time through their free Google Trends tool, which can provide a glimpse into the topics of interest among the Google user population over time.

Google Trends is a free tool provided by Google that can be used to monitor trends in public keyword search queries. Google Trends provides the "likelihood" that a Google search engine user will search for a term over a given time period or geographical location. Search term queries can be filtered by search type (i.e., web, image, news, or product), geography (i.e., country, sub-region, or metro), time range, and category (e.g., automotive, health, real estate, and travel). Google Trends data are presented as a relative scale. To compute the scale, Google uses a proportion of de-identified search data. Frequencies of each search term are then divided by the total number of searches. The data are then normalized by common variables, such as population, so terms can be compared across geographic locations (Google Trends 2011a). Once the search data are normalized, each point is divided by 100, producing a relative scale from 0–100 (Google Trends 2011b). Historical data are available from Google Trends starting January 1, 2004.

These streams have the potential to replicate health trends, often providing an earlier indication of trends than what can reasonably be supplied via surveys. For example, Eysenbach (2009) found a high correlation between clicks on sponsored search results for flu-related keywords and actual flu cases using epidemiological data from 2004–2005 and Polgreen and colleagues (2008) showed that search volume for influenza-related queries was correlated with actual reports of flu from 2004–2008. A study of the 2008 flu season found that Google search trends mapped to flu outbreak patterns (Corley et al. 2009, Corley et al. 2010).

With the data available from Google, no burden is placed on survey respondents because there are no respondents, as traditionally defined. This type of secondary analysis of organic data has been referred to in the literature as *infoveillance*. The speed at which one can investigate a topic of interest using infoveillance greatly exceeds that of a traditional survey approach. Whereas a survey requires sample identification, question construction, contact attempts, and data collection prior to analysis, infoveillance requires only access to the stream of queries and postings and a method for analyzing the content. Infoveillance suffers, however, from a high degree of obscurity around several of the most important tenets of survey methodology. The degree to which queries and postings represent the general population, let alone a specific target population for any given study, is unknown and thus far, unknowable. The lack of information on the coverage of these data makes it impossible to construct accurate population-based estimates and the inability to analyze them by respondent demographics or other characteristics prevents the researcher from gaining a more nuanced understanding of their meaning.

12.3.5 SMS AND TEXT MESSAGES

The pervasiveness, low cost, and convenience of mobile phones make short-message-service (SMS) texting an ideal application for disseminating as well as gathering health information from consumers (Fjeldsoe et al. 2009). SMS allows for the administration of health surveys immediately following some event at a predetermined periodicity. SMS can also supplement data collection and health communications and is currently being used by researchers to address health knowledge, risk reduction, social support, and patient involvement (Coomes et al. 2012, Uhrig et al. 2012).

Texting is currently being employed in a number of studies to remind sample members to complete survey tasks according to a predetermined schedule, since prior literature shows that it can be a cost-effective, low burden way to recontact sample members. In three split-half experiments in Finland, Virtanen et al. (2005) randomly assigned respondents to receive the reminder to complete a mail survey either as a conventional letter or as a text message (SMS) to their mobile telephones. In the group that received the SMS reminders, the response rate was significantly higher.

However, despite these promises, rigorous evaluations of SMS in health services research applications have been rare. The few SMS interventions that have been studied suggest that text messaging systems can effectively increase medication and appointment adherence and sustain health promotion behaviors such as smoking cessation, diabetes, asthma management, and depression (Cole-Lewis and Kershaw 2010).

Furberg (2012) describes work employing SMS to integrate daily health diary reminders, compliance prompts following incomplete or missed entries, and a suite of health promotion messaging content.

In this way, SMS and text messages have the potential to impact participant satisfaction, retention, and data quality, among other future implementations.

12.3.6 SMARTPHONES AND MOBILE DEVICES

It is worth noting that the social network platforms described above are increasingly being accessed on mobile devices. Technological advances in mobile devices and programming will continue to make such devices an increasingly useful tool for health survey researchers. Small, handheld, programmable, mobile devices, with high resolution screens, high speed data connections, text messaging, and many other features—"smartphones"—are now the device of choice for many consumers. Gone are the early days of smartphones, when early adopters suffered through agonizingly slow download speeds. By 2008, most devices automatically chose the fastest network available (GSM, GPRS, UMTS, wireless LAN, etc.) making fast, mobile access available to large proportions of a population (Fuchs and Busse 2008).

The share of Americans who can access the Internet with smart phones and other mobile devices such as tablet computers is expected to grow from 39% in 2010 to 59% in 2014, and by 2014, more Americans will access the Internet on mobile devices than on desktop computers (Lipowicz 2011). Growth in smartphone penetration is not just an American phenomenon, but is occurring worldwide, according to the United Nations: adoption of mobile cellular technology continues to grow, especially in the developing world, where average penetration surpassed the 50% mark in 2009. By early 2010, over 70 economies worldwide surpassed the 100% penetration mark, with developed countries averaging 113% by the end of last year (UN News Centre 2010).

The full-featured, programmable nature of the devices combined with their growing popularity make the smartphone an attractive tool for health survey researchers (cf Raento et al. 2009). Market and survey researchers have been experimenting with handheld devices well before they became as ubiquitous as they are now (see Shermach (2005) and Townsend (2005)). Peytchev and Hill (2010), however, note that the systematic research typically required for use of new "mode" or technological advance in health survey research has not been conducted for mobile and smartphones. Screen real estate issues, for example, more than likely require careful attention before simply transporting one's health survey questionnaire from CATI or the web onto a mobile platform. Questionnaires need to be scaled so they can be presented on various devices; for example, vertical radio buttons may be more effective than a horizontal question and answer layout (Stapleton 2013). Nonetheless, there are already numerous choices for health survey researchers wishing to collect data via mobile device, including companies such as SurveySwipe, Techneos, Vovici, and Zoomerang, among many others. A recent search of Apple's "App Store" for "mobile survey research" resulted in 62 iPad apps and 92 iPhone apps, and a search in the Android marketplace, Google Play, resulted in 61 apps. All search results included several free apps.

Smartphones and tablets also offer the potential to capture data in real time such as respondents' moods and health behaviors, food and alcohol consumption, medication adherence, and many other areas that may be important in the study of health effects and behaviors (Stone et al. 2007).

12.4 Summary

The goal of health survey research is to produce the most valid, accurate, and timely health estimates given the available resources. Traditional methods outlined at the beginning of this chapter still comprise the majority of health survey research, but new technologies and social media platforms offer opportunities to supplement the survey process and improve the validity, accuracy, and timeliness of estimates.

As these new technologies are evaluated for use in future surveys, caution should be taken to assure that survey quality is being evaluated from multiple perspectives. In the context of total survey error, health survey researchers need to consider the impact of methods on sampling error (sampling scheme, sample size, and estimator choice) and nonsampling error (specification, nonresponse, frame, measurement, and data processing) (Biemer 2011).

Ethical considerations for any type of health survey research also need to be considered when a new mode or technology is being evaluated. In the zeal to adopt and use new communications technologies and platforms, prudence is advocated in thinking about research ethics as applied to these new venues. Informed consent, of course, is a basic tenet of scientific research on human populations, and in survey research, we are continually cognizant of the need to offer both privacy and confidentiality with regard to data offered by sample members. Today, virtually all websites and social media platforms include a "privacy statement"—many of which note that "data" posted on the site may be collected and analyzed in aggregate. Facebook's privacy statement, for example, has seen intense scrutiny for its changing nature and less than transparent approach to protecting user privacy. Facebook produces revenue by selling aggregate data to advertisers who can then better target market segments based on "likes" and the like.

Whether a researcher can "mine" or "scrape" data from social media sites like Facebook, or other applications like SL, without obtaining *a priori* informed consent is a controversial issue, not yet resolved. In practice, obtaining informed consent, especially for passive research methods, is virtually impossible. And, even if one was able to obtain informed consent, doing so might well change the behavior of the individuals being observed, thus spoiling the effort.

At present, there are more questions than answers concerning the best methods for utilizing new technologies and social media for health survey research methods. For the future, these research questions regarding the use of new technologies in health survey research warrant investigation:

Quality Issues

- Looking at the entire framework of total survey error, what data quality issues must we examine when considering survey work in these new technologies?
- How reliable and valid are data collected through these platforms?
- What tools and techniques are needed to be able to assess reliability and validity in these new modes?

Adjacencies

- What additional research is being done on these new technologies in adjacent fields, such as marketing, media studies, health communications, and human–computer interaction?
- How can health survey researchers learn and benefit from this research?

Communication Preferences

- What can or will survey respondents share with survey researchers via these new tools, and how can we best tailor the request for this information? Since most social media communication is two-way or interactive, will survey researchers be expected to share information "back"?
- What information can we "share back" that attracts or motivates respondents and reduces survey error?
- How can we best make use of the interactive nature of many of these systems without sacrificing confidentiality or raising other concerns?
- What modes of communication do different types of survey respondents prefer when being contacted for or when completing a survey?
- Is there a difference between what respondents say they prefer and what methods they use to respond?

Representativeness

- What are the demographic profiles of users of different systems or technologies, and how do users differ from benchmarks?
- Can frame data be compiled and representative samples drawn from these new resources?

Despite the open questions, difficulties, and ethical considerations, the trend toward increased adoption of new technologies and forms of communication holds promise for the future of health survey research. These technologies could supplement traditional survey modes to encourage participation from respondents who may well have a high level of comfort with new technologies. Using several and varied new-technology approaches may increase participation since people may appreciate the ability to choose their preferred response mode (Dillman 2000, Schaefer and Dillman 1998). Although mode preference can lead to increased participation in that mode, its influence on response is not uniform across modes, and the effect of appealing to mode preference on nonresponse bias is still an open question (Olson et al. 2012).

While new technologies and platforms—new ways of communicating—may not ultimately replace traditional approaches, it is important to continue evaluating the potential of new technologies and social media tools and their role in health survey research to stay current during a time of fast-paced evolution in communications.

REFERENCES

Acquisti A, Gross R. Imagined communities awareness, information sharing, and privacy on the Facebook. In: Danezis G, editor. *Privacy Enhancing Technologies: 6th International Workshop, PET 2006, Cambridge, UK, June 28–30, 2006, Revised Selected Papers* (Lecture Notes in Computer Science/Security and Cryptology. Heidelberg, Germany: Springer; 2006. p 36–58.

Albrechtslund A. Online social networking as participatory surveillance. First Monday 2008;13(3)Available at http://firstmonday.org/article/view/2142/1949. Retrieved 2011 Mar 23.

Asberg P. 2009. Using social media in brand research: how brand managers can evaluate brand performance during an economic recession. Available at http://www.brandchannel.com/images/papers/433_Social_Media_Final.pdf. Retrieved 2011 Mar 23.

Balicer D. Modeling infectious diseases dissemination through online role-playing games. Epidemiology 2007;18(2):260–261.

Best SJ, Radcliff B. *Polling America: An Encyclopedia of Public Opinion.* Westport, CT: Greenwood; 2005.

Brickman Bhutta C. Not by the book: Facebook as a sampling frame. Sociol Methods Res 2012;41(1):57–88. DOI: 10.1177/0049124112440795.

Biemer P. Total survey error: design, implementation, and evaluation. Public Opin Q 2011;74:817–848.

Blumberg SJ, Luke JV. Reevaluating the need for concern regarding noncoverage bias in landline surveys. Am J Public Health 2009;99(10):1806–1810.

Boges R. 2010. Followup to my Facebook research. Skullsecurity. Available at http://www.skullsecurity.org/blog/2010/followup-to-my-facebook-research. Retrieved 2011 Mar 23.

Brenner J Smith A. 2013. 72% of online adults are social networking site users. Available at http://www.pewinternet.org/~/media//Files/Reports/2013/PIP_Social_networking_sites_update.pdf. Retrieved 2013 Aug 13.

Cassell J, Miller P. Is it self-administration if the computer gives you encouraging looks? In: Conrad FG, Schober MF, editors. *Envisioning the Survey Interview of the Future.* Hoboken, NJ: John Wiley & Sons; 2008. p 161–178.

Casteleyen J, Mottart A, Rutten K. How to use Facebook in your market research. Int J Mark Res 2009;51(4):439–447.

Castronova E, Wagner GG. Virtual life satisfaction. KYKLOS 2011;64(3):313–328.

Chew C, Eysenbach G. Pandemics in the age of Twitter: content analysis of Tweets during the 2009 H1N1 outbreak. PLoS ONE 2010;5(11):e14118. DOI: 10.1371/journal.pone.0014118.

Cole-Lewis H, Kershaw T. Text messaging as a tool for behavior change in disease prevention and management. Epidemiol Rev 2010;32(1):56–69.

Coomes CM, Lewis MA, Uhrig JD, Furberg RD, Harris JL, Bann C. Beyond reminders: a conceptual framework for using short message service to promote prevention and improve healthcare quality and clinical outcomes for people living with HIV. AIDS Care 2012;24(3):348–357.

Corley CD, Cook DJ, Mikler AR, Singh KP. Text and structural data mining of influenza mentions in web and social media. Int J Environ Res Public Health 2010;7:596–615.

Corley CD, Mikler AR, Cook DJ, Singh KP. 2009. Monitoring influenza trends through mining social media. *Proceedings of the 2009 International Conference on Bioinformatics and Computational Biology (BIOCOMP09)*; Las Vegas, NV. Available at http://www.eecs.wsu.edu/~cook/pubs/biocomp09.pdf. Retrieved 2011 Mar 23.

Curtin R, Presser S, Singer E. Changes in telephone survey nonresponse over the past quarter century. Public Opin Q 2005;69(1):87–98.

Cunningham D, Flicker L, Murphy J, Aldworth W, Myers S, Kennet J. Incidence and impact of controlled access situations on nonresponse. Presented at the Annual Conference of the American Association for Public Opinion Research; Miami Beach, FL; 2005.

Dean E, Cook SL, Keating MD, Murphy JJ. Does this avatar make me look fat? Obesity and interviewing in Second Life. J Virtual Worlds Res 2009;2(2). Available at http://journals.tdl.org/jvwr/article/view/621/495. Retrieved 2011 Mar 23).

Dean E, Cook SL, Murphy JJ, Keating MD. The effectiveness of survey recruitment methods in Second Life. Soc Sci Comput Rev 2012;30(3):324–338. DOI: 10.1177/0894439311410024.

de Heer W. International response trends: results of an international survey. J Off Stat 1999;15(2):129–142.

Dean E, Head B, Swicegood J. Virtual cognitive interviewing using Skype and Second Life. In: Hill C, Dean E, Murphy J, editors. *Social Media, Sociality, and Survey Research*. New York, NY: Wiley; 2013.

Dillman DA. *Mail and Internet Surveys: The Tailored Design Method*. New York, NY: Wiley; 2000.

Duggan M, Brenner J. 2013. The demographics of social media users – 2012. Available at http://www.pewinternet.org/~/media//Files/Reports/2013/PIP_SocialMediaUsers.pdf. Retrieved 2013 Aug 13.

Eysenbach G. Infodemiology and infoveillance: framework for an emerging set of public health informatics methods to analyze search, communication and publication behavior on the Internet. J Med Internet Res 2009;11(1):e11.

Facebook. 2013. Key facts. Available at http://newsroom.fb.com/Key-Facts. Retrieved 2013 Aug 13.

Fjeldsoe BS, Marshall AL, Miller YD. Behavior change interventions delivered by mobile telephone short-message service. Am J Prev Med 2009;36(2):165–173.

Fuchs M, Busse B. The coverage bias of mobile web surveys across European countries. Int J Internet Sci 2008;4(1):21–23.

Furberg R. 2012. SMS-adjunct to support data quality and compliance in health survey research. Presented at the Annual Conference of the American Association for Public Opinion Research; Orlando, FL.

Google Trends. 2011a. Analyzing the data: is the data normalized? Available at http://support.google.com/trends/topic/13975. Retrieved 2011 Jun 1.

Google Trends. 2011b. Analyzing the data: how is the data scaled? Available at http://support.google.com/trends/answer/87282?hl=en&. Retrieved 2011 Jun 1.

Gordon R, Björklund NK, Smith RJ, Blyden ER. Halting HIV/AIDS with avatars and havatars: a virtual world approach to modelling epidemics. BMC Public Health 2009;9(Suppl 1):S13.

Groves R. Nonresponse rates and nonresponse bias in household surveys. Public Opin Q 2006;70(5):646.

Groves RM. Three eras of survey research. Public Opin Q 2011;75(5):861–871. DOI: 10.1093/poq/nfr057.

Henning J. 2009. The phone survey in decline. Available at http://blog.vovici.com/blog/bid/19381/The-Phone-Survey-in-Decline. Retrieved 2011 Nov 29.

Heussner KM. 2009. Digital confessionals: tweeting away your vices. Available at http://abcnews.go.com/Technology/AheadoftheCurve/digital-confessionals-tweeting-vices/story?id=8830730&page=1. Retrieved 2011 Mar 13.

Holbrook AL, Green MC, Krosnick JA. Telephone versus face-to-face interviewing of national probability samples with long questionnaires. Public Opin Q 2003;67:79–125.

Iannacchione VG. The changing role of address-based sampling in survey research. Public Opin Q 2011;75(3):556–575.

Jansen BJ. *Understanding User-Web Interactions via Web Analytics* (Synthesis Lectures on Information Concepts, Retrieval, and Services). San Rafael, CA: Morgan & Claypool; 2009.

Kempf AM, Remington PL. New challenges for telephone survey research in the twenty-first century. Annu Rev Public Health 2007;28:113–126.

Keesling R. Controlled access. In: Lavrakas P, editor. *Encyclopedia of Survey Research Methods*. 2nd Vol. 1 ed. Thousand Oaks, CA: Sage; 2008. p 147–148.

Kim J, Gerhenson C, Glaser P, Smith T. Trends in surveys on surveys. Public Opin Q 2011;75(1):165–191.

Kim W, Jeong O-R, Kim C, So J. The dark side of the Internet: attacks, costs and responses. Inf Syst 2010;36(3):675–705. DOI: 10.1016/j.is.2010.11.003.

Koskela H. Webcams, TV shows and mobile phones: empowering exhibitionism. Surveill Soc 2004;2(2/3):199–215.

Linden Lab. 2009. The Second Life economy—first quarter 2009 in detail. Available at https://blogs.secondlife.com/community/features/blog/2009/04/16/the-second-life-economy--first-quarter-2009-in-detail.

Linden Lab. 2011. The Second Life economy in Q2 2011. Available at http://community.secondlife.com/t5/Featured-News/The-Second-Life-Economy-in-Q2-2011/ba-p/1035321.

Lipowicz A. 2011. Gov 2.0 on the go: agencies hit it big with mobile apps. Available at http://fcw.com/articles/2011/04/11/feat-government-mobile-apps.aspx.

Lofgren E, Fefferman N. The untapped potential of virtual game worlds to shed light on real world epidemics. Lancet Infect Dis 2007;7:625–629.

Marx G. Surveys and surveillance. In: Conrad FG, Schober MF, editors. *Envisioning the Survey Interview of the Future*. Hoboken, NJ: Wiley; 2008. p 254–266.

Morales L. 2011. Google and Facebook users skew young, affluent, and educated. Available at http://www.gallup.com/poll/146159/facebook-google-users-skew-young-affluent-educated.aspx. Retrieved 2011 Mar 23.

Moreno MA, Christakis DA, Egan KG, Brockman LN, Becker T. Associations between displayed alcohol references on Facebook and problem drinking among college students. Arch Pediatr Adolescent Med 2011;166:180.

Murphy JJ, Sha M, Flanigan TS, Dean EF, Morton JE, Snodgrass JA, Ruppenkamp JW. Using Craigslist to recruit cognitive interview respondents. Presented at Midwest Association for Public Opinion Research; Chicago, IL; 2007a.

Murphy J, Brackbill RM, Thalji L, Dolan M, Pulliam P, Walker DJ. Measuring and maximizing coverage in the World Trade Center Health Registry. Stat Med 2007b;26:1688–1701.

Murphy J, Dean E, Cook S, Keating M. *The Effect of Interviewer Image in a Virtual-World Survey* (RTI Press Publication No. RR-0014-1012). Research Triangle Park, NC: RTI Press; 2010.

Murphy J Kim A, Hagood H, Richards A, Augustine C, Kroutil L, Sage A. Twitter feeds and Google search query surveillance: can they supplement survey data collection? Presented at the Sixth International Conference of the Association for Survey Computing; Bristol, UK; 2011.

MyType. 2011. Welcome to MyType. Available at http://www.mytype.com/about. Retrieved 2011 Mar 23.

Nwadiuko J, Isbell P, Zolotor A, Hussey J, Kotch J. Using social networking sites in subject tracing. Field Meth 2011;23:77.

Nyberg S. 2010. Fake accounts in Facebook—how to counter it. Available at http://ezinearticles.com/?Fake-Accounts-in-Facebook—How-to-Counter-It&id=3703889. Retrieved 2011 Nov 23.

O'Connor B, Balasubramanyan R, Routledge B, Smith N. 2010. From Tweets to polls: linking text sentiment to public opinion time series. *Proceedings of the Fourth International AAAI Conference on Weblogs and Social Media*. Available at http://www.aaai.org/ocs/index.php/ICWSM/ICWSM10/paper/view/1536/1842. Retrieved 2011 Mar 23.

Olson K, Smyth J, Wood H. Does giving people their preferred survey mode actually increase survey participation rates? An experimental examination. Public Opin Q 2012;76(4):611–635.

Office of Management and Budget. 2006. Standards and guidelines for statistical surveys. Available at http://www.whitehouse.gov/sites/default/files/omb/inforeg/statpolicy/standards_stat_surveys.pdf. Retrieved 2011 Mar 23.

Pang B, Lee L. Opinion mining and sentiment analysis. Found Trends Inf Retrieval 2008;2(1–2):1–135.

Perkins J, Granger R, Saleska E. 2009. Data security considerations when using social networking websites for locating and contacting sample members. Presented at the International Field Directors and Technologies Conference. Available at http://www.rti.org/pubs/ifdtc09_perkins_pres.pdf. Retrieved 2011 Mar 23.

Peytchev A, Hill CA. Experiments in mobile web survey design: similarities to other modes and unique considerations. Soc Sci Comput Rev 2010;28(3):319–335.

Pew Internet and American Life Project. 2013. Pew Internet and American Life Project Poll, April 17–May 19, 2013. Available at http://pewinternet.org/Static-Pages/Trend-Data-(Adults)/Whos-Online.aspx. Retrieved 2013 Aug 20.

Polgreen PM, Chen Y, Pennock DM, Nelson FD. Using Internet searches for influenza surveillance. Clin Infect Dis 2008;47:1443–1448.

Pulliam P, Dolan M, Dean E. 2010. Methods to improve public health responses to disasters. *Proceedings of the Ninth Conference Survey on Health Survey Research Methods*. Available at http://www.cdc.gov/nchs/data/misc/proceedings_hsrm2010.pdf. Retrieved 2011 Mar 23.

Purcell K, Brenner J, Rainie L. 2012. Search engine use 2012. Available at http://www.pewinternet.org/Reports/2012/Search-Engine-Use-2012/Summary-of-findings.aspx?view=all. Retrieved 2013 Jan 18.

Raento M, Oulasvirta A, Eagle N. Smartphones: an emerging tool for social scientists. Sociol Meth Research 2009;37(2):426–454.

Rainie L, Smith A, Duggan M. 2013. Coming and going on Facebook. Available at http://pewinternet.org/Reports/2013/Coming-and-going-on-facebook.aspx. Retrieved 2013 Aug 20.

Remington T. Telemarketing and declining survey response rates. J Advert Res 1992;32:6–8.

Rhodes BB, Marks EL. Using Facebook to locate sample members. Survey Pract, October 2011. Available at http://surveypractice.wordpress.com/2011/10/ 2011. Retrieved 2011 Nov 23.

Richards AK, Dean EF, Cook SL. 2012. From microbloggers to survey respondents: utilizing Twitter for diary data collection. Presented at International Conference on Methods for Surveying and Enumerating Hard-to-Reach Populations; New Orleans, LA.

Schaefer DR, Dillman DA. Development of a standard e-mail methodology. Public Opin Q 1998;62:378–397.

Semiocast. 2012. Twitter reaches half a billion accounts: more than 140 millions [sic] in the U.S. Available at http://semiocast.com/publications/2012_07_30_Twitter_reaches_half_a_billion_accounts_140m_in_the_US. Retrieved 2013 Jan 18.

Shermach K. On-the-go polls. Sales Market Manage 2005;157(6):20.

Smith A. 2011. Twitter update 2011. Available at http://www.pewinternet.org/Reports/2011/Twitter-Update-2011/Main-Report.aspx. Retrieved 2011 Nov 23.

Smith T. Conference notes—the social media revolution. Int J Mark Res 2009; 51(4):559–561.

Smith A, Brenner J. 2012. Twitter use 2012. Available at http://pewinternet.org/~/media//Files/Reports/2012/PIP_Twitter_Use_2012.pdf. Retrieved 2013 Jan 18.

Smith A, Rainie L. 2010. Overview: the people who use Twitter. Available at http://www.pewinternet.org/Reports/2010/Twitter-Update-2010/Findings.aspx?view=all. Retrieved 2011 Mar 23.

Squiers L, Holden DJ, Doline S, Kim E, Bann CM, Renaud JM. The public's response to the U.S. Preventive Services Task Force's 2009 recommendations on mammography screening. Am J Prev Med 2011;40(5):497–504.

Socialbakers. 2013. United States Facebook statistics. Available at http://www.socialbakers.com/facebook-statistics/united-states. Retrieved 2013 Jan 18.

Stapleton C. The smartphone way to collect survey data. Survey Pract 2013;6(2).

Steeh C, Kirgis N, Cannon B, DeWitt J. Are they really as bad as they seem? Nonresponse rates at the end of the twentieth century. J Off Stat 2001;17(2):227–247.

Stone A, Shiffman S, Atienza A, Nebeling L. *The Science of Real-Time Data Capture: Self-Reports in Health Research*. USA: Oxford University Press; 2007.

Taylor TL. Living digitally: embodiment in virtual worlds. In: *The Social Life of Avatars*. Springer: London; 2002. p 40–62.

Tortora RD. Response trends in a national random digit dial survey. Metodolski zvezki 2004;1(1):21–32.

Tourangeau R. Survey research and societal change. Annu Rev Psychol 2004;55:775–801.

Townsend L. The status of wireless survey solutions: the emerging "power of the thumb." J Interact Advert 2005;6(1):52–58.

Tumasjan A, Sprenger TO, Sandner PG, Welpe IM. 2010. Predicting elections with Twitter: what 140 characters reveal about political sentiment. *Proceedings of the Fourth International AAAI Conference on Weblogs and Social Media*. Available at http://www.aaai.org/ocs/index.php/ICWSM/ICWSM10/paper/view/1441/1852. Retrieved 2011 Mar 23.

Turner CF, Forsyth BH, O'Reilly JM, Cooley PC, Smith TK, Rogers SM, Miller HG. Automated self-interviewing and the survey measurement of sensitive behaviors. In: Couper M, editor. *Computer Assisted Survey Information Collection*. Hoboken, NJ: Wiley; 1998. p 455–474.

Tynan D. *PC World*. Spam Inc; 2002.

Uhrig JD, Lewis MA, Bann C, Harris JL, Furberg R, Coomes CM, Kuhns L. Addressing HIV knowledge, risk reduction, social support, and patient involvement using SMS: a proof-of-concept study. J Health Commun 2012;17(Suppl 1):128–145.

United States Securities and Exchange Commission. 2012. Form 10-Q. Commission File Number: 001-35551. Available at http://www.sec.gov/Archives/edgar/data/1326801/000119312512325997/d371464d10q.htm. Retrieved 2013 Jan 18.

UN News Centre. 2010. Communications prices falling worldwide, UN reports. Available at http://www.un.org/apps/news/story.asp?NewsID=33867&Cr=telecom. Retrieved 2011 Nov 29.

Virtanen V, Sirkiä T, Lohikoski V, Nurmela J. Reducing nonresponse by SMS reminders in three sample surveys. Paper presented at the First Conference of the European Association for Survey Research (ESRA); Barcelona; 2005.

ONLINE RESOURCES

Pew Internet & American Life Project statistics are available at: http://pewinternet.org/Data-Tools/Get-The-Latest-Statistics.aspx.

Wireless Substitution estimates from the National Health Interview Survey can be accessed at: www.cdc.gov/nchs/data/nhis/earlyrelease/wireless201306.pdf.

RTI International's SurveyPost is available at: http://blogs.rti.org/surveypost.

Google Trends can be accessed at: www.google.com/trends.

Second Life can be accessed at:http://secondlife.com.

New World Notes blog is available at:http://nwn.blogs.com.

PART THREE

Field Issues

CHAPTER THIRTEEN

Using Survey Data to Improve Health: Community Outreach and Collaboration

Steven Whitman
Sinai Urban Health Institute, South California, Chicago, IL, USA

Ami M. Shah
UCLA Center for Health Policy Research, Los Angeles, CA, USA

Maureen R. Benjamins and Joseph West
Sinai Urban Health Institute, South California, Chicago, IL, USA

13.1 Introduction

We conduct health surveys to try to improve people's health in any number of different ways. Some surveys are conducted to carry out surveillance of health-related factors such as smoking, cancer screenings, and eating habits—all factors that can be measured only through surveys since there are no existing databases that contain such information. Another avenue for improved health via surveys derives from trying to understand how theoretical constructs such as social support, self-efficacy, and community cohesion are related to health. A third reason for conducting a health survey is to inform efforts to improve health by shaping local community plans and policies, direct funding allocations and help communities become more engaged in confronting the health challenges they are facing.

Handbook of Health Survey Methods, First Edition. Edited by Timothy P. Johnson.

It is for this third reason that, between September 2002 and April 2003, our team at the Sinai Urban Health Institute (SUHI) conducted one of Chicago's largest door-to-door health surveys. SUHI is a component of the Sinai Health System, which is located in a very poor community on the city's west side. The survey, known as the *Sinai Improving Community Health Survey (Sinai Survey)*, was conducted in an effort to understand how the Sinai Health System could better work with local communities to help them improve their health. The findings from the survey have been substantial and many programs and interventions to improve health have emanated from it. Virtually all of these programs were developed in reaction to the data through working in true partnership with various community-based organizations. The purpose of this chapter is to describe these partnership efforts. We begin by discussing our motivation for the work, we next present a few selected findings from the survey to orient the reader to the structure of our analyses, and then we provide four case studies that describe the pursuit of community partnerships. Finally, we offer some observations about how progress can be made in this essential endeavor of using survey data to improve community health.

13.2 Our Motivation

Although not all epidemiologists (or health researchers in general) take the extra step necessary to enable health-related data to motivate and guide actual changes, we believe this is a crucial task. The question about whether it is the responsibility of epidemiologists to improve health or just to do research has been debated in the literature (Rothman and Poole 1985, Weed 1999, Krieger 1999) but we find this to be an academic discussion. For us, the health of these communities must come first. Whether we do this as epidemiologists (as we consider ourselves to be) or in some other role is irrelevant. It needs to be done.

The rarity of this approach, which we have held from day one, was underscored by community reactions to our initial inquiries. Over several months we made approximately 50 presentations before starting our interviewing and at virtually every one of these, someone would say something like, "People like you come through here every now and then, ask a lot of questions, write articles and books and then are never seen again. Why should we answer YOUR questions?" We responded by saying that we were conducting this survey to gather information to improve health, that we would return, that we wanted to continue to work with the community, and that if, in the end, the health of their community did not improve, then we would have failed in achieving our goals. We meant this passionately and sometimes this explanation was accepted.

"The Sinai Model" emerged out of this orientation and associated work (see Figure 13.1). This model guides most of the rest of this chapter. It illustrates how we can move from collecting data to mounting interventions to ward improved health.

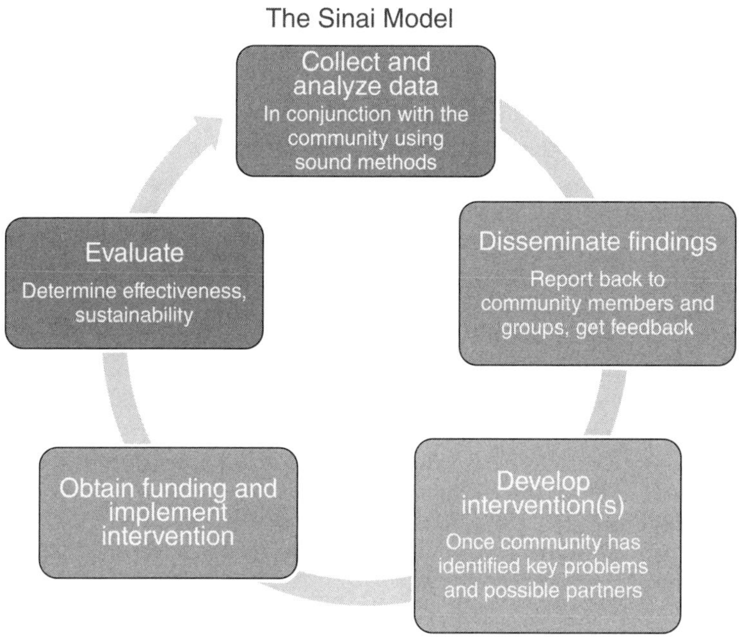

FIGURE 13.1 Sinai Model for reducing health disparities and improving health.

13.3 Our Process

At the onset of our thinking about this project, we realized that it could not succeed unless we employed a community-based participatory research (CBPR) framework (Israel et al. 2013). This entailed talking with many community members before we started (indeed before we began pursuing funding), involving them in selecting the questions that would be on the survey, in the data-collection process, in data analysis, in dissemination of results, in selection and implementation of interventions, and in evaluation of these interventions. These interactions are discussed throughout this chapter. Se interactions must be understood as essential to all that transpired, and not seen as some random steps that were taken only when convenient.

We started the whole process by speaking with several of our community partners with whom we worked on various endeavors. We explained what would be involved in the process, as well as what we thought would be the benefits and the burdens of implementing the survey. We were fully transparent in these discussions and willing to abandon the idea if our partners in other activities were not interested in pursuing a survey with us. Interestingly, they were all supportive even as they pointed out the potential problems of going into people's homes, asking them personal questions, overcoming apathy, and other barriers. On the basis of the input we received, we decided to move ahead and apply for funding.

We were fortunate to receive funding from the Robert Wood Johnson Foundation for the survey. Planning indicated that we could afford to survey 6 of Chicago's 77 community areas. We started our process by forming a Survey Design Committee (SDC) of approximately 20 people, who represented most of the six selected community areas. This SDC selected the topics to be surveyed, the phrasing of many of the questions, and the general length of the survey. The Committee also made numerous contacts for us in the communities and frequently arranged for respected community-based organizations to write letters to community members on behalf of the survey. The Committee also rejected some suggested questions and groups of questions that were proposed by some epidemiologists. For example, questions on "social capital" were seen as racist and demeaning and, questions on drug use were seen as potentially stigmatizing, especially since, according to the SDC, the authorities were never going to do anything serious about the situation (Shah and Whitman 2010). Eventually the survey comprised of 469 questions answered by a randomly selected adult in the household and 144 questions about a randomly selected child, answered by the adult in the household who knew the child best (Whitman et al. 2004).

The survey was implemented using a three-stage probability sampling design, which resulted in completed interviews describing the health of 1,699 adults (age 18-75) and 811 children (age 0-18) in these six communities. Data collection was conducted by the Survey Research Laboratory at the University of Illinois at Chicago (SRL-UIC). We have described the details of our methodology in several publications (Shah et al. 2006, Dell et al. 2005).

Consistent with the Sinai Model we started to present survey findings as soon as the data were available. At one of the first presentations, a representative of the Jewish Federation of Metropolitan Chicago jumped up and asked if we would survey a predominantly Jewish community in the city. We said we would offer all of our services for free but that they would have to raise the funds to pay for the interviewers. The Federation called the next day to say they had secured the funds and to ask when we could start (Benjamins 2010). In rather short order we were able to add surveys for a Chinese community, a Vietnamese community, and a Cambodian community (Magee et al. 2010) resulting in the sampling of 10 very diverse Chicago communities (Figure 13.2). Although the latter four communities did not use the identical survey that the first six used, there was substantial overlap and the questionnaires were only modified to tailor questions to be culturally appropriate.

13.4 A Few Findings

Table 13.1 presents the demographic characteristics of the 10 surveyed communities. As can be seen, this included communities that were all-White, all-Black, all-Asian, and mixed. Along with diversity in race and ethnicity, there was substantial diversity in socioeconomic status. For example, in North Lawndale, an all-Black community area, 73% of the respondents lived in a home where the average annual household income was less than $30,000. This may be compared with

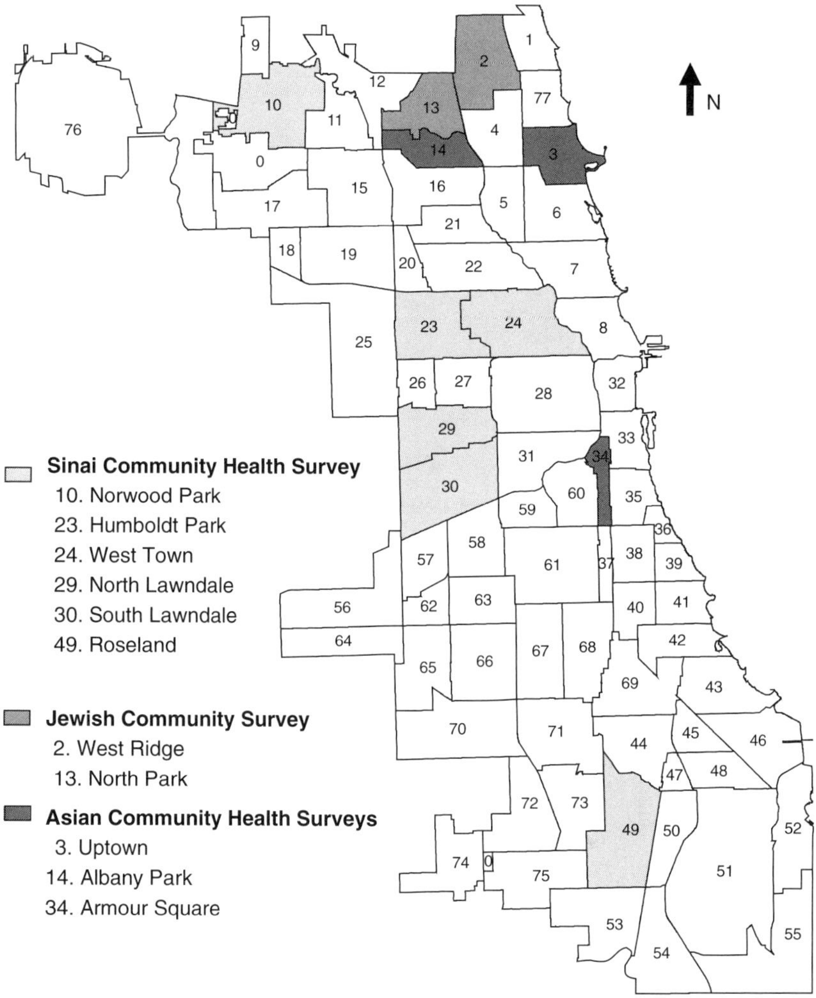

FIGURE 13.2 Chicago's 77 community areas: Chicago communities with local area health survey data.

the all-White community area of Norwood Park where only 5% of the respondents had a household income less than $30,000.

Not surprisingly, most of the health behaviors and outcomes varied substantially by community area. For example, the prevalence of adults (18–75 years) with diabetes ranged from a high of 16% in Humboldt Park (HP) to a low of 4% in the two White communities of Norwood Park and North Park/West Ridge, with the latter being an Orthodox Jewish community (see Figure 13.3). Relevantly, when the diabetes rate in HP was disaggregated, it was discovered that Puerto Ricans had the highest prevalence in the community—21%, or three times the national proportion (Whitman et al. 2006). Note also that the prevalence of diabetes was high in two of the three Asian communities.

TABLE 13.1 Demographic Characteristics of the 10 Chicago Communities Surveyed, 2002–2008

Community Area	Humboldt Park	West Town	South Lawndale	North Lawndale	Roseland	Norwood Park	North Park and West Ridge	Armour Square	Albany Park	Uptown
Total Population	65,836	87,435	91,071	41,768	52,723	37,669	270,500 [a]	7318 [b]	10199 [b]	8206 [b]
Sample size	300	303	300	304	302	190	201	368	150	250
Race/ethnicity (%)										
non-Hispanic White	3	40	10	1	0	88	100			
non-Hispanic Black	47	9	6	94	98	0				
Hispanic-Mexican	25	25	77	1	0	2				
Hispanic-Puerto Rican	18	17	1	0	0	1				
Asian-Chinese								100		
Asian-Vietnamese										100
Asian-Cambodian									100	
Female (%)	52	47	39	58	56	52	52	56	64	59
Age (%)										
18–44 yrs	68	75	78	63	54	50	39	29	49	29
45–64 yrs	24	22	19	30	30	39	41	34	33	46
65+ yrs	8	3	3	7	16	12	21	37	17	26
Annual household income (%)										
<$30,000	65	47	70	73	53	5	14	69	60	81

$30,000–$69,999	31	37	27	26	35	50	38	31[c]	40[c]	19[c]
≥$70,000	4	16	3	1	11	46	47			
HS graduate or higher (%)	60	75	44	74	78	96	99	46	45	49
% Unemployed (%)	47	33	38	49	53	34	40[d]	18	38	59
Foreign born (%)	34	31	71	1	1	20	20	93	80	100

Source: Total population estimates come from the 2000 U.S. Census; Sinai's Improving Community Health Survey 2002–2003; Jewish Community Health Survey 2003; Chicago Asian Health Surveys, 2006–2008.

All data are weighted for the probability of selection to account for the complex survey design. The Sinai Survey also includes post-stratification weights based on the 2000 U.S. Census.

Sinai Survey respondents had a maximum age of 75 years.

Percentages may not add up to 100 due to rounding.

Race/ethnicity categories do not include—other Hispanic, Hispanic origin unknown, or other from the Sinai Survey.

Race/ethnicity was self-reported as part of the screener to determine eligibility for the survey.

[a]Approximate number of Jews in the Chicago metropolitan area.

[b]Estimates from 2000 U.S. Census.

[c]Only data above and below $30,000 are available

[d]WRP estimate for unemployed does not distinguish retired persons.

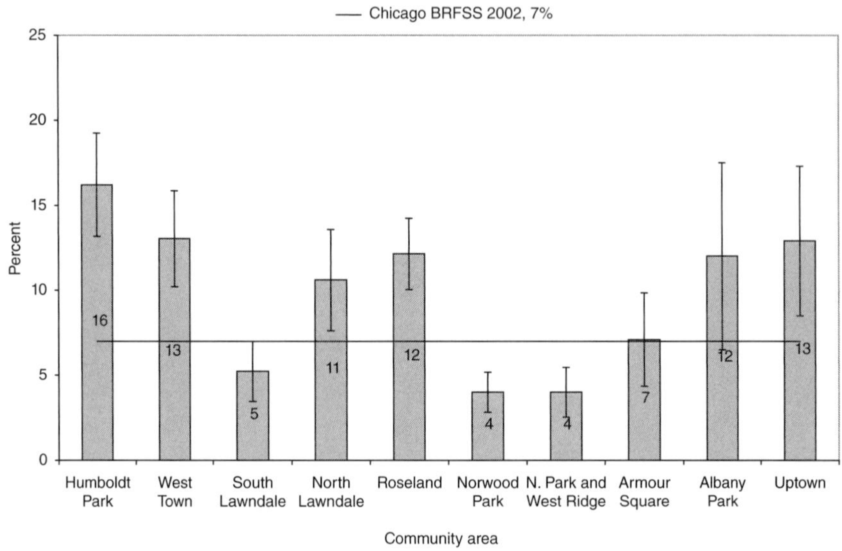

FIGURE 13.3 Diabetes prevalence in 10 Chicago communities.

Figure 13.4 presents the "current smoking" prevalence for these 10 communities. Once again, there was substantial variation. In North Lawndale, a very poor all-Black community, 39% of adults smoked, while six of the communities had prevalence proportions below the U.S. rate of 24%.

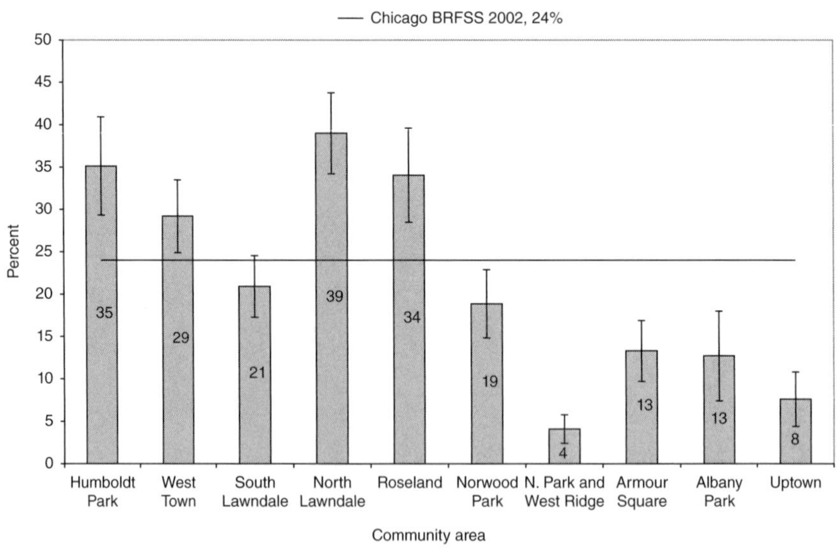

FIGURE 13.4 Smoking prevalence in 10 Chicago communities.

Because there were over 600 questions on these surveys there are literally hundreds of health-related issues that could be analyzed and discussed. We have indeed examined all of the data and have described many of the findings in peer reviewed journals, a book (Whitman et al. 2010b), and community reports (http://www.suhichicago.org/) and have presented just a few findings here to provide a sense of how we disseminated the information. It is important to emphasize that numerous other variables were available and the survey findings stimulated the local communities involved to take action on numerous issues. The effort necessary to involve a community is often substantial, usually in terms of time for listening, planning, and discussing. Such efforts are not only helpful, they are essential and, we think, ethically required. This kind of work is delineated and discussed in detail throughout the remainder of this chapter.

13.5 Case Studies of Community Engagement

We have described the basic mechanics of our survey and some of the findings. Let us now turn to the main topic of this chapter—how to work with communities to improve health once data become available. There are of course no simple rules but there are some general principles and guidelines. We first present four case studies that emerged from our work and then we delineate common themes.

13.5.1 CASE STUDY 1: HUMBOLDT PARK

Like so many communities in Chicago, Humboldt Park (HP) has seen waves of immigrants from around the world. At the time of the survey, HP was quite poor and roughly half Black, one-quarter Mexican, and one-quarter Puerto Rican (Table 13.1). One of the leading organizations in this community is the Puerto Rican Cultural Center (PRCC), which has been in existence for 40 years. The PRCC has many components ranging from an alternative high school to a preschool program to a youth café. Some members of the PRCC, notably its Executive Director Jose Lopez, were initially consulted before we undertook the survey.

When the first results from the survey became available, the HP community, already thinking about health, organized itself and, in Lopez's words, took ownership of the findings. In rapid order, the newly formed Puerto Rican Agenda Health Committee joined forces with the New Communities Program of the Local Initiatives Support Committee and the PRCC to form the Greater HP Community of Wellness (COW). (See an explication of this history by Martin and Ballesteros (2010)).

In true organizing style, one of the first actions undertaken by the COW was to call for a community discussion of the results produced by the *Sinai Survey*. At this 2004 forum, major findings of the survey (for example, obesity, diabetes, pediatric asthma, and depression) were presented to approximately 200 attendees. The attendees then split into working groups to consider these findings. In the wake of this intense community interest, the Chicago City Council Health Committee took the very unusual step of holding a meeting in the community (as opposed to the cloistered setting of City Hall) to discuss the survey results. This was again attended by over 200 people, including virtually every politician representing the community. Great emphasis was placed on what could be done to address the health problems revealed by the survey.

As noted earlier, one of the biggest health issues identified in this community was a high prevalence of diabetes. At the beginning of 2006, we learned that an article we had written about diabetes in HP for a peer-reviewed journal would be published in December (Whitman et al. 2006). Because we did not want to present only more bad news with no solutions when the article appeared, we organized the HP Diabetes Task Force, composed of 21 people, about half community members and half health professionals, and produced a substantial report entitled *Diabetes in Humboldt Park: A Call to Action.* The report was released at a press conference held on the same day the paper was published and described steps that needed to be taken to ameliorate the morbidity and mortality from diabetes (Humboldt Park Diabetes Task Force 2006).

The COW and the Task Force had discussed the best way to move ahead but no decisions had been made. However, all that became irrelevant when, at the press conference, the community demanded that we plan our next step. It was decided that we should hold a Diabetes Summit, a day-long event, which eventually took place in March, 2007 in a community church and which was attended by more than 700 people. The event was covered by all the very substantial Spanish language media in Chicago and was deemed an enormous success. Riding the wave of this event, and consistent with the Sinai Model (Figure 13.1), the Polk Bros. Foundation generously provided a planning grant for further work and this in turn led to a $2,000,000 grant (which began in 2009) from the National Institutes of Health to ameliorate the impact of diabetes in HP (Whitman et al. 2010a).

In addition to the diabetes work, other important health activities flowing from the survey findings have taken place in HP. These include (but are not limited to) interventions in pediatric asthma (Martin and Ballesteros 2010) and obesity (Becker et al. 2010). For the sake of brevity, we refer the reader to these excellent accounts rather than repeating these stories here.

The work in HP continues unabated and is expanding. For example, farmer markets now exist for the first time. The first urban greenhouse in the community has been built on the roof of the main PRCC building and it is hoped that many more will follow on Division Street, the community's main avenue. Perhaps most importantly, one can see in many instances how the ideology in the community is beginning to shift to more community-initiated activity for health improvement and the understanding that self-directed action to improve health is possible. Many people have come to us seeking avenues to increase physical activity for themselves and their children and physical activity programs are proliferating. One such program resulting from the survey data was even featured in a major article in the "New York Times" (Reaves 2010). Some community restaurants are now serving more nutritious and even diabetes-friendly dishes, and it is not unheard of for diners to be reminded by fellow patrons that they do not really need that extra piece of bread or that flan.

These activities, while of course not enough, are moving the community in the right direction. Eventually, given the motivation of area residents and organizations, HP will indeed become a COW.

13.5.2 CASE STUDY 2: WEST ROGERS PARK

Just as the *Sinai Improving Community Health Survey* revealed substantial differences between racial/ethnic groups, Jewish leaders within Chicago recognized that certain health issues may also be more (or less) prevalent within the Jewish community. They also understood that this type of health information could lead to more successful interventions and would allow the agencies serving this population to better tailor their services. Thus inspired, they began to mobilize an effort to collect similar data in two of the most densely populated Jewish neighborhoods in the city. This is how Chicago became one of the first (if not the first) city to implement a population-based health survey specifically for a Jewish community.

The leadership of this initiative came from the Jewish Federation of Metropolitan Chicago, which is the largest not-for-profit social welfare institution in Illinois and the hub of Chicago's Jewish community. They were able to secure financial support for this survey from a variety of local foundations. Following this, members of the Jewish Federation and SUHI began working together to develop the survey questionnaire. To do this in a community-focused manner, a series of meetings were held with stakeholders, community leaders, and agency professionals. During these meetings, approximately 50 additional questions were added to the *Sinai Survey* instrument to focus on health and religious issues important to the Jewish population. For example, topics such as genetic disorders, disability, and participation in Jewish religious activities were added. To make room, questions deemed less relevant or less of a priority were removed from the original survey. This included questions on Hispanic ethnicity, sexually transmitted disease (STD) testing, needle exchange programs, and selected discrimination measures, for example.

The group of community leaders and agency professionals was also in charge of selecting the target area to be surveyed. They chose a north-side community made up of two contiguous neighborhoods—West Rogers Park and Peterson Park. This community was selected because of the high concentration of Jewish individuals residing there and a presumed need for additional services and resources. The response rate and cooperation rate for this survey were high (51% and 75%, respectively). This may be at least partially due to the efforts undertaken to make the community aware of the importance of the survey. For example, before respondents were approached by the interviewers, they first received a letter explaining the survey and the importance of this type of data for the community. These letters, which were printed on letterhead from the Jewish Community Council of West Rogers Park, were signed by leaders of the community, including the chief rabbinical judge of the Chicago Rabbinical Council. In addition, the interviewers underwent rigorous training, both in general interviewing skills, as well as in relevant aspects of the Jewish culture. Care was taken to avoid conflicts, such as asking for interviews on the Sabbath or during Jewish holidays.

Because this was the first health survey ever done in these neighborhoods, all of the findings were valuable. However, certain results were particularly motivating to community members and organizations because they either revealed very serious problems or were unexpected. Perhaps most strikingly, over half of both adults and children in this community were found to be overweight or obese. For children, the prevalence of obesity (26%) was even higher than that of the overall United States. Other health problems included relatively high rates of depression, domestic violence, hypertension, and disability. It is important to note that, in addition to these problems revealed by the data, numerous findings highlighted the health-related advantages of the community. For example, almost all adults in this Jewish sample reported having health insurance, regardless of age. Also, only 4% of the sample reported being a current smoker, well below the rates of smoking seen in the general population (over 20%).

A variety of dissemination strategies were used to share these findings with community members, health service providers, and other relevant groups and individuals. To begin, these findings were shared through the publication and distribution of an in-depth report. Specifically, the report summarized the methodology and main results of the survey in layperson's terms for all interested individuals and agencies (Benjamins et al. 2006a). Since its publication, this report has been made available (free of charge) to any interested group or individual. It can also be downloaded from the SUHI website (www.suhichicago.org).

To coincide with the publication of this report, a "release event" was held at the local Jewish Community Center to present the findings and to allow community members a chance to ask questions and make comments and suggestions. All respondents to the survey were invited back, and information about the presentation was distributed through numerous avenues (including synagogue newsletters) to reach the maximum number of individuals. Unfortunately, only 40 individuals attended this session, which included opening remarks from a vice president of the Jewish Federation and the CEO of Mount Sinai Hospital. Healthy refreshments were served and the project dietitian provided healthy recipe cards and other health promotion materials. Despite the relatively low attendance, the project staff felt that this important part of the research process helped to strengthen the relationship between the research team and the community, as well as to begin generating conversations about health among individuals and organizations.

Following this, an effort was made to publish the findings in a wide variety of outlets based on the suggestions from partner organizations. To reach the community at large, a multipage article about the event and the survey findings was published in a community newspaper, the "Chicago Jewish News." For other researchers and those in the academic world, a summary article was published in the *Journal of Community Health* (Benjamins et al. 2006b). In addition, for those who provide services within the Jewish community, an article was published in the *Journal of Jewish Communal Service* (Benjamins et al. 2007).

Finally, the findings were presented to community stakeholders, including lay leaders, community agency professionals, rabbis, and school administrators, through a series of meetings held with all interested groups. Each meeting began with a presentation by the project director of the study, background, methodology, and results. The second half of each meeting was organized like an informal focus group, facilitated by a member of the project steering committee from the Jewish Federation. In particular, everyone present was asked to comment on the following questions: (i) What are the most pressing health concerns? (ii) How should these issues be addressed?, and (iii) Who should be involved? Through these sessions, health problems were prioritized, potential intervention ideas were developed, and future partners were identified.

Childhood obesity was unanimously selected as the most important issue to address. Accordingly, the first intervention launched was the Jewish Day School Wellness Initiative. This 5-year project, which used a culturally appropriate model of school wellness to reduce levels of childhood obesity within Jewish schools in Chicago, is described in detail elsewhere (Benjamins 2010, 2012, Benjamins and Whitman 2010). Although ultimately successful, there was initial resistance to the intervention from parents and school staff. Parents feared the "food police" or that the focus on being healthy might lead to eating disorders. Teachers were reluctant to add any more to their already full plates. Moreover, many members of the school community were not entirely convinced that improved student health was an appropriate objective for schools. Finally, since the Orthodox community is very insulated, bringing in new materials and outside consultants is difficult. For this reason, it was absolutely critical to the success of the program that an "insider" was available to check all materials, facilitate introductions, and generally monitor the cultural appropriateness of the intervention (and the project staff). A focus on mutual respect and a willingness to slow the project down to allow schools and individuals to move toward the goals at their own pace was also essential for the project's success. A sign of this success is that the school system involved with this intervention has continued to move forward on its own in making systemic changes to reach the goals of the wellness initiative, even after the grant ended.

In addition to this initiative, data regarding the prevalence of domestic violence factored into the creation of a pilot program targeting synagogues as a vehicle to promote safe and healthy relationships. Through this model certification program, synagogue clergy, professionals, and lay leadership participate in a series of core trainings and institutional policy review to improve their capacity to both prevent abuse, as well as their ability to effectively respond to congregants experiencing abuse. Another intervention informed by the survey data promotes health and well-being among older adults in the targeted survey community.

The survey has been a community-initiated process from sample selection to survey development and from the interventions' design to their implementation. The survey greatly increased the awareness of health issues within this community and provided an impetus for change at the individual, organization, and community level. Because the changes that have been made in response to the survey are visible throughout the community, discussions are currently underway about replicating the survey 10 years after the original one. The survey has also spurred interest in other Jewish communities around the country. Specifically, other communities have started the process to conduct a similar community survey (largely using our questionnaire) and to implement the school wellness intervention (using the culturally appropriate model and materials we developed). Overall, this is a unique and powerful example of how a community-based health survey can be used to motivate real changes.

13.5.3 CASE STUDY 3: NORTH LAWNDALE

For many years North Lawndale was a predominately White community populated in the early twentieth century in large part by Russian Jews. The community thrived on the industrial strengths of International Harvester, Sears & Roebuck, Zenith, Sunbeam, and Western Electric. Like many Chicago neighborhoods in the 1950s, there was an influx of African Americans into the community as part of the Great Black Migration, when millions of southern individuals and families migrating to the northern industrialized cities in search of greater freedoms and new opportunities.

As a result, North Lawndale experienced heavy "White flight." The White population dropped from 87,000 in 1950 to less than 11,000 in 1960 and the Black population grew from 13,000 to more than 113,000. By the 1960s, North Lawndale's population was nearly 125,000, and was 91% African American. As Whites moved away from the community, many companies left and jobs began to decline.

In 1968, rebellions followed the assassination of Martin Luther King, Jr., who in 1966 had become a resident in the community to lead his northern campaign. The unrest destroyed businesses and accelerated neighborhood decline. By 1970, African-American residents began leaving North Lawndale, beginning a precipitous population decline. This was rapidly followed by increases in crime, unemployment, and physical deterioration which led to further flight by residents and businesses (Kozol 1991, Satter 2009). Housing deteriorated or was abandoned, until North Lawndale experienced a loss of almost half of its housing units. Today, North Lawndale has 42,000 residents with 44% living below poverty, 68% living below twice the poverty level and a median household income of $18,400 (MCIC 2010).

Together, North Lawndale's social, economic, and political histories have been strong factors impacting the community's sense of social cohesion and willingness to work together to improve overall well-being. For our initiatives to be successful, SUHI has focused on drawing on community strengths and building collaboration between organizations, civic leaders, and faith-based organizations. Those strengths include engaged youth agencies, adult employment services, and a web of social services from community-based organizations with long ties to the neighborhood like the Safer Foundation, Lawndale Christian Health Center and Lawndale Christian Development Corporation, Marcy Newberry Association, Westside Association for Community Action (WACA), Better Boys Foundation, North Lawndale Family Focus, and the Sinai Community Institute. On a daily basis, these organizations help families meet their physical and social needs, while numerous churches serve their spiritual needs. SUHI has been able to establish connections through mutually beneficial partnerships.

Sinai's Improving Community Health Survey (Whitman et al. 2004) revealed significant disparities in smoking and diabetes, which led to two community-based initiatives. The first of these in North Lawndale was "Breathing Freedom," funded by the Illinois Department of Public Health. This project was a 2-year smoking cessation initiative that sought to lower North Lawndale's 39% smoking rate (West and Gamboa 2010). The second program was the North Lawndale Community Action Program (Block by Block North Lawndale), funded by the National Institutes of Health. This program sought to address the dismal North Lawndale diabetes rate that is nearly three times the national rate. Both programs have been an impetus for community-wide dialog regarding improving health one block at a time.

Although SUHI developed the form of each initiative with predetermined scientific goals, how they would function in the community was a collaborative process. Before either program was launched we began building a coalition of engaged community partners through a series of meetings with community organizations. Meetings were held with several community, health, and ministerial groups where conversations began by clearly delineating the purpose of the work, outlining scientific goals and their direct benefits to the community, and gaining trust. The meetings also emphasized the importance of engaging neighborhood partners and collaborating with other organizations. In addition, SUHI assured community stakeholders that all information would be shared with the community about each program's progress. Community stakeholders included businesses (e.g., barber shops, hair salons, and restaurants), churches, civic leaders, and community service organizations. These same stakeholders played key roles in reviewing survey, outreach, and educational materials prior to distribution in order to ensure that they were culturally appropriate and comprehendible.

One of the most unique aspects of both programs has been the training and hiring of community residents as health educators to disseminate information and assist participants with health behavior change. Having community residents be the active face of the initiative has been helpful in: (i) demonstrating SUHI's willingness to empower residents to help reach collectively derived aims; (ii) establishing residents' voices within the daily operation of the intervention; and (iii) beginning to build actionable knowledge for the community to work to improve health outcomes. Notably, for projects like the diabetes initiative "Block by Block," where health educators must go door to door, enter, and return to homes regularly for an intervention, residential status has proven to be an important factor.

North Lawndale has begun to take steps toward improving community well-being. For example, youth agencies are working harder to spread the message to prevent smoking in young people. There have been widely popular health and food fairs in the community annually, where SUHI and community partners in North Lawndale have offered health screenings and disseminated social service information and food from the Greater Chicago Food Depository. The fairs have been held in the parking lot and inside the store of Leamington Foods, a business partner that has encouraged healthy eating in the community through the placement of labels on health food, offering biweekly discounts on healthy foods, and offering space for monthly healthy eating cooking demonstrations. Another community partner, Family Focus, has been instrumental in offering meeting space for social support groups and cooking classes. The Chicago Police Department's 11th District in North Lawndale added more patrols to the park areas to help encourage recreational use and they have offered use of a Community Room for meetings regarding neighborhood safety. The Chicago Park District has offered free or reduced pricing for services, meeting space, use of recreational equipment, and program participation. Over the past four years, North Lawndale News has run a brief series of stories on issues related to community health and on the goals of each initiative. They have also placed ads for SUHI interventions, outreach, and screening at reduced pricing or free.

There are, of course, some challenges with this kind of work. One main challenge is that once trust is established, the leading agency, in this case SUHI, must work to maintain that trust. Consistent communication of findings and program progress can help with this. Also, the work requires a significant amount of incentivized engagement, namely financial incentives, with participants and in many instances with community organizations. Financial incentives can be nominal, but can play a significant role in opening both doors and conversation. Finally, although community agencies and organizations have become active assisting SUHI with meeting program goals, and in most instances integrating some of the public health aims into their own programmatic objectives, sustainability efforts by the community itself remain weak. We recognize that one reason for this is that there are competing priorities and limited resources among organizations to meet these priorities.

Community-based interventions to improve health require a number of organizations and partners with similar and often divergent interests working toward common goals. SUHI's initiatives in North Lawndale demonstrate ways not only to articulate complex, scientific public health aims to community groups so that they are readily understood, but also to make them actionable. This is necessary for any process like this to be successful.

13.5.4 CASE STUDY 4: THE ASIAN COMMUNITIES

The Asian American community of Chicago was interested in gathering local-level population health data for several reasons. For one, Asian community leaders were encouraged by the prospects of bringing greater resources to advocacy groups and local ethnic organizations serving different Asian minority populations in and around Chicago, as demonstrated by the successful efforts of the *Sinai Survey*. In addition, despite being one of the fastest growing racial/ethnic groups in the city, the Asian American population is often limited in its participation in the dialog on disparities in the Chicago because so little health data are available for it. Finally, community leaders were motivated by the growing need for disaggregated Asian data (Tao et al. 2006) that could begin to dispel the myth of the "model minority."

The Chicago Asian Community Health Surveys started with initial conversations between SUHI and the Executive Director (Dr. Hong Liu) and Board of Directors of the Asian Health Coalition (AHC—formerly known as the

AHCI—Asian Health Coalition of Illinois). This group valued the idea of gathering local data and pursued funding to replicate the *Sinai Survey* for a specific Asian population. It is because of the AHC's leadership and efforts that Chicago now has population level data for the Chinese, Vietnamese, and Cambodian communities of Chicago.

From 2006 to 2008, AHC, in collaboration with SUHI, first secured funding to conduct a population-based health survey in Chicago's Armour Square community area (better known as Chinatown) from the Illinois Department of Public Health. They partnered with the Chinese American Service League (CASL), one of the leading community organizations serving the Chinatown community for over 25 years, located in the heart of Chicago's Chinatown. Members of CASL, AHC, SUHI, and other key stakeholders and members of the community met regularly, serving as a Project Advisory Board, to develop a survey questionnaire that would best capture the health needs of the community. Using the *Sinai Survey* instrument as a base, they added, removed, or modified selected sections of the instrument to make it relevant to the Chinese community. For instance, sections on hepatitis screening were added, questions on diet/nutrition and mental health were modified, and questions on perceived racism and community violence were removed.

The next step was to identify an area from which to obtain a random sample of individuals for the Chinese community. It was decided, with technical advice and support from SRL-UIC, that households would be randomly selected from Armour Square. This area had the highest concentration of Asians, presumably Chinese, and was served by CASL, the lead community-based organization (CBO) on the project. Bilingual and native Cantonese- and Mandarin-speaking interviewers were hired from the community and trained on how to collect data and screen households. To notify the community about the project, CASL held a press conference announcing the start of the survey and posted many fliers in the local banks, restaurants, and other businesses along the main thoroughfares in Chinatown. Advance letters describing the importance of household participation in the survey were signed by the Executive Directors of AHC and CASL and sent out on AHC and CASL letterhead. Interviewers carried CASL identification with them so that residents knew that they were working in collaboration with CASL; such identification helped earn trust among residents and thus aided in data collection.

Interviewers went door-to-door and completed 385 adult interviews between two phases of the project (November 2006 and January 2007 and then again in June 2007 and March 2008). This timeline problem was due to locating adequate funding for the work. The participation rate was 86.1% and the overall response rate was 67.2% (Magee et al. 2010, p. 106). The final survey took about 45 min to complete and participants received $20 for their time. More details about the methodology of the Chinese survey are available elsewhere (Simon et al. 2008, Shah et al. 2010, Magee et al. 2010).

Not long after the Chinese survey was completed, AHC received funding from the United Way to conduct population level surveys in two additional Asian community areas of Chicago. The AHC partnered with the Chinese Mutual Aid

Association (CMAA) and the Cambodian Association of Illinois (CAI) to identify Vietnamese and Cambodian populations in the Uptown and Albany Park Community Areas of Chicago, respectively. Both organizations have a long-standing relationship serving the Asian Americans in their communities and were essential to the data collection and interpretation process, especially because these Asian communities were not as concentrated and were smaller in number.

A similar questionnaire for the Cambodian and Vietnamese communities was developed, building on lessons learned from the Chinese survey and tailored to meet community needs. For instance, response rates to the physical activity and human immunodeficiency virus (HIV) questions were low, so they recommended removing the physical activity questions for the Cambodian and Vietnamese surveys and making the HIV screening question anonymous so that response rates might increase. The Project Advisory Committee (PAC) in this case also recommended changing the diet/nutrition questions and added questions related to the sense of community to capture perception of safety and comfort in the community.

In order to obtain a random sample, AHC elected to pilot the use of a relatively new but scientifically established technique of gathering a representative sample known as *respondent-driven sampling* (RDS) (Magee et al 2010, Heckathorn 1997). This sampling method has been used for reaching populations who are traditionally hard to recruit and builds on snow-ball sampling to obtain a representative sample through network relations (see also Chapter 4 discussion of RDS). RDS required far greater support from the community organizations and was actually administered by CMAA and CAI staff. Staff from each organization were paid and trained as interviewers and participants to recruit other eligible participants and come to the community organization to complete the interview. Recruitment of the required sample size was met. It took 13 weeks to complete 150 interviews in the Cambodian community and 22 weeks to complete 250 interviews with the Vietnamese community (Shah et al. 2010, Magee et al. 2010).

As a result of these efforts, for the first time, health data, specifically disease prevalence and associated risk factor data, about three unique Asian populations in Chicago are available. The data are far more meaningful than information that existed prior because they are disaggregated and local to the populations that the community organizations serve.

Once preliminary data were analyzed, AHC reported back to the three community partners with data findings. Presentations were made to staff and community leaders outlining key health findings, which was followed by a discussion on interpretation and translation of the data. Were the survey results consistent with the perceived knowledge of the community? How could these data be used to develop health promotion and disease prevention activities?

Discussions and reactions varied across the three Asian communities but several health initiatives that have since developed share common themes. For instance, the Chinese community was initially most concerned with the low cervical and breast cancer screening rates among Chinese women and the extraordinarily high smoking rates, particularly among Chinese men. They were also surprised by the low mental health burden documented, which was not consistent with their perception of mental health needs in the community. The CMAA, working with the Vietnamese community in Uptown, was not surprised by the data and was reassured by several survey findings. For instance, for them, the data validated what they were observing in the community including low insurance rates and high diabetes rates. Lastly, the CAI was also struck by the high rates of diabetes and obesity among Cambodians they served. Although they knew diabetes was a problem in the community, they had not previously been able to quantify the prevalence. Overall, the data motivated all of them to continue their work and search for funding to enhance their efforts, particularly around access to health services.

These and other initial perceptions led to action. AHC received a one-year grant from the Chicago Community Trust to examine the data through a community lens in order to make the key findings more accessible and to build community capacity to address health inequities identified by the survey. The final purpose of the grant was to increase public knowledge about the health of Chicago Asian communities among local communities and national Asian American Pacific Islander stakeholders.

In collaboration with AHC, the community organizations were able to benefit from the survey data findings to leverage funds and support various health initiatives. To highlight some of their efforts, we describe a few examples of how the community organizations used the data findings to guide health programming around specific health topics and disseminate the survey findings to raise awareness about Asian American health issues in Chicago.

- From the Asian surveys, 31% of Chinese and 26% of Cambodian men were current smokers compared to 2% of Chinese and 8% of Cambodian women. These estimates were also substantially higher than smoking rates for most other racial/ethnic groups nationally (Magee et al. 2010, p 112). With these data, AHC applied for and received funding from the Illinois Department of Health and Human Services to increase community awareness and reduce substance abuse among Asian populations. Thereafter, AHC, along with 10 other community-based organizations, helped establish the Asian Substance Abuse Coalition to collaborate in supporting such efforts. Funding has continued for three years followed by support from the American Lung Association (now known as the *Illinois Respiratory Association*) and some federal funding.
- Another example of how data helped bring communities together around a health topic is the initiative to address cancer screening. Breast and cervical cancer screening rates were extraordinarily low among women and several projects have evolved to make sure women access screening services. For one, the CASL and AHC are working together in Chinatown with funds from the Avon Foundation and Illinois Department of Public Health to promote women's health. The Midwest Asian Health Association, a relatively young but very active community organization, also supported by the Illinois Department of Public Health, is likewise promoting breast and cervical

cancer awareness and education and providing cancer screening among the medically underserved Asian-American women in Chicago South Chinatown and Uptown. Activities take place at community sites where bilingual resources are available.

- HIV screening rates were found to be very low compared with other minority populations. On the basis of the finding, Dr. Liu has been advocating for resources for community-based culturally competent HIV programs to increase community awareness, reduce stigma, and increase HIV screening rates among underserved Asian immigrant populations.
- The diabetes prevalence documented by the survey was particularly high among the Vietnamese (13%) and Cambodian populations (12%). The CMAA and the CAI, in collaboration with AHC, received funding to implement a diabetes prevention and management program to serve adults with diabetes. Survey results motivated them to pursue funding to support this community-based diabetes initiative, which has been ongoing now for two years.
- Finally, to increase the awareness about the survey results, the Executive Director of the Midwest Asian Health Association hosted a first Asian Executive Roundtable in December 2009 to present the highlights of the health issues found from the survey. Among the attendees were Executive Directors of 10 Asian community-based organizations, Dr. Damon Arnold, Director of the Illinois Department of Public Health, Dr. Stephen Martin, Chief Operating Officer of the Cook County Department of Public Health, and Grace Hou, Assistant Secretary of the Illinois Department of Health and Human Services.

These are just a few examples of how CBOs and stakeholders responded to the data findings and are working toward improved health in their communities. While the Chinese, Vietnamese, and Cambodian communities in Chicago have only just begun to benefit from the survey data findings, it is important to recognize some common themes. The health data has been most valuable, particularly in recognizing differences among the many ethnic groups that are often grouped under the "Asian" heading. In fact, representatives of the Laotian, Japanese, and South Asian communities have already expressed interest in wanting to collect local-level health data about the populations they serve. We believe it is essential and valuable to collect such data not only because it would provide disaggregated health estimates for particular Asian ethnic groups, but also because it would be local and most relevant to guiding work in these communities. Despite a great deal of enthusiasm, no other Asian ethnic community has yet been able to raise the funds necessary to conduct such an extensive and scientific survey.

Although tremendous effort was put forth by different Asian American organizations and their community leaders, the completion of the Asian surveys was not without its challenges. Funding was one of the greatest challenges, as illustrated by the interrupted funding stream for data collection in the Chinese community. Another difficulty came from the turnover in staff and community leaders. During the 2006–2010 survey administration, data analyses and dissemination phases, there was change in programmatic staff and leadership at the community organizations that sometimes made the process seem disjointed and confusing. While the survey findings continue to be used by and for the organizations that helped collect the data, it is unclear if and how the data can further be spread through the broader Asian-American community and continue to benefit those for whom the survey was conducted.

Further work still needs to be done in advocating for greater funding, raising greater public awareness, and building community capacity for service agencies that are often on the front line serving these minority populations. Although the Asian experience is different than the other case studies, we hope the above examples illustrate how these Asian communities were successful in using local level data as a catalyst for developing health initiatives and raising awareness about the health of often overlooked populations.

13.6 Some Lessons Learned

In this chapter, we have tried to described the process of how we proceeded from wanting to improve the health of vulnerable communities in Chicago to the *Sinai Survey* to interventions. Along the way, we learned many important lessons. Primary among them was the need to effectively and meaningfully work with the communities that were involved in the survey and subsequent interventions. We are aware that this sounds obvious and straightforward and yet we know that it is neither. Although many researchers, universities, and medical centers have learned to mouth the words "community engagement" and/or "community-based participatory research," we remain surprised at how often the dictums of these theories and concepts are violated in real life.

We did not want to be part of such an insincere process (and, thus, one that was likely to fail), so we worked hard to be genuinely helpful, respectful, and available. If communities wanted raw data, reports, or presentations, we provided them. We similarly provided consultations, assistance with grant writing, and other types of technical support to help empower the communities to make the changes they sought. Unless data are placed in such hands change is unlikely to be meaningful or sustained.

Furthermore, in our experience on community advisory boards of CBO steering committees, prominent academic institutions will often come to the organization and say, "We want to have an event in X Church, can you help us get it?" rather than, "Would it be a good idea for us to hold such a program in your community?" and, "Where might be a good idea to do this?" Because we were conscious of such errors, we were almost always able to avoid them.

Another important pitfall that we constantly tried to avoid was the presentation of bad news (e.g., the diabetes rate in your community is disproportionately high) without a strategy for dealing with this problem. One more problem without a potential solution was not at all what was needed in these communities. And, after all, if we did not have a potential solution then why were we doing research to document the problem in the first place?

Of great assistance to our work was our very close relationship with the communities that we studied. For example, for the case studies described in this chapter, two of us live in the communities and all of us had close ties with the communities through constant interactions with the residents and the community organizations. We often attended community events, including parades and protest demonstrations, ate in local restaurants, and generally became known in the community. It was thus frequently the case that individuals in the interventions would mention having been taught by a relative of ours or having seen one of us speak at a near-by church or community event. While eating in restaurants, it was not at all unusual for someone having some delicious dessert to tell us spontaneously that they never did such a thing, except today because it was a birthday celebration. (Just how many birthdays one can have in a given year is another matter.) The fact that such exchanges took place just indicates that we were involved in the community, that many people knew us and what we were trying to do (Whitman et al. 2010b).

Another aspect of our work relevant to this discussion is that we spent many long hours trying to determine how best to present our data to the communities. Displays like Figures 13.2–13.4 were typical. They were easily understood by people not used to looking at graphs and they offered several comparisons at once: to other communities, to Chicago, and to the United States. Several people told us that they were surprised that they were able to "get it" since they had been "bad at math" in school. Thus, conveying the findings clearly was an essential task and we worked very hard at it, sometimes failing initially but eventually coming up with workable solutions to this important challenge. To have employed more complicated tables and graphs would have not only been unhelpful but may in fact have alienated the very people with whom we were trying to communicate.

The issue of finances and other resources is also important. Whenever it was possible we provided remuneration to our community partners. This helped them, was the ethical thing to do, and also demonstrated that we cared about our relationship with them. Again, this seems like a trivial thing to do, yet we are aware of other organizations, some with multimillion dollar grant budgets, who do not do such things.

We conducted the *Sinai Survey* to generate information that would allow us to implement interventions to improve health in vulnerable communities in Chicago. When all was said and done, that is why we were there. Overwhelmingly, people in the communities understood this and were very welcoming and understanding because of it. In fact, some of the interviewers told us that although it was difficult to get into some homes for these interviews it was often more difficult to get out of some homes because many people wanted to discuss their health and possible solutions for very long periods of time. No one, we think, was confused about why we were doing the survey. They might not have wanted to participate for any number of reasons, but we do not think it was ever because they disagreed with the mission of the project.

Perhaps the single most important question that each of us interested in conducting such a survey must answer is this: Is our main goal helping the community or individual community members and are the questions primarily designed to further that goal? All too often researchers get caught up in asking questions that are of interest to them but which might not help the community. For example, when we started the survey we proposed several questions about "social capital" to the SDC and after sustained debate they rejected the questions as being demeaning and even racist. So we omitted these questions. The group took the time and energy to review the questions and to argue with us and we listened. When this kind of spirit of collaboration is present, a survey has a chance of helping to improve the health of residents of vulnerable communities. What more could one ask of a survey?

Acknowledgments

We would like to thank the thousands of community members who took the time and energy to respond to our questions. None of this, of course, could have happened without them. We would also like to thank our colleagues in the Sinai Urban Health Institute, the Sinai Health System, and the University of Illinois at Chicago's Survey Research Laboratory who facilitated this work in a hundred different ways. We live in a collective world and this chapter and the survey it describes was a collective effort.

REFERENCES

Becker AB, Christoffel KK, Morales MA, Rodriguez JL, Lopez JE, Longjohn M. Combating childhood obesity through a neighborhood coalition: community organizing for obesity prevention in Humboldt Park. In: Whitman S, Shah AM, Benjamins MR, editors. *Urban Health: Combating Disparities with Local Data.* New York: Oxford University Press; 2010. p 171–196.

Benjamins MR. Fighting childhood obesity in a Jewish Community. In: Whitman S, Shah AM, Benjamins MR, editors. *Urban Health: Combating Disparities with Local Data.* New York: Oxford University Press; 2010. p 197–224.

Benjamins MR. Religious beliefs, diet, and physical activity among Jewish adolescents. J Sci Study Religion 2012;51(3):588–597.

Benjamins MR, Rhodes DM, Carp JM, Whitman S. *Report on the Findings of the Jewish Community Health Survey: West Rogers Park & Peterson Park.* Chicago: Jewish Federation of Metropolitan Chicago; 2006a.

Benjamins MR, Rhodes DM, Carp JM, Whitman S. A local community health survey: findings from a population-based survey of the largest Jewish community in Chicago. J Community Health 2006b;31:479–495.

Benjamins MR, Rhodes DM, Carp JM, Whitman S. Conducting a health survey: rationale, results, and advice for other Jewish communities. J Jewish Commun Serv 2007;82:83–95.

Benjamins MR, Whitman S. A culturally appropriate school wellness initiative: results of a two-year pilot intervention in two Jewish schools. J School Health 2010;80(8):378–386.

Dell JL, Whitman S, Shah AM, Silva A. Smoking in six diverse Chicago communities – a population study. Am J Public Health 2005;95:1036–1042.

Heckathorn D. Respondent-driven sampling: a new approach to the study of hidden populations. Soc Probl 1997;44(2):174–199.

Humboldt Park Diabetes Task Force. *Diabetes in Humboldt Park: A Call to Action.* Chicago: Sinai Health System; 2006.

Israel BA, Eng E, Schulz AJ, Parker EA. *Methods for Community-Based Participatory Research for Health.* 2nd ed. San Francisco: Jossey-Bass; 2013.

Krieger N. Questioning epidemiology: objectivity, advocacy, and socially responsible science. Am J Public Health 1999;89:1151–1153.

Kozol J. *Savage Inequalities*. New York: Crown Publishers, Inc.; 1991.

Magee MJ, Guo L, Shah AM, Liu H. The Chicago Asian community surveys: methodology and key findings. In: Whitman S, Shah AM, Benjamins MR, editors. *Urban Health: Combating Disparities with Local Data*. New York: Oxford University Press; 2010. p 98–124.

Martin M, Ballesteros J. Humboldt Park: a community united to challenge asthma. In: Whitman S, Shah AM, Benjamins MR, editors. *Urban Health: Combating Disparities with Local Data.* New York: Oxford University Press; 2010. p 285–306.

MCIC, Metro Chicago Information Center. 2010. Metro Chicago facts online: aggregated from EASI data set 2005/2010. Available at http://mcic3.mcfol.org/. Accessed May 2010.

Reaves J. After a Study, Healthy Changes Block by Block. New York Times; November 4, 2010.

Rothman KJ, Poole C. Science and policy making. Am J Public Health 1985;75:40–41.

Satter B. *Family Properties*. New York: Metropolitan Books; 2009.

Shah AM, Guo L, Magee M, Cheung W, Simon M, LaBreche A, Liu H. Comparing selected measures of health outcomes and health-seeking behaviors in Chinese, Cambodian, and Vietnamese communities of Chicago: results from local health surveys. J Urban Health 2010;87:813–826.

Shah AM, Whitman S. Sinai's improving community health survey: methodology and key findings. In: Whitman S, Shah AM, Benjamins MR, editors. *Urban Health: Combating Disparities with Local Data*. New York: Oxford University Press; 2010. p 37–68.

Shah AM, Whitman S, Silva A. Variations in the health conditions of 6 Chicago community areas: a case for local level data. Am J Public Health 2006;96:1485–1491.

Simon MA, Magee M, Shah AM, Guo L, Cheung W, Liu H, Dong X. Building a Chinese community health survey in Chicago: the value of involving the community to more accurately portray health. Int J Health Ageing Manage 2008;2:40–57.

Tao LS, Han J, Shah AM. Measuring state-level Asian American and Pacific Islander health disparities: the case of Illinois. Asian American Pacific Islander Nexus 2006;4:81–96.

Weed DL. Towards a philosophy of public health. J Epidemiol Public Health 1999;53:99–104.

West JF, Gamboa CJ. Working together to live tobacco-free: community-based smoking cessation in North Lawndale. In: Whitman S, Shah AM, Benjamins MR, editors. *Urban Health: Combating Disparities with Local Data.* New York: Oxford University Press; 2010. p 151–170.

Whitman S, Lopez JE, Rothschild SK, Delgado J. Disproportionate impact of diabetes in a Puerto Rican community of Chicago. In: Whitman S, Shah AM, Benjamins MR, editors. *Urban Health: Combating Disparities with Local Data*. New York: Oxford University Press; 2010a. p 225–246.

Whitman S, Shah AM, Benjamins MR. *Urban Health: Combating Disparities with Local Data*. New York: Oxford University Press; 2010b.

Whitman S, Silva A, Shah AM. Disproportionate impact of diabetes in a Puerto Rican community of Chicago. J Community Health 2006;31:521–531.

Whitman S, Williams C, Shah AM. *Sinai Health System's Improving Community Health Survey: Report I*. Chicago: Sinai Health System; 2004.

ONLINE RESOURCES

Information on the Jewish Community Health Survey is available at: www.suhichicago.org/research-evaluation/jewish-community-health-survey.

Information on the Jewish Day School Wellness Initiative is available at: www.suhichicago.org/research-evaluation/jewish-day-school-wellness-initiative.

We dedicate this chapter to Steve Whitman and his efforts to combat health disparities. If we do not use data findings to improve matters, we will have failed.

CHAPTER FOURTEEN

Proxy Reporting in Health Surveys

Joseph W. Sakshaug
Department of Statistical Methods, Institute for Employment Research, Nuremberg, Germany
Program in Survey Methodology, Institute for Social Research, University of Michigan, Ann Arbor, Michigan, USA

14.1 Introduction

This chapter offers readers a general overview of proxy reporting in health surveys. First, the rationale for collecting proxy reports as a substitute for self-reports is reviewed. Second, a description of three target populations that are commonly the focus of proxy reporting (children, elderly, and disabled) and the extent to which proxy reporting is used for each is provided. Third, examples of measures commonly collected using proxy respondents are examined. Fourth, the quality issues surrounding the collection of proxy reports and how such reports may impact the survey results are reviewed. Lastly, some general conclusions about proxy reporting in health surveys are outlined.

14.2 Background

The primary objective of health surveys is to collect high quality information from a sample of persons carefully selected from the population of interest. For various reasons it is not always possible to interview the target person directly.

Handbook of Health Survey Methods, First Edition. Edited by Timothy P. Johnson.

For example, the person of interest may lack the capacity, or be too physically or mentally impaired, to take part in a survey interview. This situation is most common when the target person is a young child, elderly, or disabled person who may be unable to complete the survey interview without assistance. This situation is not trivial. One study found that 20% of elderly persons and 50% of nursing home residents were unable (or unwilling) to provide information about their health status (Coroni-Huntley et al. 1986). Other studies have found that between 22% and 36% of respondents could not complete the questionnaires because of cognitive or linguistic impairments (De Haan et al. 1993, Magaziner et al. 1988).

To overcome the difficulties of collecting information directly from these vulnerable persons as well as the possible analytic implications of their exclusion (e.g., increased nonresponse, missing data, and bias), attempts are made to collect information indirectly through the use of proxies. Specifically, a knowledgeable proxy respondent is asked to provide information on behalf of the target respondent. Typical proxy respondents include parents who respond on behalf of their children, relatives, spouses, caretakers, household members, or anyone with detailed knowledge of the target respondents' health situation.

Proxy responses can be classified into two distinct categories (Shields 2000). "Proxy by necessity" refers to situations in which persons selected to be interviewed are unable to respond on their own behalf because of physical and/or mental conditions, or other factors that may limit their capacity to participate in a survey interview. Excluding these respondents from a health survey is likely to bias estimates. "Proxy by convenience" refers to the use of proxies for people capable of providing their own information. For example, this allows information about everyone in a household to be collected from a single respondent, thereby eliminating the need to interview each person individually. This approach typically yields significant cost savings as it avoids the need for repeated contact attempts for persons who are difficult to reach. While both types of proxy responses can be useful in certain situations, the main focus of this chapter deals with the former classification ("Proxy by necessity").

Although there are compelling reasons to collect proxy responses in health survey research—the main one being that collecting *some* data on an individual is better than collecting no data at all—survey designers must consider the possibility that proxy respondents may be less knowledgeable about the target respondent's health than the target person him- or herself. Consequently, the information collected from a proxy respondent may not be completely accurate, or directly coincide with the actual responses that would have been obtained had the target respondent been able to take part in the survey.

Inaccurate proxy responses can affect health statistics and may lead to lower rates of reported health outcomes. Proxy respondents may be unaware of asymptomatic acute or chronic conditions affecting the target respondent. They may also be unaware of their medications and functional limitations. Verbrugge (1985) proposed the hypothesis that proxy reporting may (among other reasons) explain why women report more health problems than men, but men tend to die younger than women. Since women do most of the reporting for household members, morbidity data for men may come from underreported proxy data.

The accuracy of proxy responses tend to vary by different factors, including the living situation and the intensity of the relationship between the proxy and the target respondent (e.g., parent, spouse), the level of knowledge that the proxy possesses about the target respondent's health status, the type of information being requested in the survey (e.g., factual vs subjective information), among others.

Shields (2000) highlights four potential reasons why a proxy report may be inaccurate, which are discussed in turn:

The Proxy Respondent may not be Fully Aware of the Health Situation of the Target Respondent. It is critical that proxy respondents are fully aware of the health situation of the person for whom they are responding. In some instances, this may not be possible if the individual deliberately conceals the relevant information from the proxy. For example, a husband may not tell his wife that he has been diagnosed with high blood pressure, or a teenager may not want her parents to know that she is sexually active. Furthermore, the proxy may not know about all of the health care episodes of an individual, such as the number of office visits that a spouse has had within the last 6 months.

The Proxy Respondent may not Recall Relevant Health Information. The ability of a proxy to recall relevant health information depends greatly on the importance of the information to the proxy. The most serious health conditions tend to be reported more often and accurately compared to less serious conditions (Madow 1973, Clarridge and Massagli 1989). Although a health condition is likely to be most important to the affected individual, household members are more likely to be aware of certain conditions when they are reminded of them regularly. For instance, a heart condition may be harder to forget if the household members see the individual taking medication or scheduling office visits. However, other conditions (such as allergies to certain medications) may be more easily forgotten by proxy respondents.

The Proxy Respondent may Mislabel Health Problems. Information provided by the proxy tends to be more accurate for conditions that are easily defined and labeled (National Center for Health Statistics (NCHS) 1965). For example, diabetes and heart disease tend to be easier to describe than other conditions, such as chronic muscle spasms or carpal tunnel syndrome NCHS 1965. Moreover, conditions which are not directly observable (e.g., psychological) may be reported less accurately by proxy.

The Proxy Respondent may Deliberately not Report Certain Information. There are conditions that may be perceived as sensitive or potentially embarrassing to the individual under study. Several studies have validated survey responses with medical records and found that some conditions (e.g., mental illness) tend to be under-reported by respondents (Heliövaara et al. 1993, Madow 1973). In this regard, proxy responses may be susceptible to under-reporting of certain medical conditions that are perceived to be very personal to the individual under study. Proxies may also be inclined to under-report conditions such as substance abuse or mental health that may be perceived in some cultures as reflecting poorly on the family.

14.3 Proxy Interviews for Children

Surveys which include children in their target population are faced with the dilemma of how to collect accurate information from them. Direct interviewing may be suboptimal as many children may be too young, too cognitively underdeveloped, or too ill or fatigued to complete the survey questionnaire (Eiser and Morse 2001). To address this dilemma, surveys often rely on proxy respondents to answer health-related questions on behalf of the child. Information about the child is typically collected from the mother in health surveys. Alternatively, the father, grandparents, or a caretaker of the child is interviewed in cases where it is not possible to interview the mother (Glaser et al. 1997). National child health surveys commonly use "most knowledgeable adult" as the selection rule for identifying an adult proxy respondent for children's health information (Centers for Disease Control and Prevention (CDC) 2011, Warren and Cunningham 2002). There is some evidence that suggests that when the "most knowledgeable adult" is unavailable then someone who considers him- or herself to be "sufficiently knowledgeable" about the child's health information is a good alternative in terms of response quality (Eisenhower et al. 2012).

The typical age range of children for which a proxy interview is performed varies by study and ability of the child. For example, according to printed guidelines, the National Health and Nutrition Examination Survey conducts proxy interviews for children who are 5 years or younger. Proxy-assisted interviews, which involve a mix of proxy and self-reports, are performed for children ages 6–11 (CDC 2013). Some surveys choose a higher age threshold for conducting proxy interviews with children (e.g., 15 years or younger) (Rajmil et al. 1999).

14.3.1 EXAMPLES OF MEASURES COLLECTED BY PROXY

Health-related quality of life (HRQOL) measures are the most common types of information collected by proxies on behalf of children. These measures describe how well or how poorly life is for a child at one point in time, changes in overall functioning, and a child's sense of well-being specific to a particular condition (Wallander et al. 2001, Eiser 1997). Overwhelmingly, parents have served as proxy respondents on HRQOL measures for healthy children, as well as children with chronic diseases (e.g., diabetes, asthma, and cancer) and mental disorders (Cameron 2003, leCoq et al. 2000, Ronen et al. 2003, Sawyer et al. 1999). Parents are considered to be appropriate proxy respondents to provide information regarding the child's health status and quality of life because they are usually responsible for administering medications, monitoring symptoms, and organizing health care activities for the child (Parsons et al. 1999, Saigal et al. 2000).

Recognizing the complex and multidimensional nature of the quality of life construct, there has been a growing shift toward the simultaneous and independent collection of both children's self-reports and parent proxy-reports (Sherifali and Pinelli 2007). Under this perspective, the parent proxy is viewed as a complementary component of the interview and not a substitute for a child's self-reports. The parent proxy questionnaire may include additional questions which provide extra information about a child's quality of life. Many general and disease-specific quality of life questionnaires have been developed for parallel reporting of both child and proxy parent, including the Pediatric Quality of Life Inventory™ (PedsQL™) (Varni et al. 1999, Varni et al. 2003), the Child Health and Illness Profile—Child Edition (CHIP-CE™) (Riley et al. 2004), the KINDL™ (Ravens-Sieberer et al. 2001), the Cystic Fibrosis Questionnaire (CFQ) (Modi and Quittner 2003), the Child Health Ratings Inventory (CHRI) (Parsons et al. 2005), and the How Are You? (Le Coq et al. 2000).

14.3.2 QUALITY OF PROXY REPORTS

In the absence of children's self-reports it can be difficult to assess the quality of parental proxy reports. In general, the subset of studies that have collected both children and parental proxy measurements tend to disagree over whether parents provide responses that closely resemble those given by the child. There are some studies that find parent–child agreement to be relatively high (Theunissen et al. 1998, Verrips et al. 2000, Vetter et al. 2012), while others find that agreement is poor (Ennett et al. 1991, Vogels et al. 1998). These discrepancies may be caused by various factors, including the measurement topic. Specifically, parents and children demonstrate limited agreement in areas that are considered more subjective. For example, in a literature review, Eiser and Morse (2001) found that agreement was highest for questions regarding physical health and poorer for questions regarding emotional or social well-being. Moreover, there is some evidence that parents of sick children tend to underestimate their child's quality of life compared with the children's own reports (Parsons et al. 1999). Conversely, parents of healthy children tend to overestimate quality of life compared to children's self-reports (Theunissen et al. 1998, Bruil 1999, Russell et al. 2006).

Other studies have reported that response agreement between parent proxy and child tends to differ by a child's age and the measurement topic. For example, for measurements of cognitive functioning, agreement between parent and child was reported to be higher for younger children as compared to older children (Varni et al. 1998). For physical functioning, the reverse was reported; that is, parent–child agreement was higher for adolescents as compared to younger children (Varni et al. 1998). Evidence from the obesity literature suggests that parents of obese children tend to underestimate the quality of life of their child (Pinhas-Hamiel et al. 2006). There is also some evidence that parents' own quality of life ratings may influence the ratings they provide on behalf of their child. In one study, mothers who rated their own well-being as poor tended to rate their child's quality of life as poor (Eiser et al. 2005). Goldbeck and Melches (2005) also found evidence that parental quality of life ratings interact with children's self-report ratings in predicting parent proxy reports of their children's quality of life.

14.4 Proxy Interviews for the Elderly

Elderly persons may be incapable of participating in a survey interview for various reasons, including physical or mental impairment, debilitating illness, inability to comprehend the survey questions, speech difficulties, weakness/low energy level, and so on. Moreover, many elderly persons are institutionalized and live within group quarters or an assisted-living facility. These circumstances pose challenges for conducting interviews with the target individual and may result in a greater number of contact attempts, more extensive interviewing procedures, and overall higher costs for the survey budget. Consequently, surveys must decide whether to attempt direct interviews with these elderly persons or treat them as nonrespondents and increase the missing data rate. As a compromise, some surveys perform proxy interviews to collect some information about these elderly persons. Spouses, significant others, primary caretakers, or physicians are usually asked to provide information on behalf of the elderly individual as they are considered to be "most knowledgeable" with regard to the individual's health status.

14.4.1 EXAMPLES OF MEASURES COLLECTED BY PROXY

Proxy respondents are used to collect different types of information on elderly persons. Two specific constructs that are often measured in elderly persons are HRQOL and quality of medical care received at end of life. Measures of HRQOL are usually collected for individuals who have been affected by an illness or condition that impacts their functional status and sense of well-being. These measures can be used to assess quality of life at a single point in time, longitudinally, or before and after a specific health intervention is implemented (Tamim et al. 2002). Common instruments for assessing HRQOL in the elderly (and used in proxy interviews) include the EQ-5D (EuroQoL) (The EuroQol Group 1990), the Short-Form General Health Survey (SF-36) (Ware et al. 1993), the Functional Status Questionnaire (Jette et al. 1986), the Spitzer Quality of Life Scale (Spitzer et al. 1981), and the Sickness Impact Profile (Bergner et al. 1981).

Measures of quality of care at the end of life are typically collected during the final days or weeks of a patient's life and can be collected prospectively or retrospectively after the patient's death. The purpose of collecting these data is usually to improve the quality of care for dying patients and the experiences of their family members (Fowler et al. 1999). For prospective data collection, in some cases it may be possible to directly interview the elderly individual. However, the retrospective case necessitates the need to select a knowledgeable proxy respondent to describe the patient's end of life experience. This may require the selection of more than one proxy respondent if multiple people (e.g., family members, physicians, nurses, and assistants) were involved in caring for the patient. It is important to note, however, that the individuals who are considered to be most knowledgeable about the patient's experience in his/her final days and weeks may not be the same individuals who were most knowledgeable about the patient's preceding months.

14.4.2 QUALITY OF PROXY REPORTS

It is unclear whether proxy reports of HRQOL measures collected on behalf of the elderly are accurate. Studies that have compared patient and proxy responses have reported mixed results with some studies reporting fair or poor agreement (Pierre et al. 1998, Gifford et al. 2010, Tamim et al. 2002) and other studies deeming proxy responses as an adequate substitute for patients' self-reports under various circumstances, including during chronic illness (Sneeuw et al. 2002), before hospital admission (Capuzzo et al. 2000, Elliott et al. 2006, Hofhuis et al. 2003, Badia et al. 1996), and after being discharged from an intensive care unit (Rogers et al. 1997). One study reported that the validity of proxy reports for HRQOL measures does not improve over time (Tamim et al. 2002).

In some cases, physicians are asked to serve as proxy respondents for elderly patients. However, comparisons of physician and patient ratings have not been favorable. In one study, physicians consistently underestimated the patients' health status regardless of medical condition (Pearlman and Uhlmann 1988). The authors indicated that the disagreement was due to physicians' inability to adequately assess the more subjective aspects of patients' quality of life. Another study reported that physicians did not recognize some or all of the functional disabilities that were reported by the patient, yet physicians tended to overstate disabilities for patients reporting no disabilities (Jette et al. 1986).

In general, greater agreement between proxy and patient is observed for more readily observable and objective phenomena (e.g., physical activities), while agreement tends to be worse for more subjective measurements (e.g., psychological well-being) (Wallace and Woolson 1992). Proxy responses obtained from significant others have been shown to achieve moderate-to-high agreement with regards to social activities, overall health status, and functional status, but lower agreement for emotional health and satisfaction with care (Epstein et al. 1989). Proxy agreement also seems to vary by patient characteristics. For example, agreement tends to be higher for better educated and noncognitively impaired patients (McCusker and Stoddard 1984, Rothman et al. 1991). Gender, socioeconomic status, and marital status do not seem to influence agreement (Sprangers and Aaronson 1992, Epstein et al. 1989). However, discordance tends to increase with advanced age (Rothman et al. 1991). Also, living arrangements and caregiver duties may impact concordance. For significant others, there appears to be better concordance if the proxy lives with the subject but is not responsible for providing care (Magaziner et al. 1988, McCusker and Stoddard 1984, Rothman et al. 1991).

Another line of research indicates that proxy respondents may project part of their own HRQOL ratings onto patients when assessing patient HRQOL ratings. In particular, Arons et al. (2013) found that caregivers were more likely to give patients positive overall assessments if caregivers rated themselves positively on the same HRQOL measures. The authors also found other characteristics of caregivers that were associated with their ratings of patients, including: (i) the better the financial situation of the caregiver, the lower the HRQOL ratings of patients; and (ii) caregivers who are better able to do things for fun gave higher ratings of patient functioning.

14.5 Proxy Interviews for the Disabled

Disabled persons tend to be affected by severe functional limitations that can preclude their ability to take part in survey interviews (see also Chapter 24). The size of the disabled population, at least in the United States, is not trivial. The 1994/1995 National Health Interview Survey Disability Supplement estimated that 5.8 million persons suffer from significant mobility difficulties. About 4.1 million of these persons perceive themselves to be disabled and 3.8 million thought other people see them as disabled (Iezzoni et al. 2000). Earlier population-based studies have reported divergent sizes of the disabled population, which is likely due to the use of nonstandard and study-specific definitions used to define the disabled population (Manton 1988, Kasper 1988).

The impact of having one or more disabilities can impact the likelihood of survey participation. The Woman's Health and Aging Study reported a nonresponse rate of about 30% among a screened sample of disabled women (Kasper et al. 1999). In a study of elderly hip fracture patients, 51% of patients could not be interviewed due to cognitive impairment, physical illness, or refusal (Magaziner et al. 1998). In that study, proxy respondents were able to provide information for about 84% of the patients physically or mentally incapable of responding (Magaziner et al. 1998).

14.5.1 EXAMPLES OF MEASURES COLLECTED BY PROXY

HRQOL measures are also collected for disabled persons, including the Short-Form General Health Survey (SF-36) (Ware et al. 1993) and, a shortened version, the SF-12 (Ware et al. 1995, 1996).

Many surveys accept proxy responses for disabled persons who are unable to participate directly in the survey interview. Of particular interest to researchers is the extent of one's functional limitations and quality of life. Common measures of functional limitations included in surveys are Activities of Daily Living (ADLs) and Instrumental Activities of Daily Living (IADLs). ADL items typically include a set of functional questions (e.g., transfer, dressing, and bathing), each with three response options (no help, some help, and help to do all) (Katz 1983). IADLs consist of items that assess functional limitations, such as using the telephone, meal preparation, housework, laundry, taking medication, money management, and so on. Each of these items has three response options (independent, need some assistance, and completely dependent) (Lawton 1988, Lawton and Brody 1969, Newschaffer 1998).

14.5.2 QUALITY OF PROXY REPORTS

As is the case with most assessments of proxy response quality in general, the concordance between responses obtained from both proxies and disabled patients is mixed with regard to functional limitations and overall assessment of disability. However, there are a few consistent patterns that have emerged. Self-reports and proxy reports tend to differ to a lesser extent for physical and observable dimensions and to a greater extent for subjective psychosocial dimensions (Bassett et al. 1990, Epstein et al. 1989, Rothman et al. 1991, Herjanic and Reich 1982). An important implication of this result is that easily detectable disabilities are likely to be over-reported by proxies in health surveys. Conversely, less noticeable disabilities are likely to be under-reported. For surveys which include persons younger than 65 years, the prevalence of overall and specific disability may be severely underestimated as specific disabilities may be less noticeable for this younger group.

There is also evidence of a proxy bias related to patient age. That is, proxy respondents are more likely to over-report disabilities for older persons and under-report disabilities for younger persons (Todorov and Kirchner 2000, Epstein et al. 1989, Rothman et al. 1991). The cause of this phenomenon is unknown, but one possible explanation is that proxy respondents are more likely to infer that an older person has a disability even if they have inadequate or insufficient information about the reported disability (Todorov and Kirchner 2000). This result may also lead to significant over-/underestimation of disability prevalence.

There is little evidence that characteristics of the proxy respondent influence their evaluation of a person's disablement, with the exception of the proxy respondent's involvement with the person. Proxies who have high contact or involvement with the individual (e.g., living in the same household, providing assistance, significant other/spousal arrangement) tend to provide responses that are reasonably similar with those of the disabled person. However, when the responses from these two parties' do diverge, then these close-contact proxies have a tendency to overestimate disability status (Magaziner et al. 1988).

14.6 Summary

In conclusion, proxy reporting is commonly used in health surveys to obtain information about individuals who are unable to provide information on their own. Proxy reporting is viewed as a viable and cost-effective alternative for increasing the response rate and the risk of nonresponse bias. However, proxy reports themselves are not bias-free. In fact, numerous studies have reported significant and systematic differences between proxy and self-reports. The greatest discordance tends to occur for subjective measurements of mental health and well-being. Conversely, physical ailments that are easily observable by others tend to be reported more accurately by proxy respondents. Proxy respondents are also prone to making false inferences about an individual's functional ability based on information external to the ability (e.g., age).

An important limitation to consider when reviewing studies which collect proxy and self-reports on the same individual is that the individual's responses are often considered to be the "gold standard." This may be an invalid assumption in cases where individuals are mentally impaired or are too young to accurately describe their functional status or quality of life. In some cases, it may not be possible to collect information from self-reports at all, which may lead to the collection of proxy responses for which their quality cannot be assessed.

Given the inconsistent (and, in many cases, poor) quality of proxy responses, researchers are left to decide whether to include them or exclude them from their studies altogether. While the use of proxy respondents may reduce the impact of nonresponse bias, they may instead introduce greater measurement error bias that could outweigh the potential impact of nonresponse. Whether this is likely to happen in a given study is an empirical question that needs to be considered. Along these lines, statistical approaches to reduce the impact of proxy bias are starting to be considered (Elliott et al. 2008, Reither and Utz 2009).

REFERENCES

Arons AMM, Krabbe PFM, Schölzel-Dorenbos CJM, van der Wilt GJ, Olde Rikkert MGM. Quality of life in dementia: a study on proxy bias. BMC Med Res Methodol 2013;13:110.

Badia X, Diaz-Prieto A, Rue M, Patrick DL. Measuring health and health state preferences among critically ill patients. Intensive Care Med 1996;22:1379–1384.

Bassett SS, Magaziner J, Hebel JR. Reliability of proxy response on mental health indices for aged, community-dwelling women. Psychosoc Aging 1990;5:127–132.

Bergner M, Bobbitt RA, Carter WB, Gilson BS. The sickness impact profile: development and final revision of a health status measure. Med Care 1981;19(8):787–805.

Bruil J. *Development of a Quality of Life Instrument for Children with Chronic Illness*. The Netherlands: Health Psychology, Leiden University; 1999.

Cameron FJ. The impact of diabetes on health-related quality of life in children and adolescents. Pediatr Diabetes 2003;4:132–136.

Capuzzo M, Grasselli C, Carrer S, Gritti G, Alvisi R. Quality of life before intensive care admission: agreement between patient and relative assessment. Intensive Care Med 2000;26:1288–1295.

Centers for Disease Control and Prevention (CDC). 2011. National immunization survey-child hard copy questionnaire. Available at http://ftp.cdc.gov/pub/health_statistics/nchs/Dataset_Documentation/NIS/NIS_Child_HHQuex_Q3_2011.pdf. Accessed 2013 Aug 20.

Centers for Disease Control and Prevention (CDC). 2013. Key concepts about NHANES dietary data collection. Available at http://www.cdc.gov/nchs/tutorials/dietary/SurveyOrientation/DietaryDataOverview/Info2.htm. Accessed 2013 Aug 20.

Clarridge BR, Massagli MP. The use of female spouse proxies in common symptom reporting. Med Care 1989;27(4):352–366.

Coroni-Huntley J, Brock DB, Ostfeld AM, Taylor JO, Wallace RB. *Established Populations for Epidemiological Studies of the Elderly: Resource Data Book*. NIH Publication No. 86-2443. Washington, DC: 1986.

De Haan R, Aaronson N, Limburg M, Hewer RL, Van Crevil H. Measuring quality of life in stroke. Stroke 1993;24:320–326.

Eisenhower D, Immerwahr S, Merry T, Weiss A. Using an alternative to "most knowledgeable adult" as a selection rule for proxy reporters in a child health survey. Survey Pract 2012;5(4).

Eiser C and Morse R. Quality-of-Life Measures in Chronic Diseases of Childhood. *Health Technology Assessment*, 2001;5;4:1–157.

Eiser C. Children's quality of life measures. Arch Dis Child 1997;77(4):350–354.

Eiser C, Eiser JR, Stride CB. Quality of life in children newly diagnosed with cancer and their mothers. Health Qual Life Outcomes 2005;3.

Elliott MN, Beckett MK, Chong K, Hambarsoomians K, Hyas RD. How do proxy responses and proxy-assisted responses differ from what medicare beneficiaries might have reported about their health care? Health Serv Res 2008;43(3):833–848.

Elliott D, Lazarus R, Leeder SR. Proxy respondents reliably assessed the quality of life of elective cardiac surgery patients. J Clin Epidemiol 2006;59:153–159.

Ennett S, Devellis BM, Earp JA, Kredich D, Warren RW, Wilhelm CL. Disease experience and psychosocial adjustment in children with juvenile rheumatoid arthritis: children's versus mothers' reports. J Pediatr Psychol 1991;16:557–568.

Epstein AM, Hall JA, Tognetti J, Son LH, Conant L Jr. Using proxies to evaluate quality of life: can they provide valid information about patients' health status and satisfaction with medical care? Med Care 1989;27:S91–S98.

Fowler FJ Jr, Coppola KM, Teno JM. Methodological challenges for measuring quality of care at the end of life. J Pain Symptom Manage 1999;17(2):114–119.

Gifford JM, Husain N, Dinglas V, Colantuoni E, Needham D. Baseline quality of life before intensive care: a comparison of patient versus proxy responses. Crit Care Med 2010;38(3):855–860.

Glaser AW, Davies K, Walker D, Brazier D. Influence of proxy respondents and mode of administration on health status assessment following central nervous system tumours in childhood. Qual Life Res 1997;6:43–53.

Goldbeck L, Melches J. Quality of life in families with congenital heart disease. Qual Life Res 2005;14:1915–1924.

Heliövaara M, Aromaa A, Klaukka T, Knekt P, Joukamaa M, Impivaara O. Reliability and validity of interview data on chronic diseases: the mini-Finland health survey. J Clin Epidemiol 1993;46(2):181–191.

Herjanic B, Reich W. Development of a structured psychiatric interview for children: agreement between child and parent on individual symptoms. J Abnorm Child Psychol 1982;10:307–324.

Hofhuis J, Hautvast JL, Schrijvers AJ, Bakker J. Quality of life on admission to the intensive care: can we query the relatives? Intensive Care Med 2003;29:974–979.

Iezzoni LI, McCarthy EP, Davis RB, Siebens H. Mobility problems and perceptions of disability by self-respondents and proxy respondents. Med Care 2000; 38(10):1051–1057.

Jette AM, Davies AR, Cleary PD, Calkins DR, Rubenstein LV, Fink A, Kosecoff J, Young RT, Brook RH, Delbanco TL. The functional status questionnaire: reliability and validity when used in primary care. J Gen Intern Med 1986;1:143–149.

Kasper JD. Using the long-term care surveys: longitudinal and cross-sectional analyses of disabled older people. *Proceedings of the 1987 Public Health Conference on Records and Statistics*; DHHS Pub. No. 88-1214; Hyattsville, MD: National Center for Health Statistics; 1988. p353–358.

Kasper JD, Shapiro S, Guralnik JM, Bandeen-Roche KJ, Fried LP. Designing a community study of moderately to severely disabled older women: the women's health and aging study. Ann Epidemiol 1999;9:498–507.

Katz S. Assessing self-maintenance: activities of daily living, mobility, and instrumental activities of daily living. J Am Geriat Soc 1983;31(12):721–727.

Lawton MP. Scales to measure competence in everyday activities. Psychopharmacol Bull 1988;24(4):609–614.

Lawton MP, Brody EM. Assessment of older people: self-maintaining and instrumental activities of daily living. Gerontologist 1969;9(3):179–186.

Le Coq EM, Boeke AJ, Bezemer PD, Colland VT, Van Eijk JT. Which source should we use to measure quality of life in children with asthma: the children themselves or their parents? Qual Life Res 2000;9:625–636.

LeCoq EM, Boeke AJP, Bezemer PD, Colland VT, van Eijk JTM. Which source should we use to measure quality of life in children with asthma: the children themselves or their parents? Qual Life Res 2000;9:625–636.

Madow WC. Net differences in interview data on chronic conditions and information derived from medical records. Vital Health Stat 1973;2(57):1–25.

Magaziner J, Simonsick EM, Kashner TM, Hebel JR. Patient proxy response comparability on measures of patient health and functional status. J Clin Epidemiol 1988;88(41):1065–1074.

Manton KG. A longitudinal study of functional change and mortality in the United States. J Gerontol Soc Sci 1988;43:S153–S161.

McCusker J, Stoddard AM. Use of a surrogate for the sickness impact profile. Med Care 1984;22(9):789–795.

Modi AC, Quittner AL. Validation of a disease-specific measure of health-related quality of life in children with rhinoconjunctivitis. J Pediatr Psychol 2003;28:535–546.

National Center for Health Statistics (NCHS). Health interview responses compared with medical records. Vital Health Stat 1965;2(7):1–40.

Newschaffer CJ. *Validation of the BRFSS HRQoL Measures in a Statewide Sample*. Atlanta, GA: US Department of Health and Human Services, Centers for Disease Control and Prevention; 1998.

Parsons SK, Barlow SE, Levy SL, Supran SE, Kaplan SH. Health-related quality of life in pediatric bone marrow transplant survivors: according to whom? Int J Cancer 1999;12:46–51.

Parsons SK, Shih MC, Mayer DK, Barlow SE, Supran SE, Levy SL, Greenfield S, Kaplan SH. Preliminary psychometric evaluation of the child health ratings inventory (CHRIs) and disease-specific impairment inventory-hematopoietic stem cell transplantation (DSII-HSCT) in parents and children. Qual Life Res 2005;14:1613–1625.

Pearlman RA, Uhlmann RF. Quality of life in chronic diseases: perceptions of elderly patients. J Gerontol Med Sci 1988;43:M25–M30.

Pierre U, Wood-Dauphinee S, Korner-Bitensky N, Gayton D, Hanley J. Proxy use of the canadian sf-36 in rating health status of the disabled elderly. J Clin Epidemiol 1998;51(11):983–990.

Pinhas-Hamiel O, Singer S, Pilpel N, Fradkin A, Modan D, Reichman B. Health-related quality of life among children and adolescents: associations with obesity. Int J Obes (Lond) 2006;30(2):267–272.

Rajmil L, Fernandez E, Gispert R, Rue M, Glutting JP, Plasencia A, Segura A. Influence of proxy respondents in children's health interview surveys. J Epidemiol Community Health 1999;53(1):38–42.

Ravens-Sieberer U, Thomas C, Kluth W, Teschke L, Bullinger M, Lilientahl S. A disease-specific quality of life module for children with cancer – news from the KINDL-questionnaire. Psychooncology 2001;10.

Reither EN, Utz RL. A procedure to correct proxy-reported weight in the National Health Interview Survey, 1976–2002. Popul Health Metrics 2009;7(2).

Riley AW, Forrest CB, Rebok GW, Starfield B, Green BF, Robertson JA, Friello P. The child report form of the CHIP-child edition: reliability and validity. Med Care 2004;42:221–231.

Rogers J, Ridley S, Chrispin P, Scotton H, Lloyd D. Reliability of the next of kins' estimates of critically ill patients' quality of life. Anaesthesia 1997;52:1137–1143.

Ronen GM, Streiner DL, Rosenbaum P, Canadian Pediatric Epilepsy Network. Health-related quality of life in children with epilepsy: development and validation of self-report and parent proxy measures. Epilepsia 2003;44(4):598–612.

Rothman ML, Hedrick SC, Bulcroft KA, Hickam DH, Rubenstein LZ. The validity of proxy-generated scores as measures of patient health status. Med Care 1991;29(2):115–124.

Russell KMW, Hudson M, Long A, Phipps S. Assessment of health related quality of life in children with cancer: consistency and agreement between parent and child reports. Cancer 2006;106:2267–2274.

Saigal S, Rosenbaum PL, Feeny D, Burrows E, Furlong W, Stoskopf BL, Hoult L. parental perspectives of the health status and health-related quality of life of teenaged children who were extremely low birth weight and term controls. Pediatrics 2000;105(3):569–574.

Sawyer M, Antoniou G, Rice M. A comparison of parent and adolescent reports describing the health-related quality of life of adolescents treated for cancer. Int J Cancer 1999;12:39–45.

Sherifali D, Pinelli J. Parent as proxy reporting: implications and recommendations for quality of life research. J Fam Nurs 2007;13(1):83–98.

Shields M. Proxy reporting in the national population health survey. Health Rep 2000;12(1):21–39.

Sneeuw KC, Sprangers MA, Aaronson NK. The role of health care providers and significant others in evaluating the quality of life of patients with chronic disease. J Clin Epidemiol 2002;55:1130–1143.

Spitzer WO, Dobson AJ, Hall J, Chesterman E, Levi J, Shepherd R, Battista RN, Catchlove BR. Measuring the quality of life of cancer patients: a concise QL-index for use by physicians. J Chron Dis 1981;34(12):585–597.

Sprangers MAG and Aaronson NK. The Role of Health Care Providers and Significant Others in Evaluating the Quality of Life of Patients with Chronic Disease: A Review. *Journal of Clinical Epidemiology*, 1992;45(7);743–760.

Tamim H, McCusker J, Dendukuri N. Proxy reporting of quality of life using the EQ-5D. Med Care 2002;40(12):1186–1195.

The EUROQOL Group. EUROQOL—a new facility for the measurement of health related quality of life. Health Policy 1990;16:199–208.

Theunissen NC, Vogels TG, Koopman HM, Verrips GH, Zwinderman KA, Verloove-Vanhorick SP, Wit JM. The proxy problem: child report versus parent report in health-related quality of life research. Qual Life Res 1998;7:387–397.

Todorov A, Kirchner C. Bias in proxies' reports of disability: data from the national health interview survey on disability. Am J Public Health 2000;90(8):1248–1253.

Varni JW, Burwinkle TM, Jacobs JR, Gottschalk M, Kaufman F, Jones KL. The PedsQL in Type 1 and Type 2 diabetes. Diabetes Care 2003;26(3):631–637.

Varni JW, Katz ER, Seid M, Quiggins DJL, Friedman-Bender A, Castro CM. The Pediatric Cancer Quality of Life Inventory (PCQL): I. Instrument development, descriptive statistics, and cross-informant variance. J Behav Med 1998;21:179–204.

Varni JW, Seid M, Rode CA. The PedsQL™: measurement model for the Pediatric Quality of Life Inventory. Med Care 1999;37:126–139.

Verbrugge LM. Gender and health: an update on hypotheses and evidence. J Health Soc Behav 1985;26(3):156–182.

Verrips GHW, Vogels AGC, den Ouden AL, Paneth N, Verloove-Vanhorick SP. Measuring health-related quality of life in adolescents: agreement between raters and between methods of administration. Child Care Health Dev 2000;26:457–469.

Vetter TR, Bridgewater CL, McGwin G Jr. An observational study of patient versus parental perceptions of health-related quality of life in children and adolescents with a chronic pain condition: who should the clinician believe? Health Qual Life Outcomes 2012;10.

Vogels T, Verrips GH, Verloove-Vanhorick SP, Fekkes M, Kamphuis RP, Koopman HM, Theunissen NC, Wit JM. Measuring health related quality of life in children: the development of the TACQOL parent form. Qual Life Res 1998;7:457–465.

Wallace R, Woolson R. *The Epidemiology of the Elderly*. New York, NY: Oxford University Press; 1992.

Wallander JL, Schmitt M, Koot HM. Quality of life measurement in children and adolescents: issues, instruments and applications. J Clin Psychol 2001;57(4):571–585.

Ware JE Jr, Snow KK, Kosinski M, Gandek B. *SF-36 Health Survey: Manual and Interpretation Guide*. Boston: The Health. Institute, New England Medical Center; 1993.

Ware JE, Kosinski M, Keller SD. *SF-12: How to Score the SF-12 Physical and Mental Health Summary Scales*. 2nd ed. Boston: New England Medical Center, The Health Institute; 1995.

Ware J Jr, Kosinski M, Keller SD. A 12-item short-form health survey: construction of scales and preliminary tests of reliability and validity. Med Care 1996;34(3):220–233.

Warren, P. and Cunningham, P. (2003), No. 9. 2002 National survey of America's families telephone survey methods. Urban Institute, Washington, DC. Available at http://www.urban.org/UploadedPDF/900693_2002_Methodology_9.pdf. Accessed 2013 Aug 20.

ONLINE RESOURCES

More information about the survey instruments mentioned in this chapter can be found using the links below:

Katz Activities of Daily Living (ADLs): www.tuft-healthplans.org/providers/pdf/katz_adl.pdf.

Child Health and Illness Profile—Child Edition (CHIP-CE™): www.childhealthprofile.org/index.asp?pageid=48.

Child Health Ratings Inventory (CHRIs): https://research.tufts-nemc.org/chris/.

Cystic Fibrosis Questionnaire (CFQ): www.psy.miami.edu/cfq_QLab/.

EQ 5D (EuroQoL): www.curoqol.org/.

Functional Status Questionnaire: http://web.missouri.edu/~proste/tool/funct/FSQ.pdf.

How Are You?: http://qol.thoracic.org/sections/instruments/fj/pages/hay.html.

Lawton Instrumental Activities of Daily Living (IADLs): http://tuftshealthplans.com/providers/pdf/lawton_iadl.pdf.

KINDL™: http://kindl.org/english/.

Pediatric Quality of Life Inventory™ (PedsQL™): www.pedsql.org/.

Short-Form General Health Survey (SF-12): www.sf-36.org/tools/sf12.shtml.

Short-Form General Health Survey (SF-36): www.sf-36.org/tools/sf36.shtml.

Sickness Impact Profile: www.rehabmeasures.org/Lists/RehabMeasures/DispForm.aspx?ID=955.

Spitzer Quality of Life Scale: www.rtog.org/LinkClick.aspx?fileticket=GEJNxEAm7VA%3D&tabid=118.

CHAPTER FIFTEEN

The Collection of Biospecimens in Health Surveys

Joseph W. Sakshaug
Department of Statistical Methods, Institute for Employment Research, Nuremberg, Germany; Program in Survey Methodology, Institute for Social Research, University of Michigan, Ann Arbor, Michigan, USA

Mary Beth Ofstedal and Heidi Guyer
Institute for Social Research, University of Michigan, Ann Arbor, MI, USA

Timothy J. Beebe
Department of Health Sciences Research, Mayo Clinic, Rochester, Minnesota, USA

15.1 Introduction

This chapter provides a general overview of the practical issues relevant to the collection of biomeasures in health surveys. We highlight the benefits and possible uses of survey-based biomeasure data, describe the types of biomeasure data that have and can be collected, identify the specific quality control challenges related to the collection of these data, examine the logistical, ethical, and legal issues surrounding this specialized and emerging area of survey research, and offer suggestions on possible methods for disseminating combined survey and biomeasure

Handbook of Health Survey Methods, First Edition. Edited by Timothy P. Johnson.

data post-collection. We draw upon the experiences of eight large-scale surveys to illustrate the broad range of methods currently being used to collect and disseminate such data. The primary goal of this chapter is to leave the reader with a sense of "best practices" for collecting biomeasure data in surveys.

15.2 Background

Health survey data collection has evolved significantly in recent years. While self-reported data collection has always been the primary component of health surveys, more modern surveys have complemented these data with the collection of objective physical measures, including biological materials (e.g., blood, urine), anthropometric measures (e.g., height/weight, waist circumference), physical performance assessments (e.g., grip strength, peak expiratory flow), and genetic measurements. These measurements, collectively referred to as *biomeasures*, which were once primarily limited to clinical and laboratory samples or small-scale community-based studies, have spawned new research opportunities that intersect the social and biomedical sciences and there is evidence that the use of biomeasure data in survey research is intensifying. Figure 15.1 shows a steep rise in the number of scientific publications with reference to

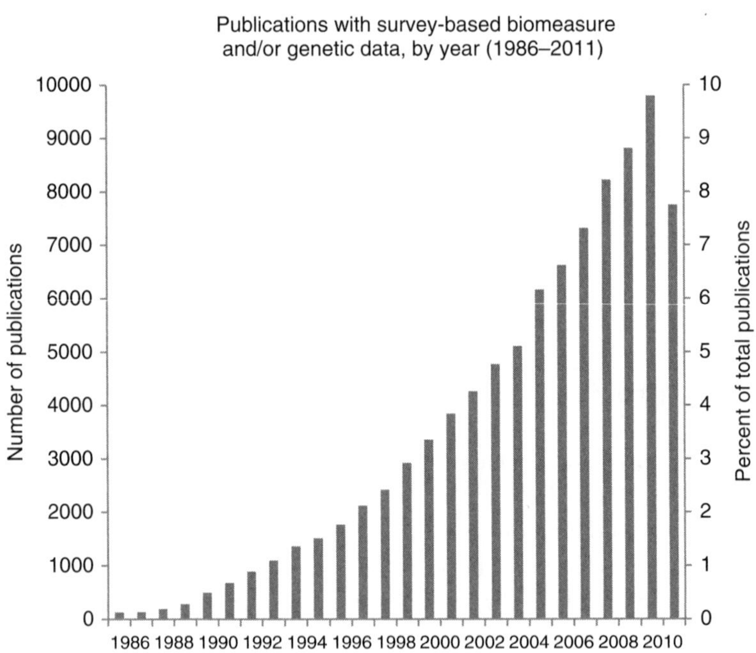

FIGURE 15.1 Number of publications and percent of total publications indicating use of survey and biomeasure data (1986–2011). PubMed search of articles using key words "(survey OR questionnaire) AND (biospecimen OR biomarker OR gene OR genotype)."

survey-based biomeasure data, both in terms of raw numbers of publications and percentage of total publications. For example, for years 2000–2010, the number of publications with reference to survey-based biomeasure collection increased threefold, with approximately 3300 publications in 2000 and 10,000 in 2010, or about 10% of the total number of publications for the latter year.

It is clear from the figure that researchers are increasingly harnessing the potential uses and benefits of incorporating biomeasures with population-based survey data. Weinstein and Willis (2000) highlight four primary uses that we describe briefly: (i) obtaining population-representative data from nonclinical samples, (ii) calibrating self-reports with other measures of health and disease, (iii) explicating pathways and elaborating causal linkages between social environment and health, and (iv) linking genetic markers with survey materials.

15.2.1 OBTAINING POPULATION-REPRESENTATIVE DATA FROM NONCLINICAL SAMPLES

An important strength of using population-based surveys as a vehicle to collect biomeasures is the ability to make generalizable inferences to the clinical and nonclinical population under study. This is possible due to the random selection mechanism used to select participants from a well-defined population of interest with known probabilities of selection. In contrast, clinic-based studies often lack randomization and participants are either self-selected or recruited into the study using nonprobability-based methods. This study design makes it difficult to generalize to the nonclinical population as the characteristics of those willing to participate in medical research studies may be different from those not willing and may in fact be correlated with the outcome(s) under study. Moreover, distinct differences between participants and nonparticipants may be unobservable and therefore impossible to control for at the analysis stage. Clearly, the survey platform offers a sound scientific rationale for making population-representative inferences from biomeasure data collected from a carefully drawn probability sample of the population. Although surveys are also susceptible to biases due to self-selection, statistical methods of adjusting for such biases are more developed for population-based samples than for clinic-based samples (Schenker et al. 2011, Brick and Kalton 1996).

15.2.2 CALIBRATING SELF-REPORTS WITH OTHER MEASURES OF HEALTH AND DISEASE

Although self-reported measures can serve as useful indicators of one's health status, health conditions, functional status, and other outcomes, they are susceptible to a variety of reporting errors. We know that survey responses can be impacted by a variety of factors, including the interviewer, mode of data collection, and by the sensitivity, format, and context of the question (Tourangeau et al. 2000, Tourangeau and Smith 1996). In contrast, biomeasures do not rely on self-reports and are therefore not subject to reporting errors. This feature makes biomeasures attractive as a reference measure for the purpose of validating and calibrating self-reported survey data as well as studying the underlying mechanisms of reporting error. For example, several studies have used measured height and weight to validate the quality of the corresponding self-reported measurements and identify patterns of misreporting (Kuczmarski et al. 2001, Brunner Huber 2007, Wang et al. 2002, Taylor et al. 2006, Zhou et al. 2010). Other studies have used biomeasure data to adjust the self-reported measurements and improve the analysis of the self-reported data (Ezzati et al. 2006, Schenker et al. 2010).

15.2.3 EXPLICATING PATHWAYS AND ELABORATING CAUSAL LINKAGES BETWEEN SOCIAL ENVIRONMENT AND HEALTH

Another potential use of survey biomeasures is to better understand how an individual's social environment can impact his or her health. Numerous studies have found evidence of a relationship between social factors (position in social hierarchies, social networks, socioeconomic status) and health outcomes (stress, illness, well-being, mortality) (Thoits 1995, Lupien et al. 1995, Smith 1999). But what is missing from these studies, which are primarily based on self-reported survey data, is explanations on how the social environment affects the physiological factors which, in turn, influence health. Survey biomeasures may be able to shed light on the biological pathways that mediate the causal relationship between social factors and health outcomes. Work in this area is already underway. For example, Weinstein et al. (2003) found strong significant effects of position in social hierarchy (education) and life challenges (recent widowhood, perception of high demands) on allostatic load, a physiological marker that mediates the effect of stress on the body. Goldman et al. (2005) studied perceived stress and its relation to physiological dysregulation in the Taiwan Biomarker Study. They found several biological markers that were significantly, albeit weakly, associated with perceptions of stress. Biomeasure data indicative of physiological dysregulation has also been shown to be a strong predictor of "downstream" health outcomes, including mortality, even after controlling for an extensive set of factors, including sociodemographic characteristics and self-reported measures of physical and mental health (Turra et al. 2005). Thus, it appears that biomeasure data can act as a useful supplement to self-reported information in understanding causal pathways and manifestation of certain health outcomes.

15.2.4 LINKING GENETIC MARKERS WITH SURVEY MATERIALS

The collection of genetic data in surveys offers many new research possibilities for understanding the role of genetics on health outcomes. Potential applications of combined genetic and survey data include the identification of previously undiscovered relationships between particular genes and health outcomes; the study of possible interactions between genes and environmental factors and their influence on the development of health conditions; and assessment of the prevalence of certain genetic traits that exist within a population. Another potential use of genetic data in a survey context is to control for genetic traits that have established links with certain health outcomes in order to determine what role nongenetic factors (e.g., environment, behaviors) play in their relationship to primary outcomes (Ryff and Singer 2005). For example, there is an established relationship between the Apolipoprotein E (ApoE) gene and risk for Alzheimer disease and cardiovascular disease (Corder et al. 1993, Hyman et al. 1996). Controlling for the ApoE gene could facilitate the identification of other factors, such as lifestyle habits (e.g., physical activity, cognitive activity, diet, social engagement), that may influence the progression of Alzheimer's disease.

Despite the many uses and foreseeable benefits of including biomeasures in surveys, there are significant logistical, ethical, and legal challenges to collecting, storing, and disseminating biomeasure-based data. In the coming sections, we explore these issues, drawing upon the experiences of eight large-scale, multipurpose surveys that, together, encompass a range of different approaches with respect to the measures that are collected, where the collection occurs and the personnel that are used to conduct the protocols. These studies also represent different target populations (children, adults, older individuals) and span a number of countries. They include the National Longitudinal Study of Adolescent Health (Add Health); the English Longitudinal Study of Ageing (ELSA); the Health and Retirement Study (HRS); the National Health and Nutrition Examination Study (NHANES); the National Social Life, Health and Aging Project (NSHAP); the Survey of Health, Aging and Retirement in Europe (SHARE); The Irish Longitudinal Study of Ageing (TILDA); and the Wisconsin Longitudinal Study (WLS)[1]. With the exception of NHANES, which is a repeated cross-sectional survey, all of the surveys are panel surveys. Some have been ongoing for many years (WLS started in 1957 and NHANES began in the 1960s), while others began more recently. WLS is primarily a telephone and mail survey,[2] whereas the other surveys conduct interviews in person. Table 15.1 provides some basic information about each of these surveys and the biomeasures they collect. We expand upon the latter in the next section. Websites for each of these studies are provided in the notes at the end of the chapter.

15.3 Biomeasure Selection

As discussed by Jaszczak et al. (2009), the decision about which biomeasures will be collected in a study is determined by the study objectives as well as practical and logistical considerations such as cost and feasibility. For example, studies interested in cardiovascular disease and risk factors might include anthropometric

[1]We acknowledge the existence of HIV- and substance abuse-focused health surveys and the multitude of biomeasures that they collect (e.g., hair, urine, saliva, sweat patches, fingernail clippings, and breathalyzer tests), but choose to focus on a set of studies that collect a broader range of biomeasures collected for multiple purposes.

[2]The first five waves of WLS used telephone and mail instruments. The most recent wave was conducted in-person.

TABLE 15.1 Selection of Eight Large-Scale Population-Based Surveys Undertaking Biomeasure Collection

Study	Population	Country	Year Survey Began	Year Biomeasures First Collected	Mode	Location of Biomeasure Collection	Personnel	Measures/ Samples Collected[a]
Add Health	Ages 12–32	United States	1994	1996	In-person	Respondent's home	Field interviewers	Blood pressure, height, weight, and waist circumference, dried blood spots, saliva
ELSA	Age 50+	England	2002	2004	In-person	R's home	Nurses	Blood pressure; pulse; grip strength; lung function; walking speed; balance stands; chair stand; height; weight; waist circumference; hip circumference; whole blood; saliva (cortisol)
HRS								
Biennial interview	Age 51+	United States	1992	2004	In-person	R's home	Field interviewers	Blood pressure; pulse; grip strength; lung function; walking speed; balance stands; height; weight; waist circumference; dried blood spots; saliva (DNA)

Diabetes mail survey	Age 51+ with diabetes	United States	2003	2003	Mail	—	None	Dried blood spot
NHANES	All ages	United States	1971	1971	In-person	Mobile clinic	Physician, medical and health technicians, dietary and health interviewers	Blood pressure; extensive anthropometrics (head, arm calf, thigh circumference, subscapular and triceps skinfold; upper arm, upper leg length; etc.); whole blood; vision; hearing; oral health; physical activity monitor; timed walk; balance test, isokinetic; lung function; bioelectrical impedence; CV fitness; dermatology; hair sample

(*continued*)

TABLE 15.1 (*Continued*)

Study	Population	Country	Year Survey Began	Year Biomeasures First Collected	Mode	Location of Biomeasure Collection	Personnel	Measures/ Samples Collected[a]
NSHAP	Born between 1920 and 1947	United States	2005	2005	In-person	R's home	Field interviewers	Blood pressure; pulse; heart rate variability; timed get up and go; walking speed; chair stands; actigraphy; smell; taste, touch, vision; height; weight; waist circumference; hip circumference; dried blood; blood spots in a microtainer; saliva; urine; vaginal swab; HIV test; DNA
SHARE	Age 50+	Europe	2004	2004	In-person	R's home	Field interviewers	Grip strength (all waves); lung function (waves 2 and 4); walking speed (waves 1 and 2); chair stand (wave 2); Germany wave 4 only: dried blood spots, height, waist circumference, blood pressure

TILDA	Age 50+	Ireland	2006	2006	In-person	Health centre (two fixed sites) or R's home (reduced protocol)	Nurses	Blood pressure; phasic blood pressure; heart rate; pulse wave velocity; heart rate variability; grip strength; timed up and go; walking speed; spatial and temporal gait assessment; height; weight; waist circumference; hip circumference; venous blood; visual acuity; contrast sensitivity; retinal photograph; macular pigment measurement; bone density; extensive cognitive testing
WLS	1957 high school graduates (and one of their siblings)	United States (Wisconsin)	1957	2007	Mail and in-person	R's home	Field interviewers	Saliva sample, height, weight, waist circumference (2 waist measures for women), hip circumference, photos, peak flow, chair rise, grip strength, walking speed, Snellen eye test

[a]List of measures is not comprehensive for all studies.

measurements, blood pressure/pulse, and blood samples for analysis of lipids (cholesterol and triglycerides), C-reactive protein, fibrinogen, and glycated hemoglobin (HbA1c, hemoglobin A1c) among others. For studies focusing on diabetes, HbA1c and anthropometry are important measures. Studies of older individuals may include strength and mobility related measures, such as gait speed, balance, grip strength, and body mass index (BMI), which have been used as markers of frailty (Cigolle et al. 2009).

Cost and feasibility of collection enter into the decision, as well. Basic anthropometric measurements (e.g., height, weight, waist and hip circumference) and some physical performance tests (e.g., walking speed, balance tests, chair stands) are relatively easy to carry out and have fairly low personnel and equipment costs. Other measures such as grip strength, lung function, and blood pressure can also be administered by a lay interviewer (with proper training), but require specialized equipment that is more expensive. The actual collection of DNA via saliva or hair samples is relatively straightforward and inexpensive; however, extraction and analysis of the samples can be quite costly. The same is true for dried blood samples, for which the collection materials are relatively cheap and the protocols (though more complex than for saliva or hair) can, at least in some countries, be carried out by lay interviewers. In contrast, the collection of whole blood intravenously requires medically trained personnel, at least in the United States and Europe, and involves more sophisticated equipment and has more restrictive shipping and storage requirements. New whole blood collection methods using a finger stick and hematocrit tube are on the horizon although immediate post-collection processing and storage requirements have inhibited the extent to which this method has been used to date.

We review the different categories of biomeasures that are commonly collected in surveys and their importance in the sections that follow.[3]

15.3.1 ANTHROPOMETRIC MEASURES

Because they are cheap and easy to collect in the context of a face-to-face survey, anthropometric measurements such as weight, height, waist and hip circumference are perhaps the most commonly collected biomeasures in surveys. The latter three measurements have minimal equipment requirements (e.g., a tape measure and rafter's square). The measurement of weight requires a scale, but reliable scales can be obtained at relatively low cost. SHARE measured height and waist circumference on a large subsample in wave 4 in Germany. This subsample consists of all panel respondents plus one-half of the refresher sample. The ELSA, NHANES, NSHAP, WLS, and TILDA studies also measure hip circumference, and NHANES includes a number of other anthropometric measurements including head, arm calf, and thigh circumference, various measures of skinfold; upper arm and upper leg length, among others. For women, WLS measures waist circumference at the narrowest point and at the navel; men are only measured at the navel.

[3] See Lindau and McDade (2008) for an earlier review of many of these measures.

Anthropometric measures are valuable as indicators of risk factors for various diseases. BMI and waist–hip ratio are two commonly used measures. High BMI is associated with hypertension, diabetes, heart disease, stroke, various forms of cancer, atherosclerosis (Folsom et al. 1993, Lapidus et al. 1984, Larsson et al. 1984, McKeigue et al. 1991), osteoarthritis (Felson et al. 1992), functional impairment, and disability (Blaum et al. 2003, Davison et al. 2002, Dey et al. 2002, Himes 2000, Jenkins 2004a, Must et al. 1999). Weight change is also an important predictor of various health outcomes such as functional impairment and disability (Ferraro et al. 2002, Jenkins 2004b, Launer et al. 1994). Waist circumference has also been shown to be an important predictor of cardiovascular risk (Dagenais et al. 2005, Ducimetiere et al. 1985).

15.3.2 PHYSICAL PERFORMANCE ASSESSMENTS

Most of the physical performance tests that are included in the surveys discussed here can be grouped into measures of strength, lung function, and mobility and balance.

Strength. Grip strength is measured with a hand dynamometer, a spring-type device that measures force. The measurement is generally conducted while the participants are standing with their arm at their side, lower arm at a 90° angle to the floor. Participants are asked to squeeze the dynamometer as hard as they can; the result is recorded in kilograms. Two to three measurements are generally taken on alternating hands, though there are some variations across studies. For example, WLS tests the same hand two times.

Grip strength is a measure of general muscle strength, as well as an indicator of the presence of arthritis and other conditions in the hand. Grip strength in midlife has been shown to predict functional limitation and disability in older ages (Giampaou et al. 1999, Rantanen et al. 1999), mortality (Snih et al. 2002), and health-related quality of life (Sayer et al. 2006). Low grip strength has also been found to predict high levels of inflammatory markers such as CRP and IL-6 (Cesari et al. 2004).

Lung Function. A lung function test provides a measure of respiratory impairment. Peak expiratory flow is a common measure of lung function that can be assessed with a peak flow meter, the device that is used in the HRS and SHARE studies. ELSA uses a spirometer, which provides more detailed measures of lung function, including forced expiratory volume in one second (FEV1) and forced vital capacity (FVC).

Peak expiratory flow provides a measure of obstructive lung disease, such as in asthma or chronic obstructive lung disease (emphysema). It has been shown to be related to mortality (Cook et al. 1991), cognitive decline (Albert et al. 1995), and physical decline (Seeman et al. 1994).

Mobility and Balance. The timed walk and timed "get up and go" tests are quick and inexpensive measures of functional mobility that can be conducted in respondents' homes. In a timed walk, participants are asked to walk a short distance (generally about 8 ft) at their normal walking pace, once in each direction. In the timed get up and go, participants start in a sitting position and the time it takes them to stand, walk a short distance at their usual pace, turn, walk back to the chair, and sit down again is measured. ELSA, HRS, NHANES, WLS, and SHARE administer the timed walk, whereas NSHAP (wave 1) and TILDA administer the timed get up and go. TILDA also assesses temporal and spatial gait patterns using the GAITRite™ system. NHANES conducts two timed walks of different lengths—one 8 ft and one 20 ft.

Walking speed is predictive of a number of health outcomes for older people including self-reported health (Jylhä et al. 2001), mortality (Corti et al. 1994, Guralnik et al. 1994, Melzer et al. 2003), disability (Guralnik et al. 1994, 1995, Ostir et al. 1998), recurrent falls (Bath and Morgan 1999), hip fracture (Dargent-Molina et al. 1996), and nursing home admission (Guralnik et al. 1994).

Balance tests are also used to assess functional mobility. Balance tests have been found to be important for predicting mortality (Guralnik et al. 1994, Laukkanen et al. 1995), disability (Guralnik et al. 1994, 1995), and institutionalization (Guralnik et al. 1994). Surveys use a variety of different tests of varying levels of difficulty, including the full tandem, semitandem, side-by-side, and one-leg stand. To make the test more challenging, participants may be asked to close their eyes while doing the task. For all of the balance tests, participants are asked to hold the position for a certain length of time, usually ranging between 10 and 60 seconds. NHANES uses a different protocol to assess balance, the "Romberg Test of Standing Balance on Firm and Compliant Support Surfaces," which is made up of four test conditions of varying difficulty (Weber and Cass 1993). ELSA, NSHAP, and SHARE also conduct a chair stand test that is separate from the timed walk. For this test, respondents are timed while standing up from a sitting position and sitting down again five times, while holding their arms crossed over their chest.

15.3.3 BLOOD PRESSURE AND PULSE

The availability of compact, portable blood pressure monitors has made it feasible to measure blood pressure and pulse in large-scale surveys. Hypertension is related to a variety of diseases such as coronary heart disease, stroke, kidney failure, and retinal disease (O'Mahoney et al. 2008, Sacco et al. 1997, United States Renal Data System (USRDS) 2007). Among older people, high blood pressure has also been shown to be associated with cognitive decline and dementia (Tzourio 2007). Pulse rate has also been used as a risk factor to predict cardiovascular disease, and to predict death and other clinical outcomes in the presence of CVD.

Blood pressure (both systolic and diastolic) and pulse are measured in all of the studies discussed here with the exception of the WLS. In the SHARE study, Germany is the only country to have measured blood pressure thus far; it was measured in wave 4 on the same subsample that received height, weight, and DBS collection. Multiple measurements are taken, generally in a resting state.

The TILDA study, which uses much more sophisticated equipment in the health center, also assesses phasic blood pressure (beat-to-beat blood pressure), heart rate variability (a powerful measure of autonomic nervous system function), and pulse wave velocity (an indicator of arterial stiffness).

15.3.4 BLOOD

The area in which recent technological advances have perhaps had the most profound impact is the collection of blood samples. In particular, the development of assays for dried blood spot (DBS) samples has made the collection of blood in population-based surveys both affordable and logistically feasible (McDade et al. 2007). The DBS protocol is minimally invasive. It involves pricking the participant's finger with a lancet and depositing drops of blood on a filter paper card. The cards are air dried, packaged, and then mailed to a lab where the assays are performed.

The Add Health, HRS, NSHAP and German-SHARE [4]studies collect blood via DBS. Whole blood was collected via venipuncture by nurses or trained medical professionals in the ELSA, NHANES, and TILDA studies. A relatively new method of blood collection that can be used in population surveys is the Demecal™ kit (Gootjes et al. 2009). This method requires only one to two drops of blood from a finger prick that are deposited in a tube containing a patented filter that separates the plasma from cells. The sample is mailed to a certified lab for analysis. This method has been used successfully in the Malawi Longitudinal Study of Families and Health (MLSFH) (http://www.malawi.pop.upenn.edu/).

The number and range of assays that are currently available from DBS and the Demecal™ method are limited compared to the results that can be obtained from venous blood samples. Some common DBS assays that are conducted for the studies discussed here include cholesterol (total and high density lipoprotein (HDL)[5]), HbA1c (which is an average measure of sugar in the blood over the last 120 days), C-reactive protein (CRP, a marker of inflammation in the blood), cystatin C (a marker of kidney function), and Epstein Barr virus (EBV, a virus of the herpes family that is associated with higher risk of autoimmune diseases). Of these, total and HDL cholesterol and HbA1c are available from the Demecal™ method. Studies that collect whole blood have conducted other assays, including fibrinogen (a protein necessary for blood clotting), ApoE (involved in transport of cholesterol in the body), and ferritin and hemoglobin (measures of iron levels in the body), among others. In addition to the blood results, DNA has been extracted from the whole blood for these studies.

---

[4]Through wave 4 of SHARE (2010), Germany was the only country that had collected DBS samples in SHARE. Plans are in place to pretest DBS collection in several more countries in SHARE wave 5 and to launch a large-scale collection in wave 6.

[5]It is possible to measure triglycerides as well, but only in fasting conditions—a limit of home-based studies, especially if included as part of an interview. LDL is a ratio of the other cholesterol measures. Thus, it is possible to get all cholesterol measures from DBS, depending on the collection conditions.

The main advantages of DBS samples over venous blood draws are the minimally invasive sample collection procedure; simplified field logistics associated with sample processing, transport, and storage; and long-term stability under freezer storage that allows for future analyses as new biomarkers of interest, such as genetic markers, emerge (McDade et al. 2007). The primary disadvantages are the relatively limited number of assays that are available from DBS samples and the need to validate and calibrate the assays against assays derived from whole blood. Another disadvantage has to do with the relatively limited quantity of sample that can be collected via DBS. Typically studies collect five to six spots of blood on the collection cards. For many purposes, this quantity may be adequate; however, depending on the number of assays to be conducted and the amount of blood needed for each, five to six spots may not be adequate and would leave little sample left over for storage for future analysis. The primary disadvantages of the Demecal™ method are the limited set of results that can be obtained from the sample and the inability to obtain DNA or to store any sample for future analysis.

15.3.5 SALIVA

The recent and rapid advances in genotyping have increased the value of DNA samples, and the collection of saliva in population-based surveys has become much more common as a result. There are numerous techniques for collecting saliva (e.g., buccal swab, mouthwash, spit method, among others), most of which are fairly straightforward to implement in the field.

Saliva samples are typically collected in order to obtain DNA for genetic analysis (as in the Add Health, HRS, NSHAP, and WLS studies), although some studies use saliva to measure cortisol levels (ELSA and NSHAP). NSHAP also uses saliva samples to test for salivary hormones including estradiol, progesterone, dehydroepiandosterone, and testosterone (Gavrilova and Lindau 2009). The protocols used to collect the samples vary depending on the purpose.

The Add Health, HRS, NSHAP, and WLS studies use the Oragene© collection kit developed by DNA Genotek for purposes of extracting DNA. For this method, the respondent simply spits into a small collection container, until the saliva reaches a marked level on the container. The cap is screwed onto the container, releasing a preservative, and the sample is mailed to a lab for extraction and storage of DNA. HRS has also collected saliva samples via buccal swabs (in the ancillary Aging, Demographics and Memory Study, ADAMS), whereas NSHAP has used salivary tubes (waves 1 and 2), OraSure© (wave 1), and salivary sponges (wave 2). For measurement of cortisol on ELSA, the collection protocol is much more complex and burdensome. Four saliva samples are collected throughout the day: when the respondent wakes up, 30 min after waking, at 7 PM and just before they go to bed. The respondent is instructed to chew on a plastic-coated cotton swab until saturated. All four samples are then packaged and mailed by the respondent. In addition, as each sample is collected, respondents are asked to complete successive pages of a log book—a self-completion that collects a range of information such as the respondent's mood at the time of each sample.

15.3.6 OTHER MEASURES

The measures described above are among the more common biomeasures collected in surveys. As indicated in Table 15.1, however, several of the surveys highlighted in this chapter also conduct other measurements, some of which are minimally invasive and easy to conduct, while others are more sensitive, technologically demanding and/or burdensome to carry out. Measures of sensory function are included in the NHANES, NSHAP, TILDA, and WLS studies. NHANES, NSHAP, and TILDA conduct vision tests and NSHAP conducts tests of smell, taste and touch. WLS has conducted a Snellen vision test on a subsample of participants. NHANES also conducts a dental examination as part of the medical examination to screen for oral health problems, such as caries, periodontal disease, and tooth loss, among others. TILDA conducts a bone density scan of the heel to test for osteoporosis. NHANES conducts a full body scan, which provides various measures of fat, both fat and lean mass, as well as bone mineral content and bone mineral density. Activity cycles and sleep can be measured by an accelerometer. In NHANES, participants were asked to wear an Actigraph accelerometer on an elastic belt around their waist during waking hours for 7 days. NSHAP and ELSA have conducted substudies to measure both activity and sleep cycles using a watch-like Actigraph accelerometer worn on the wrist. WLS has used photographs from high school yearbooks to measure facial BMI and attractiveness. Photographs were also taken in the 2011 wave to follow-up with attractiveness coding and to code perceived age. Finally, although blood and saliva are the most common biospecimens collected in the surveys highlighted here, other biospecimens that are collected in the NSHAP study include urine samples and vaginal swabs.

15.4 Methodological and Operational Considerations

Different approaches have been used for collecting biomeasures in these surveys. In this section, we expand upon ideas presented by Jaszczak and colleagues (2009). Before proceeding with data collection, each study must answer several questions. For example, what mode of data collection will be used to administer the measurements? As described in the next section, most studies conduct these measurements in a face-to-face setting, either in the respondent's home or at a clinic or other medical facility, although some studies have collected certain specimens (e.g., blood and saliva) by mail. If the biomeasures are to be collected in a face-to-face setting then who will administer them, a licensed medical specialist or a field interviewer? Having a licensed medical specialist administer the measures in a clinic offers the widest range of options with regard to biomeasure collection due to the availability of relevant biospecimen collection, analysis, and storage equipment. However, gaining cooperation from survey respondents to go to a clinic for these measurements may be a challenging task, and resistance to this request may harm the study's participation rate. Furthermore, clinic-based data collection can be prohibitively expensive for many studies. A less expensive approach is to use field interviewers to collect biomeasures in respondents' homes. Studies that have adopted this approach have had success in collecting a range of biomeasures, such as DBS samples, saliva, height, weight, waist circumference, urine, and HIV tests, among others. However, using field interviewers to collect biospecimens raises a host of questions as well. What type of interviewer is best suited to carry out both the survey interview and biomeasure collection? How should interviewers be trained to perform the latter task? How can interviewers influence the quality of the collected measurements? We touch on each of these issues in the sections that follow.

For the NHANES, detailed clinical measurements are conducted by medical professionals in a mobile examination center. This approach yields extensive physical and biological measurements in a highly standardized setting, but at a very high cost. Other studies, including TILDA, have arranged for physical examinations of respondents at a health facility (hospital, clinic, health center).[6] This approach also offers the potential for very sophisticated measurements with equipment that is not easily portable, but it is also very costly. Some studies aim for a compromise where study nurses are sent to the respondents' home (the ELSA study). Although the measurements that can be carried out in the home environment are less in depth than those that can be done in a health facility, nurses are able to conduct a wide array of measurements that require medical training, including the collection of whole blood. In contrast, an increasingly common and cost-effective approach is to have lay interviewers conduct these measurements with respondents in their homes as part of the interview. This latter approach has been adopted by the Add Health, NSHAP, and HRS studies in the United States and by the SHARE study in Europe. The measurements that can be conducted by lay interviewers are much more restricted. However, this approach has the considerable advantage of lower cost and, as technology advances, the range of measurements that can be collected in this way is likely to increase. In addition, home administration of the biomeasures facilitates participation in these measures, particularly when it is done at the same time as the interview.

The approach that is used to collect the biomeasures (mode, location, personnel, equipment) is largely dictated by the specific measures that are collected in the study. The approach is also dictated by cost and the resources available to support the collection of biomeasures in the survey context. We turn to these topics next.

15.4.1 MODE AND LOCATION OF BIOMEASURE COLLECTION

Most of the biomeasures that are collected in surveys, including the surveys highlighted here, require in-person or face-to-face administration. As noted previously,

[6]TILDA offered respondents the option of completing a reduced version of the health assessment at home if they were unable to travel to one of the study's two clinical settings. They found significant differences in the physical and cognitive health status of those who chose to complete the measures in their home. (Kearney et al. 2011)

this is typically carried out either in the participant's home (as in Add Health, ELSA, HRS, WLS, NSHAP, TILDA, and SHARE), in a health facility (TILDA), or in a mobile examination center (NHANES). Home administration limits the range of measures that can be collected, particularly for measures that require large equipment that is not practical to transport or expensive equipment that is not practical to purchase for a large field staff. In some situations, respondents prefer to complete the interview in a public setting, rather than their home, such as a church, library or restaurant. Alternative locations such as this may limit the measures conducted due to space and public health concerns. Collection in a health facility is also advantageous for blood samples, which can be spun and stored at the facility, eliminating complex protocols for packaging and shipping.

There are some exceptions to in-person collection of biomeasures. For example, WLS originally collected saliva samples from participants through the mail. In addition, the HRS collected DBS samples via mail from a sample of individuals who had reported in the survey as having been diagnosed with diabetes. Starting in 2010, WLS participants who did not donate earlier, or whose donation was of insufficient quality or quantity were invited to donate during the in-person interview. The protocol for collecting the saliva varied between leaving the collection kit behind and waiting for the participant to complete the donation on-the-spot.

Most saliva collection techniques are fairly straightforward for participants to self-administer. Both HRS and WLS use an Oragene© collection container. As part of the mail-in protocol for WLS, participants were given instructions to spit into the container until the saliva reached a marked level, seal the cap tightly on the container, and mail the sample to the lab in a pre-addressed, pre-paid mailer.

Blood samples are more difficult to self-administer and not everyone is comfortable with the procedure. In the HRS Diabetes Mail Survey, blood-collection kits (containing lancets, blood collection cards, a sanitary wipe, and bandage) were sent to participants and they were asked to mail the sample to the lab in a pre-addressed, pre-paid mailer.

As with surveys in general, participation rates tend to be lower in mail-based biomeasure collections, although that is not always the case. WLS obtained saliva samples for just under 70% of participants from the 2004 wave (Hauser and Weir 2010). Both mail and in-person collection was used during an NSHAP pretest, which yielded almost equal return rates between the two modes. In the 2008 wave of HRS 85% of participants who were asked provided a saliva sample during the in-person interview. For the HRS Diabetes Mail Survey, blood samples were obtained from 52% of people who were invited to participate in the survey (65% of those who completed the mail survey). This is fairly high for a mail survey and may be explained in large part because the selected participants (who had been diagnosed with diabetes) were accustomed to having their blood checked frequently and, at least in some cases, to monitoring it themselves. Still it is substantially lower than the blood completion rates for the core HRS survey, which range from 80–87%. Another disadvantage of mail collection is that the quality of the samples that are obtained via self-administration is likely to be lower than if an interviewer or medically trained personnel administered the measurement.

On the other hand, mail collection is by far the cheapest option, and may be the only viable one for many studies.

Looking beyond the specific observations generated by the Add Health, ELSA, HRS, WLS, NSHAP, TILDA, and SHARE studies and at the broader literature confirms that saliva is among the easiest biological specimens to self-collect in the context of a decentralized, population-based investigation. This is likely due to a general preference for the self-collection of saliva over other types of fluid specimens such as urine or blood, where issues of privacy and collection complexity come into play (Koka et al. 2008). Saliva collection strategies range from passive drool methods where participants salivate into a vial through a straw to treated cards and cotton swabs. In a recent study with a culturally and socioeconomically diverse population, Fernandes and colleagues (2012) found that through the use of direct text and telephone reminders, participants were quite willing to self-collect and correctly store multiple saliva samples over the course of 3 separate days (93.6% returned at least one sample). There is also evidence emerging from the scant literature on the topic, that various swab techniques such as vaginal, nasal, and buccal cell swabs, can be successfully obtained via self-collection (Akmatov and Pessler 2011, Chernesky et al. 2005, Lindau et al. 2009) and that mailed, home-obtained urine specimens are viable as well (Morre et al. 1999).

When deciding between self-collection versus interviewer-assisted collection of biomeasures, one must weigh a range of pros and cons. On the positive side, self-collection may increase study participation rates as some subjects are disinclined to travel to a clinic site to provide samples of saliva, blood, or urine (Rockett et al. 2004) or may not want people in their homes for such things (Koka et al. 2008). Self-collection is also less expensive but limits the range and complexity of biomeasures that can be collected.

In general, respondent capacity and motivation have some bearing on the mode and location of collection. As mentioned earlier, some respondents may be disinclined to come into a clinical setting for the interview and/or biomeasure collection. Similarly, respondents may be unwilling or unable to follow the necessary instructions for the collection of the relevant biomeasure collection, even if it is something as relatively simple as a passive drool method or buccal swab (though some of the evidence offered above suggests otherwise). Ultimately, the selection of approach requires reasoned consideration of cost, quality, and respondent capacity.

15.4.2 PERSONNEL USED FOR BIOMEASURE COLLECTION

Personnel conducting physical measures and collecting biomarkers vary by study and range from self-collection, trained interviewer or lay-person, or health professionals such as nurses or phlebotomists trained on specific study protocols. There are advantages and disadvantages related to the decision as to who will carry this collection out on a study. The decision is largely based on the location and magnitude of the study, the measures that will be conducted, and the cost and availability of personnel. In some cases it is also dictated by laws concerning who is allowed to collect certain types of specimens.[7] An advantage of using health professionals is that they are familiar with most of the measures and comfortable carrying them out. Additionally, the activities that they carry out are expected of them and consistent with their professional role; as a result, respondents may be quite comfortable having a health professional conduct the measures. This is not necessarily the case with field interviewers. Although biomeasures are becoming more common in surveys, conducting these measurements is a relatively new experience for them. Guyer and colleagues (2009, 2011) and Jaszczak and colleagues (2009) discuss the differences observed among studies that have employed different types of data collectors to collect such measures (i.e., field interviewers, nurses, medical technicians).

15.4.3 EQUIPMENT

We have already touched on the types of equipment that are used in relation to the different measures reviewed above. Depending on the specificity that is desired for a particular measure, however, the equipment requirements may differ. For example, measuring an individual's height, weight, and waist circumference using a tape measure and standard bathroom scale allows for the detection of abdominal obesity, a risk factor for cardiovascular disease, diabetes, and other diseases. However, more nuanced measures of the level and distribution of fat in the body are also possible. For example, percentage of body fat or subcutaneous fat levels can be measured using a wide range of equipment including skin calipers, bioelectrical impedance using specialized scales, dual-energy X-ray absorptiometry (DEXA), and hydrodensitometry weighing. Likewise, peak expiratory flow can be measured using a peak flow meter, a relatively cheap and highly portable device that can be used in the field and administered by a lay interviewer. More detailed measures of the volume of air inspired and expired by the lungs require a spirometer, which is best operated by a medically trained individual.

For any measurement, it is critical that the equipment is in good working order. The relevant devices (e.g., blood pressure monitors, dynamometers, stop watches, scales) should also be calibrated and/or replaced periodically, as recommended by the manufacturer.

15.4.4 COST CONSIDERATIONS

There are multiple cost drivers related to the implementation of collecting biomarkers, as well as the cost of the assays, and respondent incentives for participation. Any costs that will be incurred by a laboratory or external vendor for the processing, assaying and potentially long-term storage of samples should be negotiated during the contract phase. Additionally, a decision must be made as to whether to provide a monetary incentive for participation to respondents and, if so, whether it is pre-paid or conditional upon completion, or attempting to complete, the measure.

[7] In SHARE, field interviewers are not allowed to collect DBS samples from respondents, but they can provide instructions and guidance to the respondent for self-administration of the DBS.

The mode and location of collection and personnel used to collect the biomeasures also have major implications for costs. Most studies include a survey component in addition to the biomeasure component. There are major cost savings if a lay interviewer is able to collect the biomeasures at the time of the interview. This eliminates the need and costs involved in scheduling a separate visit, and likely leads to higher participation rates. Of course whether this is feasible depends on the measures that are being collected and the equipment needed to carry them out.

15.4.5 OTHER CONSIDERATIONS

One consideration that should be taken into account during biomeasure collection is the impact these measures may have on the behavior among panel respondents compared to cross-sectional respondents. For example, the HRS interviews respondents every 2 years and the physical measurements are repeated every 4 years. Respondents may try to improve upon a previous waves' result more so than they would in a cross-sectional study. Anecdotal accounts of this behavior have been noted (e.g., "I've been practicing," "I'm ready this time," "I'll do better this time"). Presumably the impact of this phenomenon would be different for different study populations and study designs.

Another important consideration is the complexity involving the merger of data from multiple sources. Since biological data are not part of the survey instrument, the data analyst ultimately has to merge data from multiple sources to conduct analyses. There are inevitable coding errors that crop up which may affect data quality. For example, IDs may be punched incorrectly for the biomeasures. Strategies to minimize this type of error need to be considered when designing studies employing biomeasures.

15.5 Quality Control

Quality control procedures are important for ensuring high quality data and they can be conducted at many different levels and at various points in time. Measures of quality are introduced in each phase of the study—from interviewer recruitment, hiring and training, to data collection itself and through the post-data collection phase when the biological specimens are analyzed, results reported, and data analyzed.

15.5.1 INTERVIEWER SELECTION, TRAINING PROTOCOLS, AND EFFECTS ON DATA QUALITY

There are key factors to take into account when recruiting individuals to conduct biomeasures. It is critical that the personnel who conduct or collect the measures are comfortable and confident in their ability to do so. Survey organizations that are planning to undertake biomeasure collection are well advised to note this as a requirement in their personnel recruitment materials. It is becoming a best practice among studies that collect biomeasures to use videos of the measures during the interviewer recruitment and/or interviewer training phases. As an example, HRS uses an interviewer recruitment video that prospective applicants are required to view online before applying for a position on the study. The video includes a narrative description and a demonstration of the biomeasure collection emphasizing those measures that interviewers have found to be most challenging to conduct (blood spot collection, walking speed), to gain respondent cooperation (blood spot collection) or due to the sensitivity of the results (blood pressure). Interviewers are asked several questions at the time of their in-person hiring interview to ensure that they have actually watched the video and to answer any questions they may have.

Training is critically important to ensure accuracy and consistency in the administration of measures. One of the first steps in high quality data collection is ensuring that all interviewers have completed the required training and certification or licensing necessary to conduct the measures. This is true for both lay interviewers, as well as for nurses and other medical professionals. Training may include self-study, lectures, and practice sessions. Some studies also require certification on the study-specific protocols to ensure consistent measurement and recording of all measurements conducted, as well as coding of reasons for nonparticipation. At the time of training, data collectors should be provided with clear guidelines on specimen collection and handling, both to reinforce the correct interviewer protocols in order to keep the interviewer safe and to maintain the integrity of the biomeasure samples. It should be considered a best practice to provide interviewers with training and written documentation on the Universal Precautions for the Prevention of Blood Borne Pathogens, the Centers for Disease Control and Prevention guidelines on proper hand washing, first aid tips from the American Red Cross, and information regarding vaccines that should be kept up to date when conducting in-person interviews in respondent's homes. Reinforcing safety measures and standardized protocols in the collection, handling, and shipping of biospecimens will reduce the possibility of error or loss of high quality, analyzable biological samples.

The use of nurses or other health professionals has the advantage that they may already be familiar with many of the biomeasures. However, in this situation it is important that they thoroughly review and practice the specific study protocols, rather than rely on protocols that they use in a clinical setting, as the two protocols may differ. Blood pressure is an example of this. Familiarity with the specific blood pressure cuff used for a study, the position the respondent should be in (seated, both feet flat on floor, legs uncrossed, arm on table), the position the interviewer is in (standing, sitting), the number of measures taken, the amount of time between each measure are all examples of protocols that may vary between the study and clinical settings. Also, if the biomeasure collection is conducted by a third party, or a contracted health care provider, such as a home-health company, clinic or phlebotomists, it is important to determine whether their protocols are suitable for the purposes of the study, or whether they will need to be adapted.

If adapted, additional training of the health care providers on the specific study protocols and forms will be necessary. Data confidentiality and data delivery should be addressed as well. In locations where field interviewers are not allowed to collect DBS from respondents, but can provide instructions and guidance to the respondent, additional training and quality control implications may need to be considered.

Even with highly standardized training and certification procedures, there may be variation across interviewers in the measurements. For example, Sakshaug et al. (2010) found significant between-interviewer variance in consent rates to the physical measures and biomarkers in the HRS, controlling for a range of respondent and interviewer characteristics and survey resistance indicators. The SHARE and ELSA studies have also observed interviewer variability in cooperation rates for the biomeasures, although the level of variation is generally significantly lower in ELSA for those measures that are administered by nurses (Guyer et al. 2009).

These findings reinforce the importance of adequate training and certification, continuous monitoring and feedback to the data collectors, as well as the need for ongoing training, especially if interviewers are requesting consent to participate in these measurements. Likewise, it is recommended that all data collectors who return to a study, in a follow-up year or the next wave of data collection in panel studies for example, complete the study training and certification if a certain period of time has elapsed since they were previously trained or if quality concerns existed previously. Depending on the complexity of the study protocols, or changes since the previous wave of data collection, the full training module may be necessary or a refresher may suffice. HRS and NSHAP both require returning interviewers to complete the full training module, whereas SHARE and ELSA require refresher training for returning interviewers and nurses.

15.5.2 DATA COLLECTION

Quality control is of utmost importance during the data collection phase. Study managers should be expected to generate reports on the collection status, by measurement, frequently throughout data collection. The key components to measure should be determined before data collection in order to accurately collect the necessary information from the onset of data collection. Components to measure include consent rates, completion rates, reasons for exclusion, values outside of expected ranges, and the number and rate of samples collected that are nonanalyzable. These components should be available for the study overall, by study team, by interviewer and/or geographic region, and over time. Trends in these rates by interviewer over time may indicate whether an interviewer needs to be retrained on a specific measurement, retrained in general, or removed from the study. The trends can also help identify high performing interviewers who may be able to provide input and examples to other interviewers on factors related to successful completion of the measurement.

Examples of the types of items monitored and reports generated for HRS, NSHAP, Add Health, and WLS include the following, by phase or component of collection:

Data Collection

- Consent rates—by component (physical measure, blood, saliva), overall, by week, and by interviewer
- Completion rates—by component (physical measure, blood, saliva), overall, by week, and by interviewer
- Refusal rates—by component, by interviewer
- Outliers on key measures (height, weight, waist, blood pressure)
- Rounding errors on certain measures (blood pressure, height, peak flow)

Shipping/Receipt

- Samples received/not received of those expected
- Quality of samples received (all spots filled on blood cards, spots filled properly on blood card, leakage of saliva sample, weight of saliva sample, etc.)
- Shipping delay (field to central office)
- Samples received/not received by laboratory
- Quality of samples received by laboratory
- Shipping delay (central office to laboratory)

Analysis

- Results received from laboratory
- Nonanalyzable samples by type (no sample submitted, date, quantity insufficient, etc.) overall, by week, by interviewer
- Number of blood spots filled by interviewer
- Number of assays obtained per card by interviewer
- Outliers on key measurements (total cholesterol, HbA1c)

Storage

- Whether a sample is stored after analysis (assuming sufficient remaining sample)
- Location of samples stored (freezer, package number)

- Maintenance of freezer temperature and protocol for temperature changes
- Length of time samples have been stored

15.5.3 BIOSPECIMEN STORAGE AND SHELF LIFE, SHIPMENT, AND RECONCILIATION

As indicated by the latter aspect of the previous section, it is important to consider the shipping and storage requirements, both interim and long-term, that each of the biological samples require when planning a study. Thus far, we have referred to blood, saliva, urine, vaginal swabs, and hair samples as examples of biospecimens collected in survey research. This section will focus on storage and shipping requirements for the two biospecimens most commonly collected, blood and saliva.

Shipment of biological samples is dependent on the sample collected, its intended use and the collection location. A primary consideration is the immediate processing and shipping conditions required. For example, saliva samples collected via cheek swabs, the Scope mouthwash technique, or the Oragene© method do not require immediate refrigeration nor do they need to be shipped with cold packs, dry ice, or other cooling agents. However, the amount of time during which the sample remains stable is dependent on the collection method used and the analysis performed. Differences in the stability of salivary samples maintained at room temperature and collected for DNA extraction range from a few days for buccal swabs to weeks for mouthwash salivary samples to years using the Oragene©-Discover collection kit. The effects of extreme temperatures on the stability of samples must be taken into account as well. Additionally, depending on the collection method used, shipping may need to take place quickly after collection so that the sample can be processed by the laboratory within a specific window of time in order to ensure that bacteria does not develop.

Blood samples may require cooling or maintenance of a certain temperature, again depending on the collection method used. Whole blood, collected by a phlebotomist or other trained health professional, must be shipped in cool conditions. DBS samples and blood spot samples collected using the Demecal™ method do not require immediate cooling and can be shipped or mailed in the regular mail. However, more widespread studies are needed to fully evaluate the effect of both temperature and mailing conditions on the stability of DBS samples. In wave 5 of the SHARE data collection conducted in Germany, interviewers were instructed to include temperature strips when mailing the DBS cards in order to determine the highest temperature the card was exposed to during the shipping process. A study of the stability of blood samples collected via the Demecal™ method found that samples were stable for 3 days at 4 °C (39 °F), for 2 to 3 days at room temperature and for 1 day at 37 °C (98.6 °F) (Gootjes et al. 2009). If samples are collected and processed in the same location (i.e., a clinic, lab, or hospital), shipping requirements will not be a concern, however, immediate handling should be taken into account (i.e., need to centrifuge the sample, placement on dry ice as sample is transferred from collection area to laboratory for processing).

Shipping requirements for the samples collected should be discussed both with the vendor from whom the collection supplies are procured as well as with the laboratory conducting the analysis. Shipping conditions should be determined well in advance and monitoring systems should be in place to ensure that samples meet these requirements. Additionally, federal regulations for shipping biohazardous materials must be taken into account. Packaging and labeling requirements may vary for samples shipped via regular post versus those shipped via a private carrier (FedEx, UPS). Leakage of samples is a concern as well as it can result in an insufficient quantity of material to analyze, a degradation of sample, or possibly a biohazard depending on the shipping conditions and degree of leakage.

As with shipping, storage requirements should be considered in the planning phase of biospecimen collection. If the samples are collected and shipped directly to a lab for processing, analysis, and storage, both storage upon sample receipt as well as long-term storage (if required) should be determined ahead of time. If samples are collected, shipped to a central location (survey agency for example) and periodic shipments are then made to a laboratory, storage at all three points in time must be taken into consideration: upon receipt in central location, upon receipt in laboratory, and long-term storage. Repositories are an example of long-term storage options, which allow researchers to store their study samples along with those collected by other researchers.

Upon receipt in a centralized location, samples are typically either stored in refrigerated conditions, if the processing and analysis will take place within a week or less, or in a freezer if the analysis will take place at some later point in time. Samples that are frozen can be maintained either in −30 °C conditions or in −70 °C conditions. The lower temperatures will allow for longer term storage and likely less degradation of samples. There are logistical considerations to take into account regarding storage as well. This includes the amount of storage space required (i.e., size and number of freezers required), space requirements, and availability for the freezers, the need to have a system in place to monitor the internal temperature of the freezers and an alert system when the power fails or the internal temperature drops lower than a prespecified temperature, and ventilation and power requirements for the freezers. Exposure to humidity for DBS samples is often a concern in the shipping and storage process as well. The use of desiccant packs-packs that sustain dryness-when storing blood spot samples can reduce the exposure to humidity.

Recent studies have looked at the stability and degradation of samples exposed to different freeze–thaw cycles as well as the effects of storing samples at different temperatures. In one study, the decay of DBS samples collected for RNA analysis was determined under five different storage conditions: usual transport, room temperature (25 °C), warm (37 °C), refrigerated (8 °C), and frozen (−20 °C). RNA was analyzed and compared to standardized whole blood at one, 28 and 96 days for each of the five conditions. A lower quantity of RNA was detected at 28 days in all samples, regardless of the storage method used. However, the frozen samples had the lowest rate of decay at both 28 and 92 days (Pritsch et al. 2012).

15.6 Ethical and Legal Considerations

Many of the logistical questions raised above must be answered in the context of legal and ethical considerations. For example, while some states allow field interviewers to collect blood from respondents for research purposes, the results of the analyses cannot be mailed to respondents unless a licensed phlebotomist or other medically trained person has collected the blood sample. Likewise, venous blood can be drawn only by a licensed phlebotomist or other health care professional, not by a lay interviewer. There are also respondent burden and consent issues that should be addressed by an institutional review board or an equivalently designated ethics committee. Other ethical and legal issues relate to how the data is disseminated to researchers. Anonymized biomeasure data are usually released as a public-use data product (accessible without restrictions) or as a restricted data product that is accessible only after submitting a formal application and receiving subsequent approval from the data collection agency. In the case of genetic data, further data access restrictions and a more rigorous application process may apply.

15.6.1 INFORMED CONSENT

A necessary prerequisite to collecting biological specimens and other biomeasures is obtaining informed consent from respondents. Informed consent is needed to ensure that respondents are well aware of the risks and benefits of their participation.[8] The consent step can be administered in different ways. In most cases, a consent form is given to respondents to read and sign before any biomeasures are collected. The consent form should contain information about why the specific biomeasures are being requested, how the results of the study will be reported, a description of safeguards to protect the privacy and confidentiality of the collected data, and for biological specimens, how long the samples will be stored. Separate consent forms may be administered for each biomeasure being collected or multiple biomeasures may be grouped into a single consent form. Many studies use separate consent forms for the collection of blood and saliva and a single form for all anthropometric and physical performance measurements. Separate consent may be requested for the collection versus the storage for future analyses of the samples. For example, NSHAP uses separate consent forms for DNA and future storage of remaining specimens. In ELSA, verbal consent is required for the physical measurements and a series of signed consent forms are required for blood and saliva collection, as well as for permission to send blood pressure, lung function, and blood results to the respondent's General Practitioner. In NHANES, a single, signed consent form is required to participate in the full medical examination. A single consent form is also used for SHARE interviews in Germany, on which respondents must tick a box next to each biomeasure that they consent to. However, signed consent is not required for

[8] For a detailed treatment of informed consent procedures and other ethical considerations in health surveys, refer to Chapter 19 in this Handbook.

the collection of grip strength, walking speed, chair stand, and peak flow. Likewise, WLS obtains written consent for the saliva sample and verbal consent for the functioning measures.

The percentage of respondents who consent to (or complete the) biomeasures can vary by the type and perceived sensitivity of the measure being collected. For example, in the HRS, about 90–92% of respondents consent to physical measures, about 83–84% to saliva, and about 80–87% to blood spots (Sakshaug et al. 2010, Ofstedal et al. 2010). In NSHAP, cooperation rates for physical measures range between 93% and 98%, about 90% for saliva, about 85% for blood spots, and about 67% for self-administered vaginal swabs (Jaszczak et al. 2009). In ELSA, among respondents who agreed to a nurse visit, cooperation rates vary between 87 and 98% for physical measures, 69% for saliva, and 81% for blood (Guyer et al. 2011). In TILDA, 99% of respondents who underwent a health assessment consented to blood testing.

Although consent rates to most biomeasures are relatively high, there is still a risk that certain population subgroups are disproportionately less likely to consent to physical measurements. For example, in the HRS, older, Black, and urban residents tend to be less likely to consent to blood than their younger, White, and rural counterparts (Ofstedal et al. 2010, Sakshaug et al. 2010). As a side note, diabetic respondents tend to be significantly more likely to complete the blood measure than nondiabetics, which may be due to having a greater familiarity with blood testing and interest in knowing the results (Sakshaug et al. 2010). Because there are often differences between respondents who cooperate with the biomeasure collection and those who do not, there is a concern that inferences made from biomeasure data may be biased. One way to adjust for bias due to biomeasure nonparticipation is to create adjustment weights using variables that are observed for both participants and nonparticipants, as is done in the HRS (Health and Retirement Study 2011). The advantage of this approach is that a rich source of adjustment variables can be drawn from the survey interview. Variables that are informative of the reasons for nonparticipation (e.g., self-rated functional limitation as a predictor of completing the physical performance assessment) can be especially useful for purposes of bias adjustment.

15.6.2 DNA COLLECTION

Owing to the sensitive nature of DNA, which is unique and identifiable by definition, the informed consent process can be more extensive compared to other biomeasures. The consent form should provide adequate disclosure and education about the risks involved in participation. Moreover, the form should be explicit regarding how the DNA material will be used, how long it will be stored, what other tests may be performed, and how the results will be disseminated. Ethical issues can arise later on when new genetic tests are developed after the materials have been collected. For example, as Weir (2008) points out, a new genetic test that accurately identified the possibility of an inherited disease may carry with it the ethical obligation to notify the respondent as well as any children or nonparticipants about the possibility that they too may be carriers of the inherited disease. Such a notification could be viewed as harmful to the confidentiality of the respondent. Even in less extreme cases, future and unforeseen uses of genetic data may require the survey agency to recontact respondents and seek consent to use the data for additional purposes.

15.6.3 RELAYING RESULTS BACK TO RESPONDENTS

Just as physicians are required to inform patients of exam or test results during or after an office visit, survey studies also carry the ethical responsibility to report results obtained from clinically relevant biomeasures back to respondents. For some biomeasures, the results can be relayed to respondents almost immediately. For example, results from anthropometric and physical performance measurements can be immediately shared with respondents by a medical professional or field interviewer after completion. Respondents whose test result exceeds a clinical threshold indicating a serious health condition (e.g., high blood pressure) are often given informational materials recommending that they see a doctor about their test result. For instance, HRS interviewers are instructed to administer a "high blood pressure card" if the lowest reading obtained is greater than 160 systolic or greater than 110 diastolic. The card provides the respondent with the three readings and suggests that they seek medical attention. NSHAP interviewers copy biomeasure results to a health information booklet that is left with the respondent. The booklet provides guidance on several measures, such as whether their weight (based on BMI) is below, within, or above a healthy weight, and whether their blood pressure was normal, prehypertension or high (Smith et al. 2009). There are other measures for which the results could be reported to respondents on the spot, including glucometer and cholesterol tests. However, survey agencies should consider the burden put on interviewers to report such risk to respondents in situations where glucose or cholesterol levels are indicative of other diseases.

Results that require processing at a laboratory can be relayed back to respondents through different mechanisms. In NSHAP, assays from vaginal swabs and HIV test results are provided to respondents via an anonymous toll-free results hotline (Jaszczak et al. 2009). In HRS, respondents are told that their blood test results for HbA1c and cholesterol will be reported to them by mail. However, not all test results can be relayed back to respondents. Reasons for not reporting results back to respondents could be due to (i) methods of analyzing blood and/or DNA that are not yet determined to be clinically relevant or valid at the time of data collection; (ii) using undetermined methods for future analysis of biomeasures for survey-related research purposes; (iii) and state laws that prohibit results of nonclinical data collections from being shared with respondents; (iv) concerns regarding the impact of the results on the respondent's well-being or behavior. On the SHARE project, the legal regulations of each country must be taken into consideration when determining which results to share with respondents.

15.7 Methods of Data Dissemination

After survey-based biomeasure data are collected, it is important to consider the mechanisms for dissemination. The route one takes depends upon the types of biomeasure data collected and the associated levels of sensitivity and disclosure risk properties.

15.7.1 PUBLIC-USE AND RESTRICTED DATA ACCESS

There are two primary mechanisms for disseminating survey-based biomeasure data: public use and restricted data access. A significant amount of biomeasure data can be accessed freely via the public-use model. In NHANES, nearly all exam and laboratory measurements can be accessed publicly via the project website and can be linked to other survey data. HRS and WLS also release public-use microdata for anthropometric and physical performance measurements, which can be downloaded from the project website. Other survey datasets, such as the ELSA, can be freely downloaded from the project website after registering for an online account.

Although the public-use model offers the widest possible data access to the research community, some biomarker results that are linkable to the corresponding survey data may compromise the anonymity of survey respondents and therefore can only be released as a restricted data product. Access to restricted data is usually possible via a data use agreement between the researcher and the agency responsible for managing the data. In general, the data agency may require researchers to complete a data use agreement form and indicate which data sets they wish to access and provide details about their title and employer/institutional affiliation. A signature is required to ensure that researchers agree to all conditions and stipulations regarding responsible data usage, data-reporting guidelines, and publication of results. This protocol is used by HRS to disseminate blood results and by NSHAP to release the majority of biomeasure data. Once the data use agreement has been approved researchers may still be required to access the data on-site or via a remote access server. In some cases, the data agency may send the restricted data directly to the researcher by mail under the stipulation that they do not distribute the data.

15.7.2 DISSEMINATING GENETIC DATA

There are a few different restricted-data access methods currently being used to disseminate survey-based genetic data to researchers. One method is to store the data internally and invite researchers to access the data onsite via a secure data enclave or Research Data Center (RDC). In NHANES, researchers are invited to submit proposals detailing the study aims, methods, rationale for using the genetic data, and planned outputs, among other items related to their project. Proposals take between 6 and 8 weeks to review. Once approved, researchers may access the genetic data via an RDC or remote access system. WLS has a similar procedure where proposals are reviewed by an advisory panel and approved researchers access the genetic and phenotypic data on a secure server.

Another data sharing option is to store the collected data in a genetic repository for archiving and distribution. For example, the National Institutes of Health operates a genetic repository for NIH-funded genome-wide association studies called *dbGaP*. The HRS, for example, deposits genotype data and a limited set of phenotype measures into this repository. The data are then distributed to Principal Investigators and other researchers who meet specific NIH requirements for access. The application process involves a summary of the proposed research and uses for the requested data and names of the PI and any collaborating investigators at the same institution. Once the application is approved, researchers may download individual-level data that has been de-identified. It is possible to link the genetic data to other survey data not archived in the *dbGaP* system, but this requires a separate application to the original data collection agency (e.g., HRS) in order to obtain a cross-walk reference file.

15.8 Summary

In summary, it is clear that health surveys are increasingly being supplemented with the collection of biomeasures. Survey-based biomeasures offer many potential benefits to researchers across a wide range of disciplines, including the ability to make population-representative inferences, to validate and calibrate survey self-reports, to better understand causal links between environmental exposures, physiological reactions, and health outcomes, and to study the role of genetics on human behavior and health. It is likely that additional uses and benefits of biomeasure collection will be identified in this emerging area of survey research.

There are many different types of biomeasures that one can collect in surveys, such as anthropometric (e.g., height, weight, waist circumference), physical performance measurements (e.g., grip strength, lung function) and biological specimens (e.g., blood, saliva, urine), among others. The choice of which biomeasure(s) to collect depends on many factors, including the study objectives, the location of the biomeasure collection, the person responsible for administering the measures, as well as the portability and cost of the biomeasure equipment. In future, it is likely that additional survey-based biomeasures will be introduced as the size, cost, and invasiveness of the equipment decreases.

The addition of biomeasure collection to health surveys increases both the overall complexity of data collection and the potential for error. In addition to the usual sources of survey error, there is now biomeasure-specific error associated with the selection of the appropriate interviewers and the collection and shipment of biological specimens as well as laboratory error. This increase in error sources necessitates and underscores the importance of incorporating strict quality control protocols into every phase of the survey process.

In addition to the many logistical, methodological, and quality-control challenges of biomeasure collection, there are ethical and legal challenges that must also be addressed. The extent of the informed consent process may differ depending on the particular measure to be collected. Rates of consent to biomeasure participation appear to decrease monotonically as the invasiveness and sensitivity of the measure increases. The collection of DNA in surveys, which is identifiable by definition, also carries with it special ethical, legal, and privacy issues that must be addressed. Moreover, the collection of biomeasures carries with it the ethical responsibility to relay the results back to respondents, but how this is done and whether it is permissible from a legal or data confidentiality standpoint depends on many factors.

Finally, the dissemination of combined survey and biomeasure microdata to the research community is typically handled through public-use and/or restricted data access models. The choice of model depends on the sensitivity and disclosure risk properties of the collected data. While the public-use model provides the widest possible reach to the scientific community, the restricted data access model ensures that extra precautions are made to protect the privacy of respondents by screening researchers and requiring them to agree to specific data use rules. In the case of genetic data, further stipulations and more elaborate screening criteria may be enforced before permission to use these data can be granted.

Acknowledgments

We are grateful to Timothy Johnson and an anonymous reviewer for their valuable comments and thoughtful suggestions. We are also indebted to several people affiliated with many of the surveys mentioned in this chapter for carefully reviewing this manuscript and offering numerous comments, corrections, and suggestions that greatly improved the quality of this manuscript; they include: Joyce Tabor and Ley Killeya-Jones from the National Longitudinal Study of Adolescent Health (Add Health), Meena Kumari from the English Longitudinal Study of Ageing (ELSA), David Weir from the Health and Retirement Study (HRS), Angie Jaszczak, Katie O'Doherty, and Stephen Smith from the National Social Life, Health, and Aging Project (NSHAP), Barbara Schaan from The Survey of Health, Ageing and Retirement in Europe (SHARE), Hilary Cronin from The Irish Longitudinal Study on Ageing (TILDA), and Jennifer Dykema, Ken Croes, and Kerryann DiLoreto from the Wisconsin Longitudinal Study (WLS).

REFERENCES

Akmatov MK, Pessler F. Self-collected nasal swabs to detect infection and colonization: a useful tool for population-based epidemiological studies. Int J Infect Dis 2011;15:e589–e593.

Anderson EE. Ethical considerations in collecting health survey data. In: Johnson T, editor. *Handbook of Health Survey Methods*. 20XX. p 491–515.

Albert MS, Jones K, Savage CR, Berkman L, Seeman T, Blazer D, Rowe JW. Predictors of cognitive change in older persons: Macarthur studies of successful aging. Psychol Aging 1995;10:578–589.

Bath PA, Morgan K. Differential risk factor profiles for indoor and outdoor falls in older people living at home in Nottingham, UK. Eur J Epidemiol 1999;15:65–73.

Blaum CS, Ofstedal MB, Langa KM, Wray LA. Functional status and health outcomes in older Americans with diabetes mellitus. J Am Geriatr Soc 2003;51:745–753.

Brick JM, Kalton G. Handling missing data in survey research. Stat Meth Med Res 1996;5:215–238.

Brunner Huber LR. Validity of self-reported height and weight in women of reproductive age. Matern Child Health J 2007;11:137–144.

Cesari M, Penninx B, Pahor M, Lauretani F, Corsi A, Williams GR, Guralnik JM, Ferrucci L. Inflammatory markers and physical performance in older persons: the InCHIANTI study. J Gerontol A Biol Sci Med Sci 2004;59:242–248.

Chernesky MA, Hook EW III, Martin DH, Lane J, Johnson R, Jordan JA, Fuller D, Willis DE, Fine PM, Janda WM, Schacter J. Women find it easy and prefer to collect their own vaginal swabs to diagnose Chlamydia trachomatis or Neisseria gonorrhoeae infections. Sex Transm Dis 2005;32:729–733.

Cigolle CT, Ofstedal MB, Tian Z, Blaum CS. Comparing models of frailty: the health and retirement study. J Am Geriatr Soc 2009;57:830–839.

Cook NR, Evans DA, Scherr PA, Speizer FE, Taylor JO, Hennekens CH. Peak expiratory flow rate and 5-year mortality in an elderly population. Am J Epidemiol 1991;133:784–794.

Corder EH, Saunders A, Strittmatter W, Schmechel D, Gaskell P, Small G, Roses A, Haines J, Pericak-Vance M. Gene dose of apolipoprotein-E Type 4 allele and the risk of Alzheimer's disease in late-onset families. Science 1993;261:921–923.

Corti MC, Guralnik JM, Salive ME, Sorkin JD. Serum albumin level and physical disability as predictors of mortality in older persons. JAMA 1994;272:1036–1042.

Dagenais GR, Yi Q, Mann JFE, Bosch J, Pogue J, Yusuf S. Prognostic impact of body weight and abdominal obesity in women and men with cardiovascular disease. Am Heart J 2005;149:54–60.

Dargent-Molina P, Favier F, Grandjean H, Baudoin C, Schott AM, Hausherr E, Meunier PJ, Bréart G. Fall-related factors and risk of hip fracture: the EPIDOS prospective study. Lancet 1996;348:145–149.

Davison KK, Ford ES, Cogswell ME, Dietz WH. Percentage of body fat and body mass index are associated with mobility limitations in people aged 70 and older from NHANES III. J Am Geriatr Soc 2002;50:1802–1809.

Dey DK, Rothenberg E, Sundh V, Bosaeus I, Steen B. Waist circumference, body mass index, and risk for stroke in older people: a 15-year old longitudinal population study of 70-year olds. J Am Geriatr Soc 2002;50:1510–1518.

Ducimetiere P, Richard J, Cambien F, Avous P, Jacqueson A. Relationship between adiposity measurements and the incidence of coronary heart disease in a middle aged male population: the Paris prospective study I. Am J Nutr 1985;4:31–38.

Ezzati M, Martin H, Skjold S, Vander HS, Murray CJ. Trends in national and state-level obesity in the USA after correction for self-report bias: analysis of health surveys. J R Soc Med 2006;99:250–257.

Felson DT, Zhang Y, Anthony JM, Naimark A, Anderson JJ. Weight loss reduces the risk for symptomatic knee osteoarthritis in women. Ann Intern Med 1992;116:535–539.

Fernandes A, Skinner ML, Woelfel T, Carpenter T, Haggerty KP. Implementing self-collection of biological specimens with a diverse sample. Field Meth(ePub ahead of print) 2012:1–16.

Ferraro KF, Su Y, Gretebeck RJ, Black DR, Badylak S. Body mass index and disability in adulthood: a 20-year panel study. Am J Public Health 2002;92:834–840.

Folsom AR, Kaye SA, Sellers TA, Hong C, Cerhan JR, Potter JD, Prineas RJ. Body fat distribution and 5-year risk of death in older women. JAMA 1993;269:483–487.

Gavrilova N, Lindau ST. Salivary Sex Hormone Measurement in a National, Population-Based Study of Older Adults. J Gerontol Ser B Psychol Soc Sci 2009;64B: i94–i105.

Giampaou S, Ferrucci L, Cecchi F, Noce C, Poce A, Dima F, Santaquilani A, Vescio M, Menotti A. Hand-grip strength predicts incident disability in non-disabled older men. Age Ageing 1999;28:283–288.

Goldman N, Glei D, Seplaki C, Liu I-W, Weinstein M. Perceived stress and physiological dysregulation. Stress 2005;8:95–105.

Gootjes J, Tel RM, Bergkamp FJ, Gorgels JP. Laboratory evaluation of a novel capillary blood sampling device for measuring eight clinical chemistry parameters and HbA1c. Clin Chim Acta 2009;401:152–157.

Guralnik JM, Ferrucci L, Simonsick EM, Salive ME, Wallace RB. Lower-extremity function in persons over the age of 70 years as a predictor of subsequent disability. N Engl J Med 1995;332:556–561.

Guralnik JM, Simonsick EM, Ferrucci L, Glynn RJ, Berkman LF, Blazer DG, Scherr PA, Wallace RB. A short physical performance battery assessing lower extremity function: association with self-reported disability and prediction of mortality and nursing home admission. J Gerontol 1994;49:M85–M94.

Guyer H, Ofstedal MB. Experiences with using field interviewers vs. trained health personnel to collect biomeasures in social surveys. *European Survey Research Association (ESRA) Conference*; Geneva, Switzerland; 2011.

Guyer H, Ofstedal MB, Lessof C, Cox K, Jürges H. 2009. Collecting physical measure and biomarker data on cross-national studies. *SHARE 2nd International User Conference*; Mainz, Germany; October. Available at http://paa2010.princeton.edu/download.aspx?submissionId=101058.

Hauser RM, Weir D. Recent developments in longitudinal studies of aging in the United States. Demography 2010;47:S111–S130.

Health and Retirement Study. 2011. Data description for the 2010 tracker file, early release, Version 1.0. Survey Research Center, Institute for Social Research, University of Michigan. Available at http://hrsonline.isr.umich.edu/modules/meta/tracker/desc/trk2010.pdf.

Himes CL. Obesity, disease, and functional limitation in later life. Demography 2000;37:73–82.

Hyman B, Gomez-Isla T, Briggs M, Chung H, Nichols S, Kohour F, Wallace R. Apolipoprotein E and cognitive change in an elderly population. Ann Neurol 1996; 40:55–66.

Jaszczak A, Lundeen L, Smith S. Using non-medically trained interviewers to collect biomeasures in a national in-home survey. Field Meth 2009a;21:26–48.

Jenkins KR. Obesity's effects on the onset of functional impairment among older adults. Gerontologist 2004a;44:206–216.

Jenkins KR. Body weight change and physical functioning among young old adults. J Aging Health 2004b;16:248–266.

Jaszczak A, Lundeen K, Smith S. Using nonmedically trained interviewers to collect biomeasures in a national in-home survey. Field Meth 2009b;21:26–48.

Jylhä M, Guralnik JM, Balfour J, Fried LP. Walking difficulty, walking speed, and age as predictors of self-rated health: the women's health and aging study. J Gerontol Ser A Biol Med Sci 2001;56A:M609–M617.

Kearney PM, Cronin H, O'Regan C, Kamiya Y, Whelan BJ, Kenny RA. Comparison of centre and home-based health assessments: early experience from the Irish longitudinal study on ageing (TILDA). Age Ageing 2011;40:85–90.

Koka S, Beebe TJ, Merry SP, DeJesus RS, Berlanga LD, Weaver AL, Wong DT. Towards patient-centered diagnosis: patient preferences for giving saliva, urine, or blood for clinical testing and research. J Am Dent Assoc 2008;139:735–740.

Kuczmarski MF, Kuczmarski RJ, Najjar M. Effects of age on validity of self-reported height, weight, and body mass index: findings from the Third National Health and Nutrition Examination Survey, 1988-1994. J Am Diet Assoc 2001;101:28–34.

Lapidus L, Bengtsson C, Larsson B, Pennert K, Rybo E, Sjostrom L. Distribution of adipose tissue and risk of cardiovascular disease and death: a 12 year follow up of participants in the population study of women in Gothenburg, Sweden. Br Med J 1984;289:1257–1261.

Larsson B, Svardsudd K, Welin L, Wilhelmsen L, Bjorntorp P, Tibblin G. Abdominal adipose tissue distribution, obesity, and risk of cardiovascular disease and death: 13 Year follow up of participants in the study of men born in 1913. Br Med J 1984;288:1401–1404.

Laukkanen P, Heikkinen E, Kauppinen M. Muscle strength and mobility as predictors of survival in 75–84 year-old people. Age Ageing 1995;24:468–473.

Launer LJ, Harris T, Rumpel C, Madans J. Body mass index, weight change, and risk of mobility disability in middle-aged and older women. JAMA 1994;271:1093–1098.

Lindau ST, Hoffmann JN, Lundeen K, Jaszczak A, McClintock MK, Jordan JA. Vaginal self-swab specimen collection in a home-based survey of older women: methods and applications. J Gerontol Soc Sc 2009;64B:106–118.

Lindau ST, McDade TW. Minimally invasive and innovative Methods for Biomeasure Collection in Population-Based research. In: Weinstein M, Vaupel JW, Wachter KW, editors. *Biosocial Surveys*. National Research Council (US) Committee on Advances in Collecting and Utilizing Biological Indicators and Genetic Information in Social Science Surveys. Washington, DC: National Academies Press (USA); 2008. p 251–277.

Lupien S, Gaudreau S, Sharma S, Nair NPV, Hauger RL, Meaney MJ. The effects of a psychological stress on memory performance in healthy elderly subjects: relationships with actual and past cortisol history. *International Society of Psychoneuroendocrinology Abstracts*; 1995.

McDade TW, Williams S, Snodgrass JJ. What a drop can do: dried blood spots as a minimally invasive method for integrating biomarkers into population-based research. Demography 2007;44:899–925.

McKeigue PM, Shah B, Marmot MG. Relation of central obesity and insulin resistance with high diabetes prevalence and cardiovascular in South Asians. Lancet 1991;337:382–386.

Melzer D, Lan TY, Guralnik JM. The predictive validity for mortality of the index of mobility-related limitation: results from the EPESE study. Age Ageing 2003;32:619–625.

Morre SA, van Valkengoed IGM, de Jong A, Boeke AJP, van Eijk JTM, Meijer CJLM, van den Brule AJC. Mailed, home-obtained urine specimens: a reliable screening approach for detecting asymptomatic Chlamydia trachomatis infections. J Clin Microbiol 1999;37:976–908.

Must A, Spadano J, Coakley EH, Field AE, Colditz G, Dietz WH. The disease burden associated with overweight and obesity. JAMA 1999;282:1523–1529.

Ofstedal MB, Guyer H, Sakshaug JW, Couper MP. Changes in biomarker participation rates in the HRS. Presented at the Panel Survey Methods Workshop; Mannheim, Germany; 2010.

O'Mahoney PRA, Wong DT, Ray JG. Retinal vein occlusion and traditional risk factors for atherosclerosis. Arch Ophthalmol 2008;126:692–699.

Ostir GV, Markides KS, Black SA, Goodwin JS. Lower body functioning as a predictor of subsequent disability among older Mexican Americans. J Gerontol Ser A Biol Med Sci 1998;53:M491–M495.

Pritsch M, Wieser A, Soederstroem V, Poluda D, Eshetu T, Hoelscher M, Schubert S, Shock J, Loescher T, Berens-Riha N. Stability of gametocyte-specific pfs25-mRNA in dried blood spots on filter paper subjected to different storage conditions. Malar J 2012;11:138.

Rantanen T, Guralnik J, Foley D, Masaki K, Leveille S, Curb D, White L. Midlife hand grip strength as a predictor of old age disability. JAMA 1999;281:558–560.

Rockett JC, Buck GM, Lynch CD, Perreault SD. The value of home-based collection of biospecimens in reproductive epidemiology. Environ Health Perspect 2004;112:94–104.

Ryff CD, Singer BH. Social environments and the genetics of aging: advancing knowledge of protective health mechanisms. J Gerontol Ser B Psychol Soc Sci 2005;60B:12–23.

Sacco RL, Benjamin EJ, Broderick JP, Dyken M, Easton JD, Feinberg WM, Goldstein LB, Gorelick PB, Howard G, Kittner SJ, Manolio TA, Whisnant JP, Wolf PA. American Heart Association Prevention Conference: IV: prevention and rehabilitation of stroke: risk factors. Stroke 1997;28:1507–1517.

Sakshaug JW, Couper MP, Ofstedal MB. Characteristics of physical measurement consent in a population-based survey of older adults. Med Care 2010;48:64–71.

Sayer AA, Syddall HE, Martin HJ, Dennison EM, Roberts HC, Cooper C. Is Grip Strength Associated with Health-Related Quality of Life? Findings from the Hertfordshire cohort study. Age Ageing 2006;35:409–415.

Seeman TE, Charpentier PA, Berkman LF, Tinetti ME, Guralnik JM, Albert M, Blazer D, Rowe JW. Predicting changes in physical performance in a high-functioning elderly cohort: MacArthur studies of successful aging. J Gerontol 1994;49(3):M97–108.

Schenker N, Borrud LG, Burt VL, Curtin LR, Flegal KM, Hughes J, Johnson CL, Looker AC, Mirel L. Multiple imputation of missing dual-energy X-ray absorptiometry data in the national health and nutrition examination survey. Stat Med 2011;30:260–276.

Schenker N, Raghunathan TE, Bondarenko I. Improving on analyses of self-reported data in a large-scale health survey by using information from an examination-based survey. Stat Med 2010;29:533–545.

Smith JP. Healthy bodies and thick wallets: the dual relation between health and economic status. J Econ Perspect 1999;13:145–166.

Smith S, Jaszczak A, Graber J, Lundeen K, Leitsch S, Wargo E, O'Muircheartaigh C. Instrument development, study design implementation, and survey conduct for the National Social Life, Health, and Aging Project. J Gerontol Psychol Sci 2009;64:120–129.

Snih S, Markides K, Ray L, Ostir G, Goodwin J. Handgrip strength and mortality in older Mexican Americans. J Am Geriatr Soc 2002;50:1250–1256.

Taylor AW, Dal Grande E, Gill TK, Chittleborough CR, Wilson DH, Adams RJ, Grant JF, Phillips P, Appleton S, Ruffin RE. How valid are self-reported height and weight? A comparison between CATI self-report and clinic measurements using a large cohort study. Aust N Z J Public Health 2006;30:238–46.

Thoits PA. Stress, coping, and social support processes: where are we? What next? J Health Soc Behav 1995;35:53–79.

Tourangeau R, Rips LJ, Rasinski K. *The Psychology of Survey Response*. Cambridge University Press; 2000.

Tourangeau R, Smith T. Asking sensitive questions: the impact of data collection, question format, and question context. Public Opin Q 1996;60:275–304.

Turra CM, Goldman N, Seplaki CL, Weinstein M, Glei DA, Lin Y-H. Determinants of mortality at older ages: the role of biological markers of chronic disease. Popul Dev Rev 2005;31:677–701.

Tzourio C. Hypertension, cognitive decline, and dementia: an epidemiological perspective. Dialog Clin Neurosci 2007;9:61–70.

United States Renal Data System (*USRDS*). *Annual Data Report*. Bethesda, MD: National Institute of Diabetes and Digestive and Kidney Diseases, National Institutes of Health, U.S. Department of Health and Human Services; 2007.

Wang ZM, Patterson CM, Hills AP. A comparison of self-reported and measured height, weight and bmi in Australian adolescents. Aust N Z J Public Health 2002;26:473–478.

Weber PS, Cass SP. Clinical assessment of postural stability. Am J Otolarynol 1993;14:566–569.

Weinstein M, Goldman N, Hedley A, Lin Y-H, Seeman T. Social linkages to biological markers of health among the elderly. J Biosoc Sci 2003;35:433–453.

Weinstein M, Willis R. Stretching social surveys to include bioindicators: possibilities for the health and retirement study, experience from the Taiwan study of the elderly. In: Finch C, Vaupel J, Kinsella K, editors. *Cells and Surveys: Should Biological Measures be Included in Social Science Research?* Washington, DC: National Research Council, National Academy Press; 2000. p 250–275.

Weir DR. Elastic powers: the integration of biomarkers into the health and retirement study. In: Weinstein M, Vaupel JW, Wachter K, editors. *Biosocial Surveys*. National Research Council. Washington, DC: The National Academies Press; 2008. p 78–95.

Zhou X, Dibley MJ, Cheng Y, Ouyang X, Yan H. Validity of self-reported weight, height and resultant body mass index in Chinese adolescents and factors associated with errors in self-reports. BMC Public Health 2010;10:190.

ONLINE RESOURCES

Links to each survey project described in Table 1 are provided below:

Add Health: www.cpc.unc.edu/projects/addhealth.

ELSA: www.ifs.org.uk/elsa/.

HRS: http://hrsonline.isr.umich.edu/.

NHANES: www.cdc.gov/nchs/nhanes.htm.

NSHAP: www.norc.org/Research/Projects/Pages/national-social-life-health-and-aging-project.aspx.

SHARE: www.share-project.org.

TILDA: www.tilda.tcd.ie/.

WLS: www.ssc.wisc.edu/wlsresearch/.

A link to the dbGaP genetic repository for NIH-funded genome-wide association studies is: www.ncbi.nlm.nih.gov/gap.

CHAPTER SIXTEEN

Collecting Contextual Health Survey Data Using Systematic Observation

Shannon N. Zenk
Health Systems Science Department, College of Nursing, University of Illinois at Chicago, Chicago, IL, USA

Sandy Slater
Health Policy and Administration Division, School of Public Health, University of Illinois at Chicago, Chicago, IL, USA

Safa Rashid
Health Systems Science Department, College of Nursing, University of Illinois at Chicago, Chicago, IL, USA

16.1 Introduction

Over the past decade, understanding the impact of the environments where people live, work, and play has become a major focus of research. This is consistent with the recognition of the role that social factors play in shaping health and contributing to health disparities (CSDH 2008). Research has established that health outcomes differ across *ecologic settings*, including schools, workplaces, and neighborhoods. For example, Diez Roux and colleagues found that residing in a socioeconomically disadvantaged neighborhood was associated with a 70–90%

Handbook of Health Survey Methods, First Edition. Edited by Timothy P. Johnson.

increased risk of coronary heart disease in Whites and a 30–50% higher risk among African-Americans (Diez Roux et al. 2001). A large body of research has also revealed numerous features of the physical and social environments of ecologic settings that impact health. With regard to neighborhoods, for example, research has documented that residing in a neighborhood with greater availability of healthy foods is associated with better dietary quality and lower body weight among local residents (Franco et al. 2009, Larson et al. 2009, Zenk et al. 2009). Research has established that such setting differences in and effects on health outcomes are independent of the characteristics of individuals within these settings (e.g., age, gender, socioeconomic status), or so-called "compositional" differences. These studies highlight how where you live can affect your health. Findings like these are documented for other types of ecologic settings as well. Yet there is a need to continue to develop methods to identify the underlying environmental factors that account for these health inequalities.

Investigators have employed a range of methods to collect contextual data on the environments of ecologic settings, not only self-report surveys, but also administrative sources and increasingly observational methods, or *systematic observation*. Systematic observation has emerged as a popular complement to health survey data, aided by advances of the Project on Human Development in Chicago Neighborhoods (Raudenbush and Sampson 1999), and can also be used independently of health surveys to answer questions of interest related to ecologic settings. It involves trained observers systematically and visually assessing predefined features of a setting using a standardized instrument. Systematic observation helps describe setting environments in terms of the presence, quantity, and quality of features (Brownson et al. 2009). Because systematic observation must include rules that allow replication, operational definitions for each item on the instrument are essential (Raudenbush and Sampson 1999, Reiss 1976). Other commonly used terms for systematic observation in the literature include "direct observation," "environmental audit," "environmental scan," "windshield survey," and "systematic social observation" (Schaefer-McDaniel et al. 2010b). While still in its infancy, research utilizing systematic observation is growing rapidly and has the potential to provide new insights that would not have been possible otherwise.

The purpose of this chapter is to describe the use of systematic observation to collect contextual information on ecologic settings. We begin by providing an overview of advantages and disadvantages of this method compared to others and major methodological considerations in conducting systematic observation. These include considerations for selecting an instrument or developing one (*what*); sampling (*where*); observer training; data collection approaches (i.e., direct, virtual), modes (*how*; e.g., paper forms, computer-assisted data collection, videotaping, still photography), and *who* should conduct the observations and *when*; reliability and validity assessment; and data analysis. While the information is applicable to a range of ecologic settings and health outcomes, we draw heavily on literature on neighborhoods and obesity risk to illustrate the principles and procedures. We then provide two examples of health studies in which systematic observation was used. The first study utilized systematic observation to examine associations between the neighborhood built environment and health survey data on obesity among adolescents. The second study employed systematic observation to evaluate the impact of a policy change on healthy food availability and prices at retail stores. We conclude with a summary of our key points.

16.2 Background

16.2.1 ADVANTAGES AND DISADVANTAGES

The use of systematic observation to collect information on ecologic settings has advantages and disadvantages when compared to other commonly used methods (surveys and administrative data). Some of these are summarized in Table 16.1. For example, advantages of systematic observation include avoidance of same-source bias, providing "objective" or at least independent assessment of the ecologic setting separate from a survey respondent's own assessment. However, systematic observation may be less effective in assessing some theoretical constructs, particularly related to the social environment (e.g., sense of community, discrimination). Compared to administrative data, systematic observation provides a better opportunity to capture the quality of environmental features (e.g., sidewalk maintenance) as compared to administrative data that may capture only its presence. On the other hand, systematic observation can capture only what is visible and is more resource intensive to collect. Ultimately, with research often showing low levels of agreement between and different health effects of "objective" and perceived measures of the environment (Ball et al. 2008, Hoehner et al. 2005), systematic observation can provide information that is not possible to obtain through other methods. Weaknesses associated with the approach can generally be reduced by combining it with other approaches.

16.2.2 INSTRUMENT SELECTION AND DESIGN (*WHAT*)

After settling on a theory or conceptual framework that informs how the setting's environment may influence the health outcome of interest, instrument selection is one of the first major decisions in conducting systematic observation of an ecologic setting. In many fields, numerous instruments are now available. Choice of instrument should be guided by what you want to measure (research question, ecologic setting, health outcome of interest, underlying theory) as well as the broader social context and project resources. As with survey measures, review of findings related to the instrument's reliability and validity is important. Instruments are typically designed for particular settings: childcare centers (Ward et al. 2008), schools (Baglio et al. 2004, McKenzie et al. 1991), workplaces (Oldenburg et al. 2002), restaurants (Saelens et al. 2007), food stores (Zenk et al. 2012b), parks (Bedimo-Rung et al. 2006), indoor recreation facilities (Lee et al. 2005), and neighborhood streets (Sampson and Raudenbush 1999), for example. Some instruments measure a wide range of setting features thought to influence health, while others were developed for specific health outcomes (e.g., physical

TABLE 16.1 Advantages and Disadvantages of Systematic Observation Relative to Surveys and Administrative Data to Characterize Ecologic Settings

Systematic Observation Versus Surveys		Systematic Observation Versus Administrative Data	
Advantages	Disadvantages	Advantages	Disadvantages
• Avoids same-source bias • Avoids social desirability • Can capture theoretical constructs or phenomena that are difficult for individuals to describe • Particularly effective for temporally stable phenomena	• Less effective for some theoretical constructs, particularly those that require perceptions or subjective experiences (e.g., trust, cohesion, discrimination) • Potential for misinterpretation of what is seen • Bias toward visible and readily observable • "Snapshot" in time	• Able to determine theoretical constructs of interest • Greater control over timing of data • Can assess quality, not just presence and quantity	• Generally more resource intensive to collect • Only captures what is visible

Source: Brownson et al. (2009), Dunn et al. (2010), Parsons et al. (2010), Schaefer-McDaniel et al. (2010a and 2010b), Zenk et al. (2007).

activity, smoking) (Pikora et al. 2002, Shareck et al. 2012). While a critique of observational instruments to date is that many are a-theoretical, some instruments are rooted in theories, with the broken window theory the most common for systematic observation of neighborhood streets, for example (Sampson and Raudenbush 1999, Schaefer-McDaniel et al. 2010b, Shareck et al. 2012). Instrument selection should also be guided by the broader social context (e.g., city, country) because items may have different meanings or not be relevant depending on the social context (Paquet et al. 2010, Zenk et al. 2007). Researchers have found, for example, that measures of social disorder and territoriality, commonly included in systematic observation instruments of neighborhood streets in U.S. cities, may not be applicable in Toronto or Vancouver, Canada (Paquet et al. 2010, Parsons et al. 2010). Project resources can also affect instrument selection as instruments vary in scope, length, and complexity and thus have different demands in terms of completion.

Given the considerations earlier, researchers must ultimately decide whether to use or adapt an existing instrument or develop a new instrument. Whether instruments are available and appropriate for the research question, ecologic setting and social context, outcome, theory, and resources are major factors in this decision. Designing a new instrument is time-intensive, but previous efforts have shown that content and operational definitions should be informed by theory, formative research (e.g., informal observations, focus groups or interviews with key stakeholders, expert panel review), and extensive pilot-testing (Schaefer-McDaniel et al. 2010a, Zenk et al. 2005). Developing instruments in partnership with members of ecologic settings of interest (e.g., community members) can help to ensure their relevance for the ecologic setting and broader social context and ultimately improve validity (Zenk et al. 2005).

16.2.3 SAMPLING (*WHERE*)

Researchers conducting systematic observation must weigh different options for sampling ecologic settings. In small-scale studies, it is common to conduct observations of a complete census of ecologic settings. In studies conducted in specific neighborhoods or small cities, for example, it may be possible to observe all schools or parks. Conducting observations at all ecologic settings within the study area preserves the most flexibility for researchers to examine the data later, including aggregating the data to report results. However, in larger scale settings or studies with limited resources, it may not be feasible to observe all ecologic settings in the study area given the involved time and costs. Thus, sampling strategies have received increased attention in research utilizing systematic observation. The needed sample size for ecologic settings depends on the research question, concepts of interest for the ecologic setting, and amount of variability. Using hierarchical modeling techniques to estimate the reliability of measures of physical and social disorder at the neighborhood level, for example, Raudenbush and colleagues demonstrated that more street segments were needed to reliably estimate social disorder (e.g., people selling drugs, a measure with low prevalence) than physical disorder (e.g., presence of cigarette butts or litter, measures with higher prevalence) (Raudenbush and Sampson 1999). However, the relevant information for other concepts and ecologic settings may not be known in advance. Stratified sampling is increasingly common. A study in Houston, TX found, for example, that all arterial street segments, but only a sample of 25% of the residential street segments, were sufficient to represent the pedestrian-built environment (e.g., sidewalk presence, observer ratings of attractiveness) (McMillan et al. 2010). Similar to determining the sample size for health surveys, power calculations may be useful to determine how many ecologic settings are sufficient to answer a research question of interest but have not been commonly used to date (Raudenbush and Sampson 1999) and are facilitated by publicly available software, such as Optimal Design (Raudenbush 2011).

16.2.4 OBSERVER TRAINING

As discussed in more depth later in the chapter, systematic observation depends on consistency of ratings across observers and over time. Observer training is a principle way to achieve this consistency (Zenk et al. 2007). A major focus of training is detailed instruction and explanation of the instrument items and operational definitions. Training also typically covers background information on the study, data collection procedures, technical issues, and guidelines specific to working in the ecologic setting (e.g., safety, interactions with employees of the setting). Researchers employ a range of strategies to help observers learn instrument content and operational definitions: lectures, imagery to illustrate items and response categories for items measured on Likert scales (Boarnet et al. 2006), and practice with debriefing. Practice can include the use of imagery in the "classroom," but on-site practice is essential for studies conducting direct observation (see Section 16.3.1). Some studies recommend using a certification process to help assure observers are sufficiently proficient in conducting observations (Caughy et al. 2001, Laraia et al. 2006, Zenk et al. 2007). This can consist of an observer achieving a high level of agreement (e.g., 80%) on practice observations with a trainer or other designated "gold standard." Studies using technology, such as handheld computer or cameras, require training on these elements. A study utilizing bicycles for data collection, for example, highlighted the need for training in areas such as riding technique, attire, and street hazards (Kwate and Saldaña 2011). The length of observer training varies and may depend on the length and complexity of the instrument.

16.3 Data Collection

16.3.1 APPROACHES AND MODES (*HOW*)

There are a number of methodological issues to consider in determining how to collect observational data. A variety of approaches (direct including on foot, automobile, bicycle; virtual) and modes (paper forms, computer-assisted data collection, videotaping, still photography) are used. Direct observation is a common approach that involves observers visiting ecologic settings in person. In studies of many types of settings, on-foot direct observation is the only feasible option. Yet, multiple data collection modes are possible, with studies most frequently using paper forms (which may be scannable) or computer-assisted data collection (e.g., handheld computers, smart phones) on site to record observations (Clifton et al. 2007, Hoehner et al. 2005, Zenk et al. 2007). Paper forms are simplest to implement, but collecting data via handheld computer may reduce turnaround time and possibly improve data quality (Gravlee et al. 2006, Zenk et al. 2007). Other studies use videotaping (Sampson and Raudenbush 1999) or still photography (Yancey et al. 2009) with the images coded later according to items on an instrument. While their appeal stems in part from having a permanent record that can be reexamined, videotaping and photography may raise suspicion in public settings and may require permission in private settings. Furthermore, it is important to note that use of technology (e.g., cameras, handheld computers) for data collection demands additional observer training time, as well as financial and administrative resources.

Some ecologic settings present opportunities beyond on-foot data collection. In studies collecting data on neighborhood streets, for example, researchers have most commonly conducted observations on-foot, but have also collected data in automobiles (Sampson and Raudenbush 1999) or on bicycles (Kwate and Saldaña 2011). Advantages of on-foot data collection over automobile include that it allows a 360° view of the area (Caughy et al. 2001) and permits bystanders to ask questions. Data collection via bicycle shares some of these advantages, with researchers arguing that it is also less likely to alter phenomena by virtue of observing it than on-foot observation (Kwate and Saldaña 2011). Faster data collection and enhanced observer comfort and safety are cited as advantages of data collection via automobile and bicycle over on foot. However, these approaches to data collection typically restrict researchers to videotaping as the mode of data collection.

Virtual observation is emerging as a quicker, less-expensive alternative to direct observation (Badland et al. 2010, Clarke et al. 2010, Rundle et al. 2011). Virtual observation involves using Google Street View (www.google.com/streetview), a library of video footage captured by cars driven down streets in select cities, as an alternative source of data on neighborhood streets and outdoor areas, such as parks. Similar to videotapes or still photos, images from Google Street View are coded at a computer screen using an instrument designed for systematic observation. Researchers have found high agreement between direct and virtual observations for many types of measures (Badland et al. 2010, Clarke et al. 2010, Rundle et al. 2011). Disadvantages of virtual observation include that images are available only for some locations, the timing of the imagery (generally unpublished) and study may not match (this is particularly problematic for temporally variable features), and image quality and resolution may make it less reliable for small or detailed features.

16.3.2 *WHO* CONDUCTS OBSERVATIONS AND *WHEN*

Implementing the data collection for the sampled ecologic settings (*where*) using the selected instrument (*what*) also requires decisions regarding *who* should perform the observations and *when*. We focus our discussion on those decisions related to direct observation. With regard to *who* should conduct the systematic observation, researchers have typically hired undergraduate or graduate students, but have also hired local community members (Brownson et al. 2009, Hoehner et al. 2006, Zenk et al. 2005, Zenk et al. 2012b). When conducted in conjunction with face-to-face health surveys administered in the ecologic setting (e.g., respondents' homes, schools), researchers are faced with the decision of whether observations should be conducted by interviewers while in the field or by a separate group of noninterviewers. Having interviewers conduct the observations while in the field may reduce costs. However, learning both the survey and observation instrument and their associated protocols may be taxing for interviewers. Certifying individuals for data collection would involve assuring they are equally proficient in conducting the interviews and observations. Furthermore, while some skills that make a good interviewer also make a good observer (e.g., attention to detail, organization), there are differences. An interviewer, for example, needs strong verbal communication skills while an observer needs visual acuity. Ultimately, the decision might be based in part on scope of the project and the complexity of the observational instrument.

The decision to engage members of ecologic settings (e.g., community members), students, interviewers, or others raises a variety of insider/outsider issues (Schaefer-McDaniel et al. 2010a, Zenk et al. 2005) (e.g., point of reference, safety, trust). Engaging community members or other "insiders" in data collection can take advantage of local knowledge, strengthen capacity, assist in gaining access to ecologic settings with gatekeepers (e.g., schools, stores), and enhance the likelihood that findings will be applied to bring about change (Hoehner et al. 2006, Zenk et al. 2005). However, it is important to consider what support these individuals may need to conduct systematic observation. For example, some may have additional training needs as compared with students (e.g., reading nutrition labels on food packages at stores, calculating prices at restaurants, utilizing technology) that need to be factored into the training and data collection timelines. Researchers engaging community members may also benefit from simplified observational instruments that were designed specifically for use by individuals without specialized knowledge with the subject area (Hoehner et al. 2006).

Whether to conduct observations singly or in pairs is another decision that researchers face. Assessing ecologic settings in pairs enhances observer comfort and minimizes any safety concerns. Observations may be recorded independently by each observer or arrived at by consensus between the two observers. Independent observations allows for interrater reliability assessment (discussed in more detail later). However, conducting ratings in pairs raises costs and thus should be done thoughtfully, such as in settings where safety concerns are anticipated or periodically for a subset of settings to enable interrater reliability assessment.

Another decision is *when* to conduct the systematic observation. Researchers need to consider the effect of the timing of observations on the collected data for many ecologic settings. The time of day, time of year (e.g., month, season), and timing relative to scheduled events when data are collected can affect assessments. For example, when observing parks, visible signs of social disorder (prostitution, drug dealing) may vary by time of day, more individuals may be seen during the summer months, and more litter may be present before a regularly scheduled garbage collection or after a popular community event. Researchers often control for these temporal effects in the data collection protocol. In a study of neighborhood streets, for example, Caughy and colleagues collected all data in late summer between 9:30 AM and 3:30 PM (Caughy et al. 2001). However, it is also possible to adjust for these factors during analysis. Raudenbush and colleagues, for example, adjusted for the time of day that observations were conducted on neighborhood streets when constructing scales of social and physical disorder (Raudenbush and Sampson 1999). In another study, Shareck and colleagues avoided data collection on garbage collection days (Shareck et al. 2012).

16.4 Reliability and Validity Assessment

Evaluating the reliability and validity of measures of ecologic settings derived from systematic observation is important to determine their quality. With psychometrics as the parallel in health survey research, the reliability and validity of measures of ecologic settings has been referred to as *ecometrics* (Raudenbush and Sampson 1999). As mentioned earlier, the consistency of ratings across observers and over time is essential when conducting systematic observation in order to ensure that any differences found across settings or over time are not due to variations in implementation among observers or over time (Zenk et al. 2012b). Interrater reliability is the primary type of reliability assessed (Brownson et al. 2009). Measures that are not valid may yield inappropriate conclusions. With too few extant studies rigorously testing and reporting in detail the ecometric properties, particularly validity, of their instruments, this should be a major focus of future research.

16.4.1 INTERRATER AND TEST–RETEST RELIABILITY

Interrater reliability is the extent to which the same results are obtained by different observers. Many studies have obtained high interrater reliability for the vast majority of their items (see Brownson and Shaefer for summaries). Among measures of neighborhood settings, researchers have documented lower interrater reliability for physical disorder and safety-related items as compared to land use and street characteristics, for items measuring the physical environment than the social environment, for items assessing phenomena that were large/easy to see than small/difficult to see, and for items that required judgments on quantity or quality as compared to those that did not (Brownson et al. 2009, Zenk et al. 2007).

Clearly, well-developed operational definitions for instrument items and thorough observer training are essential for promoting high interrater reliability. Zenk and colleagues have successfully used multiple training strategies to promote interrater reliability in studies of neighborhood streets and food stores: detailed instructions and operational definitions of instrument items, multiple practice opportunities in the field in groups and individually followed by group debriefings, ongoing feedback on group and individual performance as assessed by inter-rater reliability results, and certification based on individual interrater reliability results (Izumi et al. 2011, Zenk et al. 2007). Researchers have typically assessed interrater reliability by comparing results of two or more observers for the same ecologic setting or less commonly results of each observer to a "gold standard" rating of a research staff member. Ideally the observations should be conducted at the same time to minimize any problems with changing conditions. Observations conducted at different times may increase the likelihood for temporally unstable items (e.g., amount of litter, presence of children, price of milk) such that any discrepancies between observers may be due to changes in the item itself, rather than inconsistencies in implementation across observers. Studies to date have typically evaluated interrater reliability before data collection begins or at the beginning of study. However, "drift" or lack of consistency in observations over time is a common concern in studies involving observers. Therefore, evaluating interrater reliability based on data collected throughout the field period can provide a more accurate estimate of interrater reliability.

Test–retest reliability is the extent to which the same results are obtained by a single observer over a short period of time. Test–retest reliability is less commonly assessed for systematic observation measures than interrater reliability. It is important to note that test–retest reliability results may reflect change in the measurement procedure or "real" change in the phenomenon for items that are temporally unstable. Deciding the length of time between observations can be challenging. Findings can be affected by the length of time between observations, with longer intervals between observations increasing the likelihood of actual change in conditions for temporally unstable items. Some researchers have allowed the length of time to vary, while others have used a consistent timeframe. For example, when assessing the test–retest reliability of observations of food availability at retail stores, Glanz and colleagues conducted observations between 7 and 28 days apart, while Zenk and colleagues conducted observations exactly 2 weeks apart (Glanz et al. 2007, Zenk et al. 2010).

Raudenbush and colleagues' multilevel approach to reliability testing that extended typical item response models was a major innovation in the field. Exciting new advancements in the field include use of generalizability analyses and decision studies to quantify how much of the measurement error is attributable to differences in ratings across observers and over time (Shareck et al. 2012). Applying such an approach in a study of streets in four Montreal, Canada neighborhoods, Shareck and colleagues were able to determine which items had (i) good reliability, (ii) low interrater reliability, and (iii) poor test–retest reliability, as well as which items (iv) could not be measured with precision (Shareck et al. 2012). Such results are informative for determining appropriate corrective actions (Shareck et al. 2012, Zenk et al. 2007). Low interrater reliability suggests improved operational definitions or more thorough training are needed. Poor test–retest reliability may also point to the need for improved definitions and training. For temporally unstable items, it may indicate the need for multiple observations, to develop new indicators with greater temporal stability, or to use alternative methods to capture the phenomenon. Items with low interrater reliability and test–retest reliability suggest that any of the earlier corrective strategies are needed.

16.4.2 VALIDITY

Few studies have assessed the validity of measures derived from systematic observation. Yet, three types of validity are particularly relevant for ecologic measures: content validity, construct validity, and criterion-related validity (Brownson et al. 2009). Content validity is the extent to which a measure captures the domain of content (Carmines and Zeller 1979). Content validity can be enhanced through expert review and input from members of the ecologic setting in instrument design (Brownson et al. 2009). For example, Brennan Ramirez and colleagues undertook an evidence-based consensus process to identify key community indicators to enhance physical activity opportunities (Brennan Ramirez et al. 2006). The process involved: (i) a thorough literature review and (ii) a consensus review process involving academic experts, community stakeholders and grant funding agencies to review, rate, and prioritize the indicators. Construct validity is the degree to which a measure behaves according to theoretical expectations (Carmines and Zeller 1979). Convergent validity implies theoretically linked measures should be highly correlated, while divergent validity implies that theoretically unrelated measures should be weakly correlated (Raudenbush and Sampson 1999). Glanz and colleagues, for example, found that their Nutrition Environment Measures Survey for Stores (NEMS-S) performed as hypothesized related to other variables, with healthy foods more available, of higher quality, and lower priced at grocery stores as compared to convenience stores and in high income neighborhoods as compared to low income neighborhoods (Glanz et al. 2007). Gauvin and colleagues found that their measure of safety derived from systematic observation was positively associated with neighborhood affluence (Gauvin et al. 2005). In that study, density of destinations was negatively associated with affluence and positively associated with higher proportions of persons in the neighborhood walking to work. Criterion-related validity is the extent to which a measure is predictive of a gold-standard measure of the same attribute (Frost et al. 2007). Bedimo-Rung and colleagues defined the gold-standard measure of a direct observation instrument designed to measure the park environments as the assessment that was completed together by two investigators who were integrally involved in the development of the observation instrument (Bedimo-Rung et al. 2006). The results of this assessment were used to validate those of field staff trained to use the instrument. Supporting criterion-related validity, Perkins and colleagues established that community disorder as measured by the Block Environmental Inventory predicted subsequent fear of crime of local residents (Perkins and Taylor 1996).

16.5 Data Analysis

Analysis of data derived from systematic observation clearly depends on the research question of interest. Nonetheless, a few points are important to note. First, many systematic observation instruments contain numerous items and produce copious amounts of data. Data reduction techniques such as factor analysis can assist in developing scales to measure concepts of interest (Alfonzo et al. 2008). Scales can also be developed by grouping measures based on the original theoretical framework (Alfonzo et al. 2008, Alfonzo 2005). Second, consideration needs to be given to the unit of analysis. Will environmental data for restaurants, for example, be analyzed at the level of individual restaurants or will the data be aggregated to neighborhood level? Environmental data can be aggregated by simply taking an average of the measures of interest across the entire area or the process can involve the application of a predefined weighting scheme based on priority ratings, proportion to population, or some other schema. These variables can be examined as continuous variables or categorized. Again the appropriate variable construction will depend upon the distribution of the final data, as well as the research questions of interest. Third, studies utilizing systematic observation frequently have a multilevel design, with observations nested within ecologic settings. This has implications for how the data are analyzed. Hierarchical modeling, which can be used to appropriately model variance caused by within-setting versus between-setting differences, is a popular method (Bryk and Raudenbush 1992). Finally, if relevant, sampling weights will need to be developed to adjust for differential selection probabilities of the ecologic settings.

16.6 Theory and Applications

To help illustrate some of the issues earlier, we provide two examples of how systematic observation has been used in research to address health questions and discuss associated challenges and how these challenges were addressed. We selected these examples purposefully in order to illustrate studies conducted at different spatial scales and addressing different types of questions—the first on relationships between the environment and a health outcome and the second on environmental impacts of a natural policy experiment.

16.7 BTG-COMP: Evaluating the Impact of the Built Environment on Adolescent Obesity

16.7.1 BACKGROUND

The Bridging the Gap Community Measures Project (BTG-COMP) is a multiyear multisite study funded by the Robert Wood Johnson Foundation.

BTG-COMP focuses on policy and environmental factors at the community-level that are likely important determinants of healthy eating, physical activity, obesity, and tobacco use among youth. BTG-COMP developed and implemented a unique, integrated set of original data collection efforts using both systematic observation and archival data collection/analysis in a national sample of communities that surround 8th, 10th, and 12th grade schools.

Less than half of children (aged 6–11) meet the recommended minimum of at least 1 h of physical activity on most days of the week and activity levels are even lower for older age groups (Troiano et al. 2008). Many environmental, social, and individual-level factors affect physical activity and obesity rates and these factors frequently differ by demographic, economic, and cultural characteristics across populations. There is an increasing body of behavioral physical activity research that has examined associations between environmental factors and physical activity among children and adolescents, although less is known about youth obesity and the built environment (Davison and Lawson 2006, Ewing et al. 2006, Papas et al. 2007).

Associating street-related environmental measures, derived from systematic observation, with physical activity behavior is a relatively new and growing field of research. There is need to continue to develop and refine these measures and examine how they encourage and impede walking and biking behaviors across multiple populations and areas. There has been some work in associating street-level environmental measures with physical activity behavior (Alfonzo et al. 2008, McConville et al. 2011, Pikora et al. 2006, Suminski et al. 2008), but results are mixed and none of the studies examined adolescents. Therefore, Slater and colleagues designed a study utilizing systematic observation to examine the association between street-related measures of walkability and adolescent weight in a national sample of communities (Slater et al. 2013).

16.7.2 DESIGN

Data were collected in the spring and summer of 2010 from a nationally representative sample of 8th, 10th, and 12th grade students and the 154 communities surrounding the secondary schools. Built environment features of interest included mixed land use, presence of sidewalks and other sidewalk elements, street/sidewalk lighting, public transit stops, traffic calming features, and traffic control devices.

16.7.3 INSTRUMENT DESIGN

The BTG-COMP Street Segment Observation Form is a data collection tool designed to assess key street-level features of the neighborhood environment that are thought to be related to physical activity behavior. Slater and colleagues used an overarching socio-ecological framework as the foundation for the study. The two-page pen and paper BTG-COMP Street Segment Observation Form was developed by drawing upon the empirical literature to identify built environment correlates that have been associated with physical activity behavior and by using existing audit tools and input from an expert panel. All the researchers on the expert panel were previously involved in developing or using similar audit tools. Street segment measures were compiled from these existing data collection instruments (Boarnet et al. 2006, Brownson et al. 2009, Clifton et al. 2007, Emery et al. 2003, Hoehner et al. 2007, Pikora et al. 2002). After multiple calls with the experts, the list of measures was reduced to fit into the following concepts: (i) land use and opportunities for play/physical activity, which included a mix of residential and nonresidential destinations; (ii) traffic and pedestrians, which included information on the presence of sidewalks and other sidewalk elements, street shoulders, bike lanes, traffic calming, and control features; (iii) physical disorder (e.g., presence of graffiti, litter, yard debris); and (iv) aesthetics and amenities (e.g., public transportation, flowers, planters, benches). The expert panel then rated each item's level of importance for inclusion in data collection using a three-point scale (1 = high priority, 2 = low priority, 3 = drop the item). The expert panel also provided feedback including knowledge of reliability issues regarding the measures and suggested additional important items. Given the large scope of the broader BTG project, and in an attempt to minimize field staff time on the ground, Slater and colleagues chose to exclude measures that could be obtained from existing national data sources. This process resulted in the development of an 85-item instrument designed for data collection in each street segment.

16.7.4 SAMPLING

On the basis of power calculations and available project resources, a sample size of approximately 65 street segments per study community was determined. Street segments were divided into three sampling strata by street type: (i) streets located within a 2-mile buffer of the index school, (ii) residential streets, and (iii) arterial, or commercial, streets. Street segments within each stratum were then sampled proportionally to the population of youth aged 0–17 years associated with a given street segment.

16.7.5 OBSERVER TRAINING

Thirty-four employees were hired to conduct data collection for the entire project, which included street, park, physical activity facility, fast food, and food store audits. Specific to the BTG-COMP Street Segment Observation Instrument field staff underwent a 3-day training program, including classroom activities, field practice, exams, and role plays. Materials, including training manuals, data collection forms, maps, and other supplies, were developed and provided to field staff to support the data collection. Training consisted of alternating classroom-style learning and local field practice. Field staff were also required to complete and pass a certification exam.

16.7.6 DATA COLLECTION

Field staff were assigned to sites in teams of two. Multiple teams were assigned to sites with larger number of observations. All field staff were provided detailed community maps developed in ArcGIS that identified primary sample and replacement sample street segments. All observations took place on weekdays during daylight hours. Observations were recorded on scannable paper forms. Data collection occurred between April and October of 2010.

16.7.7 RELIABILITY

Interrater reliability of the BTG-COMP Street Segment Observation Form was assessed as part of a pilot project using the intraclass correlation coefficient (ICC) for continuous or ordinal variables and the Cohen's kappa statistic for dichotomous variables. The ratings system developed by Landis and Koch (1977) was used for interpreting results, where: 0.81 to 1.00 represents almost perfect agreement; 0.61 to 0.80 represents substantial agreement; 0.41 to 0.60 represents moderate agreement; 0.21 to 0.40 represents fair agreement; 0.00 to 0.20 represents slight agreement; and <0.00 represents poor agreement. Data collection on a sample of 480 street segments occurred during a 4-week period in July and August 2009. Nineteen of the thirty-four land use and opportunities for play/physical activity items had substantial or almost perfect agreement and twelve had moderate or fair agreement. Three land use items had slight/poor ICCs (presence of parking, undeveloped land use, and off-road trails). Twenty-one of the thirty-two traffic and pedestrian items had almost perfect or substantial agreement, and eight had moderate or fair agreement. The remaining three items received slight/poor scores. The four physical disorder items all had moderate or fair agreement. Eight of the thirteen aesthetics and amenities items had high agreement, four items had moderate to fair agreement, and one had slight/poor agreement. We also included two subjective items regarding how safe the segment appeared for walking and biking. The walking item had moderate agreement and the biking item had fair agreement. Overall, 57% of the measures received almost perfect or substantial agreement, 35% received moderate or fair agreement, and 8% received poor agreement.

16.7.8 DATA ANALYSIS

Slater and colleagues developed a street-level walkability index using factor analysis techniques. Sampling weights, accounting for the probability of the selection of street segments, were then applied to the data prior to aggregating the street segment data up to the community level. Statistical modeling accounting for the complex stratification and clustering of the survey sample was used for the empirical analyses. These techniques were used to correctly compute robust standard errors that adjust for the clustering of students within sites. Additionally, all statistical analyses include sampling weights to adjust for the differential selection probabilities for the schools.

16.7.9 RESULTS

Slater and colleagues found that the odds of students being overweight (adjusted odds ratio (AOR_0.98, 95% CI_0.95, 0.99) or obese (AOR_0.97, 95% CI_0.95, 0.99) decreased if they lived in communities with higher walkability index scores. Sensitivity analyses showed that the key street features associated with reduced adolescent weight included the presence of sidewalks, public transit, having a pedestrian signal at traffic lights, and marked crosswalks.

16.7.10 CHALLENGES

Slater and colleagues encountered three primary challenges when using systematic observation methods to assess street segments. First, field staff encountered many issues with the ArcGIS maps. Road files provided through ArcGIS do not accurately reflect streets on the ground. Field staff were instructed to purchase local maps when they arrived at a new site to supplement the maps provided for data collection activities. Field staff were also provided with GPS units to assist in locating all sampled streets selected for observation. Second, unsafe conditions of streets sometimes made it difficult to perform data collection activities. During debriefing sessions, field staff stated that some streets were unsafe to walk and others were unsafe to drive at a reasonable speed in order to accurately complete the observation form. Finally, weather also posed a problem. Because field staff were flying all over the country, it was difficult to plan data collection activities around poor local weather conditions. We tried to alleviate some of this by prioritizing data collection sites in southern states first during the winter months and also by conducting data collection primarily during the spring and summer.

16.8 Evaluating the Impact of a Policy Change on the Retail Fruit and Vegetable Supply

16.8.1 BACKGROUND

In 2009, the Special Supplemental Nutrition Program for Women, Infants, and Children (WIC) changed the nutritional guidelines that govern its food packages, aligning WIC foods with the 2005 Dietary Guidelines for Americans and infant feeding practice guidelines of the American Academy of Pediatrics (Institute of Medicine of the National Academies 2006, United States Department of Agriculture Food and Nutrition Service 2007). One of the most noteworthy revisions to the food packages, which are typically redeemed at authorized food retailers, or "WIC vendors," was the addition of a cash-value voucher for women and children to purchase fruits and vegetables in the amount of $8 and $6 per month, respectively.

Research in the United States has shown wide variations in the availability of healthy foods, including fruits and vegetables, by retailer type and size as well as neighborhood characteristics (Beaulac et al. 2009, Fleischhacker et al. 2011, Larson et al. 2009). Research has linked neighborhood healthy food availability to diet and weight outcomes of both adults and children (Beaulac et al. 2009, Fleischhacker et al. 2011, Larson et al. 2009). With nearly 49,000 WIC vendors nationwide (USDA 2008), the new policy requirement for these vendors to carry healthy foods including fruits and vegetables had the potential to expand healthy food availability, especially at small retailers and in rural, low income, and minority neighborhoods that may have previously offered few healthy food options.

Zenk and colleagues conducted an evaluation of the impact of this federal policy change on the retail fruit and vegetable supply using systematic observation (Zenk et al. 2012a). Specifically, they evaluated the effect of the WIC food package revisions as they were implemented in Illinois on the availability, selection, and price of fresh, frozen, and canned fruit and vegetables at WIC vendors. In this chapter, we focus on availability.

Design. The study used a quasi-experimental, one-group pre–post-design with two prepolicy observations in 2008 (baseline) and 2009 (immediately prepolicy) and one postpolicy observation in 2010 (Shadish et al. 2002). Although there was no control group, this design permitted an evaluation of a short time series in which postpolicy differences from 2009 to 2010 were examined relative to prepolicy differences occurring between 2008 and 2009. The study area spanned seven counties in northern Illinois (DeKalb, DuPage, Kane, Lee, Ogle, Winnebago, West suburban Cook).

16.8.2 INSTRUMENT DESIGN

Zenk and colleagues drew upon instruments they had used in prior studies to develop an instrument (Zenk et al. 2010, Zenk et al. 2012b, Zenk et al. 2006). The instrument included items on the availability of 62 fresh fruit and vegetable varieties, 6 canned fruits and 11 canned vegetables, and 8 frozen fruits and 10 frozen vegetables. Price and quality were assessed for a subset of 8–12 fresh fruits and vegetables. On the basis of a preselected package size but not brand, we assessed price for a subset of canned fruits, canned vegetables, frozen fruits, and frozen vegetables (five each). If more than one brand at the specified size was available, the price of the lowest cost brand was recorded. The instrument also included items on characteristics of the stores (e.g., number of cash registers, availability of scales for weighing produce).

16.8.3 SAMPLING

Zenk and colleagues attempted to complete observations at all WIC vendors in the study area. This decision was based on the limited number of vendors and concern that some data (e.g., food prices) would be available only for a subset of stores. (Many small vendors only stock some of the items, leading to "missing data" on price for these stores.) The sampling frame was based on lists of WIC vendors obtained from the Illinois Department of Human Services (IDHS), Bureau of Family Nutrition in 2008, 2009, and 2010. They included all retailers that were authorized WIC vendors in 2008, regardless of their WIC status in subsequent years. They also added all new WIC vendors that joined the program in 2009 and 2010. Three vendors refused the data collection in 2008; one vendor per year refused in 2009 and 2010. This resulted in final sample sizes of 329, 346, and 364 vendors in the 3 years.

16.8.4 OBSERVER TRAINING

Three to five undergraduate and graduate students were trained each year to conduct the observations. While the project coordinator was consistent in 2009 and 2010, different observers were used each year. Observers completed 20–25 h of training that included classroom instruction, practice sessions, debriefings, and certification. To help maintain consistency in observer training over time, one of the principal investigators assumed a lead training role at each time point. Certification consisted of achieving at least 80% agreement with the project coordinator on each section of the instrument.

16.8.5 DATA COLLECTION

Each year, WIC vendors were mailed a letter that explained the study; provided assurances that information about any individual store would not be published or shared including with IDHS, other regulatory bodies, or competitors; and requested their participation. With the exception of stores at which interrater reliability was assessed (see below), each store was visited by a single observer. Observers attempted to rate the stores on weekdays during regular business hours to minimize disrupting store operations during peak shopping times (weekends, weekday evenings). Ratings were recorded on a scannable paper form. The 2008 data collection was completed between April and October, with 38% of the stores observed in June and July and another 47% in August and September. The 2009 and 2010 data collection was completed in June and July, in order to minimize seasonal and within-season variations in food availability and prices.

16.8.6 RELIABILITY AND VALIDITY

To assess interrater reliability, in 2009 and 2010, a subset of 38–39 stores (~10% of sample) was visited by both an observer and the project coordinator during the first month of data collection. For availability, Cohen's kappa statistic values were between 0.81 and 1.00 for 93% and 97% of the fresh fruits and vegetables in 2009 and 2010, respectively. For frozen fruits and vegetables, 92% and 88% of items had Kappa values >0.80 in 2009 and 2010, respectively. In 2009 and 2010, 77% and 89% of canned items had kappa values in excess of 0.80. An additional 20% and 7% of canned items in these years had kappa values between 0.61 and 0.80. Kappa values of 0.81–1.00 correspond with "almost perfect" agreement while values of 0.61–0.80 are considered "substantial" agreement (Landis and Koch 1977). While Zenk and colleagues did not assess test–retest reliability in this study, previous research using a similar instrument showed high consistency in the availability and prices of fruits and vegetables at stores at two time points, 2 weeks apart (Zenk et al. 2010). Supporting the construct validity of the instrument, availability and selection of fresh, frozen, and canned fruits and vegetables were generally better at larger vendors than smaller vendors.

16.8.7 DATA ANALYSIS

Indices were derived for eight categories of fruits and vegetables: commonly consumed fresh fruits and vegetables, culturally specific African-American fresh fruits and vegetables, culturally specific Latino fresh fruits and vegetables, frozen vegetables, frozen fruits, canned vegetables, canned vegetables, no added salt, and canned fruits. For each of these categories, Zenk and colleagues developed an index based on a count of the number of varieties carried at the store. They then defined *availability* as the presence of one or more varieties and *selection* as the proportion of assessed varieties that were present at the vendor. *Price* was calculated for each category of fruits and vegetables as the mean of the standardized (z-scored) prices. *Quality* was the mean score.

16.8.8 RESULTS

Zenk and colleagues found that the availability and selection of some fruits and vegetables (fresh, African-American culturally specific) improved after implementation of the new policy. Small improvements were also seen for availability of canned low sodium vegetables and frozen fruits and vegetables. There were no differences by neighborhood characteristics (population density, median household income, racial/ethnic composition) in changes in fruit and vegetable availability and selection.

16.8.9 CHALLENGES

Zenk and colleagues encountered challenges in using systematic observation to evaluate the impact of the WIC food package revision on the fruit and vegetable supply at WIC vendors. A first challenge was ensuring that any changes in fruit and vegetable availability, selection, price, and quality over time were related to "actual" changes rather than the result of changes in the measurement procedure. While they would have liked to change aspects of their instrument based on what was learned, they tried to maintain consistency in items and operational definitions over time. For example, after the baseline (2008) data collection, they learned that plastic containers of "canned" fruits were allowable in the new policy, but they had only included fruits available in metal "canned" containers at baseline. Therefore, they retained their original items assessed at baseline and added items assessing presence of fruits in plastic containers in 2009 and 2010. They attempted to promote consistency in observer training by having one of two principal investigators present during each annual training. They were also able to have the same project coordinator overseeing the data collection in 2 of the 3 years. A second challenge was inconsistency in the length of the field period for the 3 time years. In 2008, data were collected over several months due to problems retaining observers and complications stemming from running the study out of two field offices. On the basis of what was learned from these experiences, Zenk and colleagues were able to collect all the data within a 2-month period in 2009 and 2010. To adjust for any seasonal or within season differences in fruit and vegetable supply characteristics, they included a control variable for the number of days from the date of data collection to July 1 of the data collection year.

16.9 Summary

Owing to interest in understanding how the environments where people live, work, and play impact health, systematic observation of ecologic settings has emerged as an important research method. Systematic observation involves trained observers systematically assessing predefined features of a setting using a standardized instrument. It can help describe environments of ecologic settings in terms of the presence, quantity, and quality of features (Brownson et al. 2009). This chapter primarily used research conducted in neighborhood settings to discuss methodological considerations and to illustrate its use; however, systematic observation has also been used in other ecologic settings including workplaces, schools, and day care facilities. There are several advantages of systematic observation over surveys and administrative records to characterize the environment of ecologic settings, but also some disadvantages. Ultimately, multimethod studies allow for the most complete picture. Researchers face a variety of methodological considerations in conducting systematic observation: what instrument; where to collect data; observer training strategies; data collection approaches and modes; who and when to collect data; reliability and validity assessment; and data analysis. The examples provided in this chapter show how data derived from systematic observation can be used to complement health survey data or independently of health surveys to answer questions of interest. Researchers interested in using systematic observations are encouraged to consult other helpful overviews and reviews of its use (Brownson et al. 2009, McKinnon et al. 2009, Schaefer-McDaniel et al. 2010b).

Acknowledgments

The authors gratefully acknowledge support from the Robert Wood Johnson Foundation: #64702 and #65852 (Healthy Eating Research Program).

REFERENCES

Alfonzo MA. To walk or not to walk? the hierarchy of walking needs. Environ Behav 2005;37:808–836.

Alfonzo M, Boarnet MG, Day K, McMillan T, Anderson CL. The relationship of neighbourhood built environment features and adult parents' walking. J Urban Des 2008;13:29–51.

Badland HM, Opit S, Witten K, Kearns RA, Mavoa S. Can virtual streetscape audits reliably replace physical streetscape audits? J Urban Health 2010;87:1007–1016.

Baglio ML, Baxter SD, Guinn CH, Thompson WO, Shaffer NM, Frye FHA. Assessment of interobserver reliability in nutrition studies that use direct observation of school meals. J Am Diet Assoc 2004;104:1385–1392.

Ball K, Jeffery RW, Crawford DA, Roberts RJ, Salmon J, Timperio AF. Mismatch between perceived and objective measures of physical activity environments. Prev Med 2008;47:294–298.

Beaulac J, Kristjansson E, Cummins S. A systematic review of food deserts, 1966-2007. Prev Chronic Dis 2009;6:A105.

Bedimo-Rung AL, Gustat J, Tompkins BJ, Rice J, Thomson J. Development of a direct observation instrument to measure environmental characteristics of parks for physical activity. J Phys Act Health 2006;3(Suppl 1):S176–S189.

Boarnet MG, Day K, Alfonzo M, Forsyth A, Oakes M. The Irvine-Minnesota inventory to measure built environments: reliability tests. Am J Prev Med 2006;30:153–159.

Brennan Ramirez LK, Hoehner CM, Brownson RC, Cook R, Orleans CT, Hollander M, Barker DC, Bors P, Ewing R, Killingsworth R. Indicators of activity-friendly communities an evidence-based consensus process. Am J Prev Med 2006;31:515–524.

Brownson RC, Hoehner CM, Day K, Forsyth A, Sallis JF. Measuring the built environment for physical activity: state of the science. Am J Prev Med 2009;36:S99–S123.

Bryk AS, Raudenbush SW. *Hierarchical Linear Models: Applications and Data Analysis Methods*. Newbury Park, CA: Sage Publications; 1992.

Carmines EG, Zeller RA. *Reliability and Validity Assessment*. Beverly Hills, CA: Sage Publications; 1979.

Caughy MO, O'Campo PJ, Patterson J. A brief observational measure for urban neighborhoods. Health Place 2001;7:225–236.

Clarke P, Ailshire J, Melendez R, Bader M, Morenoff J. Using Google Earth to conduct a neighborhood audit: reliability of a virtual audit instrument. Health Place 2010;16:1224–1229.

Clifton KJ, Smith L, Andréa D, Rodriguez D. The development and testing of an audit for the pedestrian environment. Landscape Urban Plann 2007;80:95–110.

CSDH. Closing the gap in a generation: health equity through action on the social determinants of health. Final report of the commission on social determinants of health. Geneva: World Health Organization; 2008.

Davison KK, Lawson CT. Do attributes in the physical environment influence children's physical activity? A review of the literature. Int J Behav Nutr Phys Act 2006;3:19.

Diez Roux AV, Merkin SS, Arnett D, Chambless L, Massing M, Nieto FJ, Sorlie P, Szklo M, Tyroler HA, Watson RL. Neighborhood of residence and incidence of coronary heart disease. N Engl J Med 2001;345:99–106.

Dunn JR, Schaefer-McDaniel NJ, Ramsay JT. Neighborhood chaos and children's development: questions and contradictions. In: Evans GW, Wachs TD, editors. *Chaos and its Influence on Children's Development: An Ecological Perspective*. Washington DC: American Psychological Association; 2010. p 173–189.

Emery J, Crump C, Bors P. Reliability and validity of two instruments designed to assess the walking and bicycling suitability of sidewalks and roads. Am J Health Promot 2003;18:38–46.

Ewing R, Brownson RC, Berrigan D. Relationship between urban sprawl and weight of United States youth. Am J Prev Med 2006;31:464–474.

Fleischhacker S, Evenson K, Rodriguez D, Ammerman A. A systematic review of fast food access studies. Obes Rev 2011;12:e460–e471.

Franco M, Diez-Roux AV, Nettleton JA, Lazo M, Brancati F, Caballero B, Glass T, Moore LV. Availability of healthy foods and dietary patterns: the multi-ethnic study of atherosclerosis. Am J Clin Nutr 2009;89:897–904.

Frost M, Reeve B, Liepa A, Stauffer J, Hays R, Mayo/FDA patient-reported outcomes consensus meeting group. What is sufficient evidence for the reliability and validity of patient-reported outcome measures. Value Health 2007;10(Suppl 2):S94–S105.

Gauvin L, Richard L, Craig CL, Spivock M, Riva M, Forster M, Laforest S, Laberge S, Fournel MC, Gagnon H, Gagné S, Potvin L. From walkability to active living potential: an "ecometric" validation study. Am J Prev Med 2005;28:126–133.

Glanz K, Sallis JF, Saelens BE, Frank LD. Nutrition environment measures survey in stores (NEMS-S): development and evaluation. Am J Prev Med 2007;32:282–289.

Gravlee CC, Zenk SN, Woods S, Rowe Z, Schulz A. Handheld computers for direct observation of the social and physical environment. Field Methods 2006;18:1–16.

Hoehner CM, Brennan Ramirez L, Elliott MB, Handy SL, Brownson RC. Perceived and objective environmental measures and physical activity among urban adults. Am J Prev Med 2005;28:105–116.

Hoehner CM, Ivy A, Brennan Ramirez L, Meriwether B, Brownson RC. How reliably do community members audit the neighborhood environment for its support of physical activity? Implications for participatory research. J Public Health Manag Pract 2006;12:270–277.

Hoehner CM, Ivy A, Ramirez L, Handy S, Brownson RC. Active neighborhood checklist: a user-friendly and reliable tool for assessing activity friendliness. Am J Health Promot 2007;21:534–537.

Institute of Medicine of the National Academies. *WIC Food Packages: Time for a Change*. Washington DC: National Academies Press; 2006.

Izumi B, Zenk SN, Schulz AJ, Mentz G, Wilson C. Associations between neighborhood availability and individual consumption of dark green and orange vegetables among ethnically diverse adults in Detroit. J Am Diet Assoc 2011;111:274–279.

Kwate NOA, Saldaña NT. 2011. Systematic social observation by bicycle: a new methodology for neighborhood assessment. Unpublished manuscript. Available at http://rna-lab.com/workingpapers. Retrieved 2012 Jan 19.

Landis JR, Koch GG. The measurement of observer agreement for categorical data. Biometrics 1977;33:159–174.

Laraia BA, Messer L, Kaufman JS, Dole N, Caughy M, O'Campo P, Savitz DA. Direct observation of neighborhood attributes in an urban area of the US south: characterizing the social context of pregnancy. Int J Health Geogr 2006;5:11.

Larson NI, Story MT, Nelson MC. Neighborhood environments disparities in access to healthy foods in the US. Am J Prev Med 2009;36:74–81.

Lee RE, Booth KM, Reese-Smith J, Regan G, Howard HH. The physical activity resource assessment (PARA) instrument: evaluating features, amenities and incivilities of physical activity resources in urban neighborhoods. Int J Behav Nutr Phys Act 2005;2:13.

McConville ME, Rodríguez DA, Clifton K, Cho G, Fleischhacker S. Disaggregate land uses and walking. Am J Prev Med 2011;40:25–32.

McKenzie TL, Sallis JF, Nader PR. SOFIT: system for observing fitness instruction time. J Teaching Phys Educ 1991;11:195–205.

McKinnon RA, Reedy J, Morrissette MA, Lytle LA, Yaroch AL. Measures of the food environment: a compilation of the literature, 1990-2007. Am J Prev Med 2009;36:S124–S133.

McMillan TE, Cubbin C, Parmenter B, Medina AV, Lee RE. Neighborhood sampling: how many streets must an auditor walk? Int J Behav Nutr Phys Act 2010;7:20.

Oldenburg B, Sallis JF, Harris D, Owen N. Checklist of health promotion environments at worksites (CHEW): development and measurement characteristics. Am J Health Promot 2002;16:288–299.

Papas MA, Alberg AJ, Ewing R, Helzlsouer KJ, Gary TL, Klassen AC. The built environment and obesity. Epidemiol Rev 2007;29:129–143.

Paquet C, Cargo M, Kestens Y, Daniel M. Reliability of an instrument for direct observation of urban neighbourhoods. Landscape Urban Plann 2010;97:194–201.

Parsons J, Singh G, Scott A, Nisenbaum R, Balasubramaniam P, Jabbar A, Zaidi Q, Sheppard A, Ramsay J, O'Campo P, Dunn J. Standardized observation of neighbourhood disorder: does it work in Canada? Int J Health Geogr 2010;9:6.

Perkins DD, Taylor RB. Ecological assessments of community disorder: their relationship to fear of crime and theoretical implications. Am J Community Psychol 1996;24:63–107.

Pikora TJ, Bull FC, Jamrozik K, Knuiman M, Giles-Corti B, Donovan RJ. Developing a reliable audit instrument to measure the physical environment for physical activity. Am J Prev Med 2002;23:187–194.

Pikora TJ, Giles-Corti B, Knuiman MW, Bull FC, Jamrozik K, Donovan RJ. Neighborhood environmental factors correlated with walking near home: using SPACES. Med Sci Sports Exerc 2006;38:708–714.

Raudenbush SW. 2011. Optimal design software for multi-level and longitudinal research (version 3.01). www.wtgrantfoundation.org.

Raudenbush SW, Sampson RJ. Ecometrics: toward a science of assessing ecological settings, with application to the systematic social observation of neighborhoods. Sociol Methodol 1999;29:1–41. Accessed on January 1 2012.

Reiss A. Systematic observation surveys of natural social phenomena. In: Sinaiko H, Broedling L, editors. *Perspectives on Attitude Assessment: Surveys and their Alternatives*. Champaign, IL: Pendelton; 1976.

Rundle AG, Bader MDM, Richards CA, Neckerman KM, Teitler JO. Using Google Street View to audit neighborhood environments. Am J Prev Med 2011;40:94–100.

Saelens BE, Glanz K, Sallis JF, Frank LD. Nutrition environment measures study in restaurants (NEMS-R): development and evaluation. Am J Prev Med 2007;32:273–281.

Sampson RJ, Raudenbush SW. Systematic social observation of public spaces: a new look at disorder in urban neighborhoods. Am J Sociol 1999;105:603–651.

Schaefer-McDaniel N, Dunn JR, Minian N, Katz D. Rethinking measurement of neighborhood in the context of health research. Soc Sci Med 2010a;71:651–656.

Schaefer-McDaniel N, O'Brien Caughy M, O'Campo P, Gearey W. Examining methodological details of neighbourhood observations and the relationship to health: a literature review. Soc Sci Med 2010b;70:277–292.

Shadish WR, Cook TD, Campbell DT. *Experimental and Quasi-Experimental Designs for Generalized Causal Inference*. Boston, MA: Houghton Mifflin; 2002.

Shareck M, Dassa C, Frohlich KL. Improving the measurement of neighbourhood characteristics through systematic observation: inequalities in smoking as a case study. Health Place 2012;18:671–682.

Slater SJ, Nicholson L, Chriqui J, Barker DC, Chaloupka FJ, Johnston LD. Walkable communities and adolescent weight. Am J Prev Med 2013;44:164–168.

Suminski RR, Heinrich KM, Poston WSC, Hyder M, Pyle S. Characteristics of urban sidewalks/streets and objectively measured physical activity. J Urban Health 2008;85:178–190.

Troiano RP, Berrigan D, Dodd KW, Masse LC, Tilert T, McDowell M. Physical activity in the United States measured by accelerometer. Med Sci Sports Exerc 2008;40:181–188.

United States Department of Agriculture Food and Nutrition Service. 2008. WIC and retail grocery stores. Available at http://www.fns.usda.gov/wic/WICRetailStoresfactsheet.pdf. Retrieved 2011 Dec 12.

United States Department of Agriculture Food and Nutrition Service. Special supplemental nutrition program for women, infants, and children (WIC): revisions in the WIC food packages; interim rule. Fed Regist 2007;72:68966–69032.

Ward D, Hales D, Haverly K, Marks J, Benjamin S, Ball S, Trost S. An instrument to assess the obesogenic environment of child care centers. Am J Health Behav 2008;32:380–386.

Yancey AK, Cole BL, Brown R, Williams JD, Hillier AMY, Kline RS, Ashe M, Grier SA, Backman D, McCarthy WJ. A cross-sectional prevalence study of ethnically targeted and general audience outdoor obesity-related advertising. Milbank Q 2009;87:155–184.

Zenk SN, Grigsby-Toussaint DS, Curry SJ, Berbaum M, Schneider L. Short-term temporal stability in observed retail food characteristics. J Nutr Educ Behav 2010;42:26–32.

Zenk SN, Lachance LL, Schulz AJ, Mentz G, Kannan S, Ridella W. Neighborhood retail food environment and fruit and vegetable intake in a multiethnic urban population. Am J Health Promot 2009;23:255–264.

Zenk SN, Odoms-Young A, Powell LM, Campbell RT, Block D, Chavez N, Krauss RC, Strode S, Armbruster J. Fruit and vegetable availability and selection: federal food package revisions, 2009. Am J Prev Med 2012a;43:423–428.

Zenk S, Schulz AJ, House JS, Benjamin A, Kannan S. Application of community-based participatory research in the design of an observational tool: the neighborhood observational checklist. In: Israel BA, Eng E, Schulz AJ, Parker E, editors. *Methods for Conducting Community-Based Participatory Research for Health.* San Francisco: Jossey-Bass; 2005. p 167–187.

Zenk SN, Schulz AJ, Israel BA, James SA, Bao S, Wilson ML. Fruit and vegetable access differs by community racial composition and socioeconomic position in Detroit, Michigan. Ethn Dis 2006;16:275–280.

Zenk SN, Schulz AJ, Izumi B, Sand S, Lockett M, Odoms-Young A. Development, evolution, and implementation of the food environment audit for diverse neighborhoods. In: Israel BA, Eng E, Schulz AJ, Parker E, editors. *Methods for Conducting Community-Based Participatory Research for Health.* 2nd ed. San Francisco: Jossey Bass; 2012b. p 277–304.

Zenk SN, Schulz AJ, Mentz G, House JS, Gravlee CC, Miranda PY, Miller P, Kannan S. Inter-rater and test-retest reliability: methods and results for the neighborhood observational checklist. Health Place 2007;13:452–465.

ONLINE RESOURCES

Active Living Research website provides observational tools to collect environmental data on streets, schools, parks, and other community settings that may impact physical activity. It can be accessed at: www.activelivingresearch.org/resourcesearch/toolsandmeasures.

The National Collaborative on Childhood Obesity Research website contains a searchable database of diet and physical measures relevant to childhood obesity research, including observational instruments to assess environmental features of for food stores, restaurants, schools, parks, and indoor recreational facilities. It can be accessed at: www.nccor.org/measures/.

The Project on Human Development in Chicago Neighborhoods website provides the Systematic Social Observation instrument that was used to assess physical, social, and economic characteristics of neighborhoods particularly relevant for youth violence, as well as articles published using the generated data. This website can be accessed at: www.icpsr.umich.edu/icpsrweb/PHDCN/about.jsp.

The National Cancer Institute website provides observational instruments to assess the food environment of stores, restaurants, workplaces, and schools. This website can be accessed at: https://riskfactor.cancer.gov/mfe/instruments.

CHAPTER SEVENTEEN

Collecting Survey Data on Sensitive Topics: Substance Use

Joe Gfroerer and Joel Kennet
Center for Behavioral Health Statistics and Quality, Substance Abuse and Mental Health Services Administration, Rockville, MD, USA

17.1 Introduction

This chapter addresses the collection of data on substance use, which is one of the most challenging topics for survey researchers. The large variety of types of substances and the illegality of many of them pose challenges for the design of efficient and effective survey instruments. A general discussion on the unique issues associated with substance use and how these issues affect survey design and measurement is provided in the next section. A summary of the history of survey research on substance use is included. Options for design of surveys of substance use are discussed in Section 17.3, 17.4, and 17.5 including results of methods research studies and other considerations that relate to the advantages and disadvantages of various design approaches. Section 17.6 summarizes the key points covered in this chapter.

Handbook of Health Survey Methods, First Edition. Edited by Timothy P. Johnson.

17.2 Background

Among the many aspects of health for which data are needed, substance use is one of the most important and challenging. Substance use is widespread in many countries and the negative health consequences of the use of some substances have been well established. Cigarette use has been identified as the largest single preventable cause of death in the United States, with approximately 443,000 estimated smoking-related deaths per year (CDC 2008). Alcohol, the most widely used substance, also has major health and societal consequences when used excessively. But health risks vary greatly by the type of substance and pattern of use, and there is a multitude of substances available, ranging from pharmaceuticals intended for treatment of pain or other physical and mental ailments to household products such as glue, gasoline, and aerosols. Some substances, including alcohol, may have health benefits when used appropriately, but many have potential negative health effects and some are highly addictive. Largely because of the negative health effects associated with them, certain substances have been made illegal in some countries. In the United States, illegal substances such as marijuana, cocaine, heroin, methamphetamine, and hallucinogens are of great interest to policymakers and researchers because of the substantial resources devoted to the criminal aspect of use, as well as the significant health consequences and health care costs associated with these drugs. Illegal drugs pose the biggest challenge to survey researchers attempting to estimate substance use. Nonresponse and response errors are generally thought to be greater for estimating use of illegal substances than for the use of other substances, because illicit drug users may be less willing to participate in surveys and when they do participate they may be reluctant to reveal their use. Some researchers have tried alternative approaches (discussed later in this chapter) to develop estimates of the prevalence of heroin, cocaine, and other so-called hard-core drug use, based on the contention that standard population surveys are not capable of providing valid estimates. While these concerns about the validity of survey-based prevalence estimates have merit, most researchers agree that despite limitations, properly designed surveys can provide useful data on all types of substance use, including illegal, stigmatized behaviors like heroin injection and crack cocaine use.

Large-scale health surveys have included items on alcohol and tobacco use for many years. In 1955, the Current Population Survey (CPS), conducted by the U.S. Bureau of the Census, became the first national survey to gather data on smoking prevalence in the United States. The National Health Interview Survey (NHIS), sponsored by the National Center for Health Statistics, first included questions on tobacco use in 1965 and questions on alcohol use in 1977. The Behavioral Risk Factor Surveillance System, a state-based telephone survey of adults that includes several questions on substance use, began in 1984. State and national data on youth health risk factors, including several on substance use, have been collected in the school-based Youth Risk Behavioral Surveillance System, which began in 1991.

The first national surveys with a primary focus on substance use other than alcohol and tobacco were conducted in the 1970s. In response to the rising prevalence of marijuana and other illicit drug use among young Americans in the 1960s, Congress passed the Comprehensive Drug Abuse Prevention and Control Act of 1970, which created the Commission on Marijuana and Drug Abuse and charged it to develop recommendations for legislation and administrative action. Given the lack of data on illicit drug use at that point in time, the Commission decided to conduct nationally representative household surveys in 1971 and 1972. These surveys, named the Nationwide Study of Beliefs, Information, and Experiences, were designed and carried out by Response Analysis Corporation (RAC), a small survey organization, in a very short period of time. Approximately 3000 respondents participated in each of these surveys. Methods used were based on RAC's prior experiences with small data collection efforts on sensitive topics, employing procedures that were expected to maximize respondent cooperation rates and willingness to report honestly about their illicit drug use behavior. Introductory letters and survey materials were intentionally vague, avoiding any reference to the topic of illegal drug use. Respondents were not asked to give their names, implying anonymity (despite the fact that RAC obviously knew the address and other demographic data for each respondent). Sensitive questions on substance use were asked with self-administered answer sheets, so that responses were not revealed to interviewers and other household members. The respondent inserted each answer sheet into an envelope that was sealed at the end of the interview, contained no direct identifiers, and was mailed to the contractor data processing site. Respondents were even invited to accompany the interviewer to a mailbox to ensure that it was promptly sent. These two surveys became the models for a series of surveys funded through contracts by the National Institute on Drug Abuse (NIDA) when the agency was created in 1974, as part of the Alcohol, Drug Abuse and Mental Health Administration. NIDA conducted these surveys of the U.S. civilian noninstitutionalized population aged 12 and older periodically from 1974 until 1992, when responsibility for the survey was shifted to the newly formed Substance Abuse and Mental Health Services Administration (SAMHSA). The survey, known as the *National Household Survey on Drug Abuse* (NHSDA), underwent relatively minor design changes occasionally until 1999, when the survey was converted to Audio Computer-Assisted Self Interviewing (ACASI). In 2002, the survey was renamed the National Survey on Drug Use and Health (NSDUH).

Another important substance use survey initiated in 1974 was the Monitoring the Future Study (MTF), an annual, nationally representative sample of high school students, conducted by the University of Michigan through a grant from NIDA. MTF collects data in classrooms, using self-administered answer sheets. The survey has included 12th graders since its inception, and was expanded to include 8th and 10th graders starting in 2001. MTF also has a longitudinal component, in which subsamples of 12th graders are surveyed by mail every 2 years following graduation. NSDUH and MTF are the Federal Government's two primary sources of data on illicit drug use in the United States.

In the 1980s, substance use surveys began to focus more on issues beyond just the prevalence of use. As policymakers increasingly recognized the public health aspects of substance use there was more emphasis on collecting data that addressed the need for treatment for persons with substance use problems, and the association between mental disorders and substance use. Survey researchers developed and implemented methods for assessing diagnosable mental and substance use disorders in household interviews, based on criteria established by the American Psychiatric Association (1994) in its Diagnostic and Statistical Manual of Mental Disorders (DSM). These methods were implemented in the landmark Epidemiologic Catchment Area study (ECA), a five-site study conducted in 1980–1984, and later in national surveys such as the National Comorbidity Study (NCS) and the National Longitudinal Alcohol Epidemiology Survey (NLAES) in 1990–1992. The NSDUH began including questions on DSM criteria in 1988, with full coverage of DSM-IV substance use disorders beginning in 2002. See also the discussion in Chapter 6.

The demand for data at the state level has also increased in the U.S., in part because of the large US Federal block grant that provides funds to states for substance use treatment and prevention services. There has also been increasing interest in assessing the impact of the differing state laws, policies and programs addressing tobacco, alcohol, and marijuana use.

Along with the expanded need for data on substance use, there has also been a substantial body of methodological research done to develop and improve the methods of measuring substance use through surveys. One conclusion that seems clear from this research is that survey estimates of the prevalence of substance use seem to be affected by differences in data collection methods to a greater degree than estimates of nonsensitive behaviors. This fact has also been demonstrated in practice to policymakers and other data users by the results of the variety of surveys generating estimates of the prevalence of substance use. Results from different surveys often do not agree, causing consternation, concern, and misinterpretation (Fendrich and Johnson 2001, Sudman 2001). Therefore, the next section explores options for the design of surveys of substance use, addressing specific survey design features in terms of their potential effect on estimates and the practical considerations involved in determining which features to incorporate into a substance use survey design.

17.3 Theory and Applications

Studies have addressed the potential effects on survey results associated with various design features. These design features include the setting, mode, definitions, question wording and order, sponsor and purpose of survey, confidentiality promises, and incentive payments. Each of these design characteristics is discussed below in terms of their effect on estimates of the prevalence of substance use, with an emphasis on the most widely used methods. Other factors (e.g., costs) associated with these design options are also considered. Following the discussions of each of these aspects of survey designs, sections 17.4 and 17.5 discuss validating survey responses and alternatives to standard survey estimation methods. The final summary section of this chapter briefly discusses the most important results from methodological research and gives some recommendations for best practices, including a focus on local level data collections.

It is important to note that the true effect of each of these design features cannot be easily discerned because of the complex interactions among them. Experimental studies of specific design features controlling on other factors often cannot be generalized to all types of surveys because every survey has a unique set of design characteristics that may differ from the design features employed in experimental studies. Much of what is known about the effect of survey designs on measurement error of substance use comes from analyses of large-scale survey data, including comparisons across different surveys as well as observations of the effect on survey estimates when changes are made in methods. One key assumption in most methodological research studies is that higher estimates of substance use indicate more accurate reporting.

17.3.1 SETTING

The primary settings where substance use surveys have been conducted are households and classrooms. School-based surveys of substance use have been common because of concerns about substance use among youth and because of the lower cost per interview of school surveys, compared with household surveys. Household surveys, while more expensive, provide more comprehensive coverage of youth populations, including those not enrolled in school, as well as adults. To satisfy specific needs for data on other populations of interest, surveys have also been done in substance use treatment facilities and jails. Health care providers increasingly are collecting data on substance use and other sensitive behaviors from patients in clinical settings as a part of routine screening. Each of these settings involves a different set of respondent motivations and concerns that could influence how they respond to questions about substance use. For example, it is generally assumed, and demonstrated by research, that many respondents who have used drugs are reluctant to reveal this behavior in a survey interview because of potential embarrassment or negative consequences if their drug use were to become known to others, such as friends, family members, teachers, or police. This underreporting is quite evident, as expected, for youths interviewed in their homes in the presence of their parents (Gfroerer 1985, Aquilino et al. 2000, Gfroerer et al. 2012). A study of youth (age 12–17) reporting of past year marijuana use in an ACASI interview found that 14.4% reported use when there were no other persons in the room during the interview, while 10.9% reported use when a parent was in the room during the interview (Substance Abuse and Mental Health Services Administration 2012). However, bias in the other direction (i.e., reporting of drug use by respondents who actually have not used drugs) is also assumed to occur in some situations. For example, persons seeking entry into drug treatment programs might overstate their level of substance use in order to validate their need for treatment and ensure admission. Similarly, some arrestees could also overstate their drug problem as a way of getting placement in a drug treatment program in lieu of incarceration. Also, some students participating in a survey in a classroom setting could be motivated to report use of substances that they did not use, in order to be "cool" among their friends (Percy et al. 2005, Fendrich 2005, Martino et al. 2009). Overall, it is generally held that underreporting is more common than overreporting, and that household surveys underestimate youth substance use prevalence.

Utilizing NSDUH items on age, education, and enrollment status, comparisons of prevalence rates by grade for a school (MTF) versus home (NSDUH) can be made. Both surveys are self-administered, with MTF collecting data on paper questionnaires and NSDUH employing ACASI. As shown in Table 17.1, differences between the MTF and NSDUH estimates are generally greater for the more sensitive drugs (e.g., cocaine and heroin) and for the youngest respondents (8th graders). This supports the theory that underreporting is more substantial when the respondent perceives there is a possibility that their answers could become known to others who may inflict negative consequences upon them, as would be the case in a home setting where parents are nearby.

A study that directly addressed the effect of setting on youths' reporting of substance use involved a sample of 4506 youths in grades 9 and 11 that were randomly assigned to either home or school data collection and either paper or computer-assisted self-interview (Brener et al. 2006). Consistent with the MTF–NSDUH comparisons in Table 17.1, the school setting was found to produce significantly greater reporting for 11 of 17 substance use variables, based on logistic regression models that controlled for sex, grade, and race/ethnicity. The highest odds ratios for setting were found in models for lifetime methamphetamine use (1.97), current smokeless tobacco use (1.83), lifetime cocaine use (1.63), and lifetime inhalant use (1.61). The setting effect was not statistically significant for lifetime or current cigarette use. Also consistent with Table 17.1, the Brener et al. study explored age-setting interactions and found that students aged 16 years and younger were more likely to report lifetime and past year alcohol use in the school than at home, while among older youths there was no significant setting effect. Earlier studies of school versus home data collection have found similar results (Kann et al. 2002, Gfroerer et al. 1997, Rootman and Smart 1985).

TABLE 17.1 Comparison of NSDUH and MTF Estimates of the Percentage with Lifetime Substance Use: Combined 2002–2008 Data

Substance	8th Grade		10th Grade		12th Grade	
	MTF	NSDUH	MTF	NSDUH	MTF	NSDUH
Cigarettes	25.8	19.4	38.8	37.6	50.1	51.3
Alcohol	42.2	29.7	63.2	56.6	74.8	72.3
Marijuana	16.2	9.0	33.8	26.4	44.5	39.8
Inhalants	16.1	12.0	13.1	11.6	10.9	10.4
Cocaine	3.4	0.7	5.3	3.1	7.9	6.8
Heroin	1.5	0.1	1.5	0.4	1.5	0.6

Table 17.1 also reveals two other interesting patterns that suggest reporting biases. First, note that regardless of setting, the rate of lifetime use of inhalants declines with age, which is illogical because every lifetime user at a point in time remains a lifetime user at later ages. Unless there is a general decline in new use among youths over time, the lifetime rate should always be higher among older youths than among younger youths. This illogical pattern is evidence of the reluctance among older teens to report previous use of inhalants, because inhalant use is considered to be a more immature and less cool substance use behavior, relative to the more popular marijuana and prescription drug misuse (Martino et al. 2009). The second unusual pattern is seen with heroin. As with inhalants, the expected pattern of increasing lifetime use with increasing age is not seen in MTF. But unlike inhalants, heroin is not a drug that is typically used by young teens who then move on to more popular drugs as they get older. There are at least two possible explanations, neither of which has been substantiated empirically. First, it could be evidence of overreporting by very young teens in the classroom setting. Second, it could reflect noncoverage of school dropouts in the estimates for 10th and 12th grades. In other words, a large percentage of kids who used heroin by 8th grade have dropped out of school by 10th or 12th grade and are therefore not captured in school surveys. The NSDUH data for heroin use in Table 17.1 shows the typical pattern of increasing rates with age, lending support to the first hypothesis.

Besides the effect on reporting behavior, there are other important considerations with the choice of setting, including cost and sampling error. School surveys are typically much less expensive than face-to-face household surveys (per interview) because of the reduced travel cost in school surveys, where data can be collected from large numbers of respondents at each sample unit (school). However, this sample clustering can also lead to a substantial loss of precision due to design effect, a measure of the reduced precision of a sample caused by the clustering of the sample. The loss in accuracy depends on how the particular variable of interest varies across sample units, and how big the clusters (sample units) are. For example, the MTF 12th grade estimates for 2010 are based on a sample of 15,127 students, but these respondents were selected from a sample of only 126 schools. If the school-level rates of substance use vary greatly (e.g., some schools have very high rates of drug use while other schools have very low rates) then the sampling errors of estimates based on this design will be much larger than if a simple random sample of 15,127 12th graders had been selected from all schools. It turns out that the MTF sample design produces design effects of 8 for past month marijuana use and 5 for past month cigarette or alcohol use, which means that the precision of these estimates is equivalent to that of simple random samples of 15,127/8 = 1891 and 15,127/5 = 3025, respectively (Johnston et al. 2011).

Another important distinction between school and household surveys is the nature and form of nonresponse and coverage associated with each. By design, school surveys exclude youths not enrolled in school. If data are desired for the youth population overall, this limitation of school surveys needs to be considered. The extent to which these factors make a difference depends both on the population and substance of interest, as shown in Table 17.2. Estimates for 10th graders

TABLE 17.2 Percent Reporting Past Month Substance Use by Expected Grade Level and Enrollment Status: 2002–2008 National Survey on Drug Use and Health

Substance	10th Grade			12th Grade		
	All Youths at 10th Grade Level	Enrolled Only	Not Enrolled, But Should be in 10th	All Youths at 12th Grade Level	Enrolled Only	Not Enrolled, but Should be in 12th
Cigarettes	15.3	14.1	53.4	31.4	24.3	55.3
Smokeless tobacco	3.0	3.0	4.7	4.9	4.9	4.6
Alcohol	22.3	21.3	40.9	38.6	36.7	45.0
Marijuana	9.9	9.4	26.8	17.1	15.2	23.4
Heroin (lifetime)	0.4	0.4	1.6	1.0	0.6	2.5

are similar to the total estimates because the vast majority of youths at that age are enrolled. At the 12th grade level, where not-enrolled youths have very different rates of substance use than enrolled youths, the inclusion of the not enrolled makes a significant difference.

Response rates achieved in school surveys largely depend on the cooperation of schools, which can be problematic, for example, if entire school districts decide not to participate, or if schools with more severe drug problems decline participation at a higher rate than other schools, or vice versa (Johnston et al. 2011). Response rates for students within participating schools have been very good (80–90%), particularly if follow-up interviewing of absentees is part of the survey design (Substance Abuse and Mental Health Services Administration 2012).

17.3.2 MODE

The principal modes employed in surveys of substance use are mail, in person interviewer administered, in person self-administered, and telephone interviewer administered. Self-administration has also been attempted in telephone surveys (Gribble et al. 2000). In person interviews (either self or interviewer administered) can be done using paper and pencil or with computer-assisted interviewing. Web-based data collection has also been explored (Hines et al. 2010).

Mode effects on the reporting of sensitive behaviors, including substance use, have been studied extensively. This research has established that self administration elicits higher estimates of substance use than when respondents are required to verbally provide responses to interviewer-administered questions (Aquilino 1994, Schober et al. 1992, Tourangeau and Smith 1996, Grucza et al. 2007). The effect is greater for youths than adults and also increases with the perceived sensitivity of the substance use behavior. These results are clearly seen in the data from a large ($n = 4000$) field test conducted in conjunction with the NHSDA. Half of the respondents were administered drug use questions with self-administration and half were interviewer-administered (Turner et al. 1992). In this study, ratios calculated by dividing prevalence estimates based on self-administered questions by estimates based on interviewer administered questions for past month substance use among person aged 12 and older were 2.4 for cocaine (most sensitive), 1.6 for marijuana, and 1.06 for alcohol (least sensitive). However, the ratio for alcohol reporting was 1.4 among respondents aged 12 to 17, possibly reflecting greater sensitivity toward alcohol questions among youths. An experiment embedded within the 1994 NHSDA showed similar results for reporting of current cigarette use (Brittingham et al. 1998). Researchers have surmised that these effects are driven by the effect of privacy and respondent concerns of the risk of their data being revealed to others, similar to the setting effect.

With the development of the more efficient computerized survey data collection, some researchers have hypothesized that computer-assisted self-interview (CASI) methods provide more privacy, at least as perceived by respondents, than paper-and-pencil (PAPI) self-administered questionnaires (SAQ). Several studies have explored this question, with mixed results. A few studies have found higher rates of reporting of substance use with CASI than PAPI (Turner et al. 1998, Wright et al. 1998), but others have found no differences (Webb et al. 1999, Hallfors et al. 2000). Brener et al. (2006) found the mode effect (PAPI-SAQ vs CASI) statistically significant for only 3 of the 17 substance use variables. The NHSDA converted from PAPI-SAQ to audio-CASI (ACASI) in 1999, employing a large split sample (13,809 with PAPI, 19,482 with ACASI) in 2000 sample segments that allowed study of the mode effect (Chromy et al. 2002). Although results varied by drug and age group, estimates from the ACASI sample were generally higher than estimates from the PAPI sample. However, while statistically significant, most differences were not large, and in some cases the PAPI estimate was significantly higher than the ACASI estimate. Virtually all of these studies cite other important advantages of CASI, including better cross-item consistency, less item nonresponse, faster data processing, and the ability to incorporate more complex skip patterns, respondent inconsistency resolutions and verification of unusual responses. On the other hand, there is evidence that mode may interact with setting. In clinical (Beebe et al. 2006) and school (Beebe et al. 1998) settings, adolescents reported more substance use behaviors in PAPI than in a computer-administered mode.

Another important consideration associated with the survey mode is costs. With a lower per-interview cost than face-to-face surveys, telephone surveys have been widely used to collect data on tobacco and alcohol use, but few telephone surveys have covered illicit drug use. One study found significantly lower rates of marijuana (5.2 vs 8.0%) and cocaine (1.4 vs 3.1%) use in a 1988 telephone survey than in a face-to-face (PAPI-SAQ) survey of households with telephones, largely due to underreporting in the telephone sample (Gfroerer and Hughes 1991). Another study, based on 1999 and 2001 data, found rates of adult binge alcohol use of 14.7% in the telephone-based BRFSS and 21.5% in the ACASI-based NSDUH (Miller et al. 2004). The differences were attributed primarily to the mode, with coverage and response rate differences having a small effect. However, the increasing use of call-screening devices and cellphones in recent years has raised concerns about coverage and nonresponse bias in substance use and other data collected by telephone, indicating a need for telephone surveys to include supplemental samples of cell phone numbers and addresses (Blumberg and Luke 2009).

Assuming adequate population coverage and sampling methods, web administration could become a viable mode of collecting data on substance use (Couper 2008). However, obtaining samples that are representative of the general population remains a challenge (Hines et al. 2010). Furthermore, the effect of this mode on perceived privacy and other factors associated with substance use reporting behavior is relatively unknown. A study comparing web data collection to classroom PAPI-SAQ data collection among 9th and 10th graders found more missing data and reduced privacy (both actual and perceived) in the web data collection (Denniston et al. 2010). Another study compared reported consequences associated with substance use in web and mail surveys of college students and found minimal differences (McCabe et al. 2006). These studies have limited generalizability because they were restricted to populations with high levels of web use and access. Hence, more research is needed.

17.3.3 SPONSOR AND FOCUS OF SURVEY

To achieve high response rates and accurate responses to survey questions about sensitive behaviors such as illegal drug use, it is important to convey the legitimacy of the survey, both in terms of the organizations conducting the survey, and the need for the data. The materials and presentation given to potential respondents should reflect the credibility and neutrality of the survey sponsor, the topic of the survey, why the data are needed, how long it will take to complete the survey, and how the data will be used. The goal is to gain the trust of respondents and have them perceive the survey as relevant to them and of value to the community (Groves and Couper 1998). For example, a survey of drug use that gives respondents the impression that it is connected to a law enforcement agency is less likely to yield good response rates, let alone honest reporting, than a drug use survey focused on health and conducted by a health department. This line of thinking influenced the U.S. Department of Health and Human Services to change the name of its primary drug use survey from the National Household Survey on Drug Abuse to the National Survey on Drug Use and Health in 2002. Survey staff felt that the term *use* would be more neutral than "abuse" and that "health" would also convey a more positive purpose that would be conducive to respondent participation. Beebe et al. (2008) reported that participation in health surveys was less likely among those with good health status, those with a busy schedule, and people who thought that surveys were too long. Respondents were more than twice as likely to indicate that they would participate in a future health survey if they knew the organization conducting the survey, although it was not clear whether this was associated with the survey sponsor or the organization actually collecting the data.

17.3.4 ASSURANCES OF CONFIDENTIALITY AND INFORMED CONSENT

In an era of generally declining response rates and increasing concerns about privacy and the access to and use of personal data by government and private industry, confidentiality assurances and informed consent procedures are critically important components of a survey design. They affect both response rates and accuracy of reporting by respondents. As noted earlier, substance use is a sensitive topic for many respondents, and misreporting is a potential consequence of that. Assurances of confidentiality have been studied in prior work, and continue to be a subject of interest as a means of reducing this potential source of error. Singer (1978) varied informed consent statements on the dimensions of strength and amount of information provided within a design that also examined the timing of a request for a signature on the consent document. Her findings suggested that the strength of the confidentiality assurance was positively related to item response rates and reporting rates for questions about sensitive topics. However, Singer and Couper (2010) carried out an experiment that varied the wording of the confidentiality assurance through a series of vignettes, and found no effects on reported likelihood of participation.

In school settings, Eaton et al. (2004) compared results for active versus passive parental permission for participation in the Youth Risk Behavior Survey. Active permission required a signed form to be returned to the school indicating parental approval before the child could participate, while with passive permission parents only returned a signed form if they did not want the child to participate. Lower student response rates were attained in the active permission schools (77.3% vs 86.7%), but there was no difference between passive versus active parental permission when comparing reported drug use rates. A study conducted in Kentucky in 2007 found a larger difference in response rates between active and passive consent samples (29.1% vs 78.6%), and consequently, lower rates of substance use in the active consent schools (Courser et al. 2009). In both of these studies, fewer than 3% of the active consent sample cases had returned forms with refusals to participate. Most of the nonresponse among the active consent samples was due to consent forms not being returned.

In an effort to encourage honest and complete reporting, surveys sometimes include statements stressing the importance of the survey, and asking respondents to answer truthfully. Some appeals include encouragement to skip questions that respondents feel too uncomfortable in answering. Brener et al. (2004) varied the strength of honesty appeals in a study of high school students, and found no difference in levels of reporting between standard and strong appeals for honesty. An honesty appeal experimentally tested in the NHSDA did show improvements to the accuracy of self-reports of illicit drug use behaviors (Harrison et al. 2007).

17.3.5 DEFINITIONS

Individual surveys have idiosyncratic reasons for adopting one definition over others. Survey designers should recognize that decisions regarding definitions are nontrivial, and that when attempting to measure a behavior such as substance use, focusing on concepts that are clearly defined, quantitatively, qualitatively and temporally, is usually the best approach and is most likely to yield accurate and reliable responses. It is also preferable to avoid judgmental definitions that could result in social desirability bias. For example, a simple factual definition of substance use such as any "use of marijuana at least once during the past 30 days" would usually be preferable to a definition such as "a current user."

Even slight differences in definitions of drug use among surveys can result in observable differences in the estimates that are produced. For example, the NHIS defines current smokers as those who report having smoked at least 100 cigarettes in their lifetime and specify that they now smoke on some days or every day. In this definition, not only is the act of smoking undefined in terms of quantity, but the respondent's interpretation of the word "now" also appears to be critical to the response. The definition of current smoking in NSDUH, on the other hand, is oriented toward the defined, observable behavior of the respondent. If the individual recalls (and reports) having smoked part or all of a cigarette within the past 30 days, he or she is considered a current smoker. The NSDUH consistently produces higher estimates of current smoking prevalence than NHIS does, representing a difference of about 10 million smokers. NSDUH also has a question that asks whether respondents have smoked at least 100 cigarettes in their lifetime, and subtracting those who have not does not fully account for the differences in estimates (Table 17.3). The reason for the remaining differences is not clear, but is probably due to differences in both the questions ("now smoke" vs "smoked in past 30 days") and the mode (NHIS is interviewer administered, NSDUH is self-administered) (Ryan et al. 2012). The differences may reflect the high rate of infrequent or occasional cigarette use among younger persons who apparently do not think that they "now smoke."

While it is straightforward to define some behaviors such as use of a certain drug during a specified reference period, there are also important population measures for which definitions can be complicated and controversial. Two of these are the misuse of prescription drugs and the need for treatment for a substance use problem. The choice of definitions for these topics could have major implications for organizations involved in providing services as well as government agencies responsible for regulating, monitoring, and funding services and research. Prescription drug misuse can range from simply taking a pill that was left over from

TABLE 17.3 Percentage of Population Reporting Current Smoking, by Age Group, Definition and Survey: 2008 NHIS and NSDUH

Age Group	NHIS	NSDUH	NSDUH, Excluding <100 Cigarettes
18 and older	21.0	25.5	23.6
18–25	21.5	35.5	28.2
26–34	25.2	33.8	31.5
35–49	23.4	27.6	26.4
50–64	21.5	22.1	21.7
65+	9.3	9.9	9.7

a prior prescription for dental work to alleviate current pain, all the way to "shopping" multiple doctors for prescriptions and making street purchases from drug dealers in order to support an addiction. The potential definition of misuse has multiple facets, including but not limited to reasons for use, whether the owner of the prescription is the user, dosage amounts and frequency of use in relation to what is prescribed, and timing of use in relation to the date of the prescription. Another difficulty for survey designers is the multitude of drugs on the market, some of which are sold in several dosages and formulations. It is not feasible to ask specifically about each drug, given respondent burden concerns. Some surveys, including the NSDUH, have employed visual aids such as cards with photographs of common pills to help respondents to understand the drug class definitions and recall the drugs they have used. But for surveys like NSDUH that are attempting to track trends over time, another problem is the continual changes in the prescription drugs that are available, with some being removed from the market or shifting to OTC (over-the-counter) status, and new drugs becoming available.

Defining treatment need raises similar issues, and various definitions have been used in different contexts. In this case, however, there is a general consensus among data users that an appropriate definition is one based on diagnostic criteria used in clinical practice, published by the American Psychiatric Association in the DSM. Substance dependence and substance abuse constitute substance use disorders in the (DSM-IV) manual, but an updated manual (DSM-V) was published in 2013. Survey designers have developed structured interview modules for administration by lay interviewers. These modules have been extensively tested and successfully implemented in various surveys, with results indicating that about 1 in 10 persons aged 18 and older in the United States had an alcohol or illicit drug use disorder in the past 12 months (Grucza et al. 2007).

17.3.6 QUESTION WORDING

Even with equivalent definitions, different question wordings can produce response distributions that vary widely from one another. This has been demonstrated numerous times in prior survey literature (Bradburn and Sudman 1991, Schuman and Presser 1981, Sudman and Bradburn 1982). In asking about drug use, there are several alternative strategies for wording questions, each with its own set of advantages and drawbacks. For most applications, the primary goal is to establish whether the respondent has used a given substance within a specified time period prior to the survey. More in-depth questions typically include frequency and quantity of use, patterns of use, and age at first use.

One approach to drug use questioning involves first asking about lifetime use, with "yes" or "no" response options. Respondents who report no lifetime use are skipped out of further questioning on that substance. Respondents reporting lifetime use may then be asked about recent use, such as within the past year or month, and other items of interest. This method has the advantage of asking the least sensitive question (lifetime use, as opposed to current use) first, and is not cognitively complex, at least at the outset. Disadvantages include a lack of efficiency, in that multiple questions have to be asked in order to arrive at the desired information, and the possibility that respondents will learn to answer in the negative to lifetime "gate" questions in order to avoid having to answer further questions about each substance (see discussion of interleaved vs ensemble approaches below). Another strategy is to simply ask about current use, either with "yes" and "no" response categories, or by asking for frequency of use, within the time frame of interest. In the latter case, the response option of zero is allowed, and the question would likely contain the phrase, "if any" or something similar. This method has an obvious advantage in efficiency, but in the case of the frequency method, the process of determining frequency for a substance that the respondent may or may not have used is somewhat taxing from a cognitive perspective, and may also be considered to be leading respondents, which could result in a bias toward positive responding.

Research by Kroutil et al. (2010) makes it clear that open-ended questions about drug use can produce substantial underreporting. Respondents who were asked about lifetime misuse of prescription stimulants, for example, were at least seven times less likely to report their use than when they were later queried about their use of individual stimulants, such as Adderall. The tendency to under-report in the open-ended condition was found to be inversely related to the educational level. Thus, this method would not at all be advisable for younger respondents, and is highly questionable overall.

The structure of response options is also a concern in question wording, particularly when numeric categories are the options. Careful consideration must be given to the number of categories and their relative size. Obviously, analytic needs must be taken into account, but it is also important to be aware of the body of existing research on this topic. Tourangeau et al. (2000) provide a review, and work by Tourangeau and Smith (1996) illustrates a particular point. In their study, shifting response categories from a low scale (0, 1, 2, 3, 4, 5 or more) to a higher scale (0, 1–4, 5–9, 10–49, 50–99, 100 or more) more than doubled the number of sex partners reported. Gfroerer et al. (1997) discussed this effect in their comparison of NHSDA and MTF methodologies, citing it as one of several possible reasons for the differences obtained in substance use reporting between the two surveys. In general, it is quite possible to influence the response distribution by using categories that give the impression that the norm lies toward one or the other end, and this should be avoided when possible.

Finally, the crafting of question wordings is a process that is all too often left in the hands of people whose expertise lies elsewhere. It is imperative that questionnaire design specialists are consulted and utilized early and often in the development of survey questions. Quite frequently, concepts that are clear in the minds of analysts are anything but that in the minds of respondents, and qualitative methods such as focus groups (Morgan 1997), behavior coding (van der Zouwen and Smit 2004), cognitive testing (Willis 2005), and field studies provide means through which the alignment between research questions and survey questions can best be achieved. In substance use survey research, these methods can and have been used in a variety of ways. Among other examples, focus groups consisting of experienced drug abusers can help to identify new substances being consumed, clarify street nomenclature and any regional differences therein, provide insight into unusual methods of substance administration, and quantify common street dosages, consumer quantities and pricing. Behavior coding can help to identify questions that make participants uneasy or confused, and cognitive testing should be carried out for all of the reasons above. In addition, cognitive testing helps to assure that the substance use concepts being asked about match those held by respondents, and that the questions are worded in such a way that respondents can answer them easily.

17.3.7 QUESTION ORDERING

Question order effects have been studied rather extensively in prior literature (see Tourangeau et al. 2000, for a review). With respect to survey context affecting responses to questions on sensitive topics, the question ordering can be especially problematic in ongoing surveys intended to monitor trends over time. Any questionnaire change, such as adding or removing questions, could affect the reporting on subsequent questions that may be important trend indicators. One small change that was made in the NSDUH was the removal in 2003 of an item assessing attitudes toward smoking one or more packs of cigarettes daily. This omission resulted in a large shift between 2002 and 2003 in the distribution of responses to the subsequent item, which probed attitudes toward adults trying marijuana or hashish. The shift, which was toward increased approval, was examined *post hoc* and it was determined that the omission of the cigarette item changed the anchor for subsequent responding. In other words, if respondents indicated disapproval of smoking, this created an anchoring point from which they indicated greater disapproval of trying marijuana or hashish. Without such an anchor, responses to the latter item were more approving (Wang et al. 2005).

Another type of question-ordering effect involves the ordering of filter or "gate" questions and their follow-up items (Kreuter et al. 2011, Duan et al. 2007, Bosley et al. 1999). In an interleaved format, gate questions (e.g., lifetime use items) for each substance are followed by items asking for detailed information regarding the use of the substance in question. In an ensemble, or grouped format, the gate questions are presented together, and follow-up items are delayed until after responses to all of the gate questions have been obtained. In the interleaved format, respondents learn that endorsement of a gate question results in receipt of burdensome follow-up items, and thus may tend to endorse fewer items toward the end of the list. The Kreuter et al. study was an attempt to assess response differences between the two formats, but the majority of topics covered were not sensitive. Duan et al. (2007) examined responses to mental health service use, which is likely to be considered sensitive, but neither of these studies probed drug use behavior. In both studies, however, there was a clear effect of question order format, with greater reporting occurring with the ensemble method.

17.3.8 INCENTIVE PAYMENTS

The effects of incentives on response rates have been documented in prior studies, although few have compared incentive to no-incentive with random assignment.

In general, it appears that incentives improve response rates as long as the incentive is perceived to be sufficient, not excessive, and appropriate to the target population. There is also a growing line of evidence indicating that payment of the incentive prior to participation may be more effective in gaining cooperation (Groves and Couper 1998). What is not well understood is the effect of incentives on the responses themselves.

There are a few large federal studies that provide incentives, and thus little is known about potential response effects. Willimack et al. (1995) found qualitative improvements in data (more thorough verbal responses), but no other differences besides higher response rates, when an incentive was provided prior to the interview. This research was done with open-ended questions in a face-to-face survey. In 2001, NHSDA conducted an experiment to assess the effects of varying levels (0, \$20, \$40) of incentives on unit nonresponse. Analyses of rates of the use of various substances were also conducted in this (n = 2000) experiment. As one might predict, response rates were the highest among the \$40 incentive respondents, followed by \$20, with the weakest rates in the no-incentive condition. There were no significant effects on substance-use prevalence, although there were hints that drug-use endorsement was slightly more likely among respondents who received incentives. In 2002, NSDUH adopted a \$30 incentive for all 67,500 respondents, along with several other methodological changes. Response rates increased minimally compared with 2001 for older adults, but significantly for youths aged 12 to 17. Along with increased response rates, there were increases in drug use reporting that were well beyond expectations based on the increase in response rate. Unfortunately, because multiple methodological changes were introduced simultaneously with the incentive, and because of the time lapse between survey years, it is impossible to accurately quantify the change that resulted from the incentive. It is assumed, however, that the higher levels of reported drug use reflect a greater tendency toward honesty among respondents, which would of course mean that the data were of higher quality (Kennet et al. 2005).

Explanations for higher response rates and more honest reporting when incentives are provided typically are based on reciprocity norms, social exchange theory, or simply as a result of attitudinal changes brought about by the receipt of the incentive (Groves and Couper 1998). Teasing out the exact mechanisms through which this occurs is a project for future research, as is testing the validity of the presumably more honest reporting. Another finding from the testing and implementation of incentives in NSDUH was the lower net cost of the survey once the incentives were in place. In other words, there were cost reductions in data collection efforts that exceeded the outlays of over \$2 million for providing \$30 to 67,500 respondents. The savings were due to fewer initial respondent refusals, leading to significant reductions in time and travel cost for interviewers. The net savings is a result of the particular survey design and field structure of the NSDUH, and may not be the case for other surveys, but it should be a consideration in a survey designer's decision on whether to utilize incentives (Kennet et al. 2005).

17.4 Validation

Given the skepticism regarding the veracity of self reports of substance use (Miller 1997), there has always been great interest in validation studies, particularly involving the collection of biospecimens that can be tested for the presence of substances. Blood, saliva, and urine have been collected from survey respondents and tested for cotinine, which is the principal metabolite of nicotine. Most of these studies have found very good consistency, indicating accurate reporting of tobacco use in survey interviews (Caraballo et al. 2001). Validation studies of illicit drug use have been based on urine, saliva, and hair, and many have found evidence of underreporting. However, most of these studies have been done on special populations known to have high rates of drug use (e.g., arrestees and drug treatment clients) and whose propensity to report truthfully are likely to be very different from the general population (Harrison et al. 2007). One of the few general population validation studies was conducted by SAMHSA, using a subsample of respondents in the 2000 and 2001 NHSDA (Harrison et al. 2007). Urine and hair samples were requested and obtained for later testing from about 4000 NHSDA respondents aged 12 to 25 after the completion of their ACASI interview. Respondents were given \$25 for providing a hair sample and \$25 for providing urine, and the participation rate was excellent, with 89% of persons selected providing at least one biological sample and 81% providing both. Technical problems associated with laboratory procedures precluded the use of the hair samples for validation, but urine was tested for cotinine, marijuana, cocaine, amphetamine, and opiates. Findings were not reliable for cocaine, amphetamines, and heroin due to small sample sizes and other technical problems in testing. The results showed that ACASI self-reports of tobacco were reasonably accurate, with some underreporting. Among the respondents testing positive for cotinine, 80% had self-reported tobacco use in the past 30 days. Underreporting seemed to be more prevalent for marijuana use, for which 61% of those that tested positive had reported use. For both tobacco and marijuana, congruence between the self-report and urine test was better among young adults (age 18 to 25) than youth (age 12 to 17). One of the key findings of the study was that it demonstrated the difficulties in interpreting biospecimen data linked with self-report data. Because of all of the factors that can influence whether a chemical test will be positive (e.g., cutoffs used, time since last used, amounts used, long-term use, external contaminants, metabolism of respondent) the comparison of the test result with the self report is not straightforward. For example, a person who used marijuana heavily 6 weeks ago but not within the past 30 days could potentially show a positive test result for marijuana because of the prior heavy use. Another respondent who used only a small amount of marijuana 3 weeks prior to their interview could produce a negative urine test. About 4.4% of respondents reported no marijuana use in the past 30 days but tested positive, and 5.8% reported use in the past 30 days but tested negative. The percentage that both reported use and tested positive was 6.9%, while the remaining 72.9% reported no use and tested negative.

17.5 Alternative Estimation Methods

Concern about the validity of self-report data and the ability of household surveys to achieve adequate representation of "hard-core" drug users has spawned numerous alternative approaches to estimating the prevalence of hard core use. Some examples are discussed in the following.

17.5.1 NOMINATIVE METHOD

Under the supposition that respondents would be more likely to report on drug use by anonymous persons known by the respondent than their own drug use, researchers have explored approaches within the survey framework that use proxy reporting of drug use. One application of this is the nominative technique, which is a variant of multiplicity methods developed for the purposes of studying rare diseases (Sirken 1975). Survey respondents were asked to report how many close friends they had, and then report how many of them had used heroin. With appropriate correction for duplication, an estimate of the prevalence of heroin use in the population can be derived (Miller 1985).

17.5.2 RESPONDENT-DRIVEN SAMPLING (RDS)

Like the nominative method, RDS is a method of surveying rare or hard-to-reach populations that takes advantage of the relationships between members of the population of interest. RDS applies this information in sampling and in estimation. As in "snowball" or network sampling, respondents are asked to recruit their peers, and study managers keep track of who recruited whom and their numbers of social contacts. A mathematical model of the recruitment process then weights the sample to compensate for the nonrandom recruitment procedures. RDS has been used to study injection drug users in Bangkok and Vietnam (Salganik and Heckathorn 2004). See also the discussion of RDS in Chapter 4.

17.5.3 ITEM COUNT AND OTHER RANDOMIZED QUESTIONING APPROACHES

A variety of randomized questioning techniques have been tried in surveys as a way of obtaining data on sensitive topics such that respondents do not directly reveal their answers to anyone. The randomized response approach involves having each respondent randomly select one of two questions they will answer (either the sensitive question or an innocuous question, both of which have the same response options), keeping the identity of the question secret from the interviewer or others. This allows the respondent to reveal the answer to the question without disclosing any sensitive information. The method has been problematic due to respondents either not correctly making the random selection or because of their suspicion of the process and failure to follow the protocol. An alternative method that has been attempted for estimating the prevalence of cocaine use is the item count method. With this method, the randomization of questions is controlled by the survey designers in the questionnaire administration. All respondents are given a question in which they are shown a list of behaviors and asked to report the number of the behaviors they had engaged in. For half of the sample the list would include a fixed set of items, while for the other half of the sample the list would include the same set of items, plus one more—cocaine use. A population estimate of cocaine use is derived by estimating the mean number of behaviors reported in each half-sample and subtracting the estimate based on the sample without the cocaine question from the estimate based on the sample with the cocaine question (Biemer et al. 2005).

17.5.4 RATIO ESTIMATION

The nominative and randomization approaches are designed to produce an overall prevalence estimate. But these methods are not designed to facilitate more in-depth record level analysis of substance use behavior. An approach that maintains this capability in a survey data file is ratio estimation. This method is simply an extension of the commonly used weighting adjustment procedure poststratification, which typically involves adjustment of weights to population control totals to reduce variance and account for undercoverage. The underlying assumption of poststratification is that the external control totals are benchmarks that are more accurate than the population estimates that would result just from the weighted survey data. The application to hard-core drug use estimation is based on the same criterion, but the external controls used are from data sources that are known to capture large numbers of hard-core drug users, such as arrest and drug treatment counts. Survey responses to questions on arrest and drug treatment are used to stratify the sample and then weights are adjusted by strata using the external counts. Assuming the underreporting and undercoverage of arrest and treatment is similar to the underreporting and undercoverage of hard-core drug use, hard-core drug use estimates should be improved. When this method was applied to NHSDA data, the estimate of past year heroin use increased by 82% (from 323,000 to 588,000), the estimate of injection drug use increased by 55% (from 659,000 to 1.0 million) and the estimate of weekly cocaine use increased by 29% (642,000 to 829,000) (Wright et al. 1997).

17.5.5 CAPTURE–RECAPTURE AND OTHER MODELING APPROACHES

A method that has been used to estimate the prevalence of heroin use is capture–recapture procedures, originally designed to estimate wildlife populations. For animal populations, the method involves capturing a random sample of animals, tagging them, releasing them, and then later (after the tagged animals have had time to mix with the full population) capturing another random sample of animals. On the basis of the sample sizes and the number of tagged animals in the second draw, it is possible to generate an estimate of the size of the uncaptured population. The motivation for using this method to estimate heroin prevalence was probably the availability of good data on the treatment history of heroin addicts, including data bases with information that permitted matching of person records across different treatment episodes. By making the assumption that an admission into treatment is analogous to a random selection from the total population and tagging of drug users, the data on treatment clients were exploited to produce heroin prevalence estimates at local and national levels, with no need to collect additional data (Woodward et al. 1985). The method has been used extensively to estimate the prevalence of problem drug use in European and Asian countries (Rehm et al. 2005). Simeone et al. (1995) developed an extension of the capture-recapture concept for estimating hard-core drug use in the United States, in which data from drug treatment programs, emergency departments, arrestee booking facilities, and homeless shelters were used to develop a statistical model of visit patterns to these locations among hardcore drug users. Estimates of the total number of hardcore drug users, including those with no visits to any of the locations, were generated based on the models. The method required extensive new data collection to provide input into the models. This methodology was tested in Cook County, Illinois, and produced an estimate of hardcore drug users that was approximately three times the estimate obtained from standard survey methods. However, it has never been fully implemented nationally due to its high cost and questionable validity (Office of National Drug Control Policy 1997).

17.6 SUMMARY

This chapter highlights some of the important issues to consider in designing a survey on substance use. Relevant findings of methodological research concerning the various survey design options are cited. Obviously, the studies discussed are only a small sampling of the multitude of research results available. Where appropriate, conclusions that have been consistently found across different studies are mentioned. Often the literature is not clear on the effects of certain design features under certain conditions. In sorting through the research for guidance on design decisions, it may be helpful to keep some points in mind. First, quite often the results of a particular methodological research study may not be applicable to other similar but slightly different situations. For example, interactions among different design features could change the effects of a specific factor. An example of this could be if the effects of mode (e.g., self-administered vs interviewer administered) were smaller in a survey with strong confidentiality assurances than in one where confidentiality was not promised. Or the impact of a factor such as a mode effect may differ for different age groups, drugs, or even time periods of use of the same drug. Extending this concern about generalizability, designers and analysts of substance use surveys should use caution in transferring findings from general health survey methods research to substance use surveys. In particular, recent studies suggesting that surveys can achieve acceptable levels of nonresponse bias with very low response rates have rarely been done using self-report data on illicit drug use.

While the research indicates that a face-to-face ACASI design will generally produce the most accurate estimates of substance use prevalence among adults, ACASI or other face-to-face designs are not appropriate for most situations due to high costs. In fact, the major developmental effort to create an ACASI instrument, including voice-recording the entire questionnaire, would rarely be advisable in any survey other than a large sample, high budget survey. It is impossible to prescribe a "best" survey design applicable to all situations. The key is to understand the advantages and disadvantages of each design option, including the costs, and balance these considerations with the data needs and goals of the survey.

For organizations planning to conduct small-scale local or state-level or special population surveys with limited resources, survey designers may have few options. Usually there is interest in comparing results to data from large national surveys or surveys conducted in other jurisdictions or on other special populations. These comparisons typically are confounded by the different methodologies employed. Having an understanding of research findings on the effects of design characteristics on substance use estimates is therefore important for interpreting results. This chapter provides an initial framework for designers and analysts of substance use surveys to assess these effects. The authors hope that this chapter contributes to more efficient survey designs and improved accuracy in reporting the results of surveys.

REFERENCES

American Psychiatric Association. *Diagnostic and Statistical Manual of Mental Disorders.* 4th*(DSM-IV)* ed. Washington, DC: American Psychological Association; 1994.

Aquilino WS. Interview mode effects in surveys of drug and alcohol use. Public Opin Q 1994;58:210–240.

Aquilino WS, Wright DL, Supple AJ. Response effects due to bystander presence in CASI and paper-and-pencil surveys of drug use and alcohol use. Subst Use Misuse 2000;35(6–8):845–867.

Beebe TJ, Harrison PA, McRae JA, Anderson RE, Fulkerson JA. An evaluation of computer-assisted self-interviews in a school setting. Public Opin Q 1998;62: 623–632.

Beebe TJ, Harrison PA, Park E, McRae JA, Evans J. The effects of data collection mode and disclosure on adolescent reporting of health behavior. Soc Sci Comput Rev 2006;24:476–488.

Beebe TJ, Jenkins SM, Anderson KJ, Davern ME. Survey-related experiential and attitudinal correlates of future health survey participation: results of a statewide survey. Mayo Clin Proc 2008;83(12):1358–1363.

Biemer PP, Jordan BK, Hubbard M, Wright D. A test of the item count methodology for estimating cocaine use prevalence. In: Kennet J, Gfroerer J, editors. *Evaluating and Improving Methods Used in the National Survey on Drug Use and Health.* DHHS Publication No. SMA 05-4044, Methodology Series M-5. Rockville, MD: Substance Abuse and Mental Health Services Administration, Office of Applied Studies; 2005.

Blumberg SJ, Luke JV. Reevaluating the need for concern regarding noncoverage bias in landline surveys. Am J Public Health 2009;99(10):1806–1810.

Bosley J, Dashen M, Fox J. 1999. When should we ask follow-up questions about items in lists? *Proceedings of the Survey Research Methods Section of the American Statistical Association*. Available at http://www.bls.gov.osmr/pdf.st990220.pdf.

Bradburn NM, Sudman S. The current status of questionnaire research. In: Biemer P, Groves RM, Lyberg LE, Mathiowetz NA, Sudman S, editors. *Measurement Error in Surveys*. New York: Wiley; 1991. p 29–40.

Brener ND, Eaton DK, Kann L, Grunbaum JA, Gross LA, Kyle TM, Ross J. The association of survey setting and mode with self-reported health risk behaviors among high school students. Public Opin Q 2006;70(3):354–374.

Brener ND, Grunbaum JA, Kann L, McManus T, Ross J. Assessing health risk behaviors among adolescents: the effect of question wording and appeals for honesty. J Adolescent Health 2004;35:91–100.

Brittingham A, Tourangeau R, Kay W. Reports of smoking in a national survey: data from screening and detailed interviews, and from self- and interviewer-administered questions. Ann Epidemiol 1998;8:393–401.

CDC. Smoking-attributable mortality, years of potential life lost, and productivity losses --- United States, 2000–2004. MMWR 2008;57(45):1226–1228.

Caraballo RS, Giovino GA, Pechacek TF, Mowery PD. Factors associated with discrepancies between self-reports on cigarette smoking and measured serum cotinine levels among persons aged 17 years or older. Am J Epidemiol 2001;153(8):807–814.

Chromy J, Davis T, Packer L, Gfroerer J. Mode effects on substance use measures: comparison of 1999 CAI and PAPI data. In: Gfroerer J, Eyerman J, Chromy J, editors. *Redesigning an Ongoing National Household Survey: Methodological Issues*. DHHS Pub. No. SMA 03-3768. Rockville, MD: Substance Abuse and Mental Health Services Administration, Office of Applied Studies; 2002. p 135–159.

Couper MP. *Designing Effective Web Surveys*. New York: Cambridge University Press; 2008.

Courser MW, Shamblen SR, Lavrakas PJ, Collins D, Ditterline P. The impact of active consent procedures on nonresponse and nonresponse error in youth survey data: evidence from a new experiment. Eval Rev 2009;33(4):370–395.

Denniston MM, Brener ND, Kann L, Eaton DK, McManus T, Kyle TM, Roberts AM, Flkint KH, Ross JG. Comparison of paper-and-pencil versus web administration of the youth risk behavior survey: participation, data quality, and perceived privacy and anonymity. Comput Hum Behav 2010;26:1054–1060.

Duan N, Alegria M, Canino G, McGuire TG, Takeuchi D. Survey conditioning in self-reported mental health service use: randomized comparison of alternative instrument formats. Health Serv Res 2007;42:890–907.

Eaton DK, Lowry R, Brener ND, Grunbaum JA, Kann L. Passive versus active parental permission in school-based survey research: does the type of permission affect prevalence estimates of risk behaviors? Eval Rev 2004;28:564–577.

Fendrich M. The undeniable problem of recanting. Addiction 2005;100:143–144.

Fendrich M, Johnson TP. Examining prevalence differences in three national surveys of youth: impact of consent procedures, mode, and editing rules. J Drug Iss 2001;31(3):615–642.

Gfroerer J. Underreporting of drug use by youths resulting from lack of privacy in household interviews. In: Rouse B, Kozel N, Richards L, editors. *Self-Report Methods of Estimating Drug use: Meeting Current Challenges to Validity*. National Institute on Drug Abuse Research Monograph 57. DHHS Publication (ADM) 85-104. 1985. p 22–30.

Gfroerer J, Bose J, Kroutil L, Lopez M, Kann L. Methodological considerations in estimating adolescent substance use. In: *JSM Proceedings, Survey Research Methods Section*. Alexandria, VA: American Statistical Association; 2012.

Gfroerer JC, Hughes AL. The feasibility of collecting drug abuse data by telephone. Public Health Rep 1991;106(4):384–393.

Gfroerer J, Wright D, Kopstein A. Prevalence of youth substance use: the impact of methodological differences between two national surveys. Drug Alcohol Depend 1997;47:19–30.

Gribble JN, Miller HG, Cooley PC, Catania JA, Pollack L, Turner CF. The impact of T-ACASI interviewing on reported drug use among men who have sex with men. Subst Use Misuse 2000;35(6–8):869–890.

Groves RM, Couper MP. *Nonresponse in Household Interview Surveys*. New York: John Wiley & Sons, Inc.; 1998.

Grucza RA, Abbacchi AM, Przybeck TR, Gfroerer JC. Discrepancies in estimates of prevalence and correlates of substance use and disorders between two national surveys. Addiction 2007;102:623–629.

Hallfors D, Khatapoush S, Kadushin C, Watson K, Saxe L. A comparison of paper vs computer-assisted self interview for school alcohol, tobacco, and other drug surveys. Eval Program Plann 2000;23:149–155.

Harrison LD, Martin SS, Enev T, Harrington D. *Comparing Drug Testing and Self-Report Of Drug Use Among Youths And Young Adults in the General Population*(HHS Publication No. SMA 07-4249, Methodology Series M-7). Rockville, MD: Substance Abuse and Mental Health Services Administration, Office of Applied Studies; 2007.

Hines DA, Douglas EM, Mahmood S. The effects of survey administration on disclosure rates to sensitive items among men: a comparison of an internet panel sample with a RDD telephone sample. Comput Hum Behav 2010;26:1327–1335.

Johnston LD, O'Malley PM, Bachman JG, Schulenberg JE. *Monitoring the Future National Survey Results on Drug Use, 1975-2010: Volume I, Secondary School Students*. Ann Arbor: University of Michigan, Institute for Social Research; 2011.

Kann L, Brener ND, Warren CW, Collins JL, Giovino GA. An assessment of the effect of data collection setting on the prevalence of health risk behaviors among adolescents. J Adolescent Health 2002;31:327–335.

Kennet J, Gfroerer J, Bowman KR, Martin PC, Cunningham D. Introduction of an incentive and its effects on response rates and costs in NSDUH. In: Kennet J, Gfroerer J, editors. *Evaluating and Improving Methods Used in the National Survey on Drug Use and Health*. DHHS Publication No. SMA 05-4044, Methodology Series M-5. Rockville, MD: Substance Abuse and Mental Health Services Administration, Office of Applied Studies; 2005.

Kreuter F, McCulloch S, Presser S, Tourangeau R. The effects of asking filter questions in interleafed versus grouped format. Sociol Meth Res 2011;40(1):88–104.

Kroutil LA, Vorburger M, Aldworth J, Colliver JD. Estimated drug use based on direct questioning and open-ended questions: responses in the 2006 national survey on drug use and health. Int J Methods Psychiatr Res 2010;19(2):74–87.

Martino SC, McCaffrey DF, Klein DJ, Ellickson PL. Recanting of life-time inhalant use: how big a problem and what to make of it. Addiction 2009;104:1373–1381.

McCabe SE, Couper MP, Cranford JA, Boyd CJ. Comparison of web and mail surveys for studying secondary consequences associated with substance use: evidence for minimal mode effects. Addict Behav 2006;31:162–168.

Miller JD. The nominative technique: a new method of estimating heroin prevalence. In: Rouse B, Kozel N, Richards L, editors. *Self-report Methods of Estimating Drug use: Meeting Current Challenges to Validity*. National Institute on Drug Abuse Research Monograph 57. DHHS Publication (ADM) 85-104. 1985. p 104–124.

Miller PV. Is "up" right? The national household survey on drug abuse. Public Opin Q 1997;61:627–641.

Miller JW, Gfroerer JC, Brewer RD, Naimi TS, Mokdad A, Giles WH. Prevalence of adult binge drinking: a comparison of two national surveys. Am J Prev Med 2004;27(3):197–204.

Morgan DL. *Focus Groups as Qualitative Research. 2nd.* Qualitative Research Methods Series, Vol. 16 ed. Thousand Oaks, CA: Sage Publications, Inc.; 1997.

Office of National Drug Control Policy. *A Plan for Estimating the Number of "Hardcore" Drug Users in the United States, Preliminary Findings*. Executive Office of the President, Office of National Drug Control Policy, Office of Programs, Budget, Research, and Evaluation; 1997.

Percy A, McAlister S, Higgins K, McCrystal P, Thornton M. Response consistency in young adolescents' drug use self-reports: a recanting rate analysis. Addiction 2005;100:189–196.

Rehm J, Room R, van den Brink W, Kraus l. Problematic drug use and drug use disorders in EU countries and Norway: an overview of the epidemiology. Eur Neuropsychopharmacol 2005;15:389–397.

Rootman IR, Smart RG. A comparison of alcohol, tobacco and drug use as determined from household and school surveys. Drug Alcohol Depend 1985;16:89–94.

Ryan H, Trosclair A, Gfroerer J. Adult current smoking: differences in definitions and prevalence estimates—NHIS and NSDUH, 2008. J Environ Pub Health 2012;2012, Article ID 918368.

Salganik MJ, Heckathorn DD. Sampling and estimation in hidden populations using respondent-driven sampling. Sociol Methodol 2004;34:193–239.

Schober S, Caces MF, Pergamit M, Branden L. Effect of mode of administration on reporting of drug use in the national longitudinal survey. In: Turner CF, LesslerJT, Gfroerer JC, editors. *Survey Measurement of Drug Use: Methodological Studies*. DHHS Pub. No. ADM 92-1929. Rockville, MD: National Institute on Drug Abuse; 1992. p 177–219.

Schuman H, Presser S. *Questions and Answers in Attitude Surveys: Experiments on Question Form, Wording and Context*. New York: Academic Press; 1981.

Simeone RS, Rhodes WM, Hunt DE. A Plan for Estimating the Number of "Hardcore" Drug Users in the United States. Int J Addict 1995;30(6):637–657.

Singer E. Informed consent: consequences for response rate and response quality in social surveys. Am Sociol Rev 1978;43:144–162.

Singer E, Couper M. Communicating disclosure risk in informed consent statements. J Empir Res Hum Res Ethics 2010;5(3):1–8.

Sirken MG. Network surveys of rare and sensitive conditions. In: *Advances in Health Survey Research Methods*. National Center for Health Statistics Research Proceedings Series. 1975. p 31–32.

Substance Abuse and Mental Health Services Administration. *Reliability of Key Measures in the National Survey on Drug Use and Health*HHS Publication No. SMA 09-4425, Methodology Series M-8. Rockville, MD: Substance Abuse and Mental Health Services Administration; 2010.

Substance Abuse and Mental Health Services Administration. *Comparing and Evaluating Youth Substance Use Estimates from the National Survey on Drug Use and Health and Other Surveys*, HHS Publication No. SMA 12-4727, Methodology Series M-9. Rockville, MD: Substance Abuse and Mental Health Services Administration; 2012.

Sudman S. Examining substance abuse data collection methodologies. J Drug Issues 2001;31(3):695–716.

Sudman S, Bradburn N. *Asking Questions: A Practical Guide to Questionnaire Design*. San Francisco: Jossey-Bass; 1982.

Tourangeau R, Rips LJ, Rasinski K. *The Psychology of Survey Response*. Cambridge: Cambridge University Press; 2000.

Tourangeau R, Smith TW. Asking sensitive questions: the impact of data collection mode, question format, and question context. Public Opin Q 1996;60:275–304.

Tourangeau R, Yan T. Sensitive questions in surveys. Psychol Bull 2007;133(5):859–883.

Turner CF, Lessler JT, Devore JW. Effects of mode of administration and wording on reporting of drug use. In: Turner CF, Lessler JT, Gfroerer JC, editors. *Survey Measurement of Drug Use: Methodological Studies*. DHHS Pub. No. ADM 92-1929. Rockville, MD: National Institute on Drug Abuse; 1992. p 177–219.

Turner CF, Ku L, Rogers SM, Lindberg LD, Pleck JH, Sonenstein FL. Adolescent sexual behavior, drug use, and violence: increased reporting with computer survey technology. Science 1998;280:867–873.

Van der Zouwen J, Smit JH. Evaluating survey questions by analyzing patterns of behavior codes and question-answer sequences: a diagnostic approach. In: Presser S, Rothgeb JM, Couper MP, Lessler JT, Martin E, Martin J, Singer E, editors. *Methods for Testing and Evaluating Survey Questionnaires*. Hoboken, NJ: John Wiley & Sons, Inc.; 2004.

Wang K, Baxter R, Painter D. Modeling context effects in the national survey of drug use and health (NSDUH). In: *JSM Proceedings, Survey Research Methods Section*. Alexandria, VA: *American Statistical Association*; 2005.

Webb PM, Zimet GD, Fortenberry JD, Blythe MJ. Comparability of a computer-assisted versus written method for collecting health behavior information from adolescent patients. J Adolescent Health 1999;24:383–388.

Willimack DK, Schuman H, Pennell BE, Lepkowski J. Effects of a prepaid nonmonetary incentive on response rates and response quality in a face-to-face survey. Public Opin Q 1995;59(1):78–92.

Willis GB. *Cognitive interviewing: A Tool for Improving Questionnaire Design*. Thousand Oaks, CA: Sage Publications, Inc.; 2005.

Woodward JA, Bonett DG, Brecht ML. Estimating the size of a heroin-abusing population using multiple recapture census. In: Rouse B, Kozel N, Richards L, editors. *Self-report*

Methods of Estimating Drug use: Meeting Current Challenges to Validity. National Institute on Drug Abuse Research Monograph 57. DHHS Publication (ADM) 85-104. 1985. p 158–171.

Wright DL, Aquilino WS, Supple AJ. A comparison of computer-assisted and paper-and pencil self-administered questionnaires in a survey on smoking, alcohol, and drug use. Public Opin Q 1998;62:331–353.

Wright D, Gfroerer J, Epstein J. Ratio estimation of hardcore drug use. J Off Stat 1997;13(4):401–416.

ONLINE RESOURCES

Data and methodological descriptions for the National Survey on Drug Use and Health and other SAMHSA surveys, including reports describing survey methods and methodological studies exploring mode, setting, questionnaire, and other effects in substance use surveys, are available at: http://www.samhsa.gov/data/.

The Monitoring the Future survey website contains results, descriptions of methods used, and methodological research studies of school-based surveys. It can be accessed at: http://monitoringthefuture.org/.

The website for the CDC's Office on Smoking and Health, provides descriptions of major tobacco surveys, links to websites for surveys, and results. It also includes a Question Inventory on Tobacco, a web-based tool that categorizes over 6,000 tobacco questions used in surveys. This site can be accessed at: www.cdc.gov/tobacco/.

A description of methodology used in the National Comorbidity Survey, including a complete listing of published research papers and methodological research on the measurement of substance use disorders is available at: www.hcp.med.harvard.edu/ncs/publications.php.

Information on methods and results from a variety of surveys and studies on substance use in countries of the European Union can be accessed at: www.emcdda.europa.eu/.

CHAPTER EIGHTEEN

Collecting Survey Data on Sensitive Topics: Sexual Behavior

Tom W. Smith
NORC at the University of Chicago, USA

18.1 Introduction

The total survey-error perspective (Smith 2011b) delineates the many ways in which error can undermine data quality and lower the reliability and validity of survey-based information. Chief among the sources of error are those related to (i) sampling, including (a) frame inadequacies/limitations, (b) selection, and (c) sampling variation; (ii) nonobservation, including (a) noncoverage and (b) nonresponse; and (iii) observation/measurement error, including (a) collection matters related to (a) the data-collection medium (e.g., mode, use of computers), (b) auspice (e.g., survey sponsor, data-collection organization), (c) instrument design (e.g., question wording, response options, questionnaire context/order, constructing multiitem scales), (d) interviewers, (e) respondent characteristics (e.g., cognitive processing, self-presentation/social-desirability management), (f) processing (e.g., data entry, coding, editing/cleaning, data transfer, data documentation), and (g) analysis procedures (e.g., conceptual/theoretical, statistical, presentational).

When it comes to the topic of sexual behavior, all of these standard sources of error apply and a number of these error sources are magnified by the topic.

Handbook of Health Survey Methods, First Edition. Edited by Timothy P. Johnson.

This chapter examines these sources of error and discusses how they apply to the study of sexual behavior.

18.2 Sampling

Many major studies of sexual behavior have been based on nonprobability samples that do not represent the target population that they purport to cover (Cochran et al. 1953, Ericksen 1998, Smith 2006). Examples are the Kinsey studies of the sexual behavior on men and women and the Hite reports (Kinsey et al. 1948, Kinsey et al. 1953, Miller 1995, Smith 1989b). Fortunately, over the last two decades probability samples on sexual behavior have increasingly replaced convenience and self-selected samples (Herbenick et al. 2010, Laumann et al. 1994, Miller 1995, Pollack et al. 2005, Reece et al. 2010, Smith 2006).

Many studies of sexual behavior deal with relatively small populations for which there are no high quality sample frames (Clark et al. 2014). Examples include male and female homosexuals, the transgendered, and prostitutes. In some cases, these groups can be sampled by starting with the general population samples and screening down to the target population of interest. A serious limitation of this approach is that the smaller the target group, the larger and more costly the initial sample has to be. In other cases, it is possible to sample a target group more directly. Studies of prostitutes, for example, often identify areas where prostitutes work and contact them at these locations (Brewer et al. 2000, Freund et al. 1991, Shaver 2005). While successfully used in a number of studies, this approach in effect limits the study of prostitutes to surveys of streetwalkers and omits other groups of sex workers (e.g., "massage-parlor" employees, call girls).

Another approach uses some type of node sample (also known as respondent-driven or chain referral samples; Heckathorn (2002)) in which some usually small initial "sample" of the target population is asked to nominate other group members who are then followed-up. Especially when the initial node is not a representative sample of the target population and the selection probabilities of the nominated members are not known, such "snowball" samples may be very unrepresentative. See also discussions of this topic in Chapters 4 and 23.

Respondent selection in household samples is not typically a major difficulty, but problems can arise in so-called fluid households in which the attachment of some "residents" is uncertain such as boyfriends and girlfriends who intermittently live-in (Casper and Cohen 2000, Smith 2011a).

Sampling variation can be a special problem for sexual-behavior surveys when analysis needs to focus on small groups that have a large impact on outcomes disproportionate to their sample size (e.g., the role of needle injecting, sex workers on the spread of human immunodeficiency virus (HIV) and other sexually transmitted diseases (STDs)) or when a crucial subpopulation is highly clustered leading to a substantial design effect and therefore a much less efficient sample.

18.3 Nonobservation

A number of standard sample frames undercover subpopulations of particular interest in sexual-behavior studies. For example, prostitutes not living in households would be undercovered in household samples as would employees in work camps and dormitories common in some African countries and important in the spread of AIDS.

Of even greater challenge is nonresponse bias (Catania et al. 1986, Kupeck 1999, Peterman 1995, Smith 1989a, 1992a, 1992b, 1996b, 2003, Turner 1999, Wiederman 1999b). First, among the general population there is the danger that nonresponse will be greater among those reluctant to discuss sexual behavior perhaps out of modesty or prudishness or alternatively because the person has engaged in a socially suspect behavior. Self-selected samples are, of course, especially open to such participation bias, but even probability samples with nontrivial, nonresponse, and an appreciable difference in the sexual behaviors of respondents and nonrespondents will have notable nonresponse bias.

Second, there may be subpopulations of particular interest that are prone to nonresponse. Sex workers living in households probably are undercounted because they want to avoid scrutiny. Similarly, homosexuals in societies that stigmatize such orientation would tend to avoid interviews.

18.4 Observation/Measurement Error

As serious as sampling and nonobservation error is in sexual-behavior surveys, observation or measurement error is an even greater impediment. Both intentional and unintentional misreports are made by respondents. Social-desirability effects are particularly prominent (Brody 1995, Catania et al. 2005, Fu et al. 1985, Latkin and Vlahov 1998, Smith 1992b, Tourangeau et al. 1997). People underreport sexual behaviors that reflect negatively on them (e.g., infidelity; having had an abortion), and overreport behaviors that reflect positively (e.g., safe-sex practices). As Schlesinger (1998) remarked during hearings related to the Clinton impeachment, "Gentlemen always lie about their sex lives. Only a cad tells the truth about his love affairs."

However, the problem may go well beyond general, social-desirability concerns about privacy and/or disclosing embarrassing behavior. Some sexual experiences may be deeply traumatic (e.g., being a victim of rape or child abuse) or involve admitting to illegal behaviors (e.g., homosexual behavior in some societies, sexual assaults, the use of illegal drugs during sexual encounters). Extra special steps need to be taken when surveys touch upon such matters (Karabatsos 1997). For example, studies dealing with abuse and forced sex need to train interviewers about how to handle negative reactions to such questions. Often interviewers are equipped with materials that refer respondents to hotlines and other sources of help.

Several steps can be taken to minimize the social-desirability misreporting. First, the literature clearly demonstrates that more accurate reports of sexual behavior can be collected using self-completion modes than interviewer-administered surveys (Acree et al. 1999, Biggar and Melbye 1992, Blumberg et al. 2003, Boekeloo et al. 1998, Bowling 2005, Catania et al. 1986, Clark et al. 2013, Couper and Stinson 1999, Durant and Carey 2000, Ellen et al. 2002, Hewett et al. 2008, Kissinger et al. 1999, Morrison et al. 1999, Morrison-Beedy et al. 2006, Potdar and Koenig 2005, Sonenstein 1997, Testa et al. 2005, Tourangeau et al. 1997, Tourangeau and Smith 1996, 1998, Turner et al. 1998, Van Griensven et al. 2006, Zimmerman and Langer 1995). There is also some evidence that computer-administered surveys may be more accurate than other self-completion modes (Tourangeau and Smith 1996, 1998, Turner et al. 1998).

Second, more truthful responses can be encouraged by building a rapport between interviewer and respondent, better training and supervision of interviewers (Brewer and Garrett 2001, Brewer et al. 2005, Catania et al. 1996, Huygens et al. 1996), presenting a strong rationale for accuracy (e.g., improving public health), and/or by increasing confidentiality or anonymity.

Third, special techniques can be employed to both encourage truthful reporting and to detect misreports. These include the bogus-pipeline design (Tourangeau et al. 1997), the use of lie-detection scales (Bradburn et al. 1979, Brody 1995, DeMaio 1984), and both external and internal consistency checks (Catania et al. 1993, Smith 1992a, 1992b). For example, bogus-pipeline studies convince participants that some device or test can accurately detect whether respondent reports are true or false and therefore encourage truthful answers since lies would be revealed.

In addition to intentional misreporting linked to social-desirability and privacy effects, respondents unintentionally misreport for several reasons. First, sexual behavior often takes place in conjunction with the use of alcohol and/or drugs and these substances undermine accurate recall.

Second, many questions asked about sexual behavior are cognitively demanding. For example, they may ask about behaviors over a long period of time (e.g., number of life-time sexual partners) or detailed counts of behaviors (Downey et al. 1995, Shew et al. 1997, Zenilman et al. 1995).

Third, questions may use key terms that are not understood by all respondents or are inconsistently understood by different respondents (Binson and Catania 1998, Bogart et al. 2000, Carpenter 2001, Cecil and Zimet 1998, Gillmore et al. 2001, Hunter 2005, Leonard and Ross 1997, Miller 1995, Pitts and Rahman 2001, Ramjee et al. 1999, Remez 2000, Schuster et al. 1996, Smith 1999). For example, questions about engaging in "sex" or having "sex partners" sometimes do not clearly define the behaviors being asked about. In particular, whether oral sex or mutual masturbation count as "sex" is sometimes not made explicit and people are variable in how they classify and report on such behaviors (Remez 2000, Schuster et al. 1996, Smith 1999).

Also, questions need to avoid being too technical (e.g., using only medical terms) and too colloquial (e.g., using only contemporary terms like "hooking up" or "friends with benefits" that may not have clear and consistent meanings and are unlikely to persist over time). In addition, surveys in general need to employ languages other than English. This is especially true of using Spanish since that is by far the largest non-English speaking group in the United States and is especially important among young adults and adolescents (groups of particular interest in many sexual-behavior studies), and Hispanics are known to differ from other ethnic/racial groups on some sexual attitudes and behaviors. Translations into Spanish and other languages need to be carefully done to insure functional equivalence across languages and subpopulations.

Cognitive pretest can be used to design questions that maximize the accuracy of reports and minimize variable interpretation or misunderstanding of terms (Catania et al. 1993, Hunter 2005, Sonenstein 1997).

Fourth, responses are influenced by the context or order of questions (Catania et al. 1996). The general practice is to ask the most sensitive questions last.

Finally, reports can be influenced by who sponsors a study and/or does the data collection. For example, having sponsorship by public health agencies both underscores the importance of the study and encourages accurate responses.

In addition, to misreports, there is the problem of item nonresponse to questions (Giami 1996, Kupek 1998, 1999). Item nonresponse can be reduced by various steps such as the cognitive pretesting of questions, making the questions less complex and thus easier to answer, and, in some cases, switching to self-completion.

Error also comes from coding and data-entry error. When faced with improbable outliers, researchers must decide whether to censor the data to possibly eliminate error from incorrect data at the risk that such data adjustments will actually eliminate true variation and thus distort rather than improve results (Jasso 1985, 1986, Kahn and Udry 1986).

Finally, errors can also enter at the analysis stage. These include computation mistakes, poorly designed models, misapplied statistics, and many other types of errors by analysts. Here sexual-behavior studies do not appear to materially differ from the types of mistakes that occasionally affect studies in general.

Various study designs can be employed to increase reporting accuracy such as using panels with bounded recall, timeline follow-back interviews, diaries for continuous reporting, or life history calendars for improved retrospective reports (Catania et al. 1993, Stone et al. 1999, Huygens et al. 1996, Lauritsen and Swicegood 1997, Miller 1995). Reports of attitudes can, of course, be improved by the development of reliable multivariable scales and by such other techniques as using factorial vignettes and policy capturing methodology (Daker-White 2002, Wiederman 1999a).

In addition, since numerous sources of error affect survey-based studies of sexual behavior, it is also important to cross-check survey reports both internally and externally. These include comparisons with (i) medical records (Brody 1995, Catania 1996, Catania et al. 1993, Clark 1997b, Zenilman et al. 1995), (ii) biomarkers (Hewett et al. 2008, Morris et al. 2006, Orr et al. 1997), (iii) aggregate-level indicators (e.g., condom sales and STD rates—Hewett et al. (2008)), (iv) related attitudes and/or behaviors (Smith 1992a, Metzler et al.

1992), (v) other sensitive data such as drug use (Wislar and Fendrich 2000), and (vi) multiple surveys for consistency (Kahn et al. 1988, Smith 1992a).

Specific Examples. To further illustrate issues regarding the measurement of sexual behavior in surveys, three specific examples are discussed: differences by gender in reports of heterosexual behavior, reports of same-gender orientation and behavior, and adolescent, sexual behavior.

The evidence is very mixed on the consistency of reports of heterosexual, sexual behavior by gender. On the one hand, studies have repeatedly shown that men report more opposite gender, sexual partners than women do and that even after making adjustments for various factors, the reports are inconsistent (Brewer et al. 2000, Brown and Sinclair 1999, Catania et al. 1993, Catania et al. 1996, Morris 1993, Smith 1992a, Sonenstein 1997, Wadsworth et al. 1996, Wiederman 1997). On the other hand, separate, but paired, reports by opposite gender, sex partners are often in close agreement on mutual sexual behaviors such as the frequency of sexual intercourse and the use of contraception (Catania et al. 1993, 1996, Carballo-Diéguez et al. 1999, Jaccard and Dittus 2000, Jaccard et al. 1998, Padian et al. 1995, Seal 1997, Upchurch et al. 1991).

Another specific challenge has to do with the measurement of sexual orientation and gender-related sexual behaviors (Acree et al. 1999, Blair 1999, Clark et al. 2013, Friedman et al. 2004, Laumann et al. 1994, Michaels 1998, Pathela et al. 2006, Plumb 2001, Rankow 1996, Savin-Williams 2006, Sell et al. 1995, Wight 1999). First, there is the general problem of underreporting since many gays and lesbians are not yet "out of the closet." This problem varies greatly both across societies and within societies across time as norms have changed. Second, there are several different ways to measure such orientation and behaviors. Among the chief dimensions that exist are sexual desire, sexual identity, and sexual behavior (Laumann et al. 1994, Michaels 1998). Close attention needs to be given to both the overlap and disconnect between these three dimensions and which dimensions are more relevant for the particular research questions being investigated. Third, especially when using the behavioral criteria, classification varies greatly according to the time period referenced (Laumann et al. 1994, Smith 2006). The timing and currency of sexual behaviors are very important for many research purposes. For example, a longer reference period will record more people engaged in same-gender, sexual behavior, but such a measure may be less useful in modeling the current and future spread of HIV. Finally, too little attention has been given to bisexual behavior even though most research indicates it is as common as or more common than exclusive homosexual behavior (Laumann et al. 1994, Smith 2006).

A final example concerns reports of sexual behavior by adolescents. This group is very important to study because formative patterns established at this stage have lifelong consequences and because much high risk behavior occurs during this life stage (e.g., unprotected sex leading to teenage pregnancies and STDs). In general, studies of adolescent sexual behavior have found that in well-designed and well-executed studies, data can have sufficient accuracy to allow scientifically creditable analysis to be conducted (Ansuini 1996, Boekello et al. 1998, Brener et al. 2002, 2003, 2004, Clark et al. 1997, Durant and Carey 2000, Ellen et al. 2002, Friedman et al. 2004, Hearn et al. 2003, Jaccard 1998, 2000, Kahn et al. 1998, Lauritsen and Swicegood 1997, Metzler et al. 1992, Orr et al. 1997, Potdar and Koenig 2005, Remez 2000, Rosenthal et al. 1998, Schuster et al. 1996, Shew et al. 1997, Sonenstein 1997, Turner et al. 1998, Upchurch et al. 2002, Wight 1999). In general, test/retest analyses have usually found adolescent data to be sufficiently reliable to support meaningful analysis. Data do tend to be of lower quality among younger adolescents and, in some cases, among some minority groups (see above cites).

18.5 Summary

Studying sexual behavior is an especially challenging task. There are many impediments to obtaining high quality data. But by following best practices, errors can be minimized and data that are usable, if not perfect, can be collected that will yield scientifically reliable and valid results.

REFERENCES

Acree M, Ekstrand M, Coates TJ, Stall R. Mode effects in surveys of gay men: a within-individual comparison of responses by mail and by telephone. J Sex Res 1999;36:67–75.

Ansuini CG. The source, accuracy, and impact of initial sexuality information on lifetime wellness. Adolescence 1996;31:283–89.

Biggar RJ, Melbye M. Responses to anonymous questionnaires concerning sexual behavior: a method to examine potential biases. Am J Public Health 1992;82:1506–1512.

Binson D, Catania JA. Respondent's understanding of the words used in sexual behavior questions. Public Opin Q 1998;62:190–208.

Binson D, Melbye M. Responses to anonymous questionnaires concerning sexual behavior: a method to examine potential biases. Am J Public Health 1992;82:1506–1512.

Blair J. A probability sample of gay urban males: the use of two-phase adaptive sampling. J Sex Res 1999;36:39–44.

Blumberg SJ, Cynamon ML, Osborn L, Olson L. The impact of touch-tone data entry on reports of HIV and STD risk behaviors in telephone interviews. J Sex Res 2003;40:121–128.

Boekeloo BO, Schamus LA, Simmens SJ, Cheng TL. Ability to measure sensitive adolescent behaviors via telephone. Am J Prev Med 1998;14:209–216.

Bogart LM, Cecil H, Wagstaff DA, Pinkerton SD, Abramson PR. Is it "sex"?: college students' interpretations of sexual behavior terminology. J Sex Res 2000;37:108–116.

Bowling A. Mode of questionnaire administration can have serious effects on data quality. J Public Health 2005;27:281–291.

Bradburn NM, Sudman S, Blair E, Locander W, Miles C. *Improving Interview Method and Questionnaire Design: Response Effects to Threatening Questions in Survey Research.* San Francisco, CA: Jossey-Bass; 1979.

Brener ND, Billy JO, Grady WR. Assessment of factors affecting the validity of self-reported health-risk behavior among adolescents: evidence from the scientific literature. J Adolescent Health 2003;33:436–457.

Brener ND, Kann L, Kinchen SA, Grunbaum JA, Whalen L, Eaton D, Joseph Hawkins MA, Ross JG. Methodology of the youth risk behavior surveillance system. MMWR. Recommendations and reports: morbidity and mortality weekly report. Recommendations and reports. Centers Dis Control 2004;53(RR-12):1.

Brener ND, Kann L, McManus T, Kinchen SA, Sundberg EC, Ross JG. Reliability of the 1999 youth risk behavior survey questionnaire. J Adolescent Health 2002;31:336–342.

Brewer DD, Garrett SB. Evaluation of interviewing techniques to enhance recall of sexual and drug injection partners. Sex Transm Dis 2001;28:666–677.

Brewer DD, Potterat JJ, Garrett SB, Muth SQ, Roberts JM, Kasprzyk D, Montano DE, Darrow WW. Prostitution and the sex discrepancy in reported number of sexual partners. Proc Natl Acad Sci 2000;97:12385–12388.

Brewer DD, Potterat JJ, Muth SQ, Malone PZ, Montoya P, Green DL, Rogers HL, Cox PA. Randomized trial of supplementary interviewing techniques to enhance recall of sexual partners in contact interviews. Sex Transm Dis 2005;32:189–193.

Brody S. Patients misrepresenting their risk factors for AIDS. Int J STD AIDS 1995;6: 392–398.

Brown NR, Sinclair RC. Estimating number of lifetime sexual partners: men and women do it differently. J Sex Res 1999;36:292–297.

Carballo-Diéguez A, Remien RH, Dolezal C, Wagner G. Reliability of sexual behavior self-reports in male couples of discordant HIV status. J Sex Res 1999;36:152–158.

Carpenter LM. The ambiguity of "having sex": the subjective experience of virginity loss in the United States. J Sex Res 2001;38:127–139.

Casper LM, Cohen PN. How does POSSLQ measure up? Historical estimates of cohabitation. Demography 2000;37:237–245.

Catania JA. The reliability of partner reports of sexual histories in a heterosexual STD clinic population. Sex Transm Dis 1996;23:522.

Catania JA, Binson D, Canchola J, Pollack LM, Hauck W, Coates TJ. Effects of interviewer gender, interviewer choice, and item wording on responses to questions concerning sexual behavior. Public Opin Q 1996a;60:345–375.

Catania JA, Canchola J, Pollack L. Response to "They said It couldn't be done: the National Health and Social Life Survey". Pub Opin Q 1996b;60:620–627.

Catania JA, McDermott LJ, Pollack LM. Questionnaire response bias and face-to-face interview sample bias in sexuality research. J Sex Res 1986;22:52–72.

Catania JA, Turner H, Pierce RC, Golden E, Stocking C, Binson D, Mast K. Response bias in surveys of AIDS-related sexual behavior. In: Ostrow DG, Kessler RC, editors. *Methodological Issues in AIDS Behavioral Research*. New York: Plenum Press; 1993. p 133–162.

Cecil H, Zimet GD. Meanings assigned by undergraduates to frequency statements of condom use. Arch Sex Behav 1998;27:493–505.

Clark LR, Brasseux C, Richmond D, Getson P, D'angelo LJ. Are adolescents accurate in self-report of frequencies of sexually transmitted diseases and pregnancies? J Adolescent Health 1997;21:91–96.

Clark, MA, Rosenthal, S, Boehmer, U. Surveying sexual and gender minorities. Johnson T, editor. *Handbook of Health Survey Methods*, 2014. p 589–621.

Cochran WG, Mosteller F, Tukey JW. Statistical problems of the Kinsey report. J Am Stat Assoc 1953;48:673–716.

Couper MP, Stinson LL. Completion of self-administered questionnaires in a sex survey. J Sex Res 1999;36:321–330.

Daker-White G. Reliable and valid self-report outcome measures in sexual (dys)function: a systematic review. Arch Sex Behav 2002;31:197–209.

DeMaio TJ. Social desirability and survey measurement: a review. In: Turner CFM, editor. *Surveying Subjective Phenomena*. New York: Russell Sage Foundation; 1984.

Downey L, Ryan R, Roffman R, Kulich M. How could I forget? Inaccurate memories of sexually intimate moments. J Sex Res 1995;32:177–191.

Durant LE, Carey MP. Self-administered questionnaires versus face-to-face interviews in assessing sexual behavior in young women. Arch Sex Behav 2000;29:309–322.

Ellen JM, Gurvey JE, Pasch L, Tschann J, Nanda JP, Catania J. A randomized comparison of A-CASI and phone interviews to assess STD/HIV-related risk behaviors in teens. J Adolescent Health 2002;31:26–30.

Ericksen JA. With enough cases, why do you need statistics? Revisiting Kinsey's methodology. J Sex Res 1998;35:132–140.

Freund M, Lee N, Leonard T. Sexual behavior of clients with street prostitutes in Camden, NJ. J Sex Res 1991;28:579–591.

Friedman MS, Silvestre AJ, Gold MA, Markovic N, Savin-Williams RC, Huggins J, Sell RL. Adolescents define sexual orientation and suggest ways to measure it. J Adolesc 2004;27:303–317.

Fu H, Darroch JE, Henshaw SK, Kolb E. Measuring the extent of abortion underreporting in the 1995 National Survey of Family Growth. Fam Plann Perspect 1998;30:128–138.

Giami A. Partial non-response and "don't know" responses in surveys on sexual behaviour. Soc Sci Inform 1996;35:93–109.

Gillmore MR, Gaylord J, Hartway J, Hoppe MJ, Morrison DM, Leigh BC, Rainey DT. Daily data collection of sexual and other health-related behaviors. J Sex Res 2001;38:35–42.

Hearn KD, O'Sullivan LF, Dudley CD. Assessing reliability of early adolescent girls' reports of romantic and sexual behavior. Arch Sex Behav 2003;32:513–521.

Heckathorn DD. Respondent-driven sampling II: deriving valid population estimates from chain-referral samples of hidden populations. Soc Probl 2002;49:11–34.

Herbenick D, Reece M, Schick V, Sanders SA, Dodge B, Fortenberry JD. Sexual behavior in the United States: results from a national probability sample of men and women ages 14–94. J Sex Med 2010;7:255–265.

Hewett PC, Mensch BS, Ribeiro MCSDA, Jones HE, Lippman SA, Montgomery MR, van de Wijgert JH. Using sexually transmitted infection biomarkers to validate reporting of sexual behavior within a randomized, experimental evaluation of interviewing methods. Am J Epidemiol 2008;168:202–211.

Hunter J. A report on cognitive testing of cohabitation questions. Survey Methodol 2005;6.

Huygens P, Kajura E, Seeley J, Barton T. Rethinking methods for the study of sexual behaviour. Soc Sci Med 1996;42:221–231.

Jaccard J, Dittus PJ. Adolescent perceptions of maternal approval of birth control and sexual risk behavior. Am J Public Health 2000;90:1426.

Jaccard J, Dittus PJ, Gordon VV. Parent-adolescent congruency in reports of adolescent sexual behavior and in communications about sexual behavior. Child Dev 1998;69:247–261.

Jasso G. Is it outlier deletion or is it sample truncation? Notes on science and sexuality. Am Sociol Rev 1986;51:738–742.

Jasso G. Marital coital frequency and the passage of time: estimating the separate effects of spouses' ages and marital duration, birth and marriage cohorts, and period influences. Am Sociol Revi 1985;50:224–241.

Kahn JR, Kalsbeek WD, Hofferth SL. National estimates of teenage sexual activity: evaluating the comparability of three national surveys. Demography 1988;25:189–204.

Kahn JR, Udry JR. Marital coital frequency: unnoticed outliers and unspecified interactions lead to erroneous conclusions. Am Sociol Rev 1986;51:734–737.

Karabatsos G. The sexual experiences survey: interpretation and validity. J Outcome Meas 1997;1:305.

Kinsey AC, Pomeroy WB, Martin CE. *Sexual Behavior in the Human Male*. Philadelphia: W.B. Saunders; 1953.

Kissinger P, Rice J, Farley T, Trim S, Jewitt K, Margavio V, Martin DH. Application of computer-assisted interviews to sexual behavior research. Am J Epidemiol 1999;149:950–954.

Kupek E. Determinants of item nonresponse in a large national sex survey. Arch Sex Behav 1998;27:581–594.

Kupek E. Estimation of the number of sexual partners for the nonrespondents to a large national survey. Arch Sex Behav 1999;28:233–242.

Latkin CA, Vlahov D. Socially desirable response tendency as a correlate of accuracy of self-reported HIV serostatus for HIV seropositive injection drug users. Addiction 2002;93:1191–1197.

Laumann EO, Gagnon JH, Michael RT, Michaels S. *The Social Organization of Sexuality: Sexual Practices in the United States*. Chicago: University of Chicago Press; 1994.

Lauritsen JL, Swicegood CG. The consistency of self-reported initiation of sexual activity. Fam Plann Perspect 1997;29:215–221.

Leonard L, Ross MW. The last sexual encounter: the contextualization of sexual risk behaviour. Int J STD AIDS 1997;8:643–645.

Metzler CW, Noell J, Biglan A. The validation of a construct of high-risk sexual behavior in heterosexual adolescents. J Adolescent Res 1992;7:233–249.

Michaels, SK. Queer counts: the sociological construction of homosexuality via survey research [Unpublished Ph.D. thesis]. Chicago: University of Chicago; 1998.

Miller PV. A review: they said it couldn't be done: the National Health and Social Life Survey. Pub Opin Q 1995;59:404–419.

Morris M. Telling tails explain the discrepancy in sexual partner reports. Nature 1993;365:437–440.

Morris M, Handcock MS, Miller WC, Ford CA, Schmitz JL, Hobbs MM, Cohen MS, Harris KM, Udry JR. Prevalence of HIV infection among young adults in the United States: results from the Add Health Study. J Inf 2006;96:1091–1097.

Morrison DM, Leigh BC, Gillmore MR. Daily data collection: a comparison of three methods. J Sex Res 1999;36:76–81.

Morrison-Beedy D, Carey MP, Tu X. Accuracy of audio computer-assisted self-interviewing (ACASI) and self-administered questionnaires for the assessment of sexual behavior. AIDS Behav 2006;10:541–552.

Orr DP, Fortenberry DJ, Blythe MJ. Validity of self-reported sexual behaviors in adolescent women using biomarker outcomes. Sex Transm Dis 1997;24:261–266.

Padian NS, Aral S, Vranizan K, Bolan G. Reliability of sexual histories in heterosexual couples. Sex Transm Dis 1995;22:169.

Pathela P, Hajat A, Schillinger J, Blank S, Sell R, Mostashari F. Discordance between sexual behavior and self-reported sexual identity: a population-based survey of New York City men. Ann Intern Med 2006;145:416–425.

Peterman TA. Can we get people to participate in a study of sexual behavior? Sex Transm Dis 1995;22:164–168.

Pitts M, Rahman Q. Which behaviors constitute "having sex" among university students in the UK? Arch Sex Behav 2001;30:169–176.

Plumb M. Undercounts and overstatements: will the IOM report on lesbian health improve research? Am J Public Health 2001;91:873.

Pollack LM, Osmond DH, Paul JP, Catania JA. Evaluation of the Center for Disease Control and Prevention's HIV behavioral surveillance of men who have sex with men: sampling issues. Sex Transm Dis 2005;32:581–589.

Potdar R, Koenig MA. Does audio-CASI improve reports of risky behavior? Evidence from a randomized field trial among young urban men in India. Stud Fam Plann 2005;36:107–116.

Ramjee G, Weber AE, Morar NS. Recording sexual behavior: comparison of recall questionnaires with a coital diary. Sex Transm Dis 1999;26:374–380.

Rankow EJ. Sexual identity vs sexual behavior. Am J Public Health 1996;86:1822–1823.

Reece M, Herbenick D, Schick V. Guest Editorial. J Sex Med 2010;7:243–245.

Remez L. Oral sex among adolescents: is it sex or is it abstinence? Fam Plan Perspect 2000;32:298–304.

Rosenthal SL, Burklow KA, Biro FM, Pace LC, DeVellis RF. The reliability of high-risk adolescent girls' report of their sexual history. J Pediatr Health Care 1996;10: 217–220.

Savin-Williams RC. Who's gay? Does it matter? Curr Dir Psychol Sci 2006;15:40–44.

Schlesinger AM. *Hearing before the Subcommittee on the Constitution of the Committee on the Judiciary House of Representatives, 105th Congress, Second Session, November 9, 1998*(Series No. 63). Washington, DC: GPO; 1998.

Schuster MA, Bell RM, Kanouse DE. The sexual practices of adolescent virgins: genital sexual activities of high school students who have never had vaginal intercourse. Am J Public Health 1996;86:1570–1576.

Seal DW. Interpartner concordance of self-reported sexual behavior among college dating couples. J Sex Res 1997;34:39–55.

Sell RL, Wells JA, Wypij D. The prevalence of homosexual behavior and attraction in the United States, the United Kingdom and France: results of national population-based samples. Arch Sex Behav 1995;24:235–248.

Shaver FM. Sex work research methodological and ethical challenges. J Interpers Violence 2005;20:296–319.

Shew ML, Remafedi GJ, Bearinger LH, Faulkner PL, Taylor BA, Potthoff SJ, Resnick MD. The validity of self-reported condom use among adolescents. Sex Transm Dis 1997;24:503–510.

Smith TW. *A Methodological Review of the Sexual Behavior Questions on the 1988 and 1989 GSS. GSS Methodological Report No. 65*. Chicago: NORC; 1989a.

Smith TW. Sex counts: a methodological critique of Hite's women in love. In: Turner CF, Miller HG, Moses LE, editors. *AIDS: Sexual Behavior and Intravenous Drug Use*. Washington, DC: National Academy of Sciences Press; 1989b.

Smith TW. Discrepancies between men and women in reporting number of sexual partners: a summary from four countries. Biodemography Soc Biol 1992a;39:203–211.

Smith TW. A methodological analysis of the sexual behavior questions on the General Social Surveys. J Off Stat 1992b;8:309–326.

Smith TW. *American Sexual Behavior: Trends, Socio-Demographic Differences, and Risk Behavior*. National Opinion Research Center; 2006.

Smith TW. Review: the JAMA controversy and the meaning of sex. Pub Opin Q 1999;63:385–400.

Smith TW. *A Methodological Analysis of HIV Risk Behavior from the 1988–2002 General Social Survey. GSS Methodological Report No. 97*. Chicago: NORC; 2003.

Smith TW. Questions on cohabitation status. Unpublished NORC report; 2011a.

Smith TW. Refining the total survey error perspective. Int J Pub Opin Res 2011b;23: 464–484.

Sonenstein FL. Using self reports to measure program impact*. Children Youth Serv Rev 1997;19:567–585.

Stone VE, Catania JA, Binson D. Measuring change in sexual behavior: concordance between survey measures. J Sex Res 1999;36:102–108.

Testa M, Livingston JA, VanZile-Tamsen C. The impact of questionnaire administration mode on response rate and reporting of consensual and nonconsensual sexual behavior. Psychol Women Q 2005;29:345–352.

Tourangeau R, Rasinski K, Jobe JB, Smith TW, Pratt WF. Sources of error in a survey on sexual behavior. J Off Stat 1997a;13:341–365.

Tourangeau R, Smith TW. Asking sensitive questions the impact of data collection mode, question format, and question context. Public Opin Q 1996;60:275–304.

Tourangeau R, Smith TW. Collecting sensitive information with different modes of data collection. In: *Computer-Assisted Survey Information Collection*. New York: Wiley; 1998. p 431–453.

Tourangeau R, Smith TW, Rasinski KA. Motivation to report sensitive behaviors on surveys: evidence from a bogus pipeline experiment. J Appl Soc Psychol 1997b;27:209–222.

Turner CF, Ku L, Rogers SM, Lindberg LD, Pleck JH, Sonenstein FL. Adolescent sexual behavior, drug use, and violence: increased reporting with computer survey technology. Science 1998;280:867–873.

Turner HA. Participation bias in AIDS-related telephone surveys: results from the national AIDS behavioral survey (NABS) non-response study. J Sex Res 1999;36:52–58.

Upchurch DM, Lillard LA, Aneshensel CS, Li NF. Inconsistencies in reporting the occurrence and timing of first intercourse among adolescents. J Sex Res 2002;39:197–206.

Upchurch DM, Weisman CS, Shepherd M, Brookmeyer R, Fox R, Celentano DD, Hook EW. Interpartner reliability of reporting of recent sexual behaviors. Am J Epidemiol 1991;134:1159–1166.

Van Griensven F, Naorat S, Kilmarx PH, Jeeyapant S, Manopaiboon C, Chaikummao S, Jenkins RA, Uthaivoravit W, Wasinrapee P, Mock PA, Tappero JW. Palmtop-assisted self-interviewing for the collection of sensitive behavioral data: randomized trial with drug use urine testing. Am J Epidemiol 2006;163:271–278.

Wadsworth J, Johnson AM, Wellings K, Field J. What's in a mean? an examination of the inconsistency between men and women in reporting sexual partnerships. J Roy Stat Soc Ser A Stat in Soc 1996:111–123.

Wiederman MW. The truth must be in here somewhere: examining the gender discrepancy in self-reported lifetime number of sex partners. J Sex Res 1997;34:375–386.

Wiederman MW. Policy capturing methodology in sexuality research. J Sex Res 1999a;36:91–95.

Wiederman MW. Volunteer bias in sexuality research using college student participants. J Sex Res 1999b;36:59–66.

Wight D. Poor recall, misunderstandings and embarrassment: interpreting discrepancies in young men's reported heterosexual behaviour. Cult Health Sex 1999;1:55–78.

Wislar JS, Fendrich M. Can self-reported drug use data be used to access sex risk behavior in adolescents? Arch Sex Behav 2000;20:77–89.

Zenilman JM, Weisman CS, Rompalo AM, Ellish N, Upchurch DM, Hook EW 3rd, Celentano D. Condom use to prevent incident STDs: the validity of self-reported condom use. Sex Transm Dis 1995;22:15.

Zimmerman RS, Langer LM. Improving estimates of prevalence rates of sensitive behaviors: the randomized lists technique and consideration of self-reported honesty. J Sex Res 1995;32:107–117.

ONLINE RESOURCES

Links to national studies covering sexual behavior are listed below.

NORC's General Social Survey: www3.norc.org/GSS+Website.

National Survey of Family Growth: www.cdc.gov/nchs/nsfg.htm.

National Health and Social Life Survey: http://popcenter.uchicago.edu/data/nhsls.shtml.

National Longitudinal Study of Adolescent Health: www.cpc.unc.edu/projects/addhealth.

CHAPTER NINETEEN

Ethical Considerations in Collecting Health Survey Data

Emily E. Anderson
Neiswanger Institute for Bioethics, Stritch School of Medicine, Loyola University Chicago, Chicago, IL, USA

19.1 Introduction

This chapter presents an overview of ethical and regulatory issues relevant to health survey research. First, basic ethical principles and U.S. federal regulations are reviewed. Second, the risks posed by various kinds of health survey research and researchers' ethical responsibilities to minimize these risks are examined. Third, institutional review board (IRB) review and oversight for minimal risk and greater than minimal risk survey research is discussed. Fourth, the ethical and regulatory requirements for informed consent are outlined. Considerations for the inclusion of vulnerable participants are reviewed, followed by an analysis of strategies for participant recruitment and ethical issues that may arise in conducting surveys that ask participants to answer questions about, identify, or recruit other people. Finally, issues relevant to the collection of biomeasures and the prevention of data falsification in the field (curbstoning) are discussed.

Handbook of Health Survey Methods, First Edition. Edited by Timothy P. Johnson.

The chapter ends with a comprehensive list of Internet resources related to ethics and health survey research.

19.2 Background: Ethical Principles and Federal Regulations for Research

The need for sufficient numbers of respondents in health survey research is critical. Therefore, the success of research relies upon the public's trust and willingness to participate. Although there are few examples of harm to individuals from participation in survey research, damage done by any one researcher—regardless of field—can influence public trust in all kinds of research.

In the United States, formal oversight and federal regulations for the conduct of human research—and the articulation of the ethical foundation upon which these regulations rest—developed in direct response to incidents involving severe mistreatment of research participants (National Research Council 2003). While the most notorious of these abuses come from biomedical research, there are some notable examples of questionable behavior by social scientists (Baumrind 1964, Korn 1997, Milgram 1974).

The case of Laud Humphreys and the "tearoom trade" is of particular historical importance for health survey research. During the 1960s, Humphreys was a doctoral student in sociology at Washington University in St. Louis, MO. For his dissertation, Humphreys actively observed impersonal sex between men in public restrooms, referred to as the "tearoom trade". He recorded license plate numbers as men drove away; he later visited some of their homes, claiming to be conducting a general health survey, in order to gather sociodemographic information about these men and their families (Korn 1997). Humphreys (1970) dissertation, published as *Tearoom Trade: Impersonal Sex in Public Places*, was groundbreaking in that his data did not support stereotypes of homosexual men as deviant but rather demonstrated that they were ordinary members of society. For this, his research has been commended by gay activists; however, his deceptive methods generated major controversy within the field of sociology (Babbie 2004) and lend some credence to fearful claims that survey data are used for purposes other than those stated by researchers.

In the early 1970s, the scandal of the Public Health Service (PHS)-funded Tuskegee Syphilis Study became front page news (Jones 1981, Tuskegee Syphilis Ad Hoc Advisory Panel 1974). In 1973, the Senate Labor and Public Welfare Committee, chaired by Senator Edward Kennedy (D-MA), held hearings to investigate the potential need for increased government oversight of scientific research. As a result, the National Institutes of Health (NIH) "Policies for the Protection of Human Subjects" were raised to regulatory status, forming the Code of Federal Regulations Title 45 (Public Welfare), Part 46 (Protection of Human Subjects), Subpart A (Basic HHS Policy for Protection of Human Research Subjects) (referred to as 45 CFR 46). The National Research Act

(NRA) (P.L. 93-348), enacted on July 12, 1974, required all PHS grantees and contractors to establish IRBs to review human research protocols.

The NRA also established the National Commission for the Protection of Human Subjects of Biomedical and Behavioral Research (National Commission). The charge of this 11-member multidisciplinary committee, made up of researchers, philosophers, lawyers, and others, was to (i) identify ethical principles to govern the conduct of research and ensure fair selection and treatment of research participants, and (ii) recommend revisions to the regulations that would better protect participants' rights and well-being.

The *Belmont Report*, which was the National Commission's final publication, delineated three principles that provide a basic ethical framework for human research—respect for persons, beneficence, and justice—and linked these principles to existing ethical standards and practices (National Commission for the Protection of Human Subjects of Biomedical and Behavioral Research 1979). The principle of respect for persons translates into the requirement for participant-informed consent. Beneficence requires that risks to participants be balanced against potential research benefits and that researchers minimize risk to the extent possible. Justice demands that all groups share the burdens and benefits of research equitably.

The National Commission considered the role of IRBs and ultimately retained this cornerstone of the existing regulations (Gray 1978). By this time, due to the influence of earlier NIH policies, the system of local IRB review was fairly established at institutions receiving PHS funding. In response to the *Belmont Report* and other National Commission reports, expectations for IRB composition, function, and review were fleshed out in a 1981 revision of 45 CFR 46. In 1991, the Federal Policy for the Protection of Human Subjects (10 CFR 745, also known as the *Common Rule*) was enacted. Through the Common Rule, 16 agencies that support, conduct, or otherwise regulate human research adopted 45 CFR 46 Subpart A. The Food and Drug Administration (FDA) adopted some of the provisions and promulgated additional regulations specific to clinical drug trials that collect data to be used in applications for FDA approval (see www.fda.gov for a comprehensive list). Some agencies also adopted Subparts B (Additional Protections for Pregnant Women, Human Fetuses, and Neonates Involved in Research), C (Additional Protections Pertaining to Biomedical and Behavioral Research Involving Prisoners as Subjects), and D (Additional Protections for Children Involved as Subjects in Research).

As of 2014, federal oversight for the system of human research protections falls to the US Office of Human Research Protections (OHRP), which since 2000 has been located under the Office of the Secretary of Health and Human Services (HHS). (The former Office for the Protection of Research Risks was located at NIH.) The Common Rule regulates all research conducted in the United States (and research conducted outside the country by U.S. investigators) that is sponsored by the U.S. government or by institutions that receive federal funding. These regulations also apply when investigators are employed by institutions that require them to comply with federal regulations regardless of source of research funding (which is common policy at many academic institutions). The federal regulations outline requirements for review procedures and approval criteria for research protocols, but individual IRBs have wide discretion in formulating their own institutional policies and applying the regulations to individual protocols.

Briefly, in order to be approvable, proposed research must ensure that

1. risks to participants are minimized and
2. reasonable in relation to any anticipated benefits to participants, science, and society;
3. the selection of participants is equitable;
4. informed consent will be sought from each prospective participant or their legally authorized representative, in accordance with 45 CFR 46.116 (discussed in more detail below) and
5. appropriately documented, in accordance with, and to the extent required by 45 CFR 46.117 (also discussed in more detail below);
6. when appropriate, there are adequate provisions for monitoring the data collected to ensure participant safety;
7. provisions to protect participant privacy and maintain the confidentiality of data are adequate; and
8. when potential participants may be "vulnerable to coercion or undue influence" additional safeguards are included to protect their rights and welfare (45 CFR 46.111).

Ethics codes of professional societies (e.g., the American Association for Public Opinion Research and the American Sociological Association, see "Online Resources" section) supplement federal research regulations.

The Privacy Rule of the Health Insurance Portability and Accountability Act of 1996 (HIPAA) (http://www.hhs.gov/ocr/privacy/hipaa/administrative/privacy rule/index.html) and the Family Educational Rights and Privacy Act of 1974 (FERPA) (http://www2.ed.gov/policy/gen/guid/fpco/ferpa/index.html) establish policies for the use of administrative records for research purposes. These federal regulations are germane to research linking health survey data with medical and school records, respectively, and will be discussed in more depth below.

Given this history and a focus on the biomedical context, the regulatory system for protecting research participants has been criticized by many as being a poor fit for behavioral and social science research in general and low risk survey research in particular (Gunsalus et al. 2007, Kim et al. 2009, Oakes 2002, Singer and Levine 2003). In the late 1990s and early 2000s, government shutdowns of research activities at over a dozen academic medical centers increased Congressional scrutiny of human research (Oakes 2002, Phillips 2000), making proposals for decreased oversight somewhat controversial. Fortunately, recently proposed changes to the Common Rule (see http://www.hhs.gov/ohrp/humansubjects/anprm2011page.html, will be discussed in more detail below) suggest a potential decrease in review burden for some minimal risk survey research.

19.3 Defining, Evaluating, and Minimizing Risk

Health survey research often intersects with biomedical research though recruitment of actual patients as respondents, data collection in a medical setting or in the context of clinical research, or linkage with data from medical records or biological specimens. Complex protocols can present unique challenges for IRB submission and review. However, risk should be the primary criterion considered when evaluating the ethics of any research involving human participants.

Research protocols undergo different levels of ethical review based upon the risks they pose to participants, and it is critical that level of review be commensurate with risk (National Bioethics Advisory Commission 2001). Unfortunately, there is insufficient empirical evidence to guide evaluation of risks (although this is changing), and IRBs often apply the terms *risk* and *harm* somewhat indiscriminately, conflating magnitude and probability and sometimes considering temporary discomfort to be a harm (Campbell 2003).

The federal regulations define "minimal risk" research as that in which "the probability and magnitude of harm or discomfort anticipated ... are not greater in and of themselves than those encountered in daily life or during the performance of routine physical or psychological examinations or tests" (45 CFR 46.102(i)), a definition criticized as overly vague and therefore difficult to interpret and apply (Kopelman 2000, Resnik 2005). While research that is greater than minimal risk must be reviewed by the convened IRB (usually referred to as *full board review*), federal regulations allow for streamlined approval of minimal risk research, which includes most survey research (American Association for Public Opinion Research 2005). These provisions include exemptions from review and expedited review procedures (i.e., review of studies without convening a meeting of the IRB), which are discussed in greater detail below. Unfortunately, the Common Rule does not contain any guidance regarding what kinds of survey *questions* meet the criteria for "minimal risk."

In a 2003 report, the National Research Council outlined six categories of potential harms to research participants: physical (e.g., pain, temporary or permanent disability, death), psychological (e.g., depression, altered self-concept, increased anxiety, decreased confidence in others, guilt, fear, frustration, or receiving information about oneself that is unpleasant), social (e.g., stigma, decreased opportunities, negative changes in relationships), economic (e.g., loss of employment or insurance coverage), legal (e.g., arrest, incarceration), and dignitary (e.g., shame, embarrassment) (National Research Council 2003). Boredom and inconvenience are also sometimes considered "risks" of survey research (Labott and Johnson 2004). Since social, economic, legal, and dignitary harm all result from breach of privacy and confidentiality of information collected, these can be grouped under the rubric of "informational harm."

Assessing risk in survey research is not as straightforward as assessing risk in biomedical research; psychological and social harms are not as concrete (or measurable) as physical harm, and there is limited empirical information on which to base estimates of the likelihood and magnitude of different risks in various types of research activities. Furthermore, unlike some other types of research, participation in survey research offers no prospect of direct benefit; therefore, there is no real motivation for participation beyond altruism and no potential benefits against which to weigh potential harms (Labott and Johnson 2004). Further complicating risk assessment is the fact that evaluation of risk is subjective; people vary greatly in terms of their views and imagination regarding risk. IRB members assess risk based on their own experiences or intuitions rather than hard evidence and often do so without consideration of potential participants' perceptions and views (Rid et al. 2010, Singer and Levine 2003).

19.3.1 INFORMATIONAL RISKS

Perhaps the most likely risks of survey participation are those that may result from a breach of participant privacy or of the confidentiality of their data. Participants may want their involvement in research to be private and the information they provide confidential for a variety of reasons. Researchers and IRBs are responsible for evaluating the likelihood of breach and the magnitude of harm that could result from a breach and ensuring and implementing appropriate privacy protections.

Regulatory bodies (see HIPAA Security Standards, http://www.hhs.gov/ocr/privacy/hipaa/administrative/securityrule/index.html) and scientific societies (see the American Statistical Association's Privacy and Confidentiality Committee, http://www.amstat.org/committees/pc/index.html) have developed data security standards. However, due to the human elements of research, the risk of unwanted or unintentional disclosure of personal or sensitive information collected in research can never be completely eliminated. Protecting confidentiality must be considered at every stage of the research process; best practices include

1. storing participants' identifying information separately from data collected from survey instruments;
2. restricting access to identifying and/or linking information only to those project personnel who need it;
3. ensuring that computers used for processing raw data are not connected to any (wired or wireless) networks;
4. storing raw data (paper and electronic) in a locked office;
5. avoiding transferring files containing raw data over the internet and transporting encrypted data and passwords together; and
6. destroying identifying information (shredding paper documents and completely deleting electronic files) as early as possible (Klovdahl 2005).

Privacy is breached when people are seen participating in research by individuals whom they would prefer not know about their participation. Depending upon the purpose and target population of a survey, being identified as a research participant may place respondents at risk even if individual data are not sensitive, are kept secure, or are deidentified. Different modes of data collection pose different privacy risks. Mail can be intercepted by family members or neighbors, and phone messages and conversations may be overheard by others. For example, a young adult woman living at home who is not yet "out" to her parents may not want them to find out that she has agreed to participate in a survey about lesbians' smoking behavior, so any mail or phone messages directed to her should be discreet. Additionally, certain methods of identifying and recruiting participants may threaten privacy (e.g., trying to recruit individuals seeking services at HIV clinics, hanging out at gay bars, or attending Overeaters Anonymous meetings). Even when data are recorded anonymously, when interviewers meet with participants face-to-face there is always a risk of recognition, and location matters (Sieber and Stanley 1988).

Some health surveys collect information that may be considered sensitive; in such instances, a breach could stigmatize participants, harm personal and family relationships, or cause economic harm such as the loss of a job or insurance coverage. Ultimately, the risks involved in the storage of sensitive information greatly depend upon the amount of personally identifiable information that is collected and the potential for reidentification by unauthorized parties (McCallister et al. 2010). Personally identifying information is defined by the U.S. Department of Commerce National Institute of Standards and Technology as "any information about an individual maintained by an agency, including (i) any information that can be used to distinguish or trace an individual's identity, such as name, social security number, date and place of birth, mother's maiden name, or biometric records and (ii) any other information that is linked or linkable to an individual, such as medical, educational, financial, and employment information" (McCallister et al. 2010). There have been reported instances of "statistical disclosure," that is, deducing an individual's identity despite the absence of personal identifiers on a data file through matching an individual's deidentified record against another record containing this information, although little is known about the likelihood of such disclosures (Couper et al. 2008).

Survey researchers often want to link survey data with data from other sources such as medical records or government databases. The HIPAA Privacy Rule regulates disclosure of individually identifiable information by so-called "covered entities" (e.g., health care providers, health plans, etc.). Linking survey data and medical or other administrative records necessarily involves direct identifiers (name, social security number, address) and therefore requires informed consent from research participants. This has raised concerns regarding response rates and representativeness of respondents (Sakshaug et al. 2012). Valid informed consent requires that participants are aware of the potential risks and benefits of releasing and linking records. Concerns about reidentification are particularly complicated when genetic or genomic data are collected or accessed (Lowrance and Collins 2007).

All data collection activities undertaken by federal, state, or local governments (e.g., federally funded national surveys, vital statistics, public health surveillance, etc.) are subject to rules and regulations, and government agencies may have additional (more stringent) confidentiality restrictions on data they release. Even when laws allow for the release and sharing of data, uses other than those for which the information was intentionally collected should be carefully considered, and use should not extend beyond that for which respondents initially consented (Bernstein and Sweeney 2012).

In surveys that collect no personally identifying information, confidentiality may be adequately protected through a waiver of written informed consent [45 CFR 46.117]. (Waivers will be discussed in more detail below.) In other studies, even if the likelihood of reidentification is extremely small, the information collected may be so sensitive and a breach so potentially harmful to participants that additional protective measures are necessary. Examples may include surveys on socially stigmatized behavior such as the use of alcohol or illegal drugs; surveys that ask about illegal behavior such as prostitution or gang-related activity; surveys that collect information on sexual practices or preferences; or surveys of people with HIV/AIDS, mental health diagnoses, or genetic conditions. Researchers that plan to collect such sensitive information should consider obtaining a Certificate of Confidentiality (Wolf and Zandecki 2006). This certificate ostensibly protects personally identifiable information collected in research from *forced* disclosure; this means that investigators and others who have access to research data have a legal right to refuse to disclose information about research participants in any civil, criminal, administrative, legislative, or other proceeding, whether at the federal, state, or local level (http://grants.nih.gov/grants/policy/coc/). However, the immunity of academic researchers from subpoena by the U.S. government is currently in question amidst a legal battle between the U.S. Justice Department and Boston College over access to oral history records containing interviews with former members of the Irish Republican Army (Jaschik 2011).

Survey research conducted over the Internet raises unique privacy concerns. There is no completely secure interaction online, and therefore researchers should not promise complete confidentiality to online survey participants. In the United States, Internet Protocol (IP) addresses are not considered to be personally identifiable data. European Union data protection laws however *do* consider IP addresses to be personally identifiable, and researchers have cited concerns about the potential risk of identification through IP addresses. Care should be taken in choosing an online survey tool; the privacy policies of commercially available (or free) tools may conflict with institutional policy or good research practice. Encryption of data is highly recommended and, if data being collected are sensitive, researchers should work with their institutional information technology departments to ensure appropriate safeguards at the site of data collection (Buchanan and Hvizdak 2009).

19.3.2 PSYCHOLOGICAL RISKS

Many theoretical psychological risks of participation in behavioral and social science research have been discussed in the literature. In discussing psychological risk, it is important to remember that there is always the added protection of voluntary participation; additionally, participants can and do refuse to answer particular questions.

It has been suggested that health survey participation (or even the mere invitation to participate) may increase worry or anxiety about illness in participants who may not be experiencing illness, particularly in those participants recently diagnosed (especially when diagnoses are not yet confirmed or treatment options not yet decided) (Evans et al. 2002). Certainly thinking about unpleasant or painful issues may cause some people momentary discomfort. However, evidence suggests that this distress is usually temporary and rarely if ever leads to long-lasting psychological harm (American Association for Public Opinion Research 2005, Fendrich et al. 2007).

It is often assumed by researchers and IRB members that questions about socially undesirable behavior such as drug use or risky sexual activities can cause participants embarrassment and distress. Inclusion of language in surveys and informed consent documents warning participants of potentially sensitive questions is common despite limited knowledge of participant views regarding such questions. It has been argued that these "warning clauses" may exaggerate risks and prime uncomfortable feelings; empirical research has shown potential for warnings to adversely impact response rates (Singer 2003). Fendrich et al. (2007) propose that investigators include debriefing probes and measures in surveys that ask sensitive questions and recommend that reminders about participant rights to refuse to answer certain questions be separated from statements about potential risks in order to avoid exaggerating risks of adverse reactions.

The potential for negative reactions to survey questions is most salient in research with individuals who have already experienced physical, psychological, or emotional harm (Labott and Johnson 2004). For individuals who have been traumatized by events such as childhood abuse or war, just thinking about the experience can theoretically trigger emotional distress. However, data suggest that the likelihood of this risk is fairly low, and some studies have even shown that some research participants find talking about their problems to be beneficial, even therapeutic (Newman et al. 2006, Priebe et al. 2010, Weitlauf et al. 2007). However, despite limited evidence of harm, researchers should be respectful and consider that in trauma-related research, respondent burden is much higher than a general population health survey (Aiga 2007).

Certain groups of respondents may be more vulnerable to risk from research participation than others (Kipnis 2001). These include individuals with limited decisional capacity, such as children or cognitively impaired adults, or those whose autonomy is limited due to situational imbalances of power, such as students, employees, or prisoners. The additional risks of survey participation for vulnerable individuals are primarily risks to valid, voluntary informed consent, which will be discussed in more detail below.

19.3.3 RISKS THAT ARE BEYOND IRB PURVIEW

In evaluating risks and benefits of research, IRBs "should not consider possible long-range effects of applying knowledge gained in the research (for example, the possible effects of the research on public policy)" (45 CFR 46.111). From an ethical standpoint, however, investigators should consider risks that health survey research may pose to communities (Lee and Renzetto 1990). For example, findings may suggest high rates of socially undesirable behavior such as illegal drug use or child abuse or increased prevalence of genetic diseases within specific communities or population subgroups (Ross et al. 2010, Weijer and Emanuel 2000). Where such risks are present, many would argue that some form of community engagement is ethically imperative (DuBois et al. 2011).

Nothing forbids socially sensitive research, defined by Sieber and Stanley (1988) as "studies in which there are potential social consequences or implications, either directly for participants in the research or for the class of individuals represented by the research." However, subtle social forces may work against investigators conducting research in the areas of sexuality, race, violence, or illegal or otherwise stigmatized behavior. Research has shown that topic sensitivity negatively affects willingness to participate in survey research (Couper et al. 2008). Sometimes the forces are not so subtle; for example, at least one study suggests that socially sensitive research proposals are more likely to be rejected by IRBs (Ceci et al. 1985). Although this research is over 25 years old, anecdotes of research on sensitive topics being obstructed by IRBs still abound.

19.3.4 RESEARCHER RESPONSIBILITIES

If researchers anticipate that survey questions may cause distress to participants, measures for additional assessment and referral should be put in place before survey implementation (McKeown and Weed 2004). Depending upon the topic, the qualifications and experience of the individual(s) administering the survey should also be considered (Turnbull et al. 1988). Investigators and research staff may be in a position to discover information that could reasonably prevent harm; for example, researchers' may be ethically or even legally required to breach confidentiality when certain information is discovered in the course of research—whether through formal data collection procedures or less formal interaction with participants. Some of the more straightforward examples of when a breach may be necessary are when participants report abuse, suicidal ideation, or intent to harm themselves or others (Allen 2009, Amaya-Jackson et al. 2000, Lothen-Kline et al. 2003). It is ethically imperative that information about potential breaches be included in the consent form; however, data from depression research suggest that providing participants with information about extensive follow-up may negatively impact the validity of self-report measures (Stanton et al. 1991).

Other situations are less straightforward. For example, health surveys that link questionnaire data with information from medical tests (e.g., blood tests, genetic tests), may reveal an abnormal result or an unknown medical diagnosis. In some cases it may be ethically appropriate to allow participants to decide for themselves whether or not they want to know the results, for example if health survey research includes blood tests for cholesterol or blood sugar. Disclosing results of other kinds of tests (e.g., genetic or genomic tests) is more contested as information can be of limited validity and/or clinical utility; however, the science—as well as views on the potential harms and benefits of returning different kinds of results—is changing rapidly (Bredenoord et al. 2011).

Some health surveys put researchers in the position of de facto "auditors" of health care providers and/or organizations that are known to them (Evans et al. 2002). Complicating matters, patients who complete surveys may expect feedback or advocacy on an individual level, particularly when the goal of a survey is represented as improvement of medical care or services (Mayberry 2002). Evans et al. (2002) described a breast cancer survey in which participants were invited to provide open-ended responses to questions about breast pain. Several participants' responses indicated requests for clinical advice, and another suggested a potential problem with medical services, raising questions for the authors about their responsibilities. Participants who may not understand the unique role of the researcher and seek information about health care or symptoms may experience disappointment or frustration if their questions are not answered or they feel their input did not result in change.

19.4 Ethical Review of Health Survey Research

Before discussing ethics and IRB review in the United States, it should be noted that in the United Kingdom, there is no requirement for social surveys to undergo any form of ethical review. Health surveys involving National Health Service (NHS) staff must be approved by NHS research ethics committees (RECs), and some NHS RECs have charged that what is standard practice in survey research in the U.K. violates the ethical requirements for informed consent (Martin and Marker 2007).

19.4.1 EXEMPT RESEARCH

45 CFR 46.101(b) describes certain types of research that are *exempt* from the federal regulations, which means that they are excused from certain regulatory requirements, including IRB review. However, regulatory exemption does not excuse researchers from adhering to the general ethical principles of respect for persons, beneficence, and justice and standard practices for the protection of and respect for research participants. Exempt research includes that which involves educational tests, survey procedures, interviews, or observation of public behavior *unless* information is obtained and recorded in such a manner that participants can be identified *and* disclosure of responses could place participants "at risk of criminal or civil liability or be damaging to the [their] financial standing, employability, or reputation" (45 CFR 46.101(b)(2)). Certain exempt categories do not apply to research with children, and no research involving prisoners is eligible for exemption. OHRP recommends that investigators not be given independent

authority to judge when a protocol is exempt (Exempt Research Determination FAQs, http://answers.hhs.gov/ohrp/categories/1564), therefore, at most academic research institutions, all research protocols are required to undergo initial IRB review in order to substantiate an exempt determination.

19.4.2 MINIMAL RISK SURVEY RESEARCH AND EXPEDITED REVIEW

The following types of minimal risk health surveys often require expedited review: surveys to measure the effects of behavioral or medical interventions; longitudinal studies requiring participant contact over long periods of time and significant tracking efforts; and studies collecting information that will facilitate linking of survey day to other data sets (e.g., medical records). At some institutions, health surveys involving sensitive, stigmatized, or illegal behavior or that include vulnerable categories of participants may require review by the convened IRB, even when personally identifying information is not collected or stored.

Expedited review applies the same approval criteria for research activities as review by full board, but reviews are performed by either the IRB chair or an experienced IRB member appointed by the chair rather than the full board. Two conditions must be satisfied for a protocol to be eligible for expedited review: the research must be no more than minimal risk and the proposed research activity must be included in the list of nine eligible categories established by the Department of HHS and FDA (45 CFR 46.110; http://www.hhs.gov/ohrp/policy/expedited98.html). Four of these categories pertain to biomedical research, and two pertain to continuing research previously reviewed by a convened IRB. Of the three others, category seven is most applicable to health survey research:

> Research on individual or group characteristics or behavior (including, but not limited to, research on perception, cognition, motivation, identity, language, communication, cultural beliefs or practices, and social behavior) or research employing survey, interview, oral history, focus group, program evaluation, human factors evaluation, or quality assurance methodologies (Note that some survey research that fits this description—and the two categories discussed below—may be exempt, depending upon the nature of information collected and the potential identification of participants.) (45 CFR 46.110, Category seven)

For example, a voluntary survey in which respondents are recruited in a natural setting, either in person or through another medium (mail, telephone, or Internet) and are not otherwise exempt (e.g., data are not anonymous but also not potentially sensitive) would fit in this category.

Increasingly, health survey researchers are linking survey data with data from a variety of other sources, for example, biological, treatment, or diagnostic information from medical records, biospecimens, or other observations (see also Chapter 15). Categories five and six are relevant to health survey research employing these mixed methodologies.

> Research involving materials (data, documents, records, or specimens) that have been collected, or will be collected solely for nonresearch purposes (such as medical treatment or diagnosis). (45 CFR 46.110, Category five)

For example, a study that uses medical records and survey data to compare people's weight and other medical conditions with cultural attitudes of different subpopulations toward diet and exercise would fit in this expedited category (Social and Behavioral Research Working Group, Human Subjects Research Committee, and National Science and Technology Council 2008). It is important to note that participant informed consent will be necessary to allow researcher access to medical or other administrative records, since individual identifiers are needed to make the link.

A study that compares video-recorded parent–child conversations about smoking with data from surveys about child and parental attitudes toward smoking and other health-related behaviors would fit in expedited category six:

> Collection of data from voice, video, digital, or image recordings made for research purposes. (45 CFR 446.110, Category six)

The descriptions of expedited categories are broad, and the exact kinds of research activities that fall into the various categories are not obviously discernable. Most, but not all, of these types of research activities will be eligible for expedited review, but this will ultimately depend upon the study design, specific population, circumstances, the particular information collected, and any protections proposed by the investigator that might reasonably minimize the likelihood or magnitude of potential harm (including breach of confidentiality). Decision-making criteria and guidance for researchers regarding protocols eligible for expedited review varies by institution. Further, the federal regulations do not require IRBs to provide an option for expedited review; it is optional. Therefore, some institutions that review social and behavioral research do not fully utilize the option of expedited review, resulting in unnecessary delays and researcher frustration (DeVries et al. 2004). The Social and Behavioral Research Working Group of the Human Subjects Research Committee of the National Science and Technology Council published a guidance document on Expedited Review of Social and Behavioral Research Activities (2008) in an effort to encourage use of expedited procedures.

19.4.3 RECENTLY PROPOSED CHANGES TO THE FEDERAL REGULATIONS

In summer of 2011, the Office of the Secretary of HHS issued an advance notice of proposed rulemaking (ANPRM) requesting public comment regarding proposed changes to the Common Rule (http://www.hhs.gov/ohrp/humansubjects/anprm2011page.html). Proposed reforms most relevant to health survey research are those aimed at calibrating level of review with level of risk; simplifying the informed consent process; and establishing mandatory data security standards.

Suggested changes to requirements for initial and continuing IRB review of minimal risk studies qualifying for exempt and expedited review could significantly decrease investigator burden; clarifications regarding categories of research that qualify for less than full board review could minimize investigator confusion. At the time of publication, HHS is reviewing public comments and developing specific proposed revisions to the Common Rule.

IRBs have considerable latitude in terms of applying certain provisions of the Common Rule, and particularly little guidance is given to IRBs regarding assessment of risk in health survey research. The lack of available empirical data to inform risk judgment ultimately means that investigators are not able to provide participants with meaningful information regarding the kinds of psychological or social harms that could result from research participation nor the likelihood or magnitude of these risks. It is to an investigator's advantage to provide relevant data that can support claims about risk (e.g., comfort level of population with sensitive information, cultural norms regarding written informed consent) to the extent possible (Anderson and Sieber 2009), and more scientific evidence is needed to inform decisions about risk (National Research Council 2003). There is a growing body of research on research ethics that can inform researchers, IRB members, and human research protection program administrators (for example, see the *Journal of Empirical Research on Human Research Ethics*, http://www.csueastbay.edu/jerhre/).

19.5 Informed Consent for Survey Participation

Informed consent is the cornerstone of ethical research. Much attention is focused on the signed consent form, but informed consent is a process, not a signature on a piece of paper. In biomedical research, 20-page consent forms are common due to complex multistep protocols and institutional requirements for standard language.

The federal regulations do not require that respondents sign consent forms for minimal risk survey research. Key elements of informed consent can be succinctly presented to survey participants in cover pages, introductory screens, or telephone interviewer scripts (American Association for Public Opinion Research 2005). Signed consent is often not feasible (and sometimes burdensome), particularly when participants never interact with researchers in person or when interactions are very brief. What is most important in survey research is that key elements of informed consent are provided to individuals *before* they decide whether or not to participate. Participants' autonomy is further protected by the fact that they always have the option to not answer individual questions (American Association for Public Opinion Research 2005). The full range of procedures for informed consent in survey research that are acceptable by regulatory standards has not adequately been identified. What follows is general guidance.

19.5.1 ELEMENTS OF INFORMED CONSENT

The required basic elements for valid informed consent are outlined in 45 CFR 46.116. Potential survey participants should first and foremost be informed that they are being invited to participate in a research activity and that their participation is voluntary. The purpose of the survey should be explained, and participants should be provided with an adequate description of what they will be asked to do and the approximate amount of time it will take. Foreseeable risks or discomforts should be described as well as any anticipated benefits to participants, others, or society. The procedures that will be used to maintain the confidentiality of participant data should be detailed. Contact information should be provided for those who have questions about the research or want more information about their rights as participants.

19.5.2 WAIVER OF DOCUMENTATION OF WRITTEN INFORMED CONSENT

A signed consent form is not required in research that is exempt from federal regulations. For survey research that is undergoing full board or expedited review, the documentation of informed consent (i.e., signed informed consent) may be waived by the IRB, but the researcher must request a waiver (45 CFR 46.117(c)). Signed consent may be waived if research presents no more than minimal risk and "involves no procedures for which written consent is normally required outside of the research context" or if potential harm could result from a breach of confidentiality and the signed informed consent document is the only document linking participants' name to survey participation. Studies suggest that willingness to sign is not a perfect indicator of someone's willingness to participate in survey research, supporting the argument that IRBs should allow researchers some discretion to modify the ways in which consent is documented (Singer 2003).

19.5.3 WAIVING OR ALTERING INFORMED CONSENT

Waiving a signature is not equivalent to waiving informed consent. When the signature is waived, participants should still be provided with all the usual required details for informed consent. Waiver or alteration of informed consent may be appropriate in some types of survey research (45 CFR 46.117(d)). Limiting information about the actual or complete purpose of a survey is one way that informed consent may potentially be altered. For example, there may be instances in which information provided during the informed consent process may have a profound—and possibly detrimental—effect on the goals and objectives of the research, thereby reducing the generalizability of survey results (American Association for Public Opinion Research 2005, Singer 1984). Care must be taken to ensure that information provided during the informed consent process does not "interfere with sound research practice," and survey researchers should "use information methods that do not unduly exacerbate nonresponse bias [or] jeopardize the measures of knowledge, opinion and behavior in the survey" (American Association for Public Opinion Research 2005). For example, it may bias participants' responses to explicitly explain that a survey aims to measure respondents' level of racism or adherence to nutritional guidelines. It may be appropriate to debrief participants at the end of an interview to explain the actual or complete purpose of a survey. Participants should be allowed to withdraw from participation after any debriefing.

19.5.4 CHILDREN, ADULTS LACKING DECISION-MAKING CAPACITY, AND OTHER VULNERABLE GROUPS

Individuals who lack legal decision-making capacity and therefore are considered vulnerable in research include children and some adults with developmental disabilities (Kipnis 2001, 2003). Much has been made of threats to autonomy and the potential for researchers to coerce or "unduly influence" vulnerable individuals to participate, but in minimal risk research, concerns about coercion are arguably unwarranted (Hawkins and Emanuel 2005, Wendler 2005).

Certain safeguards can protect participants who cannot provide valid informed consent and ensure their ethical inclusion in research. Subpart D of the Common Rule, Additional Protections for Children Involved as Subjects in Research, outlines requirements for parental or guardian permission and the assent of the child as well as circumstances in which parental waivers may be permissible (Diviak et al. 2004, Levine 1995). Appropriate protections for adults with intellectual and developmental disabilities are risk and context dependent (Fisher 2003). In general population surveys, exclusion of individuals who lack decision-making capacity or are otherwise vulnerable defeats the goal of a randomized sample and violates the ethical principle of justice, particularly when the purpose of a survey is to improve public health or patient care (Mayberry 2002).

In the context of low risk research, vulnerability does not necessarily result from an individual's personal traits or group membership but rather their relationship to the research and the researcher. Therefore, care should be taken when studies are being conducted or commissioned—or individuals are invited to participate—by individuals or groups with authority over potential respondents, such as teachers, church leaders, employers, or physicians (American Association for Public Opinion Research 2005).

19.5.5 RECRUITMENT, VOLUNTARINESS, AND INCENTIVES

Unlike research studying medical interventions, many health surveys are aimed at generating statistical information describing a population as a whole. Therefore, respect for individual rights to refuse survey participation must be balanced with the public good of collecting unbiased data from a representative sample, and this calls for further delineation of ethically acceptable methods of persuasion (Martin and Marker 2007). We often focus on financial incentives, but almost anything that researchers do to try to increase survey response rates has ethical ramifications. It is not uncommon for IRBs to express concern about multiple reminders or aggressive refusal conversion efforts, although neither of these practices are always ethically unacceptable (Schirmer 2009).

Paying participants in research is standard practice, and there is evidence that incentives can reduce nonresponse bias (Martin and Marker 2007). Incentive payments should not raise any particular controversy in minimal risk research (Emanuel 2004). Payment is viewed with more caution by IRBs when participation poses greater than minimal risk as the research community is somewhat uncomfortable with the idea of compensation for risk (Singer and Bossarte 2006). Providing incentives to certain hard-to-reach subgroups or only in order to convert refusals also raises concerns about fairness (Kay et al. 2001). However, empirical research has shown that higher incentive payments do not induce people to accept research risks that they otherwise would not (Singer and Couper 2008). The federal guidelines do not provide guidance for determining appropriate payment amounts; however, cash or the cash value of other incentives should be reasonable compared with participant costs of time, travel, and inconvenience. Ultimately, investigators are responsible for minimizing all risks, and the informed consent process should ensure that participants understand the risks and potential benefits of a survey, regardless of incentive payment amounts.

It has also been argued that low income individuals are particularly susceptible to undue influence even from small amounts of money and that payment to certain groups should be limited based on their potential to misuse funds (Ritter et al. 2003). However, some ethicists have countered that limiting payment based on an arbitrary delineation of an offer "too good to refuse" is unjust—particularly in the case of minimal risk research (Wertheimer and Miller 2008). Empirical data does not support concerns that paying substance users encourages them to purchase drugs (Thurstone et al. 2010) or that low income individuals are more persuaded by money than wealthy individuals (Festinger et al. 2005, Halpern et al. 2004).

19.5.6 ASKING ABOUT OTHER PEOPLE: SECONDARY SUBJECTS, SOCIAL NETWORK STUDIES, SNOWBALL SAMPLING, AND RESPONDENT-DRIVEN SAMPLING

Questions about family health history and health-related behavior that occurs in the context of social relationships are common in health surveys. Decisions to participate in research may therefore have implications for a person's family or members of their social networks, especially if private or sensitive information about another individual is shared. In 2001, an adult woman was mailed a survey as part of a twin study being conducted by researchers at Virginia Commonwealth University; her father (with whom the woman lived) read the survey instrument, viewed questions about family members' health (in this case, whether the subject's father suffered from depression or had abnormal genitalia) as intrusive, and contacted the federal agency that is now OHRP, temporarily suspending all research at VCU. This incident heightened IRBs' sensitivity to the importance of considering whether second parties are research subjects and, if so, whether it is necessary to obtain informed consent from these individuals (Botkin 2001).

Family members are the most readily identifiable individuals, although in the case of most adults who do not live with their parents, the possibility of identification is extremely unlikely. If data are collected anonymously or family member records are delinked from those of the primary participant, the risk of identification is also quite low. Social network research—particularly that which studies the spread and control of human pathogens—requires identifying information about participants' "network associates," but if comprehensive confidentiality protections are in place, such research should qualify for a waiver of consent for secondary subjects as required by the Common Rule (Klovdahl 2005).

Snowball sampling is a nonprobability, "chain-referral" sampling technique in which existing research participants recruit future participants from among their peers and acquaintances. This technique, as well as respondent-driven sampling (RDS), a variation on snowball sampling, are often used in research with hard-to-reach populations for which there is no readily available sampling frame (see also the discussion of RDS in Chapter 4). Nonrandomly selected "seeds" serve as both participants and recruiters. Research that uses snowball sampling or RDS sometimes provides financial incentives both for survey completion as well as for recruitment of others. By design, seeds should not have a preexisting professional or fiduciary relationship with other participants, and study team members, not seeds, should obtain informed consent and administer the survey. Additional ethical safeguards for employing snowball sampling and RDS include setting a limit on the number of participants each seed can recruit and limiting the amount of remuneration to seeds for recruitment (Semaan et al. 2009).

19.6 Considerations for Data Collection

19.6.1 COLLECTING BIOMEASURES IN SURVEY RESEARCH

As discussed in great detail in Chapter 15, the integration of biomeasures into survey research is becoming increasingly common. It may not always be feasible—for reasons of both cost and convenience—to collect biospecimens or other health-related measures using trained medical professionals at a central location. Mobile collection services or self-administration are other options that are less burdensome on respondents and allow in-home collection. Additionally, studies have successfully used nonmedically trained interview staff to collect biomeasures including weight, height, waist circumference, blood pressure, vision, touch sensitivity, blood spots, and saliva testing (including oral swabs for HIV testing) (Jaszczak et al. 2009). If nonmedically trained interviewers are going to collect data, methods should be quick, simple, and minimally invasive; methods should also pose minimal risk to respondents and interviewers, create minimal psychological and physical discomfort, and protect respondent privacy. Ultimately, scientific considerations must be balanced with acceptability of techniques to respondents and practical considerations. The selection and training of interviewers should be carefully planned.

Participant informed consent should include the reason for collecting the biomeasures, the procedures that will be involved, the potential risks and benefits of the procedures, and precautions taken to minimize risk. Respondents should also be told which, if any, results they will receive. It is suggested that results that are immediately available (e.g., weight, waist, blood pressure, vision screening) should be provided to respondents at the end of their interview. Participants can be offered the opportunity to call and (anonymously) receive any results that require processing (e.g., blood sugar, HIV testing); however, results that are determined not to be clinically relevant or valid should not be provided to respondents (Jaszczak et al. 2009).

19.6.2 DATA INTEGRITY

Discussions in the literature of data falsification by survey interviewers (sometimes called *curbstoning*) are rare. On the basis of experience, Turner et al. (2002) report that an unexpectedly high yield of interviews, odd household composition, unusual response patterns for substantive questions, and limited information that allows for direct verification of survey responses (e.g., telephone numbers) may serve as clues that an interviewer is falsifying survey data. Interviewer training, supervision, and verification through observation or recording are the most effective ways to prevent and detect curbstoning (Ann Arbor Summit on Interviewer Falsification 2004, Johnson et al. 2001).

19.7 Summary

To summarize the key points covered in this chapter:

- Three ethical principles provide a framework for human research: respect for persons, beneficence, and justice.
- These ethical principles provide a basis for the Code of Federal Regulations Title 45 (Public Welfare), Part 46 (Protection of Human Subjects), Subpart A (Basic HHS Policy for Protection of Human Research Subjects) (referred to as 45 CFR 46).
- The principle of respect for persons translates into the requirement for informed consent from each prospective participant or their legally authorized representative. Minimal risk research may not require a signed consent form. However, all potential survey participants should be informed of the following: that they are being invited to participate in a research activity; that their participation is voluntary; what the purpose of the survey is; what they will be asked to do and the approximate amount of time it will take; any foreseeable risks or discomforts as well as anticipated benefits; procedures that will be used to maintain the confidentiality of participant data; and contact information for investigators and institutional representatives responsible for protecting research participants.

- Beneficence requires that risks to participants be balanced against potential research benefits and that researchers minimize harm to the extent possible. Most health surveys will meet regulatory criteria for minimal risk research. However, safeguards should be in place to adequately protect participants from possible harms that could result from the breach of sensitive personal information or psychological distress.
- Justice demands that all groups share the burdens and benefits of research equitably. Respect for individual rights to refuse survey participation must be balanced with the public good of collecting unbiased data from a representative sample.
- Federal research regulations developed in response to findings of abuse of participants in risky biomedical research. As a result, they have been criticized as a poor fit for behavioral and social science research, most of which is minimal risk.
- Federal research regulations are enforced by local IRBs, which have wide discretion when developing institutional policy and applying the regulations to individual research protocols.
- Currently, much survey research will qualify as exempt from certain regulatory requirements, but most academic research institutions require all protocols to undergo initial IRB review in order to make an exemption determination.
- Proposed changes to the federal research regulations will likely decrease burden on researchers conducting minimal risk health surveys.

REFERENCES

Aiga H. Bombarding people with questions: a reconsideration of survey ethics. Bull World Health Organ 2007;85:823–824.

Allen B. Are researchers ethically obligated to report suspected child maltreatment? A critical analysis of opposing perspectives. Ethics Behav 2009;19:15–24.

Amaya-Jackson L, Socolar RR, Hunter W, Runyan DK, Colindres R. Directly questioning children and adolescents about maltreatment: a review of survey measures used. J Interpers Violence 2000;15:725–759.

American Association for Public Opinion Research. Aapor statement for Irbs; 2005.

Anderson E, Sieber J. The need for evidence-based research ethics. Am J Bioethics 2009;9:60–62.

Ann Arbor Summit on Interviewer Falsification. Interviewer falsification in survey research: current best methods for prevention, detection, and repair of its effects. Surv Res 2004;25:1.

Babbie E. Laud Humphreys and research ethics. Int J Sociol Soc Policy 2004;24:12–19.

Baumrind D. Some thoughts on ethics of research: after reading Milgram's 'behavioral studies of obedience'. Am Psychol 1964;19:421–423.

Bernstein A, Sweeney M. Public health surveillance data: legal, policy, ethical, regulatory, and practical issues. Morb Mortal Wkly Rep 2012;61:30–34.

Botkin JR. Protecting the privacy of family members in survey and pedigree research. JAMA 2001;285:207–211.

Bredenoord AL, Kroes HY, Cuppen E, Parker M, van Delden JJM. Disclosure of individual genetic data to research participants: the debate reconsidered. Trends Genet 2011;27:41–47.

Buchanan EA, Hvizdak EE. Online survey tools: ethical and methodological concerns of human research ethics committees. J Empir Res Hum Res Ethics 2009;4:37–48.

Campbell R. 2003. Risk and harm in social science research. Paper presented at the Human Subjects Policy Conference. Available at http://xtf.grainger.illinois.edu:8080/xtfEthics/data/gunsalus/risk_and_harm v2rc/risk and harm_v2rc.pdf. Accessed on 8th June 2014.

Ceci S, Peters D, Plotkin J. Human subjects review, personal values, and the regulation of social science research. American Psychol 1985;40:994–1002.

Couper M, Singer E, Conrad F, Groves R. Risk of disclosure, perceptions of risk, and concerns about privacy and confidentiality as factors in survey participation. J Off Stat 2008;24:255–275.

DeVries R, DeBruin D, Goodgame G. Ethics review of social, behavioral, and economic research: where should we go from here? Ethics Behav 2004;14:351–368.

Diviak KR, Curry SJ, Emery SL, Mermelstein RJ. Human participants challenges in youth tobacco cessation research: researchers' perspectives. Ethics Behav 2004;14:321–334.

DuBois J, Bailey-Burch B, Bustillos D, Campbell J, Cottler L, Fisher C, Hadley WB, Hoop JG, Roberts L, Salter EK, Sieber JE, Stevenson RD. Ethical issues in mental health research: the case for community engagement. Curr Opin Psychiatry 2011;24:208–214.

Emanuel EJ. Ending concerns about undue inducement. J Law Med Ethics 2004;32:100–105.

Evans M, Robling M, Maggs Rapport F, Houston H, Kinnersley P, Wilkinson C. It doesn't cost anything just to ask, does it? The ethics of questionnaire-based research. J Med Ethics 2002;28:41–44.

Fendrich M, Lippert A, Johnson T. Respondent reactions to sensitive questions. J Empir Res Hum Res Ethics 2007;2:31–37.

Festinger DS, Marlowe DB, Croft JR, Dugosh KL, Mastro NK, Lee PA, et al. Do research payments precipitate drug use or coerce participation? Drug Alcohol Depend 2005;78:275–281.

Fisher C. Goodness-of-fit ethic for informed consent to research involving adults with mental retardation and developmental disabilities. Ment Retard Dev Disabil 2003;9:27–31.

Gray BH. Institutional review boards as an instrument of assessment: research involving human subjects in the US. Sci Technol Hum Values 1978;4:34–46.

Gunsalus C, Bruner E, Burbules N, Dash L, Finkin M, Goldberg J, Greenough W, Miller G, Pratt M. Improving the system for protecting human subjects: counteracting Irb "Mission Creep" (the Illinois White Paper). Qual Inq 2007;13:617–649.

Halpern S, Karlawish J, Casarett D, Berlin J, Asch D. Empirical assessment of whether moderate payments are undue or unjust inducements for participation in clinical trials. Arch Intern Med 2004;164:801–803.

Hawkins JS, Emanuel EJ. Clarifying confusions about coercion. Hastings Cent Rep 2005;35:16–19.

Humphreys L. *Tearoom Trade: Impersonal Sex in Public Places (Observations)*. Chicago, IL: Aldine; 1970.

Jaschik S. *Oral History, Unprotected*. 2011. Inside Higher Ed. Washington, DC: Kathlene Collins.

Jaszczak A, Lundeen K, Smith S. Using nonmedically trained interviewers to collect biomeasures in a national in-home survey. Field Methods 2009;21:26–48.

Johnson T, Parker V, Clements C. Detection and prevention of data falsification in survey research. Surv Res 2001;32:1–2.

Jones J. *Bad Blood: The Tuskegee Syphilis Experiment*. New York: The Free Press; 1981.

Kay W, Boggess S, Selvavel K, McMahon M. The use of targeted incentives to reluctant respondents on response rate and data quality. Paper presented at the Proceedings of the American Statistical Association; 2001.

Kim S, Ubel P, DeVries R. Pruning the regulatory tree. Nature 2009;457:534–535.

Kipnis K. *Vulnerability in Research Subjects: A Bioethical Taxonomy*. Commissioned by the. National Bioethics Advisory Commission for Ethical and Policy Issues for Research Involving Human Participants; 2001.

Kipnis K. Seven vulnerabilities in the pediatric research subject. Theor Med Bioeth 2003;24:107–120.

Klovdahl A. Social network research and human subjects protection: towards more effective infectious disease control. Soc Netw 2005;27:119–137.

Kopelman L. Moral problems in assessing research risk. IRB Ethics Hum Res 2000;22:3–6.

Korn J. *Illusions of Reality: A History of Deception in Social Psychology*. Albany, NY: State University of New York Press; 1997.

Labott S, Johnson T. Psychological and social risks of behavioral research. IRB Ethics Hum Res 2004;26:11–15.

Lee R, Renzetto C. The problems of researching sensitive topics. Am Behav Sci 1990;33:510–528.

Levine R. Adolescents as research subjects without permission of their parents or guardians: ethical considerations. J Adolescent Health 1995;17:287–297.

Lothen-Kline C, Howard DE, Hamburger EK, Worrell KD, Boekeloo BO. Truth and consequences: ethics, confidentiality, and disclosure in adolescent longitudinal prevention research. J Adolescent Health 2003;33:385–394.

Lowrance W, Collins F. Identifiability in genomic research. Science 2007;317:600–602.

Martin J, Marker DA. Informed consent: interpretations and practice on social surveys. Soc Sci Med 2007;65:2260–2271.

Mayberry J. The cost of questionnaire based research. J Epidemiol Community Health 2002;56:956–957.

McCallister E, Grance T, Scarfone K. *Guide to Protecting the Confidentiality of Personally Identifiable Information* (No. Special Publication 800-122). National Institute of Standards and Technology, US Department of Commerce; 2010.

McKeown R, Weed D. Ethical choices in survey research. Soz-Praventivmed 2004;49:67–68.

Milgram S. *Obedience to Authority: An Experimental View*. New York: Harper and Row; 1974.

National Bioethics Advisory Commission. *Ethical and Policy Issues in Research Involving Human Participants*. 2001. Washington, DC: U.S. Government Printing Office.

National Commission for the Protection of Human Subjects of Biomedical and Behavioral Research. *The Belmont Report: Ethical Principles and Guidelines for the Protection of Human Subjects of Research*. Washington, DC: U.S. Government Printing Office; 1979.

National Research Council. *Protecting Participants and Facilitating Social and Behavioral Sciences Research*: Panel on Institutional Review Boards, Surveys, and Social Science Research. Constance F. Citro, Daniel R. Ilgen, and Cora B. Marrett. Washington, DC: National Academies Press; 2003.

Newman E, Risch E, Kassam-Adams N. Ethical issues in trauma-related research: a review. Empir Res Hum Res Ethics 2006;3:29–46.

Oakes J. Risks and wrongs in social science research: an evaluator's guide to the Irb. Eval Rev 2002;26:443–479.

Phillips D. Irbs search for answers and support during a time of change. J Am Med Assoc 2000;283:729–730.

Priebe G, Backstrom M, Ainsaar M. Vulnerable adolescent participants' experience in surveys on sexuality and sexual abuse: ethical aspects. Child Abuse Negl 2010;34:438–447.

Resnik D. Eliminating the daily life risks standard from the definition of minimal risk. J Med Ethics 2005;31:35–38.

Rid A, Emanuel E, Wendler D. Evaluating the risks of clinical research. JAMA 2010;304:1472–1479.

Ritter A, Fry C, Swan A. The ethics of reimbursing injection drug users for public health research interviews: what price are we prepared to pay? Int J Drug Policy 2003;14:1–3.

Ross L, Loup A, Nelson R, Botkin J, Kost R, Smith G, Gehlert S. Human subjects protections in community-engaged research: a research ethics framework. J Empir Res Hum Res Ethics 2010;5:5–17.

Sakshaug JW, Couper MP, Ofstedal MB, Weir DR. Linking survey and administrative records: mechanisms of consent. Sociol Meth Res 2012;41:535–569.

Schirmer J. Ethical issues in the use of multiple survey reminders. J Acad Ethics 2009;7:125–139.

Semaan S, Santibanez S, Garfein RS, Heckathorn DD, Des Jarlais DC. Ethical and regulatory considerations in HIV prevention studies employing respondent-driven sampling. Int J Drug Policy 2009;20:14–27.

Sieber J, Stanley B. Ethical and professional dimensions of socially sensitive research. Am Psychol 1988;43:49–55.

Singer E. Public reactions to some ethical issues of social research: attitudes and behavior. J Consum Res 1984;11:501–509.

Singer E. Exploring the meaning of consent: participation in research and beliefs about risks and benefits. J Off Stat 2003;19:273–285.

Singer E, Bossarte R. Incentives for survey participation: when are they "coercive"? Am J Prev Med 2006;31:411–418.

Singer E, Couper M. Do incentives exert undue influence on survey participation? Experimental evidence. J Empir Res Hum Res Ethics 2008;3:49–56.

Singer E, Levine F. Protection of human subjects of research: recent developments and future prospects for the social sciences. Public Opin Q 2003;67:148–164.

Social and Behavioral Research Working Group, Human Subjects Research Committee, and National Science and Technology Council. National Science Foundation. *Expedited Review of Social and Behavioral Research Activities*. 2008. Washington, DC: U.S. Government Printing Office.

Stanton A, Burker E, Kershaw D. Effects of researcher follow-up of distressed subjects: tradeoff between validity and ethical responsibility. Ethics Behav 1991;1:105–112.

Thurstone C, Salomensen-Sautel S, Riggs PD. How adolescents with substance use disorder spend research payments. Drug Alcohol Depend 2010;111:262–264.

Turnbull JE, McLeod JD, Callahan JM, Kessler RC. Who should ask? Ethical interviewing in psychiatric epidemiology studies. Am J Orthopsych 1988;58:228–239.

Turner C, Gribble J, Al-Tayyib A, Chromy J. *Falsification in Epidemiologic Surveys: Detection and Remediation*. Washington, DC: Research Triangle Institute; 2002.

Tuskegee Syphilis Ad Hoc Advisory Panel. *Final Report of the Tuskegee Syphilis Ad Hoc Advisory Panel*. Washington, DC: U.S. Department of Health, Education and Welfare, Public Health Service; 1974.

Weijer C, Emanuel E. Protecting communities in biomedical research. Science 2000;289:1142–1144.

Weitlauf J, Ruzek J, Westrup D, Lee T, Keller J. Empirically assessing participant perceptions of the research experience in a randomized clinical trial. J Empir Res Hum Res Ethics 2007;2:11–24.

Wendler D. Protecting subjects who cannot give consent: toward a better standard for "minimal" risks. Hastings Center Rep 2005;35:37–43.

Wertheimer A, Miller F. Payment for research participation: a coercive offer? J Med Ethics 2008;34:389–392.

Wolf LE, Zandecki J. Sleeping better at night: investigators' experiences with certificates of confidentiality. IRB Ethics Hum Res 2006;28:1–7.

ONLINE RESOURCES

Links to Federal Policies, Agencies, and Reports are listed below.

Title 45 Public Welfare, Part 46 Protection of Human Subjects, Basic HHS Policy for the Protection of Human Research Subjects (45 CFR 46) http://ohsr.od.nih.gov/guidelines/45cfr46.html.

Office for Human Research Protections, U.S. Department of Health and Human Services www.hhs.gov/ohrp/.

National Commission for the Protection of Human Subjects of Biomedical and Behavioral Research. 1979. *The Belmont Report*. http://ohsr.od.nih.gov/guidelines/belmont.html.

National Bioethics Advisory Commission. 2001. *Ethical and Policy Issues in Research Involving Human Participants*. http://bioethics.georgetown.edu/nbac/pubs.html.

National Science Foundation. *Expedited Review of Social and Behavioral Research Activities*. www.nsf.gov/pubs/2008/nsf08203/index.jsp.

Exempt Research Determination FAQs http://answers.hhs.gov/ohrp/categories/1564.

Links to several Professional Society Codes of Ethics and Reports are listed below:

American Association for Public Opinion Research (AAPOR) Code of Ethics http://aapor.org/AM/Template.cfm?Section=Standards_andamps_Ethics&Template=/CM/ContentDisplay.cfm&ContentID=2397.

American Association for Public Opinion Research (AAPOR) Statement for IRBs. www.aapor.org/Full_AAPOR_IRB_Statement1.htm.

American Sociological Association Code of Ethics www.asanet.org/about/ethics.cfm.

American Statistical Association Ethical Guidelines for Statistical Practice www.amstat.org/committees/ethics/index.html.

American Association of University Professors. 2000. *Institutional Review Boards and Social Science Research*. www.aaup.org/AAUP/comm/rep/A/protecting.htm.

Association of Internet Researchers. 2002. *Ethical decision-making and Internet research: Recommendations from the AoIR Ethics Working Committee*. www.aoir.org/reports/ethics.pdf.

Links to resources concerning confidentiality and data security can be accessed at:

American Statistical Association's Privacy, Confidentiality, and Data Security Web site www.amstat.org/committees/pc/.

Guide to Protecting the Confidentiality of Personally Identifiable Information National Institute of Standards and Technology, US Department of Commerce http://csrc.nist.gov/publications/nistpubs/800-122/sp800-122.pdf.

NIH Certificates of Confidentiality Kiosk http://grants.nih.gov/grants/policy/coc/.

Protecting Personal Health Information in Research: Understanding the HIPAA Privacy Rule http://privacyruleandresearch.nih.gov/pr_02.asp.

Health Insurance Portability and Accountability Act of 1996 (HIPAA) Privacy Rule www.hhs.gov/ocr/privacy/hipaa/administrative/privacyrule/index.html.

HIPAA Security Standards www.hhs.gov/ocr/privacy/hipaa/administrative/securityrule/index.html.

Family Educational Rights and Privacy Act (FERPA) www2.ed.gov/policy/gen/reg/ferpa/index.html.

PART FOUR

Health Surveys of Special Populations

CHAPTER TWENTY

Surveys of Physicians

Jonathan B. VanGeest
Department of Health Policy and Management, College of Public Health, Kent State University, Kent, OH, USA

Timothy J. Beebe
Department of Health Sciences Research, Mayo Clinic, Rochester, MN, USA

Timothy P. Johnson
Survey Research Laboratory and Department of Public Administration, University of Illinois at Chicago, Chicago, IL, USA

20.1 Introduction

Surveys of physicians have a long history of use as a cost-effective means to assess provider attitudes, beliefs, and practices associated with the provision of health care. Although not well documented, initial surveys likely followed the compilation of the first physician directories at the state and interstate levels in the latter half of the nineteenth century, providing potential sampling frames for researchers. National registries also appeared around the same time. Examples include Polk's Medical and Surgical Register of the United States published in 1886, the Standard Medical Directory of North America published in 1902, and the American Medical Directory published in 1906 (Weisz 2005). While the earliest directories were often unreliable, as improvements were made they expanded opportunities for survey research. Use of surveys subsequently increased in the first half of the twentieth century, with an explosion of activity beginning in the 1960s. Some topics were relatively mundane, such as the 1929 survey of the economic aspects of practicing physicians in Detroit, Michigan (Sinai and Mills

Handbook of Health Survey Methods, First Edition. Edited by Timothy P. Johnson.

1931). Results of other surveys were employed with considerable public impact, leveraging the social/cultural authority of physicians as this too was evolving during the same period. One cogent example involves the surveys of physicians conducted by tobacco companies in the early part of the twentieth century that were used to support the marketing of tobacco products, despite concerns regarding potential negative health effects (Gardner and Brandt 2006).

Today, physician surveys remain an essential component of health services and policy research, providing input on physician opinions and practices critical to ongoing efforts to improve healthcare delivery and patient health outcomes. While not all encompassing, examples of physician surveys range from studies of more routine subjects like changing physician demographics (Boukus et al. 2009) career satisfaction (Chen et al. 2012, Landon et al. 2003, McMurray et al. 2000), and knowledge of and/or compliance with evidence-based practice recommendations (Meissner et al. 2011, Mosca et al. 2005, Salinas et al. 2011), to far more sensitive issues such as substance use among physicians (Hughes et al. 1999, Kenna and Lewis 2008), physician attitudes toward euthanasia (Farber et al. 2006), the use of deception in clinical practice (Everett et al. 2011, Lezzoni et al. 2012, Werner et al. 2002), and reactions to health reform (Antiel et al. 2014). In each instance, surveys were used effectively to advance our understanding of important and emerging issues related to health services delivery, with implications for solutions at both the policy and practice levels.

While important, conducting physician surveys is often challenging, with noted difficulties contacting practicing physicians both individually and within medical groups/practices (Klabunde et al. 2012, VanGeest and Johnson 2013). Response rates, a common benchmark upon which surveys are evaluated, are typically 10% lower than nonphysician surveys (Asch et al. 1997, Asch et al. 2000) and may be declining (Cartwright 1978, Cho et al. 2013, Cook et al. 2009, Cull et al. 2005, McLeod et al. 2013). Despite being a poor single predictor of overall survey quality (Davern 2013, Johnson and Wislar 2012), low response rates raise concerns about study precision and potential nonresponse bias. Research evidence does suggest that physician surveys may be more resilient to the effects of nonresponse than other types of surveys because the population of physicians tends to be rather homogeneous regarding knowledge, training, attitudes, and behavior (Bjertnaes et al. 2008, Kellerman and Herold 2001, McFarlane et al. 2007). However, studies have identified modest differences between responders and nonresponders and between early and late respondents on demographic and/or important practice-related characteristics (Cartwright 1978, Cull et al. 2005, Flanigan et al. 2008, Kellerman and Herold 2001, Martins et al. 2012, Oremus and Wolfson 2004, Parsons et al. 1994, Stocks and Gunnell 2000, Tambor et al. 1993, Templeton et al. 1997). Survey mode and topic effects on risk of nonresponse bias may also exist (Kellerman and Herold 2001, Sibbald et al. 1994, Young 2005). For these reasons, it remains important to employ methodologies shown to improve physician survey participation.

Fortunately, there is a growing body of literature on this topic and various participation-enhancing methods have been suggested with regard to physician surveys, including applications of established design- and/or incentive-based strategies, such as elements of the Tailored Design Method (TDM) (Dillman 2008).[1] To ensure success, however, we first need to explore why physicians are less likely to respond to surveys, as this information can then be used to inform strategic application of "best practices" to maximize participation.

20.2 Why Physicians do not Respond

Little research has been conducted on motivations or barriers to physician survey participation (Klabunde et al. 2013). However, research has explored why professionals generally are more reluctant to respond to surveys, with implications for physicians specifically (Cartwright 1978, Sudman 1985). In a seminal article, Sudman (1985) identified a number of potential reasons why professionals are hesitant to participate, including time constraints, topic relevance, and concerns about confidentiality. Of these, probably the most important factor in nonresponse is time. By all accounts, physicians are busy, with increasing workloads already a significant source of professional and personal stress. In such an environment, time spent completing a survey must compete directly with arguably more important tasks (Kaner et al. 1998). A second and related issue involves the perceived value of the study. Like other professionals, physicians will not take the time to complete a survey if the value of the study is not clear or is clear but perceived to be low (Thomas et al. 2003). This is also true if research broadly is not valued. Third, physicians will generally not complete a survey when they have concerns about the confidentiality of the results. Finally, the likelihood of nonresponse is greater in cases where individual questions may appear biased or not allow the respondent a full range of choices on the subject.

Issues related to economy of time are supported by studies examining physician unwillingness to participate in research projects generally, even despite acknowledgements of the importance of research in advancing medical understanding and practice (Hummers-Pradier et al. 2008, Salmon et al. 2007). Lack of time is further compounded by the growing volume and length of surveys that physicians are asked to respond to, increasing the likelihood of survey "burnout" (Kaner et al. 1998, MacPherson and Bisset 1995, McAvoy and Kaner 1996). Finally, researchers have also identified practice settings (with their various "gatekeepers") as an additional barrier to physician participation (Flanigan et al. 2008, Heywood et al. 1995, Klabunde et al. 2013, Moore and An 2001, Parsons et al. 1994, Sudman 1985, Thran and Hixson 2000). While often envisioned as the omnipresent office secretary, equally important are office policies dictating participation in surveys (Wiebe et al. 2012). Practice settings are becoming increasingly important in designing physician surveys, as trends indicate growth in larger practice sizes and corporate ownership of medical practices (Klabunde et al. 2013).

[1]The TDM, evolved from Dillman's earlier work on the Total Design Method (Dillman 1978), specifically recommends strategies for questionnaire design, initial contacts, use of monetary and nonmonetary incentives, and follow-up contacts designed to improve response rates.

20.3 Theory and Applications: Improving Physician Participation

Key intersections in physician decisions to participate in surveys can be presented in a conceptual model (Figure 20.1). This stepwise model identifies both contextual factors (e.g., health care settings, office gatekeepers, etc.) important to access, as well as more proximate individual level factors (e.g., individual perceptions of study relevance, attitudes toward research generally, time commitment, etc.) that influence how a request is weighed/valued and—ultimately—individual decisions to participate.

The conceptual model presented incorporates elements of a decision-stage model outlining steps in the process for completing physician surveys (Albaum and Smith 2012). This decision model was based on four categories of exchange theories of survey participation: (i) social exchange theory focusing on relative balance between rewards and costs; (ii) cognitive dissonance theory linking participation to avoidance of negative feelings associated with nonparticipation; (iii) self-perception associated with whether or not the respondent considers themselves to be someone likely to complete the survey; and (iv) commitment/involvement that is associated with the extent to which a topic is considered relevant. This decision-stage model has been linked to other—more encompassing—theoretical perspectives, most notably, Leverage Salience Theory (Groves et al. 2000), which posits that participation may depend, in part, on leverage applied by the survey researcher (see Klabunde et al. 2013). Each step then represents potential "leverage points" for fostering response. Thus, Figure 20.1 also suggests key opportunities for interventions tailored to a particular individual or groups of individuals such as physicians in this case. Typically, design-based and/or incentive-based interventions are used in efforts to improve response rates and overall quality of physician surveys. Targeted interventions can be utilized across the model to address contextual or organizational opportunities and barriers, as well as individual factors, important to improving participation. Both types of interventions are discussed in greater detail in the following paragraphs.

20.4 Sampling

A key initial step in any physician survey is sampling (DiGaetano 2013, Klabunde et al. 2012). Identifying an appropriate sampling frame has significant implications for both the cost and quality of the survey; with faulty sampling frames a common source of error. Bias is often the result of poor coverage (i.e., failure to identify all of the population or subpopulation of interest) or limitations in the completeness and/or accuracy of the contact information within the frame; increasing the likelihood that contacted cases may differ from respondents on key personal/professional attributes or measures of interest and thereby limiting the generalizability of study results. A variety of sampling frames are common in physician surveys (Table 20.1).

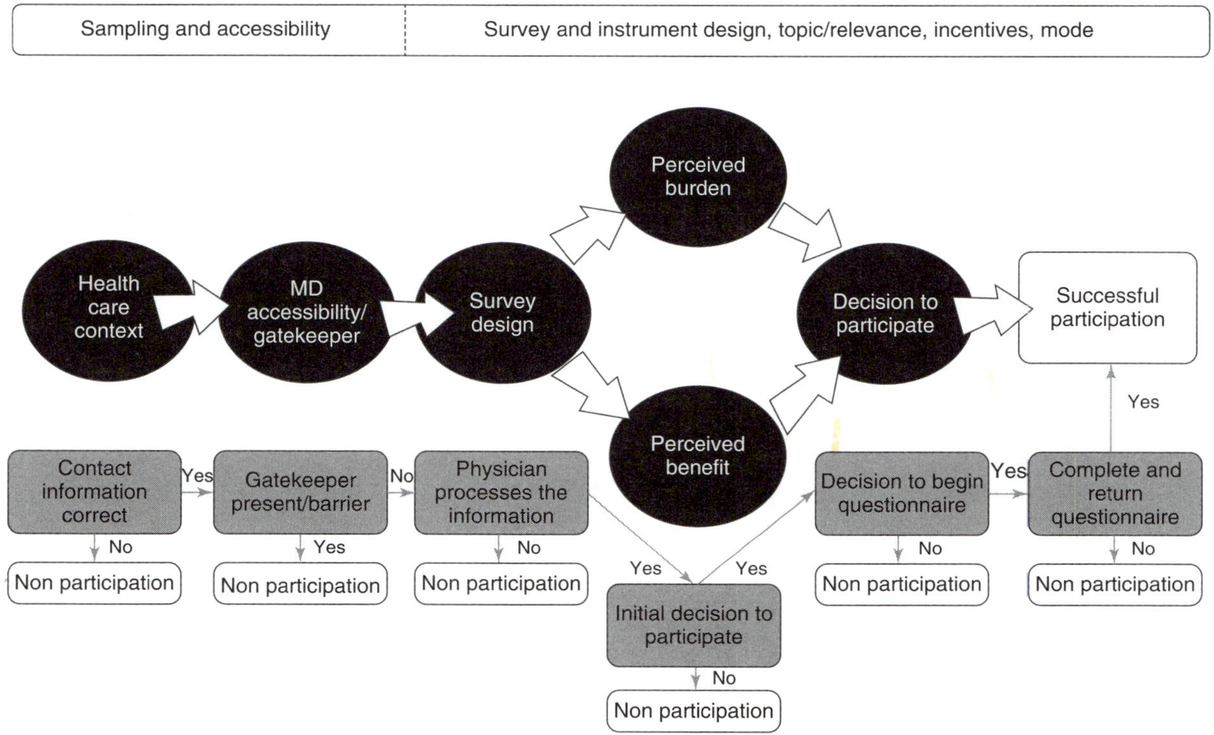

FIGURE 20.1 Conceptual model of physician decision to participate in survey request.

TABLE 20.1 Common Physician Sampling Frames

Frame	Description	Advantages	Disadvantages
American Medical Association (AMA) Masterfile	Current and historical information on all physicians, medical residents, and students in the United States. Information includes contact information as well as basic professional information (e.g., age, medical school and residency training, specialty, type of practice, etc.)	• National scope • High coverage	• Cost • Incomplete and sometimes outdated information
CMS National Plan and Provider Enumeration System (NPPES)	Data base maintained by the U.S. Centers for Medicare and Medicaid Services. Includes both clinician and organization contact information	• Cost (free) • Up-to-date contact information	• Coverage • Limited demographic and practice-related information • Duplicates
American Medical Information (AMI) database (InfoUSA)	Listing of physicians and surgeons that is updated monthly and includes information on demographics such as specialization, state of licensure, medical school attended, and office size. Information is derived from public sources, such as Yellow and White Page directories, trade publications, public records, and professional directories	• Accuracy • Up-to-date information • Good coverage (primary care)	• Poor specialty coverage • Cost

Professional association files	Information on physicians affiliated with specialty, state/regional or national (non-AMA) professional associations. Usually includes contact information as well as basic professional/practice information.	• Cost • Accuracy	• Limited scope • Coverage • Variability in timeliness
State licensing board information/Health department lists	Information on all licensed/practicing physicians. Usually includes contact information as well as basic professional information such as medical education, specialty and practice information, and so on	• Cost • Accuracy • Up-to-date information	• Limited scope • Coverage
Academic and corporate databases		• Up-to-date information	• Cost • Limited scope • Coverage

Probably the most familiar in the United States is the American Medical Association (AMA) Masterfile; a database of current and historical information on all physicians, medical residents and students in the United States, including doctors of medicine (MD) and doctors of osteopathy (DO). The AMA Masterfile is not without limitations, however, with the primary problem being delays in updating clinician information, which can impact survey response (DiGaetano 2013, Kletke 2004). Incomplete or missing information on key physician demographics is also an issue. For example, self-report data on race and ethnicity may be missing for approximately one quarter of the total U.S. physician workforce (American Medical Association 2011). This has often necessitated use of additional data to ensure updated contact information and eligibility (Martins et al. 2012, Shimizu and Hsiao 2010). In addition to the Masterfile, other common sampling frames include state licensing records, specialty association membership files, state professional association records, as well as academic and corporate databases (DiGaetano 2013). Outside the United States, physician surveys use similar sampling frames, with the Canadian National Physician Survey, for instance, utilizing a masterfile populated with information from the Canadian Medical Association (CMA) Membership System.

Choice of sampling frame can have significant implications for study results. For example, in a study of physician adoption of immunization practice recommendations, a sample drawn from member lists of the Academy of Pediatrics may have overestimated implementation, in part, because of demonstrated lower rates of agreement and adoption among nonmember pediatricians (Freed et al. 1995). Given the overall complexity of the health system and the need to improve physician surveys, alternative sampling strategies are increasingly common, especially when stratifying by medical organization, geography, or key practice characteristics. Stratifying samples by provider organizations is particularly difficult, as there are no national databases of medical organizations available. Certain national and regional professional associations maintain information on group practices that facilitate sampling frames for medical groups and healthcare institutions. Options include the AMA Group Practice database (American Medical Association 2012), as well as databases maintained by organizations such as the American Hospital Association (2012). However, most have significant limitations related to timeliness of information, coverage, and data availability. Moreover, for purposes of physician surveys, they may still need to be combined with data from the AMA Masterfile or similar datasets, using common identifiers. With regard to geography and practice data, investigators are increasingly combining the AMA Masterfile with administrative databases, such as Surveillance, Epidemiology, and End Results (SEER)-Medicare files and the Unique Physician Identification Number (UPIN) Registry (Baldwin et al. 2002). While the Masterfile provides better physician demographic information, SEER-Medicare records are a better source of information on practice ZIP code and the UPIN Registry provides better practice organization data (Baldwin et al. 2002). Combined, they are an important sampling resource for investigators assessing relationships between physicians' personal and practice characteristics and care outcomes. In another example with implications for sampling, AMA Masterfile data was linked with pharmacist data to improve identification/measures of physician supply in rural areas, which were overestimated using Masterfile data alone (Konrad et al. 2000).

Ultimately, sampling decisions require trade-offs between factors such as bias, cost, and analytic objectives (DiGaetano 2013), with no standard or preferred dataset applicable in all circumstances. Probably the most critical decision is to be clear with regard to target population(s), especially when determining which specialties to include. Additionally, both analytic objectives and precision play dominant roles in determining appropriate sample size.

20.5 Design-Based Interventions to Improve Response

Once sampling is complete, researchers must still address both contextual and individual factors important in physician survey cooperation (Figure 20.1). In particular, a number of design-based interventions have been used to overcome barriers and facilitate decisions to participate. These range from choice of survey mode to questionnaire formatting, alterations to the mailout package, to sponsorship by organizations; all of which are intended to make the survey stand out from other requests or otherwise address the identified barriers to physician survey participation. For example, mechanisms such as survey mode and registered mail are specifically designed to improve the likelihood that the survey will get through the various office "gatekeeper" filters (context/accessibility) and be prioritized for response. Results of these various methodologies are summarized by category of intervention after a brief discussion of physician accessibility and gatekeeping.

20.5.1 RESPONSE MODES

Survey mode may be particularly important in physician surveys, as the initial contact in more traditional mail and telephone surveys is often with nonphysician staff (i.e., gatekeepers) and not with the intended respondent, as indicated in the previous section. While choice of mode may alter this initial contact, each has its own methodological implications (Dykema et al. 2013). Moreover, choice of mode can significantly impact overall survey costs and the speed in which the data can be collected. We address each of these in the following paragraphs.

Electronic surveys—web surveys in particular, but also including fax and email—are attractive due to their potential for significant cost savings, reduced field periods, rapidity of data availability, and improved data quality (Dykema et al. 2013, Dykema et al. 2011, Minniear et al. 2013). However, these mode options have not proven as effective as mailed surveys with regards to physician participation (Akl et al. 2005, Braithwaite et al. 2003, Cho et al. 2013, Crouch et al. 2011, Dykema et al. 2013, Leece et al. 2004, McMahon et al. 2003, Nicholls et al. 2011, Raziano et al. 2001, Sequin et al. 2004, Thomas et al. 2003, VanDenKerkhof et al. 2004, VanGeest et al. 2007). As noted by McLeod and colleagues (2013), paper surveys may be a preferred mode for physicians, who are able to respond wherever and whenever it is convenient. In their review, the majority of studies used a mail survey, and very few (5%) relied exclusively on electronic surveys.

There exists mixed evidence on telephone interviews. In general, there is little evidence that telephone surveys are a preferred or popular mode for physician surveys, but there is evidence in the literature that telephone can be effective in combination with other modes of data collection, for example, telephone reminders (Asch et al. 1997, Flanigan et al. 2008, Martins et al. 2012, McLeod et al. 2013). It may be becoming increasingly difficult to reach physicians given their busy clinical schedules (Klabunde et al. 2012), and changes in telephone numbers in sampling frames may make contact outside the office more difficult (Thran and Hixson 2000). Studies comparing telephone with other survey modes show mixed results. In 2001, a review of published literature found similar response rates among mail and telephone modes (Kellerman and Herold 2001). However, Hocking and colleagues (2006) found significantly lower response rates in a telephone group (40.6%) compared to a mail group (59.9%). In a study by Braithwaite and colleagues (2003), it took five reminder emails to achieve a 52% response rate for an electronic survey compared to a final response rate of 63% for the telephone survey.

To increase physician response rates, researchers are increasingly turning to mixed-mode surveys (Beebe et al. 2007, Martins et al. 2012, Matteson et al. 2011, Scott et al. 2011, Sprague et al. 2009). This is, in part, because mixed modes allow individual choice in tailoring response preference to fit busy schedules. Additionally, some have demonstrated that specific modes work differentially across physician groups, making single-mode studies less preferable (Moore and Tarnai 2002, Parsons et al. 1994) though mailed surveys appear to be preferred. In a study using a mailed survey of primary care physicians, in which follow-up provided options to complete the survey by telephone, fax, email, or online, 88% of returned surveys were completed by mail, 10% were returned by fax, and only 2% were completed online (Nicholls et al. 2011).

In general, sequential mixed-mode designs are particularly promising, despite some indication of response bias (Beebe et al. 2007, Scott et al. 2011). One specific combination, an initial mail survey followed by a web survey to nonrespondents, was shown to result in both a higher response rate and a more representative sample (Beebe et al. 2007). Assessing the latter is important as there may be concerns related to sample representativeness, response bias, and item nonresponse associated with different survey modes, requiring a priori knowledge of the target population in interpreting results (Dykema et al. 2013, VanDenKerkhof et al. 2004). This is due, in large part, to variability in inclusion and accuracy of the contact information (email addresses in particular) available in sample frames and patterns of technology use among physicians (Dykema et al. 2013).

In addition to differential response propensities, the costs of the various modes may vary. Not unlike those for general health surveys, start-up costs may vary by mode. Calculating total costs for web surveys involves various fixed costs, such as potentially high programming costs, but those costs are all but removed after the initial sunk costs, leaving only marginal costs as more individuals are added to the sample. Therefore, per-survey costs for web surveys may be high with small sample sizes that cannot take advantage of efficiencies of scale. Printing costs may not be entirely eliminated in web surveys of course, as many mixed-mode survey studies begin with paper or electronic invitations and use paper or telephone reminders.

Costs for mail surveys include document formatting, printing, envelopes and reply envelopes, and postage. Once returned, mail surveys must be data entered—in contrast to web surveys that are tabulated automatically. Like web surveys, there are some economies of scale as large print jobs have lower unit costs than small jobs. Schleyer and Forrest (2000) provide an equation for finding the breakeven point between web and mail surveys—the sample size at which the cost of the two modes is the same.

Overall, health survey costs are assumed to be highest for administration that occurs face-to-face or that require interactive software, postal surveys have lower costs, and email, web, and other automated systems are least expensive of all (Wyatt 2000). However, the accounting of these costs is central to understanding which mode has the highest total cost. Off-the-shelf survey software or an existing information technology infrastructure, for example, will result in much lower web survey development costs than those for a study that is programming a novel or more complicated survey from the ground up. In a study of 805 clinicians in three practice-based research networks, the authors calculated costs per completed electronic response at $14.20 compared with $62.30 per paper response (Kroth et al. 2009). However, even though the first round of mailing for the paper version did not happen until the fourth electronic solicitation, 24% of completed surveys were completed by mail. Determining the cost-effectiveness of these strategies involves estimating not only total costs but per-survey costs in light of expected response rates, which are influenced by respondent preferences. Per-survey costs are high when used in populations where response is low (van Gelder et al. 2010). Among physicians, low response to electronic surveys may be especially problematic (Akl et al. 2005, Leece et al. 2004, McMahon et al. 2003, VanDenKerkhof et al. 2004), making per-survey costs for mail surveys more cost-competitive with web surveys.

Choice of response mode for physician surveys can also be dictated by the timeline available for data collection and the speed with which data ought to be collected. Mail, telephone, and electronic survey modes (e.g., web and email) all require time investment in development and set-up, but once the survey is ready, electronic distribution requires only a press of the button. Likewise, respondents, upon completing an electronic survey, are able to immediately make those results available to the research team. The few studies to date that estimate time to response of physician surveys typically use days as a measure of time, and those studies have found quicker response using email or web-based surveys compared to mail. In a study of residents and faculty at a university-based internal medicine residency program, response times were significantly shorter using an electronic survey relative to a postal survey (3.8 days faster among residents and 8.4 days faster among faculty; Sinclair et al. 2012). Likewise, in a study of clinicians in a practice-based research network, Kroth and colleagues (2009) found faster response times for web surveys than for postal-based paper questionnaires. However, in that study, paper questionnaires were only used for initial nonresponders.

Comparing the time (e.g., in days) for surveys to reach the research team will invariably favor electronic modes, of course, as estimates of mail survey response are subject to the vagaries of the postal delivery system. An alternative view is to consider response at each stage of reminder, with each subsequent reminder adding time to the project. In a study of family physicians in Canada, 50% of email surveys eventually returned were received very quickly—within about 24 hours of the initial distribution. Responses were slower in the postal mail group, but about half of surveys were returned after the first mailing and before the second mailing at 3 weeks (Seguin et al. 2004). In a survey of anesthesiologists conducted by VanDenKerkhof and colleagues (2004), overall response rates in the electronic survey group were only half that of the postal group, and response was lower at every reminder—even though 53% of returned electronic surveys arrived before the first follow-up reminder (1 week) compared to 36% of postal surveys at first follow-up (1 month). In a survey of pediatricians, using postal, fax, and email to solicit provider vaccine attitudes and practices, McMahon et al. (2003) found that 23% of email surveys and 18% of fax surveys were returned within a day of being sent, while none of the mail surveys were completed in a similar time frame. However, in terms of required follow-up, 50% of postal surveys eventually received were complete after only one contact, compared with 60% of fax surveys and only 24% of email surveys. The impact of ordering of a mixed-mode survey in one study found an initial boost in response to those in the web followed by mail group during the period that mail surveys would still be en route, as compared to the mail followed by web group (Beebe et al. 2007). While the median response time was 2 days lower in the web/mail group, the initial time advantage of the web/mail group disappeared after the first reminder and the difference in total response rates was not significant between the two groups at the end of data collection.

The data collection period alone for the above-mentioned studies ranged from 2 months (Akl et al. 2005, Beebe et al. 2007) to 5 months (VanDenKerkhof et al. 2004). Timeline for survey development was generally not reported but the authors did typically report pilot-testing surveys before data collection began, adding to time requirements. Nichols and colleagues (2011), in a study that gave primary care physicians a choice of modes at follow-up (telephone, fax, email, or online) to a mail survey, cite "hours of additional time in investigating options, formatting, testing the web questionnaire, and retrieving the online data"—all of which seemed unjustified given that only 2% of physicians requested a web-based survey link and none requested the email version.

20.5.2 PHYSICIAN ACCESSIBILITY AND POINTS OF CONTACT

In a summary of the 2010 Provider Survey Methods Workshop sponsored by the National Cancer Institute (NCI), Klabunde and colleagues (2013) identified gatekeeping as an area deserving future study as a way to potentially optimize initial contact, thus reducing overall burden and decrease costs. Similarly, in a review of the literature addressing ways to increase response rates among physicians, gatekeeping was cited as a potential barrier to response, particularly among those physicians in private practice settings (VanGeest et al. 2007). The hypothesized role of gatekeeping as a barrier to surveying physicians is not new (Parsons et al. 1994, Heywood et al. 1995, Thran and Hixson 2000); however, little empirical evidence documenting the prevalence and perversity of this barrier is currently available. The information that exists is rather dated and inconclusive. An ongoing study of physicians conducted by the AMA through the 1980s and 1990s reported an increase in physician gatekeepers in late 1990s as a reason for falling response rates although there was no reported data to substantiate that claim (Thran and Hixson 2000). In an earlier study, Parsons and colleagues (1994) documented that 37% of a total of 365 refusals to a physician survey were made by a gatekeeper rather than the physician. The rate at which gatekeepers were present or that gatekeepers passed the survey onto the physician were, however, not documented. In preparation for a mixed-mode survey of physicians, Beebe and colleagues conducted informal qualitative work with physicians in Mayo Clinic's Department of Medicine about potential issues in responding to surveys. The investigators found that some physicians had all emails opened by an assistant and only had those forwarded that were "deemed important." It was further hypothesized that screening occurs in the mail mode as well, but this was not documented (Beebe et al. 2007). To our knowledge, there is no clear evidence as to the extent that a survey would be screened in the presence of a gatekeeper.

With regard to type and number of contacts, issues related to prenotification and appropriate follow-up are paramount. Pre-notification has been most studied, with research showing a benefit, in that it allows for a more adequate explanation of the purpose and importance of the project as well as providing an opportunity for the respondent to plan (Dykema et al. 2011, Pirotta et al. 1999, Shiono and Klebanoff 1991, Ward and Wain 1994, Ward Bruce et al. 1998). Reminders are also important in ensuring adequate response (Cho et al. 2013, Glidewell et al. 2012, Martins et al. 2012, Olson et al. 1993, Tambor et al. 1993), although the relative influence of type of reminder (i.e., telephone call vs postcard), is not as clear (McLaren and Shelley 2000). Appropriate number of follow-up attempts has also not been empirically demonstrated, but a number of studies suggest that physician surveys may require some persistence (Parsons et al. 1994, Tambor et al. 1993, Olson et al. 1993). An important factor to consider, however, is the costs associated with follow-up contacts. While multiple cycles of recontacts increase power, they may be very inefficient; only reducing nonresponse bias minimally while substantially increasing overall survey costs (Willis et al. 2013). This finding is buttressed by evidence suggesting that recontacts may not be as important as other factors such as use of monetary incentives (Cho et al. 2013; Donaldson et al. 1999) or sponsorship (e.g., who the reminder is coming from) in predicting response (Field et al. 2002). Given the limited impact on data quality, Willis et al. (2013) recommends that it may be more effective to increase initial sample size and limit data collection to a maximum of two contacts. Finally, with regard to follow-up contacts in mail surveys, research does support inclusion of a replacement questionnaire as a means of improving participation (Ogborne et al. 1986, Vogel et al. 1983). This is considered important, as it is assumed that, because physicians are busy, they will discard the questionnaire upon receipt if they do not immediately complete the survey, making it unavailable at follow-up.

20.5.3 QUESTIONNAIRE DESIGN

Recommendations exist concerning instrument design generally, with response rates improved for surveys that are user friendly, personalized, shorter, and designed to be of interest to the target population (Dillman 2008). However, with respect to physicians specifically, relatively little is known about how survey design variations impact participation. The major element addressed, to date, is survey length. This is in large part because of the recognition of time as probably the most important factor in physician nonresponse. As might be expected, most studies have found that shorter questionnaires result in higher levels of physician participation (Burt and Woodwell 2005, Cartwright and Ward 1968, Glidewell et al. 2012, Hing et al. 2005, Jepson et al. 2005, Olmsted et al. 2005), with one systematic review estimating that physicians are twice as likely to return shorter questionnaires (VanGeest et al. 2007). Moreover, these results are independent of any other intervention employed to improve survey response (Asch et al. 1998, Thran and Berk 1993, Thran and Hixson 2000). Thus, it is recommended that researchers use economy when creating physician surveys, keeping them as short as possible.

In a recent study looking at the interplay of survey length and response incentives (covered in a latter section of this chapter), Ziegenfuss and colleagues (2013) found that in a web survey study of radiology staff, fellows, and residents at select academic medical centers in the United States, physicians chose a longer (10 min) survey accompanied by an incentive (chance to win an Apple iPad or a $5 amazon.com gift card) compared to a shorter survey (5 min) with no incentive suggesting that when given the choice, physicians may prefer a reward (either guaranteed or based on a lottery) to a less burdensome survey . Thus, researchers may need to focus more attention at increasing perceived benefits of completing a web survey compared to decreasing perceived burden.

Other design factors tested include single- versus double-sided formatting (Brehaut et al. 2006, Olmsted et al. 2005), business letter format (Gullen and Garrison 1973), standard-size (8.5 in. × 11 in.) dimensions of questionnaire booklets (Johnson et al. 1993), questionnaire order (Drummond et al. 2008), and paper quality (Clark et al. 2001b), with mixed results. Of these, only the business letter format, questionnaire order (general questions first), and use of standard-size booklets were associated with higher response rates. In terms of item formatting, one study examined open- versus closed-ended questionnaire formats on physician response, with the closed-ended format resulting in a 22% improvement in cooperation rate (Griffith et al. 1999). Benefits of closed-item formatting are twofold, in that they may be easier to answer and they make for a shorter instrument. However, caution is necessary, as choice of answer categories must allow physicians' full expression across the range of possible options so as not to appear biased.

20.5.4 PERSONALIZATION AND SPONSORSHIP

Personalization and sponsorship are also important elements of survey design. In these cases, however, rather than addressing the time barrier, personalization and sponsorship represent explicit attempts to improve the perceived value of the study, thereby increasing the likeliness of completion. As an added benefit, both represent relatively cost-effective interventions. Personalization may simply entail tailoring the mailout to be most relevant to the target population or subpopulations of interest. For mail surveys, this often includes typed salutations, handwritten postscripts thanking them for potentially completing the survey, and signed (rather than scanned) signatures; personalized email invitations and/or letters for web surveys; and personalized advance letters for telephone surveys. Overall, comparative studies suggest that personalization is effective in improving physician survey response (Leece et al. 2006, Maheux et al. 1989, Olson et al. 1993). One exception was a study by McKenzie-McHarg et al. (2005), in which hand-signed cover letters offered no benefit compared to letters with scanned signatures. Limited evidence even suggests that personalization may be particularly effective in overcoming low issue salience (Maheux et al. 1989).

Sponsorship has also been used as a means of inducing response, including institutional support, such as universities or professional associations, as well as professional backing and/or support of a trusted peer. Numerous studies have assessed effectiveness of sponsorship, with mixed results. In telephone and mixed-mode surveys, calls from a medical peer have resulted in significantly improved response (Bostick et al. 1992, Haywood et al. 1995, Martins et al. 2012, Ward et al. 1998). For postal surveys, however, while sponsorship by the AMA was effective in one study (Olson et al. 1993), neither sender recognition nor endorsement from a division of medical practice or opinion-leader was successful in others (Bhandari et al. 2003, Bonevski et al. 2011, Brehaut et al. 2006). Combined, the latter studies present evidence of potential limits related to the use of collegial and/or organizational sponsorship in improving physician survey participation.

20.5.5 POSTAGE AND COURIER SERVICES

In relation to postal surveys, a number of studies have explored the impact of various styles of postage and/or courier services (i.e., FedEx, UPS) in either the initial mailout or return mailing on physician participation rates. One strategy deemed successful is the use of first-class stamps or priority mail. Use of first-class stamps, for instance, has been shown to be more effective in many cases compared to metered or business reply envelopes in the return mailing, with total costs per completion lower as well due to the additional fees, time requirements, and logistical costs associated with business reply (Shiono and Klebanoff 1991, Streiff et al. 2001, Urban et al. 1993). With regard to the initial mailout, most studies have explored the option of courier services or certified/priority mail on physician response rates, with generally positive results. For instance, in one study, use of certified mail significantly increased participation compared to questionnaires sent via first-class mail (Del Valle et al. 1997). Similarly, another study found FedEx to be more successful compared to first-class mail (Kasprzyk et al. 2001). One exception was a recent study by Ziegenfuss et al. (2011), in which priority mail did not impact response tendency for physicians. Finally, with regard to follow-up mailings, there is limited evidence supporting the use of first-class letters over postcards (Olmsted et al. 2005). Overall, class of mail clearly has implications for survey response, as options may, to a greater or lesser extent, help personalize the survey appearance. There are notable cost considerations in making a final decision with regard to a particular survey, but evidence clearly suggests that use of business reply is less appropriate in this population.

20.6 Incentive-Based Interventions

In addition to design-based interventions, incentives have been used successfully to improve physician response to surveys. Incentive-based interventions generally fall into two categories: monetary and nonmonetary. Incentives work by increasing the salience and/or value of the survey, while at the same time engendering feelings of trust, reciprocity, and appreciation on the part of the respondent. This makes them most effective in addressing the more proximate individual level factors influencing individual decisions to participate (Cho et al. 2013). Results of the two types are summarized individually.

20.6.1 MONETARY INCENTIVES

Numerous studies have identified monetary incentives as effective in improving response in surveys of physicians and medical groups (Burns et al. 2008, Cho et al. 2013, Klabunde et al. 2012, McLeod et al. 2013, VanGeest et al. 2007). These have included cash incentives, as well as charitable donations, and opportunities to win cash lottery prizes. Generally, research suggests that even modest incentives are associated with significantly higher response in this population, more than doubling the likelihood of participation (Cho et al. 2013, Flanigan et al. 2008, VanGeest et al. 2007). Exceptions of note include a small $1 charitable donation (Olson et al. 1993), a monetary donation to a professional organization in support of research (Gattellari and Ward 2001), and a monetary lottery incentive to medical residents and students as part of the Canadian National Physician Survey (Grava-Gubins and Scott 2008). Additionally, simply alerting physicians that an incentive is included in the survey packet via placement of a "teaser" on the envelope does little to positively impact survey response (Ziegenfuss et al. 2012). Potential explanations have been offered for these discrepancies, directly related to the identified barriers to physician survey participation noted above. For instance, in the case of the charitable donation, the amount was perceived as insignificant and thus may have engendered skepticism. While not mentioned, another confounding factor may have been the more mundane focus of the survey (it was a readership satisfaction survey for the AMA). In the latter instance, the authors speculate that response may have been negatively impacted by the overarching scope of the survey, which decreased perceived relevance and, subsequently, the likelihood that physicians would respond regardless of the lottery. While this may be true in this case, others have also found lottery incentives to perform poorly in improving physician response (Halpern et al. 2011).

While clearly effective in enhancing participation, how much of a monetary incentive to offer remains an important consideration when designing physician surveys, with obvious cost implications. Results of studies exploring optimal levels of incentive are generally mixed. A systematic review conducted by VanGeest et al. (2007) graphed unweighted average effect sizes for different incentive levels; finding only small differences in serial increments over $1, suggesting that the greatest "bang for the buck" was actually at the lowest incentive levels. The implications are that incentives may be a viable option given the comparatively modest investment relative to return. These results are further supported by other experimental studies finding no or nonsignificant differences between incentive levels (Gunn and Rhodes 1981, Kasprzyk et al. 2001, Mizes et al. 1984, VanGeest et al. 2001). Exceptions include studies by Asch et al. (1998) and Halpern et al. (2002). However, their results may have been influenced by the uniqueness of the $2 bill option employed. More recently, a study by Keating et al. (2008) found a $50 check to be much more effective in inducing response compared to a $20 check, resulting in nearly a 16 percentage point increase in participation. McLeod et al. (2013), in their review of large health care provider surveys, also found that incentives over $30 were more likely to achieve a target 60% response rate compared to those offering a lower or no incentives. These latter studies might suggest that researchers may need to offer physicians larger incentives today. However, the bulk of the evidence still indicates that relatively modest incentives are capable of improving survey participation.

20.6.2 NONMONETARY INCENTIVES

With regard to nonmonetary incentives, studies have explored their effectiveness in improving physician survey participation, with mixed results. Response-enhancing techniques have included stickers, pencils, pens, informational brochures, computer programs, flash drives, CME credit, and candy (Field et al. 2002, VanGeest et al. 2007). More substantial incentives, such as trips or personal digital assistants (PDAs), have also been tried. Compared to physicians receiving no incentive, nonmonetary incentives had little or no impact on response rates (Cho et al. 2013, VanGeest et al. 2007). Even in cases where some impact is noted, results are often inconsistent. For example, with regard to using a pencil or pen, in one study, inclusion of a pencil in the second mailing resulted in significantly improved response (Sallis et al. 1984). Later studies by Ward et al. (1998) and Clark et al. (2001a), however, found no differences in overall response following inclusion of a pen. Similarly, a recent study examining the effect of an offer for a free online CME activity on physician response found the activity to be ineffective in improving participation (Viera and Edwards 2012). In fact, the offer for the free CME activity actually resulted in a lower response rate; a finding consistent across physician specialty and region of practice (Viera and Edwards 2012). Even with regard to the more substantial incentives noted above, only an opportunity to win a weekend trip resulted in a small but significant increase in physician response (Baron et al. 2001). Implications are simply that nonmonetary incentives will work only if physicians value them and, even in these cases, results will typically be small.

20.6.3 FORM AND TIMING OF INCENTIVES

When using incentives, form and timing figure prominently in enhancing physician response. For instance, as expected, at least one comparative study has found monetary incentives to be more successful compared to nonmonetary incentives (Recklitis et al. 2009). Additionally, comparative studies support cash payments as being more effective compared to other alternatives, including charity inducements, checks, gift cards, and opportunities to win cash lottery prizes (Halpern et al. 2011, Hogan and LaForce 2008, James et al. 2011, Leung et al. 2002, Tamayo-Sarver and Baker 2004). Noncontingent prepaid monetary incentives are also more effective compared to contingent post-completion rewards (Berry and Kanouse 1987, Delnevo et al. 2004, Halpern et al. 2011, James et al. 2011, Kanaan et al. 2010, Leung et al. 2004). Prepaid incentives have also been shown to improve promptness of completion (Berry and Kanouse 1987, McLaren and Shelley 2000), with one study even suggesting that higher levels of incentives may improve response times (Keating et al. 2008). Finally, it is important to address the effects of incentives on the quality of responses and representativeness of the data. The good news here is that available evidence indicates that use of incentives does not negatively impact data quality (Dykema et al. 2011, James et al. 2011, Leung et al. 2002, Leung et al. 2004, Tambor et al. 1993).

20.7 Supporting Evidence from Other Health Professions

Sudman's (1985) review of barriers to survey response addressed professionals broadly, with common factors identified that influence willingness to participate. While this chapter focuses on physician surveys, research with other medical professionals also supports many of the interventions highlighted. For example, research supporting the use of incentives in health professional surveys is consistent, with efficacy demonstrated in studies of nurses (VanGeest and Johnson 2011), pharmacists (Paul et al. 2005), and other allied health professionals (Hare et al. 1998, Hawley et al. 2009, Jamtvedt et al. 2008, Van Otterloo et al. 2011). Cho et al. (2013), in a meta-analysis of techniques to improve clinician survey response, found financial incentives to be most effective in improving participation among health care professionals. Similarly, design-based strategies akin to those discussed here have also proven successful in other health professional populations (Ho-A-Yun et al. 2011). While these results further strengthen the evidence in support of using these interventions to improve survey response, it is still not appropriate to assume that just because an intervention works in one professional population it will have similar effect in another. There are variations in autonomy, research acceptance, and work environments across different health professions. More research is necessary to verify that accepted best practices to improve survey response are generalizable across health care professions (VanGeest and Johnson 2013).

20.8 Conclusion

Despite the growing body of literature on best practices to improve physician surveys, there remains a critical need to expand on current design- and incentive-based methodologies to further advance physician surveys. The 2010 NCI Provider Survey Methods Workshop reviewed the state of the art on survey research directed toward health care providers, identifying gaps in understanding as well as outlining a research agenda for the future (Klabunde et al. 2012). Key challenges identified by the workgroup included the need to (i) identify and assemble effective sampling frames of providers within medical groups; (ii) better understand the office environment as a barrier or facilitator of physician access; (iii) identify survey and instrument design factors important to individual determinants of survey participation; and (iv) improve mechanisms to enhance contact with the respondent, especially related to optimizing use of mixed-mode surveys and follow-up approaches. Research needs to flow logically from each of these areas, with recommendations to improve sample frames, survey administration, response incentives, and questionnaire design. Additionally the workgroup recommended continued study of factors related to perceptions of benefit/burden leading ultimately to a decision to participate. This effort was expended simply because physicians play a leadership role in the delivery and improvement of health services and clinician surveys remain a vital tool in health services and policy research; obtaining information on professional practices and perspectives important to policy and practice decisions.

Finally, while this chapter focuses on improving physician response to surveys, there are fundamental questions regarding the use of response rate as a single indicator of survey quality. Nonresponse bias, which is not necessarily correlated with response rate, may be of far greater importance for evaluating the validity of survey findings (Davern 2013, Johnson and Wislar 2012). Moreover, there is applicability both at the individual and institutional level, with methods commonly employed to assess nonresponse error in individual-level surveys also applicable at the organizational level (Lewis et al. 2013). Future research should focus on the methodological correlates of nonresponse bias in surveys of physicians and whether actual substantive survey estimates differ significantly between surveys with low versus high response rates as has been done in the general survey literature (Davern et al. 2010, Holle et al. 2006, Keeter et al. 2006).

REFERENCES

Akl EA, Maroun N, Klocke RA, Montori V, Schunemann HJ. Electronic mail was not better than postal mail for surveying residents and faulty. J Clin Epidemiol 2005;58:425–429.

Albaum G, Smith SM. Why people agree to participate in surveys. In: Gideon E, editor. *Handbook of Survey Methodology for the Social Sciences*. New York: Springer; 2012. p 179–193.

American Hospital Association. 2012. AHA data and directories. Available at http://www.aha.org/research/rc/stat-studies/data-and-directories.shtml.

American Medical Association. *Demographic Characteristics of the House of Delegates and AMA Leadership*, Reports Council on Long Range Planning and Development; Chicago, IL: AMA; 2011.

American Medical Association. 2012. Physician data resources. Available at http://www.ama-assn.org/ama/pub/about-ama/physician-data-resources/surveys-primary-source-data.page.

Antiel RM, James KM, Egginton JS, Sheeler RD, Liebow M, Goold SD, Tilburt JC. Specialty, political affiliation, and perceived social responsibility are associated with U.S. physician reactions to health care reform legislation. J Gen Intern Med, 2014;29(2):299–403

Asch DA, Christakis NA, Ubel PA. Conducting physician mail surveys on a limited budget: a randomized trial comparing $2 bill versus $5 bill incentives. Med Care 1998; 36:95–99.

Asch DA, Connor SE, Hamilton EG, Fox SA. Problems in recruiting community-based physicians for health services research. J Gen Intern Med 2000;15:591–599.

Asch DA, Jedrziewski MK, Christakis NA. Response rates to mail surveys published in medical journals. J Clin Epidemiol 1997;50:1129–1136.

Baldwin L, Adamache W, Klabunde C, Kenward K, Dahlman C, Warren JL. Linking physician characteristics and Medicare claims data: issues in data availability, quality, and measurement. Med Care 2002;40:82–95.

Baron G, De Wals P, Milord F. Cost-effectiveness of a lottery for increasing physicians' responses to a mail survey. Eval Health Prof 2001;24:47–52.

Beebe TJ, Locke R III,, Barnes SA, Davern ME, Anderson KJ. Mixing web and mail methods in a survey of physicians. Health Serv Res 2007;42:1219–1234.

Berry SH, Kanouse DE. Physician response to a mailed survey: an experiment in timing of payment. Public Opin Q 1987;51:102–114.

Bhandari M, Devereaux PJ, Swiontkowski MF, Schemitsch EH, Shankardass K, Sprague S, Guyatt GH. A randomized trial of opinion leader endorsement in a survey of orthopaedic surgeons: effect on primary response rates. Int J Epidemiol 2003;32:634–636.

Bjertnaes OA, Garratt A, Botten G. Nonresponse bias and cost-effectiveness in a Norwegian survey of family physicians. Eval Health Prof 2008;31:65–80.

Bonevski B, Magin P, Horton G, Foster M, Girgis A. Response rates in GP surveys: trialling two recruitment strategies. Aust Fam Physician 2011;40:427–430.

Bostick RM, Pirie P, Luepker RV, Kofron PM. Using physician caller follow-ups to improve the response rate to a physician telephone survey: its impact and implications. Eval Health Prof 1992;15:420–433.

Boukus E, Cassil A, O'Malley AS. A snapshot of U.S. physicians: key findings from the 2008 Health Tracking Physician Survey. Data Bull (Cent Stud Health Syst Change) 2009;Sept(35):1–11.

Braithwaite D, Emery J, de Lusignan S, Sutton S. Using the internet to conduct surveys of health professionals: a valid alternative? Fam Pract 2003;20:545–551.

Brehaut JC, Graham ID, Visentin L, Stiell IG. Print format and sender recognition are related to survey completion rate. J Clin Epidemiol 2006;59:635–641.

Burns KEA, Duffett M, Kho M, Meade MO, Adhikari NKJ, Sinuff T, Cook DJ. A guide for the design and conduct of self-administered surveys of clinicians. Can Med Assoc J 2008;179:245–252.

Burt CW, Woodwell D. Tests of methods to improve response to physician surveys. Paper presented at the 2005 Federal Committee on Statistical Methodology; Arlington, VA; 2005.

Cartwright A. Professionals as responders: variations in and effects of response rates to questionnaires, 1961-77. Br Med J 1978;2:1419–1421.

Cartwright A, Ward AW. Variations in general practitioners' response to postal questionnaires. Br J Prevent Soc Med 1968;22:199–205.

Chen PG, Curry LA, Nunez-Smith M, Bradley EH, Desai MM. Career satisfaction in primary care: a comparison of international and U.S. medical graduates. J Gen Intern Med 2012;27:147–152.

Cho YI, Johnson TP, VanGeest JB. Enhancing surveys of health care professionals: a meta-analysis of techniques to improve response. Eval Health Prof 2013;36:382–407.

Clark TJ, Khan KS, Gupta JK. Provision of a pen along with questionnaire does not increase the response rate to a postal survey: a randomised controlled trial. J Epidemiol Community Health 2001a;55:595–596.

Clark TJ, Khan KS, Gupta JK. Effect of paper quality on the response rate to a postal survey: a randomised controlled trial. BMC Med Res Methodol 2001b;1:12.

Cook JV, Dickinson HO, Eccles MP. Response rates in postal surveys of healthcare professionals between 1996 and 2005: an observational study. BMC Health Serv Res 2009;9:160.

Crouch S, Robinson P, Pitts M. A comparison of general practitioner response rates to electronic and postal surveys in the setting of the National STI Prevention Program. Aust N Z J Public Health 2011;35:187–189.

Cull WL, O'Connor KG, Sharp S, Tang SS. Response rates and response bias for 50 surveys of pediatricians. Health Serv Res 2005;40:213–226.

Davern M. Nonresponse rates are a problematic indicator of nonresponse bias in survey research. Health Serv Res 2013;48:905–912.

Davern ME, McAlpine DD, Beebe TJ, et al. Are lower response rates hazardous to your health survey? An analysis of three state health surveys. Health Serv Res 2010;45:1324–1344.

Delnevo CD, Abatemarco DJ, Steinberg MB. Physician response rates to a mail survey by specialty and timing of incentive. Am J Prev Med 2004;26:234–236.

Del Valle ML, Morgenstern H, Rogstad TL, Albright C, Vickery BG. A randomized trial of the impact of certified mail on response rate to a physician survey, and a cost-effectiveness analysis. Eval Health Prof 1997;20:389–406.

DiGaetano R. Sample frame and related sample design issues for surveys of physicians and physician practices. Eval Health Prof 2013;36:296–329.

Dillman DA. *Mail and Internet Surveys: The Total Design Method*. New York: Wiley & Sons; 1978.

Dillman DA, Smyth JD, Christian LM. *Internet, Mail, and Mixed-Mode Surveys: The Tailored Design Method*. New York: John Wiley & Sons; 2008.

Donaldson GW, Moinpour CM, Bush N, Chapko M, Jocom J, Sidak M, Nielsen-Stoeck M, Bradshaw J, Bichindaritz I, Sullivan K. Physician participation in research surveys: a randomized study of inducements to return mailed research questionnaires. Eval Health Prof 1999;22:427–441.

Drummond FJ, Sharp L, Carsin AE, Kelleher T, Comber H. Questionnaire order significantly increased response to a postal survey sent to primary care physicians. J Clin Epidemiol 2008;61:177–185.

Dykema J, Stevenson J, Day B, Sellers SL, Bonham VL. Effects of incentives and prenotification on response rates and costs in a national web survey of physicians. Eval Health Prof 2011a;34:434–447.

Dykema J, Jones NR Piché TStevenson J. Surveying clinicians by web: Current issues in design and Administration. Eval Health Prof 2013;36:352–381.

Everett JP, Walters CA, Stottlemyer DL, Knight CA, Oppenberg AA, Orr RD. To lie or not to lie: resident physician attitudes about the use of deception in clinical practice. J Med Ethics 2011;37:333–338.

Farber NJ, Simpson P, Salam T, Collier VU, Weiner J, Boyer EG. Physicians' decisions to withhold and withdraw life-sustaining treatment. Arch Intern Med 2006;166:560–564.

Field TS, Cadoret CA, Brown ML, Ford M, Greene SM, Hill D, Hornbrook MC, Meenan RT, White MJ, Zapka JM. Surveying physicians: do components of the "Total Design Approach" to optimizing survey response rates apply to physicians? Med Care 2002;40:596–606.

Flanigan TS, McFarlane E, Cook S. Conducting survey research among physicians and other medical professionals — a review of current literature. *Proceeding of the Survey Research Methods Section*; American Statistical Association; 2008. p4136–4147.

Freed GL, Clark SJ, Bordley C, Konrad TR. Importance of sampling frame in physician surveys. Arch Pediatr Adolesc Med 1995;149:705.

Gardner MN, Brandt AM. "The doctors' choice is America's choice": the physician in US cigarette advertisements, 1930-1953. Am J Public Health 2006;96:222–232.

Gattellari M, Ward JE. Will donations to their learned college increase surgeons' participation in surveys? A randomized trial. J Clin Epidemiol 2001;54:645–650.

Glidewell L, Thomas R, MacLennan G, Bonetti D, Johnston M, Eccles MP, Edlin R, Pitts NB, Clarkson J, Steen N, Grimshaw JM. Do incentives, reminders, or reduced burden improve healthcare professional response rates in postal questionnaires? Two randomised controlled trials. BMC Health Serv Res, August 14 2012;12:250. DOI: 10.1186/1472-6963-12-250.

Grava-Gubins I, Scott S. Effects of various methodologic strategies: survey response rates among Canadian physicians and physicians-in-training. Can Fam Phys 2008;54:1424–1430.

Griffith LE, Cook DJ, Guyatt GH, Charles CA. Comparison of open and closed questionnaire formats in obtaining demographic information from Canadian general internists. J Clin Epidemiol 1999;52:977–1005.

Groves RM, Singer E, Corning A. Leverage-salience theory of survey participation: description and an illustration. Public Opin Q 2000;64:299–308.

Gullen WH, Garrison GE. Factors influencing physicians' response to mailed questionnaires. Health Serv Rep 1973;88:510–514.

Gunn WJ, Rhodes IN. Physician response rates to a telephone survey: effects of monetary incentive level. Public Opin Q 1981;45:109–115.

Halpern SD, Kohn R, Dornbrand-Lo A, Metkus T, Asch DA, Volpp KG. Lottery-based versus fixed incentives to increase clinicians' response to surveys. Health Serv Res 2011;46:1663–1673.

Halpern SD, Ubel PA, Berlin JA, Asch DA. Randomized trial of 5 dollars versus 10 dollars monetary incentives, envelope size, and candy to increase physician response rates to mailed questionnaires. Med Care 2002;40:834–839.

Hare S, Price JH, Flynn MG, King KA. Increasing return rates of a mail survey to exercise professionals using a modest monetary incentive. Percept Mot Skills 1998;86:217–218.

Hawley KM, Cook JR, Jensen-Doss A. Do non-contingent incentives increase survey response rates among mental health providers? A randomized trial comparison. Adm Policy Ment Health 2009;36:343–348.

Heywood A, Mudge P, Ring I, Sanson-Fisher R. Reducing systematic bias in studies of general practitioners: The use of a medical peer in the recruitment of general practitioners in research. Family Practice 1995;12:227–231.

Hing E, Schappert SM, Burt CW, Shimizu IM. Effects of form length and item format on response patterns and estimates of physician office and hospital outpatient department visits. National Ambulatory Medical Care Survey and National Hospital Ambulatory Medical Care Survey. Vital Health Stat 2005;2(139):11–32.

Hogan SO, LaForce M. Incentives in physician surveys: an experiment using gift cards and checks. *Section on Survey Research Methods, American Association for Public Opinion Research (AAPOR)*; 2008.

Holle R, Hochadel M, Reitmeir P, Meisinger C, Wichmann H-E. Prolonged recruitment efforts in health surveys. Epidemiology 2006;17:639–643.

Hughes PH, Storr CL, Brandenburg NA, Baldwin DC Jr,, Anthony JC, Sheehan DV. Physician substance use by medical specialty. J Addict Dis 1999;18:23–37.

Hummers-Pradier E, Scheidt-Nave C, Martin H, Heinemann S, Kochen MM, Himmel W. Simply no time? Barriers to GPs' participation in primary care research. Fam Pract 2008;25:105–112.

James KM, Ziegenfuss JY, Tilburt JC, Harris AM, Beebe TJ. Getting physicians to respond: the impact of incentive type and timing on physician survey response rates. Health Serv Res 2011;46:232–242.

Jamtvedt G, Rosenbaum S, Thuve Dahm K, Flottorp S. Chocolate bar as an incentive did not increase response rate among physiotherapists: a randomised controlled trial. BMC Res Notes 2008;1:34.

Jepson C, Asch DA, Hershey JC, Ubel PA. In a mailed physician survey, questionnaire length had a threshold effect on response rate. J Clin Epidemiol 2005;58:103–105.

Johnson TP, Parsons JA, Warnecke RB, Kaluzny AD. Dimensions of mail questionnaires and response quality. Sociol Focus 1993;26:271–274.

Johnson TP, Wislar JS. Response rates and nonresponse errors in surveys. JAMA 2012;307:1805–1806.

Kanaan RA, Wessely SC, Armstrong D. Differential effects of pre and post-payment on neurologists' response rates to a postal survey. BMC Neurol 2010;10:100.

Kaner EF, Haighton CA, McAvoy BR. "So much post, so busy with practice — so, no time!": a telephone survey of general practitioners' reasons for not participating in postal questionnaire surveys. Br J Gen Pract 1998;48:1067–1069.

Kasprzyk D, Montano DE, Lawrence JS, Phillips WR. The effects of variations in mode of delivery and monetary incentive on physicians' responses to a mailed survey assessing STD practice patterns. Eval Health Prof 2001;24:3–17.

Keating NL, Zaslavsky AM, Goldstein J, West DW, Ayanian JZ. Randomized trial of $20 versus $50 incentives to increase physician survey response rates. Med Care 2008;46:878–881.

Keeter S, Kennedy C, Dimock M, Best J, Craighill P. Gauging the impact of growing nonresponse on estimates from a national RDD telephone survey. Public Opin Q 2006;70:125–148.

Kellerman SE, Herold J. Physician response to surveys: a review of the literature. Am J Prev Med 2001;20:61–67.

Kenna GA, Lewis DC. Risk factors for alcohol and other drug use by healthcare professionals. Subst Abuse Treat Prevent Policy 2008;29:3.

Klabunde CN, Willis GB, Casalino LP. Facilitators and barriers to survey participation by physicians: a call to action for researchers. Eval Health Prof 2013;36:279–295.

Klabunde CN, Willis GB, McLeod CC, Dillman DA, Johnson TP, Greene SM, Brown ML. Improving the quality of surveys of physicians and medical groups: a research agenda. Eval Health Prof 2012;35(4):477–506.

Kletke PR. Physician workforce data: when the best is not good enough. Health Serv Res 2004;39:1251–1255.

Konrad TR, Slifkin RT, Stevens C, Miller J. Using the American Medical Association physician masterfile to measure physician supply in small towns. J Rural Health 2000;16:162–167.

Kroth PJ, McPherson L, Leverence R, Pace W, Daniels E, Rhyne RL, Williams RL, Prime Net Consortium. Combining Web-based and mail surveys improves response rates: a PBRN study from PRIME net. Ann Fam Med 2009;7:245–248.

Landon BE, Reschovsky J, Blumenthal D. Changes in career satisfaction among primary care and specialist physicians, 1997-2001. JAMA 2003;289:442–449.

Leece P, Bhandari M, Sprague S, Swiontkowski MF, Schemitsch EH, Tornetta P, Devereaux PJ, Guyatt GH. Internet versus mailed questionnaires: a controlled comparison. J Med Internet Res 2004;6:e39.

Leece P, Bhandari M, Sprague S, Swiontkowski MF, Schemitsch EH, Tornetta P. Does flattery work? A comparison of 2 different cover letters for an international survey of orthopedic surgeons. Can J Surg 2006;49:90–95.

Leung GM, Johnston JM, Saing H, Tin KYK, Wong IO, Ho LM. Prepayment was superior to postpayment cash incentives in a randomized postal survey among physicians. J Clin Epidemiol 2004;57:777–784.

Leung GM, Ho LM, Chan MF, Johnston JM, Wong FK. The effects of cash and lottery incentives on mailed surveys to physicians: a randomized trial. J Clin Epidemiol 2002;55:801–807.

Lewis EF, Hardy M, Snaith B. Estimating the effect of nonresponse bias in a survey of hospital organizations. Eval Health Prof 2013;36:330–351.

Lezzoni LI, Rao SR, DesRoches CM, Vogeli C, Campbell EG. Survey shows that at least some physicians are not always open or honest with patients. Health Aff 2012;31:383–391.

MacPherson I, Bisset A. Not another questionnaire!: eliciting the views of general practitioners. Fam Pract 1995;12:335–338.

Maheux B, Legault C, Lambert J. Increasing response rates in physicians' mail surveys: an experimental study. Am J Public Health 1989;79:638–639.

Martins Y, Lederman RI, Lowenstein CL, Joffe S, Neville BA, Hastings BT, Abel GA. Increasing response rates from physicians in oncology research: a structured literature review and data from a recent physician survey. Br J Cancer 2012;106:1021–1026.

Matteson KA, Anderson BL, Pinto SB, Lopes V, Schulkin J, Clark MA. Surveying ourselves: examining the use of a web-based approach for a physician survey. Eval Health Prof 2011;34:448–463.

McAvoy BR, Kaner EFS. General practice postal surveys: a questionnaire too far? Br Med J 1996;313:732–733.

McFarlane E, Olmsted MG, Murphy J, Hill CA. Nonresponse bias in a mail survey of physicians. Eval Health Prof 2007;30:170–185.

McKenzie-McHarg K, Tully L, Gates S, Ayers S, Brocklehurst P. Effect on survey response rate of hand written versus printed signature on a covering letter: randomised controlled trial. BMC Health Survey Res 2005;5:52.

McLaren B, Shelley J. Mailed survey on miscarriage: randomised trial of a prize and two forms of introduction to the research. Aust N Z J Public Health 2000;24:360–364.

McLeod CC, Klabunde CN, Willis GB, Stark D. Health care provider surveys in the United States, 2000-2010: a review. Eval Health Prof 2013;36(1):106–126.

McMahon SR, Iwamoto M, Massoudi MS, Yusuf HR, Stevenson JM, David F, Chu SY, Pickering LK. Comparison of e-mail, fax, and postal surveys of pediatricians. Pediatrics 2003;111:e299–e303.

McMurray JE, Linzer M, Konrad TR, Douglas J, Shugerman R, Nelson K. The work lives of women physicians. Results from the Physician Work Life Study. J Gen Int Med 2000;15:372–380.

Meissner HI, Klabunde CN, Han PK, Benard VB, Breen N. Breast cancer screening beliefs, recommendations and practices: primary care physicians in the United States. Cancer 2011;117:3101–3111.

Minniear TD, McIntosh EB, Alexander N, Weidle PJ, Fulton J. Using electronic surveys to gather information on physician practices during a response to a local epidemic — Rhode Island, 2011. Ann Epidemiol 2013;23:521–523.

Mizes JS, Fleece ME, Roos C. Incentives for increasing return rates: magnitude levels, response bias, and format. Public Opin Q 1984;48:794–800.

Moore D, An L. The effect of repetitive token incentives and priority mail on response to physician surveys. *Proceedings of the Annual Meeting of the American Statistical Association*; Aug 5–9; 2001.

Moore D, Tarnai J. Evaluating nonresponse error in mail surveys. In: Groves R, Dillman DA, Eltinge JL, Little RJA, editors. *Survey Nonresponse*. New York: John Wiley & Sons; 2002.

Mosca L, Linfante AH, Benjamin EJ, Berra K, Hayes SN, Walsh BW, Fabunmi RP, Kwan J, Mills T, Simpson SL. National study of physician awareness and adherence to cardiovascular disease prevention guidelines. Circulation 2005;111:499–510.

Nicholls K, Chapman K, Shaw T, Perkins A, Sullivan MM, Crutchfield S, Reed E. Enhancing response rates in physician surveys: the limited utility of electronic options. Health Serv Res 2011;46:1675–1682.

Ogborne AC, Rush R, Fondacaro R. Dealing with nonrespondents in a mail survey of professionals: the cost-effectiveness of two alternatives. Eval Health Prof 1986;9:121–128.

Olmsted MG, Murphy J, McFarlane E, Hill C. Evaluating methods for increasing physician survey cooperation. Paper presented at the annual conference of the American Association for Public Opinion Research; Miami Beach, FL; 2005.

Olson L, Schneiderman M, Armstrong RV. Increasing physician response in surveys. ASA Proceedings Survey Research Methods Section; 1993.

Oremus M, Wolfson C. Female specialists were more likely to respond to a postal questionnaire about drug treatments for Alzheimer disease. J Clin Epidemiol 2004;57:620–623.

Parsons JA, Warnecke RB, Czaja RF, Barnsley J, Kaluzny A. Factors associated with response rates in a national survey of primary care physicians. Eval Rev 1994;18:756–766.

Paul CL, Walsh RA, Tzelepis F. A monetary incentive increases postal survey response rates for pharmacists. J Epidemiol Community Health 2005;59:1099–1101.

Pirotta M, Gunn J, Farish S, Karabatsos G. Primer postcard improves postal survey response rates. Aust N Z J Public Health 1999;23:196–197.

Raziano DB, Jayadevappa R, Valenzula D, Weiner M, Lavizzo-Mourey R. E-mail versus conventional postal mail survey of geriatric chiefs. Gerontologist 2001;41:799–804.

Recklitis CJ, Campbell EG, Kutner JS, Bober SL. Money talks: non-monetary incentive and Internet administration fail to increase response rates to a physician survey. J Clin Epidemiol 2009;62:224–226.

Salinas GD, Williamson JC, Kalhan R, Thomashow B, Scheckermann JL, Walsh J, Abdolrasulnia M, Foster JA. Barriers to adherence to chronic obstructive pulmonary disease guidelines by primary care physicians. Intern J Chron Obstruct Pulmon Dis 2011;6:171–179.

Sallis JF, Fortmann SP, Solomon DS, Farquhar JW. Increasing returns of physician surveys. Am J Public Health 1984;74:1043.

Salmon P, Peters S, Rogers A, Gask L, Clifford R, Iredale W, Dowrick C, Morriss R. Peering through the barriers in GPs' explanations for declining to participate in research: the role of professional autonomy and the economy of time. Fam Pract 2007;24:269–275.

Schleyer TKL, Forrest JL. Methods for the design and administration of web-based surveys. J Am Med Inform Assoc 2000;7:416–425.

Scott A, Jeon SH, Joyce CM, Humphreys JS, Kalb G, Witt J, Leahy A. A randomised trial and economic evaluation of the effect of response mode on response rate, response bias, and item non-response in a survey of doctors. BMC Med Res Methodol 2011;11:126.

Seguin R, MacDonald S, Godwin M, McCall M. E-mail or snail mail? Randomized controlled trial on which works better for surveys. Canadian Family Physician 2004;50:414–419.

Shimizu I, Hsiao C. 2010. Survey methods for a new mail survey of office-based physicians. *Proceedings of the Joint Statistical Meetings, Survey Research Methods Section*. Available at http://www.amstat.org/sections/srms/proceedings/y2010/Files/306964_57556.pdf.

Shiono PH, Klebanoff MA. The effect of two mailing strategies in the response to a survey of physicians. Am J Epidemiol 1991;134:539–542.

Sibbald B, Addington-Hall J, Brenneman D, Freeling P. Telephone versus postal surveys of general practitioners: methodological considerations. Br J Gen Pract 1994;44:297–300.

Sinai N, Mills AB. *A Study of Physicians and Dentists in Detroit: 1929*. Washington, DC: The Committee on the Costs of Medical Care; 1931.

Sinclair M, O'Toole J, Malawaraarachchi M, Leder K. Comparison of response rates and cost-effectiveness for a community-based survey: postal, internet and telephone modes with generic or personalised recruitment approaches. BMC Med Res Methodol 2012;12.

Sprague S, Quigley L, Bhandari M. Survey design in orthopaedic surgery: getting surgeons to respond. J Bone Joint Surg 2009;91(Suppl 3):27–34.

Stocks N, Gunnell D. What are the characteristics of GPs who routinely do not return postal questionnaires: a cross sectional study. J Epidemiol Community Health 2000;54:940–941.

Streiff MB, Dundes L, Spivak JL. A mail survey of United States hematologists and oncologists: a comparison of business reply versus stamped return envelopes. J Clin Epidemiol 2001;54:430–432.

Sudman S. Mail surveys of reluctant professionals. Eval Rev 1985;9:349–360.

Tamayo-Sarver JH, Baker DW. Comparison of responses to a $2 dollar bill versus a chance to win $250 dollars in a mail survey of emergency physicians. Acad Emerg Med 2004;11:888–891.

Tambor ES, Chase GA, Faden RR, Geller G, Hofman KJ, Holtzman NA. Improving response rates through incentive and follow-up: the effect on a survey of physicians' knowledge of genetics. Am J Public Health 1993;83:1599–1603.

Templeton L, Deehan A, Taylor C, Drummond C, Strang J. Surveying general practitioners: does a low response rate matter? Br J Gen Pract 1997;47:91–94.

Thomas M, Rogers R, Maclean R. Collecting data from physicians via web-based surveys: recommendations for improving response rates. Intern J Med Inform 2003;1:ce9.

Thran SL, Berk ML. Survey of physicians: an overview. *Proceedings of the International Conference on Establishment Surveys*. Alexandria, VA: American Statistical Association; 1993.

Thran SL, Hixson JS Physician surveys: an overview. *Proceedings of the International Conference on Establishment Surveys: Survey Methods for Businesses, Farms and Institutions*. Alexandria, VA: American Statistical Association; 2000.

Urban N, Anderson GL, Tseng A. Effects on response rates and cost of stamps vs. business reply in a mail survey of physicians. J Clin Epidemiol 1993;46:455–459.

VanDenKerkhof EG, Parlow JL, Goldstein DH, Milne B. In Canada, anesthesiologists are less likely to respond to an electronic, compared to paper questionnaire. Can J Anesth 2004;51:449–454.

VanGeest JB, Johnson TP, Welch VL. Methodologies for improving response rates in surveys of physicians: a systematic review. Eval Health Prof 2007;30:303–321.

VanGeest JB, Wynia MK, Cummins DS, Wilson IB. Effects of different monetary incentives on the return rate of a national survey of physicians. Med Care 2001;39:197–201.

VanGeest J, Johnson TP. Surveying nurses: identifying strategies to improve participation. Eval Health Prof 2011;34:487–511.

VanGeest JB, Johnson TP. Surveying clinicians: an introduction to the special issue. Eval Health Prof 2013;35:275–278.

van Gelder MMHJ, Bretveld RW, Roeleveld N. Web-based questionnaires: the future in epidemiology? Am J Epidemiol 2010;172:1292–1298.

Van Otterloo J, Richards JL, Seib K, Weiss P, Omer SB. Gift card incentives and non-response bias in a survey of vaccine providers: the role of geographic and demographic factors. PLoS One 2011;6:e28108.

Viera AJ, Edwards T. Does an offer for a free online continuing medical education (CME) activity increase physician survey response rate? A randomized trial. BMC Res Notes 2012;5:129.

Vogel LL, Nowacek G, Harlan JF, Tribble A, Thorup OA Jr,. Impact of a replacement questionnaire on the response rate of practicing physicians to a mail questionnaire. J Med Educ 1983;58:905.

Ward J, Bruce T, Holt P, D'Este K, Sladden M. Labour-saving strategies to maintain survey response rates: a randomised trial. Aust N Z J Public Health 1998;22:394–396.

Ward J, Wain G. Increasing response rates of gynaecologists to a survey: a randomised trial of telephone prompts. Aust N Z J Public Health 1994;18:332–334.

Weisz G. *Divide and Conquer: A Comparative History of Medical Specialization*. New York, NY: Oxford University Press; 2005.

Ward J, Bruce T, Holt P, D'Este K, Sladden M. Labour-saving strategies to maintain survey response rates: A randomized trial. Aust N Z J Public Health, (1998);22(Suppl.), 394–396.

Werner RM, Alexander GC, Fagerlin A, Ubel PA. The "hassle factor": what motivates physicians to manipulate reimbursement rules? Arch Intern Med 2002;162:1134–1139.

Wiebe ER, Kaczorowski J, MacKay J. Why are response rates in clinician surveys declining? Can Fam Phys 2012;58:e225–e228.

Willis GB, Smith T, Lee HJ. Do additional recontacts to increase response rate improve physician survey data quality? Med Care 2013;51:945–948.

Wyatt JC. When to use web-based surveys. J Am Med Inform Assoc 2000;7:426–429.

Young J. Mail surveys of general practice physicians: response rates and non-response bias. Swiss Med Wkly 2005;135:187–188.

Ziegenfuss JY, Burmeister K, James KM, Haas L, Tilburt JC, Beebe TJ. Getting physicians to open the survey: little evidence that an envelope teaser increases response rates. BMC Med Res Methodol 2012;12.

Ziegenfuss JY, Niederhauser BD, Kallmes DF, Beebe TJ. An assessment of incentive versus survey length trade-offs in a web survey of radiologists. J Med Internet Res 2013;15:e49.

Ziegenfuss JY, Tilburt J, Beebe TJ. Increasing response rates in a survey of physicians and nurses. Presentation at the 66th Annual Conference of the American Association for Public Opinion Research, Phoenix, AZ; 2011.

ONLINE RESOURCES

The November 2010 National Cancer Institute (NCI) Provider Survey Methods Workshop reviewed and discussed methodologies in designing and fielding large-scale surveys of physicians and medical group practices. Information on the Workshop is available at: http://appliedresearch.cancer.gov/surveys/physician/.

Selected sample surveys include those listed below.

Information on the Physician Practice Information Survey supported by the American Medical Association, is available at: www.ama-assn.org/ama/pub/physician-resources/solutions-managing-your-practice/coding-billing-insurance/the-resource-based-relative-value-scale/physician-practice-information-survey.page.

Information about the Agency for Healthcare Research and Quality CAHPS Clinician & Group Surveys, including sampling guidelines and protocols, are available at: www.cahps.ahrq.gov/clinician_group/.

The Center for Studying Health System Change provides information on the CTS Physician Surveys and the Health Tracking Physician Survey (including links to technical publications) at: www.hschange.com/index.cgi?data=04.

Selected sampling resources include those listed below.

Information on the American Medical Association Physician Masterfile is available at: www.ama-assn.org/ama/pub/about-ama/physician-data-resources/physician-masterfile.page.

Information on the Centers for Medicare & Medicaid Services (CMS) National Plan and Provider Enumeration System (NPPES) is available at: https://nppes.cms.hhs.gov/NPPES/Welcome.do.

Information on the American Medical Information (AMI) database is available at: http://list.infousa.com/ami/html/about_ami_new.htm.

CHAPTER TWENTY ONE

Surveys of Health Care Organizations

John D. Loft, Joe Murphy, and Craig A. Hill
Survey, Computing, and Statistical Sciences, RTI International Chicago IL, USA

21.1 Introduction

This chapter discusses surveys of health care organizations—hospitals and other institutions that provide health care for acute or chronic conditions. From a survey research perspective, data collection efforts from these facilities are establishment surveys. Although respondents in establishment surveys are frequently individuals, there are significant distinctions between surveys of organizations and surveys of individuals or households that are important to keep in mind in survey design. Generally, respondents in establishment surveys are not reporting personal behaviors and opinions; rather they are informants about the practices of the organization where they work and their behaviors as representatives of those organizations. Moreover, although all of the design issues common to surveys of businesses, educational institutions, and other establishments are also salient in surveys of health care organizations, there are unique aspects of health care that call for special considerations.

As preface to a discussion of these design considerations, we begin with an overview of types of health care organizations and move on to outline several reasons that motivate surveys of these organizations.

Handbook of Health Survey Methods, First Edition. Edited by Timothy P. Johnson.

21.1.1 WHAT ARE HEALTH CARE ORGANIZATIONS?

In this section, we note the variety of institutions that might come under the rubric of health care organizations. A hospital is perhaps the first type that comes to mind. From an organizational perspective, hospitals are certainly not all of the same type. The American Hospital Association (AHA) reports 5795 registered hospitals in the United States (http://www.aha.org/research/rc/stat-studies/fast-facts.shtml). The AHA maintains a rich data source on both member and nonmember hospitals that includes descriptors such as ownership, specialty, and size. Most hospitals (5008) are community hospitals, defined as nonfederal, short-term general or specialty hospitals. Community hospitals can specialize in obstetrics–gynecology, eye–ear–nose–throat, rehabilitation, orthopedic, or other specialties and can include academic medical centers or other teaching/research hospitals. Community hospitals include not-for-profit hospitals, investor-owned (for-profit) hospitals, as well as hospitals owned by state or local governments. The AHA also reports 2921 community hospitals that are in a multihospital system ("two or more hospitals owned, leased, sponsored, or contract managed by a central organization") or a diversified single hospital system ("bringing into membership three or more, and at least 25%, of their owned or leased nonhospital preacute or postacute health care organizations"). The site also reports 1485 community hospitals are in a network, that is, "a group of hospitals, physicians, other providers, insurers and/or community agencies that work together to coordinate and deliver a broad spectrum of services to their community." Measures of size among community hospitals include number of beds, number of admissions, and expenses, as well as staff size. Federal hospitals are smaller in number (211) but are diverse as well in terms of federal department management (Veterans Administration and other agencies), size, and other variables. As we will note later, such diversity in the population of hospitals has implications for survey design.

There are, of course, many other types of healthcare organizations in addition to hospitals. The Joint Commission on Accreditation of Healthcare Organizations (JCAHO) offers accreditation programs for many such organizations providing long-term care, behavioral health care (including mental health and substance abuse treatment centers), ambulatory care, laboratory services, home care, and office-based surgery. In all, JCAHO accredits more than 19,000 health care organizations—an indication of the variety of organizations that might be included in the term health care organizations (http://www.jointcommission.org/about_us/). The National Center for Health Statistics has surveyed a number of health care organizations under the umbrella of the National Health Care Survey, including community health centers, ambulatory surgery centers, nursing homes, home and hospice care agencies, and residential care facilities (http://www.cdc.gov/nchs/dhcs.htm). Bazzoli et al. (1999) and Beazley (2010) discuss a number of different types of health care facilities.

21.1.2 WHY SURVEY HEALTH CARE ORGANIZATIONS?

Although health care delivery occurs between two individuals—a patient and a health care professional—the organization is context for the patient–provider relationship. Many of the decisions about diagnostic and therapeutic protocols and about availability and allocation of medical staff, equipment, and other resources are made in this context and outside of the dyadic relationship. A great deal of health care in the United States and other countries occurs in hospitals and other health care organizations and a large proportion of the dollars spent on health care pays for treatment provided in these facilities. The National Center for Health Statistics reports that 31% of U.S. health expenditures in 2008 were for hospital care and another 6% for nursing home care (National Center for Health Statistics 2011: Table 125). It is important from a health services research perspective to understand the services provided for this expenditure and the care provided under auspices of health care organizations.

In addition to providing context for understanding the relationship between provider and patients, surveys of health care organizations also serve a social accounting purpose, by documenting the geographic distribution of health care organizations relative to population distribution and describing the health services offered where services are located relative to population needs.

Another motivation for surveys of health care organizations may be to complement data derived from surveys of individuals. The care provided in hospitals and other organizations is often of a complex nature. Accurate descriptions of diagnoses and comorbidities may be beyond the ability of laypersons in household surveys. Similarly, details of therapies and prescriptions may be lacking or inaccurate in self-reports of survey respondents. Finally, complexities of health insurance arrangements and payments can contribute to error in reports of health care costs. For these reasons, household respondents may not be able to provide accurate descriptions of their own health care in household surveys. Health care organizations are an important source of information about health care delivery that can complement data obtained from household surveys. Linking data from household surveys with information obtained from the record systems of health care organizations is a design feature of several large U.S. federal surveys (e.g., the Provider Record Check Studies of the National Health Interview Survey and the National Immunization Survey, the Medical Provider Component of Medical Expenditure Panel Survey, http://www.cdc.gov/nchs/nhis/niprcs.htm, http://www.cdc.gov/nchs/nis/about_nis.htm, http://meps.ahrq.gov/mepsweb/survey_comp/mpc.jsp). See additional discussion of this topic in Chapter 27.

Independent of the patients they treat, organizations can be an important source of information about health care professions. Health care organizations can provide access to their professional staff and employees for surveys of knowledge, attitudes, and practices of physicians, nurses, and other health care professionals. Health care organizations and their employees can provide useful information about trends in health care services and the spread of medical innovation (Elkins et al. 2011, Morganthaler et al. 2012).

21.2 Examples of Health Care Organizations Surveys

In the United States, the federal government conducts several surveys of health care organizations both as data program designed to collect current information on health care resources and as one-time surveys for special purposes. Under the National Health Care Surveys, the Centers for Disease Control and Prevention's National Center for Health Statistics has conducted surveys of hospitals, ambulatory surgery centers, community health centers, nursing homes, home and hospice care agencies, and residential care facilities as well as surveys of physicians' private practices and surveys of individual professions (http://cdc.gov/nchs/dhcs.htm). The Substance Abuse, Mental Health and Services Agency (SAMHSA) supports the Drug and Alcohol Services Information System (DASIS) including three components, the National Survey of Substance Abuse Treatment Services, the Treatment Episode Data Set, and the Inventory of Substance Abuse Treatment Services (http://www.samhsa.gov/data/dasis.htm). SAMSHA also monitors hospital emergency departments and offices of medical examiners through the Drug Abuse Warning Network (http://www.samhsa.gov/data/DAWN.aspx). Several population-based health surveys include a provider component to complement household data; for example, the Medical Provider Component of the Medical Expenditure Panel Survey, sponsored by the Agency for Healthcare Research and Quality (AHRQ) and the Provider Record Check Study in the National Immunization Survey, sponsored by the Centers for Disease Control and Prevention (http://meps.ahrq.gov/mepsweb/ and http://www.cdc.gov/nchs/nis.htm).

In addition to these federal statistical programs, professional organizations may elect to conduct annual surveys of their constituent organizations. For example, the AHA has, since 1946, conducted an annual survey of member and nonmember hospitals that includes information about organizational structure, personnel, facilities and services, finances (http://www.aha.org/research/rc/stat-studies/index.shtml).

21.3 Surveys of Health Care Organizations as Establishment Surveys

The intent of the preceding discussion has been to outline the variety of health care organizations, describe the purposes of surveying these facilities, and note some important examples of ongoing surveys of these organizations. We will next discuss features of surveys of health care organizations that distinguish the design of these surveys from the design of surveys of individual patients or providers.

The literature on establishment surveys is less plentiful than exists on other types of surveys, but there are nonetheless numerous useful resources. We draw in large part on presentations, papers, and monographs resulting from the International Conference on Establishment Surveys (ICES), a series begun in 1993 to address a then-lack of published methods concerning the unique problems of business surveys. The initial conference resulted in an edited volume, *Business Survey Methods* (Cox et al. 1995) and has been followed by subsequent conferences (http://www.amstat.org/meetings/ices/2012).

21.3.1 SAMPLE DESIGN IN SURVEYS OF HEALTH CARE ORGANIZATIONS

Development of Sample Frames. Sample frames for health care organizations generally list samples developed from a single or multiple sources. Data resources available from the AHA and JCAHO may be useful sample frames for organizations represented by these entities. Frames for other types of organizations may be developed from state licensing agencies. In evaluating or developing frames, there are several features to keep in mind.

Ideally, the frame includes information to *identify* the population units as unique entities (e.g., names, addresses), *classify* the units (e.g., measures of size, type of health care services, ownership), and *contact* the units that happen to be sampled (e.g., contact persons, mailing addresses, telephone or fax numbers, email addresses). It is not unusual for health care organizations to be linked to one another (as, occurs when several facilities are owned by a local, regional, or national chain) and *linkage* data connecting the population units can be an important element of the frame (Colledge 1995).

In practice, there may be several problems with frame data. Particularly in developing national frames from state licensing agencies it is important to note that states may not have recorded data elements consistently. Thus, the assembled frame may be missing information or may be based on different definitions for some data. In addition, states are often on different cycles for updating lists of facilities so that the ages of frame data can vary by several years.

A second issue is the possibility that the reporting in the frame may not correspond consistently to the unit of analysis required in design specifications. In the case of multiestablishment organizations (that is, organizations that own or operate several establishments as branches or subsidiaries), the establishments may be listed as separate units or may not be listed separately from the organization. For example, a chain of nursing homes may be listed once as the chain or several times as the individual homes (Tomaskovic-Devey et al. 1994, Smith 2004).

The age of the data on the frame can be critical. Belonging to a class of health care organizations is a dynamic characteristic as facilities are created, change type or level of activity, merge with or split from other organizations, or go out of business (Sigman and Monsour 1995). Using a frame with relatively old data can result in excluding newly founded facilities from the survey sample. Old contact information can lead to operational difficulties in contacting facilities that might be operating under a new name or at a new address. A facility that has ceased operations completely and closed down would generally be considered ineligible. However, facilities that merge with or are purchased by another entity often continue to provide health services under the new legal entity and survey procedures need to include specifications for handling these situations consistently, possibly ineligible but possibly simply operating under a new name or new corporate identity. A related situation is a single facility that might appear on the sample list more than once, as, for example, a short-stay hospital and an ambulatory surgery center that may be departments of the same hospital.

Another potential consideration in surveys of health care organizations, especially hospitals, is whether to sample departments within the organization. A typical hospital, for example, is organized into inpatient and outpatient services and may have multiple departments within each. Depending on the topic of the survey, it may be necessary to subsample departments within the establishment in a multistage design.

Sample Design. Sigman and Monsour (1995) also note that a typical feature of list frames of businesses is skewness where a small number of businesses account for a large proportion of the population total (see also Earp and McCarthy (2012) and Thompson (2012)). For example, a small number of hospitals may account for a large proportion of patient visits in a community. Typical sample designs address this either by incorporating strata based on size, or sampling where the probability of selection is proportional to size (pps), or both. Colledge (1995) notes as well that, because of their potential impact on survey estimates, large businesses are usually sampled with certainty. Sampling large health care organizations with certainty can introduce an operational issue in repeated surveys where the same facilities are selected in each wave of survey. Even in one-time surveys it is necessary to realize that large health care organizations are often inundated with survey requests because of this feature.

Finally, sample designs for surveys of health care organizations may call for multistage designs where units are sampled at the establishment level (e.g., hospitals), at a department level within the establishment (inpatient or outpatient departments within a hospital), and even at the level of individual employees or clients of the facility (nurses or patients within a surgery department in a hospital). Balancing complex requirements at each level calls for careful optimization (see, for example, Byron et al. 2007).

21.3.2 INSTRUMENT DESIGN

In considering the design of data collection instruments, it is necessary to keep in mind that, although the data collection unit in an establishment is an organizational entity, the survey informant is a human individual who is an informant about the organization. The cognitive response model developed by Tourangeau (1984) and others is a useful guide in this respect. Extensions of the model to informants in establishment surveys have been initiated by Edwards and Cantor (1991), Biemer and Fecso (1995), and Willimack and Nichols (2010). Willimack and Nichols (2010) offer a survey response process model for establishment surveys that extends this model to surveys of businesses and other establishments. Their "hybrid" formulation explicitly recognizes features of organizations in the process of how both organizations and individuals behave as respondents to surveys. The steps in the process are the following:

1. Encoding in memory/record formation
2. Selection and identification of the informant or informants
3. Assessment of priorities
4. Comprehension of the data request
5. Retrieval of relevant information from memory and/or existing business records
6. Judgment of the adequacy of the response
7. Communication of the response
8. Release of the data

These steps summarize processes that affect both the willingness to participate in a survey (assessment of priorities) and how informants in organizations might understand survey questions and assemble responses.

This model is useful to consider in detail in the design of data collection from establishments. For our purposes, we discuss four themes suggested by the model that are particularly relevant to surveys of health care organizations.

First, the first step, encoding and record formation, was introduced by Edwards and Cantor (1991) in order to distinguish two potential sources that an informant might draw upon to gather information required by the survey. Informants in establishment surveys may choose between responding to survey questions from memory or by consulting records of one sort or another. Whether and how to guide this choice in the design of questionnaires can be a significant challenge, and may involve balancing respondent/informant burden (looking up the information vs answering from memory) and accuracy of the response.

Second, several individual informants may be called upon to respond on behalf of a single organization. Even in small organizations, information requested in a health care survey may be distributed across different departments within a single establishment. In hospitals, for example, information about inpatient services is often administratively separate from information about outpatient services. Medical records systems are often separate administratively from billing services. The possibility of multiple individual informants within a single organization means that directing the questionnaire to a knowledgeable informant or possibly several informants within the same facility is a consideration for survey design.

While the choice of the individual informant is in the hands of the responding organization, survey design can facilitate the choice by being explicit about the types of information requested and flexible in adapting the choice of informant to the particular exigencies of the organization's staffing and information systems (see also, Edwards and Cantor (1991) and Tomaskovic-Devey et al. (1994) for discussions of selecting knowledgeable informants within organizations). Willimack and Nichols (2010) note two strategies for completing data collection by multiple informants within a single organization. An individual within the responding organization might *coordinate* the survey response by delegating data collection activities to appropriate staff within the organization. Alternatively, an individual informant might *compile* the requested survey data personally by gathering the data and completing the questionnaires. Choice of one or the other of these strategies may depend on features of the organizations and willingness of a single individual to accept the survey task.

Third, while it is enticing to believe that administrative records are a "gold standard" of accuracy, survey design should note several potential sources of error in such records. Records may not contain the requested information. Records systems in health care organizations are developed to serve the needs of the organization rather than research purposes. Socioeconomic descriptors of patients are likely to be missing in medical records (Krieger 1992). In addition, records of the establishment may not be organized to match the statistical reporting units in the questionnaire. For example, a distinction between full-time and part-time staff in a particular health profession may be significant for research purposes, but not useful for an organization. Definitions of terms may vary in the records systems of different organizations. Businesses develop an internal culture that can affect how key research terms are interpreted within the organization. Finally, inaccuracies in administrative and medical records can occur through simple data entry errors made by the recorder.

Fourth, particularly for health care organizations it is important to note the development of electronic information systems. Following reports on the consequences of medical error (Kohn et al. 2000), Executive Order 13335 (2004) focused attention on the development of an interoperable health information technology infrastructure and sparked widespread initiatives to implement universal electronic health records by 2014. While health information technology offers intriguing opportunities for health services research, the field is addressing very thorny problems of costs, harmonization of data elements and security of patient information. Blumenthal (2009) reports 17% of physicians and 10% of hospitals have basic electronic health records (see also DesRoches et al. 2008, Jha et al. 2009). In organizations where such systems do exist, they may not interact fluidly with other data systems in the organization (for example, financial information systems). Nonetheless, these systems are expected to become more commonplace in the future and may be an option for organizational informants in surveys of health care organizations.

The areas listed above—responding from memory or administrative records, multiple informants within the same organization, and the suitability of either paper or electronic records as sources of data in responding to organizational surveys—are contextual features to consider in developing data collection instruments for surveys of health care organizations. Such issues point to the necessity of pretesting various aspects of survey design.

Pretests can be thought of as "small scale rehearsals of the data collection conducted before the main study" (Groves et al. 2004). The insight gathered from administering a protocol and questionnaire to a subset of eligible sample members or similar group can vastly improve the instrument and reduce the contribution of other elements of total survey error (Biemer and Lyberg 2003). Reports on other surveys of similar organizations are also valuable source of information.

Pretesting is perhaps even more important when surveying health care organizations compared to individuals or other institutions. Given the chain of communication that must be set in place to even reach the intended informant or informants at a health care organization, some tests of the survey protocol will elicit lessons learned concerning the mode of initial contact, presence of gatekeepers, and the role of incentives in gaining cooperation.

To best understand the mechanisms in place at health care organizations regarding delivery of survey materials and fulfillment of survey requests, one should consider conducting focus groups with a subset of those likely to initially receive and ultimately address the request. For instance, a survey about hospital policies or characteristics may be sent by mail to chief medical officers (CMOs) of hospitals but before reaching the desk of that person, the survey will be handled by an assistant who may make a determination of whether the request is valid or worthy of the CMO's limited and valuable time. In some cases, the CMO may not have ready access to the needed information and will need to share the survey with a department chief, financial officer, or other staff person. Speaking with one or more of these groups in advance of deploying the survey protocol could suggest optimal designs of the mailing materials or methods of contact of the likely informants to assure an efficient process that results in the collection of accurate data.

Pretesting the survey instrument itself is very important to assure that the appropriate data are gathered for the study and to reduce measurement error. While the survey may have been developed in coordination with topic or medical experts, it is often not until a real-world test of the survey is conducted that errors in the logic, definitions, or scales of certain items are identified. Often, this is addressed through cognitive interviewing, whereby an informant is administered the survey and asked to provide thoughts along the way related to the process used for determining responses. Cognitive interviewing techniques adapted to an establishment setting can be important tools in developing an understanding of how to adapt survey design elements to situations that are likely to occur with the target population (see Dippo et al. 1995). Another method is an actual test of the survey in the setting where data collection is most likely to occur. For the annual Pediatric Hospital Survey conducted by RTI International for *U.S. News & World Report* (Olmsted et al. 2011), a pretest is conducted with a subset of hospitals to test new items. This process often generates questions from responding pretest hospitals that allow for the refinement of the survey. For instance, a hospital may identify a particular procedure code that was not included in the definition for a question or report that their hospital's value on a particular question is not among the response options for that question. After the pretest, these items can be addressed so that the main study data collection will best fit the experiences and values of the participating health care organizations. Outcomes of the pretest, such as measures of respondent burden, may be useful in preparing advance materials.

Finally, pretesting can provide a set of test data for use in setting up analysis procedures. Using the pretest data, one can conduct a test analysis addressing the research questions for the study, identifying any missing elements or steps that can be addressed in advance of the actual data collection and data analysis. A "dress rehearsal" of the survey data analysis can save time when working to produce final results and improve the ultimate quality of the study.

21.3.3 DATA COLLECTION

The question of mode in surveys of health care organizations is often not clear. As noted above, informants in establishments may often need to assemble requested information from records, an activity that lends itself to a self-administered format. Depending on the nature of the survey request, the informant may need to consult several sources of information and perhaps contact several additional individuals within the company in order to complete the questionnaire. An interviewer may not be helpful in this process. On the other hand, an interviewer may be useful in getting past gatekeepers, responding to questions seeking clarification about survey terms, or even identifying possible additional points of contact. A comparison of response rate across several business surveys (Paxson et al. 1995) suggests that mixed mode approach may be the most successful.

A mixed mode approach may offer several advantages over a single mode. An interviewer might be employed to get past gatekeepers, help identify appropriate informants within the particular organizations, and respond to concerns the potential informants might have concerning participation in the survey. In addition, we noted above several kinds of questions that can occur based on the quality of frame data. An initial telephone call to the sampled organization can yield useful information clarifying whether the establishment is still eligible for the survey. A self-administered instrument might then be provided to informants in the organization, either by mail or online, to complete at their convenience.

Incentives to encourage participation in the survey may be another consideration. The literature is mixed on the effectiveness of incentives (Paxson et al. 1995). We suspect that whether or not an incentive is effective depends a great deal on situational factors in each organization. An incentive should motivate an individual to take action—decide to participate in the survey, look up information to include in a response, or convince a coworker to provide information to complete the questionnaire. As a practical matter, whether an incentive is effective can depend on whether there is a single or multiple informants in the organizations and whether the incentive goes to an individual or is shared by all of the informants. Another factor is whether the incentive goes to the individual informants in the organization or to the organization as a whole. An individual may be prevented by company policy to accept an incentive but might defer the incentive to a corporate account or an employee fund. However, this might dilute the effectiveness of the incentive. Finally, given the range in size and complexity of health care organizations, offering the same incentive is likely to have a variable effect. An incentive of equal monetary value might be significant to a small facility but trivial to a large facility. Often, the solution to these ambiguities is to reserve incentives as a step in responding to a reluctant response when a reason for refusal is cost. In this context, the incentive can be presented as reimbursement for reasonable costs of, for example, retrieving information from administrative records.

As is the case in surveys of individuals, it is important to consider potential bias due to nonresponse in surveys of health care organizations. A recent example is Lewis et al. (2013), which examined several methods of evaluating nonresponse bias in a mail survey of hospitals in the United Kingdom. The authors reported conflicting outcomes from four methods of assessing nonresponse bias but nonetheless offer useful insights concerning how methods of assessing nonresponse bias can be applicable in a survey of health care organizations.

As a final note on data collection considerations, AAPOR's revised *Standard Definitions* (American Association for Public Opinion Research 2011) for final dispositions codes includes a section on dispositions for establishment surveys that is relevant to surveys of health care organizations. The discussion notes several of the features of establishment surveys noted above including sample integrity issues, definitions of informants, and the possibility of multiple informants and multiple questionnaires for each establishment. Disposition codes and decision rules for classification of outcomes (as eligible or ineligible, respondent or nonrespondent, and so on) must be completed consistently across the sample members and reported clearly in final documentation of the survey.

21.3.4 DATA PROCESSING AND DATA MANAGEMENT

Kovar and Witridge (1995), Grandquist (1995), and Thompson (2012) make the point that because of the skewness of business survey data, errors or missing data in the responses of a small number of organizations can have a large impact on estimates based on the survey data. This point certainly applies to surveys of health care organizations and underscores the importance of post-data collection editing in data processing steps. In particular, as noted above, definitions of terminology may vary between organizations and it is important to include data in processing steps to review and edit survey data to assure that terms have been used consistently across responding organizations.

Coding information obtained from health care organizations as verbatim text fields may require specialized abilities. Examples include coding diagnosis into the International Classification for Disease (http://www.cdc.gov/nchs/icd.htm) or coding procedures into the Current Procedural Terminology (American Medical Association 2012).

Linkages of data maintained by organizations to survey data collected in patient interviews can greatly enhance the value of both. While information in administrative or medical records is generally more accurate than patient reports for variables such as diagnoses, treatment modalities, and costs, information from patient surveys are generally a better source for information on health status, socioeconomic status, and other demographic characteristics. Lillard and Farmer

(1997) and Chapter 27 discuss the advantages and challenges to linking survey data with Medicare information.

21.3.5 PARTICULAR CONCERNS IN SURVEYS OF HEALTH ORGANIZATIONS

Confidentiality of Patient Information. Identifiable patient information is protected by the Health Insurance Portability and Accountability Act (HIPAA). Along with other federal and state legislation, HIPAA prescribes requirements for both the health care organization and any organization requesting identifiable data in order to assure appropriate authorization has been obtained from the patients in question and that proper safeguards are in place for protecting patient identities (see also human subjects protections under 45 CFR 46).

Surveys of health care organizations might not call for identifiable information about patients or clients of the organizations. For example, information requested about the types of services offered at facilities or the size of staff in categories of health professions, or even numbers of visits, or overnight stays can serve as quite useful measures that do not call upon the organization to reveal the identities of individual patients. Care should always be taken to assure that patient-level information is aggregated enough to prevent accidental disclosure of individual patients.

Confidentiality of Organization Information. Although health care organizations are public entities and their identities are known, it is nonetheless important to maintain the confidentiality of the organizational data. Information sometimes collected in surveys of health care organizations—costs of services, revenues, operating costs—can be sensitive business information and should be protected in the same way as an individual survey respondent.

21.4 Conclusions

In this chapter, we have discussed surveys of health care organizations in the context of the methodological literature on establishment surveys. We acknowledge that the examples cited are drawn from the United States. Certainly, some of the considerations noted are applicable to research in other countries. However, many features of the organization of health care delivery are specific to particular countries.

In conclusion, we would like to comment on implications for future methodological research.

First, we suggest research into methods for improving the comprehensiveness of establishment lists that serve as sample frames. As health care delivery evolves, the definition of "health care organization" is expected to expand to include a more diversified array of businesses. Lists maintained by the AHA and JCAHO are comprehensive as far as their intended constituency. However, more businesses are expected to enter the market for health care services. The expansion of long-term care facilities for the elderly might serve as a case study. New types of organizations have emerged to complement traditional nursing homes, including residential care facilities, comprehensive care facilities, and other forms of long-term care organizations, yet comprehensive lists of such facilities have not been compiled by an overarching, objective body.

Similar developments are expected in the field of mental health services. Organizations are emerging to offer services in the area of mental health and rehabilitation services, yet no comprehensive lists of these organizations exist to serve as sample frames and enable population-based research. Examples of mental health care providers include outpatient and residential facilities specializing in treatment of depression, anxiety, substance addictions, or other psychopathologies.

Second, we call for investigation of effective techniques or adapting design features to known characteristics of health care organizations. Lists of health care organizations can contain valuable information to support data collection operations in the areas of unduplicating multiple records for the same corporate entity, initial contacts, identification of other points of contact in the organization. In addition, indicators of the complexity of health care organizations that may be available on sample frames or on websites can be used to formulate initial data collection approaches, such as identifying appropriate decision makers and points of contact in the organizations.

Third, although adoption of electronic health records is not universal, the potential for accessing aggregate data from this source is great. Methodological research focused on realizing this potential should address at least three areas: assuring the security and confidentiality of data obtained from such resources, assessing the comparability of data elements obtained from different EHR systems, and on concerns that health care organizations might have about transferring data from these systems for research purposes.

Fourth, the use of financial incentives in surveys of health care organizations deserves much more attention. Methodological questions include how to isolate influence of incentives on (i) the motivation to participate in the survey, (ii) encouragement to respond accurately by consulting appropriate resources within the organization, and (iii) reimbursement for costs of participating in the survey.

Fifth, we believe it is useful to the research community to develop documentation of key data collection measures such as the length of time from initial contact to final disposition; the number of contacts necessary to achieve a final disposition, and the hours per case necessary to achieve a final disposition. This information is invaluable in planning research programs for surveys of health care establishments. Moreover, it is useful to understand how these key indicators might vary by organization features available on sample frames (see, for example, Zuckerbraun et al. 2012).

Finally, it is important to document reasons for refusal to participate in surveys of health care organizations. This information is valuable for planning qualitative research about potential barriers to participation in surveys of health care organizations.

REFERENCES

American Association for Public Opinion Research. *Standard Definitions: Final Dispositions of Case Codes and Outcome Rates for Surveys. 7th* ed. AAPOR; 2011.

American Medical Association. *Current Procedure Terminology. Standard Edition* ed. Chicago: American Medical Association; 2012.

Bazzoli GJ, Shortell SM, Dubbs N, Chan C, Kralovec P. A taxonomy of health networks and systems: bringing order out of chaos. Health Serv Res 1999;33:1683–1717.

Beazley SA. *A Brief Guide to the U.S. Health Care Delivery System: Facts, Definitions, and Statistics*. 2nd ed. Chicago: American Hospital Association Resource Center; 2010.

Biemer PP, Fecso RS. Evaluating and controlling measurement error in business surveys. In: Cox BG, Binder DA, Chinnappa BN, Christianson A, Colledge MJ, Kott PS, editors. *Business Survey Methods*. New York: Wiley; 1995.

Biemer PP, Lyberg LE. *Introduction to Survey Quality*. New York: Wiley; 2003.

Blumenthal D. Stimulating the adoption of health information technology. N Engl J Med 2009;360:1477–1479.

Byron MZ, Wiener JM, Loft JD, Iannacchione VG, Greene AM. Sampling for a highly skewed population: sample design for the National Survey of Residential Care Facilities. Presented at the Third International Conference on Establishment Surveys; Montreal, Quebec; 2007.

Colledge MJ. Frames and business registers: an overview. In: Cox BG, Binder DA, Chinnappa BN, Christianson A, Colledge MJ, Kott PS, editors. *Business Survey Methods*. New York: Wiley; 1995.

Cox BG, Binder DA, Chinnappa BN, Christianson A, Colledge MJ, Kott PS. *Business Survey Methods*. New York: Wiley; 1995.

DesRoches CM, Campbell EG, Rao SR, Donelan K, Ferris TG, Jha A, Kaushal R, Levy DE, Rosenbaum S, Shields AE, Blumenthal D. Electronic health records in ambulatory care—a national survey of physicians. N Engl J Med 2008;359:50–60.

Dippo CS, Chun YI, Sander J. Designing the data collection process. In: Cox BG, Binder DA, Chinnappa BN, Christianson A, Colledge MJ, Kott PS, editors. *Business Survey Methods*. New York: Wiley; 1995.

Earp MS, McCarthy J. Non-response reduction techniques in establishment surveys: introduction overview lecture. Presented at the Fourth International Conference on Establishment Surveys (2012); Montreal; 2012.

Edwards WS, Cantor D. Toward a response model in establishment surveys. In: Biemer PP, Groves RM, Lyberg LE, Mathiowetz NA, Subman S, editors. *Measurement Errors in Surveys*. New York: Wiley; 1991.

Elkins KR, Nguyen CM, Kim DS, Meyers H, Cheung M, Huang SS. Successful strategies for high participation in three regional healthcare surveys: an observational study. BMC Med Res Methodol 2011;11:176.

Executive Order 13335. Incentives for the use of health information technology and establishing the position of the national health information technology coordinator. Fed Regist 2004;69(84):24059–20461.

Grandquist L. Improving the traditional editing process. In: Cox BG, Binder DA, Chinnappa BN, Christianson A, Colledge MJ, Kott PS, editors. *Business Survey Methods*. New York: Wiley; 1995.

Groves RM, Fowler FJ, Couper MP, Lepkowski JM, Singer E, Tourangeau R. *Survey Methodology*. New York: Wiley; 2004.

Jha AK, DesRoches CM, Campbell EG, Donelan K, Rao SR, Ferris TG, Shields A, Rosenbaum S, Blumenthal D. Use of electronic health records in U.S. hospitals. N Engl J Med 2009;360:1628–1638.

Kohn LT, Corrigan JM, Donaldson MS. *To Err is Human: Building a Safer Health System*. Washington, DC: Institute of Medicine. National Academy Press; 2000.

Kovar JG, Witridge PJ. Imputation of business survey data. In: Cox BG, Binder DA, Chinnappa BN, Christianson A, Colledge MJ, Kott PS, editors. *Business Survey Methods*. New York: Wiley; 1995.

Krieger N. Overcoming the absence of socioeconomic data in medical records: validation and application of a census-based methodology. Am J Public Health 1992;82:703–710.

Lewis EF, Hardy M, Snaith B. Estimating the effect of nonresponse bias in a survey of hospital organizations. Eval Health Prof 2013;35:330–351.

Lillard LA, Farmer MM. Linking medicare and national survey data. Ann Intern Med 1997;127:691–695.

Morganthaler TI, Lovely JK, Cima RR, Beradinelli CF, Fedraw LA, Wallerich TJ, Hinrichs DJ, Varkey P. Using a framework for spread of best practices to implement successful venous thrombembolism prophylaxis throughout a large hospital system. Am J Med Qual 2012;27:30–38.

National Center for Health Statistics. *Health, United States, 2010: With Special Feature on Death and Dying*. Hyattsville, MD: National Center for Health Statistics; 2011. . Table 125, page 388.

Olmsted MO, McFarlane E, Murphy J, Severance J, Pitts A, Bell D, Morley M (2011) Best children's hospitals 2011-12 methodology. Available at www.rti.org/besthospitals. Accessed on 6 June 2014.

Paxson MC, Dillman DA, Tarnai J. Improving response to business mail surveys. In: Cox BG, Binder DA, Chinnappa BN, Christianson A, Colledge MJ, Kott PS, editors. *Business Survey Methods*. New York: Wiley; 1995.

Sigman RS, Monsour NJ. Selecting samples from list frames of businesses. In: Cox BG, Binder DA, Chinnappa BN, Christianson A, Colledge MJ, Kott PS, editors. *Business Survey Methods*. New York: Wiley; 1995.

Smith P. Perspective on response rates and nonresponse in establishment surveys. Presented at the U.S. Federal Economic Statistics Advisory Committee, Washington, DC; 2004.

Thompson K. Nonresponse bias analysis – perspective from the US Census Bureau. Presented at the Fourth International Conference on Establishment Surveys; Montreal; 2012.

Tomaskovic-Devey D, Leiter J, Thompson S. Organizational survey nonresponse. Adm Sci Q 1994;39:439–457.

Tourangeau R. Cognitive sciences and survey methods. In: Jabine TB, Straf ML, Tanur JM, Tourangeau R, editors. *Cognitive Aspects of Survey Methodology: Building a Bridge Between Disciplines*. Washington, DC: National Academy of Sciences; 1984.

Willimack DK, Nichols E. A hybrid response process model for business surveys. J Off Stat 2010;26:3–34.

Zuckerbraun SM, LeBaron PA, Loft JD, Sengupta M. (2012). Does it pay to try again? Using production metrics from the recruiting process on an establishment survey to design recruiting protocols. Presented at Federal Conference on Statistical Methodology (FCSM) Research Conference; Washington, DC.

ONLINE RESOURCES

The American Hospital Association includes information about the association's data resources concerning hospitals and health care systems: www.aha.org.

Supported by the American Statistical Association, this site includes the proceedings of each of the International Conferences on Establishment Surveys (ICES), beginning in 1993: www.amstat.org/meetings/ices/2012/.

The Agency for Healthcare Research and Quality (AHRQ) provides information about the Medical Expenditure Panel Survey (MEPS), a set of large-scale surveys of families and individuals, their medical providers, and employers across the United States. The site includes substantive and methodological reports on the survey as well as access to public use files: http://meps.ahrq.gov/mepsweb/survey_comp/mpc.jsp.

Information on the data programs supported by the Centers for Disease Control and Prevention's National Center for Health Statistics, including provider establishment surveys conducted under the umbrella of the National Health Care Surveys: www.cdc.gov/nchs.

The Joint Commission on Accreditation of Healthcare Organizations (JCAHO) providers information about organizations providing long term care, behavioral health care (including mental health and substance abuse treatment centers), ambulatory care, laboratory services, home care, and office-based surgery: www.jointcommission.org.

Information about the Drug and Alcohol Services Information System and the Drug Abuse Warning Network: www.samhsa.gov/data/dasis.htm www.samhsa.gov/data/DAWN.aspx.

CHAPTER TWENTY TWO

Surveys of Patient Populations

Francis Fullam
Marketing Research, Rush University Medical Center, Chicago, IL, USA; Health Systems Management, Rush University, Chicago, IL, USA

Jonathan B. VanGeest
Department of Health Policy and Management, College of Public Health, Kent State University, Kent, OH, USA

22.1 Introduction

One of the most important tools in health policy and services research is the patient survey. These surveys provide a mechanism for collecting data on patient experiences with health care (Cleary 1999, Delbanco 2001, Wensing and Elwyn 2003, Press 2005), which can ultimately inform improvements in patient care outcomes. Some of the earliest health surveys conducted in the twentieth century inquired about patient access to and utilization of health care services (Falk et al. 1933). In subsequent years, the use of patient surveys has accelerated—patient satisfaction surveys in particular. There has been, for example, over a 20-fold increase in the number of quality-related patient satisfaction studies published since 1960 (Cleary 1999, Sitzia and Wood 1997). This trend has continued, with satisfaction surveys now a regular tool in quality improvement efforts.

Handbook of Health Survey Methods, First Edition. Edited by Timothy P. Johnson.

Through patient surveys, we have learned much about a range of issues, including but not limited to, patients' treatment experiences and consumer decisions about health care, individual and community health needs, and outcomes associated with health care. Many patient surveys have had direct implications for policy and practice. One of the most salient examples involves the notion of patient-centered care, defined by the Institute of Medicine (IOM) as care that is "respectful of and responsive to individual patient preferences, needs and values" (Committee on Quality Health Care in America 2001). Patient-centered care was established by the IOM as one of its six objectives for improving health care in the twenty-first century and it is a cornerstone of the 2010 Affordable Care Act. This concept is fundamentally impossible to operationalize without a generalizable and applicable understanding of the patient perspective (Wensing and Elwyn 2003). Surveys can and have been used to effectively elicit patient perceptions about care to advance changes for improvement and patient centeredness (Blackwell et al. 2013, Davies et al. 2011, Davies and Cleary 2005, Elliott et al. 2010, Marino et al. 2000, Rathert et al. 2012). In another relevant example, Medicare payments are now tied directly to patient surveys, as these surveys provide critical patient input needed to effectively reduce overall health care expenditures while at the same time improving the quality of care delivered (Petrullo et al. 2013, Wolosin et al. 2012). Finally, there is the aforementioned example of patient satisfaction surveys, which have a long history of use in clinical and service quality improvement efforts (Cleary 1999, Debono and Travaglia 2009, Press 2005).

Patient surveys have been characterized as generally falling into three broad types: epidemiological surveys, descriptive surveys, and evaluation assessments (Jones et al. 2013, Kelley et al. 2003). Further, they range considerably in scope of endeavor, from large national or international health surveys such as the European seven-country PRISMA survey on symptoms and problems experienced by cancer patients with less than 1 year to live (Bausewein et al. 2013) or the European Cancer Anaemia Survey (ECAS) defining the prevalence, incidence, and treatment of anemia in cancer patients (Ludwig et al. 2004), to state and county surveillance surveys, to small single-issue or single-institution descriptive/improvement *ad hoc* surveys. In each case, surveys are an efficient means to obtain information and feedback from the patients' perspective on key health-related topics and issues. However, while many assume patient surveys to be simple to implement, they are often challenging, requiring careful attention to construction of valid measures and sound implementation strategies (Kahn et al. 2003). This chapter addresses the challenges associated with conducting patient surveys. We begin with an overview of patients and care settings. Subsequent sections explore common types of patient survey methodologies in use today, key issues, and potential methodological limitations in survey design and administration, potential sources of measurement and nonresponse bias in patient surveys, and methodologies for improving the quality of patient surveys.

22.2 Patients and Care Settings

The Latin word "patior" means "I am suffering" and is the origin of our current use of the noun "patient" to describe a person who receives medical care. Patients are typically treated by physicians and other care providers in a variety of settings. Inpatients, for example, are patients admitted to stay in a hospital overnight or longer. Outpatients, on the other hand, are those seen by a provider but not admitted to a hospital. In the context of patient surveys, it is important to have an understanding of the treatment setting and the condition for which patients are treated. While there are thousands of specific medical conditions, they are often grossly classified into either chronic (long-term persistent illness) or acute (illnesses characterized by rapid onset and short duration) conditions. Healthy, asymptomatic patients, on the other hand, also interact with the system on a routine basis, seeking preventative care (e.g., vaccinations), routine screenings (e.g., pap smears, breast and pelvic examinations, blood testing, colonoscopies); and checkups. Nature of condition matters, in part, because it dictates patients' interactions with the health system (e.g., mobility, timing/duration of visits, treatments, etc.) and their eligibility for and/or the feasibility of survey participation (Parker and Kroboth 1991).

Increasingly, the health care paradigm is no longer one in which patients are typically treated in large facilities, but one characterized by integrated care provision in diverse—often community-based— settings (Korda and Eldridge 2012). Still, hospitals represent an important setting with regard to patient surveys, in part because they facilitate access to patients. Also important from a survey perspective, the sizes of hospitals vary considerably. Approximately, half of U.S. hospitals have less than 100 beds. Moreover, smaller hospitals tend to be in rural locations. Many of the largest, academically affiliated hospitals, on the other hand, tend to be in larger urban centers.

The paradigm shift toward supporting integrated care delivery presents new considerations to health researchers. For instance, many types of care that in the past could be provided only in an inpatient hospital setting are now performed in outpatient sites, including specialist and surgical care in free-standing ambulatory centers (Manchikanti et al. 2011, Sibbald et al. 2008). This has considerably transformed the nature and type of patient typically seen in hospital settings. At the same time, visits to hospital emergency departments (EDs) have increased precipitously (LaCalle and Rabin 2010, Pitts et al. 2008, Weber et al. 2008). While it is often assumed that the uptick in ED use was driven by increases in the numbers of uninsured, patients with a usual source of care actually drove this expansion, suggesting this trend may continue in the face of further expansion of outpatient services (Block et al. 2013, LaCalle and Rabin 2010, Weber et al. 2008). The United States, Canada, and some European countries have also experienced an expansion in a new type of outpatient care center bridging the gap between the ED and the physician's office. Urgent Care or Immediate Care

Centers increasingly are being utilized by patients who are seen on a walk-in basis, usually by a physician or allied health professional with an advanced clinical degree (Evans 2010, Hansen-Turton et al. 2007). Over the past 20 years, more than 9,000 urgent care centers have opened across the United States (McCarthy 2013). The spread of convenient care clinics accelerated following the introduction of clinical services offered by pharmacy chains (Smith 2007).

While not all-inclusive of the many changes that have occurred in health care over the past 50 years, clearly these trends point to considerable alterations in the nature of patients/conditions typically encountered in larger health centers. Moreover, institutional and patient characteristics matter in patient surveys (Aiken et al. 1997, Parker and Kroboth 1991, Young et al. 2000). Hospital and care team characteristics, in particular, are known to have an association with the patient experience (Hays et al. 2006, Young et al. 2000). In general, the type of patient, the patient's condition(s), and the setting in which a patient is seen are all interrelated and need to be taken into account in the design of a patient survey, a fact that we will explore further in subsequent sections.

22.3 Overview of Common Patient Survey Methodologies

As noted by Jones et al. (2013), descriptive surveys are used to gather information on selected phenomena, seeking to describe important characteristics of the issue in question as well as factors associated with it. Typically, they represent a cross-sectional "snapshot." Examples of descriptive surveys include those used to monitor patient experiences and outcomes (e.g., patient experience and satisfaction, and *ad hoc* hospital surveys). Epidemiological (or analytical) surveys, on the other hand, typically go beyond simply describing a phenomenon, seeking rather to illustrate and understand observed associations. This might include surveys designed to help researchers understand underlying disease epidemiology. Examples include, but are not limited to, a study of factors predicting antiretroviral regimen dosing and adherence and health outcomes for patients with HIV infection (Golin et al. 2002, Miller et al. 2003) and an examination of care-related factors associated with improvement in cancer patients (Conboy et al. 2010). While clearly not limited to patient surveys specifically, epidemiological surveys often employ prospective or retrospective designs in order to better examine associations between determinants and frequency of occurrence or severity of a disease. In cases where cross-sectional designs are employed, they are often used to examine and compare prevalence estimates between various populations and/or subsets of populations at a particular time or across geographic locations. Finally, evaluation surveys are used to study the effects of a planned program or program change (Jones et al. 2013). These too often utilize either prospective or cross-sectional study designs. An example would be the prospective evaluation of a medical home demonstration that included careful consideration of patient experiences at baseline and a 12-month follow-up (Reid et al. 2009).

Epidemiologic surveys can be further delineated into several types of studies; ranging from cohort and case control studies to observational studies of which there are several subtypes (Aschengrau and Seage 2013). Patient surveys have even been part of national health surveillance efforts, which falls under epidemiologic monitoring. For example, although designed as a general population survey, the Behavioral Risk Factor Surveillance System (BRFSS) has also been used to identify patient populations. Specifically, the BRFSS was recently used to screen the adult population to identify cancer survivors. In 2009, 45,541 adult respondents (7.2% of the sample) were identified as survivors (Underwood et al. 2012). Findings indicated that most cancer survivors have comorbid conditions and lead sedentary life styles, with approximately 15% of adults being current cigarette smokers. Another example is the Consumer Assessment of Healthcare Providers and Systems (CAHPS) surveys, a multiyear initiative of the Agency for Healthcare Research and Quality (AHRQ) to assess consumers' experiences with health care. CAHPS surveys are examples of the relatively new area of quality measurement in public health surveillance. With origins in the HEDIS® (Healthcare Effectiveness Data and Information Set) set of performance measures utilized by American health plans, CAHPS surveys are used to cover topics important to consumers; focusing on areas of quality that they are most qualified to assess, such as health communication and access to care (Hays et al. 2003).

As understood in this context, surveys are essentially a research strategy as opposed to a stand-alone research method (Kelley et al. 2003). In fact, patient surveys can utilize a range of modalities, including postal questionnaires, face-to-face interviews and phone interviews. Each of these modes has clear strengths and weaknesses, which must be offset by cost considerations when designing a patient survey (Fowler 2002). Increasingly, new media (e.g., Internet, Facebook, Twitter) are also being utilized to reach patients (Greaves et al. 2013, Hawn 2009, McKee 2013).

22.4 Key Issues in Patient Survey Design and Administration

The design and administration of patient surveys involve many of the same issues associated with health surveys generally, but they may be exacerbated by the challenges of surveying individuals recently experiencing contact (not always pleasant) with the health care system and/or the necessities of fielding a survey within health care settings themselves. Despite the widespread perception that patient surveys are easy to conduct, they have been generally underutilized. There are numerous reasons historically for this neglect. First and foremost is that patient surveys have too often been characterized by a lack of conceptual and methodological rigor (Bhandari and Wagner 2006, Cleary 1999, Draper et al. 2001, McHorney and Tarlov 1995, Sitzia and Wood 1998). Lack of rigor can introduce numerous biases, including sampling, nonresponse, measurement, and processing errors, each of which are addressed in the following sections.

22.4.1 SAMPLING AND COVERAGE ERRORS

Patient surveys often utilize convenience or haphazard sampling, which may introduce significant bias and limit their usefulness (Lin and Kelly 1995, Sitzia and Wood 1998, Lee et al. 2002). Sampling error is incurred when the characteristics of a population are estimated based on the available sample of that population. All surveys include some level of sampling error, as sample parameters generally differ from the population of interest; the degree of difference between the two determining the degree of sampling error present (Fowler 2002). Failure to adequately define and list the target population results in coverage error, which are errors that occur when the sample frame used for a survey does not completely map onto the population being studied. Ideally, the potential for sampling and coverage error are reduced through careful random selection of participants to eliminate large biases. However, there are numerous problems associated with the application of sampling theory in the context of patient surveys (Lin and Kelly 1995). Difficulties include problems with collecting sufficiently large samples of targeted patient groups and identifying target populations or subpopulations (due to disease state, patient mobility, natural disease progression, care practices, institutional case mix, etc.). Moreover, patient surveys are often triggered by health services use, itself problematic as this excludes those with the condition who are not seeking care (Lin and Kelly 1995). As a result, some have questioned whether random sampling is even appropriate in this context (Lin and Kelly 1995). The alternative is to consider carefully the limitations of the sampling plan, as convenience and nonprobability sampling still opens the possibility of spurious conclusions due to samples being selected improperly (Brown 1976, Ellenberg 1994).

While both sampling and coverage errors are a concern, nonsampling errors (e.g., nonresponse error, measurement error, etc.) may be even more problematic. While some biased samples can still be used to produce meaningful results (such as when groups are deliberately oversampled to gain sufficient precision for within group estimates), nonsampling error almost always introduces systematic bias into the data. Forms of nonsampling error, including nonresponse error and measurement error, are discussed in more detail in the following sections.

22.4.2 NONRESPONSE ERROR

Response rates for patient surveys tend to be low compared to surveys generally (Galea and Tracy 2007). This is particularly true of surveys of certain patient populations, such as those with poor health or limited functional status (Alessi et al. 2007, Ganz et al. 2009, Gourin et al. 2010). Yet, one review of response rates in the patient satisfaction literature found a mean response rate of 72.1% (Sitzia and Wood 1998). Interestingly, though, of the 200 papers reviewed, less than half reported a response rate. While a poor single indicator of overall survey quality, low survey participation may still reflect potential nonresponse bias, or the likelihood that respondents differ substantially from those who did not participate. In fact, low response rates are often, but not always, an indicator of systematic differences between patient responders and nonresponders on at least one key demographic or health-related measure (Emberton and Black 1995, Etter and Perneger 1997, Gadkari et al. 2011, Heilbrun et al. 1991, Lasek et al. 1997, Ling et al. 2001, Nieman et al. 2013). Among responders, there are also reported differences between early and late respondents (Barkley and Furse 1996, Emberton and Black 1995, Etter and Perneger 1997, Hutchings et al. 2013). For instance, Mazor et al. (2002) specifically looked at the relationship between response rate and patient satisfaction. They concluded that there was negative bias, with satisfied patients being more likely to respond than dissatisfied patients. Additionally, they found that early responders—those respondents obtained with less follow-up effort—also tended to be more satisfied with their care than late responders. These findings have been supported by other studies (Lasek et al. 1997, Perneger et al. 2005). While these differences may be small, it does necessitate that researchers take into careful consideration potential effects on estimations of results.

Variability in patient survey participation rates have also been noted among key population groups of interest, most notably racial and ethnic minorities (Boscardin and Gonzales 2013, Burrus et al. 2009, Moorman et al. 1999, Nelson et al. 2004, Nieman et al. 2013, Tadic et al. 2010). Lower response by some racial and ethnic groups are particularly problematic given demonstrated differences in patient-reported experiences of care by race and acculturation status (Boscardin and Gonzales 2013, Fongwa et al. 2008, Matthews et al. 2012, Hasnain et al. 2013, Haviland et al. 2003, Waghorn and McKee 2000). Racial and ethnic minorities of all ages are also at greater risk for disparate health and health care outcomes (Elster et al. 2003, Fiscella et al. 2002). Other patient characteristics associated with variation in experiences and/or care preferences, as well as disparate patient survey participation, include age, health status, and gender (Elliott et al. 2005, Elliott et al. 2012, Hargraves et al. 2001, Hekkert et al. 2009, Lin et al. 2007, Moret et al. 2007). Elderly patients, in particular, may be difficult to engage in the survey process due to health concerns (Ehnfors and Smedby 1993) or the challenges associated with surveying older adults in unique care settings such as nursing homes (Cohen 1989, Garrard et al. 1989). Intersections between race, gender, age, and health status pose further problems. Response rates and the potential for nonresponse bias means that patient survey data cannot be used to effectively assess or compare data in a summative way unless demonstrated differences are fully understood and appropriately considered.

22.4.3 MEASUREMENT ERROR

Historically, there has been considerable diversity of survey instruments used for assessing patient perceptions of care and health outcomes (Castle et al. 2005, Fries and Krishnan 2009, Saila et al. 2008). This significantly restricts the ability to compare and contrast survey outcomes across different patient populations, institutions, geographic areas, or time; potentially limiting their utility (Cohen et al. 1996). Moreover, patient surveys are often plagued by sizeable measurement error, which serves as an acknowledged potential barrier to use of survey results in clinical quality improvement efforts (Fries and Krishnan 2009, Lin and Kelly 1995). Measurement error usually results from the respondent's inability or unwillingness to provide accurate answers, faulty, or ambiguous wording of survey questions and/or mode effects impacting data acquisition. Indeed, available evidence suggests significant variability in measurement precision across a number of variables (e.g., pain, care satisfaction, medication compliance, health care utilization, physical activity, etc.) common to patient surveys (Barbara et al. 2012, Bhandari and Wagner 2006, Pakhomov et al. 2008, Sitzia 1999, Stone et al. 2008, Terwee et al. 2011, Wang et al. 2004). Cross-cultural sources of measurement error are also evident, with minorities less willing to disclose health-related information (Burgess et al. 2009, Neuhouser et al. 2013, Rauscher et al. 2008). This lack of precision has important implications for research studies that rely on patient self-report, as well as for the incorporation of survey results into clinical practice for individual patient application (McHorney and Tarlov 1995, Pakhomov et al. 2008). Further complicating the issue are studies identifying significant survey mode effects on the accuracy of response (Bhandari and Wagner 2006, Bower and Roland 2003, de Vries et al. 2005, Elliott et al. 2009, Fowler et al. 2002, Gribble and Haupt 2005, Hays et al. 2009, Lin et al. 2007, McBride et al. 1999, O'Cathain et al. 2010). This is consistent with population health surveys identifying genuine mode effects in survey response (Shim et al. 2013). Direction of mode bias is partly dependent on the measures and modes compared. For instance, patients asked to self-report on a stigmatized behavior or illness may be more willing to provide that information via a mailed or internet survey than one involving a survey interviewer.

Measurement error may be related, in part, to the complexity of the measures employed. Patient satisfaction is a classic example. In 2009, the University of New South Wales Centre for Clinical Governance Research conducted a review of the patient satisfaction literature. The major theme that emerged from their review was the complexity of accurately measuring patient satisfaction (Debono and Travaglia 2009). Their map of key concepts related to patient satisfaction identified over 50 associated constructs in the professional literature. Most studies were found to employ multiple criteria for the measurement of patient satisfaction. They also found patient satisfaction reports to be mediated by other variables. In addition to the aforementioned age, race/ethnicity, and gender, factors identified included health status, faith, social support, and experiences with the health system (Debono and Travaglia 2009, Dolinsky and Caputo 1990). If researchers are not clear or consistent with their own definitions, respondents may be equally challenged. This is supported by at least one systematic review of survey estimates of patient satisfaction concluding that choice of wording may be, in part, a contributor to the measurement variability observed (Cohen et al. 1996). Further support comes from studies identifying variation in the readability of survey items; again a factor in patient understanding and accuracy of response (Calderon et al. 2006, Gadkari et al. 2011, Paz et al. 2009).

Other factors also play a role in the validity of patient response. For example, patient recall is critical in ability to answer accurately. Extended reporting periods can influence the accuracy of symptom recall (Bhandari and Wagner 2006, Broderick et al. 2008, Clarke et al. 2008, Saal et al. 2005). This is consistent with earlier findings by Sudman and Bradburn (1974), who identified two types of memory error: (i) respondents forgetting completely; and (ii) respondents remembering incorrectly. Optimal recall length has yet to be determined, but those seeking longer recall periods must balance this need with the increasing likelihood of error (Clarke et al. 2008). Alternately, researchers may consider using diary measures where appropriate, as this allows respondents to record events on an ongoing basis during the reporting period in question (Stone et al. 2010). While recall is a common survey limitation, challenges associated with patient surveys are paramount due to a number of issues. Age logically plays a rolc, as older adults, especially those with chronic health issues related to dementia and other debilitating conditions may experience difficulty correctly recalling events over a relatively short period. Context also affects recall with patient anxiety, depression, and related factors associated with greater variability (Coughlin 1990, Schneider et al. 2012). Thus, it is critical to consider both reporting period and context in survey design to ensure accurate patient response (Stone et al. 2008).

22.4.4 PROCESSING ERROR

Lastly, in conducting patient surveys, researchers need to be considerate of the potential for processing error. Processing error is another type of nonsampling error resulting from the actual fielding of questionnaires and data management (e.g., handling of survey instruments, the data collection processes, and the processing of data; Groves et al. 2009). The threat of processing error is present in any patient survey. However, for those patient surveys conducted as part of ongoing clinical quality improvement efforts (limiting access of survey professionals on site), there is additional risk due to their reliance, in part, on clinical staff to assist with survey administration and data collection. The degree to which this is true and the level to which these individuals are fully trained in survey administration protocols leaves the door open to processing and other administrative errors. Clinical and administrative staff buy-in with regard to survey topic and procedures, and adequate training, will also be factors in reducing potential error.

Complexity of the study can further exacerbate many of the issues noted above. For instance, there are numerous design challenges associated with surveying hard-to-reach patients or when a patient population becomes of interest for systematic long-term study, and time has passed since their diagnosis/treatment, tracing their whereabouts is an involved process (Kahn et al. 2003, Kramer et al. 2012, Gourin et al. 2010). The project may start with a list of patient names and addresses and the challenge becomes tracking down where they are now and their status. When patients do not consent to participating in a follow-up study at the time of their diagnosis/treatment and there is no effort to track their change of address over time, a great deal of administrative effort is necessary to locate these patients. An Australian study of pediatric cancer survivors is illustrative (Wilson et al. 2009). In order to trace this population, the researchers used multiple public data sets to locate the targeted population, successfully identifying current addresses for 70% of survivors.

Most of the challenges identified can be applicable to health surveys generally. A simplified conceptual model (Figure 22.1) can be utilized to highlight

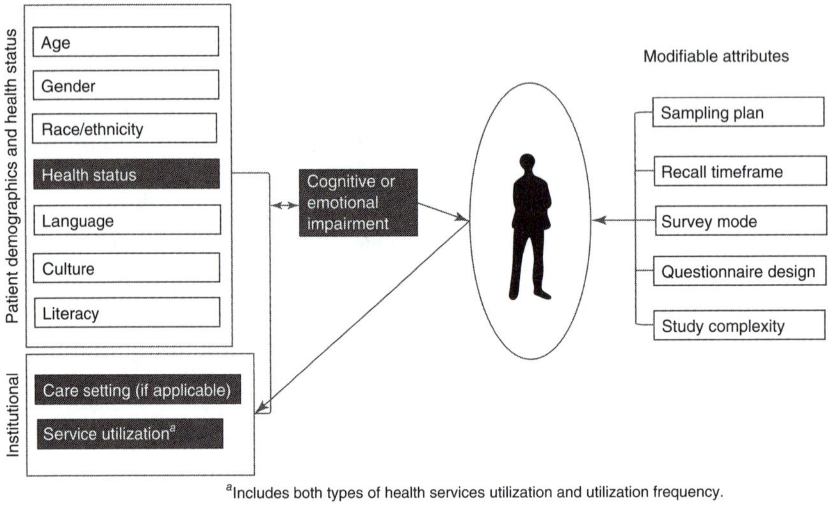

FIGURE 22.1 **Conceptual model of factors uniquely affecting patient surveys.**

those areas where patient surveys differ (e.g., patients health status and or disease state, care settings, etc.) from more general health surveys; presenting unique obstacles for researchers. Overall, given the number of challenges associated with patient surveys, it is essential that researchers use established best practices to improve survey design and administration. However, as illustrated in Figure 22.1, real challenges to improving patient surveys specifically lie in the deliberate application of best practices while fully accounting for those unique factors associated with this population. The next section turns to this topic.

22.5 Strategies for Developing Effective Patient Surveys

22.5.1 SAMPLING

Effective patient survey design and administration is basically a matter of planning, beginning with the construction of a proper sampling plan (Fowler 2002, Lin and Kelly 1995). As with surveys generally, the steps involved in recruiting a representative sample include determining the population of interest, acquiring, or developing an accurate sample frame that includes a high percentage of members of that population, drawing a probability sample from the frame, contacting the respondents from the sample, and gaining cooperation from the respondents (Fowler 2002). In patient surveys, depending on context, this may require that the researcher work closely with health care providers to develop the best possible sampling plan given the study's research questions and the available resources for data collection. This includes overcoming challenges due to policies and procedures limiting access to patient information at certain care settings (in compliance with the Health Insurance Portability and Accountability Act [HIPAA] regulations) and to patient site-specific interactions/service utilization patterns that may be dependent upon setting and their health condition and/or treatment protocols. The latter, in particular, if of short and/or infrequent in duration, can severely limit the usability of patient information.

Of course, no list is error free. Even with the best of lists, researchers need to reconfirm information about the patients (e.g., are patient demographics correct?, do individual patients have the condition(s) of interest? etc.). In addition, some contact information will inevitably be outdated. Furthermore, not all available lists will provide direct information on the patient. Examples include health plan enrollee lists where only the subscriber information is available and patient lists for minors that include the parent as contact. In these latter examples, researchers must be particularly careful to examine feasibility of respondent selection based on study eligibility and inclusion criteria, as there may be more than one "patient" in the home. For instance, a study by Gallagher et al. (1999) found that when sampling from a list of enrollees of health plans, parents were able to select eligible children for study inclusion, but only at risk of decreased overall response rates.

On the other hand, there may not a be a list from which to work to select a sample and the researcher must reach out to the general population and screen for the patients of interest. Some patient types might be relatively common and relatively easy to locate (e.g., patients who have seen a doctor anytime in the last year). Other patient types might be rarer (e.g., cancer patients with a 10-year survival rate) and will require a great deal of effort to find through an eligibility screening process. While these patients are not protected under HIPAA, researchers must keep in mind that asking about health information is a sensitive topic and care and respect must be taken in contacting these individuals.

To a large degree, the nature of the study determines the recruitment strategy. When the purpose of the research is to make inferences to the broader population to which participants belong (e.g., the percentage of African-American men who get screened for prostate cancer), it is imperative that the recruitment strategy produces a representative sample of the population. On the other hand, in a case control study of women with ovarian cancer, for example, the recruitment strategy should be designed to obtain controls who match the cancer patients on all relevant characteristics, even if the controls do not represent the broader population. Thus, the degree to which the sample needs to be truly random depends on the purpose of the study.

22.5.2 IMPROVING RESPONSE RATES

Researchers also have numerous strategies at their disposal that can be utilized to improve patient survey participation, including established design- and incentive-based elements of the Tailored Design Method (TDM; Dillman 2000). The TDM provides guidelines for instrument development, as well as comprehensive strategies to achieve high response rates. Examples of these strategies include the use of first class postage, prepaid return envelopes, personalization, and monetary and nonmonetary incentives. The TDM is the current standard for conducting mail and Internet surveys. An updated Cochrane Methodology Review verified the success of these strategies for achieving reproducible response rates in general health surveys, including patient surveys (Edwards et al. 2009). While clearly the standard, researchers must still be deliberate in their application of many techniques in patient surveys, again due to the unique situation of the target population. Use of incentives can be used to illustrate. Edwards et al. (2009) found monetary incentives generally to be the most effective method, more than doubling the odds of survey participation. However, in a review of the use of token incentives on survey participation of cancer patients, VanGeest and Johnson (2012) found that incentives did not result in improved response rates. One study reviewed actually identified a slight *decrease* in survey participation following the inclusion of a $5 incentive (Coogan and Rosenberg 2004). Many reasons exist why incentives may not work well in this population, with the most evident being the traumatic nature of the disease. Tension and emotional distress associated with a cancer diagnosis, along with the demands of disease management, have indeed been linked to higher refusal rates (Ransom et al. 2006). In this situation, monetary incentives may actually be perceived as an affront to the patient, decreasing motivation to participate (Wenemark et al. 2010).

This does not mean that incentives should always be avoided, as they may be fully appropriate in other circumstances. For example, in a medication-beliefs survey modest monetary incentives were actually successful in improving survey participation (Gadkari et al. 2011). Another very important and often unrecognized incentive for patients facing life threatening conditions to participate in survey interviews is the hope that their experience can be helpful to others who have the same condition.

22.5.3 INSTRUMENT DESIGN AND ADMINISTRATION

Finally, with regard to patient questionnaire development and administration, significant progress has been made in the development of validated instruments (Cleary 1999, Debono and Travaglia 2009). Examples include, but are not limited to, measures developed for the CAHPS surveys. Items development for the CAHPS surveys underwent considerable cognitive testing to insure that respondents could understand questions consistently and have the information necessary to answer (Dyer et al. 2012, Gallagher et al. 2009, Hargraves et al. 2003, Levine et al. 2005, Martino et al. 2009, McInnes et al. 2012). Key attributes associated with these new instruments include simplicity, consistency, organization, and clarity. These instruments are believed to provide better data, with sound psychometric properties and demonstrated improvement in relationships with technical performance data (Dyer et al. 2012, Hargraves et al. 2003, Isaac et al. 2010, Gallagher et al. 2009, Martino et al. 2009). Improved and validated measures are available across a range of health conditions and care issues, including the assessment of patient informed consent (Joffe et al. 2001).

In developing and administrating patient surveys, researchers must still be mindful of the potential for measurement error. Examples include variability on tasks that cognitive theory indicates are associated with responding to survey questions, such as basic question interpretation and response editing to overreport socially desirable behavior (Warnecke et al. 1997). Additional support is found in studies reporting some variability in measurement quality across the English and Spanish CAHPS surveys (Morales et al. 2003, Weech-Maldonado et al. 2008). Other studies have also identified cultural variability in the effects of questionnaire design features on respondent comprehension, with design strategies commonly used to improve comprehension of health questions potentially increasing cross-cultural disparities (Johnson et al. 2006). This argues for the need to carefully pretest patient survey instruments with racial and ethnic minority populations (Cho et al. 2013). Qualitative interviewing methods can also be valuable for identifying measurement problems (Suh et al. 2009).

With regard to respondent comprehension and interpretation of survey questions, it is important to go beyond the assessment of readability to purposively include the broader concept of health literacy, or the ability to understand and act on health information (Schwartzberg et al. 2005). Included in this definition is a person's ability to comment clearly on their health-related preferences, care needs, and the like. Care must be taken in questionnaire design with regard to considering patients' ability to understand health-related concepts and terms. At the very least, researchers should consider controlling for health literacy using previously developed and tested instruments (see "Online Resources" section) when interpreting results. Also important is to consider the intersection of health literacy with cultural competency. Different perceptions of health are rooted in culture and language (Kandula et al. 2007). Thus, translation processes in adapting health-related concepts and measures to diverse patient populations need to achieve full conceptual, content, semantic, and functional equivalence (Meadows 2003, Sidani et al. 2010).

Finally, researchers must consider the best or most feasible mode of data collection. Sometimes the sample frame determines the mode. When the available sample frame is a list that includes name, address, and telephone number, then several modes of administration are possible. When multiple modes are possible, the choice of which to use is typically based on respondent characteristics (education, primary language, etc.) and costs. There is support in the patient survey literature for the use of mixed survey modes as a means to reduce bias and enhance survey quality (Baines et al. 2007, Fowler et al. 2002, Zuidgeest et al. 2011).

22.6 Conclusion

Patient surveys are an important tool, especially in light of ongoing efforts to develop more patient-centered care and reform health care delivery. Patient surveys have improved considerably over the past 40 years, both in terms of design and administration. However, challenges to fully incorporate the patient perspective in quality improvement efforts remain (Davies and Cleary 2005). Most important are the methodological challenges associated with sampling and surveying patients; by definition a very special population due to their health and related circumstances. Researchers must be deliberate in efforts to design and administer effective surveys that take into account these conditions. While incorporating elements of the TDM into a patient study design, judicious application of a broad set of survey levers and identified "best practices" can reduce nonresponse bias and improve overall survey quality. The study by Gadkari et al. (2011) is again illustrative, as they used the TDM to appeal to a broad mass of potential responders; applying low cost methods such as emphasizing altruistic appeals and tailoring the questionnaire to be easy to read as well as more costly techniques such as survey prenotification and incentives to successfully improve their overall survey quality.

Sadly, even the best designed and executed patient survey will result in data that may not be accurately used in policy and practice decisions. While beyond the scope of this chapter, issues related to knowledge transfer and exchange follow, requiring some level of diligence on the part of the researcher that goes beyond the usual academic or scholarly publication of results to encourage the appropriate use of results within care processes. It starts with a basic understanding of organizational barriers to knowledge transfer of patient survey data such as clinical staff not being trained to incorporate data into clinical assessment and decision making, organizational commitment, and limited time and resources (Davies and Cleary 2005, Davies et al. 2011, Draper et al. 2001, Reeves and Seccombe 2008). Once these are understood, we can be more strategic in using patient survey data to effect real improvement in patient care.

REFERENCES

Aiken LH, Sochalski J, Lake ET. Studying outcomes of organizational change in health services. Med Care 1997;35:NS6–N18.

Alessi D, Pastore G, Zuccolo L, Mosso ML, Richiardi L, Pearce N, Magnani C, Merletti F. Analysis of nonresponse in the assessment of health-related quality of life of childhood cancer survivors. Eur J Cancer Prev 2007;16:576–580.

Aschengrau A, Seage GR. *Essentials of Epidemiology in Public Health*. Burlington, MA: Jones & Bartlett Learning; 2013.

Baines AD, Partin MR, Davern M, Rockwood TH. Mixed-mode administration reduced bias and enhanced poststratification adjustments in a health behavior survey. J Clin Epidemiol 2007;60:1246–1255.

Barbara AM, Loeb M, Dolovich L, Brazil K, Russell M. Agreement between self-report and medical records on signs and symptoms of respiratory illness. Prim Care Respir J 2012;21:145–152.

Barkley WM, Furse DH. Changing priorities for improvement: the impact of low response rates in patient satisfaction. Jt Comm J Qual Improve 1996;22:427–433.

Bausewein C, Calanzani N, Daveson BA, Simon ST, Ferreira PL, Higginson IJ, Bechinger-English D, Deliens L, Gysels M, Toscani F, Ceulemans L, Harding R, Gomes B. "Burden to others" as a public concern in advanced cancer: a comparative survey in seven European countries. BMC Cancer 2013;13:105.

Bhandari A, Wagner T. Self-reported utilization of health care services: improving measurement and accuracy. Med Care Res Rev 2006;63:217–235.

Blackwell LS, Marciel KK, Quittner AL. Utilization of patient-reported outcomes as a step towards collaborative medicine. Peadiatr Respir Rev 2013;14:146–151.

Block L, Ma S, Emerson M, Langley A, de la Torre D, Noronha G. Does access to comprehensive outpatient care alter patterns of emergency department utilization among uninsured patients in East Baltimore? J Primary Care Commun Health 2013;4:143–147.

Boscardin CK, Gonzales R. The impact of demographic characteristics on nonresponse in an ambulatory patient satisfaction survey. Jt Comm J Qual Patient Saf 2013;39:123–128.

Bower P, Roland MO. Bias in patient assessments of general practice: general practice assessment surgery scores in surgery and postal responders. Br J Gen Pract 2003;53:126–128.

Broderick JE, Schwartz JE, Vikingstad G, Pribbernow M, Grossman S, Stone AA. The accuracy of pain and fatigue items across different reporting periods. Pain 2008;139:146–157.

Brown GW. Berkson Fallacy revisited: spurious conclusions from patient surveys. Am J Dis Children 1976;130:56–60.

Burgess DJ, Powell AA, Griffin JM, Partin MR. Race and the validity of self-reported cancer screening behaviors: development of a conceptual model. Prev Med 2009;48:99–107.

Burrus C, Ballabeni P, Deriaz O, Gobelet C, Luthi F. Predictors of nonresponse in a questionnaire-based outcome study of vocational rehabilitation patients. Arch Phys Med Rehabil 2009;90:1499–1505.

Calderon JL, Morales LS, Liu H, Hays RD. Variation in the readability of items within surveys. Am J Med Qual 2006;21:49–56.

Castle NG, Brown J, Hepner KA, Hayes RD. Review of the literature on survey instruments used to collect data on hospital patients' perceptions of care. Health Serv Res 2005;40(6):1996–2017.

Cho YI, Holbrook A, Johnson TP. Acculturation and health survey question comprehension among Latino respondents in the U.S. J Immigr Minor Health 2013;15:525–532.

Clarke PM, Fiebig DG, Gerdtham UG. Optimal recall length in survey design. J Health Econ 2008;27:1275–1284.

Cleary PD. The increasing importance of patient surveys. Br Med J 1999;319:720–721.

Cohen SB. Collecting data from samples of older adults and nursing home populations. Conference Proceedings: Health Survey Research Methods, USDHHS Pub No. 89-3447; 1989.

Cohen G, Forbes J, Garraway M. Can different patient satisfaction survey methods yield consistent results? Comparison of three surveys. Br Med J 1996;313:841–844.

Committee on Quality Health Care in America. *Crossing the Quality Chasm: A New Health System for the 21st Century*. Washington, DC: National Academy Press; 2001.

Conboy LA, Macklin E, Kelley J, Kokkotou E, Lembo A, Kaptchuk T. Which patients improve: characteristics increasing sensitivity to a supportive patient-practitioner relationship. Soc Sci Med 2010;70:479–484.

Coogan PF, Rosenberg L. Impact of a financial incentive on case and control participation in a telephone interview. Am J Epidemiol 2004;160:295–298.

Coughlin SS. Recall bias in epidemiologic studies. J Clin Epidemiol 1990;43:87–91.

Davies E, Cleary PD. Hearing the patient's voice? Factors affecting the use of patient survey data in quality improvement. Qual Saf Health Care 2005;14:428–432.

Davies EA, Meterko MM, Charns MP, Seibert ME, Cleary PD. Factors affecting the use of patient survey data for quality improvement in the Veterans Health Administration. BMC Health Serv Res 2011;11:334.

Debono D, Travaglia J. *Complaints and Patient Satisfaction: A Comprehensive Review of the Literature*. Sydney, Australia: Centre for Clinical Governance Research, University of New South Wales; 2009.

Delbanco T. Hospital medicine: understanding and drawing on the patient's perspective. Am J Med 2001;111:2S–4S.

de Vries H, Elliott MN, Hepner KA, Keller SD, Hays RD. Equivalence of mail and telephone responses to the CAHPS hospital survey. Health Serv Res 2005;40: 2120–2139.

Dillman DA. *Mail and Internet Surveys: The Tailored Design Method*. New York: John Wiley & Sons; 2000.

Dolinsky AL, Caputo RK. The role of health care attributes and demographic characteristics in the determination of health care satisfaction. J Health Care Mark 1990;10:31–39.

Draper M, Cohen P, Buchan H. Seeking consumer views: what use are results of hospital patient satisfaction surveys? International J Qual Health Care 2001;13:463–468.

Dyer N, Sorra JS, Smith SA, Cleary PD, Hays RD. Psychometric properties of the Consumer Assessment of Healthcare Providers and Systems (CAHPS®) Clinician and Group Adult Visit Survey. Med Care 2012;50:S28–S34.

Edwards PJ, Roberts I, Clarke MJ, Diquiseppi C, Wentz R, Kwan I, Cooper R, Felix LM, Pratap S. Methods to increase response to postal and electronic questionnaires. Cochrane Database Syst Rev 2009;8(3). DOI: MR000008.

Ehnfors M, Smedby B. Patient satisfaction surveys subsequent to hospital care: problems of sampling, non-response and other losses. Qual Assur Health Care 1993;5:19–32.

Ellenberg JH. Selection bias in observational and experimental studies. Stat Med 1994;13:557–567.

Elliott MN, Edwards C, Angeles J, Hambarsoomians K, Hays RD. Patterns of unit and item nonresponse in the CAHPS Hospital Survey. Health Serv Res 2005;40:2096–2119.

Elliott MN, Lehrman WG, Beckett MK, Goldstein E, Hambarsoomian K, Giordano LA. Gender differences in patients' perceptions of inpatient care. Health Serv Res 2012;47:1482–1501.

Elliott MN, Lehrman WG, Goldstein EH, Giordano LA, Beckett MK, Cohea CW, Cleary PD. Hospital survey shows improvements in patient experience. Health Affairs (Millwood) 2010;29:2061–2067.

Elliott MN, Zaslavsky AM, Goldstein E, Lehrman W, Hambarsoomians K, Beckett MK, Giordano L. Effects of survey mode, patient mix, and nonresponse on CAHPS hospital survey scores. Health Serv Res 2009;44:501–518.

Elster AB, Jarosik J, VanGeest J, Fleming M. Racial and ethnic disparities in health care for adolescents: a systematic review of the literature. Arch Pediatr Adolescent Med 2003;157:867–874.

Emberton M, Black N. Impact of non-response and of late-response by patients in a multi-centre surgical outcome audit. Int J Qual Health Care 1995;7:47–55.

Etter JF, Perneger TV. Analysis of non-response bias in a mailed health survey. J Clin Epidemiol 1997;50:1123–1128.

Evans SW. Convenient care clinics: making a positive change in health care. J Am Acad Nurse Pract 2010;22:23–26.

Falk IS, Klem MC, Sinai N. *The Incidence of Illness and the Receipt and Costs of Medical Care among Representative Families: Experiences in Twelve Consecutive Months during 1928-1931.* Chicago: University of Chicago Press; 1933.

Fiscella K, Franks P, Doescher MP, Saver BG. Disparities in health care by race, ethnicity, and language among the insured: findings from a national sample. Med Care 2002;40:52–59.

Fongwa MN, Cunningham W, Weech-Maldonado R, Gutierrez PR, Hays RD. Reports and ratings of care: Black and white Medicare enrollees. J Health Care Poor Underserved 2008;19:1136–1147.

Fowler FJ. *Survey Research Methods. 3rd* ed. Thousand Oaks, CA: Sage; 2002.

Fowler FJ, Gallagher PM, Stringfellow VL, Zaslavsky AM, Thompson JW, Cleary PD. Using telephone interviews to reduce nonresponse bias in mail surveys of health plan members. Med Care 2002;40:190–200.

Fries JF, Krishnan E. What constitutes progress in assessing patient outcomes? J Clin Epidemiol 2009;62:779–780.

Gadkari A, Pedan A, Gowda N, McHorney CA. Survey nonresponders to a medication-beliefs survey have worse adherence and persistence to chronic medications compared with survey responders. Med Care 2011;49:956–961.

Galea S, Tracy M. Participation rates in epidemiologic studies. Ann Epidemiol 2007;17:643–653.

Gallagher P, Ding L, Ham HP, Schor EL, Hays RD, Cleary PD. Development of a new patient-based measure of pediatric ambulatory care. Pediatrics 2009;124:1348–1354.

Gallagher PM, Fowler FJ, Stringfellow VL. Respondent selection by mail: obtaining probability samples of health plan enrollees. Med Care 1999;37:MS50–MS58.

Ganz PA, Land SR, Antonio C, Zhenq P, Yothers G, Petersen L, Wickerham DL, Wolmark N, Ko CY. Cancer survivorship research: the challenges of recruiting adult long term cancer survivors from a cooperative clinical trials group. J Cancer Surviv 2009;3:137–147.

Garrard J, Skay C, Ratner ER, Kane RL, Chan HW. Nonresponse to survey questions by elderly in nursing homes. Conference Proceedings: Health Survey Research Methods, USDHHS Pub No. 89-3447; 1989.

Golin CE, Liu H, Hays RD, Miller LG, Beck CK, Ickovics J, Kaplan AH, Wenger NS. A prospective study of predictors of adherence to combination antiretroviral medication. J Gen Intern Med 2002;17:756–765.

Gourin CG, Kaboli KC, Boyce BJ, Burkhead LM. Factors associated with nonparticipation in one-year quality-of-life assessment in patients with head and neck squamous cell carcinoma. Laryngoscope 2010;120:1435–1443.

Greaves F, Ramirez-Cano D, Millett C, Darzi A, Donaldson L. Harnessing the cloud of patient experience: using social media to detect poor quality health care. BMJ Qual Saf 2013;22:251–255.

Gribble RK, Haupt C. Quantitative and qualitative differences between handout and mailed patient satisfaction surveys. Med Care 2005;43:276–281.

Groves R, Fowler F, Couper M, Lepkowski J, Singer E, Tourangeau R. *Survey Methodology*. 2nd ed. Hoboken, NJ: John Wiley & Sons; 2009.

Hansen-Turton T, Ryan S, Miller K, Counts M, Nash DB. Convenient care clinics: the future of accessible health care. Dis Manag 2007;10:61–73.

Hargraves JL, Hays RD, Cleary PD. Psychometric properties of the Consumer Assessment of Health Plans Study (CAHPS) 2.0 adult core survey. Health Serv Res 2003;38:1509–1527.

Hargraves JL, Wilson IB, Zaslavsky A, James C, Walker JD, Rogers G, Cleary PD. Adjusting for patient characteristics when analyzing reports from patients about hospital care. Med Care 2001;39:635–641.

Hasnain M, Schwartz A, Girotti J, Bixby A, Rivera L, UIC Experiences of Care Group. Differences in patient-reported experiences of care by race and acculturation status. J Immigr Minor Health 2013;15:517–524.

Haviland MG, Morales LS, Reise SP, Hays RD. Do health care ratings differ by race or ethnicity? Jt Comm J Qual Saf 2003;29:134–145.

Hawn C. Take two aspirin and tweet me in the morning: how Twitter, Facebook, and other social media are reshaping health care. Health Aff (Millwood) 2009;28:361–368.

Hays RD, Kim S, Spritzer KL, Kaplan RM, Tally S, Feeny D, Liu H, Fryback DG. Effects of mode and order of administration on generic health-related quality of life scores. Value Health 2009;12:1035–1039.

Hays RD, Eastwood JA, Kotlerman J, Spritzer KL, Ettner SL, Cowan M. Health-related quality of life and patient reports about care outcomes in a multidisciplinary hospital intervention. Ann Behav Med 2006;31:173–178.

Hays RD, Chong K, Brown J, Spritzer KL, Horne K. Patient reports and ratings of individual physicians: an evaluation of the DoctorGuide and Consumer Assessment of Health Plans Study provider-level surveys. Am J Med Qual 2003;18:190–196.

Heilbrun LK, Ross PD, Wasnich RD, Yano K, Vogel JM. Characteristics of respondents and nonrespondents in a prospective study of osteoporosis. J Clin Epidemiol 1991;44:233–239.

Hekkert KD, Cihangir S, Kleefstra SM, van den Berg B, Kool RB. Patient satisfaction revisited: a multilevel approach. Soc Sci Med 2009;69:68–75.

Hutchings A, Grosse Frie K, Neuburger J, van der Meulen J, Black N. Late response to patient-reported outcome questionnaires after surgery was associated with worse outcome. J Clin Epidemiol 2013;66:218–25.

Isaac T, Zaslavsky AM, Cleary PD, Landon BE. The relationship between patients' perception of care and measures of hospital quality and safety. Health Serv Res 2010;45:1024–1040.

Joffe S, Cook EF, Cleary PD, Clark JW, Weeks JC. Quality of informed consent: a new measure of understanding among research subjects. J Natl Cancer Inst 2001;17: 139–147.

Johnson TP, Cho YI, Holbrook AL, O'Rourke D, Warnecke RB, Chavez N. Cultural variability in the effects of question design features on respondent comprehension of health surveys. Ann Epidemiol 2006;16:661–668.

Jones TL, Baxter MAJ, Khanduja V. A quick guide to survey research. Ann R Coll Surg Engl 2013;95:5–7.

Kahn KL, Liu H, Adams JL, Chen WP, Tisnado DM, Carlisle DM, Hays RD, Mangione CM, Damberg CL. Methodological challenges associated with patient responses to follow-up longitudinal surveys regarding quality of care. Health Serv Res 2003;38:1579–1598.

Kandula NR, Lauderdale DS, Baker DW. Differences in self-reported health among Asians, Latinos, and non-Hispanic whites: the role of language and nativity. Ann Epidemiol 2007;17:191–198.

Kelley K, Clark B, Brown V, Sitzia J. Good practice in the conduct and reporting of survey research. International J Qual Health Care 2003;15:261–266.

Korda H, Eldridge GN. Payment incentives and integrated care delivery: levers for health system reform and cost containment. Inquiry 2012;48:277–287.

Kramer JR, Bayless ML, Lorenzi GM, Ziegler GK, Larkin ME, Lackaye ME, Harth J, Diminick LJ, Anderson KL, Braffett BH, Cleary PA. Participant characteristics and study features associated with high retention rates in a longitudinal investigation of type 1 diabetes mellitus. Clin Trials 2012;9:798–805.

LaCalle E, Rabin E. Frequent users of emergency departments: the myths, the data, and the policy implications. Ann Emerg Med 2010;56:42–48.

Lasek RJ, Barkley W, Harper DL, Rosenthal GE. An evaluation of the impact of nonresponse bias on patient satisfaction surveys. Med Care 1997;35:646–652.

Lee ML, Yano EM, Wang M, Simon BF, Rubenstein LV. What patient populations does visit-based sampling in primary care settings represent? Med Care 2002;40:761–70.

Levine RE, Fowler FJ, Brown JA. Role of cognitive testing in the development of the CAHPS Hospital Survey. Health Serv Res 2005;40:2037–2056.

Lin B, Kelly E. Methodological issues in patient satisfaction surveys. Int J Health Care Qual Assur 1995;8:32–7.

Lin OS, Schembre DB, Ayub K, Gluck M, McCormick SE, Patterson DJ, Cantone N, Soon MS, Kozarek RA. Patient satisfaction scores for endoscopic procedures: impact of a survey-collection method. Gastrointest Endosc 2007;65:775–781.

Ling BS, Moskowitz MA, Wachs D, Pearson B, Schroy PC. Attitudes toward colorectal cancer screening tests. J Gen Intern Med 2001;16:822–830.

Ludwig H, Van Belle S, Barrett-Lee P, Birgegard G, Bokemeyer C, Gascon P, Kosmidis P, Krzakowski M, Nortier J, Olmi P, Schneider M, Schrijvers D. The European Cancer Anaemia Survey (ECAS): a large, multinational, prospective survey defining the prevalence, incidence, and treatment of anaemia in cancer patients. Eur J Cancer 2004;40:2293–2306.

Manchikanti L, Parr AT, Singh V, Fellows B. Ambulatory surgery centers and interventional techniques: a look at long-term survival. Pain Physician 2011;14:E117–E215.

Marino BL, Marino EK, Hayes JS. Parents' report of children's hospital care: what it means for your practice. Pediatr Nurs 2000;26:195–198.

Martino SC, Elliott MN, Cleary PD, Kanouse DE, Brown JA, Spritzer KL, Heller A, Hays RD. Psychometric properties of an instrument to assess Medicare beneficiaries' prescription drug plan experiences. Health Care Financ Rev 2009;30:41–53.

Matthews AK, Tejeda S, Johnson TP, Berbaum ML, Manfredi C. Correlates of quality of life among African American and white cancer survivors. Cancer Nurs 2012;35:355–364.

Mazor KM, Clauser BE, Field T, Yood RA, Gurwitz JH. A demonstration of the impact of response bias on the results of patient satisfaction surveys. Health Serv Res 2002;37:1403–1417.

McBride JS, Anderson RT, Bahnson JL. Using a hand-held computer to collect data in an orthopedic outpatient clinic: a randomized trial of two survey methods. Med Care 1999;37:647–651.

McCarthy M. Consumer demand drives boom in urgent care centers, study finds. Br Med J 2013;347(47):f4632. DOI: 10.1136/bmj.f4632.

McHorney CA, Tarlov AR. Individual-patient monitoring in clinical practice: are available health status surveys adequate? Qual Life Res 1995;4:293–307.

McInnes DK, Brown JA, Hays RD, Gallagher P, Ralston JD, Hugh M, Kanter M, Serrato CA, Cosenza C, Halamka J, Ding L, Cleary PD. Development and evaluation of CAHPS questions to assess the impact of health information technology on patient experiences with ambulatory care. Med Care 2012;50:S11–S19.

McKee R. Ethical issues in using social media for health and health care research. Health Policy 2013;110:298–301.

Meadows KA. So you want to do research? 5: questionnaire design. Br J Community Nurs 2003;8:562–570.

Miller LG, Liu H, Hays RD, Golin CE, Ye Z, Beck CK, Kaplan AH, Wenger NS. Knowledge of antiretroviral regimen dosing and adherence: a longitudinal study. Clin Infect Dis 2003;36:514–518.

Moorman PG, Newman B, Millikan RC, Tse CK, Sandler DP. Participation rates in a case-control study: The impact of age, race, and race of interviewer. Ann Epidemiol 1999;9:188–95.

Morales LS, Weech-Maldonado R, Elliott MN, Weidmer B, Hays RD. Psychometric properties of the Spanish Consumer Assessment of Health Plan Survey (CAHPS). Hispanic J Behav Sci 2003;25:386–409.

Moret L, Nguyen JM, Volteau C, Falissard B, Lombrail P, Gasquet I. Evidence of a non-linear influence of patient age on satisfaction with hospital care. International J Qual Health Care 2007;19:382–9.

Nelson KM, Geiger AM, Mangione CM. Racial and ethnic variation in response to mailed and telephone surveys among women in a managed care population. Ethn Dis 2004;14:580–583.

Neuhouser ML, Di C, Tinker LF, Thomson C, Sternfeld B, Mossavar-Rahmani Y, Stefanick ML, Sims S, Curb JD, Lamonte M, Seguin R, Johnson KC, Prentice RL. Physical activity assessment: biomarkers and self-report of activity-related energy expenditure in the WHI. Am J Epidemiol 2013;177:576–585.

Nieman CL, Benke JR, Ishman SL, Smith DF, Boss EF. Whose experience is measured? A pilot study of patient satisfaction demographics in pediatric otolaryngology. Laryngoscope 2013. DOI: 10.1002/lary.24307.

O'Cathain A, Knowles E, Nicholl J. Testing survey methodology to measure patients' experiences and views of the emergency and urgent care system: telephone versus postal survey. BMC Med Res Methodol 2010;10:52.

Pakhomov SV, Jacobsen SJ, Chute CG, Roger VL. Agreement between patient-reported symptoms and their documentation in the medical record. Am J Manag Care 2008;14:520–529.

Parker SC, Kroboth FJ. Practical problems of conducting patient-satisfaction surveys. J Gen Intern Med 1991;6:430–435.

Paz SH, Liu H, Fongwa MN, Morales LS, Hays RD. Readability estimates for commonly used health-related quality of life surveys. Qual Life Res 2009;18:889–900.

Perneger TV, Chamot E, Bovier PA. Nonresponse bias in a survey of patient perceptions of hospital care. Med Care 2005;43:374–380.

Petrullo KA, Lamar S, Nwankwo-Otti O, Alexander-Mills K, Viola D. The patient satisfaction survey: what does it mean to your bottom line? J Hosp Admin 2013;2:1–8.

Pitts SR, Niska RW, Xu J, Burt CW. National Hospital Ambulatory Medical Care Survey: 2006 emergency department summary. Natl Health Stat Rep 2008;6:1–38.

Press I. *Patient Satisfaction. 2nd* ed. Chicago, IL: Health Administration Press; 2005.

Ransom S, Azzarello LM, McMillan SC. Methodological issues in the recruitment of cancer patients and their caregivers. Res Nurs Health 2006;29:190–198.

Rathert C, Williams ES, McCaughey D, Ishqaidef G. Patient perceptions of patient-centered care: empirical test of a theoretical model. Health Expect, Nov 26 2012. DOI: 10.1111/hex.12020.

Rauscher GH, Johnson TP, Cho YI, Walk JA. Accuracy of self-reported cancer-screening histories: a meta-analysis. Cancer Epidem Biomar Prevent 2008;17:748–757.

Reeves R, Seccombe I. Do patient surveys work? The influence of a national survey programme on local quality-improvement initiatives. Qual Saf Health Care 2008;17:437–447.

Reid RJ, Fishman PA, Yu O, Ross TR, Tufano JT, Soman MP, Larson EB. Patient-centered medical home demonstration: a prospective, quasi-experimental, before and after evaluation. Am J Manag Care 2009;15:e71–e87.

Saal D, Nuebling M, Husemann Y, Heidegger T. Effect of timing on the response to postal questionnaires concerning satisfaction with anaesthesia care. Br J Anaesth 2005;94:206–210.

Saila T, Mattila E, Kaila M, Aalto P, Kaunonen M. Measuring patient assessments of the quality of outpatient care: a systematic review. J Eval Clin Pract 2008;14:148–154.

Schneider S, Junghaenel DU, Keefe FJ, Schwartz JE, Stone AA, Broderick JE. Individual difference in the day-to-day variability of pain, fatigue, and well-being in patients with rheumatic disease: associations with psychological variables. Pain 2012;153:813–822.

Schwartzberg JG, VanGeest JB, Wang CC, editors. *Understanding Health Literacy: Implications for Medicine and Public Health.* Chicago, IL: American Medical Association Press; 2005.

Shim JM, Shin E, Johnson TP. Self-rated health assessed by web versus mail modes in a mixed mode survey: the digital divide effect and the genuine survey mode effect. Med Care 2013;51:774–781.

Sibbald B, Pickard S, McLeod H, Reeves D, Mead N, Gemmell I, Coast J, Roland M, Leese B. Moving specialist care into the community: an initial evaluation. J Health Serv Res Policy 2008;13:233–239.

Sidani S, Guruge S, Miranda J, Ford-Gilboe M, Varcoe C. Cultural adaptation and translation of measures: an integrated model. Res Nurs Health 2010;33:133–143.

Sitzia J. How valid and reliable are patient satisfaction data? An analysis of 195 studies. International J Qual Health Care 1999;11:319–328.

Sitzia J, Wood N. Patient satisfaction: a review of issues and concepts. Soc Sci Med 1997;45:1829–1843.

Sitzia J, Wood N. Response rate in patient satisfaction research: an analysis of 210 published studies. International J Qual Health Care 1998;10:311–317.

Smith D. Rebuilding family medicine from the foundation up. Fam Pract Manag 2007;14:9–10.

Stone AA, Broderick JE, Schwartz JE. Validity of average, minimum, and maximum end-of-day recall assessments of pain and fatigue. Contemp Clin Trials 2010;31:483–490.

Stone AA, Broderick JE, Schwartz JE, Schwarz N. Context effects in survey ratings of health, symptoms, and satisfaction. Med Care 2008;46:662–667.

Sudman S, Bradburn NM. *Response Effects in Surveys: A Review and Synthesis*. Chicago, IL: Aldine Publishing Company; 1974.

Suh EE, Kagan S, Strumpf N. Cultural competence in qualitative interview methods with Asian immigrants. J Transcult Nurs 2009;20:194–201.

Tadic V, Hamblion EL, Keeley S, Cumberland P, Lewando Hundt G, Cumberland JS. "Silent voices" in health services research: Ethnicity and socioeconomic variation in participation in studies of quality of life in childhood visual disability. Invest Ophthalmol Vis Sci 2010;51:1886–90.

Terwee CB, Schellingerhout JM, Verhagen AP, Koes BW, de Vet HC. Methodological quality of studies on the measurement properties of neck pain and disability questionnaires: a systematic review. J Manipulative Physiol Ther 2011;34:261–72.

Underwood JM, Townsend JS, Stewart SL, Buchannan N, Ekwueme DU, Hawkins NA, Li J, Peaker B, Pollack LA, Richards TB, Rim SH, Rohan EA, Sabating SA, Smith JL, Tai E, Townsend GA, White A, Fairley TL. Surveillance of demographic characteristics and health behaviors among adult cancer survivors—Behavioral Risk Factor Surveillance System, United States, 2009. MMWR Surveill Summary 2012;61:1–23.

VanGeest JB, Johnson TP. Using incentives in surveys of cancer patients: do "best practices" apply? Cancer Causes Control 2012;23:2047–2052.

Waghorn A, McKee M. Understanding patients' views of a surgical outpatient clinic. J Eval Clin Pract 2000;6:273–279.

Wang PS, Benner JS, Glynn RJ, Winkelmayer WC, Mogun H, Avorn J. How well do patients report noncompliance with antihypertensive medications? A comparison of self-report versus filled prescriptions. Pharmacoepidemiol Drug Saf 2004;13:11–19.

Warnecke RB, Johnson TP, Chavez N, Sudman S, O'Rourke DP, Lacey L, Horm J. Ann Epidemiol 1997;7:334–342.

Weber EJ, Showstack JA, Hunt KA, Colby DC, Grimes B, Bacchetti P, Callaham ML. Are the insured responsible for the increase in emergency department visits in the United States? Ann Emerg Med 2008;52:108–115.

Weech-Maldonado R, Elliott MN, Oluwole A, Cameron-Schiller KC, Hays RD. Survey response style and differential use of CAHPS rating scales by Hispanics. Med Care 2008;46:963–938.

Wenemark M, Vernby A, Norberg AL. Can incentives undermine intrinsic motivation to participate in epidemiologic surveys? Eur J Epidemiol 2010;25:231–235.

Wensing M, Elwyn G. Improving the quality of health care: methods for incorporating patients' view in health care. Br Med J 2003;326:877–879.

Wilson CL, Cohn RJ, Johnson KA, Ashton LJ. Tracing survivors of childhood cancer in Australia. Pediatr Blood Cancer 2009;52:510–515.

Wolosin R, Ayala L, Fulton BR. Nursing care, patient satisfaction, and value-based purchasing: vital connections. J Nurs Admin 2012;42:321–325.

Young GJ, Meterko M, Desai KR. Patient satisfaction with hospital care: effects of demographic and institutional characteristics. Med Care 2000;38:325–334.

Zuidgeest M, Hendriks M, Koopman L, Spreeuwenberg P, Rademakers J. A comparison of a postal survey and mixed-mode survey using a questionnaire on patients' experiences with breast care. J Med Internet Res 2011;27:13.

ONLINE RESOURCES

Information (including surveys and tools) on the Consumer Assessment of Healthcare Providers and Systems (CAHPS) is available at: http://cahps.ahrq.gov/.

Information on the CAHPS® Home Health Care Survey (HHCAHPS) is available at: https://homehealthcahps.org/.

Information on the Hospital Consumer Assessment of Healthcare Providers and Systems (HCAHPS) survey is available at: http://www.cms.gov/Medicare/Quality-Initiatives-Patient-Assessment-Instruments/HospitalQualityInits/HospitalHCAHPS.html.

The Agency for Healthcare Research and Quality (AHRQ) provides resources on developing surveys to measure hospital patient safety cultures. Information is available at: www.ahrq.gov/legacy/qual/patientsafetyculture/hospsurvindex.htm.

AHRQ's Hospital Survey Toolkit is also available at: www.ahrq.gov/professionals/quality-patient-safety/patientsafetyculture/hospital.

The Health Research and Services Administration (HRSA) Patient Satisfaction Survey can be found at: http://bphc.hrsa.gov/policiesregulations/performancemeasures/patientsurvey/satisfactionsurvey.html.

The HRSA Patient Satisfaction Survey form can be downloaded from: http://bphc.hrsa.gov/policiesregulations/performancemeasures/patientsurvey/surveyform.html.

Information on HIPAA is available at: www.hhs.gov/ocr/privacy/index.html.

The American Hospital Association also provides guidance on conducting surveys in light of HIPAA privacy regulations: www.aha.org/advocacy-issues/hipaa/conductingsurveys.shtml.

The American Association for Public Opinion Research (AAPOR) provides Institutional Review Board (IRB) facts for survey researchers at: www.aapor.org/IRB_FAQs_for_Survey_Researchers1.htm.

Resources on question design and development are available at the Duke Initiative on Survey Design and Development: http://dism.ssri.duke.edu/question_design.php.

Information on HHS patient surveys, including technical and instrument item design, and guidance on using patient and service user feedback to bring about improvements in health care, can be found at: www.nhssurveys.org/.

Validated tools for assessment of health literacy are available from the U.S. Centers for Disease Control and Prevention and from the Agency for Healthcare Research and Quality websites: www.cdc.gov/healthliteracy/researchevaluate/index.html and www.ahrq.gov/professionals/quality-patient-safety/quality-resources/tools/literacy/index.html.

The Institute of Medicine also has a workshop summary available at: www.iom.edu/Reports/2009/Measures-of-Health-Literacy.aspx.

CHAPTER TWENTY THREE

Surveying Sexual and Gender Minorities

Melissa A. Clark

Department of Epidemiology and Obstetrics & Gynecology, Public Health Program and Warren Alpert Medical School, Brown University, Providence, RI, USA

Samantha Rosenthal

Department of Epidemiology, Public Health Program, Brown University, Providence, RI, USA

Ulrike Boehmer

Department of Community Health Sciences, Boston University School of Public Health, Boston, MA, USA

23.1 Introduction

Lesbian, gay, and bisexual (LGB) individuals are often referred to as *sexual minorities*, and *transgender* (T) individuals are referred to as *gender minorities*. These labels are determined based on sexual orientation and gender identity designations. This chapter provides an overview of considerations for health-related survey research with sexual and gender minorities and is divided into three sections. The first section provides definitions of sexual orientation and gender identity, describes challenges in the measurement of sexual and gender minority status, and presents examples of questions for measuring sexual orientation and gender identity. The second section presents a summary of the probability and nonprobability

Handbook of Health Survey Methods, First Edition. Edited by Timothy P. Johnson.

sampling methods that have been used most frequently in research with sexual and gender minorities with a description of the major strengths and limitations of each approach for sampling and recruiting sexual and gender minorities. The third section provides an overview of data-collection methods that have been used in research with sexual and gender minorities. While many of the methodological issues are relevant for any medical, psychological, or social science research study, the examples in this chapter emphasize the medical and public health literatures.

23.1.1 DEFINITION OF SEXUAL ORIENTATION

Sexual orientation is a relational construct that refers to the biological sex of an individual and the sex of one's potential or actual sexual and/or romantic relationships relative to each other (Institute of Medicine 2011); this does not include isolated sexual encounters or experimentation (Peplau and Garnets 2000, Herek 2006). The most recent and generally accepted conceptualization of sexual orientation includes three components: identity, behavior, and attraction (Laumann et al. 1994, Solarz 1999, McCabe et al. 2005, Institute of Medicine 2011). Sexual orientation *identity* is generally defined as self-identification as heterosexual (e.g., straight), homosexual (e.g., gay or lesbian) or bisexual (e.g., bi). The meaning of the identity terms *homosexual*, *heterosexual*, and *bisexual* changes with cultural, social, economic, political, and historic circumstances (Lesbian Gay and Bisexual (LGB) Youth Sexual Orientation Measurement Work Group 2003). *Behavior* encompasses engagement in sexual contact with a person or people of the same sex, opposite sex, or both sexes over time. *Attraction* refers to a person's tendency to be attracted to individuals of the same sex, opposite sex, or both. Several studies have shown that engagement in same-sex sexual behaviors and/or same-sex attractions is much more common than identification as homosexual or bisexual (Laumann et al. 1994, Smith et al. 2003, Friedman et al. 2004, Mosher et al. 2005, Kerker et al. 2006, McNair et al. 2006).

Sexual orientation as a continuum was first introduced in the United States by Kinsey and colleagues (1948, 1953) and has been supported through ongoing research (Weinrich and Klein 2002, Worthington and Moreno 2005, Herek et al. 2010). The fact that sexual orientation is a multifaceted construct that operates along a continuum makes it difficult to measure sexual orientation by identity alone. For instance, because the behavior and attraction components of sexual orientation exist on a spectrum, individuals may not easily classify themselves into one of the identity categories. An individual who has engaged in sexual contact with individuals of both sexes and reports being somewhat attracted to individuals of both sexes may identify in any of the sexual identity classifications. Dissonance between the various dimensions of sexual orientation has been widely acknowledged (Ross et al. 2003, Friedman et al. 2004, McCabe et al. 2005, Savin-Williams and Ream 2007, Bauer and Jairam 2008); many more individuals report same-sex behavior or attraction than those who identify as homosexual or bisexual. Sexual orientation has also been found to change over time, adding even more of a challenge to its measurement (Diamond 2000, Diamond 2003, Kinnish et al. 2005, Savin-Williams and Ream 2007, Bauer and Jairam 2008).

To date, there have not been standard, generally accepted measures of sexual orientation. Many different measures of sexual orientation have been used over time. The Kinsey scale (Kinsey et al. 1948, 1953) was one of the first measures developed and has continued to be used in more recent studies (Rahman et al. 2008, Zietsch et al. 2008, Rubinstein 2010). This measure is typically used as a scale from 0 to 6, where 0 means exclusively heterosexual and 6 means exclusively homosexual. Values 1 through 5 represent varying degrees of bisexuality (Kinsey et al. 1948, 1953). Another older measure that has been used in recent studies is the Klein sexual orientation grid (Klein et al. 1985), a measure that views sexual orientation as a multivariable dynamic process (de Rooij et al. 2009, Colzato et al. 2010). This grid includes 21 items, each of which can be rated 1 through 7, similar to the Kinsey scale. The 21 items comprise seven dimensions of sexual orientation with three time references: lifetime history, past 12 months, and ideal preference. The seven dimensions include: attraction, behavior, fantasy, emotion, social preference, lifestyle preference, and identity (Klein et al. 1985). The Sell assessment of sexual orientation (Sell 1996, 1997) is another assessment of sexual orientation that has been used in at least one recent study (Alanko et al. 2010). This assessment considers various dimensions of sexual orientation, and consists of 12 questions about attractions, behavior, and identity. Many other multiitem measures of sexual orientation have been proposed, but none have garnered widespread support (e.g., Shively and De Cecco (1977), Storms (1980), Friedman et al. (2004), Worthington and Moreno (2005)).

Depending on the research topic, different dimensions of sexual orientation are more salient. For example, same-sex behavior is more relevant than identity for studies of HIV risk behaviors, while sexual orientation identity may be the important dimension in studies of stress or discrimination experiences. Several recent nationally representative surveys and large-scale studies, which have limited space to devote to particular constructs, have included a single measure of sexual orientation identity, with a fewer studies including questions about attraction and/or behavior. Examples of single questions used in recent large-scale surveys to measure sexual orientation dimensions are included in Table 23.1.

23.1.2 DEFINITION OF GENDER IDENTITY

Gender identity is usually defined as a person's sense of gender; being a man, woman, or another gender. *Transgender* refers to an individual whose gender identity differs from the sex originally assigned at birth, whose gender expression varies from what is traditionally associated with that sex, or who varies from or rejects traditional cultural conceptualizations of gender in terms of the male–female dichotomy (Institute of Medicine 2011). Transgender women, often referred to as *male-to-female* (MTF), are individuals who were assigned at birth as male and who self-identity as female or express their gender as female. Transgender men, often referred to as *female-to-male* (FTM), are individuals who were assigned at birth as female and who self-identify as male or express their gender as male.

TABLE 23.1 Examples of Sexual Orientation and Gender Identity Questions Used in State and National Surveys by Dimension

Dimension	Question	Example Survey
Sexual orientation-identity	Do you consider yourself to be: [ ] Heterosexual or straight, [ ] Gay or lesbian, or [ ] Bisexual?	Behavioral Risk Factor Surveillance Survey (state of Vermont) (www2a.cdc.gov/nccdphp/brfss2/coordinator.asp) HIV/AIDS Surveillance System (www.cdc.gov/hiv/stats/hasrlink.HTM) National Survey of Family Growth[a] (www.cdc.gov/nchs/nsfg.htm) National Epidemiologic Survey on Alcohol and Related Conditions[b] (http://www.niaaa.nih.gov/Resources/DatabaseResources/Pages/default.aspx) California Health Interview Survey[c] (www.chis.ucla.edu/)
	Which of the following best describes you? [ ] Heterosexual (straight) [ ] Gay or lesbian [ ] Bisexual [ ] Not sure	Youth Risk Behavior Surveillance Survey (selected states) (www.cdc.gov/HealthyYouth/yrbs/index.htm)
	Do you think of yourself as ... [ ] Heterosexual or straight (that is, sexually attract only to [opposite sex]) [ ] Homosexual or gay (that is, sexual attracted only to [same sex])	National Health and Nutrition Examination Survey[c] (www.cdc.gov/nchs/nhanes.htm)

	[ ] Bisexual (that is, sexually attracted to men and women) [ ] Something else, or [ ] Not sure?	
Sexual orientation-behavior	During the past 12 months, have you had sex with [ ] only males [ ] only females, or [ ] both males and females?	Behavioral Risk Factor Surveillance Survey (states of Vermont, Massachusetts) (www2a.cdc.gov/nccdphp/brfss2/coordinator.asp)
	During the past 12 months, have your sexual partners been [ ] male [ ] female, or [ ] both male and female?	California Health Interview Survey (www.chis.ucla.edu/)
	During your life, the person(s) with whom you have had sexual contact is (are): [ ] I have not had sexual contact with anyone [ ] Female(s) [ ] Male(s) [ ] Female(s) and male(s)	Youth Risk Behavior Surveillance Survey (selected states) (www.cdc.gov/HealthyYouth/yrbs/index.htm) National Epidemiologic Survey on Alcohol and Related Conditions[b] (http://www.niaaa.nih.gov/Resources/DatabaseResources/Pages/default.aspx)

(*continued*)

TABLE 23.1 (*Continued*)

Dimension	Question	Example Survey
	Thinking of the last 5 years, that is since (season) of (year), has the partner or partners in your sexual relationships been: [ ] only men [ ] mostly men [ ] about the same number of men and women [ ] mostly women [ ] only women, or [ ] have you not had a sexual relationship in the last five years?	National Alcohol Survey (www.arg.org/address.html)
Sexual orientation-attraction	People are different in their sexual attraction to other people. Which best describes your feelings? Are you [ ] only attracted to females [ ] mostly attracted to females [ ] equally attracted to females and males [ ] mostly attracted to males [ ] only attracted to males, or [ ] not sure?	National Survey of Family Growth (www.cdc.gov/nchs/nsfg.htm) National Epidemiologic Survey on Alcohol and Related Conditions[b] (http://www.niaaa.nih.gov/Resources/DatabaseResources/Pages/default.aspx)

Gender identity	Which of the following best describes you? [ ] Male [ ] Female [ ] Transgendered [ ] Not sure	Youth Risk Behavior Surveillance Survey (Washington, DC) (www.cdc.gov/HealthyYouth/yrbs/index.htm)
	People describe themselves as transgender when they need to express themselves, or enjoy expressing themselves in the gender role of the opposite sex. For example, this could include cross dressing, transvestitism, being transsexual, or doing drag. Do you consider yourself to be transgender? [ ] Yes-Male to female (MTF) [ ] Yes-Female to male (FTM) [ ] No	Behavioral Risk Factor Surveillance Survey (state of Vermont) (www2a.cdc.gov/nccdphp/brfss2/coordinator.asp)

[a] Includes additional response of "or something else?"
[b] Question wording varies slightly by year of administration.
[c] Second category phrased gay (lesbian) or homosexual.

Similar to sexual orientation, there have not been standard, generally accepted measures of gender identity. Some studies have included a single question to assess respondents' transgender status using a yes–no response (Almeida et al. 2009). Conron and colleagues (2008) conducted cognitive-based testing of a more complex gender identity measure with youth. Response options for this measure included (i) female; (ii) male; (iii) transgender, male to female, (iv) transgender, female to male, (v) transgender, do not identify as exclusively male or female; and (vi) not sure. The National lesbian, gay, bisexual, transgender (LGBT) Tobacco Control Network conducted cognitive-based testing of a single question that combined sexual orientation and gender identity, asking adult respondents, "Do you consider yourself to be one or more of the following," providing the answer categories: (i) straight; (ii) gay or lesbian; (iii) bisexual; (iv) transgender (Scout 2008). There have been very few large-scale surveys to date that have included items about gender identity. Examples of single items used in large-scale surveys are shown in Table 23.1. More methodological studies are needed to determine the measures of gender identity that ultimately facilitate the most valid and reliable survey responses from gender variant populations.

23.2 Prevalence Estimates of Sexual and Gender Minorities

23.2.1 SEXUAL ORIENTATION

Prevalence estimates of homosexuality and bisexuality among United States adults have ranged from 1 to 7%, increasing considerably after the 1990s (Laumann et al. 1994, Gates 2006, 2010, Herbenick et al. 2010, Gates and Cook 2011). These estimates include only adults who identify as homosexual, gay, lesbian, or bisexual. However, prevalence estimates of adults reporting same-sex partners are much higher, ranging from 4% to 12% since 1994 (Laumann et al. 1994, Mosher et al. 2005, Gates 2010, Herbenick et al. 2010). In addition to lack of consistency in definition and measurement of sexual orientation, the large variation in prevalence estimates may be due to differences in studies based on the time period of data collection, sampling methods, sample age, survey instruments used, and mode of data collection.

Differences in self-reported sexual orientation have been identified by gender, race/ethnicity, culture, age, education, income, and geography. In the first national probability survey to examine adult sexual behaviors in the United States, 2.8% of men and 1.4% of women identified as homosexual or bisexual (Laumann et al. 1994). In the 2010 National Survey of Sexual Health and Behavior, 6.8% of men identified as homosexual or bisexual, whereas only 4.5% of women did so (Herbenick et al. 2010). However, in the 2008 General Social Survey, 4.6% of women identified as homosexual or bisexual compared to only 2.9% of men (Gates 2010). These differences may be due to a large margin of error, changes over time, or differences in the sampled populations.

Self-reports of sexual orientation also differ by culture, race, and ethnicity. There is some evidence that racial/ethnic minorities who engage in same-sex behaviors are less likely to identify as gay because they fear being stigmatized by their community (Ross et al. 2003). For example, Ford and colleagues (2007) describe a culture of secret same-sex behaviors referred to as *the down low* among some African-American males that does not involve identifying as homosexual. Cultural differences in the concept of community membership, traditional gender roles, and religiosity are also known to affect reported sexual orientation identity (Institute of Medicine 2011).

Sexual orientation also differs across age groups. Among studies that have included individuals across the adult lifespan, homosexual identification is highest among young and middle-aged adults (Herek et al. 2010, Boehmer et al. 2012). Some recent data suggest that adults who identify as bisexual may be younger on average than the U.S. adult population and significantly younger than lesbians and gay men (Herek et al. 2010). Youth, despite being aware of same-sex attractions, may be less likely to self-identify as homosexual to avoid bullying and abuse (D'Augelli 2003). There is a paucity of data about older adults because only a few of the large-scale surveys that include questions about sexual orientation ask these questions of adults over age 50 years. The best projections suggest that there are 2–7 million sexual minority elders in the United States (Grant et al. 2010).

Sexual orientation differences have also been observed by socioeconomic characteristics. A 1995 study using data from the General Social Survey found that gay and bisexual male workers earned from 11 to 27% less than heterosexual counterparts with equal experience, education, marital status, and region of residence (Badgett 1995). More recent data have also documented lower incomes among gay men compared to their heterosexual counterparts (Allegretto and Arthur 2001, Black et al. 2003, Carpenter 2007). Much of this disparity has been attributed to work place discrimination. Finally, a systematic review by Black and colleagues in 2000 (Black et al. 2000) found that gay and lesbian individuals report higher average education levels than their heterosexual counterparts. However, the authors caution that this finding may be due to well-educated people being more willing to identify as homosexual.

Sexual orientation differences have also been noted across regions of the United States. The most geographically robust data on the sexual minority population is from the U.S. Census. While the Census does not measure sexual orientation directly, it includes information on same-sex partnered households, which has been used as a surrogate measure of sexual orientation (Ost and Gates 2005, Gates 2006, Carpenter and Gates 2008). Data from the 2000 Census showed that Midwestern states had disproportionately fewer same-sex couples compared to other regions of the United States (Gates 2006). However, the largest percentage increase of same-sex couples between 2000 and 2005 occurred in the Midwest region. Recent data from the 2010 Census indicate that the states with the largest numbers of same-sex couples per 1000 households include: Vermont, Massachusetts, California, Oregon, as well as the District of Columbia (Gates and Cook 2011). Congressional districts with the highest percentage of same-sex couples also tend to be more urban (Gates 2006).

There have been limited recent large-scale population-based state and national surveys that have included items about sexual orientation. Examples of these surveys are shown in Table 23.2. In general, prevalence estimates of individuals identifying as homosexual or bisexual from these surveys were consistent with other published literature. Prevalence of homosexuality ranged from 1 to 5% with men being more likely than women to identify as homosexual. Prevalence of bisexuality ranged from 1 to 3% with less consistent differences between men and women. Prevalence estimates by age and race/ethnicity varied considerably by the survey.

23.2.2 GENDER IDENTITY

One approach to obtain prevalence estimates of transgender or gender non-conforming individuals has been the use of medical record data. This approach includes the subgroup of transgender individuals who presented at medical clinics and received a diagnosis of gender dysphoria, a diagnosis in the Diagnostic and Statistical Manual of Mental Disorders, or who presented for medical services for gender-related surgery (The World Professional Association for Transgender Health 2011). Using international data, mostly from European countries, prevalence estimates range from 1 : 11,900 to 1 : 45,000 for MTF individuals and 1 : 30,400 to 1 : 200,000 for FTM individuals (The World Professional Association for Transgender Health 2011). These prevalence estimates have been criticized as underestimates, derived from biased methodology (Conway 2002). Furthermore, recent data suggest that the number of individuals seeking medical treatment to masculinize or feminize their bodies is increasing and that the prevalence of individuals identifying as transgender is likely to increase over time (Zucker and Lawrence 2009).

Very little survey research has been conducted to determine the size of the transgender population. However, the Vermont and Massachusetts Behavioral Risk Factor Surveillance Surveys (BRFSS) included a question about transgender identity, which was endorsed by 0.5% and 0.9% of Massachusetts and Vermont respondents, respectively (Conron et al. 2012). Unfortunately, there are a number of limitations with estimating the prevalence of transgender identity using population-based surveys. Household-based surveys such as the BRFSS reach only the most socially integrated transgender individuals, who have stable housing and a telephone, thereby omitting transgender individuals who are severely impoverished, homeless, or marginally housed (Conron et al. 2012). Therefore, prevalence estimates of less than 1% are likely an underestimate of the transgender population.

Differences in self-reported gender identity have been identified by sociodemographic characteristics. In a study of more than 6000 transgender adults from across the United States, Grant and colleagues (2011) found that the adult transgender population was younger and more likely to be living in poverty than the general U.S. population in the American Community Survey. These data are consistent with those from the Massachusetts BRFSS (Conron et al. 2012) and those from an Internet-based study comparing an adult transgender population to the

TABLE 23.2 Prevalence Estimates (%) and Mode of Data Collection for Self-Reported Sexual Orientation Identity from Selected Population-Based Surveys

	General Social Survey (2010)[a] $n = 2044$			National Health and Nutrition Examination Survey (2007–2008)[b, a] $n = 3265$			National Study of Family Growth (2002)[c, d] $n = 12{,}571$			California Health Interview Survey (2007)[a] $n = 41{,}157$			Behavioral Risk Factor Surveillance System: Washington, DC (2005 and 2007 combined)[e] $n = 6218$		
	Homo	Bi	Ref	Homo	Bi[f]	Ref	Homo	Bi[f]	Ref	Homo	Bi	Ref	Homo	Bi[f]	Ref
Prevalence estimates															
Overall	1.2	1.4	1.4	1.5	2.8	0.1	1.7	2.4	1.8	2.2	1.2	—	4.9	2.3	3.2
Gender															
Male	1.3	0.5	0.9	1.9	1.4	0.0	2.3	1.8	1.8	3.2	1.1	—	8.3	2.4	—
Female	1.2	2.1	1.4	1.1	4.2	0.2	1.3	2.8	1.8	1.5	1.3	—	2.0	2.2	—
Age (years)															
18–24	2.4	1.9	1.5	0.7	6.9	0.2	—	—	—	1.5	2.2	—	3.7	3.7	—
25–34	0.9	2.6	0.8	2.1	3.2	0.2	—	—	—	1.7	1.8	—	5.7	1.9	—
35–44	1.9	1.6	0.8	1.9	3.0	0.1	—	—	—	2.4	1.4	—	6.2	3.7	—
45–53	1.2	1.4	0.7	1.0	1.6	0.2	—	—	—	2.9	1.1	—	6.7	1.8	—
55–64	1.4	0.8	0.8	1.3	1.3	0.0	—	—	—	2.1	0.9	—	4.3	0.8	—
≥65	0.0	0.0	2.9	—	—	—	—	—	—	1.4	0.9	—	1.0	1.7	—
Race/ethnicity															
White	1.4	1.4	1.2	1.1	2.8	0.0	—	—	—	2.6	1.3	—	9.0	2.0	—

(continued)

TABLE 23.2 (*Continued*)

	General Social Survey (2010)[a] $n = 2044$			National Health and Nutrition Examination Survey (2007–2008)[b, a] $n = 3265$			National Study of Family Growth (2002)[c, d] $n = 12,571$			California Health Interview Survey (2007)[a] $n = 41,157$			Behavioral Risk Factor Surveillance System: Washington, DC (2005 and 2007 combined)[e] $n = 6218$		
	Homo	Bi	Ref	Homo	Bi[f]	Ref	Homo	Bi[f]	Ref	Homo	Bi	Ref	Homo	Bi[f]	Ref
Black	0.9	1.5	1.9	2.2	4.2	0.0	—	—	—	2.0	1.2	—	2.0	2.2	—
Hispanic/Latino	—	—	—	2.1	2.4	0.8	—	—	—	1.3	1.0	—	5.3	4.8	—
Asian	—	—	—	—	—	—	—	—	—	0.9	0.9	—	—	—	—
Other	0.5	1.3	0.5	2.9	1.5	0.0	—	—	—	2.3	1.3	—	5.2	1.3	—
Mode of data collection for sexual orientation questions	Computer-assisted personal interviews			Audio computer-assisted self-interviews			Audio computer-assisted self-interviews			Computer-assisted telephone interviews			Computer-assisted telephone interviews		

—, Data not available.

Homo, self-reported homosexual orientation; Bi, self-reported bisexual orientation; Ref, refused question about sexual orientation.

[a]Analysis computed for this chapter.

[b]Includes only ages 20–59.

[c]Includes only ages 15–44.

[d]Data from Mosher et al. (2005).

[e]Data from Dyer et al. (2010).

[f]Bisexual includes individuals reporting "other."

[g]Includes only ages 18–70.

general U.S. population using Census data (Rosser et al. 2007). These studies also suggest that transgender individuals were more educated than the general U.S. population (Rosser et al. 2007, Grant et al. 2011). Transgender individuals are also more likely to be unemployed than the general population. For example, in the national survey by Grant and colleagues (2011), transgender individuals were twice as likely to be unemployed as the general population, while Conron and colleagues (2012) found that the odds of being unemployed were three times higher for transgender compared to nontransgender adults in the Massachusetts BRFSS. In addition, 15–57% of transgender individuals in a sample of sexual and gender minorities reported experiencing employment discrimination with 19% reporting that they were denied a promotion based on their gender identity (Badgett et al. 2007).

Ethnicity and culture also likely influence self-identification as transgender. For example, transgender individuals were more likely to report Hispanic ethnicity in the Massachusetts BRFSS (Conron et al. 2012). Although small sample sizes have precluded specific subgroup analyses in most studies to date, many Asian and American Indian communities recognize transgender individuals as part of traditional society, unlike the dichotomous constructions of gender common in Western culture (Mayer et al. 2008), therefore, likely increasing the rates of transgender identity in those cultures.

23.3 Sampling and Recruitment

There are important considerations for sampling sexual and gender minority research participants that ultimately may affect the internal and external validity of study results. Sampling refers to the way in which research participants, a subset of individuals from the population of interest, are selected. Sampling methodologies in research with sexual and gender minorities have included probability and nonprobability approaches. Probability samples are ones from which a subset of individuals are selected from a population of interest with every person having a known nonzero probability of being included (Meyer and Wilson 2009). Nonprobability samples are ones in which a subset of individuals are selected from a population in which the probability of being selected is unknown; this is typically referred to as a *convenience* sample. To date, nonprobability sampling has been much more common than probability sampling in research with sexual and gender minorities.

There are inherent challenges in all sampling methodologies when attempting to extrapolate study findings to a broader population. However, it is even more challenging when the population of interest is considered a "hidden population." Sexual and gender minorities have frequently been referred to as a *hidden* community (Sudman et al. 1988, Watters and Biernacki 1989, Solarz 1999, Boehmer 2002). This is because LGBT individuals are not easily identifiable from any sampling frame and may be unwilling to identify as members of this population due to the sensitive nature and potential social discrimination of such an identity.

These same factors also have the potential, regardless of sampling methodology, to cause low response rates. In addition, how sexual minority status is defined may influence the sampling approach (e.g., those who identify as sexual minorities versus those who meet a behaviorally defined criterion for being a sexual minority) (Binson et al. 2007).

There are many considerations for determining a sampling method for research with sexual and gender minorities including cost, time, feasibility, generalizability, accessibility of the population, and the over-arching objective of the study. In Table 23.3, we provide an overview of the major different sampling methods that have been used in research with sexual and gender minorities and document the major strengths and limitations of each method.

23.3.1 PROBABILITY SAMPLING METHODS

In general, probability sampling is the gold standard for survey research because study findings can be extrapolated to the population from which participants were drawn (Meyer and Wilson 2009; see also Chapter 2). Probability sampling includes many different techniques including simple random sampling, stratified, and cluster sampling approaches. Unfortunately, probability sampling for studies of the sexual and gender minority population is particularly challenging due to the low prevalence of LGBT identity.

Some nationally representative surveys using probability sampling approaches have included measures of sexual orientation, including the National Health and Nutrition Examination Survey (www.cdc.gov/nchs/nhanes.htm) and the National Survey of Family Growth (www.cdc.gov/nchs/nsfg.htm). Despite their large sizes, these surveys have yielded a very small number of participants that identify as LGBT, documenting the high costs of using probability-based approaches for a population with prevalence estimates as low as 1%.

In a recent study, Herek and colleagues (2010) sampled sexual minority individuals from the Knowledge Networks panel, which is large probability sample of U.S. residents who were recruited through random-digit dialing methods. A probability sample of English-speaking adults was drawn from the subset of all panel members who had previously responded to being gay, lesbian, or bisexual. Each sampled individual then received an email invitation to complete an online survey.

A few studies have used stratified or cluster sampling to obtain probability samples of members of the LGBT community (Bowen et al. 2004, Gruskin et al. 2007, Mackesy-Amiti et al. 2008). For example, study investigators have identified neighborhoods with large numbers of sexual minorities (e.g., high gay density) and then used probability-based approaches for participant recruitment in those areas to reduce cost and increase efficiency. The use of these high gay density neighborhoods reduces the number of households that require screening to identify sexual minorities compared to other population-based approaches. For example, Gruskin and colleagues (2007) used national data to identify the California zip codes with the highest proportion of sexual minorities. Using a two-stage sampling approach with *random-digit-dialing* within the selected zip

TABLE 23.3 Strengths and Limitations of Sampling Methods Used in Studies with Sexual and Gender Minorities

Sampling Method	Strengths	Limitations	Example Studies that have Used Method
Probability sampling			
Random-digit dialing	Estimates can be extrapolated to the population from which study subjects were drawn	High costs due to low prevalence of sexual and gender minorities Low coverage of individuals with no or sporadic telephone availability	(Gruskin et al. (2007), Herek et al. (2010)
Household-based sampling	Estimates can be extrapolated to the population from which study subjects were drawn	High costs due to low prevalence of sexual minorities Potential bias toward individuals living in areas with higher densities of sexual minorities	Bowen et al. (2004)
Nonprobability sampling			
List-based sampling	Provides an easy and accessible sampling frame	Can only generalize findings to others in the list population Lists of sexual and gender minorities are generally unavailable Quality of available lists must be carefully assessed for incorrect, incomplete, and duplicate information	Solomon et al. (2004)

(continued)

TABLE 23.3 (*Continued*)

Sampling Method	Strengths	Limitations	Example Studies that have Used Method
Time-location sampling	Can help to increase sample size when recruiting sexual minorities If all relevant venues are included and all segments of population visit these venues, this can be considered a probability sampling	Appropriate venues for recruitment may change over time and must be reevaluated continually Venues and times selected for data collection may not include certain segments of the population Nonresponse may be a problem at stigmatized venues	MacKellar et al. (1996), Muhib et al. (2001), Cai et al. (2010)
Snowball sampling	Can help to increase sample size when recruiting sexual minorities May be able to better recruit hard-to-reach individuals not enrolled through other sampling schemes	Members of the same social network are likely to be more socially connected and thus more similar than the broader sexual and gender minority population	Warner et al. (2004), Browne (2005), Kendall et al. (2008), Balsam et al. (2010), Feng et al. (2010), Lehavot and Simoni (2011), Prado Cortez et al. (2011)
Respondent-driven sampling	Can help to increase sample size when recruiting sexual minorities	Assumptions of the methodology must be met	Ramirez-Valles et al. (2005), Johnston et al. (2008), Kendall et al. (2008), Lauby et al.

	Associated with lower costs than time-location sampling Can be used to derive valid, unbiased population estimates	May not be able to reach an adequate sampling size in subgroups of sexual and gender minority population with limited social connections	(2008), Ramirez-Valles et al. (2008) Richards et al. (2008), Wheeler et al. (2008), Evans et al. (2011)
Web-based sampling	Can help to increase sample size when recruiting sexual minorities May be particularly effective for recruiting younger populations	Samples are not likely representative of the broader sexual and gender minority population	Rosser et al. (2007), Johnston et al. (2008), Chesir-Teran and Hughes (2009), Evans et al. (2011)
Advertising	Can help to increase sample size when recruiting sexual minorities	Samples are not likely representative of the broader sexual and gender minority population	Silvestre et al. (2006), Chesir-Teran and Hughes (2009)

codes, they recruited participants who identified as sexual minorities. Next, using prevalence rates of LGB individuals, the average numbers of LGB adults per household, and the numbers of households per zip code from the 2000 census data, they constructed weights to account for the unequal probabilities of selection. Similarly, a study by Bowen and colleagues (2004) identified zip codes in Massachusetts with high proportions of female same-sex partnered households using census data. They then conducted *door-to-door household sampling* in those zip codes to screen for female participants. Finally, Mackesy-Amiti and colleagues (2008) identified two zip codes in Chicago, Illinois with known high concentrations of gay men and then used face-to-face screening to select eligible respondents.

Boehmer and colleagues (2010) used a similar approach to obtain representative samples of sexual minority and heterosexual individuals with a particular health condition. Using Census data, they defined areas in Massachusetts with the highest density of sexual minority women and then obtained data on female cancer cases in those areas from the Massachusetts Cancer Registry. Next, they used telephone screening of the cancer cases from the Cancer Registry to identify a sample of sexual minority women and a comparison sample of heterosexual women. Another recent novel approach by Boehmer and colleagues (2011) was to combine the geographic density of sexual minorities identified by the Census with cancer incidence and mortality data from the Surveillance, Epidemiology, and End Results (SEER) Program. Combining these data allowed for ecological analyses of differences in cancer incidence and mortality by county, resulting in county-level prevalence estimates of cancer disparities by sexual orientation.

Focusing on areas with a high density of sexual minorities has the advantage of reducing costs and increasing efficiency of sampling small or hidden populations. However, potential biases with this approach remain. For example, sexual minorities living in high density LGB areas may be different than those that do not live in such areas. In addition, these high density areas are most likely to be in large, urban metropolitan areas, leaving substantial challenges for probability-based sampling in nonmetropolitan areas. Finally, potential biases remain if there are differential response rates by sexual orientation or within the sexual minority population.

23.3.2 NONPROBABILITY SAMPLING

Using nonprobability samples, it is not possible to estimate population measures such as the prevalence of sexual and gender minorities. However, it is possible to examine factors within a specific target group. In fact, Boehmer and colleagues (2008, 2010) demonstrated that characteristics and experiences of participants from nonprobability samples were representative of the sexual minority communities of interest when carefully selected inclusion criteria were applied.

Many different types of nonprobability methods have been used in research with sexual and gender minorities. The most commonly used methods include: list-based sampling, time-location sampling (TLS), snowball sampling, respondent-driven sampling (RDS), web-based sampling, and advertising. A general discussion of several of these techniques is also provided in Chapter 4.

List-Based Sampling. List-based sampling involves the use of a preexisting list of members of the population of interest to select potential study participants. This sampling method may be very efficient when information about individuals is in the public record such as drivers' licenses, marriage licenses, and birth and death certificates. However, there are very few lists of individuals in the LGBT community from which to sample. In addition, the quality of the lists must be carefully assessed due to the potential for incorrect, incomplete, and duplicate information in available lists (Kalton and Anderson 1986). In one novel study, Solomon and colleagues (2004) used a list of all civil union certificates from the Vermont Office of Vital Records to select adults in same-sex civil unions for research about their experiences during the first year after civil union legislation passed in Vermont. Unfortunately, this approach is limited to states that have same-sex civil union and marriage legislation. Furthermore, study findings cannot be generalized beyond individuals in legally recognized relationships in the limited number of states for which same-sex relationships have been officially sanctioned.

Time-Location Sampling. TLS, also known as *time-space sampling*, *venue-based* or *venue-day-time* sampling, is another nonprobability sampling method (MacKellar et al. 1996, Muhib et al. 2001) that has been used in research with sexual minorities. Using TLS, study investigators recruit from venues (e.g., sites) where the population of interest tends to gather. Prior to study implementation, venues are enumerated and used as a sampling frame. A probability sample of venues is selected from the sampling frame and data collection is implemented at all or some of the sites. Data are collected at a predetermined time period at each site. In a study by Cai and colleagues (2010) examining HIV risk behaviors among male sex workers in China, TLS was used to sample 32 venue-date-times from 43 venues, yielding a total sample size of 456 individuals. The analysis included a weighting scheme that adjusted for the probability of selection of venue-date-times and the homogeneity of participants sampled at each venue-date-time. TLS approximates a random cluster sampling method, so unlike other nonprobability methods, it provides somewhat known probabilities of selection and is considered by some to be a probability sampling method (Magnani et al. 2005). Others argue, however, that while the probability of selection can be determined for each venue-date-time, the probability of selection for a specific individual cannot necessarily be established. In addition, nonresponse bias may be particularly problematic at venues that have stigma associated with them.

Snowball Sampling. Snowball sampling, also referred to as *chain sampling*, *chain-referral sampling*, or *referral sampling* is another nonprobability method that has been used in studies of sexual and gender minorities. In this method, participants are not recruited from a sampling frame. Rather, study eligibility is defined, several eligible individuals are approached for participation, and each is asked to recruit other individuals in his/her social network that also meet the study eligibility criteria. The additionally recruited participants are then asked to recruit other individuals in their social network, and this referral approach continues until the designated sample size is met. For example, Kendall and colleagues (2008) used snowball sampling to recruit men who have sex with men (MSM) in Fortaleza, Brazil. Initial recruits were recruited from venues around the city where MSM were likely to meet. Snowball sampling can result in samples of participants who are similar to one another given their connectedness in a broader social network, and as a result, the sample is not necessarily representative of the broader target population. Therefore, snowball sampling may be a useful way to increase the sample size in studies of sexual and gender minorities, but caution should be used in making generalizations about study findings.

Respondent-Driven Sampling. RDS is a method that is similar to snowball sampling. The approach, initially used for research on HIV/AIDS and injection drug use, is becoming increasingly more common among studies of other topics in the LGBT community (Ramirez-Valles et al. 2005, Abdul-Quader et al. 2006, Frost et al. 2006, Robinson et al. 2006, Lauby et al. 2008, Ramirez-Valles et al. 2008, Richards et al. 2008, Wheeler et al. 2008, Abramovitz et al. 2009, Townsend et al. 2010). Unlike snowball sampling, RDS provides the opportunity to derive valid, unbiased population estimates, as well as measures of precision around those estimates (Heckathorn 1997, 2002). In RDS, respondents recruit their peers and study investigators monitor who recruited whom and the numbers of each participant's social contacts. Then, using a mathematical model to apply weights to the sample, a weighting scheme is applied to compensate for the nonrandom sampling approach. RDS is useful because it allows for the calculation of selection probabilities and therefore is considered by some to be a probability sampling method. It also has more external validity than other nonprobability sampling methods because it is not limited to subgroup members who access venues such as is necessary for TLS. In a comparison of snowball sampling, TLS, and RDS to recruit MSM, Kendall and colleagues (2008) found that RDS produced a sample with greater inclusion of individuals of lower socioeconomic status than snowball sampling or TLS. RDS also achieved the sample size faster and at lower cost. In addition, RDS can contribute to a more inclusive sample and strengthen community participation in research (Tiffany 2006).

Unfortunately, there are a number of limitations of RDS. RDS can be challenging due to small network sizes, lack of ties among members of the target population, and high levels of perceived stigma and fear of participation in studies. In addition, there are inherent assumptions that must be met for RDS to be used in deriving valid and unbiased population estimates: (i) the number of people that each person is associated with in the target population is measured accurately; (ii) relationships are reciprocal; (iii) sampling is with replacement, that is, each person in the population may be included in the sampling more than once; (iv) seeds (e.g., recruiters) choose who to recruit randomly from their associates within the target population; (v) a sufficient number of waves of data collection can be collected such that seeds are independent of the subsequent waves of recruits; and (vi) each person in the population is connected to every other person in the population through a chain of associations. In order to best use RDS, these assumptions must be tested and/or addressed in implementation. For example, in a study examining recruitment methods of central and eastern European migrant MSM in London, study investigators found that RDS was ineffective due to small sample size and/or little connectedness of this population (Evans et al. 2011). A similar study conducted in Estonia found that RDS did not adequately recruit a large enough sample, and the sample recruited was fairly homogenous by demographics (Johnston et al. 2009).

Web-Based Sampling and Advertising. Other convenience sampling methods that have been used in LGBT research include web-based sampling and advertising. In web-based sampling, individuals are recruited through the Internet. Advertising is typically done using print ads such as flyers, posters, or magazines. In a Four-City study examining different ways to recruit minority MSM for HIV research, Silvestre and colleagues (2006) used city and minority newspapers, news releases, and magazines to advertise for participation. A study by Chesir-Teran and Hughes (2009) of LGB and questioning high school students used both online and print advertising to sample participants. A study of the transgender community was also conducted by web-based sampling. Rosser and colleagues (2007) used banners on transgender community websites, chat rooms, online mailing lists, journals, and forums to recruit participants for a transgender health survey. In two separate recent studies comparing recruitment of MSM via the Internet to RDS, study investigators found that recruitment via the Internet was the more successful method at recruiting an adequate, more diverse sample (Johnston et al. 2009, Evans et al. 2011). While advertising by print or web can increase samples of sexual and gender minorities, there may be volunteer bias. In addition, individuals frequenting particular websites may not be representative of the broader population of interest.

23.3.3 OTHER RECRUITMENT CONSIDERATIONS

Given the challenges and limitations for recruiting representative samples of sexual and gender minorities, other analytic methods have been proposed to determine prevalence estimates. One analytical method that has been attempted is the capture-recapture method. This method originated to estimate the prevalence of wildlife populations where organisms were captured, marked and released back into the population. Organisms were then captured again by the same procedure. The proportion of marked organisms among those recaptured was assumed to be the same as the proportion of those initially captured among the entire population (Sudman et al. 1988). Using this method, Aaron and colleagues (2003) attempted to estimate the lesbian population prevalence in Allegheny County, Pennsylvania. A total of 2185 lesbian women were identified from four organizations that served the lesbian and gay population in the county. Using the proportion of overlap of the lesbian population across the four organizations and log-linear modeling of heterogeneity and dependence across sources, it was estimated that 7031 lesbian women lived in Allegheny County. Bias could result from this type of model if there is a high rate of immigration or emigration into the region or if the probabilities of being sampled by these sources are not equal for all individuals. Assuming these biases are minimal, the capture–recapture method may be a valid alternative to otherwise costly representative probability samples.

In addition to specific challenges with sampling, there are other recruitment considerations for LGBT research. One limitation of many prior health studies among LGB participants has been that there has rarely been a control group with which to compare results. In large-scale national probability studies, there are sufficiently large sample sizes to construct subgroups to compare sexual minorities to majority groups. However, smaller studies directed at particular topic areas must define and recruit the most appropriate control group. One alternative that has been used in studies of risk factors for breast cancer among lesbians has been the use of heterosexual siblings as controls (Rothblum and Factor 2001, Rothblum et al. 2004). Unfortunately, while some research topics are conducive to siblings as controls (i.e., effect of genetic and familial risk factors on health outcomes; relationship of childhood environment on subsequent adult health outcomes), this approach has many limitations for other topics. Another alternative is to compare a sample of sexual minority women recruited through convenience sampling strategies with women from nationally representative samples of adults. In a study of alcohol use behaviors, Wilsnack and colleagues (2008) compared lesbians recruited by convenience sampling to women in the National Study of Health and Life Experiences of Women. Women in the national sample were selected for the study based on age and geographic criteria that maximized comparability with the convenience sample.

23.4 Data Collection

Two questions arise when considering mode of data collection for studies of sexual and gender minorities. One question is the best mode for eliciting information about sexual orientation to determine prevalence estimates and to classify individuals based on identity, behavior, or attraction. A second question is the extent to which there are mode differences in studies specific to sexual and gender minorities and/or with sexual orientation or gender identity specific objectives. To date, more research has been conducted to address the question about methods to elicit sensitive information such as sexual orientation. Results from these studies suggest that self-administered questionnaires (SAQ) are more likely to give participants a sense of anonymity as compared to telephone and face-to-face interviews. However, paper-and-pencil SAQs tend to have more missing data, lower response rates, and are more challenging to use when incorporating skip patterns. Computer-assisted self-interviews (CASIs) have been shown to have better data quality and allow for more complex questionnaire structures relative to paper-and-pencil SAQs (Tourangeau et al. 2000). Despite these advantages, studies comparing CASI to other modes for reports of sensitive behaviors have had mixed results (Epstein et al. 2001, Gerbert et al. 1999, Hasley 1995, Macalino et al. 2002, Metzger et al. 2000, Newman Jarlais et al. 2002, Saris 1991, Webb et al. 1999, Wright et al. 1998).

There have been a limited number of randomized control trials that have accessed reporting differences in measures of sexual orientation by survey mode. Metzger and colleagues (2000) evaluated audio-CASI (ACASI) versus interviewer-administered assessment for the reporting of sensitive HIV-risk behaviors among gay men and male injection drug users. They found that significantly more men reported engaging in risky sexual behaviors when interviewed by ACASI versus interviewer-administered assessments. They concluded that ACASI can improve data quality of behavioral assessments, particularly when attempting to elicit the disclosure of sensitive and/or risky behaviors. In a similar randomized controlled trial, Macalino and colleagues (2002) compared ACASI and interviewer-administered questionnaires among injection drug users. Participants who were interviewed with ACASI were more likely to report engagement in risky sexual behaviors and HIV-seropositive status. Given that most studies of mode differences in reports of sensitive behaviors, including the randomized control trials were conducted at least 10 years ago, additional research is needed to determine the extent to which these findings are still valid.

As shown in Table 23.2, recent national and state surveys that have included items about sexual orientation have used many different modes, including computer-assisted telephone interviewing (CATI), computer-assisted personal interviewing (CAPI), and audio computer-assisted self-interviewing (ACASI). Unfortunately, it is challenging to compare prevalence and nonresponse estimates from these surveys due to inconsistent ways of measuring sexual orientation and lack of information in the public use data. In addition, some surveys such as the National Health and Examination Survey and the National Study of Family Growth did not ask questions related to sexual orientation of older adults. Regardless, prevalence estimates and nonresponse rates in these surveys do not differ greatly by method of data collection.

Unfortunately, there is less data about mode differences in studies specific to sexual minorities and/or with sexual orientation-specific objectives. Of the available studies, several different survey modes have been used. For example, in a study among high school students that examined emotional distress among LGBT youth, a paper-and-pencil survey was administered in classrooms. Less than 1% of students were prohibited by their parents from participating, and an additional 5.3% of students declined to participate (Almeida et al. 2009). A similar study was conducted nationally among a convenience sample of the same age group and administered only via the Internet. Nonresponse rates could not be computed because all participants volunteered and therefore were self-selected for survey completion (Chesir-Teran and Hughes 2009). A study by McCabe and colleagues (2003) examined associations between sexual identity and substance use among undergraduate students. Half of the participants were randomly assigned to receive mailed SAQ, and the other half were assigned to a web survey. The response rate was 63% for the web survey, and only 40% for the mailed SAQ. However, identification as homosexual did not differ by survey mode. In 2002, a study was conducted among sexual minority homeless adolescents (Cochran et al. 2002). Private, face-to-face structured interviews were conducted with a response rate of 95%. However, this was a convenience sample with a $25 incentive for participation. In a recent cross-sectional survey, investigators used personal digital assistants to collect information from young adult homosexual males regarding attitudes and behaviors toward sex parties in New York City in an attempt to emulate ACASI in a venue-based recruitment environment (Solomon et al. 2011). Finally, in a sample of MSM, Fendrich and colleagues (2008) examined agreement between self-reported past month drug use by ACASI and urine and saliva drug testing and found that self-reports among MSM were at least as valid as those provided by a general population sample of men.

Although several modes of data collection have been used to conduct research with younger members of the LGBT community, there have been limited studies that have directly compared response rates and data quality by mode. To date, available data suggests that self-administered computer-assisted technology may optimize response rates among younger adults and result in comparable or higher data quality than other survey modes (McCabe et al. 2003, Turner et al. 1998). However, more research is needed to determine how response rates or data quality might be affected by mode in studies with varying sampling designs, eligibility criteria, and incentives.

Much less research has been done with middle-aged and older LGBT populations, and fewer survey modes have been used. In conducting a perceptions and needs assessment of older LGBT individuals in the greater Chicago area in 2003, mailed SAQs were used. Of approximately 2500 surveys distributed, 11% were received and assessed (Beauchamp et al. 2003). In a 2001 study examining mental health and victimization history of LGB individuals older than 60 years old in the United States, investigators obtained 416 SAQs from a convenience sample of participants recruited through social support groups and social service agencies (D'Augelli and Grossman 2001). In one of the few randomized trials of mode differences among middle-aged and older sexual minorities, Clark and colleagues (2008) randomly assigned 599 heterosexual and sexual minority women aged 40–75 to three different survey modes: self-administered mailed questionnaire (SAMQ), CATI, and the computer-assisted self-interview (CASI) for collecting data about cancer screening behaviors. Response rates were comparable across mode, and method of data collection had little effect on reports of breast, cervical or colorectal cancer screening behaviors.

23.5 Conclusions

With the exception of studies of HIV prevention among MSM, limited numbers of population-based surveys and longitudinal cohort studies of sexual and gender minorities have been conducted. Population-based state-level data about sexual orientation has increased in the past few years due to surveys such as the California Health Interview Survey (www.chis.ucla.edu/ and state-specific BRFSS (www2a.cdc.gov/nccdphp/brfss2/coordinator.asp. However, population-based data at the national level have been very limited. The consistent inclusion of robust measures of sexual orientation in all state and national population-based surveys is necessary to ultimately determine and address health disparities facing sexual minorities (Institute of Medicine 2011). To date, none of these surveys oversample sexual minorities, resulting in small actual numbers of LGB individuals in these surveys. As a result, subgroup analyses by age and race are essentially impossible unless a survey consistently ask questions about sexual orientation, and researchers wait until they can pool data from several years of the survey (Boehmer et al. 2012). These problems are particularly compounded for gender minorities because only a few surveys include at least one measure of gender identity.

To date, the majority of studies of sexual and gender minorities have used nonprobability sampling methods. While nonprobability sampling can cause biased estimates and prevent generalizations, many early studies that used nonprobability sampling made it possible to learn about disparities in the LGBT population and prepared the field for studies using probability sampling. Unfortunately, the significant effort spent critiquing early studies that used nonprobability methods at times delayed devoting resources to the disparities that were highlighted and later confirmed by more methodologically rigorous studies (Meyer 2001).

The considerable strengths of probability-based methods are well known. However, ultimately, the sampling procedure used when conducting research with sexual and gender minorities should take into account the particular research question. Specifically, consideration should be given to whether the findings are intended to be extrapolated to a larger population or if the intended analyses involve examination of differences between subgroups within the sexual and gender minority population. In addition, feasibility, cost, sample size requirements and time should be considered when choosing a method. Finally, when considering sampling methods that rely on social networks, the likely connectedness of the underlying population of interest should be considered.

To date, no data collection method has been determined to be superior for conducting research with the LGBT population. Rather, the particular research question of interest, the segment of the population, recruitment strategy, and the sensitivity of questions asked must all be considered when determining the most appropriate data collection method for a particular study. Other measures such as efficiency and cost-effectiveness of the method should also be considered in study development.

REFERENCES

Aaron DJ, Chang YF, Markovic N, LaPorte RE. Estimating the lesbian population: a capture-recapture approach. J Epidemiol Community Health 2003;57:207–209.

Abdul-Quader A, Heckathorn D, Sabin K, Saidel T. Implementation and analysis of respondent driven sampling: lessons learned from the field. J Urban Health 2006;83:1–5.

Abramovitz D, Volz EM, Strathdee SA, Patterson TL, Vera A, Frost SDW, for Proyecto ElCuete. Using respondent-driven sampling in a hidden population at risk of HIV infection: who do HIV-positive recruiters recruit? Sex Transm Dis 2009;36:750–756.

Alanko K, Santtila P, Harlaar N, Witting K, Varjonen M, Jern P, Johnansson A, von der Pahlen B, Sandnabba N. Common genetic effects of gender atypical behavior in childhood and sexual orientation in adulthood: a study of Finnish twins. Arch Sex Behav 2010;39:81–92.

Allegretto SA, Arthur MM. An empirical analysis of homosexual/heterosexual male earnings differentials: unmarried and unequal? Indus Labor Relat Rev 2001;54:631–646.

Almeida J, Johnson R, Corliss H, Molnar B, Azrael D. Emotional distress among LGBT youth: the influence of perceived discrimination based on sexual orientation. J Youth Adolesc 2009;38:1001–1014.

Badgett MVL. The wage effects of sexual orientation discrimination. Indus Labor Relat Rev 1995;48:726–739.

Badgett MVL, Lau H, Sears B, Ho D. 2007. Bias in the workplace: consistent evidence of sexual orientation and gender identity discrimination. Available at http://wiwp.law.ucla.edu/wp-content/uploads/Badgett-Sears-Lau-Ho-Bias-in-the-Workplace-Jun-2007.pdf.

Balsam KF, Lehavot K, Beadness B, Circo E. Childhood abuse and mental health indicators among ethnically diverse lesbian, gay, and bisexual adults. J Consult Clin Psychol 2010;78:459–468.

Bauer GR, Jairam JA. Are lesbians really women who have sex with women (WSW)? Methodological concerns in measuring sexual orientation in health research. Women Health 2008;48:383–408.

Beauchamp D, Skinner J, Wiggins P. *LGBT Persons in Chicago: A Survey of Needs and Perceptions*. Chicago, IL: Chicago Task Force on LGBT Aging; 2003.

Binson D, Blair J, Huebner DM, Woods WJ. Sampling in surveys of lesbian, gay, and bisexual people. In: Meyer IH, Northridge ME, editors. *The Health of Sexual Minorities: Public Health Perspectives on Lesbian, Gay, Bisexual and Transgender Populations*. New York: Springer; 2007. p 375–418.

Black D, Gates G, Sanders S, Taylor L. Demographics of the gay and lesbian population in the United States: evidence from available systematic data sources. Demography 2000;37:139–154.

Black DA, Makar HR, Sanders SG, Taylor LJ. The earnings effects of sexual orientation. Ind Labor Relat Rev 2003;56:449–469.

Boehmer U. Twenty years of public health research: inclusion of lesbian, gay, bisexual, and transgender populations. Am J Public Health 2002;92:1125–1130.

Boehmer U, Clark M, Glickman M, Timm A, Sullivan M, Bradford J, Bowen DJ. Using cancer registry data for recruitment of sexual minority women: successes and limitations. Journal of Womens Health (Larchmont) 2010;19:1289–1297.

Boehmer U, Clark M, Timm A, Ozonoff A. Two means of sampling sexual minority women: how different are the samples of women? J LGBT Health Res 2008;4:143–151.

Boehmer U, Miao X, Linkletter C, Clark M. Adult health behaviors over the life course by sexual orientation. Am J Public Health 2012;102:292–300.

Boehmer U, Ozonoff A, Miao X. An ecological analysis of colorectal cancer incidence and mortality: differences by sexual orientation. BMC Cancer 2011a;11:400.

Boehmer U, Ozonoff A, Timm A. County-level association of sexual minority density with breast cancer incidence: results from an ecological study. Sexuality Res Soc Policy 2011b;8:139–145.

Bowen DJ, Bradford JB, Powers D, McMorrow P, Linde R, Murphy BC, Han J, Ellis J. Comparing women of differing sexual orientations using population-based sampling. Women Health 2004;40:19–34.

Browne K. Snowball sampling: using social networks to research non-heterosexual women. Int J Soc Res Methodol 2005;8:47–60.

Cai W, Zhao J, Zhao J, Raymond HF, Feng Y, Liu J, McFarland W, Gan Y, Yang Z, Zhang Y, Tan J, Wang X, He M, Cheng J, Chen L. HIV prevalence and related risk factors among male sex workers in Shenzhen, China: results from a time–location sampling survey. Sex Transm Infect 2010;86:15–20.

Carpenter C, Gates GJ. Gay and lesbian partnership: evidence from California. Demography 2008;45:573–590.

Carpenter CS. Revisiting the income penalty for behaviorally gay men: evidence from NHANES III. Labour Econ 2007;14:25–34.

Chesir-Teran D, Hughes D. Heterosexism in high school and victimization among lesbian, gay, bisexual, and questioning students. J Youth Adolesc 2009;38:963–975.

Clark M, Rogers M, Armstrong G, Rakowski W, Kviz F. Differential response effects of data collection mode in a cancer screening study of unmarried women ages 40-75 years: a randomized trial. BMC Med Res Methodol 2008;8:10.

Cochran BN, Stewart AJ, Ginzler JA, Cauce AM. Challenges faced by homeless sexual minorities: comparison of gay, lesbian, bisexual, and transgender homeless adolescents with their heterosexual counterparts. Am J Public Health 2002;92:773–777.

Colzato LS, Van Hooidonk L, Van Den Wildenberg W, Harinck F, Hommel B. Sexual orientation biases attentional control: a possible gaydar mechanism. Front Psychol 2010;1:1–5.

Conron KJ, Scott G, Stowell GS, Landers SJ. Transgender health in Massachusetts: results from a household probability sample of adults. Am J Public Health 2012;102:118–122.

Conron KJ, Scout , Austin SB. "Everyone has a right to, like, check their box": findings on a measure of gender identity from a cognitive testing study with adolescents. J LGBT Health Res 2008;4:1–9.

Conway L. 2002. How frequently does transsexualism occur? Available at http://ai.eecs.umich.edu/people/conway/TS/TSprevalence.html. Accessed 2011 Nov 23.

D'Augelli AR. Lesbian and bisexual female youths aged 14 to 21: developmental challenges and victimization experiences. J Lesbian Stud 2003;7:9–29.

D'Augelli AR, Grossman AH. Disclosure of sexual orientation, victimization, and mental health among lesbian, gay, and bisexual older adults. J Interpers Violence 2001;16:1008–1027.

de Rooij S, Painter R, Swaab D, Roseboom T. Sexual orientation and gender identity after prenatal exposure to the Dutch famine. Arch Sex Behav 2009;38:411–416.

Diamond LM. Sexual identity, attractions, and behavior among young sexual-minority women over a 2-year period. Dev Psychol 2000;36:241–250.

Diamond LM. What does sexual orientation orient? a biobehavioral model distinguishing romantic love and sexual desire. Psychol Rev 2003;110:173–192.

Dyer C, Garner T, Opoku J. *A Report of Lesbian, Gay and Bisexual Health in the District of Columbia*. Washington, DC: Mayor's Office of Gay, Lesbian, Bisexual and Transgender Affairs; 2010.

Epstein JF, Barker PR, Kroutil LA. Mode effects in self-reported mental health data. Public Opin Quart 2001;65:529–49.

Evans AR, Hart G, Mole R, Mercer CH, Parutis V, Gerry CJ, Imrie J, Burns FM. Central and east European migrant men who have sex with men: an exploration of sexual risk in the UK. Sex Transm Infect 2011;87:325–330.

Fendrich M, Mackesy-Amiti ME, Johnson TP. Validity of self-reported substance use in men who have sex with men: comparisons with a general population sample. Ann Epidemiol 2008;18:752–759.

Feng Y, Wu Z, Detels R, Qin G, Liu L, Wang X, Wang J, Zhang L. HIV/STD prevalence among men who have sex with men in Chengdu, China and associated risk factors for HIV infection. J Acquir Immune Defic Syndr 2010;53(Supplement 1):S74–80.

Ford CL, Whetten KD, Hall SA, Kaufman JS, Thrasher AD. Black sexuality, social construction, and research targeting 'the down low' ('the DL'). Ann Epidemiol 2007;17:209–216.

Friedman MS, Silvestre AJ, Gold MA, Markovic N, Savin-Williams RC, Huggins J, Sell RL. Adolescents define sexual orientation and suggest ways to measure it. J Adolesc 2004;27:303–317.

Frost S, Brouwer K, Firestone Cruz M, Ramos R, Ramos ME, Lozada R, Magis-Rodriguez C, Strathdee S. Respondent-driven sampling of injection drug users in two U.S.–Mexico border cities: recruitment dynamics and impact on estimates of HIV and syphilis prevalence. J Urban Health 2006;83:83–97.

Gates GJ. 2006. Same-sex couples and the gay, lesbian, bisexual population: new estimates from the American Community Survey. Los Angeles, CA: The Williams Institute, UCLA School of Law, University of California-Los Angeles. Available at http://escholarship.org/uc/item/8h08t0zf. Accessed 2011 Nov 23.

Gates GJ. 2010. Sexual minorities in the 2008 general social survey: coming out and demographic characteristics. Los Angeles, CA: The Williams Institute, University of California-Los Angeles. Available at http://papers.ccpr.ucla.edu/papers/PWP-CCPR-2010-015/PWP-CCPR-2010-015.pdf. Accessed 2011 Nov 23.

Gates GJ, Cook AM. 2011. United States Census Snapshot 2010. Los Angeles, CA: The Williams Institute. Available at http://williamsinstitute.law.ucla.edu/wp-content/uploads/Census2010Snapshot-US-v2.pdf. Accessed 2011 Nov 23.

Gerbert B, Bronstone A, Pantilat S, McPhee S, Allerton M, Moe J. When asked, patients tell: disclosure of sensitive health-risk behaviors. Med Care 1999;37(1):104–11.

Grant JM, Koskovich G, Frazer MS, Bjerk S, Services & Advocacy for GLBT Elders (SAGE). *Outing Age: Public Policy Issues Affecting Gay, Lesbian, Bisexual, and Transgender Elders*. Washington, DC: The Policy Institute of the National Gay and Lesbian Task Force Foundation; 2010.

Grant JM, Mottet LA, Tanis J, Harrison J, Herman JL, Keisling M. *Injustice At Every Turn: A Report of the National Transgender Discrimination Survey*. Washington, DC:

National Center for Transgender Equality and National Gay and Lesbian Task Force; 2011.

Gruskin EP, Greenwood GL, Matevia M, Pollack LM, Bye LL. Disparities in smoking between the lesbian, gay, and bisexual population and the general population in California. Am J Public Health 2007;97:1496–1502.

Hasley S. A comparison of computer-based and personal interviews for the gynecologic history update. Obstet Gynecol 1995;84(4):494–8.

Heckathorn D. Respondent-driven sampling: a new approach to the study of hidden populations. Soc Probl 1997;44:174–199.

Heckathorn DD. Respondent-driven sampling ii: deriving valid population estimates from chain-referral samples of hidden populations. Soc Probl 2002;49:11–34.

Herbenick D, Reece M, Schick V, Sanders SA, Dodge B, Fortenberry JD. Sexual behavior in the united states: results from a national probability sample of men and women ages 14-94. J Sex Med 2010;7:255–265.

Herek GM. Legal recognition of same-sex relationships in the United States: a social science perspective. Am Psychol 2006;61:607–621.

Herek GM, Norton AT, Allen TJ, Sims CL. Demographic, psychological, and social characteristics of self-identified lesbian, gay, and bisexual adults in a US probability sample. Sex Res Soc Policy 2010;7:176–200.

Institute of Medicine. *The Health of Lesbian, Gay, Bisexual, and Transgender People: Building a Foundation for Better Understanding*. Washington, DC: The National Academies Press; 2011.

Johnston L, Khanam R, Reza M, Khan SI, Banu S, Alam MS, Rahman M, Azim T. The effectiveness of respondent driven sampling for recruiting males who have sex with males in Dhaka, Bangladesh. AIDS Behav 2008;12:294–304.

Johnston LG, Trummal A, Lohmus L, Ravalepik A. Efficacy of convenience sampling through the internet versus respondent driven sampling among males who have sex with males in Tallinn and Harju County, Estonia: challenges reaching a hidden population. AIDS Care 2009;21:1195–1202.

Kalton G, Anderson DW. Sampling rare populations. J Roy Stat Soc Ser A 1986;149:65–82.

Kendall C, Kerr L, Gondim R, Werneck G, Macena R, Pontest M, Johnston L, Sabin K, McFarland W. An empirical comparison of respondent-driven sampling, time location sampling, and snowball sampling for behavioral surveillance in men who have sex with men, Fortaleza, Brazil. AIDS Behav 2008;12:97–104.

Kerker BD, Mostashari F, Thorpe L. Health care access and utilization among women who have sex with women: sexual behavior and identity. J Urban Health 2006;83:970–979.

Kinnish K, Strassberg D, Turner C. Sex differences in the flexibility of sexual orientation: a multidimensional retrospective assessment. Arch Sex Behav 2005;34:173–183.

Kinsey AC, Pomeroy WB, Martin CEoriginally published. *Sexual Behavior in the Human Male*. Bloomington, IN: Indiana University Press; 1948, reprinted 1998.

Kinsey AC, Pomeroy WB, Martin CE, Gebhard PHoriginally published. *Sexual Behavior in the Human Female*. Bloomington, IN: Indiana University Press; 1953, reprinted 1998.

Klein F, Sepekoff B, Wolf TJ. Sexual orientation: a multi-variable dynamic process. J Homosex 1985;11:35–49.

Lauby J, Millett G, LaPollo A, Bond L, Murrill C, Marks G. Sexual risk behaviors of HIV-positive, HIV-negative, and serostatus-unknown black men who have sex with men and women. Arch Sex Behav 2008;37:708–719.

Laumann E, Gagnon JH, Michael RT, Michaels S. *The Social Organization of Sexuality: Sexual Practices in the United States*. Chicago, IL: University of Chicago Press; 1994.

Lehavot K, Simoni JM. The impact of minority stress on mental health and substance use among sexual minority women. J Consult Clin Psychol 2011;79:159–170.

Lesbian Gay and Bisexual (LGB) Youth Sexual Orientation Measurement Work Group. *Measuring Sexual Orientation of Young People in Health Research*. San Francisco, CA: Gay and Lesbian Medical Association; 2003.

Macalino GE, Celentano DD, Latkin C, Strathdee SA, Blahoy D. Risk behaviors by audio computer-assisted self-interviews among HIV-seropositive and HIV-seronegative injection drug users. AIDS Educ Prevent 2002;14:367–378.

MacKellar D, Valleroy L, Karon J, Lemp G, Janssen R. The young men's survey: methods for estimating HIV seroprevalence and risk factors among young men who have sex with men. Public Health Rep 1996;3(Supplement):138–144.

Mackesy-Amiti ME, Fendrich M, Johnson TP. Prevalence of recent illicit substance use and reporting bias among MSM and other urban males. Addict Behav 2008;33:1055–1060.

Magnani R, Sabin K, Saidel T, Heckathorn D. Review of sampling hard-to-reach and hidden populations for HIV surveillance. AIDS 2005;19:S67–S72.

Mayer KH, Bradford JB, Makadon HJ, Stall R, Goldhammer H, Landers S. Sexual and gender minority health: what we know and what needs to be done. Am J Public Health 2008;98:989–995.

McCabe SE, Boyd C, Hughes T, d'Arcy H. Sexual identity and substance use among undergraduate students. Subst Abus 2003;24:77–91.

McCabe SE, Hughes TL, Bostwick W, Boyd CJ. Assessment of difference in dimensions of sexual orientation: implications for substance use research in a college-age population. J Stud Alcohol Drugs 2005;66:620–629.

McNair R, Gleitzman M, Hillier L. Challenging research: methodological barriers to inclusion of lesbian and bisexual women in Australian population-based research. Gay Lesbian Issues Psychol Rev 2006;2:114–127.

Metzger DS, Koblin B, Turner C, Navaline H, Valenti F, Holte S, Gross M, Sheon A, Miller H, Cooley P, Seage GR. Randomized controlled trial of audio computer-assisted self-interviewing: utility and acceptability in longitudinal studies. HIVNET Vaccine Preparedness Study Protocol Team. Am J Epidemiol 2000;152:99–106.

Meyer IH. Why lesbian, gay, bisexual, and transgender public health? Am J Public Health 2001;91:856–859.

Meyer IH, Wilson PA. Sampling lesbian, gay, and bisexual populations. J Couns Psychol 2009;56:23–31.

Mosher WD, Chandra A, Jones J. Sexual behavior and selected health measures: men and women 15-44 years of age, United States, 2002. Adv Data 2005;362:1–55.

Muhib FB, Lin LS, Stueve A, Miller RL, Ford WL, Johnson WD, Smith PJ. A venue-based method for sampling hard-to-reach populations. Public Health Rep 2001;116(Supplement 1):216–222.

Newman JC, Des Jarlais DC, Turner CF, Gribble J, Cooley P, Paone D. The differential effects of face-to-face and computer interview modes. Am J Public Health 2002;92(2):294–7.

Ost J, Gates GJ. *The Gay and Lesbian Atlas*. Washington, DC: The Urban Institute Press; 2005.

Peplau LA, Garnets LD. A new paradigm for understanding women's sexuality and sexual orientation. J Soc Iss 2000;56:329–350.

Prado Cortez FC, Boer DP, Baltieri DA. A psychosocial study of male-to-female transgendered and male hustler sex workers in Sao Paulo, Brazil. Arch Sex Behav 2011;40:1223–1231.

Rahman Q, Collins A, Morrison M, Orrells J, Cadinouche K, Greenfield S, Begum S. Maternal inheritance and familial fecundity factors in male homosexuality. Arch Sex Behav 2008;37:962–969.

Ramirez-Valles J, Garcia D, Campbell RT, Diaz RM, Heckathorn DD. HIV infection, sexual risk behavior, and substance use among Latino gay and bisexual men and transgender persons. Am J Public Health 2008;98:1036–1042.

Ramirez-Valles J, Heckathorn D, Vazquez R, Diaz R, Campbell R. From networks to populations: the development and application of respondent-driven sampling among IDUs and Latino gay men. AIDS Behav 2005;9:387–402.

Richards JE, Risser JM, Padgett PM, Rehman HU, Wolverton ML, Arafat RR. Condom use among high-risk heterosexual women with concurrent sexual partnerships, Houston, Texas, USA. Int J STD AIDS 2008;19:768–771.

Robinson W, Risser J, McGoy S, Becker A, Rehman H, Jefferson M, Griffin V, Wolverton M, Tortu S. Recruiting injection drug users: a three-site comparison of results and experiences with respondent-driven and targeted sampling procedures. J Urban Health 2006;83:29–38.

Ross MW, Essien EJ, Williams ML, Fernandez-Esquer ME. Concordance between sexual behavior and sexual identity in street outreach samples of four racial/ethnic groups. Sex Transm Dis 2003;30:110–113.

Rosser B, Oakes J, Bockting W, Miner M. Capturing the social demographics of hidden sexual minorities: an Internet study of the transgender population in the United States. Sex Res Soc Policy 2007;4:50–64.

Rothblum ED, Balsam KF, Mickey RM. Brothers and sisters of lesbians, gay men, and bisexuals as a demographic comparison group. J Appl Behav Sci 2004;40:283–301.

Rothblum ED, Factor R. Lesbians and their sisters as a control group: demographic and mental health factors. Psychol Sci 2001;12:63–69.

Rubinstein G. Narcissism and self-esteem among homosexual and heterosexual male students. J Sex Marital Ther 2010;36:24–34.

Saris WE. *Computer-assisted interviewing*. Newbury Park, CA: Sage; 1991.

Savin-Williams R, Ream G. Prevalence and stability of sexual orientation components during adolescence and young adulthood. Arch Sex Behav 2007;36:385–394.

Scout. 2008. LGBT surveillance and data collection briefing paper. National LGBT Tobacco Control Network. Available at http://www.lgbttobacco.org/files/09FCH_DataCollection.pdf. Accessed 2011 Nov 23.

Sell RL. The Sell assessment of sexual orientation: background and scoring. J Gay Lesbian Bisexual Ident 1996;1:295–310.

Sell RL. Defining and measuring sexual orientation: a review. Arch Sex Behav 1997;26:643–658.

Shively MG, De Cecco JP. Components of sexual identity. J Homosex 1977;3:41–48.

Silvestre AJ, Hylton JB, Johnson LM, Houston C, Witt M, Jacobson L, Ostrow D. Recruiting minority men who have sex with men for HIV research: results from a 4-city campaign. Am J Public Health 2006;96:1020–1027.

Smith AM, Rissel CE, Richters J, Grulich AE, de Visser RO. Sex in Australia: sexual identity, sexual attraction and sexual experience among a representative sample of adults. Aust N Z J Public Health 2003;27:138–145.

Solarz AL. *Lesbian Health: Current Assessment and Directions for the Future*. Washington, DC: National Academy Press; 1999.

Solomon SE, Rothblum ED, Balsam KF. Pioneers in partnership: lesbian and gay male couples in civil unions compared with those not in civil unions and married heterosexual siblings. J Fam Psychol 2004;18:275–286.

Solomon T, Halkitis P, Moeller RM, Siconolfi DE, Kiang MV, Barton SC. Sex parties among young gay, bisexual, and other men who have sex with men in New York city: attendance and behavior. J Urban Health 2011;88:1063–1075.

Storms MD. Theories of sexual orientation. J Pers Soc Psychol 1980;38:783–792.

Sudman S, Sirken MG, Cowan CD. Sampling rare and elusive populations. Science 1988;240:991–996.

The World Professional Association for Transgender Health. 2011. The standards of care for transsexual, transgender, and gender nonconforming people, 7th version. Minneapolis, MN: The World Professional Association for Transgender Health, Inc. http://www.wpath.org/documents/Standards%20of%20Care%20V7%20-%202011%20WPATH.pdf. Accessed 2011 Nov 23.

Tiffany J. Respondent-driven sampling in participatory research contexts: participant-driven recruitment. J Urban Health 2006;83:113–124.

Tourangeau R, Rips LJ, Rasinski K. *The Psychology of Survey Response*. Cambridge, UK: Cambridge University Press; 2000.

Townsend L, Rosenthal SR, Parry CDH, Zembe Y, Mathews C, Flisher AJ. Associations between alcohol misuse and risks for HIV infection among men who have multiple female sexual partners in Cape Town, South Africa. AIDS Care 2010;22:1544–1554.

Turner CF, Ku L, Rogers SM, Lindberg LD, Bleck JH, Sonenstein FL. Adolescent sexual behavior, drug use, and violence: increased reporting with computer survey technology. Science 1998;280:867–873.

Warner J, McKeown E, Griffin M, Johnson K, Ramsay A, Cort C, King M. Rates and predictors of mental illness in gay men, lesbians and bisexual men and women: results from a survey based in England and Wales. Br J Psychiatry 2004;185:479–485.

Watters JK, Biernacki P. Targeted sampling: options for the study of hidden populations. Soc Probl 1989;36:416–430.

Webb PM, Zimet GD, Fortenberry JD, Blythe MJ. Comparability of a computer-assisted versus written method for collecting health behavior information from adolescent patients. J Adolesc Health 1999;24(6):383–8.

Weinrich JD, Klein F. Bi-gay, bi-straight, and bi-bi. J Bisexuality 2002;2:109–139.

Wheeler D, Lauby J, Liu K, Van Sluytman L, Murrill C. A comparative analysis of sexual risk characteristics of black men who have sex with men or with men and women. Arch Sex Behav 2008;37:697–707.

Wilsnack SC, Hughes TL, Johnson TP, Bostwick WB, Szalacha LA, Benson P, Aranda F, Kinnison KE. Drinking and drinking-related problems among heterosexual and sexual minority women. J Stud Alcohol Drugs 2008;69:129–139.

Worthington RL, Moreno MV. Beyond Kinsey and Klein: measuring sexual orientation and identity. Washington, DC: *Annual Convention of the American Psychological Association*; 2005.

Wright DL, Aquilino WS, Supple AJ. A comparison of computer assisted and paper-and-pencil self-administered questionnaires in a survey on smoking, alcohol, and drug use. Public Opin Quart 1998;62:331–53.

Zietsch BP, Morley KI, Shekar SN, Verweij KJH, Keller MC, Macgregor S, Wright MJ, Bailey JM, Martin NG. Genetic factors predisposing to homosexuality may increase mating success in heterosexuals. Evol Hum Behav 2008;29:424–433.

Zucker KJ, Lawrence AA. Epidemiology of gender identity disorder: recommendations for the standards of care of the World Professional Association for Transgender Health. Int J Transgenderism 2009;11:8–18.

ONLINE RESOURCES

A website, created and maintained by Dr. Rondall Sell, serves as an open-access clearinghouse for collection of sexual orientation and gender identity data and measures, including recommendations for how to collect sexual orientation data: www.lgbtdata.com.

Below is the link to the website for the Williams Institute, a national think tank, which conducts independent research on sexual orientation and gender identity law and public policy. Much of the research includes analysis of Census data to estimate prevalence of the lesbian, gay, and bisexual population as well as relevant health and social issues. http://williamsinstitute.law.ucla.edu.

The website below is maintained by the Inter-university Consortium for Political and Social Research. It allows access to data sets that have collected sexual orientation data and allows for comparisons of variables across datasets. www.icpsr.umich.edu/icpsrweb/landing.jsp.

Below is the website for Fenway Health, including the Fenway Institute, which conducts research and evaluation, education and training, and public health advocacy for lesbian, gay, bisexual, and transgender individuals. www.fenwayhealth.org/.

CHAPTER TWENTY FOUR

Surveying People with Disabilities: Moving Toward Better Practices and Policies

Rooshey Hasnain

Asian Studies Program and Department of Disability and Human Development, University of Illinois at Chicago, Chicago, IL, USA

Carmit-Noa Shpigelman

Department of Community Mental Health, Faculty of Social Welfare and Health Sciences, University of Haifa, Haifa, Israel

Mike Scott

Division of Rehabilitation Services of the Illinois Department of Human Services, Chicago, IL, USA

Jon R. Gunderson and Hadi B. Rangin

Assistive Communication and Information Technology Accessibility in the Division of Disability Resources and Education Services (DRES), University of Illinois, Champaign/Urbana, IL, USA

Ashmeet Oberoi

Department of Disability and Human Development, University of Illinois at Chicago, Chicago, IL, USA

Liam McKeever

Department of Disability and Human Development, University of Illinois at Chicago, Chicago, IL, USA

Handbook of Health Survey Methods, First Edition. Edited by Timothy P. Johnson.

24.1 Introduction

When social scientists design health surveys, they take special care to ensure that the survey will reach individuals who are representatives of the target population. However, disability researchers and scholars note that some local and national survey research initiatives partly or completely exclude people who have disabilities (e.g., hearing, visual, cognitive/intellectual, and mobility impairments). There are multiple reasons for this problem, including the "lack of alternative formats in the survey administration, inappropriate handling of proxy responses, insufficient interviewer training to accommodate people with disabilities and under sampling" (Keer 2007; Kroll et al. 2007, p. viii).

It has been estimated that more than one billion people in the world (~15% of the total population) have some type of significant disability (World Health Organization [WHO] 2011). According to the U.S. Census Bureau (2010), more than 50 million people in the United States, including 40% of Americans over the age of 65 (~20% of the total population) have one or more disabilities. Because the U.S. population is aging, these numbers will continue to rise. Their inclu-dion, which is important, is particularly valuable in general population surveys because social scientists can use their input to expand target populations and thereby increase surveys' representativeness.

24.1.1 SURVEY DATA COLLECTION TECHNIQUES

Research on people with disabilities has usually been conducted through direct in-person interviews (Day & Campbell 2003). Paper-and-pencil surveys are not a popular method of collecting data from this population because high cognitive demands are placed on the respondents for both comprehending the written questions and communicating responses in writing (Mitchell et al. 2006). Paper-and-pencil surveys are also associated with lower complete-item response rates than electronic methods of data collection such as computer-assisted, self-completion questionnaires and telephone and web surveys (Bowling 2005). By contrast, face-to-face interviews place the least burden on respondents because this format requires them to have only basic verbal and listening skills (Bowling 2005).

Face-to-face interviewing is also advantageous in establishing the identities of interviewers and respondents. When surveys are taken by telephone and on the web, the influence of third parties on interviewee responses cannot be ruled out. Face-to-face interviewing, and (to a lesser degree) interviews by telephone, allow interviewer and respondent to form a rapport; such a connection may be important when information is being gathered from stigmatized disability groups such as people with issues that are psychiatric or have resulted from violence (Cook et al. 2007, Fenig et al. 1993). Although face-to-face interviews have been commonly used for collecting physical and mental health data, the high costs and labor associated with this mode restrict its usage (Day & Campbell 2003) unless the full sample consists of disabled persons.

Telephone surveys are one of the most common ways to collect population health data on and from people with disabilities (Mitchell et al. 2006). This mode is also highly reliable in the review of their experiences with conducting three large-scale surveys exclusively with people with disabilities, Mitchell et al. (2006) concluded that "it provided information that appeared to be consistent with that collected by in-person interviews" (p. 38). Wright et al. (2012) reported that telephone and face-to-face respondents with disabilities show the same levels of item nonresponse and nondifferentiation; however, telephone respondents are more likely to provide shorter answers to open-ended questions because the format places higher cognitive demands on them. These researchers also concluded that with appropriate accommodations, there would be few differences between data obtained from this population by telephone versus in-person interviews.

In recognition of the fact that not all people with disabilities can complete a telephone interview, and considering that in-person interviewing can be substantially more expensive than telephone interviewing, Wright et al. (2012) recommended a mixed-mode approach that attempts telephone interviews first and uses face-to-face interviewing for people with disabilities who do not or cannot respond by telephone. Cook et al. (2007) utilized Computer Assisted Telephone Interviewing (CATI) to assess the effectiveness of a wellness program on subjects with serious mental illness and Barnett and Franks (1999) used CATI for telephone surveys with deaf people. These approaches created opportunities to collect data without the expense of in-person interviews.

24.1.2 ONLINE SURVEYS AND TECHNOLOGY TOOLS

Adaptive technology, which has opened many doors for people with disabilities, is increasingly being applied to surveys. Online surveys in particular provide valuable opportunities to reach people with disabilities who might otherwise be excluded. Although not all disabilities affect a person's ability to complete online surveys, certain disabling conditions can make it difficult or impossible for some individuals to respond to some survey instruments. For instance, a person who is blind or sight-impaired may not be able to read survey questions in print or on a computer screen, and someone who cannot use his or her hands may not be able to mark an answer by using a pencil or clicking a computer mouse. Consider the following scenario:

> Amina, who is deaf, is completing an online survey that presents scenarios in short video clips. The instructions are to watch the videos and then respond to a set of related questions. Amina clicks "play" on the first video and watches as two people appear to be conversing. She checks the video player controls for a button to display captions, but doesn't find one.

Developments in computer technology and telecommunications continue to provide new mechanisms for access to the Internet and the web that take into account literacy, vision, and physical disabilities. Examples of such technologies include onscreen keyboards with head pointers, voice command systems, teletypewriter (TTY), and software that offer graphic representations of concepts. Multisensory surveys can be problematic, however, because—unlike face-to-face and telephone interviews—a live person is not present to help determine if respondents are having problems understanding the questions or following the survey process (Pendergrass et al. 2001). This type of drawback is particularly relevant when the groups being surveyed are from minority, non-English-speaking, and/or low reading-ability populations.

The Internet has noteworthy benefits over other methods of data collection, including reduced data entry errors and lower costs. Any type of questionnaire is easily translated into a web format and can include error-reduction features such as checkboxes, numeric entry boxes, selection lists, and pull-down menus that also facilitate ease of data entry for respondents (Rhodes et al. 2003). Some of these features cannot be built into self- or interviewer-administered paper surveys. Unlike paper-and-pencil questionnaires, web surveys allow researchers to keep respondents from skipping questions or selecting multiple responses to questions that require one answer, and to restrict the format in which responses are entered (e.g., by date, numeric). Interviewer effects, including bias, are also eliminated in web surveys because respondents' interactions with the survey instrument are standardized. In addition, because data entry occurs automatically, online surveys eliminate the cost of field staff salaries and the amount of staff training that is required before data can be collected and entered (Rhodes et al. 2003). Collecting data by web does have its challenges, however; these are discussed below.

24.1.3 INCLUSIVE PRACTICES AND PURPOSE

In this chapter we examine how survey modes can help or hinder survey participation by individuals with disabilities. We also explore how to make surveys accessible to a wider audience, including people with hearing, sight, cognitive/intellectual, and mobility impairments. In this context, *accessible* means "usable by people with disabilities." Although it may seem like a simple concept, its implications are as varied and complex as are the needs of people with disabilities. Our concern is with inclusion in all kinds of surveys, but much of our discussion in this chapter is focused on participation in web and other electronic surveys.

We use the term *disability* very broadly because many circumstances can decrease an individual's functioning or create a special need. The ways that people with disabilities can access information on the Internet vary greatly, according to their individual conditions. For the purposes of this chapter, disabilities are organized into the following categories: vision, hearing, combination blind and deaf, musculoskeletal or neurologic, learning and cognitive.

24.2 Setting a Foundation: The Importance of Inclusion for Web-Based Surveys

Since the early 2000s, the Internet has grown from an information source to a broad-based social environment in which people communicate, work, learn, play, shop, and develop relationships (Bargh & McKenna 2004). The Internet has made a wide range of communication, education, employment, and entertainment opportunities available to people with disabilities (Bowker & Tuffin 2007). Vicentea and Lópeza (2010) found that although adults (18 years and older) with disabilities tend to use many of the same Internet applications as nondisabled adults (e.g., for sending email, making purchases, finding training information, and taking courses), their rates of use are lower than the rest of the population. According to a report from the Pew Internet and American Life Project, only 54% of disabled adults use the Internet, compared to 81% of nondisabled adults (Fox 2011a, 2011b). This gap is due in part to the web's accessibility issues.

The term *accessibility* refers to the ability to gain access to, understand, or approach something or someone. In terms of accessibility laws and standards, *accessibility* refers to what the law requires for compliance (WHO 2011). For people with disabilities, *accessibility* is used more often in the context of the physical environment and less often in the context of information access and retrieval (Iwarsson & Stahl 2003). Since 2003, more legislation has been introduced in the United States to ensure full access to online information by people with disabilities.

As the Internet and its diversity of users continue to expand, the Internet's power as an educational and information-gathering tool will also grow (Pealer & Dorman 1997). Consequently, web surveys will be commonly used for data collection. What remains to be determined is whether people with disabilities will be proportionately represented in future iterations of the web revolution, and if they are, whether the full range of disabilities will be considered instead of only certain disability types or disabilities within certain demographic or socioeconomic subgroups. Ten years ago, in 2003, the American Academy of Physical Medicine and Rehabilitation posited that the technology available via the Internet had the potential to improve the quality of life of people with disabilities and to increase their participation in and integration into community activities. Inasmuch as people with disabilities and those in the disability field have never stopped advocating for inclusion in the new Internet communities, it is also important to examine who has social, technical, and legal responsibilities for these populations' web accessi.

Relevant social issues include the role of web accessibility in providing equal opportunities for people with disabilities, as well as issues (e.g., how the digital divide impacts older populations). For example, because a significant number of people develop disabilities later in life, persons with disabilities may be older than today's average Internet user. Therefore, as a matter of course, general surveys intended for older populations should be made accommodative to persons with disabilities. Although most issues of accessibility are applicable to people with and without disabilities, in developing ease-of-use components for web surveys, designers should be especially careful to consider the range of respondents' experiences with and uses of the Internet.

In terms of recruitment, persons with disabilities have been considered as rare or hard-to-reach populations (Burgstahler & Comden 1997). Still, simply uploading a survey to the web does not guarantee sufficient response. Surveys that specifically target persons with disabilities should avoid using gloomy or piteous language; instead, they should convey a accepting tone and use positive examples. In addition, positive feedback should be offered to respondents who complete surveys, as some might grow fatigued or have other issues with lengthy questionnaires (Mitchell et al. 2006). Comments such as "Your responses are very helpful to this study" can be made to appear at frequent intervals. Additionally, respondents should be allowed several sessions for completion, so that they can log off, return, sign in, and finish surveys at an individual pace. Reminders can be sent to those who elect not to complete an entire survey during a single session.

In their review of the implementation and results of three large-scale surveys done exclusively with people with disabilities, Mitchell et al. (2006) carefully planned and pretested modifications to the survey instruments and data collection procedures. Their intent was to remove barriers to participation that would affect this population. They recommended three guiding principles for the design of survey instruments: use simple but positive language; keep questions brief; and keep recall periods short. They also suggested that careful pretesting and review by experts who self report a disability are necessary to address the tremendous intra-group diversity within this population in terms of "disability types, severity and age, education and employment, living situation (e.g., in group homes, assisted living centers, nursing homes), and environmental supports" (p. 38).

24.3 Promoting Participation with Web Accessibility

The design of access forms is relevant to individuals with various disabilities such as sensory impairment, learning difficulties, cognitive limitations, limited movement, speech difficulties, and photosensitivity. These populations can benefit from, be disadvantaged by, or be excluded due to a web page's design[1] (Web Accessibility Initiative 2012). For example, people with manual repetitive stress injuries are faced with design barriers when an Internet is, or a software application is not, fully supported by spoken commands and instead requires them to use of a keyboard or mouse. Another barrier is posed when an online survey with a video clip or a podcast does not include captioning or sign language interpretation for respondents who are deaf (Web Accessibility Initiative 2012). These are just a few examples of how Internet survey designs can present barriers

[1] For details on web accessibility needs and barriers of people with different types of disabilities, see "How People with Disabilities Use the Web" at http://www.w3.org/WAI/intro/people-use-web/diversity

for people with disabilities, regardless of assistive technology. The main point is that these types of barriers can be ameliorated (National Council on Disability 2001).

An array of tools and assistive technologies are available to help people with disabilities access the Internet. However, "assistive technology alone cannot overcome the barriers that are created at a more basic level: the format in which content is presented" (Schmetzke 2003, p. 147). Therefore, in designing online survey instruments, Internet tools, applications, and software, it is important to consider the broad diversity of users' functional needs and to incorporate the necessary tools and technologies to fulfill them.

Over the past 25 years various laws have been enacted in the United States to mandate web accessibility for people with disabilities, as described below (Yu 2002).

- The *Americans with Disabilities Act (ADA) of 1990* is a sweeping piece of civil rights legislation that requires public entities and places of public accommodation to ensure that their services and communications are accessible to people with disabilities. Although the ADA does not specifically mention online surveys, numerous lawsuits regarding the accessibility of a range of websites and web-based services have been based on unequal access to online survey participation.
- The *Rehabilitation Act of 1973*, (as amended), introduced some of the first provisions requiring accessibility for people with disabilities. Section 504 requires U.S. federal agencies and some recipients of federal funding to ensure general accessibility and effective communications for people with disabilities. Section 508 adds specific requirements for federal agencies to make electronic information technologies accessible.
- The *Telecommunications Act of 1996* established new standards of information transmission that cover voice (telephone), video, and Internet communication services (Yu 2002).
- The *Web Accessibility Initiative (WAI)* was launched in 1997 by the World Wide Web Consortium (W3C) with endorsement by the U.S. government. The WAI brought together representatives from industry, disability organizations, government, and research labs around the world to develop guidelines and resources to help make the web accessible to people with disabilities (http://www.w3.org/WAI). In 1999, the release of Web Content Accessibility Guidelines (WCAG) 1.0 began to define technical and design guidelines for web content authors so that difficulties faced by users with disabilities could be minimized.

The specific requirements of these laws depend largely upon the nature of the organizations that enact them (e.g., whether they receive government funding or employ individuals with disabilities). Ultimately, organizations are responsible for deciding if and how accessibility laws apply to their particular businesses or services. WCAG specified 14 guidelines; which have been further divided into more than 60 compliance checkpoints. Each guideline has been assigned to one of three priority levels, priority 1 being the highest. In 2008, W3C released WCAG 2.0 and broadened the 1.0 guidelines. All of the guidelines are broadly grouped under four basic principles known as POUR, which stands for:

- *P*erceivable: Information and user interface components must be presented to users in ways they can sense and understand;
- *O*perable: User interface components and navigation must be doable;
- *U*nderstandable: Information and the operation of the user interface must be comprehensible; and
- *R*obust: Content must be sufficient to be interpreted reliably by a wide variety of users and agents, including assistive technologies.

POUR has been divided into 12 guidelines, which have in turn been divided into more than 60 specific points of compliance. The three levels of priority in version 1.0 have been replaced by levels A, AA, and AAA (Gottliebson et al. 2010).

Despite these laws, initiatives, and guidelines, there are still barriers that impede the implementation of a fully accessible Internet, including online surveys that are accessible to people with disabilities. In response to a reporter's question in April 2011 about its supposed "refusal" to include people with disabilities in its polling, the Pew Research Center (PRC) released this response (S. Keeter, email communication with author, February 21, 2013):

> It is not accurate to say that we refuse to include people with disabilities in our polling. We periodically ask about this in our surveys, so we know that our samples definitely include people with disabilities—at least as many as in government surveys ...
>
> However, it is also true that people with certain disabilities may not be able to take some of our surveys. For example, we do not include TDD or related technologies in our phone surveys. Known to be a nonpartisan, non-advocacy fact tank, PRC conducts research on a range of issues—politics, media, religion, technology and more. Technology use by people with chronic disease and disabilities has been part of our research on the social impact of the Internet since 2002. In fact, the most recent report by Fox (2012) was released in January, 2011, which highlights Internet access and use among people living with a disability (http://www.pewinternet.org/Reports/2011/Disability.aspx).

24.4 Testing the Accessibility of Some Web-Based Survey Tools

In his evaluation of the extent of such oversights, Ken Petri reported on August 13, 2012 that Survey Monkey is the most accessible online platform and the only one "where the survey creation process could be achieved relatively easily using a screen reader" (from http://webaim.org/discussion/mail_thread?thread=5445).

Alternatively, in November 2008, the Web Accessibility Center at Ohio State University (OSU; http://wac.osu.edu) assessed the degree to which online survey tools are accessible by keyboard alone and by a screen reader. This project compared six online tools (Survey Gizmo, Survey Monkey, Zoomerang, Checkbox, Lime Survey, and Snap Survey Professional Edition) and rated their relative levels of accessibility for users by assigning letter grades (A, B, C, D); a grade of "A" meant that the tool was fully accessible; "D" meant that the tool had severe access problems. The highest grade (B+) was awarded to Survey Gizmo for its screen reader and accessible keyboard. In 2003, the Great Lakes ADA Center in Chicago began to use Survey Gizmo. They found it to be the most robust and accessible tool, based on the OSU analysis as well as its own research. However, many of today's survey tools are generally more accessible than they were in 2008 (J. Peters, email communication with author, March 8, 2013).

A group of Australian researchers compared the accessibility and usability of 11 online survey tools, including Only a Survey, Our Web Survey, Question Pro, Survey Monkey, Survey Gizmo, Opinio (Gottliebson et al. 2010). The term *usability* refers to how well the design of the environment or service enables functioning, performance, and well-being, mainly from the user's perspective (Iwarsson & Stahl 2003). The Australian researchers found that while many of the online survey tools claimed to be accessible by users with disabilities (primarily sensory and physical disabilities) this was not the case. In fact, many users found insurmountable difficulties and could not complete the surveys.

In contrast to the OSU survey, Gottliebson and colleagues (2010) found that Survey Monkey struck a reasonable compromise between accessibility and functionality and complied with most points that were examined in this assessment, although screen reader users still reported some usability issues. The researchers concluded that the voices of a large proportion of people living with disabilities are absent from the data collected by online surveys, and also that current accessibility guidelines, even when they are implemented according to laws and guidelines, continue to fall short of ensuring usable survey tools.

These findings highlight the need to lessen the gap between legislative directives and the implementation of standards for web accessibility, particularly online survey tool accessibility and usage. This need can be addressed through a range of approaches that includes raising public awareness, targeted training, government monitoring, mandatory reporting protocols, and technical support (WHO 2011, Yu 2002). Accessible online survey tools should meet the varied needs of people with disabilities. On the basis of the preceding literature review, we have produced a list of recommendations that should be considered when developing an accessible online survey (Table 24.1).

The new definition of *disability* framed by the International Classification of Functioning, Disability and Health (ICF) views disability as a contextual variable, meaning that it is dynamic over time and in relation to circumstances (WHO 2011). The ICF provides a platform that supports universal design as an international priority for reducing the experience of disability and enhancing everyone's experience and performance. This concept of universal design calls for all products

TABLE 24.1 Recommendations for Developing an Accessible Online Survey

Recommendation	Description
Font size and color	Users must be able to enlarge the font size, change the font colors, and use contrasting font colors to adapt survey questions to their needs. These changes should not affect the survey interface.
Keyboard input	Users with physical or motor disabilities may not be able to use a mouse to complete an online survey. To be fully accessible, a survey should not rely only on the mouse but should provide all functionality via a keyboard and/or voice-activated commands.
Logical page organization	Survey questions should be organized in an order that seems logical to users with intellectual or cognitive disabilities. Including a scale that demonstrates the progress users are making through the surveys (i.e., a progress indicator) is also recommended.
Use of images	When for users with visual disabilities, images that might not be presentable by screen readers should be avoided. If images are needed to make the survey accessible for users with intellectual or cognitive disabilities or hearing impairments, developers should consider providing accurate alternative text descriptions for images (in simplified text). When equivalent alternative text is provided, the information is available to everyone.
Text-to-speech	Accessible surveys should include a text-to-speech function (i.e., an automatic screen reader with adjustable volume) that reads the survey content. This would serve users with visual or intellectual disabilities.
Testing	It is important to have people with disabilities test the survey and participate in its design.

and services to be contrived so that all people, including those with disabilities, can use them (Iwarsson & Stahl 2003).

Gottliebson et al. (2010) have presented an inclusive approach for designing online surveys in which they suggest that rather than creating a single "compromise" page for the sake of accessibility, web designers should create single, richly functional pages with complex layouts, and leave issues of accessibility adaptation to the web server. With this approach, selective adaptations would become the norm. For example, a visually impaired user could access a page that displays with a simplified layout and larger text and a user who is sighted but cannot use a mouse could access a page that is graphically rich and can be navigated with clearly marked, keyboard-accessible alternatives. Users with different types of disabilities could be accommodated with an extension to the way the pages are created that ensures adequate separation between design layout and content (text and graphics).

24.5 Ensuring Web Accessibility at Various Levels of Disability

Obviously, not every disability affects a person's ability to surf the Internet or complete an online survey. For example, a sighted non-quadriplegic person who uses a wheelchair to ambulate is not likely to have any difficulty filling out an online survey. For someone who has limited vision, however, completing an online survey may require magnifying text or changing text and background colors; someone who is blind may need survey questions and answer options read aloud; and someone who has difficulty using his or her hands may require a way to provide answers via voice. From a practical standpoint, we can group people with disabilities into several broad categories based on their online accessibility needs. These categories include people:

- with low vision
- who are blind
- who have limited use of their hands
- who are hard of hearing or deaf
- who have learning or cognitive disabilities

Specific characteristics and needs of people in these categories are considered below. It should be noted that the information in this section was obtained from WAI (www.W3.org/WAI), a group dedicated to making the Internet accessible to everyone.

24.5.1 PEOPLE WITH LOW VISION

Low vision includes any visual impairment short of total blindness. It may involve limitations in field of view, such as blind spots and tunnel vision, and can include a wide range of color perception deficits, including color blindness. It may be caused by a range of conditions including cataracts, diabetic retinopathy, glaucoma, macular degeneration, and retinitis pigmentosa, or simply by advancing age. Regardless of the condition or cause, the key characteristic of individuals in this category is that they have a visual loss but are still primarily using their vision to read printed or on-screen information.

People with low vision must magnify and/or change the colors of text and images displayed on a page or screen. A number of computer-based tools are available to assist them, including:

- Text-size settings built into computer operating systems and programs (e.g., Microsoft Word's "enlarge font") and, web browsers (e.g., Internet Explorer's "Zoom" setting, and Safari's "Zoom In" option).
- Simple magnification options included in computer operating systems, such as Windows' Magnifier and Apple Mac's Zoom.

- Powerful screen magnifier programs that can enlarge all or part of the screen, change colors, increase contrast, and more, such as Ai Squared's ZoomText and Freedom Scientific's MAGic.

From an accessibility perspective, the key to accommodating the needs of people with low vision is realizing that using one of these tools may display a survey differently from the way it was designed. In such cases, the goal is to ensure that the survey remains usable when text size is increased and contrast and/or color are changed.

24.5.2 PEOPLE WHO ARE BLIND

In this chapter, the term *blindness* includes any visual impairment that renders vision impossible or impractical. Individuals who are blind may in fact have a fair amount of vision but are unable to effectively read printed and on-screen information even with magnification. People who are blind rely on specialized software to interpret the information displayed on a computer screen and translate it to speech or Braille. The main tools that enable these tasks include:

- Screen reader programs that monitor the information displayed on computer screens and recite it aloud using computer-synthesized speech. Such products include free open-source software, Freedom Scientific's JAWS, GW Micro's Window-Eyes, NVDA (Non-Visual Desktop Access) for Windows, and Apple's "VoiceOver" (a screen reader built into Apple's Mac OS, iOS, and iPod operating systems).
- Refreshable Braille devices that use arrays of movable plastic pins to translate onscreen text into Braille that users can read by touch. Such devices include HumanWare's ALVA and Focus from Freedom Scientific.

Screen readers and refreshable Braille devices are truly remarkable technologies that enable individuals who are blind to read information from a computer screen efficiently and effectively. However, these assistive technologies are among the most difficult to adjust for the purposes of accommodation because they rely on web page codes to present information in a meaningful way. Some of the key abilities of screen readers are:

- *Provision of text alternatives* for images, figures, maps, diagrams, videos, and other nontext graphical elements so that a screen reader can interpret them. HTML, the web's programming language, offers a number of ways to provide text by screen readers.
- *Identification of structure and semantics*. Screen readers have to do more than just read the text; among other tasks, they must identify headlines, parts of a list, and cells in a table. For surveys, they must also be able to indicate which text is a question and where to type the answer. Again, HTML, the web's

"native" language, can provide all this behind-the-scenes information, but a survey has to implement it.

- *Support of standard keyboard commands.* Because individuals who are blind cannot see a mouse pointer moving on a computer screen, they cannot make use of a mouse. However, screen reader users can interact with web pages and online surveys using only keyboard commands. Most computer operating systems and web browsers facilitate this option by programming standard keyboard commands; for example, the tab key can be used to move among questions in a form and the up/down arrows to move among choices in a list. A survey, however, must be specifically programmed to work with these standard commands.

24.5.3 PEOPLE WITH LIMITED USE OF THEIR HANDS

A wide range of conditions can limit an individual's ability to use his or her hands, from arthritis and carpal tunnel syndrome to cerebral palsy, stroke, multiple sclerosis, amyotrophic lateral sclerosis, quadriplegia, and amputation. Clearly, any disability that affects the hands will make it difficult to respond to surveys using a computer. Even a mild impairment of fine motor control can make it virtually impossible to point, click, and drag a computer mouse.

Fortunately, a wide range of devices are available to replace computer keyboards and mouses:

- Alternate mouse devices can be operated by fingers, palms, feet, and even eyes.
- Onscreen keyboards, such as those available for Windows and Mac OS, enable mouse users to type letters by pointing and clicking on a picture of a keyboard on the screen.
- Keyboard commands can enable, for example, the tab key to move between questions and the up/down arrows to select options.
- Alternate keyboards have been enlarged or reduced to accommodate individual needs.
- Speech recognition software, such as Nuance's Dragon NaturallySpeaking, can control computer functions by voice alone and allow voice-dictation of text.

The key principle in accommodating individuals who use any of these devices is to ensure that a survey is "device independent," meaning that it can be accessed and used either by keyboard or by mouse alone. In order to create such surveys, designers must build pages around the U.S. Rehabilitation Act Section 508 standards. The Section 508 website (http://www.section508.gov) contains links to specialized trainings in both accessible web design and accessible software design. For those who are less design-savvy, software programs such as Survey Monkey offer templates that are compliant with Section 508 (www.help.surveymonkey.com).

24.5.4 PEOPLE WHO ARE HARD OF HEARING OR DEAF

Hearing loss can vary from mild to profound. In most cases, hearing impairment may not affect a person's his or her ability to complete self-administered questionnaires on paper or online. However, the increasing use of multimedia on the web can pose problems for deaf and hearing-impaired individuals. Surveys that incorporate audio or video in questions, instructions, and/or supporting materials must be modified (if they are not already) to accommodate the needs of people who are hard of hearing or deaf. The primary means of accommodation is to provide the equivalent information as text or via TTY machines (see Wilson et al. 1998, for details of TTY usage). Text transcripts usually suffice for audio clips but for video that contains speech, synchronized captions must be provided. Although, the specific techniques for providing these accommodations are outside the scope of this chapter, it is easy enough to determine whether they are needed and if they are being provided.

Margellos-Anast and colleagues (2005) have found that deaf individuals who primarily communicate via American Sign Language (ASL) are excluded from health surveys due to limited literacy skills (English reading and writing skills), that is, they may not be able to fully comprehend the written health information they encounter in their doctors' offices or the captioning for health-related programs that appear on television. Such situations may lead to significant gaps in knowledge about important area of knowledge, including health, healthy living, and how to negotiate their role as patients within the health care system. In response to this challenge, the authors have developed an accessible and standardized interview tool administered in ASL for deaf individuals. Although the developed survey was conducted in face-to-face settings, it promotes our understanding of the online needs of deaf users who might have difficulties with written language. In such cases, video clips using a visual–manual (i.e., sign) language such as ASL can make communication and participation accessible for this population.

24.5.5 PEOPLE WITH LEARNING OR COGNITIVE DISABILITIES.

This is by far the largest category of disability; it includes more people than all the previous categories combined. Unfortunately, the specific needs of this population and the means of accommodating the wide range of their disabilities are also the least well understood. It is well known, however, that people with learning disabilities, including dyslexia and ADD may have some of the same needs as the other disability categories. For example, someone with dyslexia may use reading software to read a survey aloud, and someone with ADD may benefit by being able to customize colors displayed on a screen.

Some cases may require a caregiver to act as proxy for the participant and answer the survey questions for him or her. This option has been generally accepted for participants with certain cognitive impairments or intellectual disabilities, but it must be noted that it may introduce considerable error into a study (Todorov & Kirschner 2000). For example, it has been shown that proxies consistently underreport disabilities pertaining to activities of daily living if the participant is between 18 and 65 years of age, but overreport the disability if the participant is over 65 years (Todorov & Kirchner 2000).

Underreporting may be corrected, at least to an extent, by assessing participants' agreements with their proxies. Determining whether a proxy survey is appropriate probably depends in large part on the ability of the participant to interact directly with the interviewer, as well as the nature of the subject matter (Parsons et al. 2000). Considering the high likelihood of flaws when the proxy method is used, researchers should determine its necessity on a case-by-case basis. For additional discussion of this topic, see also Chapter 14.

Beyond the techniques described above, survey designers can help accommodate people with learning or cognitive disabilities by avoiding unnecessary distractions, such as gratuitous graphics and animations, and by keeping survey designs and language as clear, concise, and simple as possible.

24.6 Problems Posed By Inaccessible Web-Based Surveys for People with Disabilities

To delineate the impact that lack of accessibility can have on a person with a disability, the following examples describe some experiences of people attempting to complete an inaccessible online survey.

> *Jae, who has low vision.* Jae has retinitis pigmentosa. He is 30 years old and the condition is not yet severe. He has increased the size of text on his computer to 150% and switched to a white-on-black color scheme to reduce the effects of glare. While filling out an online survey, Jae notices that some of the text is overlapping and running off the edge of the screen. He has little difficulty seeing the text and thinks he can figure out the parts he cannot see. He comes to the last page, which contains some demographic questions. The instructions at the top of the page indicate that only the questions highlighted in red are required. He scans down the page, but everything is white on black.
>
> *Ki, who is blind.* Ki has been blind from birth and is a proficient user of screen readers. She is asked to complete a survey on the web, easily browses to the survey page, reads the instructions using her screen reader, and begins the survey. When she gets to the first question, her screen reader says, "Edit box." She tries again and hears the same message. Not sure what to enter, she moves on. The next question reads, "One, radio button, checked." She presses the down arrow key and hears, "Two, radio button, checked" and so on through "Five, radio button, checked." Having no idea what the survey is asking for or telling her, she closes her web browser and gives up.

John, who has limited hand use. John has a mild hand tremor that makes it difficult to use a regular mouse. He has a trackball but prefers to use keyboard commands to operate his computer. While filling out an online survey, he successfully uses the tab key to move from question to question and the down arrow to select answers from drop-down lists. He encounters a new question that asks him to rate the strength of his opinion using a slider, but nothing happens when he presses the tab key to get to the slider. He tries pressing the right and left arrow keys to select a value, but again nothing happens. Nonetheless, he tries both approaches several times. Eventually, he does his best to use his trackball, but positioning the arrow on the small control box while simultaneously holding a button and rolling the ball proves to be too frustrating. He leaves the question set to a value he did not choose, and abandons the questionnaire.

Hugo, who has a learning disability. Although Hugo has dyslexia and attention deficit disorder, he has learned coping strategies and has been successful at both school and work. He is asked to complete an online survey as part of a college research project. When he gets to the survey website, he discovers that the instructions are five pages long. He skims the beginning and quickly skips ahead to the survey. The survey questions are not only wordy and hard to understand, they also jump back and forth between topics in no apparent order. Hugo is additionally distracted by an animation of a pencil scribbling on a piece of paper that appears to the right of each question. Hugo rushes though the remainder of the survey without caring if he has answered completely or correctly.

The next section examines how survey designers can evaluate whether they have addressed these technical components for users with disabilities.

24.7 Applications: How to Ensure that Web-Based Surveys are Accessible

The frustrations and failings described in the previous section can and should be avoided. How to do so, however, involves a depth of technical detail that is likely to go beyond the scope of what most readers will ever need or be asked to do. Our goal in this section, therefore, is to help readers ask the right questions and communicate intelligently with computer experts and programmers, who will do the actual work of ensuring that your online surveys are accessible to users with disabilities.

24.7.1 ACCESSIBILITY STANDARDS

The most basic answer to the question, "How do we make online surveys accessible?" is "Follow the standards." In other words, pay close attention to the technical guidelines that tell programmers what they need to know in order to ensure that their software, websites, and online forms, including questionnaires, are accessible. As described in Section 24.3, two sets of standards are widely accepted and used: The WCAG 2.0, developed and published by W3C, and Section 508 of the U.S. Rehabilitation Act.

Both sets of standards, which overlap are intended to achieve the same end—accessibility for persons with disabilities—and they overlap. The choice of which set to use when developing an online survey depends mainly on the organization that is developing it or for which it is being developed. If it is being developed for a U.S. government entity, it must comply with Section 508. If it is not, a choice must be made; as of early 2014, the WCAG 2.0 is probably the better option because the Section 508 standard is undergoing revision. Either way, determining which set of accessibility standards to follow is less important than ensuring accessibility standards have been taken into consideration and systematically implemented.

24.7.2 QUESTIONS TO ASK

The most important ways to ensure that an online survey tool is accessible are: (i) Ask the right questions of the person or team programming the survey; and (ii) Make sure that the survey tool has the capacities to program and build the survey. It is also critical to ask about accessibility *before* committing to use a particular company or tool. Asking these questions first makes it easier to determine which company or tool to use.

1. *Check the relevant websites for accessibility information.* Look for information about accessibility in the company's list of product features. If nothing prominent appears, use the site's search tool to search for the terms *accessibility*, *disability*, and *Section 508*. Look for statements showing that the company is committed to making their surveys accessible to people with disabilities and find out what steps they have taken to accomplish this goal. There are no guarantees but the more information about accessibility you find on a company's website, the more likely it is that you will be able to use their products or tools to construct an accessible survey.
2. *Ask which accessibility standards the firm adheres to.* If this information is not on their website, call or e-contact the company and ask which accessibility standards their surveys can incorporate. Ideally, they will answer with one of the two standards mentioned earlier: W3C's WCAG or Section 508 of the Rehabilitation Act. If they do not answer, or do not mention one of these standards by name, be wary.
3. *Ask if, when, and how the firm's accessibility tools/programs have been tested.* The answer may be that they use an automated accessibility testing tool, such as the University of Illinois' Functional Accessibility Evaluator (FAE), WebAIM's WAVE, or another commercial accessibility testing tool. Ideally, testing has also been done by accessibility experts and/or people with disabilities.

4. *If you receive positive responses to the above questions, ask if any special instructions or additional steps are necessary* to develop an accessible survey using their tool. For example, is additional information needed to enter or are there certain types of questions that must be avoided? Special steps may not be necessary, but if any are, it is important to know about them up front.

24.7.3 TESTS TO EVALUATE ACCESSIBILITY OF A SURVEY TOOL

As a final step in evaluating the accessibility of a survey tool that you are considering, a good practice is to create a sample survey that researchers can personally test. Although researchers should not attempt to test a survey with a screen reader or speech recognition software if they are not already proficient in their use, the simple tests outlined below can help identify some obvious accessibility errors.

- *Text size.* As discussed earlier, some users with low vision rely on text-size settings built into computer operating systems and/or web browsers. Researchers can easily test whether these tools will work for users by activating certain settings in their own browsers:
  For Internet Explorer, open the Page menu, pick Zoom, and set it to 150% or 200%. For Safari, open its Page menu, and click Zoom In two or three times. Once the text size has been increased, researchers can go through the survey and make sure that no text disappears, overlaps, or runs off the page.
- *High contrast.* Just as users can increase text size in a web browser, researchers can try a high contrast color scheme. This strategy makes text more legible for visually impaired users.
  In Windows 7, right click on the desktop, and choose Personalize. Next, scroll down to the Basic and High Contrast Themes, and click on High Contrast Black. As Windows 8 becomes more widely used, it will be updated to include assistive technologies optimized for touch-enabled devices. The most important changes involve the adoption of industry standards, including those from the WAI, Accessible Rich Internet Applications, HTML5, and XAML.
  In Mac OS X, open System Preferences, choose Universal Access, and click White on Black. When the colors have been set to white-on-black, test the survey to make sure that everything is still visible and that there is no important text that cannot be seen.
- *Keyboard operation.* Optimal keyboard operability is a key principle in ensuring accessibility for blind or visually impaired users and for users who have limited use of their hands. Researchers can test directly for operability with the same techniques a person with a disability would use:
  Start by setting the mouse aside, preferably out of reach. Complete the survey using the following keyboard commands:
- Press the tab key (Option + Tab in Safari) to move from one form field to the next.

- Use the up and down arrows to select options in list boxes, drop-down lists, or radio button groups.
- Use the space bar to check and uncheck check boxes and to click buttons.
- Ensure that every question can be answered and the survey can be completed without touching the mouse.

Testing a survey in these ways will provide some sense of how it will work for users with disabilities. If a researcher has problems completing the survey while performing these tests, inform the survey tool company, and negotiate with them about how they can correct the issue.

24.8 Summary and Conclusions

24.8.1 OVERVIEW OF SURVEY PLATFORMS AND CURRENT PRACTICES

Surprisingly little research has been done on efforts to make surveys more accessible for people with disabilities through the use of assistive technologies. Such efforts seem to take one of two forms: some try to change the way the survey is administered by using a model that is more inclusive, whereas others rely on the possibility that people with disabilities have the technology they need to translate the survey into something they can work with. Although the latter is more common, evidence demonstrates that both are necessary to resolve the problem of accessibility (Gottliebson et al. 2010).

Despite this lack of research, today's rapidly evolving assistive technologies enable people with disabilities to achieve greater inclusion. They allow those with disabilities to translate information from a sense they do not possess to a sense they do possess. Visual inputs can be changed to auditory inputs through screen-reading software or text that can be enlarged through screen-magnifying software; audio data can appear as visual data through transcription software; and visual as well as audio data can become tactile through refreshable Braille devices. Overall, there are many ways for willing participants to achieve greater inclusion (www.w3.org/WAI/). Ideally, these home devices can open doors for people with disabilities to participate more effectively in online survey research, where they can express their unique needs and views both individually and collectively. In reality, however, significant barriers remain.

The W3C and WCAG standards for making web content accessible to everyone provide the tools to build websites and surveys that flow seamlessly with all the assistive technologies currently in use by people with disabilities. The problem is that very few researchers are choosing to follow the guidelines. When Gottliebson et al. (2010) assessed 11 popular online survey engines for compliance with WCAG and general practical accessibility, only one was found to reliably translate survey questions to a screen-reading software program without difficulty. The rest, despite their claims of screen-reader accessibility, had varying degrees of noncompliance and were difficult to navigate with assistive technologies.

In most cases, noncompliance was due to complex layouts and heavy reliance on JavaScript, an ubiquitous software that adds cosmetic flair to websites and applications. Although interfacing seamlessly with various assistive technologies might cost a survey designer some cosmetic appeal, it could also grant access to vast numbers of people with disabilities. When Gottliebson's research team tested WCAG by using them to create a survey system entitled "The Equipment Survey," they found that by following the guidelines they were able to create a survey that the screen reader could interpret with ease.

24.8.2 CONCLUSION

The responsibility for including people with disabilities in surveys is shared by the survey designer, who must comply with the necessary code to make surveys accessible to a diverse group of users, and with users themselves, who must obtain the necessary devices to translate text from the senses they do not have into the senses they do have. The technologies to do all of these things are in place. It is simply researchers' willingness to comply (or not) that keeps surveys from finding disabled community, and users vice versa. Survey researchers and web designers must be educated on the needs of disabled population for inclusion and on the appropriate methods to make their work accessible to the disabled community.

REFERENCES

American Academy of Physical Medicine and Rehabilitation. 2003. Access to assistive technologies. Retrieved from http://www.aapmr.org/hpl/legislation/AT03.htm

Bargh JA, McKenna KYA. The Internet and social life. Annu Rev Psychol 2004;55:573–590. DOI: 10.1146/annurev.psych.55.090902.141922.

Barnett S, Franks P. Telephone ownership and deaf people: implications for telephone surveys. Am J Public Health 1999;89(11):1754–1756.

Bowker NI, Tuffin K. Understanding positive subjectives made possible online for disabled people. New Zeal J Psychol 2007;36(2):63–71.

Bowling A. Mode of questionnaire administration can have serious effects on data quality. J Public Health 2005;27(3):281–291.

Braithwaite DO, Waldron VR, Finn J. Communications of social support in computer-mediated media for people with disabilities. Health Commun 1999;11(2): 123–151 EASI http://people.rit.edu/easi/index.htm.

Burgstahler S, Comden D. World wide access: focus on libraries. J Inf Tech Disabilities 1997;4(1–2http://staff.washington.edu/sherylb/fol.html. Accessed 2014 Jun 06.).

Chicago Community Trust. 2010. A quest for equality: breaking the barriers for people with disabilities. Retrieved from http://www.cct.org/impact/partnerships-initiatives/strengthening-communities/persons-with-disabilities/quest-for-equality. Accessed 2014 Jun 06.

Comden D, Burgstahler S. 2012. World wide access: accessible Web design. Retrieved from http://www.washington.edu/doit/Brochures/PDF/universal.design.pdf. Accessed 2014 Jun 06.

Cook JA, Grey DD, Fitzgibbon G, Batteiger D, Caras S, Dansky H, Priester F. Challenges in defining respondent populations in a Web survey of individuals with psychiatric disabilities. In: Kroll T, Keer D, Placek P, Cyril J, editors. *Towards Best Practices for Surveying People with Disabilities*. Vol. 1. New York: Nova Science; 2007.

Day HY, Campbell KA. Is telephone assessment a valid tool in rehabilitation research and practice? Disabil Rehabil 2003;25(19):1126–1131.

Fenig S, Levav I, Kohn R, Yelin N. Telephone vs. face-to-face interviewing in a community psychiatric survey. Am J Public Health 1993;83(6):896–898.

Finn J, Holden G. *Human services online: A new arena for service delivery*. New York: Haworth; 2000.

Flowers CP, Bray M, Algozzine RF. Accessibility of special education program home pages. J Spec Educ Tech 1999;14(2):21–26.

Fox S. 2011a. Americans living with disability and their technology profile. The Pew Research Center's Internet & American Life Project. Retrieved from http://www.pewinternet.org/Reports/2011/Disability.aspx. Accessed 2014 Jun 06.

Fox S. 2011b. Americans living with disability and their technology profile. Pew Internet & American Life Project. Retrieved from http://www.pewinternet.org/~/media//Files/Reports/2011/PIP_Disability.pdf. Accessed 2014 Jun 06.

Gibson J, Pennington R, Stenhoff D, Hopper J. Using desktop videoconferencing to deliver interventions to a preschool student with autism. Top Early Child Spec 2010;29(4):214–225.

Gottliebson D, Layton N, Wilson E. Comparative effectiveness report: Online survey tools. Disabil Rehabil Assist Technol 2010;5(6):401–410.

Irwin MM, Gerke JD. Web-based information and prospective students with disabilities: a study of liberal arts colleges. Educause Q 2004;4:51–59.

Iwarsson S, Stahl A. Accessibility, usability, and universal design: Positioning and definition of concepts describing person-environment relationships. Disabil Rehabil 2003;25(2):57–66. DOI: 10.1080/0963828021000007969.

Keer D. Best practices for surveying people with disabilities: an introduction. In: Kroll T, Keer D, Placek P, Cyril J, editors. *Towards Best Practices for Surveying People with Disabilities*. Vol. 1. New York: Nova Science; 2007.

Kroll T, Keer D, Placek P, Cyril J. *Towards Best Practices For Surveying People with Disabilities*. Vol. 1. New York: Nova Science; 2007.

Margellos-Anast H, Hedding T, Perlman T, Miller L, Rodgers R, Kivland L, DeGutis D, Giloth BE, Whitman S. Developing a standardized comprehensive health survey for use with deaf adults. Am Ann Deaf 2005;150(4):388–396.

Mitchell S, Ciemnecki A, CyBulski K, Markesich J. *Removing Barriers to Survey Participation for Persons with Disabilities*. Washington, DC: Mathematica Policy Research; 2006.

Mitchel W, Sloper P. Making choices in my life: listening to the ideas and experiences of young people in the UK who communicate non-verbally. Child Youth Serv Rev 2011;33:521–527.

National Council on Disability. 2001. The accessible future. Retrieved from http://www.ncd.gov/publications/2001/June_2001. Accessed 2014 Jun 06.

National Institute on Disability & Rehabilitation Research. 2009. Disability statistics: online resource for U.S. disability statistics. http://www.disabilitystatistics.org/reports/acs.cfm. Accessed 2014 Jun 06.

Parsons JA, Baum S, Johnson TP. 2000. Inclusion of disabled populations in social surveys: review and recommendations. Retrieved from http://www.srl.uic.edu/Publist/StdyRpts/838disability/DisabledPops.pdf. Accessed 2014 Jun 06.

Pealer LN, Dorman SM. Evaluating health-related web sites. J School Health 1997;67(6):232–235.

Pendergrass S, Nosek MA, Holcomb JD. Design and evaluation of an Internet site to educate women with disabilities on reproductive health care. Sex Disabil 2001;19(1):71–83.

Rhodes SD, Bowie DA, Hergenrather KC. Collecting behavioral data using the World Wide Web: considerations for researchers. J Epidemiol Community Health 2003;57:68–73.

Schmetzke A. Web accessibility at university libraries and library schools: 2002 follow-up study. In: Hricko M, editor. *Design and Implementation of Web-Enabled Teaching Tools*. Hershey, PA: Information Science; 2003. p 145–186.

Stern SM. n.d. Counting people with disabilities: how survey methodology influences estimates in Census 2000 and the Census 2000 Supplementary Survey. Retrieved from https://www.census.gov/people/disability/files/finalstern.pdf. Accessed 2014 Jun 06.

Todorov A, Kirchner C. Bias in proxies' reports of disability: data from the National Health Interview Survey on Disability. Am J Public Health 2000;90(8):1248–1253.

U.S. Census Bureau. 2010. Disability.http://www.census.gov/hhes/www/disability/sipp/disable05.html. Accessed 2014 Jun 06.

U.S. Census Bureau. 0000a Survey methodology. Retrieved from http://www.census.gov/acs/www/methodology/methodology_main/. Accessed 2014 Jun 06.

Web Accessibility Initiative. 0000 Retrieved from http://www.w3.org/WAI/. Accessed 2014 Jun 06.

Web Accessibility Initiative. 2012. How people with disabilities use the web. Retrieved from http://www.w3.org/WAI/EO/Drafts/PWD-

Wilson BF, Senda B, Whitaker K, Beatty P, Hendershot G. (May, 1998) Improving the feasibility of including deaf respondents in telephone surveys. Paper presented at the Annual Conference of the American Association for Public Opinion Research, St. Louis, MO.

Wright D, Sloan M, Barrett K. *Is There a Trade-Off between Quality and Cost? Telephone Versus Face-to-Face Interviewing of Persons with Disabilities*. Washington, DC: Mathematica Policy Research; 2012.

Vicentea MR, Lópeza AJ. A multidimensional analysis of the disability digital divide: some evidence for Internet use. Inform Soc 2010;26:48–64. DOI: 10.1080/01615440903423245.

World Health Organization. *World Report on Disability*. Geneva: World Health Organization; 2011.

Yu H. Web accessibility and the law: recommendations for implementation. Library High Tech 2002;20(4):406–419. DOI: 10.1108/07378830210452613abstract.

ONLINE RESOURCES

The Americans with Disabilities Act of 1990 provides information and technical assistance. As one of America's most comprehensive pieces of civil rights legislation, the ADA prohibits discrimination and guarantees that people with disabilities have the same opportunities as everyone else to participate in the mainstream of American life. www.usdoj.gov/crt/ada/adahom1.htm.

Access Web provides a variety of resources that serve as good starting points for anyone interested in learning more about web accessibility. www.washington.edu/doit/Resources/accessweb.html.

EASI (Equal Access to Software and Information) is the premier provider of online training on accessible information technology for people with disabilities. http://people.rit.edu/easi/index.htm.

Electronic and Information Technology Accessibility Standards (Section 508) provide standards issued under Section 508 of the Rehabilitation Act cover access to electronic and information technology procured by federal agencies. www.access-board.gov/sec508/standards.htm.

The International Center for Disability Resources on the Internet includes a knowledge base of quality disability resources and best practices and provides education, outreach and training based on these core resources. www.icdri.org/.

The National Center for Accessible Media (NCAM) resources is a nonprofit R&D organization dedicated to achieving media access equality for people with disabilities. http://ncam.wgbh.org/.

The National Center on Accessible Information Technology in Education (AccessIT) promotes the use of electronic and information technology (E&IT) for students and employees with disabilities in educational institutions at all academic levels. This website features the AccessIT Knowledge Base, a searchable database of questions and answers about accessible E&IT. It is designed for educators, policy makers, librarians, technical support staff, students and employees with disabilities, and their advocates. www.washington.edu/accessit/.

The Rehabilitation Act of 1973 (amended) empowered individuals with disabilities to maximize employment, economic self-sufficiency, independence, and inclusion and integration into society through research, training, guarantees of equal opportunity, and so forth. www.access-board.gov/enforcement/rehab-act-text/intro.htm.

Section 508 Standards requires that when federal agencies develop, procure, maintain, and use electronic and information technology, federal employees with disabilities must have access to and use of information and data that is comparable to the access and use by federal employees who are not individuals with disabilities, unless an undue burden would be imposed on the agency. www.section508.gov/index.cfm?fuseAction=stdsdoc.

Surveying Persons with Disabilities: A Source Guide, Version II (2008). Princeton, NJ: Mathematica Policy Research, October 2008, Jason Markesich. Document

No. PR08-48, 229 pp. In an effort to provide the public with an up-to-date and easily accessible source of research on the methodological issues associated with surveying persons with disabilities, Mathematica Policy Research, Inc. has prepared a source guide of material related to this topic. www.mathematica-mpr.com/publications/PDFs/surveypersons_ver2.pdf.

Trace Research and Development Center is a part of the College of Engineering, University of Wisconsin-Madison. A pioneer in the field of technology and disability, Trace developed the first set of accessibility guidelines for web content as well as the Unified Web Access Guidelines, which became the basis for the World Wide Web Consortium's Web Content Accessibility Guidelines 1.0. http://trace.wisc.edu/.

Universal Design: Principles, Process, and Applications. Universal Design (UD) "is the design of products and environments to be usable by all people, to the greatest extent possible, without the need for adaptation or specialized design." When UD principles are applied, products and environments meet the needs of potential users with a wide variety of characteristics. UD resources are available at: www.washington.edu/doit/Brochures/Programs/ud.html.

W3C's Web Accessibility Initiative (WAI) develops guidelines that widely regarded as the international standard for web accessibility and offers support materials to help understand and implement web accessibility. http://www.w3.org/WAI/.

Web Accessibility in Mind (WebAIM) offers complete web accessibility services. They specialize in developing and retrofitting web content for accessibility; their accessibility approach empowers clients to maintain accessibility into the future. http://webaim.org/.

Web Content Accessibility Guidelines (WCAG) 2.0 cover a wide range of recommendations for making web content more accessible. Following these guidelines will make content accessible to a wider range of people with disabilities, including blindness and low vision, deafness and hearing loss, learning disabilities, cognitive limitations, limited movement, speech disabilities, photosensitivity, and combinations of these conditions. www.w3.org/TR/WCAG/.

PART FIVE

Data Management and Analysis

CHAPTER TWENTY FIVE

Assessing the Quality of Health Survey Data Through Modern Test Theory

Adam C. Carle
University of Cincinnati, Cincinnati, OH, USA

25.1 Introduction

Health surveys frequently rely on fallible self-report data. Participants report on their own health, health-related outcomes, environment, and experiences (hereafter collectively called health outcomes). Thus, health surveys typically only indirectly measure health outcomes. Additionally, health surveys often ask a set of questions about health outcomes with the intention of aggregating responses to the questions into a single descriptor of an individual's health (i.e., a score). Both these situations lead to challenges.

As one challenge, surveys frequently use sets of questions to measure one or more latent (indirectly observed) constructs. With respect to each construct, a single summary score of responses often serves as an estimate of the construct. However, the possibility exists that, although a survey's developers intended a set of questions to measure a single (unidimensional) construct, the questions may seem to measure more than one construct (multidimensionality). If this occurs, the measure lacks internal validity. The questions do not measure the construct of interest as expected. And (depending on the type of multidimensionality), one should not create a single score from the responses. It may make more sense to

Handbook of Health Survey Methods, First Edition. Edited by Timothy P. Johnson.

create several scores from the questions. Health survey research too infrequently addresses this possibility and rarely describes methods for assessing it. This leaves unaddressed whether scores derived from health surveys validly measure health outcomes.

As another challenge, even when a measure's dimensionality does not differ from *a priori* expectations, the possibility exists that participants respond to questions about themselves differently depending on their social and economic (SES) backgrounds or other variables. This possibility, a form of systematic measurement error often labeled differential item functioning (DIF) or measurement bias, refers to the fact that two individuals with an identical underlying health outcome status may nevertheless respond to questions asking about their health differently. This may occur because of cultural differences in differential perceptions of the questions. Among other complexities, this leads to the possibility that observed health outcome disparities may reflect measurement bias rather than true differences. Yet, health survey research has not adequately acknowledged this challenge or adopted methods to evaluate and mitigate it. This leaves unclear whether the results of health surveys across subpopulations reflect true differences or systematic measurement error.

When survey research has addressed these issues (which is rarely), it has tended to use the more traditional measurement approach of classical test theory (Carle et al. 2011a). Classical test theory (also labeled true score theory) considers responses to questions as consisting of an individual's true level on the variable the question measures and random measurement error. Classical test theory has a long history and has led to statistics with which many readers are likely familiar, like Chronbach's Alpha. However, classical test theory has limits. For example, it treats reliability as a constant and does not allow for the possibility that some questions may provide more reliable measurement at higher (or lower) health outcome levels (Embretson and Reise 2000). Classical test theory's approaches to measurement bias also suffer from theoretical limitations (Millsap 2011). And, classical test theory does not well address issues of dimensionality (Bollen 1989). Modern test theory overcomes many of these problems.

Modern test theory, which includes item response theory (IRT), confirmatory factor analysis (CFA), and structural equation modeling (SEM)-based models (e.g., multiple group (MG) multiple cause multiple indicator (MIMIC)), offers a powerful set of tools that can tackle the challenges identified above. Each uses mathematical measurement models to describe how individuals respond to questions. Equations describe the relations among item responses and equations' parameters provide empirical assessments of the questions' measurement properties. With them, one can make empirically based decisions about measurement quality.

However, little work integrates modern test theory into health survey research, impeding the advances that modern test theory and measurement models could bring to the field. This chapter addresses two relatively unaddressed measurement issues in health survey research, internal validity and DIF, and discusses how modern test theory can provide important empirical insight into these data quality issues. It will discuss how modern test theory can address the challenges identified in the chapter. It will develop the primary statistical measurement models and describe how one interprets them. Finally, the discussion will use applied examples with real data to more concretely demonstrate modern test theory's ability to advance health outcomes measurement.

25.2 Internal Validity and Dimensionality

Validly interpreting participants' reports of their health outcomes depends on valid scoring systems. Surveys frequently use sets of questions to measure one or more latent (indirectly observed) constructs. A single summary score of responses often serves as an estimate of each construct. However, the possibility exists that, although a survey's developers intended a set of questions to measure a single construct, the questions measure more than one. If the questions measure multiple constructs, one should not create a single score, as the single score would be an amalgamation of multiple constructs. Rather, one should create an individual score for each identified construct (McDonald 1999). Thus, before generating summary scores based on a question set (or recommending that users create summary scores), investigators should first ask whether empirical data support the hypothesis that a question set measures a single construct.

Psychometricians call this internal validity. Internal validity exists when responses to a set of questions measure a construct (or constructs) as expected. With respect to a survey that is expected to measure a single, continuous construct (e.g., depressive symptomatology), internal validity would exist if the data support the expectation that the questions selected to measure the continuous construct do indeed measure a common continuous construct (McDonald 1999). Too frequently, researchers have created surveys and scores without empirically examining whether derived scores appear to measure the construct as intended (Carle et al. 2011b).

Psychometricians call data measuring a single construct unidimensional and data measuring multiple constructs multidimensional (Bollen 1989, McDonald 1999). CFA offers a tool to empirically evaluate the dimensionality of question sets (Bollen 1989). CFA (like SEM) uses a mathematical model to describe how individuals tend to respond to questions. Let's consider the model. Let Y_{ij} equal the ith individual's score on the jth ordered-categorical item (question), let the number of items equal p ($j = 1, 2, \ldots, p$), and let the number of item responses range $(0, 1, \ldots, s)$. For simplicity, consider a dichotomous item (i.e., responses 0 or 1). The model assumes that a latent response variate, Y_{ij}^*, determines responses. The variate corresponds to the idea that, although observed responses fall into discrete categories (e.g., no=0/yes=1), an underlying continuum represents the possible responses. A threshold value on the variate determines responses. If an individual's value on the latent response variate is less than the threshold, the individual would not endorse the item (i.e., will say "no"), but if their value is greater than the threshold, they will endorse the item. Formally:

$$Y_{ij} = m \quad \text{if} \quad \tau_{jm} \leq Y_{ij}^* \leq \tau_{j(m+1)} \tag{25.1}$$

where, τ_{j1} is the latent threshold parameters for the *j*th dichotomous item. As noted above, one can use the thresholds to estimate the level of the construct at which individuals will likely endorse an item.

Now, suppose that some factor(s), η, causes item responses. Y_{ij}^* relates to the factor(s) as follows:

$$\mathbf{Y}_i^* = \boldsymbol{\upsilon} + \boldsymbol{\Lambda}_y \boldsymbol{\eta}_i + \boldsymbol{\varepsilon}_i \tag{25.2}$$

$\boldsymbol{\upsilon}$ is a matrix of the latent intercept parameters, $\boldsymbol{\Lambda}_y$ is an $r \times r$ matrix of factor loadings, $\boldsymbol{\eta}_i$ is the matrix of factor scores for the *i*th person, and $\boldsymbol{\varepsilon}_i$ is a matrix of the unique factors. The loadings, like correlations, represent the degree to which an item relates to the factor(s). Higher factor loading values indicate a strong relation between the item and the latent variable. As noted above, the loadings provide an indication of reliability. Intercept parameters give the expected value of an item when the value of the underlying factor(s) is zero. Uniqueness includes sources of variance not attributable to the factor(s). As a result, the uniqueness also provides information about reliability. As the uniqueness value increases, the reliability of an item decreases (Bollen 1989, Carle 2010). One additional matrix is worth noting in this context: $\boldsymbol{\Psi}$, the matrix of the factor variances and covariances. In a unidimensional model, η_i is a scalar rather than a vector. And, similarly, $\boldsymbol{\Psi}$ includes only one element. One does not expect multiple factors in the unidimensional model.

In CFA, one uses empirical fit indices to evaluate the validity of a hypothesized measurement structure for a scale. The fit indices describe the extent to which the model-implied covariance matrix ($\hat{\boldsymbol{\Sigma}}$, i.e., the implied covariance among item responses) differs from the observed covariance matrix ($\boldsymbol{\Sigma}$, i.e., the observed covariance among item responses). The more similar these two are to each other, the better the model fits the data. Though detailing these indices falls beyond the scope of this chapter, research (Hu and Bentler 1998, Hu and Bentler 1999) has established standard guidelines for evaluating fit. If the model fails to support unidimensionality, one needs to consider multidimensional models as an alternative. Multidimensional models allow for multiple factors. If necessary, items can load on multiple factors. And, typically, these models allow the factors to correlate. By modifying the model using empirically guided techniques (e.g., exploratory factor analysis (EFA), examination of the single factor model's residuals, modification indices), one can often generate a multidimensional model that fits the data well. However, in practice, real data are often "messy." They fail tests of unidimensionality but, simultaneously, identified multidimensionality may not be substantively meaningful (Reise et al. 2007, Reise et al. 2010, Carle et al. 2011b, Reise et al. 2011b).

For example, consider a survey measure of depression, generally considered a single (unidimensional) construct (see Figure 25.1a) (APA 1994). The survey may ask several questions specifically related to cognitive aspects of depression and several related to somatic aspects of depression. Each set will include common wording related to cognitive and somatic symptoms and this can lead to

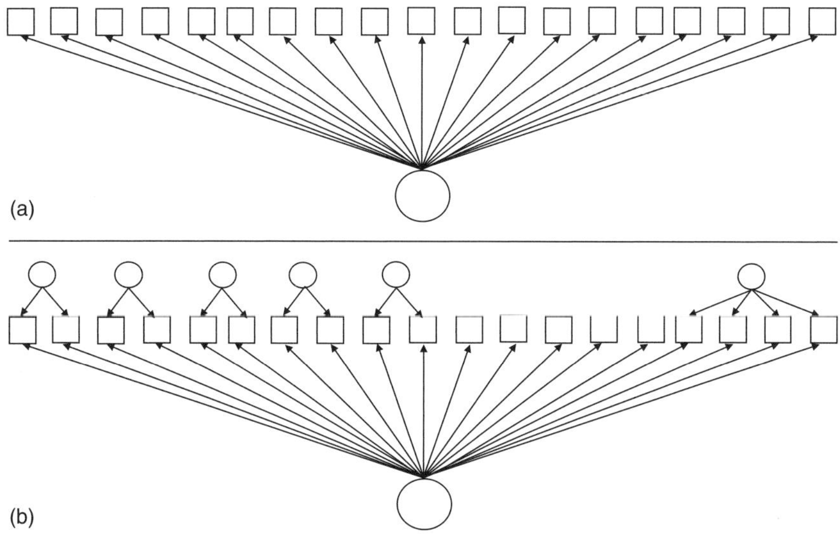

FIGURE 25.1 An example unidimensional model (a) and an example bifactor model (b). Suppose the survey questions measure depression. Then, the 19 small squares represent observed responses to the items. In the undimensional model, the presence of a single large circle indicates that the responses measure one and only one factor. In the bifactor model, the large circle represents a genearl depression factor. However, the smaller circles represent specific factors that measure narrower facets of depression (e.g., questions asking about thoughts about death). In both models, the arrows from the large and small circles to the squares indicate that the item responses measure the latent variables (for simplicity's sake and to minimize clutter, this figure does not depict all of the factor analysis parameters (e.g., uniquenesses, thresholds, etc.)).

specific factors. These "clusters" may result in a model with several "smaller" factors (see Figure 25.1b). In a strict sense, the scale appears multidimensional. This would argue against a single score. However, responses to the questions may still measure a single depression construct (a general factor) and the item clusters may measure "specific," substantively less meaningful factors. Essentially the scale does measure a single construct. The multidimensionality reflects "specific" factors (also labeled "grouping" and "nuisance" factors). As in the example, these can occur because of shared item content, but they can occur because of context effects, item location, and so on (Carle and Weech-Maldonado 2012).

When specific factors occur in the presence of a single general factor, one can more appropriately create a single score from the entire item set (Reise et al. 2007; Reise et al. 2010; Carle et al. 2011b; Reise et al. 2011b). This is because the data appear sufficiently unidimensional (Lai et al. 2006; Reeve et al. 2007; Reise et al. 2010). From a scoring perspective, then, when data fail unidimensionality tests the question becomes: does the scale "essentially" measure one construct (as well as one or more specific factors) or does it measure multiple meaningful constructs? If it sufficiently measures one construct, this provides evidence for the validity of a single score. If it measures multiple meaningful constructs, one has evidence in favor of multiple scores rather than a single score.

In order to create valid scoring systems, one should always conduct empirical analyses to address whether a scale's measurement structure is consistent with a single construct, multiple constructs, or single construct with specific factors. Three general types of factor models correspond to these structures: pure unidimensional models, multidimensional models, and bifactor models (a special case of multidimensional models), respectively. One can use factor analyses to examine the extent to which these models are consistent with the data. Unlike unidimensional and multidimensional models, bifactor models have not seen much use in survey research.

The bifactor model (Holzinger and Swineford 1937) explicitly models a general factor and then one or more specific factors. All items load on the general factor. And, each item can load on one of the specific factors (though not all items need to load on a specific factor). In addition, the bifactor model does not allow any of the factors to correlate. This specification allows one to unambiguously interpret scores on the general factor uninfluenced by the specific factors. Thus, when a test of pure unidimensionality fails and a bifactor model fits well, the item set's data structure is consistent with a single construct and scores from the entire item set measure that construct.

Few published examples in health survey research address internal validity, measurement models to investigate dimensionality generally, and the bifactor model specifically. This is unfortunate because (when appropriate) the bifactor model can resolve potentially thorny dimensionality issues (Reise et al. 2007, Reise et al. 2010, Carle et al. 2011b, Reise et al. 2011a, Reise et al. 2011b) and subsequent difficulty regarding the interpretability of health outcome measures. Thus, consider the following empirical example that examines the internal validity of creating a single "depression" score from a set of items intended to measure depression on a large, nationally representative survey of the non-institutionalized US population. Generally, researchers consider depression a single construct (APA 1994). However, depression encompasses several specific areas of symptomatology (e.g., cognitive aspect of depression, somatic aspects, etc.). Thus, the data may not support a single summary depression score. The example uses data from the National Epidemiologic Survey on Alcohol and Related Conditions (NESARC) (Grant et al. 2003b) and explores the validity of a single summary score using a bifactor model.

25.3 Dimensionality and Bifactor Model Example

25.3.1 METHODS

Participants. Participants (n = 11,678) were a subset of the 2001-2002 NESARC data designed and sponsored by the National Institute for Alcohol Abuse and Alcoholism. The original sample consisted of 43,093 individuals 18 years and older representing the non-institutionalized US adults. The complex, multistage design oversampled Black, Hispanics, and adults aged 18-24. Sample weights adjust the data to make it representative (Grant et al. 2003b). My analyses included all participants with complete data who reported on their depressive symptomatology in the past 12 months.

Measures. *Depression* is marked by a 2-week period that includes either (i) depressed mood most of the day, nearly every day, or (ii) markedly diminished interest or pleasure in daily activities. In addition, it includes at least three of the following nearly every day: (i) significant weight loss, or significant weight gain, or decrease in appetite, or increase in appetite; (ii) insomnia or hypersomnia; (iii) psychomotor agitation or retardation; (iv) fatigue or loss of energy; (v) feelings of worthlessness or excessive or inappropriate guilt; (vi) diminished ability to think or concentrate or indecisiveness; (vii) recurrent thoughts of death, recurrent suicidal ideation without a specific plan, or a suicide attempt or plan (APA 1994). The NESARC's Alcohol Use Disorder and Associated Disabilities Interview Schedule-IV, (Grant et al. 1995, Grant 1997, Hasin et al. 1997, Hasin and Paykin 1999, Grant 2000, Grant et al. 2001, Harford and Muthén 2001, Grant et al. 2003a) uses 19 dichotomous items (0 = Yes, 1 = No) to operationalize these criteria. The analyses reported below used all items.

Analytical Approach. The analyses proceeded in steps. First, they tested a unidimensional model's fit. Second, given the failure of the unidimensional model to fit well (see below), analyses sought to develop a bifactor model. All analyses used empirically validated fit indices and associated levels suggested by Hu and Bentler: (Hu and Bentler 1998, Hu and Bentler 1999) root mean square error of approximation (RMSEA) values less than 0.05, and comparative fit index (CFI) and Tucker-Lewis Index (TLI) values greater than 0.95. All analyses used Mplus (6.1), (Muthén and Muthén 2009), its theta parameterization and robust weighted least squares estimator, and missing data estimation capability to estimate the means and covariances (rather than item level imputation) for all analyses (Little and Rubin 2002).

25.3.2 RESULTS

Unidimensional Model. To test whether responses appeared to measure a single depression construct, analyses first tested a unidimensional model's fit. In this model, each item loaded on only a single factor (i.e., cultural competence). For statistical identification, the model had a factor mean of zero and factor variance of one. The model allowed no correlations among the uniqueness. This model did not fit well (RMSEA = 0.12; TLI = 0.64; CFI = 0.68) indicating that a single depression factor did not well account for the covariance among the item responses. Subsequently, analyses turned to developing and comparatively examining the fit of multidimensional and bifactor models.

Bifactor Model. A number of potential methods exist for developing bifactor models. One could examine the modification indices that result from the unidimensional model. Modification indices indicate the change in the chi-square that would result if one freed a specific constraint. Thus, the modification indices for the uniqueness will reveal potential patterns indicative of specific factors. One could also conduct an EFA and develop a bifactor model based on the EFA's results. Several other potential model development possibilities exist, (Carle and Weech-Maldonado 2012) including examining item content and theory to develop a bifactor model. The current analyses took the latter approach. By definition, (APA 1994) to measure depression, one will require several questions to get at each of the specific content areas (e.g., cognition, weight, etc.). Thus, the item content was a "good" place to start.

Analyses estimated a bifactor model that included a general depression factor and also included six specific factors; one for gaining weight or appetite; one for losing weight or appetite; one for difficulty in sleeping; one for feeling tired; one for restlessness; and one for thoughts about death. The thoughts about death specific factor included four items. The remainder included two items each (see Figure 25.1). This model fit the data well (RMSEA = 0.051; TLI = 0.94; CFI = 0.95).

25.4 Dimensionality Discussion

Confirmatory unidimensional and bifactor models addressed the internal validity of using responses to the 19 depression questions on the NESARC to derive a single depressive symptomatology score. The results provide evidence that despite some multidimensionality (as modeled by specific factors), responses to the questions do seem to measure a general depressive symptomatology construct. These results provide evidence that investigators can use responses to these questions on the health survey to form a single depressive symptomatology construct and derive a single depression score from this item set.

These results demonstrate the need for researchers to empirically examine the apparent dimensionality of data resulting from scales. Despite best efforts, a set of questions may not appear to measure a construct (or constructs) as expected (Carle et al. 2011a). Scoring systems following theoretical rather than empirical measurement structure (when they differ) may result in spurious and invalid conclusions. In these data, one can see that the initially hypothesized structure of a single domain did not appear to describe question responses well, suggesting users may not be able to validly create a single depression score. However, the bifactor findings indicated that, while responses to these questions seem to measure six specific factors each measuring relatively specific facets of depression, the evidence does support deriving a single depression score from item responses. Given the potential for real data to fail to correspond to theoretical expectations, investigators should always evaluate dimensionality.

The interpretability and validity of scores derived from measurement instruments depends upon whether the questions included in a composite score measure a single coherent construct. If developers or users of a scale intend to measure a single construct, but models suggest a measurement structure more consistent with multiple substantive constructs and not a bifactor structure, one should not create a single summary score from the entire set of questions. This can lead to spurious results and invalid conclusions. Rather, one should create subscale scores for each of the constructs measured by the questions on the scale (Holzinger and Swineford 1937, Bollen 1989, Reise et al. 2007, Reise et al. 2010, Carle et al. 2011a, Reise et al. 2011a, 2011b).

Before concluding this section, one should note some limitations. First, one should not consider this brief treatment as a definitive step-by-step guide. Rather, one should see this as an applied perspective on the importance of evaluating dimensionality and the use of bifactor model in that pursuit. Second, this chapter has focused on the internal validity of creating a single summary score from an item set. Although this addresses vital questions vis-à-vis score development and interpretability, this does not address how to best derive the subsequent scores (e.g., sum of observed responses, IRT-based methods, etc.). Although sum scores can provide reasonable construct estimates, other methods (i.e., IRT) generally provide more precise estimates. Third, the chapter has focused on establishing dimensionality rather than IRT scaling. Finally, before making strong conclusions about a model's general acceptability, researchers should attempt to replicate findings in a separate sample.

Summarily, the previous section shows the importance of examining dimensionality. These analyses demonstrate the critical importance of empirically evaluating dimensionality using measurement models that allow one to distinguish whether or not responses to a set of questions seem to essentially measure a single construct or not. Without conducting these analyses, the validity of scores derived from item sets remains in doubt. However, as noted earlier, establishing an internally valid scoring system is not the only challenge facing health survey research. The possibility also exists that participants respond to questions about themselves differently depending on their SES backgrounds or other variables, even when a measure's dimensionality does not differ from a priori expectations. Let the discussion now turn to measurement bias.

25.5 Measurement Bias

Not only should health surveys be internally valid in general, they should have equivalent internal validity and psychometric properties across various subpopulations (e.g., Whites, Blacks, and Hispanics). The possibility exists that participants respond to questions about themselves differently depending on their SES backgrounds or other characteristics. This possibility, a form of systematic measurement error often labeled measurement bias or DIF, refers to the fact that two individuals with an identical underlying health status may nevertheless respond to questions asking about their health differently. For example, two people with equivalent alcohol dependence behavior levels may respond to questions about their alcohol use differently due to culturally divergent beliefs about discussing their alcohol use. One may feel free to discuss their behavior, while the other does not. Thus, despite equivalent pathology, the two individuals would appear dissimilar based on their responses to these questions. As a result, efforts to understand individuals' health based on their responses to questions about their health would include systematic flaws (see Figure 25.2).

Measurement bias leads to the possibility that observed health disparities may not reflect true differences. This leaves unclear whether the results of health surveys across subpopulations reflect true differences or bias. Bias can obscure differences, decrease reliability and validity, and render group comparisons impossible (Carle 2009b, 2009c). Without establishing equivalent measurement, the field cannot: (i) draw strong conclusions about disparate outcomes, (ii) support evidence-based practice and policy, and (iii) address health disparities.

Modern test theory and related measurement models offer a powerful set of tools capable of addressing the challenges identified above (Muthén 1989, Carle 2010). However, like bifactor models and dimensionality, little work integrates these models into health survey research, impeding the advances they could bring. In addition to investigating bias, these methods can correct for bias, allowing more valid comparisons across groups. These models have seen few applications in health survey research methods. Thus, the next section briefly describes them

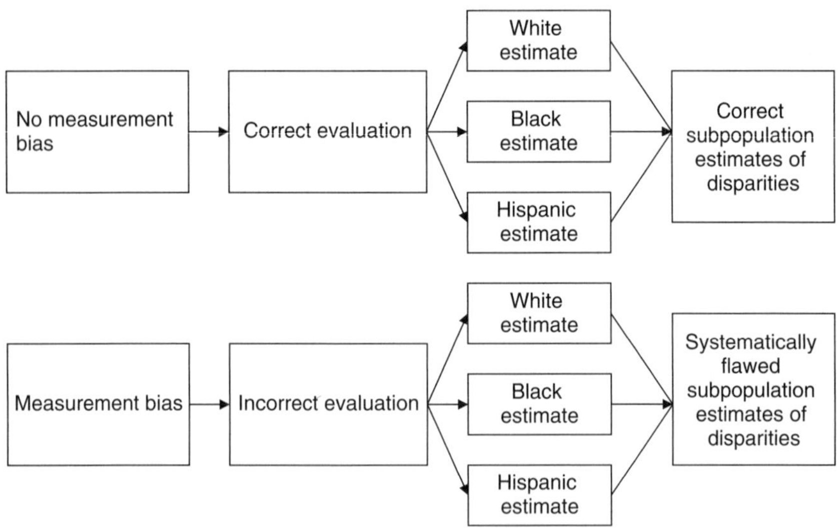

FIGURE 25.2 An example of measurement bias' influence on population health measurement.

and then provides an example using them to evaluate a set of survey questions asking about alcohol dependence, again using data from the NESARC.

25.6 Multiple Group Multiple Indicator Multiple Cause Models

SEM-based MG-MIMIC models offer a potent method to investigate the psychometric properties of health surveys, including whether one can form a single summary score based upon responses and whether responses to questions provide suitable reliability and internal validity, both generally and equivalently across subpopulations. MG-MIMIC models extend "traditional" models by incorporating additional background variables as covariates in SEM (Muthén 1989, Jones 2003, Jones 2006, Carle 2010). Rather than limiting analyses to a single variable as traditional approaches do, the MG-MIMIC approach simultaneously controls for differences in responses due to some variables (e.g., education and income) and allows an investigation of bias across another (e.g., race and ethnicity) (Jones 2006, Carle 2010). Moreover, MG-MIMIC provides empirical measures of internal validity (Bollen 1989). With them, one can directly examine the validity of creating a single summary score.

MG-MIMIC models build on the factor analytic model developed earlier. Through two equations, MG-MIMIC models expand the earlier equation 25.2 to include background covariate(s). These covariate(s) can directly influence the latent variable's measurement and the latent variable itself. The first allows the covariate to directly influence the measurement of the latent trait:

$$\mathbf{Y}_i^* = \boldsymbol{\upsilon} + \boldsymbol{\Lambda}_y \boldsymbol{\eta}_i + \boldsymbol{\Gamma}_y \mathbf{x}_i + \boldsymbol{\varepsilon}_i \tag{25.3}$$

The second, a structural equation, allows the covariate to predict the latent variable:

$$\boldsymbol{\eta}_i = \boldsymbol{\alpha} + \boldsymbol{\Gamma}_\eta \mathbf{x}_i + \boldsymbol{\zeta}_i \tag{25.4}$$

$\boldsymbol{\alpha}$ describes the latent trait's mean value, $\boldsymbol{\zeta}$ indicates residuals in the structural model, and $\boldsymbol{\Gamma}_\eta$ captures the covariate's influence on the latent variable.

To investigate bias, one subscripts measurement parameters to allow for group differences. Then, one constrains some or all of the measurement parameters to equality across groups and tests the constrained model's fit compared to a less constrained model. If fit indices indicate the constraints' acceptability, measurement equivalence exists. If not, bias presents. Once one has developed a final model, one can use model-based estimates to compare the health of various groups, removing the error that bias introduces.

The remainder of the section, again using data from the NESARC, (Grant et al. 2003b) describes an MG-MIMIC analysis. It shows how measurement bias as a function of income, educational attainment, and minority status can lead to erroneous conclusions about alcohol dependence. It also shows how model-based estimates can mitigate this error (Carle 2010).

25.6.1 METHODS

Participants. Participants (16,109 non-Hispanic White (hereafter White), 4072 non-Hispanic Black/African-Americans (hereafter Black), and 4819 Hispanic) were a subset of the 2001-2002 NESARC data. These analyses included White, Black, and Hispanic participants with complete data who reported on their alcohol consumption in the past 12 months.

Measures.

Alcohol Dependence. Alcohol dependence is a maladaptive alcohol use pattern that leads to significant impairment or distress. It demonstrates at least three of seven criteria identified by the DSM-IV (APA 1994). The NESARC's Alcohol Use Disorder and Associated Disabilities Interview Schedule-IV, (Grant et al. 1995, Grant 1997, Hasin et al. 1997, Hasin and Paykin 1999, Grant 2000, Grant et al. 2001, Harford and Muthén 2001, Grant et al. 2003a) uses 27 dichotomous items (0 = Yes, 1 = No) to operationalize these criteria. These analyses used all 27 items.

Ethnicity. Five options coded race. A single item allowed Hispanic self-identification. Individuals were considered White if they identified as White and non-Hispanic, Black/African-American if they identified as Black/African-American and non-Hispanic, and anyone who self-identified as Hispanic a Hispanic.

Income. Participants reported their total past 12 months' personal and family incomes. From this, the NESARC estimated household income (hereafter income). As in regression, (Cohen et al. 2003) centering a variable (i.e., subtracting the mean from all scores), can increase the interpretability of coefficients. By centering income, one can interpret bias attributable to this variable in terms of differences relative to those at average income level. Thus, the analyses used centered income.

Educational Attainment. The analyses used centered years of education.

Analytical Approach. The analyses examined measurement invariance following the method described by Millsap and Yun-Tein (2004), Carle (2010), and Woods (2009). All preferred fit index levels corresponded to those identified by the literature: (Hu and Bentler 1998, Steiger 1998, Hu and Bentler 1999). After identifying bias using omnibus fit criteria, item level comparisons were used to identify bias' source and modify the model accordingly. Constraints that led to significantly decreased fit identified bias. Subsequent models freed these constraints to develop a partial invariance model. All analyses used Mplus (Muthen and Muthen 2009), its theta parameterization and robust weighted least squares estimator, and appropriately incorporated the complex sampling design and weights in Mplus (Muthén and Muthén 2009). The zero-weighting (Korn and Graubard 2003) technique allowed full incorporation of the complex survey design (which resulted in correct standard errors) while only analyzing the subsample of interest (Korn and Graubard 2003; Carle 2009a).

25.6.2 RESULTS

Evaluating Internal Validity. Analyses first examined whether the question set measured a single construct. This provided a test of whether data reflected the theoretical assumption that responses measured alcohol dependence only and whether alcohol dependence appears to be a single construct (Muthén 1995, Harford and Muthén 2001). Thus, analyses tested a single factor alcohol dependence model (Model 1) across Whites, Blacks, and Hispanics. Model 1 allowed income and educational attainment each to have direct effects on each of the items (within statistical identification limits) and allowed income and educational attainment to correlate.

For statistical identification, Model 1 fixed the factor mean and variance at one and zero for Whites, while freely estimating the Black/African-American and Hispanic means and variances. Additional statistical identification constraints required constraining all groups' item intercepts to zero, fixing the direct effect of income and educational attainment on the "usual number of drinks had less effect" item to zero in all groups, constraining the loading for the "drinks" item to equality across the groups, constraining the threshold for the "drinks" item to equality across the groups, and fixing the uniqueness to one for all groups. This method used the "anchoring" method described by Woods (2009). Model 1 included no other constraints. Model 1 fit the data well (RMSEA = 0.014, CFI = 0.98, TLI = 0.98, $\chi^2 = 2918.43$, 1151, $n = 25{,}000$, $p < 0.01$). This provided evidence for internal validity within and across the groups.

Evaluating Measurement Bias. Given good fit, analyses proceeded to Model 2, which constrained the direct effects of income and educational attainment to zero across all groups. These constraints led to statistically significant misfit ($\Delta\chi^2 = 355.197$, 156 $n = 25{,}000$, $p < 0.01$), indicating bias as a function of income and educational attainment. Item-level analyses showed that 14 equality constraints led to misfit. Table 25.1, which provides the parameters for the final model, details the differences across the groups. Model 2b relaxed the misfitting constraints. Model 3 modified Model 2b to constrain the loadings to equivalence across groups. This examined whether the items provided similar reliability and related similarly to alcohol dependence across Whites, Blacks, and Hispanics, after accounting for bias due to income and educational attainment. Constraining the loadings resulted in statistically significant misfit ($\Delta\chi^2 = 94.646$, 52, $n = 25{,}000$, $p < 0.01$) indicating bias as a function of race/ethnicity. Analyses indicated that 5 equality constraints led to the misfit (see Table 25.1). Model 3b relaxed these constraints. Model 4 modified Model 3b to constrain the thresholds to equality across Whites, Blacks, and Hispanics. This examined whether affirmative

TABLE 25.1 Final Partially Invariant Measurement Model (Bolded Values Correspond to Statistically Significantly Different Values Across Groups)

Whites Item	Loadings	Thresholds	Income's Effect	Education's Effect
Usual number of drinks had less effect	1.301	−2.662	0	0
Needed to drink more to get desired effect	1.975	−4.141	0	0
Drank equivalent of fifth of liquor in one day	1.11	−2.862	0	0
Increased use to get desired effect	2.006	−4.563	0	0
More than once wanted to stop or cut down	1.109	**−2.033**	**−0.067**	0
More than once tried unsuccessfully to stop or cut down	1.253	**−3.49**	0	0
Ended up drinking more than intended	2.033	**−2.86**	**−0.081**	**−0.108**
Kept drinking longer than intended	**2.103**	**−3.181**	**−0.117**	0
Trouble falling asleep when alcohol's effects wore off	**1.083**	**−2.563**	**−0.129**	**−0.298**
Shook when alcohol's effects wore off	1.52	**−3.839**	0	**0.008**
Felt anxious or nervous when alcohol's effects wore off	1.666	**−3.986**	0	0
Nausea when effects of alcohol wearing off	1.262	−2.146	0	**−0.083**
Felt unusually restless when alcohol's effects wore off	1.416	**−3.155**	**−0.064**	0
Sweat/heart beat fast when alcohol's effects wore off	1.268	**−2.997**	**−0.085**	0
See, felt, heard things when alcohol's effects wore off	1.089	−3.809	**0.272**	0
Had fits or seizures when alcohol's effects wore off	1.037	−4.51	0	0
Had bad headaches when alcohol's effects wore off	1.16	**−1.846**	**−0.046**	**−0.172**

Drank or used drugs to get over alcohol's bad effects	1.152	−3.055	0	**−0.108**
Drank or used other drugs to avoid to get over alcohol's bad effects	**1.224**	**−3.489**	0	0
Spent lot of time drinking	1.633	−3.787	0	0
Spent lot of time getting over drinking's aftereffects	1.466	−4.206	0	0
Gave up or cut down important activities to drink	**2.344**	**−6.215**	0	0
Gave up or cut down pleasurable activities to drink	2.548	−6.949	0	0
Continued to drink though made depressed	1.766	−4.433	0	0
Continued to drink even though causing health problem	1.284	−3.271	0	0
Continued to drink despite prior blackout	1.404	**−3.427**	**−0.063**	0
Found could drink less than before to get desired effect	0.567	−1.369	0	0
Alcohol Dependence Factor Mean	0			
Alcohol Dependence Factor Variance	1			
Black/African-Americans				
	Loadings	**Thresholds**	**Income's Effect**	**Education's Effect**
Usual number of drinks had less effect	1.301	−2.662	0	0
Needed to drink more to get desired effect	1.975	−4.141	0	0
Drank equivalent of fifth of liquor in one day	1.11	−2.862	0	0
Increased use to get desired effect	2.006	−4.563	0	0
More than once wanted to stop or cut down	1.109	**−1.686**	0	0
More than once tried unsuccessfully to stop or cut down	1.253	**−3.071**	0	0

(continued)

TABLE 25.1 ***(Continued)***

Whites Item	Loadings	Thresholds	Income's Effect	Education's Effect
Ended up drinking more than intended	2.033	**−3.079**	0	0
Kept drinking longer than intended	**1.79**	−3.181	0	0
Trouble Falling Asleep when alcohol's effects wore off	**1.225**	**−3.082**	0	0
Shook when alcohol's effects wore off	1.52	**−4.327**	**0.739**	0
Felt anxious or nervous when alcohol's effects wore off	1.666	**−4.477**	**1.186**	0
Nausea when effects of alcohol wearing off	1.262	−2.146	**0.008**	0
Felt unusually restless when alcohol's effects wore off	1.416	**−3.381**	0	0
Sweat/heart beat fast when alcohol's effects wore off	1.268	−2.997	0	0
See, felt, heard things when alcohol's effects wore off	1.089	−3.809	0	0
Had fits or seizures when alcohol's effects wore off	1.037	−4.51	0	0
Had bad headaches when alcohol's effects wore off	1.16	**−2.193**	0	0
Drank or used drugs to get over alcohol's bad effects	1.152	−3.055	0	0
Drank or used other drugs to avoid to get over alcohol's bad effects	1.224	−3.489	0	0
Spent lot of time drinking	1.633	−3.787	0	0
Spent lot of time getting over drinking's aftereffects	1.466	−4.206	0	0
Gave up or cut down important activities to drink	**3.88**	**−10.325**	0	0
Gave up or cut down pleasurable activities to drink	2.548	−6.949	0	0
Continued to drink though made depressed	1.766	−4.433	0	0
Continued to drink even though causing health problem	1.284	−3.271	0	0
Continued to drink despite prior blackout	1.404	**−3.889**	0	0

Found could drink less than before to get desired effect	0.567	−1.369	0	0
Alcohol dependence factor mean	0.019			
Alcohol dependence factor variance	1.042			
Hispanics				
	Loadings	**Thresholds**	**Income's Effect**	**Education's Effect**
Usual number of drinks had less effect	1.301	−2.662	0	0
Needed to drink more to get desired effect	1.975	−4.136	0	0
Drank equivalent of fifth of liquor in one day	1.11	−2.876	0	0
Increased use to get desired effect	2.006	−4.516	0	0
More than once wanted to stop or cut down	1.109	−1.911	0	**0.168**
More than once tried unsuccessfully to stop or cut down	1.253	**−3.139**	0	**0.285**
Ended up drinking more than intended	2.033	**−3.453**	0	0
Kept drinking longer than intended	2.103	**−3.806**	0	0
Trouble falling asleep when alcohol's effects wore off	1.083	**−2.91**	0	0
Shook when alcohol's effects wore off	1.52	−4.065	0	0
Felt anxious or nervous when alcohol's effects wore off	1.666	−4.213	0	**0.278**
Nausea when effects of alcohol wearing off	1.262	−2.274	0	0
Felt unusually restless when alcohol's effects wore off	1.416	−3.217	0	0
Sweat/heart beat fast when alcohol's effects wore off	1.268	**−3.33**	**−0.126**	0
See, felt, heard things when alcohol's effects wore off	1.089	−3.886	0	0

(continued)

TABLE 25.1 (*Continued*)

Whites Item	Loadings	Thresholds	Income's Effect	Education's Effect
Had fits or seizures when alcohol's effects wore off	1.037	−4.652	0	0
Had bad headaches when alcohol's effects wore off	1.16	−1.928	0	0
Drank or used drugs to get over alcohol's bad effects	1.152	−2.998	0	0
Drank or used other drugs to avoid to get over alcohol's bad effects	**1.224**	**−3.574**	0	0
Spent lot of time drinking	1.633	−4.1	**−0.15**	0
Spent lot of time getting over drinking's aftereffects	1.466	−4.286	**−0.163**	0
Gave up or cut down important activities to drink	**2.344**	**−6.21**	0	0
Gave up or cut down pleasurable activities to drink	2.548	−6.874	0	0
Continued to drink though made depressed	1.766	−4.485	0	0
Continued to drink even though causing health problem	1.284	−3.388	0	0
Continued to drink despite prior blackout	1.404	−3.667	0	0
Found could drink less than before to get desired effect	0.567	−1.546	0	0
Alcohol dependence factor mean	**−0.18**			
Alcohol dependence factor variance	1.022			

item endorsements had similar likelihoods across race and ethnicity. Constraining the thresholds resulted in statistically significant misfit ($\Delta\chi^2 = 280.608$, 52, $n = 25{,}000$, $p < 0.01$), indicating bias. Analyses showed that 17 equality constraints led to misfit (see Table 25.1). The final model relaxed these constraints. Summarily, analyses revealed statistically significant bias across race, ethnicity, income, and education.

Mitigating Measurement Bias. The presence of significant bias indicates that one should not use unadjusted scores to measure alcohol dependence. Rather, one should use model-based estimates of alcohol dependence levels to mitigate systematic error. Analyses compared model-based estimates that resulted from the final model incorporating measurement differences to estimates that resulted from a model ignoring bias. Under the model ignoring bias, Whites served as the reference group and had a mean of zero (for statistical identification). Both Blacks and Hispanics had greater means ($M_{\text{Black}} = -0.07 : z = -2.86; M_{\text{Hispanic}} = -0.211 : z = -8.88$) than White, where negative values reflect more use. However, under the model mitigating bias, Blacks no longer differed significantly from Whites ($M_{\text{Black}} = 0.019 : z = 0.28$) and, while Hispanics still had greater alcohol dependence levels ($M_{\text{Hispanic}} = -0.18 : z = -2.325$), the disparity was somewhat smaller.

Measurement Bias Discussion. This study provides an example of how measurement models can provide an empirically informed method of meeting some of the challenges facing health survey research methodologists. It aimed to show how to use an SEM-based model (MG-MIMIC) to evaluate internal validity. And, it aspired to show the importance of empirically evaluating measurement bias. Additionally, it sought to demonstrate how bias can influence analytic results and how model-based techniques can mitigate this.

In the current example, results supported the notion that one can create a summary score of severity from these questions. Individuals lower on this score will have greater levels of alcohol use behavior related to dependence. Second, income, educational attainment, and race and ethnicity all directly influenced alcohol dependence measurement. Without accounting for this bias, one would conclude that Hispanics and Black demonstrate significantly greater amounts of alcohol dependence behavior than Whites. However, after using model-based estimates that corrected for bias, model-based estimates clarified that only Hispanics demonstrate greater amounts of alcohol dependence behavior in comparison to Whites and that Blacks do not differ significantly from Whites. These findings highlight that research must consider whether group differences (or similarities) reflect true differences or result from bias. And, the findings highlight that measurement models can effectively address measurement bias when it occurs, allowing users to include biased items in a survey by estimating scores using the partially invariant measurement model.

25.7 Additional Challenges to Health Survey Data Quality

In addition to the overarching themes addressed in this chapter, one must still confront several important issues investigating the quality of health survey data. First, stakeholders often require dichotomous indicators. The method for combining and dichotomizing the aggregate all affect reliability and validity. Health survey research has not sufficiently attended to this. Carle et al. (in press) describes model-based methods for creating and evaluating cut-points. Second, the validity of developing contextual-level measures using individuals' self-reports remains relatively unexplored. For example, how can (or should) a set of responses describing contextual aspects of an individual's environment be used to develop a contextual-level measure? Multilevel (ML) SEM uses individuals' responses to estimate contextual-level variables (Muthén 1991, Lüdtke et al. 2008). This approach explicitly recognizes that individuals' responses include measurement error. In essence, ML-SEM capitalizes on the aspects of using model-based estimates of reliability as described above and generalizes them to the ML setting.

Third, survey research organizations often must make decisions about the number of questions to include. For example, while it may be ideal to include 27 questions, respondent burden may require a smaller set. By using the measurement parameters from the full question set, a methodologist could make an empirically informed choice about which questions to include. The parameters allow methodologists to target the construct levels of interest and maintain reliability. Finally, investigators should always seek to demonstrate external as well as internal validity. External validity refers to whether a set of questions actually measure the construct they purport to measure (McDonald 1999). Though a description falls beyond this paper's scope, SEM-based measurement work can also address external validity (Bollen 1989).

25.8 Overall Conclusion

In sum, health survey research faces a number of challenges with respect to measurement quality. Given the number of potential directions in which measurement quality analyses can lead, it is difficult to describe exact step-by-step procedures to evaluate measurement quality. However, one can make some high-level suggestions. First, survey developers should carefully consider the constructs they intend to measure. Do they expect responses to the questions to measure one or more constructs? Once one has developed a hypothesis specifying the number of constructs and which questions measure these constructs, one should use measurement models (e.g., CFA) to test the validity of the proposed measurement hypothesis. The results will either support the proposed measurement model, or they will prove useful in guiding the development of a modified, empirically based and theory-drive alternative model. After identifying a model that appears valid, one should then test for measurement bias using model-based methods. These analyses will address whether one can use the measure equivalently across individuals of different backgrounds, or whether additional steps are needed to achieve an appropriate scoring system given measurement bias before comparing people of different backgrounds.

As one can see, model-based methods provide a powerful conceptual and analytical framework for addressing these challenges. They provide an empirical scaffold for addressing the validity of creating summary scores based on item responses and for evaluating the extent to which measurement bias influences efforts to evaluate health statuses across subpopulations. Importantly, model-based methods offer a tool to mitigate DIF if it occurs. Hopefully, future work will see these methods more frequently integrated in health survey research.

REFERENCES

APA. *Diagnostic and Statistical Manual of Mental Disorders*. 8th ed. Washington, DC: American Psychiatric Association; 1994.

Bollen K. *Structural Equations with Latent Variables*. New York, NY: John Wiley & Sons, Inc.; 1989.

Carle AC. Assessing the adequacy of self-reported alcohol abuse measurement across time and ethnicity: cross-cultural equivalence across Hispanics and Caucasians in 1992, non-equivalence in 2001–2002. BMC Public Health 2009a;9:60.

Carle AC. Fitting multilevel models in complex survey data with design weights: recommendations. BMC Med Res Methodol 2009b;9(49).

Carle AC. Tolerating inadequate alcohol dependence measurement: cross-cultural invalidity of alcohol dependence across hispanics and caucasians in 2001 and 2002. Addict Behav 2009c;34:43–50.

Carle AC. Mitigating systematic measurement error in comparative effectiveness research in heterogeneous populations. Med Care 2010;48(6):S68.

Carle AC, Blumberg SJ, et al. Advanced psychometric methods for developing and evaluating cut-point-based indicators. Child Indi Res 2011a:1–26.

Carle AC, Cella D, et al. Advancing PROMIS's methodology: results of the Third Patient-Reported Outcomes Measurement Information System (PROMIS®) Psychometric Summit. Expert Rev Pharmacoecon Outcomes Res 2011b;11(6):677–684.

Cohen J, Cohen P, et al. *Applied Multiple Regression/Correlation Analysis for the Behavioral Sciences*. Hillsdale, NJ: Lawrence Erlbaum Associates; 2003.

Carle AC, Weech-Maldonado R. Validly interpreting patients' reports: using bifactor and multidimensional models to determine whether surveys and scales measure one or more constructs. Med Care 2012;50:S42–S48.

Embretson S, Reise SP. Item response theory for psychologists. 2000 (Journal Article).

Grant BF. Convergent validity of DSM-III-R and DSM-IV alcohol dependence: results from the national longitudinal alcohol epidemiologic survey. J Subst Abuse 1997;9:89–102.

Grant BF. Theoretical and observed subtypes of DSM-IV alcohol abuse and dependence in a general population sample. Drug Alcohol Depend 2000;60(3):287–293.

Grant BF, Dawson DA, et al. *The Alcohol Use Disorder and Associated Disabilities Interview Schedule-DSM-IV Version (AUDADIS-IV)*. Bethesda, MD: National Institute of on Alcohol Abuse and Alcoholism; 2001.

Grant BF, Dawson DA, et al. The Alcohol Use Disorder and Associated Disabilities Interview Schedule-IV (AUDADIS-IV): reliability of alcohol consumption, tobacco use, family history of depression and psychiatric diagnostic modules in a general population sample. Drug Alcohol Depend 2003a;71(1):7–16.

Grant BF, Harford TC, et al. The Alcohol Use Disorder and Associated Disabilities Interview Schedule (AUDADIS): reliability of alcohol and drug modules in a general population sample. Drug Alcohol Depend 1995;39(1):37–44.

Grant BF, Kaplan K, et al. *Source and Accuracy Statement for Wave 1 of the 2001–2002 National Epidemiologic Survey on Alcohol and Related Conditions*. Bethesda MD: National Institute on Alcohol Abuse and Alcoholism; 2003b.

Harford TC, Muthén BO. The dimensionality of alcohol abuse and dependence: a multivariate analysis of DSM-IV symptom items in the National Longitudinal Survey of Youth. J Stud Alcohol 2001;62:150–157.

Hasin D, Paykin A. Alcohol dependence and abuse diagnoses: concurrent validity in a nationally representative sample. Alcohol Clin Exp Res 1999;23:144–150.

Hasin DS, Grant B, et al. Nosological comparisons of alcohol and drug diagnoses: a multisite, multi-instrument international study. Drug Alcohol Depend 1997;47:217–226.

Holzinger KJ, Swineford F. The bi-factor method. Psychometrika 1937;2(1):41–54.

Hu L, Bentler P. Cutoff criteria for fit indexes in covariance structure analysis: conventional criteria versus new alternatives. Struct Equ Modeling 1999;6(1):1–55.

Hu L, Bentler PM. Fit indices in covariance structure modeling: sensitivity to underparameterized model misspecification. Psychol Methods 1998;3(4):424–453.

Jones RN. Racial bias in the assessment of cognitive functioning of older adults. Aging Ment Health 2003;7(2):83–102.

Jones RN. Identification of measurement differences between English and Spanish language versions of the Mini-Mental State Examination. Detecting differential item functioning using MIMIC modeling. Med Care 2006;44(11 Suppl 3):S124–133.

Korn E, Graubard B. Estimating variance components by using survey data. J Roy Stat Soc B 2003;65(1):175–190.

Lai J-S, Crane PK, et al. Factor analysis techniques for assessing sufficient unidimensionality of cancer related fatigue. Qual Life Res 2006;15(7):1179–1190.

Little R, Rubin DB. *Statistical Analysis with Missing Data*. New York: John Wiley & Sons, Inc.; 2002.

Lüdtke O, Marsh HW, et al. The multilevel latent covariate model: a new, more reliable approach to group-level effects in contextual studies. Psychol Methods 2008;13(3):203–229.

McDonald RP. *Test Theory: A Unified Treatment*. Mahwah, NJ: Erlbaum; 1999.

Millsap RE. *Statistical Approaches to Measurement Invariance*. Routledge; 2011.

Millsap RE, Yun-Tein J. Assessing factorial invariance in ordered-categorical measures. J Multivariate Behav Res 2004;39:479–515.

Muthén BO. Latent variable modeling in heterogeneous populations. Psychometrika 1989;54(4):557–585.

Muthén B. Multilevel factor analysis of class and student achievement components. J Educ Meas 1991;28(4):338–354.

Muthén BO. Factor analysis of alcohol abuse and dependence symptom items in the 1988 National Health Interview Survey. Addiction 1995;90(5):637–645.

Muthén LK, Muthén BO. *Mplus User's Guide*. Los Angeles, CA: Muthén & Muthén; 2009.

Reeve BB, Hays RD, et al. Psychometric evaluation and calibration of health-related quality of life item banks: plans for the Patient-Reported Outcomes Measurement Information System (PROMIS). Med Care 2007;45(5 Suppl 1):S22–31.

Reise S, Moore T, et al. Bifactor models and rotations: exploring the extent to which multidimensional data yield univocal scale scores. J Pers Assess 2010;92(6):544–559.

Reise S, Moore T, et al. Target rotations and assessing the impact of model violations on the parameters of unidimensional item response theory models. Educ Psychol Meas 2011a;71(4):684–711.

Reise SP, Morizot J, et al. The role of the bifactor model in resolving dimensionality issues in health outcomes measures. Qual Life Res 2007;16(Suppl 1):19–31.

Reise SP, Ventura J, et al. Bifactor and item response theory analyses of interviewer report scales of cognitive impairment in schizophrenia. Psychol Assess 2011b;23(1):245–261.

Steiger J. A note on multiple sample extensions of the RMSEA fit index. Struct Equ Modeling 1998;5(4):411–419.

Woods CM. Empirical selection of anchors for tests of differential item functioning. Appl Psych Meas 2009;33(1):42.

ONLINE RESOURCES

A site run by the National Cancer Institute that includes some basic IRT information can be accessed at: http://appliedresearch.cancer.gov/areas/cognitive/item.html.

PROMIS® stands for Patient Reported Outcomes Measurement Information System. PROMIS is a part of the National Institutes of Health (NIH) Roadmap for Medical Research. To create the next generation of patient-reported outcome (PRO) measures, PROMIS utilizes IRT and other advanced measurement techniques (SEM, CFA, etc.). This site provides an excellent review of PROMIS methodology, several examples of patient reported outcome measures, software, item banks, and more. www.nihpromis.org/.

CHAPTER TWENTY SIX

Sample Weighting for Health Surveys

Kennon R. Copeland and Nadarajasundaram Ganesh
NORC at the University of Chicago, Statistics and Methodology
Bethesda, MD, USA

26.1 Objectives of Sample Weighting

This chapter presents guidelines for weighting samples from health surveys, both household and establishment (e.g., physician, hospital, clinic). The objective of sample weighting is to allow generation of estimates from survey data that represent the values for the target population. The sample weighting methodology should yield estimates subject to as little variance and bias as possible given the survey sample design, data collection, and information available concerning the target population. For probability sample designs, sample weighting involves calculating base weights to incorporate probabilities of selection, accounting for noncontacts and nonresponse, and adjusting for relevant differences between the sample and population distributions. These weighting steps are carried out so as to reflect the sample design used in the survey, and control variance and bias associated with survey estimates. Weighting is not advised for nonprobability sample designs and the data will not support statistical inference of survey results; however, weights may be desired so as to allow examination of survey results with some adjustment to account for differences between the responding sample and population distributions and are hence also briefly covered.

Handbook of Health Survey Methods, First Edition. Edited by Timothy P. Johnson.

26.2 Sample Weighting Stages (Probability Sample Designs)

Sample weighting requires information from the sampling frame, the selected sample, the observed sample, and the target population. The more information available from these data sources, both at the sampling unit and aggregate levels, the greater the ability to construct a weighting methodology that controls variance and bias of the resultant survey estimates.

The sample weighting methodology must take into account the sample design and the survey tabulation and analysis requirements. In addition, the sample weighting methodology should be informed by the data collection process and, where appropriate, prior survey results.

The major stages of sample weighting are:

- Calculate base weights that reflect probabilities of selection;
- Account for noncontact and nonresponse;
- Adjust to independent population controls.

The flow chart in Figure 26.1 reflects the weighting stages.

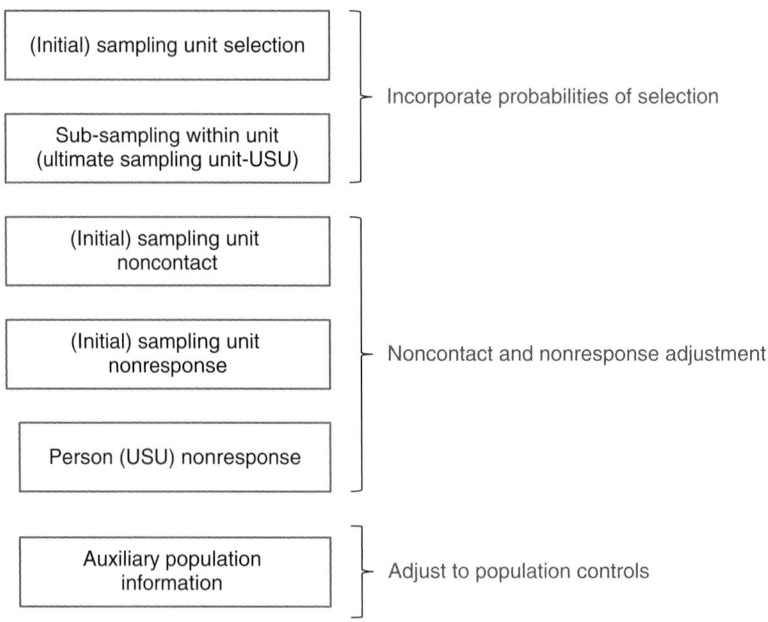

FIGURE 26.1 Survey weighting stages.

26.3 Calculating Base Weights

The first stage of weighting is to calculate base weights which reflect the probabilities of selection for the sampled units and which, when summed, yield the total count from the sampling frame. The sample design utilized for the survey may involve multiple stages of selection and a complex design. In selecting units for inclusion in the survey, it is critical that the probabilities of selection at each stage are tracked and available for use in the initial weighting stage.

26.3.1 SAMPLING UNIT SELECTION

The initial, or base, weight for each sampled unit is defined as the inverse of the probability of selecting the sample unit

$$W_{0i} = \frac{1}{\pi_i} \tag{26.1}$$

where π_i = probability of selecting the ith unit into the sample. For a complex sample design with multiple stages of selection, π_i will reflect the cumulative probability of selection for the ith unit.

Note that the sum of the base weights across all sampled units will be equal to the total number of units in the sampling frame, N'.

$$\sum_{i \in s} W_{0i} = N' \tag{26.2}$$

where s = set of units selected into the sample.

26.3.2 SUB-SAMPLING WITHIN UNITS

In some surveys, the sampled unit is not the unit of interest (referred to as the *ultimate sampling unit*, or USU) for which information is to be collected for the survey. These situations typically arise when there does not exist an appropriate sampling frame from which to select USUs, or it is deemed inefficient to select USUs directly. Rather, initial sampling units (e.g., housing units, hospitals) are selected and USUs (e.g., persons, doctors) are selected from within the selected initial sampling units. The sample design may call for any number of USUs from a given larger unit, from one to all USUs within the larger unit. The probability of selecting the USU must be accounted for as part of the weighting methodology, through calculation of a within-unit adjustment factor, defined as

$$A_{1ij} = \frac{1}{\pi_{ij}} \tag{26.3}$$

where π_{ij} = probability of selecting for interview the jth USU in the ith initial sampling unit.

Often, simple random sampling without replacement is used to select the USUs within each initial sampling unit, and thus, the probability of selecting the jth USU in the ith initial sampling unit is simply the ratio of the number of USUs in the ith initial sampling unit that were selected for interview (n_i) to the total number of USUs in the ith initial sampling unit (N_i), or $\pi_{ij} = \frac{n_i}{N_i}$. However, in some surveys of health care establishments, USUs are selected with probability proportional to a measure of size, M_{ij}, in which case the probability of selecting the jth USU in the ith initial sampling unit is

$$\pi_{ij} = \frac{n_i M_{ij}}{\sum_{j \in S_i} M_{ij}} \tag{26.4}$$

where S_i is the set of USUs in the ith initial sampling unit.

In some cases, the within-unit adjustment factor can be extremely large (e.g., if selecting one adult from a household containing 10 adults). Such adjustments can create unusually large weights and result in increased variance in survey estimates. It is generally desirable to cap such adjustments to reduce variability, even though capping may introduce some bias. Setting a value for the cap is generally ad hoc with a focus on controlling unusually large adjustments. In some cases, the cap value may be established arbitrarily at a level intended to keep adjustments from having too large an effect (e.g., set cap value at 5, so no single case has its weight adjusted upward by more than a factor of five). Note that this capping is different from weight trimming, which is discussed in Section 26.7.3.

Thus, the within-unit sampling adjustment factor becomes

$$\acute{A}_{1ij} = \min(A_{1ij}, \text{cap}(A_1)) \tag{26.5}$$

where $\text{cap}(A_1)$ = defined cap for the within-unit adjustment factor.

Typically, within-unit sampling adjustment factors are derived and applied after adjustments for noncontact and initial sampling unit nonresponse (discussed below) are complete, as that is the point in the survey process at which information becomes available upon which to derive the within-unit sampling adjustment factors.

26.4 Accounting for Noncontact and Nonresponse

As part of survey data collection, multiple steps may be required before obtaining a completed response: sample units must be located; an appropriate individual within each unit must be contacted; eligibility of the unit for inclusion in the survey must be determined; determination of target within-unit respondents be made (for surveys in which within-unit sampling is carried out); and the survey instrument be completed by the respondent(s). Successful completion of survey data collection in each of these steps for all sample units is almost never accomplished. As a result, adjustments must be made to survey weights to account for this incomplete information.

Unit nonresponse is defined as " … a complete failure to obtain data from a sample unit … " (Office of Management and Budget 2001). In addition to the increased variability due to respondent sample sizes being smaller than selected sample sizes, nonresponse can result in bias in survey estimates to the extent that nonrespondents differ from respondents. The variance increase for a sample mean from a simple random sample (SRS) can be expressed as (ignoring the finite population correction) the ratio of the total to the responding sample counts.[1]

$$\frac{\mathrm{Var}(\bar{y}_r)}{\mathrm{Var}(\bar{y}_n)} = \frac{S_Y^2/(n-n_{\mathrm{NR}})}{S_Y^2/n} = \frac{n}{n-n_{\mathrm{NR}}} \tag{26.6}$$

where $\bar{y}_r$ = mean for sample respondents, $\bar{y}_n$ = mean for all sample units, S_Y^2 = population variance for variable Y, n = number of sample units, and n_{NR} = number of nonrespondents.

Nonresponse bias for a sample mean from a SRS can be expressed assuming two models of the nonresponse mechanism: (i) deterministic, in which each unit in the population will either respond or not respond; or (ii) stochastic, in which each unit in the population has a given response propensity (Bethlehem 2002).

Under the deterministic model, nonresponse bias can be expressed as the product of two components: the nonresponse rate and the difference of the means of the respondents and the nonrespondents.

$$\mathrm{Bias}(\bar{y}_r) = E(\bar{y}_r - \bar{y}_n) = \frac{n_{\mathrm{NR}}}{n}(E(\bar{y}_r) - E(\bar{y}_{n_{\mathrm{NR}}})) \tag{26.7}$$

where $\bar{y}_{n_{NR}}$ = mean for sample nonrespondents, $\frac{n_{\mathrm{NR}}}{n}$ = nonresponse rate.

Under the stochastic model, nonresponse bias can be expressed as the ratio of the covariance between the variable of interest and the response propensity, and the mean response propensity.

$$\mathrm{Bias}(\bar{y}_r) = \frac{\sigma_{y,\rho}}{\bar{\rho}} \tag{26.8}$$

Thus, reducing the difference between nonrespondents and respondents relative to the variables of interest should serve to lessen nonresponse bias. Making adjustments utilizing information on the correlation between response probability and variables of interest can also serve to lessen nonresponse bias. Adjustments should be made to the survey weights in an attempt to reduce nonresponse bias.

The number of adjustment steps required for a particular survey will depend upon the nature of the sample design and data collection methodology. A schematic of the data collection methodology should be prepared, so as to guide the determination of and approach to the noncontact/nonresponse weighting adjustments. The discussion below presents details for weighting class adjustments (Oh and Scheuren 1983)[2] given a specified data collection method-

[1]Although most sample designs are not SRS, formula 26.6 provides a rough measure of the potential impact of nonresponse on the variance of survey estimates.

[2]An alternative approach is response propensity adjustment, discussed in Section 26.10.2.

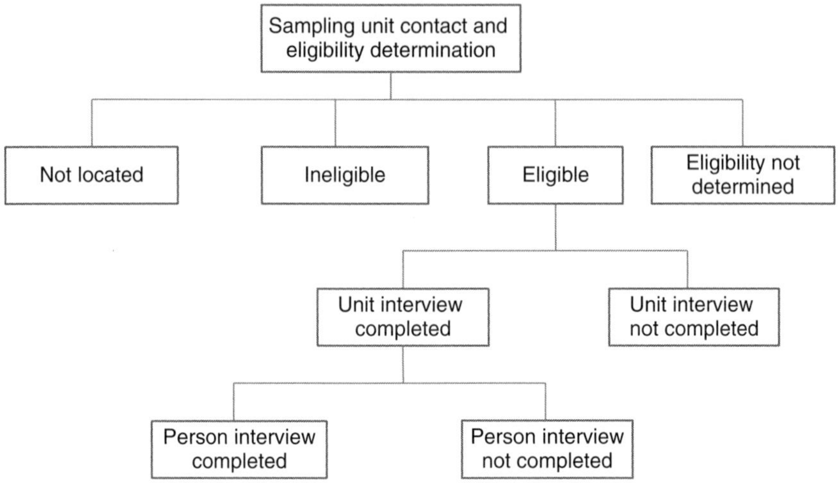

FIGURE 26.2 Illustration of noncontact/nonresponse adjustments.

ology in which there are three potential points at which noncontact/nonresponse can occur, as illustrated in Figure 26.2.

26.4.1 SAMPLING UNIT NONCONTACT

At the first stage of survey contact, the interviewer should try to determine the eligibility of each sampled unit. If cases refuse to cooperate, the eligibility will remain unknown.

An adjustment to the survey weights for sampled units for which eligibility status was determined, regardless of eligibility outcome, must be made to account for those sample units for which determination was not able to be made. This eligibility nonresolution adjustment is typically carried out within adjustment cells and is defined as

$$A_{2i} = \frac{\sum_{k \in c_2} W_{0k}}{\sum_{k \in c_2, k \in R_2} W_{0k}}, \quad i \in c_2 \tag{26.9}$$

where R_2 = the set of sampling units for which eligibility was determined (includes both eligible and ineligible sample units), and c_2 = the eligibility nonresolution adjustment cell.

Eligibility nonresolution adjustment cells are defined based upon characteristics known for all sampling units and which have been determined to be or are believed to be correlated with response propensity and the survey variables of interest. Generally, this means adjustment cell definitions make use of information only available from the sampling frame. Further information related to defining adjustment cells is provided in Section 26.7.1.

On the basis of this eligibility nonresolution adjustment, the survey weight at this stage of weighting becomes

$$W_{2i} = A_{2i} W_{0i} \tag{26.10}$$

Note that the sum of the eligibility nonresolution-adjusted weights across all sampled units for which eligibility was determined will be equal to the total number of units in the sampling frame.

$$\sum_{i \in R_2} W_{2i} = N' \tag{26.11}$$

In addition, the sum of the eligibility nonresolution-adjusted weights across all sampled units determined to be eligible will yield an estimate of the total number of eligible units on the sampling frame, $\widehat{N}'_E$.

$$\sum_{i \in R_2 \cap E} W_{2i} = \widehat{N}'_E \tag{26.12}$$

where E = set of sample units determined to be eligible for the survey.

26.4.2 SAMPLING UNIT NONRESPONSE

For units determined to be eligible, the initial contact at the sampling unit may not cooperate in providing basic information about the sampling unit. An adjustment to the survey weights for sampled units for which cooperation was obtained must be made to account for those sample units for which survey cooperation was not obtained. This sampling unit nonresponse adjustment is typically carried out within adjustment cells and defined as

$$A_{3i} = \frac{\sum_{k \in c_3} W_{2k}}{\sum_{k \in c_3, k \in R_3} W_{2k}}, \qquad i \in c_3 \tag{26.13}$$

where R_3 = the set of sampling units determined to be eligible and for which sampling unit cooperation was obtained, and c_3 = the sampling unit nonresponse adjustment cell.

Sampling unit nonresponse adjustment cells are defined based upon characteristics known for all eligible sampling units and which have been determined to be or are believed to be correlated with sampling unit cooperation propensity and the survey variables of interest. Generally, this means adjustment cell definitions make use of information only available from the sampling frame.

On the basis of this sampling unit nonresponse adjustment, the survey weight at this stage of weighting becomes

$$W'_{3i} = A_{3i} W_{2i} \tag{26.14}$$

The sum of the sampling unit nonresponse-adjusted weights across all eligible sampled units for which cooperation was obtained will be equal to the estimate of the total number of eligible units on the sampling frame.

$$\sum_{i \in R_3} W'_{3i} = \widehat{N}'_E \tag{26.15}$$

It is at this stage in the weighting that the within-unit sampling adjustment factor is applied. If within-unit sampling is carried out, the survey weight for the jth USU in the ith initial sampling unit becomes

$$W_{3ij} = \acute{A}_{1ij} W'_{3i} \tag{26.16}$$

If within-sampling unit selection of survey respondents is not carried out (i.e., if the USU is the initial sampling unit), the survey weight remains unchanged, that is,

$$W_{3ij} = W'_{3i} \tag{26.17}$$

The sum of the survey weights at this stage will provide an estimate of the total number of USUs in the population.[3]

$$\sum_{i \in R_3} W_{3ij} = \widehat{N} \tag{26.18}$$

26.4.3 PERSON INTERVIEW NONRESPONSE

After contacting the sampling unit and determining eligibility and collecting some basic information about the sampling unit, the interviewer will seek to complete an interview with designated or sampled persons within the sampling unit. Some identified survey respondents will inevitably refuse to participate. An adjustment to the survey weights for ultimate sampled units for which a sufficient survey response was obtained must be made to account for those ultimate sample units for which a survey response was not obtained. This survey nonresponse adjustment is typically carried out within adjustment cells and defined as

$$A_{4ij} = \frac{\sum_{k,j \in c_4} W_{3kj}}{\sum_{k,j \in c_4, k,j \in R_4} W_{3kj}}, \qquad i,j \in c_4 \tag{26.19}$$

where R_4 = the set of USUs for which a survey response was obtained, and c_4 = the survey nonresponse adjustment cell.

[3]Note that this estimate will be a slight underestimate if USUs are subsampled and the adjustment factors were capped.

On the basis of this survey nonresponse adjustment, the survey weight at this stage of weighting becomes

$$W_{4ij} = A_{4ij} W_{3ij} \tag{26.20}$$

The sum of the survey nonresponse-adjusted weights will be equal to the estimate of the total number of USUs in the population.

$$\sum_{i \in R_4} W_{4ij} = \widehat{N} \tag{26.21}$$

26.5 Adjusting to Independent Population Controls

Estimates derived from the survey nonresponse-adjusted weights are subject to coverage bias, resulting from coverage error in the sampling frame and/or differences between the true population distribution and the weighted sample distribution. A final stage in survey weighting is to adjust the weighted survey counts to agree with independent population counts on select characteristics. The characteristics used in adjustment should be selected on the basis of correlation with survey variables of interest and/or publication requirements. In addition, prior weighting stages may yield variability among survey weights, which can result in excessive variability in survey estimates. Reduction in variance will occur when the variables used in adjustment to population controls are strongly correlated with the survey outcome variables.

Adjustment to population controls is generally carried out through one of two calibration methods: post-stratification ratio adjustment or raking ratio adjustment.[4] Both methods achieve agreement between weighted survey estimates and population controls for selected characteristics; however, post-stratification achieves this agreement for cells defined by the cross-classification of all designated characteristics, while raking ratio adjustment achieves this agreement for cells defined by the marginals associated with each designated characteristic.

26.5.1 POST-STRATIFICATION RATIO ADJUSTMENT

Post-stratification is typically used when the number of characteristics available for adjustment is small, and independent population counts are available for all cross-classified cells resulting from the post-stratification. In post-stratification ratio adjustment, cells are created based on the cross-classification of the categories for characteristics to be used as population controls (Smith 1991). For example, if in controlling survey weights from a sample of physicians, the characteristics specialty (primary care, specialist), type of practice (hospital, office/clinic), and

[4]Alternative calibration methods are discussed in Section 26.10.3.

geography (four Census regions) were used, there would be 16 post-stratification cells, defined by the cross-classification of specialty by type of practice by Census region.

Post-stratification ratio adjustments are defined by the ratio of the population control for a cell to the weighted survey count for that cell

$$A_{5ij} = \frac{N_{\mathrm{PS}_c}}{\sum\limits_{k,j \in PS_c} W_{4kj}}, \qquad i,j \in \mathrm{PS}_c \tag{26.22}$$

where PS_c = post-stratification cell c, and N_{PS_c} = population control for post-stratification cell c.

Based upon the post-stratification ratio adjustment, the final survey weight becomes

$$W_{5ij} = A_{5ij} W_{4ij}, \qquad i,j \in \mathrm{PS}_c \tag{26.23}$$

The sum of the W_{5ij} across all survey respondents will equal the true population total, N; in addition, the sum of the W_{5ij} across all survey respondents within post-stratification cell c will equal the true population total for post-stratification cell c, N_{PS_c}.

$$\sum_{i,j} W_{5ij} = N, \qquad \sum_{i,j \in PS_c} W_{5ij} = N_{\mathrm{PS}_c} \tag{26.24}$$

26.5.2 RAKING RATIO ADJUSTMENT

Raking ratio adjustment is typically used when the number of characteristics available for adjustment is large and, thus, use of post-stratification would yield an unacceptably large number of cross-classification cells. In addition, raking ratio adjustment is advised when independent population counts are not available for all cross-classification cells resulting from prost-stratification. In raking ratio adjustment (Deming and Stephan 1940), survey weights are adjusted to marginal totals or distributions for each defined characteristic in turn, using the weights from the immediately prior adjustment. Adjustments are iterated until weighted counts for all characteristics converge to their corresponding population control.

In terms of the survey nonresponse weights, the raking ratio adjustment can be described as follows. Assume there are L characteristics (such as type of practice, geography, etc.) denoted by $C_1, \ldots, C_l, \ldots, C_L$, and characteristic C_l has H_l categories, designated by $C_{l1}, \ldots, C_{lh}, \ldots, C_{lH_l}$.

First Iteration. Control sum of survey nonresponse adjusted weights to equal population total within each category for characteristic C_1

$$W_{5ij}^{(1.1)} = \frac{N_{C_{1h}}}{\sum\limits_{k,j \in C_{1h}} W_{4kj}} W_{4ij}, \qquad i,j \in C_{1h} \tag{26.25}$$

where NC_{1h} = population control for category h of characteristic C_1.

Control sum of prior weights, $W_{5ij}^{(1.1)}$, to equal population total within each category for characteristic C_2

$$W_{5ij}^{(1.2)} = \frac{NC_{2h}}{\sum\limits_{k,j \in D_{2h}} W_{5kj}^{(1.1)}} W_{5ij}^{(1.1)}, \quad i,j \in D_{2h} \tag{26.26}$$

where NC_{2h} = population control for category h of characteristic C_2.

Control sum of prior weights, $W_{5ij}^{(1.2)}$, to equal population total within each category for characteristic C_3

$$W_{5ij}^{(1.3)} = \frac{N_{C_{3h}}}{\sum\limits_{k,j \in C_{3h}} W_{5kj}^{(1.2)}} W_{5ij}^{(1.2)}, \quad i,j \in C_{3h} \tag{26.27}$$

where NC_{3h} = population control for category h of characteristic C_3.

Continue adjustment through the last characteristic, C_L, used in the raking ratio adjustment.

Control sum of prior weights, $W_{5ij}^{(1.L-1)}$, to equal population total within each category for characteristic C_L

$$W_{5ij}^{(1.L)} = \frac{N_{C_{Lh}}}{\sum\limits_{k,j \in C_{Lh}} W_{5kj}^{(1.L-1)}} W_{5ij}^{(1.L-1)}, \quad i,j \in C_{Lh} \tag{26.28}$$

where NC_{Lh} = population control for category h of characteristic C_L.

This ends the first iteration. At this point weighted sample counts will equal population controls for characteristic C_L, but not for the other L-1 characteristics. Thus, the steps need to be repeated.

Second Iteration. Control sum of prior weights, $W_{5ij}^{(1.L)}$, to equal population total within each category for characteristic C_1

$$W_{5ij}^{(2.1)} = \frac{N_{C_{1h}}}{\sum\limits_{k,j \in C_{1h}} W_{5kj}^{(1.L)}} W_{5ij}^{(1.L)}, \quad i,j \in C_{1h} \tag{26.29}$$

Control sum of prior weights, $W_{5ij}^{(2.1)}$, to equal population total within each category for characteristic C_2

$$W_{5ij}^{(2.2)} = \frac{N_{C_{2h}}}{\sum\limits_{k,j \in C_{2h}} W_{5kj}^{(2.1)}} W_{5ij}^{(2.1)}, \quad i,j \in C_{2h} \tag{26.30}$$

Continue adjustment through the last characteristic, C_L, used in the raking ratio adjustment, which will conclude the second iteration.

26.5.3 FINAL RAKING RATIO-ADJUSTED WEIGHTS

Continue iterating until the difference between the weighted counts and population controls for each characteristic are suitably small (e.g., the relative difference between the weighted counts and the population controls for all categories of all characteristics used in raking is less than 0.5%).[5] Assuming the raking ratio estimation went through I iterations, the final survey weights can then be expressed as

$$W_{5ij} = W_{5ij}^{(I.L)} \tag{26.31}$$

The sum of the W_{5ij} across all survey respondents will equal the true population total, N; in addition, the sum of the W_{5ij} across all survey respondents within a given category of one of the characteristics used in raking will equal (or nearly equal) the true population total for that category, $N_{C_{lh}}$.

$$\sum_{i,j} W_{5ij} = N, \quad \sum_{i,j \in C_{lh}} W_{5ij} = N_{C_{lh}} \tag{26.32}$$

26.6 Sample Weighting for Nonprobability Sample Designs

For nonprobability sample designs, probabilities of selection are not known. Thus, base weights cannot be determined. In addition, information concerning outcomes of the data collection process is typically unavailable and thus noncontact/nonresponse adjustments cannot be made. As a result, inferences about the target population based upon statistical theory cannot be made.

However, researchers may be interested in using the survey data to come to some better understanding of the population by adjusting for differences in the distributions between the sample units and the population to which these sample units belong. In these situations, sample units are designated with a base weight of 1.0, and ratio adjustment to population counts is carried out. The characteristics used in the ratio adjustment are those for which it is determined the sample has a skewed distribution relative to the population and for which it is believed the survey variables of interest are correlated. Note that this approach merely adjusts the responding sample distribution to agree with the population distribution, but does not allow for statements of variability or bias.

26.7 Issues in Sample Weighting

The prior discussion assumes no unusual situations are encountered and that adjustment cells are predefined. Below is a brief discussion of issues which must

[5]In some cases, convergence may not be achieved, in which case, collapsing of planned post-strata will need to be carried out.

be addressed in implementing a weighting methodology. Further information on these topics can be found in the earlier mentioned survey weighting references.

26.7.1 ADJUSTMENT CELL CREATION

Cells for use in noncontact and nonresponse adjustment should be defined so as to yield groups of units with similar response rates and/or similar values for selected variables of interest. This can be accomplished through analysis of the survey data or analysis of results from prior rounds of the survey or related surveys. Note that one objective is to create cells for which the values for selected variables of interest are similar between respondents and nonrespondents. While this obviously cannot be accomplished based upon available data, basing cells upon similarity of values for variables known for the total sampling frame and known or believed to be correlated with the variables of interest is an appropriate proxy.

Adjustment cells can be defined only on the basis of information known for both respondents and nonrespondents. This typically limits adjustment cells to be defined upon the basis of a small number of characteristics.

26.7.2 COLLAPSING ADJUSTMENT CELLS

In some instances, specific noncontact/nonresponse cells may contain a very small number of contacts/respondents upon which to derive a stable adjustment factor. In these situations (general guidelines are when the number of available contacts/respondents is less than 20 or 30), cells with small numbers should be collapsed with an adjacent cell. Determination of which cell to collapse with should be based upon the same information used in defining the adjustment cells initially—response rates and values for selected variables from the sampling frame.

26.7.3 EXTREME WEIGHTS

Adjustments may occasionally result in some sample units having substantially larger weights than other sample units. To the extent that the survey weights vary widely among sample respondents, survey estimates will have large variances. Thus, checks should be made to identify extreme weights and trim them to reduce variance. Weight trimming refers to the process of identifying outlier weights and changing those weights to make them more similar to the weights for other units. Weight trimming will introduce some bias, but it is generally felt that the reduction in variance is more beneficial.

One common approach is to identify weight adjustments that exceed the median weight plus six times the interquartile range (IQR) of the adjustments for all sample cases. If the adjustment for any sample case exceeds that threshold, that weight is truncated so the cumulative adjustment equals the cutoff value. The aim is to reduce the impact on the variance of large weight adjustments, but at the same time to limit the amount of truncation because of the bias it could introduce into the estimates. The overall goal of truncation is to reduce the mean squared error of the estimates.

26.7.4 POPULATION CONTROLS

Independent population counts are required for use in weighting adjustments to achieve agreement with population controls. Unless the sampling frame is known to be complete and accurate, population controls should be based upon some independent source which is complete and accurate. Examples include population estimates from the Census Bureau, natality records, administrative records on licensed providers, and so on. In creating population controls, one objective is to determine counts by selected characteristics known or believed to be correlated with the survey variables of interest, and/or for which published estimates are to be generated from the survey data.

26.8 Estimation

Survey estimates are derived by applying the final survey weights to the survey data. An estimate of the total for a given variable, *Y*, is defined as

$$\hat{Y} = \sum_{i,j} W_{5ij} Y_{ij} \tag{26.33}$$

where the Y_{ij} represent the value for variable *Y* reported by the *j*th USU in the *i*th initial sampling unit.

Similarly, when deriving an estimate of the total for a given variable, *Y*, within a specified domain, *d* (e.g., by physician specialty, by race/ethnicity), the estimate is defined as

$$\hat{Y}_d = \sum_{i,j \in d} W_{5ij} Y_{ij} \tag{26.34}$$

Estimates for means can likewise be derived. The estimate of the mean for the variable *Y* for the total population can be written as

$$\hat{\bar{Y}} = \frac{\sum_{i,j} W_{5ij} Y_{ij}}{N} \tag{26.35}$$

The estimate of the mean for variable *Y* for domain *d* will be derived as

$$\hat{\bar{Y}} = \frac{\sum_{i,j \in d} W_{5ij} Y_{ij}}{N_d} \tag{26.36}$$

if domain d was used in the adjustment to population controls (where N_d is the population total for domain d), or

$$\hat{\bar{Y}} = \frac{\sum_{i,j \in d} W_{5ij} Y_{ij}}{\sum_{i,j \in d} W_{5ij}} \tag{26.37}$$

if domain d was not used in the adjustment to population controls. The reason for the difference in denominators is that for domains used in adjustment to population controls, the population size is a fixed number, whereas for domains not used in adjustment to population controls, the population size is an estimate dependent upon the number of sample cases in the domain and their corresponding final survey weights.

26.9 Variance Estimation

Sample survey estimates contain uncertainty due to the sample design, resultant responding sample, and survey weighting approach, as well as from nonsampling error sources. A variety of methods are available for use in deriving variance estimates. Design-based variance estimates utilize the sample design to define the form of the variance estimator. However, adjustments to the base weights, which reflect the sample design, to account for nonresponse and coverage error result in the need for other approaches to fully represent the error in survey estimates. Approaches that can be used include Taylor Series expansion, Jackknife variance estimation, and replication methods. Extensive discussion of variance estimation for sample surveys can be found in Wolter (2007). This topic is also discussed in Chapter 29.

26.10 Special Topics

In this section, we provide a brief review of some important topics that can be of particular importance when constructing sample weights for health survey data files. These include the challenge of dual-frame weighting, response propensity weighting adjustments, alternative calibration methods, and developing weights for longitudinal and panel designs.

26.10.1 DUAL-FRAME SAMPLE WEIGHTING

Some sample designs make use of multiple sampling frames, in which the sampling frames have some degree of overlap in terms of the population covered by each, and therefore some units have a chance of being selected from more than one sampling frame. An obvious example is the use of both landline and cell telephone sampling frames, in which households may be on both sampling frames. The objectives in developing the dual-frame weighting approach are to account for overlap between the two sample frames and to minimize mean squared error at the estimation area level. Discussion of dual-frame weighting may be found in Wolter et al. (2010), Brick et al. (2011), and Schaible (1979).

26.10.2 RESPONSE PROPENSITY WEIGHTING ADJUSTMENTS

An alternative to creation of noncontact/nonresponse weighting class adjustment cells based upon variables available for all sample units is to utilize response propensity models (Little 1986). In this approach, response propensities are estimated using a generalized linear model appropriate to response rate, such as logistic, probit, or complementary log–log models (Valliant et al. 2013). Weights are adjusted based upon either by calculating the inverse of the estimated response propensities or by creating response propensity cells by quintiling the estimated response propensities and calculating the noncontact/nonresponse weight adjustment within each quintile as described previously.

26.10.3 ALTERNATIVE CALIBRATION METHODS

Post-stratification and raking ratio estimation belong to a larger class of adjustments called *calibration estimators* (Deville and Särndal 1992), which utilize auxiliary information from the sampling frame population controls, independent measures of survey variables of interest, and so on, to improve the efficiency of estimators. These estimators seek to minimize some defined measure of the distance between the weights prior to and following adjustment subject to selected constraints concerning weighted counts of the survey data.

Alternative calibration methods include generalized regression estimators, or GREGs (Särndal 2007), and generalized raking estimators (Deville et al. 1993). In addition, if independent estimates for some survey variables exist and are deemed of sufficient accuracy, these independent estimates may be used in the constraints to which weighted counts are controlled.

26.10.4 WEIGHTING FOR LONGITUDINAL AND PANEL SURVEYS

Longitudinal and panel surveys, which collect measurements across time, involve complete overlap of the sample across time, rotation of the sample units across time, or a combination of complete overlap and rotation of the sample across time. Given overlap and rotation of the sample, along with the issue of nonresponse across time, weighting for longitudinal and panel surveys differs from that for cross-sectional surveys. For discussion of weighting and nonresponse adjustment for longitudinal and panel surveys, refer to Lynn (2009), Binder (1998), Kasprzyk et al. (1989), and Duncan and Kalton (1987).

26.10.5 SURVEY WEIGHTING SOFTWARE

Given the customization of sample design and data collection methodology, analysts often write survey specific code for calculating survey weights. Statistical software packages Stata® (www.stata.com), SAS® (www.sas.com), SPSS® (http://www-01.ibm.com/software/analytics/spss/) R® (www.r-project.org) are widely used by statisticians in processing and analyzing survey data, with R software being available for free. Software developed specifically for survey applications to allow for accurate variance estimation, but which also provide for survey weighting include SUDAAN® (www.rti.org/sudaan) and WesVar® (www.westat.com/Westat/expertise/information_systems/WesVar/index.cfm)

26.11 Example: Weighting for the 2010 National Immunization Survey

26.11.1 INTRODUCTION

The National Immunization Survey (NIS) has been conducted quarterly since 1994 by the Centers for Disease Control and Prevention (CDC), to estimate the vaccination coverage rates among children aged 19–35 months in the United States within geographic areas (called *estimation areas*) consisting of 50 states, the District of Columbia, and several sub-state areas. The NIS collects vaccination data on the following childhood vaccines: diphtheria, tetanus toxoids, and pertusis (DTaP) vaccine; poliovirus (polio) vaccine; measles, mumps and rubella (MMR) vaccine; *Haemophilus influenza* type b (Hib) vaccine; hepatitis B (Hep B) vaccine; varicella zoster (chicken pox) vaccine; pneumococcal vaccine; hepatitis A (Hep A) vaccine; influenza vaccine; and rotavirus vaccine.

The NIS uses a two-phase survey design where the first phase is a random digit-dial (RDD) survey that identifies the households with age-eligible children and collects information on vaccinations and vaccination providers of the eligible children.[6] In the second phase a mail survey of providers, called the *provider record check (PRC)*, collects detailed vaccination histories for the children for whom the RDD-phase interview was complete and consent to contact providers was received. In 2010, the NIS included 23,605 children with complete household interviews and 16,798 children with adequate provider data.

The remainder of this section is adapted from the 2010 National Immunization Survey Data User's Guide (NCHS 2011). The 2010 NIS sample design selected a sample of landline telephone numbers for the survey. Further information concerning the sample design and collection methodology associated with the NIS is also contained in the Data User's Guide.

[6] NIS utilized a landline telephone number sampled design through 2010. A dual frame, landline and cell telephone number sample design was implemented beginning Q4/2010.

26.11.2 OVERVIEW OF NIS WEIGHTING APPROACH

Each of the two phases of NIS data collection results in a separate sampling weight for each child who has data at that phase. The household-phase sampling weights permit analyses of data from children with completed household interviews. Each child with adequate provider data (the subset on which official estimates of vaccination coverage are based) has a provider-phase sampling weight.

A sampling weight controlled to population totals may be interpreted as the approximate number of children in the target population that a child in the sample represents. Thus, for example, the sum of the sampling weights of children who are up-to-date (on a particular vaccine or series of vaccines) yields an estimate of the total number of children in the target population who are up-to-date. Dividing this sum by the total of the sampling weights for all children gives an estimate of the corresponding vaccination coverage rate.

The following section describes how these weights are developed and adjusted so as to achieve an accurate representation of the target population.

Base Sampling Weight. In each quarterly NIS sample, each child with a completed household interview receives a base sampling weight. This weight is equal to the total of telephone numbers in the sampling frame for the estimation area divided by the total of telephone numbers that were randomly sampled from that sampling frame and released for interview during that quarter.

$$W_{1k} = \frac{1}{\pi_k} = \frac{N_{aq}}{n_{aq}}, \quad k \in a, q \qquad (28.38)$$

where,

π_k probability of selecting the *k*th telephone number in the estimation area
n_{aq} sample size (in released replicates) in estimation area a in quarter q
N_{aq} total telephone numbers on the sampling frame in estimation area a in quarter q

Adjustments for Nonresolution of Telephone Numbers, Screener Nonresponse and Interview Nonresponse. Figure 26.3 illustrates the data collection flow for the NIS. First, selected telephone numbers are called to determine if they are associated with a residential household. Second, residential households are asked screening questions to determine if there are any age-eligible children in the household. Finally, those residential households with age-eligible children are asked to complete the household interview. To compensate for the unit nonresponse that can occur at each of these stages, the sampling weights of children with a completed household interview are adjusted to account for the estimated number of age-eligible children in households whose telephone numbers are never determined to be residential, the estimated number of age-eligible children in households that fail to complete the screening interview, and the number of identified age-eligible children for whom the household interview is not completed.

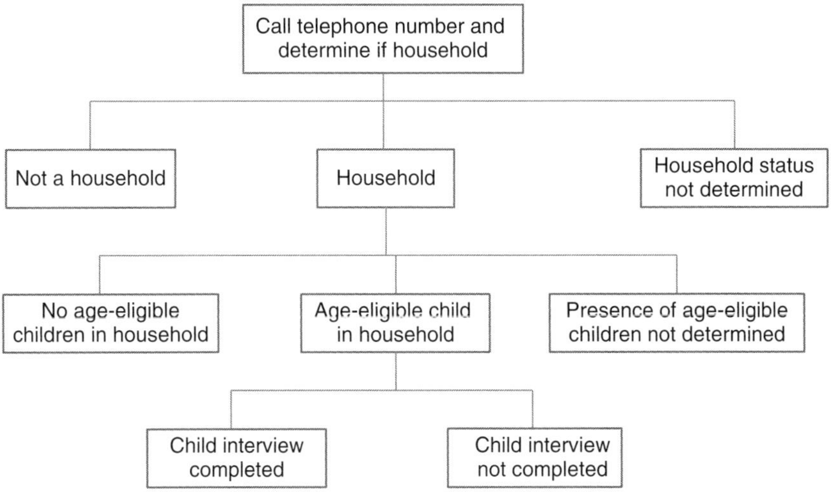

FIGURE 26.3 NIS data collection flow.

Telephone Number Nonresolution Adjustment. The telephone numbers selected for the NIS contain some that are not associated with a household. All selected telephone numbers are called to determine whether they are associated with a residential household. However, some telephone numbers remain unresolved, and the survey weights are adjusted to account for this nonresolution.

$$\begin{aligned} W_{2k} &= \frac{W_{1k}}{R_{2\ell}}, \quad \text{if } k \text{ is a resolved telephone number in adjustment cell } \ell \\ &= 0, \quad \text{otherwise} \end{aligned} \tag{26.39}$$

where $R_{2\ell}$ is the resolution rate, computed using weights W_{1k}, in adjustment cell ℓ.

Screener Nonresponse Adjustment. The target population for the NIS is children 19–35 months of age. As not all households contain an age-eligible child, a set of screening questions are asked to identify households eligible for the survey. As some households do not respond to the screener, the survey weights are adjusted to account for this nonresponse.

$$\begin{aligned} W_{3k} &= \frac{W_{2k}}{R_{3\ell}}, \quad \text{if } k \text{ is a screener completed telephone number in adjustment} \\ &\quad \text{cell } \ell, \\ &= 0, \quad \text{otherwise} \end{aligned} \tag{26.40}$$

where $R_{3\ell}$ is the screener response rate, computed using weights W_{2k}, in cell ℓ.

Interview Nonresponse Adjustment. Finally, the NIS questionnaire is attempted to be completed for eligible children 19–35 months of age. As the questionnaire is not completed for some age-eligible children, the survey weights are adjusted to account for this nonresponse.

$$W_{4k} = \frac{W_{3k}}{R_{4\ell}}, \quad \text{if } k \text{ is an interview completed telephone number in adjustment cell } \ell$$
$$= 0, \quad \text{otherwise} \tag{26.41}$$

where $R_{4\ell}$ is the interview completion rate, computed using weights W_{3k}, in cell ℓ.

Each of these adjustments is carried out within estimation areas by forming weighting cells based on the residential directory-listed status of the sample telephone number, percent of the population that is White in the telephone exchange, and MSA (i.e., Metropolitan Statistical Area) status of the telephone exchange. Cells with an insufficient number of responding cases are collapsed with neighboring cells. Within each adjustment cell, the weights of the unresolved/non-responding records from the previous adjustment step are distributed to the weights of the resolved/responding records within each cell.

Adjustment for Multiple Telephone Lines and Deriving Annual Weights. Once the nonresponse-adjusted interview weights for households are computed, these weights are adjusted for additional telephone landlines in the household. Because households with multiple landline telephone lines have a greater chance of being sampled, each child's household interview weight is adjusted by dividing it by the total number of residential landline telephone lines reported in the household (up to a maximum of 3).

$$W_{5k} = \frac{W_{4k}}{t_k} \tag{26.42}$$

where

t'_k number of telephone landlines for home use, excluding lines used only for fax or computer communication, reported by the kth household in the completed interview, and

t_k min $(3, t'_k)$.

Adjustment for Combining Study Quarters. Through the previous step, the sampling weights are adjusted separately for each quarter and the weights in each quarter pertain to the entire target population. However, annual vaccination coverage estimates are obtained from data for four consecutive quarters, so the weights in each quarterly file are adjusted when the data from the four quarters are combined. The adjustment factor is proportional to the number of households with completed household interviews in each quarter within an estimation area.

$$W_{6k} = W_{5k}/R_{6k}, \quad \text{for} \quad k \in q, a \tag{26.43}$$

where

$$R_{6k} = \frac{\sum_{q'=1}^{4} n_{q'a}}{n_{qa}}$$

n_{qa} number of households with a complete interview in quarter q in estimation area a.

Initial Adjustment to Population Controls. To derive survey weights that yield estimates representing the total population of age-eligible children in the United States, the combined survey weights from the prior step must be controlled to independent estimates of the target population. This is accomplished through a three-step process intended to address known undercoverage and control for potential differential coverage bias.

Adjustment for Sampling Frame Noncoverage. The 2010 NIS sampling frame included only households with landline telephones. Because the target population consists of all children ages 19–35 months living in households, regardless of whether they have landline telephones, nonresponse-adjusted base sampling weights need to be adjusted to compensate for the noncoverage of children living in households without landline telephones. The noncovered children include children from both cell phone-only and phoneless households. Data from the NHIS suggest that, of children under the age of 18, approximately 2.0% lived in phoneless households and approximately 31.8% lived in cell phone-only households in July–December, 2010.

Adjustment for sampling frame noncoverage builds on findings that households that have a landline telephone at the time of the survey but have experienced an interruption of more than 1 week in their landline telephone service during the previous year are often similar to households that do not have a landline telephone (Keeter 1995, Frankel et al. 2003). In essence, the resulting adjustment projects from the interruption part of the sample to both the interruption and non-landline-telephone parts of the population, and from the non-interruption part of the sample to the non-interruption part of the population.

A post-stratification adjustment is used, with two cells within each estimation area formed based on the interruption status in landline telephone service. Weights are adjusted to control totals within each estimation area—weights of the children with interruption in landline telephone service are adjusted to the control total representing themselves and the children in non-landline-telephone households, while the weights of the children without interruption in landline telephone service are adjusted to the control total representing themselves only, that is, the children in households without interruption in telephone service

$$W_{7j} = \left(\frac{T_{ma}}{\sum_{j' \in F,m,a} \delta_{7j'm} W_{6k}} \right) W_{6k}, \quad \textit{for} \quad j \in F, m, a, k \tag{26.44}$$

where

W_{6k} the weight associated with the household containing the *j*th child (from the previous step)

F the set of children for whom the household interview is complete

m corresponds to the adjustment cells based on interruption status

$$\delta_{7jm} = 1, \quad \text{if the } j\text{th child is in cell } m,$$
$$= 0, \quad \text{otherwise,}$$

The control totals used for the NIS are derived from current natality data from the National Center for Health Statistics, adjusted for infant mortality, immigration, and migration between estimation areas. Because the Vital Statistics data give the counts of all live births in the United States, regardless of whether the household has landline telephone service, the control totals include children in both landline-telephone and non-landline-telephone households. The control total for children in non-landline-telephone households or in landline-telephone households with interruption are derived from the estimation area-level control totals by estimating the percentage of children in non-landline-telephone households and the percentage of children in landline telephone households with interruption within each estimation area.

Post-stratification Ratio Adjustment. The next step in the adjustment is a simple post-stratification that separates the sample of completed interviews into cells defined by characteristics related to noncoverage—race/ethnicity of the child's mother, level of educational attainment of the child's mother, and age of the child.

$$W_{8j} = \left(\frac{T_m}{\sum_{j \in F} \delta_{8jm} W_{7j}} \right) W_{7j}, \quad \text{for} \quad j \in F, m \tag{26.45}$$

where

$$\delta_{8jm} = 1, \quad \text{if the } j\text{th child is in the } m\text{th post-stratum}$$
$$= 0, \quad \text{otherwise}$$

To reduce sampling variability and improve the precision of estimation, extreme weights are trimmed and then recalibrated to control totals. Sampling weight values exceeding the median weight plus six times the IQR of the weights within an estimation area are then truncated to that threshold.

Raking Ratio Adjustment. The final step in adjusting the household-phase sampling weights is a raking ratio adjustment of the trimmed, post-stratified weights. The raking procedure uses estimation area-level control totals for maternal education categories, maternal race/ethnicity, age group of the child, and gender of the child, as described in Section 26.5.2. The raked weights can be expressed as:

$$W_{9j} = \varphi_j W_{8j}, \quad \text{for} \quad j \in F \tag{26.46}$$

where, ϕ_j is the raking adjustment factor for the *j*th child derived through the iteration process.

The raking process yields survey sampling weights which constitute the household-phase weights and can be used with data from the household interview to derive estimates.

Adjustment for Provider Nonresponse. Among the children with a completed household interview, approximately 70% had adequate provider data. Failure to obtain adequate provider data for the remaining roughly 30% was attributable to a variety of factors, including parent or guardian not giving consent to contact the child's vaccination provider(s), children with one or more identified provider but provider(s) did not respond, or responding providers did not report sufficient information to determine the child's vaccination status.

Empirical results suggest that children with adequate provider data have characteristics believed to be associated with a greater likelihood of being up-to-date, compared with children who had missing provider data (Smith et al. 2001, Smith et al. 2005). If no adjustment is made to the household-phase sample weights to account for these differences, estimated vaccination coverage rates may be biased.

To reduce potential bias in estimators of vaccination coverage attributable to partial nonresponse, a weighting-class adjustment is used in each estimation area (Brick and Kalton 1996). This adjustment involves three steps. In the first step, sampled children are classified according to the quintile of their estimated probabilities of having adequate provider data, referred to as *response propensities* (Rosenbaum and Rubin 1983, 1984, Rosenbaum 1987). Children who have similar response propensities will also be similar with respect to variables that are strongly associated with the probability of having adequate provider data. In this important respect, children in each class are comparable. Because of this comparability, any sub-sample of children in a class may represent all children in the class. Therefore, the weighting-class adjustment uses the children with adequate provider data to represent all children in the class.

In the second step of this weighting-class adjustment, within each class an adjustment factor redistributes the household-phase sample weights of the children with missing provider data to the weights of the children who have adequate provider data. These adjusted sample weights of children with adequate provider data are initial nonresponse-adjusted provider-phase weights.

$$
\begin{aligned}
W_{10j} &= \frac{W_{9j}}{R_{10\ell}}, \quad \text{if } j \text{ is a child with adequate provider data in adjustment cell } \ell \\
&= 0, \quad \text{otherwise}
\end{aligned} \tag{26.47}
$$

where $R_{10\ell}$ is the adequate provider data rate, computed using weights W_{9j}, in cell ℓ.

Final Adjustment to Population Controls. Within an estimation area, the sums of provider nonresponse adjusted weights of children with adequate provider data for the various levels of important socio-demographic variables (such as race/ethnicity) may not be equal to corresponding population totals. To reduce bias attributable to these differences, raking was used in the third step to adjust the nonresponse adjusted weights to match estimation area control totals.

These raked weights of children with adequate provider data are called *final provider-phase weights.*

$$W_{11j} = \eta_j W_{10j}, \quad \text{for} \quad j \in F \tag{26.48}$$

where, η_j is the raking adjustment factor for the jth child derived through the iteration process.

The raking process yields survey sampling weights which constitute the provider-phase weights and can be used with data from the provider interview to derive estimates.

26.12 Summary

Survey weighting allows analysts to extrapolate data collected for a random sample of a population to make inferences for the full population. Survey weighting must account for the probabilities of selection of the sample units, adjust for noncontact and nonresponse, and adjust for differences between the weighted sample counts and independent population counts. Adjustments should be defined so as to lessen the potential for variance and bias in the resulting survey estimates. Additional and more extensive discussions of weighting for sample surveys can be found in such texts as Valliant et al. (2013), Lohr (2010), Groves et al. (2009), Hidiroglou et al. (1995), and Kalton (1983).

REFERENCES

Bethlehem J. Weighting nonresponse adjustments based on auxiliary information. In: Groves RM, Dillman DA, Eltinge JL, Little RJA, editors. *Survey Nonresponse*. New York: John Wiley & Sons, Inc.; 2002.

Binder D. Longitudinal surveys: why are these surveys different from all other surveys? Surv Method 1998;24:101–108.

Brick JM, Cervantes IF, Lee S, Norman G. Nonsampling errors in dual frame telephone surveys. Surv Method 2011;37:1–12.

Brick JM, Kalton G. Handling missing data in survey research. Stat Methods Med Res 1996;5:215–238.

Deming WE, Stephan FF. On a least squares adjustment of a sample frequency table when the expected marginal totals are known. Ann Math Stat 1940;11:428–444.

Deville JC, Särndal CE. Calibration estimators in survey sampling. J Am Stat Assoc 1992;87:376–382.

Deville JC, Särndal CE, Sautory O. Generalized raking procedures in survey sampling. J Am Stat Assoc 1993;88:1013–1020.

Duncan GJ, Kalton G. Issues of design and analysis of surveys across time. Int Stat Rev 1987;55:97–117.

Frankel MR, Srinath KP, Hoaglin DC, Battaglia MP, Smith PJ, Wright RA, Khare M. Adjustments for non-telephone bias in random-digit-dialing surveys. Stat Med 2003;22:1611–1626.

Groves RM, Fowler FJ Jr,, Couper MP, Lepkowski JM, Singer E, Tourangeau R. *Survey Methodology*. New York: John Wiley & Sons, Inc.; 2009.

Hidiroglou MA, Särndal CE, Binder DA. Weighting and estimation in business surveys. In: Cox BG, Binder DA, Chinnappa BN, Christianson A, Colledge MJ, Kott PS, editors. *Business Survey Methods*. New York: John Wiley & Sons, Inc.; 1995. p 477–502.

Kalton G. *Introduction to Survey Sampling*. Newbury Park, CA: Sage Publications, Inc.; 1983.

Kasprzyk D, Duncan G, Kalton G, Singh MP, editors. *Panel Surveys*. New York: John Wiley & Sons, Inc.; 1989.

Keeter S. Estimating noncoverage bias from a telephone survey. Public Opin Q 1995;59:196–217.

Little RA. Survey nonresponse adjustments for estimates of means. Int Stat Rev 1986;54:139–157.

Lohr SL. *Sampling Design and Analysis*. 2nd ed. Boston: Brooks/Cole; 2010.

Lynn P. *Methodology of Longitudinal Surveys*. New York: John Wiley & Sons, Inc.; 2009.

National Centers for Health Statistics. 2011. 2010 National Immunization Survey Data User's Guide. Available at http://www.cdc.gov/nchs/nis/data_files.htm. Accessed 2014 Jun 08.

Office of Management and Budget. Measuring and reporting sources of error in surveys, Statistical Policy Working Paper 31, Springfield, VA: National Technical Information Service; 2001.

Oh HL, Scheuren F. Weighting adjustment for unit nonresponse. In: Madow WG, Olkin I, Rubin DB, editors. *Incomplete Data in Sample Surveys*. Theory and Bibliography. Vol. 2. New York: Academic Press, Inc.; 1983. p 143–184.

Rosenbaum PR. Model-based direct adjustment. J Am Stat Assoc 1987;82:387–394.

Rosenbaum PR, Rubin DB. The central role of the propensity score in observational studies for causal effects. Biometrika 1983;70:467–474.

Rosenbaum PR, Rubin DB. Reducing bias in observational studies using subclassification on the propensity score. J Am Stat Assoc 1984;79:516–524.

Särndal CE. The calibration approach in survey theory and practice. Surv Method 2007;33:99–119.

Schaible WL. Choosing weights for composite estimators for small area statistics. Proceedings of the Section on Survey Research Methods, American Statistical Association; 1979. p 741–746.

Smith TMF. Post-stratification. Statistician 1991;40:315–323.

Smith PJ, Hoaglin DC, Battaglia MP, Khare M, Barker LE. Statistical methodology of the National Immunization Survey, 1994–2002. Vital Health Stat 2 2005;(138(DHHS Publication No. (PHS) 2005–1338). Hyattsville, MD: National Center for Health Statistics):1–55.

Smith PJ, Rao JNK, Battaglia MP, Ezzati-Rice TM, Daniels D, Khare M. Compensating for provider nonresponse using response propensities to form adjustment cells: the National Immunization Survey. Vital Health Stat 2 2001;(133(DHHS Publication No. (PHS) 2001–1333). Hyattsville, MD: National Center for Health Statistics.):1–17.

Valliant R, Dever JA, Kreuter F. *Practical Tools for Designing and Weighting Survey Samples*. New York: Springer-Verlag; 2013.

Wolter KM. *Introduction to Variance Estimation*. 2nd ed. New York: Springer-Verlag; 2007.

Wolter KM, Smith P, Blumberg SJ. Statistical foundations of cell-phone surveys. Surv Method 2010;36:203–215.

ONLINE RESOURCES

The National Health and Nutrition Examination Survey, Survey Weighting Tutorial can be accessed at: www.cdc.gov/nchs/tutorials/nhanes/surveydesign/Weighting/intro.htm.

The National Ambulatory Medical Care Survey Estimation Procedures are available at: www.cdc.gov/nchs/ahcd/ahcd_estimation_procedures.htm#namcs_procedures.

The Medical Expenditure Panel Survey Household Component Estimation Procedures are available at: http://meps.ahrq.gov/mepsweb/data_files/publications/mr24/mr24.pdf.

CHAPTER TWENTY SEVEN

Merging Survey Data with Administrative Data for Health Research Purposes

Michael Davern
NORC at the University of Chicago, Chicago, IL, USA

Marc Roemer
Agency for Healthcare Research and Quality, Survey Statistician formerly at the US Census Bureau, Rockville, MD, USA

Wendy Thomas
Minnesota Population Center, University of Minnesota, Minneapolis, MN, USA

27.1 Introduction

High quality demographic and program participation data are crucial to health research, health surveillance, and monitoring the impact of public policy. General population health surveys have long met this need, but have limitations. For example, surveys often produce counts of public program enrollment or participation that vary greatly from the administrative enrollment data (US Census Bureau 2004, Davern et al. 2009a). Surveys are often unable to measure program specific benefits accurately such as healthcare utilization, cost, size of benefit received, and type of treatment received. On the other hand, administrative data have the significant deficiency that they do not include the robust socio-demographic and

Handbook of Health Survey Methods, First Edition. Edited by Timothy P. Johnson.

economic information of persons enrolled. They do not contain any information on those eligible for a public program but unenrolled, nor those who would be eligible if the program rules changed. To enhance both sources of data for health research, researchers have linked survey and administrative data for health research and analysis (Hotz et al. 1998).

Survey data[1] are widely used for health research because they seek to cover entire populations of people, not just those eligible or participating in a program, and they contain policy-relevant information on people, families, and households. This information includes people's characteristics such as relationships to other household members, employment, income sources, income amounts, program participation, and much more. As a result, a survey constitutes a robust set of data not only on people enrolled in public programs but people who are eligible and not participating, and people whose eligibility could change depending on program rules. This information can be used to simulate effects of changes in a policy or program (e.g., does the Earned Income Tax Credit result in more labor force participation?), as well as to evaluate the effectiveness of a particular program in achieving its goals (e.g., does the State Children's Health Insurance Program result in lower rates of uninsurance for low income children?).

Survey data are crucial to health policy makers, and despite their limitations, continue to be widely used because they are the only source of information rich enough to provide broad population surveillance and to predict the impact of changes in policy on the entire population. Combining survey data with data gleaned from public program administration that track payments to beneficiaries, such as Social Security checks and payments to providers by Medicare and Medicaid, creates a linked data product with superior analytic capabilities than either source of data by itself. The potential uses of these linked data products in health research are tremendous, but without basic research into data quality, the potential for deriving incorrect inferences from these data is also great.

27.2 Potential Uses of Linked Data[2]

Administrative data typically entail records collected or maintained by federal, state, tribal, or local government agencies, or commercial entities; not for the purpose of demographic statistics, public health surveillance, or policy analysis, but for administering programs or providing services. For this reason, an administrative data set such as the Medicaid Statistical Information System (MSIS) contains basic information about persons enrolled in state Medicaid programs, but lacks

[1]Through this chapter we shorten demographic household surveys to simply "surveys" and public program administrative data is often shortened to "administrative data".

[2]In this chapter we are dealing with after-the-fact linking. The survey and administrative data were independently collected and linked after the fact. This chapter is still relevant in some areas for cases where administrative data themselves were used as the survey sampling frame (such as is done with the Medicare Current Beneficiaries Survey) but not all the issues discussed will apply to these data collection efforts.

the socioeconomic and demographic details provided by surveys and needed for health research (Hotz et al. 1998). Conceptually, therefore, combining the survey and the enrollment information from the MSIS records might provide a richer, more complete, and more accurate view of the Medicaid program, its participants, and the eligible but unenrolled population. A list of selected administrative data sources that could potentially be used for linking to surveys can be found in Table 27.1.

Other applications include correcting bias in imputation, direct editing of survey items, evaluating the accuracy of survey responses, editing and imputing survey data, improving the coverage of sampling frames (e.g., Chappell et al. 2005, National Research Council 2004a), and reducing unit nonresponse bias (Czajka 2013). For example, the U.S. Census Bureau has linked its Current Population Survey (CPS) data to Internal Revenue Service (IRS) and Social Security Administration (SSA) data in order to compare survey reports of income to the IRS and SSA records measuring similar concepts. Now in the CPS, the U.S. Census Bureau adjusts interest income upwardly for individuals for whom the amount was imputed (not reported), based on the relationships observed in a CPS and IRS linked data file (Nelson 1985). With linked data sets, data providers could develop similar adjustments for other survey items.

Linked data files can enhance data quality directly. Research has documented that a significant proportion of enrollees in Medicaid and the Food Stamp Program do not report being enrolled when responding to survey questions (U.S. Census Bureau 2004, Call et al. 2002, Klerman et al. 2005).[3] This discrepancy could be attenuated through the use of linked data by editing each person's self-reported status to be consistent with the administrative data. The resulting linked data would better simulate the impact of Medicaid program changes (Davern et al. 2009b).

If not used to edit the survey data, at least linked data files could be used to evaluate the quality of survey responses about public program participation. For example, these files can help assess how well respondents answer questions about participation in Medicaid, Food Stamps, Temporary Assistance for Needy Families (TANF), and Supplemental Security Income (SSI). Such research could lead to better survey questions that extract more accurate information from respondents and build models that could be used for imputation (e.g., Davern et al. 2009b).[4] Furthermore, comparing survey and administrative data can lead to better-informed imputation methodologies for survey data and perhaps even model-based imputation methodologies to generate more accurate estimates regarding program participation. Research with these linked data files could improve the accuracy of surveys by identifying who is likely to make errors and how these errors can influence estimates (those enrolled in a program, as well as those eligible and not enrolled).

[3]Furthermore, some people who cannot be found on the administrative data file report receiving some of these benefits. These respondents might have given an incorrect answer to the question, although it could also be a problem with the linking information.

[4]Administrative data cannot be used to directly edit or correct the survey data because of disclosure issues (Chappell et al. 2005).

TABLE 27.1 Basic Information on Selected Administrative Data that Could be Potentially linked to Survey Data

Source Data Description	Linkage Unit	Provider	Requirements to Access	Source Website
CMS Medicare Research Identifiable Files	Person	Centers for Medicare & Medicaid Services	Funded study + DUA	http://www.resdac.org/cms-data/request/research-identifiable-files
District Data on Annual Performances School	Person	State Education Agencies	Application	http://nces.ed.gov/programs/slds/summary.asp
InfoUSA Databases	Person, Address and Geographic	InfoUSA Inc.	Fee	http://www.infousa.com
Medicaid Analytic eXtract (MAX)	Person	Centers for Medicare & Medicaid Services	Funded study + DUA	http://www.cms.gov/MedicaidDataSourcesGenInfo/MAX/list.asp
Medicaid Statistical Information System	Person	Centers for Medicare & Medicaid Services	Funded study + DUA	http://www.cms.gov/MedicaidDataSourcesGenInfo/MAX/list.asp
National Child Abuse and Neglect Data System (NCANDS)	Person	Children's Bureau, Department of Health and Human Services	See terms of use (http://www.ndacan.cornell.edu/ndacan/Datasets/Abstracts/DatasetAbstract_NCANDS_General.html)	http://www.ndacan.cornell.edu/ndacan/Datasets/Abstracts/DatasetAbstract_NCANDS_General.html
National Death Index	Person	Vital Statistics, National Center for Health Statistics, CDC	See http://www.cdc.gov/nchs/data/ndi/APPROVAL%20CRITERIA_FINAL_3-12-07_.pdf	http://www.cdc.gov/nchs/ndi.htm
NCHS Vital Statistics: Birth Data	Person	Vital Statistics, National Center for Health Statistics, CDC	DUA	http://www.cdc.gov/nchs/births.htm

Linked data files have great potential to improve data collection by building better survey sampling frames; for example, improving the Master Address File used for many sampling purposes at the Census Bureau (National Research Council 2004a). Administrative data that include address information can be especially informative if they contain addresses of individuals who are likely to be missing from the current sampling frames. Research into sample coverage error shows that the sampling frames are likely to miss the addresses of low income people, precisely the people targeted by public programs such as Medicaid, Food Stamps, and TANF (U.S. Census Bureau 2002). The U.S. Census Bureau sampling frames could be systematically missing these low income households, and therefore undercount the number of poor people and the number of people participating in public programs. Linking addresses contained in such programs' administrative data files to the sampling frames would allow the U.S. Census Bureau to identify addresses that may have otherwise remained missing from the frames.

Linked data files can also improve administrative data. For example, many administrative data elements such as race, ethnicity, education, and marital status are of suspect quality because they are not essential fields for the administration of programs, and therefore not collected consistently. Survey data could shed light on the nature of the data missing from administrative data sets within these domains. In particular, survey data could improve the outdated race and ethnicity information in some systems that was collected before Office of Management and Budget Directive 15 went into effect in 1997. For example, the SSA has collected race and ethnicity information for many years, during which time official definitions have changed repeatedly. Race and ethnicity information conforming to current definitions and applied to SSA data and Centers for Medicare and Medicaid Services (CMS) data sets could greatly improve research in the field of health disparities (National Research Council 2004b, p. 83).

27.3 Limitations and Strengths of Survey Data

One of the great strengths of survey data (ironically) is the accumulated knowledge about their limitations. Much research has studied the components of survey error, including sampling and non-sampling errors. Survey sampling frames have problems with population coverage (Groves 2004). The CPS, the U.S. Census Bureau's premier demographic survey, estimates sampling frame coverage to be only 93% (U.S. Census Bureau 2002). Additionally, surveys suffer from growing nonresponse. Over the last decade, response rates for personal interview surveys such as the CPS and the National Health Interview Survey (NHIS) have declined markedly. For the NHIS the household response rate fell from 90% in 1998 to 82% in 2011 (National Center for Health Statistics, Division of Health Interview Statistics 2000, 2012). For telephone surveys such as the Behavioral Risk Factor Surveillance System (BRFSS) and the Survey of Consumer Attitudes, response rates fell even faster (Curtin et al. 2005).

Research has also established that surveys with complex sample designs have sampling error that can be easily underestimated (Korn and Graubard 1999, Davern et al. 2006). Furthermore, surveys have serious measurement problems with key concepts. For example, they produce widely varying estimates of the number of people without health insurance. The estimate of full-year uninsurance in 2001 from the U.S. Census Bureau's Survey of Income and Program Participation (SIPP) is 22 million individuals, half the size of the 44 million estimate from the CPS (Peterson 2005). Surveys also tend to undercount enrollment in public programs such as Medicaid and the Food Stamp Program (U.S. Census Bureau 2004, Lewis et al. 1998), partially as a result of enrolled people not answering questions correctly. There are also problems with editing, imputing, and processing survey data (Davern et al. 2004, Davern et al. 2007, Bollinger and Hirsch 2006). Finally, data users often wish survey data were released more quickly and that broader access is given to the microdata, including key elements that are often suppressed for confidentiality reasons (Blewett et al. 2004, Davern et al. 2006).

Knowledge of these limitations from past research has led to significant improvements in survey data, as well as a better informed community of data users about inferential limitations. In response to research conducted by government agencies and outside researchers, data providers have improved data products (e.g., Boudreaux and Turner 2011). Survey data have improved greatly for analytic purposes as a result of well-researched limitations and high quality documentation available in the public domain.

27.4 Limitations and Strengths of Administrative Data

The strength of administrative data lies in the reuse of an existing data resource, full coverage of the target population, and accuracy of programmatic details that are important for understanding the functioning of the program. Administrative data captures transaction information including payments and type of service more accurately and in greater detail than self-reporting and self-recall. For example, a Medicare patient may know they had a "bypass surgery" but will likely be unable to report the specific medical procedures performed and the associated cost. The temporal coverage of data collection coincides with the period of agency activity, providing a complete record of individual transactions as well as agency development and change over time. Changes in information technology and increased use of administrative data have improved both data retention activities (archiving) and data quality (Holenbeck et al. 2003).

However, the original purpose of administrative data is internally focused on program administration—not on the creation, dissemination and archiving of a data product to be used for statistical purposes, or for linking to survey data. Focus is on program eligibility, current and recent transactions, and information directly related to the provision of service and the efficiency of the agency. Administrative data may contain data elements that are not essential to administering the program such as background socio-demographic information and enrollment in other programs, but these elements can have significant limitations such as large amounts of "missingness." Low availability of data items such as educational level and other important covariates can greatly limit analystic utility. Inter-state and intra-state data availability and consistency may also vary (Holenbeck et al. 2003).

Lack of documentation of concepts, data item definitions, the collection and cleaning processes, changes in data management systems over time, and local variations that may affect data accuracy and consistency is a major issue for administrative data (Reidy et al. 1998). It is difficult to identify and locate the individuals able to provide this metadata after the fact. This is even more problematic for programs that rely on highly variable state and local data submitted to a national level database. The data crosses multiple points where actions affecting data quality may take place. Ideally, programmatic documentation as well as information about local variations in data collection, cleaning and processing should be available to the researcher, but this is rarely the case for administrative data, and makes the type of data quality assessment commonly done for survey data extremely difficult to perform (Reidy et al. 1998).

27.5 A Research Agenda into Linked Data File Quality

All data—whether administrative, survey, or linked—have limitations for answering health research questions. As discussed earlier, problems with survey data are well-known to the research community because these data are in the public domain and heavily used. The data themselves are better because the limitations are known—even quantified—and improvements often follow research findings. Moreover, if a research paper using survey data fails to consider important issues or limitations, peer review often informs the author of the omission.

A problem with most linked data files is that they are usually constructed for the purpose of answering a limited set of research questions, are available to a small number of researchers, and cannot be released to the public according to the Inter-Agency Agreement (IAA), Data Use Agreement (DUA), or Memorandum of Understanding (MOU) that allows the linkage (Cox et al. 2006, Obenski 2006, Hotz et al. 1998, National Research Council 2000). For example, the Medicare Current Beneficiary Survey (MCBS) which is designed to link administrative data from Medicare claims and enrollment files to survey data on enrollees creates two major linked data products, the Cost and Utilization files and the Health Care Coverage files. These files are available only to researchers through a DUA which can take up to 9 months to negotiate, and only allows access to the data for answering the research question specified in the DUA application. Similarly, to work with the National Center for Health Statistics (NCHS's) linked National Health and Nutrition Examination Survey (NHANES) or NHIS data files, researchers must submit a Research Data Center (RDC) application, pay a fee or "seat charge", travel to an RDC site, and have all output reviewed for disclosure risk before publishing. In addition, the application process can take up to 12 months depending on the number of reviews needed and complexity of the proposal.

Such restrictions are necessary because of the risk of disclosing the identities of sampled persons. The linking process most often uses identifiers such as name, address, and Social Security number, so when the U.S. Census Bureau links a file they remove all this information immediately and replace it with a Protected Identity Key (PIK). Even with this step, only authorized researchers working on an approved project can view the linked data, and only for the approved purposes. Furthermore, the U.S. Census Bureau requires the research to demonstrate a clear benefit to ongoing statistical programs (often called a Title *13 Benefit*). Extensive research into the quality of the linked data file for broad-based health research is normally not undertaken because it is not part of the core research question the data were linked to answer. The highly restricted access to these data presents a serious challenge to the methodological research community who might wish to explore quality issues.

How the federal statistical system balances the competing interests of providing access to data on one hand, and ensuring the privacy of individuals on the other, creates uncertainty about how much the research community will be able to learn about linked data sets. With growing privacy concerns, it seems that more and more data fall under access restrictions and linked data files are unlikely to ever enter the public domain, hindering the growth of knowledge (Lane and Schur 2010). At the same time, because these data sets constitute such a rich and novel resource, a researcher who does gain access risks misusing them if he or she undertakes substantive analysis before conducting a thorough quality review.

This chapter attempts to outline a research agenda for assessing the quality of linked data files, using the sources of survey error as a guide. These concerns about the quality of survey data, familiar to all researchers who use survey data, will navigate us through the following potential problems and some possible solutions associated with linked data files: coverage error in the sampling frame, sampling error, nonresponse error, measurement error, data processing issues, imputation procedures, editing rules, documentation, dissemination, and timeliness.

27.5.1 COVERAGE ERROR IN THE SAMPLING FRAME

Sample coverage error in a linked data set is largely a function of the coverage error in the survey data that persists in the linked data file. To the extent that the sampling frame fails to properly represent the population of interest, the linked data file inherits this problem. For example, survey data tend to have poor coverage of minority members, males, and young adults; the group with the lowest sample coverage ratio in the CPS is Black males aged 20–29, who only have a 0.66 coverage ratio, while people over 60 have coverage ratios much closer to 1.0 (U.S. Census Bureau 2002). Weighting and post-stratification adjustments to the survey weights attempt to minimize the impact, but to the extent that these adjustments are inadequate, the linked data file will also have issues of sampling frame coverage.

The administrative data themselves do not have to contend with coverage issues because everyone covered or "administered" by a program should have a record on the administrative file. However, not everyone administered by a program is part of the survey's sampling frame. For example, prisons and skilled nursing facilities are often excluded from survey sample frames. Biased conclusions about aggregate discrepancies between survey estimates and administrative data can result from a poorly defined set of individuals who, because they belong to the survey sampling frame, are eligible to be linked to the survey. Even if the sampling frame is available, enforcing a survey universe on administrative data is difficult because the administrative data may lack the detail necessary for identifying the appropriate set of records. These difficulties may apply also to decedents (those who die before the survey is conducted), people living overseas, military personnel, or people without any regular place of residence.

Two examples demonstrate this problem. First, administrative data and survey sampling frames can entail different concepts of institutional group quarters. People living in such places are excluded from some survey sampling frames. Individuals in the administrative data may belong to the survey sampling frame because they are not living in an institutional group quarters according to the administrative agency's definition, but they could, in fact, be living in institutional group quarters by the survey's definition (U.S. Census Bureau 2008b). The reverse is possible as well. Someone's address in the administrative data could be a mailing address for a guardian or relative, while the individual actually lives in an institutional group quarter such as a skilled nursing facility (U.S. Census Bureau 2008b). Second, the administrative data could contain more than one address for an individual, and it is difficult to determine from the information available when the person lived at each address, or where they lived at the time of the survey (U.S. Census Bureau 2008b).

An important measure of quality for linked data files is a "linkable universe ratio." This statistic is the ratio of the weighted number of linked individuals to the number of people in the administrative data who are in the survey's sampling frame. This linkable universe ratio is imperfect because there often will not be enough information in the administrative data to reconstruct the survey sampling frame and target population (e.g., Davern et al. 2009a).

27.5.2 SAMPLING ERROR

Sampling error is not typically a problem for research on administrative records because all the records are available and a sample is not necessary. However, when linking survey data to administrative records, the linked data file carries with it the limitations of the survey's complex sample design. Estimates derived from the linked file need to take the complex sample design into account when calculating standard errors and variances for statistical inferences (Korn and Graubard 1999). Procedures for estimating design-based sampling errors are available in most statistical packages such as SAS, STATA, SUDAAN, and SPSS, and should be invoked. See also the discussion in Chapter 29.

27.5.3 NONRESPONSE ERROR

Surveys have unit and item nonresponse, which imputation and post-stratification weighting adjustments account for in order to make the responding population more representative of the population as a whole. Imputation and post-stratification weighting techniques have been evaluated for survey data and have been found to perform well when the critical assumptions are met (Little and Rubin 2002). The most critical assumption is that the responding sample is representative of the full population after controlling for key demographic characteristics (i.e., any missing data is Missing at Random) through post-stratification for unit and person nonresponse, and multivariate modeling and imputation for item nonresponse.

This issue is complicated when linking survey and administrative data because survey and administrative data often lack linking identifiers, and they can be missing systematically, not at random. For example, Figure 27.1 shows results from a data linkage study conducted by the U.S. Census Bureau, the CMSs, the State Health Access Data Center, and the Department of Health and Human Services Assistant Secretary for Planning and Evaluation. Nationwide, 90% of the identifiers (i.e., SSNs (Social Security Number)) in the MSIS are verified, but this figure is much lower in certain states and counties. California and Montana in particular stand out with respect to missing identifiers (U.S. Census Bureau 2007). People from these states who are enrolled in Medicaid have a lower probability of being linked.

In addition to the missing SSNs in the MSIS data, over 26% of CPS persons lacked linking identifiers. This occurs for two reasons. First, respondents who refuse to provide the linking information (the SSN) are interpreted as refusing to have their data linked. Consequently the U.S. Census Bureau disallows linking their data to administrative records. This accounts for about 20% points of the missing identifiers in the CPS, which can be dealt with in the usual manner assuming that those who refuse to provide the identifier are missing at random. The remaining 6% are cases in which the SSN provided could not be validated and the correct identifier could not be found (Davern 2007). It is quite possible this group is not "missing at random" in Little and Rubin's (2002) terminology, because some people such as very young children and recent immigrants may not have an SSN yet when they are sampled for the CPS. This group is not well represented by those in the data set with validated SSNs.

When working with linked data files, it is essential to understand whether systematic differences exist between those cases that were linked and those that were not linked. Both the survey and the administrative data likely have systematically missing identifiers used for linking. Agencies that have access to linked data files must endeavor to understand these sources of sample loss and how they can influence or bias any analysis. In the case of the CPS-MSIS linked data file, 10% of the MSIS cases could not be linked because they were missing SSNs and 26% of the CPS data could not be linked because they refused to provide the SSN or one could not be found to match the person. This is a large sample loss and needs investigation to better delineate the limitations of the linked data file for research purposes (U.S. Census Bureau 2007, Davern 2007).

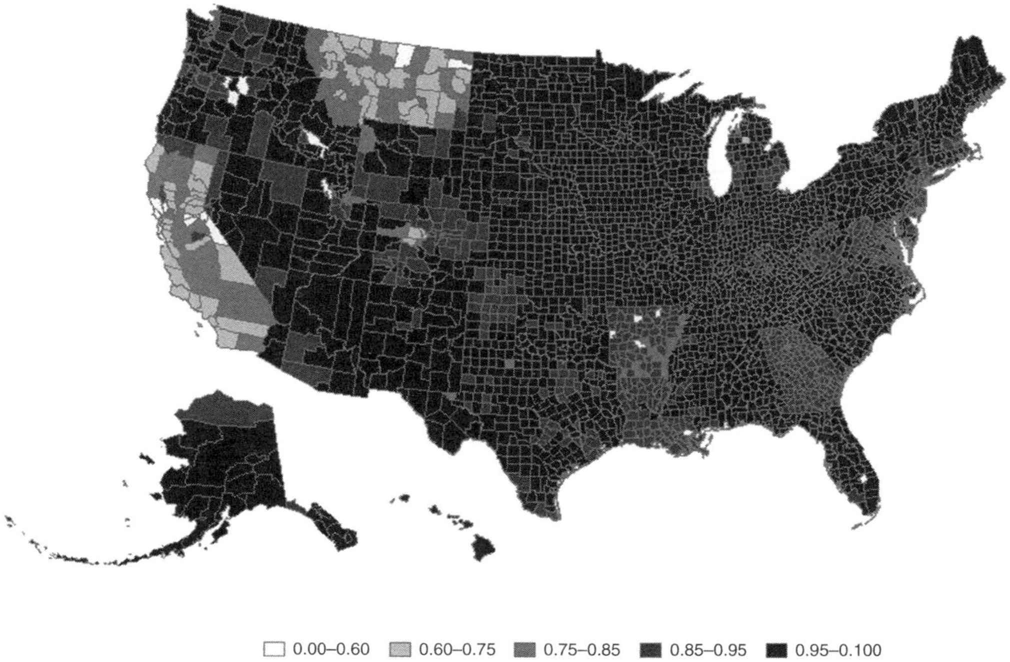

FIGURE 27.1 U.S. Counties by their rate of validated social security numbers in the Medicaid Statistical Information System (MSIS): 2001.

Under some circumstances, understanding for whom the linking identifier from the survey and administrative file tends to be missing allows some control over minor differences between the populations represented by the linked and unlinkable cases (i.e., those cases with and without linking identifiers). It may be appropriate to create a post-stratified "linked" record weight that adjusts for sample loss. One way to accomplish this is to increase the survey weights of those linkable cases (i.e., those with verified linkable information, not just those that are linked) to the full weighted sample size for the survey, treating the unlinkable cases similarly to survey non-respondents, and stratifying by the characteristics of greatest interest (e.g., Davern et al. 2009a).

27.5.4 MEASUREMENT ERROR

Surveys have extensive measurement error issues that have been the subject of many investigations (Groves 2004, Dillman 2000). Survey measurement errors can be impacted by mode of interview, question wording, question appearance on the page, survey question order, reference period of the question, incentives for completion, interviewer effects, and proxy response. All of these errors could impact administrative data as well, and investigation into this possibility is critical for working with and understanding linked data files.

Administrative data are designed to track critical programmatic details. For example, there is little reason to dispute that an SSI recipient or an SSA recipient was sent a check in the amount on the administrative data file on the date specified. However, the administrative data contain many more items besides programmatic details such as timing and amount of payments. They contain information on age, sex, marital status, addresses, telephone numbers, race, ethnicity, and other program-relevant variables. For example, Medicaid data contain information on participation in complementary public programs such as the Special Supplemental Nutrition Program for Women, Infants, and Children (WIC), Food Stamps, and TANF. In addition, the values reported to some administrative agencies for program purposes, such as the IRS for tax reporting, may systematically differ from a value the same person would report when asked in a survey. The incentives and application of the rules (e.g., who is a dependent child) associated with reporting income are different. Reporting less income to the IRS or to the Medicaid office reduces taxes owed or can qualify someone for program benefits, whereas there is no direct incentive to understate income in a survey. Therefore, income amounts from the two sources on a linked data file could represent systematically different things.

Administrative data can be collected through many modes (i.e., interviewer or self-administered), during more than one wave of interviewing, and using various instruments. Very little information is kept on the origin of variable values. This information is an important issue that managers of administrative data systems should address. In a survey, information on where each data element came from is called *paradata* and it is useful for research (Couper 2005). Survey research has demonstrated that the answers to questions can vary by survey mode, and this could be the case for administrative data as well. For example, if the data are taken as part of a facilitated interview with a professional case worker instead of completed on paper by the person applying for the program, the information could be affected. For example, a hospital employee responsible for helping patients fill out forms for Medicaid is an expert in eligibility, as are tax accountants who fill out IRS tax forms for clients. Forms filled out by professionals may vary in systematic ways from those filled out by someone who completes their own application for Medicaid or files their own taxes. How the information enters the administrative database, or paradata, should be recorded so researchers can look for variation by the mode of data collection. In an examination of birth certificate data, Wilson (2012) conducted cognitive interviews with people responsible for collecting and entering the data and found wide variability in how the data were entered. Investigations like these are essential in better understanding these administrative systems and the quality of the data they contain.

Self-administered data collection forms often fail to be user-friendly or to incorporate the advances made in survey questionnaire design developed over many years (e.g., Dillman 2000). Administrative data collectors are not as concerned about usability of their forms, because the applicant generally has a strong incentive to complete the form in order to collect benefits such as Medicaid, child-care assistance, or TANF. However, the forms can cause measurement errors in key pieces of demographic information, and research should be conducted on how to create user-friendly self-administered instruments that ensure high quality supplemental demographic data on age, date of birth, sex, marital status, race and ethnicity. This is an area where the research on surveys greatly surpasses the research on administrative data. Knowledge about the quality of administrative data is essential for properly exploiting linked data files, and a necessary first step is to collect better paradata in administrative systems.

Measurement error can also indicate programmatic problems. Another potentially strong contribution of linked data files is helping evaluate how well state and local public programs serve their clients. Many state-run programs have complicated enrollment and renewal procedures and it may not always be obvious to the enrollee that they are in fact enrolled. The survey respondent's report of program enrollment may be at fault in part because of the way in which the program is administered in a specific area. One way to determine whether this is the case is to assume a general level of response error in national surveys regarding program enrollment (controlling for basic socio-demographics and survey administration issues such as proxy reporting for non-relatives), then examine the degree to which the quality of reporting varies by state.

In the example of the CPS' Annual Social and Economic Supplement (CPS) linked to the MSIS, research has found differences by state in patterns of reporting enrollment. The analysis generated two logistic regression models predicting whether the CPS case accurately represented Medicaid coverage in the CPS. The first model (results shown in Figure 27.2) shows the odds ratios for each state (the reference category is the national average) of not having Medicaid in the CPS given that the MSIS shows enrollment. The second model (results shown in Figure 27.3) produces odds ratios for each state (the reference category is the national average) of being uninsured according to the CPS for respondents linked

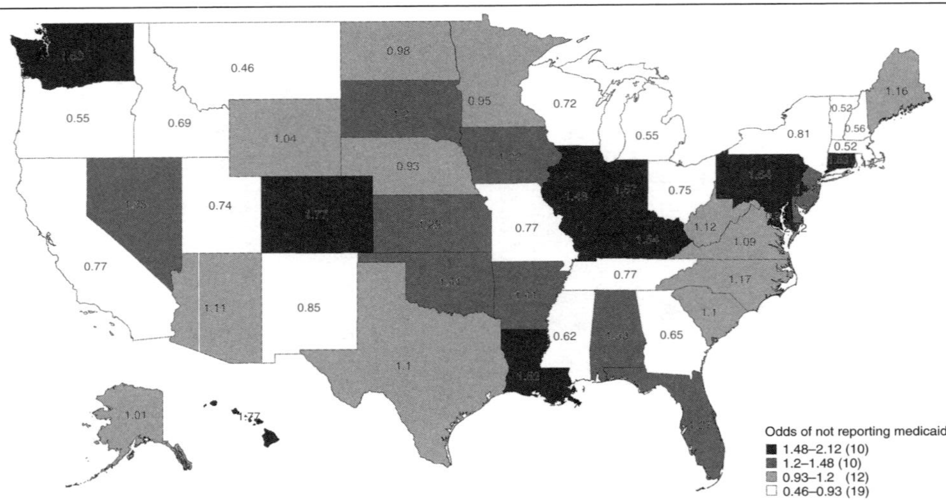

Source: Odds ratios taken from the full model 1a on pages 217-219 in the following report: U.S. Census Bureau. (2008a). Phase II research results: Examining discrepancies between the national medicaid statistical information system (MSIS) and the current population survey (CPS) annual social and economic supplement (ASEC). Report of the research project to understand the medicaid undercount: The university of Minnesota's state health access data assistance center, the centers for medicare and medicaid services, the department of health and human services office of the assistant secretary for planning and evaluation, and the U.S. census bureau. Washington DC: U.S census bureau. http://www.census.gov/did/www/snacc/docs/SNACC_Phase_II_Full_Report.pdf

FIGURE 27.2 State odds ratios for NOT reporting medicaid on the CPS for respondents who are linked to the MSIS and show full medicaid benefit enrollment at some point in the reference period: CY 2000–2001.

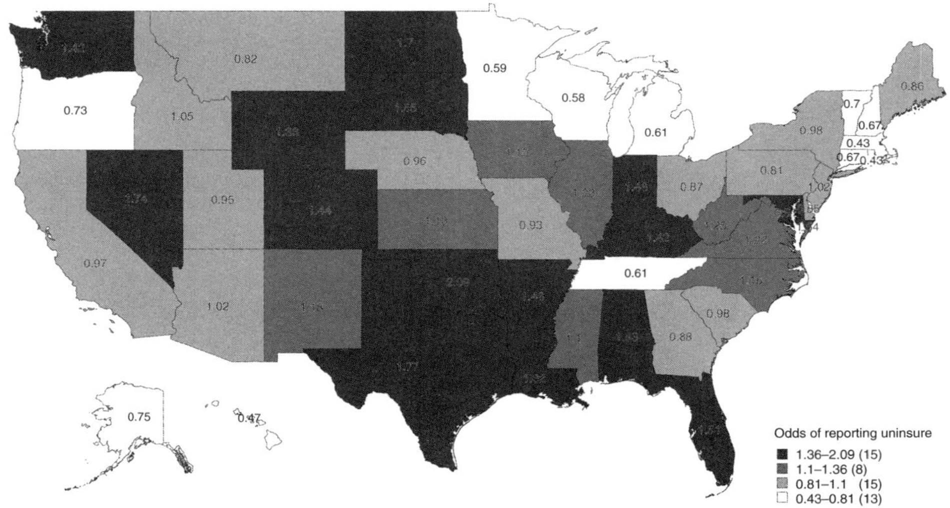

Source: Odds ratios taken from the full model 2 on pages 217-219 in the following report: U.S. Census Bureau. (2008a). Phase II research results: Examining discrepancies between the national medicaid statistical information system (MSIS) and the current population survey (CPS) annual social and economic supplement (ASEC). Report of the research project to understand the medicaid undercount: The university of Minnesota's state health access data assistance center, the centers for medicare and medicaid services, the department of health and human services office of the assistant secretary for planning and evaluation, and the U.S. census bureau. Washington DC: U.S census bureau. http://www.census.gov/did/www/snacc/docs/SNACC_Phase_II_Full_Report.pdf

FIGURE 27.3 State odds ratios for reporting being uninsured on the CPS for respondents who are linked to the MSIS and show full medicaid benefit enrollment at some point in the reference period: CY 2000–2001.

to MSIS showing enrollment in Medicaid. Both models show socio-demographic characteristics: the relationship to the household reference person, utilization of services, and state of residence (see US Census Bureau 2008b for model details). The variation in the first model shown in Figure 27.2, estimating whether someone was correctly classified as having Medicaid, could be caused by many things such as stigma or confusion over the exact plan name (e.g., SCHIP vs Medicaid). However, as shown in Figure 27.3, falsely reporting no coverage at all (meaning the person is classified as uninsured) is more serious as it demonstrates that covered people do not know they are enrolled. Perhaps such people are more likely to behave like the uninsured and have health outcomes like the uninsured. In Figure 27.3, there is wide variability between states in the probability of being classified in the CPS as uninsured despite an administrative record of Medicaid enrollment. A high probability could partly reflect problems in the state Medicaid programs rather than pure "survey error," and signal that states such as Oklahoma, which has twice the national average rate of false reporting of uninsurance, could do a better job of communicating to people that they are enrolled. The enrollees then might have health outcomes more consistent with those who both have and report coverage.

27.5.5 DATA PROCESSING, EDITING RULES, AND IMPUTATION PROCEDURES

Survey data and administrative data are routinely edited and imputed, but unlike survey data there is little documentation in the public domain regarding the editing and imputation procedures applied to administrative data. Because imputation and editing can influence estimates substantially it is important to know how the procedures work. A process that makes perfect sense from one point of view (e.g., administering a program) may not be appropriate for certain research purposes (for examples of such instances see, Davern et al. 2004, Davern et al. 2007, Bollinger and Hirsch 2006). In order for linked data files to fulfill their potential, custodians of administrative data need to produce appropriate metadata on how information has been processed and altered.

By the same token, data missing from a survey may be imputed or edited in a sensible way from the survey perspective but suboptimal for directly comparing to administrative data in an individual linked record. The purpose of imputation is to make population and subpopulation estimates accurate, not the individual-level values. Probabilistic, model-based, imputed values in the survey agree much less with the administrative data than the values reported by respondents do. A linked MSIS-CPS individual that had Medicaid coverage imputed in the CPS is less likely to be in the MSIS data than an individual with a reported value (Davern 2007). Imputation does not necessarily aim to accurately put an individual into the "correct" category; rather, it is an attempt to make the estimates for certain classes of people correct. That is, imputation may not correctly classify a single 15-year-old Hispanic girl, but a statistic for 15-year-old Hispanic girls should be more accurate in the aggregate, based on reported and imputed data. Distinguishing reported and imputed data is essential in work with linked data files, depending on the purpose of the research.

Furthermore, administrative data can often systematically lack information in some non program-specific fields. For example, in the 2003 MSIS, race and ethnicity information was listed as "unknown" for more than one in five Medicaid enrollees in Rhode Island, New York, and Vermont. A recent National Academy of Sciences panel that reviewed the quality of data available to study race and ethnic health disparities concluded that the "CMS does not yet have any information on the quality of the racial and ethnic data collected through the MSIS" (National Research Council 2004b, p. 83). In the fiscal year 2000, the race and ethnicity of three million of the total 44.5 million Medicaid enrollees (about 7%) were reported as "unknown" (National Research Council 2004b). In addition, some cross-reference program information can be systematically missing from administrative data. For example, the variable for the receipt of TANF in the MSIS shows no one in Los Angeles County, California receiving TANF, clearly an anomaly (Centers for Medicare and Medicaid Services 2007). Using a variable without taking such anomalies into account can obviously lead to incorrect conclusions.

27.5.6 DISSEMINATION AND TIMELINESS

Significant time delays, availability, and disclosure issues complicate disseminating linked data files. For example, the U.S. Census Bureau received the 2003 MSIS data file in the summer of 2006. Moreover, linked data files are highly protected due to the sensitive nature of both the survey data and the administrative data, and only a few people in a restricted environment typically have access. The IRS-U.S. Census Bureau linked data file, for example, has especially tight restrictions on who can access it and for what purposes. Most data linkage projects are for a specific purpose only and tightly controlled according to the negotiated IAA, DUA, or MOU between federal agencies (Hotz et al. 1998, National Research Council 2000, Cox et al. 2006, Obenski 2006).

In many cases, tabular data produced using linked data files also require clearance through both the agency that conducted the survey and the agency that provided the administrative data. So not only are the data obsolescent and generally inaccessible to outside researchers, but analyses are subject to lengthy clearance procedures.

It is possible that as agencies begin to understand better ways of protecting confidentiality, some access restrictions may be lifted (Reiter 2012). And even though public use of these data files may not be possible without sophisticated disclosure-proofing procedures, perhaps they could be housed at a secure data access facility or system such as the U.S. Census Bureau's RDCs, the NORC data Enclave, or the NCHS RDC. The RDC model is one in which trusted researchers access data at a secure computing facility. The Data Enclave model supplies researchers a secure remote connection for accessing the data (Lane and Schur 2010). In both the RDC and Enclave model, researchers could perform analyses on linked data files in a protected computing environment, and the collaborating agencies enforce their standards for disclosure review.

Some secure access systems, such as the U.S. Census Bureau's RDC also require that research projects provide a direct benefit to the U.S. Census Bureau. Researchers could meet this requirement by producing a report about the data quality issues they encountered during the course of their research and how they overcame these difficulties. To the extent that the issues of data quality raised in this paper pertain to a particular linked data file, a researcher at an RDC can justify a project by investigating them in more detail as part of the research agenda.

27.6 Conclusions

Linked survey and administrative data constitute a valuable tool for health research. These files are being created by a variety of federal agencies such as the U.S. Census Bureau, the SSA, the NCHS, the IRS and the CMS, to name a few (National Committee on Vital and Health Statistics 2006). Some of these projects are ongoing partnerships with strong linked data research agenda (e.g., the linked NHIS and Medicare Claims data, or the LEHD program at the US Census Bureau) while many others are more *ad hoc*. Each source of data has limitations by itself that the other can potentially help overcome. Survey data are very strong because their limitations are well-understood and the research is widely disseminated. Similar research into administrative data is necessary to better understand the limitations and possibilities of using linked survey and administrative data in health research.

Although linked microdata itself cannot be released to the public without substantial alteration, publicly available documentation of the files would nevertheless maximize the usefulness of the research based on them. One way to achieve this level of documentation would be to consider a linked data file a "data product" and to systematically conduct research into its quality. The results of this research could be assembled into a coherent set of metadata in the public domain, allowing researchers to understand the file's usefulness and idiosyncrasies. The documentation should attempt to develop and use a systematic standard such as the Data Documentation Initiative developed for survey data (Data Documentation Initiative 2014). Creating an ongoing linkage program takes a considerable amount of resources and the costs of producing a high quality linked data product should not be underestimated.

Investigators aiming to perform their own data linkage are warned not to underestimate the time, resources, patience and persistence necessary to apply for access and obtain permission to merge survey data with administrative data. They should consider partnerships with the organizations responsible for the data sets. Working together with the data sets' sponsors can facilitate data access and enhance the research. A collaborative work facility that meets federal FISMA standards for security such as the NORC Data Enclave can also ease data access.

The technical aspects of data linkage are non-trivial as well. The linkage itself is imperfect, and dealing with the uncertainty in the linkage is imperative from a statistical point of view (Fellegi and Sunter 1969). Researchers should take advantage of the many statistical guides on how to merge survey data with administrative data using identifying information, whether geographic or individual (Fellegi and Sunter 1969).

Finally, as this chapter has outlined, analysis needs to recognize the limitations of the various sources of data which have been combined in the linked data set. Notionally, the survey and administrative sources might measure the same concept, but the two can actually represent quite distinct windows on it. Considering one data set a "gold standard" by which to judge the others may not always be appropriate. A properly framed analysis of the two measures that takes these factors into account can greatly enrich the research community's understanding of the concept, the difficulties of measuring it, and the analytic rigor of the investigation.

The issues presented in this chapter serve as a summary of the opportunities and challenges associated with linking survey data and administrative data to produce resources for health research. Extensive experience with public-use survey data has allowed the research community to develop a wealth of information on working within limitations, and similar knowledge is necessary for administrative data as a stand-alone source of information or in combination with a survey. This statement should not deter researchers from creating and analyzing linked files. Rather, it is an invitation to pursue data linkage projects and establish a system of sharing information on methodologies for exploiting them intelligently. Combined with improvements to the quality of administrative data, such projects can provide rigorous analyses, high quality information, and ultimately much more robust data infrastructure supporting health research.

REFERENCES

Blewett LA, Good MB, Call KT, Davern M. Monitoring the uninsured: a state policy perspective. J Health Polit Policy Law 2004;29:107–145.

Bollinger CR, Hirsch BT. Match bias from earnings imputation in the current population survey: the case of imperfect matching. J Labor Econ 2006;24(3):483–519.

Boudreaux M, Turner J 2011 "Modifications to the Imputation Routine for Health Insurance in the CPS ASEC: Description and Evaluation." SHADAC Working Paper. Minneapolis, MN: University of Minnesota. Available at: http://www.shadac.org/files/shadac/publications/CPS_Imputation_Dec2011.pdf.

Call KT, Davidson G, Sommers AS, Feldman R, Farseth P, Rockwood T. Uncovering the missing Medicaid cases and assessing their bias for estimates of the uninsured. Inquiry 2002;38:396–408.

Centers for Medicare and Medicaid Services (CMA). 2007. Medicaid data sources – general information, MSIS data web page. http://www.cms.hhs.gov/MedicaidDataSourcesGenInfo/02_MSISData.asp. Accessed 2014 Jun 08.

Chappell G, Obenski S, Farber J. Research to improve census imputation methods: item results and conclusions. Presentation at the Joint Statistical Meetings of the American Statistical Association, Survey Research Methods Section. Minneapolis MN; 2005 August 10.

Couper MP. Technology trends in survey data collection. Soc Sci Comput Rev 2005;23:486–501.

Cox C, Berning M, Wilkie Martinez S. Data policy and legal issues in creating and managing integrated data sets. Presentation to the Federal Committee on Statistical Methodology, Statistical Policy Seminar, Washington DC; 2006 November 28.

Curtin R, Presser S, Singer E. Changes in telephone survey nonresponse over the past quarter century. Public Opin Q 2005;69:87–98.

Czajka J. Can administrative records be used to reduce nonresponse bias. Ann Am Acad Polit 2013;645:171–184.

Data Documentation Initiative. 2014. http://www.ddialliance.org/

Davern M, Klerman JA, Baugh D, Call K, Greenberg G. An examination of the medicaid undercount in the current population survey (CPS): preliminary results from record linking. Health Serv Res 2009a;44:965–987.

Davern M, Klerman J, Ziegenfuss J, Lynch V, Greenberg G. A partially corrected estimate of medicaid enrollment and uninsurance: results from an imputational model developed off linked survey and administrative data. J Econ Soc Meas 2009b;34:219–240.

Davern M, Blewett LA, Bershadsky B, Arnold N. Missing the mark? examining imputation bias in the current population survey's state income and health insurance coverage estimates. J Off Stat 2004;20:519–549.

Davern M, Jones A Jr,, Lepkowski J, Davidson G, Blewett LA. Unstable inferences? An examination of complex survey sample design adjustments using the current population survey for health services research. Inquiry 2006;43:283–297.

Davern M, Rodin H, Call KT, Blewett LA. Are the CPS uninsurance estimates too high? An examination of imputation. Health Serv Res forthcoming, 2007;42:2038–2055. DOI: 10.1111/j.1475-6773.2007.00703.x.

Davern M. Fitting square pegs into round holes: linking medicaid and current population survey data to understand the 'Medicaid Undercount'. Presentation to the Office of Research, Development, and Information Seminar Series, Centers for Medicare and Medicaid Services, Baltimore MD; 2007 February 15.

Dillman D. *Mail and Internet Surveys: The Tailored Survey Design*. 2nd ed. New York: John Wiley & Sons, Inc.; 2000.

Fellegi I, Sunter A. A theory for record linkage. J Am Stat Assoc 1969;64(328):1183–1210.

Groves R. *Survey Errors and Survey Costs*. New York: John Wiley & Sons, Inc.; 2004.

Holenbeck K, King CT, Schroeder D. Preliminary WIA net impact estimates: administrative records opportunities and limitations. New Tools for a New Era! Symposium. Washington, DC: Bureau of Labor Statistics & the Workforce Information Council; 2003.

Hotz JV, Goerge R, Balzekas J., Margolin F, editors. A Report of the Advisory Panel on Research Uses of Administrative Data of the Northwestern University/University of Chicago Joint Center for Poverty Research. Administrative Data for Policy-Relevant Research: Assessment of Current Utility and Recommendations for Development; 1998. http://www.econ.ucla.edu/hotz/working_papers/adm_data.pdf. Accessed 2014 jun 08.

Klerman JA, Ringel JS, Roth B. Under-reporting of medicaid and welfare in the current population survey. *Working Paper*. Santa Monica CA: RAND; 2005.

Korn EL, Graubard BI. *Analysis of Health Surveys*. New York: John Wiley & Sons, Inc.; 1999.

Lane J, Schur C. Balancing access to data and privacy. A review of the issues and approaches for the future. Health Serv Res 2010;45(5):1456–1467.

Lewis K, Elwood M, Czajka JL. Counting the uninsured: a review of the literature. Washington DC: Urban Institute; 1998. http://www.urban.org/url.cfm?ID=308032. Accessed 2014 Jun 08.

Little RA, Rubin DB. *Statistical Analysis with Missing Data*. New York: John Wiley & Sons, Inc.; 2002.

National Committee on Vital and Health Statistics (NCVHS). Meeting of the subcommittee on populations. Transcript and presentation web page. Washington DC; 2006 November 18–19. http://www.ncvhs.hhs.gov/060918ag.htm. Accessed 2014 Jun 08.

National Center for Health Statistics (NCHS), Division of Health Interview Statistics. National Health Interview Survey (NHIS) public use data release. 1998 NHIS survey description. Hyattsville, MD: Centers for Disease Control and Prevention; 2000 October. http://ftp.cdc.gov/pub/Health_Statistics/NCHS/Dataset_Documentation/NHIS/1998/srvydesc.pdf. Accessed 2014 Jun 08.

National Center for Health Statistics (NCHS), Division of Health Interview Statistics. National Health Interview Survey (NHIS) public use data release. 2011 NHIS survey description. Hyattsville, MD: Centers for Disease Control and Prevention; 2012 June. ftp://ftp.cdc.gov/pub/Health_Statistics/NCHS/Dataset_Documentation/NHIS/2011/srvydesc.pdf. Accessed 2014 Jun 08.

National Research Council. Improving access to and confidentiality of research data: report of a workshop. Washington, DC, The National Academics Press; 2000.

National Research Council. *Reengineering the 2010 Census: Risks and Challenges*. Washington, DC: The National Academics Press; 2004a.

National Research Council. *Eliminating Health Disparities: Measurement and Data Needs*. Washington, DC: The National Academics Press; 2004b.

Nelson C. Adjusting imputed interest amounts based on results of the CPS-IRS exact match. Unpublished memorandum for Chief of Income Statistics, U.S. Bureau of the Census; 1985.

Peterson C. Survey estimates of the uninsured and of medicaid/SCHIP enrollees. Presentation at the American Enterprise Institute's event, "9 Million Less Uninsured?" Washington DC; 2005 April 8.

Obenski S. How recent advances have facilitated comparing, analyzing and jointly using large-scale survey and administrative data to answer big policy questions. Presentation to the Federal Committee on Statistical Methodology, Statistical Policy Seminar, Washington DC; 2006, November 28.

Reidy M, George R, Lee BJ. Developing an integrated administrative database. In: *Exploring Research Methods in Social Policy Research*. Asldershot, UK: The Ashgate Publishing Company; 1998.

Reiter JP. Statistical approaches to protecting confidentiality for microdata and their effects on the quality of statistical inferences. Public Opin Q 2012;76:163–181.

Urban Institute. 2014. Transfer income model 3 (TRIM3) project website. http://trim3.urban.org/T3Welcome.php.

U.S. Census Bureau.Current population survey: design and methodology. Technical Paper #63RV. Washington, DC: U.S. Census Bureau; 2002.

U.S. Census Bureau. Current population survey 2005 annual social and economic supplement: technical documentation. Washington, DC: U.S. Census Bureau; 2005.

U.S. Census Bureau. Difference in estimates of Food Stamp Program participation between surveys and administrative records. U.S. Census Bureau: Washington DC; 2004. http://www.ubalt.edu/jfi/jfi/reports/fstampfinrept273004.pdf

U.S. Census Bureau. Phase I research results: overview of National Medicare and Medicaid Files. Report of the research project to understand the Medicaid undercount: The University of Minnesota's State Health Access Data Assistance Center, the Centers for Medicare and Medicaid Services, the Department of Health and Human Services Office of the Assistant Secretary for Planning and Evaluation, and the U.S. Census Bureau. Washington DC: U.S. Census Bureau; 2007.

U.S. Census Bureau. Phase III research results: refinement in the analysis of examining discrepancies between the National Medicaid Statistical Information System (MSIS) and the current population survey (CPS) Annual Social and Economic Supplement (ASEC). Report of the research project to understand the Medicaid undercount: The University of Minnesota's State Health Access Data Assistance Center, the Centers for Medicare and Medicaid Services, the Department of Health and Human Services Office of the Assistant Secretary for Planning and Evaluation, and the U.S. Census Bureau. Washington DC: U.S. Census Bureau; 2008b.

Wilson S. The use of cognitive interviewing to evaluate data quality in administrative records. Proceedings of the 10th Health Survey Methods Conference. Session 4; 2012. http://www.srl.uic.edu/hsrm/HSRM10_session4.pdf. Accessed 2014 Jun 08.

ONLINE RESOURCES

Please see Table 27.1 for links to data available for linkage.

Please see the National Center for Health Statistic's data linkage program's web site for an example of a robust data linkage program: www.cdc.gov/nchs/data_access/data_linkage_activities.htm.

For information on linking mechanics and linking software information please see William Winkler's paper: www.vrdc.cornell.edu/info7470/2011/Readings/rr2001-03.pdf.

For a good example of data governance procedures for a linked data set please see the SEER-Medicare website: http://healthservices.cancer.gov/seermedicare/obtain/requests.html.

CHAPTER TWENTY EIGHT

Merging Survey Data with Aggregate Data from Other Sources: Opportunities and Challenges

Jarvis T. Chen
Department of Social and Behavioral Sciences, Harvard School of Public Health, Boston, MA, USA

28.1 Background

In real life, even the best designed, best planned, and best executed health surveys can lack important variables of interest for future researchers. Whether the omission is due to a lack of foresight, instrumentation, or time for administering an already lengthy survey, researchers often find themselves in the position of wishing that the survey had included additional questions about exposures and covariates. Given the cost and effort involved in organizing and implementing population-based surveys, *post hoc* linkage of survey data to data from other sources provides a means of maximizing the usefulness of population surveys by supplementing existing survey data with data on other variables of interest.

Data linkage can take place at the level of the individual, as addressed in Chapter 27 of this Handbook, which discusses merging of survey data with administrative data for health research. The individual-level linkage can also be conceptualized as deterministic, whereby identifiers in the survey data

Handbook of Health Survey Methods, First Edition. Edited by Timothy P. Johnson.

enable exact identification of the same individual in the administrative dataset, or probabilistic, whereby there is uncertainty in the linkage process. In the deterministic setting, supplemental variables are treated as fixed and known. When the linkage is probabilistic and subject to error, the data linkage has the flavor of missing data imputation, which can provide a framework for thinking about uncertainty or mismeasurement in the linked variables and the potential effect on inferences using such data.

Data on individuals in surveys can also be linked to shared characteristics of groups or areas to which the individuals belong. Such linkages are often motivated by an interest in the contextual effects of the environments in which individuals are embedded, with these environmental exposures conceptualized as having "neighborhood," "place," or "ecologic" effects (Macintyre et al. 2002, Krieger et al. 2003, Macintyre and Ellaway 2003, Sampson 2003, Diez-Roux 2004a, Diez-Roux 2004b). In other situations, when data on individual-level exposures are not available, aggregations of these exposures defined at the group or area level are sometimes used as proxies for the missing individual-level data (Geronimus and Bound 1998). In both settings, linkage to aggregated group- or area-level data from other data sources serves to enrich the original survey dataset with these types of ecologic variables. Because these variables are so often conceptualized based on area (especially, area of subject's residence), and because the data linkage is usually accomplished by means of geocoding, this chapter will also use the term "area-level measure" to describe these types of variables. One possible source of ecologic data on survey subjects' neighborhoods of residence is systematic observation, whereby a supplemental dataset of relevant contextual variables is collected *de novo* (Raudenbush and Sampson 1999). This approach is discussed in Chapter 16 of this Handbook. Given that such novel data collection can be costly and require significant time and effort, another strategy is to link to routinely collected aggregated data from administrative or census datasets. This chapter focuses on this strategy.

The use of aggregate data, whether as proxies for missing individual variables or to capture contextual effects, presents certain challenges for inference, and these have been extensively debated in the social science, economics, epidemiologic, and biostatistical literature. Indeed, since Robinson's seminal 1950 paper on the problems of drawing individual-level inferences from group-level correlations (Robinson 1950), researchers have been wary of using group-level measures, especially with respect to the potential for ecologic fallacy (Greenland and Robins 1994). At the same time, a growing number of researchers have argued that it is equally problematic to ignore the effects of contextual factors on health (Diez-Roux 1998, Diez-Roux 2000). The aim of this chapter is to summarize some of these issues and offer concrete suggestions for analytic strategies.

The outline of this chapter is as follows. First, the process of geocoding and data linkage is described. Second, issues related to the conceptualization and operationalization of typical ecologic measures are discussed, using area-based measures of socioeconomic position as an example. Third, a brief summary of issues related to inference and interpretation involving ecologic variables follows, including possible sources of ecologic bias; the goal is to offer practical recommendations for analysis and interpretation, given the extensive and at times contentious debates in the literature on this subject. Fourth, analytic strategies are presented for analyzing survey data with ecologic variables, including some practical recommendations for multilevel modeling when using data from complex survey designs.

28.2 Geocoding and Linkage to Area-Based Data

In order to link individual survey records to area-level data, the study subject's address (typically, residential address) is *geocoded*: that is, the spatial location of the address is identified and the geographic coordinates are assigned to the record (Krieger et al. 2001, Waller and Gotway 2004). Typically this involves matching a street address to a reference geographic base file that contains both addresses and the geographic coordinates of these addresses. An example of a reference geographic base file in the United States are the Census TIGER (Topologically Integrated Geographic Encoding and Referencing)/Line files, which provide address ranges and street segment records for the 50 states, the District of Columbia, Puerto Rico, the Virgin Islands, and U.S. territories, all geographically referenced by latitude and longitude coordinates (U.S. Census Bureau 2013b). Some type of interpolation is usually necessary to provide the actual location of the address within the street segment. For example, it is necessary to assume an "offset" (a small geographic distance by which the subject's dwelling is assumed to be set back from the street), and to know whether the subject resides on the even or odd numbered side of the street, as this affects which area a person is in when their address is on the border of two adjacent areas. As a result, there is often some location error remaining in most geocoded addresses, even when "complete" street address (number, street name, street type) are available, and this error can be quite large for rural areas containing few street segments. In addition to the official U.S. Census TIGER/Line files, there are now a variety of commercially available geographic base files available for use.

Ideally, the street address permits identification of latitude and longitude coordinates, which further permits locating these coordinates within political or administrative boundaries (e.g., census block groups, census tracts, counties, states) for linking with aggregate data. Thus, we may speak of geocoding records to the block group, census tract, or county level. The boundaries for these administrative units often coincide with streets or other geographic features. Care has to be taken when using geographic reference base files from different sources that the street maps and geographic polygons are in agreement, as mismatch between the base files can result in geographic misclassification. In some cases, it may not be possible to identify the exact latitude and longitude of an address, but, depending on the desired level of aggregation, it may still be possible to geocode the address to, say, the census tract level with certainty (e.g., in general, having the ZIP+4 code permits geocoding to the census tract level).

Researchers involved in primary collection of survey data have several options for geocoding of data. Geocoding can be performed "in house" using GIS software such as ESRI's ArcGIS. Some preprocessing of address data ("address cleaning") is recommended, for example, to check for misspellings of addresses, abbreviations, or poorly formatted street numbers and street type, and so on. In general, geocoding will be facilitated if the cleaned address retains only the key address elements needed (house/building number; street name; street type), with all extraneous characters removed (e.g., "BSMT," "REAR," "APT 1," "UNIT 3," etc.). It is usually helpful to have some knowledge of the local geography to do this. Given reasonably clean data, batch geocoding of thousands of records is now relatively easily implemented using ArcGIS. A key advantage is that privacy concerns are minimized since the address data are geocoded in house.

For extremely large datasets with millions of records (e.g., public health surveillance records), researchers may have to resort to outsourcing geocoding to a commercial geocoding firm. Cost and turnaround time can vary widely across firms, so researchers are encouraged to compare several vendors before choosing a particular company (Krieger et al. 2001). To preserve subject confidentiality, residential addresses should be stripped of any identifiers or associated health or covariate data before being transferred to the geocoding firm for processing.

For both "in house" and outsourced geocoding, Krieger et al. (2001) recommend evaluation of geocoding *completeness* and *accuracy*. *Completeness* refers to the proportion of records that can be geocoded with certainty to a desired level of aggregation. For example, in a study using geocoded mortality data from Massachusetts (1988–1992), Krieger et al. found that 94% of mortality records could be geocoded to the block group level with certainty, but that virtually 100% of records could be geocoded to the census tract level (Krieger et al. 2002a). *Accuracy* refers to the proportion of addresses with known geocodes that are correctly geocoded when put through the geocoding process. Particularly, when selecting a commercial geocoding vendor, it may be a good idea to evaluate the accuracy of the geocoding process before expending time and money on geocoding a large number of addresses.

28.3 Geographic Levels of Aggregation

There are practical and conceptual considerations that govern the choice of geographic level of aggregation for data linkage. First, in practical terms, the choice of level of aggregation may be determined by the available data from other sources. For example, a survey of smoking behaviors that seeks to supplement data on individuals with aggregated data about the tobacco sales environment may be limited to using ZIP code level data sales data are only available at this level. Second, as noted above, geocoding completeness may be affected by the level of aggregation. A researcher might prefer to analyze block group-level data, but if a large proportion of the residential addresses in the survey dataset cannot be geocoded to this level with certainty, this may result in a large proportion of missing data. In this case, the choice of a level of aggregation, which gives greater completeness of geocoding, may have to be weighed against conceptual considerations about the most meaningful level of aggregation for analysis.

The choice of level of aggregation is also influenced by how the area-level variable is conceptualized. For example, if an area-level socioeconomic variable is conceptualized as a proxy for individual socioeconomic position, it might be reasonable to choose a smaller level of aggregation. Since smaller areas are more likely to be socioeconomically homogeneous (Krieger 1992, Davey Smith et al. 1998), assigning the aggregate mean for the area as a proxy for the individual-level variable will be less subject to error (however, see the cautions below in the discussion of aggregate measures as proxies). On the other hand, if the area-level measure is conceptualized as a contextual or ecologic measure, the choice of level of aggregation should be driven by theoretical considerations about the level at which social processes are taking place. For example, a measure of socioeconomic inequality may have little meaning at the block group level, but more meaning at the county, city, or state level.

Many sources of aggregated data used for linkage to individual survey data in the United States are organized by census-defined administrative units. It is therefore helpful to review the U.S. census geographic hierarchy here (U.S. Census Bureau 2013a, Messer and Kaufman 2006). As represented in Figure 28.1, all census geographic entities can be defined as aggregations of *census blocks*, the smallest geographic unit for which the Census Bureau tabulates 100% data. The central axis of Figure 28.1 presents the key hierarchy of nested census geographic units: the United States is divided into four census regions (Northeast, Midwest, South, and West), each of which contains two or three divisions. Divisions are divided into states, which are further divided into counties (the primary legal subdivision in most states). Counties are divided into *census tracts*, which are small, "relatively permanent" statistical subdivisions of counties containing on average 4000 residents. Tract boundaries are delineated by a local committee of census data users for the purpose of representing data and are designed to be relatively homogeneous with respect to sociodemographic characteristics and living conditions. Areas experiencing rapid population growth or decline may become heterogeneous during the decennial census period, and census tract boundaries may be adjusted between censuses (Chen et al. 2008). *Census block groups* are nested within census tracts and generally contain between 600 and 3000 people with an optimal size of 1500. This is generally the smallest level for which socioeconomic data are available.

In addition to this nested hierarchy, other subdivisions of states and counties are possible (Messer and Kaufman 2006). For example, states may be divided into school districts, congressional districts, or state legislative districts, which may be of interest for studies of health and aggregated data on educational policy or political representation. Counties may be divided into voting districts, traffic analysis zones, or county subdivisions. The Census Bureau also defines urban areas and core-based statistical areas (including metropolitan statistical units). Linkable aggregated data may be available for these entities as well; however, as these

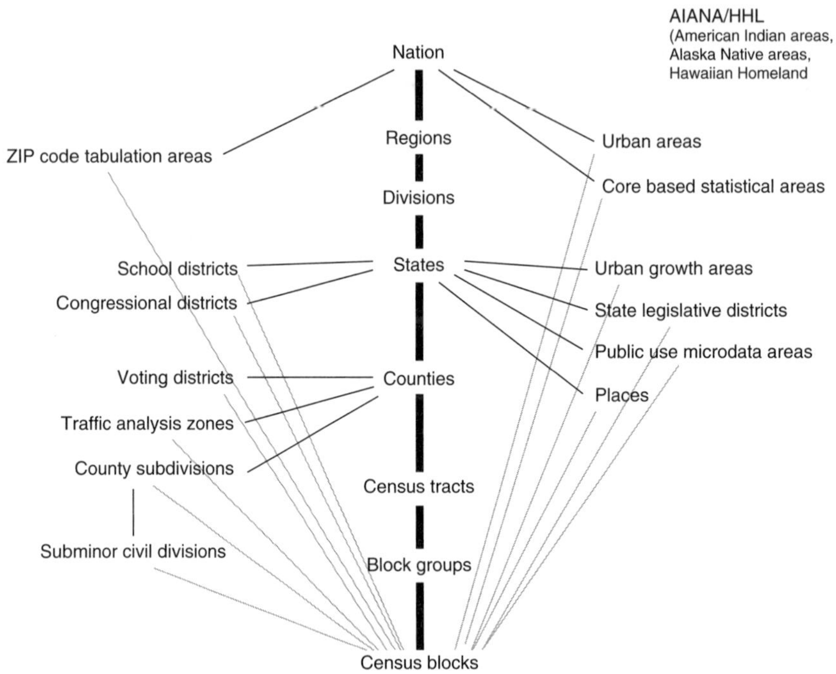

FIGURE 28.1 U.S. Census geography.

subdivisions do not exhaustively cover the entire United States, linkable aggregate data defined on these units may not be available for study subjects living outside of these areas.

ZIP codes deserve special mention here. The U.S. Postal Service uses ZIP codes to identify the individual post office or metropolitan area delivery station associated with mailing addresses. USPS ZIP Codes are thus technically not administrative or statistical units, but a collection of mail delivery routes established for the most efficient delivery of mail. They may be large areas cutting across states, or a single building with a high volume of mail; carrier routes for one ZIP code may intertwine with those of one or more ZIP codes, such that "this area is more conceptual than geographic" (Krieger et al. 2002a). The Census does release data for what they call ZIP Code Tabulation Areas (ZCTAs), which are "generalized areal representations of United States Postal Service (USPS) ZIP Code service areas" (U.S. Census Bureau 2013c). In most cases, these ZCTAs line up with USPS defined ZIP codes, but they need not always do so. Moreover, ZIP codes may change substantially over time in response to changes in postal service needs, such that analyses based on ZIP code level data can be unstable (Krieger et al. 2002b).

In most applications linking to aggregated data from the census and similar data sources, census geography is used by default as a convenient means to delineate geographically defined neighborhoods (Sampson et al. 2002). However, researchers interested in neighborhood effects should consider how appropriately a given level of census aggregation captures the level at which the hypothesized neighborhood effects operate. In densely populated areas, neighborhoods seem well approximated by census tracts or clusters of census tracts; however, in areas with low population density, such as rural areas, census tracts may be overly large in terms of geographic space, and block groups may provide a better approximation.

28.3.1 EXAMPLE: NCHS DATASETS CONTAINING GEOCODES

The National Center for Health Statistics makes geocodes available for several national surveys. Geographic identifiers are considered "Indirect Identifiers," in that these variables, when combined with other data, could lead to identification of study subjects. Therefore, NCHS restricts access to these confidential variables via the Research Data Centers (RDC) system (CDC/NCHS 2009a). Researchers can apply to the NCHS to work with these restricted data at these data centers. The main use of these geocodes is to permit the appending of variables from external sources of data to add contextual information or information on policy. Typically, following the merge, the geographic variables are removed, although the NCHS acknowledges that if these variables need to be retained for analytic purposes as well, researchers can request this (CDC/NCHS 2013). The suppression of small area identifiers in public use versions of these datasets can mean that researchers have access to linked area-level measures for analysis but may not be able to specify fully multilevel models that include random area effects. This limits the kinds of analytic approaches available (see Section 28.9.1).

Important national survey datasets with census tract and block group geographic identifiers include the National Health and Nutrition Examination Surveys (NHANES III and Continuous NHANES; CDC/NCHS 2011), the National Health Interview Survey (1997 to present; there also exists a special project geocode file with similar information for NHIS households from 1995 to 2005; CDC/NCHS 2012), and the National Survey of Family Growth (Cycle 2 onward; CDC/NCHS 2009b). Published studies using geocoded NHANES data include: Stimpson et al. (2007), Merkin et al. (2009), Do et al. (2007), Finch et al. (2010).

28.4 Types of Area-Level Measures

Numerous authors (Susser 1994, Diez-Roux 1998, 2000, Blakely and Woodward 2000, Blakely and Subramanian 2006) have described typologies of ecological variables, noting in particular the distinction that can be made between variables based on individual-level data aggregated up versus variables that directly measure properties of groups (and for which there is no individual-level analog). For example, Macintyre (1997) refers to the former as "collective" and the latter as "contextual," while Diez-Roux (1998) uses the terms "derived" and "integral."

Derived variables summarize the characteristics of individuals in the group (means, medians, proportions, or measures of dispersion). *Integral variables* describe characteristics of the group that are not derived from characteristics of its members (e.g., the existence of certain types of regulations, availability of health care, social organization, political regime, legal status of women). Integral variables do not have analogs at the individual level. While derived and integral variables are often presented as conceptually distinct, they are closely interrelated (Diez-Roux 1998). For derived variables, the distinction between group-level and individual-level becomes particularly important when the variable has analogs at both levels, but both measure different constructs. For example, an individual may be characterized as living in a household with annual income below the poverty line, which reflects information about that individual's access to material resources, but the census tract level measure percentage of persons living below the poverty line reflects additional information about that individual's exposure to conditions driven by the social processes occurring in communities with concentrated deprivation. These conditions might include, for example, lack of access to resources or economic opportunity, exposure to environmental pollutants, exposure to violence, and so on. Moreover, these factors may affect everyone in the neighborhood regardless of individual-level poverty status.

Blakely and Subramanian (2006) compared further subcategorizations of ecological variables, as discussed in the epidemiologic and social science literature; Table 28.1 shows the variety of terminology used to describe these concepts.

While numerous authors have argued for the greater use of "integral" variables to capture characteristics of neighborhoods, including directly observing neighborhoods and groups themselves (Macintyre and Ellaway 2003, Raudenbush and Sampson 1999), "derived" variables based on aggregations of individual-level data remain extremely popular in studies of neighborhoods and health due to their availability and relative ease of calculation from census or other administrative data. Here, individual and household responses to particular census questions are aggregated to multiple geographic units (census block groups, census tracts, etc.) to produce summary data (typically, means, medians, or proportions) on various characteristics, including age composition, racial/ethnic composition, and socioeconomic and housing characteristics. These can be linked by geographic level to geocoded survey data. As discussed below, however, special care must be taken in interpreting these measures because they likely reflect a mix of individual- and contextual-level effects (Greenland 1992).

28.5 Sources of Aggregated Data

The most common source of aggregated data for linkage to health survey data is the U.S. Census Bureau's Census of Population and Housing. As mandated by the U.S. Constitution, the census is administered every 10 years, and, up until

TABLE 28.1 Classification and Examples of Ecological Variables, Showing the Different Terminology Applied to Similar Concepts

Ecological Variable		Description	Examples
Derived	(Diez-Roux)	Aggregate of attributes measured at the individual level. Often expressed as a measure of central tendency (e.g., mean, median, proportion), but may be extended to include measures of variation of individual variables.	Mean income
Aggregate	(Morgenstern)		Percentage less than high school proportion smoking
Contextual	(Susser)		Area-based composite indices of deprivation
Analytical	(Lazarfeld and Menzel)		Income inequality
Contagion	(Susser)	Aggregate of the individual-level outcome, rather than exposure(s), that in turn affect the probability of the same outcome in individuals in the same population who are not yet affected.	Prevalence of infectious disease, suicide rate.
Endogenous	(Manksi)		
Peer	(Dietz)		

(*continued*)

TABLE 28.1 (*Continued*)

Ecological Variable		Description	Examples
Environmental	(Morgenstern)	Physical characteristics of a place, with an individual level analog that usually varies between individuals (though it may remain unmeasured at the individual level).	Hours of sunlight, environmental pollutant.
Structural	(Lazarfeld and Menzel)	Measure the pattern of relationships and interactions between individuals belonging to the group.	Social networks
Integral	(Susser, Diez-Roux)	Measure attributes of groups, organizations or places, and are not reducible to the individual level. They are fixed for all, or nearly all, individual group members.	Social (dis)organization, social capital, legislation or regulation.
Global	(Morgenstern, Lazarfeld, and Menzel)		

Susser 1994, Lazarfeld and Menzel 1961, Morgenstern 1998, Manski 1993, Diez-Roux 2000, Dietz 2002.
Source: Adapted from Blakely and Subramanian (2006).

2000, consisted of a short-form questionnaire and a long-form questionnaire. The short-form questionnaire queries the type of household and number of people included, as well as the name and phone number of the head of household and sex and race of up to 12 people in the household. The long form, which was administered to a sample of households, asked additional questions about age, education, language, citizenship, residential stability, disabilities, military status, employment, sources of income and employer, household type and condition, and expenses.

As of their 2005–2009 data release, ongoing national data collection via the American Community Survey (ACS) replaces the Census long-form questionnaire (U.S. Census Bureau 2008). The ACS is a nationwide, continuous survey designed to provide communities with reliable and timely demographic, housing, social, and economic data every year. A key advantage of these data is that they are now available on an ongoing basis instead of every 10 years. Data at the block group and census tract level are released as 5 year rolling averages, beginning with the 2005–2009 data release. Five-year ZCTA data are also available, beginning with the 2012 release of 2007–2011 5-year estimates.

While the Census 2000 long-form sample represented approximately a 1-in-6 household sample at one point in time (April 1, 2000), the ACS represents approximately 1-in-40 households on a rolling sample basis. Accordingly, along with ACS estimates of population characteristics, the Census Bureau reports a margin of error (MOE) that captures the variability of the estimate due to sampling error (U.S. Census Bureau 2010). Though researchers have usually treated linked aggregated data as fixed and known in most analyses, the availability of MOE information and the greater variability associated with ACS estimate raises the possibility of incorporating measurement error models into analyses of neighborhood effects (Richardson and Best 2003).

28.5.1 EXAMPLE: AREA-BASED MEASURES OF SOCIOECONOMIC POSITION

Area-based measures of socioeconomic characteristics are among the most commonly linked aggregated measures used in health research. This is motivated on the one hand by the relative paucity of individual-level socioeconomic measures in routinely collected health surveillance data (Krieger et al. 1997a, Krieger et al. 2002b) and, at the same time, by interest in how neighborhood level socioeconomic context influences health.

Recognizing that socioeconomic position is a multidimensional construct predicated on the social relationship of social class (Krieger et al. 1997b), researchers have identified multiple domains of socioeconomic position that can be captured through aggregations of individual-level census variables. These include measures that capture economic resources (including income, poverty, and wealth), educational attainment, occupational class, and housing characteristics. Examples of some of these measures are given in Table 28.2.

TABLE 28.2 Examples of U.S. Census-Based Measures of Socioeconomic Position and Relevant Domains of Socioeconomic Position

Construct	Operational definition
Income	
Median household income	Median household income in the year prior to the census
Low income	Percentage of households with an income <50% of the U.S. median household income (Gordon and Spicker 1999)
High income	Percentage of households with an income ≥400% of the U.S. median household income
Poverty	
Below U.S. poverty line	Percentage of persons below the federally defined poverty line, a threshold that varies by the size and age composition of the household
Wealth	
Expensive homes	Percentage of owner-occupied homes >400% of the median value of owned homes
Educational level	
Low: less than high school	Percentage of persons aged ≥25 years with less than a high school education
High: ≥4 years of college	Percentage of persons aged ≥25 years with at least 4 years of college
Occupational class	
Working class (Krieger et al. 2002b)	Percentage of persons employed in predominantly working-class occupations, that is, as nonsupervisory employees. Operationalized as percentage of persons employed in the following 8 of 13 census-based occupational groups: administrative support; sales; private household service; other service (except protective); precision production, craft, and repair; machine operators, assemblers, and inspectors; transportation and material moving; handlers, equipment cleaners, and laborers.
Crowding	
Crowded households	Percentage of households containing more than one person per room
Income inequality	
Gini coefficient	A measure of income inequality summarizing the distribution of shares of the income distribution across the population

Source: Adapted from Krieger et al. (2002).

While measures based on single census items are widely used, particularly in the United States, composite indicators using aggregates of several individual-level indicators have been widely used in the United Kingdom, where these area-based measures are termed "indices of deprivation" (Lee et al. 1995, Gordon 1995). In the United Kingdom, these indicators have important policy applications, as they serve to allocate public resources to areas. Two of the most commonly used indices are:

1. The Townsend deprivation index (Townsend 1990; Townsend et al. 1990), which measures deprivation with four variables from the British census: the proportion of unemployment (proportion of economically active residents age 16–64 who are unemployed), the proportion of households with no car, the proportion of households that are not owner occupied, and the proportion of households with overcrowding (>one person per room).
2. The Carstairs deprivation index (Carstairs and Morris 1991), which uses the proportion of unemployed males, proportion of households with no car, the proportion of households with overcrowding (>one person per room), and the proportion of low social class occupations (proportion individuals in households with head in social class IV/V according to the U.K. Registrar General's social class scale).

For each, the component elements are standardized using a z-score transformation and summed to yield a continuous score (Lee et al. 1995).

The summed z-score approach to deprivation indices gives equal weighting to each of the component items that go into the index. Researchers have also taken a more empirically driven latent variable approach to developing area-based socioeconomic measures by employing factor analysis or principal components analysis as a data reduction technique. These techniques allow for unequal weighting of specific area-based socioeconomic measures. For example, Singh and colleagues developed a factor-based deprivation scale consisting of 11 census-based socioeconomic indicators, with factor loadings ranging from 0.9 for median family income to 0.57 for unemployment rate. They have published numerous analyses of U.S. mortality trends in relation to this scale (Singh 2003, Singh and Siahpush 2002, 2006, Singh et al. 2002).

The advantage of such data reduction techniques is that they enable researchers to capture the multidimensional construct of socioeconomic position in a single measure (Galobardes et al. 2006). Having done so, however, it becomes difficult to disentangle the contribution of a specific domain of socioeconomic position (e.g., poverty, education) with the outcome or to explore explicit interactions between measures. Moreover, relationships between specific measures of socioeconomic position can change over time (Chen et al. 2013), drawing into question the stability of factor-based measures over time. Finally, given the diversity of specific socioeconomic measures employed by researchers, reliance on such measures contributes to a lack of comparability across studies.

28.6 Aggregate Data Measures as Proxies for Individual Data

Aggregate measures are often used in studies because data on relevant individual-level covariates are missing (Krieger 1997b). In this situation, the implicit rationale for including aggregate measures is that they function as proxies for the unobserved individual-level data. Empirical research using area-based socioeconomic measures shows that these measures do capture socioeconomic gradients in the expected direction for many health outcomes (Krieger et al. 2002b, 2003b, 2003c, 2003d, 2005). However, it is important to consider potential biases arising from the use of these variables as proxies.

Some have argued that when area-level measures of socioeconomic position (SEP) are used as proxies for individual-level indicators, the estimate of the association with SEP and the health outcomes is likely to be an underestimate of the true individual-level effect (Davey Smith et al. 1998, Galobardes et al. 2006), since the area-based measure is essentially a "mismeasured" version of the individual variable. Under this logic, the larger the area, the greater the underestimate is likely to be. Moreover, the variability in SEP captured by the area aggregate indicator will always be smaller than that of the individual-level indicator (Galobardes et al. 2006). On the other hand, if the area socioeconomic characteristics have an effect on health outcomes independent of individual SEP but in the same direction, the association of individual SEP will be overestimated when area-level indicators are used to predict individual-level effect, because the area effect will be interpreted as the individual-level effect (Galobardes et al. 2006).

These two bias mechanisms are explored by Geronimus et al. (1996). Their arguments are similar to those pertaining to ecologic bias (see Section 28.8). First, they identify what they call an "errors-in-variables type bias," which arises because the aggregate variable is only imperfectly correlated with the individual-level variable that it is representing. The second, an aggregation bias, arises because the "aggregate variable may itself be correlated with the residual in the microlevel equation"—that is, there may be an additional contextual effect above and beyond the effect of the missing individual-level variable. In such situations, a purely individual-level analysis and a purely ecological analysis will produce different results (Firebaugh 1978). Geronimus et al. (1996) suggest that, although this is not a mathematical necessity, these two biases may work in opposite directions: the errors-in-variables bias tends to exert a downward bias on the estimated coefficient for the aggregate proxy, while the additional contextual effect picked up by the aggregated variable results in inflation of the estimated coefficient. At the same time, the fact that the aggregated variable is imperfectly correlated with the individual-level variable implies that estimates of other individual-level variables will be affected by residual confounding. Whether underestimation (or overestimation) and its magnitude affect a given study will depend on the specific health outcomes, the area measures, and area size (Davey Smith et al. 1998, Geronimus and Bound 1998).

An additional concern pertains when applying aggregated area summaries based on the total population to selected individuals within areas. Consider an area with a population that is 80% White and 20% Black, and in which the Black population is significantly poorer than the White population. If the median household income measure for the total population in the area is applied to all individuals equally, it is more likely to be closer to the individual-level value for a randomly selected White person from the area than for a Black person from the same area. That is to say, it is a more accurate proxy of individual SEP for a White person from this area than a Black person. As a result, the extent of bias stemming from the "errors-in-variables" mechanism described above will be greater for the Black population in this example than the White, drawing into question the validity of comparing socioeconomic associations across racial/ethnic groups.

Where interest is in using an aggregate measure as a proxy, a possible solution is to use covariate-specific aggregate summaries instead of those based on the total population. For example, more recent data from the ACS includes key socioeconomic variables stratified by sex, gender, and race/ethnicity (U.S. Census Bureau 2008). For analyses where the intention is to control as best as possible for individual socioeconomic position using an area-level proxy, it is reasonable to think it is preferable to use a covariate-specific aggregate measure instead of the area-level marginal value.

28.7 Aggregate Measures as Contextual Variables

A now substantial literature in social epidemiology has argued for the inclusion of area- or group-level variables in analyses as measures of social context in their own right (Macintyre et al. 2002, Diez-Roux 1998, Diez-Roux 2000). This is based on the recognition that group-level variables often provide information about social processes occurring at the community level that is not captured by individual-level data alone (Diez-Roux 1998, Diez-Roux 2000) and that exploring these group-level phenomena is vital to our understanding of population patterns of health, disease, and well-being. In particular, concepts such as income inequality, social cohesion, social disorganization, social capital, and so on, that are defined at the level of communities cannot be reduced to individual-level variables. From this perspective, the "atomistic" (or "individualistic" fallacy) of making inferences about group level associations based solely on individual data is as much a danger as the better-known ecologic fallacy (Schwartz 1994, Diez-Roux 1998, Diez-Roux 2000, Subramanian et al. 2009).

The issues here are conceptual, and not just methodological, and pertain to what variables, at multiple levels, can and should be included in an analysis to permit estimation of the associations of interest. Thus, even when data on individual outcomes and exposure are available, are there additional group-level variables that should be included in an analysis, both as exposures in their own right, as well as to permit unbiased estimation of individual associations of interest? In addition to the ecologic and atomistic fallacies already mentioned, Diez-Roux

(1998), drawing on Riley (1963), points out two additional fallacies relevant to this kind of multilevel thinking. The "psychologistic" fallacy ignores relevant group-level variables in a study of individual-level associations, assuming that individual-level outcomes can be explained exclusively in terms of individual-level characteristics. Analogously, the "sociologistic fallacy" may arise when ignoring the role of individual-level factors in a study of group-level effects. Diez-Roux (1998) points out that both the psychologistic and sociologistic fallacies can be thought as types of confounding, whereby relevant variables from other levels have been excluded from the model. Indeed several authors have used the more general term "cross-level confounding" to refer to biases that arise from omitting key variables at different levels (Alker 1969 p. 78; Greenland 2001).

When contextual effects are the focus of an investigation, the sociological fallacy (omission of relevant individual-level variables) is of particular concern. Care should therefore be taken to include relevant individual-level confounders in the model. However, because aggregate variables are themselves derived from group-level summaries of individual-level variables, an effect estimate based on an aggregated variable will necessarily be confounded by its own individual-level analog. Thus, it is rarely possible to tell whether the effect of a variable operates at the individual level or through its area-level average (a contextual effect), when only the area-level variable is available (Greenland 1992, 2001, Sheppard 2003).

Empirically, when studies have been able to adjust for individual-level and area-level SEP, most have found a relatively small (in comparison with individual-level variables) independent area-level effect of SEP on various health outcomes and health behaviors (Pickett and Pearl 2001). In many cases, however, studies have adjusted for only one measure of individual SEP, whereas when life course individual SEP was accounted for, area SEP was no longer associated with mortality (Davey Smith et al. 1997). By contrast, in a study of British women, 60–79 years of age, area-level SEP and individual life course SEP both contributed to CHD prevalence (Lawlor et al. 2005). It remains an empirical question to what extent observed associations between area-level measures of SEP and health outcomes are related to the socioeconomic characteristics of the area *independent* of the (lifetime) characteristics of the people living within these areas. From a life course epidemiologic perspective, historical socioeconomic information on both areas and individuals would be required to understand how contextual processes affect health over time independently of individual SEP. Thus, it is unlikely that adjustment for only one or two adult indicators of individual SEP, as is employed in most research, would be sufficient for capturing the full extent of individual SEP effects (Galobardes et al. 2006).

28.8 The Components of Ecological Bias

In a seminal paper, Robinson (1950) warned sociologists of the dangers of using aggregate data to make inferences about individual relationships, showing that correlations between variables at the aggregate level can differ from correlations between the same variables at the individual level. The nature of this bias and examples of how the aggregate associations can vary substantially in both magnitude and direction from individual associations have been extensively discussed in the scientific literature (Richardson et al. 1987, Greenland and Robins 1994, Greenland 2001), and generations of social scientists and epidemiologists have been warned of the dire consequences of committing the "ecologic(al) fallacy" (Selvin 1958). Nevertheless, social scientists continue to use aggregate measures, often because the desired individual-level data are not available. As noted above, the issue is not resolved merely by eschewing individual-level interpretations, since estimation of the contextual level effect is also biased by the individual-level associations.

The fundamental problem of ecologic inference is that the loss of information due to aggregation prevents identification of associations of interest in the underlying individual-level model (Wakefield 2008). A distinction may be drawn between "purely" ecological studies, in which *both* the exposure and outcome data are available only as aggregated data, and study designs in which outcome (and possibly covariate) data on individuals are linked to aggregated measures of exposures. The latter design has been called "semi-ecological" (or, more optimistically, "semi-individual") (Künzli Tager 1997, Sheppard 2003, Richardson and Best 2003, Wakefield 2008). While some forms of bias that occur in purely ecological designs do not occur in the semi-ecological setting, interpretation of the estimated effect of the ecological exposure must still be made with caution, as shown below. Given that researchers continue to use aggregated measures, it is perhaps more useful to enumerate the possible sources of ecological bias, so that informed interpretations can be made of effect estimates based on ecological variables.

A vast literature on the sources of ecological bias has identified key elements that may contribute, including: (i) pure specification bias, (ii) within- and between-area confounding, (iii) contextual effects, and (iv) effect modification (Richardson et al. 1987, Greenland and Robins 1994, Lasserre et al. 2000, Wakefield 2003; Salway and Wakefield 2004, Wakefield 2008). We present a summary of these concepts here, while referring the interested reader to Greenland and Robins (1994), Sheppard (2003), Richardson and Best (2003), Wakefield (2003), Salway and Wakefield (2004), and Wakefield (2008) for more detailed and mathematically rigorous explications.

An important concept in understanding ecological bias is that such bias is relative to a particular individual-level model. Thus, when trying to understand ecological bias, it is useful to specify the underlying individual-level model of interest and to aggregate up in order to determine the consequences (Wakefield 2008). Note that this is not the same thing as saying that only individual-level variables are of interest: such an individual-level model may include individual-level as well as contextual effects. Aggregation of the individual-level model to the area level helps us to understand the relationship between the underlying data generating process and the observed, area-level data.

Taking this approach here, suppose that we are interested in the relationship between an outcome Y and an exposure X, possibly conditional on a cofounder Z, and we have collected data on a disjoint set of m areas, with area i containing

N_i individuals, $i = 1, \ldots, m$. The outcome Y is a Bernoulli random variable, Y_{ij}, with $Y_{ij} = 1$ corresponding to a case and $Y_{ij} = 0$ to a non-case. To illustrate the possible sources of ecologic bias, we assume that, at the individual level, the true relationship between outcome and exposure follows some probability model, $q_{ij} = P(Y_{ij}|X_{ij}, Z_{ij}, X_i)$, where

$$g(q_{ij}) = \beta_{0i} + \beta_{1i}(X_{ij} - X_i) + \beta_2 X_i + \gamma Z_{ij} \tag{28.1}$$

and X_i represents the mean exposure in area i. Note that, in this general model, there is the possibility of area-specific intercepts, β_{0i}, and area-specific exposure effects, β_{1i}. Linearity is assumed on a scale determined by the link function, $g(\cdot)$, which allows for a nonlinear risk-exposure relationship. Typical link functions in epidemiologic applications include a logit link or log link, with the latter appropriate when q_{ij} is small (i.e., the disease is rare; the logit link for nonrare events is, unfortunately, less amenable to analytic study, Salway and Wakefield 2005). We focus on the linear and log-linear models in the discussion here. Note that the identity link and a linear model for q_{ij} is not very realistic, insofar as no constraints are placed on the probability q_{ij} (which should properly be bounded by 0 and 1). However, certain results are more clearly explained for the linear model, as noted below.

In an ecological study, we only observe area-level summaries of data, for example, area means Y_i, X_i, and Z_i, or the area-level count of cases, $Y_{i+} = \sum_j^{N_i} Y_{ij}$. To derive the model induced at the ecological level by Model 28.1, we aggregate over individuals within each area,

$$\begin{aligned} E[Y_i|X_i, Z_i] &= \frac{1}{N_i}\sum_j^{N_i} E[Y_{ij}|X_i, Z_i] \\ &= \frac{1}{N_i}\sum_j^{N_i} E_{(X_{ij},Z_{ij})|X_i,Z_i}\left\{E\left[Y_{ij}|X_{ij}, Z_{ij}\right]\right\} \\ &= \frac{1}{N_i}\sum_j^{N_i} E_{(X_{ij},Z_{ij})|X_i,Z_i}\left\{q_{ij}\right\} \end{aligned}$$

where the expectation is with respect to the joint distribution of $(X_{ij}, Z_{ij})|X_i, Z_i$ (Elliott and Wakefield 2000). Note that, in general, the form of the ecological model depends on the joint within-area distribution of X_{ij}, Z_{ij}; because this joint within-area distribution is unobserved for ecological data, the parameters of the ecological model are generally unidentified without further assumptions.

28.8.1 PURE SPECIFICATION BIAS

First, consider the situation where there are no contextual effects ($\beta_2 = 0$) and no confounders ($\gamma = 0$), and where the intercept and exposure effects do not vary by area ($\beta_{0i} = \beta_0$ and $\beta_{1i} = \beta_1$). If we have a linear model, that is, $g(q_{ij}) = \beta_0 + \beta_1 X_{ij}$, then aggregation gives

$$E[Y_i|X_i] = \frac{1}{N_i}\sum_j^{N_i} E_{X_{ij}|X_i}(\beta_0 + \beta_1 X_{ij}) = \beta_0 + \beta_1 X_i$$

which shows that, in this particular case of a linear model, an ecological analysis will give an unbiased estimate of the individual-level relationship.

If, however, a nonlinear model applies, then so-called specification bias will occur. For example, if $g(q_{ij}) = e^{\beta_0+\beta_1 X_{ij}}$ then we must evaluate

$$E_{X_{ij}|X_i}[e^{\beta_0+\beta_1 X_{ij}}]$$

to see the effects of aggregation. To proceed further, an assumption about the form of the exposure distribution within the area is required. If we assume $X_{ij}|X_i \sim N(X_i, \sigma_i^2)$, then

$$E[Y_i|X_i] = e^{\beta_0+\beta_1 X_i + 0.5\beta_1^2\sigma_i^2} \tag{28.2}$$

In contrast, in many settings, researchers fit a naïve ecological model,

$$E[Y_i|X_i] = e^{\beta_0^* + \beta_1^* X_i} \tag{28.3}$$

where β_0^* and β_1^* have been superscripted with "*" to distinguish them from the individual-level parameters in Model 28.1. Clearly, the parameters in Model 28.2 do not correspond to those in 28.3, and bias results. The distinction between Models 28.2 and 28.3 may be succinctly stated as follows: whereas Model 28.2 averages the risk across the individual exposures in area i, Model 28.3 gives the risk corresponding to the average exposure (Wakefield 2008).

If X_{ij} is a binary exposure indicator, then the aggregated model is

$$E(Y_i|X_i) = (1 - X_i)e^{\beta_0} + X_i e^{\beta_0+\beta_1} \tag{28.4}$$

Again, if we fit the "naïve" Model 28.3, $e^{\beta_1^*}$ does not correspond to e^{β_1}. However, it is interesting to note that, in the case of a binary exposure, as long as we have the area summaries X_i, we can fit the aggregated model (as opposed to the "naïve" model) and obtain unbiased estimates (Lasserre et al. 2000, Sheppard 2003, Jackson et al. 2006, Wakefield 2008).

There are situations when pure specification bias does not apply. First, as noted above, in the case of a simple linear model (i.e., an additive risk model), there is no specification bias. Second, if there is no within-area variability in exposure (i.e., $X_{ij} = X_i$ for all individuals in an area and thus $\sigma_i^2 = 0$), then one can expect that $e^{\beta_1} = e^{\beta_1^*}$; this is, however, unlikely in practice. Third, if exposure does vary within areas, there is no bias if the within area means are independent of all higher moments; this can occur, for example, if the within-area distribution is normal and the within-area variances are constant. Otherwise, the bias depends on the form of the risk-exposure model, the size of the exposure effect, the amount of within-area variability, and the within-area exposure distribution.

28.8.2 UNMEASURED CONFOUNDING

Confounding is an important source of ecological bias, and has been extensively discussed in the literature (Greenland and Robins 1994, Greenland 2001, Salway and Wakefield 2004). Because of the nature of ecological data, it is important to recognize that bias may be due to within- or between-area confounding. Between-area confounding is analogous to the confounding that may arise in all epidemiologic studies, and can be addressed in ecological analyses if data on area-level confounders is collected and analyzed. In contrast, within-area confounding is more problematic in ecological analyses, since typically only marginal summaries of exposure and confounder distributions (X_i and Z_i) are available, and the joint distribution of X_{ij} and Z_{ij} is unobserved. We illustrate confounding here under the linear risk model, so that the implications of aggregation can be appreciated independent of pure specification bias.

Figure 28.2 illustrates the effect of different sources of ecological bias for three areas, A, B, and C. This graphical description, which appears in Salway and Wakefield (2004), gives an accessible summary of these biases. In each of the four scenarios, the dotted lines represent the individual-level relationships between disease risk and exposure within each area, while the dashed line presents the observed ecological relationship. The relationships are based on the individual-level model in Model 28.1 with a linear link function. Figure 28.2a presents the simple case where there are no confounding or contextual effects and where the parameters do not vary between areas. As a result, there is no ecological bias, and the ecological regression line is identical to the individual regression line.

Figure 28.2b,c shows two situations in which the individual-level relationships are the same for all areas (thus, the dotted lines are parallel), but the baseline risk (the area-specific intercepts) vary. This can be due to between-area or within-area confounding, confounding by group, or contextual effects. In Figure 28.2b, the relationship between individual-level exposure and disease is positive, but the ecological effect is negative, so that negative bias has been induced. In Figure 28.2c, both the individual-level and ecological relationships are positive, so the ecological regression yields an overestimate of the individual-level effect. As shown in Table 28.3, each of these sources of bias (between-area confounding, within-area confounding, confounding by group, or contextual effects) can be conceptualized as resulting in area-specific intercepts in the aggregated model. In particular, a contextual effect can be viewed as acting in the same way as a between area confounder, since β_{0i} is explicitly correlated with X_i and thus ecological bias results. Notably, if the baseline risk β_{0i} varies *randomly* due to unmeasured factors between areas, then it can be modeled as a random effect in a multilevel framework (see Section 28.9.2). However, if β_{0i} varies systematically between areas (referred to as confounding by group,

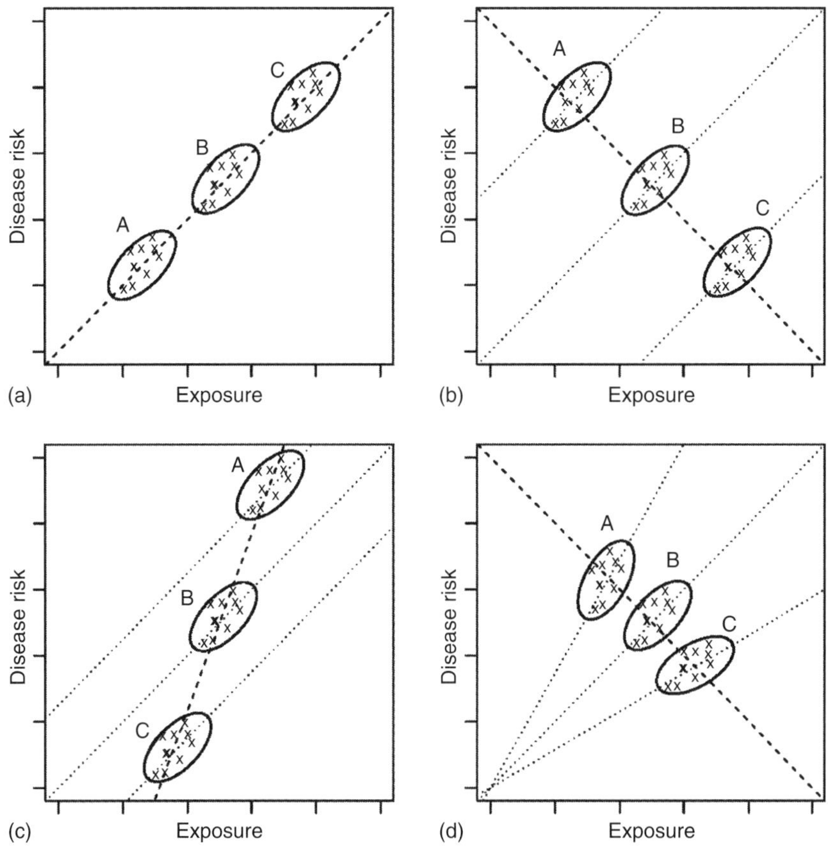

FIGURE 28.2 Examples of ecological bias induced by confounding and effect modification (see Table 28.3). A, B, and C are areas, the dotted lines show the within-area relationship between exposure and disease risk, and the dashed lines show the estimated ecological regression line. (a) No bias, (b) Negative bias, (c) Positive bias, (d) Effect modification.

Greenland and Morgenstern 1989), then the inclusion of random effects cannot in general control for confounding (Salway and Wakefield 2004).

The third example in Table 28.3, under the linear model, shows the effect of an unmeasured within-area confounder. What happens if we have an area-level summary of a within-area confounder, for example, $Z_i = \frac{1}{n_i}\sum_j^{n_i} Z_{ij}$? In the linear setting, controlling for the area summaries Z_i is sufficient to permit unbiased estimation of β_1, but in the nonlinear setting, this does not hold. Consider the example of a binary exposure (e.g., poor vs nonpoor socioeconomic position) and a binary confounder (e.g., White vs non-White race/ethnicity), along with a log linear model for q_{ij}:

$$E(Y_{ij}|X_{ij}, Z_{ij}) = e^{\beta_0+\beta_1 X_{ij}+\gamma Z_{ij}}$$

TABLE 28.3 Examples of Biases Induced by Aggregation, Assuming a Linear Individual-Level Model

Source of Bias	Individual Model	Ecological Model Under Aggregation
Bias due to area variation in baseline risk (e.g., data anomalies in population or disease counts)	$E[Y_{ij} \mid X_{ij}] = \beta_{0i} + \beta_1 X_{ij}$	$E[Y_i \mid X_i] = E[\beta_{0i} \mid X_i] + \beta_1 X_i$ If β_{0i} is negatively correlated with X_i, then negative bias results. If β_{0i} is positively correlated with X_i then positive bias results.
Bias due to unmeasured between-area confounding	$E[Y_{ij} \mid X_{ij}, Z_i] = \beta_0 + \beta_1 X_{ij} + \gamma Z_i$	$E\left[Y_i \mid X_i\right] = \beta_0 + \beta_1 X_i + \gamma E[Z_i \mid X_i] = \beta_{0i} + \beta_1 X_i$ where $\beta_{0i} = \beta_0 + \gamma E[Z_i \mid X_i]$. This shows how variation in baseline risk is induced. Since β_{0i} and X_i are by definition correlated if Z_i is a between-area confounder, bias results as above if Z_i is unobserved.
Bias due to unmeasured within-area confounding	$E[Y_{ij} \mid X_{ij}] = \beta_0 + \beta_1 X_{ij} + \gamma Z_{ij}$	$E\left[Y_i \mid X_i\right] = \beta_0 + \beta_1 X_i + \gamma E[Z_{ij} \mid X_i] = \beta_{0i} + \beta_1 X_i$ where $\beta_{0i} = \beta_0 + \gamma E[Z_{ij} \mid X_i]$. β_{0i} and X_i are correlated since Z_{ij} is a within-area confounder, so bias results as above.

<table>
<tr>
<td>Bias due to contextual effects</td>
<td>If the individual effect is centered around the contextual effect,
$E\left[Y_{ij}|X_{ij}, X_i\right] = \beta_0 + \beta_1(X_{ij} - X_i) + \beta_2 X_i = \beta_{0i} + \beta_1 X_{ij}$
with
$\beta_{0i} = \beta_0 + (\beta_2 - \beta_1)X_i$
If the model is written as:
$E[Y_{ij}|X_{ij}, X_i] = \beta_0 + \beta_1 X_{ij} + \beta_2^* X_i$</td>
<td>$E\left[Y_i|X_i\right] = \beta_{0i} + \beta_1 X_i = \beta_0 + (\beta_2 - \beta_1)X_i + \beta_1 X_1 = \beta_0 + \beta_2 X_i$
which shows that only the contextual effect can be estimated.
Under aggregation we obtain:
$E[Y_i|X_i] = \beta_0 + (\beta_1 + \beta_2^*)X_i$
showing that we are estimating the combined effect of individual and contextual effects.</td>
</tr>
</table>

The ecological model under aggregation shows the effect of aggregating and shows the information necessary to obtain an unbiased estimate of β_1 when only group data are available.

The joint within-area distribution for a generic area is depicted in Table 28.4. The complete joint distribution can be described by three proportions (with the fourth being 1 minus the sum of the other three), but with ecological data we only observe the marginal proportion poor (X_i) and proportion non-White (Z_i). The aggregated model is:

$$
\begin{aligned}
E(Y_i) &= p_{00}e^{\beta_0} + p_{10}e^{\beta_0+\beta_1} + p_{01}e^{\beta_0+\gamma} + p_{11}e^{\beta_0+\beta_1+\gamma} \\
&= (1 - X_i - Z_i + p_{11})e^{\beta_0+\beta_1} + (X_i - p_{11})e^{\beta_0+\beta_1} + (Z_i - p_{11}) + p_{11}e^{\beta_0+\beta_1+\gamma}
\end{aligned}
$$

(Wakefield 2008). The presence of p_{11} in this expression shows that the marginal proportions X_i and Z_i are not sufficient to characterize the joint distribution (unless X_{ij} and Z_{ij} are independent, in which case Z_{ij} is not a confounder). The implication is also that controlling for the area-level proportion non-White in the naïve ecological model

$$E(Y_i|X_i, Z_i) = e^{\beta_0^* + \beta_1^* X_i + \gamma^* Z_i}$$

is not sufficient to eliminate bias in the socioeconomic estimate due to within-area confounding.

28.8.3 EFFECT MODIFICATION

Figure 28.2d illustrates ecological bias due to effect modification (Greenland and Morgenstern 1989, Morgenstern 1995, Salway and Wakefield 2004). Here, the individual-level effect parameter β_{1i} is different in each area, as shown by different slopes for each of the dotted lines. In each area, the relationship is positive; however, the ecological regression estimates the dashed line, and concludes that the relationship is negative because (in this example) β_{1i} is negatively correlated with X_i (i.e., the slopes decrease with increasing mean exposure).

28.8.4 SOLUTIONS TO THE ECOLOGICAL INFERENCE PROBLEM

In the above examples, it is clear that, given the most common epidemiologic models for exposure-outcome relationships, data on within-area distributions of exposures and covariates is required to overcome ecological bias (Richardson

TABLE 28.4 **Joint Distribution of Race/Ethnicity and Socioeconomic Position in a Generic Area: X_i is the Proportion Non-White and Z_i is the Proportion Poor; p_{00}, p_{01}, p_{10}, p_{11} are the Within-Area Cross-Classified Proportions**

	Nonpoor	Poor	
White	p_{00}	p_{01}	$1 - X_i$
Non-White	p_{10}	p_{11}	X_i
	$1 - Z_i$	Z_i	1.0

et al. 1987, Prentice and Sheppard 1995, Wakefield and Salway 2001). For example, Prentice and Sheppard (1995) describe a semiparametric model for supplementing ecological data with within-area samples of covariate measurements, and Wakefield and Salway (2001) describe parametric models for supplementing group-level data with individual-level samples of covariates. Best et al. (2001) apply these ideas to a study of childhood leukemia incidence, using within-area measures of environmental benzene exposure.

Even greater improvements can be gained by using individual data on covariates and outcomes (Wakefield 2004, Jackson et al. 2006, 2008). For example, Jackson et al. (2006, 2008) describe a framework they term hierarchical related regression (HRR), whereby ecological data can be combined with small samples of individual level data on covariates and outcomes, and show that small individual-level samples can substantially improve inference, reducing bias in cases where analyses based on ecological data alone would be biased. They caution that, when the true model is complex, it is most important to make sure that the model is correctly specified, as no amount of individual-level data can help if the model is misspecified.

28.8.5 SEMI-ECOLOGICAL INFERENCE

In an ecological study design, both the exposure and outcome are aggregated at the area or group level, leading to the forms of ecological bias noted above. In many survey settings, however, data on outcomes and covariates may be available for individuals, and it is the exposure variable that is aggregated to the group level. This can arise with health survey data linked to area-based socioeconomic measures and also in environmental epidemiologic settings, where survey data on individuals may be linked to environmental data (e.g., air pollution) defined at the area level (Richardson and Best 2003). This type of design has been called "semi-ecological" or "semi-individual" (Künzli and Tager 1997).

Künzli and Tager (1997) argue that the semi-ecological design is free from ecological bias, but Wakefield (2008) shows otherwise. Consider the risk for an individual in confounder stratum c. Under aggregation, the semi-ecological risk in stratum c is

$$E(Y_k|Z_k = c) = e^{\beta_0+\gamma_c} \frac{1}{n_c} \sum_{k}^{n_c} e^{\beta_1 X_{ck}}$$

where X_{ck} are the exposures of individuals within stratum c, $k = 1, \ldots, n_c$ and γ_c is the baseline risk in stratum c. In contrast, a naïve semi-ecological model might be

$$E(Y_k|Z_k = c) = e^{\beta_0^*+\gamma_c^*+\beta_1^*\overline{X}_g}$$

where $\overline{X}_g$ is some summary exposure measure defined at the group level. Wakefield (2008) points out that there are two possible sources of bias here. First, there is the possibility of pure specification bias because we have not acknowledged the within-area variability in exposures. Second, there is within-area confounding because we have not allowed the exposure to vary by confounder stratum.

As a result, researchers must still be wary of bias when using aggregated measures in semi-ecological designs.

28.9 Analytic Approaches to the Analysis of Survey Data with Linked Area-Based Measures

The choice of modeling approach depends on the inferential targets, the design of the survey, and the availability of identifiers of the grouping or area-level units, as well as the availability of software for fitting the model.

28.9.1 SINGLE LEVEL MODEL

A single level model ignores clustering by geographic area. This is equivalent to pooling over geographic areas, into strata defined by a (categorical) group-level variable. When area-level identifiers are not included in the dataset, this is the only option available. In addition, when there are a limited number of actual areas represented or when there are a very small number of observations per area, multilevel approaches may not be feasible (Diez-Roux 2000). However, Clarke (2008) suggests that even with only five observations per area, a multilevel approach is preferable to a single level model. In practical terms, it may be advisable to fit a multilevel model, and, if the area-level variance component is negligible, to proceed with a single-level model.

28.9.2 MULTILEVEL HIERARCHICAL MODELS

Especially when the effects of individual versus contextual exposures on health are the focus, multilevel hierarchical models are used to partition variation in the outcome and to explore the effects of covariates at each of the specified levels of interest (Blakely and Subramanian 2006, Goldstein 2011). Also known as *hierarchical, mixed, random effects, variance components,* or *random coefficient regression models,* such models can also be used to explore variation in individual-level effects across areas.

A justification often given for multilevel models is that, through the random effects structure, they account for the effect of unidentified or unmeasured confounders that vary across areas (Richardson and Monfort 2000) and that induce correlation between observations from the same area. For example, in the section above, Model 28.1 is a multilevel model with two levels (individual, indexed by j, and area, indexed by i) and with area-level variation in both the intercept (β_{0i}) and the individual-level effect (β_{1i}).

At Level 1:

$$g(q_{ij}) = \beta_{0i} + \beta_{1i}(X_{ij} - X_i) + \beta_2 X_i + \gamma Z_{ij}$$

At Level 2:

$$\beta_{0i} = \beta_0 + u_{0i}\,, \quad \beta_{1i} = \beta_1 + u_{1i}$$

where

$$\begin{bmatrix} u_{0i} \\ u_{1i} \end{bmatrix} \sim \text{MVN}\left[0, \begin{bmatrix} \sigma^2_{u_0} & \sigma_{u_0u_1} \\ \sigma_{u_0u_1} & \sigma^2_{u_1} \end{bmatrix}\right]$$

This model has random intercepts (β_{0i}) and random slopes (β_{1i}). As noted in Table 28.3, unmeasured confounding can often be seen as inducing area variation in the baseline risk parameter, $\beta_{0i} = \beta_0 + u_{0i}$, so that taking a multilevel approach to modeling a random intercept when Z_{ij} is unobserved is an attractive idea in order to account indirectly for the aggregated effect of unobserved risk factors (Richardson and Monfort 2000). However, it should be noted that, in the multilevel model, the $\{u_{0i}\}$ are assumed to be independent of the fixed effects, so that control for confounding may be incomplete.

Hierarchical models are also used extensively in spatial epidemiology and disease mapping, where estimation of the spatial structure is of interest (Chen 2013). In this case, the normal model for the distribution of the random effects is replaced by a spatially structured model, for example, the popular Besag–York–Mollié (BYM) model (convolution model) which decomposes the area-level variation into a spatially clustered component and an unstructured heterogeneity component (Besag et al. 1991, Lawson et al. 2003).

28.9.3 POPULATION AVERAGED OR MARGINAL MODELS

Population averaged or marginal models are an alternative to random or mixed models for estimating associations between area characteristics and individual-level health outcomes. These models, typically using a generalized estimating equation (GEE) approach, describe changes in the population mean given changes in the covariates, while accounting for the within-area nonindependence of observations when deriving the variability estimates of these coefficients. Whereas the hierarchical multilevel model approach explicitly models and partitions the covariance structure of the outcomes within and between areas, the GEE approach treats estimation of the mean of the dependent variable conditional on the covariates separately from estimation of the correlations between outcomes, with the latter usually based on a robust variance estimator (Hubbard et al. 2010). Thus, while random effects models model the dependent variable conditional on the random effects, marginal models model the marginal expectation of the dependent variables across the population (that is to say, averaged across the random effects). While for linear models and log-linear models, the GEE approach and the random effects model approach often yield similar results with similar interpretations, the two approaches diverge for logistic models (Diggle et al. 2002), for which the marginal parameter values will usually be smaller in absolute value than their random effects analogs.

Proponents of the marginal model approach for estimating associations between neighborhood risk factors and health argue that mixed models involve "unverifiable assumptions on the data generating distribution, which leads to potentially misleading estimates and biased inference" (Hubbard et al. 2010). That is, inference for mixed models is conditional on correct specification of the regression models for the fixed effects coefficients as well as distributional assumptions and regression models for the random effects. In particular, regression parameters in mixed effects models are more sensitive to random effects assumptions than are their counterparts in the population-averaged model. In contrast, the GEE approach allows robust inference even if the correlation model is misspecified, provided that the number of neighborhoods is sufficiently large. Thus, if the focus of an investigation is the estimation of mean effect as well as the estimation of the inference of the coefficients in the model, then a marginal model approach via GEE provides an attractive alternative to the mixed model approach. On the other hand if there is interest in estimating area-specific effects or in prediction (i.e., conditional on area), then the marginal model approach is not appropriate.

28.9.4 MULTILEVEL MODELS FOR COMPLEX SURVEY DATA

For analyses of complex survey data that include area-level variables and area-level geographic identifiers, the question of how to deal with clustering due to survey design along with multilevel structure arises. It is well recognized that multistage complex sampling designs result in nonindependence of data within clusters. This can result in biased standard errors and parameters when the analytical techniques do not take the clustered nature of the data into account. This leads to increased Type I errors, leading analysts to incorrectly reject the null hypothesis. Traditionally, modeling techniques have treated the clustered nature of the complex survey data as a nuisance by adjusting the standard errors for the sampling design (e.g., SUDAAN). Because complex survey designs often involve unequal selection probabilities of clusters and/or people within clusters, traditional models incorporate design weights to account for these unequal selection probabilities (see also Chapter 25).

The problem of clustering and nonindependence of observations is similar to what multilevel models set out to address: conceptually, it seems appealing to simply add the primary sampling unit as an additional level in the multilevel hierarchy. However, while the standard multilevel model can properly estimate parameters and standard errors in clustered data that resulted from equal probability sampling, the standard multilevel model may lead to biased estimates when employed in samples that include unequal probability of selection. To address this problem, statisticians have recommended incorporating design weights in the likelihood function, where the design weights account for unequal selection probabilities (Asparouhov 2005, 2006, Graubard and Korn 1996; Longford 1996, Pfeffermann et al. 1998, Rabe-Hesketh and Skrondal 2006; Carle 2009). As has been noted, though, one cannot simply use the "raw" weights when estimating multilevel models with unequal probabilities of selection (Carle 2009). Rather, to properly include design weights in the likelihood function requires scaling the weights. Numerous scaling methods have been proposed and several authors have undertaken simulation work to examine the behavior of the scaling methods in simulated data in an attempt to identify a scaling method that provides the least biased estimates in most situations (Asparouhov 2005, 2006, Rabe-Hesketh and Skrondal 2006).

Carle (2009) summarizes key findings from this area of active research as follows. First, simulations indicate that most scaling methods consistently provide better estimates than using unweighted analyses (Asparouhov 2006, Rabe-Hesketh and Skrondal 2006, Carle 2009). Second, two scaling methods appear to provide the least biased results. (Table 28.5): Method A, scales the weights so that the new weights sum to the cluster sample size. Method B, scales the weights so that the new weights sum to the effective cluster size (Asparouhov 2006). Third, various features of the design and data can affect the scaling method's adequacy. For example, as cluster sizes increase, the estimates generally become less biased. The number of clusters, size of clusters, type of outcome (categorical vs continuous), size of correlation between outcome and design weight, and the design weight's informativeness can all independently and jointly affect the scaling method's results. Fourth, simulations do point to a need for some type of scaling if using weights, especially with small cluster sizes (Rabe-Hesketh and Skrondal 2006). Notably, if one cannot scale the weights and include them properly in the estimation, *analyzing the data without weights provides the next best option.* Including the weights, but failing to scale them (i.e., including them as raw weights) results in biased parameters and standard errors, especially with small cluster sizes (Rabe-Hesketh and Skrondal 2006).

It should be pointed out that few publicly available data sets include weights for each level of analysis (Rabe-Hesketh and Skrondal 2006, Carle 2009). Rather, publicly available data usually include a single overall level 1 weighting variable that incorporates level 2 design issues. This confounding of level 1 (individual) and level 2 (cluster) design issues in a single weight can result in biased estimates.

TABLE 28.5 Recommended Methods for Rescaling Weights for Multilevel Analysis of Complex Survey Data

Method A	$w_{ij}^* = w_{ij}\left(\dfrac{n_j}{\sum_i w_{ij}}\right)$
Method B	$w_{ij}^* = w_{ij}\left(\dfrac{\sum_i w_{ij}}{\sum_i w_{ij}^2}\right)$

where
w_{ij}^* scaled weight for individual i in cluster j
w_{ij} unscaled weight for individual i in cluster j
n_j number of sample units in cluster j

Thus, along with choosing the appropriate scaling method, one must also decide whether to use the level 1 weights to estimate higher level weights or whether to leave the higher levels unweighted. However, the choice of the scaling of the level 2 weights will not influence parameter estimates or the standard errors associated with these estimates if level 2 corresponds to the highest level of the model and the same scale factor applies to all units. Finally, different estimation procedures and convergence criteria may lead to dissimilar results even when using identical scaling methods (Carle 2009).

Carle (2009) concludes that, based on the simulation work, one should *not* rely on a single scaling method, suggesting that analysts should fit the multilevel model using both scaling methods (A and B) and unweighted data and compare the results across methods. When the inferential decisions diverge, Carle (2009) suggests that analysts conduct detailed sensitivity analyses (Asparouhov 2006, Rabe-Hesketh and Skrondal 2006, Carle 2009). Additionally, the simulation work suggests that, for point estimates (e.g., intercepts, odds ratios, etc.), method A will often provide the least biased estimates (Asparouhov 2006). Thus, analysts who wish to discuss point estimates should report results based on weighting method A. For analysts more interested in residual between-cluster variance, method B may generally provide the least biased estimates. However, as cluster sizes increase ($n > 20$), the performance of method A improves more rapidly, though bias decreases substantially for all methods as cluster sizes become sufficiently large (Pfeffermann et al. 1998, Asparouhov 2006, Rabe-Hesketh and Skrondal 2006). Thus, when working with cluster sizes larger than $n = 20$ and when concerned that insufficient cluster size may lead to biased estimates, analysts may prefer to report method A's results.

Carle (2009) also notes the need for flexible software that can accommodate user-defined weights. The dedicated multilevel modeling packages Mplus, MLwiN, and GLLAMM allow this. However, user-defined scaled weights are not allowed in HLM and SAS procedures treat the weights as frequency weights instead of sampling weights. Grilli and Pratesi developed a complicated method to "trick" SAS NLMIXED into properly handling weights in models with no more than 2 levels (Grilli and Pratesi 2004). Meanwhile, SAS Survey procedures that do accommodate weighting generally fit a population averaged model, and do not allow proper fitting of multilevel models.

28.10 Summary

Linkage of survey records to aggregate area-based measures allows researchers to supplement their datasets with rich data on the social environment, permitting more extensive adjustment for covariates as well as exploration of the relationships between contextual factors and health. This is aided by the increasing availability and accessibility of georeferenced datasets with area-based characteristics summarized at multiple geographic levels, including, in the United States, the decennial U.S. Census and the ACS.

Enthusiasm for linked aggregate measures must be tempered by an awareness of the limitations of inferences based on such measures. The use of aggregate variables entails careful conceptualization and operationalization of the measures, including attention to level of geographic aggregation, timeframe, and potential causal mechanisms by which the area-level measure is hypothesized to influence health. In particular, whether using area-based measures as proxies for unobserved individual-level variables or exploring the contextual effect of area-based measures in the absence of individual-level variables, careful attention must be paid to the potential for cross-level confounding and resulting biases.

Ecological bias can arise due to pure specification bias (whereby a nonlinear underlying risk model is aggregated to the area level), within- and/or between-area confounding, contextual effects, or effect modification; the common feature is a lack of information concerning the within-area variability of exposures and confounders. Even when individual-level data on outcomes and covariates are linked to aggregate measures (as in a semi-ecological design), some sources of ecological bias may still apply. In both ecological and semi-ecological settings, it is therefore useful to posit an underlying individual-level model of interest, and to examine the effects of aggregation in order to understand the potential sources of bias. In general, ecological bias can only be removed by combining ecological and individual-level data.

While data linked to aggregate measures can be analyzed using traditional regression models, a number of modeling strategies are often used to address particular features of the data. Depending on the targets of inference and the availability of geographic identifiers, researchers may choose to fit multilevel hierarchical models or population averaged (marginal) models. As models become more complex, model results will be more sensitive to model assumptions, and care must be taken in the interpretation of parameter estimates. When aggregated measures are linked to complex survey data, additional concerns about appropriate weighting schemes may arise. As this is an area of ongoing research, researchers are encouraged to explore the sensitivity of their results to different weighting methods.

While there are numerous conceptual and methodological challenges to using aggregated variables in studies of health, whether in ecological, semi-ecological, or multilevel designs, these data are worth exploring, especially when they can be combined with high quality individual-level survey data on exposures, covariates, and outcomes. Furthermore, as Greenland (2001) points out, "the *possibility* of bias does not demonstrate the presence of bias," nor does a conflict between associations based on individual-level variables and those based on aggregate variables demonstrate that the ecological association is necessarily the one that is biased. Ecological variables encourage health researchers to think about the context in which individuals live their lives and the relationship between individuals and the aggregated entities to which they belong, whether defined by shared geography, shared characteristics, or shared covariate histories. As such, they can provide important insights into population patterns of health, disease, and well-being.

REFERENCES

Alker HA. A typology of ecological fallacies. In: Dogan M, Rokkan S, editors. *Quantitative Ecological Analysis*. Cambridge, Massachusetts: Massachusetts Institute of Technology; 1969. p 69–86.

Asparouhov T. Sampling weights in latent variable modeling. Struct Equ Model 2005;12(3):411–434.

Asparouhov T. General multi-level modeling with sampling weights. Commun Stat Theory 2006;35(3):439–460.

Besag J, York J, Mollié A. Bayesian image restoration with two applications in spatial statistics. Ann Inst Stat Math 1991;43:1–59.

Best N, Cockings S, Bennett J, Wakefeld J, Elliott P. Ecological regression analysis of environmental benzene exposure and childhood leukaemia: sensitivity to data inaccuracies, geographical scale and ecological bias. J Roy Stat Soc A Stat 2001;164(1):155–174.

Blakely T, Woodward A. Ecological effects in multi-level studies. J Epidemiol Community Health 2000;54:367–374.

Blakely T, Subramanian SV. Multilevel studies. In: Oakes JM, Kaufman JS, editors. *Methods in Social Epidemiology*. San Francisco: Jossey-Bass; 2006. p 316–340.

Carle AC. Fitting multilevel models in complex survey data with design weights: recommendations. BMC Med Res Methodol 2009;9:49.

Carstairs V, Morris R. *Deprivation and Health in Scotland*. UK.: Aberdeen University Press; 1991.

CDC/NCHS. 2009a. NCHS research data center (RDC). Available at http://www.cdc.gov/rdc/index.htm. Accessed 2014 Jun 08.

CDC/NCHS. 2009b. National survey of family growth (NSFG) geocodes. Available at http://www.cdc.gov/rdc/index.htm. Accessed 2014 Jun 08.

CDC/NCHS. 2011. National health and nutrition examination survey (NHANES) geocodes. Available at http://www.cdc.gov/rdc/geocodes/geowt_nhanes.htm. Accessed 2014 Jun 08.

CDC/NCHS. 2012. National health interview survey (NHIS) geocodes. Available at http://www.cdc.gov/rdc/geocodes/geowt_nhis.htm. Accessed 2014 Jun 08.

CDC/NCHS. 2013. Geocodes. Available at http://www.cdc.gov/rdc/B1DataType/Dt123Geocod.htm. Accessed 2014 Jun 08.

Chen JT. Multilevel and hierarchical models for disease mapping. In: Boscoe F, editor. *Geographic Health Data: Fundamental Techniques for Analysis*. Wallingford, UK: CABI; 2013.

Chen JT, Beckfield J, Waterman PD, Krieger N. Can changes in the distributions of and associations between education and income bias temporal comparisons of health disparities? An exploration with causal graphs and simulations. Am J Epidemiol 2013;177(9):870–881. DOI: 10.1093/aje/kwt041.

Chen JT, Coull BA, Waterman PD, Schwartz J, Krieger N. Methodologic implications of social inequalities for analyzing health disparities in large spatiotemporal data sets: an example using breast cancer incidence data (Northern and Southern California, 1988– 2002. Stat Med 2008;27:3957–3983.

Clarke P. When can group level clustering be ignored? Multilevel models versus single-level models with sparse data. J Epidemiol Community Health 2008;62:752–758. DOI: 10.1136/jech.2007.060798.

Davey Smith D, Hart C, Blane D, Gillis C, Hawthorne V. Lifetime socioeconomic position and mortality: prospective observational study. Br Med J 1997;314:547–552.

Davey Smith G, Hart CL, Watt G, Hole DJ, Hawthorne VM. Individual social class, area-based deprivation, cardiovascular disease risk factors, and mortality: the renfrew and paisley study. J Epidemiol Community Health 1998;52:399–405.

Dietz R. The estimation of neighborhood effects in the social sciences: an interdisciplinary approach. Soc Sci Res 2002;31:539–575.

Diez-Roux AV. Multilevel analysis in public health research. Annu Rev Public Health 2000;21:171–192.

Diez-Roux AV. Bringing context back into epidemiology: variables and fallacies in multilevel analysis. Am J Public Health 1998;88:216–222.

Diez-Roux AV. Estimating neighborhood health effects: the challenges of causal inference in a complex world. Soc Sci Med 2004a;58(10):1953–1960.

Diez-Roux AV. The study of group-level factors in epidemiology: rethinking variables, study designs, and analytical approaches. Epidemiol Rev 2004b;26:104–111.

Diggle PJ, Heagerty PJ, Lee K-Y, Zeger SL. *Analysis of Longitudinal Data,* 2nd Edition. Oxford UK: Oxford University Press; 2002.

Elliott P, Wakefield JC. Bias and confounding in spatial epidemiology. In: Elliott P, Wakefield J, Best N, Briggs D, editors. *Spatial Epidemiology*. Oxford: Oxford University Press; 2000. p 68–84.

Do DP, Dubowitz T, Bird CE, Lurie N, Escarce JJ, Finch BK. Neighborhood context and ethnicity differences in body mass index: a multilevel analysis using the NHANES III survey (1988-1994). Econ Hum Biol 2007;5(2):179–203.

Finch BK, Do DP, Heron M, Bird C, Seeman T, Lurie N. Neighborhood effects on health: concentrated advantage and disadvantage. Health Place 2010;16(5):1058–1060.

Firebaugh G. A rule for inferring individual-level relationships from aggregate data. Am Sociol Rev 1978;43:557–572.

Galobardes B, Shaw M, Lawlor DB, Davey Smith G, Lynch J. Indicators of socioeconomic position. In: Oakes JM, Kaufman JS, editors. *Methods in Social Epidemiology*. San Francisco: Josey-Bass; 2006. p 47–85.

Geronimus AT, Bound J, Niedert LJ. On the validity of using census geocode characteristics to proxy individual socioeconomic characteristics. J Am Stat Assoc 1996;91(434):529–537.

Geronimus AT, Bound J. Use of census-based aggregate variables to proxy for socioeconomic group: evidence from national samples. Am J Epidemiol 1998;148:475–486.

Goldstein H. *Multilevel Statistical Models* (4th edition). John Wiley & Sons; 2011.

Gordon D. Census based deprivation indices: their weighting and validation. J Epidemiol Community Health 1995;49(suppl 2):S39–S44.

Gordon D, Spicker P, editors. *The International Glossary on Poverty*. London: Zed Books; 1999.

Graubard BI, Korn EL. Modeling the sampling design in the analysis of health surveys. Statistical Methods in Medical Research 1996;5:263–281.

Greenland S. Divergent biases in ecologic and individual-level studies. J Natl Cancer Inst 1992;11:1209–1223.

Greenland S. Ecologic versus individual-level sources of bias in ecologic estimates of contextual health effects. Int J Epidemiol 2001;30:1343–1350.

Greenland S, Morgenstern H. Ecological bias, confounding and effect modification. Int J Epidemiol 1989;18:269–284.

Greenland S, Robins J. Ecological studies—biases, misconceptions and counterexamples. Am J Epidemiol 1994;139:747–760.

Grilli L, Pratesi M. Weighted estimation in multilevel ordinal and binary models in the presence of informative sampling designs. Surv Method 2004;30:93–103.

Hubbard AE, Ahern J, Fleischer NL, Van der Laan M, Lippman SA, Jewell N, Bruckner T, Satariano WA. To GEE or not to GEE: comparing population average and mixed models for estimating the associations between neighborhood risk factors and health. Epidemiology 2010;21:467–474.

Jackson C, Best NG, Richardson S. Improving ecological inference using individual-level data. Stat Med 2006;25(12):2136–2159.

Jackson C, Best NG, Richardson S. Hierarchical related regression for combining aggregate and individual data in studies of socio-economic disease risk factors. J Roy Stat Soc A Stat 2008a;171(1):159–178.

Jackson C, Richardson S, Best NG. Studying place effects on health by synthesising individual and area-level outcomes. Soc Sci Med 2008b;67:1995–2006.

Krieger N. Overcoming the absence of socioeconomic data in medical records: validation and application of a census-based methodology. Am J Public Health 1992;92:703–710.

Krieger N. A century of census tracts: health and the body politic (1906-2006). J Urban Health 2006;83(3):355–361.

Krieger N, Chen JT, Ebel G. Can we monitor socioeconomic inequalities in health? A survey of US health departments' data collection and reporting practices. Public Health Rep 1997a;112:481–491.

Krieger N, Williams DR, Moss NE. Measuring social class in U.S. public health research: concepts, methodologies, and guidelines. Annu Rev Public Health 1997b;18:341–378.

Krieger N, Chen JT, Waterman PD, Rehkopf DH, Subramanian SV. Painting a truer picture of US socioeconomic and racial/ethnic health inequalities: The Public Health Disparities Geocoding Project. Am J Public Health 2005;95:312–323.

Krieger N, Waterman PD, Chen JT, Soobader MJ, Subramanian S. Monitoring Socioeconomic Inequalities in Sexually Transmitted Infections, Tuberculosis, and Violence: Geocoding and Choice of Area-Based Socioeconomic Measures–The Public Health Disparities Geocoding Project (US). Public Health Rep 2003;118:240–260.

Krieger N, Chen JT, Waterman PD, Soobader MJ, Subramanian SV, Carson R. Choosing area based socioeconomic measures to monitor social inequalities in low birth weight and childhood lead poisoning: The Public Health Disparities Geocoding Project (US). J Epidemiol Community Health 2003;57:186–199.

Krieger N, Chen JT, Waterman PD, Rehkopf DH, Subramanian SV. Race/ethnicity, gender, and monitoring socioeconomic gradients in health: a comparison of area-based socioeconomic measures–The Public Health Disparities Geocoding Project. Am J Public Health 2003;93:1655–1671.

Krieger N, Waterman P, Chen JT, Soobader M-J, Subramanian SV, Carson R. ZIP Code caveat: bias due to spatiotemporal mismatches between ZIP Codes and US census-defined areas—The Public Health Disparities Geocoding Project. Am J Public Health 2002a;92:1100–1102.

Krieger N, Chen JT, Waterman PD, Soobader MJ, Subramanian SV, Carson R. Geocoding and monitoring of US socioeconomic inequalities in mortality and cancer incidence: does the choice of area-based measure and geographic level matter?: the public health disparities geocoding project. Am J Epidemiol 2002b;156:471–482.

Krieger N, Waterman P, Lemieux K, Zierler S, Hogan JW. On the wrong side of the tracts? Evaluating the accuracy of geocoding in public health research. Am J Public Health 2001;91:1114–1116.

Krieger N, Zierler S, Hogan JW, Waterman P, Chen J, Lemieux K, Gjelsvik A. Geocoding and measurement of neighborhood socioeconomic position. In: Kawachi I, Berkman LF, editors. *Neighborhoods and Health*. New York: Oxford University Press; 2003. p 147–178.

Künzli N, Tager IB. The semi-individual study in air pollution epidemiology: a valid design as compared to ecologic studies. Environ Health Perspect 1997;105:1078–1083.

Lawlor DA, Davey Smith G, Patel R, Ebrahim S. Life-course socioeconomic position, area deprivation, and coronary heart disease: findings from the British Women's Heart and Health Study. Am J Public Health 2005;95:91–97.

Lawson A, Browne WJ, Vidal Rodeiro CL. *Disease Mapping with WinBUGS and MLwiN*. Chichester, UK: John Wiley & Sons, Ltd; 2003.

Lazarfeld P, Menzel H. On the relation between individual and collective properties. In: Etzioni A, editor. *Complex Organization*. New York: Holt, Reinhart and Winston; 1961. p 422–440.

Lee P, Murie A, Gordon D. *Area Measures of Deprivation: A Study of Current Methods and Beast Practices in the Identification of Poor Areas in Great Britain*. Birmingham, UK: Centre for Urban and Regional Studies, University of Birmingham; 1995.

Longford NT. Model-based variance estimation in surveys with stratified clustered designs. Aust J Stat 1996;38:333–352.

Manski C. Identification problems in the social sciences. Sociol Methodol 1993;23:1–56.

Merkin SS, Basurto-Dávila R, Karlamangla A, Bird CE, Lurie N, Escarce J, Seeman T. Neighborhoods and cumulative biological risk profiles by race/ethnicity in a national sample of US adults: NHANES III. Ann Epidemiol 2009;19(3):194–201.

Messer LC, Kaufman JS. Using census data to approximate neighborhood effects. In: Oakes JM, Kaufman JS, editors. *Methods in Social Epidemiology*. San Francisco: Josey-Bass; 2006.

Morgenstern H. Uses of ecologic analysis in epidemiologic research. Am J Public Health 1982;72:1336–1344.

Morgenstern H. Ecologic studies in epidemiology: concepts, principles, and methods. Annu Rev Public Health 1995;16:61–81.

Morgenstern H. Ecologic studies. In: Rothman K, Greenland S, editors. *Modern Epidemiology*. Philadelphia: Lippincott-Raven; 1998. p 459–480.

Macintyre S, Ellaway A. Neighborhoods and health: an overview. In: Kawachi I, Berkman L, editors. *Neighborhoods and Health*. New York: Oxford Press; 2003. p 20–42.

Macintyre S, Ellaway A, Cummins S. Place effects on health: how can we conceptualise, operationalize and measure them? Soc Sci Med 2002;55:125–139.

Macintyre S. What are spatial effects and how can we measure them?. In: Dale A, editor. *Exploiting national survey data: the role of locality and spatial effects*. Manchester: Faculty of Economic and Social Studies, University of Manchester; 1997b. pp. 1–17.

O'Campo P. Invited commentary: advancing theory and methods for multilevel models of residential neighborhoods and health. Am J Epidemiol 2003;157:9–13.

Oakes JM. The (mis)estimation of neighborhood effects; causal inference for a practicable social epidemiology. Soc Sci Med 2004;58(10):1929–1952.

Pfeffermann D, Skinner CJ, Holmes DJ, Goldstein H, Rasbash J. Weighting for unequal selection probabilities in multilevel models. J R Stat Soc Ser B Stat Methodol 1998;60:23–40.

Pickett KE, Pearl M. Multilevel analyses of neighbourhood socioeconomic context and health outcomes: a critical review. J Epidemiol Community Health 2001;55(2):111–22.

Prentice RL, Sheppard L. Aggregate data studies of disease risk factors. Biometrika 1995;82:113–125.

Rabe-Hesketh S, Skrondal A. Multilevel modelling of complex survey data. J Roy Stat Soc A Stat 2006;169:805–827.

Raudenbush SW, Sampson RJ. 'Ecometrics': toward a science of assessing ecological settings, with application to the systematic social observation of neighborhoods. Sociol Methodol 1999;29:1–41.

Richardson S, Best N. Bayesian hierarchical models in ecological studies of health-environment effects. Environmentrics 2003;14:129–147.

Richardson S, Monfort C. Ecological correlation studies. In: Elliott P, Wakefield J, Best N, Briggs D, editors. *Spatial Epidemiology*. Oxford: Oxford University Press; 2000. p 205–220.

Richardson S, Stucker I, Hémon D. Comparison of relative risks obtained in ecological and individual studies: some methodological considerations. Int J Epidemiol 1987;16(1):111–120.

Riley MW. Special problems of sociological analysis. In: *Sociological Research I: A Case Approach*. New York, NY: Harcourt, Brace & World Inc; 1963. p 700–725.

Robinson WS. Ecological correlations and the behavior of individuals. Am Sociol Rev 1950;15:351–357.

Salway R, Wakefield J. A common framework for ecological inference in epidemiology, political science, and sociology. In: King G, Rosen O, Tanner MA, editors. *Ecological Inference: New Methodological Strategies*. Cambridge, UK: Cambridge University Press; 2004. p 303–332.

Salway RA, Wakefield JC. Sources of bias in ecological studies of nonrare events. Environ Ecol Stat 2005;12:321–347.

Sampson RJ, Morenoff JD, Gannon-Rowley T. Assessing "neighborhood effects": social processes and new directions in research. Annu Rev Sociol 2002;28:443–478.

Sampson R. The neighborhood context of well-being. Perspect Biol Med 2003; 46:S53–S64.

Schwartz S. The fallacy of the ecological fallacy: the potential misuse of a concept and the consequences. Am J Public Health 1994;84:819–824.

Selvin HC. Durkheim's suicide and problems of empirical research. Am J Soc 1958;63:607–619.

Sheppard L. Insights on bias and information in group-level studies. Biostatistics 2003;4:265–278.

Singh GK. Area deprivation and widening inequalities in US mortality, 1969-1998. Am J Public Health 2003;93:1137–1143.

Singh GK, Siahpush M. Increasing inequalities in all-cause and cardiovascular mortality among US adults aged 25–64 years by area socioeconomic status, 1969–1998. Int J Epidemiol 2002;31:600–613.

Singh GK, Siahpush M. Widening socioeconomic inequalities in US life expectancy, 1980-2000. Int J Epidemiol 2006;35:969–979.

Singh GK, Miller BA, Hankey BF, Feuer EJ, Pickle LW. Changing area socioeconomic patterns in U.S. cancer mortality, 1950–1998: part I—all cancers among men. J Natl Cancer Inst 2002;94:904–915.

Stimpson JP, Ju H, Raji MA, Eschbach K. Neighborhood deprivation and health risk behaviors in NHANES III. Am J Health Behav 2007;31(2):215–222.

Subramanian SV, Jones K, Duncan C. Multilevel methods for public health research. In: Kawachi I, Berkman L, editors. *Neighborhoods and Health*. Oxford: Oxford University. Press; 2003. p 65–111.

Subramanian SV, Jones K, Kaddour A, Krieger N. Revisiting Robinson: the perils of individualistic and ecologic fallacy. Int J Epidemiol 2009;38:1–19.

Susser M. *Causal Thinking in the Health Sciences*. New York: Oxford University Press; 1973. [Susser p. 20].

Susser M. The logic in ecological: I. The logic of analysis. Am J Public Health 1994;84(5):825–829.

Lasserre V, Guihenneuc-Jouyaux C, Richardson S. Biases in ecological studies: utility of including within-area distribution of confounders. Stat Med 2000;19:45–59.

Townsend P. *The International Analysis of Poverty*. New York: Harvester/Wheatsheaf; 1990.

Townsend P, Davidson N, Whitehead M. *Inequalities in Health: The Black Report and the Health Divide*. London, UK: Penguin Books; 1990.

Townsend P. Deprivation. J Soc Policy 1987;16:125–146.

Townsend P, Phillimore P, Beattie A. *Health and Deprivation: Inequalities and the North*. London: Croom Helm; 1988.

U.S. Census Bureau. *A Compass for Understanding and Using American Community Survey Data: What General Data Users Need to Know*. Washington, DC: US Government Printing OfficeAvailable at http://www.census.gov/acs/www/Downloads/handbooks/ACSGeneralHandbook.pdf. Accessed 2014 Jun 08.; 2008.

U.S. Census Bureau. *"Variance Estimation," Design and Methodology American Community Survey*. Washington, DC: US Government Printing Office; 2010. p 12-4–12-5.

U.S. Census Bureau. 2013a. Standard hierarchy of census geographic entities. http://www.census.gov/geo/reference/pdfs/geodiagram.pdf. Accessed 2014 Jun 08.

U.S. Census Bureau. 2013b. TIGER products. http://www.census.gov/geo/maps-data/data/tiger.html. Accessed 2014 Jun 08.

U.S. Census Bureau. 2013c. Zip code tabulation areas (ZCTAs) http://www.census.gov/geo/reference/zctas.html. Accessed 2014 Jun 08.

Wakefield JC. Sensitivity analyses for ecological regression. Biometrics 2003;59:9–17.

Wakefield JC. Ecological inference for 2x2 tables (with discussion). J R Stat Soc Ser A 2004;167:385–445.

Wakefield J, Salway R. A statistical framework for ecological and aggregate studies. J R Stat Soc Ser A 2001;164:119–137.

Waller LA, Gotway CA. *Applied Spatial Statistics for Public Health Data*. New York: John Wiley & Sons, Inc.; 2004.

ONLINE RESOURCES

For additional information regarding geocoding and area-based socioeconomic measures, consult the Public Health Disparities Geocoding Project Monograph, which provides background, methods, and examples of using geocoding to link health records to Census-derived area-based socioeconomic measures: www.hsph.harvard.edu/thegeocodingproject/.

There are several sources for additional information regarding US Census data concepts. For information regarding the standard hierarchy of census geographic entities: www.census.gov/geo/reference/pdfs/geodiagram.pdf.

For information regarding the Census TIGER Shapefiles: www.census.gov/geo/maps-data/data/tiger.html.

For information regarding the American Community Survey: www.census.gov/acs/www/Downloads/handbooks/ACSGeneralHandbook.pdf.

There are also several useful sources for US Census Data download. One is the US Census Bureau's American FactFinder: http://factfinder2.census.gov/faces/nav/jsf/pages/index.xhtml.

The Missouri Census Data Center is another useful resource for Census data, extracted and made available in machine readable datasets: http://mcdc.missouri.edu/.

Examples of US national surveys with geocodes are available from the National Center for Health Statistics Surveys with Geocodes: www.cdc.gov/rdc/B1DataType/Dt123Geocod.htm.

Software for ecologic inference is available from several sources. The EI: A(n R) Program for Ecologic Inference by Gary King and Margaret Roberts is available at: http://gking.harvard.edu/eiR.

Additional ecological inference software, including R package ecoreg and WinBUGS code, can be accessed at The Bias Project (UK): www.bias-project.org.uk/software/.

CHAPTER TWENTY NINE

Analysis of Complex Health Survey Data

Stanislav Kolenikov
Abt SRBI, Silver Spring, MD, USA

Jeff Pitblado
StataCorp LP, College Station, TX, USA

29.1 Introduction

This final chapter of the handbook outlines the basic principles of how complex health survey data are to be analyzed. The preceding chapters talked at length about how to plan and design a health study, how to collect the data, and how to prepare them for subsequent analytical work. Analysis of the data thus obtained is the ultimate goal of most studies, and while the specific methods differ from study to study, there are some common themes in the analysis of complex survey data.

The standard textbooks such as those written by Pagano and Gauvreau (2000), Rosner (2010), and Hosmer et al. (2013) or Harrell (2010) deal with describing and modeling the *outcomes*, with statistical models attempting to remove uncertainty about the values of these outcome variables for specific persons in the study. Such models may describe the probability of an individual having medical insurance as a function of their sociodemographic characteristics, or the probability of an individual having high blood pressure as a function of their health history. Procedures of statistical inference explained in these books (estimates, standard errors, tests, and diagnostics) operate with respect

Handbook of Health Survey Methods, First Edition. Edited by Timothy P. Johnson.

to the assumed distribution of the outcomes; if covariates were used to model the outcomes, then this implies variation that remains unaccounted for by the covariates. Such data are often said to be *i.i.d.*—independent, identically distributed. This means that they have a common model, and they were sampled independently of one another. The sampling distribution of the statistic of interest, such as the estimate of prevalence of high blood pressure, derives from the random draws of the random variables which are the outcomes for the sampled individuals, given their characteristics. We shall refer to this approach to inference as *model-based inference*.

The starting point of sample surveys is very different. A sampling statistician dealing with a finite population treats the values of outcomes as *fixed*, as, indeed, in any given point in time, every individual in the population can be characterized as having or not having health insurance, or as being diagnosed or not diagnosed with high blood pressure. There is no uncertainty about these measurements. The randomness in data comes from the sampling procedure. If the researcher could collect the data on the health conditions from everybody in the population, this *census* prevalence would be the true population quantity. With a census being prohibitively expensive, a sample survey is conducted instead, in which a relatively small proportion of the population is asked the relevant health questions. The uncertainty related to this sample estimate (or, to be precise, the sampling error) then stems from the fact that not every population member was surveyed. The magnitude of such error can be quantified through the methods of sample surveys (Hansen et al. 1953). The distribution of the sample statistic derives from different samples that can be drawn. Statistical procedures that operate on this sampling distribution are referred to as *design-based inference*, as opposed to model-based inference described in the preceding paragraph (Binder and Roberts 2003, 2009).

A shaky bridge between inference for the flat i.i.d. data and inference for the complex survey data is the simplest sampling design, the simple random sample (SRS), in which every sample of size n from the population of size N has the same probability, $\binom{N}{n}^{-1}$. Some of the basic formulae, such as the sample mean, its variance, and the confidence intervals surrounding it, are identical for i.i.d. data and for the SRS with replacement design. However, the analogies start breaking down and produce different formulae when other types of sampling designs are used, even when the designs have a desirable property of equal probability of selection, or *epsem* designs, for short.

As discussed in Chapters 2–4, the complex survey designs arise because in nearly all data collection efforts, simplicity of statistical analysis afforded by the i.i.d. assumptions plays a minor role compared to the cost efficiencies that these complex designs can provide. An efficient stratification scheme can reduce variances, especially in situations when good correlates of the outcome of interest are available on the frame. Multistage cluster samples in face-to-face surveys allow one to economize on interviewer travel costs. An SRS may not even be a feasible "gold standard" design in a number of practical situations. When a health study is aimed at a rare population whose membership is not available on the frame (e.g., children 0–3 years of age, or adults diagnosed with diabetes), the researchers need to screen for eligibility, and if the target population prevalence is known ahead of time, SRS may not be the most efficient design (Kalton and Anderson 1986, Srinath 2013). For some frames, an SRS of the frame units may not generate the SRS of the analysis units. While phone samples widely used in health research can often be thought of as SRSs of phone numbers (at least within a given frame, either cell phone or landline), different adults have different probabilities of selection as they may be covered by landline service, cell phone service, only one of them, both of them, and may have multiple phone numbers that they can be reached at (Wolter et al. 2010).

Design-based paradigms suited well the descriptive and enumerative purposes of basic sample surveys. However, advances in statistical modeling, such as regression analysis, generalized linear models, and survival analysis, generated demand for inferential procedures that would combine statistical models and survey design to protect against violations of i.i.d. assumptions imposed by the sampling designs. The existing theory of design-based variance estimation was extended to regression (Fuller 2002), generalized linear models (Binder 1983), survival analysis models (Binder 1992, Lawless 2003), and general maximum quasilikelihood estimates (Skinner 1989). Further steps have been made to build inferential paradigms that assume a super-population model from which a given finite population was generated, and appropriate estimation techniques have been developed (Binder and Roberts 2003, Demnati and Rao 2010, Rubin-Bleuer and Kratina 2005). Sill, design-based estimation that incorporates the design features through sampling weights and design-consistent variance estimation techniques provides the benefits of being robust to model misspecifications. It can provide correct inference for the census model parameters that would have been obtained should a model, however imperfect, be fit to all units in the population (Binder and Roberts 2003, Pfeffermann 1993).

In the following sections, we shall outline how traditional statistical methods need to be modified to accommodate complex survey data structures. Most health researchers who are interested in substantive effects will thus be interested in Section 29.3 that covers the basics of survey estimation and analysis. Researchers who collect their own data, or those otherwise responsible for describing the methodology of health surveys, will benefit from Section 29.4 which describes how the existing statistical methods can be used to analyze the quality of the survey data, quantify the survey errors, and identify the sources of error.

In our examples, we shall use the data from the 2012 wave of the National Health Interview Survey (Botman et al. 2000, NHIS).[1] NHIS is a continuously operating face-to-face survey concerning the health of the U.S. civilian noninstitutionalized population collected in household interviews throughout the United States. The survey documentation states that "the first stage of the current sampling plan consists of a sample of 428 primary sampling units (PSUs) drawn from approximately 1900 geographically defined PSUs that cover the 50 States and the District of Columbia. A PSU consists of a county, a small group of contiguous counties, or a metropolitan statistical area." A *primary sampling unit* is a subset of

[1] See http://www.cdc.gov/nchs/nhis.htm.

population units that can be potentially drawn together in the sampling process with a single random draw at the very top level of a multistage sample. In the case of National Health Interview Survey (NHIS), the population of the United States was split into geographic *strata*, that is, nonoverlapping population groups, of several PSUs each. Samples were taken independently within each stratum: 2 PSUs were sampled from each stratum. At subsequent stages of selection, finer geographic units like census tracts or blocks may have been sampled, until ultimately the sampling process would reach dwelling units, households, and individuals within households. NHIS annually reaches about 35,000 households containing about 87,000 persons, collects the family and dwelling unit information on these units, as well as detailed health information for one randomly sampled adult and one randomly sampled child (if children are present in the HH). The publicly released data contain several hundred variables concerned with health behaviors and experiences of families, adults, and children. This is an exemplary survey both in terms of methodological rigor and the variety of analyses it can support.

EXAMPLE 29.1 NHIS example

In this and other examples in this chapter, we shall use Stata 13 statistical software (Stata Corp. 2013) to analyze the NHIS 2012 sampled adult data set. This data set contains information on one randomly selected adult within each sampled household. In subsequent analyses, we shall use demographic variables, such as gender, race, and age, and explore their relations to allergies, a variable that we will construct later from several variables containing specific allergic reactions. These analyses are not intended to be conclusive from a substantive, scientific perspective, but rather are used to demonstrate typical features of the complex survey data analysis, and what is expected to be seen in the related software output.

```
. describe sex mracrpi2 age_p respalyr dgstalyr sknalyr othalyr

               storage  display    value
variable name    type   format     label      variable label
-------------------------------------------------------------------------------
sex              byte   %8.0g      sap013x    HHC.110_00.000: Sex
mracrpi2         byte   %48.0g     sap016x     HHC.200_01.000: Race coded to
                                                   single/multiple race group
age_p            byte   %15.0g     sap018x    HHC.420_00.000: Age
respalyr         byte   %17.0g     sap028x    ACN.125_00.010: Had respiratory
                                                   allergy, past 12 months
dgstalyr         byte   %17.0g     sap028x    ACN.125_00.020: Had digestive
                                                   allergy, past 12 months
sknalyr          byte   %17.0g     sap028x    ACN.125_00.030: Had eczema/skin
                                                   allergy, past 12 months
othalyr          byte   %17.0g     sap028x    ACN.125_00.040: Had other
                                                   allergy, past 12 months
```

```
. tabulate sex

HHC.110_00.  |
    000: Sex |      Freq.     Percent        Cum.
-------------+-----------------------------------
      1 Male |     15,273       44.24       44.24
    2 Female |     19,252       55.76      100.00
-------------+-----------------------------------
       Total |     34,525      100.00


. codebook mracrpi2

-------------------------------------------------------------------------------
mracrpi2             HHC.200_01.000: Race coded to single/multiple race group
-------------------------------------------------------------------------------

                  type:  numeric (byte)
                 label:  sap016x

                 regna:  [1,17]                      units:  1
         unique values:  9                       missing .:  0/34525

            tabulation:  Freq.   Numeric  Label
                         26214         1  01 White
                          5452         2  02 Black/African American
                           413         3  03 Indian (American), Alaska
                                          Native
                           408         9  09 Asian Indian
                           449        10  10 Chinese
                           518        11  11 Filipino
                           849        15  15 Other Asian (See file layout)
                           102        16  16 Primary race not releasable
                                          (See file layout)
                           120        17  17 Multiple race, no primary
                                           race selected


. codebook respalyr

-------------------------------------------------------------------------------
respalyr             ACN.125_00.010: Had respiratory allergy, past 12 months
-------------------------------------------------------------------------------

                  type:  numeric (byte)
                 label:  sap028x

                 range:  [1,9]                       units:  1
         unique values:  4                       missing .:  0/34525

            tabulation:  Freq.   Numeric  Label
                          3906         1  1 Yes
                         30571         2  2 No
                             6         7  7 Refused
                            42         9  9 Don ´t know
```

29.2 Inference with Complex Survey Data

As outlined in Section 29.1, for the findings of a complex survey analysis to be generalizable to the target population, the specific design features have to be taken into account. Several major software packages, such as R, SAS, or Stata, provide sufficient support for most analyses. Specialized packages that were designed by survey statisticians for their specific complex survey data related tasks (SUDAAN, WesVar) may provide additional functionality.

Many publicly released microdata files simplify the actual design that was used to collect the data, and their methodological documentation suggests that the data can be analyzed as if derived from a two-stage stratified sampling design. That is, the population was broken down into strata (usually at a high level of geography, such as a U.S. state); *primary sampling units* (PSUs) were listed and sampled from these strata (at a lower level of geography; if states were used as strata, then counties or groups of counties of roughly equal sizes may serve as PSUs); and the ultimate observation units (households or individuals) were sampled from these PSUs. The intermediate levels of sampling (e.g., tracts within counties, blocks within tracts, and housing units within block) are ignored, which is mathematically correct when the PSUs are sampled with replacement, and leads to conservative standard errors if the PSUs are sampled without replacement. The observation units typically have analysis weights attached to them. These weights account for (potentially different) probabilities of selection, as well as nonresponse patterns that may be different between different demographic groups (Groves 2006). See Chapter 26 for a description of typical steps in weight construction for a two-stage sampling survey with nonresponse and calibration to the known population totals. The documentation for NHIS public use microdata suggests a similar specification of weights and the design: the 2012 data set is specified to have 300 pseudostrata with two PSUs in each.

29.2.1 POINT ESTIMATION

The most general developments of statistical theory for sample surveys are based on the *Horvitz–Thompson* estimator

$$t[y] = \sum_{j\in\mathcal{S}} \frac{y_j}{\pi_j} \equiv \sum_{j\in\mathcal{S}} w_j y_j \tag{29.1}$$

where $\mathcal{S}$ denotes the sample π_j is the probability of selection of unit j, and $w_j = 1/\pi_j$ is the weight of the jth unit. Rao (2005) refers to equation (29.1) as Narain–Horvitz–Thompson estimator giving credit to the parallel developments of this estimator. Survey statisticians think about weighted means, proportions, ratios, and regression coefficients as functions of the survey totals. Thus, the weighted mean

$$\bar{y}_w = \frac{\sum_{j\in\mathcal{S}} w_j y_j}{\sum_{j\in\mathcal{S}} w_j} \tag{29.2}$$

can be thought of as the ratio $t[y]/t[1]$ where the denominator of equation (29.2) is represented as $\sum_{j\in\mathcal{S}} w_j \times 1$. In a similar manner, the researcher can obtain the estimates of the ratio of two survey variables x and y,

$$\hat{r} = \frac{\sum_{j\in\mathcal{S}} w_j y_j}{\sum_{j\in\mathcal{S}} w_j x_j} \equiv \frac{t[y]}{t[x]} \qquad (29.3)$$

or regression coefficients

$$\hat{\beta} = (X'WX)^{-1}X'Wy, \quad W = \mathrm{diag}(w_1, \ldots, w_n) \qquad (29.4)$$

The latter are functions of the multivariate totals $\sum_j w_j x_{jk} x_{jl}$ of the products of the explanatory variables x_k and x_l, as well as products of these variables with response y, $\sum_j w_j y_j x_{jk}$. Hence, the theoretical books written by Särndal et al. (1992), Thompson (1997), and Fuller (2009) discuss the general theory of estimating the survey totals, and present estimation of ratios, proportions, and regression coefficients by expressing these statistics as functions of totals.

Weights. The weights that appear in expressions such as equations (29.2), (29.3), or (29.4) may come with a variety of names attached to them. We have encountered "sampling weights," "probability weights", "analysis weights," "final weights," and "expansion weights" as generic terms. Other qualifiers, such as "nonresponse adjusted weights," "poststratified weights," "raked weights," or "calibrated weights," point to specific weight adjustment procedures similar to those described in Chapter 26.

Two clarifying comments can be made on the use of these terms. First, the specific terms "sampling weights" and "probability weights" refer specifically to the inverse probabilities of selection that appear in the Narain–Horvitz–Thompson estimator (29.1). If additional adjustments are made, then the adjective describing the weights should technically be something other than "sampling" or "probability."

Second, the specific term *poststratified weight* refers to the particular method for adjusting sample-based estimates to account for any imbalance of the population groups relative to the known population totals or proportions. In this method, the sample is split into groups such that (i) the groups do not overlap; (ii) the group information is not available before sampling (otherwise it would be used to define proper strata rather than poststrata); and (iii) total counts of these groups are available to the researcher (usually, from administrative data sources such as Census data). Then the poststratification adjustment (Holt and Smith 1979) entails multiplying the weights within a poststratification cell by the ratio of the total population of this cell over the sum of weights in the cell. In other words, the weighted total of that cell is made equal to the population count for the cell.

Thus, to avoid methodological confusion, we refer to the weights used in complex survey analysis as "final weights," to highlight that they reflect all of the adjustments that the survey data provider has incorporated. In relation to that, the probability weights are sometimes referred to as the *base weights*, as they serve as inputs to further weight adjustments.

Without specifying the weights, the analyst will get biased estimates that would not be generalizable to the population of interest (Pfeffermann 1993). The weights correct for informative sampling designs, in which the probability of selection may depend on important survey variables of interest, for coverage errors on the frame, and for nonresponse encountered in the field. While one can speculate about settings where the analysis weights can be omitted (an equal probability of selection design with no nonresponse), these settings are hardly practical. Hence, weights should be used for all analyses that the researcher wants to generalize to the target population of the study.

Major statistical packages usually support weights for most commands, procedures, and functions. Researchers unfamiliar with the specific details should locate the help file(s) explaining the exact syntax for their preferred package(s). An incorrect interpretation of weights is that of *frequency weights*, that is, that each observation in the data set reflects w_i cases in the sample that have identical values of all survey variables, and are collapsed into a single record to save on storage memory. Specification of sampling weights as frequency weights leads the software to treat the sample of size n, typically in hundreds or thousands, as a sample of size N which may be in millions or even hundreds of millions, and produce grossly large test statistics and grossly small standard errors.

29.2.2 VARIANCE ESTIMATION

Having produced the point estimates, researchers usually need to provide a measure of uncertainty about these estimates, either in the form of a standard error, or by surrounding the estimate with confidence intervals. A comprehensive reference on all aspects of variance estimation with complex survey data is Wolter (2007).

Variance estimates fall roughly into three major categories. First, simple statistics, like survey totals, usually afford explicit variance estimates based on standard sampling theory. Second, variance estimates for moderately complicated statistics, like ratio or correlation parameters, are often obtained through approximations known as *Taylor series linearization*. Third, as such derivations are getting prohibitively difficult for the final weights obtained via multiple adjustment steps, replicate variance estimation methods are finding greater use by statistical agencies. At a conceptual level, replicate variance estimation methods interpret the question of sampling variance estimation rather literally: they treat the full sample as the population and take subsamples from it using a sampling design that matches the sampling design of the original survey as closely as possible.

EXAMPLE 29.2 NHIS example

The final weights in the Sampled Adult file of NHIS represent probabilities of selection of the households and adults in them, as well as adjustments for nonresponse and calibration for the census population totals. They sum up to 234,920,670, which is the estimate of the size of eligible adult population of the United States in 2012. Distribution of the weights demonstrates skewness typical of the weight distributions (Figure 29.1).

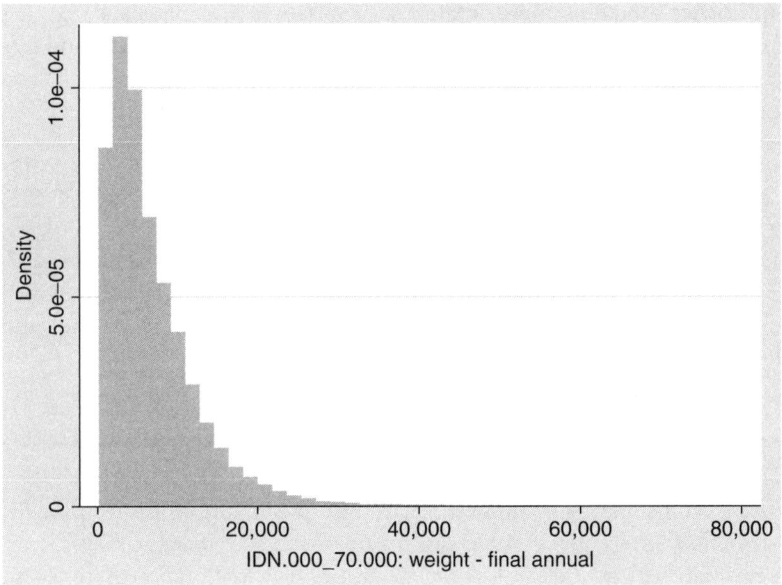

FIGURE 29.1 Distribution of the final weights in 2012 Sampled Adult NHIS data.

```
. summarize wtfa_sa, detail

            IDN.000_70.000: Weight - Final Annual
-------------------------------------------------------------

      Percentiles      Smallest
 1%        577            224
 5%       1083            230
10%       1580            234       Obs                34525
25%       2849            241       Sum of Wgt.        34525

50%       5238                      Mean            6804.364
                        Largest     Std. Dev.       5674.817
75%       9161          71723
90%      13811          71887       Variance        3.22e+07
95%      17553          79062       Skewness        2.233534
99%      26827          80870       Kurtosis        12.63891
```

■

An approach that is sometimes used for stabilizing design-based variance estimates, which is often helpful for statistics based on small sample sizes in subpopulations, as well as in mass production of tables with point estimates and standard errors, is the method of variance functions (Cho et al. 2014). Generalized variance functions approximate design variances by expressions that involve *ad hoc* functions of the point estimates, approximate design effects, and sample sizes of subgroups. Consider the SRS expression

$$v_{\text{SRS}}[\hat{p}_k] = \frac{p_k(1-p_k)}{n_k} \tag{29.5}$$

where p_k is the target proportion in domain k, n_k is the domain size, and $v_{\text{SRS}}[\hat{p}_k]$ is the variance of an estimated survey proportion $\hat{p}_k$ under SRS. Then by taking logs of both sides, one can consider a generalized variance function for the variance $v[\hat{p}_k]$ under the true design that has a functional form of

$$\ln v[\hat{p}_k] = \alpha_0 + \alpha_1 \ln \hat{p}_k + \alpha_2 \ln(1-\hat{p}_k) + \alpha_3 \ln n_k + \alpha_4 \ln z_k + \nu_k \tag{29.6}$$

where ν_k is the approximation error with zero mean, and z_k is the approximate design effect in domain k. One can reasonably expect that the coefficients are approximately $\alpha_1 \approx 1, \alpha_2 \approx 1, \alpha_3 \approx -1$, and $\alpha_4 \approx 1$. Calibration of this equation with accurate design variances as dependent variables may reveal overdispersion, where variances do not go to zero as quickly as equation (29.5) would imply, that is, $\alpha_1 < 1, \alpha_2 < 1$, and $\alpha_3 > -1$.

Explicit Formulae for Totals. An exact, although rarely usable, expression for the variance of the survey total (equation 29.1) involves the first-order selection probabilities π_i and the second-order selection probabilities π_{ij} (i.e., the probability that given two units i and j both appear in the sample) known as the *Yates–Grundy–Sen estimator*:

$$v\{t[y]\} = \frac{1}{2} \sum_{j\in\mathcal{S}} \sum_{k\in\mathcal{S}} \frac{\pi_i\pi_k - \pi_{jk}}{\pi_{jk}} \left(\frac{y_j}{\pi_j} - \frac{y_k}{\pi_k}\right)^2 \tag{29.7}$$

Practical application of this expression is usually prohibitively complicated. First, the second-order probabilities of selection are often difficult to compute. Second, the double summation involves approximately n^2 terms, where n is the sample size, and becomes computationally expensive even for relatively small samples of the size of several hundreds, let alone large surveys like NHIS with tens of thousands of sampled units. Thus, for practical applications, simpler expressions are desirable.

For a commonly used (approximate) two-stage design with simple random sampling at each stage, variance of the survey total can be approximated by the

Hansen–Hurwitz variance estimator (Hansen et al. 1953):

$$v\{t[y]\} = \sum_{h=1}^{L}(1-f_h)\frac{n_h}{n_h-1}\sum_{i=1}^{n_h}(y_{hi}-\bar{y}_h)^2$$
$$+\sum_{h=1}^{L} f_h \sum_{i=1}^{n_h}(1-f_{hi})\frac{m_{hi}}{m_{hi}-1}\sum_{j}(y_{hij}-\bar{y}_{hi})^2,$$
$$\bar{y}_{hi} = \frac{\sum_{j=1}^{m_{hi}} w_{hij}y_{hij}}{\sum_{j=1}^{m_{hi}} w_{hij}} \qquad \bar{y}_h = \frac{1}{n_h}\sum_{i=1}^{n_h} y_{hi} \tag{29.8}$$

where y_{hij} is the observed value from a sampled individual in strata $h = 1, \dots, L$, PSU $i = 1, \dots, n_h$, secondary sampling unit $j = 1, \dots, m_{hi}$; $f_h = n_h/N_h$ is the sampling fraction for stratum h in the first stage; and $f_{hi} = m_{hi}/M_{hi}$ is the sampling fraction in the second stage. A careful look at this expression sheds some light on how survey design features affect sampling variances. First, in multistage samples, only the first stage matters when sampling fractions f_h are negligibly small. Also, stratification helps reduce the variances when units in the strata are similar to one another, so that $(y_{hi} - \bar{y}_h)$ are small in magnitude (compared to, say, the deviations from the overall mean, $(y_{hi} - \bar{y})$, that would appear in an SRS sample variance).

Design Effects. Since design-based variances of survey statistics tend to be more complicated than those obtained in the model-based paradigm for i.i.d. data, these differences need to be properly discussed and accounted for. Kish (1995) introduced the concept of *design effect* (DEFF) to quantify these differences:

$$\text{DEFF} = \frac{\mathbb{V}[\text{design}]}{\mathbb{V}[\text{SRS}]} \tag{29.9}$$

Here, $\mathbb{V}[\text{design}]$ is the variance of a statistic computed from the design perspective incorporating the appropriate design components (such as equation (29.8)), and $\mathbb{V}[\text{SRS}]$ is the variance of the same statistic assuming the data were collected via a simple random sampling without replacement design. Conceptually, design effects measure gain or loss of precision that is associated with the sampling design, at least the way it was introduced by Kish (1995). In practice, it is used to measure the impact of other components of survey error, including, for instance, nonresponse and calibration weighting. A concept that is related to design effects is the *effective sample size*:

$$n_{\text{eff}} = \frac{n}{\text{DEFF}} \tag{29.10}$$

It shows the number of observations that could have been collected by SRS that would yield the same precision as the actual sample size with the actual design of the health survey.

By construction, design effects are specific to the particular quantity being estimated. Design effects for the means and proportions of different variables can (and do) vary within the same survey, and design effects for other analytical statistics such as regression coefficients may be very different from design effects for means and proportions.

All of the design components have an effect on variances, increasing or decreasing the design effects. Let us review them in turn; however, to get closed-form expressions of the design effects due to weights, stratification, and clustering, very simplistic sampling designs have to be studied that only deviate from SRS in one specific aspect.

Design Effect of Weights. Application of weights comes at a cost of loss of statistical efficiency. Korn and Graubard (1999) (Section 4.4) analyze the weighted mean (equation 29.2) under the model assuming y_i are i.i.d. with mean μ and variance σ^2. In this model, the design effect of the weighted mean due to unequal weighting (*uwe* for short) is given by

$$\text{DEFF}_{\text{uwe}} = \frac{n\sum_{i=1}^{n} w_i^2}{(\sum_{i=1}^{n} w_i)^2} \approx 1 + \text{CV}_w^2 \tag{29.11}$$

where the approximation ignores the factor $1 - 1/n$, where n is the sample size.

There are however situations where unequal probability of selection is very beneficial. If (i) the analytical goal of a study is to estimate population totals (e.g., total number of patients with a certain diagnosis, or total medical expenditures for a given kind of surgery); (ii) the target population exhibits a natural structure with PSUs of known size, and (iii) the variable of interest can be characterized by the ratio per individual that is reasonably stable between PSUs, then sampling with *probability proportional to size* (PPS; Brewer and Hanif (1983)) leads to highly efficient estimates of the totals of interest. If x_i is the *measure of size* of the PSU i that is known in the sampling frame, and t_i is the total (known or unknown) of the variable of interest in that PSU, then the design effect for the estimates of the population total $t = \sum_{i\in\mathcal{U}} t_i$ is $1 - R^2$, where R^2 is the determination coefficient in the (population) regression through the origin $t_i = rx_i + e_i$.

Design Effect of Stratification. Stratification is effective when there are large differences between strata on the primary survey outcomes of interest. In a single-stage stratified design, the design variance of the stratified mean, $\bar{y}_{\text{str}} = \sum_{h=1}^{L} W_h y_h$, where $W_h = N_h/N$ is the fraction of the total population in stratum h, and $\bar{y}_h$ is the estimated mean in stratum h, is (Hansen et al. 1953)

$$\mathbb{V}[\bar{y}_{\text{str}}] = \sum_{h=1}^{L} W_h^2 \frac{1 - f_h}{n_h} S_h^2, \tag{29.12}$$

where $f_h = n_h/N_h$ is the sampling fraction in stratum h, and S_h^2 is the within-stratum variance of the outcome of interest. In a *proportional allocation* epsem design, $f_h = f$ is the same for all strata, so that $n_h = fN_h = nW_h$, and equation (29.12) can be further simplified to

$$\mathbb{V}[\bar{y}_{\text{str}}] = \frac{1-f}{n} \sum_{h=1}^{L} W_h S_h^2, \tag{29.13}$$

Hence the design effect due to stratification for this design is

$$\text{DEFF}_{\text{str}} = \frac{\sum_{h=1}^{L} W_h S_h^2}{S^2} \approx \frac{S_w^2(1 + 1/\bar{N})}{S_b^2 + S_w^2} \tag{29.14}$$

where S^2 is the overall population variance of the response, $S_b^2 = \sum_h N_h(\bar{Y}_h - \bar{Y})^2/N$ is the population variance between strata, $S_w^2 = \sum_h \sum_{i=1}^{N_h} (Y_{hi} - \bar{Y}_h)^2/N = \sum_h N_h S_h^2/N$ is the population variance within the strata, and $\bar{N} = N/L$ is the average strata size. From equation (29.14), it is clear that the greatest gains from stratification come when the strata are uniform, so that S_w^2 is sufficiently small.

In practice, stratification is often used to oversample important population groups such as racial and ethnic minorities, and/or to reach the target population when screening is required (Srinath 2013). Here, the simple expression (29.14) no longer applies, as other considerations in survey design overshadow the simplistic goal of minimizing the overall variance.

Design Effect of Clustering. Clustering of observations into larger sampling units is usually done when there is a natural hierarchy in the population (such as patients nested in hospitals) or in the frames that are used to draw samples (such as historic use of 100-banks in the way landline telephone numbers were being assigned, Mitofsky (1970), Waksberg (1978)). In single-stage epsem cluster samples, the design effect due to clustering is (Lohr 2009, Korn and Graubard 1999)

$$\text{DEFF}_{\text{cl}} = 1 + \text{ICC}_y(\bar{m} - 1) \tag{29.15}$$

where $\bar{m}$ is the average number of observations per cluster (PSU), and ICC is the intraclass correlation, or the share of the between-cluster component in total variance of the response variable y due to the cluster structure (Lohr 2009, sec. 5.2):

$$\text{ICC} \approx 1 - \frac{\sum_{i=1}^{N} \sum_{j=1}^{M_i} (Y_{ij} - \bar{Y}_i)^2}{\sum_{i=1}^{N} \sum_{j=1}^{M_i} (Y_{ij} - \bar{Y})^2} \tag{29.16}$$

where $\bar{Y}_i$ is the cluster mean, $\bar{Y}$ is the overall population mean, and the approximation involves large and approximately balanced cluster sizes.

Realistic cluster sample designs usually involve $\bar{m}$ ~dozens of observations taken from a geographic PSU or an administrative health unit. When combined with high ICC, these values of $\bar{m}$ may lead to notable increases in design effects. Adams et al. (2004) report meta-analysis of a broad set of practice-based studies, and found most ICCs to be in single digit percentage points. Their interquartile range of ICCs found in 31 studies on 1039 variables was [0,0.032], with 5% of reported ICCs exceeding 0.07, and 1% exceeding 0.21. Thompson et al. (2012) report ICCs of 0.1–0.25 on variables such as age, race, smoking, and unhealthy diet for patients nested in general practices in the United Kingdom. In the authors' experience working with Demographic and Health Survey data,[2] an ICC=1 can be encountered on an access to tap water variable for respondents nested in villages that serve as the survey PSUs: either the whole village would have tap water, or nobody would. For this variable, the effective sample size is naturally the number of villages rather than the number of respondents.

A source of intraclass correlations that is rarely if ever accounted for in variance estimation are intraclass correlations due to interviewers. In both phone and face-to-face surveys, responses that a specific interviewer obtains from survey respondents may have an ICC in low single digit percentages (O'Muircheartaigh and Campanelli 1998). However, in some phone surveys where interviewer workload can be as high as dozens to low hundreds of interviews, equation (29.15) predicts a notable design effect of about 2 due to interviewer effects when ICC=1% and the average workload is $\bar{m} = 100$ which is not unheard of in massive data collection efforts.

In more complex models, the effects of clustering are attenuated due to the explanatory power of the covariates. In a bivariate regression model, Scott and Holt (1982) demonstrated the effect of clustering on the standard error of a regression coefficient estimate to be

$$\mathrm{DEFF}_{\mathrm{cl}} = 1 + \mathrm{ICC}_x \mathrm{ICC}_e (\bar{m} - 1) \tag{29.17}$$

where ICC_x and ICC_e are the intraclass correlations of the explanatory variable and residuals, respectively. While, as mentioned earlier, the ICC_x may be relatively high, when the regression model is working well, the ICC_e of residuals is likely to be fairly low, with the overall DEFF in equation (29.17) being barely above 1.

EXAMPLE 29.3 NHIS example

Let us now tabulate the demographic variables and explore their design effects. To analyze the complex survey data in Stata, the researcher needs to declare the survey design using **svyset**, and use **svy:** prefix in subsequent analyses.

```
. svyset psu_p [pw=wtfa_sa] , strata(strat_p)

      pweight: wtfa_sa
          VCE: linearized
  Single unit: missing
     Strata 1: strat_p
         SU 1: psu_p
        FPC 1: <zero>
```

[2] See http://www.dhsprogram.com/.

```
. svy: tabulate sex, count se ci deff format(%12.0g)
(running tabulate on estimation sample)

Number of strata   =       300              Number of obs      =      34525
Number of PSUs     =       600              Population size    =  234920670
                                            Design df          =        300

--------------------------------------------------------------------------------
HHC.110_0 |
0.000:    |
Sex       |      count           se           lb           ub          deff
----------+---------------------------------------------------------------------
   1 Male |  113070897  1471455.596  110175215.1  115966578.9   5.425501254
 2 Female |  121849773  1395324.466  119103909.8  124595636.2   4.878608458
          |
    Total |  234920670
--------------------------------------------------------------------------------
  Key:  count      =  weighted counts
        se         =  linearized standard errors of weighted counts
        lb         =  lower 95% confidence bounds for weighted counts
        ub         =  upper 95% confidence bounds for weighted counts
        deff       =  deff for variances of weighted counts

. svy: tabulate mracrpi2, count se ci deff format(%12.0g)
(running tabulate on estimation sample)
Number of strata   =       300              Number of obs      =      34525
Number of PSUs     =       600              Population size    =  234920670
                                            Design df          =        300

--------------------------------------------------------------------------------
HHC.200_0 |
1.000:    |
Race      |
coded to  |
single/mu |
ltiple    |
race      |
group     |      count           se           lb           ub          deff
----------+---------------------------------------------------------------------
 01 White |  190205036  2133166.629    186007171    194402901    18.4709514
 02 Black |   28701548  623339.9492  27474875.44  29928220.56   2.266401121
 03 India |    2240430  223118.3122  1801354.802  2679505.198   3.296861155
 09 Asian |    2569197  185687.5828  2203781.847  2934612.153   1.994086518
 10 Chine |    2447896  186307.3913  2081261.124  2814530.876   2.105795616
 11 Filip |    3067658  229899.3828  2615238.312  3520077.688   2.565529637
 15 Other |    4677088  243222.6548  4198449.405  5155726.595   1.896557799
 16 Prima |     400589  81027.80894  241134.1308  560043.8692    2.41273844
 17 Multi |     611228    83792.396  446332.6916  776123.3084   1.692533586
          |
    Total |  234920670
--------------------------------------------------------------------------------
  Key:  count      =  weighted counts
        se         =  linearized standard errors of weighted counts
        lb         =  lower 95% confidence bounds for weighted counts
        ub         =  upper 95% confidence bounds for weighted counts
        deff       =  deff for variances of weighted counts
```

```
. svy: tabulate sex, se ci deff
(running tabulate on estimation sample)

Number of strata    =      300          Number of obs      =      34525
Number of PSUs      =      600          Population size    =  234920670
                                        Design df          =        300
```

HHC.110_0 0.000: Sex	proportions	se	lb	ub	deff
1 Male	.4813	.0037	.4741	.4886	1.874
2 Female	.5187	.0037	.5114	.5259	1.874
Total	1				

```
  Key:  proportions  =  cell proportions
        se           =  linearized standard errors of cell proportions
        lb           =  lower 95% confidence bounds for cell proportions
        ub           =  upper 95% confidence bounds for cell proportions
        deff         =  deff for variances of cell proportions
```

The design effects for totals of the sex categories are relatively high at 4–5, and reflect the complexity of the sampling design. While the design effects due to unequal weighting, given by equation (29.11), would be expected to be approximately $1 + (5675/6804)^2 \approx 1.70$, the actual design effects are higher due to clustering of observation units (adults) in PSUs, SSUs, ..., households. Compared to the DEFFs of the sex categories, the DEFFs of the race categories reflect oversampling of minorities built into the design. (Technically speaking, the race of an individual is not available on the frame *per se*. However, the existing tendencies of members of different racial groups to live in relatively compact clusters makes it possible for sample designers to oversample the geographic areas where these minorities are known to reside.) While the design effect for Whites is much larger than those for males or females, the design effects for minority races are notably smaller, that is, the proportions of these groups are estimated with relatively better precision than would be the case for a sampling design that would reach the different racial groups equally.

Finally, it is worth observing that the design effects for the ratio (proportion, rather than the total, of males and females) is smaller than the design effect for the total, and in closer agreement with the design effect due to unequal weighting (DEFF=1.70). The variance inflating effect of clustering appears to act in an approximately equal manner in the numerator (the count of males; the count of females) and denominator (the total count of population).

As this analysis demonstrates, there is no single design effect applicable to all statistics and all analyses. Modern statistical software allows researchers to compute the design effects specific to any given analysis. ■

Power and Sample Size Considerations. In planning their health surveys, researchers need to be aware of the issues of design effects and the impacts they have on precision, power, and the required sample size. The mainstream techniques of power analysis (Ryan 2013) are generally designed for, and applicable to, "flat" i.i.d. data only. To project the sample sizes derived under i.i.d. assumptions to complex survey data, design effects discussed above need to be incorporated into the sample size calculations. The simplest approach is to assume that the various design effects act multiplicatively, and to obtain the overall design effect by multiplying the individual design effects (e.g., from clustering and unequal weighting). While some of these DEFFs can come from the preliminary sampling plan (unequal weighting effect, prospective interviewer load), others may need to be identified in the literature for similar studies (ICCs of key variables, screening rates and prevalences of conditions if only a specific population is of interest; see Chapter 4). Once all of the design effects are combined, equation (29.10) can be inverted to obtain the sample sizes that need to be fielded. A sensitivity analysis with different values of ICC, interviewer effects, unequal weighting effects needs to be conducted, as well, to explore sensitivity of the power and sample size calculations to the underlying assumptions made by the health researcher and the sample designer.

Linearization for Nonlinear Statistics. For statistics more complicated than totals, the standard errors can often be obtained by an approximation called *linearization*, also known as *Taylor series expansion* and the delta method in other branches of statistical literature (van der Vaart 1998). It can be applied in two ways.

If the parameter of interest θ can be expressed as a function of one or more survey totals, $\theta = f(T_1, \dots, T_K)$, and estimators of these totals $t_1, \dots, t_k$ along with their estimated variance–covariance matrix $v\{t_1, \dots, t_k\}$ are available, then the approximate variance of $\hat{\theta}$ is given by

$$v(\hat{\theta}) = D_f' v\{t_1, \dots, t_k\} D_f \tag{29.18}$$

where D_f is the vector of partial derivatives of f. Examples where this approach is applicable include the standard errors of a ratio estimator (equation 29.3), which is a function of two totals, or correlation, which is a function of five totals, including three second-order moments.

To be precise, equation (29.18) is the estimate of *mean squared error* (MSE) rather than the variance. The difference is what the quantity is being centered at. The variance of an estimator $\hat{\theta}$ is

$$\mathbb{V}[\hat{\theta}] = \mathbb{E}[(\hat{\theta} - \mathbb{E}\hat{\theta})^2]$$

centered at the expected value of $\hat{\theta}$, while the MSE is defined as

$$\text{MSE}[\hat{\theta}] = \mathbb{E}[(\hat{\theta} - \theta_0)^2],$$

centered at the true value θ_0. The two expressions coincide when the estimator is unbiased, $\mathbb{E}\hat{\theta} = \theta_0$. However, nearly every estimator discussed in this chapter (except the Horvitz–Thompson estimator (29.1) of the population total) is biased, although biases are generally small and are ignored in practical work (see however a more explicit treatment of bias in small area models, Section 29.3.6). Thus, the MSE expressions are arguably more appropriate in quantifying the average distance from the estimator to the true value.

While equation (29.18) involves direct application of Taylor series expansion, it does not necessarily solve the issue with even more complicated statistics such as regression estimates. To obtain variance estimates for these statistics, they need to be expressed in the form of estimating equations (Godambe and Thompson 1978, Godambe and Thompson 2009) $\mathbb{E}[\mathbf{g}(X, \theta_0)] = 0$ evaluated at the true parameter θ_0. Examples include normal equations for linear regression,

$$\sum_j w_j(y_j - \mathbf{x}_j'\beta)\mathbf{x_j} = 0 \tag{29.19}$$

or score equations in models fit by pseudolikelihood (Skinner 1989). Once that is done, the first-order Taylor series expansion for the estimating equations,

$$\mathbf{g}(X, \hat{\theta}) = \mathbf{g}(X, \theta_0) + D_\theta(\hat{\theta} - \theta_0) + \ \dots$$

where D_θ is the matrix of derivatives of $\mathbf{g}(X, \theta)$ with respect to θ (Hessian matrix at the solution for the pseudo-ML models), is inverted to express $\hat{\theta} - \theta_0$, and the MSE of the parameter estimate is then obtained as

$$v(\hat{\theta}) = D_\theta^{-1} v[\mathbf{g}(X, \theta)] D_\theta^{-1} \tag{29.20}$$

where $v[\mathbf{g}(X, \theta)]$ is the variance–covariance matrix estimator for the estimating equations computed from the first principles, such as equation (29.8). Similar estimators are known in other areas as the Huber (1967) or White (1982) estimator.

Linearization is considered to be the gold standard method for statistics to which it is applicable. However, it can have poor performance for some types of estimates that lack "smoothness" (such as the Gini index of inequality) or may be too complicated to derive and code (e.g., two-step estimators in which intermediate results from one model are fed into another model).

Note that application of equation (29.18) or (29.20) requires specification of sampling strata and PSUs. Owing to privacy concerns, statistical agencies may not be able to release the true strata and sampling unit information in public use data, and produce synthetic strata and PSUs that are generally related to, but do not exactly coincide with, the actual design specification. Alternatively, some public use microdata sets are distributed with weight variables for use with the replication methods discussed next.

EXAMPLE 29.4 NHIS example

In NHIS public use microdata, the suggested method of variance estimation is linearization. In the Sampled Adult data set we are using, the weights are **wtfa_sa**, the strata are **strat_p**, and the PSUs are **psu_p**. ■

Replicate Variance Estimation. Replicate variance estimation methods shift the burden of computing the squared differences from paper-and-pencil analytical derivations to the computer. They do so by representing the required differences with an alternative weighting system. Consider, for instance, the formula for the variance of the SRS sample mean,

$$v(\bar{y}) = \frac{1-f}{n}s^2 = \frac{1-f}{n}\frac{1}{n-1}\sum_{j=1}^{n}(y_j - \bar{y})^2$$

The first term in the formula for s^2 can be represented as

$$\begin{aligned}\frac{1}{n-1}(y_1 - \bar{y})^2 &= \frac{1}{n-1}[n\bar{y} - (n-1)\bar{y}_{(-1)} - \bar{y}]^2 \\ &= \frac{1}{n-1}[(n-1)\bar{y} - (n-1)\bar{y}_{(-1)}]^2 \\ &= (n-1)(\bar{y}_{(-1)} - \bar{y})^2 \qquad (29.21)\end{aligned}$$

where

$$\bar{y}_{(-1)} = \frac{1}{n-1}\sum_{j=2}^{n} y_j$$

is the average of the observations with the first one excluded, and $y_1 = n\bar{y} - (n-1)\bar{y}_{(-1)}$. Expression (29.21) motivates the *jackknife* method: the jackknife pseudovalues $\bar{y}_{(-j)}$ are obtained by excluding the jth sampled unit, and the variance estimator is obtained by summing up the scaled squared differences of these pseudovalues minus the overall sample estimate. While the idea may be somewhat silly for the purposes of computing the variance of $\bar{y}$, it proves very useful when the analytical expressions or the linearization method prove untractable.

In general, replicate variance estimation methods (Krewski and Rao 1981, Rust and Rao 1996, Shao 1996, Kolenikov 2010) for a statistic $\hat{\theta}$

1. take a subsample $r = 1, \ldots, R$ from the original data using the design that resembles the original sampling plan;
2. compute the replicate value $\hat{\theta}_{(r)}$ using exactly the same procedure as the one used for the quantity of interest $\hat{\theta}$;
3. repeat the process R times; and

4. form the squared differences (scaled as needed) and sum them up to obtain the variance estimator:

$$v(\hat{\theta}) = \frac{A}{R} \sum_{r=1}^{R} \{\hat{\theta}_{(r)} - \bar{\theta}_{(.)}\}\{\hat{\theta}_{(r)} - \bar{\theta}_{(.)}\}'$$

or the MSE estimator

$$v(\hat{\theta}) = \frac{A}{R} \sum_{r=1}^{R} \{\hat{\theta}_{(r)} - \hat{\theta}\}\{\hat{\theta}_{(r)} - \hat{\theta}\}',$$

where $\bar{\theta}_{(.)}$ is the average of the replicate values, and A is a scaling factor if necessary.

When multistage sampling designs are used, the replication scheme typically runs at the level of the PSUs, that is, entire PSUs are omitted from the sample when a subsample is taken.

The replication schemes (units to be included or omitted in the subsample), the number of replicates R and scaling factors are chosen so that in the simple cases like sample means or totals the expressions will algebraically coincide with the known formulae like equation (29.8).

Instead of shuffling the data in computer memory (or reading them in and out from the hard drive), replicate variance estimation can be cast in terms of weighted estimation with alternative weights. If a sampling unit is omitted from a replicate, it receives a weight of zero; if it is used twice, it receives a weight that is double its sampling weight, and so on. Thus, a practical implementation of a replicate variance estimation method would call for a set of R weights that incorporate the patterns of units omitted from and included into the replicate subsamples.

Several replicate weighting schemes have found wide use.

Balanced Repeated Replication. Introduced by McCarthy (1969) for designs with two PSU per stratum, balanced repeated replication (BRR) creates replicates by dropping a PSU from each stratum and doubling the weight of the remaining one. A balanced subset of the 2^L replicates can be found with a much smaller number $R, L \leq R < L + 4$, by using a Hadamard matrix of order R (Hedayat et al. 1999). Balance here means that each PSU is used the same number of times and each pair of PSUs (across strata) is used the same number of times.

Given that half of the sample is removed in any given replicate, i.e., half of the observations receive zero weights, two problems may arise. First, a potential confidentiality intruder may be able to identify the units that go together as a PSU, and thus partially recover geographic information that may be sensitive. Second, a small subpopulation with low incidence may disappear completely in a replicate if all the subpopulation units receive zero weights. To ameliorate these problems, the weight of a sampling unit can be reduced by a fraction, rather than set to zero. This procedure is known as *Fay's adjustment* (Judkins 1990).

Thus, if H_R is a Hadamard matrix for R replicates (i.e., the matrix with ± 1 entries that form orthogonal columns, $H_R' H_R = R\mathrm{I}$), then the BRR weight in replicate r for unit j in PSU $i = 1, 2$ of stratum h is formed as

$$w_{ij}^{(r)} = \begin{cases} f w_{ij}, & \text{if } H_R[r,h] = (-1)^i \\ (2-f) w_{ij}, & \text{if } H_R[r,h] = (-1)^{i+1} \end{cases} \tag{29.22}$$

where $0 \leq f < 1$ is the Fay's adjustment, with $f = 0$ for no adjustment. The BRR variance estimator is then

$$v(\hat{\theta}) = \frac{1}{R(1-f)^2} \sum_{i=r}^{R} \{\hat{\theta}_{(r)} - \bar{\theta}_{(.)}\}\{\hat{\theta}_{(r)} - \bar{\theta}_{(.)}\}' \tag{29.23}$$

and the MSE estimator is

$$v(\hat{\theta}) = \frac{1}{R(1-f)^2} \sum_{r=1}^{R} \{\hat{\theta}_{(r)} - \hat{\theta}\}\{\hat{\theta}_{(r)} - \hat{\theta}\}' \tag{29.24}$$

where $\hat{\theta}$ are the point estimates for the original survey data, $\hat{\theta}_{(r)}$ is the rth replicate value, and $\bar{\theta}_{(.)}$ is the average of the replicate values. Note how the variance of the pseudovalues is inflated by a factor of $(1-f)^{-2}$ when Fay's adjustment is being used.

Extensions of BRR for other designs have been proposed by Wu (1991) and Sitter (1993), and BRR is sometimes considered to be a special case of a balanced bootstrap (Nigam and Rao 1996).

The Jackknife. The jackknife method omits one PSU at a time, calculates the value of the statistic on thus formed subsample, and repeats the process for every PSU. Unlike BRR, the jackknife is not restricted to a specific design. If in the rth replicate, the PSU i^* from stratum h^* (one out of $R_h = n_{h^*}$ PSUs in that stratum) is being dropped, then the adjusted sampling weight is

$$w_{hij}^{(r)} = \begin{cases} 0, & \text{if } h = h^* \text{and} i = i^* \\ \dfrac{n_h}{n_h - 1} w_{hij}, & \text{if } h = h^* \text{and} i \neq i^* \\ w_{hij}, & \text{otherwise} \end{cases} \tag{29.25}$$

As was shown in the motivation explanation, the jackknife variance formula needs to employ scaling factors:

$$v(\hat{\theta}) = \sum_{h=1}^{L} (1-f_h)\, k_h \sum_{r=1}^{R_h} \{\hat{\theta}_{(r)} - \bar{\theta}_h\}\{\hat{\theta}_{(r)} - \bar{\theta}_h\}' \tag{29.26}$$

The MSE formula is

$$v(\hat{\theta}) = \sum_{h=1}^{L}(1 - f_h)\, k_h \sum_{r=1}^{R_h}\{\hat{\theta}_{(r)} - \hat{\theta}\}\{\hat{\theta}_{(r)} - \hat{\theta}\}' \tag{29.27}$$

where $\hat{\theta}_{(r)}$ is the rth replicate value, $\bar{\theta}_h$ is the average of replicate values from stratum h, and $k_h = (n_h - 1)/n_h$ is the jackknife scaling multiplier for stratum h.

Given that this method disturbs the data the least compared to other methods, it tracks the linearization estimator more closely compared to other replicate variance estimation methods. The jackknife variance estimates are sometimes even preferrable to the linearization estimates from the model-based perspective (Valliant 1996). However, jackknife has two serious limitations. A methodological one is that the jackknife may fail to provide correct standard errors for statistics that are not smooth, such as percentile estimates, the Gini coefficient of income inequality, or matching estimators in causal inference. A computational limitation is that the number of replicates must equal the number of PSUs, and in some types of list surveys this may require thousands or tens of thousands of replicates. To overcome that, pseudodesigns can be created that collapse some strata and some PSUs together in a delete-a-group jackknife procedure (Kott 2001, Valliant et al. 2008); however, doing so may lead to further methodological complications such as lack of consistency (Shao 1996).

The Bootstrap. In mainstream statistics for "flat" i.i.d. data, the bootstrap method takes a sample with replacement from the original data (Efron and Tibshirani 1994). In the survey statistics world, the bootstrap subsamples have to be taken independently within strata, and then in some designs, the number of units to be resampled may be as low as $n_h = 2$ PSUs per stratum. Moreover, a sample size that is this low uncovers the small sample biases of the bootstrap as a variance estimation method. Having considered these issues, Rao and Wu (1988) proposed the following bootstrap scheme:

- Choose the resampling scheme parameters: number of replicates R and the number of units m_h to be resampled in stratum h, $0 < m_h \leq n_h$.
- To form the rth replicate, take a subsample of size m_h PSUs from stratum h, or equivalently assign the bootstrap frequencies $f_{hi}^{(*r)} = 0, 1, 2, \ldots$ to the unit i in stratum h so that $\sum_{i=1}^{n_h} f_{hi}^{(*r)} = m_h$.
- Form specially scaled replicate values of the statistic of interest (details are omitted, but the resulting weight expressions will be given later).
- Repeat the process R times.
- Form the variance or MSE estimates using a simple variance of the replicate values.

Rao and Wu (1988) demonstrated that the choice $m_h = n_h - 1$ removes the need for the otherwise awkward scaling, while the choice $m_h = n_h - 3$ may help removing the skewness of the distribution of the estimates. Rao et al. (1992) provided the equivalent formulation for the rth bootstrap replicate weight of unit j in PSU i of stratum h as follows:

$$w_{hij}^{(r)} = \left\{ 1 - \left(\frac{m_h}{n_h - 1} \right)^{1/2} + \left(\frac{m_h}{n_h - 1} \right)^{1/2} \frac{n_h}{m_h} f_{hi}^{(*r)} \right\} w_{hij} \tag{29.28}$$

A modification of the bootstrap method that is similar in motivation (i.e., to avoid zero replicate weights) and execution to Fay's adjustment for jackknife is the mean bootstrap (Yung 1997) in which the bootstrap frequencies $f_{hi}^{(*r)}$ are formed by averaging b consecutive replicates, and thus are fractional. This modification, just as is Fay's adjustment, calls for an additional scaling factor when the replicate values are aggregated. In general, the variance estimate is

$$v(\hat{\theta}) = \frac{b}{R} \sum_{r=1}^{R} \{\hat{\theta}_{(r)} - \bar{\theta}_{(.)}\}\{\hat{\theta}_{(r)} - \bar{\theta}_{(.)}\}' \tag{29.29}$$

and the (MSE) estimate is

$$v(\hat{\theta}) = \frac{b}{R} \sum_{r=1}^{R} \{\hat{\theta}_{(r)} - \hat{\theta}\}\{\hat{\theta}_{(r)} - \hat{\theta}\}' \tag{29.30}$$

where $\hat{\theta}$ are the point estimates based on the original survey data, $\hat{\theta}_{(r)}$ is the rth replicate value of the point estimates, $\bar{\theta}_{(.)}$ is the average of the replicate values, and b is the number of bootstrap samples used to generate each replicate-weight variable in the mean bootstrap method ($b = 1$ for the original bootstrap).

The bootstrap method is the least restrictive on both the design and statistics compared to other replicate variance estimation methods. It is the variance estimation method of choice that is used by Statistics Canada for nearly all of their work. Its greater flexibility spans additional classes of statistics that it can be applied to; Shao (1996) provides the proof of consistency of the bootstrap for percentiles, which no other replicate variance estimation method can provide.

Other Replicate Methods. Besides the jackknife, BRR and the bootstrap that are generally used for variance estimation and provide variance estimates that are in agreement with linearization estimates, other variance estimation methods can be encountered. The U.S. Census Bureau uses *successive difference replication* for variance estimation with the Current Population Survey (CPS) and American Community Survey (ACS) public use microdata. The sampling designs of these studies involve systematic sampling of units, and while there is no unbiased estimator available for the systematic sampling designs, successive difference estimators (Ash 2011, Wolter 2007) demonstrate reasonable performance.

The most general treatment of replicate variance estimation is provided by Kim and Wu (2013). They demonstrate an approach that allows converting the most general Yates–Grundy–Sen variance estimator (29.7) into an algebraically equivalent set of replicate weights, and demonstrate how an optimal subset of these weights can be chosen to minimize the computational cost.

29.2.3 DEGREES OF FREEDOM

As is the case with "flat" i.i.d. data, most arguments that justify sampling distributions of statistics of interest are asymptotic in their nature. To construct confidence intervals surrounding the point estimates of interest, researchers can refer to the large sample standard normal distribution of the ratio $(\hat{\theta} - \theta_0)/\text{s.e. of } \hat{\theta}$. The question however may be raised as to what constitutes a large sample in the complex survey context.

The theory of single-stage stratified sampling suggests that the degrees of freedom of the variance estimators for these designs is $n - L$, where n is the sample size, and L is the number of strata. A natural extension to more complex designs would be the same expression where n would now be interpreted as the number of PSUs. In this situation, we may experience a severe loss of degrees of freedom: in designs with say 30 strata and 2 PSUs per stratum, the degrees of freedom is 30 no matter how large the sample size of the ultimate observation units is.

This reduction of degrees of freedom is often undesirable. For instance, it limits the number of variables that the researcher can use in regression models, and the number of domains, or subpopulations (see Section 29.2.4), that can be analyzed at once.

Korn and Graubard (1999), Sec. 5.2, discuss some strategies for *ad hoc* increases in degrees of freedom. The most conservative method is to ignore stratification, thus increasing the degrees of freedom from $n - L$ to $n - 1$. For a common design with 2 PSUs per stratum (such as the public use version of NHIS), this allows doubling the degrees of freedom.

More advanced treatments of the issue of degrees of freedom are available for descriptive statistics like means, totals, and proportions. Potthoff et al. (1992) and Valliant and Rust (2010) relate the degrees of freedom to the kurtosis of the study variable, and demonstrate that a higher kurtosis leads to fewer effective degrees of freedom:

$$\text{d.f.} = \frac{2(\sum_h \frac{\sigma_h^2}{n_h})^2}{\sum_h \frac{\sigma_h^4}{n_h^3}(\kappa_h - \frac{n_h-3}{n_h-1})} \tag{29.31}$$

where σ_h^2 is the variance of the variable of interest specific to stratum h, and $\kappa_h = \mu_{4h}/\sigma_h^4$ is the normalized kurtosis. The upper bound $n - L$ is only attained for normal data with $\kappa_h = 3$. Also, in the case of binary response, the kurtosis is

$\kappa_h = (1 - 6p_h + 6p_h^2)/p_h(1 - p_h) + 3$ for a binary variable with proportion p_h in stratum h grows arbitrarily large when the events become rare, $p_h \to 0$ or $p_h \to 1$.

29.2.4 SUBPOPULATION ANALYSIS

One of the important points where special caution should be exercised in ensuring that correct estimation procedures are used is analysis of domains, or subpopulations (Skinner 1989, West et al. 2008). A *domain* is a subset of the population that is of substantive interest to the health researcher, such as a special demographic group (e.g., young adults, females, or an ethnic minority), or a group of respondents in a specific geography, and so on. In other words, the researcher disaggregates the overall target population into several categories, and analyzes the categories separately, or compares them to one another.

The statistical caveat that arises with analysis of domains is that the domain sample size is random, since domain membership may not be known in advance (except when the domain is also a stratification variable, such as geographic region). In some situations, estimating the size of the domain may be a question of its own substantive interest (e.g., how many people with diabetes are there in the United States?). Thus, in forming the estimate of the mean in domain $\mathscr{D}$,

$$\bar{y}_a = \frac{\sum_{j \in \mathscr{S} \cap \mathscr{D}} w_j y_j}{\sum_{j \in \mathscr{S} \cap \mathscr{D}} w_j} \tag{29.32}$$

both numerator and denominator are random, and the extra randomness coming from the denominator must be properly accounted for. If the data outside of the domain are simply excluded from the analysis, and the resulting restricted data set is analyzed, even with the correct specifications of weights, strata, and sampling units, several effects may jeopardize estimation. First, the statistical package may incorrectly assume that the sample size is fixed rather than random, thus producing inappropriately small standard errors. Second, some PSUs may not contain the domain members, and thus would be dropped from analysis. This could produce a very undesirable effect of single PSUs per stratum, especially in the deeply stratified designs that have many strata and as few as two PSUs per stratum (as is the case with the NHIS example).

Fortunately, all packages that support design-based estimation also support analysis of domains, usually with options referred to as *subpopulation* or *domain*.

It is worth noting that the domain analysis may incur additional losses of degrees of freedom. The standard formula $n - L$ needs to be modified to become $n_d - L_d$, where L_d is the number of strata that have at least one member of the domain, and n_d is the number of PSUs in these strata. All other strata contribute zero to all the sums of squares such as those in equation (29.8), which means zero degrees of freedom in terms of how much the sample statistic can vary.

Sometimes, subpopulation estimation may run into problems when a replicate variance estimation method produces zero weights for some PSUs, and thus makes it possible that some rare subpopulation members are excluded. Handling of this situation will likely vary between different software packages. If the researcher has the available design information, variance estimation methods that do not suffer from zero replicate weights, such as Fay's BRR or the mean bootstrap, can be used.

EXAMPLE 29.5 NHIS example

Let us demonstrate some of the specific features of subpopulation analysis by concentrating on the Hispanic subpopulation:

```
. tabulate hispan_i

      HHC.180_00.000: Hispanic subgroup |
                                 detail |      Freq.     Percent        Cum.
----------------------------------------+-----------------------------------
                  00 Multiple Hispanic |        110        0.32        0.32
                        01 Puerto Rico |        578        1.67        1.99
                            02 Mexican |      2,226        6.45        8.44
                   03 Mexican-American |      1,358        3.93       12.37
               04 Cuban/Cuban American |        291        0.84       13.22
               05 Dominican (Republic) |        189        0.55       13.76
          06 Central or South American |        945        2.74       16.50
07 Other Latin American, type not speci |         10        0.03       16.53
                      08 Other Spanish |        152        0.44       16.97
         12 Not Hispanic/Spanish origin |     28,666       83.03      100.00
----------------------------------------+-----------------------------------
                                  Total |     34,525      100.00

. gen hispanic = hispan_i < 12

. svy, subpop(hispanic): proportion sex
(running proportion on estimation sample)

Survey: Proportion estimation

Number of strata =     289         Number of obs     =      33660
Number of PSUs   =     578         Population size   =  228222685
                                   Subpop. no. obs   =       5859
                                   Subpop. size      =   34946432
                                   Design df         =        289

      _prop_1: sex = 1 Male
      _prop_2: sex = 2 Female

--------------------------------------------------------------
             |             Linearized
             |  Proportion   Std. Err.     [95% Conf. Interval]
-------------+------------------------------------------------
sex          |
     _prop_1 |    .500907    .0082969      .4845818    .5172302
     _prop_2 |    .499093    .0082969      .4827698    .5154182
--------------------------------------------------------------
Note: 11 strata omitted because they contain no subpopulation
      members.
```

```
. estat effects

      _prop_1: sex = 1 Male
      _prop_2: sex = 2 Female
```

	Proportion	Linearized Std. Err.	DEFF	DEFT
sex				
_prop_1	.500907	.0082969	1.41415	1.18918
_prop_2	.499093	.0082969	1.41415	1.18918

Several additional bits of output are of note.

1. 11 strata did not have any Hispanic respondents: Stata issued a note below the output about this. These strata were fully excluded from estimation, and contributed neither to the point estimates nor to the standard errors.
2. Because of that, the degrees of freedom changed to (# of PSU in strata containing at least one Hispanic respondent−# of strata containing at least one Hispanic respondent). With 11 strata excluded, there are $300 - 289 = 11$ strata left, with 2 PSUs per stratum in each, producing 289 degrees of freedom.
3. Reported separately are the total number of observations used in the analysis (33,660) and the number of units in the domain of interest (5859). The former may have been fixed by the design, while the latter is a random variable.
4. Likewise, reported separately are the population size in the strata used for this analysis (i.e., excluding the 11 strata with no Hispanic respondents), and the (estimated) population size of the subpopulation of interest. ■

29.2.5 SINGLETON PSUS

Sometimes, researchers may find themselves analyzing the data from a design that has only one PSU in some (or all) strata, often called *singleton PSUs*. This may be done by design, where the sample designer aimed at *deep stratification* with many strata, and only one PSU was being used from each stratum. Technically speaking, systematic sampling with only one seed produces a cluster sample with one cluster (Thompson 1997, Lohr 2009). Alternatively, missing data can cause entire sampling units to be dropped from the analysis, possibly leaving a single sampling unit in the estimation sample. Finally, in sampling with probability proportional to size (PPS), some large units may be selected into the sample with certainty, which is sometimes denoted as a single certainty PSU per stratum. Strata with single PSUs is a big issue for variance estimation, as effectively we need to estimate variances from a sample with only 1 observation. Equation (29.8) clearly shows the problems that arise, as the term $n_h - 1$ in the denominator of this expression leads to an undetermined division 0/0.

Several options are usually provided in survey software packages, and researchers need to be aware of defaults and behaviors appropriate for their sampling designs and analysis.

1. If the singleton PSU is a certainty unit, then it does not contribute sampling variance to the resulting estimates. The survey software package may support corresponding design specifications in which the certainty units have zero contribution to the total variance. When the sampling design had more than one stage, the next level units, SSUs, may be specified as nominal PSUs.
2. In other situations, the singleton PSUs present a generic methodological problem. The best *ad hoc* solution appears to be to combine two or more such singleton PSUs into separate stratum or several strata, matching the singleton PSUs that are similar in the variables of substantive interest (Rust and Kalton 1987).
3. Other *ad hoc* solutions, although less well justified, include using deviations from the grand mean $\bar{y}$ instead of the stratum mean y_h in computing equation (29.8), or using the average of variances from other strata, assuming that these variances are approximately homogeneous. There is little if any methodological research to support these options.
4. Lacking any better guidance from the user, some software packages may produce zero or missing standard errors when encountering singleton PSUs. When missing standard errors appear in survey estimation output, the researcher may need to review the design and sample structure, and if there are no strata with a single PSU intended by design, inspect the estimation sample as it may have been restricted by missing data. Respecifying designs with alternative settings for singelton PSUs, or conducting analysis as if analyzing a subpopulation with nonmissing data (see Section 29.2.4) would be good analytical alternatives.

EXAMPLE 29.6 NHIS example

Note that should we have analyzed Hispanics using the restricted sample approach, we would have run into the singleton strata issue:

```
. svydescribe if hispanic, single

Survey: Describing strata with a single sampling unit in stage 1

      pweight: wtfa_sa
          VCE: linearized
  Single unit: missing
     Strata 1: strat_p
         SU 1: psu_p
        FPC 1: <zero>
```

```
                                            #Obs per Unit
                                       ----------------------------
 Stratum     #Units      #Obs        min        mean        max
 --------   --------   --------   --------   --------   --------
        2         1*          2          2        2.0          2
   (output omitted)
      264         1*          2          2        2.0          2
 --------   --------   --------   --------   --------   --------
                 58
```

We would find 58 strata with only one PSU containing any Hispanics, leading the software to believe that there is only one PSU in these strata:

```
. svy : proportion sex if hispanic
(running proportion on estimation sample)

Survey: Proportion estimation

Number of strata =       289         Number of obs     =        5859
Number of PSUs   =       520         Population size   =    34946432
                                     Design df         =         231

       _prop_1: sex = 1 Male
       _prop_2: sex = 2 Female

--------------------------------------------------------------
             |             Linearized
             |  Proportion   Std. Err.     [95% Conf. Interval]
-------------+------------------------------------------------
sex          |
     _prop_1 |    .500907          .            .           .
     _prop_2 |    .499093          .            .           .
--------------------------------------------------------------
Note: missing standard errors because of stratum with single
      sampling unit.
```

Once again, this is an incorrect analysis, and researchers need to use the appropriate subpopulation estimation features. ■

29.2.6 CALIBRATED WEIGHTS

As described in Section 26.5, weighting adjustments commonly include raking ratio adjustments to known control totals. Deville and Särndal (1992) present a very general theory for a class of *weight calibration* procedures, including raking, when the only source of survey error is the sampling error (i.e., there is no nonresponse). They demonstrate asymptotic equivalence of the calibrated estimator of a survey total $t_{\text{cal}}[y]$ to the *generalized regression* estimator (Särndal et al. 1992):

$$t_{\mathrm{GREG}}[y] = t[y] + (T[X] - t[x])'b \tag{29.33}$$

where b is the coefficient estimate in the sample regression (equation 29.4), $T[X]$ is the known population total of the calibration variables, and $t[x]$ is the sample total (such as Horvitz–Thompson total (29.1)) of the same variables. Deville and Särndal (1992) demonstrate the efficiency gains of calibration to be

$$\mathrm{DEFF}_{\mathrm{cal}} = 1 - R_y^2 \tag{29.34}$$

where R_y^2 is the coefficient of determination, or the proportion of variance explained by the calibration variables, in regression (29.4).

While the original developments of Deville and Särndal (1992) are aimed at removing the sampling imbalances associated with the pure sampling error, D'Arrigo and Skinner (2010) study how the calibrated estimators perform in the presence of nonresponse. They demonstrate that while the general form (29.34) of the estimator holds, the final nonresponse adjusted weights must be used in computing the variance estimator to reduce its bias.

What if calibration or poststratification information is incomplete? When calibrated weights are specified as if they were probability weights, while calibration variables (or poststratification identifiers and poststrata sizes) are not available, the point estimates reflect additional accuracy gains obtained by weight calibration or poststratification, but the variance estimates will be those of the basic, noncalibrated (nonpoststratified) estimator. Similar considerations apply to other forms of calibrated weights (e.g., raking and other marginal adjustment procedures). On technical differences between poststratification and calibration, see Section 29.2.1.

29.3 Substantive Analyses

In this section, we describe how several mainstream statistical methods need to be modified in order to take complex survey designs into account. Typically, the presence of complex survey design features makes it impossible to use tests and diagnostics that assume i.i.d. data, although in some cases, these tests can be modified to produce analyses that are consistent with complex survey data. We assume that readers are familiar with these models, as we do not have room to explain them, other than to provide the main references.

29.3.1 TWO-WAY TABLES

In analysis of two-way tables (Agresti 2012), one of the basic analyses that the researcher can undertake is to test whether there are interactions between the margins, that is, whether the conditional distributions of say the row variable are the same for different values of the column variable. With i.i.d. data, such a test can be performed using the standard Pearson test for proportions: under the null hypothesis of independence, the cell proportions are obtained as a product of the marginal proportions; and the variances of the cell counts can be obtained from the corresponding multinomial distribution. With complex survey data, the variances of these cell counts will be affected by the non-i.i.d. design. Rao and Scott (1981) (see also Rao and Thomas (2003)) demonstrate that with complex survey data, instead of the regular χ^2, the asymptotic distribution of the test statistic becomes

$$\sum_k \lambda_k \chi_1^2$$

where λ_k are *generalized design effects*, that is, the (estimated) eigenvalues of the matrix $(\mathbb{V}_{\text{SRS}}[\hat{p}])^{-1}\mathbb{V}_{\text{design}}[\hat{p}]$. While this distribution is not tractable analytically, the Satterthwaite (1946) approximation by the first two moments can be used to generate p-values. The **survey** package in R (Lumley 2010) also produces a saddlepoint approximation (Smith and Young 2005) to the tail p-value.

Similar behavior occurs with other tests that have asymptotic χ^2 distributions with "flat" data. While Rao–Scott tests are conceptually applicable more broadly, implementation depends on the particular test in question, and whether the generalized design effects can be obtained from underlying estimates.

EXAMPLE 29.7 NHIS example

Let us now create the health outcome variable of interest, presence of any kind of allergies, and tabulate it against demographics.

```
. gen allergy = respalyr == 1 | dgstalyr == 1 | sknalyr == 1 | othalyr == 1

. svy : tabulate mracrpi2 allergy, row se
(running tabulate on estimation sample)

Number of strata   =       300              Number of obs      =      34525
Number of PSUs     =       600              Population size    =  234920670
                                            Design df          =        300

----------------------------------------------
HHC.200_0 |
1.000:    |
Race      |
coded to  |
single/mu |
ltiple    |
race      |          allergy
group     |         0          1     Total
----------+-----------------------------------
 01 White |     .7706      .2294         1
          |   (.0035)    (.0035)
          |
 02 Black |     .8144      .1856         1
          |    (.007)     (.007)
```

```
 03 India |   .7708     .2292        1
          |  (.024)    (.024)
          |
 09 Asian |   .8503     .1497        1
          | (.0196)   (.0196)
          |
 10 Chine |   .7584     .2416        1
          | (.0248)   (.0248)
          |
 11 Filip |    .795      .205        1
          |  (.024)    (.024)
          |
 15 Other |   .8175     .1825        1
          | (.0138)   (.0138)
          |
 16 Prima |   .7815     .2185        1
          | (.0643)   (.0643)
          |
 17 Multi |   .7892     .2108        1
          | (.0402)   (.0402)
          |
    Total |    .778      .222        1
          | (.0031)   (.0031)
-----------------------------------------

  Key:  row proportions
        (linearized standard errors of row proportions)

  Pearson:
    Uncorrected   chi2(8)          =   60.5220
    Design-based  F(7.39, 2217.18)=     6.2604     P = 0.0000
```

We see clear differences between racial groups in prevalence of allergy conditions. Thus, we should not be surprised to see that the test of independence of the margins is strongly rejected. The design-based F-statistic is the statistic of Rao and Scott (1981) test. It has fractional degrees of freedom in both the numerator and the denominator. The numerator degrees of freedom is the corrected degrees of freedom of the "flat" i.i.d. analysis (7.39 degrees of freedom instead of 8), while the denominator degrees of freedom represent somewhat extended design degrees of freedom (2217 instead of $600 - 17 = 583$). It can be shown that the numerator degrees of freedom are always smaller than those in the i.i.d. analysis. ■

29.3.2 REGRESSION ANALYSIS

Equation (29.4) shows that obtaining regression coefficient estimates in complex surveys entails inserting the matrix of final weights in the manner similar to generalized least squares (which, however, has a different motivation of heteroskedastic or dependent data). Obtaining standard errors requires combining equations (29.19) and (29.20). In the context of linear regression, $D_\theta = (X'X)^{-1}$, and the variance estimator (29.20) becomes

$$v(\hat{\beta}) = (X'X)^{-1} v[\mathbf{x}\varepsilon](X'X)^{-1} \tag{29.35}$$

which can be thought of as the complex survey generalization of the White (1980) heteroskedasticity-robust estimator.

Fuller (2002) gives a comprehensive treatment of how regression models are utilized in survey statistics in both substantive analyses and to generate more efficient estimates of descriptive statistics such as totals.

The linear regression model can support a relatively straightforward test for whether the analysis must include survey weights, or can proceed without them. Fuller (2009) (Sec. 6.3) suggests adding weights and their interactions with the explanatory variables in the regression of interest:

$$y = X\beta + Z\gamma + e, \quad \mathbf{z}_{jk} = w_j \mathbf{x}_{jk} \tag{29.36}$$

Then the test for whether the weights are necessary is given by $H_0 : \gamma = 0$. An ordinary least square (OLS) estimation and testing of equation (29.36) is only reasonable when the data are homoskedastic, and observations are independent. Since both of these assumptions are questionable in typical survey data, regression (29.36) needs to be estimated using equations (29.4) and (29.35).

Extensions of the traditional regression influence and residual diagnostics (Belsley et al. 1980) have been proposed by Li and Valliant (2009, 2011). One of the important modifications is that the influence of an observation depends not only on the geometry of the space of regression variables, as is the case with i.i.d. data, but also on the final weights of the observations.

29.3.3 LOGISTIC REGRESSION

Execution and implementation of logistic regression analysis, as well as interpretation (e.g., odds ratio interpretation of the exponentiated coefficients) remains the same as with "flat" data. The point estimates need to be obtained using final weights, and the standard errors need to be corrected for complex survey designs. However, the concepts of likelihood and deviance are not applicable with complex survey data. Thus, instead of likelihood ratio tests for nested models, researchers need to use Wald tests (Buse 1982) that only involve the full model and the estimated variance–covariance matrix of the estimated coefficients.

EXAMPLE 29.8 NHIS example

Let us now regress our health outcome of interest, known allergies, on the demographic variables:

```
. svy : logistic allergy i.sex i.mracrpi2 age_p, baselevels
(running logistic on estimation sample)

Survey: Logistic regression

Number of strata   =        300              Number of obs      =      34525
Number of PSUs     =        600              Population size    =  234920670
                                             Design df          =        300
                                             F(  10,     291)   =      19.29
                                             Prob > F           =     0.0000

------------------------------------------------------------------------------
             |             Linearized
     allergy | Odds Ratio   Std. Err.      t    P>|t|     [95% Conf. Interval]
-------------+----------------------------------------------------------------
         sex |
     1 Male  |          1  (base)
   2 Female  |   1.478707   .0491499    11.77   0.000      1.38508    1.578663
             |
    mracrpi2 |
    01 White |          1  (base)
 02 Black/.. |   .7623883   .0384156    -5.38   0.000     .6904174    .8418616
 03 Indian.. |   1.008865   .1377978     0.06   0.949     .7710796    1.319979
 09 Asian .. |   .6147153   .0966087    -3.10   0.002     .4511878    .8375114
  10 Chinese |   1.061252   .1490081     0.42   0.672     .8050426    1.399001
 11 Filipino |   .8561493    .128176    -1.04   0.300      .637673    1.149479
 15 Other..) |   .7484601   .0705674    -3.07   0.002     .6217121     .901048
 16 Prima..) |   .9725542   .3598414    -0.08   0.940     .4695662    2.014331
 17 Multip.. |   .9468009   .2353393    -0.22   0.826     .5805301    1.544161
             |
       age_p |   1.003188   .0009828     3.25   0.001     1.001256    1.005124
       _cons |    .207078   .0111811   -29.16   0.000     .1862033    .2302928
------------------------------------------------------------------------------

. estat gof

Logistic model for allergy, goodness-of-fit test

                   F(9,292) =            1.86
                   Prob > F =          0.0571
```

Stata specifically indicated that it used the linearization variance estimation method (see "linearized standard errors" heading). As with the previous complex survey estimation commands, the main features of the design are reported (# of strata, # of PSUs, design degrees of freedom, population size). The females appear to have higher prevalence of allergies than males (OR=1.48, 95% CI (1.39, 1.58)). Whites appear to have higher prevalence of allergies than most minorities, given that none of the odds ratios against Whites is significantly greater than 1, but some are significantly less than 1. Prevalence of allergies grows with age. Goodness of fit of this regression is borderline as demonstrated by the Archer–Lemeshow test p-value of 0.057. ■

A popular diagnostic test for goodness of fit of logistic regression is the Hosmer–Lemeshow test (Hosmer et al. 2013). This is the Pearson χ^2 test for proportions where the predicted proportions come from the estimated logistic model. As is the case with two-way tables for categorical variables (Section 29.3.1), the distribution of the test statistic does not follow χ^2 with complex survey data. The necessary modifications are provided by Archer and Lemeshow (2006). If all the predictors are categorical, the traditional Hosmer–Lemeshow test is conducted based on estimated versus empirical proportions for all combinations of regressors. This may not be feasible with complex survey data that may have at most a few dozen degrees of freedom (Section 29.2.3). For this reason, Archer and Lemeshow (2006) advocate the version of the Hosmer–Lemeshow test in which the sample is broken into percentile groups of the estimated probability of the positive response. For example, 10 groups corresponding to deciles of the predicted probability can be formed; the average predicted probability can be computed within each group; and this average predicted probability can be compared with the empirical probability.

Estimation and inference for the class of generalized linear models were discussed in Binder (1983), which is arguably the most cited paper in survey statistics.

29.3.4 SURVIVAL ANALYSIS

Survival analysis, also known as *analysis of failure time data* or duration data, concerns analysis of a time to event, and how covariates or random effects can make this time shorter or longer (Kalbfleisch and Prentice 2002). Rather than operating on the density of the response variable, time to event T, as is done in generalized linear models (GLMs), survival models operate with the survivor function, $S(t) = \text{Prob}[T > t]$, where T is the random variable of the survival time, and with the hazard function (the conditional failure rate, or the intensity function), $h(t) = f(t)/S(t) = -S'(t)/S(t) = -\text{d}/\text{d}t \ln S(t)$. The staple model of survival analysis is the Cox proportional hazards model in which the hazard is postulated to depend on the unspecified baseline hazard $h_0(t)$, and depends on covariates x_j only through a multiplicative factor $\exp\ [x_j'\beta]$.

The extension of the Cox model to survey data is due to Binder (1992), with later treatments, among others, by Lin (2000) and Boudreau and Lawless (2006). Lawless (2003) provides a discussion of estimation and testing issues that arise due to complex survey data. Some of them are mathematical: complex correlation structures due to clustered designs preclude some effective diagnostic computations, like Schoenfeld residual plots; or analysis units must be fully nested in the sampling design. Other methodological issues are more of a substantive nature due to the differences in how typical complex survey data and typical survival data are collected. While "classic" survival data typically have frequent observations on subjects, with accurate information on changes in risk exposures, treatments, and event times, complex health survey data tend to be population-wide studies with infrequent, if any, follow-up. Thus, the violations of the "standard" survival model assumptions may include the following:

- Left truncation: individuals enter the study when sampled, not at onset of exposure.
- Losses to follow-up may not be independent of survival experience.
- Few observation points (often just one), may be long periods apart.
- Recall errors in exposure and risk factors history.
- Exposure and risk factors may be unknown between the last observation and death.
- Truncation and censoring time may depend on design.

Also, the two literatures use the terminology of stratified samples in different ways. In survey statistics, units are grouped into strata for sampling efficiency. In survival analysis, stratified analysis consists of fitting separate baseline hazard estimates for substantively different population groups that may cut across the sampling strata.

29.3.5 MULTILEVEL ANALYSIS

Multilevel models (Raudenbush and Bryk 2002) and mixed models (Demidenko 2004) are used for populations and data sets that have hierarchical structures. A typical social science application of multilevel models are studies of students nested in teachers, classrooms, or schools. A typical medical application of mixed models are studies of repeated measures nested in patients. Thus, the two strands of literature have developed similar but somewhat different models. The multilevel models of the "social science" variety pay greater attention to the unique characteristics of the units at the lowest level of hierarchy, and interactions between levels (i.e., whether teacher's education or experience are predictive of how students of different race or socioeconomic status perform). Other medical applications may involve patients nested in doctors, practices, or hospitals, as well as spatial random effects that commonly affect individuals who live in the same geographic area.

For simplicity, let us consider a two-level model. Let j enumerate the lowest level units, or level-1 units (students in a class, visits within a patient), and i enumerate the level-2 units (classes; patients). Note that the numbering of levels goes in the direction opposite to sampling nomenclature, which would refer to classes as primary sampling units, and to students, as secondary sampling units. Then, biostatistics mixed models are usually formulated as

$$g(\theta_{ij}) = X'_{ij}\beta + Z'u_i, \quad y_{ij} \sim \text{exp. family}(\theta_{ij}) \qquad (29.37)$$

where y_{ij} is the response of level-1 unit j within the level-1 unit i; X_{ij} are explanatory variables at level 1; u_i are unobserved random effects of unit i; Z is the design matrix that designates the random effects to the level-1 units; $g(\cdot)$ is a link function; θ_{ij} is the canonical parameter of an exponential family distribution. Thus, the formulation (29.37) is explicitly allowing for generalized linear model-type extensions, that is, binary or count responses.

A typical way to represent a social science multilevel model is

$$\begin{cases} y_{ij} = b_i' x_{ij} + \varepsilon_{ij} \\ b_i = \gamma' z_i + u_i \end{cases} \tag{29.38}$$

Each unit i is allowed to have its own set of regression coefficients b_i, and in turn b_i can be explained by level-2 characteristics z_i. This is a hierarchical linear model formulation; generalized linear model extensions with link functions are also feasible.

Estimation with multilevel models typically proceeds by assuming a (mulitvariate) normal distribution of the level-2 effects u_i, and integrating the likelihoods of the level-2 observations with respect to this distribution (which may lead to a closed-form solution in linear models that involve the matrices of within- and between-unit i variances).

Hierarchical populations can be sampled in ways that naturally reflect the existing hierarchy. However, if sampling is informative, and different units within a given level have different probabilities of selection, then the unweighted sample distributions of the random effects u_i are likely to be misleading, and proper use of weights at different levels would be required to obtain consistent parameters of fixed effects β in equation (29.37), or γ in equation (29.38), as well as the parameters of the distribution of variance components u_i (variance σ_u^2 for scalar u_i, which is the most common model).

Pfefferman et al. (1998) discuss different choices of weighting schemes in informative hierarchical sampling designs. Namely, they consider weighting schemes in which the level-2 units enter the pseudolikelihood with their probability weights $w_{1i} = \frac{1}{\pi_{1i}}$, and the weights of the level-1 units can be scaled to optimize the bias of the variance component estimate σ_u^2, that is, $w_{2j|i} = \frac{\lambda_j}{\pi_{2j|i}}$. They argue in favor of scaling the weights so that within a level-2 unit, they sum up either to the nominal sample size ($\lambda_j = n_j / \sum_j w_{2j|i}$), or to the effective sample size ($\lambda_j = \sum_j w_{2j|i} / \sum_j w_{2j|i}^2$), that is, nominal sample size divided by the unequal weighting DEFF (29.11), with a slight preference to the effective sample size scaling approach. Instead of solving the likelihood maximization problem iteratively, as was done in Pfefferman et al. (1998), Kovacevic and Rai (2003) proposed an alternative method based on explicitly stating the census equations, expressing the model parameters from them, and generating the design-based variance estimator for these parameter estimates in a manner similar to equation (29.20). In a way, they exploit the hierarchical structure of the population to define the population parameters of variances at different levels of hierarchy, and provide design-based inference for these well-defined population quantities. Advancing the estimation methods further, Rao et al. (2013) proposed a method of moments estimator based on the concept of composite likelihood that involves pairwise contrasts of observations within unit i, thus increasing the number of degrees of freedom available for estimation, and helping to achieve less biased estimates of variance components.

Switching to a different paradigm, Rabe-Hesketh and Skrondal (2006) gave an example of a fully model-based approach in which the hierarchical elements of the sample are fully modeled as random components at the levels of strata, PSU and subsequent sampling units. While this approach can provide more efficient estimates when the statistical model describing the response variable is correctly specified, it is highly sensitive to this assumption of correct specification, and may have limited applicability in situations where not all of the design variables are known (or released in the public use version of the data).

29.3.6 SMALL AREA ESTIMATION

In many community health studies, there may be interest in obtaining estimates at relatively small geographic scales. In a national study, estimates of health condition prevalence at the state or county level may be required. In city-wide studies, estimates for specific neighborhoods may be needed. In many cases, the sample sizes that would be collected in these small areas will be inadequately small to support meaningful statistical analysis. Even with a national sample of the U.S. population of size 10,000, each of the 3144 counties of the United States would have on average only three observations; and given that the 590 counties with a population of 100,000 or more are home to 250 million population out of 314 million population, most counties are small and would likely have zero counts in the sample.

To yield usable estimates and accompanying mean squared error, small area estimation (SAE) models (Rao 2003) combine the design-based and the model-based approaches that were discussed in Section 29.1. These SAEs seek a trade-off in precision and accuracy between mixed models (see Section 29.3.5) that explain survey outcomes in terms of the available demographic data, on one hand, and direct design-based survey estimates of the local prevalence, on the other.

One class of SAE models are *area models* where the survey estimates are available at the level of the areas of interest. For a continuous outcome Y, a standard model links the average outcome of interest $\bar{Y}_i$ in area i with the area-level explanatory variables z_i as

$$\theta_i = g(\bar{Y}_i) = z_i'\beta + v_i \tag{29.39}$$

where $g(\cdot)$ is a link function, which may be used to transform the range of Y or stabilize the variance, and v_i is the remaining error model term with $\mathbb{E}_m[v_i] = 0, \mathbb{V}_m[v_i] = \sigma_v^2 \geq 0$. The direct estimates $\hat{\bar{Y}}_i$ are available, at least for some areas, and with the identical transformation, we obtain the direct estimates of θ_i as

$$\hat{\theta}_i = g(\hat{\bar{Y}}_i) = \theta_i + e_i \tag{29.40}$$

where e_i is the sampling error with the known variance based on the sampling design, $\mathbb{E}_p[e_i|\theta_i] = 0, \mathbb{V}_p[e_i|\theta_i] = \psi_i$. The subscript p denotes the expectations and variances with respect to *p*robability sampling, while the subscript m refers to expectations and variances with respect to the *m*odel. The two approaches are then combined to arrive at the model for the observed direct estimates:

$$\hat{\theta}_i = z_i'\beta + v_i + e_i \tag{29.41}$$

Note that equation (29.41) involves both the design-induced sampling errors e_i as well as the model errors v_i. The latter are used to cover the model misspecifications and the consequent biases of the predicted values $z_i'\hat{\beta}$. The model (29.41) is treated as a linear mixed/multilevel model, and can be estimated using the methods described in the previous section. Once the estimates $\tilde{\beta}$ are obtained, the final estimate (referred to as the *best linear unbiased estimate*, or BLUP, as it is derived by minimizing the mean squared error) is given by

$$\tilde{\theta}_i = \gamma_i\hat{\theta}_i + (1 - \gamma_i)z_i'\tilde{\beta}) \tag{29.42}$$

where

$$\gamma_i = \frac{\sigma_v^2}{\sigma_v^2 + \psi_i} \tag{29.43}$$

is the fraction of information that the small area model takes from direct estimates. (If an area does not have any observations in the sample data, then $\psi_i = +\infty$, $\gamma_i = 0$, and the reported estimate is the synthetic estimate $Z_i'\tilde{\beta}$.)

In other types of small area applications, the unit-level data on respondents in their specific areas may be available. If that is the case, then the *unit model* for responses is formulated at an individual level:

$$y_{ij} = x_{ij}'\beta + v_i + \varepsilon_{ij} \tag{29.44}$$

where i still enumerates the areas, and j enumerates individuals in areas. When the sampling fractions are small, the BLUP estimator for the area mean based on the model estimates $\tilde{\beta}$, assuming the covariates are known for all units in the area, is given by

$$\tilde{\mu}_i = \gamma_i[\bar{y}_i + (\bar{X}_i - \bar{x}_i)\tilde{\beta}] + (1 - \gamma_i)X_i'\tilde{\beta} \tag{29.45}$$

where

$$\gamma_i = \frac{\sigma_v^2}{\sigma_v^2 + \sigma_e^2/n_i} \tag{29.46}$$

Just as is the case with the estimates for simpler models conflated by the complex survey design, estimation of variance in small area models is even more complicated than estimation of the parameters of interest. The estimates of uncertainty for the estimated area means are cast in terms of MSE, since the model component may contain misspecification errors. These MSEs have the terms that account for sampling variability of the direct estimator ($\gamma_i\psi_i$ in the area model BLUP (29.42); $\gamma_i\sigma_e^2/n_i$ in the unit model BLUP (29.45)), uncertainty in the model parameter estimates $\tilde{\beta}$, and uncertainty in the variance components σ_v^2, ψ_i, and σ_e^2. The latter term is usually the most difficult to assess, and the bootstrap methods have been found to be of value for these purposes (Lahiri 2003).

SAE is arguably the most active area of statistical methodology research related to health survey statistics from the 1990s through the current period (mid-2010s). New developments appear regularly, and overviews are published on a regular basis (Ghosh and Rao 1994, Pfeffermann 2002, Pfeffermann 2013).

A number of large-scale SAE projects have been executed by the U.S. federal statistical agencies. The early developments of the SAE models (Fay and Herriot 1979) came from the statistical program for income for small places which is now the Model-based Small Area Income and Poverty Estimates (SAIPE) for School Districts, Counties and States.[3] The Census Bureau website states that "the main objective of this program is to provide estimates of income and poverty for the administration of federal programs and the allocation of federal funds to local jurisdictions. In addition to these federal programs, state and local programs use the income and poverty estimates for distributing funds and managing programs." SAIPE uses Bayesian techniques to combine regression predictions, direct estimates from the ACS, the prior Census data and administrative data at local levels. Another high profile Census small area data product is the Model-based Small Area Health Insurance Estimates (SAHIE) for Counties and States.[4] SAHIE relies on an area-type model similar in spirit to equations (29.39)–(29.43).

There are several important health data products that rely on SAE methods. The Small Area Estimates for Cancer Risk Factors and Screening Behaviors[5] combines the data from the NHIS and the Behavioral Risk Factors Surveillance System (BRFSS[6]) from 1997 to 2003. The model takes into account the different coverage properties of NHIS, which is conducted face-to-face, and BRFSS which is collected on the phone (Raghunathan et al. 2007). While BRFSS is by design representative at the state level, it is often used to produce more detailed estimates, like the Diabetes Interactive Atlas,[7] which is also based on Bayesian methods (Cadwell et al. 2010).

A small area data product of great importance beyond the health discipline that comes out of NHIS are the state-level estimates of wireless substitution (Blumberg et al. 2013). These estimates are the only reliable estimates of phone use patterns in the United States. They are invaluable for survey statisticians who need to design phone surveys and optimize allocations between the cell phone and the landline frames (Chapter 2). These data are also used for weight calibration if phone usage acts as one of the control margins using the methods described in Chapter 26.

An entirely different class of small area models is derived from combining multiple data sets in a situation where none of the data sets would have all the

[3] See http://www.census.gov/did/www/saipe/.

[4] See http://www.census.gov/did/www/sahie/.

[5] See http://sae.cancer.gov/.

[6] See http://www.cdc.gov/brfss/.

[7] See http://www.cdc.gov/diabetes/atlas/countydata/atlas.html.

necessary pieces. Battaglia et al. (2010) fit a multinomial model of phone use using NHIS data, and applied the model coefficient to a larger, more geographically detailed ACS data set to estimate the control totals of phone usage in a New York city-wide study.

29.4 Quality Control Analyses

The preceding discussion has mostly been concerned with getting the point estimates and the standard errors right, that is, quantifying the sampling error component of the total survey error (Biemer 2010, Groves and Lyberg 2010). In this section, we present several types of analysis that a health researcher who collects their own data may want to do as part of a quality control and assurance process. In other words, these analyses attend to other components of the total survey error, including nonresponse error, interviewer effects, and mode differences. These analyses may not necessarily concern health outcomes and population prevalences. They rather address the issues of internal validity of the study by looking at how the data were collected, rather than what the data tell about health conditions. For the most part, though, the statistical models that these additional analyses will rely upon are the same as those covered in Section 29.3. One important difference, however, is that some of these quality control analyses require the use of the base weights rather than the final weights, keeping all other design information such as stratification and clustering structure.

For comprehensive reviews of these and other issues in survey quality, see Biemer and Lyberg (2003) and Groves et al. (2009).

29.4.1 NONRESPONSE BIASES

The problem of declining response rates and nonresponse has been in the center of attention in survey methodology since the 1990s (Groves 2006). While sampling contributes representation error with a magnitude that can be quantified based on sampling theory, and generally has a mean equal to or close to zero, nonresponse tends to produce systematic errors with nonzero means that lead to biases in descriptive statistics and parameter estimates. Thus, keeping nonresponse at low levels is often considered a necessary condition for high quality survey data. The American Association for Public Opinion Research has developed a set of standards for computing and reporting response rates (AAPOR 2011). These standards should be followed by all researchers who collect data on human populations and report response rates as a measure of survey quality. The response rate version RR3 appears to be the one that is most frequently reported.

If auxiliary information exists on both respondents and nonrespondents from a sampling frame, survey paradata such as interviewer observations, or outcomes in prior waves in a longitudinal study, the two groups of respondents and nonrespondents can be compared on these variables using two-way tables (Section 29.3.1). Such analysis should employ the base weights and sampling design structure (strata, clusters). It can identify important correlates of nonresponse that can later be used in constructing response propensity models or nonresponse adjusted weights. Once such weights are constructed, the tabulations can be run again, now comparing the results based on final weights with those based on the population or the complete sample, to see whether nonresponse adjustments have reduced the nonresponse biases.

Bethlehem (2002) demonstrates that in a model-based setting, the nonresponse bias of a sample mean is

$$\text{Bias}[\bar{y}] = \frac{\text{Cov}[y_i, \rho_i]}{\bar{\rho}} \tag{29.47}$$

where ρ_i = Prob[unit i reponds] is the response propensity, and $\bar{\rho}$ is its population mean (i.e., the response rate). Thus, a survey statistic may have little or no bias even when $\bar{\rho}$ is low provided that $\text{Cov}[y_i, \rho_i]$ is small in magnitude. In turn, this can happen in two circumstances: when the outcome y_i and response propensity ρ_i are uncorrelated; and when $\mathbb{V}[\rho_i]$ is small, that is, all response propensities are about the same.

The role response propensity plays in equation (29.47) suggests that modeling and analyzing it will likely shed some light on potential response biases. Little and Vartivarian (2003) argue that both demographic and sampling design variables should be used in such a propensity modeling. Schouten et al. (2009) propose a descriptive statistic related to variance of response propensities, dubbed the R-indicator, and provide bounds on nonresponse bias based on it. The R-indicator varies from 0 to 1, with the value of 1 indicating no variability in ρ_i, and hence no bias, according to equation (29.47). Witt (2010) demonstrates how the risk of nonresponse bias, and mitigation of that risk through nonresponse adjusted weighting can be quantified with partial and semipartial correlations of survey outcomes and estimated response propensities. Typically, a nonresponse propensity model is built by fitting a logistic regression model (Section 29.3.3) with a 0/1 indicator of unit response as the dependent variable, and the available information on sampled units, which can come from the sampling frame, survey paradata such as interviewer observations, or prior waves in a longitudinal study.

29.4.2 INTERVIEWER EFFECTS

The presence of an interviewer in person in face-to-face studies, or on the phone in phone studies, and unique interviewer characteristics and interviewing style can affect whether a sampled person will respond to the survey, and the answers they will provide (Groves et al. 2009, Ch. 9).

O'Muircheartaigh and Campanelli (1998) demonstrated how classic multilevel models (Section 29.3.5) can be used to quantify interviewer effects by expressing one of the random effects in the model as interviewer-specific random effects. While quantitatively small, interviewer effects may matter both qualitatively for the face validity of a study, and quantitatively for computing design effects (29.15). Technically speaking, the use of random effects for interviewers in multilevel models may not be entirely appropriate, as it assumes an entirely random allocation of cases to interviewers. In practice, more experienced interviewers tend to be assigned to more complicated cases that require refusal conversions, and field managers often match the interviewer demographic characteristics, such as race, gender, and age, with those of the selected respondents. West and Olson (2010) look deeper into sources of interviewer effects, and argue that the observed differences between interviewers may arise because different interviewers successfully obtain cooperation from different pools of respondents, rather than from systematic measurement error in the answers that the respondents provide to a given interviewer.

29.4.3 MODE EFFECTS

When a health survey is conducted using more than one mode of data collection (e.g., on the Web and on the phone), it is likely that distributions of responses obtained in different modes will differ. Different individuals may prefer, or have access to, different modes. For example, those with no Internet access cannot complete a web survey; and those with hearing difficulties may not be able to complete a survey by phone. Thus different modes may be populated by respondents with different demographic characteristics.

Beyond that, Groves et al. (2009) discuss some of the reasons why the same respondents may provide different responses in different modes. One prominent reason is social desirability, when the presence of an interviewer entices respondents to provide fewer reports of socially undesirable behaviors (e.g., illicit drug use), and/or greater reporting of socially desirable behaviors (e.g., political engagement). Respondents may be taking cognitive shortcuts when they are under the time pressure of a phone interview, and provide the minimally satisfactory rather than the most accurate answer. Finally, presentation of the survey instrument in different modes may lead to different perceptions of questions and response categories. For instance, while respondents taking the survey on paper or on the Web may be able to assess all items in long lists, administering such long lists on the phone will likely lead to primacy or recency effects, with respondents only able to map their answers to the first few or the last few response categories. All these effects are undesirable, and responsible survey design involves optimizing the survey instrument to the mode(s) in which the survey will be administered.

While comparisons of survey responses between modes is relatively straightforward using two-way tabulation methods (Section 29.3.1), this comparison is only meaningful when mode choice is free from confounders such as demographics. Arguably, this is only possible when respondents are randomized into survey mode in an interpenetrating samples design. If this is not the case, corrections should be made for different demographic mixes in different modes. Elliott et al. (2009) report substantial mode effects in a study with four modes (phone, mail, interactive voice response, and mixed mail with phone follow-up) where each hospital collects data in one mode only, and provide a regression adjustment that equates the modes (and adjusts for nonresponse that is related to the same demographic variables that are controlled for in the mode effect adjustments). Kolenikov and Kennedy (2014) discuss the various counterfactuals in mode comparisons, and compare regression adjustments with various types of multiple imputation.

29.5 Discussion

Let us conclude this chapter with some suggestions for further reading.

There are a great variety of books covering different topics in survey statistics, some of them devoting considerable attention specifically to health applications. A good introduction to the basic building blocks of sample surveys, as well as the main aspects of the analysis of complex survey data, is Lohr (2009). These foundations can be built up with more theoretical books written by Särndal et al. (1992), Thompson (1997), and Fuller (2009).

A good introduction to the analysis of survey data with step-by-step recommendations demonstrated in Stata software is given by Heeringa et al. (2010). A somewhat more advanced treatment that is aimed specifically at health researchers is provided by Korn and Graubard (1999). Methodological foundations of analytical work for some mainstream as well as nonstandard models are nicely covered in edited volumes by Skinner et al. (1989) and Chambers and Skinner (2003). A comprehensive high level coverage of nearly all aspects of survey statistics and analytical methodology is provided in *The Handbook of Statistics*, vol. 29 (Pfeffermann and Rao 2009a, b).

There is no doubt that the novel ways to analyze survey data will continue to appear in survey literature. Journals devoted specifically to new methodological contributions in survey statistics and methodology include *Survey Methodology* published by Statistics Canada; *Journal of Official Statistics* published by Statistics Sweden—both freely available online; *Journal of Survey Statistics and Methodology* published jointly by the American Statistical Association (ASA) and the American Association for Public Opinion Research (AAPOR); *Public Opinion Quarterly* published by AAPOR; and *Survey Research Methods* published by the European Survey Research Association. Applied recommendations and reviews can often be found in *Statistics in Medicine* and other substantive health research journals.

29.5.1 ACKNOWLEDGMENTS

The authors would like to thank Tim Johnson for organizing this volume and for his encouragement during our work. Trent Buskirk and Heather Hammer provided helpful comments and suggestions. We would also like to thank our respective employers, Abt SRBI and Stata Corp., for providing some release time to work on this chapter. The opinions expressed in this chapter are the authors' own and do not reflect the views of Abt SRBI nor Stata Corp.

REFERENCES

AAPOR. *Standard Definitions: Final Dispositions of Case Codes and Outcome Rates for Surveys*. 7th ed. The American Association for Public Opinion Research; Deerfield, IL, USA 2011. Available online at http://aapor.org/Content/NavigationMenu/AboutAAPOR/StandardsampEthics/StandardDefinitions/StandardDefinitions2011.pdf. Accessed 23 July 2014.

Adams G, Gulliford MC, Ukoumunne OC, Eldridge S, Chinn S, Campbell MJ. Patterns of intra-cluster correlation from primary care research to informstudy design and analysis. J Clin Epidemiol 2004;57(8):785–794.

Agresti A. *Categorical Data Analysis*. Wiley series in probability and statistics. 3rd ed. Hoboken, NJ: John Wiley and Sons; 2012.

Archer KJ, Lemeshow S. Goodness-of-fit test for a logistic regression model fitted using survey sample data. Stata J 2006;6(1):97–105.

Ash S. Using successive difference replication for estimating variances. In: *Proceedings of Survey Research Methods Section*. Alexandria (VA): American Statistical Association; 2011.

Battaglia MP, Eisenhower D, Immerwahr S, Konty K. Dual-frame weighting of RDD and cell phone interviews at the local level. In: *Proceedings of Survey Research Methods Section*. Alexandria (VA): The American Statistical Association; 2010.

Belsley DA, Kuh E, Welsch RE. *Regression Diagnostics: Identifying Influential Data and Sources of Collinearity*. New York: Wiley-Interscience; 1980.

Bethlehem J. Weighting nonresponse adjustments based on auxiliary information. In: Groves RM, Dillman DA, Eltinge JL, Little RJA, editors. *Survey Nonresponse*. New York: John Wiley and Sons; 2002. p 375–288.

Biemer PP. Total survey error: design, implementation, and evaluation. Public Opin Q 2010;74(5):817–848.

Biemer PP, Lyberg LE. *Introduction to Survey Quality*. Wiley series in survey methodology. Hoboken, NJ: Wiley-Interscience; 2003.

Binder DA. On the variances of asymptotically normal estimators from complex surveys. Int Stat Rev 1983;51:279–292.

Binder DA. Fitting Cox's proportional hazards models from survey data. Biometrika 1992;79(1):139–147.

Binder DA, Roberts GR. Design-based and model-based methods for estimating model parameters. In: Chambers RL, Skinner CJ, editors. *Analysis of Survey Data*. Chapter 3. New York: John Wiley and Sons; 2003.

Binder DA, Roberts GR. Design- and model-based inference for model parameters. In: Pfeffermann D, Rao CR, editors. *Handbook of Statistics*. Volume 29B, Sample surveys: inference and analysis. Chapter 24. Oxford: Elsevier; 2009.

Blumberg SJ, Ganesh N, Luke JV, Gonzales G. Wireless substitution: state-level estimates from the National Health Interview Survey, 2012. Technical Report 70. Hyattsville, MD: National Center for Health Statistics; 2013.

Botman S, Moore T, Moriarity C, Parsons V. Design and estimation for the National Health Interview Survey, 1995–2004. Technical Report 130. Hyattsville, MD: National Center for Health Statistics; 2000.

Boudreau C, Lawless JF. Survival analysis based on the proportional hazards model and survey data. Can J Stat 2006;34(2):203–216.

Brewer K, Hanif M. *Sampling with Unequal Probabilities*. New York: Springer-Verlag; 1983.

Buse A. The likelihood ratio, Wald, and Lagrange multiplier tests: an expository note. Am Stat 1982;36(3):153–157.

Cadwell BL, Thompson TJ, Boyle JP, Barker LE. Bayesian small area estimates of diabetes prevalence by U.S. county, 2005. J Data Sci 2010;8(1):173–188.

Chambers RL, Skinner CJ, editors. *Analysis of Survey Data*, Wiley series in survey methodology. New York: John Wiley and Sons; 2003.

Cho M, Eltinge JL, Gershunskaya J, Huff LL. Evaluation of generalized variance functions in the analysis of complex survey data. J Off Stat 2014;30(1):63–90.

D'Arrigo J, Skinner C. Linearization variance estimation for generalized raking estimators in the presence of nonresponse. Surv Methodol 2010;36(2):181–192.

Demidenko E. *Mixed Models: Theory and Applications with R*, 2nd edition Wiley series in probability and statistics. Hoboken, NJ: Wiley-Interscience; 2004.

Demnati A, Rao JNK. Linearization variance estimators for model parameters from complex survey data. Surv Methodol 2010;36(2):193–202.

Deville JC, Särndal CE. Calibration estimators in survey sampling. J Am Stat Assoc 1992;87(418):376–382.

Efron B, Tibshirani RJ. 1994, *An Introduction to the Bootstrap*. Boca Raton, FL: Chapman and Hall/CRC.

Elliott MN, Zaslavsky AM, Goldstein E, Lehrman W, Hambarsoomians K, Beckett MK, Giordano L. Effects of survey mode, patient mix, and nonresponse on CAHPS hospital survey scores. Health Serv Res 2009;44(2 Pt 1):501–518.

Fay RE, Herriot RA. Estimates of income for small places: an application of James-Stein procedures to census data. J Am Stat Assoc 1979;74(366):269–277.

Fuller WA. Regression estimation for survey samples (with discussion). Surv Methodol 2002;28(1):5–23.

Fuller WA. *Sampling Statistics*. Hoboken (NJ): John Wiley and Sons; 2009.

Ghosh M, Rao JNK. Small area estimation: an appraisal. Stat Sci 1994;9(1):55–76.

Godambe VP, Thompson M. Some aspects of the theory of estimating equations. J Stat Plann Inference 1978;295–104.

Godambe VP, Thompson ME. Estimation functions and survey sampling. In: Pfeffermann D, Rao CR, editors. *Handbook of Statistics*. Volume 29B, Sample surveys: inference and analysis. Amsterdam: North Holland; 2009.

Groves RM. Nonresponse rates and nonresponse bias in household surveys. Public Opin Q 2006;70(5):646–675.

Groves RM, Fowler FJ, Couper MP, Lepkowski JM, Singer E Tourangeau R. *Survey Methodology*, Wiley series in survey methodology. 2nd ed. New York: John Wiley and Sons; 2009.

Groves RM, Lyberg L. Total survey error: past, present, and future. Public Opin Q 2010;74(5):849–879.

Hansen M, Hurwitz WN, Madow WG. *Sample Survey Methods and Theory*. New York: John Wiley and Sons; 1953.

Harrell F. *Regression Modeling Strategies: With Applications to Linear Models, Logistic Regression, and Survival Analysis*. 2nd ed. New York: Springer-Verlag; 2010.

Hedayat A, Sloane NJA, Stufken J. *Orthogonal Arrays: Theory and Applications*, Springer series in statistics. New York: Springer-Verlag; 1999.

Heeringa SG, West BT, Berglund PA. *Applied Survey Data Analysis (Chapman and Hall/CRC Statistics in the Social and Behavioral Science)*. Boca Raton, FL: Chapman and Hall/CRC; 2010.

Holt D, Smith TMF. Post stratification. J R Stat Soc, Ser A 1979;142(1):33–46.

Hosmer DW, Lemeshow S, Sturdivant RX. *Applied Logistic Regression*, Wiley series in probability and statistics. 3rd ed. Hoboken, NJ: John Wiley and Sons; 2013.

Huber P. The behavior of the maximum likelihood estimates under nonstandard conditions. In: *Proceedings of the 5th Berkeley Symposium on Mathematical Statistics and Probability*. Volume 1. Berkeley: University of California Press; 1967. p 221–233.

Judkins DR. Fay's method for variance estimation. J Off Stat 1990;6(3):223–239.

Kalbfleisch JD, Prentice RL. *The Statistical Analysis of Failure Time Data*, Wiley series in probability and statistics. 2nd ed. New York: Wiley-Interscience; 2002.

Kalton G, Anderson D. Sampling rare populations. J R Stat Soc Ser A (Gen) 1986;149(1):65–82.

Kim JK, Wu C. Sparse and efficient replication variance estimation for complex surveys. Surv Methodol 2013;39(1):91–120.

Kish L. *Survey Sampling*. 3rd ed. New York: John Wiley and Sons; 1995.

Kolenikov S. Resampling inference with complex survey data. Stata J 2010;10:165–199.

Kolenikov S, Kennedy C. Evaluating three approaches to statistically adjust for mode effects. J Surv Stat Methodol 2014;2(2):126–158.

Korn EL, Graubard BI. *Analysis of Health Surveys*. New York: John Wiley and Sons; 1999.

Kott PS. The delete-a-group jackknife. J Off Stat 2001;17(4):521–526.

Kovacevic MS, Rai SN. A pseudo maximum likelihood approach to multilevel modelling of survey data. Commun Stat - Theory Methods 2003;32(1):103–121.

Krewski D, Rao JNK. Inference from stratified samples: properties of the linearization, jackknife and balanced repeated replication methods. Ann Stat 1981;9(5):1010–1019.

Lahiri P. On the impact of bootstrap in survey sampling and small area estimation. Stat Sci 2003;18199–210.

Lawless JF. Event history analysis and longitudinal surveys. In: Chambers RL, Skinner CJ, editors. *Analysis of Survey Data*. Chapter 15. John Wiley and Sons; 2003. p 221–243.

Li J, Valliant R. Survey weighted hat matrix and leverages. Surv Methodol 2009;35(1):15–24.

Li J, Valliant R. Linear regression influence diagnostics for unclustered survey data. J Off Stat 2011;27(1):99–119.

Lin DY. On fitting Cox's proportional hazards models to survey data. Biometrika 2000;87(1):37–47.

Little RJ, Vartivarian S. On weighting the rates in non-response weights. Stat Med 2003;22(9):1589–1599.

Lohr SL. *Sampling: Design and Analysis*. 2nd ed. Pacific Grove, CA: Duxbury Press; 2009.

Lumley TS. *Complex Surveys: A Guide to Analysis Using R*. Wiley series in survey methodology. New York: John Wiley and Sons; 2010.

McCarthy PJ. Pseudo-replication: half samples. Rev Int Stat Inst 1969;37(3):239–264.

Mitofsky W. Sampling of telephone households, *unpublished CBS News memorandum*; 1970.

Nigam AK, Rao JNK. On balanced bootstrap for stratified multistage samples. Stat Sin 1996;6(1):199–214.

O'Muircheartaigh C, Campanelli P. The relative impact of interviewer effects and sample design effects on survey precision. J R Stat Soc Ser A (Stat Soc) 1998;161(1):63–77.

Pagano M, Gauvreau K. 2000, *Principles of Biostatistics (with CD-ROM)*, 2nd ed. Pacific Grove, CA: Cengage Learning.

Pfefferman D, Skinner CJ, Holmes DJ, Goldstein H, Rasbash J. Weighting for unequal selection probabilities in multilevel models. J R Stat Soc Ser B 1998;60(1):23–40.

Pfeffermann D. The role of sampling weights when modeling survey data. Int Stat Rev 1993;61:317–337.

Pfeffermann D. Small area estimation—new developments and directions. Int Stat Rev 2002;70(1):125–143.

Pfeffermann D. New important developments in small area estimation. Stat Sci 2013;28(1):40–68.

Pfeffermann D, Rao CR, editors. *Handbook of Statistics*. Volume 29A, Sample surveys: design, methods and applications. Amsterdam: North Holland; 2009a.

Pfeffermann, D, Rao CR, editors. *Handbook of Statistics*. Volume 29B, Sample surveys: inference and analysis. Amsterdam: North Holland; 2009b.

Potthoff RF, Woodbury MA, Manton KG. Equivalent sample size and equivalent degrees of freedom refinements for inference using survey weights under superpopulation models. J Am Stat Assoc 1992;87(418):383–396.

Rabe-Hesketh S, Skrondal A. Multilevel modelling of complex survey data. J R Stat Soc Ser A (Stat Soc) 2006;169(4)):805–827.

Raghunathan TE, Xie D, Schenker N, Parsons VL, Davis WW, Dodd KW, Feuer EJ. Combining information from two surveys to estimate county-level prevalence rates of cancer risk factors and screening. J Am Stat Assoc 2007;102(478):474–486.

Rao JNK *Small Area Estimation*, Wiley series in survey methodology. New York: John Wiley and Sons; 2003.

Rao JNK. Interplay between sample survey theory and practice: an appraisal. Surv Methodol 2005;31(2):117–138.

Rao J, Scott A. The analysis of categorical data from complex sample surveys: chi-squared tests for goodness of fit and independence in two-way tables. J Am Stat Assoc 1981;76:221–230.

Rao JNK, Thomas DR. Analysis of categorical response data from complex surveys: an appraisal and update. In: Chambers RL, Skinner CJ, editors. *Analysis of Survey Data*. Chapter 7. Chichester: John Wiley and Sons; 2003.

Rao JNK, Verret F, Hidiroglou MA. A weighted composite likelihood approach to inference for two-level models from survey data. Surv Methodol 2013;39(2):263–282.

Rao JNK, Wu CFJ. Resampling inference with complex survey data. J Am Stat Assoc 1988;83(401):231–241.

Rao JNK, Wu CFJ, Yue K. Some recent work on resampling methods for complex surveys. Surv Methodol 1992;18(2):209–217.

Raudenbush S, Bryk A. *Hierarchical Linear Models*. 2nd ed. Thousand Oaks (CA): SAGE; 2002.

Rosner B. *Fundamentals of Biostatistics*. 7th ed. Pacific Grove, CA: Cengage Learning; 2010.

Rubin-Bleuer S, Kratina IS. On the two-phase framework for joint model and design-based inference. Ann Stat 2005;33(6):2789–2810.

Rust K, Kalton G. Strategies for collapsing strata for variance estimation. J Off Stat 1987;3(1):69–81.

Rust KF, Rao JN. Variance estimation for complex surveys using replication techniques. Stat Methods Med Res 1996;5(3):283–310.

Ryan TP. *Sample Size Determination and Power*. Hoboken (NJ): John Wiley and Sons; 2013.

Särndal C-E, Swensson B, Wretman J. *Model Assisted Survey Sampling*. New York: Springer; 1992.

Satterthwaite FE. An approximate distribution of estimates of variance components. Biometrics Bull 1946;2(6):110–114.

Schouten B, Cobben F, Bethlehem J. Indicators for the representativeness of survey response. Surv Methodol 2009;35(1):101–113.

Scott AJ, Holt D. The effect of two-stage sampling on ordinary least squares methods. J Am Stat Assoc 1982;77(380):848–854.

Shao J. Resampling methods in sample surveys (with discussion). Statistics 1996;27:203–254.

Sitter RR. Balanced repeated replications based on orthogonal multi-arrays. Biometrika 1993;80(1):211–221.

Skinner CJ. Domain means, regression and multivariate analysis. In: Skinner CJ, Holt D, Smith TM, editors. *Analysis of Complex Surveys*. Chapter 3. New York: John Wiley and Sons; 1989. p 59–88.

Skinner CJ, Holt D, Smith TM. *Analysis of Complex Surveys*. New York: John Wiley and Sons; 1989.

Smith RL, Young GA. *Essentials of Statistical Inference*. Cambridge, UK: Cambridge University Press; 2005.

Srinath KP. Design effects in surveys that require oversampling of certain subpopulations. In: *Proceedings of Survey Research Methods Section*. Alexandria (VA): The American Statistical Association; 2013.

Stata Corp. *Stata Statistical Software: Release 13*. College Station (TX); 2013.

Thompson ME. *Theory of Sample Surveys*. Volume 74, Monographs on statistics and applied probability. New York: Chapman and Hall/CRC; 1997.

Thompson DM, Fernald DH, Mold JW. Intraclass correlation coefficients typical of cluster-randomized studies: estimates from the Robert Wood Johnson prescription for health projects. Ann Family Med 2012;10(3):235–240.

Valliant R. Discussion of "resampling methods in sample surveys" by J. Shao. Statistics 1996;27:247–251.

Valliant R, Brick JM, Dever JA. Weight adjustments for the grouped jackknife variance estimator. J Off Stat 2008;24(3):469–488.

Valliant R, Rust KF. Degrees of freedom approximations and rules-of-thumb. J Off Stat 2010;26(4):585–602.

van der Vaart AW. *Asymptotic Statistics*. New York: John Wiley and Sons; 1998.

Waksberg J. Sampling methods for random digit dialing. J Am Stat Assoc 1978;73(361):40–46.

West BT, Berglund P, Heeringa SG. A closer examination of subpopulation analysis of complex-sample survey data. Stata J 2008;8(4):520–531(12).

West BT, Olson K. How much of interviewer variance is really nonresponse error variance? Public Opin Q 2010;74(5):1004–1026.

White H. A heteroskedasticity-consistent covariance-matrix estimator and a direct test for heteroskedasticity. Econometrica 1980;48(4):817–838.

White H. Maximum likelihood estimation of misspecified models. Econometrica 1982;50(1):1–26.

Witt MB. Estimating the R-indicator, its standard error and other related statistics with SAS and SUDAAN. In: *Proceedings of the Survey Research Methods Section*. Alexandria (VA): The American Statistical Association; 2010.

Wolter KM. *Introduction to Variance Estimation*. 2nd ed. New York: Springer; 2007.

Wolter K, Smith P, Blumberg SJ. Statistical foundations of cell-phone surveys. Surv Methodol 2010;36(2):203–215.

Wu CFJ. Balanced repeated replications based on mixed orthogonal arrays. Biometrika 1991;78(1):181–188.

Yung W. Variance estimation for public use files under confidentiality constraints. In: Proceedings of Statistics Canada Symposium, Statistics Canada; 1997. p 434–439.

ONLINE RESOURCES

Review of survey software packages at the webpage of Alan Zaslavsky: www.hcp.med.harvard.edu/statistics/survey-soft/.

Different types of weights and their specification in software can be reviewed at: www.ats.ucla.edu/stat/stata/faq/weights.htm.

Public use data files and methodology documents of the National Health and Nutrition Examination Survey (NHANES), the National Health Interview Survey (NHIS), the National Survey of Family Growth (NSFG), the State and Local Area Integrated Telephone Survey (SLAITS) and other data products of the National Center For Health Statistics: www.cdc.gov/nchs/surveys.htm.

Webinars of the Survey Research Methods Section of the American Statistical Association; some joint with the American Association for Public Opinion Research; include several webinars on analysis of survey data: www.amstat.org/sections/srms/webinar_archive.cfm.

Proceedings of the Survey Research Methods Section (SRMS) of the American Statistical Association are short publications based on presentations given at Joint Statistical Meetings and other conferences organized by SRMS: www.amstat.org/sections/srms/Proceedings.

Index

Handbook of Health Survey Methods, First Edition. Edited by Timothy P. Johnson.